This is Volume 21 of WEST'S NEW YORK PRACTICE SERIES

West's New York Practice Series

Vol. 1	Walker, et al., New York Limited Liability Companies and Partnerships: A Guide to Law and Practice
Vols. 2-4	Haig, et al., Commercial Litigation in New York State Courts
Vol. 5	Barker and Alexander, Evidence in New York State and Federal Courts
Vol. 6	Greenberg, Marcus, et al., New York Criminal Law
Vol. 7	Marks, et al., New York Pretrial Criminal Procedure
Vol. 8	Davies, Stecich, Gold, et al., New York Civil Appellate Practice
Vol. 9	Ginsberg, Weinberg, et al., Environmental Law and Regulation in New York
Vol. 10	Sobie, et al., New York Family Court Practice
Vols. 11-12	Scheinkman, et al., New York Law of Domestic Relations

Vol. 13	Taber, et al., Employment Litigation in New York
Vols. 14-16	Kreindler, Rodriguez, et al., New York Law of Torts
Vols. 17-19	Field, Moskin, et al., New York and Delaware Business Organizations: Choice, Formation, Operation, Financing and Acquisitions
Vols. 20-25	Ostertag, Benson, et al., General Practice in New York
Vol. 26	Borchers, Markell, et al., New York State Administrative Procedure and Practice
Vol. A	Borges, et al., Enforcing Judgments and Collecting Debts in New York
Vols. B-C	Bensel, Frank, McKeon, et al., Personal Injury Practice in New York
Vols. D-E	Preminger, et al., Trusts and Estates Practice in New York
Vols. F-G	Finkelstein and Ferrara, Landlord and Tenant Practice in New York

COORDINATED RESEARCH IN NEW YORK FROM WEST

New York Practice 2d
David D. Siegel

Handling the DWI Case in New York
Peter Gerstenzang

New York Elder Law Practice
Vincent J. Russo and Marvin Rachlin

WEST'S McKINNEY'S FORMS

Civil Practice Law and Rules

Uniform Commercial Code

Business Corporation Law

Matrimonial and Family Law

Real Property Practice

Estates and Surrogate Practice

Criminal Procedure Law

Not-For-Profit Corporation Law

Tax Practice and Procedure

Local Government Forms

Selected Consolidated Law Forms

McKinney's Consolidated Laws of New York Annotated

West's New York Legal Update

New York Digest

New York Law Finder

PAMPHLETS

New York Civil Practice Law and Rules

New York Sentence Charts

WESTLAW®

COORDINATED RESEARCH FROM WEST

WEST*Check*® and WESTMATE®

West CD–ROM Libraries™

To order any of these New York practice tools, call your West Representative or 1–800–328–9352.

> **NEED RESEARCH HELP?**
>
> **If you have research questions concerning WESTLAW or West Publications, call West's Reference Attorneys at 1–800–733–2889.**

GENERAL PRACTICE IN NEW YORK

By

ROBERT L. OSTERTAG
HON. JAMES D. BENSON

Sections 7.1 to 12.98

ST. PAUL, MINN.
WEST GROUP
1998

GENERAL PRACTICE IN NEW YORK FORMS ON DISK™

The **Forms on Disk**™ which accompany these volumes provide instant access to WordPerfect 5.1/5.2 versions of the forms included in *General Practice in New York*. These electronic forms will save you hours of time drafting legal documents. The electronic forms can be loaded into your word processing software and formatted to match the document style of your law firm. These electronic forms become templates for you to use over and over without having to retype them each time.

The forms in Volumes 20, 21, 22, 23, 24 and 25 that are included on the accompanying disks are marked with the following disk icon for easy identification. 💾

COPYRIGHT © 1998 By WEST GROUP
          610 Opperman Drive
          P.O. Box 64526
          St. Paul, MN 55164–0526
          1–800–328–9352

All rights reserved
Printed in the United States of America
ISBN 0–314–23142–0

 TEXT IS PRINTED ON 10% POST CONSUMER RECYCLED PAPER

WESTLAW® ELECTRONIC RESEARCH GUIDE

Coordinating Legal Research with WESTLAW

The *New York Practice Series* is an essential aid to legal research. WESTLAW provides a vast, online library of over 8000 collections of documents and services that can supplement research begun in this publication, encompassing:

- Federal and state primary law (statutes, regulations, rules, and case law), including West's editorial enhancements, such as headnotes, Key Number classifications, annotations

- Secondary law resources (texts and treatises published by West Group and by other publishers, as well as law reviews)

- Legal news

- Directories of attorneys and experts

- Court records and filings

- Citators

Specialized topical subsets of these resources have been created for more than thirty areas of practice.

In addition to legal information, there are general news and reference databases and a broad array of specialized materials frequently useful in connection with legal matters, covering accounting, business, environment, ethics, finance, medicine, social and physical sciences.

This guide will focus on a few aspects of WESTLAW use to supplement research begun in this publication, and will direct you to additional sources of assistance.

Databases

A database is a collection of documents with some features in common. It may contain statutes, court decisions, administrative materials, commentaries, news or other information. Each database has a unique identifier, used in many WESTLAW commands to select a database of interest. For example, the database containing New York cases has the identifier NY-CS.

The WESTLAW Directory is a comprehensive list of databases with information about each database, including the types of documents each

WESTLAW ELECTRONIC RESEARCH GUIDE

contains. The first page of a standard or customized WESTLAW Directory is displayed upon signing on to WESTLAW, except when prior, saved research is resumed. To access the WESTLAW Directory at any time, enter DB.

Databases of potential interest in connection with your research include:

NY-AG	New York Attorney General Opinions
NYETH-EO	New York Ethics Opinions
NYETH-CS	Legal Ethics & Professional Responsibility - New York Cases
WLD-NY	West's Legal Directory - New York
LAWPRAC	The Legal Practice Database

For information as to currentness and search tips regarding any WESTLAW database, enter the SCOPE command SC followed by the database identifier (e.g., SC NY-CS). It is not necessary to include the identifier to obtain scope information about the currently selected database.

WESTLAW Highlights

Use of this publication may be supplemented through the WESTLAW Bulletin (WLB), the WESTLAW New York State Bulletin (WSB-NY) and various Topical Highlights. Highlights databases contain summaries of significant judicial, legislative and administrative developments and are updated daily; they are searchable both from an automatic list of recent documents and using general WESTLAW search methods for documents accumulated over time. The full text of any judicial decision may be retrieved by entering FIND.

Consult the WESTLAW Directory (enter DB) for a complete, current listing of highlights databases.

Retrieving a Specific Case

The FIND command can be used to quickly retrieve a case whose citation is known. For example:

FI 616 A.2d 1336

Updating Case Law Research

There are a variety of citator services on WESTLAW for use in updating research.

Insta-Cite® may be used to verify citations, find parallel citations, ascertain the history of a case, and see whether it remains valid law. References are also provided to secondary sources, such as Corpus Juris Secundum®, that cite the case. To view the Insta-Cite history of a displayed case, simply enter the command IC. To view the Insta-Cite history of a selected case, enter a command in this form:

IC 574 A.2d 502

Shepard's® Citations provides a comprehensive list of cases and publications that have cited a particular case, with explanatory analysis to indicate how the citing cases have treated the case, e.g., "followed," "explained." To view the Shepard's Citations about a displayed case, enter the command SH. Add a case citation, if necessary, as in the prior Insta-Cite example.

For the latest citing references, not yet incorporated in Shepard's Citations, use Shepard's PreView® (SP command) and QuickCite™ (QC command), in the same way.

To see a complete list of publications covered by any of the citator services, enter its service abbreviation (IC, SH, SP or QC) followed by PUBS. To ascertain the scope of coverage for any of the services, enter the SCOPE command (SC) followed by the appropriate service abbreviation. For the complete list of commands available in a citator service, enter its service abbreviation (IC, SH, SP or QC) followed by CMDS.

Retrieving Statutes, Court Rules and Regulations

Annotated and unannotated versions of the New York statutes are searchable on WESTLAW (identifiers NY-ST-ANN and NY-ST), as are New York court rules (NY-RULES) and New York Administrative Code (NY-ADC).

The United States Code and United States Code - Annotated are searchable databases on WESTLAW (identifiers USC and USCA, respectively), as are federal court rules (US-RULES) and regulations (CFR).

In addition, the FIND command may be used to retrieve specific provisions by citation, obviating the need for database selection or search. To FIND a desired document, enter FI, followed by the citation of the desired document, using the full name of the publication, or one of the abbreviated styles recognized by WESTLAW.

If WESTLAW does not recognize the style you enter, you may enter one of the following, using US, NY, or any other state code in place of XX:

FI XX-ST	Displays templates for codified statutes
FI XX-LEGIS	Displays templates for legislation
FI XX-RULES	Displays templates for rules
FI XX-ORDERS	Displays templates for court orders

Alternatively, entering FI followed by the publication's full name or an accepted abbreviation will normally display templates, useful jump

WESTLAW ELECTRONIC RESEARCH GUIDE

possibilities, or helpful information necessary to complete the FIND process. For example:

FI USCA	Displays templates for United States Code - Annotated
FI FRAP	Displays templates for Federal Rules of Appellate Procedure
FI FRCP	Displays templates for Federal Rules of Civil Procedure
FI FRCRP	Displays templates for Federal Rules of Criminal Procedure
FI FRE	Displays templates for Federal Rules of Evidence
FI CFR	Displays templates for Code of Federal Regulations
FI FR	Displays templates for Federal Register

To view the complete list of FINDable documents and associated prescribed forms, enter FI PUBS.

Updating Research in re Statutes, Rules and Regulations

When viewing a statute, rule or regulation on WESTLAW after a search or FIND command, it is easy to update your research. A message will appear on the screen if relevant amendments, repeals or other new material are available through the UPDATE feature. Entering the UPDATE command will display such material.

Documents used to update New York statutes are also searchable in New York Legislative Service (NY-LEGIS). Those used to update rules are searchable in New York Orders (NY-ORDERS).

Documents used to update federal statutes, rules, and regulations are searchable in the United States Public Laws (US-PL), Federal Orders (US-ORDERS) and Federal Register (FR) databases, respectively.

When documents citing a statute, rule or regulation are of interest, Shepard's Citations on WESTLAW may be of assistance. That service covers federal constitutional provisions, statutes and administrative provisions, and corresponding materials from many states. The command SH PUBS displays a directory of publications which may be Shepardized on WESTLAW. Consult the WESTLAW manual for more information about citator services.

Using WESTLAW as a Citator

For research beyond the coverage of any citator service, go directly to the databases (cases, for example) containing citing documents and use standard WESTLAW search techniques to retrieve documents citing specific constitutional provisions, statutes, standard jury instructions or other authorities.

Fortunately, the specific portion of a citation is often reasonably distinctive, such as 22:636.1, 301.65, 401(k), 12-21-5, 12052. When it is, a search on that specific portion alone may retrieve applicable documents

WESTLAW ELECTRONIC RESEARCH GUIDE

without any substantial number of inapplicable ones (unless the number happens to be coincidentally popular in another context).

Similarly, if the citation involves more than one number, such as 42 U.S.C.A. §1201, a search containing both numbers (e.g., 42 +5 1201) is likely to produce mostly desired information, even though the component numbers are common.

If necessary, the search may be limited in several ways:

A. Switch from a general database to one containing mostly cases within the subject area of the cite being researched;

B. Use a connector (&, /S, /P, etc.) to narrow the search to documents including terms which are highly likely to accompany the correct citation in the context of the issue being researched;

C. Include other citation information in the query. Because of the variety of citation formats used in documents, this option should be used primarily where other options prove insufficient. Below are illustrative queries for any database containing New York cases:

> N.Y.Const.! Const.! Constitution /s 6 VI +3 3

will retrieve cases citing the New York State Constitution, Art. 6, §3; and

> "Criminal Procedure Law" CPL /s 30.30

will retrieve cases citing Criminal Procedure Law §30.30.

Alternative Retrieval Methods

WIN® (WESTLAW Is Natural™) allows you to frame your issue in plain English to retrieve documents:

> Does new trial motion extend (toll) the time for filing (taking) appeal?

Alternatively, retrieval may be focused by use of the Terms and Connectors method:

> TO(30) /P DI(NEW +1 TRIAL /P EXTEND!
> EXTENSION TOLL! /P APPEAL)

In databases with Key Numbers, either of the above examples will identify Appeal and Error ⟴345.1 as a Key Number collecting headnotes relevant to this issue if there are pertinent cases.

Since the Key Numbers are affixed to points of law by trained specialists based on conceptual understanding of the case, relevant cases that were not retrieved by either of the language-dependent methods will often be found at a Key Number.

WESTLAW ELECTRONIC RESEARCH GUIDE

Similarly, citations in retrieved documents (to cases, statutes, rules, etc.) may suggest additional, fruitful research using other WESTLAW databases (e.g., annotated statutes, rules) or services (e.g., citator services).

Key Number Search

Frequently, case law research rapidly converges on a few topics, headings and Key Numbers within West's Key Number System that are likely to contain relevant cases. These may be discovered from known, relevant reported cases from any jurisdiction; Library References in West publications; browsing in a digest; or browsing the Key Number System on WESTLAW using the JUMP feature or the KEY command.

Once discovered, topics, subheadings or Key Numbers are useful as search terms (in databases containing reported cases) alone or with other search terms, to focus the search within a narrow range of potentially relevant material.

For example, to retrieve cases with at least one headnote classified to Appeal and Error ⇨345.1, sign on to a caselaw database and enter

    30k345.1   [use with other search terms, if desired]

The topic name (Appeal and Error) is replaced by its numerical equivalent (30) and the ⇨ by the letter k. A list of topics and their numerical equivalents is in the WESTLAW Reference Manual and is displayed in WESTLAW when the KEY command is entered.

Using JUMP

WESTLAW's JUMP feature allows you to move from one document to another or from one part of a document to another, then easily return to your original place, without losing your original result. Opportunities to move in this manner are marked in the text with a JUMP symbol (▶). Whenever you see the JUMP symbol, you may move to the place designated by the adjacent reference by using the Tab, arrow keys or mouse click to position the cursor on the JUMP symbol, then pressing Enter or clicking again with the mouse.

Within the text of a court opinion, JUMP arrows are adjacent to case cites and federal statute cites, and adjacent to parenthesized numbers marking discussions corresponding to headnotes.

On a screen containing the text of a headnote, the JUMP arrows allow movement to the corresponding discussion in the text of the opinion,

    ▶ (3)

WESTLAW ELECTRONIC RESEARCH GUIDE

and allow browsing West's Key Number System beginning at various heading levels:

- ▶ 30   APPEAL AND ERROR
- ▶ 30VII   Transfer of Cause
- ▶ 30VII(A)   Time of Taking Proceedings
- ▶ 30k343   Commencement of Period of Limitation
- ▶ 30k345.1 k.   Motion for new trial.

To return from a JUMP, enter GB (except for JUMPs between a headnote and the corresponding discussion in opinion, for which there is a matching number in parenthesis in both headnote and opinion). Returns from successive JUMPs (e.g., from case to cited case to case cited by cited case) without intervening returns may be accomplished by repeated entry of GB or by using the MAP command.

General Information

The information provided above illustrates some of the ways WESTLAW can complement research using this publication. However, this brief overview illustrates only some of the power of WESTLAW. The full range of WESTLAW search techniques is available to support your research.

Please consult the WESTLAW Reference Manual for additional information or assistance or call West's Reference Attorneys at 1-800-REF-ATTY (1-800-733-2889).

For information about subscribing to WESTLAW, please call 1-800-328-9352.

*

SUMMARY OF CONTENTS

Volume 20

		Page
Chapter		
1.	Business Organizations: Corporations	2
2.	Non-corporate Entities: Limited Liability Companies and Partnerships	253
3.	Municipal Law	403
4.	Administrative Law	468
5.	Commercial Sales Contracts	594
6.	Buying and Selling a Small Business	670

Volume 21

7.	Consumer Law	2
8.	Enforcement of Money Judgments	181
9.	Bankruptcy	253
10.	Mechanic's Liens	541
11.	Mortgage Foreclosure	683
12.	Purchase and Sale of Real Estate	792

Volume 22

13.	Landlord–Tenant Law	2
14.	Eminent Domain	108
15.	Environmental Law	212
16.	New York Land Use Law	296
17.	New York Employment Law	467
18.	Civil Rights Law	609
19.	Immigration and Nationality Law—Permanent Residence Applications	733
20.	Adoptions	857

Volume 23

21.	Domestic Relations	2
22.	Guardianship	162
23.	Elder Law	329
24.	Estate Planning	448
25.	Probate and Estate Administration	545
26.	Personal Injury	638

SUMMARY OF CONTENTS

Chapter | **Page**
27. Products Liability — 722

Volume 24

28. Legal Malpractice — 2
29. Medical Malpractice — 92
30. Damages — 166
31. Insurance — 251
32. Workers' Compensation — 315
33. Local Criminal Court Practice — 382
34. Social Security Disability Cases — 452
35. Income Tax — 551
36. Alcoholic Beverage Control Law — 653
37. Civil Appellate Practice Before the Appellate Division and Other Intermediate Appellate Courts — 738

Volume 25

38. Criminal Appellate Practice Before the Appellate Division and Other Intermediate Appelllate Courts — 2
39. Civil and Criminal Appeals to the Court of Appeals — 145

Table of Jury Instructions — 235
Table of Forms — 236
Table of Statutes — iii
Table of Rules — iii
Table of Cases — iii
Index — iii

XVI

TABLE OF CONTENTS

Volume 20

CHAPTER 1. BUSINESS ORGANIZATIONS: CORPORATIONS

Sec.
1.1 Scope Note.
1.2 Strategy.
1.3 Strategy Checklist.
1.4 Overview.
1.5 Definitions.
1.6 Formation of Corporations.
1.7 ____ Certificates; Notices.
1.8 ____ Corporate Seal.
1.9 ____ Corporate Purposes.
1.10 ____ ____ Upholding and Disregarding the Corporate Entity.
1.11 ____ ____ General Powers.
1.12 ____ ____ Defense of *Ultra Vires*.
1.13 ____ Corporate Name.
1.14 ____ ____ Reservation of Name.
1.15 ____ Service of Process.
1.16 ____ ____ Records and Certificates of Department of State.
1.17 ____ ____ Statutory Designation of Secretary of State as Agent for Service of Process.
1.18 ____ ____ Registered Agent for Service of Process.
1.19 ____ ____ Upon Unauthorized Foreign Corporation.
1.20 ____ Incorporators and Promoters.
1.21 ____ Certificate of Incorporation.
1.22 ____ Bylaws.
1.23 ____ Organization Meeting; Biennial Statement; Franchise Tax.
1.24 ____ Formation of Corporations Summary.
1.25 ____ Formation of Corporations Checklist.
1.26 Capital Structure.
1.27 ____ Authorized Shares.
1.28 ____ Preferred Shares in Series.
1.29 ____ Subscription for Shares.
1.30 ____ Consideration and Payment for Shares.
1.31 ____ Rights to Purchase Shares.
1.32 ____ Stated Capital.
1.33 ____ Corporate Bonds; Convertible Securities.
1.34 ____ Federal Income Taxation Aspects.
1.35 ____ Capital Structure Summary.
1.36 ____ Capital Structure Checklist.
1.37 Distributions.
1.38 ____ Dividends; Share Distributions and Changes.
1.39 ____ Purchase or Redemption of Shares.

XVII

TABLE OF CONTENTS

Sec.
1.40 ——— Federal Income Tax Aspects.
1.41 ——— Distributions Summary.
1.42 ——— Distributions Checklist.
1.43 Shareholders' Meetings and Agreements—Generally.
1.44 ——— Notice Requirements.
1.45 ——— Voting.
1.46 ——— Quorum Requirements.
1.47 ——— Agreements; Voting Trusts.
1.48 ——— Action Without a Meeting.
1.49 Shareholders' Meetings and Agreements Summary.
1.50 Shareholders' Meetings and Agreements Checklist.
1.51 Shareholders' Rights.
1.52 ——— Preemptive Rights.
1.53 ——— Inspection of Books and Records.
1.54 ——— Shareholders' Rights Summary.
1.55 ——— Shareholders' Rights Checklist.
1.56 Shareholders' Liabilities.
1.57 ——— Shareholders' Liabilities Summary.
1.58 ——— Shareholders' Liabilities Checklist.
1.59 Directors.
1.60 ——— Vacancies; New Directorships.
1.61 ——— Removal.
1.62 ——— Meetings.
1.63 ——— ——— Quorum and Voting Requirements.
1.64 ——— Executive Committee; Other Committees.
1.65 ——— Fiduciary Duties.
1.66 ——— Liabilities.
1.67 ——— Directors Summary.
1.68 ——— Directors Checklist.
1.69 Officers.
1.70 ——— Officers Summary.
1.71 ——— Officers Checklist.
1.72 Amendment of Certificate of Incorporation.
1.73 ——— Procedure.
1.74 ——— Class Vote.
1.75 ——— Certificate of Amendment.
1.76 ——— Certificate of Change.
1.77 ——— Restated Certificate of Incorporation.
1.78 ——— Reorganization Under Act of Congress.
1.79 Amendment of Certificate of Incorporation Summary.
1.80 Amendment of Certificate of Incorporation Checklist.
1.81 Business Combinations.
1.82 ——— Mergers and Consolidations.
1.83 ——— ——— Procedures.
1.84 ——— ——— Effect.
1.85 ——— Sale, Lease, Exchange, or Other Disposition of Assets.
1.86 ——— ——— Mortgage or Security Interest in Assets.
1.87 ——— ——— Guarantee Authorized by Shareholders.
1.88 ——— Share Exchanges.
1.89 ——— Takeover Bids.

TABLE OF CONTENTS

Sec.	
1.90	―――― Right of Shareholder to Receive Payment for Shares.
1.91	―――― Federal Income Taxation Aspects.
1.92	Business Combinations Summary.
1.93	Business Combinations Checklist.
1.94	Dissolution.
1.95	―――― Non-judicial Dissolution.
1.96	―――― ―――― Authorization.
1.97	―――― ―――― Certificate of Dissolution.
1.98	―――― ―――― Notice to Creditors.
1.99	―――― Judicial Dissolution.
1.100	―――― ―――― Attorney General's Action.
1.101	―――― ―――― Directors' Petition.
1.102	―――― ―――― Shareholders' Petition.
1.103	―――― ―――― Petition Upon Deadlock Among Directors or Shareholders and in Other Circumstances.
1.104	―――― ―――― Procedures.
1.105	―――― ―――― Preservation of Assets; Appointment of Receiver.
1.106	―――― ―――― Certain Transfers and Judgments Void; Injunction.
1.107	―――― Liquidation Distributions.
1.108	―――― ―――― Federal Income Tax Aspects.
1.109	―――― Dissolution Summary.
1.110	―――― Dissolution Checklist.
1.111	Receivership.
1.112	Receivership—Summary.
1.113	―――― Checklist.
1.114	Foreign Corporations.
1.115	―――― Authorization to Do Business in New York.
1.116	―――― Application for Authority.
1.117	―――― ―――― Effect of Filing.
1.118	―――― Surrender of Authority.
1.119	―――― Termination of Existence.
1.120	Foreign Corporations Summary.
1.121	Foreign Corporations Checklist.
1.122	Professional Service Corporations.
1.123	Professional Service Corporations Summary.
1.124	Professional Service Corporations Checklist.
1.125	Foreign Professional Service Corporations.
1.126	Foreign Professional Service Corporations Summary.
1.127	Foreign Professional Service Corporations Checklist.
1.128	Transactional Checklist—Generally.
1.129	―――― Formation ("Birth").
1.130	―――― Operation ("Growth").
1.131	―――― Business Combinations ("Marriage").
1.132	―――― Spin-offs and Split-offs ("Children" and "Divorce").
1.133	―――― Repurchase of Shares ("Redemption").
1.134	―――― Dissolution; Liquidation ("Death").
1.135	Procedural Checklist—Generally.
1.136	―――― Notices.
1.137	―――― Reservation of Corporate Name.
1.138	―――― ―――― Foreign Corporations.

TABLE OF CONTENTS

Sec.

1.139 ____ Mandatory and Permissive Provisions in Certificate of Incorporation.
1.140 ____ Incorporation.
1.141 ____ Filing Certificate of Incorporation.
1.142 ____ Bylaws.
1.143 ____ Organization Meetings.
1.144 ____ Share Certificate.
1.145 ____ Shareholder Approval Requirements.
1.146 ____ Shareholder's Right to Receive Payment for Shares.
1.147 ____ Close Corporations.
1.148 ____ Foreign Corporations.
1.149 Drafting Checklist.
1.150 Form—Application to Reserve Corporate Name. 💾
1.151 ____ Certificate of Incorporation. 💾
1.152 ____ Bylaws. 💾
1.153 ____ Subscription Agreement. 💾
1.154 ____ Certificate of Amendment. 💾
1.155 ____ Certificate of Dissolution. 💾

CHAPTER 2. NON-CORPORATE ENTITIES: LIMITED LIABILTY COMPANIES AND PARTNERSHIPS

2.1 Scope Note.
2.2 Strategy—Choice of Entity.
2.3 Tax Classification.
2.4 ____ Eagerly–Awaited Simplification.
2.5 ____ Former Corporate Characteristics Test.
2.6 ____ ____ Limited Liability.
2.7 ____ ____ Continuity of Life.
2.8 ____ ____ Free Transferability of Interests.
2.9 ____ ____ Centralized Management.
2.10 Partnership vs. LLC.
2.11 ____ Tax Implications.
2.12 ____ Liability.
2.13 ____ Flexibility.
2.14 Limited Liability Companies.
2.15 ____ Governing Law.
2.16 ____ Formation.
2.17 ____ ____ Articles of Organization.
2.18 ____ ____ Publication.
2.19 ____ ____ Operating Agreement.
2.20 ____ ____ Other Issues.
2.21 ____ Members.
2.22 ____ ____ Admission of New Members.
2.23 ____ ____ Liability.
2.24 ____ ____ One-member LLCs.
2.25 ____ Management.
2.26 ____ ____ Members vs. Managers.
2.27 ____ ____ Voting: Members.
2.28 ____ ____ Voting: Managers.

TABLE OF CONTENTS

Sec.		
2.29	__ __	Non-waivable Requirements.
2.30	__ __	Delegation of Responsibility.
2.31	__ __	Standard of Care.
2.32	__ __	Agency Authority.
2.33	__	Assignment of Interests.
2.34	__ __	Default Rules.
2.35	__ __	Vote Required to Admit Assignee as Member.
2.36	__	Dissolution.
2.37	__ __	Events.
2.38	__ __	Continuation of Business after Dissolution Event.
2.39	__ __	Winding Up.
2.40	__	Conversions/Mergers.
2.41	__ __	Procedures.
2.42	__ __	Dissenters' Rights.
2.43	__	PLLCs.
2.44		General Partnerships.
2.45	__	Governing Law.
2.46	__	Formation.
2.47	__ __	Agreement.
2.48	__ __	Business Certificate.
2.49	__ __	Publication.
2.50	__ __	Other Issues.
2.51	__	Partners.
2.52	__ __	Admission of New Partners.
2.53	__ __	Liability.
2.54	__ __	Contribution Issues.
2.55	__	Management.
2.56	__ __	Voting.
2.57	__ __	Non-waivable Requirements.
2.58	__ __	Delegation of Responsibility.
2.59	__ __	Standard of Care.
2.60	__ __	Agency Authority.
2.61	__	Assignment of Interests.
2.62	__ __	Default Rules.
2.63	__ __	Vote Required to Admit New Partner.
2.64	__	Dissolution.
2.65	__ __	Events.
2.66	__ __	Continuation of Business after Dissolution Event.
2.67	__ __	Winding Up.
2.68	__	Conversions/Mergers.
2.69	__ __	Procedures.
2.70	__ __	Dissenters' Rights.
2.71	__	Professional Organizations.
2.72		Limited Liability Partnerships.
2.73	__	Governing Law.
2.74	__	Comparison with General Partnerships.
2.75	__	Formation/Registration.
2.76	__	Other Issues.
2.77		Limited Partnerships.
2.78	__	Governing Law.

TABLE OF CONTENTS

Sec.
2.79 ____ Formation.
2.80 ____ ____ Certificate of Limited Partnership.
2.81 ____ ____ Publication.
2.82 ____ ____ Agreement.
2.83 ____ ____ Other Issues.
2.84 ____ Partners.
2.85 ____ ____ Admission of New Partners.
2.86 ____ ____ Liability.
2.87 ____ Contribution Issues.
2.88 ____ Management.
2.89 ____ ____ Voting: General Partners.
2.90 ____ ____ Voting: Limited Partners.
2.91 ____ ____ Delegation of Responsibility.
2.92 ____ ____ Standard of Care.
2.93 ____ ____ Agency Authority.
2.94 ____ Assignment of Interests.
2.95 ____ ____ Default Rules.
2.96 ____ ____ Vote Required to Admit New Partner.
2.97 ____ Dissolution.
2.98 ____ ____ Events.
2.99 ____ ____ Continuation of Business after Dissolution Event.
2.100 ____ ____ Winding Up.
2.101 ____ Conversions/Mergers.
2.102 ____ ____ Procedures.
2.103 ____ ____ Dissenters' Rights.
2.104 ____ Professional Organizations.
2.105 Due Diligence Issues.
2.106 Securities Laws Issues.
2.107 Summary.
2.108 Chart Comparing New York Entities.
2.109 Drafting Checklist.
2.110 Forms.
2.111 ____ LLC Articles of Organization.
2.112 ____ Operating Agreement: Member–Managed LLC.
2.113 ____ Registration as LLP.
2.114 ____ Certificate of Limited Partnership.
2.115 ____ Limited Partnership Agreement.

CHAPTER 3. MUNICIPAL LAW

3.1 Scope Note.
3.2 Strategy.
3.3 Municipal Corporations.
3.4 ____ Creation.
3.5 ____ Consolidation, Annexation and Dissolution.
3.6 ____ ____ Annexation Checklist.
3.7 Powers of Municipal Corporations.
3.8 ____ Governmental v. Proprietary Powers.
3.9 ____ Police Powers.
3.10 Legislative Enactments.

TABLE OF CONTENTS

Sec.
3.11 ____ Resolutions.
3.12 ____ Ordinances.
3.13 ____ Rules and Regulations.
3.14 ____ Local Laws.
3.15 ____ Referendum Requirements.
3.16 Acquisition and Disposition of Property.
3.17 Officers and Employees.
3.18 ____ Qualifications.
3.19 ____ Terms.
3.20 ____ Removal.
3.21 ____ Collective Bargaining.
3.22 ____ Conflicts of Interest.
3.23 ____ ____ Checklist.
3.24 Contracts.
3.25 ____ Competitive Bidding.
3.26 Municipal Finance.
3.27 ____ Municipal Borrowing.
3.28 Public Meetings.
3.29 Access to Records.
3.30 Tort Claims Against Municipalities.
3.31 ____ Checklist.
3.32 Challenges to Governmental Determinations.
3.33 Special Purpose Units of Government.
3.34 ____ Industrial Development Agencies.
3.35 ____ Public Authorities.
3.36 Forms.
3.37 ____ Notice of Claim.
3.38 ____ Verified Complaint in Tort Action.

CHAPTER 4. ADMINISTRATIVE LAW

4.1 Scope Note.
4.2 Strategy.
4.3 ____ Checklist.
4.4 Procedural Due Process.
4.5 ____ Individualized State Action.
4.6 ____ Protected Interests.
4.7 ____ The Process Due.
4.8 ____ Summary.
4.9 ____ Checklist.
4.10 Adjudicatory Proceedings.
4.11 ____ Definition of an Adjudicatory Proceeding.
4.12 ____ Notice.
4.13 ____ Discovery.
4.14 ____ Right to Counsel.
4.15 ____ Evidence.
4.16 ____ Cross-Examination and Witness Attendance.
4.17 ____ Official Notice.
4.18 ____ Statement of Decision and Decisional Record.
4.19 ____ Burden of Proof.

TABLE OF CONTENTS

Sec.	
4.20	____ Intervention.
4.21	____ Unreasonable Agency Delay.
4.22	____ Agency Duty to Decide Consistently.
4.23	____ Intra-agency Review.
4.24	____ Checking Agency Bias.
4.25	____ *Res Judicata* and Collateral Estoppel Effect.
4.26	____ Special Rules Applicable to Licensing Matters.
4.27	____ Special Issues in Handling Licensing Matters.
4.28	____ ____ Basic License Information.
4.29	____ ____ The Role of SAPA and SEQRA in the Licensing Process.
4.30	____ ____ Accuracy and Completeness in Applications.
4.31	____ ____ Opportunities to Expedite the Process.
4.32	____ ____ Opportunities for Variances from Standard Approaches.
4.33	____ ____ Renewal, Suspension and Revocation Issues.
4.34	____ Special Issues in Handling Enforcement Matters.
4.35	____ ____ Strategies to Minimize Violations.
4.36	____ ____ Agency Fact–Finding in the Pre-enforcement Phase.
4.37	____ ____ Agency Enforcement Options.
4.38	____ ____ The Settlement Process.
4.39	____ ____ The Hearing Process.
4.40	____ ____ Post–Hearing Issues.
4.41	____ Summary.
4.42	____ Checklist.
4.43	Administrative Rulemaking.
4.44	____ Rulemaking Compared With Other Agency Action.
4.45	____ Rulemaking Notice.
4.46	____ Comments and Agency Assessment of Comments.
4.47	____ Agency Duty to Reveal Underlying Information.
4.48	____ Notice of Adoption and Effective Date of Rules.
4.49	____ Ancillary Documentation and the Role of GORR.
4.50	____ Rule Filing and Publication.
4.51	____ Declaratory Rulings Regarding Rules.
4.52	____ Overlapping State and Federal Rules.
4.53	____ Special Strategic Considerations in Handling Administrative Rulemaking Matters.
4.54	____ ____ Basic Sources of Information on Rulemaking.
4.55	____ ____ Participating in the Rulemaking Process.
4.56	____ ____ Special Issues in Negotiated Rulemakings.
4.57	____ ____ Special Issues in Emergency Rulemakings.
4.58	____ ____ Agency Guidance Documents.
4.59	____ Summary.
4.60	____ Checklist.
4.61	Agency Information–Gathering.
4.62	____ Administrative Searches.
4.63	____ Administrative Subpoenas.
4.64	____ Reporting and Recordkeeping Requirements.
4.65	____ Summary.
4.66	____ Checklist.
4.67	Judicial Review.
4.68	____ Delegation of Authority to Agencies.

TABLE OF CONTENTS

Sec.
4.69 ____ Standing to Seek Judicial Review.
4.70 ____ Ripeness.
4.71 ____ Final Order and Relief in the Nature of Prohibition.
4.72 ____ Exhaustion of Administrative Remedies.
4.73 ____ Primary Jurisdiction.
4.74 ____ Statutory Preclusion of Judicial Review.
4.75 ____ Article 78 and the Consolidation of the Common Law Prerogative Writs.
4.76 ____ Standards of Review.
4.77 ____ ____ Review of Agency Determinations of Law.
4.78 ____ ____ Review of Agency Determinations of Fact Under the Substantial Evidence Test.
4.79 ____ ____ Review of Agency Determinations of Fact Under the Arbitrary and Capricious Test.
4.80 ____ ____ Review of Administrative Rules.
4.81 ____ ____ Review of Administrative Discretion.
4.82 ____ Statutes of Limitation Applicable to Judicial Review of Agency Action.
4.83 ____ Venue in Article 78 Proceedings.
4.84 ____ Subject Matter Jurisdiction in Article 78 Proceedings.
4.85 ____ Summary.
4.86 ____ Checklist.
4.87 Forms.
4.88 ____ Notice of Appearance in Licensing or Permitting Matter. 💾
4.89 ____ Notice for Discovery and Inspection in an Administrative Proceeding. 💾
4.90 ____ Notice of Deposition in an Administrative Proceeding. 💾
4.91 ____ Notice to Permit Entry Upon Real Property. 💾

CHAPTER 5. COMMERCIAL SALES CONTRACTS

5.1 Scope Note.
5.2 Strategy.
5.3 Transactional Checklist—Breach of Contract.
5.4 Defining a Contract.
5.5 Governing Law.
5.6 ____ Freedom to Contract—Generally.
5.7 ____ ____ Presumption of Legality.
5.8 ____ ____ ____ Burden of Proof.
5.9 ____ ____ ____ Determining the Contract's Validity.
5.10 ____ ____ ____ Not All Illegal Contracts Are Unenforceable.
5.11 ____ Public Policy Issues.
5.12 ____ Unconscionability.
5.13 ____ ____ Elements.
5.14 ____ ____ Codification in UCC.
5.15 ____ Duty of Good Faith—Generally.
5.16 ____ ____ Codification in UCC.
5.17 The Written Contract—Statute of Frauds.
5.18 ____ ____ General Rules.
5.19 ____ ____ Formal Requirements.

XXV

TABLE OF CONTENTS

Sec.
5.20 ___ ___ Nature of the Writing.
5.21 ___ Parol or Extrinsic Evidence.
5.22 ___ Offer.
5.23 ___ Acceptance.
5.24 ___ ___ Additional Terms.
5.25 ___ Indefiniteness.
5.26 ___ Use of Open Terms.
5.27 Warranties.
5.28 ___ Warranty of Title Against Infringement.
5.29 ___ Express Warranty.
5.30 ___ Implied Warranty of Merchantability.
5.31 ___ Implied Warranty of Fitness for a Particular Purpose.
5.32 Assumption of the Risk of Loss.
5.33 ___ In the Absence of Breach.
5.34 ___ In the Event of a Breach.
5.35 Performance.
5.36 ___ Buyer's Response to Tender of Delivery.
5.37 ___ ___ Acceptance.
5.38 ___ ___ Rejection.
5.39 ___ ___ Revocation of Acceptance.
5.40 Breach of Contract.
5.41 ___ Seller's Remedies.
5.42 ___ ___ Action for the Price.
5.43 ___ ___ Withholding the Goods and Stopping Delivery.
5.44 ___ ___ Recovery of Goods Delivered.
5.45 ___ ___ Resale.
5.46 ___ ___ Damages for Non-acceptance or Repudiation.
5.47 ___ Buyer's Remedies.
5.48 ___ ___ Cover.
5.49 ___ ___ Damages for Non-delivery.
5.50 ___ ___ Damages for Breach Regarding Accepted Goods.
5.51 ___ ___ Specific Performance or Replevin.
5.52 ___ Liquidated Damages.
5.53 ___ Mitigation of Damages.
5.54 Third-Party Interests.
5.55 ___ Subsequent Buyers.
5.56 ___ Other Creditors.
5.57 Drafting Checklists—Order of Goods for Resale by Buyer.
5.58 ___ Verified Complaint On Account Stated for Goods, Services and Wares Delivered.
5.59 ___ Plaintiff's Notice of Motion for Summary Judgment in Contract Action.
5.60 ___ Affidavit of Officer of Plaintiff Company in Support of Summary Judgment Motion in Contract Action.
5.61 ___ Notice of Petition for Order Staying Arbitration in Dispute Over Contract for Sale of Goods.
5.62 ___ Petition for Order Staying Arbitration in Dispute Over Contract for Sale of Goods.
5.63 ___ Affidavit in Opposition to Petition for Order Staying Arbitration in Dispute Over Contract for Sale of Goods.

TABLE OF CONTENTS

Sec.
- 5.64 ____ Answer to Petition for Order Staying Arbitration in Dispute Over Contract for Sale of Goods.
- 5.65 Forms—Order of Goods for Resale by Buyer. 💾
- 5.66 ____ Verified Complaint On Account Stated for Goods, Services and Wares Delivered. 💾
- 5.67 ____ Plaintiff's Notice of Motion for Summary Judgment in Contract Action. 💾
- 5.68 ____ Affidavit of Vice President of Plaintiff Purchaser in Support of Summary Judgment Motion in Contract Action. 💾
- 5.69 ____ Notice of Petition for Order Staying Arbitration in Dispute Over Contract for Sale of Goods. 💾
- 5.70 ____ Petition for Order Staying Arbitration in Dispute Over Contract for Sale of Goods. 💾
- 5.71 ____ Affidavit in Opposition to Petition for Order Staying Arbitration in Dispute Over Contract for Sale of Goods. 💾
- 5.72 ____ Answer to Petition for Order Staying Arbitration in Dispute Over Contract for Sale of Goods. 💾

CHAPTER 6. BUYING AND SELLING A SMALL BUSINESS

- 6.1 Scope Note.
- 6.2 Strategy: Representing the Buyer—Introduction.
- 6.3 ____ The Attorney's Role.
- 6.4 ____ Different Considerations Depending on the Type of Transaction.
- 6.5 ____ General Stages of the Transaction.
- 6.6 Representing the Buyer—Investigating the Business.
- 6.7 ____ Nature and Operation of Business.
- 6.8 ____ Geographic Location.
- 6.9 ____ The Negotiating Team.
- 6.10 ____ The Letter of Intent.
- 6.11 ____ Confidentiality Agreements.
- 6.12 ____ Drafting the Agreement.
- 6.13 Due Diligence Investigation.
- 6.14 ____ Legal Issues.
- 6.15 ____ ____ Organizational Documents.
- 6.16 ____ ____ Ownership Documents.
- 6.17 ____ ____ Existing Contracts.
- 6.18 ____ ____ Liens and Security Interests.
- 6.19 ____ ____ Corporate and Trade Names.
- 6.20 ____ ____ Real Estate.
- 6.21 ____ ____ Compliance With Law.
- 6.22 ____ ____ Litigation Investigation.
- 6.23 ____ Financial Issues—General Considerations.
- 6.24 ____ ____ Seller's Records From the Buyer's Position.
- 6.25 ____ ____ Buyer's Records From the Seller's Position.
- 6.26 ____ ____ Public Records.
- 6.27 ____ ____ Financial Statements.
- 6.28 ____ ____ The Need for Other Professionals.
- 6.29 ____ ____ Valuation of the Business.

TABLE OF CONTENTS

Sec.
6.30 —— —— Tax Returns.
6.31 Tax Issues for Buyer.
6.32 —— Asset Purchase.
6.33 —— —— Allocation of Purchase Price.
6.34 —— —— Depreciation of Assets.
6.35 —— —— Land.
6.36 —— —— Good Will and Covenants Not to Compete.
6.37 —— —— Inventory.
6.38 —— —— Cash.
6.39 —— —— Supplies.
6.40 —— —— Patents, Franchises, Trademarks, Trade Names.
6.41 —— Stock Purchase.
6.42 —— —— Basis of Stock.
6.43 —— —— Basis of Corporate Assets.
6.44 —— —— Election to Treat Stock Purchase as Asset Purchase.
6.45 —— Mergers, Consolidations, and Exchanges.
6.46 Structuring the Buyer's Transaction.
6.47 —— Type of Payment.
6.48 —— Assumption of Seller's Liabilities.
6.49 —— Security to Seller.
6.50 —— Notes.
6.51 —— Escrow Arrangements and Agreements.
6.52 Drafting the Buyer's Asset Purchase Agreement.
6.53 —— Identification of the Parties.
6.54 —— Recitals.
6.55 —— Assets and Property to Be Conveyed.
6.56 —— Retained Assets of Seller.
6.57 —— Purchase Price and Method of Payment.
6.58 —— Closing.
6.59 —— Representations, Warranties and Covenants of Seller.
6.60 —— Representations, Warranties and Covenants of Buyer.
6.61 —— Conduct of Business Prior to Closing.
6.62 —— Indemnifications.
6.63 —— Corporate or Other Name.
6.64 —— —— Notice to Customers and Suppliers.
6.65 —— —— UCC Bulk Sale Notices or Escrow Agreement in Lieu of UCC Bulk Sale Notice.
6.66 —— —— NYS Sales Tax and Bulk Sale Notification.
6.67 —— —— Covenant Not to Compete.
6.68 —— Matters Respecting Real Property.
6.69 —— Conditions Precedent to Purchaser's Obligations.
6.70 —— Conditions Precedent to Seller's Obligations.
6.71 —— Nature and Survival of Representations and Warranties.
6.72 —— Non-disclosure Provisions.
6.73 —— Miscellaneous Agreements Between Buyer and Seller.
6.74 —— Documents to Be Delivered to Purchaser at Closing.
6.75 —— Documents to Be Delivered to Seller at Closing.
6.76 —— Notices, Severability and Other General Provisions.
6.77 —— Documents to Be Prepared or Reviewed Prior to Closing.
6.78 Drafting the Buyer's Stock Purchase Agreement.

TABLE OF CONTENTS

Sec.	
6.79	____ Identification of the Parties.
6.80	____ Recitals.
6.81	____ Sale of Shares.
6.82	____ Purchase Price and Method of Payment.
6.83	____ Closing.
6.84	____ Representations, Warranties and Covenants of Seller.
6.85	____ Representations, Warranties and Covenants of Buyer.
6.86	____ Conduct of Business Prior to Closing.
6.87	____ Indemnifications.
6.88	____ Covenant Not to Compete.
6.89	____ Matters Respecting Real Property.
6.90	____ Nondisclosure Provisions.
6.91	____ Conditions Precedent to Purchaser's Obligations.
6.92	____ Conditions Precedent to Seller's Obligations.
6.93	____ Nature and Survival of Representations and Warranties.
6.94	____ Documents to Be Delivered to Purchaser at Closing.
6.95	____ Documents to Be Delivered to Seller at Closing.
6.96	____ Notices, Severability and Other General Provisions.
6.97	____ Documents to Be Prepared or Reviewed Prior to Closing.
6.98	Post–Contract and Pre-closing.
6.99	____ Bulk Sales Act—UCC Article 6.
6.100	____ NYS Sales Tax and Bulk Sale Notification.
6.101	____ Plant Closing Notice.
6.102	____ Environmental Searches and Testing.
6.103	____ Certificate of Good Standing.
6.104	____ Real Property Transfer Gains Tax.
6.105	Closing and Post–Closing.
6.106	Strategy: Representing the Seller—Introduction.
6.107	____ The Attorney's Role.
6.108	____ Different Considerations Depending on the Type of Transaction.
6.109	____ General Stages of the Transaction.
6.110	Representing the Seller—General Investigation.
6.111	____ Investigating the Buyer.
6.112	____ The Negotiating Team.
6.113	____ The Letter of Intent.
6.114	____ Confidentiality Agreements.
6.115	____ Drafting the Agreement.
6.116	Tax Issues for the Seller—General Overview.
6.117	____ Asset Sale.
6.118	____ ____ Allocation of Purchase Price.
6.119	____ ____ Depreciation Recapture.
6.120	____ ____ Capital Gains or Losses.
6.121	____ ____ Ordinary Income.
6.122	____ ____ Income to Corporation.
6.123	____ ____ Real Property Transfer Gains Tax.
6.124	____ ____ Covenant Not to Compete and Consulting Agreements.
6.125	____ Stock Sale—General Advantages.
6.126	____ ____ Capital Gain or Loss.
6.127	____ ____ No Concern for Income to a Corporate Entity.

XXIX

TABLE OF CONTENTS

Sec.

6.128	___ ___	Real Property Transfer Gains Tax.
6.129	___ ___	Consulting and Non-compete Agreements.
6.130	___ ___	I.R.C. § 1244 Stock and Qualified Small Business Stock.
6.131	___ ___	Stock Transfer Tax.
6.132	___ ___	Collapsible Corporation.
6.133	___ ___	Mergers, Consolidations and Exchanges.
6.134		Structuring the Seller's Transaction—General Overview.
6.135	___	Purchase Price and Payment Terms.
6.136	___	Security to Seller.
6.137	___	Notes.
6.138	___	Escrow Arrangements.
6.139		Drafting the Seller's Asset Sale Agreement.
6.140	___	Identification of the Parties.
6.141	___	Recitals.
6.142	___	Assets and Property to Be Conveyed.
6.143	___	Assets Retained by Seller.
6.144	___	Sale Price and Method of Payment.
6.145	___	Closing.
6.146	___	Representations, Warranties and Covenants of Buyer.
6.147	___	Representations, Warranties and Covenants of Seller.
6.148	___	Conduct of Business Prior to Closing.
6.149	___	Indemnifications.
6.150	___	Matters Respecting Real Property.
6.151	___	Notice to Customers and Suppliers.
6.152	___	Covenant Not to Compete and Consulting Agreements.
6.153	___	UCC Bulk Sale Notices or Escrow Agreements in Lieu of UCC Bulk Sale Notice.
6.154	___	New York State Sales Tax and Bulk Sale Notification.
6.155	___	Nature and Survival of Representations and Warranties.
6.156	___	Non-disclosure Provisions.
6.157	___	Conditions Precedent to Seller's Obligations.
6.158	___	Conditions Precedent to Buyer's Obligations.
6.159	___	Documents to Be Delivered to Seller at Closing.
6.160	___	Documents to Be Delivered to Buyer at Closing.
6.161	___	Notices, Severability and Other General Provisions.
6.162	___	Documents to Be Prepared or Reviewed Prior to Closing.
6.163		Drafting the Seller's Stock Sale Agreement.
6.164	___	Identification of the Parties.
6.165	___	Recitals.
6.166	___	Sale of Shares.
6.167	___	Sale Price and Method of Payment.
6.168	___	Closing.
6.169	___	Representations, Warranties and Covenants of Buyer.
6.170	___	Representations, Warranties and Covenants of Seller.
6.171	___	Conduct of Business Prior to Closing.
6.172	___	Indemnifications.
6.173	___	Matters Respecting Real Property.
6.174	___	Non-disclosure Provisions.
6.175	___	Covenants Not to Compete and Consulting Agreements.
6.176	___	Notice to Customers and Suppliers.

TABLE OF CONTENTS

Sec.
6.177 ____ Conditions Precedent to Seller's Obligations.
6.178 ____ Conditions Precedent to Buyer's Obligations.
6.179 ____ Nature and Survival of Representations and Warranties.
6.180 ____ Documents to Be Delivered to Seller at Closing.
6.181 ____ Documents to Be Delivered to Buyer at Closing.
6.182 ____ Notices, Severability and Other General Provisions.
6.183 ____ Documents to Be Prepared or Reviewed Prior to Closing.
6.184 Post–contract and Pre-closing.
6.185 Closing and Post–Closing.
6.186 Forms.
6.187 ____ Asset Purchase and Sale Agreement. 💾
6.188 ____ Agreement of Purchase and Sale of Stock. 💾

Volume 21

CHAPTER 7. CONSUMER LAW

7.1 Scope Note.
7.2 Strategy—Generally.
7.3 ____ Automobile Sales Cases.
7.4 ____ Automobile Leasing Cases.
7.5 ____ Credit Reporting.
7.6 ____ Debt Collection.
7.7 ____ Deceptive Business Practices.
7.8 ____ Information to Obtain at Outset of Case.
7.9 Lemon Laws.
7.10 ____ New Cars.
7.11 ____ Used Cars.
7.12 ____ Arbitration or Plenary Action?
7.13 ____ Arbitration Procedure.
7.14 ____ ____ Preparation for the Hearing.
7.15 ____ ____ The Hearing.
7.16 ____ ____ Appeals and Confirmation Proceedings.
7.17 ____ ____ Scope of Review.
7.18 ____ Source Materials.
7.19 Automobile Leasing—Overview.
7.20 ____ Statutory Protection Overview.
7.21 ____ The Consumer Leasing Act.
7.22 ____ The Motor Vehicle Retail Leasing Act.
7.23 Motor Vehicle Installment Sales.
7.24 Repossession—Overview.
7.25 ____ Prevention and Avoidance.
7.26 ____ Defending Deficiency Claims.
7.27 Automobile Repairs.
7.28 Automobile Repair Shop Liens—Overview.
7.29 ____ Statutory Challenges.
7.30 Credit Reporting—Overview.
7.31 ____ Consumer Rights.
7.32 ____ Non-litigation Strategies.
7.33 ____ Litigating Credit Reporting Matters.

TABLE OF CONTENTS

Sec.
- 7.34 Debt Collection—History and Overview.
- 7.35 ____ Claims for Intentional Infliction of Emotional Distress.
- 7.36 ____ Statutory Overview.
- 7.37 ____ FDCPA—Contacts With Third Parties.
- 7.38 ____ ____ Contacts With a Debtor.
- 7.39 ____ ____ Prohibited Tactics.
- 7.40 ____ ____ Improper Omissions and Disclosures.
- 7.41 ____ ____ Harassment or Abuse.
- 7.42 ____ ____ Improper Demands.
- 7.43 ____ ____ Judicial Enforcement.
- 7.44 ____ State Law.
- 7.45 Deceptive Practices Act—Overview.
- 7.46 ____ Elements of the Claim.
- 7.47 ____ Types of Recovery Available.
- 7.48 Drafting Checklist—List of Essential Allegations.
- 7.49 Forms—Lemon Law Document Request Pursuant to 13 NYCRR § 300.9(a). 💾
- 7.50 ____ Notice of Petition to Vacate Lemon Law Arbitration Award Pursuant to CPLR Article 75. 💾
- 7.51 ____ Petition to Vacate Lemon Law Arbitration Award Pursuant to CPLR Article 75. 💾
- 7.52 ____ Complaint for Fraud, Breach of Warranties, Deceptive Business Practices, Used Car Lemon Law, Rescission and Revocation of Acceptance for Fraudulent Leasing Practices. 💾
- 7.53 ____ Answer and Third-party Complaint Alleging Fraud, Deceptive Practices, Breach of Warranty, and Federal Odometer Law Claims in Fraudulent Automobile Lease Case. 💾
- 7.54 ____ Answer to Complaint by Automobile Leasing Company for Deficiency Following Repossession, Alleging Commercially Unreasonable Resale and Deceptive Business Practices. 💾
- 7.55 ____ Affirmation in Opposition to Lessor's Motion for Summary Judgment and in Support of Lessee's Cross-motion for Summary Judgment Alleging Commercially Unreasonable Resale. 💾
- 7.56 ____ Notice of Rescission And/or Revocation of Acceptance and Demand for Restitution Pursuant to UCC 2–601 and 2–608. 💾
- 7.57 ____ Order to Show Cause in Proceeding under Lien Law § 201–a to Vacate Garageman's Lien. 💾
- 7.58 ____ Verified Petition in Proceeding under Lien Law § 201–a to Vacate Garageman's Lien. 💾
- 7.59 ____ Affirmation in Support of Petition in Proceeding under Lien Law § 201–a to Vacate Garageman's Lien. 💾
- 7.60 ____ Complaint Against Credit Reporting Agency Alleging Violations of the Fair Credit Reporting Act and the New York State Fair Credit Reporting Act and Deceptive Business Practices. 💾
- 7.61 ____ Stipulation of Settlement of Plaintiff's Lemon Law Claims Providing for Cancellation of Lease and Deletion of Any Derogatory Credit Information. 💾

TABLE OF CONTENTS

Sec.
7.62 ____ Complaint Alleging Violations of the Fair Debt Collection Practices Act and the Deceptive Practices Act. 💾
7.63 ____ Order to Show Cause with Temporary Restraining Order, Seeking Preliminary Injunction in Action Alleging Fraud, Deceptive Business Practices and Breach of Warranties. 💾
7.64 ____ Affirmation in Support of Temporary Restraining Order and Preliminary Injunction in Action Alleging Fraud, Deceptive Business Practices and Breach of Warranties. 💾
7.65 ____ Complaint in Action Alleging Fraud, Deceptive Business Practices and Breach of Warranties. 💾

CHAPTER 8. ENFORCEMENT OF MONEY JUDGMENTS

8.1 Scope Note.
8.2 Strategy.
8.3 Judgments—Generally.
8.4 ____ Methods to Obtain.
8.5 ____ Form of Judgment—Judgment-Roll.
8.6 ____ Interest.
8.7 ____ Fees, Costs and Disbursements.
8.8 ____ Entry.
8.9 ____ Transcript of Judgment.
8.10 Matters Affecting Judgment—Vacatur.
8.11 ____ Satisfaction By Payment or Otherwise.
8.12 ____ Assignment.
8.13 ____ Death of Judgment Debtor.
8.14 ____ Amendment or Correction.
8.15 Actions on Judgments.
8.16 Entry of a Foreign Judgment—Sister-State Judgments.
8.17 ____ Federal Court Judgments.
8.18 ____ Foreign Country Judgments.
8.19 Judgment Enforcement Against Property—Definition of Property.
8.20 ____ Exemptions.
8.21 ____ Property in the Possession of Others.
8.22 ____ Disclosure of Property.
8.23 ____ ____ Subpoenas.
8.24 Article 52 Enforcement Devices—Introduction.
8.25 ____ Restraining Notices—Nature and Use.
8.26 ____ ____ Formal Requirements.
8.27 ____ ____ Service and Punishment for Disobedience.
8.28 ____ Execution.
8.29 ____ ____ Property Execution With Regard to Personal Property.
8.30 ____ ____ ____ Sale, Distribution and Priority In Proceeds.
8.31 ____ ____ Property Execution With Regard to Real Property.
8.32 ____ ____ ____ Notice and Sale of Real Property.
8.33 ____ ____ ____ Distribution of Proceeds of Sale and Conveyance of Title.
8.34 ____ Income Execution.
8.35 ____ Installment Payment Order—Nature and Purpose.
8.36 ____ ____ Form of Application and Service.

XXXIII

TABLE OF CONTENTS

Sec.
8.37 —— Receiver.
8.38 —— —— Application, Appointment and Extension.
8.39 —— Turnover Orders For Property or Debts.
8.40 —— —— Turnover Against the Judgment Debtor.
8.41 —— —— Turnover Against A Garnishee.
8.42 —— Contempt.
8.43 —— Arrest of the Judgment Debtor.
8.44 Protective Orders.
8.45 Proceeding To Determine Adverse Claims.
8.46 Forms.
8.47 —— Statement For Judgment (Default Judgment), Affidavit of Facts Constituting the Claim, the Default and the Amount Due.
8.48 —— Affidavit of Confession of Judgment and Judgment by Confession.
8.49 —— Notice to Judgment Debtor [or Obligor].
8.50 —— Subpoena (*Duces Tecum*) To Take Deposition of Judgment Debtor With Restraining Notice.
8.51 —— Subpoena (*Duces Tecum*) To Take Deposition of Witness With Restraining Notice.
8.52 —— Information Subpoena.
8.53 —— Restraining Notice to Judgment Debtor.
8.54 —— Execution.
8.55 —— Income Execution.
8.56 —— Affirmation and Order To Show Cause To Punish Judgment Debtor—Witness For Contempt.

CHAPTER 9. BANKRUPTCY

9.1 Scope Note.
9.2 Strategy.
9.3 —— Checklist for Representing a Debtor.
9.4 —— Checklist for Representing a Creditor.
9.5 Governing Law.
9.6 Nature of Cases Under Each Chapter of the Bankruptcy Code.
9.7 Eligibility to File.
9.8 Commencement of a Case—Voluntary Cases.
9.9 —— Involuntary Cases.
9.10 —— —— Procedure.
9.11 —— Additional Requirements.
9.12 —— First–Day Orders.
9.13 Joint Administration.
9.14 Substantive Consolidation.
9.15 Types of Proceedings in Cases Under the Bankruptcy Code.
9.16 —— Adversary Proceedings.
9.17 —— Contested Matters.
9.18 Jurisdiction of the Bankruptcy Court.
9.19 —— Types of Jurisdiction.
9.20 —— Case Ancillary to Foreign Proceedings.
9.21 Venue.
9.22 Withdrawal of Reference.

TABLE OF CONTENTS

Sec.	
9.23	Abstention.
9.24	Removal.
9.25	Appeals—To District Court and Bankruptcy Appellate Panel From Bankruptcy Court.
9.26	___ To Court of Appeals From District Court.
9.27	The Debtor in Possession.
9.28	___ Rights, Powers and Duties.
9.29	Employment of Professionals.
9.30	___ Compensation.
9.31	___ ___ Fee Applications.
9.32	U.S. Trustee.
9.33	___ Duties Owed by Debtors and Trustees.
9.34	Bankruptcy Trustee.
9.35	Mediators.
9.36	Creditors.
9.37	___ Meeting of Creditors.
9.38	___ ___ Scope of Examination.
9.39	Examinations Under Bankruptcy Rule 2004.
9.40	___ Notice Requirements.
9.41	___ Subpoena.
9.42	Right of Parties in Interest to Be Heard.
9.43	Statutory Committees.
9.44	___ Function and Duties.
9.45	___ Right to Bring Litigation.
9.46	___ Fiduciary Duty.
9.47	___ Removal of Members.
9.48	___ Organizational Meeting.
9.49	Property of the Estate.
9.50	Automatic Stay.
9.51	___ Exceptions.
9.52	___ Obtaining Relief.
9.53	___ ___ Strategy.
9.54	___ ___ Hearing.
9.55	___ ___ Single Asset Real Estate Debtor.
9.56	Adequate Protection.
9.57	___ Types.
9.58	___ Strategy.
9.59	___ Objections and Hearing.
9.60	Use, Sale, or Lease of Property.
9.61	___ Ordinary Course of Business.
9.62	___ Outside Ordinary Course of Business.
9.63	___ Sales Free and Clear of Liens.
9.64	___ Appeals from Order Authorizing Sale.
9.65	Cash Collateral.
9.66	___ Strategy.
9.67	___ Hearing.
9.68	___ Postpetition Proceeds.
9.69	___ ___ Security Interests in Rents and Hotel Revenues.
9.70	Abandonment of Property.
9.71	Postpetition Financing.

TABLE OF CONTENTS

Sec.
9.72 —— Hearing.
9.73 —— Appeals From Order Authorizing.
9.74 Executory Contracts and Unexpired Leases.
9.75 —— Strategy.
9.76 —— Time for Assumption or Rejection.
9.77 —— Nonresidential Real Property Leases.
9.78 —— Assumption by the Debtor.
9.79 —— Assumption and Assignment.
9.80 —— Exceptions to Assumption and Assignment.
9.81 —— Rejection by Debtor.
9.82 —— Damages Arising From Rejection: Debtor as Tenant/Lessee.
9.83 —— Calculation of Allowed Real Property Lease Rejection Damages.
9.84 —— Debtor as Landlord/Lessor.
9.85 —— Unexpired Personal Property Leases.
9.86 Collective Bargaining Agreements.
9.87 Retired Employees' Insurance Benefits.
9.88 —— Procedure for Modifying.
9.89 Utility Services.
9.90 Claims Procedures.
9.91 —— Filing Proofs of Claim or Interest.
9.92 —— —— Bar Dates.
9.93 —— Late-Filed Proofs of Claim.
9.94 —— Amendment of Proofs of Claim or Interest.
9.95 —— Withdrawal of Claims.
9.96 —— Allowance of, and Objections to, Claims or Interests.
9.97 —— Compromise and Settlement of Claims.
9.98 —— Allowance of Administrative Expense Claims.
9.99 —— Secured Claims.
9.100 —— —— Bifurcation of Claims.
9.101 —— —— Avoidance of Liens.
9.102 —— Interest on Claims and Charges Against Secured Claims.
9.103 —— Valuation of Collateral.
9.104 —— —— Methods of Valuation.
9.105 —— Reclamation Claims.
9.106 Priorities.
9.107 Subordination.
9.108 —— Strategy.
9.109 Setoff.
9.110 —— Strategy.
9.111 —— Characteristics of Claims.
9.112 Recoupment.
9.113 The Avoiding Powers.
9.114 —— Strategy.
9.115 —— Strong Arm Powers.
9.116 —— Avoidance of Certain Statutory Liens.
9.117 —— Preferences.
9.118 —— Exceptions to the Avoidance of Preferential Transfers.
9.119 —— Fraudulent Conveyances.
9.120 —— Liability of Transferee of Avoided Transfer.

TABLE OF CONTENTS

Sec.
9.121 ____ Statute of Limitations and Standing.
9.122 ____ Relation–Back Provision.
9.123 ____ Reclamation.
9.124 Return of Goods by Debtor.
9.125 Exemptions.
9.126 ____ Procedure.
9.127 ____ Objections.
9.128 ____ Lien Avoidance.
9.129 ____ Liens on Exempt Property.
9.130 Reaffirmation of Debts.
9.131 ____ Strategy.
9.132 Protection Against Discriminatory Treatment.
9.133 Tax Considerations.
9.134 Conversion and Dismissal of Cases Under Title 11.
9.135 Effect of Conversion.
9.136 Effect of Dismissal.
9.137 Closing and Reopening Cases.
9.138 Chapter 11—Appointment of a Trustee.
9.139 ____ Duties of a Trustee.
9.140 ____ Appointment of an Examiner.
9.141 ____ Duties of an Examiner.
9.142 ____ Exclusivity—Right to File a Plan.
9.143 ____ ____ Small Businesses.
9.144 ____ ____ Strategy: Representing a Debtor.
9.145 ____ ____ Strategy: Representing a Creditor.
9.146 ____ ____ Appealability of Orders.
9.147 ____ Plan.
9.148 ____ ____ Mandatory Provisions.
9.149 ____ ____ Discretionary Provisions.
9.150 ____ ____ Exemption from Securities Registration.
9.151 ____ ____ Retention of Jurisdiction by the Court.
9.152 ____ Classification of Claims.
9.153 ____ ____ Effect on Voting.
9.154 ____ ____ Substantially Similar Claims.
9.155 ____ ____ Convenience Class.
9.156 ____ Recourse and Nonrecourse Claims: The § 1111(b) Election.
9.157 ____ ____ Strategy.
9.158 ____ Impairment of Claims or Interests.
9.159 ____ ____ Rights Are Altered.
9.160 ____ ____ Defaults Are Not Cured.
9.161 ____ Disclosure and Solicitation.
9.162 ____ Acceptance of a Plan.
9.163 ____ Prepackaged and Prenegotiated Plans.
9.164 ____ Modification of a Plan.
9.165 ____ Confirmation.
9.166 ____ Cramdown.
9.167 ____ Effect of Confirmation.
9.168 ____ Discharge.
9.169 ____ ____ Limitations.
9.170 ____ ____ Release of Nondebtor.

XXXVII

TABLE OF CONTENTS

Sec.
9.171 ____ Channelling Injunctions: Asbestos–Related Cases.
9.172 ____ Plan Implementation.
9.173 ____ Small Business Reorganizations.
9.174 ____ Conversion or Dismissal of Cases.
9.175 ____ ____ Procedure.
9.176 ____ Closing and Reopening Cases.
9.177 Chapter 7—Overview.
9.178 ____ Commencement of a Case.
9.179 ____ Fees.
9.180 ____ Appointment of an Interim Trustee.
9.181 ____ Election of a Permanent Trustee.
9.182 ____ Duties of a Trustee.
9.183 ____ Employment of Professionals.
9.184 ____ Creditors' Committee.
9.185 ____ Protection Against Discriminatory Treatment.
9.186 ____ The Debtor's Statement of Intention.
9.187 ____ Exemptions.
9.188 ____ Redemption of Property.
9.189 ____ ____ Procedure.
9.190 ____ Reaffirmation of Debts.
9.191 ____ Abandonment of Property.
9.192 ____ Debtor's Surrender of Property and Records.
9.193 ____ Trustee's Turnover Powers.
9.194 ____ Liability of General Partners.
9.195 ____ Trustee's Operation of the Business.
9.196 ____ Executory Contracts.
9.197 ____ Adversary Proceedings to Avoid Liens and Transfers.
9.198 ____ ____ Statute of Limitations.
9.199 ____ Treatment of Certain Liens.
9.200 ____ Trustee's Sale of Assets.
9.201 ____ Disposition of Property Subject to the Interest of Another.
9.202 ____ Priorities.
9.203 ____ Special Tax Provisions.
9.204 ____ Discharge.
9.205 ____ ____ Exceptions to General Discharge of the Debtor.
9.206 ____ ____ Procedure for Objections to General Discharge of the Debtor.
9.207 ____ ____ Exceptions to Discharge of Particular Debts.
9.208 ____ ____ Procedure for Objections to Discharge of Particular Debts.
9.209 ____ Conversion or Dismissal of Cases.
9.210 ____ ____ Procedure.
9.211 ____ Closing and Reopening Cases.
9.212 Chapter 12—Overview.
9.213 ____ Rights and Powers of Debtor.
9.214 ____ Appointment of a Trustee.
9.215 ____ Duties of a Trustee.
9.216 ____ Automatic Stay.
9.217 ____ Property of the Estate.
9.218 ____ Sales Free of Interests.

TABLE OF CONTENTS

Sec.
9.219 ____ Adequate Protection.
9.220 ____ Exclusivity—Right to File a Plan.
9.221 ____ Plan.
9.222 ____ ____ Mandatory Provisions.
9.223 ____ ____ Discretionary Provisions.
9.224 ____ ____ Modification.
9.225 ____ ____ Confirmation.
9.226 ____ ____ Confirmation: Objections.
9.227 ____ Disbursements.
9.228 ____ Effect of Confirmation.
9.229 ____ Discharge.
9.230 ____ Modification after Confirmation.
9.231 ____ Special Tax Provisions.
9.232 ____ Revocation of Confirmation Order.
9.233 ____ Conversion or Dismissal of Cases.
9.234 ____ ____ Procedure.
9.235 ____ Closing and Reopening Cases.
9.236 Chapter 13—Overview.
9.237 ____ Eligibility.
9.238 ____ Rights and Powers of Debtor.
9.239 ____ Appointment of a Trustee.
9.240 ____ Duties of a Trustee.
9.241 ____ Automatic Stay.
9.242 ____ ____ Relief.
9.243 ____ Property of the Estate.
9.244 ____ ____ Use, Sale, or Lease.
9.245 ____ Exclusivity—Right to File a Plan.
9.246 ____ Plan.
9.247 ____ ____ Mandatory Provisions.
9.248 ____ ____ Discretionary Provisions.
9.249 ____ ____ Discretionary Provisions: Debtor's Principal Residence.
9.250 ____ ____ Modification.
9.251 ____ ____ Confirmation.
9.252 ____ ____ Confirmation: Objections.
9.253 ____ ____ Confirmation: Effect.
9.254 ____ Payments.
9.255 ____ Discharge.
9.256 ____ ____ Exceptions.
9.257 ____ ____ Objections.
9.258 ____ ____ Revocation.
9.259 ____ Postconfirmation Modification of a Plan.
9.260 ____ Revocation of Confirmation Order.
9.261 ____ Conversion or Dismissal of Cases.
9.262 ____ ____ Procedure.
9.263 ____ Closing and Reopening Cases.
9.264 Procedural Checklist—Commencing a Voluntary Case.
9.265 ____ Lists and Schedules to be Filed at the Commencement of a Case Under Chapter 7, 11, 12, or 13.
9.266 ____ Commencing an Adversary Proceeding.
9.267 ____ Commencing a Contested Matter.

TABLE OF CONTENTS

Sec.

9.268	____ Appeal from an Interlocutory Judgment, Order, or Decree of a Bankruptcy Judge.
9.269	____ Creditor's Motion to Request Relief from the Automatic Stay.
9.270	____ Creditor's Motion to Obtain Adequate Protection.
9.271	____ Debtor's Motion to Use, Sell, or Lease Property of the Estate.
9.272	____ Debtor's Motion to Request Use of Cash Collateral.
9.273	____ Cash Collateral Stipulation.
9.274	____ Debtor's Motion to Obtain Postpetition Financing.
9.275	____ Request to Assume, Reject, or Assign an Executory Contract or Unexpired Nonresidential Real Property Lease.
9.276	____ Debtor's Motion to Reject or Modify a Collective Bargaining Agreement.
9.277	____ Debtor's Motion to Obtain Approval of a Compromise and Settlement of a Claim.
9.278	____ Claiming Exemptions.
9.279	____ Debtor's Motion to Avoid a Judicial Lien or a Nonpossessory, Nonpurchase–Money Security Interest that Impairs Exempt Property.
9.280	____ Debtor's Motion to Obtain Court Approval of a Reaffirmation Agreement.
9.281	____ Debtor's Motion to Request an Extension of Exclusivity.
9.282	____ Filing a Chapter 11 Plan and Disclosure Statement.
9.283	____ Soliciting Acceptance of a Chapter 11 Plan.
9.284	____ Filing a Chapter 12 or 13 Plan of Debt Adjustment.
9.285	____ Objection to a Chapter 12 or 13 Plan.
9.286	____ Debtor's Motion to Request Modification of a Chapter 12 or 13 Plan after Confirmation
9.287	Drafting Checklist—General Rules for all Motions, Applications, and Complaints.
9.288	____ Complaint in an Adversary Proceeding.
9.289	____ Motion for Leave to Appeal From an Interlocutory Judgment, Order, or Decree of a Bankruptcy Judge.
9.290	____ Motion for a Stay of a Bankruptcy Court Judgment or Order Pending Appeal.
9.291	____ Application of Debtor or Statutory Committee to Retain Professionals.
9.292	____ Creditor's Motion to Request Relief From the Automatic Stay.
9.293	____ Creditor's Motion to Obtain Adequate Protection.
9.294	____ Debtor's Motion to Use, Sell, or Lease Property of the Estate.
9.295	____ Debtor's Motion to Request Use of Cash Collateral.
9.296	____ Cash Collateral Stipulation.
9.297	____ Debtor's Motion to Obtain Postpetition Financing.
9.298	____ Motion to Assume or Reject an Executory Contract or Unexpired Non-residential Real Property Lease.
9.299	____ Debtor's Motion to Reject or Modify a Collective Bargaining Agreement (CBA).
9.300	____ Debtor's Motion to Obtain Approval of a Compromise and Settlement of a Claim.

TABLE OF CONTENTS

Sec.
9.301 ____ Debtor's Motion to Avoid a Judicial Lien or a Nonpossessory, Nonpurchase–Money Security Interest that Impairs Exempt Property.
9.302 ____ Reaffirmation Agreement.
9.303 ____ Debtor's Motion for Approval of a Reaffirmation Agreement.
9.304 ____ Debtor's Motion to Request an Extension of Exclusivity.
9.305 Forms—Notice of Appearance and Demand for Service of Documents. 💾
9.306 ____ Contested Matter—Motion. 💾
9.307 ____ ____ Notice of Motion. 💾
9.308 ____ ____ Proposed Order. 💾
9.309 ____ Adversary Proceeding—Complaint. 💾
9.310 ____ Retention of Professionals—Application. 💾
9.311 ____ ____ Affidavit. 💾
9.312 ____ Plan Provision for Retention of Jurisdiction. 💾

CHAPTER 10. MECHANIC'S LIENS

10.1 Scope Note.
10.2 Strategy.
10.3 Nature of Mechanic's Lien.
10.4 Creation of Mechanic's Lien—Elements.
10.5 ____ ____ Protected Class.
10.6 ____ ____ Improvements to Real Property.
10.7 ____ ____ Consent or Request of Owner.
10.8 Extent of Lien—Ownership Interest at Time of Filing.
10.9 ____ Sale of Property.
10.10 ____ Insurance Proceeds.
10.11 ____ Amount.
10.12 ____ Loss of Profits.
10.13 Subcontractors and Materialmen—Derivative Rights.
10.14 ____ ____ Statutory Protections.
10.15 Procedure—Notice of Lien.
10.16 ____ ____ Contents.
10.17 ____ ____ Filing.
10.18 ____ ____ Service.
10.19 Amendment of Notice of Lien.
10.20 Lien for Private Improvements—Checklist.
10.21 Liens Under Contract for Public Improvements—Extent of Lien.
10.22 ____ Notice of Lien.
10.23 ____ Filing of Notice of Lien.
10.24 ____ Notice of Completion and Acceptance.
10.25 ____ Checklist.
10.26 Lien Priorities—Private Improvements—Parity of Mechanic's Liens.
10.27 ____ ____ Assignments of Contract Rights.
10.28 ____ ____ Building Loan Mortgages.
10.29 ____ ____ Contracts of Sale.
10.30 ____ ____ Seller's Mortgage.
10.31 ____ ____ Deeds.

XLI

TABLE OF CONTENTS

Sec.
10.32 —— Contracts for Public Improvements.
10.33 Assignment of Liens.
10.34 Assignments of Contracts for Private Improvements and Orders to be Filed—Filing of Notice of Assignment.
10.35 —— Contents of Notice of Assignment.
10.36 —— Extension of Term of Notice of Assignment.
10.37 Assignment of Contracts and Orders for Public Improvements.
10.38 Duration of Lien for Private Improvements—Notice of Pendency.
10.39 —— Extensions.
10.40 Duration of Lien Under Contract for a Public Improvement—Notice of Pendency.
10.41 —— Extension of Lien.
10.42 Discharge of Lien for Private Improvement—Satisfaction of Lien.
10.43 —— Expiration of Term.
10.44 —— Termination of Notice of Pendency.
10.45 —— Failure to Prosecute.
10.46 —— Undertaking.
10.47 —— Judgment.
10.48 —— Defective Lien.
10.49 —— Deposit of Money with County Clerk or Court.
10.50 Discharge of Lien for Public Improvement—Satisfaction of Lien.
10.51 —— Expiration of Lien.
10.52 —— Satisfaction of Judgment.
10.53 —— Deposit of Money.
10.54 —— Undertaking.
10.55 —— Retention of Credit.
10.56 —— Invalidity of Lien.
10.57 —— Failure to Prosecute.
10.58 —— Procedures.
10.59 Building Loan Contracts—Filing Requirements.
10.60 —— Checklist.
10.61 Subordination of Liens—Agreement with Owner.
10.62 —— —— Postponement of Judgments.
10.63 Subordination of Liens to Subsequent Mortgage.
10.64 Subordination of Notices of *Lis Pendens*.
10.65 Discharge of Liens on Sale of Real Property.
10.66 Limitations on Waiver of Mechanic's Lien.
10.67 Effect of Filing of Notice of Lien on Right of Arbitration.
10.68 Bond to Discharge Liens—Effect of Bond.
10.69 —— Requirements of Bond.
10.70 —— Claim Against Bond.
10.71 —— Notice of Claim.
10.72 —— Action on Bond.
10.73 —— Discharge of Liens and Notices of Claims.
10.74 Protecting the Owner—Itemized Statement.
10.75 —— Lien Wilfully Exaggerated.
10.76 Repossession of Materials Not Used.
10.77 Enforcement of Mechanic's Liens—Courts.
10.78 —— Courts of Record—Procedures.
10.79 —— —— Necessary Parties.

TABLE OF CONTENTS

Sec.
10.80 —— Actions in a Court Not of Record—Summons and Complaint.
10.81 —— —— Proceedings Upon Return of Summons.
10.82 —— —— Judgments and Transcripts.
10.83 —— Costs and Disbursements.
10.84 —— Effect of Failure to Establish Lien.
10.85 —— Deposit of Money or Securities to Discharge Lien—Procedures.
10.86 —— —— Effect of Order.
10.87 —— —— Preference Over Contractors.
10.88 —— —— Delivery of Property in Lieu of Money.
10.89 —— Deficiency Judgment.
10.90 —— Vacating of Mechanic's Lien, Cancellation of Bond or Return of Deposit.
10.91 —— Public Improvements.
10.92 —— New Parties.
10.93 —— Service of Answer on State or Public Corporation.
10.94 Trust Funds—Purpose.
10.95 —— Creation.
10.96 —— Contractors and Subcontractors.
10.97 —— Beneficiaries.
10.98 Diversion of Trust Assets.
10.99 Notice of Lending.
10.100 Record Keeping Obligations.
10.101 Right of Beneficiaries to Examine Books or Records.
10.102 Action to Enforce Trust—Standing and Procedure.
10.103 —— Remedies.
10.104 —— Preferences.
10.105 Relief After Judgment on Obligation Constituting Trust Claim; Effect on Mechanic's Liens.
10.106 Misappropriation of Trust Funds.
10.107 Procedural Checklist.
10.108 Forms.
10.109 —— Notice of Mechanic's Lien—General Form.
10.110 —— Notice of Lien for Public Improvement.
10.111 —— Form For Demand for Terms of Contract.
10.112 —— Demand for Notice of Completion and Acceptance of Public Improvement.
10.113 —— Petition to Amend Notice of Mechanic's Lien—Correct Name of Owner of Property.
10.114 —— Assignment of Lien for Public Improvement.
10.115 —— Assignment of Mechanic's Lien.
10.116 —— Assignment of Moneys Due or to Become Due Under Public Improvement Contract.
10.117 —— Affidavit for Continuance of Mechanic's Lien.
10.118 —— Affidavit for Continuance of Lien for Public Improvement.
10.119 —— Petition to Discharge Mechanic's Lien Where Notice of Lien Defective.
10.120 —— Petition for Order Discharging Mechanic's Lien Upon Filing of Undertaking.

TABLE OF CONTENTS

Sec.
10.121 —— Undertaking to Discharge Mechanic's Lien.
10.122 —— Petition for Order Fixing Amount of Undertaking to Discharge Mechanic's Lien.
10.123 —— Approval by Lienors of Subordination of Mechanic's Liens to Trust Bond or Note and Mortgage.
10.124 —— Affidavit for Order Fixing Amount of Bond to Discharge All Mechanic's Liens.
10.125 —— Petition for Order Requiring Itemized Statement.
10.126 —— Notice of Application for Order Requiring Itemized Statement.
10.127 —— Demand for Itemized Statement.
10.128 —— Affidavit in Support of Application to Cancel Mechanic's Lien for Failure to Furnish Itemized Statement.
10.129 —— Notice Requiring Lienor to Commence Action to Enforce Mechanic's Lien.
10.130 —— Affidavit in Support of Application to Cancel Notice of Mechanic's Lien for Failure to Commence Action.
10.131 —— Notice Requiring Lienor to Commence Action to Enforce Lien for Public Improvement.
10.132 —— Affidavit in Support of Application to Cancel Notice of Lien for Public Improvement for Failure to Commence Action.
10.133 —— Complaint for Foreclosure of Lien for Public Improvement.
10.134 —— Complaint for Foreclosure of Mechanic's Lien—Contractor.
10.135 —— Defense and Counterclaim Based on Wilful Exaggeration of Mechanic's Lien.
10.136 —— Affidavit in Support of Motion to Consolidate Actions for Foreclosure of Mechanic's Liens.
10.137 —— Notice of Motion to Consolidate Actions to Foreclose Mechanic's Liens.
10.138 —— Acceptance of Offer to Pay Money Into Court in Discharge of Mechanic's Lien.
10.139 —— Offer to Pay Money Into Court in Discharge of Mechanic's Lien.
10.140 —— Judgment of Foreclosure and Sale—Mechanic's Lien.
10.141 —— Judgment of Foreclosure—Lien for Public Improvement—Where Lien Discharged and Fund Retained for Payment.
10.142 —— Affidavit in Support of Motion for Summary Judgment—Foreclosure of Lien for Public Improvement.
10.143 —— Demand for Verified Statement from Trustee.
10.144 —— Petition for Verified Statement from Trustee of Trust Funds.
10.145 —— Complaint by Subcontractor to Enforce Trust Against Funds Received by Contractor or Assignee of Contractor.
10.146 —— Complaint by Surety to Have Parties Declared Trustees of Subcontract Moneys and for Accounting.
10.147 —— Affidavit in Support of Motion to Determine if Class Action Can be Maintained—Action to Impress and Enforce Trust.

XLIV

TABLE OF CONTENTS

CHAPTER 11. MORTGAGE FORECLOSURE

Sec.
- 11.1 Scope Note.
- 11.2 Strategy—Initial Client Interview.
- 11.3 ____ First Review of Loan Documents.
- 11.4 ____ Foreclosure Title Certificate.
- 11.5 New York Mortgage Foreclosure Law.
- 11.6 ____ Choice of Remedies: Foreclosure Action or Money Action.
- 11.7 ____ Partial Foreclosure Action.
- 11.8 ____ Non-Judicial Foreclosure.
- 11.9 Representing Subordinate Lienors.
- 11.10 Pre-commencement Procedure.
- 11.11 ____ Notice of Default.
- 11.12 ____ Notice of Acceleration.
- 11.13 ____ Foreclosure Title Certificate.
- 11.14 Determining the Necessary Defendants.
- 11.15 ____ The United States As a Necessary Defendant.
- 11.16 Starting the Foreclosure Action.
- 11.17 ____ Notice of Pendency of Action.
- 11.18 ____ Summons.
- 11.19 ____ Venue.
- 11.20 ____ Complaint.
- 11.21 ____ Allegations Regarding Parties.
- 11.22 ____ Allegations Regarding Loan, Note and Mortgage.
- 11.23 ____ References to Pertinent Terms of Note and Mortgage.
- 11.24 ____ Asserting Default(s).
- 11.25 ____ Reserving Right to Add Advances Made by Plaintiff to Indebtedness Secured by Mortgage.
- 11.26 ____ Allegation Regarding Subordinate Interest of Defendant(s).
- 11.27 ____ Whether There Has Been or is Pending Another Action Regarding the Mortgage Debt.
- 11.28 ____ Amendments.
- 11.29 Receivers.
- 11.30 ____ Considerations in Determining Whether to Seek Appointment of Receiver.
- 11.31 ____ *Ex Parte* Motion for Appointment of Receiver.
- 11.32 ____ Compensation.
- 11.33 ____ Opposing Appointment of Receiver.
- 11.34 ____ Discharging Receiver.
- 11.35 Defendant's Response.
- 11.36 ____ Motion to Dismiss Complaint.
- 11.37 ____ Answer and Defenses.
- 11.38 ____ Notice of Appearance and Waiver.
- 11.39 Obtaining Judgment.
- 11.40 ____ Motion for Judgment.
- 11.41 ____ Opposing Motion for Judgment.
- 11.42 Reference to Compute.
- 11.43 ____ Hearing Before Referee to Compute.
- 11.44 ____ Report of Referee to Compute.
- 11.45 ____ Motion to Confirm Referee's Computation Report and for Judgment of Foreclosure and Sale.

TABLE OF CONTENTS

Sec.
11.46 Judgment of Foreclosure and Sale.
11.47 Foreclosure Sale.
11.48 ____ Noticing and Advertising the Sale.
11.49 ____ Conducting the Sale.
11.50 ____ Vacating the Sale.
11.51 Referee's Deed, Other Closing Documents and Referee's Report of Sale.
11.52 Deficiency Judgment.
11.53 Surplus Money Proceedings.
11.54 Eviction of Tenants and Other Occupants After Foreclosure Sale.
11.55 Drafting Checklists.
11.56 ____ Notice of Default.
11.57 ____ Notice of Acceleration.
11.58 ____ Notice of Pendency of Action.
11.59 ____ Summons.
11.60 ____ Complaint.
11.61 ____ Order Appointing Receiver.
11.62 ____ Affidavit in Support of *Ex Parte* Application for Receiver.
11.63 ____ Notice of Motion for Summary Judgment and Related Relief.
11.64 ____ Affidavit of Regularity and in Support of Plaintiff's Motion for Summary Judgment and Related Relief.
11.65 ____ Judgment of Foreclosure and Sale.
11.66 ____ Notice of Sale.
11.67 ____ Terms and Memorandum of Sale.
11.68 Forms.
11.69 ____ Notice of Default.
11.70 ____ Notice of Acceleration.
11.71 ____ Notice of Pendency of Action.
11.72 ____ Summons.
11.73 ____ Verified Complaint for Foreclosure of Mortgage Affecting Single Family Residence.
11.74 ____ Verified Complaint for Foreclosure of Mortgage Affecting Commercial, Multi–Unit Residential or Mixed Property.
11.75 ____ Order Appointing Receiver.
11.76 ____ Affidavit in Support of Motion for Appointment of Receiver.
11.77 ____ Notice of Motion for Summary Judgment and Related Relief.
11.78 ____ Affidavit of Regularity and in Support of Motion for Summary Judgment.
11.79 ____ Judgment of Foreclosure and Sale.
11.80 ____ Notice of Sale.
11.81 ____ Terms and Memorandum of Sale.

CHAPTER 12. PURCHASE AND SALE OF REAL ESTATE

12.1 Scope Note.
12.2 Strategy.
12.3 ____ Pre-contract Checklist.
12.4 Contract of Sale.

TABLE OF CONTENTS

Sec.
12.5	⎯⎯ Preparation and Delivery
12.6	⎯⎯ Recordation.
12.7	Residential Contract of Sale.
12.8	⎯⎯ Parties.
12.9	⎯⎯ Premises.
12.10	⎯⎯ Personal Property.
12.11	⎯⎯ Purchase Price and Method of Payment.
12.12	⎯⎯ ⎯⎯ Down Payment.
12.13	⎯⎯ ⎯⎯ Assumption of Existing Mortgage.
12.14	⎯⎯ ⎯⎯ Purchase Money Mortgage.
12.15	⎯⎯ ⎯⎯ Mortgage Contingency.
12.16	⎯⎯ ⎯⎯ Acceptable Funds.
12.17	⎯⎯ Permitted Exceptions.
12.18	⎯⎯ Governmental Violations and Orders.
12.19	⎯⎯ Seller's Representations.
12.20	⎯⎯ Condition of Property.
12.21	⎯⎯ Insurable and Marketable Title.
12.22	⎯⎯ Closing, Deed and Title.
12.23	⎯⎯ Closing Date and Place.
12.24	⎯⎯ Conditions to Closing.
12.25	⎯⎯ Deed Transfer and Recording Taxes.
12.26	⎯⎯ Apportionments.
12.27	⎯⎯ Allowance for Unpaid Taxes.
12.28	⎯⎯ Title Examination; Seller's Inability to Convey; Limitation of Liability.
12.29	⎯⎯ Defaults and Remedies.
12.30	⎯⎯ Assignment.
12.31	⎯⎯ Broker.
12.32	⎯⎯ Risk of Loss.
12.33	Condominium Contract of Sale.
12.34	⎯⎯ Comparisons to the Residential Contract of Sale.
12.35	⎯⎯ Homeowner's Associations.
12.36	Contract of Sale for Office, Commercial and Multi-family Residential Premises.
12.37	Contract of Sale for Cooperative Apartment
12.38	⎯⎯ Standard Form.
12.39	Contract of Sale for New Construction.
12.40	Title Insurance.
12.41	⎯⎯ The Buyer's Obligation.
12.42	⎯⎯ Role of the Title Insurer.
12.43	⎯⎯ Duration and Cost.
12.44	⎯⎯ Basic and Extended Coverage.
12.45	Title Insurance Policy.
12.46	⎯⎯ Loan Policy Coverage.
12.47	⎯⎯ New York Modifications of Loan Policy.
12.48	⎯⎯ Owner's Policy Coverage.
12.49	⎯⎯ New York Modifications of Owner's Policy.
12.50	⎯⎯ Standard Exceptions.
12.51	⎯⎯ Endorsements.
12.52	⎯⎯ Exclusions.

TABLE OF CONTENTS

Sec.
12.53 Title Examination: Recording Title and the Torrens System.
12.54 ____ Objections to Be Disposed of Prior to Closing.
12.55 ____ ____ Checklist.
12.56 The Survey Map.
12.57 ____ What it May Disclose.
12.58 ____ Effect on Marketability of Title.
12.59 ____ ____ Where Contract Is Silent on the Matter of Survey.
12.60 ____ ____ Where Contract Subject to Any State of Facts an Accurate Survey May Show.
12.61 ____ ____ Where Contract Subject to Any State of Facts an Accurate Survey May Show Provided Same Does Not Render Title Unmarketable.
12.62 ____ ____ Where Contract Subject to Specific Encroachments or to Facts Shown on a Specific Survey.
12.63 ____ ____ Suggested Clause.
12.64 Marketability of Title.
12.65 ____ What Renders Title Unmarketable.
12.66 ____ ____ Encroachments Due to Adverse Possession.
12.67 ____ ____ Party Walls.
12.68 ____ Driveway Easements.
12.69 ____ Other Covenants and Restrictions.
12.70 ____ Reservations for Public Utilities.
12.71 ____ Land Abutting Bodies of Water and the Federal Navigational Servitude.
12.72 Closing of Title.
12.73 ____ Checklist.
12.74 ____ Recording Fees and Filings.
12.75 ____ Disclosure and Other Requirements.
12.76 ____ ____ Foreign Investors Real Property Tax.
12.77 ____ ____ Form 1099–S Federal Requirement for One to Four Family Residence.
12.78 ____ ____ Form 1099–S Federal Requirement for One to Four Family Residence—Checklist.
12.79 ____ ____ Cash Payments Received by Businesses in Excess of $10,000.
12.80 ____ ____ Lead Paint Hazards.
12.81 ____ ____ Agricultural Foreign Investment Disclosure Act.
12.82 ____ Payment of Taxes.
12.83 ____ ____ New York State Real Estate Transfer Tax and Mansion Tax.
12.84 ____ ____ Article 31-B—Real Property Transfer Gains Tax.
12.85 ____ ____ New York City Real Property Transfer Tax.
12.86 ____ ____ Cities of Mount Vernon and Yonkers.
12.87 ____ ____ Real Estate Investment Trusts.
12.88 ____ ____ Mortgage Recording Tax Outside New York City.
12.89 ____ ____ Mortgage Recording Tax Rate in New York City.
12.90 ____ Method of Payment.
12.91 ____ Other Required Forms and Information.
12.92 Forms.
12.93 ____ Residential Contract of Sale.

TABLE OF CONTENTS

Sec.
12.94	____ Contract of Sale—Condominium Unit.
12.95	____ ____ Office, Commercial and Multi–Family Residential Premises.
12.96	____ ____ Cooperative Apartment.
12.97	____ Durable General Power of Attorney. 💾
12.98	____ Power of Attorney to Take Effect at a Later Time. 💾

Volume 22

CHAPTER 13. LANDLORD–TENANT LAW

13.1	Scope Note.
13.2	Strategy.
13.3	____ Checklists.
13.4	Summary Proceedings.
13.5	____ Venue and Jurisdiction.
13.6	____ Service of Process.
13.7	____ ____ Personal Delivery.
13.8	____ ____ Substituted Service.
13.9	____ ____ Conspicuous Place Service.
13.10	____ ____ New York City Civil Court "Postcard Requirement."
13.11	Non-payment Proceedings.
13.12	____ Rent Demands.
13.13	____ Notice of Petition.
13.14	____ ____ Form of Notice.
13.15	____ ____ Content of Notice.
13.16	____ ____ Defects in the Notice.
13.17	____ The Petition.
13.18	____ ____ Defects in the Petition.
13.19	____ ____ Verification.
13.20	____ ____ Defects in the Verification.
13.21	Responding to the Non-payment Petition.
13.22	____ The Answer.
13.23	____ The Motion to Dismiss.
13.24	____ The RPAPL § 755 Motion to Stay.
13.25	Tenant Defenses to the Non-payment Proceeding.
13.26	____ No Landlord Tenant Relationship.
13.27	____ Tenant Out of Possession.
13.28	____ Statutory Noncompliance.
13.29	____ Illegal Rent.
13.30	____ Actual Eviction.
13.31	____ Constructive Eviction.
13.32	____ Warranty of Habitability.
13.33	____ Laches.
13.34	____ Payment.
13.35	Holdover Proceedings.
13.36	____ Predicate Notices.
13.37	____ ____ Month-to-Month Tenants.
13.38	____ ____ Illegal Use.
13.39	____ ____ Rent–Controlled Tenants.

XLIX

TABLE OF CONTENTS

Sec.
- 13.40 ____ ____ Rent–Stabilized Tenants.
- 13.41 ____ ____ The Notice of Petition.
- 13.42 ____ ____ Defects in the Notice.
- 13.43 ____ Holdover Petition—Form and Content.
- 13.44 ____ ____ Defects in the Petition.
- 13.45 ____ ____ Verification and Verification Defects.
- 13.46 Responding to the Holdover Petition.
- 13.47 ____ The Answer.
- 13.48 ____ The Motion to Dismiss.
- 13.49 Tenant Defenses to the Holdover Proceeding.
- 13.50 ____ Acceptance of Rent After Expiration or Termination of Tenancy.
- 13.51 ____ Defective Predicate Notice.
- 13.52 ____ ____ Rent–Regulated Apartments.
- 13.53 ____ Waiver.
- 13.54 ____ Equitable Estoppel.
- 13.55 ____ Succession Rights to Rent–Regulated Apartments.
- 13.56 Counterclaims.
- 13.57 Bill of Particulars.
- 13.58 Discovery.
- 13.59 ____ Notice to Admit.
- 13.60 ____ Freedom of Information Law.
- 13.61 The Trial—Adjournments.
- 13.62 ____Amending Petition and Burden of Proof.
- 13.63 Stipulations—Overview.
- 13.64 ____ Non-payment Proceedings.
- 13.65 ____ Holdover Proceedings.
- 13.66 ____ Enforcement and Vacatur.
- 13.67 The Judgment and Warrant.
- 13.68 ____ Staying the Warrant in Non-payment Proceedings.
- 13.69 ____ Staying the Warrant in New York City Residential Holdover Proceedings.
- 13.70 Yellowstone Actions.
- 13.71 ____ Obtaining the Injunction.
- 13.72 Article 7-A Proceedings.
- 13.73 Rent Regulatory Proceedings.
- 13.74 ____ Rent Overcharge.
- 13.75 ____ Service Reduction.
- 13.76 ____ Major Capital Improvement Rent Increase.
- 13.77 Checklist of Essential Allegations.
- 13.78 ____ Petition Non-payment.
- 13.79 ____ Holdover Petition.
- 13.80 ____ Stipulation Settling Non-payment Proceeding.
- 13.81 ____ Stipulation Settling Holdover Proceeding.
- 13.82 Forms.
- 13.83 ____ Petition Non-payment. 💾
- 13.84 ____ Petition Holdover. 💾
- 13.85 ____ Individual Verification. 💾
- 13.86 ____ Corporate Officer Verification. 💾
- 13.87 ____ Partnership Verification. 💾

L

TABLE OF CONTENTS

Sec.
13.88 ____ Attorney Verification. 💾
13.89 ____ Stipulations. 💾
13.90 ____ ____ Settling Non-payment Proceeding. 💾
13.91 ____ ____ Settling Non-payment Proceeding With Final Judgment in Favor of Petitioner. 💾
13.92 ____ ____ Settling Holdover Proceeding Where Tenant Agrees to Cure Lease Violation. 💾
13.93 ____ ____ Settling Holdover Proceeding Where Tenant–Respondent Agrees to Vacate Premises. 💾

CHAPTER 14. EMINENT DOMAIN

14.1 Scope Note.
14.2 Strategies for Condemnors and Condemnees.
14.3 Exercise of the Power of Eminent Domain.
14.4 ____ The State as Condemnor.
14.5 ____ Other Public Entities as Condemnor.
14.6 ____ Private Entities.
14.7 Property Rights Subject to Acquisition.
14.8 ____ Real Property.
14.9 ____ Easements.
14.10 ____ Leases.
14.11 ____ Personal Property.
14.12 ____ Public Property/Priority of Taking.
14.13 ____ Excess Property.
14.14 *De Facto* Taking.
14.15 Public Use, Benefit or Purpose.
14.16 ____ Particular Uses.
14.17 ____ Incidental Private Benefit.
14.18 Just Compensation.
14.19 Summary.
14.20 The First Stage: The Condemnation Phase.
14.21 Public Hearing.
14.22 Exemptions From the Public Hearing Requirement.
14.23 ____ Overlap with Other Governmental Requirements.
14.24 ____ Overlap with Issuance of a Certificate of Environmental Compatibility and Public Need.
14.25 ____ Alternate Public Hearing.
14.26 ____ *De Minimis* Acquisition or Emergency Situation.
14.27 ____ Section 41.34 of the Mental Hygiene Law.
14.28 Notice.
14.29 Conduct of the Public Hearing and Requirement of a Record.
14.30 Determination and Findings.
14.31 ____ Publication of Synopsis.
14.32 ____ Interplay with SEQRA.
14.33 ____ Amendments for Field Conditions.
14.34 Judicial Review of Determination and Findings.
14.35 ____ Prerequisite Determination.
14.36 ____ Persons Entitled to Review.
14.37 ____ 30-Day Statute of Limitations.

TABLE OF CONTENTS

Sec.
14.38 —— Scope of Review.
14.39 Summary.
14.40 The Second Stage—The "Offer and Negotiation" Phase.
14.41 —— Pretaking Appraisals.
14.42 —— Pretaking Discovery.
14.43 —— Offer as Payment in Full.
14.44 —— Advance Payment.
14.45 Use and Occupancy by Condemnee After Taking.
14.46 Summary.
14.47 The Third Stage—The Acquisition Phase.
14.48 —— Court of Claims v. Supreme Court Jurisdiction.
14.49 —— Statute of Limitations for Bringing an Acquisition Proceeding.
14.50 —— —— Acquisition in Stages.
14.51 —— Acquisition Map.
14.52 Acquisition of Property—Court of Claims Jurisdiction.
14.53 —— Condemnors Subject to Court of Claims Jurisdiction.
14.54 —— Filing and Notice Requirements.
14.55 —— Vesting of Title.
14.56 Acquisition of Property—Supreme Court Jurisdiction.
14.57 —— Notice of Pendency.
14.58 —— Petition in Condemnation.
14.59 —— —— Content.
14.60 —— —— Additional Content Rules for Certain Non-governmental Condemnors.
14.61 —— Notice.
14.62 —— —— Certification of Names of Reputed Condemnees.
14.63 —— Answer by Condemnee.
14.64 —— —— Defenses.
14.65 —— Vesting of Title and Order of Condemnation.
14.66 Notice of Acquisition.
14.67 Immediate Entry.
14.68 Summary.
14.69 The Fourth Stage—The Compensation Phase.
14.70 —— Court of Claims.
14.71 —— —— Time to File Claim.
14.72 —— —— Service.
14.73 —— Supreme Court.
14.74 —— —— Time to File Claim.
14.75 —— —— Service.
14.76 Content of Claim.
14.77 Scope of Just Compensation.
14.78 —— "Highest and Best Use."
14.79 —— Total Taking.
14.80 —— —— Direct Damages.
14.81 —— —— —— Improvements.
14.82 —— Partial Taking.
14.83 —— Temporary Taking.
14.84 —— —— Easements.
14.85 Methods of Valuation to Determine Compensation.

TABLE OF CONTENTS

Sec.
14.86 ____ Market Approach to Value.
14.87 ____ Income Approach to Value.
14.88 ____ Cost Approach to Value.
14.89 Specialty Property.
14.90 Effect of Environmental Contamination on Property Value.
14.91 Fixtures.
14.92 ____ Compensable Fixtures.
14.93 ____ Valuation of Fixtures.
14.94 Leasehold Interests.
14.95 ____ Valuation and Compensation.
14.96 Loss of Business and Goodwill.
14.97 Going Concern Value.
14.98 Moving and Relocation Expenses.
14.99 Conflicting Claims by Condemnees.
14.100 ____ Conflicting Claims to the Condemnor's Offer.
14.101 ____ Conflicting Claims to the Award.
14.102 The Trial on Compensation.
14.103 ____ Preference.
14.104 ____ Filing and Exchange of Appraisals.
14.105 ____ Expert Testimony.
14.106 ____ Viewing of the Property.
14.107 ____ Joint or Consolidated Trials.
14.108 ____ Interest.
14.109 Setoff for Indirect Benefit.
14.110 Incidental Expenses and Proration of Taxes.
14.111 Abandonment of Procedure by Condemnor.
14.112 Finding that Condemnor is Not Legally Authorized to Acquire the Property.
14.113 Finding Contrary to Claim by Condemnor That it Did Not Take Property.
14.114 Decision By the Court and Entry of Judgment.
14.115 Additional Allowances for Costs and Expenses.
14.116 Payment Pending Appeal.
14.117 Small Claims Proceedings.
14.118 Summary.
14.119 Procedural Checklist.
14.120 Forms—Demand on Condemnor to File Copy of Proceedings to Determine Need and Location of Public Project with Appellate Division for Purpose of Judicial Review.
14.121 ____ Petition for Review of Determination and Finding that Public Use, Benefit or Purpose Will be Served by Proposed Acquisition.
14.122 ____ Judgment of Appellate Division Rejecting the Determination and Finding that Public Use, Benefit or Purpose Will be Served by Proposed Acquisition.
14.123 ____ Complaint by Condemnee to Establish Fair and Reasonable Value for Temporary Use and Occupancy After Acquisition by Eminent Domain.

TABLE OF CONTENTS

Sec.
14.124 ____ Notice of Pendency of Proceeding in Supreme Court to Acquire Property by Eminent Domain and File Acquisition Map. 💾
14.125 ____ Notice of Petition in Proceeding in Supreme Court to Acquire Property by Eminent Domain and File Acquisition Map. 💾
14.126 ____ Petition in Proceeding in Supreme Court to Acquire Property by Eminent Domain and File Acquisition Map. 💾
14.127 ____ Petition in Proceeding in Supreme Court to Acquire Property by Eminent Domain and File Acquisition Map—Petitioner Exempt from Compliance with Eminent Domain Procedure Law Article 2. 💾
14.128 ____ Answer to Petition in Proceeding in Supreme Court to Acquire Property by Eminent Domain and File Acquisition Map. 💾
14.129 ____ Order to Show Cause Why Condemnor Should Not be Permitted to Enter Immediately upon Real Property and Devote It Temporarily to Public Use Specified in Petition Upon Deposit of a Fixed Sum with the Court. 💾
14.130 ____ Order to Show Cause Why Condemnor Should Not be Permitted to File Acquisition Maps or Enter upon Real Property. 💾
14.131 ____ Order in Proceeding in Supreme Court to Acquire Property by Eminent Domain and File Acquisition Map. 💾
14.132 ____ Notice of Acquisition by Eminent Domain Where Supreme Court Has Jurisdiction. 💾
14.133 ____ Claim for Damages Arising from Acquisition by Eminent Domain—General Form. 💾
14.134 ____ Judgment Awarding Compensation in Claim for Acquisition of Property by Eminent Domain. 💾
14.135 ____ Notice of Motion for Additional Allowance to Condemnee for Expert Witnesses. 💾
14.136 ____ Affidavit in Support of Motion for Additional Allowance to Condemnee for Expert Witnesses. 💾
14.137 ____ Order Granting Additional Allowance to Condemnee for Expert Witnesses. 💾

CHAPTER 15. ENVIRONMENTAL LAW

15.1 Scope Note.
15.2 Strategy.
15.3 State Environmental Quality Review Act.
15.4 ____ Determination of Significance.
15.5 ____ The Environmental Impact Statement and Findings Statement.
15.6 ____ Judicial Review.
15.7 ____ Checklist.
15.8 Water Pollution Control.
15.9 ____ SPDES Permit Program.
15.10 ____ Stormwater Discharges and Oil Spills.
15.11 ____ Enforcement.

TABLE OF CONTENTS

Sec.
15.12 ____ Strategy: Clean Water Act Citizen Suit Checklist.
15.13 Wetlands Protection.
15.14 ____ Strategy: Checklist.
15.15 ____ The Federal Scheme.
15.16 ____ New York Tidal and Freshwater Wetlands Law.
15.17 ____ Permit Procedure and Criteria.
15.18 ____ Penalties.
15.19 Air Pollution Control.
15.20 ____ The 1990 CAA Amendments.
15.21 ____ New York State Requirements.
15.22 ____ Enforcement.
15.23 Regulation of Solid and Hazardous Waste.
15.24 ____ New York Hazardous Waste Regulation.
15.25 ____ Enforcement.
15.26 Regulation of Underground Storage Tanks and Petroleum Storage Tanks—Federal Law.
15.27 ____ New York Law.
15.28 Regulation of Inactive Hazardous Waste Sites—CERCLA.
15.29 ____ CERCLA Section 107(a).
15.30 ____ Lender Liability, Contribution and Indemnification Under CERCLA.
15.31 ____ New York Law.
15.32 Relevant Common Law Doctrines—Nuisance.
15.33 Common Law Doctrines—Trespass.
15.34 Regulatory Takings.
15.35 Drafting Checklist—Clean Water Act Citizen Suit Notice Letter.
15.36 ____ Clean Water Act and Resource Conservation and Recovery Act Citizen Suit Notice Letter.
15.37 ____ Clean Water Act Complaint.
15.38 ____ Nuisance and Trespass Complaint.
15.39 ____ Oil Spill Complaint.
15.40 Forms—Clean Water Act Citizen Suit Notice Letter. 💾
15.41 ____ Clean Water Act and Resource Conservation and Recovery Act Citizen Suit Notice Letter. 💾
15.42 ____ Clean Water Act Complaint. 💾
15.43 ____ Nuisance and Trespass Complaint. 💾
15.44 ____ Oil Spill Complaint. 💾

CHAPTER 16. LAND USE LAW

16.1 Scope Note.
16.2 Strategy.
16.3 Local Land Use Law.
16.4 ____ Delegated Authority.
16.5 ____ Enabling Acts.
16.6 ____ ____ New York City.
16.7 ____ Home Rule Authority.
16.8 ____ ____ Flexibility.
16.9 ____ ____ Floating Zone.
16.10 ____ Summary.

LV

TABLE OF CONTENTS

Sec.
16.11 Comprehensive Plan.
16.12 ____ Judicial Definition.
16.13 ____ Statutory Definition.
16.14 ____ Preparation and Adoption.
16.15 ____ Protects Zoning Against Challenge.
16.16 ____ Summary.
16.17 Substantive Limits—Illustrative Case.
16.18 ____ Substantive Due Process.
16.19 ____ Procedural Due Process.
16.20 ____ Equal Protection.
16.21 ____ *Ultra Vires*.
16.22 ____ Regulatory Takings.
16.23 ____ Vested Rights.
16.24 ____ Preemption.
16.25 ____ First Amendment.
16.26 ____ Summary.
16.27 Local Process.
16.28 ____ Structure of Local Regulations.
16.29 ____ Adoption.
16.30 ____ Amendment.
16.31 ____ Other Regulations/Official Map.
16.32 ____ Building Regulations and Permits.
16.33 ____ Summary.
16.34 Local Boards and Practices.
16.35 ____ Local Legislature.
16.36 ____ Planning Board.
16.37 ____ Zoning Board of Appeals.
16.38 ____ Freedom of Information.
16.39 ____ Open Meetings.
16.40 ____ Conflict of Interests.
16.41 ____ Summary.
16.42 Judicial Review.
16.43 ____ Procedures.
16.44 ____ Standards.
16.45 ____ ____ Local Legislature.
16.46 ____ ____ Zoning Board of Appeals.
16.47 ____ ____ Planning Board.
16.48 ____ Standing.
16.49 ____ Exhaustion.
16.50 ____ Remedies.
16.51 ____ Summary.
16.52 Local Environmental Review.
16.53 ____ Actions Subject to SEQRA.
16.54 ____ ____ Building Permits.
16.55 ____ ____ Variances.
16.56 ____ ____ Subdivisions.
16.57 ____ ____ Site Plans.
16.58 ____ ____ Rezoning.
16.59 ____ Summary.
16.60 Zoning Law—In General.

LVI

TABLE OF CONTENTS

Sec.

16.61	As of Right Use.
16.62	Nonconforming Use—Definition and Application.
16.63	____ Changes.
16.64	____ Reconstruction and Restoration.
16.65	____ Enlargement, Alteration or Extension.
16.66	____ Changes to Another Nonconforming Use.
16.67	____ Termination.
16.68	____ Abandonment.
16.69	____ Amortization.
16.70	____ Transfer of Ownership.
16.71	____ Procedures.
16.72	____ Summary.
16.73	Use Variance.
16.74	____ Statutory Standard.
16.75	____ ____ Reasonable Return.
16.76	____ ____ Unique Hardship.
16.77	____ ____ Protect Essential Neighborhood Character.
16.78	____ ____ Self–Created Hardship.
16.79	____ Minimum Variance Needed.
16.80	____ Procedure.
16.81	____ Summary.
16.82	Area Variance.
16.83	____ Statutory Balancing Test.
16.84	____ ____ Guiding Principles from Case Law.
16.85	____ ____ Balancing Factors.
16.86	____ Minimum Variance Needed.
16.87	____ Procedure.
16.88	____ Summary.
16.89	Conditions Imposed on Use and Area Variances.
16.90	Special Use Permits.
16.91	____ Imposition and Use of Standards.
16.92	____ Findings and Determination of Board.
16.93	____ Limitation on Imposition of Conditions.
16.94	____ Procedure.
16.95	____ Summary.
16.96	Subdivision Approval.
16.97	____ Procedure.
16.98	____ ____ How Affected By SEQRA.
16.99	____ Provision of Essential Services.
16.100	____ Parkland.
16.101	____ Decisions and Conditions.
16.102	____ Summary.
16.103	Site Plans.
16.104	____ Responsible Agency.
16.105	____ ____ Procedure.
16.106	____ ____ Standards for Review.
16.107	____ ____ Conditions Imposed.
16.108	____ Summary.
16.109	Particularized Actions.
16.110	____ Spot Zoning.

TABLE OF CONTENTS

Sec.
16.111 ____ ____ Challenge Dismissed.
16.112 ____ ____ Challenge Successful.
16.113 ____ Rezoning.
16.114 ____ ____ Conditions.
16.115 ____ ____ Contract Zoning.
16.116 ____ ____ Development Agreements.
16.117 ____ Summary.
16.118 Special Regulations.
16.119 ____ Accessory Uses.
16.120 ____ Accessory Apartments.
16.121 ____ Home Offices.
16.122 ____ Definition of Family.
16.123 ____ Affordable Housing.
16.124 ____ Mobile Homes.
16.125 ____ Aesthetics.
16.126 ____ ____ Architectural Review.
16.127 ____ ____ Historic Preservation.
16.128 ____ Public Uses.
16.129 ____ ____ Public Utilities.
16.130 ____ ____ Cellular Transmission Facilities.
16.131 ____ ____ Religious Uses.
16.132 ____ Summary.
16.133 Forms—Environmental Assessment—Short Form. 💾
16.134 ____ Environmental Assessment—Long Form. 💾

CHAPTER 17. EMPLOYMENT LAW

17.1 Scope Note.
17.2 Strategy.
17.3 ____ Plaintiff's Counsel's Investigation.
17.4 ____ Defendant's Counsel's Investigation.
17.5 ____ Pre-litigation Settlement Process.
17.6 ____ Negotiating With Opposing Counsel.
17.7 ____ Alternative Dispute Resolution ("ADR").
17.8 ____ ____ Mediation.
17.9 ____ ____ Arbitration.
17.10 ____ Settlement and Severance Agreements.
17.11 ____ ____ Older Workers Benefit Protection Act ("OWBPA").
17.12 ____ ____ COBRA.
17.13 ____ ____ Pay.
17.14 ____ ____ Income Taxes.
17.15 ____ ____ Benefits.
17.16 ____ Other Severance Issues.
17.17 ____ Independent Contractor vs. Employee.
17.18 ____ Checklist: Initial Considerations for Plaintiff.
17.19 ____ Checklist: Terminating an Employee.
17.20 Causes of Action.
17.21 ____ Tort–Assault.
17.22 ____ ____ Battery.
17.23 ____ ____ Conspiracy.

LVIII

TABLE OF CONTENTS

Sec.
- 17.24 ____ ____ Conversion.
- 17.25 ____ ____ Defamation.
- 17.26 ____ ____ False Imprisonment; Malicious Prosecution.
- 17.27 ____ ____ Fraud, Negligent Misrepresentation and Fraudulent Inducement.
- 17.28 ____ ____ Intentional Infliction of Emotional Distress.
- 17.29 ____ ____ Interference with Business Relations.
- 17.30 ____ ____ Negligence.
- 17.31 ____ ____ *Prima Facie* Tort.
- 17.32 ____ ____ Wrongful Discharge.
- 17.33 ____ Contract.
- 17.34 ____ ____ Express Promises.
- 17.35 ____ ____ Implied Promises.
- 17.36 ____ ____ Estoppel.
- 17.37 Statutory Causes of Action—Age Discrimination.
- 17.38 ____ Anti-reprisal Provisions of Various Statutes.
- 17.39 ____ Arrest Records.
- 17.40 ____ Bankruptcy.
- 17.41 ____ Convictions.
- 17.42 ____ Credit Information.
- 17.43 ____ Disability.
- 17.44 ____ Equal Pay.
- 17.45 ____ Family and Medical Leave Act (FMLA).
- 17.46 ____ Health Plan Coverage (COBRA).
- 17.47 ____ Legal Off Duty Activities.
- 17.48 ____ Marital Status Discrimination.
- 17.49 ____ Discrimination on the Basis of Race, Color or National Origin.
- 17.50 ____ Pension Plans.
- 17.51 ____ Plant Closing, Mass Layoffs.
- 17.52 ____ Polygraphs.
- 17.53 ____ Public Employees.
- 17.54 ____ Pregnancy.
- 17.55 ____ Privacy.
- 17.56 ____ Religious Discrimination.
- 17.57 ____ Sex Discrimination, Harassment.
- 17.58 ____ Sexual Orientation Discrimination.
- 17.59 ____ Title VII, Burdens of Proof.
- 17.60 ____ Unemployment Insurance.
- 17.61 ____ Unionization, Rights Within Unions.
- 17.62 ____ Unsafe Workplace.
- 17.63 ____ Wages; Unpaid Compensation; Overtime.
- 17.64 ____ Whistleblowing/*Qui Tam*.
- 17.65 ____ Workers' Compensation.
- 17.66 Procedure—Anti-discrimination Agency Practice.
- 17.67 ____ Filing and Responding to Administrative Charges.
- 17.68 ____ Election of Remedies.
- 17.69 ____ Statutes of Limitations and Prerequisites to Private Lawsuits.
- 17.70 Private Lawsuits.

TABLE OF CONTENTS

Sec.
17.71 —— Discovery—General Considerations.
17.72 —— —— Plaintiff's Strategy.
17.73 —— Summary Judgment.
17.74 —— Trial.
17.75 —— Fee Application.
17.76 —— Post–Trial Motions and Appeal.
17.77 —— Checklist: Statutes of Limitations.
17.78 —— Checklist: Commencement of New York State Actions.
17.79 —— Checklist: Commencement of Federal Court Actions.
17.80 Miscellaneous Practice Issues—OFCCP/Glass Ceiling Audits.
17.81 —— Employment Policies and Handbooks.
17.82 Drafting the Complaint.
17.83 Drafting Checklist—Complaint.
17.84 Drafting the Answer.
17.85 Drafting Checklist—Answer
17.86 Forms—Client (Plaintiff) Intake Questionnaire.
17.87 —— Severance/Release Agreement.
17.88 —— Letter to EEOC Requesting "Mohasco" Waiver of State Processing.
17.89 —— Charge of Discrimination—New York State Division of Human Rights (Official Form).
17.90 —— Information Sheet—New York State Division of Human Rights (Official Form).
17.91 —— SDHR Information Sheet.
17.92 —— Charge of Discrimination—Equal Employment Opportunity Commission (Official Form).
17.93 —— Affidavit for a Charge of Discrimination—Equal Employment Opportunity Commission (Official Form).
17.94 —— EEOC Filing Cover Letter Requesting EEOC Processing of Dual-filed Charge.
17.95 —— Letter Requesting Administrative Convenience Dismissal from State or City Administrative Agency.
17.96 —— Pleadings—New York State Complaint.
17.97 —— —— New York State Answer.
17.98 —— —— Federal Complaint.
17.99 —— —— Federal Answer.

CHAPTER 18. CIVIL RIGHTS

18.1 Scope Note.
18.2 Strategy.
18.3 —— Checklist.
18.4 Overview of New York and Federal Civil Rights Provisions.
18.5 Jurisdiction over Civil Rights Actions.
18.6 New York Bill of Rights.
18.7 —— Overview.
18.8 —— Comparison With Federal Bill of Rights.
18.9 —— Search and Seizure.
18.10 —— —— Civil Liability.
18.11 —— —— Return of Seized Property.

TABLE OF CONTENTS

Sec.
18.12 ____ Rights of Persons Accused of Crimes.
18.13 ____ ____ Public Trial/Closure of Courtroom.
18.14 ____ ____ Exclusion of Public or Press.
18.15 ____ Rights of Jurors.
18.16 General Federal Civil Rights Provisions.
18.17 ____ 42 U.S.C.A. § 1981.
18.18 ____ 42 U.S.C.A. § 1983.
18.19 ____ Other Federal Civil Rights Provisions.
18.20 Police and Prosecutorial Misconduct.
18.21 ____ Excessive Force.
18.22 ____ False Arrest.
18.23 ____ False Imprisonment.
18.24 ____ Search and Seizure.
18.25 ____ Malicious Prosecution.
18.26 First Amendment.
18.27 ____ Freedom of Speech.
18.28 ____ Freedom of Religion.
18.29 Rights of Prisoners.
18.30 Defenses to Federal Actions.
18.31 ____ Absolute Immunity.
18.32 ____ Qualified Immunity.
18.33 ____ Eleventh Amendment.
18.34 ____ *Monell* and Its Progeny.
18.35 ____ *Respondeat Superior*.
18.36 ____ Abstention.
18.37 ____ *Res Judicata* and Collateral Estoppel.
18.38 ____ Statute of Limitations.
18.39 Housing.
18.40 ____ Prohibition Against Discrimination in Publicly Assisted Housing.
18.41 ____ ____ Owners and Lessors.
18.42 ____ ____ Real Estate Agents and Brokers.
18.43 ____ ____ Remedies for Discrimination.
18.44 ____ Prohibition Against Discrimination in Private Housing.
18.45 ____ ____ Owners and Lessors.
18.46 ____ ____ Real Estate Agents and Brokers.
18.47 ____ ____ Cooperatives.
18.48 ____ ____ Remedies for Discrimination.
18.49 ____ ____ ____ Administrative Proceedings.
18.50 ____ ____ ____ Actions in State and Federal Court.
18.51 ____ *Prima Facie* Case and Burden of Proof.
18.52 ____ Summary of Procedure for Filing an Administrative Claim and Challenging an SDHR Order.
18.53 Education.
18.54 Equal Rights in Places of Public Accommodation and Amusement.
18.55 ____ General Provisions.
18.56 ____ Private Clubs.
18.57 ____ Persons With Disabilities Accompanied by a Guide Dog, Hearing Dog or Service Dog.
18.58 ____ Remedies for Discrimination.

TABLE OF CONTENTS

Sec.
- 18.59 Employment Discrimination Provisions Exclusive to the New York Civil Rights Law.
- 18.60 ____ In General.
- 18.61 ____ Persons With Disabilities.
- 18.62 ____ Persons With Genetic Disorders.
- 18.63 Right of Privacy.
- 18.64 ____ Generally.
- 18.65 ____ Police Officers, Corrections Officers and Firefighters.
- 18.66 ____ Victims of Sex Offenses.
- 18.67 Changing One's Name.
- 18.68 ____ Procedure for Petition to Change Name.
- 18.69 ____ ____ Contents of Petition.
- 18.70 ____ ____ Special Procedures for Infants.
- 18.71 ____ Factors to Be Considered by the Court.
- 18.72 ____ Publication Requirement.
- 18.73 ____ Checklist.
- 18.74 Heart Balm Statute.
- 18.75 ____ Penalty for Bringing Action.
- 18.76 ____ Action for Return of Gifts Made in Contemplation of Marriage.
- 18.77 ____ ____ Procedure.
- 18.78 Miscellaneous Rights and Immunities.
- 18.79 ____ Frivolous Litigation.
- 18.80 ____ ____ Protection from SLAPP Suits.
- 18.81 ____ Libel and Slander.
- 18.82 ____ ____ Defenses.
- 18.83 ____ Breast Feeding.
- 18.84 ____ Suspension of Rights Due to Imprisonment.
- 18.85 ____ Shield Law.
- 18.86 ____ Performing Abortion.
- 18.87 ____ "Good Samaritan" Law Provisions.
- 18.88 Drafting Checklists.
- 18.89 ____ Framing the Federal Court § 1983 Complaint.
- 18.90 ____ Petition to Change One's Name.
- 18.91 Forms.
- 18.92 ____ Complaint for False Arrest, False Imprisonment and Malicious Prosecution.
- 18.93 ____ Complaint for Excessive Force.
- 18.94 ____ Complaint for Return of Seized Property.
- 18.95 ____ Complaint Against Landlord for Housing Discrimination.
- 18.96 ____ Complaint Against Cooperative for Discrimination.
- 18.97 ____ Notice of Commencement of Action for Discrimination.
- 18.98 ____ Complaint for Discrimination in Place of Public Accommodation.
- 18.99 ____ Petition to Change Name.

CHAPTER 19. IMMIGRATION AND NATIONALITY LAW —PERMANENT RESIDENCE APPLICATIONS

- 19.1 Scope Note.

TABLE OF CONTENTS

Sec.	
19.2	Strategy.
19.3	____ Flowchart.
19.4	Overview of the U.S. Immigration System.
19.5	____ Numerical Limitations on Immigrant Selection.
19.6	____ Implementation: Foreign State Chargeability and Quota Allocation.
19.7	Family–Based Immigration.
19.8	____ Immediate Relative Categories.
19.9	____ Family Preference Categories.
19.10	____ Qualifying as a Relation.
19.11	____ ____ "Child" and "Parent" Issues.
19.12	____ ____ "Marriage" Issues.
19.13	____ Petitioning Procedures and Documentation.
19.14	____ ____ I–130 Petition.
19.15	____ Orphans and Amerasians.
19.16	____ Abused Spouse and Children.
19.17	Employment–Based Immigration.
19.18	____ First Employment Preference Applicants (Priority Workers).
19.19	____ ____ Extraordinary Ability Aliens.
19.20	____ ____ Outstanding Professors and Researchers.
19.21	____ ____ Managerial or Executive Intracompany Transferees.
19.22	____ Second Employment Preference Applicants.
19.23	____ ____ Exceptional Ability Aliens.
19.24	____ ____ Advanced Degree Professionals.
19.25	____ ____ The Role of "National Interest."
19.26	____ Third Employment Preference Applicants.
19.27	____ ____ Professional and Skilled Workers.
19.28	____ ____ Unskilled Workers.
19.29	____ I–140 Petition, Procedures and Documentation.
19.30	____ ____ Checklist.
19.31	____ Labor Certification.
19.32	____ ____ Procedures.
19.33	____ ____ Legal Issues.
19.34	____ ____ Job Description.
19.35	____ ____ Business Necessity.
19.36	____ ____ Recruitment.
19.37	____ ____ Approvals.
19.38	____ ____ Notices of Findings.
19.39	____ ____ Denials and Administrative Appeal.
19.40	____ Fourth Employment Preference Applicants.
19.41	____ ____ Religious Workers and Ministers.
19.42	____ Fifth Employment Preference Applicants (Immigrant Investors).
19.43	____ Petition Procedures and Requirements.
19.44	____ ____ Special Immigrant Investor Programs.
19.45	Special Categories.
19.46	____ The Diversity (Lottery) Program.
19.47	____ Registry.
19.48	____ Cancellation of Removal.
19.49	____ Legislatively Created Programs.

TABLE OF CONTENTS

Sec.
19.50 ____ Asylum and Refugee Status.
19.51 Applying for Permanent Residence.
19.52 ____ Exclusionary Grounds.
19.53 ____ Immigrant Visa Processing.
19.54 ____ ____ Framework of the Immigrant Visa Processing System.
19.55 ____ ____ Special Requirements, Public Law No. 103–317.
19.56 ____ ____ Checklist of Required Documents.
19.57 ____ Adjustment of Status.
19.58 ____ ____ General Requirements.
19.59 ____ ____ Special Provisions of Section 245(i).
19.60 ____ ____ Discretionary Factors.
19.61 ____ ____ Application Process.
19.62 ____ ____ Concurrent Filing of Petition and Adjustment of Status.
19.63 ____ ____ Completion of the Process.
19.64 ____ ____ Administrative and Judicial Review.
19.65 ____ ____ Checklist.
19.66 ____ Tactical Considerations.
19.67 ____ ____ Nonimmigrant Status as a Factor.
19.68 ____ ____ Immigrant Visa Processing Versus Adjustment of Status.
19.69 ____ ____ Flowchart.
19.70 The Green Card and its Limitations.
19.71 ____ Conditional Residence.
19.72 ____ ____ Marriage Cases, Removal of Condition.
19.73 ____ ____ Immigrant Investors, Removal of Condition.
19.74 ____ Unconditional Permanent Residence.
19.75 Forms.
19.76 ____ Form I–130.
19.77 ____ Form I–140.
19.78 ____ Form I–485.
19.79 ____ Form OF–230.

CHAPTER 20. ADOPTIONS

20.1 Scope Note.
20.2 Strategy.
20.3 ____ Checklist: Pre-adoption—Counsel for Parents.
20.4 ____ Checklist: Interview With Birth Mother.
20.5 Adoptions—Generally.
20.6 ____ Defined.
20.7 ____ Rationale.
20.8 ____ Judicial Construction of Statutes.
20.9 ____ Concurrent Jurisdiction.
20.10 ____ ____ Where to File Adoption Proceedings.
20.11 ____ Choice of Venue.
20.12 ____ Types.
20.13 ____ Effect of Adoption.
20.14 ____ Who May Adopt—Statutory Mandates.
20.15 ____ ____ Separated Persons.

LXIV

TABLE OF CONTENTS

Sec.	
20.16	———— —— Foster Parents: Preference to Adopt.
20.17	———— —— Second Parent Adoptions.
20.18	———— —— Unwed Putative Fathers.
20.19	———— —— Citizens and Aliens.
20.20	———— —— Age as a Factor.
20.21	———— —— Extended Family as Factor.
20.22	———— —— Adult Unmarried Person.
20.23	———— Who May Be Adopted——In General.
20.24	———— —— Adult Adoptions.
20.25	———— —— Aliens.
20.26	———— —— Non-marital Children.
20.27	———— —— Interracial Adoptions.
20.28	———— —— Religion as a Factor.
20.29	———— Consents Required—Statutory Mandate.
20.30	———— —— Rights of Unwed Fathers.
20.31	———— —— When Consent Not Required.
20.32	———— —— Notice of a Proposed Adoption.
20.33	———— —— Checklist of Fathers to Receive Notice of Adoption.
20.34	———— Persons Excluded from Notice.
20.35	———— Purpose of Notice.
20.36	———— Procedure.
20.37	Private Placement Adoptions—In General.
20.38	———— Terminating Parental Rights Based Upon Abandonment.
20.39	———— Terminating Parental Rights Based Upon Mental Retardation.
20.40	———— Dual Representation Prohibited.
20.41	———— Independent Counsel.
20.42	———— Permissible Dual Representation.
20.43	———— Independent Representation of the Child.
20.44	———— The Attorney's Fee.
20.45	———— Locating an Infant for Adoption—The Attorney's Responsibility.
20.46	———— Illegal Sale of Babies.
20.47	———— Advertisement.
20.48	———— Foreign Infants.
20.49	———— Readoption of Foreign Infants.
20.50	———— Native American Children.
20.51	———— Residency Requirements.
20.52	———— Permissible Payments by Adoptive Parents.
20.53	———— Interstate Compact on the Placement of Children.
20.54	———— Pre-certification of Adoptive Parents—In General.
20.55	———— —— Requirement of Pre-certification.
20.56	———— —— Procedure.
20.57	———— —— Checklist of Documents Needed for Certification.
20.58	———— Hospital Procedures—Physical Transfer of Custody of the Infant to the Adoptive Parents.
20.59	———— —— Certification Procedures.
20.60	———— Petition for Temporary Guardianship—Legislative Background.
20.61	———— —— Impact of Pre–placement Certification.

TABLE OF CONTENTS

Sec.
20.62 —— Procedure Upon Filing Petition for Temporary Guardianship.
20.63 —— Consent of Birth Parents.
20.64 —— —— Extra–Judicial Consent.
20.65 —— —— Judicial Consents.
20.66 —— —— Personal Appearances Required.
20.67 —— —— Step-Parent Adoptions.
20.68 —— Foreign Born Children.
20.69 —— Petition for Adoption.
20.70 —— The Agreement of Adoption.
20.71 —— Affidavit of Attorney Representing Adoptive Parents.
20.72 —— Confidential Affidavit.
20.73 —— Attorney's Affidavit of Financial Disclosure.
20.74 —— Notification of Order of Adoption; Report of Adoption.
20.75 —— Order of Adoption.
20.76 —— Birth Mother's Affidavit Regarding Putative Father.
20.77 —— Affidavit of Intermediary.
20.78 —— Attorney's Affidavit Regarding Legal Fees.
20.79 —— Affidavit of Explanation of Criminal Activity.
20.80 —— Investigation by Disinterested Person.
20.81 —— The Hearing.
20.82 —— Certificate of Adoption.
20.83 —— The New Birth Certificate.
20.84 —— Checklist of Documents Required for Private Placement Adoption.
20.85 Agency Adoptions—Defined.
20.86 —— Definition of "Authorized Agency."
20.87 —— Venue.
20.88 —— Child's Entry into the System.
20.89 —— —— Voluntary Transfer of Legal Custody of Children to the Authorized Agency.
20.90 —— —— Judicial Surrender.
20.91 —— —— Extra–Judicial Surrender.
20.92 —— —— Court Approval of Extra–Judicial Surrender.
20.93 —— —— Assigned Counsel.
20.94 —— —— Required Notice of Application.
20.95 —— —— Notification to Court.
20.96 —— —— Court Order.
20.97 —— —— Conditional Surrender.
20.98 —— —— Recording a Surrender.
20.99 —— —— Revocation of Surrender.
20.100 —— —— Proceedings Subsequent to Execution of Extra–Judicial Surrender.
20.101 —— —— Court Ordered Transfer of Children to Authorized Agency.
20.102 —— Procedures.
20.103 —— The Petition.
20.104 —— The Agreement of Adoption.
20.105 —— Verified Schedule.
20.106 —— Affidavit of Financial Disclosure.
20.107 —— Confidential Affidavit.

TABLE OF CONTENTS

Sec.
20.108 ____ Marital Affidavit.
20.109 ____ Child's Medical History.
20.110 ____ Supplemental Affidavit.
20.111 ____ Notification of Order of Adoption; Report of Adoption.
20.112 ____ Doctor's Certificate of Health.
20.113 ____ Authorization and Approval for Subsidized Adoption.
20.114 ____ Adoption Homestudy.
20.115 ____ Affidavit Identifying Party.
20.116 ____ Order of Adoption.
20.117 ____ Certificate of Adoption.
20.118 ____ Abuse Clearance Form.
20.119 ____ Unavailability of Abuse Clearance Form and Criminal Conviction Check.
20.120 ____ Attorney's Affidavit of Legal Fees.
20.121 ____ Checklist of Other Required Supporting Documentation.
20.122 ____ The Adoption Hearing.
20.123 Post-adoption Issues—The Open Adoption.
20.124 ____ Visitation With Siblings.
20.125 ____ Sealing Adoption Records.
20.126 ____ ____ Constitutionality of Laws Relating to Sealing Records.
20.127 ____ ____ Good Cause for Unsealing Records.
20.128 ____ ____ ____ Criminal Investigation and Probation Department.
20.129 ____ ____ ____ Requirement of Medical Information.
20.130 ____ ____ ____ Religion.
20.131 ____ Abrogation of Order.
20.132 Checklist of Facts and Allegations to be Included in the Petition for a Private Placement Adoption.
20.133 Forms—Private Placement Adoptions—Petition for Certification as a Qualified Adoptive Parent.
20.134 ____ ____ Petition for Temporary Guardianship.
20.135 ____ ____ Judicial Consent of Natural Parent.
20.136 ____ ____ Extra-Judicial Consent of Natural Parent.
20.137 ____ ____ Petition for Adoption.
20.138 ____ ____ Order of Adoption (Private Placement).
20.139 ____ Agency Adoptions—Petition for Adoption.
20.140 ____ ____ Verified Schedule.
20.141 ____ ____ Marital Affidavit.
20.142 ____ ____ Marital Affidavit Dispensing With Consent of Spouse After Three Year Separation.
20.143 ____ ____ Confidential Affidavit.
20.144 ____ ____ Affidavit Pursuant to Section 111–a of the Domestic Relations Law.
20.145 ____ ____ Agreement of Adoption and Consent.
20.146 ____ ____ Affidavit Identifying Party.
20.147 ____ ____ Affidavit of Financial Disclosure by Parents.
20.148 ____ ____ Order of Adoption.

Volume 23

CHAPTER 21. DOMESTIC RELATIONS

21.1 Scope Note.

TABLE OF CONTENTS

Sec.
21.2 Strategy.
21.3 Jurisdiction.
21.4 ____ Residence Requirements.
21.5 ____ Uniform Child Custody Jurisdiction Act.
21.6 Competency of the Court to Grant Relief.
21.7 ____ Equitable Distribution.
21.8 ____ Support.
21.9 ____ Custody and Visitation.
21.10 Jurisdiction Over the Defendant's Person or Property.
21.11 ____ Personal Jurisdiction.
21.12 ____ Long Arm Jurisdiction.
21.13 ____ *In Rem* Jurisdiction.
21.14 *Quasi in Rem* Jurisdiction.
21.15 Venue.
21.16 ____ Changing Venue.
21.17 Joinder, Consolidation and Joint Trials.
21.18 Grounds for Divorce.
21.19 ____ No Official No–Fault Ground.
21.20 ____ Cruel and Inhuman Treatment.
21.21 ____ ____ Defenses.
21.22 ____ Abandonment.
21.23 ____ ____ Defenses.
21.24 ____ ____ Effect of Separation Agreement.
21.25 ____ Imprisonment.
21.26 ____ Adultery.
21.27 ____ ____ Defenses.
21.28 ____ ____ Effect of Separation Agreement.
21.29 ____ Divorce Action Based Upon Living Apart Pursuant to Separation Decree or Judgment.
21.30 ____ Divorce Action Based Upon Living Apart Pursuant to Separation Agreement.
21.31 ____ Dual Divorce.
21.32 Effect of Sister State Divorce Judgment.
21.33 Equitable Distribution.
21.34 ____ When Available.
21.35 ____ Identification of Property.
21.36 ____ Characterization of Property.
21.37 ____ ____ Marital Property.
21.38 ____ ____ ____ Pensions.
21.39 ____ ____ ____ Professional Practices, Licenses, Degrees and Careers.
21.40 ____ ____ Separate Property.
21.41 ____ ____ ____ Increase in Value of Separate Property.
21.42 ____ Valuation Dates.
21.43 ____ Valuation Methods.
21.44 ____ Distribution Factors.
21.45 ____ Tax Considerations.
21.46 Maintenance.
21.47 ____ Legislative Factors.
21.48 ____ Effect of Fault.

TABLE OF CONTENTS

Sec.
21.49 ___ Current Trends.
21.50 ___ Payments Fixed by Agreement.
21.51 ___ Tax Consequences.
21.52 Child Support.
21.53 ___ Child Support Standards Act.
21.54 ___ ___ Where Statutory Percentages Are Unfair or Inappropriate.
21.55 ___ ___ Recent Trends.
21.56 ___ Effect of Agreement or Stipulation.
21.57 Health and Life Insurance.
21.58 Custody.
21.59 ___ Visitation.
21.60 ___ Relocation of Custodial Parent With the Child.
21.61 ___ Joint Custody.
21.62 ___ Proceedings in Which Custody Dispositions Are Available.
21.63 Financial Disclosure.
21.64 Disclosure on Matters Going to the Merits of the Case.
21.65 Net Worth Statement.
21.66 Statement of Proposed Disposition.
21.67 Findings of Fact and Conclusions of Law; Judgments.
21.68 Modification.
21.69 ___ Maintenance.
21.70 ___ Child Support.
21.71 ___ Custody.
21.72 Enforcement.
21.73 ___ Plenary Action to Enforce Agreement.
21.74 ___ Defenses.
21.75 Practice Considerations.
21.76 ___ Procedure for Attorneys in Domestic Relations Matters.
21.77 ___ Disciplinary Rules.
21.78 ___ Fee Arbitration Rules.
21.79 ___ Rules Regarding Case Management.
21.80 Procedural Checklist—Calendar Control.
21.81 Drafting Checklist—Retainer Agreements.
21.82 ___ Complaint in Action for Divorce.
21.83 ___ Statement of Proposed Disposition.
21.84 Forms.
21.85 ___ Retainer Agreement. 💾
21.86 ___ Complaint for Divorce. 💾
21.87 ___ Statement of Net Worth. 💾
21.88 ___ Statement of Proposed Disposition. 💾
21.89 ___ Findings of Fact and Conclusions of Law. 💾
21.90 ___ Matrimonial Judgments. 💾
21.91 ___ Referee's Report on Findings of Fact and Conclusions of Law. 💾
21.92 ___ Matrimonial Judgment Entered Upon Referee's Report. 💾

CHAPTER 22. GUARDIANSHIP

22.1 Scope Note.

TABLE OF CONTENTS

Sec.
22.2 Strategy.
22.3 Checklists.
22.4 Prior Law—Generally.
22.5 ____ Role of Committees and Conservators.
22.6 ____ Problems Encountered.
22.7 ____ Impact of *Matter of Grinker (Rose)*.
22.8 Legislative Purpose of Mental Hygiene Law Article 81.
22.9 Definitions.
22.10 Summary.
22.11 Power to Appoint Guardian—Generally.
22.12 ____ Elements.
22.13 ____ Incapacity.
22.14 ____ Primary Considerations.
22.15 ____ Jurisdiction.
22.16 ____ Venue.
22.17 ____ Standing to Commence Proceeding.
22.18 ____ Summary.
22.19 Proceeding to Appoint Guardian.
22.20 ____ Time and Method of Service of Notice.
22.21 ____ Persons Entitled to Notice.
22.22 ____ Notice Requirements.
22.23 ____ Petition.
22.24 ____ Summary.
22.25 Court Evaluator—Persons Eligible for Appointment.
22.26 ____ Duties.
22.27 ____ Compensation.
22.28 ____ Appointment of Counsel for the Alleged Incapacitated Person.
22.29 ____ Summary.
22.30 Hearing and Order—An Overview.
22.31 ____ Procedure.
22.32 ____ Presence of Person Alleged to be Incapacitated.
22.33 ____ Evidence.
22.34 ____ Findings of the Court.
22.35 ____ ____ Voluntary Appointment.
22.36 ____ ____ Personal Needs.
22.37 ____ ____ Property Management.
22.38 ____ Dispositional Alternatives.
22.39 ____ Award of Counsel Fees to Petitioner.
22.40 ____ Person to be Appointed Guardian.
22.41 ____ Priority and Criteria for Appointment.
22.42 ____ Requirement of Bond.
22.43 ____ Designation of Clerk and Issuance of Commission.
22.44 ____ Summary.
22.45 Role of Guardian—Overview.
22.46 ____ Duties.
22.47 ____ Powers; Property Management.
22.48 ____ Substituted Judgment.
22.49 ____ Petition for Authorization to Transfer Property.
22.50 ____ ____ Notice of Application.

TABLE OF CONTENTS

Sec.
22.51 ____ ____ Considerations of Court.
22.52 ____ ____ Granting Petition.
22.53 ____ Powers; Personal Needs.
22.54 ____ Effect of Appointment on Incapacitated Person.
22.55 ____ Summary.
22.56 Provisional Remedies.
22.57 ____ Temporary Guardian.
22.58 ____ Injunction and Temporary Restraining Orders.
22.59 ____ Notice of Pendency.
22.60 ____ Summary.
22.61 Compensation of Guardian.
22.62 Reports by Guardian.
22.63 ____ Initial Report.
22.64 ____ Annual Report.
22.65 ____ Examination; Court Examiners.
22.66 ____ Intermediate and Final Reports.
22.67 ____ Decree Upon Approving Accounts.
22.68 ____ Summary.
22.69 Removal, Discharge and Resignation of Guardian—Removal.
22.70 ____ Discharge or Modification of Powers.
22.71 ____ Resignation or Suspension of Powers.
22.72 ____ Vacancy in Office; Appointment of Interim and Successor Guardians.
22.73 ____ Standby Guardian.
22.74 ____ Summary.
22.75 Education Requirements—Generally.
22.76 ____ Guardian Training.
22.77 ____ Court Evaluator Training.
22.78 ____ Court Examiner Training.
22.79 ____ Compliance.
22.80 ____ Summary.
22.81 Proceedings to Discover Property Withheld.
22.82 ____ Petition and Supporting Papers.
22.83 ____ Grounds For Inquiry.
22.84 ____ Answer.
22.85 ____ Trial.
22.86 ____ Decree.
22.87 ____ Summary.
22.88 Drafting Checklists.
22.89 ____ Order to Show Cause.
22.90 ____ Petition.
22.91 ____ Court Evaluator's Report.
22.92 ____ Order and Judgment.
22.93 ____ Initial Report of the Guardian.
22.94 ____ Annual Report.
22.95 ____ Decree Approving Accounts.
22.96 ____ Petition on Proceeding to Discover Property Withheld.
22.97 Forms.
22.98 ____ Order to Show Cause. 💾
22.99 ____ Petition. 💾

TABLE OF CONTENTS

Sec.
22.100 ____ Court Evaluator's Report. 💾
22.101 ____ Order and Judgment Appointing Guardian of the Person and Property. 💾
22.102 ____ Oath and Designation of Guardian. 💾
22.103 ____ Commission of Guardian. 💾
22.104 ____ Initial Report of Guardian. 💾
22.105 ____ Annual Report and Inventory of Guardian. 💾
22.106 ____ Decree Upon Approving Accounts. 💾
22.107 ____ Petition on Proceeding to Discover Property Withheld. 💾

CHAPTER 23. ELDER LAW

23.1 Scope Note.
23.2 Strategy.
23.3 Ethical Considerations.
23.4 ____ Identifying the Client.
23.5 ____ Confidentiality.
23.6 ____ Diminished Capacity.
23.7 Social Security Benefits.
23.8 ____ Quarters of Coverage.
23.9 ____ Insured Status.
23.10 ____ Calculation of Benefits.
23.11 ____ Retirement Benefits.
23.12 ____ Benefits for Spouses, Survivors and Dependents.
23.13 ____ Reduction in Benefits Due to Earned Income.
23.14 ____ Overpayments and Underpayments.
23.15 ____ Administrative and Judicial Appeals.
23.16 ____ Representation by Attorneys.
23.17 Supplemental Security Income for the Elderly.
23.18 ____ Categorical Eligibility.
23.19 ____ Financial Eligibility.
23.20 ____ Benefit Calculation.
23.21 ____ Underpayments and Overpayments.
23.22 ____ Administrative and Judicial Appeals.
23.23 ____ Representation by Attorneys.
23.24 Retirement Income from Qualified Plans.
23.25 ____ Eligibility, Vesting and Accrual.
23.26 ____ Contribution Limitations.
23.27 ____ Payment of Benefits.
23.28 ____ Alienation and Assignment.
23.29 ____ Spousal Rights.
23.30 ____ Qualified Domestic Relations Orders.
23.31 ____ Waiver of Spousal Rights.
23.32 ____ Taxation of Contributions.
23.33 ____ Distributions.
23.34 ____ Termination or Merger.
23.35 ____ Appeals.
23.36 Railroad Retirement Benefits.
23.37 Benefits for Federal Employees.
23.38 ____ Federal Employees Retirement System ("FERS").

TABLE OF CONTENTS

Sec.
23.39 ____ Civil Service Retirement Act ("CSRA").
23.40 ____ Appeals.
23.41 Veterans' Benefits.
23.42 Medicare.
23.43 ____ Eligibility and Enrollment.
23.44 ____ Part A Benefits.
23.45 ____ ____ Hospital Services.
23.46 ____ ____ Skilled Nursing Facilities.
23.47 ____ ____ Home Health Care.
23.48 ____ ____ Hospice Care.
23.49 ____ Part B Supplementary Medical Insurance.
23.50 ____ ____ Deductibles and Coinsurance.
23.51 ____ ____ Assignment of Claims/Participating Physicians.
23.52 ____ ____ Limitations on Balance Billing.
23.53 ____ Administrative and Judicial Appeals.
23.54 ____ ____ Eligibility for Benefits.
23.55 ____ ____ Part A Fiscal Intermediary Decisions.
23.56 ____ ____ Part A Peer Review Organization Decisions.
23.57 ____ ____ Part B Determinations.
23.58 Supplemental Medical Insurance (Medigap Plans).
23.59 ____ Gaps in Medicare Coverage.
23.60 ____ Federal and State Regulation of the Industry.
23.61 ____ Ten Standard Plans.
23.62 ____ Criteria for Choosing the Right Plan.
23.63 Long Term Care Insurance.
23.64 ____ Regulation Under New York Law.
23.65 ____ Relationship to Medicaid Eligibility.
23.66 ____ The Partnership For Long Term Care/Robert Wood Johnson Program.
23.67 ____ Choosing a Policy.
23.68 ____ Tax Issues.
23.69 Medicaid.
23.70 ____ Covered Services.
23.71 ____ Basic Eligibility Requirements.
23.72 ____ Surplus Income Program for the "Medically Needy."
23.73 ____ Income.
23.74 ____ Resources.
23.75 ____ Exempt Resources.
23.76 ____ Transfer of Resources.
23.77 ____ Treatment of Trusts.
23.78 ____ ____ Self Settled Trusts.
23.79 ____ ____ Third Party Trusts.
23.80 ____ Spousal Budgeting: Protection of Resources and Income for the Community Spouse.
23.81 ____ Recoveries Against Estates.
23.82 ____ Liens.
23.83 ____ Administrative and Judicial Appeals.
23.84 Home Care Coverage.
23.85 ____ Medicare.
23.86 ____ Medicaid.

LXXIII

TABLE OF CONTENTS

Sec.
23.87 ___ Expanded In-Home Services for the Elderly Program ("EISEP").
23.88 ___ Private Insurance.
23.89 Hospital Patients Rights.
23.90 ___ Bill of Rights.
23.91 ___ Discharge Planning.
23.92 Nursing Home Resident Rights.
23.93 ___ Admission to a Facility.
23.94 ___ Bill of Rights.
23.95 ___ Financial Rights.
23.96 ___ Transfer and Discharge.
23.97 ___ Bed Hold Policy.
23.98 ___ Remedies for Violation of Rights or Improper Treatment.
23.99 Housing Issues.
23.100 ___ Real Property Tax Exemption.
23.101 ___ Real Property Tax Credit.
23.102 ___ Tax Assistance Loans.
23.103 ___ Home Repair Assistance.
23.104 ___ Reverse Mortgages and Home Equity Loans.
23.105 ___ Home Energy Assistance Program ("HEAP").
23.106 ___ Tenant Protections.
23.107 ___ Life Care Retirement Communities.
23.108 ___ Community Based Services.
23.109 Health Care Decision Making.
23.110 ___ Health Care Proxy.
23.111 ___ The Living Will.
23.112 ___ Do Not Resuscitate Orders.
23.113 ___ Physician Assisted Suicide.
23.114 Tax Issues.
23.115 ___ Additional Standard Deduction for the Aged and Blind.
23.116 ___ Incapacity.
23.117 ___ Sale of a Principal Residence.
23.118 ___ Medical Deductions.
23.119 Miscellaneous Programs.
23.120 ___ Elderly Pharmaceutical Insurance Coverage ("EPIC").
23.121 ___ Life Line Telephone Service.
23.122 Forms.
23.123 ___ Documentation Letter.
23.124 ___ Consultation Letter.
23.125 ___ Health Care Proxy Statutory Form.
23.126 ___ Sample Living Will.

CHAPTER 24. ESTATE PLANNING

24.1 Scope Note.
24.2 Strategy.
24.3 Wills.
24.4 ___ Execution Requirements.
24.5 ___ ___ Signature.
24.6 ___ ___ Publication.

TABLE OF CONTENTS

Sec.
24.7 ____ ____ Witnesses.
24.8 ____ ____ Self Proving Affidavit.
24.9 ____ Provisions—Personal Property Dispositions.
24.10 ____ ____ Debts and Taxes.
24.11 ____ ____ Real Property.
24.12 ____ ____ Residuary Estate.
24.13 ____ ____ Dispositions in Trust.
24.14 ____ ____ Guardianships.
24.15 ____ ____ Appointment of Executors and Trustees.
24.16 ____ ____ Fiduciary Powers.
24.17 ____ ____ Miscellaneous.
24.18 Federal Estate and Gift Taxes.
24.19 ____ Rates.
24.20 New York State Estate and Gift Tax.
24.21 Estate Tax Planning—Utilizing the Unified Credit.
24.22 ____ Utilizing the Marital Deduction.
24.23 ____ Formula Clauses.
24.24 Generation Skipping Transfer Tax.
24.25 ____ Taxable Termination.
24.26 ____ Direct Skip.
24.27 ____ Taxable Distribution.
24.28 ____ Generation Assignment.
24.29 ____ Multiple Skips.
24.30 ____ Exemption.
24.31 ____ "Reverse QTIP."
24.32 Charitable Bequests.
24.33 Planning With Certain Assets.
24.34 ____ Life Insurance.
24.35 ____ ____ Life Insurance Trusts.
24.36 ____ ____ ____ "Crummey Powers."
24.37 ____ Retirement Benefits.
24.38 ____ Closely Held Business Interests.
24.39 ____ ____ Buy-Sell Agreements.
24.40 ____ ____ Liquidity Issues.
24.41 ____ ____ Minority Discounts.
24.42 ____ Farms and Business Real Property.
24.43 ____ Installment Obligations.
24.44 Lifetime Planning.
24.45 ____ Valuation of Gifts.
24.46 ____ ____ Grantor Retained Trusts.
24.47 ____ ____ Residence Trusts.
24.48 ____ ____ ____ Income Tax Considerations.
24.49 ____ Annual Gift Tax Exclusion.
24.50 ____ ____ Section 2503(c) Trusts.
24.51 ____ ____ Uniform Transfers to Minor's Act Accounts.
24.52 ____ ____ Crummey Trusts.
24.53 ____ ____ Family Limited Partnerships.
24.54 ____ Charitable Remainder Trusts.
24.55 ____ Charitable Lead Trusts.
24.56 Planning in Special Situations—Terminally Ill.

TABLE OF CONTENTS

Sec.
24.57 ____ ____ Self-Canceling Installment Notes.
24.58 ____ Non-citizen Spouses.
24.59 ____ Multiple Marriages.
24.60 ____ Spousal Rights.
24.61 ____ ____ Joint Wills and Contracts to Make Wills.
24.62 ____ ____ Long Term Care.
24.63 ____ Separation.
24.64 ____ Divorce.
24.65 ____ ____ Death During Divorce Proceeding.
24.66 ____ Unmarried Couples.
24.67 Postmortem Planning.
24.68 ____ Disclaimers.
24.69 ____ ____ Disclaimer Trusts.
24.70 ____ ____ Creditor Avoidance.
24.71 ____ ____ New York Statutory Requirements.
24.72 ____ Partial QTIP Election.
24.73 ____ Electing Alternate Valuation Date.
24.74 ____ Allocation of Income and Expenses.
24.75 ____ ____ U.S. Savings Bonds.
24.76 ____ ____ Expenses.
24.77 ____ Choosing the Fiscal Year of the Estate.
24.78 ____ Electing to File Joint Return with Decedent's Spouse.
24.79 ____ Waiving Commissions.
24.80 Probate Avoidance.
24.81 ____ Revocable Trusts.
24.82 ____ Totten Trusts.
24.83 ____ Jointly Held Assets.
24.84 Asset Protection.
24.85 ____ Statutory Exemptions.
24.86 ____ Family Partnerships.
24.87 ____ Domestic Trusts.
24.88 ____ Foreign Trusts.
24.89 Powers of Attorney.
24.90 Advance Directives.
24.91 ____ Health Care Proxy.
24.92 ____ Living Will.
24.93 Ethical Considerations in Estate Planning.
24.94 ____ Multiple Clients.
24.95 ____ Attorney/Draftsman as Fiduciary or Beneficiary.
24.96 Forms
24.97 ____ Estate Planner's Checklist. 💾
24.98 ____ Sample Information Request Letter. 💾
24.99 ____ Client Questionnaire. 💾
24.100 ____ "Durable" Power of Attorney Form. 💾
24.101 ____ Crummey Notice. 💾
24.102 ____ Spousal Conflicts Letter. 💾

CHAPTER 25. PROBATE AND ESTATE ADMINISTRATION

25.1 Scope Note.

TABLE OF CONTENTS

Sec.
- 25.2 Explanation of Basic Legal Terms in Estate Practice.
- 25.3 Strategy.
- 25.4 Who May Commence the Estate of a Person Who Dies Without a Will.
- 25.5 Who Is Entitled to Letters of Administration.
- 25.6 Who May Commence the Estate of a Person Who Dies With a Will.
- 25.7 Documents Required on Application for Letters of Administration.
- 25.8 Who Must Be Cited on an Application for Letters of Administration.
- 25.9 When a Guardian *Ad Litem* Must be Appointed.
- 25.10 Denial or Revocation of Letters of Administration.
- 25.11 Letters of Temporary Administration.
- 25.12 Venue.
- 25.13 Duty of the Fiduciary to Expeditiously Seek Probate.
- 25.14 When a Beneficiary Should Petition for Probate.
- 25.15 When a Creditor Should Petition for Probate.
- 25.16 When a Person in Litigation with an Estate Should Petition for Probate.
- 25.17 Information to Be Gathered by Attorney.
- 25.18 Contents of Petition for Probate.
- 25.19 Documents Required to Accompany Probate Petition.
- 25.20 What to Do If Your Client Cannot Produce the Original Will.
- 25.21 Requirements and Procedure for Proving a Will Where the Original Is Lost.
- 25.22 How to Get a Will Admitted to Probate If None of the Witnesses to the Will are Available.
- 25.23 When a Court Must Appoint a Guardian *Ad Litem* in a Probate Proceeding.
- 25.24 Who May Oppose the Admission to Probate of a Will By Filing Objections.
- 25.25 When Objections Must Be Filed.
- 25.26 How to Start an Estate Administration Where There Will Be a Delay in Getting a Will Admitted to Probate.
- 25.27 Form of Objections to Probate.
- 25.28 Burden of Proof
- 25.29 Requirement of a Notice of Objections to Complete Jurisdiction in a Contested Probate.
- 25.30 Right to a Trial by Jury.
- 25.31 Right to Discovery in a Probate, Administration or Accounting Proceeding.
- 25.32 Who Is Entitled to Letters of Administration When a Person Dies Without a Will.
- 25.33 Procedures to Follow in Administering the Estate.
- 25.34 How to Force an Estate Administration to Be Completed—Compelling an Accounting.
- 25.35 Concluding an Estate Administration Without an Accounting Proceeding.
- 25.36 Obtaining a Decree Concluding the Estate Based on Filed Receipts and Releases.
- 25.37 Concluding an Estate by a Formal Judicial Accounting.

TABLE OF CONTENTS

Sec.
25.38 Objections to an Account.
25.39 Prosecuting Objections to an Account.
25.40 Claims Against an Estate by a Creditor.
25.41 Representing a Claimant Against an Estate.
25.42 Obtaining Information About Estate Assets and Recovering Estate Property.
25.43 How to Proceed When Your Client Has a Claim Against an Estate.
25.44 A Special Provision for an Estate Beneficiary Obtaining Funds for Education.
25.45 Who Is Entitled to Assets When Two or More Fiduciaries Are in Dispute.
25.46 Compensation of Executor and Administrator, When Payable.
25.47 Attorney's Fees.
25.48 Declining to Serve as an Executor or Trustee.
25.49 Renouncing an Inheritance.
25.50 Construction of a Will.
25.51 Forms.
25.52 ____ Probate Petition.
25.53 ____ Affidavit Proving Correct Copy of Will.
25.54 ____ Citation in Probate.
25.55 ____ Affidavit of Service of Citation.
25.56 ____ Affidavit of Mailing Notice of Application for Letters of Administration.
25.57 ____ Waiver and Consent.
25.58 ____ Notice of Probate.
25.59 ____ Deposition Affidavit of Subscribing Witness.
25.60 ____ Objections to Probate.
25.61 ____ Decree Granting Probate.
25.62 ____ Receipt and Release Agreement Concluding an Estate Without an Accounting Proceeding.
25.63 ____ Receipt and Release (Legacy).
25.64 ____ Petition to Judicially Settle Executor's Account.
25.65 ____ Citation to Executor to Show Cause Why Judicially Executor Should Not Account.
25.66 ____ Accounting Form.
25.67 ____ Petition for Letters of Administration or Limited Letters of Administration or Temporary Administration.
25.68 ____ Decree Appointing Administrator.
25.69 ____ Affidavit Asking Court to Fix Amount of Administrator's Bond.
25.70 ____ Waiver of Citation, Renunciation of Signer's Claim to Letters and Consent to Appointment of Administrator.
25.71 ____ Notice of Application for Letters of Administration.
25.72 ____ Citation That Can Be Adopted for Use in Any Proceeding.

CHAPTER 26. PERSONAL INJURY

26.1 Scope Note.
26.2 Strategy.

LXXVIII

TABLE OF CONTENTS

Sec.
26.3 ____ Client Interview.
26.4 ____ Valuing the Case.
26.5 ____ Skills and Ethics.
26.6 ____ Retainer.
26.7 ____ ____ Retainer Statement.
26.8 ____ Expenses.
26.9 Investigation.
26.10 ____ Premises Liability.
26.11 ____ Medical Malpractice.
26.12 ____ ____ Hospital.
26.13 ____ ____ Dental and Podiatric Malpractice.
26.14 ____ Products Liability.
26.15 ____ Dog Bites.
26.16 ____ Chemical Exposure.
26.17 ____ Automobile Accidents.
26.18 ____ ____ Police Report.
26.19 ____ ____ Witness Statements.
26.20 ____ ____ MV104.
26.21 ____ ____ Application of No-Fault.
26.22 ____ ____ Medical Records.
26.23 ____ ____ Photographs.
26.24 ____ ____ Insurance Policies and Coverage.
26.25 Claims Procedure for Automobile Accidents.
26.26 ____ Filing Notice of Claim With the Motor Vehicle Accident Indemnity Corporation.
26.27 ____ ____ Procedure for Cases in Which There Is No Insurance.
26.28 ____ ____ Procedure for Cases in Which There Is No Insurance and the Identity of the Wrongdoer Is Not Ascertainable (Hit and Run).
26.29 ____ ____ Procedure for Cases in Which Insurance Initially Is Believed to Exist, But There Is No Insurance After Later Disclaimer.
26.30 ____ ____ Late Claims.
26.31 Theories of Liability.
26.32 Filing the Action.
26.33 ____ When.
26.34 ____ Where.
26.35 ____ Potential Defendants.
26.36 The Summons and the Complaint.
26.37 The Answer.
26.38 Actions Against Municipal Corporations.
26.39 ____ Notice of Claim.
26.40 ____ ____ Content.
26.41 Actions Against the State.
26.42 Discovery—Generally.
26.43 ____ Depositions.
26.44 ____ Interrogatories.
26.45 ____ Document Discovery and Inspection.
26.46 ____ Bills of Particulars.
26.47 ____ Demand for a Bill of Particulars.

LXXIX

TABLE OF CONTENTS

Sec.
26.48 Settlement.
26.49 Liens.
26.50 Alternative Dispute Resolution.
26.51 Trial Preparation: Introductory Note.
26.52 Trial.
26.53 ____ Subpoenas.
26.54 ____ Exhibits.
26.55 ____ *Voir Dire.*
26.56 Disbursement of Proceeds of Settlement or Recovery.
26.57 Drafting Checklists.
26.58 ____ Complaint.
26.59 ____ Answer.
26.60 ____ Demand for Bill of Particulars.
26.61 ____ Responses to Demand for Bill of Particulars.
26.62 Forms—Client's Retainer Agreement. 💾
26.63 ____ Retainer Statement. 💾
26.64 ____ Department of Motor Vehicles MV104 Form.
26.65 ____ Summons and Complaint. 💾
26.66 ____ Amended Answer, Counterclaim and Cross Claim. 💾
26.67 ____ Defendant's Demand for a Verified Bill of Particulars. 💾
26.68 ____ Defendant's CPLR 3101 Demands. 💾
26.69 ____ Plaintiff's Demand for a Verified Bill of Particulars. 💾
26.70 ____ Plaintiff's CPLR 3101 Demands. 💾
26.71 ____ Closing Statement. 💾

CHAPTER 27. PRODUCTS LIABILITY

27.1 Scope Note.
27.2 Strategy.
27.3 Historical Overview.
27.4 Bases of a Products Liability Claim.
27.5 Theories of Liability.
27.6 ____ Manufacturing Defect or Mistake in the Manufacturing Process.
27.7 ____ Defective Design.
27.8 ____ ____ Burden of Proof.
27.9 ____ ____ Defense.
27.10 ____ Failure to Warn or Inadequate Warnings.
27.11 ____ ____ Burden of Proof.
27.12 ____ ____ Duty to Warn.
27.13 ____ ____ Adequacy of Warning.
27.14 ____ ____ Jury Question.
27.15 ____ ____ Informed Intermediary Defense.
27.16 ____ ____ Duty to Warn the Unusually Sensitive.
27.17 ____ ____ Non-Commercial Cases.
27.18 ____ Failure to Test.
27.19 ____ ____ FDA Approval.
27.20 ____ ____ Jury Question.
27.21 ____ ____ Preemption Defense.
27.22 Distributors' or Sellers' Liability.

LXXX

TABLE OF CONTENTS

Sec.
27.23	____ Sale Must Be Part of Ordinary Business.
27.24	____ Service v. Sales.
27.25	____ Medical Care Providers.
27.26	Successor Liability.
27.27	____ Burden of Proof.
27.28	____ Punitive Damages.
27.29	Liability of the Manufacturer of Component Parts.
27.30	Liability of the Manufacturer of the Complete Product.
27.31	Introducing Evidence of Post Accident Modification or Repairs.
27.32	Introducing Evidence of Other Incidents.
27.33	Effect of Destruction of the Product Upon Plaintiff's Ability to Prove a Defect.
27.34	Proof of Causation.
27.35	____ Question for the Jury or Question for the Judge.
27.36	Foreseeability of Harm.
27.37	Discovery Issues.
27.38	____ Confidentiality Orders or Stipulations.
27.39	Statute of Limitations.
27.40	Intervening Acts of Negligence—Plaintiff's Misuse of the Product.
27.41	____ Alteration of the Product After it Has Left the Hands of the Manufacturer.
27.42	Preemption of Private Claims.
27.43	____ Old Rule.
27.44	____ New Rule.
27.45	____ National Traffic & Motor Vehicle Safety Act and Its Savings Clause.
27.46	____ Public Health Cigarette Labeling & Advertising Act of 1965 and the Public Health Cigarette Smoking Act of 1969—The *Cipollone* Decision.
27.47	____ Federal Insecticide, Fungicide and Rodenticide Act (FIFRA) and Its Impact on Labeling Requirements.
27.48	____ Medical Device Amendments to FDA Regulations.
27.49	____ Limits on Preemption and Statutory Defenses.
27.50	____ Validity of the Safety Standard or Regulatory Statute.
27.51	____ Checklist.
27.52	Imposing Liability when the Manufacturer of a Fungible or Generic Product Is Unknown (Concert of Action/Market Share Liability).
27.53	Collateral Estoppel in Products Liability Cases.
27.54	Proof of Allegations Checklist.
27.55	Drafting Checklist—Complaint.
27.56	____ Answer.
27.57	Forms—Products Liability Complaint.
27.58	____ Products Liability Answer.

Volume 24

CHAPTER 28. LEGAL MALPRACTICE

28.1   Scope Note.

TABLE OF CONTENTS

Sec.	
28.2	Strategy.
28.3	The Duty of Care.
28.4	____ Specific Acts—Erroneous Advice.
28.5	____ ____ Incompetent Tax Advice.
28.6	____ ____ Proper Withdrawal.
28.7	____ ____ Detecting Fraud.
28.8	____ Causation.
28.9	____ ____ The Doctrine of Compelled Settlement.
28.10	____ Damages.
28.11	____ Defenses—The Privity Rule.
28.12	____ ____ Lawyer's Judgment Rule.
28.13	____ ____ Statute of Limitations.
28.14	____ ____ Continuous Representation Tolling Doctrine.
28.15	____ ____ Extension by Estoppel.
28.16	____ ____Standard Negligence Defenses of Lack of Foreseeability and Supervening Act.
28.17	____ ____ Concealment of Malpractice Not a Separate Cause of Action.
28.18	____ ____ Need for Consistent Positions.
28.19	The Duty of Loyalty.
28.20	____ Conflict of Interest.
28.21	____ Disqualification.
28.22	____ Misappropriation of Client Funds.
28.23	Liability for Negligence of Independent Contractors.
28.24	Statutory Liability Under Judiciary Law § 487.
28.25	Vicarious Liability for Partner's Misdeeds.
28.26	Liability for Indemnity and Contribution.
28.27	Fee Disputes.
28.28	____ Alternative Dispute Resolution.
28.29	____ ____ Retainer Agreements Given Strict Scrutiny.
28.30	____ ____ Arbitration Clause in Retainer Agreement May Waive Other Client Rights.
28.31	____ Statutory Limitations.
28.32	____ Account Stated.
28.33	____ A Standard of Reasonableness.
28.34	Limited Liability Companies and Limited Liability Partnerships.
28.35	Lawyers Professional Liability Insurance.
28.36	____ Extended Reporting Period.
28.37	____ What Is a "Claim" and When Is It "Made"?
28.38	____ Professional Capacity and Typical Exclusions.
28.39	____ Limits, Deductibles and Defense.
28.40	____ Notice of Claim and Notice of Occurrence.
28.41	____ Cancellation.
28.42	____ Innocent Partner Coverage.
28.43	____ Application for Coverage and Rescission of Policy.
28.44	____ Bad Faith.
28.45	____ Cautions for Dissolving Law Firms.
28.46	Conclusion.
28.47	Drafting Checklist—Retainer Agreement.
28.48	____ Malpractice Complaint Against Attorney.

TABLE OF CONTENTS

Sec.
28.49 ___ Answer to Malpractice Complaint on Behalf of Attorney.
28.50 Forms—Retainer Agreement With ADR Clause.
28.51 ___ Retainer Agreement Without ADR Clause.
28.52 ___ Complaint for Malpractice: Commercial Transaction.
28.53 ___ Complaint for Malpractice: Personal Injury Action.
28.54 ___ Answer: Commercial Transaction.
28.55 ___ Answer: Personal Injury Action.

CHAPTER 29. MEDICAL MALPRACTICE

29.1 Scope Note.
29.2 Strategy.
29.3 ___ Determining the Presence or Absence of Medical Malpractice.
29.4 ___ The Nature and Degree of Damages.
29.5 ___ Interviewing the Client.
29.6 ___ ___ History of the Current Condition.
29.7 ___ ___ Past Medical Conditions.
29.8 ___ ___ Current Medical Condition.
29.9 ___ ___ Miscellaneous Issues.
29.10 The Common Law Standards.
29.11 ___ The Standard of Care.
29.12 ___ ___ Hospitals' *Respondeat-Superior* Liability.
29.13 ___ ___ Hospitals' Direct Liability.
29.14 ___ Informed Consent.
29.15 ___ Health Maintenance Organizations.
29.16 ___ Expert Witnesses.
29.17 ___ Defenses in Medical Malpractice Cases.
29.18 Regulatory Standards.
29.19 ___ Qualifications of Nurse Midwives.
29.20 ___ Clinical Laboratories.
29.21 ___ Blood Banks.
29.22 ___ Testing for Phenylketonuria and Other Diseases and Conditions/Early Intervention Program.
29.23 ___ Hospitals.
29.24 Damages.
29.25 Procedure.
29.26 ___ Statutes of Limitation.
29.27 ___ Steps for Filing an Action.
29.28 ___ ___ Certificate of Merit.
29.29 ___ ___ Notice of Medical Malpractice Action.
29.30 ___ ___ Pre-calendar Conferences.
29.31 ___ Periodic Payment of Large Verdicts.
29.32 Hospital Operations and Medical Negligence—Credentialling of Physicians.
29.33 ___ Quality Assurance and Risk Management.
29.34 ___ Departmentalization of Services—Departmental Chairs.
29.35 Training and Education of Physicians.
29.36 ___ Medical School.
29.37 ___ PGY–1 (Internship).
29.38 ___ Residency.

TABLE OF CONTENTS

Sec.
29.39 ____ Fellowships.
29.40 ____ Board Certification & Re-certification.
29.41 ____ Associations, Societies, and Continuing Medical Education.
29.42 ____ National Practitioner Data Bank.
29.43 Medical Literature.
29.44 ____ Obtaining Medical Literature.
29.45 ____ Sources.
29.46 ____ Using Medical Literature to Evaluate a Case.
29.47 ____ Preparing for Depositions.
29.48 ____ Preparing for Trial.
29.49 ____ Use of Treatises in State Court.
29.50 ____ Use of Treatises in Federal Court.
29.51 Evaluating and Understanding Medical Records—Physician's Records.
29.52 ____ Hospital Records.
29.53 ____ ____ Informed Consent Forms.
29.54 ____ ____ Progress Notes.
29.55 ____ ____ Order Sheets.
29.56 ____ ____ Consultation Records.
29.57 ____ ____ Operative Records.
29.58 ____ ____ Medication Records.
29.59 ____ ____ Intake and Output Records.
29.60 ____ ____ Radiographic Records.
29.61 ____ ____ Obstetrical Records.
29.62 ____ ____ ICU/CCU Records.
29.63 ____ ____ Nurses' Notes.
29.64 Discovery.
29.65 ____ Obtaining and Identifying Relevant Records.
29.66 ____ ____ Physician's Records.
29.67 ____ ____ Hospital Records.
29.68 ____ ____ Billing Records.
29.69 ____ ____ Pharmacy Records.
29.70 ____ ____ Allied Health Provider Records.
29.71 ____ ____ Workers' Compensation Claims File.
29.72 ____ ____ Autopsy Report.
29.73 ____ ____ Workers' Compensation Actions.
29.74 ____ ____ Medical Malpractice Actions.
29.75 Trial Preparation.
29.76 Drafting Checklists.
29.77 ____ Order to Show Cause to Obtain Medical Records.
29.78 ____ Affirmation in Support of Order to Show Cause.
29.79 ____ Certificate of Merit.
29.80 Forms
29.81 ____ Order to Show Cause to Obtain Medical Records. 💾
29.82 ____ Affirmation in Support of Order to Show Cause. 💾
29.83 ____ Certificate of Merit. 💾

CHAPTER 30. DAMAGES

30.1 Scope Note.

LXXXIV

TABLE OF CONTENTS

Sec.
30.2 Strategy.
30.3 ____ Pretrial Stage.
30.4 ____ Trial Stage.
30.5 The Nature of Damages.
30.6 Compensatory Damages.
30.7 ____ Personal Injury.
30.8 ____ ____ Physical Pain and Suffering.
30.9 ____ ____ Mental or Emotional Pain and Suffering.
30.10 ____ ____ Loss of Earnings and Impairment of Future Earning Ability.
30.11 ____ ____ Aggravation of Pre-existing Injuries.
30.12 ____ Wrongful Death.
30.13 ____ ____ Damages Sustained Before Death.
30.14 ____ ____ Damages Sustained After Death.
30.15 ____ Loss of Consortium.
30.16 ____ Property Damage.
30.17 ____ ____ Real Property.
30.18 ____ Personal Property.
30.19 ____ Breach of Contract.
30.20 ____ ____ Contract Price and Actual Loss.
30.21 ____ ____ Delay in Performance.
30.22 ____ ____ Defective Performance.
30.23 ____ ____ Anticipatory Breach.
30.24 ____ ____ Damages Within the Contemplation of the Parties, and Loss of Profits.
30.25 ____ ____ Building and Construction.
30.26 ____ Minimizing and Mitigating Damages.
30.27 ____ ____ Contracts.
30.28 ____ ____ Personal Injury.
30.29 ____ Excessive or Inadequate Damages.
30.30 ____ ____ Specific Awards.
30.31 Punitive Damages.
30.32 ____ Intentional Torts.
30.33 ____ Negligence.
30.34 ____ Contract.
30.35 ____ Awards.
30.36 ____ Mitigation.
30.37 Nominal Damages.
30.38 Statutory Damages.
30.39 Liquidated Damages and Penalties.
30.40 Interest.
30.41 Attorney Fees.
30.42 ____ Statutory.
30.43 ____ Agreements and Miscellaneous.
30.44 Periodic Payment of Judgments.
30.45 Forms.
30.46 ____ *Ad Damnum* Clause in Ordinary Complaint.
30.47 ____ *Ad Damnum* Clause in Complaint in Medical or Dental Malpractice Action or in Action Against Municipal Government (Supreme Court).

TABLE OF CONTENTS

Sec.
30.48 _____ Clauses in Complaint in Action Involving Automobile Accident.
30.49 _____ Request for Supplemental Demand for Relief in Medical or Dental Malpractice Action or Action Against Municipal Corporation.
30.50 _____ Defense of Culpable Conduct in Answer.
30.51 _____ Defense of Failure to Use Seat Belt Contained in Answer.
30.52 _____ Defense of Indemnification From Collateral Sources.
30.53 _____ Partial Defense; Mitigation of Damages.
30.54 _____ Partial Defense; Mitigation of Damages in Libel Action.
30.55 _____ Partial Defense; Inability to Convey Property.
30.56 _____ Notice of Motion to Amend Verdict (or Judgment) to Add Interest.
30.57 _____ Affidavit in Support of Motion to Amend Verdict (or Judgment) to Add Interest.
30.58 _____ Notice of Motion to Fix Date From Which Interest is to Be Computed.
30.59 _____ Affidavit in Support of Motion to Fix Date From Which Interest is to Be Computed.
30.60 Pattern Jury Instructions.
30.61 _____ Personal Injury—Subsequent Injury, Accident.
30.62 _____ _____ Loss of Earnings.
30.63 _____ Damages—Personal Injury—Shock and Fright and Physical Consequences.
30.64 _____ _____ Aggravation of Injury.
30.65 _____ Payment of Income Taxes on Damages for Personal Injury.
30.66 _____ Reduction to Present Value.
30.67 _____ Wrongful Death—Conscious Pain and Suffering.
30.68 _____ Personal Injury—Collateral Sources—Itemized Verdict (CPLR 4111).
30.69 _____ Damages—Property Without Market Value.
30.70 _____ Damages—Property With Market Value.
30.71 _____ Contracts—Damages—Generally.
30.72 _____ _____ Damages—Employment Contract.

CHAPTER 31. INSURANCE

31.1 Scope Note.
31.2 Strategy.
31.3 _____ Checklist.
31.4 Sources of New York Insurance Law.
31.5 Third Parties Involved in the Placement and Administration of the Insurance Contract.
31.6 _____ Insurance Brokers.
31.7 _____ Insurance Agents.
31.8 Nature of Insurance.
31.9 Interpreting an Insurance Policy.
31.10 Notice.
31.11 The Cooperation Clause.

TABLE OF CONTENTS

Sec.
- 31.12 The Insurer's Duty to Defend.
- 31.13 ____ Responding to a Request for a Defense.
- 31.14 ____ Damages for Breach of the Duty.
- 31.15 Reservations of Rights By an Insurer.
- 31.16 Disclaiming/Denying Coverage.
- 31.17 The Insurer's Duty of Good Faith and Fair Dealing.
- 31.18 Rescission of Insurance Policies.
- 31.19 Reformation.
- 31.20 Lost Policies.
- 31.21 Nature of Relief.
- 31.22 Service of Process.
- 31.23 Pre-answer Security.
- 31.24 Arbitration Clauses.
- 31.25 Choice of Law.
- 31.26 Statutes of Limitation.
- 31.27 Burden of Proof.
- 31.28 Insolvent Insurers.
- 31.29 Subrogation.
- 31.30 Allocation of Losses Between Co-insurers.
- 31.31 Checklist of Essential Allegations.
- 31.32 Forms—Complaint By Policyholder for Declaratory Relief and Breach of Contract.
- 31.33 ____ Complaint By Insurer for Declaratory Relief.
- 31.34 ____ Complaint By Insurer for Rescission.
- 31.35 ____ Affirmative Defenses Asserted By Insurer in a Coverage Action.

CHAPTER 32. WORKERS' COMPENSATION

- 32.1 Scope Note.
- 32.2 Strategy.
- 32.3 ____ Employer's Counsel's Checklist.
- 32.4 ____ Employee's Counsel's Checklist.
- 32.5 Introduction to The Workers' Compensation Law.
- 32.6 ____ History and Theory.
- 32.7 ____ ____ Workmen's Compensation Law of 1910.
- 32.8 ____ ____ Constitutional Amendment.
- 32.9 ____ ____ Workmen's Compensation Law of 1914.
- 32.10 ____ ____ Statutory Changes.
- 32.11 Workers' Compensation Board.
- 32.12 Employer's Obligations and Methods of Coverage.
- 32.13 Compensable Injury.
- 32.14 Exclusive Remedy Doctrine.
- 32.15 ____ Exceptions.
- 32.16 Pre-hearing Conference.
- 32.17 Hearings.
- 32.18 ____ Statute of Limitations.
- 32.19 ____ Burden of Proof, Presumptions and Defenses.
- 32.20 ____ Conciliation Process.
- 32.21 Benefits.

TABLE OF CONTENTS

Sec.	
32.22	____ Classification of Disability.
32.23	____ Wage Replacement.
32.24	____ ____ Schedule vs. Non-schedule Awards.
32.25	____ ____ Rehabilitation.
32.26	____ ____ Industrially Disabled.
32.27	____ ____ Special Disability Fund.
32.28	____ Medical Benefits.
32.29	____ Facial Disfigurement.
32.30	____ Death Awards.
32.31	____ ____ Funeral Expenses.
32.32	____ Assignments, Liens and Lump-sum Settlements.
32.33	Board Review of Decisions, Orders and Awards.
32.34	Appeal to Court.
32.35	Reopening Closed Claims.
32.36	Discrimination.
32.37	Licensed Representative.
32.38	Attorney's Fees.
32.39	Posted Notice of Coverage.
32.40	Uninsured Employers' Fund.
32.41	Insurance Policy for Workers' Compensation.
32.42	State Insurance Fund.
32.43	Federal Workers' Compensation Laws and Benefits.
32.44	Disability Benefits Law.
32.45	____ Employer's Obligations.
32.46	____ Exempt Employees.
32.47	____ Benefits and Employee Contribution.
32.48	____ Special Fund.
32.49	____ Employee Eligibility.
32.50	____ Claim Filing.
32.51	____ Pregnancy.
32.52	____ End Note.
32.53	Forms.
32.54	____ Workers' Compensation Board Employee's Claim For Compensation. (C–3 7–97)
32.55	____ Workers' Compensation Board Employer's Report of Work–Related Accident/Occupational Disease. (C–2 10–97)
32.56	____ Workers' Compensation Board Attending Doctor's Report and Carrier/Employer Billing. (C–4 3–97)
32.57	____ Workers' Compensation Board Notice that Right to Compensation is Controverted. (C–7 2–97)
32.58	____ Workers' Compensation Board Notice that Payment of Compensation for Disability has Been Stopped or Modified. (C–8/8.6 4–97)
32.59	____ Notice and Proof of Claim for Disability Benefits. (DB–450 3–97)
32.60	____ Notice of Total or Partial Rejection of Claim for Disability Benefits. (DB–451 3–97)

CHAPTER 33. LOCAL CRIMINAL COURT PRACTICE

33.1	Scope Note.

LXXXVIII

TABLE OF CONTENTS

Sec.
33.2 Strategy.
33.3 Overview of Local Criminal Court Process.
33.4 Police/Citizen Encounters.
33.5 ____ Vehicle Stops.
33.6 ____ The Parked Car.
33.7 ____ Arrest Without Warrant.
33.8 Accusatory Instruments.
33.9 ____ Information.
33.10 ____ Simplified Information.
33.11 ____ Prosecutor's Information.
33.12 ____ Misdemeanor and Felony Complaints.
33.13 ____ Supporting Depositions.
33.14 ____ ____ Procedure.
33.15 ____ ____ When Must They Be Provided?
33.16 ____ ____ Who Must Be Served?
33.17 ____ ____ Service of Request Must be Timely.
33.18 ____ ____ Request By Attorney Requires Service on Counsel.
33.19 ____ ____ Dismissal For Failure to Serve.
33.20 ____ ____ Motion Must Be In Writing.
33.21 ____ ____ Motion to Dismiss Must Be Timely.
33.22 ____ ____ Factual Insufficiency Not Jurisdictional: Plea Waives Defect.
33.23 ____ ____ Superseding Information Disallowed.
33.24 ____ ____ People May File New Information Upon Dismissal of Supporting Deposition.
33.25 ____ ____ Failure to Serve Not An Amendable Defect.
33.26 ____ ____ Verification.
33.27 Probable Cause Hearing.
33.28 Plea Bargaining.
33.29 ____ Plea Bargain Can Be Conditioned Upon Waiver of Right to Appeal.
33.30 ____ Plea Bargaining—No Penalty for Asserting Right to Trial.
33.31 Pretrial Discovery.
33.32 ____ Applicable to Simplified Informations.
33.33 ____ Applicable to Traffic Infractions.
33.34 ____ Subpoenas.
33.35 ____ Demands to Produce/Bills of Particulars.
33.36 ____ ____ Must Be Filed Within 30 Days.
33.37 ____ ____ Response Within 15 Days.
33.38 ____ ____ People's Failure to Comply With Time Limits.
33.39 ____ *Brady* Material.
33.40 ____ ____ Prosecutor Need Not Be Aware of Evidence.
33.41 ____ ____ Timely Disclosure.
33.42 Evidence.
33.43 ____ Motions to Suppress.
33.44 ____ *Sandoval* Issues—Prior Convictions.
33.45 ____ ____ Procedure.
33.46 ____ ____ *Sandoval* Criteria.
33.47 ____ ____ Defendant's Presence at *Sandoval* Hearing.
33.48 ____ *Miranda*.

LXXXIX

TABLE OF CONTENTS

Sec.	
33.49	___ ___ Applicable to Misdemeanor Traffic Offenses.
33.50	___ ___ Stop and Frisk Does Not Constitute Custodial Interrogation.
33.51	___ ___ Sobriety Checkpoint Stops Are Non-custodial.
33.52	___ ___ Interrogation Defined.
33.53	___ ___ Public Safety Exception.
33.54	___ ___ Pedigree Exception.
33.55	___ ___ Waiver Following Assertion of Right to Remain Silent.
33.56	___ ___ Waiver Following Request for Counsel.
33.57	___ Involuntary Statements.
33.58	___ ___ May Not Be Used to Impeach.
33.59	___ ___ Applicability of Harmless Error Doctrine.
33.60	___ The Use of Defendant's Pre-arrest Silence.
33.61	___ Corroboration of Admission or Confession Required.
33.62	Trial.
33.63	___ Modes of Trial.
33.64	___ Order of Jury Trial Proceedings.
33.65	___ Order of Bench Trial Proceedings.
33.66	___ Trial of Speeding Tickets.
33.67	___ ___ Discovery.
33.68	___ ___ People's *Prima Facie* Case.
33.69	___ ___ When Not to Request a Supporting Deposition.
33.70	___ ___ Speeding Trial Summary.
33.71	Speedy Trial Pursuant to CPL § 30.20.
33.72	___ Application to Traffic Infractions.
33.73	___ Criteria.
33.74	CPL § 30.30.
33.75	___ Vehicle and Traffic Law Violations Generally Excluded.
33.76	___ ___ Unless Combined With Felony, Misdemeanor or Violation.
33.77	___ People's Readiness Rule.
33.78	___ Requirements for An Assertion of Readiness.
33.79	___ ___ Actual Readiness for Trial.
33.80	___ Guilty Plea Waives CPL § 30.30 Motion.
33.81	___ Burden of Proof.
33.82	___ Commencement of Criminal Action—Appearance Tickets.
33.83	___ Uniform Traffic Tickets.
33.84	___ Excludable Time.
33.85	___ ___ Motions.
33.86	___ ___ Defective Accusatory Instrument.
33.87	___ ___ Adjournments.
33.88	___ ___ Delays by the Court.
33.89	___ ___ Effect of Defendant's Unavailability.
33.90	___ Post Readiness Delay.
33.91	Procedural Checklists.
33.92	___ Notice of Motion to Dismiss For Failure to Serve a Timely Supporting Deposition/Attorney Affirmation in Support of Motion.
33.93	___ Demand to Produce: Speeding Ticket.
33.94	Drafting Checklists.

TABLE OF CONTENTS

Sec.
- 33.95 ____ Notice of Motion to Dismiss For Failure to Serve a Timely Supporting Deposition.
- 33.96 ____ Attorney Affirmation in Support of Motion to Dismiss For Failure to Serve a Timely Supporting Deposition.
- 33.97 ____ Demand to Produce: Speeding Ticket.
- 33.98 Forms.
- 33.99 ____ Notice of Motion to Dismiss For Failure to Serve a Timely Supporting Deposition. 💾
- 33.100____ Attorney Affirmation in Support of Motion to Dismiss For Failure to Serve a Timely Supporting Deposition. 💾
- 33.101____ Demand to Produce: Speeding Ticket. 💾

CHAPTER 34. SOCIAL SECURITY DISABILITY CASES

- 34.1 Scope Note.
- 34.2 Strategy.
- 34.3 The Law of Disability.
- 34.4 ____ Statutory Definition of Disability.
- 34.5 ____ Judicial Definitions.
- 34.6 ____ Durational Requirements.
- 34.7 ____ Comparison to Workers' Compensation.
- 34.8 ____ Assessing Disability: The Sequential Evaluation.
- 34.9 ____ ____ Substantial Gainful Activity.
- 34.10 ____ ____ Severity.
- 34.11 ____ ____ Listings of Impairments.
- 34.12 ____ ____ Ability to Do Past Relevant Work.
- 34.13 ____ ____ Ability to Do Other Work.
- 34.14 ____ ____ Dispensing With Individualized Assessment.
- 34.15 Financial Consideration of The Two Federal Programs: Social Security Disability Insurance Benefits and Supplemental Security Income.
- 34.16 ____ Income.
- 34.17 ____ Assets.
- 34.18 ____ Amount of Benefits.
- 34.19 ____ SSI: Based on Financial Need.
- 34.20 ____ SSDIB: Based on FICA Withholding.
- 34.21 ____ Eligibility for Both SSI and SSDIB.
- 34.22 ____ Retroactivity of Benefits.
- 34.23 Administrative Procedure.
- 34.24 ____ Application.
- 34.25 ____ Reconsideration.
- 34.26 ____ Termination of Benefits.
- 34.27 ____ Administrative Hearing.
- 34.28 ____ Appeals Council.
- 34.29 ____ Federal District Court.
- 34.30 ____ Court of Appeals, Second Circuit.
- 34.31 Handling the Case—Generally.
- 34.32 ____ Initial Interview.
- 34.33 ____ Retainer Agreements.
- 34.34 ____ Social Security Administration's Records.

TABLE OF CONTENTS

Sec.
34.35 —— Medical Evidence.
34.36 —— —— Hospital Records.
34.37 —— —— Reports from Treating Physicians.
34.38 —— Other Evidence.
34.39 —— —— Former Co-workers and Employers.
34.40 —— —— Family Members.
34.41 —— Preparing for the Hearing.
34.42 —— —— Preparing the Claimant.
34.43 —— —— Other Witnesses or Documents.
34.44 —— Conducting the Hearing.
34.45 —— —— Testimony of the Claimant.
34.46 —— —— Medical Advisors.
34.47 —— —— Vocational Experts.
34.48 —— Post-hearing Evidence and Memoranda.
34.49 Implementing Favorable Decisions.
34.50 —— Collecting SSDIB Benefits.
34.51 —— Collecting SSI Benefits.
34.52 —— Collecting Fees.
34.53 —— —— Fee Applications.
34.54 —— —— Fee Agreements.
34.55 Appealing Unfavorable Decisions.
34.56 —— Strategic Considerations Regarding Unfavorable Decisions.
34.57 —— Strategic Considerations Regarding Partially Favorable Decisions.
34.58 Reopening Prior Applications.
34.59 —— Reopening SSDIB.
34.60 —— Reopening SSI.
34.61 —— Review of Grants of Reopening.
34.62 —— Review of Denials of Reopening.
34.63 —— Court Decisions Requiring Reopening.
34.64 —— Statutes and Regulations Requiring Reopening.
34.65 Procedural Checklist.
34.66 Checklists of Allegations—Medical Claims.
34.67 —— Psychiatric Claims.
34.68 Forms—Claimant Questionnaire. 💾
34.69 —— Retainer Agreement. 💾
34.70 —— Retainer Agreement: Concurrent Benefits. 💾
34.71 —— Fee Agreement: Maximum Fee. 💾
34.72 —— Request for Medical Records. 💾
34.73 —— Medical Release. 💾
34.74 —— Medical Questionnaire for Treating Physician. 💾
34.75 —— Psychiatric Questionnaire. 💾
34.76 —— Cover Letter to Treating Physician. 💾
34.77 —— Thank-you Letter to Treating Physician. 💾
34.78 —— Request for Appeals Council Review. 💾

CHAPTER 35. INCOME TAX

35.1 Scope Note.
35.2 Strategy.

TABLE OF CONTENTS

Sec.	
35.3	___ Checklist.
35.4	Personal Income Tax.
35.5	___ Computing Federal Adjusted Gross Income.
35.6	___ Computing Federal Taxable Income.
35.7	___ Definition of New York Taxable Income.
35.8	___ Computing New York Adjusted Gross Income.
35.9	___ Computing New York Taxable Income.
35.10	___ New York Personal Exemptions.
35.11	___ Itemized Deductions for Married Couple.
35.12	___ Exclusion of Pension and Disability Distributions From New York Income.
35.13	___ New York Minimum Tax.
35.14	___ Definition of Residency.
35.15	___ Burden of Proving Non-residency.
35.16	___ Domicile and Change of Domicile.
35.17	___ New York Income Tax on Non-resident Individuals.
35.18	___ Checklist.
35.19	New York Corporate Franchise Tax.
35.20	___ Comparison With Federal Taxation.
35.21	___ Initial Tax on Corporate Capital Structure.
35.22	___ Foreign Corporations.
35.23	___ Corporations Subject to Tax.
35.24	___ Corporations Exempt From Tax.
35.25	___ Necessary Level of Activity.
35.26	___ Calculation.
35.27	___ Tax on Net Income Base.
35.28	___ ___ Subtractions From Federal Taxable Income.
35.29	___ Items From Subsidiaries.
35.30	___ Tax on Capital Base.
35.31	___ ___ Definition of Capital Base.
35.32	___ ___ Exemption for Small Businesses.
35.33	___ Minimum Taxable Income Base.
35.34	___ Fixed Dollar Minimum Tax.
35.35	___ Apportionment of Tax Bases to New York.
35.36	___ ___ Business Allocation Percentage.
35.37	___ ___ Investment Allocation Percentage.
35.38	___ Definition of Subsidiary Capital.
35.39	___ Franchise Tax Checklist.
35.40	Department of Taxation and Finance.
35.41	___ Role of Office of the Counsel.
35.42	___ Taxpayer Services Division.
35.43	___ Office of Revenue and Information Management.
35.44	___ Office of Tax Operations.
35.45	___ ___ Audit Division.
35.46	___ ___ Tax Compliance Division.
35.47	___ ___ Revenue Opportunity Division.
35.48	___ ___ Office of Tax Enforcement.
35.49	___ ___ Division of Tax Appeals.
35.50	___ Summary.
35.51	Filing Returns.

XCIII

TABLE OF CONTENTS

Sec.	
35.52	____ Where to File.
35.53	____ Keeping Records of Returns.
35.54	____ Extensions of Time for Filing.
35.55	____ Obtaining New York Tax Forms.
35.56	____ Filing Claims for Refund.
35.57	____ Time Limitations.
35.58	____ Where to File.
35.59	____ Special Refund Authority.
35.60	____ Claim Based on Federal Changes.
35.61	____ Petitions for Refund.
35.62	____ Judicial Review of Denied Refund Claims.
35.63	____ Checklist.
35.64	Statutes of Limitation.
35.65	____ General Statutes for Income Tax Assessment.
35.66	____ Effect.
35.67	____ Exceptions.
35.68	____ Request for Prompt Assessment.
35.69	____ Waiver.
35.70	Penalties.
35.71	____ Late Filing.
35.72	____ Late Payment.
35.73	____ Reasonable Cause.
35.74	____ Negligence.
35.75	____ Substantial Understatement.
35.76	____ Underpayment of Estimated Taxes.
35.77	____ ____ Exceptions.
35.78	____ Fraud.
35.79	____ ____ Elements.
35.80	____ ____ Specific Determination Methods.
35.81	____ ____ Common Cases.
35.82	____ ____ Creative Methods of Proof.
35.83	____ Interest on Underpayment or Overpayment.
35.84	____ Checklist.
35.85	Audits and Appeals.
35.86	____ Audit Methods.
35.87	____ Taxpayer Bill of Rights.
35.88	____ Representation of Taxpayer.
35.89	____ Audit Results.
35.90	____ Bureau of Conciliation and Mediation Services.
35.91	____ ____ Requesting a Conciliation Conference.
35.92	____ ____ Conferences.
35.93	____ ____ Conference Orders.
35.94	____ Petition to Division of Tax Appeals.
35.95	____ ____ Referral to Bureau of Conciliation and Mediation Services.
35.96	____ ____ Small Claims Hearings.
35.97	____ Summary.
35.98	____ Checklist.
35.99	Judicial Actions.
35.100	____ Appeal by Article 78 Proceeding.

TABLE OF CONTENTS

Sec.
35.101 ___ ___ Payment of Taxes.
35.102 ___ ___ Initiation.
35.103 ___ ___ Burden of Proof.
35.104 ___ Declaratory Judgment Actions.
35.105 ___ Appeal to New York Court of Appeals.
35.106 ___ Summary.
35.107 ___ Checklist.
35.108 Assessment and Collection of Tax.
35.109 ___ Summary Assessment.
35.110 ___ Deficiency Assessment.
35.111 ___ Statute of Limitations.
35.112 ___ Jeopardy Assessment.
35.113 ___ Collection of Tax.
35.114 ___ ___ Lien.
35.115 ___ ___ Duration of Lien.
35.116 ___ Collection by Levy or Warrant.
35.117 ___ Installment Payment Agreements.
35.118 ___ Offer in Compromise.
35.119 ___ Bankruptcy as an Option.
35.120 ___ Checklist.
35.121 Criminal Tax Provisions.
35.122 ___ Failure to File Return.
35.123 ___ False or Fraudulent Return.
35.124 ___ Aiding or Assisting in False Return or Statement.
35.125 ___ Failure to Pay Tax.
35.126 ___ Failure to Properly Withhold Taxes.
35.127 Forms.
35.128 ___ Power of Attorney to Represent an Individual.
35.129 ___ Application for Automatic Extension of Time for Filing Return.
35.130 ___ Application For Additional Extension of Time to File for Individuals.
35.131 ___ Notice of Exception to Tax Tribunal.
35.132 ___ Petition to Division of Tax Appeals.
35.133 ___ Petition for Advisory Opinion.
35.134 ___ Statement of Financial Condition.
35.135 ___ Petition for Declaratory Ruling.
35.136 ___ Request for Conciliation Conference.
35.137 ___ Offer in Compromise.

CHAPTER 36. ALCOHOLIC BEVERAGE CONTROL LAW

36.1 Scope Note.
36.2 Strategy.
36.3 ___ Checklist.
36.4 Historical Background of State and Federal Regulations.
36.5 Jurisdiction.
36.6 New York State Liquor Authority.
36.7 Licenses.
36.8 ___ Retail Licenses.

TABLE OF CONTENTS

Sec.
36.9 —— —— On-Premises Licenses.
36.10 —— —— Off-Premises Licenses.
36.11 —— Wholesale Licenses.
36.12 —— Manufacturing Licenses.
36.13 —— General Application Requirements.
36.14 —— Special Qualifications for Licensees.
36.15 Permits.
36.16 —— Temporary Permits.
36.17 —— Other Permits.
36.18 Brand and/or Label Registration.
36.19 Penal and Tax Bonds.
36.20 Application Form (Retail) Reviewed.
36.21 —— Lease Information.
36.22 —— Applicant Information.
36.23 —— Information Regarding Premises.
36.24 —— Financial Information and Criminal Background.
36.25 —— Community Notification.
36.26 —— Landlord Information.
36.27 —— Additional Requirements for On–Premises Consumption Licenses.
36.28 —— —— Neighborhood.
36.29 —— —— Premises Exterior.
36.30 —— —— Premises Interior.
36.31 —— —— Bars.
36.32 —— —— Kitchen.
36.33 —— —— Permits.
36.34 —— —— Hotel.
36.35 —— Proposed Method of Operation.
36.36 —— Additional Requirements for Off–Premises Liquor Store Applicants.
36.37 —— Additional Requirements for Grocery Store Applicants.
36.38 —— Liquidators Permit.
36.39 —— Affidavit Requirements.
36.40 —— Personal Questionnaire.
36.41 —— On–Premises Liquor Applications 500 Foot Verification.
36.42 —— Miscellaneous Requirements.
36.43 —— Checklist.
36.44 Record–Keeping Requirements.
36.45 Reporting Changes.
36.46 —— Application for Endorsement Certificate.
36.47 —— Application for Approval of Corporate Change.
36.48 —— Alteration of Premises.
36.49 —— Removal of Premises.
36.50 —— Financing and Method of Operation.
36.51 Renewals.
36.52 Trade Practices.
36.53 Enforcement.
36.54 Penalties.
36.55 —— Revocation Order.
36.56 —— Cancellation Order.

XCVI

TABLE OF CONTENTS

Sec.
36.57 ____ Suspension Order.
36.58 ____ ____ Forthwith.
36.59 ____ ____ Deferred.
36.60 ____ ____ Combined Forthwith and Deferred Suspension.
36.61 ____ Letters of Warning.
36.62 ____ Suspension Proceedings.
36.63 ____ Revocation Notice of Pleading.
36.64 Pleadings and Procedure.
36.65 ____ Hearings.
36.66 ____ Judicial Review.
36.67 Forms.
36.68 ____ Application for Alcoholic Beverage Control Retail License.
36.69 ____ Application for Endorsement Certificate.
36.70 ____ Application for Approval of Corporate Change.
36.71 ____ Application for Permission to Make Alterations.
36.72 ____ Application for Wholesale License.
36.73 ____ Retail License and Filing Fee Schedule.

CHAPTER 37. CIVIL APPELLATE PRACTICE BEFORE THE APPELLATE DIVISION AND OTHER INTERMEDIATE APPELLATE COURTS

37.1 Scope Note.
37.2 Strategy.
37.3 Judiciary Structure.
37.4 Administration of the Appellate Division.
37.5 Administrative Powers of the Appellate Division.
37.6 ____ Admission, Removal and Disciplinary Jurisdiction.
37.7 ____ Administration of the Courts.
37.8 ____ Law Guardian Program.
37.9 ____ Mental Hygiene Legal Service Oversight.
37.10 ____ Assigned Counsel.
37.11 ____ Powers Relating to Appellate Term.
37.12 ____ Marshals.
37.13 An Overview of the Statutory Framework of the Appellate System and the Rules of the Court.
37.14 Appeals to the Appellate Division.
37.15 ____ Courts of Original Jurisdiction From Which Appeals Lie.
37.16 ____ ____ Supreme Court and County Court.
37.17 ____ ____ Court of Claims.
37.18 ____ ____ Surrogate's Court.
37.19 ____ ____ Family Court.
37.20 ____ Appeals From Other Appellate Courts.
37.21 ____ Who May Appeal.
37.22 ____ ____ Aggrieved Parties.
37.23 ____ ____ ____ Defaulters; Orders or Judgments on Consent.
37.24 ____ ____ ____ Intervenors.
37.25 ____ ____ ____ Substitution of Parties.
37.26 ____ ____ ____ Third Party Defendants.
37.27 ____ Scope of Review.

XCVII

TABLE OF CONTENTS

Sec.
37.28 ____ ____ Questions of Law.
37.29 ____ ____ Questions of Fact and the Exercise of Discretion.
37.30 ____ ____ Limitations in Notice of Appeal or Brief.
37.31 ____ ____ Mootness.
37.32 ____ ____ Change in Law While Case Is Pending.
37.33 ____ Appeals as of Right.
37.34 ____ ____ Appeals From Final and Interlocutory Judgments.
37.35 ____ ____ Appeals From Orders.
37.36 ____ Appeals by Permission.
37.37 ____ Non-appealable Matters.
37.38 ____ Appealable Paper.
37.39 ____ Time for Taking the Appeal.
37.40 ____ ____ Appeal as of Right.
37.41 ____ ____ Appeal by Permission.
37.42 ____ ____ Cross-Appeal.
37.43 ____ ____ Extensions; Omissions.
37.44 ____ ____ Other Statutory Provisions.
37.45 ____ Notice of Appeal—Form and Content.
37.46 ____ ____ Service and Filing Requirements.
37.47 ____ Reargument; Subsequent Orders.
37.48 ____ Assignment of Counsel.
37.49 ____ Perfecting the Appeal.
37.50 ____ ____ Time.
37.51 ____ ____ Methods of Perfection.
37.52 ____ ____ Briefs.
37.53 ____ ____ Consolidation.
37.54 ____ What to File; Number of Copies.
37.55 ____ ____ First Department.
37.56 ____ ____ Second Department.
37.57 ____ ____ Third Department.
37.58 ____ ____ Fourth Department.
37.59 ____ Location; Transfer Plan.
37.60 ____ Calendars.
37.61 ____ Preferences.
37.62 ____ Oral Arguments.
37.63 ____ Disposition of the Appeal.
37.64 ____ ____ Affirmance.
37.65 ____ ____ Reversal or Modification.
37.66 ____ ____ Dismissal.
37.67 ____ ____ Costs and Disbursements; Attorneys' Fees.
37.68 ____ Post-disposition Proceedings.
37.69 ____ ____ Reargument.
37.70 ____ ____ Leave to Appeal to the Court of Appeals.
37.71 ____ ____ Enforcement.
37.72 ____ ____ Resettlement or Clarification.
37.73 ____ ____ *Certiorari* to the U.S. Supreme Court.
37.74 ____ Motion Practice—Generally.
37.75 ____ ____ First Department.
37.76 ____ ____ Second Department.
37.77 ____ ____ Third Department.

TABLE OF CONTENTS

Sec.
37.78 ___ ___ Fourth Department.
37.79 ___ ___ Interim Relief.
37.80 ___ ___ Stays.
37.81 ___ ___ *Amicus Curiae.*
37.82 ___ ___ Miscellaneous Motions.
37.83 ___ Sanctions.
37.84 ___ Preargument Conferences.
37.85 ___ Unperfected Appeals.
37.86 Other Proceedings in the Appellate Division.
37.87 ___ CPLR Article 78 Proceedings.
37.88 ___ Writs of *Habeas Corpus.*
37.89 ___ CPLR 5704 *Ex Parte* Order Review.
37.90 ___ Miscellaneous Proceedings.
37.91 Appeals to Other Intermediate Courts.
37.92 ___ Appeals from Justice Courts.
37.93 ___ ___ Courts to Which Appeals Are Taken.
37.94 ___ ___ Applicability of CPLR Article 55.
37.95 ___ ___ Appeals as of Right and by Permission.
37.96 ___ ___ Taking the Appeal: Settlement of Case and Return on Appeal.
37.97 ___ ___ Perfection of Appeal.
37.98 ___ ___ Costs on Appeal.
37.99 ___ ___ Small Claims Review.
37.100 ___ ___ Rule Governance by Administrative Board.
37.101 ___ Appeals From City Courts.
37.102 ___ ___ Courts to Which Appeals Are Taken.
37.103 ___ ___ Applicability of CPLR Article 55.
37.104 ___ ___ Appeals as of Right and by Permission.
37.105 ___ ___ Taking the Appeal: Settlement of Case and Return on Appeal; Variations from CPLR.
37.106 ___ ___ Perfection of Appeal.
37.107 ___ ___ Costs on Appeal.
37.108 ___ ___ Small Claims Review.
37.109 ___ Appeals From District Courts.
37.110 ___ ___ Court to Which Appeals Are Taken.
37.111 ___ ___ Applicability of CPLR Article 55.
37.112 ___ ___ Appeals as of Right and by Permission.
37.113 ___ ___ Taking the Appeal: Settlement of Case and Return on Appeal.
37.114 ___ ___ Perfecting the Appeal.
37.115 ___ ___ Costs on Appeal.
37.116 ___ ___ Small Claims Review.
37.117 ___ Appeals from the Civil Court of the City of New York.
37.118 ___ ___ Courts to Which Appeals Are Taken.
37.119 ___ ___ Applicability of CPLR Article 55.
37.120 ___ ___ Appeals as of Right and by Permission.
37.121 ___ ___ Appeals to the Court of Appeals.
37.122 ___ ___ Taking the Appeal: Settlement of Case and Return on Appeal; Variations From CPLR.
37.123 ___ ___ Perfecting the Appeal.

TABLE OF CONTENTS

Sec.
37.124 ___ ___ Costs on Appeal.
37.125 ___ ___ Small Claims Review.
37.126 ___ Appeals from County Courts.
37.127 Procedural Checklist.
37.128 Forms.
37.129 ___ Notice of Appeal.
37.130 ___ Notice of Motion for a Stay of Proceedings.
37.131 ___ Order to Show Cause for a Stay of Proceedings.
37.132 ___ Affirmation in Support of Motion or Order To Show Cause for a Stay of Proceedings.
37.133 ___ Notice of Motion for a Preference to Expedite the Appeal.
37.134 ___ Affirmation in Support of Motion for a Preference to Expedite the Appeal.
37.135 ___ Notice of Motion to Enlarge Time for (Appellant to Perfect Appeal)(Respondent To File Brief).
37.136 ___ Affirmation in Support of Motion to Enlarge Time for (Appellant to Perfect Appeal) (Respondent to File Brief).
37.137 ___ Notice of Motion to Strike Matter *Dehors* the Record (Appendix)(Brief).
37.138 ___ Affirmation in Support of Motion to Strike Matter *Dehors* the Record(Appendix)(Brief).
37.139 ___ Notice of Motion for Reargument or Leave to Appeal to the Court of Appeals.
37.140 ___ Affirmation in Support of Motion for Reargument or Leave to Appeal to the Court of Appeals.

Volume 25

CHAPTER 38. CRIMINAL APPELLATE PRACTICE BEFORE THE APPELLATE DIVISION AND OTHER INTERMEDIATE APPELLATE COURTS

38.1 Scope Note.
38.2 Strategy.
38.3 Appeals to the Appellate Division—General Principles.
38.4 ___ Courts of Original Jurisdiction From Which Appeals Lie.
38.5 ___ Who May Appeal.
38.6 ___ ___ Status as Aggrieved by "Adverse" Determination.
38.7 ___ ___ Appeals by the Defendant From Superior Courts.
38.8 ___ ___ ___ As of Right.
38.9 ___ ___ ___ Appeals by Permission.
38.10 ___ ___ Appeals by the People.
38.11 ___ ___ Appeals from Orders Accepting or Sealing Grand Jury Reports; Appeals by Prosecutors; Appeals by Public Servants.
38.12 ___ Appeal Process—Appeals as of Right.
38.13 ___ ___ Appeals by Permission: Certificate Granting Leave.
38.14 ___ ___ Extensions of Time.
38.15 ___ ___ Stay of Judgment or Order.
38.16 ___ ___ Poor Person Relief and Assignment of Counsel.

TABLE OF CONTENTS

Sec.
- 38.17 ___ ___ Perfecting and Calendaring the Appeal.
- 38.18 ___ Scope of Review.
- 38.19 ___ ___ Questions of Law.
- 38.20 ___ ___ Questions of Fact; Weight of Evidence.
- 38.21 ___ ___ Interest of Justice/Discretion.
- 38.22 ___ ___ Change in Law While Case Pending.
- 38.23 ___ Disposition of Appeal.
- 38.24 ___ ___ Affirmance.
- 38.25 ___ ___ Modification.
- 38.26 ___ ___ Reversal.
- 38.27 ___ ___ Character of Order of Reversal or Modification: On the Law, On the Facts, in the Interest of Justice.
- 38.28 ___ ___ Corrective Action.
- 38.29 ___ Post-disposition Proceedings.
- 38.30 ___ ___ Responsibilities of Counsel.
- 38.31 ___ ___ Reargument.
- 38.32 ___ ___ Leave to Appeal.
- 38.33 ___ ___ *Certiorari* to U.S. Supreme Court.
- 38.34 ___ ___ *Coram Nobis*—Ineffective Assistance of Appellate Counsel.
- 38.35 ___ ___ Clarification/Resettlement.
- 38.36 ___ Motions in Connection With Appeals—Generally.
- 38.37 ___ ___ *Pro Se* Supplemental Brief.
- 38.38 ___ ___ *Anders* Brief.
- 38.39 ___ ___ Dismissal.
- 38.40 ___ ___ Reconstruction Hearing; Summary Reversal.
- 38.41 ___ ___ Death or Absence of a Defendant.
- 38.42 ___ ___ Assignment of New Counsel.
- 38.43 ___ ___ Expanding the Judgment Roll.
- 38.44 ___ ___ Briefs.
- 38.45 ___ ___ Withdrawal of Appeal.
- 38.46 Appeals to Intermediate Appellate Courts Other Than the Appellate Division.
- 38.47 ___ Appeals From Village Courts, Town Courts, City Courts and District Courts.
- 38.48 ___ Appeals From Criminal Court of the City of New York.
- 38.49 ___ ___ New York and Bronx County Branches.
- 38.50 ___ ___ Kings, Queens, Richmond County Branches.
- 38.51 ___ Orders, Sentences and Judgments Appealable.
- 38.52 ___ Taking the Appeal—Appeal as of Right.
- 38.53 ___ ___ Appeals by Permission.
- 38.54 ___ Stays Pending Appeal.
- 38.55 ___ Perfecting the Appeal.
- 38.56 ___ Determination of the Appeal.
- 38.57 Governance of the Appellate Term.
- 38.58 Original Application to County Court for Change of Venue.
- 38.59 Procedural Checklist for Appeals to Appellate Division.
- 38.60 Forms—Notice of Motion for a Stay of Execution of Judgment. 💾

TABLE OF CONTENTS

Sec.
38.61 ____ Affirmation in Support of Motion for a Stay of Execution of Judgment. 💾
38.62 ____ Notice of Motion for an Extension of Time to Take an Appeal. 💾
38.63 ____ Affirmation in Support of Motion for an Extension of Time to Take an Appeal. 💾
38.64 Chart.

CHAPTER 39. CIVIL AND CRIMINAL APPEALS TO THE COURT OF APPEALS

39.1 Scope Note.
39.2 Strategy.
39.3 Civil Appeals.
39.4 ____ Finality.
39.5 ____ Non-appealable Orders.
39.6 ____ Appealable Paper.
39.7 ____ Scope of Review.
39.8 ____ Appeal as of Right.
39.9 ____ ____ Appellate Division Orders or Judgments.
39.10 ____ ____ Final Judgment of Court of Original Instance.
39.11 ____ ____ Judgment of Court of Original Instance to Review Prior Non-final Determination of the Appellate Division.
39.12 ____ Appeals by Permission of the Appellate Division or the Court of Appeals.
39.13 ____ ____ Judgment of Court of Original Instance to Review Prior Non-final Determination of the Appellate Division.
39.14 ____ ____ Final Order of the Appellate Division Determining the Action.
39.15 ____ ____ Non-final Appellate Division Orders in Proceedings by or Against Public Officers or Others.
39.16 ____ Appeals by Permission of the Appellate Division.
39.17 ____ Form, Content and Service of Motions for Leave to Appeal.
39.18 ____ ____ Motions Filed in the Appellate Division.
39.19 ____ ____ Motions Filed in the Court of Appeals.
39.20 ____ Time for Taking the Appeal or Moving for Leave to Appeal—Appeals as of Right.
39.21 ____ ____ Motions for Leave to Appeal.
39.22 ____ ____ Cross Appeals.
39.23 ____ ____ Extensions of Time.
39.24 ____ ____ Omissions.
39.25 ____ Notice of Appeal—Form and Content.
39.26 ____ The Jurisdictional Statement.
39.27 ____ Jurisdictional Inquiry.
39.28 ____ Perfecting and Readying the Appeal.
39.29 ____ ____ Full Briefing and Oral Argument.
39.30 ____ ____ *Sua Sponte* Merits Consideration ("SSM").
39.31 ____ Determination of the Appeal—*Remittitur*.
39.32 ____ Motion Practice.
39.33 ____ ____ Motion for a Stay.

TABLE OF CONTENTS

Sec.
39.34 ____ ____ Motion to File an *Amicus* Brief.
39.35 ____ ____ Motion for Poor Person Relief.
39.36 ____ ____ Motion for Reconsideration.
39.37 Criminal Appeals.
39.38 ____ Definition of Criminal Case.
39.39 ____ Orders and Judgments From Which Appeals May Be Taken.
39.40 ____ By the Defendant in Death Penalty Cases.
39.41 ____ By the Prosecution in Death Penalty Cases.
39.42 ____ Intermediate Appellate Courts.
39.43 ____ Additional Limitations on Appealability.
39.44 ____ Appeals by Permission.
39.45 ____ ____ Obligation of Intermediate Appellate Court Counsel.
39.46 ____ ____ Who May Grant Leave to Appeal.
39.47 ____ ____ Criminal Leave Application ("CLA") Practice.
39.48 ____ ____ Stays and Continuation of Bail.
39.49 ____ Appeals Practice.
39.50 ____ Scope of Review.
39.51 ____ Disposition of Appeal.
39.52 ____ Motion Practice.
39.53 ____ ____ Poor Person Relief and Assignment of Counsel.
39.54 ____ ____ Extension of Time to Seek Leave to Appeal.
39.55 ____ ____ Dismissal of Appeal.
39.56 ____ ____ Withdrawal of Appeal.
39.57 ____ ____ Reargument.
39.58 Other Proceedings in the Court of Appeals.
39.59 ____ Review of Determinations of the Commission on Judicial Conduct.
39.60 ____ Certified Questions From Other Courts.
39.61 ____ Matters Regarding Admission of Attorneys and Licensing of Foreign Legal Consultants.
39.62 *Certiorari* to the Supreme Court of the United States.
39.63 Procedural Checklists.
39.64 ____ Civil Appeals as of Right.
39.65 ____ Civil Appeals by Permission of Court of Appeals.
39.66 ____ Criminal Appeals by Leave of a Court of Appeals Judge.
39.67 ____ Civil Appeals by Leave of the Appellate Division and Criminal Appeals by Leave of an Appellate Division Justice.
39.68 ____ Appeals Selected for Expedited Review Pursuant to Rule 500.4
39.69 ____ Appeals Tracked to Full Briefing and Oral Argument.
39.70 Drafting Checklists.
39.71 ____ Notice of Appeal.
39.72 ____ Rule 500.2 Jurisdictional Statement.
39.73 ____ Motion for Leave to Appeal to Court of Appeals Filed in Court of Appeals.
39.74 ____ Application for Leave to Appeal in Criminal Case Filed in Court of Appeals.
39.75 ____ Appellant's Brief on the Merits.
39.76 ____ Respondent's Brief on the Merits.

TABLE OF CONTENTS

Sec.
39.77 Forms—Notice of Appeal to Court of Appeals From Order of Appellate Division Finally Determining Action With Two Dissents on Question of Law.
39.78 ____ Notice of Appeal to Court of Appeals From Order of Appellate Division Finally Determining Action Where Construction of Constitution is Directly Involved.
39.79 ____ Notice of Appeal to Court of Appeals From Judgment of Supreme Court Where Constitutionality of Statute is Directly Involved.
39.80 ____ Notice of Appeal to Court of Appeals From Appellate Division Order of Reversal Granting New Trial With Stipulation for Judgment Absolute.
39.81 ____ Notice of Appeal to Court of Appeals From Judgment of Supreme Court to Review Prior Non-final Determination of Appellate Division.
39.82 ____ Rule 500.2 Jurisdictional Statement.
39.83 ____ Notice of Motion in Court of Appeals for Leave to Appeal to Court of Appeals From Order of Appellate Division.
39.84 ____ Affidavit in Support of Motion in Court of Appeals for Leave to Appeal to Court of Appeals From Order of Appellate Division.
39.85 ____ Notice of Motion in Court of Appeals for Reargument of Motion for Leave to Appeal.
39.86 ____ Notice of Motion in Court of Appeals for Leave to Appear *Amicus Curiae.*
39.87 ____ Notice of Motion to Dismiss Appeal as Untimely Taken.
39.88 ____ Affidavit in Support of Motion to Dismiss Appeal as Untimely Taken.
39.89 ____ CPLR 5531 Statement.
39.90 ____ Letter Seeking Leave to Appeal in Criminal Case.

	Page
Table of Jury Instructions	235
Table of Forms	236
Table of Statutes	iii
Table of Rules	iii
Table of Cases	iii
Index	iii

WEST'S NEW YORK PRACTICE SERIES

GENERAL PRACTICE IN NEW YORK

Volume 21

Chapter 7

CONSUMER LAW

by
James B. Fishman

Table of Sections

7.1	Scope Note.
7.2	Strategy—Generally.
7.3	___ Automobile Sales Cases.
7.4	___ Automobile Leasing Cases.
7.5	___ Credit Reporting.
7.6	___ Debt Collection.
7.7	___ Deceptive Business Practices.
7.8	___ Information to Obtain at Outset of Case.
7.9	Lemon Laws.
7.10	___ New Cars.
7.11	___ Used Cars.
7.12	___ Arbitration or Plenary Action?
7.13	___ Arbitration Procedure.
7.14	___ ___ Preparation for the Hearing.
7.15	___ ___ The Hearing.
7.16	___ ___ Appeals and Confirmation Proceedings.
7.17	___ ___ Scope of Review.
7.18	___ Source Materials.
7.19	Automobile Leasing—Overview.
7.20	___ Statutory Protection Overview.
7.21	___ The Consumer Leasing Act.
7.22	___ The Motor Vehicle Retail Leasing Act.
7.23	Motor Vehicle Installment Sales.
7.24	Repossession—Overview.
7.25	___ Prevention and Avoidance.
7.26	___ Defending Deficiency Claims.
7.27	Automobile Repairs.
7.28	Automobile Repair Shop Liens—Overview.
7.29	___ Statutory Challenges.
7.30	Credit Reporting—Overview.
7.31	___ Consumer Rights.
7.32	___ Non-litigation Strategies.
7.33	___ Litigating Credit Reporting Matters.
7.34	Debt Collection—History and Overview.
7.35	___ Claims for Intentional Infliction of Emotional Distress.
7.36	___ Statutory Overview.

7.37	____ FDCPA—Contacts With Third Parties.
7.38	____ ____ Contacts With a Debtor.
7.39	____ ____ Prohibited Tactics.
7.40	____ ____ Improper Omissions and Disclosures.
7.41	____ ____ Harassment or Abuse.
7.42	____ ____ Improper Demands.
7.43	____ ____ Judicial Enforcement.
7.44	____ State Law.
7.45	Deceptive Practices Act—Overview.
7.46	____ Elements of the Claim.
7.47	____ Types of Recovery Available.
7.48	Drafting Checklist—List of Essential Allegations.
7.49	Forms—Lemon Law Document Request Pursuant to 13 NYCRR § 300.9(a).
7.50	____ Notice of Petition to Vacate Lemon Law Arbitration Award Pursuant to CPLR Article 75.
7.51	____ Petition to Vacate Lemon Law Arbitration Award Pursuant to CPLR Article 75.
7.52	____ Complaint for Fraud, Breach of Warranties, Deceptive Business Practices, Used Car Lemon Law, Rescission and Revocation of Acceptance for Fraudulent Leasing Practices.
7.53	____ Answer and Third-party Complaint Alleging Fraud, Deceptive Practices, Breach of Warranty, and Federal Odometer Law Claims in Fraudulent Automobile Lease Case.
7.54	____ Answer to Complaint by Automobile Leasing Company for Deficiency Following Repossession, Alleging Commercially Unreasonable Resale and Deceptive Business Practices.
7.55	____ Affirmation in Opposition to Lessor's Motion for Summary Judgment and in Support of Lessee's Cross-motion for Summary Judgment Alleging Commercially Unreasonable Resale.
7.56	____ Notice of Rescission And/or Revocation of Acceptance and Demand for Restitution Pursuant to UCC 2–601 and 2–608.
7.57	____ Order to Show Cause in Proceeding under Lien Law § 201–a to Vacate Garageman's Lien.
7.58	____ Verified Petition in Proceeding under Lien Law § 201–a to Vacate Garageman's Lien.
7.59	____ Affirmation in Support of Petition in Proceeding under Lien Law § 201–a to Vacate Garageman's Lien.
7.60	____ Complaint Against Credit Reporting Agency Alleging Violations of the Fair Credit Reporting Act and the New York State Fair Credit Reporting Act and Deceptive Business Practices.
7.61	____ Stipulation of Settlement of Plaintiff's Lemon Law Claims Providing for Cancellation of Lease and Deletion of Any Derogatory Credit Information.
7.62	____ Complaint Alleging Violations of the Fair Debt Collection Practices Act and the Deceptive Practices Act.
7.63	____ Order to Show Cause with Temporary Restraining Order, Seeking Preliminary Injunction in Action Alleging Fraud, Deceptive Business Practices and Breach of Warranties.

§ 7.1 CONSUMER LAW Ch. 7

7.64 ____ Affirmation in Support of Temporary Restraining Order and Preliminary Injunction in Action Alleging Fraud, Deceptive Business Practices and Breach of Warranties. 💾

7.65 ____ Complaint in Action Alleging Fraud, Deceptive Business Practices and Breach of Warranties. 💾

WESTLAW Electronic Research

See WESTLAW Electronic Research Guide preceding the Summary of Contents.

---

§ 7.1 Scope Note

This chapter involves Consumer Law matters that most often arise in areas relating to automobiles, credit, and general consumer transactions. The chapter discusses the following areas of Consumer Law: sale and leasing of new and used automobiles, including the new car and used car "Lemon Laws";[1] the Motor Vehicle Installment Sales Act;[2] the Motor Vehicle Retail Leasing Act;[3] automobile repossessions; the New York Automobile Repair Shop Registration Act;[4] garagemen's liens;[5] credit reporting;[6] debt collection abuses;[7] and deceptive business practices.[8]

The chapter provides advice on how one should represent consumers involved in each of the listed topics, including discussion of the basic statutory requirements of each area of law, leading case law, litigation, and negotiation strategies. Litigation forms, as well as helpful sources of more detailed analysis are provided. When a particular consumer law problem requires more in-depth analysis, the attorney should refer to some of the other listed sources for assistance.[9]

§ 7.1

1. General Business Law §§ 198–a, 198–b; *see infra*, §§ 7.9 *et seq*.

2. Personal Property Law Art. 9; *see infra*, § 7.23.

3. Personal Property Law Art. 9–A; *see infra*, § 7.19.

4. Vehicle & Traffic Law §§ 398 *et seq*.; *see infra*, §§ 7.24 *et seq*.

5. Lien Law § 201–a; *see infra*, § 7.28.

6. Fair Credit Reporting Act (hereafter "FCRA") 15 U.S.C.A. §§ 1681 *et seq*.; *see infra*, § 7.30 for a discussion of recent amendments to FCRA.

7. Fair Debt Collection Practices Act (hereafter "FDCPA") 15 U.S.C.A. §§ 1692 *et seq*.; *see infra*, § 7.34.

8. General Business Law Art. 22–A; *see infra*, § 7.45.

9. Probably the best, and most exhaustive, materials available for attorneys on consumer law are the Consumer Litigation Series, written and published by the National Consumer Law Center ("NCLC"), located at 18 Tremont Street, Boston, MA, (617) 523–8010. This thirteen-volume series includes manuals entitled *Fair Debt Collection*, *Unfair and Deceptive Acts and Practices*, *Sales of Goods and Services* (which includes a Lemon Law chapter), *Fair Credit Reporting Act*, *Consumer Bankruptcy Law and Practice*, *Credit Discrimination*, *Odometer Law* (which includes discussion of car fraud), *Truth in Lending* (which includes retail installment sales of cars and other goods), *Consumer Class Actions: A Practical Litigation Guide*, *Repossessions and Foreclosures*, *Truth in Lending* (which includes a chapter on automobile leasing), *The Cost of Credit: Regulation and Legal Challenges* (which covers usury claims), and *Consumer Law Pleading With Disk* (vols. 1 and 2). The manuals are available directly from the NCLC and are also available at most law school libraries.

Practitioners should always be aware that consumer law matters derive from, and are intertwined with, many other substantive areas of law. For example, virtually all consumer law matters involving the sale or lease of personal property are grounded in the law of contracts[10] and sales.[11] When dealing with a client facing debt collection or credit reporting problems, the practitioner should consult materials pertaining to collection procedures, which describe the mechanisms available to creditors,[12] mortgage foreclosure,[13] as well as bankruptcy issues.[14] Defective car cases involving personal injury are treated under the law of products liability.[15]

Despite all of the recent technological advances, defective automobiles continue to roll off assembly lines both in the United States and abroad. After a home, an automobile is usually the most costly purchase a consumer will make. An automobile that does not operate properly is not only an annoyance, but often is dangerous as well. New York's new and used car "Lemon Laws" contain important rights and protections for consumers. The chapter first provides an overview of these laws[16] and then discusses: how one commences either a lawsuit or an arbitration proceeding under the Lemon Law,[17] preliminary procedural matters in preparing a Lemon Law case, such as discovery, expert witnesses, and evidence preparation,[18] Lemon Law arbitration hearing procedures,[19] and appeals from arbitration hearings and the types of issues that can result in a vacatur of an arbitrator's award.[20] The Lemon Law also provides remedies for consumers who win their cases but cannot secure voluntary compliance with the arbitrator's award from the manufacturer or dealer, and the chapter discusses the procedures available to confirm an arbitration award so that it is enforceable as a court-issued money judgment.[21]

The NCLC also provides consulting services in consumer law to private attorneys, for a reasonable hourly fee. NCLC staff attorneys will review contracts, leases, sales materials, debt collection notices, credit reporting materials and other documents for compliance with applicable laws, provide case cites from around the country dealing with the particular issue, and offer strategic advice on the best way to approach a problem. Any attorney who is interested in handling consumer law problems should be familiar with the NCLC's services and manuals.

New York practitioners should also refer to Newman and Imholz, *Caveat Venditor: A Manual for Consumer Representation in New York* (2d ed. 1994) for an excellent overview of how to litigate virtually all areas of consumer law, including a discussion of procedure and tactics, common consumer claims and defenses, statutory regulation of consumer contracts, special statutes and rules, credit and debt collection problems and creditors remedies.

10. Chapter 5, "Commercial Sales Contracts," *supra*.

11. UCC Art. 2.

12. Chapter 8, "Enforcement of Money Judgments," *infra*. See also, Borges et al., *Enforcing Judgments and Collecting Debts in New York* (West 1997).

13. Chapter 11, "Mortgage Foreclosure," *infra*.

14. Chapter 9, "Bankruptcy," *infra*.

15. Chapter 27, "Products Liability," *infra*. See also, Kreindler, Rodriguez, et al., *New York Law of Torts* (West 1997).

16. See infra, §§ 7.9—7.11.

17. See infra, § 7.12.

18. See infra, §§ 7.13—7.14.

19. See infra, § 7.15.

20. See infra, §§ 7.16—7.17.

21. See infra, § 7.16.

§ 7.1   CONSUMER LAW   Ch. 7

Leasing is a rapidly growing option for consumers seeking to obtain a new or used automobile, because it generally offers lower monthly payments than sale financing. Automobile leasing is, however, fraught with risks for consumers who do not understand basic leasing terminology and concepts. The chapter covers automobile leasing issues under both federal and state law.[22] The statutes in this area primarily involve disclosure of lease terms, termination penalties, and costs imposed on consumers, and the chapter explains the legal remedies available to consumers whose rights have been violated by lessors.[23]

Consumers who finance an automobile purchase may also face problems caused by dishonest dealers and lending institutions. Thus, a discussion of the Motor Vehicle Installment Sales Act, which contains important consumer rights, is included.[24]

When consumers fall behind in making their car payments, repossession, or the threat of repossession, becomes a reality. Practitioners can help either to prevent repossession altogether or to force the creditor to return the vehicle to the consumer after repossession has taken place. The chapter includes a discussion of consumer rights with regard to repossession, as well as defenses against post-repossession deficiency claims.[25]

Often, automobile problems do not begin until long after purchase, when repairs are needed and the manufacturer's warranty has expired. Many consumers fall victim to dishonest repair shops, either those that are independently run or those connected to a dealership. Consumer rights and remedies under the New York Repair Shop Registration Act are discussed.[26]

When disputes over automobile repairs escalate, consumers often find that their automobile is held "hostage" by the repair shop, which claims a lien for the cost of "repairs" and seeks to exact exorbitant storage charges. Statutory lien requirements and consumer remedies and strategies to vacate them to recover possession of the vehicle are discussed.[27]

For many consumers, credit reporting problems can be a nightmare that will not go away. All too often credit reports containing erroneous and obsolete information are used by potential creditors in making credit decisions. Consumer credit reports are produced and maintained by large, faceless credit reporting agencies. Credit reports are maintained on virtually every person in the United States over 18 years old. Consumers have certain rights in dealing with credit reporting agencies, such as obtaining the deletion of inaccurate or obsolete information. Attorneys practicing in this area, however, must be aware of the specific

22.   See infra, §§ 7.19—7.21.
23.   See infra, §§ 7.20—7.21.
24.   See infra, § 7.22.
25.   See infra, §§ 7.24—7.26.
26.   See infra, § 7.27.
27.   See infra, §§ 7.28—7.29.

limitations placed on those rights by the courts in order to advise and represent their clients properly. Thus, the chapter includes discussions of the particular rights and remedies available to consumers under the Fair Credit Reporting Act, pre-litigation steps to take to correct erroneous credit reports, filing a dispute statement on the report, and issues arising in litigation against credit reporting agencies.[28]

Consumers are also sometimes victimized by abusive and harassing debt collection practices employed by collection agencies, creditors, and collection attorneys. When attempts are made to collect bills that are either disputed or have already been paid, the matter can be particularly problematic. Even more troubling are cases in which consumers are subjected to repeated abusive and harassing telephone calls at home and at work. Such practices often cause severe emotional and physical distress for consumers. The Fair Debt Collection Practices Act outlaws a long list of abusive and deceptive debt collection practices, and it provides specific rights and remedies for consumers. Consumer-debtor rights and remedies, as well as specific strategies to combat illegal collection practices, are discussed.[29] Also covered are litigation of debt collection claims and the legal remedies available.[30]

Perhaps the most important consumer protection statute is New York's Deceptive Practices Act.[31] This statute permits consumers to sue businesses that engage in deceptive practices and to obtain injunctive relief, actual and statutory damages, as well as attorney's fees. The most significant part of the statute is its authorization for consumers to act as "private attorneys general" to seek to enjoin deceptive practices on behalf of all consumers. The chapter includes discussions of the coverage of the statute, the standards used by the courts in evaluating deceptive practices claims, and examples of particular business practices that have triggered successful resort to the deceptive practices act.[32]

Finally, a checklist of various litigation forms written for actual cases in the above areas is provided, offering practitioners a useful starting point in commencing or defending consumer law cases.[33]

§ 7.2 Strategy—Generally

Consumer law is a field that affects everyone. In one respect or another, we are all consumers who shop for and acquire goods and services in the marketplace. In most instances our dealings in the marketplace are satisfactory, and legal recourse to enforce our rights does not become necessary. Unfortunately, for a variety of reasons, something may go wrong with either the goods or services that form the basis of a particular transaction. Very often, consumers are completely

28. *See infra*, §§ 7.30—7.33.
29. *See infra*, §§ 7.34—7.42.
30. *See infra*, § 7.43.
31. General Business Law Art. 22–A.
32. *See infra*, §§ 7.45—7.47.
33. *See infra*, § 7.48.

§ 7.2 CONSUMER LAW Ch. 7

unaware of their rights in particular situations and how to enforce them. Even most lawyers do not have a rudimentary knowledge of basic consumer rights and how to enforce them.

Fortunately, there are many tools available to attorneys who seek to assist victimized consumers. Since the 1970's there has been a virtual explosion of federal and state laws protecting consumers. In addition, many court decisions have been rendered, recognizing and expanding upon the rights of consumers. Despite the availability of these tools, however, there are judges who are unfamiliar with consumer law and therefore are not willing to recognize important consumer rights. A good consumer lawyer must be prepared to educate judges, who typically handle personal injury, matrimonial, and business dispute cases, in consumer law.

For most consumers, a reasonably priced, reliable automobile and a good credit rating have crucial importance in their daily lives. The ability to obtain an automobile, to find a job, to get to work, to keep a job, and to obtain a mortgage or other credit, is directly affected by the issues discussed in this chapter. Without either one, a consumer's life can be severely disrupted, often without much notice. A lawyer presented with a problem arising in any of these areas must be able to analyze the problem quickly, develop a range of possible solutions, and obtain a positive result for his or her client. Very often, consumers do not have extensive resources available to pay a lawyer to enforce their rights. Fortunately, most federal and state consumer laws provide for the recovery of attorney's fees by a successful plaintiff. For this reason, it is *crucial* that attorneys keep accurate and contemporaneous time records at every stage of a consumer matter.

In addition, there are many types of consumer law problems that simply do not involve a sufficient amount of money to justify hiring a private attorney to handle them, even with the possibility of recovering statutory attorney's fees. Many such small matters can be handled by the consumer without an attorney, by commencing an action in small claims court.[1] Other types of consumer problems may be referred to an appropriate government agency for investigation and possible mediation or enforcement. For example, the New York State Attorney General's Office, Bureau of Consumer Frauds and Protection, which has regional offices throughout the state, mediates certain consumer disputes.[2] Historically, that office has enjoyed a strong reputation for aggressive consumer law enforcement. Many lawsuits brought by that office have

---

§ 7.2

1. The Small Claims Court Acts are found in the court acts for the particular jurisdictions involved. For example, in New York City, where the monetary jurisdiction is currently $3,000, the New York City Civil Court Act ("NYCCCA"), Art. 18, covers small claims court procedures. Outside of New York City, small claims court procedures are found in Art. 18 of the Uniform District Court Act, the Uniform Justice Court Act, and the Uniform City Court Act.

2. In New York City, the telephone number is (212) 416–8000.

involved issues brought to the Attorney General's attention by victimized consumers.

Consumers may also be referred to the appropriate local consumer protection agencies. In New York City, the Department of Consumer Affairs[3] ("DCA") not only receives and investigates thousands of consumer complaints each year, it also licenses many specific categories of businesses, *i.e.,* used car dealers, debt collection agencies, etc. By having the power to revoke a business' license, the DCA can serve as a very effective tool to enforce the rights of consumers who have been taken advantage of by dishonest businesses. A private attorney can also represent a consumer at a DCA hearing involving a licensed business.

Federal agencies can also be helpful in attempting to resolve consumer problems. For example, the Federal Trade Commission[4] receives complaints involving improper debt collection practices, credit reporting problems, deceptive advertising and sales practices, and many others.[5] Complaints about federally chartered banks should be directed to the Federal Reserve Board.

§ 7.3 Strategy—Automobile Sales Cases

Consumer problems are often multi-faceted. It is not uncommon for a client to present a problem like the following scenario:

Client "A" responds to a newspaper advertisement placed by a car dealer. The advertisement announces a particularly low interest rate and purchase price for a new car that the consumer is interested in purchasing. In response to the advertisement and the salesman's representations, the consumer purchases a new car from the dealer, which obtains "dealer financing" from a bank or finance company. The consumer is not given a copy of the installment sales contract until several weeks after taking delivery of the car. At that time, the consumer notices that the interest rate in the contract is five percent higher than was advertised in the newspaper and that the selling price is three thousand dollars more than was advertised. After carefully examining the sales invoice, the consumer notices that she was charged for rustproofing, pinstriping, and an extended service contract, which she neither requested nor needed. Shortly thereafter the car breaks down, and the manufacturer either refuses, or is unable, to repair it. The consumer brings the car to an independent mechanic, who tells her that the vehicle's frame is bent, probably from a pre-sale collision, and that the odometer likely was rolled back to hide it. Since the consumer can no longer use the car, she stops making her payments on it to the bank. The bank reports the account as delinquent to a credit reporting agency, and that information

3. Telephone number: (212) 487–4444.
4. New York City telephone number: (212) 264–1207.

5. *See also,* Borges, et al., *Enforcing Judgments and Collecting Debts in New York* (West 1997) Ch.2.

§ 7.3   CONSUMER LAW   Ch. 7

appears on the client's credit report. The bank also refers the account to a collection agency, which begins a series of harassing telephone calls to the consumer at both her home and job. The bank threatens to repossess the car. The client contacts an attorney, seeking help.

The preceding example involves at least nine different substantive and procedural areas of consumer law: false advertising,[1] deceptive business practices,[2] the New Car Lemon Law,[3] the Motor Vehicle Retail Installment Sales Act,[4] the Truth in Lending Act,[5] the Federal Odometer Act,[6] the Fair Debt Collection Practices Act,[7] the federal and state Fair Credit Reporting Acts,[8] and secured transactions and repossessions.[9] Each area of law must be distilled and evaluated.

As with any consumer law problem, the first thing that an attorney must do is have the client produce *every* document he or she has that is, or may be, relevant to the entire problem, including all advertisements, contracts, repair orders, correspondence, etc. The attorney must then review all of the documents, separating them according to the particular problem involved, *i.e.*, automobile purchase, repairs, payments, credit reports, collection letters.

The attorney should first analyze the problem for possible new or used car Lemon Law coverage.[10] If it is determined that the Lemon Law does apply, the attorney and client should consider whether to commence an arbitration proceeding or a lawsuit.[11] Next, the attorney should review the purchase documents to determine if they comply with the Motor Vehicle Retail Installment Sales Act.[12]

Library References:

West's Key No. Digests, Consumer Protection ⊂=9.

§ 7.4   Strategy—Automobile Leasing Cases

The first, and most obvious, focus in analyzing an automobile leasing problem is on the lease itself.[1] The practitioner must have a basic understanding of each of the terms to which the consumer initially agreed, and, in particular, those terms that directly impact on the particular problem.

§ 7.3
1. General Business Law § 350.
2. General Business Law § 349.
3. General Business Law § 198–a.
4. Personal Property Law Art. 9.
5. 15 U.S.C.A §§ 1601 *et seq.*
6. 15 U.S.C.A. §§ 1901, 1981–1991.
7. 15 U.S.C.A. §§ 1692 *et seq.*
8. 15 U.S.C.A. § 1681; General Business Law § 380.
9. UCC Art. 9.

10. See *infra*, §§ 7.9—7.18.
11. See *infra*, § 7.22.
12. Personal Property Law Art. 9. The attorney should also send this and other sales documents to the National Consumer Law Center for review. See *supra*, § 7.1 note 9.

§ 7.4
1. See *infra*, § 7.19.

Some of the more typical leasing problems presented by consumers are the following: the vehicle is defective, and the consumer wants to know how to rectify the problem when the leasing company and the manufacturer refuse to do so; the consumer can no longer afford the monthly payments and wants to cancel the lease before its scheduled termination; the consumer has fallen behind in making payments, the leasing company has repossessed the vehicle and is now demanding payment of exorbitant charges; or the consumer is facing a lawsuit by the leasing company following her default in making payments.[2]

As with all consumer problems, the practitioner must determine, early on, exactly what result the consumer seeks. If the lease violates specific mandatory statutory protections, it may be possible to cancel it altogether, with no further obligation to the consumer. Other violations may trigger a claim for actual and statutory damages, as well as attorney's fees, the assertion of which might result in an agreed settlement of the lessor's claims.

§ 7.5 Strategy—Credit Reporting

If the client does not have a copy of a recent credit report from Experian[1], Equifax, and Trans Union (the three major credit reporting agencies) he or she should either obtain them directly or should provide counsel with a notarized written authorization to obtain them on his or her behalf. Once the reports have been obtained, the attorney should go over them very carefully with the client to determine if all of the information in them is complete and accurate. Particular attention should be paid to the manner in which the automobile loan is reported. If it is listed as delinquent, or otherwise adversely, the client should exercise the right to demand the insertion of a dispute statement outlining the problems with the vehicle and that it is being handled by an attorney.[2] If a Lemon Law claim, or other claim, is ultimately successful, the attorney should demand that the bank delete the account completely from its reports to the consumer reporting agencies.

§ 7.6 Strategy—Debt Collection

All written dunning notices from a collection agency should be

---

2. PRACTICE POINTER: If the primary problem presented by the consumer is that the vehicle is defective, the practitioner should first determine if the problem can be handled under either the New Car or Used Car Lemon Laws. See infra, §§ 7.9— 7.18. If the consumer is successful in a Lemon Law claim when the vehicle is a leased vehicle, the remaining lease payments must be fully paid off by the manufacturer or dealer, the consumer must be refunded all payments made, and the lease will be deemed terminated, with no penalty owed by the consumer for early termination. General Business Law § 198-a(c)(2); General Business Law § 198-b(c)(1).

§ 7.5
1. Formerly known as TRW.
2. See infra, § 7.30.

§ 7.6   CONSUMER LAW   Ch. 7

reviewed for compliance with the Fair Debt Collection Practices Act.[1] The attorney should also obtain detailed information from the client about the date, time, and place of all collection calls, including the specific words used by the caller.[2]

The next step the attorney should consider is providing written notice to the collection agency to cease all further communication with the consumer[3] and to direct all further communication concerning the alleged debt to the attorney.[4] This step should eliminate the collection agency from the problem. The attorney should consider asserting claims under the FDCPA against a collection agency or collection attorney engaging in illegal collection practices. Claims against creditors cannot, in most instances, be asserted under the FDCPA.

§ 7.7   Strategy—Deceptive Business Practices

All of the acts and omissions of the dealer in the example set out above[1] should be analyzed for deceptive business practices/false advertising issues.[2] Basically, any material misrepresentation made in connection with a consumer transaction that causes harm to consumers and that would likely mislead a reasonable consumer is actionable under either the Deceptive Practices Act[3] or the related False Advertising Act[4] Both statutes provide a very powerful weapon in the consumer lawyer's arsenal: the ability to act as a "private attorney general" and to seek injunctive relief on behalf of the client, as well as on behalf of all consumers, without the need to bring a class action.[5] These statutes are also valuable in that they permit the consumer to recover both damages and attorney's fees.[6]

§ 7.6

1. 15 U.S.C.A. §§ 1692 et seq. In particular the notices should be reviewed for compliance with Section 1692g, which requires that certain "Miranda"-type warnings be given by collection agencies. See infra, § 7.37.

PRACTICE POINTER: If the attorney suspects that the collection agency's dunning notices are improper, counsel should send them to the National Consumer Law Center for review. See supra, § 7.1, note 9.

2. It is not illegal for a consumer to tape record calls from collection agencies. Most telephone answering machines can easily be used for this purpose. Tape recording is the most effective way to prove that abusive or harassing collection calls took place.

3. 15 U.S.C.A. § 1692c(c). See infra, § 7.37.

4. 15 U.S.C.A. § 1692c.

§ 7.7

1. See supra, § 7.3.

2. This chapter does not specifically cover the false advertising statute, General Business Law §§ 350 et seq., however the case law interpreting the Deceptive Practices Act, General Business Law § 349, is generally applicable to such claims as well. As a general rule, deceptive practices and false advertising, to the extent they have the capacity or tendency to mislead a reasonable consumer, are analyzed under the same standard. Guggenheimer v. Ginzburg, 43 N.Y.2d 268, 401 N.Y.S.2d 182, 372 N.E.2d 17 (1977); Geismar v. Abraham & Strauss, 109 Misc.2d 495, 439 N.Y.S.2d 1005 (Dist.Ct., Nassau County, 1981).

3. General Business Law § 349.

4. General Business Law § 350.

5. General Business Law § 349(h); See infra, § 7.46.

6. General Business Law §§ 349(h), 350.

§ 7.8 Strategy—Information to Obtain at Outset of Case

In any consumer law matter, the attorney should obtain the following information from the client and should ask the following questions at the outset:

How did you first learn about the merchant?

What advertisements or other materials did you rely upon in deciding to go to the particular merchant?

Describe all oral statements made by the merchant, in chronological order.[1]

Provide all written materials pertaining or connected to the problem.

In addition, the attorney should write to the local Better Business Bureau and request a copy of any reports prepared about the particular merchant.

The attorney should also send requests under the Freedom of Information Law ("FOIL")[2] to all government agencies that either license the particular merchant or that investigate consumer complaints. Counsel should request both the "license file" and the "complaint file" pertaining to the merchant, as well as any previously entered "cease and desist" agreements.[3]

Counsel should also review the defendant index in the local court, both the lower level court as well as the supreme court, to determine if other consumers have previously sued the particular merchant.[4]

Once the various elements of the problem have been sorted out, the attorney should develop a game plan with the consumer. The most important question the attorney can ask a client is, "What type of relief are you seeking?" The client can then advise which of the particular problems is most pressing, *i.e.*, stopping the collection agency's harassment, getting the car fixed or replaced, getting a refund of the money paid, or clearing up an adverse credit report. The following sections

---

§ 7.8

1. **PRACTICE POINTER:** Probably the most valuable source of information that the consumer can provide to the attorney is a written chronological description of *all* events, conversations, correspondence, etc., that pertain to the matter. The client should be encouraged to include anything and everything that is even remotely connected to the problem. For example, if the consumer has suffered emotional distress, such as nervousness, sleeplessness, depression or anxiety, as a result of debt collection abuses or erroneous credit reporting, this should be included and documented.

2. Public Officer's Law Art. 6.

3. This strategy is particularly helpful because a court will be much more impressed with the severity of a particular allegation if the merchant has engaged in similar practices with other consumers. Also, businesses that are required to have a license issued by a particular government agency are generally more likely to respond and to resolve consumer complaints.

4. **PRACTICE POINTER:** If any other cases are located, each court file should be reviewed. This step can be particularly useful both to learn about other victims of the same practices, as well as to see how the defendant had responded to litigation in general.

address, in more detail, the approaches to take on each of these topics. Very often the client's financial situation will play a major role in determining the most logical and efficient course of action. If the client is unable to afford even modest attorney's fees, and if the attorney is unable to proceed *pro bono* or only on the basis of a hope of recovering statutory attorney's fees, it will become necessary to explore alternative ways to obtain relief for the client. Often this may mean attempting to resolve the client's problem informally, without commencing litigation, advising the client how to handle the matter *pro se*, or referring the client to a government consumer protection office that may be able to assist the client in solving the problem.

§ 7.9 Lemon Laws

Both the New Car Lemon Law[1] and the Used Car Lemon Law[2] provide substantial protections to consumers who purchase or lease defective motor vehicles. Most states now have Lemon Laws, and New York's statutes are among the most comprehensive and widely used in the country. After the purchase of a house, an automobile is probably the largest single expense most consumers have. When an automobile proves to be substantially defective, that purchase can be seriously jeopardized. Fortunately, New York has a relatively simple, cost efficient mechanism to address the problem.

Prior to enactment of the Lemon Laws, purchasers of defective automobiles in New York could not look far beyond the Uniform Commercial Code for redress. However, in many cases, reliance on UCC provisions provided little, if any, consolation for consumers when faced with the extensive resources of motor vehicle manufacturers and dealers. Before enactment of the Lemon Laws, consumers could assert, pursuant to the UCC, a breach of the implied warranty of merchantability,[3] breach of an implied warranty of fitness for a particular purpose,[4] rejection,[5] or revocation of acceptance,[6] as well as common law claims alleging failure of consideration and breach of contract.

These remedies, however, have proven inadequate in most cases, because most consumers are unaware of them and the UCC remedies are not specifically related to defective conditions in automobiles. Moreover, these remedies are, at best, both expensive and time consuming, and they do not provide consistent and uniform standards for review. Few consumers could be expected to be aware of particular sections of the UCC. Few lawyers, even those who are generally familiar with consumer law, would undertake representation in such matters on a contingency basis. Finally, the absence of provisions for awards of attorney's fees to

---

§ 7.9
1. General Business Law § 198–a.
2. General Business Law § 198–b.
3. UCC § 2–314.
4. UCC § 2–315.
5. UCC § 2–601.
6. UCC § 2–608.

victorious consumers has resulted in few cases being brought pursuant to the UCC or the common law by consumers unable to pay extensive legal costs.

New York's New Motor Vehicle Lemon Law, enacted in 1983, and its subsequent amendments, created a revolutionary new mechanism for consumers. At the same time, it provided a uniform set of rules and procedures for manufacturers to follow. The enactment of the Lemon Law leveled the playing field for consumers in their dealings with manufacturers and dealers. Since 1983, the Lemon Law has evolved on an almost annual basis, with newly enacted amendments designed to remedy problems and to close loopholes not originally foreseen.

The most significant amendments to the Lemon Law have been the enactment of the *Used Car* Lemon Law[7] in 1984 and the creation of a state-run arbitration mechanism in 1986. At the same time, an extensive body of case law has developed throughout the state.

The purpose of the following sections is to provide the practitioner with the basic tools necessary for understanding both the New and Used Car Lemon Laws and the procedures involved under each law. Also, source materials are identified for more in-depth analysis. Finally, practice tips will be included throughout to give the practitioner the type of information necessary to advise clients with defective vehicles and to enable counsel to use the Lemon Law successfully.

For the most part, the coverage and procedures in both the New Car and Used Car Lemon Laws are very similar, with the major distinction being that the new car law applies to the manufacturer only, and the used car law applies to the dealer only.[8] To the extent that they are similar, they will be discussed simultaneously. The major differences both in coverage and procedure will be highlighted.

§ 7.10 Lemon Laws—New Cars

The New Car Lemon Law is designed to provide a legal remedy when a motor vehicle does not conform to the terms of the manufacturer's written warranty, and the problem cannot be cured after reasonable effort. If a consumer successfully establishes that his/her car is a lemon within the meaning of the law, he or she is entitled either to a full refund of the purchase price (including sales tax paid[1] and any rebate

---

7. General Business Law § 198–b.
8. References to a manufacturer generally apply to the new car lemon law. References to a dealer generally apply to the used car lemon law.

§ 7.10
1. The statute only addresses New York State sales tax and not any other taxes, like the federal luxury tax. Despite this omission from the statute, there is no reason why a successful consumer should not be able to recover that tax as well from the federal government.

§ 7.10   CONSUMER LAW   Ch. 7

applied to the purchase price) or to replacement with a comparable car.[2]

In order to qualify for Lemon Law protection, the consumer must establish initially that the vehicle was covered by a written manufacturer's express warranty at the time of original delivery and that it was purchased *or* leased in New York State *or* was registered in New York State, at the time the Lemon Law is invoked.[3] Thus, consumers who purchase vehicles in other states, such as New Jersey or Connecticut, and then register them in New York, may qualify for protection under the statute.[4]

Additionally, the Lemon Law applies not only to traditional "passenger cars," but also to increasingly popular vehicles, such as vans, sport utility vehicles, four-wheel-drive vehicles and light trucks.[5] The only requirement in this regard is that the vehicle be used primarily for "personal, family or household purposes."[6] The Lemon Law also applies to recreational vehicles and Motor Homes.[7] The practitioner is referred to the language of the statute for specific coverage.[8] The Lemon Law does *not* apply to motorcycles or purely off-road vehicles or to vehicles that are used primarily for business purposes.[9]

2. General Business Law § 198–a(c)(1).
PRACTICE POINTER: Although the statute permits the consumer to elect between a refund and a comparable replacement vehicle, it rarely makes sense to choose the latter. In Volvo North America Corp. v. DePaola, 156 A.D.2d 40, 554 N.Y.S.2d 835 (1st Dep't 1990), the court held that a "comparable replacement vehicle" means one with as many miles as the consumer's. Given that the Statute of Limitations in a Lemon Law case is four years (General Business Law § 198–a(j); General Business Law § 198–b(f)(2), (5)), by the time the consumer wins the case it may be difficult, if not impossible, even to find a comparable replacement vehicle. Fortunately, this problem does not arise too often. By the time a consumer successfully brings a Lemon Law claim, he or she has usually become so soured by that particular manufacturer that the consumer usually does not want even to consider another one. By choosing the refund option, the consumer is free to buy any other manufacturer's vehicle.

3. General Business Law § 198–a(a)(2).

4. This was not always the case. When the Lemon Law was first enacted, the vehicle had to have been purchased or leased *and* registered in New York, thereby precluding protection for New Yorkers who were lured to neighboring New Jersey, Pennsylvania or Connecticut to buy their cars. The statute was amended in 1990 to correct this flaw.

5. The 1986 amendment to the Lemon Law eliminated the term "passenger" from the definition of a motor vehicle.

6. General Business Law § 198–a(a)(1).

7. As with most such vehicles, the engine, drive train and chassis are produced by one manufacturer, and the body and furnishings by another, and the latter then assembles the final product and sells it under its brand name. In Safari Motor Coaches, Inc. v. Corwin, 162 Misc.2d 449, 617 N.Y.S.2d 289 (Sup.Ct., Saratoga County, 1994), aff'd as modified 225 A.D.2d 921, 638 N.Y.S.2d 992 (3d Dep't 1996), the consumer had purchased a new motor home. When the engine and other mechanical components proved defective, the consumer commenced a Lemon Law proceeding against the ultimate manufacturer, rather than against the manufacturer of the particular defective component. The court held that this was proper and that since the consumer was only in privity with the ultimate manufacturer, Lemon Law liability was properly laid at the doorstep of that defendant.

8. General Business Law § 198–a(n).

9. **CAVEAT**: There has been substantial litigation over this aspect of Lemon Law coverage, much of which deals with vehicles that have been purchased or leased by a business. *See* Parlato v. Chrysler Corp., 170 A.D.2d 442, 565 N.Y.S.2d 230 (2d Dep't 1991) (corporate lessee is a "consumer");

§ 7.10 LEMON LAWS—NEW CARS

A "lemon" under the new car law is defined as a motor vehicle that fails to conform to the manufacturer's express warranty during the first 18,000 miles of operation or during the first two years from original delivery, whichever comes first.[10] In the Lemon Law, this is referred to as the "period of nonconformity."[11] A vehicle is presumed to be a lemon if there have been at least *four* attempts by the manufacturer to correct a particular defect during the period of nonconformity (the "repeated repair rule"),[12] *or* the vehicle has been "out of service" because of one or more defects for a cumulative total of 30 days or more during that period (the "out of service rule"),[13] *or* the manufacturer refuses to make repairs to correct a defect under the warranty within 20 days after receipt of written notice from the consumer (the "refusal to repair rule").[14]

In addition, in order to qualify for coverage under the statute, the defect complained of cannot be the result of abuse, neglect, or unauthorized modification, and it must "substantially" impair the vehicle's value.[15] Finally, the defect(s) must continue to exist at the time the matter is heard.[16]

Matter of Mercedes–Benz of North America, Inc. v. Yoon, N.Y.L.J., 4/26/94, p.21, col.5 (Sup.Ct., N.Y. County)(same); *See infra*, § 7.20 note 1.

The courts have essentially held that the focus in this inquiry is not whether the vehicle is owned by a natural person or a business, but rather the purpose for which the vehicle is primarily used. In this regard, the courts have required consumers to produce relevant business tax returns, so it can be determined if a business deduction was taken for the cost of the vehicle. If a client presents a Lemon Law claim, and the registered owner or lessee is a business, the attorney must inquire into whether a tax deduction was taken by the business for the vehicle. If it was, the client should be advised that a Lemon Law claim might not be viable.

10. General Business Law §§ 198–a(a)(2), (b)(1).

11. General Business Law § 198–a(b)(1).

12. General Business Law § 198–a(d)(1).

13. General Business Law § 198–a(d)(2).

14. General Business Law § 198–a(b)(2).

CAVEAT: Unlike the "repeated repair rule" and the "out of service rule," the "refusal to repair rule" only applies when the vehicle was both purchased *and* registered in New York. General Business Law § 198–a(b)(1).

15. General Business Law §§ 198–a(c)(3)(i), (ii).

PRACTICE POINTER: The consumer is not required to prove that the value of the vehicle has been substantially impaired. Merely establishing either the repeated repairs, that the vehicle was out of service for the required period, or a refusal to repair is sufficient to find that the vehicle is a "lemon." Instead, under the statute, the absence of substantial impairment is an affirmative defense that the manufacturer or dealer has the burden of proving. General Business Law § 198–a(c)(3)(i); General Business Law § 198–b(c)(a). Walker v. General Motors Corp., Pontiac Motor Div., 159 Misc.2d 651, 606 N.Y.S.2d 125 (Civ.Ct., N.Y. County, 1993)(New Car Lemon Law); Jandreau v. LaVigne, 170 A.D.2d 861, 566 N.Y.S.2d 683, 685 (3d Dep't 1991) (Used Car Lemon Law).

16. General Business Law § 198–a(d)(1); General Business Law § 198–b(c)(2)(a).

PRACTICE POINTER: As a result, if, after the 25th effort to fix the problem, the dealer finally locates its source and cures it, the vehicle is not a "lemon," and the consumer has no right to recover under the Lemon Law. There is no requirement, however, that the consumer allow more than four repair attempts to fix the same problem or wait more than the 30 day out-of-service period before using the law. Consumers should therefore be advised that if

§ 7.10

Conditions that prevent the vehicle from operating or that substantially affect its major components, *i.e.*, engine, transmission, electrical systems, are clearly "substantial" under the statute. More minor conditions that do not substantially impair the vehicle's value are not considered "defects" under the Lemon Law, unless a number of such minor conditions, taken as a whole, result in substantial impairment.[17]

Neither manufacturers nor dealers are permitted to charge for repairs of conditions arising during the period of nonconformity. Also, charging a deductible has been expressly found to violate the New Car Lemon Law.[18] As a result, the Lemon Law effectively extends the "bumper-to-bumper" warranty on all new cars to at least two years or 18,000 miles from delivery, regardless of the length of the manufacturer's actual warranty.[19]

§ 7.11 Lemon Laws—Used Cars

Coverage under the Used Car Lemon Law[1] is substantially similar to the New Car Lemon Law, with the following significant differences:

A used car is defined under the Used Car Lemon Law as a motor vehicle that was purchased or leased *after* the earlier of 18,000 miles of they have made sufficient attempts to solve the problem, allowing further repair efforts may actually jeopardize their ability to recover under the Lemon Law, and they are under no legal obligation to permit such additional attempts. Despite, or perhaps because of, this statutory provision, many manufacturers and dealers will persistently ask for another repair attempt after an attorney has contacted them pursuant to the Lemon Law. Attorneys should be aware that permitting an additional repair attempt not only is *not* required but could also jeopardize the client's claim. At the very least, the additional attempt will only give the manufacturer or dealer free discovery to which it is not entitled.

Notwithstanding the above, the requirement that the defect continue to exist at the time the claim is heard *only* applies to cases brought under the "repeated repair rule." The statute imposes no such requirement for claims brought under the "out of service rule."

17. PRACTICE POINTER: Under the new and used car Lemon Laws, absence of substantial impairment is an affirmative defense that must be established by the manufacturer or the dealer. General Business Law § 198–a(c)(3)(i); General Business Law § 198–b(c)(1)(a). Walker v. General Motors Corp., Pontiac Motor Div., 159 Misc.2d 651, 606 N.Y.S.2d 125 (Civ.Ct., N.Y. County, 1993)(New Car Lemon Law); Jandreau v. LaVigne, 170 A.D.2d 861, 566 N.Y.S.2d 683, 685 (3d Dep't 1991)(Used Car Lemon Law).

As such, the initial burden of proof rests with the manufacturer or dealer. The consumer should be prepared to rebut any effort by the manufacturer or dealer to show the absence of substantial impairment. In less obvious cases, the consumer can present evidence of the diminished value of the vehicle by having it appraised by a different dealer, showing that the vehicle has less value because of the defect. In this regard, it may be necessary to subpoena the dealer who makes the appraisal.

18. State by Abrams v. Ford Motor Co., 74 N.Y.2d 495, 549 N.Y.S.2d 368, 548 N.E.2d 906 (1989).

19. PRACTICE POINTER: Vehicles with slightly less than 18,000 miles, or slightly less than two years removed from original delivery, are considered "new" for Lemon Law purposes. Accordingly, consumers can actually receive greater statutory protection if the vehicle has more than 18,000 miles or two years from delivery, because they then qualify under the Used Car Lemon Law, which could, under certain circumstances, provide a longer statutory warranty period.

§ 7.11

1. General Business Law §§ 198–b *et seq.*

operation *or* two years from the original delivery.[2] Cars purchased or leased before both of these cut-offs are defined as "new" and are handled under the New Car Lemon Law.[3]

The law applies to a purchase *or* lease of a car, with a total cost of at least $1,500.00, from a New York dealer,[4] except if the vehicle is transferred by the purchaser during the statutory warranty period. Sales by private parties are otherwise not covered. A dealer is defined as a seller of at least three cars in the preceding twelve months.[5] Finally, cars sold or leased with more than 100,000 miles[6] or that are not used primarily for personal, family, or household purposes,[7] are not covered.

Dealers are required to provide a written warranty at or before the time of the transaction. The duration of the warranty is determined by the car's mileage at the time of the transaction:[8]

Miles	Duration of the Warranty the earlier of:
18,000 to 36,000	90 days or 4,000 miles
36,001 to 79,999	60 days or 3,000 miles
80,000 to 100,000	30 days or 1,000 miles

The above periods are tolled while a vehicle is being repaired under the warranty.[9] The warranty must cover all major components set forth in the statute, including engine, transmission and drive train, brakes, radiator, steering, and electrical system.[10] Dealers are permitted to exclude coverage under the warranty for various acts and conditions, such as defects caused by the consumer's lack of maintenance, collision, abuse, negligence, theft or vandalism, or where the odometer has been tampered with.[11] In addition, the statute does not cover normal maintenance, tuneups, defects caused by racing, defects caused by towing a trailer, vehicles used for hire, vehicles rented to someone else, repair of valves or rings to correct low compression and/or oil consumption that are considered normal wear, property damage arising from the failure of a covered part, loss of use, inconvenience, or consequential damages.[12]

A used car is presumed to be a lemon if there have been at least three attempts to correct a particular defect during the applicable

---

2. General Business Law § 198–b(a)(2).

3. **PRACTICE POINTER:** Because of this arbitrary limitation, a consumer who purchases a car with slightly less than 18,000 miles or slightly less than two years from original delivery may have little protection if it proves to be defective. A consumer is therefore well advised to purchase a car that slightly exceeds these cut-offs in order to have the maximum protection available.

4. General Business Law § 198–b(d)(3).
5. General Business Law § 198–b(a)(3).
6. General Business Law § 198–b(d)(3).
7. General Business Law § 198–b(a)(1).
8. General Business Law § 198–b(b).
9. General Business Law § 198–b(c)(3).
10. General Business Law § 198–b(b)(2).
11. General Business Law § 198–b(b)(4).
12. General Business Law § 198–b(b)(4).

period[13] *or* the vehicle has been "out of service" because of one or more defects for a cumulative total of fifteen days or more during that period.[14] Under the Used Car Lemon Law, a dealer may elect to reimburse the consumer for the "reasonable cost of the repair," rather than make the repair itself.[15] If the dealer refuses to correct a defect after a reasonable period, it must accept the return of the vehicle and refund the purchase price to the consumer.[16]

§ 7.12 Lemon Laws—Arbitration or Plenary Action?

Two of the major advantages of using the Lemon Laws are their simplicity and the relatively short time between commencement and resolution of a claim. The primary reason for these attributes is that most cases are heard in an arbitration process described in the statute. The law also gives consumers the choice of commencing suit in court, without first going through arbitration, as long as the manufacturer or dealer does not participate in a dispute resolution system that complies with the regulations enacted pursuant to the federal Magnuson–Moss Warranty Act.[1] If the manufacturer or dealer does participate in such a program, it is not required to provide a refund to the consumer in a court action, unless the consumer first participates in the federal program or in the New York State administered arbitration program.[2]

There are also benefits to commencing an action under the Lemon Law instead of submitting a claim to arbitration. Consequential or other damages can be sought and recovered in a court action but not in arbitration. A separate action must be commenced to seek such a recovery; usually, this can be done in small claims court. Attorney's fees can be recovered by "successful plaintiffs" who sue under the statute or by consumers who successfully challenge or defend cases arising from an

---

13. General Business Law § 198–b(c)(2)(a).
14. General Business Law § 198–b(c)(2)(b).
15. General Business Law § 198–b(b)(2).
16. General Business Law § 198–b(c)(1).

§ 7.12
1. 16 CFR Pt. 703.
2. General Business Law §§ 198–a(g), 198–b(f)(1). **PRACTICE POINTER:** The obvious advantage to the consumer of going through the arbitration process is that it is far quicker and much less costly than litigation. Generally, a consumer will receive a final result within 90 days of filing a claim. When a defective car is at issue, this alone can be a substantial factor militating in favor of arbitration. Arbitration hearings generally take no more than a few hours, although more complicated factual issues may take longer. Hearings also tend to take longer when there are attorneys on both sides. Less time and a quicker resolution means that total attorney's fees are generally lower in arbitration. The major trade-off to the client in arbitration is that the cost of an attorney cannot be recovered, unless a court proceeding arises from the arbitration, either to overturn the award or to enforce compliance with it.

CAVEAT: The Statute of Limitations for any Lemon Law claim is four years from the date of original delivery of the vehicle to the consumer. General Business Law §§ 198–a(j), 198–b(f)(5).

arbitrator's award.[3] There is no provision in the Lemon Law, however, that requires the client to pay the manufacturer's attorney's fees if the client's claim is not successful.

On balance, with few exceptions, consumers are well advised to pursue their Lemon Law claims through the state-run arbitration program rather than through a plenary lawsuit. However, the following are examples of situations in which a lawsuit would make more sense than arbitration: If the dealer is about to go out of business, and a provisional remedy, such as attachment under CPLR Article 63, is needed to maintain the status quo; and when there is a possibility of recovering substantial punitive damages, *e.g.*, if a used car has a serious collision damage history that was not disclosed to the buyer *or* if the odometer has been rolled back by the seller.[4]

The Lemon Laws provide for the establishment of a state-run arbitration program pursuant to regulations promulgated by the Attorney General,[5] which program consumers can choose to use instead of either commencing an action in court or using a manufacturer's or dealer's "informal dispute settlement" mechanism.[6] The Attorney General has designated the American Arbitration Association ("AAA") as the administrator of the state-run arbitration program.

§ 7.13 Lemon Laws—Arbitration Procedure

Consumers that want to participate in the program should obtain either the New or Used Car Lemon Law "Request for Arbitration Form" from the State Attorney General's office.[1] After completing the form, it must be submitted to the Attorney General's Bureau of Consumer Frauds for review. The Attorney General's function in this regard is *solely* to determine if the claim meets the bare minimum under the Lemon Law. The Attorney General's approval of the claim does not lessen or diminish the consumer's burden of proof during the arbitration proceeding. The consumer is permitted to choose from over a dozen locations throughout the state for the hearing *or* may choose to have the

---

3. General Business Law §§ 198–a(*l*), 198–b(f)(5).

4. *See* Federal Odometer Act, 15 U.S.C.A. §§ 1901, 1981–1991. *See infra,* §§ 7.52 and 7.53 for sample form Complaints alleging these claims.

5. 13 NYCRR Pt. 300 *et seq.*; General Business Law §§ 198–a (k), 198–b(f)(3).

6. General Business Law §§ 198–a(g), 198–b(f)(3).

§ 7.13

1. **CAVEAT:** It is preferable for the attorney to help the client to fill out the form after a thorough interview with the client. Inaccurate statements, as well as omissions made in the form, can and will be used against the consumer by the manufacturer at the hearing. The attorney should also attach all relevant documents to the form, including all repair orders pertaining to the defect(s), the original invoice for the vehicle, the lease (if any), and the retail installment agreement with the bank (if any).

§ 7.13 CONSUMER LAW Ch. 7

case heard on the documents only, provided the manufacturer consents to this procedure.[2]

Finally, the consumer can elect, if successful at this stage, to receive either a full refund or a comparable replacement car.[3] Upon approval of the claim, the form will be sent to the AAA, which requires payment of a $250.00 fee before processing it.[4] The amount of time necessary for an attorney to handle the typical "no frills" Lemon Law case, from completion of the necessary forms through the hearing, should be roughly ten hours. Obviously, there are many variables that may alter this estimate.[5]

§ 7.14 Lemon Laws—Arbitration Procedure—Preparation for the Hearing

After reviewing the claim and evaluating the consumer's evidence, the attorney should take the following steps: Notify the AAA Lemon Law Case Administrator of your retention in the matter to insure that you receive all notices; draft a request for documents from the manufacturer or dealer, pursuant to 13 NYCRR § 300.9, for submission to the arbitrator (the parties do not make discovery demands directly to each other);[1] arrange for an independent inspection and evaluation of the vehicle by an expert familiar with the vehicle;[2] discuss settlement possibilities with the client.[3]

---

2. 13 NYCRR § 300.7(b).

3. 13 NYCRR § 300.4(c).

4. 13 NYCRR §§ 300.4 (e), (f), (g).

5. **CAVEAT:** Clients should be advised of the types of situations that might result in their case requiring more time. For example, if there is a question concerning whether a client qualifies for arbitration, *i.e.,* if the client's vehicle is owned or leased by a business, the manufacturer or dealer might commence a proceeding under CPLR Article 75 to block arbitration altogether. If this occurs, obviously additional time and expense will be involved in the case.

§ 7.14

1. All letters and notices to the AAA should be copied to the manufacturer or dealer or to its attorney. *See infra,* § 7.49 for a sample form discovery request under the Lemon Law.

2. **PRACTICE POINTER:** Obtaining an expert who is willing to testify at the hearing can mean the difference between winning and losing in many cases. Be certain that the expert has sufficient experience and training in handling the particular type of vehicle and defect involved.

3. **PRACTICE POINTER:** As with any type of litigation, the client should be advised of the pros and cons of settling. If the case is particularly problematic, *i.e.,* it is arguable whether the defect substantially impairs the value of the vehicle, or the client does not make a credible witness, it is not a bad idea to discuss settlement possibilities. Obviously, as in any settlement, the client would recover less than if successful at the hearing.

PRACTICE POINTER: Many manufacturers and dealers will not consider settling the consumer's claim until an attorney with a demonstrated understanding of the Lemon Law has appeared on the scene. Also, settlements are generally more available when the consumer is willing to accept a replacement vehicle instead of a refund. In this regard, the negotiations will generally start with the price difference between the consumer's car and a comparable new car. The practitioner's goal in this negotiation is to narrow the gap as much as possible or to determine if the consumer is interested in accepting a less fancy model. Practitioners should be leery of manufacturers or dealers who condition such settlements upon a prior inspection of the vehicle. This may be a ploy to obtain unauthorized pre-hearing discovery in order to bolster a claim at the hearing that a recent inspection shows that the vehicle is not defective. Counsel should

§ 7.14 PREPARATION FOR THE HEARING

As a general rule, settlements are most likely to occur when lower-end vehicles are involved. The increased cost involved in buying back a higher-end car, which can cost upwards of $50,000.00 to $100,000.00, or more, makes manufacturers much less likely to settle. For the same reason, the increased expense makes it much more worthwhile to fight the claim. Finally, some high-end manufacturers consider the consumer's claim that their vehicle is defective to be an affront. Counsel should be prepared to dig in for an extended battle if the vehicle involved is very expensive.[4] It is not uncommon for manufacturers even to try an end run in this type of case and seek to prevent arbitration altogether by bringing a preemptive proceeding, pursuant to CPLR 7503, to stay the hearing. Such a maneuver can, of course, substantially add to the consumer's legal expense and will likely make the process more time consuming. However, if the consumer successfully repels the effort, he or she may be entitled to an award of attorney's fees, because the proceeding arises out of an arbitration proceeding.[5]

Assuming that the matter cannot be settled, the practitioner will have to prepare quickly for the hearing. The document request should be drafted as broadly as possible, as long as it seeks relevant information.[6] If a party fails to provide documentation that has been ordered by the arbitrator, a negative inference may be drawn concerning any issue involving such documents or information.[7] The practitioner should request that the manufacturer or dealer produce any work orders that the consumer does not have. Dealers who fail to provide repair orders are in violation of the Vehicle and Traffic Law[8] and should be reported to the Department of Motor Vehicles. Manufacturers should be asked to provide any recall notices or technical service bulletins involving the vehicle,

---

protect against this by having the manufacturer stipulate that such an inspection will not be admissible at the hearing in the event the settlement is unsuccessful.

CAVEAT: Vehicle & Traffic Law § 417–a requires manufacturers who take back a vehicle under the Lemon Law to disclose this fact to any subsequent purchaser. (This provision does not apply to subsequent lessees, an obvious oversight on the part of the Legislature). Some manufacturers take the position that Vehicle & Traffic Law § 417–a is not triggered until a Lemon Law hearing has actually taken place. Others take the position that it is triggered simply by the client's filing of the Lemon Law arbitration request with the Attorney General and/or AAA. In any event, if the disclosure provision is not triggered, the client will have a chance of obtaining a much greater settlement because "branding the title" substantially reduces the re-sale value. Despite this, many manufacturers continue to evade this provision by simply shipping the vehicle to a state that does not require such "branding."

4. PRACTICE POINTER: Used car cases generally do not settle before a hearing. A major reason for this is that used car dealers generally have less incentive to maintain customer good will. Another reason is that used car dealers tend to have more parochial views and may consider "consumer rights" to be an oxymoron. Counsel should be prepared to negotiate with a dealer but not to expect to do as well as with a manufacturer.

5. General Business Law § 198–a(l); *but see,* Matter of Mercedes–Benz v. Yoon, N.Y.L.J., 4/26/94, p.21, col.5 (Sup.Ct., N.Y. County).

6. *See infra,* § 7.49 for a sample form discovery request under the Lemon Law.

7. 13 NYCRR § 300.9(c).

8. *See, infra,* § 7.26.

§ 7.14   CONSUMER LAW   Ch. 7

as well as all notes, reports, and communications made by either the dealer or manufacturer's representatives in connection with the condition of the vehicle.

Either the consumer or the practitioner should arrange to have the vehicle inspected (not repaired) by a mechanic who would qualify as an expert in the particular problem and who is familiar with the particular vehicle.[9]

§ 7.15 Lemon Laws—Arbitration Procedure—The Hearing

If the client has chosen the state run arbitration program, the hearing will likely take place at the office of the AAA. Arbitrators are chosen at random from a panel of those who have undergone special Lemon Law training.[1] The parties will receive a brief biography of the arbitrator in advance. Arbitrators are not necessarily attorneys. They are, however, required to be objective.[2]

Hearings must be scheduled no later than 35 days from the date the claim is filed with the AAA.[3] The hearing can be adjourned, however, if an application is made in writing on at least two business days notice.[4] The consumer can appear *pro se* or with any other representative, including a non-lawyer.[5]

All testimony at the hearing is given under oath,[6] although the arbitrator is permitted to receive affidavits instead of live testimony. In

9. **PRACTICE POINTER:** There are many repair shop "boutiques" that repair only certain makes of vehicles. Very often, these shops are run by former manufacturer's employees who have undergone specialized training with regard to the particular vehicle.

PRACTICE POINTER: Certain defects, such as intermittent stalling or electrical malfunctions, may not be evident at all times. Yet most arbitrators require (and if they do not, the manufacturers will demand), that the consumer produce the vehicle at the hearing for examination and/or a test drive. *See, e.g.,* 13 NYCRR § 300.12 (f). If the car does not stall or otherwise demonstrate the particular defect at that time, the arbitrator might conclude that the problem has been corrected and that it is no longer a lemon and thereby rule against the consumer. In order to avoid this result, practitioners should consider introducing expert testimony on the unpredictable nature of such intermittent problems. Emphasis should also be placed on the sudden and unpredictable nature of the defect, which increases the impairment of the vehicle's value.

§ 7.15
1. 13 NYCRR § 300.6(e).
2. General Business Law § 198–a(k).
3. 13 NYCRR § 300.7(e).
4. 13 NYCRR § 300.8.
5. **PRACTICE POINTER:** Clients should be advised that they are better off retaining an attorney experienced in the Lemon Law for the hearing, rather than proceeding on their own and risking a loss because of their inexperience. It is certainly less expensive and more productive to hire a lawyer for the hearing than for an appeal. In addition, since it can be very difficult to overturn an arbitrator's award, it is better to lessen the possibility of losing at the hearing by having a competent lawyer handle it. And, since the manufacturer will likely be represented by an attorney at the hearing, *pro se* consumers may find themselves at a distinct disadvantage if they proceed without an attorney.
6. 13 NYCRR § 300.12.

such case, the arbitrator is free to assign appropriate weight to affidavits.[7] The rules of evidence do not apply at the hearing; the standard of admissibility is purely one of relevance.[8] There is no requirement that hearings be recorded or transcribed.

The consumer has the burden of proof at the hearing on all elements of the Lemon Law *other than* the issue of whether the defect has substantially impaired the value of the vehicle. The absence of substantial impairment is an affirmative defense that must be established by the dealer or manufacturer.[9]

Once the consumer has satisfied the burden of proof with relevant evidence, the manufacturer or dealer bears the burden of rebutting the claim. The hearing will continue even if one party does not appear. In that case, a decision will be rendered based upon the evidence actually presented.

A written decision must be issued within 40 days after the claim is filed.[10] The arbitrator is required to state the grounds upon which the decision is based and summarize the contentions of the parties. If the arbitrator rules in favor of the consumer, the award must state the amount of the refund (provided that the consumer has elected to receive one). The arbitrator is permitted to reduce the award if the vehicle has excess mileage, under a formula set forth in the Lemon Law,[11] or to reduce the award if the vehicle has abnormal damage.[12]

§ 7.16 Lemon Laws—Arbitration Procedure—Appeals and Confirmation Proceedings

Post-arbitration proceedings are "special proceedings" brought pursuant to CPLR Article 75. An application to vacate or modify an award

---

7. 13 NYCRR § 300.12(d).

8. 13 NYCRR § 300.12(c).

9. Walker v. General Motors Corp., Pontiac Motor Div., 159 Misc.2d 651, 606 N.Y.S.2d 125 (Civ.Ct., N.Y. County, 1993) (New Car Lemon Law); Jandreau v. LaVigne, 170 A.D.2d 861, 566 N.Y.S.2d 683, 685 (3d Dep't 1991) (Used Car Lemon Law).

10. 13 NYCRR § 300.16(a).

11. General Business Law § 198-a (a)(4). The statute is completely silent, however, on the specific time when the mileage deduction should be calculated. Nor is there any case law that directs when the mileage should be measured for this purpose. It can be argued that for purposes of determining if there is an applicable mileage deduction, the mileage should be measured at the time that the vehicle is shown to have been defective, *i.e.*, when the fourth unsuccessful repair attempt took place. It can also be argued that the mileage should be measured at the time the client filed for arbitration.

Conversely, manufacturers will argue that the mileage reading should be taken at the latest possible time, *i.e.*, at the time the vehicle was returned.

The absence of any statutory guidance on this subject should result in judicial or legislative resolution of the issue. Given the legislative history and purpose of the Lemon Law, it arguably should be broadly interpreted to protect consumers, and a court would thus have ample basis to find that the mileage deduction should be measured from the earliest possible time.

12. General Business Law § 198-a (c)(1).

must be made within 90 days after it is issued and delivered.[1] A consumer who is successful at the arbitration may also have to commence a CPLR Article 75 proceeding to confirm the award, if the losing side refuses to comply with the award. Such a proceeding must be brought within one year of issuance of the award.[2] Upon confirmation, the consumer will receive a judgment, which can then be enforced like any other judgment.[3] If the consumer is compelled to bring a confirmation proceeding, the relief requested should also include attorney's fees incurred in that proceeding under the Lemon Law.[4]

If the losing party fails to comply with the arbitrator's award within thirty days, the consumer is entitled to an additional penalty of $25.00 per day, up to a $500.00 maximum.[5] This relief should be demanded in the confirmation proceeding as well.[6]

The purpose of attorney's fee awards in Lemon Law cases is "to protect consumers from being worn down by protracted post-arbitration litigation."[7] Accordingly, fees can be recovered not only by a successful plaintiff but by a successful consumer as well.[8]

§ 7.17 Lemon Laws—Arbitration Procedure—Scope of Review

In general, proceedings to vacate or modify arbitration awards pursuant to CPLR Article 75 are extremely difficult to win. To vacate the award, the moving party must show, with a high level of certainty,

§ 7.16

1. CPLR 7511(a). See infra, §§ 7.50 and 7.51 for a sample Notice of Petition and Petition in an Article 75 proceeding to vacate or modify a Lemon Law arbitration award.

PRACTICE POINTER: It is not necessary to bring an Article 75 proceeding in the supreme court. As long as the amount sought does not exceed the monetary jurisdiction of a lower court, the matter can be brought there. See, e.g., NYCCCA § 206.

2. CPLR 7510.

3. CPLR 7514.

4. Reyes v. Talley Motors, Inc., N.Y.L.J., 8/20/92, p.23, col.8 (Sup.Ct., N.Y. County). See also, General Business Law § 198–a(l); General Business Law § 198–b(f)(5).

5. General Business Law § 198–a(h).

6. **PRACTICE POINTER:** If the consumer wins the arbitration hearing, and the losing side does not comply with it, it is best to wait at least 91 days from the date of the award to bring a confirmation proceeding. By doing so, the consumer will cut off the possibility of a cross-motion to vacate or modify the award, which must be made within 90 days.

PRACTICE POINTER: In used car cases, even after losing the hearing many dealers will refuse to accept the arbitrator's decision and will refuse to accept return of the car and pay the refund. This scenario is not likely in a new car case because manufacturers are more willing to accept the loss and pay the award. If the award is not paid as required, and the consumer is forced to retain an attorney to collect the award, the consumer will be entitled to recover the attorney's fees incurred in doing so, even if the dealer eventually settles and satisfies the award before an Article 75 proceeding to confirm is brought. Reyes v. Talley Motors, Inc., N.Y.L.J., 8/20/92, p.23, col.8 (Sup. Ct., N.Y. County). In addition, under Reyes, a consumer can recover the attorney's fees incurred in recovering attorney's fees. ("fees on fees").

7. R. Givens, Supplementary Practice Commentaries, General Business Law § 198–a, p.94.

8. Reyes v. Talley Motors, Inc., N.Y.L.J., 8/20/92, p.23, col.8 (Sup.Ct., N.Y. County).

some form of fraud, partiality, or corruption in the arbitrator's rendering of the award.[1] An arbitration award may also be modified if the arbitrator made a minor error in calculation or if the award goes beyond the scope of the matter submitted for decision.[2]

In order to obtain a vacatur of the award, the moving party must establish that the award is "irrational." In this regard, courts are extremely reluctant to substitute their own judgment for that of the arbitrator, even if the arbitrator's decision is legally or factually erroneous. The reason for this stringent standard is that arbitration is generally intended to be final and binding, without the possibility of lengthy and expensive appeals.

CPLR Article 75 proceedings brought by consumers appealing Lemon Law decisions are not, however, governed by the extremely narrow scope of review applicable to most arbitrations. Typically, arbitration hearings are conducted pursuant to a written agreement to arbitrate disputes, as in many labor agreements. These "contractual" arbitration hearings are also termed "consensual." However, Lemon Law arbitrations are neither contractual nor consensual; instead, they are "compulsory."[3]

Judicial review of compulsory arbitration is subject to the far broader "arbitrary and capricious" standard.[4] Consumer appeals from Lemon Law arbitration awards are therefore more akin to proceedings brought pursuant to CPLR Article 78, challenging actions taken by governmental authorities. Further, "... Lemon Law arbitrators are not given broad powers and it is thus essential that they follow the *exact procedure set forth in the statute and regulation* ...."[5] "The standard of judicial review to be applied in an arbitration case under the Lemon Law, inasmuch as it is compulsory arbitration, is broad, requiring that the award be supported by adequate evidence in the record. The award must be rational and must not be arbitrary and capricious. *If the arbitrator neglects to follow these standards, the award will be vacated.*"[6]

---

§ 7.17

1. CPLR 7511(b).

2. CPLR 7511(c).

3. Motor Vehicle Mfrs. Ass'n of U.S., Inc. v. State of New York, 146 A.D.2d 212, 540 N.Y.S.2d 888 (3d Dep't 1989), aff'd 75 N.Y.2d 175, 551 N.Y.S.2d 470, 550 N.E.2d 919 (1990); Walker v. General Motors Corp., Pontiac Motor Div., 159 Misc.2d 651, 606 N.Y.S.2d 125 (Civ.Ct., N.Y. County, 1993); Baker v. Ford Motor Company, N.O.R., Index No. 29505/91 (Sup.Ct., N.Y. County) ("It is well settled that Lemon Law arbitration is a *compulsory* process."); Scolza v. GMC Truck & Coach, N.O.R., Index No. 21702/89 (Sup.Ct., Suffolk County) (Lemon Law arbitration is *compulsory* arbitration.); Homer v. Ford Motor Company, N.O.R., Index No. 62427/88 (Sup.Ct., Herkimer County) (The Lemon Law provides for *compulsory* arbitration).

4. Mount St. Mary's Hosp. of Niagara Falls v. Catherwood, 26 N.Y.2d 493, 311 N.Y.S.2d 863, 260 N.E.2d 508 (1970); Chrysler Motors Corp. v. Schachner, 166 A.D.2d 683, 561 N.Y.S.2d 595 (2d Dep't 1990).

5. Scolza v. GMC Truck & Coach, N.O.R., Index No. 21702/89 (Sup.Ct., Suffolk County) (emphasis added).

6. *Id.*, citing Motor Vehicle Mfrs. Ass'n of U.S., Inc. v. State of New York, 75 N.Y.2d 175, 551 N.Y.S.2d 470, 550 N.E.2d 919 (1990). (emphasis added) (failure to follow proper procedure resulted in vacatur of

§ 7.17   CONSUMER LAW   Ch. 7

If "the arbitrator fails to follow the statutory standards, the award should be vacated for exceeding the legislative grant of authority."[7]

In addition, a consumer who successfully challenges an arbitrator's award in an Article 75 proceeding is entitled to an award of attorney's fees,[8] *even if the successful challenge results in a remand for a new hearing and not a reversal.*[9] In *Walker v. General Motors Corp., Pontiac Motor Div. (Walker II)*,[10] the court found that under these circumstances the consumer had "prevailed" within the meaning of General Business Law § 198–a(*l*) and that the legislative history of the 1988 attorney's fee amendment to the Lemon Law mandated this result. "(T)he denial of attorney's fees to (the consumer) in this proceeding, after successfully vacating a clearly erroneous arbitration decision, would obviously frustrate the legislative purpose."[11]

§ 7.18   Lemon Laws—Source Materials

Numerous materials providing a more detailed analysis of both the New York Lemon Law and Lemon Laws in general are available to the general public. The New York Attorney General's Office, Bureau of Consumer Frauds and Protection, is probably the best source of material and information on the New and Used Car Lemon Laws. That office publishes *New York's New Car Lemon Law: A Guide For Consumers*, as well as *New York's Used Car Lemon Law: A Guide For Consumers*. Persons may call or write for a free copy of either publication.[1]

In addition, the Consumer Frauds Bureau issues annual reports, as well as Appendices, each year, containing all written court decisions under the Lemon Law, including unreported decisions submitted by practitioners from around the state. These sources might not otherwise be available to the public.

---

the award and remand); Clark v. Chrysler Motors Corporation, N.O.R., Index No. 27638/89 (Sup.Ct., N.Y. County).

7. Motor Vehicle Mfrs. Ass'n of U.S., Inc., *supra* note 6, 551 N.Y.S.2d at 476, citing Mount St. Mary's Hosp. of Niagara Falls v. Catherwood, 26 N.Y.2d 493, 311 N.Y.S.2d 863, 260 N.E.2d 508 (1970); Walker v. General Motors Corp., Pontiac Motor Div., 159 Misc.2d 651, 606 N.Y.S.2d 125 (Civ.Ct., N.Y. County, 1993).

8. General Business Law § 198–a(*l*).

9. Walker v. General Motors Corp., Pontiac Motor Div., 160 Misc.2d 903, 611 N.Y.S.2d 741 (Civ.Ct., N.Y. County, 1994) ("Walker II").

10. *Id.*

11. *Id.*, 611 N.Y.S.2d at 742.

PRACTICE POINTER: Despite the lesser standard of review for Lemon Law appeals, judges are sometimes reluctant to issue a flat out *vacatur*. Instead, if it can be shown that the hearing either did not comply with the Lemon Law regulations or that the arbitrator acted in an arbitrary manner, the court is more likely to remand the matter for a new hearing. In this regard, the practitioner should, if appropriate, request that the remand be made to a different arbitrator. CPLR 7511(d).

§ 7.18

1. 120 Broadway
New York, New York
(212) 416–8000.

The National Consumer Law Center[2] ("NCLC") publishes an excellent set of consumer law manuals, entitled *The Consumer Credit and Sales Legal Practice Series*. These manuals, which cover virtually every major consumer law topic, are a must for any practitioner planning to handle consumer cases.[3] For Lemon Law cases, the NCLC manual, *Sales of Goods and Services*, contains an entire section devoted to this topic.

§ 7.19 Automobile Leasing—Overview

Leasing, as opposed to purchasing, of automobiles has become more and more popular among consumers and automobile dealers. Over the past twenty-five years, the percentage of automobile lease transactions has grown steadily to the point where it is estimated that in the not-too-distant future, the number of leases will equal the number of sales of new motor vehicles. The primary reason consumers consider leasing is that it usually means a lower monthly expense than with a financed purchase. Dealers and leasing companies find that leasing provides greater profits than sales, as well as greater opportunities to exact additional charges from consumers. Unfortunately, for many consumers, leasing can be fraught with problems when the consumer discovers, to his or her dismay, that the lease actually costs more in the end than if the vehicle had been purchased outright or even if the purchase had been financed.

The primary reason that leasing may cost more than a purchase is that leases often contain numerous charges and fees above the actual monthly lease payments, which are either hidden in prolix and lengthy lease agreements, or which are not disclosed at all until it is too late to object. And, many consumers are not familiar with basic leasing terminology, which is often very different from seemingly similar concepts found in financing agreements. Consumers are typically denied the opportunity to study complicated lease provisions, to have them reviewed by an attorney in advance, or to shop around and compare terms with other lessors, even if the consumer understands the terms. Automobile dealers and leasing companies have long taken advantage of consumer ignorance in this regard. Until recently, there has been little statutory protection for consumers with leasing problems. What little protection that did exist often proved to be of little use in many situations and of no use in many others. Fortunately, the New York Legislature has enacted perhaps the most sweeping and complex legislation in the nation in this

---

2. 11 Beacon Street Boston, MA 02108.

3. *See supra,* § 7.1 note 9. Other publications include, Billings, *Handling Automobile Warranty and Repossession Cases* (Lawyers Co-op 1984); Nader and Ditlow, *The Lemon Book* (Center for Auto Safety, Moyer Bell Ltd. 1990); Kaye, *Lemon Aid* (Tele-Travel Network, Inc. 1991); and Newman and Imholz, *Caveat Venditor: A Manual for Consumer Representation in New York* (2d ed. 1994).

area.[1]

The following section discusses and identifies the most important statutory protections available to consumers with automobile leasing problems and suggests strategies for the practitioner in dealing with them.

§ 7.20 Automobile Leasing—Statutory Protection Overview

The starting point for the practitioner is an analysis of the terms and purpose of the lease. Is the vehicle to be used primarily for personal, family, or household purposes or is it to be used primarily for business purposes? Most leases contain a statement indicating which of these purposes applies to the particular transaction. The inquiry should not end there, however. Lease forms are often filled out by dealers who encourage the consumer to select business, rather than consumer, use of the vehicle. At other times, the business-purpose designation is made without the consumer's knowledge or consent. Dealers who induce consumers to select a business purpose on the lease form do so by promising that the lease payments will be tax deductible, even if the actual use of the vehicle will not be for business purposes. If the consumer agrees to this scenario, he or she may later be disappointed when the deduction is disallowed by the government. The benefit to the dealer and leasing company of the business-use designation is substantial; it could result in complete immunity from any of the statutory protections afforded consumers. For example, a vehicle leased for business purposes, and in fact used solely for business purposes, would probably not be covered by the Lemon Law if the vehicle should prove defective. Nor would the lessee be protected under the Consumer Leasing Act. If, however, the lease designates a business purpose, but the vehicle is actually used primarily for personal purposes, the Lemon Law and other consumer protection statutes *will* apply, even if the nominal lessee is a business.[1] While the designation of business use on a lease may create a presumption of such use, it can be rebutted with evidence that the actual use is not for business purposes.

Fortunately, the deceptive practice of some dealers in persuading consumers to select a business purpose for the vehicle on the lease form

---

§ 7.19

1. Motor Vehicle Retail Leasing Act ("MVRLA"), codified at Personal Property Law Art. 9–A. This statute took effect on August 31, 1995 and applies to leases entered on or after that date.

§ 7.20

1. *See* Parlato v. Chrysler Corp., 170 A.D.2d 442, 565 N.Y.S.2d 230 (2d Dep't 1991) (corporate lessee is a "consumer"); Matter of Mercedes–Benz of North America, Inc. v. Yoon, N.Y.L.J., 4/26/94, p.21, col.5 (Sup.Ct., N.Y. County) (same). *See also, supra,* § 7.9.

is one of the areas covered by legislation recently enacted in New York.[2] However, if the vehicle is truly to be used for business purposes, and the practitioner is convinced that consumer protection laws will not apply, attention must be directed to other possible sources of applicable law.[3]

If the transaction at least arguably involves a personal, family, or household purpose, the next step for the practitioner should be to analyze the lease itself for possible statutory violations.[4]

Once statutory violations have been identified, the practitioner must next decide the best course of action to take. If the matter is not yet in litigation, and the consumer wishes to avoid the time and expense invariably involved, it might be wise to approach the leasing company's counsel's office in an effort to resolve the matter informally. If the practitioner has identified one or more provisions in a lessor's "boilerplate" lease agreement that violate statutory provisions, a leasing company may be willing to resolve the matter without litigation on terms favorable to the consumer, thereby avoiding the possibility of an adverse finding that would otherwise ultimately affect many other identical leases.

If the matter cannot be resolved without litigation (either defense of a suit brought by a lessor or commencement of affirmative litigation by the consumer), the practitioner and the consumer must be prepared to pursue all possible claims aggressively or to defend any action brought by the lessor.[5] If the matter involves a lessor's claim against the consumer, the client should understand that more than that dispute is ultimately at issue. In all likelihood, if the consumer is in default of the lease, that fact has already been reported to a credit reporting agency as

---

2. Motor Vehicle Retail Leasing Act ("MVRLA"), codified at Personal Property Law § 336. *See infra,* § 7.22.

3. Such other sources include the recently enacted UCC Art. 2–A, the common law, and, in some instances, basic landlord-tenant principles.

4. PRACTICE POINTER: As with most types of consumers problems, practitioners who are not familiar with automobile leasing should not hesitate to seek guidance from one or more of the available resources in the field. The National Consumer Law Center's *Truth in Lending* manual contains an excellent discussion of the Consumer Leasing Act, 15 U.S.C.A. § 1667. Another valuable source in this area is Billings, *Handling Automobile Financing and Leasing Cases* (Lawyers Co-op 1988).

Practitioners can also consult with a staff attorney at the National Consumer Law Center, for a reasonable hourly fee, on this and many other consumer law topics. The NCLC staff will review lease agreements and other documents for statutory violations and other concerns. The NCLC consulting service is an invaluable tool for practitioners who are not familiar with this field.

5. *See infra,* § 7.52 for a sample Complaint alleging fraud, breach of warranties, deceptive business practices, Lemon Law violations, rescission, revocation of acceptance, and fraudulent leasing practices. *See infra,* § 7.53 for a sample Answer and Third–Party Complaint alleging fraud, deceptive business practices, breach of warranty, and federal odometer claims in a fraudulent lease case. *See infra,* § 7.54 for a sample Answer to a complaint by a leasing company following repossession, alleging commercially unreasonable resale and deceptive business practices.

§ 7.20　　　　　　　　CONSUMER LAW　　　　　　　　Ch. 7

a derogatory item. Once the claim results in a lawsuit by the lessor, its mere filing will likely also be reported on the consumer's credit report.[6]

§ 7.21　Automobile Leasing—The Consumer Leasing Act

Enacted in 1976 as a part of the Truth in Lending Act,[1] the Consumer Leasing Act ("CLA") is the first statutory response to the growing field of leasing and the associated problems faced by consumers. The primary purpose of the CLA, like the Truth in Lending Act generally, is to provide consumers with greater disclosure of lease terms and provisions in the hope and expectation that a more informed consumer will be able to avoid more onerous lease terms by shopping around and bargaining for a better deal. Unfortunately, this purpose is probably more accurate in theory than in practice. For, even with greater disclosure, few lessors actually bargain over lease terms, and few consumers who attempt to bargain actually understand the meaning of most of the lease terms.

The following is a summary of the basic scope of the CLA, the primary disclosures required by the act, and the remedies available for statutory violations. The CLA applies to leases of "personal property"[2] for a period longer than four months,[3] where the "total contractual obligation" under the lease is less than $25,000.00.[4]

The CLA does not apply if the transaction is actually a "disguised credit sale," which occurs when the lease payments are substantially equal to the value of the vehicle and the consumer has a purchase option for nominal consideration.[5] A determination of this coverage issue is not a "bright-line test," but rather is one that requires the weighing of various factors.[6] If the CLA does not apply because the transaction is

---

6. PRACTICE POINTER: The practitioner should also inquire whether anyone co-signed or guaranteed payment under the lease. Because such persons have the same liability as the lessee, and a default will likely affect such person's credit report as well, such person may wish to consult counsel as well. *See infra*, §§ 7.30—7.32.

§ 7.21

1. 15 U.S.C.A. §§ 1601 *et seq.*

2. 15 U.S.C.A. § 1667(1). This includes not just motor vehicles, but many other types of personal property as well.

3. 15 U.S.C.A. § 1667(1).

4. 15 U.S.C.A. § 1667(1).

PRACTICE POINTER: Many long-term leases for high-end automobiles are therefore excluded from the act. Practitioners should carefully examine the total "contractual obligation," which generally means the total of lease payments plus any trade-in allowance or initial payment of the lease, to determine CLA coverage. The "contractual obligation" should not be confused with the "total lease obligation," which also includes the estimated value of the property at the termination of the lease.

5. *See* Sheffield Commercial Credit Corporation v. Clemente, 792 F.2d 282 (2d Cir. 1986); Credit Car Leasing Corp. v. DeCresenzo, 138 Misc.2d 726, 525 N.Y.S.2d 492 (Civ.Ct., N.Y. County, 1988) (where the lease had all of the indicia of a sale, it created a security interest, and the lessor became obligated to comply with UCC Art. 9 in disposing of the vehicle after repossession).

6. PRACTICE POINTER: The practitioner should carefully analyze the lease terms, using the factors described in *Sheffield Commercial Credit Corporation v. Clemente, supra,* and *Credit Car Leasing*

actually a "disguised credit sale," then the practitioner must look to the statutes applicable to those types of transactions.[7]

The CLA not only exempts transactions with a business, or non-consumer purpose, it also exempts lessees who are not natural persons, such as corporations, trusts, estates, partnerships, etc.[8]

Under the CLA, lessors are required to make certain disclosures to lessees in the lease agreement itself. Lessors are liable for statutory damages of $1,000.00, actual damages, and attorneys fees for failing to make *any* of the required disclosures, without any requirement of proof that the lessee was actually misled by the violation.[9]

The CLA requires disclosure of fifteen separate and distinct terms prior to consummation of the lease. The CLA regulations require that a copy of the lease be given to the consumer at that time, with all blank spaces filled out, and the disclosures must be clear, conspicuous, and in meaningful sequence, so as to be in a reasonably understood form in at least 10–point type. The CLA mandates disclosure of the following terms:[10]

1. Description of the property;
2. Payments made at lease consummation;
3. The schedule and amount of lease payments;
4. Official fees and taxes;
5. Other charges;
6. Insurance;
7. Identification of express warranties;

Corp. v. DeCresenzo, supra, in determining whether the transaction is really a lease or a sale. In defending an action by a lessor, or in bringing an action under the "lease," describing the transaction as a "disguised sale" can and should be pled in the alternative. See *infra,* § 7.54, for a sample form answer to a complaint by a leasing company for a deficiency claim following repossession, alleging, *inter alia,* UCC Art. 9 affirmative defenses, and see *infra,* § 7.55, for a form affirmation in opposition to a lessor's summary judgment motion, alleging UCC Art. 9 violations by the lessor.

7. For example, the main portion of the Truth-in-Lending Act ("TILA") (15 U.S.C.A. §§ 1601 *et seq.*), which has the same initial coverage criteria as the CLA, applies to credit sales and the mandatory disclosures required by lenders. In New York, the Motor Vehicle Retail Installment Sales Act (Personal Property Law Art. 9) tracks most of the TILA provisions on the state level.

PRACTICE POINTER: In many instances, as long as the consumer purpose, the number of payments, and the $25,000.00 cap are met, it makes little difference if the transaction is ultimately characterized as a lease or a sale. Many of the protections and remedies will be the same, with few differences. For this reason, if the practitioner is not sure how properly to characterize the transaction, both should be pled alternatively in any litigation.

If the transaction is actually a sale, other statutes should apply as well, *i.e.,* UCC Art. 2 and Art. 9 on sales and disposition of secured collateral.

8. 15 U.S.C.A. § 1667(1).

9. 15 U.S.C.A. § 1667d(a).

10. The practitioner should refer to the language of the regulation itself, as well as the Official Staff Commentaries, for a definition of each term. Reg. M, 12 C.F.R. §§ 213 *et seq.*

§ 7.21   CONSUMER LAW   Ch. 7

8. Party responsible for maintenance and excess wear and use;
9. Security Interest;
10. Late payment and default charges;
11. Purchase option;
12. Early termination and default charges;
13. Liability for the difference between the estimated and realized value of the property;
14. The right to an appraisal; and
15. Lessee's liability upon termination of an open-ended lease.

Even if all of the above disclosures are made by the lessor, there is no requirement that the consumer actually demonstrate an understanding of them. Instead, the disclosures are only required to be in a "reasonably understood form." Many consumers, and even many attorneys, will be hard pressed actually to explain the meaning of a particular lease provision.[11] If a required disclosure is not made at all, or if it is not made in a manner that can reasonably be understood, the lessor can be held liable in an action under the CLA for the actual damages sustained by the consumer,[12] plus statutory damages of up to $1,000.00,[13] plus costs and reasonable attorney's fees.[14]

§ 7.22   Automobile Leasing—The Motor Vehicle Retail Leasing Act

Up until 1995, consumers could not look far beyond the CLA for protection from onerous or incomprehensible lease provisions. And, as a disclosure statute, the CLA simply does not prohibit onerous, unfair, or deceptive lease provisions, as long as they are properly disclosed. Given the absence of any real bargaining in the marketplace over lease terms, many of the CLA protections are thus of little value to consumers.

Recognizing this deficiency, the New York Legislature, in 1994, enacted the Motor Vehicle Retail Leasing Act ("MVRLA").[1] The MVRLA is landmark consumer legislation which greatly supplements both the CLA and the recently adopted Uniform Commercial Code Article 2–A. Rather than simply requiring the disclosure of certain lease terms, the

---

11. Lease provisions that are incomprehensible, even to attorneys, violate the CLA and will not be enforced. Lundquist v. Security Pacific Automotive Financial Services Corp., 993 F.2d 11 (2d Cir.1993), cert. denied 510 U.S. 959, 114 S.Ct. 419, 126 L.Ed.2d 365 (1993).

12. 15 U.S.C.A § 1640 (a)(1).
13. 15 U.S.C.A § 1640(a)(2)(A)(ii).
14. 15 U.S.C.A. § 1640(a)(3).

PRACTICE POINTER: The above remedies can be sought not only in an affirmative suit by the consumer, but as a counterclaim in an action brought by the lessor under the lease.

CAVEAT: The Statute of Limitations under the CLA is one year from termination of the lease. 15 U.S.C.A. § 1667(c).

§ 7.22

1. Personal Property Law Art. 9–A, §§ 330 *et seq.*

MVRLA affirmatively prohibits some of the more pernicious lease provisions altogether. And the MVRLA goes beyond the requirements of the CLA by mandating certain disclosures not required by federal law, providing important information to lessees.

The MVRLA incorporates many of the statutory provisions that protect purchasers of vehicles under retail installment sales agreements[2] and supplements that protection with other provisions applying only to lease transactions.[3] The following is a summary of the major provisions of the MVRLA.

Leases must be in a single document,[4] printed in certain prescribed type sizes, with specific captions and notices.[5] Sample blank copies of the lessor's lease form must be made available to consumers in advance of the transaction.[6] Lessees are not obligated under a lease, and may unconditionally cancel it, until the lessor provides the lessee with a complete copy of it, signed by the lessor.[7] The lease must contain all of the information required to be disclosed under the CLA,[8] with the express provision that the MVRLA also applies to consumer leases in which the total contractual obligation is in excess of twenty-five thousand dollars.[9]

The MVRLA also seeks to remedy the deceptive practices of some dealers and leasing companies that insert a business-purpose use of the vehicle in the lease form without the lessee's knowledge or that dishonestly seek to convince the lessee to make such an election. Under the MVRLA, the Legislature clearly intended to eliminate such practices by adding safeguards designed to ensure that a business-purpose election is accurate. Under the MVRLA, a pre-printed lease provision setting forth a business use of the vehicle is inadmissible in evidence in any action or proceeding, unless it is contained in a separate document, signed by the lessee, in which the lessee describes the actual nature of the business and the following statement is set forth, in at least 8-point bold type: **"WARNING: Important consumer protections may not apply if this agreement indicates that you are leasing the vehicle primarily for agricultural, business or commercial use."**[10] However, if the consumer indicates a business purpose for leasing the vehicle, after receiving this warning, this knowing designation will still not necessarily

---

2. Personal Property Law §§ 301—316.

3. **PRACTICE POINTER:** Because the MVRLA is so new, as of this writing there are no reported decisions interpreting it. However, because many of the MVRLA's protections are based upon similar ones found in the MVRISA, case law interpreting that statute, where applicable, should be applied by analogy to leasing cases.

4. Personal Property Law § 337(1).

5. Personal Property Law § 337(2).

6. Personal Property Law § 333.

7. Personal Property Law § 337(3).

8. 15 U.S.C.A. § 1667. See supra, § 7.21.

9. Personal Property Law § 337(5)(a).

10. Personal Property Law § 336.

be dispositive of the issue. Instead, the courts are directed to consider "any other factors relevant to that determination."[11]

Under the MVRLA, leases must disclose the "capitalized cost" of the vehicle[12] and must contain a statement indicating that the lessee has the right to terminate the agreement voluntarily at any time after fifty percent of the payments have been made.[13] Lessors must also provide a notice that such early termination may require payment of a substantial early termination charge.[14] The MVRLA places substantial restrictions, however, on assessing and calculating any early termination liability, and it provides a simple method for determining the components of such liability.[15] Moreover, if a consumer terminates a lease early, the lessor is not permitted to report that fact to a credit reporting agency as a derogatory item, unless the consumer fails to satisfy the early termination obligations under the lease.[16] Lessors are also required to provide conspicuous notice to lessees of their potential liability if the vehicle is stolen or totally damaged during the lease term.[17] This notice relates to the "gap amount," which is the difference between the gross early termination liability under the lease and the "actual cash value" of the vehicle under a collision or comprehensive insurance policy applicable to the vehicle. Often, when the vehicle is stolen or totally damaged, the insurance proceeds are not sufficient to pay off the lessee's liability for the value of the vehicle. Typically, the lessee is left responsible for this "gap amount." The MVRLA requires the lessor to highlight this possibility to the lessee so that the lessee can arrange to purchase "gap insurance." A failure to provide this notice voids any obligation the lessee might otherwise have to pay this amount.[18] In the alternative, the MVRLA requires a lessor to waive the lessee's obligation for the "gap amount" if gap insurance coverage is available to the lessor.[19]

The MVRLA also adds a significant protection for consumers in cases in which the lessor has breached the lease. This provision is similar in purpose and effect to a provision found in the MVRISA,[20] applicable to financed purchases of automobiles. Automobile leases are frequently assigned to an assignee without any requirement of consent by the lessee. Such leases often contain provisions that preclude lessees from asserting any claims or defenses against any subsequent assignee of the

11. Personal Property Law § 336(3). See supra, § 7.10 note 9 and § 7.20 note 1.
12. Personal Property Law § 337(5)(b). Under Personal Property Law § 331(11), this is defined as "the agreed upon amount which serves as the basis for determining the base rental payment and a portion of the early termination liability of the lessee." Disclosure of this amount, which includes the amount paid for the vehicle by the lessor, is one of the most important terms a consumer can use in determining if the lease is a reasonable one.
13. Personal Property Law § 337(5)(g).
14. Personal Property Law § 337(5)(h).
15. Personal Property Law § 341.
16. Personal Property Law § 342.
17. Personal Property Law § 335.
18. Personal Property Law § 335(1).
19. Personal Property Law § 335(2).
20. Personal Property Law Art. 9.

lease, regardless of the vehicle's condition and regardless of whether the lessor has breached the lease. These provisions require lessees to assert any such claims against the original lessor only, or against the manufacturer, if applicable, and they present a substantial obstacle to a consumer lessee's ability to obtain redress.[21] The MVRLA expressly bars such clauses, providing:

> No retail lease agreement shall contain any provision by which the lessee agrees not to assert against a holder a claim or defense or require or entail the execution of any note or series of notes which, when separately negotiated, will cut off as to third parties any right of action or defense which the lessee may have against the lessor. The holder of a retail lease agreement shall be subject to all claims and defenses of the lessee against the lessor arising from the lease notwithstanding any agreement to the contrary, but the holder's liability under this subdivision shall not exceed the amount owing to the holder at the time the claim or defense is asserted against the holder. The holder shall have recourse against the lessor to the extent of any liability incurred by the holder pursuant to this subdivision regardless of whether the assignment of the agreement was with or without recourse.[22]

As a result of this statutory provision, lessees can defend a claim by an assignee by asserting the lessor's breach of the lease.[23]

A lessee who falls behind in the periodic payments under a lease also has an opportunity, under the statute, to cure the default and to reinstate the lease. Unlike the case with financed purchases of automobiles,[24] prior to enactment of the MVRLA lessors were under no obligation to reinstate a lease when it was terminated for non-payment. In those instances, the lessee could not only lose possession of the vehicle, but he or she could be held liable for all remaining payments due under the lease as well. The MVRLA requires leases to state that if a default occurs solely as the result of the lessee's failure to make timely pay-

---

21. CAVEAT: This provision should not be confused with the lessee's rights under the New Car or Used Car Lemon Laws (General Business Law § 198–a and General Business Law § 198–b), applicable if the vehicle proves defective. Under those laws, the lessee can assert his or her rights directly against the manufacturer or dealer without regard to the lessor or any subsequent assignee. Both statutes mandate that if the consumer is successful in a Lemon Law claim involving a leased vehicle, the lease is declared terminated, and the consumer has no further obligation under the lease.

22. Personal Property Law § 337(10).

23. PRACTICE POINTER: Note that the MVRLA, like the MVRISA, contains a substantial limitation on the right to assert such claims; it is expressly limited to the amount owing at the time. Therefore, if a dispute arises well into the lease, after numerous payments have been made, the assignee's liability to the lessee may be severely limited. The practitioner should assert claims against the original lessor in a third-party complaint in order to avoid this limitation. *See infra*, § 7.53 for a sample Answer and Third–Party Complaint in an action by a leasing company against a consumer alleging, *inter alia*, fraud, deceptive practices, and federal odometer law violations.

24. Personal Property Law § 316.

ments, the lessee must be given an opportunity to cure that default, without losing any rights or options under the lease, by paying all past due amounts, applicable late fees, and actual and reasonable repossession charges, within 25 days after receipt of written notice of such rights.[25] The lessor may permit only one such reinstatement during the term of the lease.[26] If the lessor declares a default under the lease solely for non-payment, regardless of whether the vehicle is repossessed, it must, within 10 days of such declaration, send a notice to the lessee advising of the reinstatement rights set out above.[27] If the lessee does not exercise this right of reinstatement, and the lessor proceeds to dispose of the vehicle, it must do so in a "commercially reasonable manner."[28]

When a lease is terminated prior to its scheduled end, either voluntarily or otherwise, lessees often find it difficult, if not impossible, to determine the amount of the early termination liability. Prior to enactment of the MVRLA, early termination clauses typically applied formulas that were so complicated that they required both an accountant and an actuary using a computer to figure them out. Under the CLA, the lessor was only required to disclose the method for determining the amount of any penalty or charge for early termination.[29] The CLA also requires that the disclosed method be "reasonable."[30] Even with these protections, however, no obligation was imposed mandating that the lease provision dealing with early termination penalties be understandable. The MVRLA attempts to correct this omission by requiring the standardized disclosure of a dollar amount, called the "initial early termination charge."[31] The statute sets forth explicit restrictions on early termination liability and spells out the specific components a lessor may include in determining it.[32]

Many leasing abuses continue even after termination, voluntary or scheduled, when the lessee is presented with a bill by the lessor for "excess wear and damage" to the vehicle.[33] Many leasing companies have

25. Personal Property Law § 337(5)(i).
26. Personal Property Law § 337(5)(i).
27. **PRACTICE POINTER:** The practitioner should be prepared to act quickly when presented with a repossession in a case in which the lessor has failed to comply with this provision. If the consumer wants to reinstate the lease, the practitioner should be prepared to commence an action immediately, by Order to Show Cause, seeking an injunction barring the lessor from disposing of the vehicle, directing it to comply with Personal Property Law § 339, and permitting the lessee to reinstate the lease. The Order to Show Cause should contain a Temporary Restraining Order, barring the lessor from disposing of the vehicle pending determination of the application.
28. This language is identical to the requirement imposed upon a secured party who disposes of collateral following a default in a sales transaction. UCC § 9–504(3). The practitioner should refer to cases interpreting that section for guidance in determining whether a particular disposition was commercially reasonable.

29. Reg. M, 12 CFR § 213.4(g)(12).
30. 15 U.S.C.A. § 1667b(b).
31. Personal Property Law § 331(7).
32. Personal Property Law § 341.
33. **PRACTICE POINTER:** This should not be confused with excess mileage charges. Virtually all leases permit the lessee a specified number of miles over the course of its term. Leases usually contain an "excess mileage charge," which is the amount the lessor will charge the lessee at termination for each mile above the total

been accused of grossly inflating the nature and extent of wear and damage allegedly found on the vehicle or the dollar amount that such damages cost it to repair. Large leasing companies usually do not pay retail rates for such work, if they have it done at all. It is not common, however, for the leasing company to pass on its actual cost of repair to the lessee. In short, excess wear and damage clauses have become nothing more than another way for leasing companies to squeeze out additional profits from lessees.

The MVRLA provides a detailed mechanism designed to eliminate the worst abuses in excess wear and damage assessments and to eliminate it as a source of profit for leasing companies.[34] The provision basically puts the lessee on a far more level playing field with the lessor by flatly prohibiting the charging or collecting of any charge for excess wear and damage that exceeds the actual wholesale cost to the lessor of making the repairs or the true itemized estimate by a licensed appraiser.[35] The act also provides an objective basis for determining the actual extent and cost of any wear and damage that is beyond normal and requires the lessor to give the lessee a conspicuous notice, just prior to the scheduled lease termination, of the lessee's rights in this regard.[36] The law permits the lessee to submit an itemized appraisal of any damage to the vehicle. If the parties cannot thereafter agree on the dollar amount for excess wear and damage, the act provides for an informal dispute resolution mechanism, or, at the lessee's option, submission of the dispute to an arbitration mechanism set up by the Attorney General's office.[37]

The MVRLA also provides a variety of remedies and penalties for violation of its various provisions, as well as general remedies for any violation of the act. Lessees can sue to recover any actual damages suffered as a result of a violation of any provision of the act.[38] If a lessor fails to provide a timely refund of any payment made following the cancellation of a lease, it is liable for twice the amount of the refund.[39] Lessors are liable for the value of any traded-in vehicle and for all costs and expenses incurred by the lessee if it fails to return such vehicle upon the cancellation of the lease by the lessee.[40] In addition, where any violation of the act is found, the court is required to award a civil penalty

number permitted under the lease. Leases usually do not provide for a credit if the lessee returns the vehicle with less than the permitted mileage. If the lessee anticipates that the total mileage will be less than the amount permitted under the lease, he or she can attempt to negotiate a lower lease cost in exchange for a higher excess mileage charge that, in all likelihood, will not be exceeded.

34. Personal Property Law § 343.
35. Personal Property Law § 343(1)(a).
36. Personal Property Law § 343(2)(a).
37. Personal Property Law § 343(2)(e)-(5). In all likelihood, the arbitration procedure will be similar to the one established under the New and Used Car Lemon Laws. See supra, § 7.13.
38. Personal Property Law § 346(1).
39. Personal Property Law § 346(2).
40. Personal Property Law § 346(3).

of $100.00 plus the costs and disbursements of the action and attorney's fees.[41]

Another major remedy available to consumers under the MVRLA is the express recognition that a lessor's violation of any one of nine specific prohibitions, which bar the more pernicious lease clauses,[42] is a *per se* deceptive trade practice under General Business Law § 349.[43]

While the MVLRA offers many valuable protections for lease consumers, the act's penalty provisions are subject to two major provisions that could potentially eviscerate a consumer's ability to obtain relief from the courts. First, before a consumer can sue a lessor, the consumer must give the lessor sixty days written notice of the violation. If the violation is not corrected within such time, the consumer may sue.[44]

A second major weakness of the act is the provision that a "lessor ... may not be held liable ... for a violation ... that was unintentional and resulted from a bona fide error notwithstanding the maintenance of

---

41. Personal Property Law § 346(4), (5).

PRACTICE POINTER: The act specifically provides that in "determining the award of attorney's fees, the amount of recovery on behalf of the lessee is not controlling." Personal Property Law § 346(5)(a). This provision is particularly beneficial to consumers, because some courts have been reluctant, and wrongfully so, to award the actual attorney's fees incurred when the consumer's recovery is relatively small. The legislative purpose here, like that found in other consumer statutes that provide statutory attorney's fees, *i.e.*, the Lemon Law, is to encourage the private bar to take such cases when the consumer might not otherwise be able to afford an attorney. By encouraging private enforcement of the act, the Legislature clearly intended that the availability of attorneys' fees would be the primary mechanism to insure compliance by the leasing community.

42. The nine prohibited practices are set forth in Personal Property Law § 337(14)(a)–(i).

43. Personal Property Law § 346(6)(a). *See infra*, §§ 7.45—7.47.

PRACTICE POINTER: This is a particularly important remedy because General Business Law § 349 not only permits individuals to sue businesses for deceptive business practices and to recover actual and statutory damages and attorney's fees, but it also permits individual consumers, acting as "private attorneys general," to obtain injunctive relief on behalf of all consumers, without the need to bring a class action. In some General Business Law § 349 cases, consumers have found it difficult to convince a court that the practice complained of was in fact deceptive. Personal Property Law § 346(6) completely removes this obstacle and, in effect, imposes strict liability for a violation of any of the proscribed practices.

Like virtually all state consumer protection laws, the MVRLA also provides for enforcement by the Attorney General, who can obtain an injunction and restitution on behalf of aggrieved consumers. Personal Property Law § 346(7). Given the limited resources available to the Attorney General, however, that office generally takes action only in the most egregious cases. Primary enforcement of this and other consumer protection statutes rests largely with the private bar.

44. **PRACTICE POINTER:** It is likely that this provision will only create more, not less, litigation, as lessors will undoubtedly claim either that they did not receive the notice (there is no requirement as to the means of giving the notice) or that the violation was in fact corrected following receipt of the notice. Practitioners should be careful to send such notices early in their representation of consumer lessees, and they should do so by certified, return receipt mail. In the notice, the practitioner should expressly demand that the lessor promptly advise of all steps taken to rectify

procedures reasonably adapted to avoid any such error."[45]

Finally, the MVRLA expressly does not preempt the field in consumer leasing litigation. Consumers are free to assert any other statutory or common law claims or defenses in any action arising out of a lease transaction.[46]

§ 7.23 Motor Vehicle Installment Sales

New York's Motor Vehicle Retail Installment Sales Act[1] ("MVRISA") was first enacted in 1956, and it is one of the oldest statutes of its kind in the country. The MVRISA provides the primary source of protection for consumers who finance the purchase of an automobile, and it expressly prohibits some of the most onerous contractual provisions.[2]

The act, like virtually all consumer protection laws, applies only to the sale of vehicles used primarily for personal, family, or household

the violation and should demand proof of these actions.

45. Personal Property Law § 346(9).

PRACTICE POINTER: This provision presents a possible affirmative defense that can be asserted by a lessor in defense of an action brought by a lessee. The consumer is not obligated to plead the absence of *bona fide* error affirmatively; the obligation is on the lessor to assert the defense affirmatively. As with any affirmative defense, the burden of proof rests with the party asserting it. The consumer is, of course, free to challenge the defense and should be freely granted discovery of all of the lessor's business practices and procedures in order to do so.

CAVEAT: The *bona fide* error provision also raises a fundamental inconsistency with well-established case law. It has long been held that violations of General Business Law § 349 do not require a showing of knowledge or intent by the defendant. Under that section, a deceptive practice that harms a consumer and that has the capacity to deceive is actionable. Guggenheimer v. Ginzburg, 43 N.Y.2d 268, 401 N.Y.S.2d 182, 372 N.E.2d 17 (1977); Geismar v. Abraham & Strauss, 109 Misc.2d 495, 439 N.Y.S.2d 1005 (Dist.Ct., Nassau County, 1981); R. Givens, *Practice Commentaries,* General Business Law § 349. *See infra,* § 7.46. It is difficult to understand, therefore, how a bona fide, unintentional error can be a defense to a violation of any of the nine proscribed practices set forth in Personal Property Law § 337(14)(a)–(i), since Personal Property Law § 346(6) provides that any such violation is a *per se* deceptive practice in violation of General Business Law § 349. At best it appears that the creation of this inconsistency was itself unintentional and should be rectified by the courts or the Legislature.

46. Personal Property Law § 351.

PRACTICE POINTER: Practitioners can and should assert whatever other statutory or common law claims that are available, such as claims pursuant to the Consumer Leasing Act, UCC Art. 2A, and any of the various theories set forth in Personal Property Law § 351. In addition, in any affirmative action against a lessor, the practitioner should consider claims for rescission and/or reformation of the lease, if applicable, as well as declaratory relief.

§ 7.23

1. Personal Property Law Art. 9, §§ 301—316.

2. PRACTICE POINTER: The MVRISA is similar in many respects to the provisions of the Retail Installment Sales Act ("RISA") (Personal Property Law Art. 10, §§ 401—422), which applies to the financed purchase of consumer goods other than motor vehicles. That article is outside the scope of this chapter and should be referred to by the practitioner in handling any non-automobile finance problem.

The MVRISA is also analogous to the Federal Truth-in-Lending Act (15 U.S.C.A. §§ 1601 *et seq.*). Practitioners should review and analyze any automobile financing case

§ 7.23   CONSUMER LAW   Ch. 7

purposes and it defines such use as being "other than for a commercial or business use or for the purpose of resale ..."[3] The act further requires that the transaction involve payment of two or more installments and that the payments thereunder be secured by a retail installment contract.[4]

Unlike lease transactions, which typically involve complex terms and concepts,[5] financing terms and concepts are generally much easier to understand and compare to those offered by different dealers.

The act requires that all contracts for the purchase and financing of an automobile be in writing and contain the entire agreement of the parties.[6] The contract must contain a specific notice advising the buyer of certain rights, such as the right to: pay off the full amount due and receive a refund of the unearned finance charge, redeem the vehicle if it is repossessed,[7] require that the seller resell the vehicle and apply the proceeds to the balance due under the contract, and purchase insurance for the vehicle from the broker of the buyer's choosing.[8]

The MVRISA also contains a significant protection for consumers when the seller breaches the contract. Automobile installment contracts are frequently sold to an assignee, often simultaneously with the initial sale, without any requirement of consent by the buyer. Under common law, the buyer would generally be precluded from asserting any claims or defenses against the assignee, regardless of the vehicle's condition and regardless of whether the seller has breached the contract. Under that theory, a buyer would be required to assert any such claims against the original seller only, or against the manufacturer, if applicable, and this would present a substantial obstacle to a consumer's ability to obtain redress.[9] The MVRISA, expressly barring such clauses, provides:

> No retail installment contract shall contain any provision by which the buyer agrees not to assert against an assignee a claim or defense arising out of the sale or require or entail the execution of any note or series of notes which, when separately negotiated, will cut off as to third parties any right of action or defense which the buyer may have against the seller. The assignee of a retail installment contract or obligation shall be subject to all claims and defenses of the buyer against the seller arising from the sale notwithstanding any agreement to the contrary, but the assignees's liability under this subdivi-

---

under both statutes and plead violations of both in any action arising out of a motor vehicle retail installment sales contract.

3. Personal Property Law § 301(4).
4. Personal Property Law § 301(4).
5. *See supra*, §§ 7.19—7.22.
6. Personal Property Law § 302(1).
7. *See* Personal Property Law § 316.
8. Personal Property Law § 302(2)(c).

9. **CAVEAT:** This provision should not be confused with the buyer's rights under the New Car or Used Car Lemon Laws, applicable if the vehicle proves defective. Under those laws, the buyer can assert rights directly against the manufacturer or dealer without regard to the seller or any subsequent assignee. Both statutes mandate that if the consumer is successful in the Lemon Law claim involving a financed vehicle, the contract is paid off by the losing

sion shall not exceed the amount owing to the assignee at the time the claim or defense is asserted against the assignee.[10]

As a result of this provision of the statute, a buyer can defend a claim by an assignee by asserting the seller's breach of the contract.[11]

Under the act, any contract provisions having the following effects are void:

1. Arbitrary acceleration of the balance due;[12]
2. Confession of judgment or a wage assignment;[13]
3. Advance authority to the seller to unlawfully enter the buyer's premises or to commit any breach of the peace in repossessing the vehicle;[14]
4. Buyer's waiver of any claims for illegal repossession;[15]
5. Requiring the buyer to execute a power of attorney appointing the seller as agent for collection of payments;[16]
6. Waiver of liability against the seller "for any legal remedy which the buyer may have had against the seller";[17]
7. Any acceleration of the balance due after repossession when the buyer timely tenders the past due payments;[18]
8. Waiver of a jury trial in any action arising out of the contract;[19]
9. Creation of a security interest in any property other than the vehicle that is the subject of the transaction;[20]

party, and the consumer has no further obligation under it. See supra, §§ 7.9—7.11.

10. Personal Property Law § 302(9).

11. PRACTICE POINTER: The MVRISA contains a substantial limitation on the right to assert such claims; it expressly limits such claims to the amount owing at the time of the claim. Therefore, if a dispute arises well into the contract, after numerous payments have been made, the assignee's liability to the buyer may be severely limited. In any such case, even those occurring early in the contract, the practitioner should assert claims against the seller as well, in a Third–Party Complaint, in order to avoid this limitation. See infra, § 7.53 for a sample Answer and Third–Party Complaint in an action by a leasing company against a consumer alleging, inter alia, fraud, deceptive practices, and federal odometer law violations, which can easily be adapted to a sale case. See also, infra, § 7.52 for a sample form Complaint against a leasing company and automobile dealer alleging fraud, breach of warranties, deceptive business practices, Lemon Law violations, rescission, and revocation of acceptance in a case that can also easily be adapted to a case involving a sale.

12. Personal Property Law § 302(13)(a).

13. Personal Property Law § 302(13)(b).

14. Personal Property Law § 302(13)(c).

15. Personal Property Law § 302(13)(d).

16. Personal Property Law § 302(13)(e).

17. Personal Property Law § 302(13)(f).

18. Personal Property Law § 302(13)(g). See also, General Obligations Law § 7–401(1), which bars contractual provisions that provide for the acceleration of remaining payments so as to prevent the buyer's right of redemption. General Obligations Law § 7–401(2) requires the creditor to send a notice, similar to the one required by Personal Property Law § 316. See also, infra, § 7.26.

19. Personal Property Law § 302(13)(h).

20. Personal Property Law § 314.

§ 7.23 CONSUMER LAW Ch. 7

10. A provision permitting the collection of a late charge at a rate in excess of the rate agreed to in the contract;[21] and

11. A provision permitting the seller to collect attorney's fees from the buyer in an action arising under the contract in an amount in excess of 15% of the amount due.[22]

If a buyer pays off the loan prior to maturity, he or she is entitled to a rebate of the unearned finance charge, as well as a rebate of any unearned premium for credit life insurance that was purchased through the lender.[23]

The MVRISA provides the following penalties for violations of its provisions: A wilful violation of any provision of the act is a misdemeanor punishable by a $500.00 fine.[24] A wilful violation of any of the disclosure provisions results in a bar to the creditor's collection of any interest or finance charge under the note.[25] The seller or assignee may raise as a defense to an action brought under the act that the buyer failed to provide a 10–day written notice of the violation.[26]

21. Personal Property Law § 302(7).
22. Personal Property Law § 302(7).
23. Personal Property Law § 305(2)–(3).
24. Personal Property Law § 307(1).
25. Personal Property Law § 307(2).
26. Personal Property Law § 307(3).

PRACTICE POINTER: In most cases, violations of the MVRISA will be asserted defensively, in response to an action by the lender for a deficiency following default, repossession, and re-sale, or in response to an action for default under the contract. Note that Personal Property Law § 307(2), which bars the collection of any interest charge, provides primarily for an affirmative defense to such charges. It does not suggest, however, that the buyer cannot affirmatively counterclaim for interest already paid. The practitioner should always consider asserting a counterclaim for violation of the Truth-in-Lending Act (15 U.S.C.A. § 1637; 12 CFR §§ 226.5 *et seq.*). This statute provides additional remedies beyond the MVRISA, including statutory damages equal to twice the finance charge, up to $1,000.00, actual damages, and attorney's fees. Although the TILA has a one-year Statute of Limitations, a violation may be asserted as a counterclaim even beyond that period.

PRACTICE POINTER: Even though the MVRISA does not expressly authorize the consumer to seek an award of attorney's fees in connection with an action arising out of a retail installment contract, there are at least two statutes under which such a claim can be made. General Obligations Law § 5–327 provides:

Whenever a consumer contract provides that the creditor, seller or lessor may recover attorney's fees and expenses incurred as the result of a breach of any contractual obligation by the debtor, buyer or lessee, it shall be implied that the creditor, seller or lessor shall pay the attorney's fees and expenses of the debtor, buyer or lessee incurred as the result of a breach of any contractual obligation by the creditor, seller or lessor, or in the successful defense of any action arising out of the contract commenced by the creditor, seller or lessor. Any limitations on the attorney's fees recoverable by the creditor or seller shall also be applicable to attorney's fees recoverable by the debtor or buyer under this section. Any waiver of this section shall be void as against public policy.

The practitioner should therefore assert a claim or counterclaim under General Obligations Law § 5–327 in any action in which the contract permits the creditor to recover attorney's fees. The section does, however, limit the amount of attorney's fees that the consumer can recover to the 15% limitation on sellers under Personal Property Law § 302(7).

In addition, under General Business Law § 349, a consumer can recover attorney's fees in an action alleging that the creditor

If an automobile purchased pursuant to a motor vehicle retail installment contract is repossessed, either voluntarily or involuntarily, the holder of the contract is required to send the buyer a notice, within 72 hours after such repossession, advising the buyer of the right to redeem the vehicle, setting forth the amount necessary to redeem, and providing information pertaining to the location and manner of exercising the redemption right.[27]

§ 7.24 Repossession—Overview

Repossession is a self-help right of a creditor by which it seizes property covered by a security interest, without a prior judgment or even the commencement of a lawsuit. By definition, since repossession does not take place within the context of a pending or completed legal action there is no court overseeing the process. As a result, a consumer who wishes to challenge the propriety of a repossession must initiate some form of action, either to prevent it from taking place or to undo it after it occurs. Even if affirmative action is taken to challenge a repossession, a consumer can also defend a resulting deficiency claim by asserting that the repossession was unwarranted or otherwise improper or that a resulting resale was not "commercially reasonable."

This section does not deal with a related, but distinctly different, seizure of property by creditors—seizure of personal property pursuant to CPLR Article 52. Seizures under that statute differ in several major respects. They are made by either a sheriff or city marshal[1] and only occur in connection with the enforcement of a money judgment after the consumer has already been sued and lost, either after trial or on default. More importantly, Article 52 seizures can apply to almost any property owned by the debtor[2] and are not limited simply to property covered by a security agreement.

A security agreement or security interest is defined as "an interest in personal property or fixtures which secures payment or performance of an obligation."[3] Security agreements are commonly used in connection with the sale of automobiles, where the purchase is financed by a bank or other lending institution. Security agreements are found in documents called "retail installment contracts."[4]

engaged in deceptive business practices. This claim can also be asserted in an affirmative action or in a counterclaim. *See infra*, § 7.47.

27. Personal Property Law § 316; General Obligations Law § 7–401. *See supra*, note 17 and *see infra*, § 7.26.

§ 7.24

1. County sheriffs have general authority to enforce money judgments in New York State. Judgments arising from the New York City Civil Court can be enforced by a marshal, who has the same powers and authorities as sheriffs in such cases. NYCCCA § 1609.

2. Subject to the property exemptions found in CPLR 5205. *See also*, Borges, *et al.*, *Enforcing Judgments and Collecting Debts in New York* (West 1997) Ch.7.

3. UCC § 1–201(37).

4. Personal Property Law §§ 301(5), 401(6).

§ 7.24 CONSUMER LAW Ch. 7

Because they can be more easily located and removed from public places and tend to have higher resale value, automobiles are the most common subject of repossession. Even though personal property purchased under a security agreement is subject to repossession, such actions are rare because property, such as furniture, electronic equipment, and major appliances, is generally located inside private property and therefore may not easily be seized without a "breach of the peace." In addition, this type of property depreciates in value quickly, has a lower resale value, and does not have the same well-established re-sale market as do automobiles. Creditors who threaten repossession of personal property other than automobiles often do so for the *in terrorem* effect, without any actual intent of following through with the repossession.[5]

The law of repossessions and security interests is found in various places, primarily UCC §§ 9–503 to 9–506, the Motor Vehicle Retail Installment Sales Act,[6] and the Truth-in-Lending Act.[7] Repossession problems generally arise in one of the following three contexts: (1) the consumer has recently defaulted on a loan payment, and the bank is threatening to repossess; (2) repossession has already taken place, but no deficiency action has been commenced, or (3) a deficiency action has been commenced or has already been reduced to judgment. The course of action that the practitioner should take will depend upon which of these three scenarios counsel faces.

---

5. PRACTICE POINTER: Consumers who are threatened with pre-judgment repossession of personal property located in their home should be advised that while a creditor may have the legal right to carry out this threat, the likelihood of the creditor actually doing so is relatively slight. In counseling a client who wishes to avoid repossession, the practitioner should advise the client that debtors do not have to consent to the seizure, nor are they required to permit entry onto their private property for the purpose of conducting a repossession.

Both the MVRISA and the RISA prohibit contract clauses that allow creditors to enter the buyer's premises unlawfully or to commit a breach of the peace in carrying out a repossession. Personal Property Law §§ 302(13)(c), 403(2)(d). In addition, such practices are unconscionable. Kosches v. Nichols, 68 Misc.2d 795, 327 N.Y.S.2d 968 (Civ.Ct., N.Y. County, 1971); Sturman v. Polito, 161 Misc. 536, 291 N.Y.S. 621 (Rochester City Ct., 1936).

A creditor determined to seize secured property that is not easily subject to self-help repossession can bring an action to recover chattel, commonly called a replevin action, pursuant to CPLR Art. 71. A court-awarded judgment of possession can be enforced by a sheriff or marshal, who have greater authority to enter onto private property. Replevin seizures are, however, subject to both the Fourth and Fourteenth Amendments, barring unreasonable searches and seizures and deprivation of property without due process. Laprease v. Raymours Furniture Co., 315 F.Supp. 716 (N.D.N.Y.1970); Jefferds v. Ellis, 127 Misc.2d 477, 486 N.Y.S.2d 649 (Sup.Ct., Cattaraugus County, 1985), rev'd on other grounds 122 A.D.2d 595, 505 N.Y.S.2d 15 (4th Dep't 1986).

6. Personal Property Law Art. 9, §§ 301—316.

7. 15 U.S.C.A. §§ 1601 *et seq.*

CAVEAT: In evaluating and preparing any repossession case, the practitioner must carefully review the latest case law on the particular issues involved. Typically, in litigating UCC issues, New York courts do not always follow the view taken by the majority of courts in other states. Indeed, even within New York, unless settled by the Court of Appeals, there may be issues upon which different appellate divisions have reached opposite results.

§ 7.25 Repossession—Prevention and Avoidance

If repossession is being threatened, the practitioner must be prepared to advise the consumer properly concerning the most effective action to pursue. Initially, the practitioner should determine whether the creditor even has a valid security interest.[1] The practitioner should also determine whether the creditor has a present intent actually to repossess.[2]

In some instances, the consumer might be well advised to consider voluntarily surrendering the secured collateral to the creditor, especially if the consumer's financial situation makes retention of the property problematic. Factors to be considered in this regard include the potential savings to the consumer of repossession expenses, attorney's fees, damage to the property incurred during repossession, and the possible loss of personal property contained in a motor vehicle at the time of repossession. In addition, voluntary repossession expedites the process, thereby increasing the possibility that the property will suffer less depreciation and thereby realize a higher selling price.

Voluntary repossession should not be considered, however, without obtaining some concessions from the creditor. For example, in exchange for voluntarily surrendering the property, it is not uncommon for the practitioner to seek either a waiver of any deficiency claim by the creditor or an agreement not to report derogatory information on any credit report.[3] Another tactic is to negotiate an agreement permitting the debtor to sell the property privately, which, in all likelihood, will result in a greater sales price than the amount the creditor might obtain at a wholesale auction. Under this scenario, the creditor receives more money sooner than it would otherwise receive through a drawn-out repossession process.[4] When voluntary repossession is neither feasible nor justified,

---

§ 7.25

1. **PRACTICE POINTER:** In this regard, the practitioner should carefully study Chapter 3 of the National Consumer Law Center's manual entitled, *Repossessions.* If it is determined that the creditor does not in fact have a valid security interest, every effort should be made to resist repossession and, if it has already taken place, to sue for conversion and/or replevin.

2. **PRACTICE POINTER:** In this regard, the threat of repossession may be false, especially when the amount in default is relatively small, when the debt is disputed, when repossession is not even authorized, or when the security interest is defective. If it turns out that the threat of repossession is not valid, the practitioner should consider asserting a claim for false, deceptive, or misleading debt collection practices under the "Fair Debt Collection Practices Act," 15 U.S.C.A. §§ 1692 *et seq.*

See infra, §§ 7.36—7.41. In addition or in the alternative, counsel could bring a deceptive practices claim under General Business Law § 349. *See infra,* §§ 7.45—7.47.

3. **PRACTICE POINTER:** Without such an agreement, the creditor invariably will report the account simply as a "repossession," which carries with it all of the negative connotations of an involuntary repossession. Most potential creditors viewing such reports have little interest in the substantial distinction between a voluntary and an involuntary repossession and will view any repossession as a seriously negative entry on the report. *See generally infra,* §§ 7.30—7.31.

4. **CAVEAT:** Voluntary surrender should not be seriously considered if there is a substantial likelihood that the creditor will not be able to recover a deficiency judgment, for whatever reason, such as

§ 7.25 CONSUMER LAW Ch. 7

the practitioner must examine other options to prevent repossession or to recover property already seized involuntarily.

Repossession sometimes occurs even though the consumer is current on all payments. As long as the installment contract permits it, and most do, creditors can declare a default and an acceleration of the balance due, and then repossess the collateral, for a variety of reasons unrelated to non-payment, such as the debtor's failure to properly insure the collateral, removal of it from the state without permission, sale, transfer, or other encumbrance of the collateral, filing of a bankruptcy petition, seizure of the property by a governmental entity,[5] or other acts that cause the creditor to reasonably believe that "the prospect of payment or performance is impaired."[6]

Despite the above, creditors cannot legally declare a default and then repossess unless the specific grounds for the alleged default have previously been spelled out in the contract. Both the Motor Vehicle Retail Installment Sales Act, governing the sale of automobiles, and the Retail Installment Sales Act, governing the sale of other goods, prohibit creditors from accelerating the maturity of the balance due "arbitrarily and without reasonable cause."[7]

If the consumer wishes to avoid repossession, the safest way to do so is to ensure that the property is not left out in the open in a public place. For an automobile, this requires keeping it in a locked garage. The UCC bars creditors from "breaching the peace" in carrying out any repossession.[8] Both the MVRISA and the RISA bar installment contract provi-

when the security interest is defective or non-existent. In these instances, instead of seeking a voluntary surrender, the practitioner should consider initiating an action against the creditor, or asserting a counterclaim in a deficiency action, for statutory damages. See UCC § 9–507(1).

5. This typically occurs with regard to automobiles towed by a city for non-payment of parking tickets, as long as the unpaid tickets were issued for the subject vehicle.

6. UCC § 1–208.

7. Personal Property Law §§ 302(13)(a), 403(4).

PRACTICE POINTER: New York, unlike states that have adopted the Uniform Consumer Credit Code, does not provide a statutory right to cure any of these non-payment defaults. If, however, the consumer is notified of the default and promptly cures it, a substantial argument can be made that the creditor has thereby waived any right to repossess the collateral in that it no longer has the "reasonable cause" required by Personal Property Law § 302(13)(a) and § 403(4).

8. UCC § 9–503. Depending on the severity of the breach of the peace, the repossession agent and the creditor can be liable for substantial actual and punitive damages. See, e.g., Roberson v. Ammons, 477 So.2d 957 (Ala.1985) (award of $1,380 in compensatory damages and $100,000 in punitive damages upheld; evidence showed that defendants acted in known violation of law, as well as of borrower's rights, so as to permit award of punitive damages); First and Farmers Bank of Somerset, Inc. v. Henderson, 763 S.W.2d 137 (Ky.Ct.App. 1988) (court upheld $75,000 punitive damages award to debtor against secured creditor who had breached the peace while repossessing debtor's boat); Hinton v. State Farm Mut. Auto. Ins. Co., 741 S.W.2d 696 (Mo.Ct.App.1987) (award of $27,500 in punitive damages in an action for trover and conversion); Villella v. Waikem Motors, Inc., 45 Ohio St.3d 36, 543 N.E.2d 464 (1989) (award of $250 in actual damages and $150,000 in punitive damages upheld for wrongful repossession and conversion); Mitchell v. Ford Motor Credit Co., 688 P.2d 42 (Okla.1984) (award of $60,000 in puni-

sions that authorize unlawful entry onto property or any breach of the peace in carrying out any repossession.[9] Consumers who wish to avoid repossession of property from private property should be advised that they are not obligated to permit entry onto their property for such a purpose, and they should instruct other family members not to permit such entry in their absence.[10]

If the vehicle proves to be defective, or if the seller breaches the contract of sale in any material way, repossession can legally be prevented by the buyer's revocation of acceptance or rejection of the property, pursuant to UCC § 2-608 or § 2-601. Under this analysis, the creditor's security interest is extinguished by the buyer's cancellation of the contract.[11]

§ 7.26 Repossession—Defending Deficiency Claims

Once an automobile repossession takes place, certain obligations of the creditor are triggered. The repossessor is required to notify both the owner and the local police department within 24 hours of the seizure.[1] In addition, if an automobile is repossessed, either voluntarily or involun-

tive damages upheld for conversion and wrongful repossession); Lee County Nat. Bank v. Nelson, 761 S.W.2d 851 (Tex.Ct. App.1988) (award of $75,000 in punitive damages upheld for unlawful conversion of title to borrower's automobile; punitive award was not excessive even though borrower suffered only $2,000 in actual damages).

9. Personal Property Law §§ 302(13)(c), 403(2)(d).

10. PRACTICE POINTER: Practitioners can further protect the consumer by issuing, or directing their client to issue, a letter to the creditor advising that the consumer does not consent to repossession or to entry onto private property. Such a letter will likely cause the creditor to attempt a negotiated resolution of the problem.

11. PRACTICE POINTER: If the facts warrant it, the practitioner should promptly issue a "Notice of Rejection and/or Revocation of Acceptance" both to the seller and to the assignee holder of the note/security interest, unequivocally asserting the consumer's rejection and/or revocation of acceptance and further advising that any attempt at repossession would therefore be illegal, and any actual repossession would constitute a conversion. A sample form notice of rejection and/or revocation of acceptance of an automobile, pursuant to UCC §§ 2-601 and 2-608, containing such a demand, may be found *infra*, § 7.56.

At the same time, the consumer should take steps to insure that the vehicle cannot be easily seized from a public place.

CAVEAT: Penal Law § 185.05(2) provides, "A person is guilty of fraud involving a security interest when, having executed a security agreement creating a security interest in personal property securing a monetary obligation owed to a secured party, and ...having under the security agreement no right of sale or other disposition of the property, he knowingly secretes, withholds or disposes of such property in violation of the security agreement."

Criminal prosecutions under this section are rare, except in extreme instances. In order for a debtor to be held in violation of this section, it must be shown that the debtor acted with intent to defraud the creditor. A rightful assertion of a right to revoke acceptance or to reject the property should vitiate any such allegation. Practitioners should be aware of the possibility of a creditor threatening the consumer with a criminal prosecution for wrongfully concealing secured property. A false or misleading threat of criminal prosecution by a collection agency (but not by a creditor) violates the FDCPA. 15 U.S.C.A. §§ 1692e(4), 1692e(5), 1692e(10). *See infra*, § 7-39.

§ 7.26

1. Vehicle & Traffic Law § 425.

§ 7.26   CONSUMER LAW   Ch. 7

tarily, the holder of the contract is required to send the buyer a notice, within 72 hours after such repossession, advising the buyer of the right to redeem the vehicle, setting forth the amount necessary to redeem, and providing information pertaining to the location and the manner of exercising the redemption right.[2] Perhaps the most important protection the consumer has in the redemption process is the right to recover possession of the vehicle by paying only the amount in default, plus the creditor's reasonable repossession expense. Creditors are expressly barred from requiring acceleration of the full outstanding balance of the loan as a condition of returning the vehicle.[3] Creditors who either fail to issue a timely and proper notice of redemption or who refuse to return the vehicle upon a proper tender of the amount lawfully due under General Obligations Law § 7–401 are subject to liability for conversion, replevin, as well as deceptive business practices under General Business Law § 349.[4]

If the buyer does not seek to redeem the property following repossession, the creditor is permitted to sell the property and to sue the buyer for any resulting deficiency between the realized price and the remaining balance under the note, together with repossession expenses.[5] Any such resale must be performed in a "commercially reasonable" manner.[6] Under certain circumstances, this obligation extends to leases as well. Numerous courts around the country have held that the repossession of a leased automobile is governed by UCC Article 9 if the lease "is intended as security."[7] There are various factors to be considered in determining whether a lease is truly a lease or is instead a disguised credit sale that triggers coverage of Article 9.[8]

If the procedures employed by the creditor in conducting the resale or in complying with its other obligations under UCC § 9–504 are found

---

2. Personal Property Law § 316; General Obligations Law § 7–401.

3. Personal Property Law §§ 302(13)(g), 403(4); General Obligations Law § 7–401. While UCC § 9–506 provides for a debtor's right of redemption, which requires the payment of the full accelerated balance, that provision is superseded by the above protections under state law. UCC § 9–201. See supra, § 7.23 note 17.

4. See infra, §§ 7.45—7.47.

5. UCC § 9–504(2); Personal Property Law § 422.

6. UCC §§ 9–504(3), 9–507(2).

7. UCC § 1–201(37).

8. Sheffield Commercial Credit Corp. v. Clemente, 792 F.2d 282 (2d Cir.1986); Credit Car Leasing Corp. v. DeCresenzo, 138 Misc.2d 726, 525 N.Y.S.2d 492 (Civ.Ct., N.Y. County, 1988) (where lease had all of the indicia of a sale, it created a security interest, and the lessor became obligated to comply with UCC Article 9 in disposing of the vehicle after repossession). See supra, § 7.21 note 4.

PRACTICE POINTER: The practitioner should carefully evaluate the particular circumstances of the lease to determine whether it can be deemed to create a security interest in the lessor, or if it is actually a disguised sale. With consumer leases entered after August 31, 1995, the Motor Vehicle Retail Leasing Act (Personal Property Law Art. 9A) renders this exercise unnecessary because that statute includes a requirement that lessors dispose of repossessed vehicles in a commercially reasonable manner. Personal Property Law § 339. See supra, § 7–22.

to be commercially unreasonable, some courts have held that the creditor is barred from recovering any deficiency whatsoever.[9] Other courts have held that a creditor is not automatically barred from recovering on a deficiency claim when it violates UCC § 9–504. Instead, the burden is shifted to the creditor to establish that despite the commercially unreasonable resale, or violation of § 9–504, the value of the collateral was less than the deficiency claim.[10]

In defending against a deficiency claim, the practitioner should assert all possible defenses, including: strict foreclosure (if the creditor improperly retained the collateral instead of disposing of it and applying the proceeds to the balance due), commercially unreasonable disposition in violation of UCC § 9–504(3), absence of default (*i.e.*, where the creditor had previously accepted late payments and thereby waived its right to declare a default for this reason), arbitrary acceleration in violation of Personal Property Law § 302 (13)(a) or § 403(4), incorrect calculation of the deficiency claim, revocation of acceptance pursuant to UCC § 2–608, rejection pursuant to UCC § 2–601,[11] fraud, and violation of applicable provisions of the MVRISA or the RISA.

In addition, all possible counterclaims should be asserted, including: conversion of the repossessed property due to a defective or invalid security interest, conversion of personal property left in the vehicle, breach of the peace in conducting the seizure, statutory damages under UCC § 9–507, deceptive business practices in violation of General Business Law § 349,[12] violation of applicable provisions of the MVRISA[13] or the RISA,[14] violation of the Truth-in-Lending Act,[15] violation of the Fair

9. Mack Financial Corp. v. Knoud, 98 A.D.2d 713, 469 N.Y.S.2d 116 (2d Dep't 1983); Long Island Trust Co. v. Porta Aluminum, Inc., 63 A.D.2d 670, 404 N.Y.S.2d 682 (2d Dep't 1978); Central Budget Corp., v. Garrett, 48 A.D.2d 825, 368 N.Y.S.2d 268 (2d Dep't 1975); Credit Car Leasing Corp. v. DeCresenzo, 138 Misc.2d 726, 525 N.Y.S.2d 492, 497 (Civ.Ct., N.Y. County, 1988); Fitzpatrick v. Bank of New York, 125 Misc.2d 1069, 480 N.Y.S.2d 864 (Civ.Ct., Queens. County, 1984); Long Island Bank v. Knight, 122 Misc.2d 878, 473 N.Y.S.2d 901 (Sup.Ct., App. Term., 2d & 11th Jud.Dist., 1983); International Paper Credit Corp. v. Columbia Wax Products Co., Inc., 102 Misc.2d 738, 424 N.Y.S.2d 827 (Sup.Ct., Queens County, 1980), rev'd on other grounds 79 A.D.2d 700, 434 N.Y.S.2d 270 (2d Dep't 1980); Marine Midland Bank–Central v. Watkins, 89 Misc.2d 949, 392 N.Y.S.2d 819 (Sup.Ct., Onondaga County, 1977); Avis Rent–A-Car System, Inc. v. Franklin, 82 Misc.2d 66, 366 N.Y.S.2d 83 (Sup.Ct., App. Term, 2d & 11th Jud.Dist., 1975).

10. Paco Corp. v. Vigliarola, 611 F.Supp. 923 (E.D.N.Y.1985), aff'd 835 F.2d 1429 (2d Cir.1987); Kohler v. Ford Motor Co., 93 A.D.2d 205, 462 N.Y.S.2d 297 (3d Dep't 1983).

CAVEAT: The New York Court of Appeals has not ruled on this issue. As a result, New York has a patchwork of decisions, some applying the automatic bar to a deficiency claim and others applying the shifting-of-the-burden-of-proof theory. As a general rule, the Second Department follows the absolute bar theory. Practitioners should carefully read the applicable case law in order to apply the factual setting of their case to the facts of the absolute bar case law.

11. See *infra*, § 7.56 for a sample form notice of rescission and/or revocation of acceptance.

12. See *infra*, §§ 7.45—7.47.

13. See *supra*, § 7.23.

14. Personal Property Law Art. 9.

15. 15 U.S.C.A. §§ 1601 *et seq.*

§ 7.26 CONSUMER LAW Ch. 7

Debt Collection Practices Act,[16] and violation of the New or Used Car Lemon Law.[17] In addition, consumers can assert a counterclaim for attorney's fees under General Obligation Law § 5–327, as long as the underlying contract with the seller permits the creditor to seek attorney's fees from the consumer.

§ 7.27 Automobile Repairs

When an automobile breaks down or is damaged in a collision, consumers sometimes are subjected to deceptive and fraudulent repair practices by motor vehicle repair shops. Most consumers are not familiar with the complicated mechanical workings of automobiles, particularly those with the latest electronic and computer technology. Historically, consumers have been victimized by unscrupulous repair shops that have found it easy to prey on such unfamiliarity. In an effort to stem such practices and to provide consumers with greater protection in this area, the State Legislature, in 1974, enacted the Motor Vehicle Repair Shop Registration Act.[1]

The legislation has a two-prong focus: it mandates registration with the Department of Motor Vehicles of all repair shops[2] and sets forth a motor vehicle repair "bill of rights" for consumers.[3] The statute is enforceable by the Commissioner of the Department of Motor Vehicles, who has the authority to revoke or suspend a repair shop registration and/or assess civil penalties and restitution to an aggrieved complainant.

In enacting the MVRSRA, the Legislature stated:

> The purposes of this article are to further highway safety by promoting the proper and efficient repair of malfunctioning or disabled motor vehicles and to protect the consumers of this state from dishonest, deceptive and fraudulent practices in the repair of such motor vehicles. These purposes will be accomplished by the enactment of legislation which requires the registration of those engaged in the business of repairing malfunctioning or disabled motor vehicles and to exclude from that business those persons who engage in dishonest or fraudulent practice or who otherwise demonstrate unfitness for that business. That further, the purpose of this article is to protect the motoring public from improper repairs made to its vehicles to set standards for quality repairs to be made to motor vehicles for fair and reasonable fees and to eliminate unquali-

---

16. 15 U.S.C.A. §§ 1692 *et seq.* See *infra*, §§ 7.37—7.43.
17. General Business Law §§ 198–a, 198–b. See *supra*, §§ 7.9—7.11.

§ 7.27
1. Vehicle & Traffic Law Art. 12–A.
2. Vehicle & Traffic Law § 398–c.
3. Vehicle & Traffic Law § 398–d.

PRACTICE POINTER: The MVRSRA is broader in scope than most other consumer protection statutes in that it protects not only the traditional consumer, who contracts with a merchant for "personal, family or household purposes," but also any "customer," which would include business customers as well.

fied automotive repair shops from engaging in the business of automotive repair to malfunctioning or disabled vehicles.[4]

Consumers are given the following rights by the statute:

1. to receive a written invoice describing all work to be done;[5]
2. to inspect all work performed prior to making payment;[6]
3. to inspect all replaced parts;[7] and
4. to receive a written estimate of all work to be performed and not to be charged for any work done or parts supplied in excess of the estimate without consent.[8]

The DMV has the authority to revoke or suspend a repair shop's license if the shop:

1. engages in fraud, fraudulent or deceptive practices;[9]
2. is grossly negligent in making repairs or grossly overcharges for its services;[10]
3. wilfully fails to comply with the provisions of the MVRSRA;[11]
4. knowingly issues a false or misleading estimate;[12] or
5. interferes with a consumer's recovery under an insurance policy.[13]

A consumer who has been victimized by a dishonest repair shop has two primary options. The consumer can file a complaint with the DMV or an action can be brought directly against the shop, either in small claims court or in any other court with the appropriate monetary and subject matter jurisdiction.[14]

4. Vehicle & Traffic Law § 398–a.
5. Vehicle & Traffic Law § 398–d(1).
6. Vehicle & Traffic Law § 398–d(1).
7. Vehicle & Traffic Law § 398–d(1).
8. Vehicle & Traffic Law § 398–d(2).
9. Vehicle & Traffic Law § 398–e(1)(g).
10. Vehicle & Traffic Law § 398–e(1)(h).
11. Vehicle & Traffic Law § 398–e(1)(i).
12. Vehicle & Traffic Law § 398–e(1)(j).
13. Vehicle & Traffic Law § 398–e(1)(k).
14. The monetary jurisdiction in small claims court in New York City is $3,000.00. NYCCCA § 1801.

PRACTICE POINTER: There are several advantages to advising a consumer to file a complaint with the DMV, rather than bringing an action in court. The DMV will have one of its inspectors examine the vehicle and the invoice to determine if the repair was properly performed and properly documented. There is no charge to the consumer for a DMV investigation and proceeding, if necessary. If the DMV finds a violation by the repair shop, it can order restitution to the consumer in lieu of a civil penalty. Vehicle & Traffic Law § 398–e(3). Such restitution orders cannot be made, however, if the consumer has already commenced an action against the repair shop, so the consumer must elect a remedy in advance. Vehicle & Traffic Law § 398–e(3).

Consumers are not, however, precluded from commencing an action against a repair shop *after* a restitution order has been made, for consequential or punitive damages. Although the MVRSRA does not include an express private right of action, the statute's prohibition against deceptive business practices is the equivalent of such a claim under General Business Law § 349. Allstate Ins. Co. v. Foschio, 93 A.D.2d 328, 462 N.Y.S.2d 44 (2d Dep't 1983). A successful claim under that statute also will result

Although the DMV has brought numerous actions against repair shops for violations of the act,[15] abuses in this area continue.

§ 7.28 Automobile Repair Shop Liens—Overview

As described in the previous section, automobile repair shops sometimes engage in dishonest and deceptive business practices. It is not uncommon for consumers to be charged for shoddy, non-existent, or unauthorized repairs to their vehicles. Although the Motor Vehicle Repair Shop Registration Act[1] expressly grants the consumer the right to inspect his or her vehicle at the repair shop before paying for repairs, it does not permit the consumer to remove the vehicle from the premises before payment is made. Thus, when disputes over payment between consumers and repair shops arise, a lien problem usually follows.

Under the New York Lien Law,[2] a repair shop "has a lien upon such motor vehicle ... for the sum due for ... towing, storing ... or repairing of such motor vehicle ... and may detain such motor vehicle ... at any time it may lawfully be in (its) possession until such sum is paid ..."[3] The Lien Law expressly bars the assertion of a lien by any unregistered repair shop operating in violation of the MVRSRA.[4]

A properly asserted lien is a very potent enforcement device for a repair shop. If a consumer refuses to pay for any agreed charges incurred for repair, storage, towing, or parts, the repair shop is permitted, under certain circumstances, to sell the vehicle and to apply the proceeds of such sale to the outstanding charges.[5] As detailed below, the charges must, however, be agreed upon by the consumer. Without such consent, the lien is subject to challenge. Like self-help repossession, the law permits the assertion of a lien without first requiring resort to judicial

---

in an award of statutory attorney's fees. A finding by the DMV of a violation may be considered, but is not binding upon a court in any such action. Vehicle & Traffic Law § 398–e(3)(e).

CAVEAT: The MVRSRA has strict filing requirements for consumer complaints. A complaint must be filed within 90 days or 3,000 miles of the complained-of repair or conduct in order for the DMV to investigate. Practitioners presented with repair problems that do not qualify under this rule because of untimeliness can still commence an action, using the standards set forth in Vehicle & Traffic Law § 398 as a reference for the court and can also bring common-law fraud and breach of contract actions, as well as an action pursuant to General Business Law § 349, for deceptive business practices.

15. *See, e.g.,* De Cillis Auto Service Center, Inc. v. New York State Dept. of Motor Vehicles, 212 A.D.2d 700, 622 N.Y.S.2d 787 (2d Dep't 1995); Kel–Car Assoc. Ltd. v. Adduci, 176 A.D.2d 942, 575 N.Y.S.2d 554 (2d Dep't 1991); Leon's Collision Shop, Inc. v. Adduci, 167 A.D.2d 986, 562 N.Y.S.2d 316 (4th Dep't 1990); Little Reb Auto Corp. v. New York State Dept. of Motor Vehicles, 93 A.D.2d 821, 460 N.Y.S.2d 618 (2d Dep't 1983); Sholz Buick, Inc. v. Melton, 92 A.D.2d 871, 459 N.Y.S.2d 829 (2d Dep't 1983).

§ 7.28
1. Vehicle & Traffic Law § 398.
2. Lien Law § 184.
3. Lien Law § 184(1).
4. Lien Law § 184(4).
5. Lien Law § 200.

intervention.[6] As a creature of statute in derogation of the common law, however, garagemen's liens are strictly construed, and a lienor is required to establish that it has fully complied with each and every obligation of the statute.[7]

Perhaps the most fundamental requirement of a garageman's lien under Lien Law § 184 is the requirement that the claimed services have been rendered at the express request of the consumer or with the consumer's express consent.[8] The interplay between a garageman's lien and a repair shop's obligations under the MVRSRA is pivotal. Under MVRSRA § 398–d(2), a repair shop is not permitted to charge for any repairs that the consumer has not authorized. As a result, by definition, any unauthorized repairs not only cannot properly be the subject of a lien, but they cannot be the subject of any claim by the repair shop whatsoever.

Another key element of a garageman's lien is that the lienor must have lawful possession of the vehicle. If the repair shop relinquishes possession, or obtains possession unlawfully, the lien is waived or nonexistent.[9]

In order to assert and enforce a lien properly, a lienor is required to personally serve a notice of sale upon the owner of the vehicle.[10] If service cannot be made personally, "with due diligence," the lienor is permitted to serve it by certified mail.[11] The notice must set forth a verified statement, which includes the following:

1. Facts giving the nature of the debt or agreement under which the lien arose, with an itemized statement of the claim and the time when due;[12]

6. Like repossession, enforcement of claims by foreclosure on a lien is not the equivalent of enforcement of a money judgment under CPLR Article 52, which permits a judgment creditor to cause a levy to be served on property owned by the judgment debtor and then force the sale of such property by a sheriff or marshal.

7. Slank v. Sam Dell's Dodge Corp., 46 A.D.2d 445, 363 N.Y.S.2d 138 (4th Dep't 1975); Manufacturers Trust Co. v. Stehle, 1 A.D.2d 471, 151 N.Y.S.2d 384 (1st Dep't 1956); Wyche v. New Amsterdam Garage Corp., 82 Misc.2d 956, 371 N.Y.S.2d 754 (Civ.Ct., New York City, 1975).

8. Lien Law § 184(1). Campbell v. WABC Towing Corp., 78 Misc.2d 671, 356 N.Y.S.2d 455 (Sup.Ct., N.Y. County, 1974); Hartford Fire Ins. Co. v. Albertson, 59 Misc.2d 207, 298 N.Y.S.2d 321 (Westchester County Ct., 1969).

9. ITT Commercial Finance Corp. v. Kallmeyer & Sons Truck Tire Service Inc., 156 Misc.2d 505, 593 N.Y.S.2d 951 (Sup.Ct., Suffolk County, 1993); Owl Wet Wash Laundry Co. v. Karish, 188 N.Y.S. 782 (Sup. Ct., N.Y. County, 1921); Thourot v. Delahaye Import Co., 69 Misc. 351, 125 N.Y.S. 827 (Sup.Ct., N.Y. County, 1910).

PRACTICE POINTER: Practitioners should be aware of this crucial requirement in advising a client faced with a lien claim. A motor vehicle left out in the open on public property can lawfully be "seized" by an owner, thereby vitiating the possessory requirement of the lien. This "reverse repossession" does not extinguish the repair shop's right to sue for unpaid charges, however it would no longer have any basis to either assert or enforce a lien.

10. Lien Law § 201.

11. Lien Law § 201.

12. Lien Law § 201(1).

2. A brief description of the personal property against which the lien exists;[13]

3. The estimated value of the property;[14] and

4. The amount of the lien asserted.[15]

The notice must further advise the consumer that if the lien is not satisfied within ten days after the notice, the property will be sold, setting forth the time and place of such sale.[16] Additionally, the notice must apprise the consumer of the consumer's right to commence a proceeding to challenge the validity of the lien.[17]

§ 7.29 Automobile Repair Shop Liens—Statutory Challenges

Prior to 1980, lienors were given free rein to enforce liens under the Lien Law without any oversight whatsoever by a court. Abuses of the rights conveyed by the Lien Law were rampant, and liens were commonly misused by unscrupulous repair shops to exact exorbitant fees and charges from unsuspecting consumers. In 1980, following a declaration by the Court of Appeals that the *ex parte* sale of vehicles under the Lien Law violated consumers' rights to due process under the New York State Constitution,[1] the Legislature enacted a statutory mechanism for consumers to challenge the validity of such liens.[2]

The new provision, Lien Law § 201–a, authorizes a consumer to commence a special proceeding to determine the validity of the lien in any court that would have monetary jurisdiction equal to the amount of the asserted lien.[3] If the consumer shows that the lien is improper, the court is required to vacate it and issue a judgment providing for the return of the vehicle to the consumer. If the lienor establishes the validity of the lien, the court may permit the sale to take place five days after service of the judgment.

Although Section 201–a provides a mechanism for consumers to seek relief from a lien, in practice the procedure is severely flawed, and, in many cases, it is of little actual value to consumers. Thus, Lien Law § 201–a is a statutory "protection" that cries out for legislative reform to make its promise a reality.

---

13. Lien Law § 201(2).
14. Lien Law § 201(3).
15. Lien Law § 201(4).
16. Lien Law § 201.
17. Lien Law § 201.

§ 7.29
1. Sharrock v. Dell Buick–Cadillac, Inc., 45 N.Y.2d 152, 408 N.Y.S.2d 39, 379 N.E.2d 1169 (1978).

2. Lien Law § 201–a.

3. *See infra*, §§ 7.57—7.59 for sample forms, including an Order to Show Cause, Petition, and Supporting Affirmation for commencing a Lien Law § 201–a proceeding.

The Section 201-a process is inherently problematic. Often, consumers do not receive the notice required by Section 201 at all, or it is received too late to challenge it. Even when the notice is timely received, it is difficult, if not impossible, for most consumers to take the steps necessary to challenge it in time. Consumers who attempt to commence a special proceeding *pro se* quickly discover that the courts are not set up to assist them with forms and procedural advice.[4] Many court clerks are simply unfamiliar with the entire Section 201-a procedure and are unable to provide any assistance to *pro se* consumers. Even if a consumer is willing to obtain an attorney to commence a Section 201-a proceeding, few attorneys are familiar with it, the lien amount or the value of the vehicle often does not justify the expenditure of more than nominal legal fees, and the statute does not provide for an award of attorney's fees to the successful consumer. Given all of these drawbacks, it is not surprising that few Section 201-a proceedings are brought. The consumer in this position either abandons the vehicle to the repair shop or pays inflated and improper charges to rescue the vehicle that is being held hostage.

A knowledgeable practitioner can provide substantial assistance to a consumer faced with a garageman's lien, often without spending a large amount of time. Because of the very limited time constraints imposed on the bringing of a Section 201-a proceeding, the first step the practitioner should take is to secure a stipulation from the repair shop, extending the consumer's time to challenge the lien. If the possibility of settling the claim without further expense is presented, most repair shops, or their attorneys, should be willing to enter into such an agreement. Once that agreement is reached, the practitioner has far greater leeway in preparing a Section 201-a challenge, if the matter cannot be settled.[5]

---

4. This differs greatly from the substantial assistance given to *pro se* litigants, particularly in New York City, in small claims court, housing court, and even in the Special Term of Civil Court when orders to show cause are brought to vacate default judgments. Because Section 201-a requires a consumer to commence a proceeding, where none existed before, they are often completely overwhelmed by the procedure.

5. **PRACTICE POINTER:** Because few Section 201-a proceedings are ever commenced, the auctioneers who prepare and serve sale notices are generally less concerned with ensuring full compliance with the requirements of Section 201. The practitioner must first analyze the notice of sale to determine if it complies with Lien Law § 201, both in substance and in the manner in which it was served. Repair shops typically fail to provide the "facts giving the nature of the debt or agreement under which the lien arose, with an itemized statement of the claim." Next, the underlying repair documents must be carefully reviewed to determine if the consumer either authorized or consented to the charges asserted by the lienor. Garagemen's liens usually include claims for unpaid storage charges accruing from the time the repairs were supposedly completed. Repair shop invoices typically attempt to indicate consent to such charges in the fine print in pre-printed authorizations on the forms. However, repair shops often neglect to secure a signature on the authorization. Even if it is signed, the pre-printed language usually does not include the storage charge amount; therefore consent is clearly lacking. Even if the consent is signed, *and* the form sets forth the storage charge amount, the form is usually printed in such small type that it is inadmissible in any court proceeding. CPLR 4544.

§ 7.29   CONSUMER LAW   Ch. 7

Although Section 201-a expressly provides that the proceeding to challenge the validity of the lien can be brought in any court that would have jurisdiction to render a money judgment equal to the amount of the lien, at least one New York City Civil Court judge has ruled that full relief can only be obtained in the supreme court. In *Maloney v. Rincon*,[6] the court stated that while it could determine the validity of the lien, and even could issue a judgment directing the vehicle's return to the owner, it lacked subject matter jurisdiction to restrain the sale of the vehicle pending the court's determination of the application. As a result, a Section 201-a proceeding may constitute an empty promise if it is brought in any court other than the supreme court, because the court may be powerless to stop the sale until the parties can be heard.[7]

§ 7.30 Credit Reporting—Overview

The importance of consumer credit, the ability to obtain it, and the need to use it, cannot be underestimated. In today's economy, access to credit, *i.e.*, credit cards, automobile loans, home mortgages, and many other types, is no longer a luxury; it is a fundamental necessity. In the fifty years since World War II, outstanding consumer debt has increased over one-hundred fold from six billion dollars to over seven hundred billion dollars, equal to thirty-thousand dollars of debt for every man, woman and child in America.[1] If credit is the lifeblood of the consumer economy, credit reports are the scorecard by which our ability to obtain it is measured.

One of the most frequent, and most difficult to resolve, problems faced by consumers is the presence of inaccurate or erroneous information on their credit report. For many consumers, credit reporting problems can be a nightmare that will not go away. All too often credit reports containing erroneous and obsolete information are used by potential creditors to make credit decisions. Otherwise creditworthy consumers routinely find themselves turned down for credit as a result of a potential creditor's reliance on information, contained in a credit report, which is either erroneous, incomplete, or obsolete. As a result of such false negative, or incomplete, information, lenders often deny credit to those to whom they would otherwise be willing to lend. Consumer

---

6. 153 Misc.2d 162, 581 N.Y.S.2d 120 (Civ.Ct., N.Y. County, 1992).

7. The *Maloney* decision cries out for the Legislature to amend either Section 201-a or the NYCCCA, as well as the UCCA, the UDCA and the UJCA, to expand those courts' equitable jurisdiction so that consumers do not have to proceed in supreme court to obtain full relief. So far, the Legislature has not acted. Fortunately, not all judges have chosen to follow *Maloney*. A practitioner faced with a potential *Maloney* problem would be wise to inquire of the clerks in Special Term as to whether the duty judge tends to follow or disregard *Maloney*. If it is the former, the practitioner might be well advised either to commence the proceeding in the supreme court or to wait for a different duty judge, in order to avoid having a restraining order stricken, thereby rendering the ultimate relief moot.

§ 7.30

1. S. Rep. 103-209, 103d Cong., 1st Sess. 2-3 (1993).

credit reports are produced and maintained by large, faceless, credit reporting agencies. The three largest credit reporting agencies in the United States are Experian (formerly known as TRW), Trans Union Credit Information Corporation, and Equifax Credit Information Services. Credit reporting agencies maintain files on virtually every person in the United States over 18 years old; over 450 billion credit files are maintained on over 110 million people, and these agencies process almost 2 billion pieces of data per month.[2] It has been estimated that almost half of all credit reports contain inaccurate information.[3] It is not difficult to understand, therefore, how credit reporting problems can become pervasive.

Consumers have certain rights in dealing with credit reporting agencies, such as the right to force the deletion of inaccurate or obsolete information or to force the agency to publish more complete information about them. Often, however, consumers find themselves unable, after extensive effort, to enforce even the most basic rights under the law. The Federal Trade Commission reports that consumers spend, on average, 23 weeks trying to resolve credit reporting disputes directly with the credit reporting agency before either giving up or seeking legal assistance.[4]

Attorneys may be of assistance to consumers facing these problems, but counsel must be aware of the specific limitations placed on consumer rights by the courts in order properly to advise and represent a client.

Extensive amendments to FCRA. Effective September 30, 1997, extensive amendments to the FCRA took effect.[5] While the amendments do not, in large part, diminish consumer rights under existing law, they add many important new ones. The practitioner should review the applicable amendments before pursuing any FCRA claim. The amendments pertain to three primary areas: (1) accuracy of information which can be reported about individuals; (2) access to credit reports and privacy; and (3) enforcement rights. A summary of the new amendments follows.

1) **Accuracy.** The FCRA now imposes accuracy requirements on businesses that supply information to reporting agencies. However, these requirements are not privately enforceable; they may only be enforced by federal and state officials. Businesses must properly reinvestigate items disputed by consumers and can be liable in a private suit if they do not. New rules also expressly restrict the reinsertion of previously deleted information. Accounts that are voluntarily closed at the consumer's request must be accurately reported as such. The period of measuring the obsolescence of an account is shortened to commence 180 days after it becomes delinquent, rather than from the time collection activity began.

2. *Id.,* p.3.
3. *Id.*
4. *Id.,* p.6.
5. Pub. L. No. 90–321.

Reporting agencies must complete investigations of disputed accuracy claims within 30 days. In doing so, reporting agencies are required to promptly notify the supplier of the disputed information of the dispute so that it can conduct its own investigation.

2) **Privacy.** Consumer privacy rights have been cut back under the new FCRA amendments which allow wider access to consumer credit reports by third parties than before. Commonly owned companies are now permitted to freely share credit information about consumers among themselves without having to meet the stringent requirements of need previously found in the statute.

The new FCRA also clarifies judicial confusion in the area of permissible purpose of third parties obtaining credit reports.[6] Previously, some courts have treated the "legitimate business need" category of 15 USCA § 1681b as a catch-all resulting in a complete evisceration of any privacy protection under the statute. The new amendments clarify and adopt the lead suggested by some courts and require that the consumer initiate any transaction which is used by a subscriber to justify obtaining their credit report.

3) **Enforcement.** Like other areas of the new FCRA, consumer rights are both expanded and decreased in the area of private enforcement. For the first time, consumers can now recover minimum statutory damages for wilful violations of the FCRA, or actual damages, instead of just actual damages as before. This amendment may alleviate the problem in the Second Circuit created by the *Casella* case.[7] The amendments do not affect availability of punitive damages for wilful violations.

In addition, companies that furnish information to credit reporting agencies (such as creditors and collection agencies) are liable for the first time under the FCRA, but only in limited ways. While the amendments impose extensive obligations on such information providers, violations of most of those requirements are not privately enforceable. Instead, consumers can only seek civil damages from furnishers who fail to properly reinvestigate consumer disputes filed with reporting agencies.

Finally, the new FCRA requires courts to award attorney's fees to any prevailing party on a motion, pleading "or other paper" which was filed in bad faith or for purposes of harassment. While this provision appears to restate FRCP 11, it should send a strong message to credit reporting agencies and their attorneys who may feel that they can wear down consumers with baseless litigation tactics.[8]

6. *See supra* note 6.
7. *See infra* § 7.33 note 7.
8. **CAVEAT**: As with any sweeping amendment, it remains to be seen how the courts will interpret the new FCRA. Hopefully, the new consumer rights and protections intended by Congress will result in actual judicial enforcement, rather than the blind refusal to follow the law as was seen previously in many cases.

§ 7.31 Credit Reporting—Consumer Rights

Both the federal Fair Credit Reporting Act[1] and the New York Fair Credit Reporting Act[2] provide, in theory at least,[3] fundamental consumer protections with regard to the accuracy and dissemination of credit information.[4] In enacting the FCRA, Congress found that:

> Consumer reporting agencies have assumed a vital role in assembling and evaluating consumer credit and other information on consumers. 15 U.S.C.A. § 1681(a)(3) ... It is the purpose of this title to require that consumer reporting agencies adopt reasonable procedures ... in a manner which is fair and equitable to the consumer, with regard to the confidentiality, accuracy, relevancy and proper utilization of such information ... 15 U.S.C.A. § 1681(b).

The FCRA requires credit reporting agencies to comply with its mandates by: maintaining and following "reasonable procedures" to avoid reporting obsolete information about a consumer,[5] to prevent consumer reports from being obtained by third parties for impermissible purposes,[6] and to assure "maximum possible accuracy of the information

---

§ 7.31

1. 15 U.S.C.A. §§ 1681 *et seq.*

2. General Business Law Art. 25 (§§ 380 *et seq.*).

3. **PRACTICE POINTER:** As discussed *infra*, although the statutory language appears to provide certain rights and protections to consumers, various court decisions have diminished those rights in certain key respects. The practitioner is advised to review all applicable case law carefully before assuming that a statutory protection can actually be enforced.

4. Although the federal and state statutes are similar in many respects, state law provides substantially greater rights in certain areas. Major differences between the two laws are discussed *infra*. References to similar provisions are cited to both statutes.

5. 15 U.S.C.A. § 1681e(a). Under Section 1681c, obsolete information is generally defined to include adverse information about the consumer that is more than seven years old. 15 U.S.C.A. § 1681c(a)(2)-(6). Bankruptcies can generally be reported for ten years. 15 U.S.C.A. § 1681c(a)(1). The prohibition against reporting obsolete information does not apply to credit reports used in connection with credit or life insurance applications with a principal amount in excess of $50,000.00. § 1681c(b). *See also,* General Business Law § 380–j(f)(1)-(2).

6. 15 U.S.C.A. § 1681b permits credit reporting agencies to disclose credit reports only to a party designated by the consumer to whom it relates (15 U.S.C.A. § 1681b(2)) or to any other person who intends to use the information in connection with a credit transaction, employment, or an insurance policy involving the consumer, or who "otherwise has a legitimate business need for the information in connection with a business transaction involving the consumer" (15 U.S.C.A. § 1681b(3)(E)). *See also,* General Business Law § 380–b.

PRACTICE POINTER: The "permissible purpose" provision of the FCRA is one of the few aspects of the statute that applies to persons who are not credit reporting agencies, such as creditors. Typically, creditors subscribe to one or more credit reporting agencies and thereby have the ability to receive credit reports, so long as the purpose for obtaining a particular report is one of those listed in Section 1681b. The FCRA permits suits against such "user(s) of information" who violate the act by obtaining a credit report for an impermissible purpose, under Sections 1681n and 1681o, or who knowingly obtain any information under false pretenses (15 U.S.C.A. § 1681q). *See also,* General Business Law §§ 380–b and 380–o.

The impermissible acquisition of credit reports by third parties is a growing problem. Many businesses, not realizing that

concerning the individual about whom the report relates."[7]

Consumers who find inaccurate, obsolete, or incomplete information on their report have certain rights to correct it. Section 1681i(a) of the Act requires a consumer to advise a credit reporting agency of any dispute regarding the "completeness or accuracy of any item of information contained in his file." Upon receipt of a dispute, the credit reporting agency is required, within a reasonable time, to reinvestigate the information and promptly delete it if it cannot be verified.[8]

If the reinvestigation does not resolve the dispute, the consumer is permitted to file a statement with the credit reporting agency outlining the dispute, and that statement must be included in any subsequently issued credit report.[9]

A substantial body of case law has developed over claims of disputed accuracy. Some courts have held that as long as the information contained in the report is technically accurate, although incomplete or misleading, there is no violation of the FCRA.[10] Some examples of "technically accurate" information border on the ridiculous. For exam-

the FCRA prohibits such conduct, obtain such information without a legitimate business purpose. Too often, credit reports are viewed simply as a source of information no different from motor vehicle records, which are generally available to the public. Businesses do this at substantial risk. Courts in New York have addressed this issue in a variety of contexts. Boothe v. TRW, 557 F.Supp. 66 (S.D.N.Y.1982) (obtaining credit report under false pretenses resulted in $15,000.00 punitive damage award); Klapper v. Shapiro, 154 Misc.2d 459, 586 N.Y.S.2d 846 (Sup.Ct., N.Y. County, 1992) (obtaining credit report to impeach a party in pending litigation is an impermissible purpose); People v. Warmus, 148 Misc.2d 374, 561 N.Y.S.2d 111 (Sup.Ct., Westchester County, 1990) (prosecutor does not have a permissible purpose to obtain a credit report on a criminal defendant).

Landlords sometimes obtain credit report information to determine if a tenant truly resides in a particular apartment. In New York City, for example, if a rent-stabilized or rent-controlled tenant does not maintain the apartment as a primary residence, the tenant is subject to eviction. A strong case can be made that obtaining such information for the purpose of establishing a cause of action of this nature is improper under both the federal and state FCRA's. *See* Chapter 13, "Landlord–Tenant Proceedings," *infra. See also,* Finkelstein and Ferrara, *Landlord and Tenant Practice in New York* (West 1997).

Inquiries by subscribers who obtain a credit report are listed on the report itself. Consumers should be advised to obtain and review their credit reports, from all three reporting agencies, at least annually and more often if they suspect someone might be accessing it improperly.

7. 15 U.S.C.A. § 1681e(b). *See also,* General Business Law § 380–j(e).

8. 15 U.S.C.A. § 1681i(a). *See also,* General Business Law § 380–f.

9. 15 U.S.C.A. § 1681i(b)-(c). *See also,* General Business Law § 380–f(c).

PRACTICE POINTER: If a credit reporting agency either deletes information or publishes a dispute statement as a result of a consumer's complaint, it is required to advise the consumer of his or her right to request notification of any person who received the consumer's report containing the deleted or disputed information within the previous six months or, if the report was used for employment purposes, within the previous two years. 15 U.S.C.A. § 1681i(d). *See also,* General Business Law § 380–f(b)(3), which expands the six-month federal period to one year.

10. Colletti v. Credit Bureau Services, 644 F.2d 1148 (5th Cir.1981); Todd v. Associated Credit Bureau Services, Inc., 451 F.Supp. 447 (E.D.Pa.1977), aff'd 578 F.2d 1376 (3d Cir.1978), cert. denied 439 U.S. 1068, 99 S.Ct. 834, 59 L.Ed.2d 33 (1979); Austin v. BankAmerica Service Corp., 419 F.Supp. 730 (N.D.Ga.1974).

ple, if a consumer is sued but successfully defends the action, and even recovers a judgment on a counterclaim against the plaintiff, it would be "technically accurate" to report simply that the suit was brought, although it is not difficult to argue that such a report would be so misleading and incomplete as to be inaccurate. Under the "technical accuracy" line of cases, a credit reporting agency might not be liable for failing to report the complete story. Fortunately, this appears to be the minority view. Other courts have questioned, and even rejected, the "technical accuracy" approach, instead focusing on the completeness of the information and whether it is obsolete or misleading.[11]

For example, it may be technically accurate to report the filing of a bankruptcy petition, but if the petition was withdrawn prior to discharge, it should not be the basis of a negative inference about the person. At the very least, reporting of the filing of the petition, without the withdrawal, is incomplete and misleading. A consumer faced with a situation like this should write to the credit reporting agency and demand a reinvestigation of the item, providing documentary proof of this position. If the information is not deleted, or at the very least amended, a suit under the FCRA should be considered.[12]

§ 7.32 Credit Reporting—Non-litigation Strategies

Consumers with inaccurate or incomplete credit reports generally have a single goal: to correct the report so that they can obtain credit. Often, consumers learn of erroneous information on their report as a result of having a credit application declined. When a credit application is denied, the creditor is required to advise the consumer that a particular credit report was used "wholly or partly" as a basis for the denial.[1] A

---

11. Henson v. CSC Credit Services, 29 F.3d 280 (7th Cir.1994); Pinner v. Schmidt, 805 F.2d 1258 (5th Cir.1986), cert. denied 483 U.S. 1022, 107 S.Ct. 3267, 97 L.Ed.2d 766 (1987); Koropoulos v. Credit Bureau Inc., 734 F.2d 37 (D.C.Cir.1984); Thompson v. San Antonio Retail Merchants Ass'n, 682 F.2d 509 (5th Cir.1982); Houston v. TRW Information Services, Inc., 707 F.Supp. 689 (S.D.N.Y.1989); Swoager v. Credit Bureau of Greater St. Petersburg, 608 F.Supp. 972 (M.D.Fla.1985); Bryant v. TRW, Inc., 487 F.Supp. 1234 (E.D.Mich.1980), aff'd 689 F.2d 72 (6th Cir.1982).

12. The failure to demand a reinvestigation resulted in a dismissal of a FCRA claim in McPhee v. Chilton Corp., 468 F.Supp. 494 (D.Conn.1978), where the reporting of the filing of a bankruptcy petition was technically accurate, even though not complete. The court distinguished between the credit reporting agency's obligation under Section 1681e(b) to prepare a report using maximum possible accuracy and the duty under Section 1681i to reinvestigate when completeness of the information is challenged.

PRACTICE POINTER: Given the state of the case law under the FCRA, consumers must exercise continual vigilance concerning their credit reports. If a consumer is planning to apply for credit, particularly a major loan, such as a mortgage, the consumer would be well advised to obtain copies of the most recent reports from all three reporting agencies well in advance of making an application. The consumer can then take steps to have inaccurate information deleted or incomplete information corrected, and, if necessary, to file a dispute statement.

§ 7.32

1. 15 U.S.C.A. § 1681m(a). *See also*, General Business Law § 380–i(a), which goes beyond the express terms of the FCRA and includes the denial of any residential lease, based at least partially on a credit

§ 7.32   CONSUMER LAW   Ch. 7

consumer is entitled to obtain a copy of his or her credit report, without charge, from the agency that provided it to the creditor within thirty days of the denial.[2] If, after reviewing the report, the consumer finds items that are either incomplete or inaccurate, the consumer should follow the procedures outlined in Section 1681i.[3]

Attorneys can provide substantial assistance to consumers who have damaging information on their credit reports. Very often the easiest way to obtain the deletion of an adverse entry on a credit report is to negotiate a resolution of the underlying claim directly with the creditor involved. Consumers often find a negative entry on their credit report when they are involved in a dispute with a creditor involving the underlying transaction. For example, the purchase of a defective automobile[4] or a financed sale or lease transaction that was misrepresented by the dealer or was otherwise deceptive[5] can result in the refusal by the consumer to make payments until the matter is resolved. An attorney faced with this type of problem must not only seek to resolve the underlying problem directly with the merchant and/or bank, but must treat the credit reporting problem as well.[6]

In handling such a dispute, once the underlying transaction is resolved an attorney may frequently secure an agreement by the creditor to direct the complete deletion of the transaction from the credit report or at least to report it as having been paid satisfactorily. A credit reporting agency receiving such an instruction is obligated to comply with it.[7] Even if the successful resolution of the underlying dispute does

report, as triggering the obligation to disclose the identity of the credit reporting agency supplying the report.

2.   15 U.S.C.A. § 1681j. *See also,* General Business Law § 380–d(c).

3.   PRACTICE POINTER: As a general rule, all communications with credit reporting agencies should be in writing and sent by certified mail, return receipt requested. The consumer should also provide copies of any documentary evidence that supports his or her complaint.

4.   *See supra,* §§ 7.9—7.18.

5.   *See supra,* §§ 7.19—7.23.

6.   PRACTICE POINTER: When a consumer disputes a debt, General Business Law § 601(5) prohibits a creditor from reporting any adverse information to a credit reporting agency pertaining to the debt without also reporting the dispute. Similarly, when the consumer's dispute is conveyed to a third-party collection agency, it is barred from adversely reporting the debt to a reporting agency without also advising that the debt is disputed. 15 U.S.C.A. § 1692e(8). *See infra,* § 7.40.

In notifying a creditor of a dispute pertaining to the underlying transaction, the attorney should demand that it refrain from submitting any adverse information to a credit reporting agency without also disclosing that the information is disputed by the consumer. A sample form notice of rejection and/or revocation of acceptance of an automobile, pursuant to UCC §§ 2–601, 2–608, containing such a demand, is contained in § 7.56.

7.   Written instructions to credit reporting agencies to delete, alter, or modify information pertaining to a particular creditor are conveyed on "Universal Data Forms" or "UDFs."

PRACTICE POINTER: In settling disputes with creditors that include a deletion or modification of the entry on a credit report, attorneys should require that they receive a copy of any UDF submitted to the reporting agency to insure that the agreement is followed. A sample form agreement used in settling a fraudulent automobile lease transaction is contained in § 7.61.

Attorneys should also be aware that adverse information can also be obtained from

not expressly include an agreement to delete the information, the attorney should demand its deletion from the reporting agency and provide a copy of the agreement establishing the resolution of the dispute. If the matter cannot be resolved informally, without litigation, the practitioner should consider commencing legal action under either the federal or state credit reporting acts.[8]

§ 7.33 Credit Reporting—Litigating Credit Reporting Matters

Not all credit reporting problems can be resolved without litigation. If the practitioner is unable to resolve a problem of erroneous credit reporting with the agency privately, counsel may wish to consider commencing an action to recover damages under federal and/or state law.[1]

Under the FCRA, the most common causes of action allege that the reporting agency failed to "follow reasonable procedures to assure maximum possible accuracy" of its reports,[2] that it failed to delete inaccurate information following a dispute filed by a consumer,[3] or that it failed or refused to publish the consumer's dispute statement following its refusal to delete the information.[4] A consumer may seek an award of actual damages resulting from the negligent failure to comply with the statute[5] and/or punitive damages based upon a willful failure to comply.[6] Also, public record sources, such as court clerks. For example, if the consumer's refusal to make payment results in a suit being filed, such filing may be reported independently of the creditor's transmission of that information to the reporting agency. In that situation, a creditor's agreement to file a UDF deleting the creditor's report would probably not cause deletion of the public record report. In order to obtain a deletion of the latter, the attorney should write directly to the reporting agency, enclosing a copy of the settlement agreement, and direct that the public record information be deleted as well.

Most importantly, attorneys should recognize that reporting agencies are either unable or unwilling to block previously deleted information from reappearing in later reports, if it is subsequently re-reported by the creditor via their automated computer tapes. A settlement agreement should therefore include a provision whereby the creditor agrees either to delete the information from its own records or otherwise agrees not to report it in the future.

8. See infra, § 7.33.

§ 7.33

1. A sample federal court Complaint, alleging violations of the federal FCRA, the state FCRA, and the Deceptive Practices Act may be found infra, § 7.60.

2. 15 U.S.C.A. § 1681e(b). See also, General Business Law § 380–j(e).

3. 15 U.S.C.A. § 1681i(a). See also, General Business Law § 380–f.

4. 15 U.S.C.A. § 1681i(b)-(c). See also, General Business Law § 380–f(c).

5. 15 U.S.C.A. § 1681o. See also, General Business Law § 380–m.

6. 15 U.S.C.A. § 1681n. See also, General Business Law § 380–l, which requires that the conduct be both willful and knowing. See Nitti v. Credit Bureau of Rochester, Inc., 84 Misc.2d 277, 375 N.Y.S.2d 817 (Sup.Ct., Monroe County, 1975).

CAVEAT: The Statute of Limitations for an action under the FCRA is two years from the date of the violation, regardless of when the consumer discovers it. 15 U.S.C.A. § 1681p. If, however, the consumer claims that the defendant materially and willfully misrepresented any information required to be disclosed under the FCRA, and such misrepresentation is material to the defendant's liability, the action may be brought within two years of discovery of the misrepresentation by the consumer. 15 U.S.C.A. § 1681p.

§ 7.33   CONSUMER LAW   Ch. 7

attorney's fees may be awarded in connection with a successful action to enforce the statute.

A major obstacle to enforcement of the FCRA was recently provided by a decision of the Second Circuit Court of Appeals. In *Casella v. Equifax Credit Information Services and Trans Union Corporation*,[7] the court held that in order to recover damages for emotional distress caused by a reporting agency's failure and refusal to delete erroneous information, the consumer's credit report must have been transmitted to a third party—for example, in connection with a credit application. The court held that, in the absence of such publication, a consumer cannot recover damages under the FCRA, even if the reporting agency had substantial reason to believe its files contained seriously erroneous information about the consumer.

The Second Circuit's decision is directly in conflict with FCRA decisions from at least two other federal circuit courts. In *Guimond v. Trans Union Credit Information Co.*,[8] the Ninth Circuit upheld an emotional distress claim under the FCRA, even without evidence of a credit denial or other publication of the report to a third party. In *Stewart v. Credit Bureau, Inc.*,[9] the District of Columbia Circuit similarly held that the FCRA does not limit recovery to damages caused by publication to third parties.

In *Casella*, the plaintiff also claimed that the defendant's failure to publish his dispute statement pursuant to Section 1681i(b) was actionable. The court disagreed.[10] The court did, however, recognize that, even in the absence of a showing of actual damages, a plaintiff can recover punitive damages for a willful violation of the FCRA.[11]

The *Casella* obstacle can likely be overcome by completely avoiding the FCRA and bringing an action under the New York Fair Credit

---

The Statute of Limitations under state law is identical to the federal provisions. General Business Law § 380–n.

7. 56 F.3d 469 (2d Cir.1995), cert. denied ___ U.S. ___, 116 S.Ct. 1452, 134 L.Ed.2d 571 (1996). This author represented the appellant in Casella.

8. 45 F.3d 1329 (9th Cir.1995).

9. 734 F.2d 47 (D.C.Cir.1984).

10. The Second Circuit's disagreement with this claim is puzzling at best since it was based upon the discredited notion that the plaintiff had not requested publication of his dispute statement. In the same decision, the court recognized that the plaintiff *had* in fact requested such publication, and the defendant reporting agency never fully explained why it had failed to publish it.

11. *But see supra*, § 7.30 for a discussion of recent change in the law that may alleviate the problem in the Second Circuit created by Casella. *See also,* Boothe v. TRW Credit Data, 557 F.Supp. 66, 71–72 (S.D.N.Y.1982).

PRACTICE POINTER: While the *Casella* case can be limited to its facts in many ways, it presents an important lesson to practitioners up against a reporting agency that stubbornly refuses to delete erroneous information. Despite the fact that, in the short term at least, additional harm might be caused to the consumer, the consumer should be advised to apply for credit even though the report contains erroneous information. Assuming that the application for credit is then denied, based upon a report that presumably contains the erroneous information, which the reporting agency knew was erroneous, the *Casella* obstacle will be obviated, and the claim should withstand a summary judgment motion.

Reporting Act.[12] That statute is far broader in its protections of consumers in several key respects.[13] For example, state law not only bars reporting agencies from reporting information "which it has reason to know is inaccurate,"[14] it also prohibits them from "maintain(ing) (such information) in the file on a consumer."[15] Thus, by its very terms, state law can be enforced even if the erroneous information was not the basis for a credit denial or even when the consumer never applied for credit, assuming that the consumer communicated to the reporting agency his or her dispute with regard to the accuracy of the information. Under Section 380-j(a)(3), the knowing maintenance by the reporting agency of the erroneous information in its files is actionable.[16]

If an erroneous credit report *has* caused the consumer to be denied credit, and therefore the *Casella* case is not an obstacle, the practitioner must decide where and how to bring the action. While claims under the federal FCRA and the state act can be maintained in the same action, if the case is brought in state court the defendant will likely bring a motion to remove the action to federal court. The practitioner should thus either

---

12. General Business Law Art. 25 (§§ 380 *et seq.*).

13. Nor can reporting agencies claim that the FCRA preempts state law, as 15 U.S.C.A. § 1681t provides that the FCRA "does not annul, alter, affect, or exempt any person subject to the provisions of this title from complying with the laws of any state with respect to the collection, distribution, or use of any information on consumers, except to the extent that those laws are inconsistent with any provision of this title, and then only to the extent of the inconsistency." Thus, any state law provision that is *more* protective of consumers is not preempted by the FCRA.

14. General Business Law § 380-j(a)(3).

15. General Business Law § 380-j(a).

16. **PRACTICE POINTER:** A consumer under a deadline to obtain a mortgage or other credit could be placed in the untenable position of either submitting the application, knowing his or her file contains the erroneous information, with the resulting likelihood that the application will be denied, or making repeated time-consuming efforts to convince all three credit reporting agencies to delete the information. Either choice could likely result in loss of the opportunity to purchase a home, either because of a denial of the mortgage or because of expiration of the time to obtain financing.

General Business Law § 380-j(a)(3) provides a reasonably expeditious solution to this dilemma. The consumer or the attorney should immediately issue dispute statements to all three reporting agencies, providing detailed factual and documentary information fully supporting the consumer's side of the dispute. The reporting agencies should be advised of the special circumstances of the request and that time is of the essence. The reporting agency is then required to "promptly re-investigate" the dispute and then "promptly notify the consumer of the result." General Business Law § 380-f(a). Hopefully, this exercise will result in the desired goal of having the erroneous information deleted, in which case the credit application can then be filed.

If this effort is not successful, the practitioner should consider immediately commencing an action under General Business Law § 380 in supreme court, by Order to Show Cause, seeking a Temporary Restraining Order barring the continued reporting of the erroneous information. In order to do so, the practitioner will have to show that the continued violation of Section 380-j(a)(3) will cause the consumer to suffer irreparable harm. CPLR 6301, 6313. In any event, this action will quickly get the reporting agency's attention and will likely make it necessary for it to appear before a judge on short notice to explain its unwillingness to delete the information. In all probability, the information will then quickly be deleted.

commence the action in federal court or bring the action in state court raising state claims only.

Certain types of credit reporting lawsuits are far easier to prove than others—for example, a case in which the claim of inaccuracy cannot seriously be challenged. This type of claim most often exists when the reporting agency has merged the information of two or more people, with similar names, into the plaintiff's report. In this case, the plaintiff can easily establish that he or she never had, or even applied for, a particular credit account.[17]

In order to establish a FCRA claim effectively, the practitioner must be prepared to engage in extensive discovery, including document requests, interrogatories, and depositions. The focus of the discovery should not be on the highly technical computer systems used by the reporting agency. Instead, the practitioner should concentrate on how the consumer's complaint was handled, how the dispute was investigated, and whether that conduct was reasonable. If the inquiry is directed to whether the reporting agency's actions showed common sense, or if its actions were arbitrary, unreasonable, or callous in disregarding the consumer's rights, it will be far easier for the trier of fact to find for the plaintiff. A plaintiff should always seek a jury trial in credit reporting actions. It will be extremely difficult for the reporting agency to find many jurors who have not had credit reporting problems themselves. Many jurors also are likely to have friends or relatives who have suffered from experiences similar to the plaintiff's.

§ 7.34   Debt Collection—History and Overview

Abusive and harassing debt collection practices have plagued consumers as long as credit has existed. For decades, creditors seeking to collect overdue bills have employed various tactics and devices to convince reluctant debtors to pay their bills. Many creditors, unwilling to limit their collection practices to the bounds of civility, have crossed the line into abuse, harassment, and deception. Sometimes consumers have been dunned for bills they simply did not owe, that were already paid, or that were subject to a valid defense to payment. Studies have repeatedly found that abusive and harassing debt collection practices play a major role in increasing the loss of jobs, marital and familial instability, bankruptcies, and invasions of privacy.

Unfortunately, the judicial system was initially slow to respond to the plight of consumers victimized by improper collection practices. Many judges, more sympathetic to business interests, turned a deaf ear to the plight of the abused debtor. During the 1930's, when many

---

17. Many people assume that files cannot be merged, because they erroneously believe that reporting agencies require an exact match of at least the full name, date of birth, and social security number of the consumer before placing information in the file. Unfortunately, reporting agencies require far less information in order to find a match. As a result, merged files are relatively common.

Americans were out of work and unable to pay their bills, creditors found themselves competing for fewer and fewer dollars. Collectors quickly found that some debtors paid those who were making their lives the most miserable and ignored the rest. Soon, it became apparent to many collection agencies who had sprung up all over the country that the quickest way to squeeze a payment out of a debtor was to call him repeatedly, threaten him and his family, yell and curse at him, until he paid.

The courts were generally unsympathetic to such abuses, because those who did not pay their bills, regardless of the reason, were viewed as "deadbeats" who threatened the economic survival of businesses. Businesses claimed that these "deadbeats" caused "legitimate" consumers to pay more to make up for their losses. These theories were not, however, based upon serious analysis. Studies performed by social researchers found that, in reality, the "deadbeat debtor" who incurred debt without any expectation of ever paying it back was actually quite rare. It was also found that most debtors honestly wanted to pay their debts and simply found themselves in situations, such as illness, divorce, or unemployment, that either temporarily or permanently prevented them from being able to make their payments. Collection agencies, concerned only with bringing in payments, began treating all debtors the same—as "deadbeats" who did not deserve to be treated with civility and respect. Debt collection abuses flourished as a result.

§ 7.35 Debt Collection—Claims for Intentional Infliction of Emotional Distress

Prior to the enactment of legislation protecting abused debtors, consumers could resort only to common-law remedies, such as claims for intentional infliction of emotional distress, defamation, and invasion of privacy. The courts, however, were not quick to allow debtors to pursue these remedies, except in the most egregious situations.

The first reported New York appellate decision to address and define intentional infliction of emotional distress arising out of the debtor-creditor relationship was *Long v. Beneficial Finance Co. of New York, Inc.*[1] The *Long* decision, which has been extensively followed by other courts, held that this cause of action must meet the standards set forth in the *Restatement (Second) Torts*.[2] The plaintiff in *Long* alleged that the creditor's employee regularly contacted her at work, called her neighbors, and visited her house, causing her to lose her job and to suffer mental distress and a serious heart attack. The court upheld part of the complaint, saying that these facts were sufficient under the *Restatement*, which requires that the offending conduct be "so outrageous in charac-

§ 7.35
1. 39 A.D.2d 11, 330 N.Y.S.2d 664 (4th Dep't 1972).

2. *Restatement (Second) Torts*, § 46.

ter, and so extreme in degree, as to go beyond all bounds of decency, and to be regarded as atrocious, and utterly intolerable in a civilized society."[3]

Following *Long*, courts in New York have repeatedly rejected intentional infliction of emotional distress claims arising out of abusive debt collection practices. It was not until the late 1970's that statutory prohibitions against such practices were first enacted.

§ 7.36 Debt Collection—Statutory Overview

Debt collection practices are covered by federal and New York State law. The federal "Fair Debt Collection Practices Act"[1] ("FDCPA") was enacted in 1978 as part of the Truth-in-Lending Act.[2] The New York "Debt Collection Procedures Act"[3] was enacted in 1973. Both laws protect consumers only, and do not cover debts owed by businesses.[4]

The FDCPA applies to agencies in the business of collecting debts owed to others,[5] creditors who collect debts owed to themselves but who do not use their own names in doing so,[6] and attorneys engaged in the business of collecting consumer debts.[7]

The FDCPA applies primarily to third-party collectors and generally does not cover creditors collecting debts in their own names.[8] State law, however, applies both to third-party collectors as well as to creditors themselves.[9] The FDCPA does not apply to a person who only occasionally collects debts.[10]

§ 7.37 Debt Collection—FDCPA—Contacts With Third Parties

Under the FDCPA, a debt collector cannot contact a third party, except a credit reporting agency, for any information other than to

3. *Restatement (Second) Torts*, § 46, comment d.

§ 7.36

1. 15 U.S.C.A. §§ 1692 *et seq. See also,* Borges *et al., Enforcing Judgments and Collecting Debts in New York* (West 1997) Ch.2 "Liability for Unfair Collection Practices."

2. 15 U.S.C.A. §§ 1601 *et seq.*

3. General Business Law Art. 29–H (§§ 600 *et seq.*).

4. 15 U.S.C.A. § 1692a(5); General Business Law § 600(1).

5. 15 U.S.C.A. § 1692a(6).

6. 15 U.S.C.A. § 1692a(6).

7. *See generally,* Heintz v. Jenkins, 514 U.S. 291, 115 S.Ct. 1489, 131 L.Ed.2d 395 (1995); Clomon v. Jackson, 988 F.2d 1314 (2d Cir.1993). *See infra,* § 7.62 for a sample form Complaint against an attorney, alleging violations of the FDCPA. Borges *et al., Enforcing Judgments and Collecting Debts in New York* (West 1997) ¶¶ 2:16–2:24.

8. 15 U.S.C.A. § 1692a(6). The primary exception here is that the FDCPA does apply to a creditor who collects its own debts by using a name that suggests that it is a third-party collector. 15 U.S.C.A. § 1692a(6).

9. General Business Law § 601 provides that the act's prohibitions apply to a "principal creditor . . . or his agent."

10. 15 U.S.C.A. § 1692a(6)(F).

PRACTICE POINTER: State law is broader in this regard in that it covers any "agent" of a "principal creditor," without any limitation with regard to the frequency with which such agent engages in debt collection. General Business Law §§ 600(3), 601.

obtain location information about the debtor.[1] When attempting to locate a debtor, collectors are limited in how they may communicate with third parties. They may only ask for the debtor's residence, telephone number, and place of employment.[2] They must identify themselves by their own name to third persons, but must not disclose the name of their employer, unless the person contacted asks them to. The collector must not communicate with that person more than once, unless reasonably necessary, and must not reveal the debt to the third party. However, if the collector knows the debtor has retained an attorney, the collector is prohibited from communicating with any third party except that attorney.[3]

§ 7.38 Debt Collection—FDCPA—Contacts With a Debtor

Under state law, a collector is prohibited from disclosing or threatening to disclose false information about a consumer's creditworthiness.[1] State law also prohibits the collector from communicating or threatening to communicate the nature of a debt to the consumer's employer before obtaining a judgment.[2] Even after obtaining a judgment, the collector's communications must not disparage the consumer.[3]

A collector may make reasonable efforts to discuss a debt with a consumer, but he cannot overstep certain legal bounds, and the consumer has the right to restrict these discussions.

The FDCPA permits a collector to call a debtor only between 8 a.m. and 9 p.m.[4] Moreover, a collector may not call at a time or place known to be inconvenient to the debtor.[5] The collector may not call a debtor at a place of employment if it is known that the employer prohibits such calls.[6] If the collector knows the debtor is represented by an attorney, only the attorney may be contacted, and not the debtor directly, unless the attorney fails to respond to such contacts.[7]

Under the FDCPA, a debtor can stop all debt collection communications by demanding in writing that the collector refrain from further contact or by advising the collector that he or she refuses to pay the debt. After receiving such written notice, the collector may contact the

---

§ 7.37

1. 15 U.S.C.A. § 1692c(b). Borges et al., Enforcing Judgments and Collecting Debts in New York (West 1997) ¶¶ 2:78–2:92.
2. 15 U.S.C.A. §§ 1692b, 1692a(7).
3. 15 U.S.C.A. § 1692b.

§ 7.38

1. General Business Law § 601(3). Borges et al., Enforcing Judgments and Collecting Debts in New York (West 1997) ¶¶ 2:58–2:77.
2. General Business Law § 601(4).
3. General Business Law § 601(3).
4. 15 U.S.C.A. § 1692c(a)(1).
5. 15 U.S.C.A. § 1692c(a)(1).
6. 15 U.S.C.A. § 1692c(a)(3).
7. 15 U.S.C.A. §§ 1692b(6), 1692c(a)(2).

debtor again only to explain that a lawsuit or other legal action may be commenced.[8]

Within five days of an initial communication from a collection agency, the agency must send a written notice to the debtor, which notice includes: the amount of the debt, the name of the creditor, a statement that unless the debtor disputes the validity of the debt within thirty days it will be assumed to be valid, and a statement that if the debt is disputed in writing the collector will obtain verification of it and provide it to the debtor.[9] If a debtor exercises his or her rights under the federal statute and either disputes the validity of the debt or demands verification of it, the collection agency is required to cease all collection activity until it provides the required information.[10]

§ 7.39 Debt Collection—FDCPA—Prohibited Tactics

The FDCPA prohibits a collector from making false or misleading representations.[1] Conduct of this nature includes false, deceptive, or misleading representations about the collector's identity,[2] falsely stating the name of the collector's employer,[3] falsely stating or implying that the collector is connected with any governmental body or that written communications originated from, or have been approved by, any court or official agency,[4] falsely stating or implying that the collector is an attorney,[5] falsely stating the amount, character, or legal status of the debt,[6] and threatening any action that cannot legally be taken or that is

---

8. 15 U.S.C.A. § 1692c(c).

PRACTICE POINTER: This provision is one of the most significant for debtors under the FDCPA. It permits a debtor to "shut off" all further communications from the collection agency. The debtor must exercise this right in writing, and, like all communications from consumers to businesses, this notice should be sent by certified mail, return receipt requested. The practitioner can assert this right on behalf of a client, and the Section 1692c(c) demand should be made in conjunction with a demand, under Section 1692c(a)(2), to address any further communication regarding the debt to the attorney. This demand does not, however, constitute an agreement to accept service of process on behalf of the client.

CAVEAT: Both the client and the practitioner should be aware that, depending on the amount of the debt involved, the assertion of a "shut-off" demand may accelerate the commencement of a lawsuit against the consumer. If the consumer is suffering from abusive or harassing collection practices, however, this right should be asserted regardless of the possibility of suit.

9. 15 U.S.C.A. § 1692g(a).

10. 15 U.S.C.A. § 1692g(b).

PRACTICE POINTER: A consumer asserting rights under Section 1692g should also be advised to demand the cessation of all collection activity under Section 1692c(c). If the notice is sent by the attorney, a demand that there be no further communication with the debtor, pursuant to Sections 1692b(6) and 1692c(b), should also be made.

§ 7.39

1. 15 U.S.C.A. § 1692e. Borges *et al.*, *Enforcing Judgments and Collecting Debts in New York* (West 1997) ¶¶ 2:93–2:121.

2. 15 U.S.C.A. §§ 1692d(6), 1692e(1), 1692e(3), 1692e(14).

3. 15 U.S.C.A. § 1692e(14).

4. 15 U.S.C.A. § 1692e(9).

5. 15 U.S.C.A. § 1692e(3).

6. 15 U.S.C.A. § 1692e(2)(A).

not intended to be taken.[7]

§ 7.40 Debt Collection—FDCPA—Improper Omissions and Disclosures

Collection agencies are prohibited from failing to provide adequate disclosure of the reason for contacting a consumer,[1] from communicating by post card or from using any symbol or language, other than the collector's return address, on any envelope sent to a consumer.[2] The collection agency's name may appear on the envelope of mail sent to a debtor only if the agency does not indicate that it is in the debt collection business.[3] A collection agency may not disclose the debt to a third party or provide false information about the debt to a credit reporting agency.[4]

---

[7]. 15 U.S.C.A. § 1692e(5). This is one of the most commonly violated provisions of the FDCPA, particularly when collection agencies threaten to commence suit over relatively small sums of money. If it can be shown that a particular creditor rarely, if ever, commences suit for an amount below a certain threshold, a "boiler-plate" threat of suit for such amount is illegal. *See infra*, § 7.62 for a sample complaint against an attorney, alleging deceptive debt collection practices in violation of the FDCPA.

PRACTICE POINTER: Suits cannot be commenced in New York directly by collection agencies unless the claim has been assigned to it by the creditor. And, collection agencies are barred from purchasing accounts from creditors solely for the purpose of commencing suit. Such conduct constitutes champerty, in violation of Judiciary Law § 489. Thus, a collector that threatens suit directly, without an intent to purchase the debt from the creditor, is acting in violation of Section 1692e(5).

If a collection agency has the right to sue on a particular debt, Section 1692i(a)(2) provides that such suit can only be brought in the county where the consumer signed the contract being sued upon or where the consumer lives at the time of the commencement of the action. In New York, the CPLR provides a similar provision for any "consumer credit transaction" lawsuit. CPLR 105(f); 503(f). These provisions were designed to prevent "distant forum abuse," whereby large numbers of consumers are sued by large creditors in a distant location, with the expectation of obtaining default judgments. *See generally*, Spiegel, Inc. v. FTC, 540 F.2d 287 (7th Cir.1976).

§ 7.40

[1]. 15 U.S.C.A. § 1692e(11). This section requires collection agencies to disclose in all communications with the debtor, including oral communications, that it is attempting to collect a debt and that any information obtained will be used for that purpose.

[2]. 15 U.S.C.A. § 1692f(8).

[3]. 15 U.S.C.A. § 1692f(7)-(8). The primary purpose of these provisions is the preservation and protection of the debtor's privacy.

[4]. 15 U.S.C.A. § 1692c(b). Collection agencies may, however, discuss the debt with a third party, if consent to do so is given by the debtor, a court orders it, or it is reasonably necessary to effectuate a post-judgment remedy. In addition, collection agencies are permitted to discuss the debt with an attorney representing either the debtor, the creditor, or the collection agency. Collection agencies are also permitted to disclose accurate information about the debt to a credit reporting agency.

PRACTICE POINTER: Many of the larger collection agencies are subscribers to one or more credit reporting agencies and regularly report unpaid debts to them. 15 U.S.C.A. § 1692e(8) prohibits a collection agency from either communicating or threatening to communicate credit information to "any person," including a credit reporting agency, that it knows or should know is false, and it also prohibits them from failing to advise the credit reporting agency that a disputed debt is disputed. It is therefore essential for a consumer who disputes the validity of any debt to advise the collection agency in writing at the earliest possible opportunity, under Section 1692g(b).

§ 7.41 Debt Collection—FDCPA—Harassment or Abuse

The FDCPA prohibits the use of any conduct, "the natural consequence of which is to harass, oppress, or abuse any person in connection with the collection of a debt."[1] This includes the following conduct: (1) using or threatening violence or harm to the consumer, the consumer's reputation, or the consumer's property;[2] (2) using obscene language;[3] (3) placing annoying or repetitive telephone calls to any person;[4] (4) placing anonymous telephone calls;[5] (5) falsely stating that the result of nonpayment will be arrest, imprisonment, seizure of property, or salary garnishment, unless such action would be lawful and the creditor actually intends to take it;[6] (6) advertising the sale of the debt to coerce payment;[7] (7) claiming that the collector is a "holder-in-due-course" and thus misleading the consumer into believing that the consumer will be unable later to assert defenses in court concerning the debt; or (8) falsely claiming that a transfer of the debt will result in subjecting the consumer to any practice prohibited by the FDCPA.[8]

§ 7.42 Debt Collection—FDCPA—Improper Demands

Collection agencies are barred under the FDCPA from the following practices: (1) soliciting or accepting checks that have been postdated by up to five days, if the collector intends to deposit a check prior to its date or to threaten criminal prosecution;[1] (2) collecting an additional fee or interest charge not expressly allowed by law or by the contract creating the debt;[2] and (3) charging the debtor with collect calls or telegram fees.[3]

§ 7.43 Debt Collection—FDCPA—Judicial Enforcement

Under the FDCPA, an individual may bring an action either in state or federal court within one year of the alleged violation.[1] In such an action, the consumer may recover actual damages, statutory damages of $1,000.00, and attorney's fees.[2] A collection agency may raise an affirmative defense to a claim if it can show that the violation of the FDCPA

§ 7.41
1. 15 U.S.C.A. § 1692d.
2. 15 U.S.C.A. § 1692d(1).
3. 15 U.S.C.A. § 1692d(2).
4. 15 U.S.C.A. § 1692d(5).
5. 15 U.S.C.A. § 1692d(6).
6. 15 U.S.C.A. § 1692e(4).
7. 15 U.S.C.A. § 1692d(4).
8. 15 U.S.C.A. § 1692e(6)(A)-(B).

§ 7.42
1. 15 U.S.C.A. § 1692f(2)-(3).
2. 15 U.S.C.A. § 1692f(1). Even the demand for such a fee or charge, without actually collecting it, would violate Section 1692e(5), if such a charge cannot legally be collected, or Section 1692e(2), which prohibits the false representation of any compensation that may lawfully be received by a collection agency.
3. 15 U.S.C.A. § 1692f(5).

§ 7.43
1. 15 U.S.C.A. § 1692k(d). Borges *et al.*, *Enforcing Judgments and Collecting Debts in New York* (West 1997) ¶¶ 2:214–2:215.
2. 15 U.S.C.A. § 1692k(a).

CAVEAT: The Statute of Limitations under the FDCPA is one year from the date of the occurrence of the violation. 15 U.S.C.A. § 1692m(g).

was not intentional and that it resulted from a *bona fide* error, notwithstanding the maintenance of procedures reasonably designed to avoid any such error.[3]

The response by the courts to claims under the FDCPA has been mixed, at best. In the Second Circuit, however, FDCPA claims have generally fared well. In *Clomon v. Jackson*,[4] for example, the court affirmed a $1,000.00 statutory penalty, plus attorney's fees, in an action brought against an attorney who had allowed his name to be used by a collection agency that sent out a mass mailing to collect allegedly overdue magazine subscriptions. The defendant's dunning letters indicated that the attorney had actually reviewed the file of each debtor who received the letters. The court found this practice to be illegal, in violation of the FDCPA's proscription against any false, deceptive, or misleading representations.

The court in *Clomon* also confirmed that the standard of review in determining if collection practices are misleading is whether the "least sophisticated consumer," rather than the average or "reasonable" consumer, would be deceived by the practice. This standard complies with the generally accepted standard of deception in consumer protection matters.

In another case, the Second Circuit court held, in *Bentley v. Great Lakes Collection Bureau, Inc.*,[5] that a collection agency that threatened suit against a debtor, when the creditor had not authorized such action, was in violation of the FDCPA.

In yet another Second Circuit case, *Paulemon v. Tobin*,[6] the court applied the FDCPA to a pre-litigation letter that was sent to a debtor by an attorney, where the letter falsely suggested that suit was imminent. The ruling confirmed that the FDCPA applies to a broad range of activities by attorneys attempting to collect debts on behalf of creditors and that, as a general rule, attorneys are treated no differently under the FDCPA than are collection agencies. Recently, the United States Supreme Court held that the FDCPA applies to attorneys who regularly engage in debt collection activity, including litigation.[7] In this case, *Heintz v. Jenkins*,[8] the attorney had sent a false, deceptive, and misleading letter to the debtor's attorney. This letter allegedly sought collection of an amount not authorized by the underlying contract, in violation of 15 U.S.C.A. § 1692f(1). The court refused to find an exemption from the FDCPA on behalf of attorneys who seek to collect debts through litigation.[9]

3. 15 U.S.C.A. § 1692k(c).
4. 988 F.2d 1314 (2d Cir.1993).
5. 6 F.3d 60 (2d Cir.1993).
6. 30 F.3d 307 (2d Cir.1994).
7. Heintz v. Jenkins, 514 U.S. 291, 115 S.Ct. 1489, 131 L.Ed.2d 395 (1995).
8. *Id.*
9. **CAVEAT:** As a result of the *Jenkins* decision, *all* attorneys who regularly attempt to collect consumer debts must be aware of and comply with the FDCPA. Following the court's decision, a number of bar associations and private organizations have

§ 7.44 Debt Collection—State Law

The New York State Debt Collection Procedures Law[1] is far less expansive than the federal statute in its prohibition of certain practices, as well as in its applicability to individual actions, yet it is more expansive in its coverage.

Unlike the FDCPA, the state law applies not only to third-party collectors but to creditors as well.[2] The state statute bars the following conduct: (1) communications with the debtor or the debtor's family so frequently, at such an unusual hour, or in a manner that reasonably could be expected to abuse or harass the debtor;[3] (2) falsely stating or implying that a collector is a law enforcement officer or a representative of a government agency, or using written communications that simulate legal or judicial papers or imply official authorization;[4] (3) charging the debtor a fee or cost not legally chargeable against them;[5] (4) disclosing or threatening to disclose a debt, known to be disputed, to a third party without also disclosing the dispute;[6] and (4) threatening any action that the collector does not intend to take and that would not be taken in the ordinary course of business.[7] Similarly, collectors may not threaten any action that the creditor or collector has no legal right to take.[8]

The courts have held that the state debt collection law cannot be enforced by private individuals seeking redress for illegal collection practices, *unless* the conduct was deceptive.[9] In that event, the consumer can assert a claim under the Deceptive Practices Act.[10] As a result, consumers in New York cannot sue creditors, for even the most egregious debt collection practices, under any statutory theory. As shown above,[11] common law claims are not easily asserted, either.

Consumer advocates have long lobbied for an amendment to the New York law to extend the protections of the FDCPA to claims against creditors, without success. To date, creditors have prevented the enact-

---

begun to offer FDCPA compliance training sessions and materials. Consumer debt collection should not be attempted by attorneys who have not familiarized themselves with such materials.

§ 7.44

1. General Business Law Art. 29–H. Borges *et al.*, *Enforcing Judgments and Collecting Debts in New York* (West 1997) ¶¶ 2:248–2:279.

2. General Business Law § 601 provides that the act's prohibitions apply to a "principal creditor ... or his agent."

3. General Business Law § 601(6).

4. General Business Law § 601(1), (9).

5. General Business Law § 601(2).

6. General Business Law § 601(5).

7. General Business Law § 601(7).

8. General Business Law § 601(8).

9. Varela v. Investors Insurance, 81 N.Y.2d 958, 598 N.Y.S.2d 761, 615 N.E.2d 218 (1993). *See* General Business Law § 602(2), which permits only the Attorney General or any district attorney to enforce the statute.

10. General Business Law Art. 22–A. *See infra*, §§ 7.45—7.47. *See infra*, § 7.62 for a sample form complaint alleging deceptive collection practices in violation of General Business Law Art. 29–H and General Business Law § 349.

11. *See supra*, § 7.45.

ment of comprehensive legislation designed to close this glaring loophole.[12]

§ 7.45 Deceptive Practices Act—Overview

Perhaps the most important consumer protection statute in New York is the Deceptive Practices Act, formally known as "Consumer Protection From Deceptive Acts and Practices."[1]

General Business Law § 349(a) provides:

Deceptive acts or practices in the conduct of *any business, trade or commerce or in the furnishing of any service* in this state are hereby declared unlawful. (emphasis added)

General Business Law § 349(g) provides:

This section shall apply to *all deceptive acts or practices* declared to be unlawful, *whether or not subject to any other law of this state*, and shall not supersede, amend or repeal any other law of this state under which the attorney general is authorized to take any action or conduct any inquiry. (emphasis added)

General Business Law Article 22-A, which includes the Deceptive Practices Act as well as the False Advertising Act,[2] is similar to "Unfair and Deceptive Acts and Practices" statutes, or "UDAPs," found in 45 other states.[3] UDAP's are modeled after, and given complimentary construction with, Section 5 of the FTC Act.[4] The Deceptive Practices Act is also given parallel construction to Executive Law § 63(12), which permits the Attorney General to prosecute consumer fraud when a business engages in "persistent fraud or illegality."[5]

Unlike UDAP's in many other states, the Deceptive Practices Act is not limited to any particular conduct, businesses, or activity. Instead, the

---

12. *See,* Fishman, *New York Needs A Private Right of Action for Debt-Collection Abuse,* N.Y.L.J., 6/23/83, p.1, col.1; *Creating a Private Cause of Action Under the New York Fair Debt Collection Practices Act,* 50 Rec. Ass'n Bar City N.Y. #3 (April 1995).

§ 7.45

1. General Business Law Art. 22-A (§§ 349 et seq.).

2. General Business Law § 350.

3. Strictly speaking General Business Law § 349 is not a UDAP because, unlike UDAP's in most states, the statute does not specifically bar conduct that is "unfair" as opposed to conduct that is "deceptive." Despite this, many courts in New York have interpreted Section 349 as implicitly barring conduct that is unfair as well.

4. 15 U.S.C.A. § 45(a)(1).

PRACTICE POINTER: As a result, practitioners and courts can, and should, look to FTC trade regulations, guides, cease and desist and consent orders, FTC commentaries, and judicial decisions under Section 5 in analyzing a claim under the Deceptive Practices Act. Oswego Laborers' v. Marine Midland Bank, 85 N.Y.2d 20, 623 N.Y.S.2d 529, 647 N.E.2d 741 (1995); State v. Colorado State Christian College, 76 Misc.2d 50, 346 N.Y.S.2d 482 (Sup.Ct., N.Y. County, 1973). In addition, since UDAP's in every other state are also modeled after the FTC Act, the practitioner should review relevant decisions from other states as well. An excellent source of nationwide UDAP material, both commentary and case law, is Sheldon, *Unfair and Deceptive Acts and Practices,* National Consumer Law Center, 18 Tremont Street, Boston, MA.

5. Colorado State Christian College, *supra* note 4.

§ 7.46 Deceptive Practices Act—Elements of the Claim

The basis for a claim that the defendant violated the Deceptive Practices Act is simply that the complained-of practice was deceptive or misleading in a material respect and that the person asserting the claim was injured as a result.[1] The plaintiff is not required to show that any actual damages were incurred, as the act permits the recovery of statutory minimum damages of fifty dollars.[2] It is also not necessary that the claimant establish that he or she actually relied upon the defendant's misrepresentation or deceptive practice, or even that the claimant was actually deceived.[3] Instead, the challenged conduct must have had the "capacity, tendency or effect in deceiving or misleading (consumers)."[4]

It has been held that the defendant's conduct need only have had the capacity or tendency to deceive the "vast multitude which includes the ignorant, the unthinking and the credulous ... The test is not whether the average (person) would be deceived."[5] However, it has also been said that in determining whether the average consumer would be deceived by the challenged conduct, the court must determine if it is "likely to mislead a reasonable consumer acting reasonably under the circumstances."[6]

The Deceptive Practices Act is a particularly valuable tool because, unlike a common-law fraud claim, it is not necessary that the claimant either allege or establish that the defendant's conduct was intentional or reckless;[7] instead the Act is a strict liability statute.

It is apparent that the Legislature intended the Deceptive Practices Act to be a "powerful remedy to right commercial wrongs," far easier to employ than a common-law fraud claim, which requires a showing of

---

6. Because the statute is limited to "business" activity, it cannot, under any theory, be used against consumers or against anyone engaging in non-business activity.

§ 7.46

1. General Business Law § 349(h). McDonald v. North Shore Yacht Sales, Inc., 134 Misc.2d 910, 513 N.Y.S.2d 590 (Sup.Ct., Nassau County, 1987); Geismar v. Abraham & Strauss, 109 Misc.2d 495, 439 N.Y.S.2d 1005 (Dist.Ct., Nassau County, 1981). See also, Givens, *Practice Commentaries*, General Business Law § 349, p.565.

2. General Business Law § 349(h).

3. Oswego Laborers' v. Marine Midland Bank, 85 N.Y.2d 20, 623 N.Y.S.2d 529, 647 N.E.2d 741 (1995).

4. Guggenheimer v. Ginzburg, 43 N.Y.2d 268, 401 N.Y.S.2d 182, 372 N.E.2d 17 (1977); Geismar, *supra* note 1.

5. People v. Volkswagen of America, Inc., 47 A.D.2d 868, 366 N.Y.S.2d 157 (1st Dep't 1975); Guggenheimer, *supra* note 4.

6. Oswego Laborers', *supra* note 3, 623 N.Y.S.2d at 533.

7. Allstate Insurance Co. v. Foschio, 93 A.D.2d 328, 462 N.Y.S.2d 44, 47 (2d Dep't 1983); State v. Colorado State Christian College, 76 Misc.2d 50, 346 N.Y.S.2d 482 (Sup.Ct., N.Y. County, 1973); Geismar, *supra* note 1. If the plaintiff establishes that the defendant acted wilfully, however, the court is permitted to treble the plaintiff's actual damages, up to a maximum of $1,000.00. General Business Law § 349(h); Oswego Laborers', *supra* note 3.

intent and reliance by the claimant. As a remedial statute, the Deceptive Practices Act is therefore afforded a broad application.[8]

In order to be actionable under the statute, however, the conduct must be "consumer oriented."[9] Although a consumer is not required to establish that the conduct was engaged in repeatedly, either to the same plaintiff or to other consumers, or that it constitutes a "pattern of deceptive behavior," it must be shown that the practices are of a "recurring nature," which "have a broader impact on consumers at large."[10] The statute is not applicable to a "private commercial dispute" or a "single shot transaction" that is not likely to affect any other party.[11]

§ 7.47 Deceptive Practices Act—Types of Recovery Available

The Deceptive Practices Act was initially enacted in 1970. As originally written, the statute was only enforceable by the Attorney General. In such an action, the Attorney General was empowered to seek an injunction against deceptive business practices, as well as to obtain restitution for victimized consumers.[1]

In 1980, the Legislature dramatically expanded coverage of the

---

8. Hart v. Moore, 155 Misc.2d 203, 587 N.Y.S.2d 477, 479 (Sup.Ct., Westchester County, 1992) ("Legislative intent and history also indicate that GBL Sec. 349 was meant to have a broad application ...It seems that remedial statutes are interpreted liberally in order to eliminate injustice on as broad a scale as possible.").

9. New York University v. Continental Insurance Co., 87 N.Y.2d 308, 639 N.Y.S.2d 283, 662 N.E.2d 763 (1995); Oswego Laborers', *supra* note 3.

PRACTICE POINTER: The requirement of "consumer oriented" conduct does not mean that it is limited to transactions that are "primarily for personal, family or household purposes," as opposed to transactions entered by businesses. Indeed, the statute has repeatedly been applied to business plaintiffs harmed by other businesses. Associates Capital Services Corp. of New Jersey v. Fairway Private Cars, Inc., 590 F.Supp. 10 (E.D.N.Y.1982); Oswego Laborers', *supra* note 3; Sulner v. General Accident Fire and Life Assurance Corp., 122 Misc.2d 597, 471 N.Y.S.2d 794 (Sup.Ct., N.Y. County, 1984); Givens, *Supplementary Practice Commentaries*, General Business Law § 349, p.171. *See also,* Memorandum for the Governor of Attorney General Robert Abrams, May 21, 1980, submitted in support of legislation adding the private right of action under Section 349(h): "It is also noted that a business itself will be able to use the private right of action against another business engaged in deceptive practices and thereby obtain increased legal protection."

10. Oswego Laborers', *supra* note 3; Hart v. Allstate Insurance Co., 201 A.D.2d 621, 608 N.Y.S.2d 241 (2d Dep't 1994).

11. Genesco Entertainment v. Koch, 593 F.Supp. 743 (S.D.N.Y.1984); Holmes Protection of New York, Inc. v. Provident Loan Society of New York, 179 A.D.2d 400, 577 N.Y.S.2d 850 (1st Dep't 1992); Quail Ridge Assoc. v. Chemical Bank, 162 A.D.2d 917, 558 N.Y.S.2d 655 (3d Dep't 1990). *But see,* People v. Empyre Inground Pools, Inc., 227 A.D.2d 731, 642 N.Y.S.2d 344 (3d Dep't 1996) (pattern of individual complaints about various interconnected businesses are not "single shot" transactions).

§ 7.47

1. General Business Law § 349(b). The Attorney General is also required to issue a five-day warning notice to the defendant before commencing the action. General Business Law § 349(c).

statute by creating an express private right of action.[2] This section provides:

> In addition to the right of action granted to the attorney general pursuant to this section, *any person* who has been injured by reason of any violation of this section may bring an action in his own name to enjoin such unlawful act or practice, an action to recover his actual damages or fifty dollars, whichever is greater, or both such actions. The court may, in its discretion, increase the award of damages up to one thousand dollars, if the court finds the defendant willfully or knowingly violated this section. The court may award reasonable attorney's fees to a prevailing plaintiff. (emphasis added)

The private right of action thus provides a powerful opportunity for any individual, acting as a "private attorney general," to prosecute illegal conduct by businesses.[3] In addition to the ability to recover an individual consumer's actual damages, or 50 dollars if no actual damages are incurred, the statute permits the recovery of attorney's fees, and a plaintiff can obtain a broad injunction to prevent the deceptive practices from recurring.[4] The injunction remedy is of particular importance to attorneys representing consumers in that it permits an individual to enjoin a business not only from engaging in such practices with respect to the plaintiff, but with regard to *all* consumers as well.[5]

---

2. General Business Law § 349(h).

3. Moldovan, *New York Creates a Private Right of Action to Combat Consumer Fraud: Caveat Venditor*, 48 Brooklyn L. Rev. 509 (1982). *See infra,* §§ 7.63—7.65 for a sample form Order to Show Cause with Temporary Restraining Order, Supporting Affirmation and Complaint in an action alleging ongoing deceptive business practices.

4. **CAVEAT:** The Deceptive Practices Act does not contain an express Statute of Limitations. It is therefore covered by the six-year Statute of Limitations found in CPLR 213.

5. **PRACTICE POINTER:** A practitioner representing a consumer victimized by a deceptive practice should not overlook the possibility of obtaining this type of broad-based injunction, which has an effect similar to that of a class action but without the need for class certification under CPLR Art. 9. If it can be shown that the complained-of conduct is not only ongoing but likely to cause irreparable harm to consumers during the pendency of the action, an application may be made pursuant to CPLR Art. 63 for a temporary restraining order, followed by a preliminary injunction. In an ordinary case, a plaintiff seeking to temporarily restrain conduct *pendente lite* is required to post a bond in an amount set by the court to protect the defendant from any damage caused by a wrongfully issued order. CPLR 63. An individual seeking a temporary injunction under the Deceptive Practices Act is not, however, required to first secure such a bond. Since the Attorney General is exempt from the bonding requirement, a plaintiff acting as a "private attorney general," seeking redress for consumers at large, is similarly exempt. McDonald v. North Shore Yacht Sales, Inc., 134 Misc.2d 910, 513 N.Y.S.2d 590 (Sup.Ct., Nassau County, 1987).

CAVEAT: Injunctive relief claims cannot, however, be sought in a court of limited jurisdiction and must instead be brought in the supreme court. If the claim is for damages and attorney's fees only, the action can be brought in any court that would otherwise have monetary jurisdiction over the claim, even small claims court. While a consumer can sue for an injunction and damages, he or she is not required to seek both in the same action but instead may elect to sue for either or both. Beslity v. Manhattan Honda, 120 Misc.2d 848, 467 N.Y.S.2d 471 (Sup.Ct., App. Term, 1st Dep't, 1983).

Suits can also be brought under the Deceptive Practice Act as a class action to recover the actual damages suffered by class members, as well as injunctive relief, although statutory damages cannot be recovered in a class action under the Act.[6]

Very often, deceptive business people disband a particular company when the number of consumer complaints reaches a high level and then re-open the same business in a different name in an effort to avoid detection. The Deceptive Practices Act can also be a potent weapon against such individuals, who attempt to hide behind a corporate shell.[7]

The Deceptive Practices Act is expressly applicable to businesses that are otherwise regulated by government agencies in that the statute applies "whether or not subject to any other law of this state."[8] In *Riordan v. Nationwide Mutual Insurance Co.*,[9] an insurance company's settlement practices were alleged to be deceptive and in violation of the Deceptive Practices Act. The defendant argued that the Deceptive Practice Act could not "be used against insurance companies because of the pervasive statutory scheme regulating unfair and deceptive acts and practices by insurance companies."[10]

The Second Circuit Court of Appeals rejected this contention in *Riordan* "because it ignores the plain language of GBL § 349(g), which provides that '(t)his section shall apply to all deceptive acts or practices declared to be unlawful, whether or not subject to any other law of this state.' ...GBL § 349 applies to acts and practices of *every business* operating in New York ... Nowhere does GBL § 349 provide an exception for insurance companies ... from the reach of GBL § 349." Moreover, the statute contains no exemption excepting its coverage over any other type of business.

§ 7.48 Drafting Checklist—List of Essential Allegations

1. New Car Lemon Law claims.

    - Vehicle purchased with a written warranty. (*See* § 7.10)
    - Vehicle purchased, leased, or registered in New York. (*See id.*)
    - Vehicle used primarily for personal, family, or household purposes. (*See id.*)
    - Four or more repair attempts for the same problem within first two years or 18,000 miles (*see id.*) *or*

---

6. Weinberg v. Hertz Corp., 69 N.Y.2d 979, 516 N.Y.S.2d 652, 509 N.E.2d 347 (1987).

7. People v. Empyre Inground Pools, Inc., 227 A.D.2d 731, 642 N.Y.S.2d 344 (3d Dep't 1996); *see also* Meachum v. Outdoor World Corp., 235 A.D.2d 462, 652 N.Y.S.2d 749 (2d Dep't 1997).

8. General Business Law § 349(g).

9. 977 F.2d 47 (2d Cir.1992), cert'd quest. withdrawn 984 F.2d 69 (2d Cir.1993).

10. *See* Insurance Law §§ 2401 *et seq.*, 2601 (and that this statutory scheme) preempts the use of GBL § 349 by private individuals against insurance companies.

§ 7.48   CONSUMER LAW   Ch. 7

- Vehicle out of service for 30 days or more during statutory warranty period. (*See id.*)
- Defect not caused by consumer's abuse or neglect. (*See id.*)
- Defect substantially impairs vehicle's value. (*See id.*)

2. Used Car Lemon Law claims.
   - Vehicle purchased or leased *and* registered in New York. (*See* § 7.11)
   - Vehicle purchased or leased after earlier of 18,000 or two years from original delivery. (*See id.*)
   - Vehicle purchased or leased from a "dealer" for more than $1500.00. (*See id.*)
   - Vehicle had less than 100,000 miles at time of purchase or lease. (*See id.*)
   - Vehicle used primarily for personal, family, or household purposes. (*See id.*)
   - Warranty duration: 90 days or 4,000 miles for vehicles with 18,000–36,000 miles; 60 days or 3,000 miles for vehicles with 36,001–79,999 miles; 30 days or 1,000 miles for vehicles with 80,000–100,000 miles. (*See id.*)
   - Only certain components covered. (*See id.*)
   - Defect not caused by consumer's abuse or neglect. (*See id.*)
   - Defect substantially impairs vehicle's value. (*See id.*)

3. Lemon Law—Suit or Arbitration.
   - Suit.

     (i) Statute of Limitations for any Lemon Law claim is four years from date of original delivery of the vehicle to the consumer. (*See* § 7.12)

     (ii) Can recover consequential damages and attorney's fees. (*See id.*)

     (iii) Can combine Lemon Law claim with other claims in the same action. (*See* § 7.52)

   - Arbitration.

     (i) Statute of Limitations for any Lemon Law claim is four years from date of original delivery of the vehicle to the consumer. (See *id.*)

     (ii) Process is generally quicker and less expensive. (*See id.*)

   - Arbitration Preparation.

(i) Prepare and file Request for Arbitration with Attorney General. (*See* § 7.14)

(ii) After acceptance and filing with AAA, prepare and file document request. (*See* §§ 7.14, 7.49)

(iii) Discuss settlement possibilities with both client and adverse party.

4. Lemon Law Arbitration appeals and confirmation proceedings.
   - Procedure covered by CPLR Article 75.
   - Application to vacate or modify award must be made within 90 days. (*See* § 7.16)
   - Confirmation must be requested within 1 year. (*See id.*)
   - Standard of review is "arbitrary and capricious." (*See id.*)
   - Proceeding can be brought in limited jurisdiction courts. (*See id.*)
   - Request attorney's fees in any CPLR Article 75 proceeding.

5. Leasing Cases.
   - Generally.
       (i) State and federal statutes apply to leases for primarily personal, family, or household purposes. (*See* § 7.20, § 7.21, § 7.22)
   - Consumer Leasing Act.
       (i) UCC, not federal law, applies to leases that are "disguised credit sales." (*See* § 7.21)

       (ii) Federal law applies to leases for more than four months and less than $25,000. (*See id.*)

       (iii) Review lease for violations of federal disclosure violations. (*See id.*)

       (iv) Statute of Limitations under the CLA is one year from lease termination. (*See id.*)
   - Motor Vehicle Retail Leasing Act.
       (i) MVRLA applies to leases entered after August 31, 1995. (*See* § 7.19)

       (ii) Procedure used by dealer in procuring lease must comply with MVRLA. (*See* § 7.22)

       (iii) Lease terms must comply with all disclosure requirements of MVRLA. (*See id.*)

       (iv) Statutory violations can be asserted against assignees. (*See id.*)

       (v) Lessees have the right to cure default. (*See id.*)

§ 7.48   CONSUMER LAW   Ch. 7

       (vi) Early termination charges must be disclosed. (*See id.*)

       (vii) Excess damage claims are strictly scrutinized. (*See id.*)

       (viii) Statutory damages and attorney's fees available for MVRLA violations. (*See id.*)

       (ix) Many MVRLA violations are *per se* deceptive business practices. (*See id.*)

       (x) Lessee must give 60 days notice before suing lessor in most cases. (*See id.*)

       (xi) Lessors have *bona fide* error defense. (*See id.*)

       (xii) Lessees can assert all other statutory or common law claims. (*See id.*)

6. Motor Vehicle Installment Sales.

   - MVRISA applies to vehicles purchased for personal, family, or household purposes. (*See* § 7.23)
   - Applies to vehicles purchased in two or more installments. (*See id.*)
   - Applies to vehicles secured by a retail installment contract. (*See id.*)
   - Installment sales contracts must be in writing. (*See id.*)
   - Installment sales contracts are required to include all statutory notices. (*See id.*)
   - Installment contracts are barred from including certain prohibited terms. (*See id.*)
   - Claims can be asserted against assignees of the contract. (*See id.*)
   - Buyer has a right to redeem after default and repossession. (*See id.*)
   - Lender cannot accelerate balance due on default without first providing opportunity to redeem. (*See id.*)
   - Penalties for violations include bar to collection of any finance charges. (*See id.*)

7. Repossessions.

   - Self-help right without the need for a judgment. (*See* § 7.24)
   - Only property covered by a security interest can be repossessed. (*See id.*)
   - Repossession cannot be done in violation of the contract or "arbitrarily and without good cause." (*See id.*)

- Creditor may not "breach the peace" in repossessing property. (*See id.*)
- Repossession can be blocked by revoking acceptance, rejecting the property, and declaring a security interest in it for payments made. (*See* § 7.25)
- Creditor must provide right to redeem for arrearage after repossession. (*See* § 7.26)
- Resale following repossession must be "commercially reasonable." (*See id.*)
- If resale is not commercially reasonable, right to deficiency claim may be barred. (*See id.*)

8. Automobile Repairs.
    - Motor Vehicle Repair Shop Registration Act applies to any customer, including business customers. (*See* § 7.27)
    - MVRSRA requires a written invoice with authorization for all repairs. (*See id.*)
    - Consumers can either sue or file complaint with DMV. (*See id.*)
    - DMV complaints must be made within 90 days or 3,000 miles of the repair. (*See id.*)

9. Repair Shop Liens.
    - Enforcement of lien requires lawful possession of the vehicle. (*See* § 7.28)
    - Lien cannot be enforced by any unlicensed repair shop. (*See id.*)
    - Goods and services creating the lien must be rendered with the consumer's express consent. (*See id.*)
    - Lien notice must state supporting facts, the amount of the lien, a description of the vehicle, and its value. (*See id.*)
    - Consumers have a right to challenge liens by commencing a special proceeding. (*See id.*)
    - Proceeding must be brought within 10 days of the lien notice. (*See id.*)
    - Proceeding can be brought in any court with monetary jurisdiction over the claim. (*See id.*)
    - Limited jurisdiction court might not grant order restraining sale pending determination of the claim. (*See id.*)

10. Credit Reporting.
    - Federal and state credit reporting acts apply only to credit issued for consumer, not business purposes.

- Credit reporting agencies must follow "reasonable procedures" to avoid reporting obsolete information. (*See* § 7.31)
- Credit reporting agencies must follow "reasonable procedures" to prevent consumer reports from being obtained by third parties for impermissible purposes. (*See id.*)
- Credit reporting agencies must follow "reasonable procedures" to assure "maximum possible accuracy" of credit reports. (*See id.*)
- Consumers should dispute any inaccurate information in writing and demand its deletion from both the credit reporting agency as well as the reporting source. (*See id.*)
- Credit reporting agencies are required to publish any written dispute statement filed by a consumer unless it is plainly frivolous. (*See id.*, § 7.33)
- Some courts require publication of erroneous credit information to a third party before the consumer can recover damages. (*See* § 7.33)
- State law prohibits reporting erroneous credit information *or* even maintaining erroneous information in reporting agency's files. (*See id.*)
- Negligent violation of federal or state law entitles the consumer to recover actual damages and attorney's fees. (*See id.*)
- Willful violation of federal or state law entitles the consumer to recover actual damages, punitive damages, and attorney's fees. (*See id.*)
- Actions under either federal and/or state credit reporting acts can be brought in federal or state court. (*See id.*)
- Action can be commenced by Order to Show Cause with a Temporary Restraining Order if the erroneous information will cause immediate and irreparable harm to the consumer. (*See id.*)
- Statute of Limitations under federal and state law is generally one year from violation. (*See id.*)

11. Debt Collection.
    - Common Law claims.
        (i) Intentional infliction of emotional distress claim requires proof of conduct that is outrageous and beyond all bounds of decency. (*See* § 7.35)
    - Statutory claims.

(i) Fair Debt Collection Practice Act only applies to third-party collectors and attorneys who regularly collect debts, not creditors. (*See* § 7.36)

(ii) Federal and state debt collection laws only apply to debts incurred for personal, family, or household, not business, purposes. (*See* § 7.36)

(iii) Federal and state law strictly limit contacts with third parties. (*See* §§ 7.36, 7.43)

(iv) Federal law can be enforced privately by any consumer. State law does not include an express private right of action. (*See* §§ 7.36, 7.43)

(v) Federal and state law prohibit false, deceptive, or misleading collection practices. (*See* §§ 7.38, 7.39, 7.43)

(vi) Federal law permits a debtor to demand the collector cease all further collection activity. (*See* § 7.38)

(vii) Federal law requires disclosure of the consumer's right to dispute the validity of a debt and obtain verification of it. (*See id.*)

(viii) Federal and state law prohibit any abusive or harassing collection conduct. (*See* § 7.40)

(ix) FDCPA claims can be brought in state or federal court. (*See* § 7.42)

(x) Statute of Limitations for FDCPA claims is one year. (*See id.*)

(xi) Consumers can recover actual damages, statutory damages of $1,000.00, and attorney's fees. (*See id.*)

(xii) Collection agencies have a *bona fide* error defense for certain claims. (*See id.*)

(xiii) Deceptive debt collection claims can be brought under General Business Law § 349. (*See* § 7.43)

12. Deceptive Practices Act.
    - Applies to any business, even if regulated by any other state law. (*See* § 7.44)
    - Deceptive Practices Act is given parallel construction with the FTC Act, as well as with similar statutes in 45 other states. (*See id.*)
    - Conduct must be deceptive or misleading in a material respect. (*See id.*)
    - Statute applies to conduct directed at all consumers, including businesses. (*See* § 7.45)

§ 7.48 CONSUMER LAW Ch. 7

- Consumers can recover actual damages or $50.00, whichever is greater, plus attorney's fees. (*See* §§ 7.45, 7.46)
- Consumers need not show actual reliance on the deceptive conduct, or actual deception, just that the conduct has the capacity to deceive a reasonable consumer. (*See* § 7.45)
- Deceptive Practices Act is a remedial statute and is afforded broad application. (*See id.*)
- Challenged conduct must be "consumer oriented." (*See id.*)
- Consumers need not show repeated conduct, just a "pattern of deceptive behavior." (*See id.*)
- Deceptive Practices Act does not apply to "private commercial disputes" of a "single shot" nature. (*See id.*)
- Consumers can also seek broad injunctive relief on behalf of all consumers, acting as "private attorneys general." (*See id.*)
- "Private attorneys general" are not required to post an undertaking to temporarily enjoin deceptive conduct. (*See id.*)
- Deceptive Practices Act can be used to pierce the corporate veil. (*See id.*)
- Statute of Limitations for Deceptive Practices Act claims is six years. (*See* § 7.46)

§ 7.49 Forms—Lemon Law Document Request Pursuant to 13 NYCRR § 300.9(a)

Case Administrator
American Arbitration Association
[*666 Old County Road Suite 603*
Garden City, New York 11530–
6447]

    Re: [*Consumer v. Acme Motor Company*
        No. 17–178–0184–95
        AG No. 20029
        D/F]

Dear Sir/Madam,

Please be advised that I represent the consumer in the above referenced matter, which has been noticed for a hearing on _____ before Arbitrator _____.

Pursuant to 13 NYCRR § 300.9(a), request is hereby made that the arbitrator direct the manufacturer to produce, within the time required by § 300.9(b), the following documents and information:

(xiv) Each and every repair order for work performed by any manufacturer-authorized dealer on the subject vehicle;

(xv) Any service bulletin, technical service bulletin, recall notice, voluntary or involuntary, issued by, or on behalf of, the manufacturer that relates, or may relate, to any of the defects as set forth in the consumer's Request for Arbitration Form duly filed with the New York State Department of Law;

(xvi) Any and all reports, notes, correspondence, communications or other written materials that describe or pertain to the consumer's vehicle;

(xvii) Any and all other documentation, not described above, that relates, or that may relate, to this proceeding.

Your prompt attention to this matter is appreciated.

Very truly yours,
[ATTORNEY]

cc: [consumer
Acme Motor Company]

§ 7.50 Forms—Notice of Petition to Vacate Lemon Law Arbitration Award Pursuant to CPLR Article 75

CIVIL COURT OF THE CITY OF NEW YORK
COUNTY OF NEW YORK

In the Matter of the Application of

[JOHN SMITH],

      Petitioner,

For an Order and Judgment Pursuant to CPLR Article 75

   -against-

[ACME MOTORS CORP., ZENITH MOTOR DIVISION],

      Respondent.

NOTICE OF PETITION

Index No.

§ 7.50   CONSUMER LAW   Ch. 7

PETITIONING PARTY: The petitioner, by his attorney, [ATTORNEY], Esq.;

DATE, TIME, AND PLACE OF PETITION: _____, 9:30 AM; Civil Court of the City of New York, Special Term Part I, Room 325, 111 Centre, New York, New York;

RELIEF REQUESTED: An order pursuant to CPLR Article 75, vacating and reversing the _____ arbitration decision and award which denied the petitioner's claim for a refund of the purchase price of his vehicle pursuant to GBL § 198–a and 13 NYCRR §§ 300 et seq., an award of reasonable attorney's fees pursuant to Gen. B. L. § 198–a and for such other relief as may be just;

SUPPORTING PAPERS: Petition of [JOHN SMITH], verified on _____, with Exhibits attached, Memorandum of Law;

ANSWERING PAPERS: If any, shall be served at least seven (7) days before the return date pursuant to CPLR 403(b);

NOTICE GIVEN TO: [Acme Motors Corp. Detroit, Michigan]

DATED: New York, New York

Yours, etc.,
[ATTORNEY], Esq.
Attorney for the Petitioner
[ADDRESS]

§ 7.51   Forms—Petition to Vacate Lemon Law Arbitration Award Pursuant to CPLR Article 75

CIVIL COURT OF THE CITY OF NEW YORK
COUNTY OF NEW YORK

_____
In the Matter of the Application of

[JOHN SMITH],

                 Petitioner

For an Order and Judgment Pursuant to CPLR Article 75   VERIFIED PETITION

                 -against-   Index No.

[ACME MOTORS CORP., ZENITH MOTOR DIVISION],

                 Respondent
_____

Ch. 7 VACATE LEMON LAW ARBITRATION AWARD § 7.51

The Petitioner, [*JOHN SMITH*], (hereinafter the "petitioner"), by his attorney, _____, Esq., alleges as follows:

PRELIMINARY STATEMENT

1. This is a special proceeding brought pursuant to CPLR Article 75 in which the petitioner seeks the vacatur and reversal of the _____ arbitration decision and award of [*Arbitrator*], which denied the petitioner's claim for a refund of the purchase price of his vehicle pursuant to General Business Law § 198–a (the "New Car Lemon Law") and 13 NYCRR Pts. 300 *et seq.* ("New York State Lemon Law Regulations").

2. The petitioner alleges that such decision must be vacated and reversed pursuant to CPLR § 7511(b), on the grounds that:

   A. The Arbitrator's decision is irrational, arbitrary and capricious; and

   B. The Arbitrator's decision is not supported by evidence produced at the hearing.

3. In the alternative, the Petitioner requests that the Court vacate the Arbitrator's decision and, pursuant to CPLR 7511(d), remand the matter for a rehearing and determination of the issues between the parties before a different arbitrator.

PARTIES, JURISDICTION, AND VENUE

4. The petitioner is a natural person residing at _____.

5. Upon information and belief, the respondent, [*ACME MOTORS CORP., ZENITH MOTOR DIVISION*] (hereinafter the "respondent"), is a corporation authorized to do business in New York State, having a principal place of business in New York County.

6. The Court has subject matter jurisdiction over this proceeding pursuant to CPLR Article 75 and NYCCA § 206(b).

7. Venue is properly laid in New York County pursuant to CPLR 7502(a), as a County where the respondent is doing business as well as the County where the underlying arbitration proceeding took place.

STATEMENT OF FACTS

8. On or about _____, the petitioner purchased a new [*1991 Pontiac "Grand Prix"*] (hereinafter the "vehicle"), manufactured by, or on behalf of, the respondent, from (dealer). The total sale price of the vehicle, including state and local sales tax, was $_____ .

9. Shortly after the petitioner took possession of the vehicle, it began experiencing serious and persistent mechanical problems.

10. Between _____ and _____, the petitioner was compelled to have repairs made to the vehicle on at least _____ occasions for mechanical problems, including: drained and dead battery, broken starter, transmission failure, and persistent and serious wiring and electrical problems, which caused the vehicle to become inoperable.

11. On or about December ___, 19__, the petitioner completed a "New Car Lemon Law Request for Arbitration Form" for arbitration under GBL § 198–a(k) and filed it with the New York State Attorney General, pursuant to 13 NYCRR § 300.4, together with copies of the five (5) repair orders pertaining to the vehicle. (Application and repair invoices annexed hereto as Exhibit "A".)

12. Pursuant to the New Car Lemon Law, GBL § 198–a(c)(1), a motor vehicle is *presumed* to be a "lemon" if, *inter alia*, there have been four or more attempts to correct the same defect during the warranty period and the problem still exists *or* the vehicle is out of service for a cumulative total of thirty days or more for a series of defects during the statutory warranty period (GBL § 198–a(d)(1)and(2)).

13. In [*his/her*] Lemon Law application, the petitioner claimed that the subject vehicle had been out of service for over thirty days as a result of a series of defects that substantially impaired its value.

14. In [*his/her*] application, the petitioner requested, pursuant to 13 NYCRR § 300.4(c), that his purchase price be refunded as provided by GBL § 198–a(c)(1).

15. Upon information and belief, the Attorney General reviewed and approved the petitioner's application for arbitration.

16. On or about _____, the petitioner was advised by the American Arbitration Association ("AAA") that [*his/her*] request for arbitration was approved and accepted and that his case was assigned to the AAA New York Regional Office for administration. (Annexed hereto as Exhibit "B".)

17. On or about _____, the AAA advised the parties that the petitioner's request for arbitration was approved and accepted and that _____, Esq. had been appointed as the Arbitrator to hear the matter. (Annexed hereto as Exhibit "C".)

18. On or about _____, the parties were notified that a hearing on the petitioner's claim was scheduled for February ___, 19__ before Arbitrator _____. (Annexed hereto as Exhibit "D") The hearing was later rescheduled for _____.

19. On or about _____, the respondent requested that the Arbitrator direct the petitioner to produce numerous documents pursuant to 13 NYCRR § 300.9. (Annexed hereto as Exhibit "G") At that time, the

respondent further requested that the petitioner produce the vehicle for inspection by the Arbitrator at the hearing. (See Exhibit "G".)

20. On or about _____, the petitioner responded to the respondent's request for documents. (Attached hereto as Exhibit "H".)

21. A hearing was held on ____ before the Arbitrator. The petitioner produced the vehicle for inspection by the Arbitrator. The hearing was not recorded, either stenographically or otherwise, and no transcript was produced.

22. At the commencement of the hearing the Arbitrator stated that petitioner bore the burden of establishing that the vehicle's defects constituted a substantial impairment of its value.

23. Counsel for the petitioner objected to this mischaracterization of the Lemon Law, which provides that the respondent has the burden of proving the absence of substantial impairment, as an affirmative defense. The Arbitrator refused to modify the burden of proof set out above and instead reiterated his contention that the petitioner had the burden of proving substantial impairment.

24. At the hearing, the petitioner produced six (6) repair invoices for the vehicle occurring during the statutory warranty period (an additional repair attempt was made subsequent to the petitioner's filing of the claim), and [he/she] testified as to the nature and extent of the problems with the vehicle as described above in paragraph 10. (See repair invoices annexed hereto as Exhibit "A" and Exhibit "M")

25. The petitioner further testified that the vehicle had been out of service for over 33 days during the statutory warranty period due to defects, as was indicated by the repair invoices. (See Exhibit "A")

26. The petitioner further testified that the defects in the vehicle continue to exist and that such defects constitute a substantial impairment of the value of the vehicle.

27. At the hearing the respondent's only witness, a service manager for (dealer), testified as to the repairs performed on the vehicle but conceded that he had no personal knowledge of the facts.

28. On _____, the arbitrator issued a decision in favor of the respondent on the *sole* basis that "The problems(s) which still exists [sic] does *not* substantially impair the value of the car to the consumer." (Annexed hereto as Exhibit "N", ¶ 3)

AS AND FOR A FIRST CAUSE OF ACTION

29. The petitioner repeats and realleges each and every paragraph above with the same force and effect as if restated here.

30. The Arbitrator found that the vehicle was subject to four or more repair attempts for the same defect *and* was out of service due to

repairs for a series of defects for 30 or more days within 18,000 miles or 24 months of delivery. (Exhibit "N", ¶ 1)

31. The Arbitrator further found that the vehicle is used primarily for personal, family, or household purposes and that the problems with the vehicle continue to exist. (Exhibit "N", ¶ 1)

32. The Arbitrator ruled in favor of the respondent *solely* upon the finding that the vehicle's defects do not substantially impair the value of the vehicle. (Exhibit "N", ¶ 3)

33. The Arbitrator stated in support of his decision that "The *consumer* failed to establish that the vehicle had a substantial defect which impaired its use, value or safety." (Emphasis added.) (See Exhibit "N", ¶ 2) The Arbitrator further stated that " ... the *consumer* did not satisfy the statutory requirement that the problem(s) which still exist substantially impaired the value of the car to the consumer." (Exhibit "N", ¶ 2) (Emphasis added.)

34. GBL § 198–a(c)(3) states, in pertinent part,

It shall be an *affirmative defense* to any claim under this section that:

the nonconformity, defect or condition does not substantially impair such value (emphasis added);

35. Under GBL § 198–a(c)(3), the manufacturer has the burden of proving that the defect, which does exist, does *not* substantially impair the value of the vehicle.

36. By finding that the *petitioner* "failed to establish that the vehicle had a substantial defect which impaired its use, value or safety," the Arbitrator expressly disregarded the law by improperly shifting the burden of proof on this issue.

37. The Arbitrator's decision is therefore irrational, arbitrary, and capricious, and the Arbitrator evidenced a manifest disregard for the law in unilaterally imposing the burden of proof of substantial impairment on the petitioner.

38. As a result, the award must be vacated and reversed pursuant to CPLR 7511(b)(iii).

AS AND FOR A SECOND CAUSE OF ACTION

39. The petitioner repeats and realleges each and every paragraph above with the same force and effect as if restated here.

40. At the hearing, the petitioner testified that the vehicle's electrical problems caused the battery to completely drain, thereby rendering the vehicle inoperable. The petitioner thereby established that the defective condition substantially impaired the value of the vehicle.

41. Although the decision indicates that the Arbitrator was presented with numerous repair bills and towing receipts, the Arbitrator inexplicably disregarded this evidence, which establishes the severity of the vehicle's defects.

42. As a result, the defects complained of substantially impair the value of the vehicle. The Arbitrator's decision is therefore baseless, irrational, arbitrary and capricious and not supported by the record or evidence, and must be vacated and reversed pursuant to CPLR 7511(b)(iii).

AS AND FOR A THIRD CAUSE OF ACTION

43. The petitioner repeats and realleges each and every paragraph above with the same force and effect as if restated here.

44. The petitioner is entitled to an award of attorney's fees pursuant to GBL § 198–a(*l*).

WHEREFORE, it is respectfully requested that the Court issue an Order and Judgment reversing and vacating the Arbitrator's decision herein, or in the alternative, vacating such decision and remanding the matter to the American Arbitration Association for rehearing before a different Arbitrator, awarding the petitioner attorney's fees pursuant to GBL § 198–a(*l*), and the costs and disbursements of this proceeding, and granting such other relief as may be just.

Dated: _____, New York

> [*ATTORNEY*], Esq.
> Attorney for Petitioner
> [*ADDRESS AND TELEPHONE NUMBER*]

[*VERIFICATION*]

§ 7.52 Forms—Complaint for Fraud, Breach of Warranties, Deceptive Business Practices, Used Car Lemon Law, Rescission and Revocation of Acceptance for Fraudulent Leasing Practices

SUPREME COURT OF THE STATE OF NEW YORK
COUNTY OF NEW YORK

_____
TODD STONE,   )
)
)
              Plaintiff,   )
)

§ 7.52   CONSUMER LAW   Ch. 7

-against-	)
	)
ABC LEASING GROUP, INC.,	) VERIFIED COMPLAINT
	)
ABC MOTOR GROUP, INC.,	) Index No.
ROBERT AMES, individually and as	)
an officer of ABC LEASING	)
GROUP, INC., and/or ABC MOTOR	)
GROUP, INC., and ALLSOP	)
BANK,	)
	)
Defendants.	)
	)

The plaintiff TODD STONE, (the "plaintiff") by his attorney, _____, Esq., as and for his complaint against the defendants, alleges as follows:

PRELIMINARY STATEMENT

1. This is an action for actual, compensatory, consequential, statutory, and punitive damages for fraud, breach of warranties, and deceptive business practices, in violation of General Business Law Art. 22–A ("Deceptive Business Practices"), and violations of General Business Law § 198–b ("Used Car Lemon Law"). The complaint also seeks injunctive and declaratory relief for rescission and restitution, revocation of acceptance and deceptive business practices, as well as for statutory attorney's fees pursuant to GBL § 349(h), GBL § 198–b (f)(5) and GOL § 5–327.

PARTIES

2. The plaintiff is a natural person over eighteen years of age and maintains a residence in the City, County and State of New York.

3. Upon information and belief, the defendant ABC LEASING GROUP, INC., ("Leasing Group") is a domestic corporation having a place of business at _____, New York.

4. Upon information and belief, Leasing Group is engaged in the business of, *inter alia*, leasing new and used motor vehicles to members of the general public.

5. Upon information and belief, the defendant ABC MOTOR GROUP, INC., ("Motor Group") is a domestic corporation having a place of business at _____, New York.

6. Upon information and belief, Motor Group is engaged in the business of, *inter alia*, purchasing and selling new and used motor vehicles to be leased to members of the general public by Leasing Group.

7. Upon information and belief, Leasing Group and Motor Group share common ownership and have common officers, directors, shareholders, and/or employees.

8. Upon information and belief, the defendant ROBERT AMES ("Ames") is the President or other officer of Leasing Group and/or Motor Group and maintains a place of business at 100 Jericho Turnpike, Woodbury, New York. Ames is sued herein both in his individual and corporate capacities.

9. Upon information and belief, ALLSOP Bank ("ALLSOP") is a banking institution duly chartered by the State of New York and maintains a place of business at _____, New York.

STATEMENT OF FACTS

10. On or about _____, the plaintiff entered a motor vehicle lease agreement (the "lease") with Leasing Group for the lease of a 1990 Ferrari, VIN ZFFFK1234K1234567 (the "Ferrari") for a term of 35 months with a first payment of $2598.00, followed by 34 monthly payments of $1299.00.

11. Upon information and belief, the lease was financed by ALLSOP pursuant to a promissory note and lease assignment dated July ___, 19__ in the amount of $40,000.00.

12. On or about _____, Leasing Group agreed to accept the return of the Ferrari from the plaintiff and substitute a 1993 Mercedes-Benz 500 SEL VIN WDBGA12F1YS123456 (the "subject vehicle") in its place under the remaining term of the lease.

13. Leasing Group did not in any manner alter or modify the financial terms of the lease to reflect the lower value or price of the subject vehicle as compared to the Ferrari.

14. Upon information and belief, on or about _____, Leasing Group executed a "Substitution of Collateral" agreement with ALLSOP whereby it agreed that the subject vehicle be substituted for the Ferrari under the lease. In that agreement, Leasing Group affirmatively stated that the subject vehicle is a "Car" as defined in the Loan and Security Agreement with ALLSOP. In the agreement, Leasing Group further granted ALLSOP a purchase money security interest in the subject vehicle.

15. Upon information and belief, on or about _____, Leasing Group leased the Ferrari to The Avriell Group, Inc. _____, New York pursuant to a lease agreement which was assigned to ALLSOP.

16. Prior to accepting the subject vehicle from Leasing Group, the plaintiff and his wife, Glenda Stone, were expressly advised by the defendants, Leasing Group, Motor Group and/or Ames, in response to their inquiry, *inter alia*, that the subject vehicle had never been involved in an accident and that it was in excellent mechanical condition. Leasing

§ 7.52 CONSUMER LAW Ch. 7

Group and/or Ames further advised the plaintiff and his wife that the vehicle had been purchased by Leasing Group from an individual residing in Jericho, New York.

17. Based upon the above representations, the plaintiff agreed to accept the subject vehicle from Leasing Group. Thereafter, the plaintiff registered the subject vehicle with the New York State Department of Motor Vehicles. ("DMV")

18. Between _____ and _____ the plaintiff made each and every monthly lease payment to ALLSOP in the amount of $1,299.00, for a total of at least $7,794.00.

19. Almost immediately after taking possession of the subject vehicle, the plaintiff and his wife discovered that it had serious mechanical defects involving, *inter alia*, the transmission, power steering, electrical components, and brakes.

20. The plaintiff immediately advised Leasing Group of such problems and defects. Leasing Group and Ames advised the plaintiff to bring the subject vehicle to Mercedes-Benz Manhattan, Inc. ("MBM") an authorized Mercedes–Benz dealer, for service under the manufacturer's warranty. The plaintiff took the subject vehicle to MBM for warranty service on at least seven occasions between _____ and _____. Upon information and belief, the dealership performed substantial repairs to the vehicle on such occasions. Despite such repairs, the subject vehicle continues to be substantially defective and is not safe to operate.

21. On _____, the plaintiff and his wife learned, for the first time, from the Used Car Sales Manager for MBM that, after inspection, the subject vehicle had previously been involved in a serious front-end collision, that the entire front end of the vehicle had been redone and that its frame was damaged.

22. At no time during the plaintiff's possession of the subject vehicle was it ever involved in any collision of any nature.

23. The plaintiff immediately advised Leasing Group, Ames and ALLSOP of the findings of MBM and demanded that the lease be canceled and the return of the vehicle accepted. Despite such demand, the defendants failed and refused to take any steps whatsoever to resolve the matter.

24. Thereafter, the plaintiff retained counsel who issued a "NOTICE OF RESCISSION AND/OR REVOCATION OF ACCEPTANCE AND DEMAND FOR RESTITUTION", dated _____, to Leasing Group and ALLSOP. Despite such demand, both Leasing Group and ALLSOP have failed and refused to cancel the lease and return the lease payments made by the plaintiff.

25. Despite such notice, the defendants have failed and refused to acknowledge the plaintiff's rightful revocation of acceptance of the subject vehicle and rescission of the lease.

26. In connection with such notice, the plaintiff advised the defendants that he would make no further payments under the lease.

27. In response, ALLSOP has continued to bill the plaintiff for payment under the lease and has, upon information and belief, reported such refusal to pay to one or more credit reporting agencies without disclosing that the plaintiff disputes the defendants' claim for payment.

A. *The history of the subject vehicle*

28. According to DMV records the subject vehicle was first sold by Mercedes-Benz of North America, Inc. to Knox Pontiac, Inc., pursuant to a Certificate of Origin dated _____. The records further disclose that the vehicle was sold by Knopf to Rondo Motors, Inc., _____, New York, on _____.

29. Thereafter, according to DMV records, the vehicle was sold by Rondo to MBM. On or about _____, the subject vehicle was purchased by Mercedes-Benz Credit Corporation ("MBCC") and simultaneously leased to Abraham A. Josephs _____, New York, for a three year term commencing that date.

30. According to DMV records, on _____, the subject vehicle, while being operated by Mr. Josephs in Nassau County, was involved in a serious collision causing personal injury.

31. Upon information and belief, the subject vehicle suffered serious physical damage as a result of the collision, in particular to its front end.

32. Upon information and belief, Mr. Joseph's insurance carrier, Interstate Insurance Company, adjusted the physical damage loss to the subject vehicle at $79,269.87.

33. Upon information and belief, the collision required the complete replacement of numerous parts, components and systems of the subject vehicle including, *inter alia*, the engine, transmission, front end, air bags, brakes and electrical systems.

34. Upon information and belief, the subject vehicle was brought to Vehicle City Motorworks, Inc. ("Vehicle City"), _____, New York, for repair of the collision damage.

35. According to DMV records, the subject vehicle was purchased by Vehicle City from MBCC on or about _____. The title issued to Vehicle City by the DMV at that time stated that the vehicle was "TOTALED."

36. On _____, according to DMV records, Vehicle City sold the subject vehicle to Motor Group. On _____, according to DMV records, Motor Group sold the subject vehicle to Leasing Group, who thereafter leased it to the plaintiff.

37. In transferring the subject vehicle to Leasing Group, Motor Group affirmatively certified to the DMV under penalty of perjury, and thereby to the general public, that it was in a "condition and repair to render satisfactory and adequate service on the public highway under normal use," as required by Vehicle and Traffic Law § 417.

38. Upon information and belief, Leasing Group, Motor Group and/or Ames had discussions and/or correspondence with MBCC prior to Motor Group's purchase of the subject vehicle from Vehicle City.

39. Upon information and belief, the subject of such discussions and/or correspondence included, *inter alia*, the prior collision history of the subject vehicle. As a result of such discussions, Motor Group secured a retraction from MBCC of the "TOTALED" notation on the title for the subject vehicle. Motor Group did so as part of a scheme to conceal such information from any subsequent purchaser and/or lessee.

40. All of the defendants knew, or reasonably should have known, that the subject vehicle had been seriously damaged in a prior collision at the time possession was transferred to the plaintiff.

41. All of the defendants knew, or reasonably should have known, that the subject vehicle's mechanical condition was defective and that it was not safe to operate at the time possession was transferred to the plaintiff.

AS AND FOR A FIRST CAUSE OF CAUSE OF ACTION:
Breach of Express Warranty

42. The plaintiff repeats and realleges each and every allegation above.

43. The First Cause of Action is asserted against the defendants for breach of contract, due to Leasing Group's, Motor Group's and Ames's breach of express warranties, and in the alternative to the plaintiff's cause of action for revocation of acceptance.

44. Leasing Group, Motor Group and Ames made certain representations and express warranties, as described above, regarding the condition and prior history of the subject vehicle prior to the plaintiff's agreement to accept it.

45. Leasing Group, Motor Group and Ames breached such express warranties in that the vehicle had in fact been involved in a prior collision in which it suffered serious physical damage and had serious mechanical defects which rendered it unfit for normal use.

46. As a result of the defendants' breach, the plaintiff has sustained damage in the amount of $250,000.00, for which he is entitled to recover from Leasing Group, Motor Group and Ames.

AS AND FOR A SECOND CAUSE OF ACTION:
Breach of Implied Warranty of Merchantability

47. The plaintiff repeats and realleges each and every allegation above.

48. The Second Cause of Action is asserted against the defendants Leasing Group, Motor Group and Ames, for breach of contract, due to their breach of the implied warranty of merchantability, and in the alternative to the plaintiff's cause of action for revocation of acceptance.

49. Leasing Group and/or Motor Group were, at all relevant times, merchants of motor vehicles.

50. A warranty that the subject vehicle was in merchantable condition is implied by law.

51. The subject vehicle was not in merchantable condition when delivered to the plaintiff or at any time thereafter, and was not fit for the ordinary purpose for which the vehicle was to be used.

52. The defendants thereby breached the warranty of merchantability implied by law in the instant transaction.

53. As a result of the defendants' breach, the plaintiff has sustained damage in the amount of $250,000.00, for which he is entitled to recover from Leasing Group, Motor Group and Ames.

AS AND FOR A THIRD CAUSE OF ACTION:
Breach of Implied Warranty of Fitness

54. The plaintiff repeats and realleges each and every allegation above.

55. The Third Cause of Action is asserted against the defendants, Leasing Group, Motor Group and Ames, for breach of contract due to their breach of the implied warranty of fitness, and in the alternative to the plaintiff's cause of action for revocation of acceptance.

56. A warranty that the subject vehicle was fit for the particular purpose for which it was intended, *i.e.*, as a motor vehicle to be operated on the highways and to provide safe and reliable operation is implied by law in the instant transaction.

57. The subject vehicle was not fit for the particular purpose for which it was intended to be used.

58. Leasing Group, Motor Group and Ames breached the warranty of fitness for a particular purpose implied by law in the instant transaction.

59. As a result of the defendants' breach, the plaintiff has sustained damage in the amount of $250,000.00, for which he is entitled to recover from the defendants.

AS AND FOR A FOURTH CAUSE OF ACTION:
Revocation of Acceptance

60. The plaintiff repeats and realleges each and every allegation above.

61. The Fourth Cause of Action is asserted against the defendants, Leasing Group and ALLSOP, to cancel the lease and to recover damages based upon the defendants' breach of express and implied warranties.

62. The above described non-conformities of the subject vehicle resulting from defendants' breach of warranty substantially impaired the value of the subject vehicle to the plaintiff.

63. The plaintiff accepted the subject vehicle on the reasonable assumption that the non-conformities resulting from the breach of warranty above would be cured.

64. The non-conformities of the subject vehicle resulting from the breaches of warranty described above were not seasonably, or ever, cured.

65. The plaintiff accepted the subject vehicle without discovery of all the non-conformities resulting from the breach of warranty described above.

66. The plaintiff's acceptance of the subject vehicle was reasonably induced by the defendants' assurances of the subject vehicle's condition.

67. The plaintiff justifiably and effectively revoked acceptance of the subject vehicle on _____.

68. At all relevant times, Leasing Group and ALLSOP have refused to comply with the plaintiff's revocation of acceptance of the subject vehicle and have refused to return any monies paid by the plaintiff under the lease.

69. Further, at all relevant times, Leasing Group and ALLSOP have refused to discontinue billing the plaintiff for payment under the lease. In addition, upon information and belief, Leasing Group and/or ALLSOP have reported the plaintiff's refusal to make additional payments under the lease to one or more credit reporting agencies without disclosing to such agencies that the plaintiff disputes the validity of their claim.

70. As a result, the plaintiff has suffered damage in the amount of the down payment and all other monies paid pursuant to the lease and is entitled to recover therefor from Leasing Group and ALLSOP.

71. The plaintiff is further entitled to a judgment declaring the lease involved herein canceled.

AS AND FOR A FIFTH CAUSE OF ACTION:
Rescission

72. The plaintiff repeats and realleges each and every allegation above.

73. The plaintiff elected to rescind the lease with Leasing Group and ALLSOP based upon Leasing Group's, Motor Group's and/or Ames's material breach of the lease and their false, fraudulent, and misleading representations and/or omissions of fact, as described above.

74. In the alternative, the plaintiff elected to rescind the lease based upon his unilateral mistake in that he would not have agreed to accept the subject vehicle if he had knowledge of its prior history.

75. In the alternative, the plaintiff elected to rescind the lease based upon failure of consideration in that the value, condition and quality of the subject vehicle was substantially less than what was represented to him by Leasing Group, Motor Group and/or Ames.

76. On or about _____, the plaintiff duly notified Leasing Group and ALLSOP that based upon the above, he had elected to rescind the lease.

77. The plaintiff has duly demanded the return of all monies paid under the lease from the defendants.

78. Leasing Group and ALLSOP have continually failed and/or refused to comply with the plaintiff's rescission of the lease and have failed and/or refused to return any amounts paid by the plaintiff under the lease.

79. As a result, the plaintiff has suffered damage in the amount of all monies paid to Leasing Group and ALLSOP pursuant to the lease and is entitled to recover therefor from Leasing Group and ALLSOP.

80. The plaintiff is further entitled to a judgment declaring the lease herein rescinded.

AS AND FOR A SIXTH CAUSE OF ACTION:
Deceptive Business Practices: Damages

81. The plaintiff repeats and realleges each and every allegation above.

82. The Sixth Cause of Action is asserted against the defendants and alleges that the plaintiff suffered damages as a result of the defendants' deceptive business practices in violation of Gen. B. L. Art. 22-A.

83. In the course of the within transaction, the defendants committed and/or engaged in the following acts or conduct and/or made the following misrepresentations:

    a. misrepresenting and/or failing to disclose the true mechanical condition of the subject vehicle prior and subsequent to the plaintiff taking possession;

    b. misrepresenting and/or failing to disclose the true history of the subject vehicle prior and subsequent to the plaintiff taking possession;

c. wrongfully failing and refusing to adjust the terms of the lease following the substitution of the vehicles to accurately reflect the difference in value of the subject vehicle;

d. failing and/or refusing to acknowledge the plaintiff's rightful notice of rescission and/or revocation of acceptance and his resulting security interest;

e. wrongfully claiming a right to report derogatory credit information to credit reporting agencies without disclosing that the plaintiff disputed such information;

f. failing to comply with the requirements of the New York Used Car Lemon Law by, *inter alia*, failing to provide a written warranty for the subject vehicle as required by GBL § 198–b(b)(1).

84. Some or all of the above misrepresentations, acts and/or conduct involved material elements of the transaction between the parties and were unfair, illegal, false, deceptive and/or misleading.

85. Additionally, such representations had the capacity and tendency to, and in fact did, harm, deceive or mislead the plaintiff.

86. The conduct and actions described herein are directed at the general public and are not isolated or unique to the transaction between the parties.

87. The aforementioned conduct constitutes deceptive business practices, in violation of General Business Law Art. 22–A.

88. As a result of such violation, the plaintiff suffered damage in the amount of $250,000.00, and the plaintiff is entitled to recover therefor from the defendants pursuant to GBL § 349(h).

89. Such conduct was also willful, malicious and/or reckless, and/or the result of gross negligence, and, as a result, the plaintiff may recover additional damages in the amount of ONE THOUSAND DOLLARS ($1,000.00) per violation of law from the defendants pursuant to GBL § 349(h).

90. The plaintiff is entitled to recover attorney's fees from the defendants pursuant to GBL § 349(h).

AS AND FOR A SEVENTH CAUSE OF ACTION:
Deceptive Business Practices: Injunction

91. The plaintiff repeats and realleges each and every allegation above, and in particular, the allegations set forth in the Sixth Cause of Action alleging deceptive business practices in violation of GBL Art. 22–A, which are hereby incorporated by reference.

92. Pursuant to GBL § 349(h), the plaintiff is entitled to an injunction barring the defendants from:

a. misrepresenting and/or failing to disclose the true mechanical condition of any vehicle prior and subsequent to the sale and/or lease of any such vehicle;

b. misrepresenting and/or failing to disclose the true history of any vehicle prior and subsequent to the sale and/or lease of any such vehicle;

c. wrongfully failing and/or refusing to acknowledge any rightful notice of rescission and/or revocation of acceptance and resulting security interest;

d. wrongfully claiming a right to report derogatory credit information to any credit reporting agencies without disclosing that the consumer/lessee disputed such information;

e. failing to comply with the requirements of the New York Used Car Lemon Law by, *inter alia*, failing to provide a written warranty as required by GBL § 198–b(b)(1).

93. The plaintiff is entitled to an award of attorney's fees pursuant to GBL § 349(h).

AS AND FOR AN EIGHTH CAUSE OF ACTION:
Fraud

94. The plaintiff repeats and realleges each and every allegation above.

95. The Eighth Cause of Action is asserted against the defendants for actual and punitive damages based upon fraud.

96. The conduct referred to in the Sixth Cause of Action above, as well as in the paragraphs set forth above, constitute misrepresentations, concealment and/or omissions by the defendants of fact.

97. The misstatements, concealment and/or omissions were material to the transaction.

98. Upon information and belief, the defendants made the above described misrepresentations, concealment and/or omissions of material fact with full knowledge of their falsity and/or with reckless disregard of the truth.

99. Upon information and belief, the defendants intended that the plaintiff rely upon the aforementioned misrepresentations, concealment and/or omissions.

100. The plaintiff did rely on the defendants' aforementioned misrepresentations, concealment and/or omissions to his detriment.

101. As a result of the defendants' conduct, the plaintiff was injured in the amount of $250,000.00 for which he is entitled to recover from the defendants.

102. In addition, in transferring the subject vehicle to Leasing Group, Motor group affirmatively certified, under penalty of perjury, to the DMV, and thereby to the general public, that it was in a "condition and repair to render satisfactory and adequate service on the public highway under normal use," as required by Vehicle and Traffic Law § 417.

103. Such representations were known, or reasonably should have been known, to be false when made.

104. In addition, by wilfully, wantonly and recklessly engaging in the above conduct, the defendants' actions and omissions directly impacted on public safety by causing and allowing a motor vehicle to be operated by the plaintiff and his family upon public highways with actual knowledge that such vehicle was not safe.

105. Upon information and belief, the above mentioned acts were committed by the defendants willfully, wantonly and with reckless disregard of the rights of the plaintiff and the general public.

106. In order to punish the defendants for engaging is such morally and legally reprehensible conduct and to deter them from engaging in such conduct in the future, the Court should impose an award of punitive damages in the amount of not less than ONE MILLION DOLLARS ($1,000,000.00).

AS AND FOR A NINTH CAUSE OF ACTION:
Violation of the Used Car Lemon Law

107. The plaintiff repeats and realleges each and every allegation above.

108. The plaintiff is a "Consumer" within the meaning of GBL § 198–b(a)(1) ("Used Car Lemon Law").

109. Upon information and belief, Leasing Group is a "Dealer" within the meaning of GBL § 198–b(a)(3).

110. The subject vehicle is a "Used Motor Vehicle" within the meaning of GBL § 198–b(a)(2).

111. Pursuant to GBL § 198–b(b)(1), Leasing Group was required to provide a written warranty to the plaintiff applying for at least ninety days or four thousand miles from delivery of the subject vehicle, whichever came first.

112. At no time did Leasing Group ever comply with GBL § 198–b(b)(1) and § 198–b(e) by providing a written warranty to the plaintiff for the subject vehicle. Pursuant to GBL § 198–b(d)(1), Leasing Group is deemed to have provided such written warranty to the plaintiff as a matter of law.

113. The above notwithstanding, within ninety days or four thousand miles from the date of delivery, the plaintiff notified Leasing Group of the failure of "covered part[s]," as defined by GBL § 198–b(b)(2).

114. Following such notification, Leasing Group and/or its agent failed or refused to correct the malfunction or defective conditions of the subject vehicle, despite having been provided a reasonable opportunity to do so.

115. The same condition[s] were subject to repair at least three times by Leasing Group and/or its agent within the warranty period and such condition[s] continue to exist despite such repair attempts.

116. The subject vehicle was out of service by reason of repair or malfunction or defect for a cumulative total of at least fifteen days during the warranty period.

117. On several occasions, and most recently on _____, the plaintiff demanded that Leasing Group and ALLSOP accept the return of the subject vehicle and refund all payments made under the lease and to cancel the lease, pursuant to GBL § 198–b(c)(1). To date, the defendants have failed and refused to comply with any such obligations.

118. Pursuant to GBL § 198–b (f)(5), the plaintiff is entitled to: a) recover all payments made under the lease from Leasing Group and ALLSOP; b) cancellation of the lease; and c) an award of attorney's fees.

AS AND FOR A TENTH CAUSE OF ACTION:
Attorney's Fees Pursuant to GOL § 5–327

119. The plaintiff repeats and realleges each and every allegation above.

120. The lease is a "Consumer Contract" within the meaning of GOL § 5–327(1)(a).

121. Leasing Group is a "Lessor" within the meaning of GOL § 5–327(1)(d).

122. The lease between Leasing Group and the plaintiff purports to permit Leasing Group to recover its reasonable attorney's fees incurred in any action arising out of the lease.

123. Pursuant to GOL § 5–327(2), a reciprocal right to recover attorney's fees, in favor of the plaintiff, is implied as a matter of law upon a breach of any contractual obligation by Leasing Group.

124. Leasing Group breached the lease with the plaintiff as set forth above.

125. The plaintiff is entitled to an award of attorney's fees pursuant to GOL § 5–327(2).

WHEREFORE, the plaintiff demands judgment against the defendants, as set forth above, awarding relief as follows:

§ 7.52   **CONSUMER LAW**   Ch. 7

a. On the First Cause of Action, TWO HUNDRED AND FIFTY THOUSAND DOLLARS ($250,000.00);

b. On the Second Cause of Action, TWO HUNDRED AND FIFTY THOUSAND DOLLARS ($250,000.00);

c. On the Third Cause of Action, TWO HUNDRED AND FIFTY THOUSAND DOLLARS ($250,000.00);

d. On the Fourth Cause of Action, an amount equal to all monies paid pursuant to the lease and declaring the lease canceled;

e. On the Fifth Cause of Action, an amount equal to all monies paid pursuant to the lease and declaring the lease canceled;

f. On the Sixth Cause of Action, TWO HUNDRED AND FIFTY THOUSAND DOLLARS ($250,000.00), ONE THOUSAND DOLLARS per violation of law and attorney's fees;

g. On the Seventh Cause of Action, an injunction barring the defendants from engaging in the conduct set forth therein and an award of attorney's fees;

g. On the Eighth Cause of Action, TWO HUNDRED AND FIFTY THOUSAND DOLLARS ($250,000.00) and ONE MILLION DOLLARS ($1,000,000.00) in punitive damages;

h. On the Ninth Cause of Action, an amount equal to all monies paid pursuant to the lease, declaring the lease canceled and attorney's fees;

i. On the Tenth Cause of Action, an award of attorney's fees;

j. The interest, costs and disbursements of this action; and

k. Such other relief as may be just.

Dated: _____ New York

                                                Yours, etc.

                                                [ATTORNEY], Esq.
                                                Attorneys for the Plaintiff
                                                [ADDRESS AND TELEPHONE NUMBER]

TO: **ABC LEASING GROUP, INC.,**
760 Jericho Turnpike
Woodbury, New York 11797

ABC MOTOR GROUP, INC.,
760 Jericho Turnpike
Woodbury, New York 11797

ROBERT AMES
c/o ABC Leasing Group, Inc.
760 Jericho Turnpike
Woodbury, New York 11797

ALLSOP BANK
1 ALLSOP Plaza
Uniondale, New York 11555–9572

[*VERIFICATION*]

Library References:
West's Key No. Digests, Consumer Protection ⚖=38.

§ 7.53 Forms—Answer and Third–Party Complaint Alleging Fraud, Deceptive Practices, Breach of Warranty, and Federal Odometer Law Claims in Fraudulent Automobile Lease Case

SUPREME COURT OF THE STATE OF NEW YORK
COUNTY OF NEW YORK

TREMONT LEASING ASSOCIATES, L.P.,)
                  Plaintiff,)
                  -against-)
MARIA SHELDON, also known as MARIA)
FRANCIS SHELDON, and HERBERT FERRIS,)
                  Defendants.) VERIFIED ANSWER
                  -and-) Index No.
MARIA SHELDON AND HERBERT FERRIS,)
                  Third–Party Plaintiffs,)
                  -against-)
MAYER MOTORS INC.,)
                  Third–Party Defendants.)

---

§ 7.53   CONSUMER LAW   Ch. 7

PLEASE TAKE NOTICE that the defendants, **GEORGE C. FERRIS and MARIA SHELDON** sued herein as MARIA FRANCIS SHELDON ("Mr. Ferris," "Ms. Sheldon," and/or "the defendants"), hereby appear in this action by their attorney, _____, Esq., and demand that all papers in this action be served on him at the address below.

PLEASE TAKE FURTHER NOTICE that the defendants, as and for their answer to the complaint, assert the following:

1. The defendants lack information sufficient to form a belief concerning the allegations stated in paragraphs 1, 2, 8, 10 and 14 of the complaint.

2. The defendants deny the allegations stated in paragraphs 5, 6, 7, 9, 10, 11, 13 and both paragraphs numbered 16 of the complaint.

3. The defendants admit the allegations in paragraphs 3 and 4 of the complaint.

4. The defendants admit so much of paragraph 15 that alleges that the defendants have not returned the subject vehicle.

HISTORY AND BACKGROUND OF THIS MATTER

5. Upon information and belief, the plaintiff TREMONT LEASING ASSOCIATES, L.P. ("TREMONT" or "the plaintiff") is in the business of leasing automobiles to consumers.

6. Upon information and belief, TREMONT, as principal, uses Mayer Motors Inc., ("Mayer") as its agent, in connection with its business of automobile leasing.

7. Upon information and belief, at all times mentioned herein TREMONT used Mayer as its disclosed and undisclosed agent to lease the subject vehicle, a 1987 Mercedes-Benz automobile, VIN WDBEA30DXHA566520. (The "subject vehicle")

8. In or about, _____, Mayer, acting as TREMONT's agent, procured a lease of the subject vehicle, on TREMONT's behalf, with Mr. Ferris. Prior to such time the defendants had no contact with, or knowledge of, TREMONT.

9. In or about _____, Mr. Ferris was shown the subject vehicle by an employee(s) of Mayer, acting as TREMONT's agent.

10. At that time, Mr. Ferris was quoted a purchase price of $25,000.00 for the subject vehicle, was told that it had traveled 33,960 miles (which its odometer corroborated) and that a full warranty for two years was included in the purchase price.

11. Upon information and belief, TREMONT, through its agent, knew, or should have known, that the odometer reading at that time was not accurate, that the odometer understated the subject vehicle's actual

mileage by more than 20,000 miles, and that in fact it had incurred in excess of 56,000 miles of use at that time. At no time did Mayer or TREMONT ever advise the defendants that the odometer reading on the subject vehicle was in fact substantially understated.

12. Mr. Ferris sought to purchase the vehicle from Mayer. Mayer, however, induced Mr. Ferris to lease, rather than purchase, the subject vehicle, claiming that this arrangement would result in an improvement of his credit rating.

13. The terms of the lease offered by Mayer, on TREMONT's behalf were as follows:

   a. Mr. Ferris was to be the lessee;
   b. The purchase price of the subject vehicle under the lease was to be $25,000.00;
   c. The lessee was to tender $15,000 as a down payment on the lease;
   d. The balance of the lease price was to be paid in 48 equal, monthly installments of approximately $200.00;
   e. The lease was to include an option to purchase the subject vehicle at the end of the lease for $2,000.00;
   f. The lease was to include a two-year full warranty for the subject vehicle.

14. At the request of Mayer and TREMONT, Mr. Ferris secured Ms. Sheldon as a guarantor of the lease.

15. On or about _____, Mayer, on behalf of, and as agent for, TREMONT, presented Mr. Ferris and Mr. Sheldon with an incomplete, proposed lease.

16. The defendants signed the proposed agreement whereby TREMONT would lease the subject vehicle to Mr. Ferris, and Ms. Sheldon would guaranty the lease.

17. Mr. Ferris paid the sum of $15,000.00 to TREMONT's agent when he signed the lease.

18. The lease did not contain any acknowledgment of the $15,000.00 down payment, any notation of the balance remaining, the terms upon which the balance was payable, nor any reference to a manufacturer's warranty.

19. An employee of Mayer advised the defendants that Mr. Ferris would receive a copy of the fully executed lease with TREMONT, along with a payment coupon book, vehicle registration and the car's maintenance record.

20. At no time has Mayer or TREMONT delivered true copies of the executed leases to the defendants.

21. At no time has Mayer or TREMONT delivered any of the other documentation to Mr. Ferris, except for maintenance records pertaining to the subject vehicle.

22. Mayer and/or TREMONT have delivered altered or forged documents to the defendants purporting to be the leases.

23. The documents state, incorrectly, that Ms. Sheldon is the lessee, rather than the guarantor. The plaintiff, or its agents, have also made her the primary obligor on the lease, thus negating the express intent of the parties to use a transaction that would result in a rehabilitation of Mr. Ferris's credit rating.

AS AND FOR A FIRST DEFENSE

24. The complaint fails to state a cause of action upon which relief can be granted and therefore must be dismissed pursuant to CPLR 3211(a)(8).

AS AND FOR A SECOND DEFENSE AND FIRST COUNTERCLAIM: FRAUD

25. Each paragraph and allegation above is repeated and realleged.

26. TREMONT, acting through its agent, made material representations concerning the subject vehicle, including, but not limited to, the actual mileage of the subject vehicle and its value at the time of the transaction.

27. Such representations concerned a material aspect of the transaction and were false and misleading.

28. The plaintiff knew, or should have known, that such representations were false and misleading.

29. The plaintiff, through its agents, thereby intended to deceive the defendants.

30. The defendants believed and relied upon the misrepresentations.

31. The defendants have thereby been harmed in the amount of $20,000.00, any contract or lease they were induced to sign is thereby void, and the complaint should therefore be dismissed.

32. The plaintiff acted knowingly, recklessly and maliciously. In order to punish and deter the plaintiff from engaging in such acts in the future, the Court should award punitive damages to the defendants in the amount of $500,000.00.

AS AND FOR A SECOND COUNTERCLAIM: REFORMATION

33. Each allegation above is repeated and realleged.

34. The defendants demand reformation of the lease to reflect the intent of the parties and the terms set forth in paragraph 13 above.

AS AND FOR A THIRD COUNTERCLAIM:
FEDERAL ODOMETER LAW

35. Each allegation above is repeated and realleged.

36. The plaintiff is a "transferor" within the meaning of the federal Odometer Law, 15 U.S.C.A. §§ 1980 *et seq.*

37. The plaintiff violated 15 U.S.C.A. § 1988(b) by failing to disclose the actual mileage of the subject vehicle and by providing a false statement concerning the mileage.

38. The defendants have thereby been damaged in an amount in excess of $20,000.00.

39. Pursuant to 15 U.S.C.A. § 1989(a)(1), the defendants are entitled to an award of treble damages, as well as attorney's fees to be determined at the conclusion of this action.

AS AND FOR A FOURTH COUNTERCLAIM:
ILLEGAL AND DECEPTIVE ACTS AND PRACTICES

40. Each allegation above is repeated and realleged.

41. The conduct and actions described herein are directed at the general public and are not isolated or unique to the transaction between the parties.

42. The plaintiffs' acts and practices, as described above, were illegal and deceptive, in violation of New York General Business Law Article 22–A.

43. The defendants have suffered damage in an amount in excess of $20,000.00 and may recover therefore under GBL § 349(h).

44. The acts and practices of the plaintiff were wilful, and, as a result, the defendants are entitled to an award of additional damages in the amount of $1,000.00 per violation of law pursuant to GBL § 349(h).

45. In addition, the defendants are entitled to an award of reasonable attorney's fees pursuant to GBL § 349(h) in an amount to be determined at the conclusion of this action.

AS AND FOR A FIFTH COUNTERCLAIM:
BREACH OF WARRANTY

46. Each allegation above is repeated and realleged.

47. The plaintiff, directly or indirectly, created an express warranty as to the subject vehicle's mileage, pursuant to UCC §§ 2–313 and 2–318. The plaintiff, directly, and/or through its agent, breached such warranty by misrepresenting the subject vehicle's actual mileage.

48. The defendants are entitled to an award of damages equal to the difference between the value of the subject vehicle as represented to

§ 7.53   CONSUMER LAW   Ch. 7

them, and its actual value, together with an award of consequential damages in an amount in excess of $20,000.00.

AS AND FOR A SIXTH COUNTERCLAIM: ATTORNEY'S FEES PURSUANT TO GOL § 5-327

49. Each allegation above is repeated and realleged.

50. The purported lease, which is the subject of this action, contains a clause purportedly providing for an award of attorney's fees to the plaintiff if it is successful in an action to enforce the lease.

51. Pursuant to General Obligations Law § 5-327(2) a provision providing for the recovery of attorney's fees to the defendants is therefore implied as well.

52. Based upon the foregoing, if the defendants are successful in this action, they are entitled to an award of attorney's fees pursuant to GOL § 5-327.

WHEREFORE, the defendants demand judgment as follows:

a. Dismissing the complaint with prejudice;

b. On the first counterclaim and defense, that the lease be declared void, the complaint be dismissed, and that they be awarded $20,000.00 in compensatory damages as well as punitive damages in an amount to be determined by the Court;

c. On the second counterclaim, reformation of the lease;

d. On the third counterclaim, an award of $20,000.00 together with treble damages and reasonable attorneys' fees;

e. On the fourth counterclaim, an award of damages in excess of $20,000.00 together with additional damages of $1,000.00 per violation of law and attorneys' fees;

f. On the fifth counterclaim, an award of damages in an amount to be determined by the Court;

g. On the sixth counterclaim, an award of attorney's fees;

h. Awarding the defendants the costs and disbursements of this action as well as the interest accrued on all damages incurred; and

i. Such other relief that the Court may deem just and proper.

Dated: _____, New York

                                                           Yours, etc.

                                                           [ATTORNEY], Esq.
                                                           Attorney of Defendants
                                                           [*ADDRESS AND TELEPHONE NUMBER*]

TO: ZELIG & SCHWARTZ
    Attorneys for Plaintiff
    TREMONT LEASING
    ASSOCIATES, L.P.
    305 Lexington Avenue
    New York, New York 10174

[VERIFICATION]

SUPREME COURT OF THE STATE OF NEW YORK
COUNTY OF NEW YORK

TREMONT LEASING ASSOCIATES, L.P.,

    Plaintiff,

-against-

MARIA SHELDON, also known as MARIA FRANCIS SHELDON, and HERBERT FERRIS,

    Defendants.

-and-

MARIA SHELDON AND HERBERT FERRIS,

    Third–Party Plaintiffs,

-against-

MAYER MOTORS INC.,

    Third–Party Defendants.

VERIFIED THIRD–PARTY COMPLAINT

THIRD PARTY COMPLAINT AGAINST MAYER MOTORS INC.

PLEASE TAKE FURTHER NOTICE, that **GEORGE FERRIS and MARIA SHELDON** ("Mr. Ferris," "Ms. Sheldon" and/or the "third-party plaintiffs"), the third-party plaintiffs, by their attorney, as and for their third-party complaint against MAYER MOTORS, INC., allege as follows:

    1. The third-party plaintiff's are both natural persons, over the age of 18, and residents of New York State.

    2. Upon information and belief, the third-party defendant, Mayer Motors Inc. ("Mayer" or the "third-party defendant"), is a domestic corporation with offices at 15–34 Northern Blvd., Long Island City, N.Y.

§ 7.53   CONSUMER LAW   Ch. 7

11101 and is in the business of automobile sales and arranging automobile leases between third parties.

3. At all times relevant here, the third-party defendant acted as a disclosed and undisclosed agent for TREMONT Leasing Associates, L.P. ("TREMONT"), the owner of an equipment lease for, and titleholder, to a 1987 Mercedes–Benz automobile, VIN# WDBEA29XDWQ123456 (the "subject vehicle").

4. In or about _____, Mayer, acting as TREMONT's agent, procured a lease of the subject vehicle, on TREMONT's behalf, with Mr. Ferris.

5. In or about _____, Mr. Ferris was shown the subject vehicle by an employee(s) of Mayer.

6. At that time, Mr. Ferris was quoted a purchase price of $25,000.00 for the subject vehicle, was told that it had traveled 33,960 miles (which its odometer corroborated) and that a full warranty for two years was included in the purchase price.

7. Upon information and belief, Mayer knew, or should have known, that the odometer reading at that time was not accurate, that the odometer understated the subject vehicle's actual mileage by more than 20,000 miles, and that in fact it had incurred in excess of 56,000 miles of use at that time. At no time did Mayer ever advise the defendants that the odometer reading on the subject vehicle was in fact substantially understated.

8. Mr. Ferris sought to purchase the subject vehicle from Mayer. Mayer, however, induced Mr. Ferris to lease, rather than purchase, the subject vehicle, claiming that this arrangement would result in an improvement of his credit rating.

9. The terms of the lease offered by Mayer were as follows:

a. Mr. Ferris was to be the lessee;

b. The purchase price of the subject vehicle under the lease was to be $25,000.00;

c. The lessee was to tender $15,000 as a down payment on the lease;

d. The balance of the lease price was to be paid in 48 equal, monthly installments of approximately $200;

e. The lease was to include an option to purchase the subject vehicle at the end of the lease for $2,000.00;

f. The lease was to include a two-year full warranty for the subject vehicle.

10. At the request of Mayer, Mr. Ferris secured Ms. Sheldon as a guarantor of the lease.

11. On or about _____, Mayer, on behalf of, and as agent for, TREMONT, presented Mr. Ferris and Mr. Sheldon with an incomplete, proposed lease.

12. The third-party plaintiffs signed the proposed agreement whereby TREMONT would lease the subject vehicle to Mr. Ferris and Ms. Sheldon would guaranty the lease.

13. Mr. Ferris paid the sum of $15,000.00 to Mayer when he signed the lease.

14. The lease did not contain any acknowledgment of the $15,000.00 down payment, any notation of the balance remaining, the terms upon which the balance was payable, nor any reference to a warranty.

15. An employee of Mayer advised the third-party plaintiffs that Mr. Ferris would receive a copy of the fully executed lease with TREMONT, along with a payment coupon book, vehicle registration and the car's maintenance record.

16. At no time have Mayer or TREMONT delivered true copies of the executed leases to the third-party plaintiffs.

17. At no time have Mayer or TREMONT delivered any of the other documentation to Mr. Ferris, except for maintenance records pertaining to the subject vehicle.

18. Mayer and/or TREMONT have delivered altered or forged documents to the third-party plaintiffs purporting to be the leases.

19. The documents state, incorrectly, that Ms. Sheldon is the lessee, rather than the guarantor. The third-party defendant, or its principal, has also made her the primary obligor on the lease, thus negating the express intent of the parties to a transaction, which would result in a rehabilitation of Mr. Ferris's credit rating.

AS AND FOR A FIRST CAUSE OF ACTION: FRAUD

20. Each paragraph and allegation above is repeated and realleged.

21. Mayer, on its own behalf, and on behalf of its principal, TREMONT, made material representations concerning the subject vehicle, including, but not limited to, the actual mileage of the subject vehicle and its value at the time of the transaction.

22. Such representations concerned a material aspect of the transaction and were false and misleading.

23. The third-party defendant knew, or should have known, that such representations were false and misleading.

24. The third-party defendant, through its agents, thereby intended to deceive the third-party plaintiffs.

25. The third-party plaintiffs believed and relied upon the misrepresentations.

26. The third-party plaintiffs have thereby been harmed in the amount of $20,000.00.

27. The third-party defendant acted knowingly, recklessly and maliciously. In order to punish and deter it from engaging in such acts in the future, the Court should award punitive damages to the defendants in the amount of $500,000.00.

AS AND FOR A SECOND CAUSE OF ACTION: REFORMATION

28. Each allegation above is repeated and realleged.

29. The third-party plaintiffs demand reformation of the lease to reflect the intent of the parties and the terms set forth in paragraph 10 above.

AS AND FOR A THIRD CAUSE OF ACTION: FEDERAL ODOMETER LAW

30. Each allegation above is repeated and realleged.

31. The third-party defendant is a "transferor" within the meaning of the federal Odometer Law, 15 U.S.C.A. §§ 1980 *et seq.*

32. The third-party defendant violated 15 U.S.C.A. § 1988(b) by failing to disclose the actual mileage of the subject vehicle and by providing a false statement concerning the mileage.

33. The third-party plaintiffs have thereby been damaged in an amount in excess of $20,000.00.

34. Pursuant to 15 U.S.C.A. § 1989(a)(1), the third-party plaintiffs are entitled to an award of treble damages, as well as attorney's fees to be determined at the conclusion of this action.

AS AND FOR A FOURTH CAUSE OF ACTION: INDEMNIFICATION

35. Each allegation above is repeated and realleged.

36. The third-party plaintiffs are currently defendants in an action brought by TREMONT Leasing Associates L.P., in which they may be found to have defaulted on the subject lease and thereby be liable for money found to be due TREMONT (Complaint attached hereto).

37. Should the third-party plaintiffs be found liable to TREMONT, it would be solely due to the fraud, misrepresentations and/or malfeasance of Mayer.

38. The third-party defendants will thereby be harmed in an amount to be determined, and they demand judgment against Mayer in an amount sufficient to make them whole.

AS AND FOR A FIFTH CAUSE OF ACTION:
ILLEGAL AND DECEPTIVE ACTS AND PRACTICES

39. Each allegation above is repeated and realleged.

40. The conduct and actions described herein are directed at the general public and are not isolated or unique to the transaction between the parties.

41. The third-party defendant's acts and practices were illegal, unfair and deceptive, in violation of New York General Business Law Article 22–A.

42. The third-party plaintiffs have suffered damage in an amount in excess of $20,000.00 and may recover therefor under GBL § 349(h).

43. The acts and practices of the third-party defendants were wilful, and, as a result, the third-party plaintiff's are entitled to an award of additional damages in the amount of $1,000.00 per violation of law pursuant to GBL § 349(h).

44. In addition, the third-party plaintiffs are entitled to an award of reasonable attorney's fees pursuant to GBL § 349(h) in an amount to be determined at the conclusion of this action.

AS AND FOR A SIXTH CAUSE OF ACTION:
BREACH OF WARRANTY

45. Each allegation above is repeated and realleged.

46. The third-party defendant created an express warranty as to the subject vehicle's mileage, pursuant to UCC §§ 2–313 and 2–318. The third-party defendant breached such warranty by misrepresenting the subject vehicle's actual mileage.

47. The third-party plaintiffs are entitled to an award of damages equal to the difference between the value of the subject vehicle as represented to them and its actual value, together with an award of consequential damages, in an amount in excess of $20,000.00.

WHEREFORE, the third-party plaintiffs demand judgment against the third-party defendant as follows:

a. On the first cause of action, $20,000 as actual damages and $500,000.00 in punitive damages;

b. On the second cause of action, that the lease between the third-party plaintiffs and the defendant's principal be reformed;

c. On the third cause of action, $20,000.00 plus treble damages and attorney's fees;

d. On the fourth cause of action, that judgment be rendered for them against the third-party defendant in any amount for which they are found liable to the plaintiff in the main action;

§ 7.53   CONSUMER LAW   Ch. 7

  e. On the fifth cause of action, an award of damages in excess of $20,000.00, together with additional damages of $1,000.00 per violation of law, and attorney's fees;
  f. On the sixth cause of action, an award of damages in an amount to be determined by the court;
  g. Awarding the third-party plaintiffs the costs and disbursements of this action as well as the interest accrued on all damages incurred; and
  h. Such other relief that the court may deem just and proper.

Dated: _____, New York

Yours, etc.
[ATTORNEY], Esq.
Attorney of Third–Party Plaintiffs
[ADDRESS AND TELEPHONE NUMBER]

TO: Mayer Motors, Inc.
Third-party Defendants
34–11 Northern Blvd.
Long Island City, N.Y. 11101

[VERIFICATION]

Library References:

West's Key No. Digests, Consumer Protection ⇔38.

§ 7.54 Forms—Answer to Complaint by Automobile Leasing Company for Deficiency Following Repossession, Alleging Commercially Unreasonable Resale and Deceptive Business Practices

SUPREME COURT OF THE STATE OF NEW YORK
COUNTY OF NASSAU

————————————————————————————)
)
LOW CLASS AUTO LEASING CORP.,   )
)
                      Plaintiff,)
) VERIFIED
         -against-   ) ANSWER
)
FIRST HUDSON EQUIPMENT LEASING CORP.) Index No.
and MARTIN FRANK,   )
)
                     Defendants.)
————————————————————————————)

120

PLEASE TAKE NOTICE, that the defendants hereby appear in this action by their attorney, _____, Esq., and demand that all papers be served upon the undersigned at the address set forth below.

PLEASE TAKE FURTHER NOTICE, that the defendants, as and for their answer to the complaint, state as follows:

1. The defendants lack knowledge or information sufficient to admit or deny the allegations set forth in paragraph "1" of the complaint.

2. The defendants deny the allegations set forth in paragraphs "3", "4", "5", "6", "7", "8", "9", "10", "12" and "13" of the complaint and respectfully refer the Court to the document(s) themselves for their contents.

AS AND FOR A FIRST DEFENSE

3. The plaintiff failed to serve the summons and complaint upon the individual defendant in the manner required by CPLR Art. 3. Such papers were sent by certified mail only. As a result, the Court lacks personal jurisdiction over the individual defendant. The complaint against such defendant must be dismissed.

AS AND FOR A SECOND DEFENSE

4. The complaint fails to state a cause of action and must therefore be dismissed pursuant to CPLR 3211a(7).

AS AND FOR A FIRST AFFIRMATIVE DEFENSE

5. The purported lease between the parties is unconscionable and ambiguous and is therefore unenforceable.

AS AND FOR A SECOND AFFIRMATIVE DEFENSE

6. Accord and satisfaction.

AS AND FOR A THIRD AFFIRMATIVE DEFENSE

7. The plaintiff's conduct and actions constitute strict foreclosure under UCC § 9–505(2). The plaintiff therefore cannot recover from the defendants.

AS AND FOR A FOURTH AFFIRMATIVE DEFENSE

8. Upon information and belief, the plaintiff sold the subject vehicle without providing any notice of such sale to the defendants in violation of UCC § 9–504(3). As a result, the plaintiff may recover any sum from the defendants.

§ 7.54

AS AND FOR A FIFTH AFFIRMATIVE DEFENSE

9. Upon information and belief, the plaintiff's sale of the subject vehicle was not commercially reasonable, in violation of UCC § 9–504(3). As a result, the plaintiff may recover any sum from the defendants.

AS AND FOR A SIXTH AFFIRMATIVE DEFENSE

10. Upon information and belief, the plaintiff's claim is improper because the plaintiff failed to credit the defendants with the full re-sale value of the subject vehicle, the plaintiff failed to credit the defendants for all payments made, and the plaintiff failed to credit the defendants with unearned interest charges.

11. As a result the complaint must be dismissed.

AS AND FOR A SEVENTH AFFIRMATIVE DEFENSE

12. The plaintiff's claim is barred by the doctrine of unjust enrichment.

AS AND FOR AN EIGHTH AFFIRMATIVE DEFENSE

13. The amount sought by the plaintiff amounts to a penalty and unenforceable liquidated damages.

AS AND FOR A FIRST COUNTERCLAIM

14. Upon information and belief, the plaintiff, by its conduct and actions, engaged in illegal and deceptive business practices in violation of GBL Art. 22–A. The defendants are entitled to an award of actual damages pursuant to GBL § 349(h) as well as an award of attorney's fees.

15. Upon information and belief, the plaintiff's conduct and actions were wilful, and, as a result, the defendants are entitled to an award of additional damages in the amount of $1,000.00 pursuant to GBL § 349(h).

WHEREFORE, the defendants demand judgment dismissing the complaint in its entirety and with prejudice and awarding them the costs, disbursements and attorney's fees of this action together with such other relief as may be just.

Dated: _____, New York

                        Yours, etc.

                        [ATTORNEY], Esq.
                        Attorney for Defendants
                        [ADDRESS AND TELEPHONE NUMBER]

TO:

[ATTORNEY], Esq.
Attorney for the Plaintiff
575 Madison Avenue
Suite 508
New York, New York 10022

[VERIFICATION]

Library References:

West's Key No. Digests, Consumer Protection ⚖=38.

§ 7.55 Forms—Affirmation in Opposition to Lessor's Motion for Summary Judgment and in Support of Lessee's Cross–Motion for Summary Judgment Alleging Commercially Unreasonable Resale

SUPREME COURT OF THE STATE OF NEW YORK
COUNTY OF NASSAU

———————————————————
LOW CLASS AUTO LEASING CORP.,   )
)
                            Plaintiff,)
) AFFIRMATION
            -against-   )
) Index No.
ELLWOOD EQUIPMENT LEASING CORP.   )
and MARTIN FRANK,   )
)
                            Defendants.)
———————————————————

_____, an attorney duly admitted to practice before the Courts of the State of New York, affirms the truth of the following:

1. I am the attorney for the defendants herein. This affirmation is offered in opposition to the plaintiff's motion for summary judgment and in support of the defendants' cross-motion for summary judgment, dismissing the complaint.

2. For a variety of reasons, its clear that the plaintiff's motion must be denied in its entirety and with prejudice. For the same reasons, the defendant's cross-motion for summary judgement dismissing the complaint must be granted.

3. The summons and complaint is attached to the plaintiff's moving papers as Exhibit "A." The defendants' verified answer is attached

§ 7.55   **CONSUMER LAW**   Ch. 7

to the moving papers as Exhibit "B." The plaintiff's reply is attached to the moving papers as Exhibit "C."

THE PLAINTIFF FAILED TO SERVE A PROPER SALE NOTICE

4. As set forth in the within affidavit of the individual defendant MARTIN FRANK, ("Frank affidavit"), neither he nor the corporate defendant received any notice whatsoever from the plaintiff advising of the sale of the subject vehicle following repossession. (Frank affidavit, para. 5).

5. U.C.C. § 9–504(3) requires a secured party, after default, to, *inter alia*, provide the debtor with "reasonable notification of the time and place of any public sale . . ."

6. Here, no such notice was given. Nor has the plaintiff provided an affidavit from anyone with personal knowledge that the notices were even sent. For this reason alone, the complaint must be dismissed because failure to send a sale notice bars the plaintiff from recovering a deficiency judgment. *Long Island Trust Co. v. Porta Aluminum*, 63 A.D.2d 670, 404 N.Y.S.2d 682 (2d Dep't 1978); *Security Trust Co. v. Thomas*, 59 A.D.2d 242, 399 N.Y.S.2d 511 (4th Dep't 1977); *Manufacturers Hanover Trust Co. v. Goldstein*, 25 A.D.2d 405, 270 N.Y.S.2d 261 (1966); *Leasco Data Processing Equip. Corp. v. Atlas Shirt Co.*, 66 Misc.2d 1089, 323 N.Y.S.2d 13 (1971); *Avis Rent-A-Car System, Inc. v. Franklin*, 82 Misc.2d 66, 366 N.Y.S.2d 83 (App. Term 2d & 11th Jud. Dists., 1975); *Credit Car Leasing Corp. v. DeCresenzo*, 138 Misc.2d 726, 525 N.Y.S.2d 492 (Civ. Ct., N.Y. County, 1988); *Long Island Trust Co. v. Williams*, 133 Misc.2d 746, 507 N.Y.S.2d 993 (Civ. Ct., N.Y. County, 1986), aff'd, 142 Misc.2d 4, 539 N.Y.S.2d 612 (App. Term 1st Dept., 1988).

7. In addition, and more importantly, even if the notices were sent, they are patently defective on their face and the result is therefore the same.

8. The notices state:

> The above leased vehicle will be offered for sale at the Statewide Auto Auction in Plainview, New York after _____. The vehicle will be stored at that facility from until it is sold. You are invited to purchase the vehicle. Any proceeds received from the sale will be credited to your termination liability as per Article 10 of the lease. (See Exhibit "1")

9. The notices do not state the date, time or place of the proposed sale. Instead they refer only to a date sometime in the future after _____. In fact, according to the affidavit of Stephen Schultz, the vehicle

was sold at a public auction some 19 days after that date.[1] (See Schultz Affidavit, para. 12)

10. Although § 9–504(3) permits a secured party to dispose of collateral by either public or private sale, if it elects to use a public sale it must comply with the notice requirements therein by providing "reasonable notification of the time and place" of the sale.

Even if the secured party gives notice to debtor ...his 'notice' may not contain the correct message. *Note that notice of a public sale must contain different information from that announcing an intent to sell privately. In the latter case, the notice need only state 'the time after which' the collateral is to be sold; in the case of a public sale, it must state 'the time and place' at which the sale will occur. A creditor who uses his private sale form for a public sale violates 9–504(3).* White and Summers, *Handbook of the Law Under the Uniform Commercial Code*, West Publishing Co., 1972, Sec. 26–10, p. 986 (emphasis added).

11. Here, it is readily apparent that if the plaintiff sent a sale notice, it used one that applies only to a private sale, not a public auction. The notices are therefore deficient on their face as a matter of law and are a nullity.

12. Moreover, the notices here also do not meet the strict requirements of U.C.C. § 9–504(3) by failing to provide "reasonable notification of the time and *place*" of such sale. By omitting the location of the auction the plaintiff did not even provide notification of the place of the sale. "[A]t a minimum, the notice must be sent so that the persons entitled to receive it have sufficient time to take appropriate action to protect their interests (54 N.Y. Jur., Secured Transactions, § 286; *Marine Midland Bank–Rochester v. Vaeth*, 88 Misc.2d 657, 388 N.Y.S.2d 548)." *Fitzpatrick v. Bank of New York*, 124 Misc.2d 732, 480 N.Y.S.2d 157 (App. Term. 2d Dept., 1983), on remand, 125 Misc.2d 1069, 480 N.Y.S.2d 864 (1984).

13. For the foregoing reasons, the complaint must be dismissed because the plaintiff undeniably failed to comply with the notice provisions of U.C.C. § 9–504(3).

THE PLAINTIFF BREACHED THE LEASE

14. Paragraph 10 of the lease describes the plaintiff's obligations following an alleged default and sets forth the explicit steps that the plaintiff was required to take at that time. Paragraph 10(f) provides that

---

§ 7.55

1. Mr. Baron refers to a Bill of Sale that was apparently signed under oath by him as proof of the sale of the vehicle on March 19, 1991. (See Exhibit "G" to Mr. Baron's affidavit). This document too is patently defective on its face because Mr. Baron's signature on the document was notarized on *February* 19, 1991, some thirty days *before* the sale allegedly took place.

the "The price (the lessor) can sell the vehicle after default" is to be deducted from any deficiency claim.

15. Paragraph 10(f) further provides:

The price for which we can sell the vehicle may be set within 10 days after we get the vehicle back if you and we can agree on a price or if you and we can agree on a professional appraiser picked and paid for by you to appraise the WHOLESALE value of the vehicle. If you and we can't agree on a price or an appraiser within 10 days, we will obtain 3 written cash bids for purchase of the vehicle at WHOLESALE. The highest of the 3 bids will be the price for which we can sell the vehicle even if we decide not to sell the vehicle. (Attached hereto as Exhibit "B").

16. The plaintiff does not contend that it complied with any of the provisions of paragraph 10(f). Indeed, the plaintiff fails to acknowledge that it made any effort whatsoever to set a price of the vehicle with the defendants. Nor does the plaintiff claim that it made any effort to select an appraiser or to obtain any written cash bids for the vehicle.

17. It is undisputed that the plaintiff violated its own lease agreement by failing to take any of the steps required by paragraph 10(f). In *Chrysler Credit Corp. v. Smith*, N.Y.L.J. April 1, 1993 p.27, col.1, (Civ. Ct. Kings Co., Friedman, J.) the court recently held that a lessor of a motor vehicle cannot recover any amount from a lessee if it fails to comply with the lease terms governing default and termination.

18. For this reason as well, the plaintiff's claim must be dismissed.

THE PLAINTIFF'S CLAIM IS AN UNENFORCEABLE PENALTY

19. In order to constitute enforceable liquidated damages, as opposed to an unenforceable penalty, the amount sought must bear a reasonable proportion to the actual losses sustained by the plaintiff. *Truck Rent–A–Center v. Puritan Farms*, 41 N.Y.2d 420, 425, 393 N.Y.S.2d 365, 370, 361 N.E.2d 1015 (1977); *Barco Auto Leasing Corp., v. Atlas*, 165 A.D.2d 851, 560 N.Y.S.2d 314 (2d Dep't 1990).

20. No such reasonable proportion exists here. In fact, it is clear that the plaintiff has *already* received over $8,000.00 *more* than it could possibly have paid for the vehicle when it was originally purchased in 1984.

21. According to the Frank affidavit, the defendants have made payments totaling $24,407.48 for the subject vehicle. (See Frank affidavit, para. 17) In addition, the plaintiff claims that it received an additional $1,800.00 for the vehicle at the auction. The plaintiff has therefore received a total of at least $26,207.48 for the vehicle.

22. In 1984, the plaintiff stated that the vehicle's market value was $17,900.00. (See Frank affidavit, para. 18 and Exhibit "4"). Upon

information and belief, the plaintiff paid an amount far less than this when it purchased the vehicle. However, even if it paid retail, it has already received over $8,000.00 more than it paid for the vehicle.

23. The plaintiff cannot therefore reasonably argue that the sum it is seeking here bears a reasonable relation to its damage. At the very least, the Court should set the matter down for trial and require the plaintiff to prove its actual damage, if any. *Vanguard Commercial Leasing Corp. v. Dayanzadeh*, 147 A.D.2d 557, 538 N.Y.S.2d 492 (2d Dep't 1989).

WHEREFORE, it is respectfully requested that the Court issue an order denying the plaintiff's motion in its entirety and with prejudice and granting the defendants' cross-motion for summary judgment dismissing the complaint with prejudice and granting such other relief as may be just.

Dated: _____, New York

[ATTORNEY], Esq.

Library References:

West's Key No. Digests, Consumer Protection ⚖︎38.

§ 7.56 Forms—Notice of Rescission And/Or Revocation of Acceptance and Demand for Restitution Pursuant to UCC 2–601 and 2–608

VIA FAX TO: (914) 555–5555
and CERTIFIED MAIL
RETURN
RETURN RECEIPT
REQUESTED
ABC ACURA
985 East 79th Street
New York, New York 10038

VIA FAX TO: (516) 444–4444
and CERTIFIED MAIL
RETURN
RETURN RECEIPT
REQUESTED
JEFFERSON ACCEPTANCE
CORP.
900 Smallhollow Road
Ishmael, New York 13747

§ 7.56   CONSUMER LAW   Ch. 7

Re: Claribel Jones
Account No. 0000000
1992 Acura Legend
VIN JH4LM122333331237
Date of transaction: 10/12/95

NOTICE OF RESCISSION AND/OR REVOCATION OF ACCEPTANCE AND DEMAND FOR RESTITUTION

Dear Sir/Madam,

Please be advised that I represent Claribel Jones, the purchaser of a used 1992 Acura Legend VIN JH4LM122333331237 from ABC Acura ("Acura"), on or about _____.

Please be further advised that my client hereby demands rescission of the transaction and/or revokes acceptance of the vehicle and further demands the return of all payments, including the down payment made since the time of the transaction. The basis for such demand is described as follows.

The vehicle has, and continues to have, from the outset of the transaction, numerous defects and has required service on numerous occasions.

More significantly, prior to my client taking possession of the vehicle it had been involved in at least one serious collision, and, as a result, the vehicle has frame damage and is not safe to operate. In addition, the damage to the vehicle is so apparent that, even upon a cursory inspection, an automobile dealer would know or should know of this condition. Despite this, no disclosure whatsoever was made by Acura to my client at any time. To the contrary, Acura affirmatively advised my client that the vehicle had not previously been involved in an accident. Under these circumstances, had my client been advised of the prior history of this vehicle she would not have agreed to purchase it.

Moreover, in the event that Franklin was not aware of this information prior to agreeing to take an assignment of the retail installment contract, I do not believe that it would have entered such agreement.

The condition of the vehicle is such that it is not in condition and repair to render satisfactory and adequate service upon the public highway, in violation of V & T Law § 417.

In addition, the failure to disclose the prior collision damage to the vehicle constitutes a deceptive business practice in violation of GBL Art. 22–A, as well as common law fraud. Further, the vehicle is defective within the meaning of GBL § 198–b ("Used Car Lemon Law").

In the event that the contract is not canceled and all payments for the vehicle made by my client refunded, within seven (7) business days, an action will be commenced seeking all appropriate relief including, but not necessarily limited to, rescission, actual, statutory, compensatory and punitive damages and statutory attorneys fees.

Pursuant to UCC § 2–711(3), my client has a security interest in the vehicle for the return of the payments made. Please be advised that any attempt by you or your agents to repossess the vehicle will be wrongful and will subject you to liability for conversion and wrongful repossession under UCC §§ 9–503 and 9–507.

Finally, pursuant to GBL § 601(6), both Acura and Franklin are barred from disclosing or threatening to disclose any information pertaining to this account without disclosing that it is disputed by my client.

If you wish to resolve this matter without the need for litigation I suggest that you contact me.

Very truly yours,
[ATTORNEY], Esq.

JBF:lr
cc: Claribel Jones

Library References:

West's Key No. Digests, Sales ⇔112, 177, 180.

§ 7.57 Forms—Order to Show Cause in Proceeding Under Lien Law § 201–a to Vacate Garageman's Lien

CIVIL COURT OF THE CITY OF NEW YORK
COUNTY OF NEW YORK

———————————————————
In the Matter of the Application of   )
)
KATHLEEN SMITH,   )
)
            Petitioner,   )
) ORDER TO SHOW CAUSE
For an Order and Judgment Pursuant   )
to Lien Law § 201–a Canceling   ) Index No.:
a Lien Asserted by   )
)
ROY OLDSMOBILE INC.,   )
)
            Respondent.   )
———————————————————

UPON the annexed petition of KATHLEEN SMITH, verified on _____, with exhibits attached, and the affirmation of [ATTORNEY],

§ 7.57

Esq., dated _____, and upon all prior proceedings had herein, LET the respondent, or its attorney, show cause before me or one of the Judges of the Court, at a Special Term Part _____, Room ___, thereof, at the Courthouse located at 111 Centre Street, New York, New York on the ___ day of _____, at 9:30 a.m., or as soon thereafter as counsel can be heard, for an order and judgment pursuant to Lien Law § 201-a canceling a lien on a motor vehicle owed by the petitioner, claimed by the respondent pursuant to Lien Law § 201, and for such other and further relief as may be just and proper.

SUFFICIENT CAUSE APPEARING, pending the hearing of this application, LET the respondent, its agents, officers, employees, assignees, and any auctioneer, including but not necessarily limited to Fred Jones, Inc., 535 Marina Avenue, Woodmere, New York 11598, its agents, officers, employees and assignees, be stayed from conducting an auction or other sale of the subject vehicle or in any way disposing of, transferring or removing the subject vehicle from the premises of ROY OLDSMOBILE INC. or from taking any steps to enforce a lien against the petitioner, including but not necessarily limited to, sending, serving, or causing to be sent or served, any Notice of Lien and/or Sale of the subject motor vehicle, and it is further

ORDERED, that service by certified mail of a copy of this order together with the supporting papers upon ROY OLDSMOBILE INC., 245 West Holland Road, Bronx, New York 10468, and upon Fred Jones, Inc., 535 Marina Avenue, Woodmere, New York 11598 on or before _____, be sufficient.

Dated: _____, New York

_____
J.C.C.

Library References:

West's Key No. Digests, Automobiles ⚷374.

§ 7.58 Forms—Verified Petition in Proceeding Under Lien Law § 201-a to Vacate Garageman's Lien

CIVIL COURT OF THE CITY OF NEW YORK
COUNTY OF NEW YORK

_____
)
In the Matter of the Application of)
)
KATHLEEN SMITH,   )
)
                       Petitioner,)
) VERIFIED PETITION

For an Order and Judgment Pursuant)
to Lien Law § 201–a Canceling   ) Index No.:
a Lien Asserted by   )
)
ROY OLDSMOBILE INC.,   )
)
                  Respondent.)
_____)

The Petition of KATHLEEN SMITH, by her attorney, [ATTORNEY], Esq., respectfully alleges:

PARTIES, JURISDICTION, AND VENUE

1. The petitioner resides at 700 West 159th Street, New York, New York.

2. Upon information and belief, the respondent ROY OLDSMOBILE INC. is a New York corporation engaged in the business of selling and servicing new and used motor vehicles at 245 West Holland Road, Bronx, New York 10468. Upon information and belief, the respondent is an authorized sales agent of the Oldsmobile Motor Division of the General Motors Corporation (hereinafter "OLDSMOBILE").

3. The Civil Court of the City of New York has jurisdiction to hear this proceeding pursuant to Lien Law § 201–a, which provides that "(T)he special proceeding (to determine the validity of the lien) may be brought in any court which would have jurisdiction to render a judgment for a sum equal to the amount of the lien." The amount of the lien alleged herein is $5,290. Venue is properly laid in New York County pursuant to CPLR 503(a), as well as NYCCA § 301(a) as the County of the petitioner's residence.

BACKGROUND OF THIS PROCEEDING

4. The petitioner is the owner of a 1988 Renault Medallion, VIN No. VF1FF45CX00004, New York State Plate No. XYZ 123, purchased from the respondent on or about _____ (hereinafter, "the subject vehicle"). Upon information and belief, the subject vehicle is presently worth in excess of $9,000.

5. Shortly after the petitioner took possession of the subject vehicle, it began experiencing serious and persistent mechanical problems, including: no brakes; inoperable electrical system; passenger door came off of its hinges; inoperative hand brake; front axle separated from the ball joint; and repeated and unexplained stalling.

6. On or about _____ while driving the subject vehicle on the Whitestone Expressway in Queens, New York, the front axle fell apart, causing it to go into a 360–degree spin. The subject vehicle suffered severe collision damage.

§ 7.58 CONSUMER LAW Ch. 7

7. Following that accident the petitioner brought the subject vehicle to the respondent, where it has remained ever since.

8. At no time did the petitioner authorize or agree to the payment of any storage charges to the respondent, nor did the respondent advise the petitioner that storage charges would be incurred.

9. The first time the petitioner received any written indication that the respondent was claiming storage charges in excess of $5,290 was upon receipt, by regular mail only, of a copy of an unverified "Notice of Lien and Sale" and an invoice purporting to describe storage charges (hereinafter the "notice" and the "invoice"). (Attached hereto as Exhibit A.)

THE LIEN ASSERTED BY THE RESPONDENT

10. The respondent's alleged lien and the lien notice are defective and improper and, pursuant to Lien Law §§ 184, 201 and 201–a, they must be vacated.

11. The purported lien for "storage" in the amount of $5,290 must be vacated because no such service was ever requested by the petitioner, she never consented to such a charge, and the amount charged is unconscionable and excessive.

12. Before a valid garageman's lien can be properly asserted under Lien Law § 184, all of the necessary elements required by such section must be present. As a creature of statute, not found in the common law, § 184 must be strictly construed.

13. The essential elements of a valid § 184 lien (consent or request of the owner of the vehicle to incur the charge) do not exist here. As a result, the lien is defective and it must be vacated.

14. The invoice attached to the notice served by the respondent does not have the petitioner's signature and therefore there is no express consent to incur the storage charges.

15. While the invoice states "customer agrees to pay storage," there is no written evidence of such consent, and the amount for such storage, "$4,000," clearly indicates that such written entries were added to the invoice on or about _____, long after the invoice was prepared.

16. Additionally, the portion of the invoice attached to the notice that refers to the creation of a mechanic's lien is inadmissible in this proceeding. The section of the invoice above the blank signature line is not printed in at least eight-point type, as required by CPLR 4544.

17. Attached hereto as Exhibit B1 is a copy of a transparent standard printer's type-size gauge superimposed over the invoice at issue here. The gauge clearly indicates that the type size of the portion of the invoice purportedly creating the lien herein and authorizing storage

charges is printed in less than 6–point type. In fact, the type size herein is only in 4–point type (See Exhibit B2).

18. The invoice herein is a purported "contract or agreement involving a consumer transaction" within the meaning of CPLR 4544.

19. The invoice is a contract or agreement that was, upon information and belief, either "printed or prepared" or was "caused ... to be printed or prepared" by the respondent. CPLR 4544.

20. Such contracts or agreements that are not printed in at least 8–point type are not admissible "in any trial, hearing or proceeding" on behalf of the respondent. CPLR 4544. This matter is a "proceeding" under Lien Law § 201–a, and therefore the invoice is not admissible here.

21. As a result, any purported lien for storage charges here is a nullity because there is no admissible document providing for such a lien or charges, and there is no contract, signed by the petitioner, acknowledging or agreeing to any such lien or charges. In the absence of these basic elements necessary for the creation of a lien, it cannot exist. Lien Law § 184.

22. Additionally, the respondent took no steps whatsoever to assert a lien before the alleged storage charges had grown to $5,290. The respondent is therefore guilty of gross laches because of its failure to assert any storage charges whatsoever for almost seven months. Instead the respondent chose to sit back and allow the charges to accrue daily until the petitioner could be compelled to pay $5,290, on only ten days notice, or lose her vehicle at an auction sale.

23. The notice must also be vacated because it violates Lien Law § 201 on the following grounds:

   a. The notice was not personally served as required by § 201;

   b. The respondent made no showing whatsoever of exercising "due diligence" before resorting to regular mail service, as required by § 201;

   c. The notice is not verified by the lienor, in violation of § 201.

24. Based upon all of the above, the respondent's purported lien is invalid and defective and the petitioner is entitled to an order and judgment canceling same pursuant to Lien Law § 201–a.

WHEREFORE, it is respectfully requested that the Court issue an Order and Judgment, pursuant to Lien Law § 201–a, canceling the lien asserted by the respondent over the subject vehicle, awarding the petitioner the costs, disbursements, and attorney's fees of this proceeding and granting such other relief as may be just.

Dated: _____, New York

Respectfully submitted,

§ 7.58   CONSUMER LAW   Ch. 7

> KATHLEEN SMITH
> Petitioner
>
> Yours etc.,
>
> [ATTORNEY], Esq.
> Attorney for Petitioner
> [ADDRESS AND TELEPHONE NUMBER]

[VERIFICATION]

Library References:

West's Key No. Digests, Automobiles ⟐374.

§ 7.59 Forms—Affirmation in Support of Petition in Proceeding Under Lien Law § 201–a to Vacate Garageman's Lien

CIVIL COURT OF THE CITY OF NEW YORK
COUNTY OF NEW YORK

In the Matter of the Application of

KATHLEEN SMITH,

                 Petitioner,   AFFIRMATION IN SUPPORT

For an Order and Judgment Pursuant
to Lien Law § 201–a Canceling   Index No.:
a Lien Asserted by

ROY OLDSMOBILE INC.,

                 Respondent.

[ATTORNEY], an attorney duly admitted to practice before the Courts of the State of New York, hereby affirms the truth of the following:

    1. I am the attorney for the petitioner. I am fully familiar with the facts and circumstances stated herein.

    2. This affirmation is offered in support of the within petition brought pursuant to Lien Law § 201–a to vacate and cancel the lien asserted by the respondent herein.

3. At the outset, the respondent's undated Notice of Lien and Sale (the "notice") (See Exhibit A) violates Lien Law § 201 in that it was not verified by the lienor, it was not personally served upon the petitioner, it does not include an agreement under which the lien allegedly arose, and there has been no showing by the respondent that it exercised "due diligence" to make personal service of the notice before resorting to service by mail as required by Lien Law § 201.

4. Based upon these violations of Lien Law § 201, the lien herein must be vacated.

5. There are additional compelling reasons for the Court to vacate and cancel the lien.

6. Lien Law § 184 provides, in pertinent part, that in order to create a valid lien for charges arising out of repairs or storage of a motor vehicle, such repairs or storage must be done "at the request of or with the consent of the owner."

7. As a result, the lien asserted by the respondent is completely improper and defective in that the petitioner, as the owner of the subject vehicle, neither requested nor consented to the charges asserted and it must therefore be vacated and canceled. Campbell v. WABC Towing Corp., 78 Misc.2d 671, 356 N.Y.S.2d 455 (1974); Hartford Insurance Co. v. Alberston, 59 Misc.2d 207, 298 N.Y.S.2d 321 (1969); Bankers Commercial Corp. v. Mittleman, 21 Misc.2d 1096, 198 N.Y.S.2d 184 (1960); Manufacturers Trust Co. v. Stehle, 1 A.D.2d 471, 151 N.Y.S.2d 384 (1956); Goodrich Silvertown Stores of B.F. Goodrich Co. v. Valentine, 10 N.Y.S.2d 447 (1939); New York Yellow Cab Co. Sales Agency, Inc. v. Laurel Garage, Inc., 219 App. Div. 329, 219 N.Y.S. 671 (1927).

8. Additionally, the portion of the invoice referring to the creation of a mechanic's lien is not signed by the petitioner. However, even if it were, it is not admissible in this proceeding. The section of the invoice, above the blank signature line, is not printed in at least eight-point type, as required by CPLR 4544.

9. As is shown in the within verified petition (paragraphs 15–20) the invoice is printed in only 4–point type, and it is therefore inadmissible here.

10. As a creature of statute in derogation of common law, a garageman's lien and the elements necessary to create it must be strictly construed. Slank v. Sam Dell's Dodge Corp., 46 A.D.2d 445, 363 N.Y.S.2d 138 (1975); Manufacturers Trust Co., *supra*.

11. The lien asserted here is defective for numerous reasons, as shown above and in the within verified petition. It must therefore be vacated and canceled.

WHEREFORE, it is respectfully requested that the Court issue an order and judgment, pursuant to Lien Law § 201–a, canceling the lien asserted by the respondent over the subject vehicle, awarding the costs, disbursements and attorney's fees of this proceeding and granting such other relief as may be just.

Dated: _____, New York

[ATTORNEY]

§ 7.60 Forms—Complaint Against Credit Reporting Agency Alleging Violations of the Fair Credit Reporting Act and the New York State Fair Credit Reporting Act and Deceptive Business Practices 💾

UNITED STATES DISTRICT COURT
DISTRICT OF NEW YORK

JANE DOE AND JOHN DOE,

    Plaintiffs,

    -against-

XYZ CREDIT REPORTING CO.,

    Defendant.

COMPLAINT

Docket No.

The plaintiffs, JANE F. DOE (hereafter "Jane Doe") and JOHN DOE (hereafter "John Doe") (hereafter collectively the "plaintiffs"), by their attorney, [ATTORNEY], Esq., as and for their Complaint against the defendant, allege as follows:

PRELIMINARY STATEMENT

1. This is an action for actual, statutory and punitive damages, costs and attorney's fees, brought pursuant to 15 U.S.C.A. §§ 1681 *et seq.* (Federal Fair Credit Reporting Act) and New York General Business Law arts. 25 (State Fair Credit Reporting Act) and 22–A (Deceptive Business Practices).

2. The plaintiffs contend that the defendant has violated such laws by repeatedly and wilfully issuing false consumer credit reports concerning the plaintiff Jane Doe, resulting in the denial of credit to them, actual damages, and damage to their reputation, and causing the plaintiffs humiliation, mental anguish, and emotional distress.

JURISDICTION

3. The jurisdiction of this Court is conferred by 15 U.S.C.A. § 1681(p).

4. The plaintiff Jane Doe is a natural person and is a resident of the State of New York, County of Kings. She is a "consumer" as defined by 15 U.S.C.A. § 1681a(c) and New York General Business Law § 380–a(b).

5. The plaintiff John Doe is a natural person and is a resident of the State of New York, County of Kings. He is a "consumer" as defined by 15 U.S.C.A. § 1681a(c) and New York General Business Law § 380–a(b).

6. Upon information and belief, the defendant XYZ Credit Information Co. is a corporation incorporated under the laws of the State of Delaware and is authorized to do business in the State of New York, and is actually doing business at 897 East Broadway Astoria, New York.

7. Upon information and belief, the defendant is a "consumer reporting agency," as defined in 15 U.S.C.A. § 1681(f) and New York General Business Law § 380–a(e). Upon information and belief, the defendant is regularly engaged in the business of assembling, evaluating, and dispersing information concerning consumers for the purpose of furnishing consumer reports, as defined in 15 U.S.C.A. § 1681(d) and N.Y. Gen. Bus. Law § 380–a(c)(1), to third parties. Upon information and belief, the defendant dispenses such consumer reports to third parties under contract for monetary compensation.

8. Venue is properly laid pursuant to 28 U.S.C.A. § 1391(b) in the judicial district where the claim arose.

FACTS

9. In or about _____, the plaintiff Jane Doe applied for credit from J.C. Penney, Inc. In or about _____, the plaintiff Jane Doe received a letter from J.C. Penney advising that her request for a credit was denied based, in whole or in part, on a credit report obtained from the defendant pertaining to the plaintiff Jane Doe.

10. The plaintiff Jane Doe immediately requested a copy of the credit report relied upon by J.C. Penney from the defendant.

11. On or about _____, the defendant sent the plaintiff Jane Doe a copy of her credit report as requested. The report contained many inaccuracies, the most significant of which was the false statement that the plaintiff Jane Doe had previously defaulted on a student loan. Upon information and belief, the credit report issued by the defendant and relied upon by J.C. Penney in making its credit determination contained erroneous information, including, but not necessarily limited to the student loan described above.

12. The plaintiff Jane Doe has never defaulted on or even obtained a student loan of any kind.

§ 7.60   CONSUMER LAW   Ch. 7

13. On or about _____, the plaintiff Jane Doe sent the defendant a letter detailing the inaccuracies in the credit report and demanding that the report be corrected.

14. On or about _____, the defendant sent the plaintiff Jane Doe a letter stating that her credit file had been reinvestigated and revised, together with a credit report that no longer included the inaccurate information.

15. In or about _____, the plaintiffs applied to the Lincoln Savings Bank for a $5,000.00 loan in order to make certain home improvements.

16. After the plaintiffs submitted the application to Lincoln, the mother of the plaintiff Jane Doe and the wife of the plaintiff John Doe was diagnosed as having cancer. The plaintiffs' family did not have sufficient funds available to pay for the medical care that was immediately required. The plaintiffs therefore decided that the proceeds of the loan they had applied for from Lincoln would go towards the medical bills. Given the plaintiffs' excellent credit history, they had no reason to believe that their loan application would be declined.

17. On or about _____, Lincoln advised the plaintiffs that their loan application was declined because of a credit report provided by the defendant that stated that the plaintiff Jane Doe had been delinquent in her credit obligations to others. Upon information and belief, Lincoln did not request or receive a credit report from the defendant pertaining to the plaintiff John Doe and instead relied solely on a credit report issued by the defendant, relating to the plaintiff Jane Doe, in making its credit determination. Upon information and belief, the credit report issued by the defendant, relied upon by Lincoln in making its credit determination, contained erroneous information, including, but not necessarily limited to the student loan described above.

18. On or about _____, the plaintiff Jane Doe obtained a copy of her credit report issued by the defendant containing the information that the defendant had issued to Lincoln. Notwithstanding the correct information that plaintiff had provided the defendant a year earlier, the report again contained many inaccuracies, including the false statement that the plaintiff Jane Doe had previously defaulted on a student loan.

19. On or about _____, the plaintiff Jane Doe sent a letter to the New York State Department of Law, complaining of the defendant's repeated, gross and damaging errors, providing all correct information pertaining to her credit history, and requesting the State to intervene. The plaintiff Jane Doe forwarded a copy of the letter to the defendant.

20. On or about _____, the defendant sent the plaintiff Jane Doe a letter stating that her credit file had been reinvestigated and revised

and provided an updated credit report that no longer included the inaccurate information.

21. By that time, the plaintiffs' family had been compelled to borrow the necessary emergency funds from a neighbor to pay for the medical bills described above, and they had begun receiving insurance benefits. The plaintiffs were profoundly distressed and humiliated at not being able to assist their family in a time of great need.

22. In or about _____, the plaintiff Jane Doe applied for credit from World Financial Network National Bank on behalf of a store entitled Sizes Unlimited. On or about _____, World Financial notified the plaintiff Jane Doe that her application for credit was denied on the basis of an "unsatisfactory" credit history as reported by the defendant. Upon information and belief, the credit report issued by the defendant, and relied upon by World Financial in making its credit determination, contained erroneous information, including, but not necessarily limited to the student loan described above.

23. From in or about to in or about _____, the plaintiff Jane Doe repeatedly wrote to the defendant supplying all of the correct information pertaining to her credit history. In response, the defendant repeatedly sent the plaintiff Jane Doe credit reports containing multiple errors, including, once again, the false statement that she had defaulted on a student loan.

FIRST CLAIM FOR RELIEF

24. The plaintiffs repeat and reallege each paragraph above.

25. The defendant violated 15 U.S.C.A. § 1681e(b) by failing to follow reasonable procedures to assure maximum possible accuracy in the preparation of the consumer reports concerning the plaintiff Jane Doe.

26. As a result of the defendant's conduct, actions and inaction, the plaintiff Jane Doe, who in fact had an impeccable credit history, was unable to secure credit privileges at stores where she regularly shopped and was unable to secure the credit she needed to help her family during her mother's medical emergency.

27. As a result of the defendant's conduct, actions and inaction, the plaintiff Jane Doe was unable to secure favorable credit privileges. As a result, the plaintiff Jane Doe incurred interest and finance charges relating to credit far in excess of what she would have otherwise incurred had she been able to secure credit elsewhere.

28. As a result of the defendant's conduct, actions and inaction, the plaintiff John Doe was unable to secure the credit he needed to help his wife during her medical emergency.

29. As a result of the defendant's conduct, actions and inactions, the plaintiff John Doe suffered actual damages in the form of extreme mental anguish and emotional distress and humiliation.

30. As a result of the defendant's conduct, actions and inactions the plaintiff Jane Doe suffered actual damages in the form of additional interest, expense and finance charges as well as extreme mental anguish and emotional distress, humiliation, and damage to her reputation for creditworthiness.

31. The defendant's conduct, actions and inactions were willful, rendering the defendant liable for punitive damages in an amount to be determined by the Court pursuant to 15 U.S.C.A. § 1681n.

32. The plaintiffs are entitled to recover costs and attorney's fees from the defendant in an amount to be determined by the court pursuant to 15 U.S.C.A. §§ 1681n and 1681o.

SECOND CLAIM FOR RELIEF

33. The plaintiffs repeat and reallege each paragraph above.

34. The defendant violated 15 U.S.C.A. § 1681i(a) by failing to delete inaccurate information in the plaintiff Jane Doe's credit file after receiving actual notice of such inaccuracies and conducting a reinvestigation.

35. As a result of the defendant's conduct, actions and inaction the plaintiffs suffered damage as described above.

36. The defendant's conduct, actions and inaction were willful, rendering the defendant liable for punitive damages in an amount to be determined by the Court pursuant to 15 U.S.C.A. § 1681n.

37. The plaintiffs are entitled to recover costs and attorney's fees from the defendant in an amount to be determined by the court pursuant to 15 U.S.C.A. §§ 1681n and 1681o.

THIRD CLAIM FOR RELIEF

38. The plaintiffs repeat and reallege each paragraph above.

39. The defendant violated New York General Business Law § 380–j(e) by failing to maintain reasonable procedures designed to assure maximum possible accuracy of the information concerning the plaintiff Jane Doe.

40. As a result of the defendant's conduct, actions and inaction, the plaintiffs suffered damage as described above.

41. The defendant's failure to comply with GBL § 380–j(e) was willful and knowing, rendering the defendant liable for punitive damages in an amount to be determined by the Court pursuant to GBL § 380–l.

42. The plaintiffs are entitled to recover costs and attorney's fees from the defendant in an amount to be determined by the court pursuant to GBL §§ 380–l(c) and 380–m(b).

FOURTH CLAIM FOR RELIEF

43. The plaintiffs repeat and reallege each paragraph above.

44. The defendant violated GBL § 380–j(a)(3) by reporting and maintaining in the plaintiff Jane Doe's file information that it knew or had reason to know was inaccurate.

45. As a result of the defendant's conduct, actions and inaction the plaintiffs suffered damage as described above.

46. The defendant's failure to comply with GBL § 380–j(e) was willful and knowing, rendering it liable for punitive damages in an amount to be determined by the Court pursuant to GBL § 380–l.

47. The plaintiffs are entitled to recover costs and attorney's fees from the defendant in an amount to be determined by the court pursuant to GBL §§ 380–l(c) and 380–m(b).

FIFTH CLAIM FOR RELIEF

48. The plaintiffs repeat and reallege each paragraph above.

49. The defendant violated GBL § 380–f by failing to delete inaccurate information in the plaintiff Jane Doe's file after allegedly conducting a reinvestigation.

50. As a result of the defendant's conduct, actions and inaction, the plaintiffs suffered damage as described above.

51. The defendant's failure to comply with GBL § 380–f was willful and knowing, rendering the defendant liable for punitive damages in an amount to be determined by the Court pursuant to GBL § 380–l.

52. The plaintiffs are entitled to recover costs and attorney's fees from the defendant in an amount to be determined by the court pursuant to GBL §§ 380–l(c) and 380–m(b).

SIXTH CLAIM FOR RELIEF

53. The plaintiffs repeat and reallege each paragraph above.

54. The defendant's conduct, actions and inaction constitute false, deceptive and/or illegal business practices in violation of GBL Art. 22–A. Such practices include, but are not necessarily limited to:

   a) the failure to maintain and follow reasonable procedures to assure maximum possible accuracy of information contained in the plaintiff Jane Doe's credit file;

   b) the failure to delete inaccurate information from such file after receiving actual notice of such inaccurate information;

§ 7.60　　　　　　　　CONSUMER LAW　　　　　　　　Ch. 7

　　c) the failure to conduct a proper investigation after receiving notice that information contained in its file on the plaintiff Jane Doe was inaccurate;

　　d) the reporting to third parties of information affecting the plaintiff Jane Doe's reputation for credit worthiness, with knowledge or reason to know such information was false.

　55. As a result of such violations, the plaintiffs suffered damage as described above and may recover such damages pursuant to GBL § 349(h).

　56. The defendant's conduct and actions were willful, malicious, and/or reckless, and/or the result of gross negligence, rendering the defendant liable for additional damages in the amount of $1,000.00 per violation pursuant to GBL § 349(h).

　57. The plaintiffs are entitled to recover attorney's fees from the defendant pursuant to GBL § 349(h).

　WHEREFORE, the plaintiffs respectfully demand that the Court enter judgment in favor of each of them, against the defendant as follows:

　　a) actual damages in the amount of $250,000.00;

　　b) punitive damages in the amount of $1,000,000;

　　c) statutory damages in the amount of $1,000 for each violation of law as alleged in the Sixth Claim for Relief;

　　d) attorney's fees;

　　e) interest, costs and disbursements; and

　　f) such other relief as may be just.

Dated: New York, New York

　　　　　　　　　　　　　　　　Yours, etc.

　　　　　　　　　　　　　　　　[ATTORNEY], Esq.
　　　　　　　　　　　　　　　　Attorneys for the Plaintiff
　　　　　　　　　　　　　　　　[ADDRESS AND TELEPHONE NUMBER]

Library References:

West's Key No. Digests, Credit Reporting Agencies ⚖4.

§ 7.61 Forms—Stipulation of Settlement of Plaintiff's Lemon Law Claims Providing for Cancellation of Lease and Deletion of Any Derogatory Credit Information

SUPREME COURT OF THE STATE OF NEW YORK
COUNTY OF NEW YORK

TODD STONE,

               Plaintiff,

    -against-

ABC LEASING GROUP, INC.,
ABC MOTOR GROUP, INC.,
ROBERT AMES, individually and as an officer of ABC LEASING GROUP, INC., and/or ABC MOTOR GROUP, INC., and ALLSOP BANK,

              Defendants.

STIPULATION OF SETTLEMENT

Index No.

IT IS HEREBY STIPULATED AND AGREED, by and between the plaintiff TODD STONE, and the defendants ABC LEASING GROUP, INC., ("Leasing Group") ABC MOTOR GROUP, INC., ("Motor Group"), ROBERT AMES ("Ames"), individually and as an officer of LEASING GROUP, INC., and MOTOR GROUP, INC. (collectively, the "ABC defendants"), and ALLSOP BANK, ("ALLSOP") all of whom are represented by counsel, as follows:

1. No party hereto is an infant, incompetent person for whom a committee has been appointed or conservatee, and no person not a party has an interest in the subject matter of the action.

2. The above-entitled action, including the plaintiff's claim for relief under the "Used Car Lemon Law" (GBL §§ 198–b *et seq.*) and all claims asserted by ALLSOP against the ABC defendants, are discontinued, with prejudice, without costs to any party, upon the terms and conditions set forth herein.

3. This stipulation may be filed without further notice with the Clerk of the Court.

4. In consideration of such discontinuance, the ABC defendants agree to pay to the plaintiff the sum of FIFTEEN THOUSAND DOLLARS ($15,000.00) in full satisfaction of all claims against such defendants, except as set forth below in paragraph "11." The plaintiff hereby

§ 7.61   CONSUMER LAW   Ch. 7

acknowledges receipt of such payment, which is currently held in escrow by the plaintiff's attorney. The defendants hereby consent to the immediate and unconditional release of such funds to the plaintiff.

5. The ABC defendants represent that they have inspected the vehicle that is the subject of this action, that they are satisfied with its condition and that they have received possession of same from the plaintiff. The receipt of possession of the vehicle by such defendants shall not, in any manner, be deemed a repossession, voluntary or otherwise.

6. The lease that is the subject of this action is hereby canceled, and any liability of the plaintiff thereunder is hereby terminated.

7. Upon execution of this stipulation, the plaintiff shall provide a release to all of the defendants releasing them from all claims asserted in the complaint in this action as well as any other claim arising out of the facts asserted in the complaint. Such release shall expressly exclude any claim for sales tax under the provisions of paragraph "11" below.

8. Upon execution of this stipulation, the ABC defendants shall provide the plaintiff with a release releasing him from all claims arising out of the lease which is the subject of this action as well as from all claims pertaining to the condition of the vehicle.

9. Upon execution of this stipulation ALLSOP shall issue a release to the plaintiff releasing him from any liability under the motor vehicle lease that is the subject of this action and from any other claims arising out of such lease.

10. The defendants agree that they shall not report any derogatory information to any third party, including any credit reporting agency, concerning the lease that is the subject of this action. In the event that any such information has been, or is discovered to have been, reported, the defendant that caused such reporting shall, within five (5) days written notice to its attorney, forthwith issue written instructions to any such third party to delete any and all reference to the matter from its records. A copy of any such instructions shall be forthwith provided to the plaintiff's attorney.

11. The plaintiff acknowledges receipt from the ABC defendants of certain documentation pertaining to the collection and payment of sales tax to New York State in connection with the lease, in the amount of $3,974.94. The plaintiff shall use his best efforts and due diligence to obtain a refund of such sales tax from the State and shall provide copies to such defendants of all correspondence in this regard, including any written determination by the State. In the event that such efforts are not successful, such defendants shall, upon five (5) days written notice to their attorney, pay to the plaintiff the sum of $3,974.94. In no event shall such notice be given prior to _____. Such amount shall be in addition to the payment set forth in paragraph "4" above. In the event

such payment is not made by such defendants as provided herein, the plaintiff shall be entitled to enter judgment, without further notice, against the ABC defendants in the amount of $3,974.94, and in such event, the plaintiff shall have execution therefor.

12. This agreement may be signed in counterpart and filed in such manner with the Court without further notice.

Dated: New York, New York

_____, Esq. _____, Esq.
Attorney for the ABC   Attorneys for the Plaintiff
Defendants

_____   _____
ROBERT AMES, Individually   **TODD STONE**
and as an officer of the ABC
Defendants

ABC LEASING GROUP, INC.
By:
    President

ABC MOTOR GROUP, INC.
By:
    President

ALLSOP BANK   _____, Esq.
By: Attorney for ALLSOP

Library References:

West's Key No. Digests, Consumer Protection ⚖9.

§ 7.62 Forms—Complaint Alleging Violations of the Fair Debt Collection Practices Act and the Deceptive Practices Act

SUPREME COURT OF THE STATE OF NEW YORK
COUNTY OF NEW YORK

JUDITH A. JONES,

        Plaintiff,

-against-

ALLEN M. SMITH,

        Defendant.

VERIFIED COMPLAINT

Index No.

The plaintiff, JUDITH A. JONES, by her attorney, [ATTORNEY], Esq., as and for her Complaint against the defendant, alleges as follows:

PRELIMINARY STATEMENT

1. This is an action for actual, compensatory, statutory and punitive damages and attorney's fees brought pursuant to 15 U.S.C.A. §§ 1692 et seq. ("Fair Debt Collection Practices Act" or "FDCPA") and New York General Business Law Arts. 29–H (Debt Collection Procedures Law) and 22–A (Deceptive Business Practices) and the common law of the State of New York.

2. The plaintiff contends that the defendant has engaged in repeated and persistent violations of the above laws in collecting and attempting to collect a consumer debt allegedly owed by the plaintiff to Ladies' Store, Inc. Division of YZ Credit Service, Inc. ("Ladies' Store"), and, as a result, she is entitled to the relief requested in this action.

PARTIES AND VENUE

3. The plaintiff, JUDITH A. JONES, is a natural person residing in the County of New York, City and State of New York. The plaintiff is a "consumer" within the meaning of 15 U.S.C.A. § 1692a(3) as well as a "debtor" within the meaning of General Business Law § 600.2.

4. Upon information and belief, the defendant ALLEN M. SMITH is an attorney duly licensed to practice law in the State of New York and maintains a place of business for such purpose at 141 Livingston Street, Brooklyn, New York. The defendant is also a "debt collector" within the meaning of 15 U.S.C.A. § 1692a(6) as well as an "agent" of a "principal

creditor" within the meaning of General Business Law Art. 29–H and § 600.3.

5. Venue is properly laid pursuant to CPLR § 503(a) in the County of the plaintiff's residence.

STATEMENT OF FACTS

6. On or about _____, the defendant sent a letter to the plaintiff which demanded that she immediately send a check in the amount of $335.53, "including attorney's fees," based upon an alleged indebtedness to Ladies' Store (Attached as Exhibit A.) The alleged indebtedness to Ladies' Store, as described herein, is a "debt" within the meaning of 15 U.S.C.A. § 1692a(5) as well as a "consumer claim" within the meaning of General Business Law § 600.1.

7. The letter stated that the alleged debt had been "turned over to this firm for immediate legal action." (Exhibit A).

8. The letter further stated that unless the plaintiff sent payment "within ten days, our client has authorized us to commence legal proceedings." (Exhibit A).

9. The letter further stated that "(S)uch action will result in additional expenses . . .". (Exhibit A).

10. The letter further stated that the plaintiff had thirty days to dispute the validity of the debt and that if she did so, the defendant would provide verification of it and mail it to her. (Exhibit A).

11. The letter further stated that the plaintiff's failure to pay within ten days "may result in issuance of a SUMMONS AND COMPLAINT by an attorney in your area and the commencement of legal proceedings." (Exhibit A). (Emphasis in original).

12. Despite the defendant's threat to commence or cause the commencement of a lawsuit within ten days, no such suit was so commenced or caused to be commenced, nor, upon information and belief, did the defendant intend to so do so.

13. In _____, shortly after receiving the letter, the plaintiff contacted the defendant's office and spoke with an employee of the defendant who advised her that she had to pay $335.53 to satisfy the Ladies' Store claim. Upon information and belief, the plaintiff agreed to pay $167.76 on or before _____ and the remaining $167.76 on or before _____, in full satisfaction of the Ladies' Store claim. The plaintiff only agreed to make such payments because the defendant's employee insisted the sum was owed and demanded that she make the payments.

14. On or about _____, the defendant sent a letter to the plaintiff, which stated in large block letters, "SECOND NOTICE" and demanded that she immediately send payment in the amount of $335.53 "including attorney's fees," based upon the same alleged indebtedness to

Ladies' Store. (Attached as Exhibit B). The letter further stated, "Our previous request for payment was ignored. Unless we hear from you on receipt of this letter as to your intention in liquidating this indebtedness, we may have no other alternative but to request authorization from our client to commence legal action against you." (Exhibit B).

15. Despite the defendant's threat to "request authorization from (his) client to commence legal action" following the plaintiff's receipt of the letter, upon information and belief, no such request was made or intended to be made.

16. The plaintiff made the agreed upon payments to the defendant on the dates described above in paragraph 14 (Attached as Exhibits C1 and D1). The plaintiff wrote her Ladies' Store account number, as stated in Exhibits A and B, on the face of each check.

17. On the face of the second check (Exhibit D1), the plaintiff wrote "Final Payment." On the reverse side of that check the plaintiff wrote, "Upon receipt of this check, account will be paid in full." (Exhibit D2).

18. The reverse side of the checks establishes that they were deposited into the "Allen M. Smith Brooklyn, Spec. Account" at Chemical Bank and subsequently paid by the plaintiff's bank. (See Exhibits C2 and D2).

19. On or about _____, the defendant sent a letter to the plaintiff similar to the letter described above in paragraphs 6–11, again demanding payment of the same indebtedness allegedly owed to Ladies' Store. The amount demanded by the defendant in the letter was $167.77 "including attorney's fee." (Attached as Exhibit E).

20. Once again, despite the defendant's threat to commence or cause the commencement of a lawsuit if payment was not received within ten days, no such suit was commenced or caused to be commenced, nor, upon information and belief, did the defendant intend to so do so.

21. On or about _____, the plaintiff contacted the defendant's office and advised one of the defendant's employees that she had received another dunning letter (Exhibit E) even though she had fully satisfied the Ladies' Store claim. The employee stated that the letter had been sent erroneously and assured the plaintiff that she would receive no further letters.

22. On or about the defendant sent a letter to the plaintiff, again demanding payment of the same indebtedness allegedly owed to Ladies' Store, in the amount of $335.53 "including attorney's fee." (Attached as Exhibit F1).

23. The letter stated "(Y)ou have failed to respond to our previous communication with regard to the above claim against you." (Exhibit F1). The letter further stated, "(E)nclosed is a copy of a summons, which

Ch. 7 VIOLATIONS OF FAIR DEBT ACT § 7.62

may be issued to a process server to be served upon you unless you contact my office within three days ... ". (Exhibit F1).

24. The letter further stated, "It is in your best interest to remit payment in full within the time aforesaid in order to avoid commencement of legal proceedings against you." (Exhibit F1).

25. Despite the defendant's threat to once again commence a lawsuit, if contact was not made within three days, no such suit was commenced, nor, upon information and belief, did the defendant intend to so do so.

26. A summons was enclosed in the same envelope that contained the letter annexed as Exhibit F1. (Attached as Exhibit F2).

27. The summons stated in 12–point bold type, "IMPORTANT!! YOU ARE BEING SUED!! THIS IS A COURT PAPER—A SUMMONS. DON'T THROW IT AWAY!! TALK TO A LAWYER RIGHT AWAY! ....". (Exhibit F2). (Emphasis in original).

28. The caption in the summons described the action as "LADIES' STORE, INC., DIV OF YZ CREDIT SERVICE, INC., Plaintiff, against JUDITH A. JONES," Defendant, and listed the Court where such suit was to be heard as the "CIVIL COURT OF THE CITY OF NEW YORK, COUNTY OF KINGS." (Exhibit F2).

29. The summons further stated: YOU ARE HEREBY SUMMONED to appear in the Civil Court of the City of New York, County of Kings ... upon your failure to answer, judgment will be taken against you for the sum of $335.53 .... (Exhibit F2). The summons further stated that it had been issued by "ALLEN M. SMITH 123 LIVINGSTON STREET BROOKLYN, N.Y. 11201 Attorneys (sic) for Plaintiff."

30. On or about _____, the plaintiff wrote to the defendant, enclosing a copy of her canceled check (Exhibit C) and explained that her check would be returned by her bank with the monthly statement. (Attached as Exhibit G).

31. The letter stated, "I have kept my part of the bargain, now let's hope you can, and please clear my account instead of continually sending me dunning notices. I'm still getting them." (Exhibit G).

32. On or about _____, the defendant, by an authorized employee, sent the plaintiff a pre-printed form letter. (Attached as Exhibit H). The letter stated, "(P)lease be advised that the above stated debt has been satisfied via payment in full as of _____. No legal action was initiated, therefore, no formal letter of satisfaction is necessary. We have instructed our client upon clearance of you (sic) check, to inform the appropriate credit reporting agencies of voluntary amiable satisfaction of this debt ...". (Exhibit H).

§ 7.62   CONSUMER LAW   Ch. 7

33. On or about _____, the defendant sent the plaintiff a letter, once again demanding payment of the same indebtedness allegedly owed to Ladies' Store in the amount of $335.53. (Attached as Exhibit I).

34. The letter stated in large bold print, "FINAL DEMAND." The letter further stated that it "concerns a matter of great importance to you ... your CREDIT RATING with our client." (Exhibit I). (Emphasis in original).

35. The letter further stated, "(T)he record of this delinquency will remain on file with our client. We have recorded the fact that you have ignored our previous correspondence. Therefore, we must assume that this is a just debt. You have an obligation to pay! At this point your account is SERIOUSLY DELINQUENT. Only full payment of the amount shown above or a prompt explanation of why you have not paid this bill will halt further collections." (Exhibit I). (Emphasis in original).

36. In _____, shortly after receipt of the letter, the plaintiff once again contacted the defendant's office and again stated that even though she had fully satisfied the Ladies' Store claim she had received another dunning letter. The employee stated that the letter had been sent erroneously and assured the plaintiff that she would receive no further letters.

37. On or about _____, the plaintiff, once again, wrote to the defendant enclosing a copy therewith of the defendant's letter (Exhibit I). (Attached as Exhibit J).

38. The plaintiff stated in her letter, "Kindly inform your staff that this bill was paid in full on _____ and to please stop sending me these annoying letters." (Exhibit J).

39. On or about _____, the defendant sent a letter, once again demanding payment of the same indebtedness allegedly owed to Ladies' Store and demanded that she pay the amount of $167.77 "included (sic) attorneys (sic) fee." (Attached as Exhibit K).

40. The letter stated "(O)ur previous request for payment was ignored. Unless we hear from you on receipt of this letter as to your intentions in liquidating this indebtedness, we may have no other alternative but to request authorization from our client to commence legal action." (Exhibit K).

41. Despite the defendant's threat to "request authorization from (his) client to commence legal action" following the plaintiff's receipt of the letter, upon information and belief, no such request was made or intended to be made.

42. Shortly after receipt of the letter, the plaintiff, once again, contacted the defendant's office and again stated that even though she had fully satisfied the Ladies' Store claim she had received another dunning letter. The employee stated that the letter had been sent

150

Ch. 7   VIOLATIONS OF FAIR DEBT ACT   § 7.62

erroneously and assured the plaintiff that she would receive no further letters.

43. On or about _____, the defendant sent to the plaintiff a letter once again demanding payment of the same indebtedness allegedly owed to Ladies' Store in the amount of $167.77. (Attached as Exhibit L).

44. The letter further stated "(A)ccording to our records, the last payment due on the above mentioned account was not made. Kindly forward your next payment so that we may update our account. Your previous balance is indicated above." (Exhibit L).

45. Upon receipt of the letter, the plaintiff contacted the New York County District Attorney's Office in an effort to obtain relief from the continued harassment and intimidation from the defendant. That office referred her to the New York City Department of Consumer Affairs ("DCA").

46. On or about _____, the plaintiff filed a complaint against the defendant with the DCA. (Attached as Exhibit M).

47. In her complaint the plaintiff stated that she had paid the Ladies' Store debt in full on _____, and "(S)ince then I have been inundated with letters from this irresponsible agency. It took me two months after many, many phone calls to receive a letter from the manager, Don Juan, ... stating that my account was satisfied ... Please stop these people. It is very upsetting to come home from a hard day's work and be greeted by something that I am no longer responsible for." (Exhibit M).

48. Upon information and belief, on or about _____, the DCA sent a notice to the defendant advising him of the plaintiff's complaint and enclosing a copy of it. (Attached as Exhibit N). The letter requested that the defendant respond to the plaintiff's complaint.

49. Upon information and belief, in response to the plaintiff's complaint, the defendant sent a reply to the DCA stating, "The paid in full information was not properly and timely put into our computer, so complainant received additional letters. This has now been corrected and the account marked as 'Paid in Full' ". (Attached as Exhibit N).

50. The response to the DCA was, upon information and belief, signed personally by the defendant. (Exhibit N).

51. On or about _____, approximately one month after the defendant had *personally* assured the DCA that the matter had been "corrected," he sent the plaintiff a letter that stated in large black letters "SECOND NOTICE" and demanded that she immediately send payment in the amount of $335.53 based upon the same alleged indebtedness to Ladies' Store. (Attached as Exhibit O).

52. The letter further stated, "(O)ur previous request for payment was ignored. Unless we hear from you on receipt of this letter ... we

may have no other alternative but to turn your account over to an attorney in your local area for further legal action." (Exhibit O).

53. Despite the defendant's threat to "turn (the) account over to an attorney in (her) local area for further legal action," upon information and belief, no such referral was made or intended to be made.

54. On or about _____, the defendant sent a letter to the plaintiff once again demanding that she pay the sum of $167.77 allegedly owed to Ladies' Store. (Attached as Exhibit P).

55. The letter stated, "According to our records, the last payment due on the above mentioned account was not made. Please be advised that there is a balance due on your account in the amount of $167.77. It is imperative that you pay the amount due to save any additional costs." (Exhibit P).

56. As described above, the defendant and/or his authorized employee(s) repeatedly assured the plaintiff and the DCA, both orally (see paragraphs 21, 136, 42 and 49) and in writing (See Exhibits H and N), that she owed nothing. However, such assurances were meaningless because, despite them, the defendant willfully, maliciously, and/or recklessly and/or with gross negligence, persisted in making repeated demands for payment of the same sum.

57. As a direct result of the defendant's repeated and persistent acts and conduct, as described above in paragraphs 6–56, the plaintiff suffered severe headaches, fear, anxiety, loss of sleep, loss of appetite, loss of concentration, irritability, intimidation, indignation, and mental anguish.

58. As a direct result of the defendant's repeated and persistent acts and conduct, as described above, the plaintiff incurred expense for medication, telephone charges, stationery, postage, and personal time spent in repeatedly and unnecessarily responding to the defendant's letters.

AS AND FOR A FIRST CAUSE OF ACTION

59. Each paragraph above is repeated and realleged.

60. The defendant's conduct and actions, as described above in paragraphs 6–12, 14–15, 19–20, 22–25, 26–29, 33–35, 39–41, 43–44, 51–53 and 54–55, (See Exhibits A, B, F1, F2, I, K, L, O and P) constitutes ten separate and distinct violations of 15 U.S.C.A. § 1692e(2)(A) in that each such letter and oral communication described above unlawfully demanded the payment of a sum that, upon information and belief, was not in fact due and owing to Ladies' Store at the time each such demand was made and thereby constituted a false representation of the amount of such debt.

61. As a result of such conduct and actions, the plaintiff suffered damage in an amount to be determined by the Court, and the plaintiff may recover therefore pursuant to 15 U.S.C.A. § 1692k(a)(1).

62. The defendant's conduct was willful, malicious, and/or reckless, and/or the result of gross negligence, and, as a result, the defendant is liable to the plaintiff for statutory damages in the amount of One Thousand Dollars ($1,000) per violation, pursuant to 15 U.S.C.A. § 1692k(a)(2)(A).

63. The plaintiff is also entitled to attorneys's fees from the defendant pursuant to 15 U.S.C.A. § 1692k(a)(3).

AS AND FOR A SECOND CAUSE OF ACTION

64. Each paragraph above is repeated and realleged.

65. The defendant's conduct and actions, as described above in paragraphs 22–25, 33–35, 39–41, 51–53, and 54–55, (See Exhibits F1, I, K, L, O and P) constitute six separate and distinct violations of 15 U.S.C.A. § 1692d in that by sending such letters, after receiving full payment of the claim, the defendant engaged in conduct, the natural consequence of which, was to harass, oppress or abuse the plaintiff.

66. As a result of such conduct and actions, the plaintiff suffered damage in an amount to be determined by the Court, and the plaintiff may recover therefore pursuant to 15 U.S.C.A. § 1692k(a)(1).

67. The defendant's conduct was willful, malicious, and/or reckless, and/or the result of gross negligence, and, as a result, the defendant is liable to the plaintiff for statutory damages in the amount of One Thousand Dollars ($1,000) per violation, pursuant to 15 U.S.C.A. § 1692k(a)(2)(A).

68. The plaintiff is also entitle to attorney's fees from the defendant pursuant to 15 U.S.C.A. § 1692k(a)(3).

AS AND FOR A THIRD CAUSE OF ACTION

69. Each paragraph above is repeated and realleged.

70. The defendant's conduct and actions as described above in paragraphs 22–25, 33–35, 39–41, 51–53, and 54–55, (See Exhibits F1, I, K, L, O and P) constitute six separate and distinct violations of 15 U.S.C.A. § 1692k in that each such letter demanding payment, after the plaintiff had made such payment, constitutes an unfair or unconscionable means to collect or attempt to collect a debt.

71. As a result of such conduct and actions, the plaintiff suffered damage in an amount to be determined by the Court, and the plaintiff may recover therefore pursuant to 15 U.S.C.A. § 1692k(a)(1).

72. The defendant's conduct was willful, malicious, and/or reckless, and/or the result of gross negligence, and, as a result, the defendant is

liable to the plaintiff for statutory damages in the amount of One Thousand Dollars ($1,000) per violation, pursuant to 15 U.S.C.A. § 1692k(a)(2)(A).

73. The plaintiff is also entitled to attorney's fees from the defendant pursuant to 15 U.S.C.A. § 1692k(a)(3).

AS AND FOR A FOURTH CAUSE OF ACTION

74. Each paragraph above is repeated and realleged.

75. The defendant's conduct and actions, as described above in paragraphs 22–25, 33–35, 39–41, 51–53, and 54–55, (See Exhibits F1, I, K, L, O and P) constitute six separate and distinct violations of 15 U.S.C.A. § 1692e(2)(A) in that each such letter described above includes a demand for payment of a sum that had already been paid and thereby constitutes a false representation of the character, amount or legal status of a debt.

76. As a result of such conduct and actions, the plaintiff suffered damage in an amount to be determined by the Court, and the plaintiff may recover therefore pursuant to 15 U.S.C.A. § 1692k(a)(1).

77. The defendant's conduct was willful, malicious, and/or reckless, and/or the result of gross negligence, and, as a result, the defendant is liable to the plaintiff for statutory damages in the amount of One Thousand Dollars ($1,000) per violation, pursuant to 15 U.S.C.A. § 1692k(a)(2)(A).

78. The plaintiff is also entitled to attorney's fees from the defendant pursuant to 15 U.S.C.A. § 1692k(a)(3).

AS AND FOR A FIFTH CAUSE OF ACTION

79. Each paragraph above is repeated and realleged.

80. The defendant's conduct and action, as described above in paragraphs 26–29, (See Exhibit F2), in sending a notice that purports to be a summons, constitutes a violation of 15 U.S.C.A. § 1692e(13) in that the use of such notice creates a false representation or implication that the notice is legal process.

81. As a result of such conduct and action, the plaintiff suffered damage in an amount to be determined by the Court, and the plaintiff suffered damage in an amount to be determined by the Court, and the plaintiff may recover therefore pursuant to 15 U.S.C.A. § 1692k(a)(1).

82. The defendant's conduct was willful, malicious, and/or reckless, and/or the result of gross negligence, and, as a result, the defendant is liable to the plaintiff for statutory damages in the amount of One Thousand Dollars ($1,000) per violation, pursuant to 15 U.S.C.A. § 1692k(a)(2)(A).

83. The plaintiff is also entitled to attorney's fees from the defendant pursuant to 15 U.S.C.A. § 1692k(a)(3).

AS AND FOR A SIXTH CAUSE OF ACTION

84. Each paragraph above is repeated and realleged.

85. The defendant's conduct and action, as described above in paragraphs 26–29, (See Exhibit F2), in sending a notice that falsely purports to be a summons, constitutes a violation of 15 U.S.C.A. § 1692e(9) in that such notice is a written communication that unlawfully simulates or is falsely represented to be a document authorized, issued or approved by a Court and/or that creates a false impression as to its source, authorization or approval.

86. As a result of such conduct and action, the plaintiff suffered damage in an amount to be determined by the Court, and the plaintiff may recover therefore pursuant to 15 U.S.C.A. § 1692k(a)(1).

87. The defendant's conduct was willful, malicious, and/or reckless, and/or the result of gross negligence, and, as a result, the defendant is liable to the plaintiff for statutory damages in the amount of One Thousand Dollars ($1,000) per violation, pursuant to 15 U.S.C.A. § 1692k(a)(2)(A).

88. The plaintiff is also entitled to attorneys fees from the defendant pursuant to 15 U.S.C.A. § 1692k(a)(3).

AS AND FOR A SEVENTH CAUSE OF ACTION

89. Each paragraph above is repeated and realleged.

90. The defendant's conduct and action, as described above in paragraphs 26–29, (See Exhibit F2), in sending a notice that falsely purports to be a summons, constitutes a violation of 15 U.S.C.A. § 1692e(10) in that the use of such notice constitutes a false representation or deceptive means to attempt to collect a debt.

91. As a result of such conduct and action, the plaintiff suffered damage in an amount to be determined by the Court, and the plaintiff may recover therefore pursuant to U.S.C.A. § 1692k(a)(1).

92. The defendant's conduct was willful, malicious, and/or reckless, and/or the result of gross negligence, and, as a result, the defendant is liable to the plaintiff for statutory damages in the amount of One Thousand Dollars ($1,000) per violation, pursuant to 15 U.S.C.A. § 1692k(a)(2)(A).

93. The plaintiff is also entitled to attorney's fees from the defendant pursuant to 15 U.S.C.A. § 1692k(a)(3).

AS AND FOR AN EIGHTH CAUSE OF ACTION

94. Each paragraph above is repeated and realleged.

95. The defendant's conduct and actions, as described in paragraphs 6–12, 14–15, 19–25, 39–41 and 51–53, (See Exhibits A, B, E, F1, K and O) constitute six separate and distinct violations of 15 U.S.C.A. § 1692e(5) in that each such letter described above contains a threat to take certain specified action within a specific time period when no such action was actually taken or intended to be taken.

96. As a result of such conduct and actions, the plaintiff suffered damage in an amount to be determined by the Court, and the plaintiff may recover therefore pursuant to 15 U.S.C.A. § 1692k(a)(1).

97. The defendant's conduct was willful, malicious, and/or reckless, and/or the result of gross negligence, and, as a result, the defendant is liable to the plaintiff for statutory damages in the amount of One Thousand Dollars ($1,000) per violation, pursuant to 15 U.S.C.A. § 1692k(a)(2)(A).

98. The plaintiff is also entitled to attorney's fees from the defendant pursuant to 15 U.S.C.A. § 1692k(a)(3).

AS AND FOR A NINTH CAUSE OF ACTION

99. Each paragraph above is repeated and realleged.

100. On or about _____, the plaintiff fully paid the sum demanded by the defendant that was allegedly owed to Ladies' Store, as described above in paragraphs 16–18.

101. After such payment, the defendant, in violation of 15 U.S.C.A. § 1692e(8), communicated to Ladies' Store and/or to a credit reporting agency that such debt had not been paid and/or failed to report that it had been paid, and thereby reported information to such third party that was known, or that should have been known, to be false.

102. As a result of such conduct and actions, the plaintiff suffered damage in an amount to be determined by the Court, and the plaintiff may recover therefore pursuant to 15 U.S.C.A. § 1692k(a)(1).

103. The defendant's conduct was willful, malicious, and/or reckless, and/or the result of gross negligence, and, as a result, the defendant is liable to the plaintiff for statutory damages in the amount of One Thousand Dollars ($1,000) per violation, pursuant to 15 U.S.C.A. § 1692k(a)(2)(A).

104. The plaintiff is also entitled to attorney's fees from the defendant pursuant to 15 U.S.C.A. § 1692k(a)(3).

AS AND FOR A TENTH CAUSE OF ACTION

105. Each paragraph above is repeated and realleged.

106. The defendant's conduct and actions, as described above in paragraphs 33–35, 39–41, 43–44, 51–53, and 54–55, (See Exhibits I, K, L, O and P) constitute five separate and distinct violations of 15 U.S.C.A.

§ 1692c(c) in that each such letter described above constitutes a communication with the plaintiff with respect to a debt claimed to be owed to Lane Bryant sent after the plaintiff had previously requested, in writing, that the defendant cease further communication with her with respect to such debt.

107. As a result of such conduct and actions, the plaintiff suffered damage in an amount to be determined by the Court, and the plaintiff may recover therefore pursuant to 15 U.S.C.A. § 1692k(a)(1).

108. The defendant's conduct was willful, malicious, and/or reckless, and/or the result of gross negligence, and, as a result, the defendant is liable to the plaintiff for statutory damages in the amount of One Thousand Dollars ($1,000) per violation, pursuant to 15 U.S.C.A. § 1692k(a)(2)(A).

109. The plaintiff is also entitled to attorney's fees from the defendant pursuant to 15 U.S.C.A. § 1692k(a)(3).

AS AND FOR AN ELEVENTH CAUSE OF ACTION

110. Each paragraph above is repeated and realleged.

111. The defendant's conduct and actions, as described above in paragraphs 6, 13, and 16–18, (See Exhibits A, B, C1, C2, D1, and D2) constitute a violation of 15 U.S.C.A. § 1692f(1) in that the defendant unlawfully demanded and received a pre-judgment attorney's fee when such fee was not, upon information and belief, expressly authorized by the agreement creating the debt, or otherwise permitted by law.

112. As a result of such conduct and actions, the plaintiff suffered damage in an amount to be determined by the Court, and the plaintiff may recover therefore pursuant to 15 U.S.C.A. § 1692k(a)(1).

113. The defendant's conduct was willful, malicious, and/or reckless, and/or the result of gross negligence, and, as a result, the defendant is liable to the plaintiff for statutory damages in the amount of One Thousand Dollars ($1,000) per violation, pursuant to 15 U.S.C.A. § 1692k(a)(2)(A).

114. The plaintiff is also entitled to attorney's fees from the defendant pursuant to 15 U.S.C.A. § 1692k(a)(3).

AS AND FOR A TWELFTH CAUSE OF ACTION

115. Each paragraph above is repeated and realleged.

116. The defendant's conduct and actions, as described above in paragraphs 6–12, 14–15, 19–20, 22–25, 33–35, 39–41, 43–44, 51–53, and 54–55, (See Exhibits A, B, E, F1, I, K, L, O and P) constitute nine separate and distinct violations of 15 U.S.C.A. § 1693e(10) in that each such letter described above unlawfully demands the payment of a sum that includes pre-judgment attorney's fees that, upon information and belief, are not expressly authorized by the contract creating the debt, or

permitted by law, and therefore constitute a deceptive means to collect or attempt to collect a debt.

117. As a result of such conduct and actions, the plaintiff suffered damage in an amount to be determined by the Court, and the plaintiff may recover therefore pursuant to 15 U.S.C.A. § 1692k(a)(1).

118. The defendant's conduct was willful, malicious, and/or reckless, and/or the result of gross negligence, and, as a result, the defendant is liable to the plaintiff for statutory damages in the amount of One Thousand Dollars ($1,000) per violation, pursuant to 15 U.S.C.A. § 1692k(a)(2)(A).

119. The plaintiff is also entitled to attorney's fees from the defendant pursuant to 15 U.S.C.A. § 1692k(a)(3).

AS AND FOR A THIRTEENTH CAUSE OF ACTION

120. Each paragraph above is repeated and realleged.

121. The defendant's conduct and actions, as described above in paragraphs 6–12, 14–15, 19–20, 22–25, 33–35, 39–41, 43–44, 51–53, and 54–55 (See Exhibits A, B, E, F1, I, K, L, O and P) constitute nine separate and distinct violations of 15 U.S.C.A. § 1692e(2)(B) in that each letter described above unlawfully includes a demand for the payment of a sum that includes pre-judgment attorney's fees and therefore constitutes a false representation of the compensation that may lawfully be received for the collection of a debt.

122. As a result of such conduct and actions, the plaintiff suffered damage in an amount to be determined by the Court, and the plaintiff may recover therefore pursuant to 15 U.S.C.A. § 1692k(a)(1).

123. The defendant's conduct was willful, malicious, and/or reckless, and/or the result of gross negligence, and, as a result, the defendant is liable to the plaintiff for statutory damages in the amount of One Thousand Dollars ($1,000) per violation, pursuant to 15 U.S.C.A. § 1692k(a)(2)(A).

124. The plaintiff is also entitled to attorney's fees from the defendant pursuant to 15 U.S.C.A. § 1692k(a)(3).

AS AND FOR A FOURTEENTH CAUSE OF ACTION

125. Each paragraph above is repeated and realleged.

126. All of the letters sent by the defendant to the plaintiff, as described above in paragraphs 6–12, 14–15, 19–20, 22–25, 26–29, 33–35, 39–41, 43–44, 51–53, and 54–55, (See Exhibits A, B, E, F1, F2, I, K, L, O, and P) fail to disclose that the defendant was attempting to collect a debt and that any information obtained would be used for that purpose. Such failures constitute ten separate and distinct violations of 15 U.S.C.A. § 1692e(11), which requires that such disclosures be made "in all communications made to collect a debt . . .".

127. As a result of such conduct and actions, the plaintiff suffered damage in an amount to be determined by the Court, and the plaintiff may recover therefore pursuant to 15 U.S.C.A. § 1692k(a)(1).

128. The defendant's conduct was willful, malicious, and/or reckless, and/or the result of gross negligence, and, as a result, the defendant is liable to the plaintiff for statutory damages in the amount of One Thousand Dollars ($1,000) per violation, pursuant to 15 U.S.C.A. § 1692k(a)(2)(A).

129. The plaintiff is also entitled to attorney's fees from the defendant pursuant to 15 U.S.C.A. § 1692k(a)(3).

AS AND FOR A FIFTEENTH CAUSE OF ACTION

130. Each paragraph above is repeated and realleged.

131. The defendant's conduct and actions as described above in paragraphs 22–25, 39–41, and 51–53, (See Exhibits F1, K and O), in threatening to serve a summons upon the plaintiff, or commence legal action, or turn the account over to another attorney for "further legal action," after the debt allegedly owed to Ladies' Store had been fully paid, constitute three separate and distinct violations of General Business Law § 601.8 in that the defendant thereby claimed, attempted or threatened to enforce a right with knowledge or reason to know that such right did not exist.

132. Such violation also constitutes a deceptive business practice in violation of General Business Law Art. 22–A.

133. As a result of such violation, the plaintiff suffered damage in an amount to be determined by the Court, and the plaintiff may recover therefore pursuant to General Business Law § 349(h).

134. Such conduct was also willful, malicious, and/or reckless, and/or the result of gross negligence, and, as a result, the plaintiff may recover additional damages of One Thousand Dollars ($1,000) per violation, pursuant to General Business Law § 349(h).

135. The plaintiff is also entitled to attorney's fees from the defendant pursuant to General Business Law § 349(h).

AS AND FOR A SIXTEENTH CAUSE OF ACTION

136. Each paragraph above is repeated and realleged.

137. The defendant, in sending a notice to the plaintiff that falsely purported to be a summons (See paragraphs 26–29; Exhibit F2) engaged in an unlawful collection practice in violation of Penal Law § 190.50.

138. Such violation is a deceptive business practice in violation of General Business Law Art. 22–A.

139. As a result of such violation, the plaintiff suffered damage in an amount to be determined by the Court, and the plaintiff may recover therefore pursuant to General Business Law § 349(h).

140. Such conduct was also willful, malicious, and/or reckless, and/or the result of gross negligence, and, as a result, the plaintiff may recover additional damages of One Thousand Dollars ($1,000) per violation, pursuant to General Business Law § 349(h).

141. The plaintiff is also entitled to attorney's fees from the defendant pursuant to General Business Law § 349(h).

AS AND FOR AN SEVENTEENTH CAUSE OF ACTION

142. Each paragraph above is repeated and realleged.

143. The defendant's conduct and action, as described above in paragraphs 26–29, (See Exhibit F2) constitute a violation of General Business Law § 601.9 in that the use of a notice, which falsely purports to be a summons, constitutes a communication that unlawfully simulates legal or judicial process.

144. Such violation and the use of such notice also constitutes a deceptive business practice in violation of General Business Law Art. 22–A.

145. As a result of such violation, the plaintiff suffered damage in an amount to be determined by the Court, and the plaintiff may recover additional damages of One Thousand Dollars ($1,000) per violation, pursuant to General Business Law § 349(h).

146. Such conduct was also willful, malicious, and/or reckless, and/or the result of gross negligence, and, as a result, the plaintiff may recover additional damages of One Thousand Dollars ($1,000) per violation, pursuant to General Business Law § 349(h).

147. The plaintiff is also entitled to attorney's fees from the defendant pursuant to General Business Law § 349(h).

AS AND FOR AN EIGHTEENTH CAUSE OF ACTION

148. Each paragraph above is repeated and realleged.

149. After receipt of full payment of the alleged claim of Ladies' Store from the plaintiff, the defendant, upon information and belief, communicated to Ladies' Store and/or to a credit reporting agency that such debt had not been paid and/or failed to correct a prior report(s) to such entities concerning the plaintiff and thereby reported information affecting the debtor's reputation for credit worthiness, with knowledge or reason to know such information was false, in violation of General Business Law § 601.3.

150. Such violation also constitutes a deceptive business practice in violation of General Business Law Act. 22–A.

151. As a result of such violation, the plaintiff suffered damage in an amount to be determined by the Court, and the plaintiff may recover therefore pursuant to General Business Law § 349(h).

152. Such conduct was also willful, malicious, and/or reckless, and/or the result of gross negligence, and, as a result, the plaintiff may recover additional damages of One Thousand Dollars ($1,000) per violation, pursuant to General Business Law § 349(h).

153. The plaintiff is also entitled to attorney's fees from the defendant pursuant to General Business Law Sec, 349(h).

AS AND FOR A NINETEENTH CAUSE OF ACTION

154. Each paragraph above is repeated and realleged.

155. The defendant's conduct and actions as described above in paragraphs 6–12, 14–15, 19–20, 22–25, 33–35, 39–41, 43–44, 51–53, and 54–55, (See Exhibits A, B, E, F1, I, K, L, O and P) constitute nine separate and distinct violations of New York General Business Law § 601.2 in that the defendant, by sending each such letter or notice described above, knowingly attempted to collect, and asserted a right to a pre-judgment attorney's fee, when such fee was not justly due and legally chargeable against the plaintiff.

156. Such violations also constitute deceptive business practices in violation of General Business Law Art. 22–A.

157. As a result of such violations, the plaintiff suffered damage in an amount to be determined by the Court, and the plaintiff may recover therefore pursuant to General Business Law § 349(h).

158. Such conduct was also willful, malicious, and/or reckless, and/or the result of gross negligence, and, as a result, the plaintiff may recover additional damages of One Thousand Dollars ($1,000) per violation, pursuant to General Business Law § 349(h).

159. The plaintiff is also entitled to attorney's fees from the defendant pursuant to General Business Law § 349(h).

AS AND FOR A TWENTIETH CAUSE OF ACTION

160. Each paragraph above is repeated and realleged.

161. The defendant's conduct and actions as described above in paragraphs 6, 13 ad 16–18, (See Exhibit A, B, C1, C2, D1 and D2) constitute a violation of General Business Law § 601.2 in that the defendant demanded and received a pre-judgment attorney's fee that was not justly due and legally chargeable against the plaintiff.

162. Such violation also constitutes a deceptive business practice in violation of General Business Law Art. 22–A.

163. As a result of such violation, the plaintiff suffered damage in an amount to be determined by the Court, and the plaintiff may recover therefore pursuant to General Business Law § 349(h).

164. Such conduct was also willful, malicious, and/or reckless, and/or the result of gross negligence, and, as a result, the plaintiff may recover additional damages of One Thousand Dollars ($1,000) per violation, pursuant to General Business Law § 349(h).

165. The plaintiff is also entitled to attorneys' fees from the defendant pursuant to General Business Law § 349(h).

AS AND FOR A TWENTY-FIRST CAUSE OF ACTION

166. Each paragraph above is repeated and realleged.

167. The defendant, in engaging in the conduct and actions described above, engaged in unfair, illegal and deceptive acts and practices in the conduct of business in violation of General Business Law Art. 22–A.

168. As a result of such violations, the plaintiff suffered damage in a amount to be determined by the Court, and the plaintiff may recover therefore pursuant to General Business Law § 349(h).

169. Such conduct was also willful, malicious, and/or reckless, and/or the result of gross negligence, and, as a result, the plaintiff may recover additional damages of One Thousand Dollars ($1,000) per violation, pursuant to General Business Law § 349(h).

170. The plaintiff is also entitled to attorney's fees from the defendant pursuant to General Business Law § 349(h).

AS AND FOR A TWENTY-SECOND CAUSE OF ACTION

171. Each paragraph above is repeated and realleged.

172. The defendant's conduct and actions, as set forth above, occurred as the result of repeated and persistent negligence by the defendant, and/or an authorized employee(s) of the defendant, acting within the scope of his/her employment.

173. As a direct and proximate result of such negligent conduct, the plaintiff suffered damage in an amount to be determined by the Court.

AS AND FOR A TWENTY-THIRD CAUSE OF ACTION

174. Each paragraph above is repeated and realleged.

175. The defendant's conduct, and/or that of his authorized employee(s), as described above, was willful, malicious, and/or reckless, and/or the result of gross negligence.

176. As a direct and proximate result of such willful, malicious, and/or reckless, and/or grossly negligent conduct, the plaintiff suffered damage in an amount to be determined by the Court.

177. In addition, in order to penalize the defendant and deter him from engaging in such willful, malicious, and/or reckless, and/or grossly negligent conduct in the future, with respect to the plaintiff and/or the general public, the Court should award substantial punitive damages to the plaintiff.

WHEREFORE, the plaintiff respectfully demands that the Court enter judgment against the defendant as follows:

(i) Awarding damages, in an amount to be determined by the Court, pursuant to 15 U.S.C.A. § 1692k(a)(1) on the FIRST, SECOND, THIRD, FOURTH, FIFTH, SIXTH, SEVENTH, EIGHTH, NINTH, TENTH, ELEVENTH, TWELFTH, THIRTEEN, and FOURTEENTH causes of action;

(ii) Awarding statutory damages pursuant to 15 U.S.C.A. sec. 1692k(a)(2)(A) in the amount of one thousand dollars ($1,000) for each violation of law as alleged in the FIRST SECOND, THIRD, FOURTH FIFTH, SIXTH, SEVENTH, EIGHTH, NINTH, TENTH, ELEVENTH, TWELFTH, THIRTEENTH, and FOURTEENTH causes of action;

(iii) Awarding attorney's fees to the plaintiff pursuant to 15 U.S.C.A. § 1692k(a)(3) on the FIRST, SECOND, THIRD, FOURTH, FIFTH, SIXTH, SEVENTH, EIGHTH, NINTH, TENTH, ELEVENTH, TWELFTH, THIRTEENTH, and FOURTEENTH causes of action;

(iv) Awarding damages in an amount to be determined by the Court, pursuant to General Business Law § 349(h) on the THIRTEENTH, FOURTEENTH, SIXTEENTH, SEVENTEENTH, EIGHTEENTH, NINETEENTH, TWENTIETH, TWENTY–FIRST and TWENTY–SECOND causes of action;

(v) Awarding statutory damages pursuant to General Business Law § 349(h) in the amount of one thousand dollars ($1,000) for each violation of law as alleged in the THIRTEENTH FOURTEENTH, FIFTEENTH, SIXTEENTH, SEVENTEENTH, EIGHTEENTH, NINETEENTH, TWENTIETH, TWENTY–FIRST and TWENTY-SECOND causes of action;

(vi) Awarding attorney's fees to the plaintiff pursuant to General Business Law § 349(h) on the THIRTEENTH, FOURTEENTH, FIFTEENTH, SIXTEENTH, SEVENTEENTH, EIGHTEENTH, NINETEENTH, TWENTIETH, TWENTY–FIRST and TWENTY-SECOND causes of action;

(vii) Awarding damages, in an amount to be determined by the Court, on the TWENTY–THIRD cause of action;

§ 7.62   CONSUMER LAW   Ch. 7

    (viii) Awarding damages, in the amount to be determined by the Court, and punitive damages, on the TWENTY–FOURTH cause of action; and

    (ix) Granting such other relief as may be proper.

Dated: _____, New York

                        Yours etc.

                        [*ATTORNEY*], Esq.
                        Attorney for the
                        Plaintiff
                        [*ADDRESS AND TELEPHONE NUMBER*]

Library References:

West's Key No. Digests, Consumer Protection ⇐10, 38.

§ 7.63   Forms—Order to Show Cause With Temporary Restraining Order, Seeking Preliminary Injunction in Action Alleging Fraud, Deceptive Business Practices and Breach of Warranties

I

SUPREME COURT OF THE STATE OF NEW YORK
COUNTY OF NEW YORK

JANE DOE,

                Plaintiff,   ORDER TO SHOW CAUSE FOR TEMPO-
           -against-   RARY RESTRAINING ORDER AND PRELIMI-

A.B.C. JEWELERS LTD. d/b/a   NARY INJUNCTION
ROSINI FINE JEWELRY and JOHN ROE,
individually and as President of   Index No.:
A.B.C. JEWELERS LTD.,

                Defendants.

    Upon reading and filing the affirmation of [*ATTORNEY*], Esq., dated _____, the attorney for the plaintiff, the affidavit of the plaintiff, **JANE DOE**, sworn to on _____, the affidavit of Warren Brown, sworn to on _____, the affidavit of Robert Jones, sworn to on _____, the affidavit of Herman Smith, sworn to on _____, and the within sum-

164

Ch. 7   DECEPTIVE BUSINESS PRACTICES   § 7.63

mons and complaint, verified by the plaintiff on _____, together with the exhibits annexed hereto, it is hereby

ORDERED, that the defendants show cause at an IAS Part _____, Room _____, of the Supreme Court of the State of New York, County of New York, at the Courthouse located at 60 Centre Street, New York, New York, on the _____ day of at _____ o'clock in the _____ noon of that day, or as soon thereinafter as counsel may be heard, why an order should not be made pursuant to General Business Law Art. 22-A and CPLR 6301 and 6311, enjoining the defendants, pendente lite, from selling, offering for sale or otherwise distributing or attempting to distribute any "Art Deco" figurine the same or similar to any of the figurines sold by the defendants to the plaintiff, (hereinafter the "figurines") without first truthfully and completely disclosing, in writing, and providing such writing to any purchaser or prospective purchaser:

    a) the name of the actual artist who created such work;

    b) that such figurine is a reproduction and not a work created during the "Art Deco" period, if in fact such is the case; and

    c) whether documents exist that certify the authenticity of such work, and if such documents exist,

enjoining the defendants, *pendente lite*, from completing any sale of figurines without first providing such documents to the prospective purchaser, and pursuant to CPLR 6301 and 6311, enjoining the defendants, *pendente lite*, from destroying any and all documents, books, records, files and papers of any kind, (hereinafter the "records") pertaining to the sale of figurines to the plaintiff, as well as any such records pertaining to the purchase or sale of the same or similar figurines to other members of the public and enjoining and prohibiting the defendants, *pendente lite*, from altering, tampering with or removing any such records from the business address of the defendants in New York County.

SUFFICIENT CAUSE APPEARING, demonstrating that immediate and irreparable harm is likely to result if a temporary restraining order against the defendants is not issued, it is hereby

ORDERED, that pending the hearing and determination of this application, the individual defendant and his agents, and the officers and agents of the corporate defendants herein, be and hereby are temporarily restrained from selling, offering for sale or otherwise distributing or attempting to distribute any "Art Deco" figurine the same or similar to any of the figurines sold by the defendants to the plaintiff (hereinafter the "figurines"), without first truthfully and completely disclosing, in writing, and providing such writing to any purchaser or prospective purchaser:

    a) the name of the actual artist who created such work;

    b) that such figurine is a reproduction and not a work created during the "Art Deco" period, if in fact such is the case; and

c) whether documents exist that certify the authenticity of such work, and, if such documents exist,

enjoining the defendants, *pendente lite*, from completing any sale of figurines without first providing such documents to the prospective purchaser, and pursuant to CPLR 6301 and 6311, enjoining the defendants, *pendente lite*, from destroying any and all documents, books, records, files and papers of any kind, (hereinafter the "records") pertaining to the sale of figurines to the plaintiff, as well as any such records pertaining to the purchase or sale of the same or similar figurines to other members of the public and enjoining and prohibiting the defendants, *pendente lite*, from altering, tempering with or removing any such records from the business address of the defendants in New York County.

SUFFICIENT CAUSE APPEARING, LET service of a copy of this Order and the supporting papers, upon the defendants, on or before _____ be deemed good and sufficient service hereof.

_____
J.S.C.

Library References:

West's Key No. Digests, Consumer Protection ⌐41.

§ 7.64 Forms—Affirmation in Support of Temporary Restraining Order and Preliminary Injunction in Action Alleging Fraud, Deceptive Business Practices and Breach of Warranties

I

SUPREME COURT OF THE STATE OF NEW YORK
COUNTY OF NEW YORK

JANE DOE,	)
Plaintiff,	)))
-against-	) AFFIRMATION)
A.B.C. JEWELERS LTD. d/b/a ROSINI FINE JEWELRY and JOHN ROE, individually and as President of A.B.C. JEWELERS LTD.,	) Index No.:))))
Defendants.	))

[*ATTORNEY*], an attorney duly admitted to practice before the Courts of the State of New York, hereby affirms the truth of the following:

1. I am the attorney for the plaintiff herein. I am fully familiar with the facts and circumstances alleged herein.

INTRODUCTION

2. This is a consumer fraud action brought by the plaintiff on her own behalf, and as a "Private Attorney General," as provided by New York General Business Law (hereinafter "GBL") Article 22-A (the "Deceptive Business Practices Act").

3. The plaintiff alleges that the defendants have engaged in a massive art fraud scam in which she was defrauded of $55,000.00. As alleged herein, the defendants sold the plaintiff eight (8) bronze and ivory or bronze "Art Deco" figurines by representing that they were created by well known artists and had substantial value.

4. In reality, as is set forth herein, such figurines were forgeries, fakes and/or counterfeit reproductions with little or no value as investments.

5. The plaintiff, in her verified complaint (attached hereto and served herewith), is seeking actual, consequential, incidental, statutory and punitive damages against the defendants in seven separate causes of action, alleging deceptive business practices, fraud, breach of express warranties, breach of implied warranties, and unconscionability.

6. In addition, the plaintiff, acting on her own behalf, as well as a "Private Attorney General," as provided by the Deceptive Business Practices Act, is seeking a permanent injunction barring the defendants from engaging in the acts and practices complained of herein with respect to herself as well as on behalf of the general public.

THE TEMPORARY RESTRAINING ORDER AND PRELIMINARY INJUNCTION

7. This affirmation is offered in support of the plaintiff's motion for a Temporary Restraining Order, followed by a Preliminary Injunction, barring the defendants, during the pendency of this action, from selling, offering for sale or otherwise distributing or attempting to distribute any "Art Deco" figurine the same or similar to any of the figurines sold by the defendants to the plaintiff (hereinafter the "figurines"), without first truthfully and completely disclosing, in writing, and providing such writing to any purchaser or prospective purchaser:

  (i) the name of the actual artist who created such work;

  (ii) that such figurine is a reproduction and not a work created during the "Art Deco" period, if in fact such is the case; and

  (iii) whether documents exist that certify the authenticity of such work.

8. If such documents or authenticity exist, the plaintiff further requests that the defendants be enjoined, *pendente lite*, from completing

§ 7.64 CONSUMER LAW Ch. 7

any sale of figurines without first providing such documents to the prospective purchaser.

9. This affirmation is also offered in support of the plaintiff's motion for a Temporary Restraining Order, followed by a Preliminary Injunction, enjoining the defendants, *pendente lite*, from destroying any and all documents, books, records, files and papers of any kind, (hereinafter the "records") pertaining to the sale of figurines to the plaintiff, as well as any such records pertaining to the purchase or sale of the same or similar figurines to other members of the public and, pursuant to CPLR 6301 and 6311, enjoining and prohibiting the defendants, *pendente lite*, from altering, tampering with or removing any such records from the business address of the defendants in New York County.

10. In support of the relief requested herein, the plaintiff offers her within affidavit (the "Doe affidavit"), which describes the transaction involving the sale of the figurines; the affidavit of Warren Brown, (the "Brown affidavit"), and "Art Deco" expert and consultant for Christies, who examined the figurines purchased from the defendants and determined that they were counterfeit; the affidavit of Robert Jones (the "Jones affidavit"), an investigator who visited the defendants' place of business subsequent to the plaintiff's purchase and was offered for purchase a figurine virtually identical to one of the figurines purchased by the plaintiff; and the affidavit of Herman Smith (the "Smith affidavit"), the former president of the Appraisers Association of America, who recently visited the defendant's place of business and observed at least one "Art Deco" figurine, similar in style to the figurines purchased by the plaintiff, being offered for sale as an original piece. According to Mr. Smith, that piece was in fact a reproduction.

11. It is apparent from the Jones and Smith affidavits that the defendants are continuing in the same course of conduct used to victimize the plaintiff.

12. It is also apparent that unless the Court issues a Temporary Restraining Order and a Preliminary Injunction enjoining the defendants, *pendente lite*, from engaging in such practices, numerous other consumers will be victimized in a similar manner.

13. The plaintiff, acting as a "Private Attorney General," is both authorized and mandated by GBL Art. 22–A, to obtain injunctive relief on behalf of *all* consumers who may be subjected to future illegal and/or deceptive business practices by the defendants. *McDonald v. North Shore Yacht Sales, Inc.*, 134 Misc.2d 910, 513 N.Y.S.2d 590, 595 (Sup. Ct., Nassau County, 1987).

14. Such consumers will, upon information and belief, suffer irreparable harm if preliminary relief is not granted.

15. Based upon the amply documented claims in the verified complaint, supported by the affidavits of the plaintiff, Brown, Jones and

Smith, there is a substantial likelihood of success on the merits of this action.

16. The plaintiff's First Cause of Action in her complaint alleges that the defendants have engaged in unfair, illegal and deceptive business practices in connection with the sale of the figurines to her and that such conduct is actionable under GBL § 349(h).

17. The elements of a deceptive business practices claim under GBL Art. 22–A are "merely (1) that the act or practice was misleading in a material respect, and (2) that the plaintiff was injured." *McDonald, supra*; *Geismar v. Abraham & Strauss*, 109 Misc.2d 495, 439 N.Y.S.2d 1005 (Dist. Ct., Nassau County, 1981); Note, *New York Creates A Private Right of Action to Combat Consumer Fraud: Caveat Venditor*, 48 Brooklyn L. Rev. 509 (1982); Richard A. Givens, *McKinney's Practice Commentaries*, GBL § 349, 1988 ed., p. 565.

18. Therefore, unlike a claim for common law fraud, it is unnecessary for the plaintiff to plead or prove an intent to deceive or reliance upon such deception in order to establish a cause of action under GBL Art. 22–A.

19. By showing a violation of GBL Art. 22–A, together with a demonstration that the complained of conduct is ongoing and therefore likely to harm others, the plaintiff has established a right to a Preliminary Injunction. *McDonald, supra*.

20. GBL § 349(h) permits any individual who has suffered damage as a result of a deceptive business practice to recover their actual damages, plus treble damages, if the conduct was wilful, up to a cap of $1,000.00. The plaintiff is also entitled to an award of attorney's fees pursuant to that section.

21. More importantly, in order to prevent businesses who defraud the public from simply writing off a restitution damage award as a "cost of doing business," the Legislature, in adopting GBL § 349(h) in 1980, expressly permitted any individual victimized by deceptive business practices, acting as a "Private Attorney General," to obtain an injunction against the recurrence of such practices. As then Governor Carey stated:

> " ... by authorizing private actions, providing for a minimum damage recovery and permitting attorney's fees (we) will encourage private enforcement of these consumer protection statutes (GBL §§ 349, 350), add a strong deterrent against deceptive business practices and the prosecution of consumer fraud complaints." Governor's Approval Memorandum, N.Y. Legis. Ann. 1980, p. 147.

22. The injunctive relief available under GBL Art. 22–A is therefore clearly intended to protect the plaintiff as well as the general public.

23. As the Court stated in *McDonald, supra*,

"Given the ... purpose the (GBL Art. 22–A), to encourage private enforcement of consumer protection, to strongly deter deceptive business practices, and to supplement the activities of the New York State Attorney General in prosecuting consumer fraud complaints, I hold that *the Legislature intended the irreparable injury issue to be irreparable injury to the public at large, not just to one consumer.*" 513 N.Y.S.2d at p. 595. (Emphasis added).

24. At this juncture, the plaintiff seeks a Temporary Restraining Order, followed by a Preliminary Injunction, barring the defendants, *pendente lite*, from selling the same or similar figurines without truthfully and completely disclosing whether such works are original or reproductions.

25. The proposed order does not bar the defendants from selling reproduced "Art Deco" figurines as long as they are not offered as original pieces.

26. Therefore, the defendants will not suffer any prejudice as the order simply requires them to comply with the law.

27. If, however, such relief is not granted, unknown numbers of people may suffer irreparable harm. As alleged herein, the defendants are clearly engaged in an ongoing consumer fraud scheme by offering and receiving tens of thousands of dollars for reproduced artwork while falsely representing that it has substantial value. Unless temporary injunctive relief is granted, untold other consumers may suffer a fate similar to the plaintiff.

28. The plaintiff also seeks a Temporary Restraining Order, followed by a Preliminary Injunction, requiring the defendants to retain, *pendente lite*, their books and records pertaining to the sale of the figurines to the plaintiff as well as to the general public.

29. The plaintiff will likely suffer substantial and irreparable harm if such documents are not available for discovery and inspection in this case.

30. The defendants' prior conduct in this matter supports the belief that the above described documents may be destroyed without the Court's intervention.

31. The defendants, as described in the Verified Complaint (paragraph 7) and in the Doe affidavit (paragraph 3) have engaged in a massive scheme to defraud the plaintiff by offering and selling eight (8) "Art Deco" figurines for $55,000.00 by:

(i) falsely representing that they were original pieces created by well known artists;

(ii) falsely representing that the figurines had a substantial monetary value in excess of $250,000.00;

(iii) falsely representing that at least one of the figurines had recently been sold at auction at Sotheby's and/or Christies and that it realized in excess of $50,000.00;

(iv) falsely representing that as authentic works by well known artists, the figurines had excellent investment potential; and

(v) falsely representing that documents certifying the authenticity of the figurines existed and would be provided to the plaintiff.

32. And, as is shown in the within Jones and Smith affidavits, this illegal conduct is ongoing.

33. In addition, as alleged in the Doe affidavit (paragraphs 13–15) a detective from the Special Fraud Division of the New York City Police Department visited the defendants' store on her behalf and the defendants denied any knowledge of the plaintiff or her purchase of the figurines. As a result, the defendants, who have already displayed an effort to conceal their fraudulent conduct, may continue to do so by destroying records pertaining to this or other similar transactions.

34. The plaintiff, by simply seeking to have the defendants obey the law and not engage in deceptive practices in offering the figurines to other members of the public, is not preventing the defendants from engaging in any lawful business.

35. Accordingly, it is neither necessary nor appropriate for the Court to require the plaintiff to post a bond.

36. Moreover, the interim relief requested by the plaintiff does not require the posting of a bond. As the Court stated in *McDonald, supra,*

> As to the posting of a bond, such a requirement would be impossible for almost every consumer seeking relief under (GBL Art. 22–A), rendering it a nullity ... As consumers here stand in the shoes of the Attorney General who is not required to post a bond, I find they are also not required to do so. 513 N.Y.S.2d at p. 595.

37. As shown herein the injunctive relief available here is no different from the relief that would be available in an action brought by the New York State Attorney General under GBL Art 22.

38. And, the defendants cannot possibly suffer any prejudice or damage based upon the narrow scope of the Temporary Restraining Order and Preliminary Injunction requested here. Even if the defendants were ultimately successful, it is unlikely that they will have suffered any damage by having had to truthfully disclose the origin of the figurines and not deceive potential new purchasers of their actual value. Nor can there be any claim of prejudice by a requirement to retain the requested records.

39. No prior request has been made for the relief sought herein.

WHEREFORE, it is respectfully requested that the Court issue an Order pursuant to GBL Art. 22–A and CPLR 6301 and 6311 granting a

§ 7.64   CONSUMER LAW   Ch. 7

Preliminary Injunction, barring the defendants, *pendente lite*, from selling, offering for sale or otherwise distributing or attempting to distribute any "Art Deco" figurine of the same or similar medium as any of the figurines sold by the defendants to the plaintiff, without first truthfully and completely disclosing, in writing, and providing such writing to any purchaser or prospective purchaser:

    (i) the name of the actual artist who created such work;

    (ii) that such figurine is a reproduction and not a work created during the "Art Deco" period, if in fact such is the case;

    (iii) whether documents exist that certify the authenticity of such work, and if such documents exist,

enjoining the plaintiffs, *pendente lite*, from completing any sale of figurines without providing such documentation, requiring the defendants to retain, *pendente lite*, any and all documents, books, records, files and papers of any kind, pertaining to the sale of figurines to the plaintiff, as well as any such records pertaining to the purchase or sale of the same or similar figurines to other members of the public and, pursuant to CPLR 6301 and 6311, enjoining and prohibiting the defendants, *pendente lite*, from destroying, altering, tampering with or removing any such records from the business address of the defendants in New York County.

Dated: _____, New York

                                                     [*ATTORNEY*]

Library References:
West's Key No. Digests, Consumer Protection ⚖=41.

§ 7.65   Forms—Complaint in Action Alleging Fraud, Deceptive Business Practices and Breach of Warranties

SUPREME COURT OF THE STATE OF NEW YORK
COUNTY OF NEW YORK
_____
JANE DOE,   )
)
                          Plaintiff,   )
)
               -against-   )   VERIFIED COMPLAINT
)
A.B.C. JEWELERS LTD. d/b/a   )
ROSINI FINE JEWELRY and JOHN ROE,)   Index No.:
individually and as President of   )
A.B.C. JEWELERS LTD.,   )
)
                      Defendants.)
_____

172

The plaintiff, **JANE DOE** (hereinafter the "plaintiff"), by her attorney, [*ATTORNEY*], Esq. as and for her complaint against the defendants, alleges as follows:

PRELIMINARY STATEMENT

1. This is an action for actual, consequential, incidental, statutory and punitive damages, attorney's fees, cancellation and injunctive relief brought pursuant to New York General Business Law (hereinafter "GBL") Article 22–A (Deceptive Business Practices), New York Arts and Cultural Affairs Law (hereinafter "ACAL") Title C, Article 13 (Breach of Express Warranty), the Uniform Commercial Code and the common law of the State of New York.

2. The plaintiff contends that the defendants sold her various items, for a total price of $55,000.00, which were represented to be authentic or original bronze and ivory or bronze "Art Deco" figurines created by certain well known artists and which were represented to have substantial value, when in fact such items were forgeries, fakes and/or counterfeit reproductions having little or no value in the antique market. The plaintiff further contends that the defendants knew or should have known that such representations were false, misleading, deceptive and dishonest.

3. The plaintiff further contends that the defendants have engaged, and are continuing to engage, in a similar course of conduct on a repeated and persistent basis with respect to other consumers. Pursuant to the authority provided by GBL Art. 22–A, the plaintiff is therefore also acting as a "Private Attorney General" and asks that the Court enjoin the defendants from engaging in such conduct in the future on her behalf and on behalf of such other consumers.

PARTIES

4. The plaintiff is a natural person residing in the City and State of New York.

5. Upon information and belief, the defendant **A.B.C. JEWELERS LTD., d/b/a ROSINI FINE JEWELRY** (hereinafter "ROSINI") is a New York corporation engaged in the business of buying and selling new and second-hand jewelry and items purported to be antiques. Upon information and belief, ROSINI maintains retail stores for the purpose of conducting such business at 503 Fifth Avenue and at the Royal Arms Hotel, both of which are located in the County and City of New York. Upon information and belief, ROSINI possesses a Second–Hand Dealer's

License issued by the New York City Department of Consumer Affairs, License No. 57264, pursuant to Title 20, Chapter 2, Subchapter 11, §§ B20–264 *et seq.* of the Administrative Code of the City of New York. Upon information and belief, ROSINI employs sales personnel who are authorized to engage in the sale or attempted sale of such goods to the public (hereinafter "sales personnel").

6. Upon information and belief, the defendant **JOHN ROE** (hereinafter "Roe") is a natural person and the President of ROSINI, residing at 123 East 85th Street, New York, New York. Upon information and belief, Roe's duties and responsibilities include, but are not limited to, the sale or attempted sale of such products to the public (hereinafter ROSINI and Roe are collectively termed "the defendants").

STATEMENT OF FACTS

7. On or about _____, the plaintiff visited the ROSINI store located at 503 Fifth Avenue. At or about that time the defendant Roe and/or other of the defendants' sales personnel exhibited various items to her and represented that:

(i) they were "Art Deco" figurines made by certain well known artists;

(ii) such figurines had substantial momentary value in excess of $250,000.00;

(iii) at least one of such figurines had recently been sold at auction at Sotheby's and/or Christies and that it had realized in excess of $50,000.00 at such auction(s);

(iv) such figurines were authentic and/or original works created by well known artists in the field such as Demetre H. Chiaparus and Ferdinand Preiss, and, as such, had excellent investment potential;

(v) documents certifying the authenticity of such figurines existed, and that the defendants possessed, or were about to obtain, such documents and that such documentation would be provided to the plaintiff after completion of the sale; and

(vi) such figurines had been purchased from the estate of the late Dorothy Socialite in Palm Beach, Florida.

8. Roe and/or other sales personnel offered to sell eight such figurines to the plaintiff for a total of $60,000.00 if payment were made in cash.

9. In reliance upon the representations made by Roe and/or other sales personnel, as described above, the plaintiff offered to purchase such figurines for $55,000.00.

10. Roe and/or other sales personnel agreed to sell the figurines to the plaintiff for such amount, and the plaintiff paid such amount to them.

11. Roe and/or other sales personnel prepared a bill of sale for such figurines that listed the eight items sold and that stated their authors. Such bill of sale was then provided to the plaintiff upon payment in full of $55,000.00 to the defendants.

12. Following the completion of the sale, the plaintiff repeatedly requested that the defendants provide the documents certifying the authenticity of the figurines, as promised.

13. Despite such repeated requests, the defendants have failed and refused to provide such documentation to the plaintiff.

14. After the completion of the sale and after making full payment, the plaintiff learned that the figurines sold to her by the defendants were in fact forgeries, fakes and/or counterfeit, that they are neither authentic nor original, that they were not in fact created by the artists as stated by the defendants, and that they do not in fact have investment value as antiques or otherwise.

15. Shortly thereafter, the plaintiff advised the defendants that she had learned that the figurines sold to her were neither authentic nor original pieces and demanded a return of the money paid to the defendants. The defendants have failed and refused to return such money to the plaintiff.

AS AND FOR A FIRST CAUSE OF ACTION

16. Each paragraph is repeated and realleged.

17. The representations described above in the paragraphs 7a–7e concerned material elements of the transaction between the parties and were false, deceptive and misleading and had the capacity and tendency to, and in fact did, deceive or mislead the plaintiff.

18. The conduct and actions described herein are directed at the general public and are not isolated or unique to the transaction between the parties.

19. The defendants' conduct and actions as described above constitute unfair, illegal and deceptive business practices in violation of General Business Law Art. 22–A.

20. As a result of such illegal conduct the plaintiff suffered actual damage in the amount of FIFTY–FIVE THOUSAND DOLLARS ($55,000.00) and may recover therefore pursuant to GBL § 349(h).

21. Such conduct was also wilful, and, as a result, the plaintiff may recover additional damage in the amount of ONE THOUSAND DOLLARS ($1,000.00) pursuant to GBL § 349(h).

22. The plaintiff is also entitled to an award of attorney's fees pursuant to GBL § 349(h).

AS AND FOR A SECOND CAUSE OF ACTION

23. Each paragraph above is repeated and realleged.

24. The defendants made material representations to the plaintiff concerning the figurines, as described above in paragraphs 7a–7e.

25. Such material representations were made to the plaintiff as statements of fact.

26. Such material representations were falsely and fraudulently made by the defendants.

27. Such material representations were made by the defendants with the intent to deceive the plaintiff.

28. Such material representations were made with the intent to induce the plaintiff into purchasing the figurines.

29. The plaintiff did not discover the falsity of such representations and was thereby induced into purchasing the figurines.

30. The plaintiff justifiably relied upon the defendants' representations and was thereby induced into purchasing the figurines.

31. As a result of the defendants' fraudulent conduct as described above, the plaintiff suffered damage in the amount of FIFTY–FIVE THOUSAND DOLLARS ($55,000.00) and is entitled to recover such sum from the defendants.

32. The defendants intentionally and wilfully engaged in the shocking, outrageous and unconscionable conduct and action described above.

33. In order to punish the defendants and to properly deter them, and others, from engaging in similar conduct in the future, the Court should award the plaintiff punitive damages in the amount of FIVE MILLION DOLLARS ($5,000,000.00).

AS AND FOR A THIRD CAUSE OF ACTION

33. Each paragraph above is repeated and realleged.

34. The defendants are "Art Merchants" within the meaning of Arts and Cultural Affairs Law § 11.01.2.

35. The figurines described above are works of "Fine Art" within the meaning of ACAL Section 11.01.9.

36. The bill of sale prepared by the defendants and furnished to the plaintiff as described above is a "Written Instrument" within the meaning of ACAL Section 11.01.20.

37. The defendants expressly warranted the truth of their representations to the plaintiff.

38. The defendants breached the express warranty provided to the plaintiff under ACAL Art 13.

39. As a direct and proximate result of such breach, the plaintiff suffered damage in the amount of FIFTY-FIVE THOUSAND DOLLARS ($55,000.00) and is entitled to recover such sum from the defendants.

40. In addition, the plaintiff suffered incidental and consequential damages as a proximate result of such breach, in the sum of ONE MILLION DOLLARS ($1,000,000.00).

AS AND FOR A FOURTH CAUSE OF ACTION

41. Each paragraph above is repeated and realleged.

42. The misrepresentations stated above in paragraphs 7a–7e were affirmations of fact or promise made by the defendants to the plaintiff.

43. Such representations relate to the figurines sold by the defendants to the plaintiff.

44. Such representations became part of the basis of the bargain between the plaintiff and the defendants.

45. The representations were false in that the figurines do not conform to such representations and the defendants thereby breached their express warranty to the plaintiff under UCC § 2–313.

46. The plaintiff gave the defendants timely notice of such breach, and they have failed and refused to cure same.

47. As a direct and proximate result of such breach, the plaintiff suffered damage in the amount of FIFTY-FIVE THOUSAND DOLLARS ($55,000.00) and is entitled to recover such sum from the defendants.

48. In addition, the plaintiff suffered incidental and consequential damages as a proximate result of such breach in the sum of ONE MILLION DOLLARS ($1,000,000.00).

AS AND FOR A FIFTH CAUSE OF ACTION

49. Each paragraph above is repeated and realleged.

50. The defendants are or were merchants engaged in the business of selling goods of the kind purchased by the plaintiff.

51. The defendants warranted to the plaintiff that the figurines sold by them were merchantable and could thereby pass without objection in the trade under the contract description and that they were fit for the ordinary purposes for which they are used.

52. The figurines are not merchantable in that they are fake, forgeries or counterfeit. They thereby do not conform to the standards of merchantability as required by UCC § 2–314.

53. The defendants thereby breached their implied warranty of merchantability to the plaintiff.

54. As a direct and proximate result of such breach, the plaintiff suffered damage in the amount of FIFTY-FIVE THOUSAND DOLLARS ($55,000.00) and is entitled to recover such sum from the defendants.

55. In addition, the plaintiff suffered incidental and consequential damages as a proximate result of such breach in the sum of ONE MILLION DOLLARS ($1,000,000.00).

AS AND FOR A SIXTH CAUSE OF ACTION

56. Each paragraph above is repeated and realleged.

57. The defendant impliedly warranted to the plaintiff that the figurines sold to her had substantial investment value and thereby impliedly warranted that they were fit for such purpose pursuant to UCC § 2-315.

58. The figurines are not fit for an investment purpose because they are fakes, forgeries or counterfeit and thereby have no value in the antique market.

59. The defendants thereby breached their implied warranty to the plaintiff that the figurines were fit for a particular purpose.

60. As a direct and proximate result of such breach, the plaintiff suffered damage in the amount of FIFTY-FIVE THOUSAND DOLLARS ($55,000.00) and is entitled to recover such sum from the defendants.

61. In addition, the plaintiff suffered incidental and consequential damages as a proximate result of such breach in the sum of ONE MILLION DOLLARS ($1,000,000.00).

AS AND FOR A SEVENTH CAUSE OF ACTION

62. Each paragraph above is repeated and realleged.

63. The transaction between the parties, as described above, including, but not necessarily limited to, the material misrepresentations made by the defendants and the excessive price charged, was unconscionable, in violation of UCC § 2-302.

64. Based upon such unconscionability, the Court should cancel the contract between the parties and award restitution to the plaintiff in the sum of FIFTY-FIVE THOUSAND DOLLARS ($55,000.00).

AS AND FOR AN EIGHTH CAUSE OF ACTION

65. Each paragraph above is repeated and realleged.

66. Upon information and belief, the defendants' illegal conduct and actions, as described above, have been and continue to be directed at numerous consumers in that the defendants have deceptively sold and continue to sell or attempt to sell the same or similar figurines to others using the unfair, illegal and deceptive business practices described above.

Ch. 7   DECEPTIVE BUSINESS PRACTICES   § 7.65

67. The plaintiff, on her own behalf, and that of the general public, acting as a "Private Attorney General" pursuant to General Business Law Art. 22–A, demands that the defendants be enjoined from engaging in further conduct, as described above in paragraphs 7a-7e, in violation of GBL Art. 22–A.

68. The plaintiff is also entitled to an award of attorney's fees pursuant to GBL § 349(h).

WHEREFORE, the plaintiff demands judgment against the defendants, jointly and severally, as follows:

(i) Awarding the sum of FIFTY–FIVE THOUSAND DOLLARS ($55,000.00) in actual damages, ONE THOUSAND DOLLARS ($1,000.00) in additional damages, plus attorney's fees, on the FIRST CAUSE OF ACTION;

(ii) Awarding the sum of FIFTY–FIVE THOUSAND DOLLARS ($55,000.00) in damages plus the sum of FIVE MILLION DOLLARS ($5,000,000.00) in punitive damages on the SECOND CAUSE OF ACTION;

(iii) Awarding the sum of FIFTY–FIVE THOUSAND DOLLARS ($55,000.00) in damages plus ONE MILLION DOLLARS ($1,000,-000.00) in incidental and consequential damages on the THIRD CAUSE OF ACTION;

(iv) Awarding the sum of FIFTY–FIVE THOUSAND DOLLARS ($55,000.00) in damages plus ONE MILLION DOLLARS ($1,000,-000.00) in incidental and consequential damages on the FOURTH CAUSE OF ACTION;

(v) Awarding the sum of FIFTY–FIVE THOUSAND DOLLARS ($55,000.00) in damages plus ONE MILLION DOLLARS ($1,000,-000.00) in incidental and consequential damages on the FIFTH CAUSE OF ACTION;

(vi) Awarding the sum of FIFTY–FIVE THOUSAND DOLLARS ($55,000.00) in damages plus ONE MILLION DOLLARS ($1,000,-000.00) in incidental and consequential damages on the SIXTH CAUSE OF ACTION;

(vii) Canceling the contract between the parties and awarding restitution in the sum of FIFTY–FIVE THOUSAND DOLLARS ($55,000.00) on the SEVENTH CAUSE OF ACTION;

(viii) Enjoining the defendants from engaging in the same or similar deceptive business practices on behalf of the general public on the EIGHTH CAUSE OF ACTION;

(ix) Awarding the costs, disbursements and attorney's fees of this action, together with the interest on all sums awarded from the date of accrual to the date of entry of judgment;

(x) Granting such other and further relief as may be just.

§ 7.65　　　　　CONSUMER LAW　　　　　Ch. 7

Dated: _____, New York

　　　　　　　　Yours, etc.

　　　　　　　　[ATTORNEY], Esq.
　　　　　　　　Attorneys for Plaintiff
　　　　　　　　[ADDRESS AND TELEPHONE NUMBER]

Library References:
　West's Key No. Digests, Consumer Protection ⇌38.

Chapter 8

ENFORCEMENT OF MONEY JUDGMENTS

by
Arthur M. Neiss

Table of Sections

Sec.	
8.1	Scope Note.
8.2	Strategy.
8.3	Judgments—Generally.
8.4	____ Methods to Obtain.
8.5	Form of Judgment—Judgment–Roll.
8.6	____ Interest.
8.7	____ Fees, Costs and Disbursements.
8.8	____ Entry.
8.9	____ Transcript of Judgment.
8.10	Matters Affecting Judgment—Vacatur.
8.11	____ Satisfaction By Payment or Otherwise.
8.12	____ Assignment.
8.13	____ Death of Judgment Debtor.
8.14	____ Amendment or Correction.
8.15	Actions on Judgments.
8.16	Entry of a Foreign Judgment—Sister–State Judgments.
8.17	____ Federal Court Judgments.
8.18	____ Foreign Country Judgments.
8.19	Judgment Enforcement Against Property—Definition of Property.
8.20	____ Exemptions.
8.21	____ Property in the Possession of Others.
8.22	____ Disclosure of Property.
8.23	____ ____ Subpoenas.
8.24	Article 52 Enforcement Devices—Introduction.
8.25	____ Restraining Notices—Nature and Use.
8.26	____ ____ Formal Requirements.
8.27	____ ____ Service and Punishment for Disobedience.
8.28	____ Execution.
8.29	____ ____ Property Execution With Regard to Personal Property.
8.30	____ ____ ____ Sale, Distribution and Priority In Proceeds.
8.31	____ ____ Property Execution With Regard to Real Property.
8.32	____ ____ ____ Notice and Sale of Real Property.
8.33	____ ____ ____ Distribution of Proceeds of Sale and Conveyance of Title.
8.34	____ Income Execution.
8.35	____ Installment Payment Order—Nature and Purpose.

8.36 ____ ____ Form of Application and Service.
8.37 ____ Receiver.
8.38 ____ ____ Application, Appointment and Extension.
8.39 ____ Turnover Orders For Property or Debts.
8.40 ____ ____ Turnover Against the Judgment Debtor.
8.41 ____ ____ Turnover Against A Garnishee.
8.42 ____ Contempt.
8.43 ____ Arrest of the Judgment Debtor.
8.44 Protective Orders.
8.45 Proceeding To Determine Adverse Claims.
8.46 Forms.
8.47 ____ Statement For Judgment (Default Judgment), Affidavit of Facts Constituting the Claim, the Default and the Amount Due.
8.48 ____ Affidavit of Confession of Judgment and Judgment by Confession.
8.49 ____ Notice to Judgment Debtor [or Obligor].
8.50 ____ Subpoena (*Duces Tecum*) To Take Deposition of Judgment Debtor With Restraining Notice.
8.51 ____ Subpoena (*Duces Tecum*) To Take Deposition of Witness With Restraining Notice.
8.52 ____ Information Subpoena.
8.53 ____ Restraining Notice to Judgment Debtor.
8.54 ____ Execution.
8.55 ____ Income Execution.
8.56 ____ Affirmation and Order To Show Cause To Punish Judgment Debtor—Witness For Contempt.

WESTLAW Electronic Research

See WESTLAW Electronic Research Guide preceding the Summary of Contents.

§ 8.1 Scope Note

This chapter on creditors' rights and remedies addresses the practice and procedures available for the enforcement of money judgments. As a litigator, there is perhaps no greater professional satisfaction than the successful conclusion of a case when, by verdict, motion, or even default, you cause the entry of a money judgment in your client's favor. After a long and difficult struggle, all of the time and energy spent on diligent investigation, legal research, briefing or actually trying a case has finally culminated in a "win" for your client. The client now believes that its rights have been vindicated; and you, not unjustifiably, are feeling like a hero. For its part, the judgment debtor, having succumbed to your extraordinary legal onslaught, will now do the honorable thing and pay the judgment, immediately and in full, and the entire matter will be behind everybody.

Great scenario. More often, however, the judgment debtor's immediate payment in full is simply a fantasy.

Although no reliable statistics exist in New York, it is a safe assumption that the lion's share of money judgments go unpaid. Whether because the judgment debtor has made himself "judgment proof" and/or simply can't pay, or because he wishes to delay and/or avoid payment of the judgment as a strategic maneuver designed to drive up the costs of litigation and lessen the judgment creditor's (or its attorney's) resolve to collect the full amount, it is probable that collection problems will be encountered.

Fortunately, New York's Civil Practice Law and Rules (CPLR), unlike the procedural statutes of many states, provide relatively powerful judgment enforcement tools which can be employed and timed at your discretion and usually without judicial involvement. Unfortunately, these measures are often cumbersome, time-consuming and may later require judicial intervention for more complete enforcement. Further, because some of the devices require efforts by persons outside your direct control (e.g., recipients of enforcement devices and enforcement officers such as sheriffs and city marshals), you may encounter frustrating delays and, occasionally, feelings of powerlessness.

This chapter addresses the enforcement of a money judgment. Structurally, it begins with a review of the basics of a judgment,[1] the methods by which judgments are obtained in litigation,[2] and the format of judgments, including the factors—interest, fees, costs and disbursements—that increase the judgment's value.[3]

Before judgments are enforceable, they must be entered.[4] Occasionally, the record of a judgment must be transferred to another court or county for lien purposes; this "transcripting" procedure is discussed in Section 8.9.

Although the purpose of any judgment is to conclude most or all matters between the parties, judgments are not necessarily immutable. Judgments may be vacated for a number of reasons.[5] Judgments, of course, may be satisfied.[6] Judgments are also affected by their assignment,[7] by the death of the judgment debtor,[8] or by amendment or correction.[9]

Sometimes an earlier judgment proves inadequate. Section 8.15 discusses the reasons for commencing suit on an earlier judgment.

It is not unusual to learn that a judgment debtor has moved his residence (or property which can be used to satisfy a judgment) from one country or state to another, or that he simply owns property in another

§ 8.1

1. See infra, § 8.3. See generally, Borges et al., Enforcing Judgments and Collecting Debts in New York (West 1997).
2. See infra, § 8.4.
3. See infra, §§ 8.5—8.7.
4. See infra, § 8.8.
5. See infra, § 8.10.
6. See infra, § 8.11.
7. See infra, § 8.12.
8. See infra, § 8.13.
9. See infra, § 8.14.

state. Note that the reach of New York's judgment enforcement statute does not exceed its grasp: this chapter and the enforcement techniques discussed herein apply only when the judgment debtor or his property may be found in New York. Accordingly, this chapter contains a discussion of the methods by which a sister state,[10] federal[11] or foreign country[12] judgment may be recorded as a New York judgment in aid of its enforcement.

Because judgments are satisfied from the property of the judgment debtor, an understanding of the nature of the property interests reachable,[13] those that are exempt and those in the possession of others[14] are reviewed. Statutory process used in discovering the location of the debtor's property is addressed in Sections 8.22—8.23.

Finally, the primary focus of this chapter is to provide the practitioner with a working knowledge of each of the statutory devices available for the enforcement of money judgments. Each procedure is discussed in turn and the purposes, service and methods of enforcement of each are reviewed.[15] For humility as well as for completeness, we conclude with a discussion of the steps the judgment debtor can take to protect, at least to some extent, against a judgment creditor's harassment,[16] and an explanation of the steps others can take when their interests, as creditors or otherwise, are affected by judgment enforcement proceedings.[17]

This chapter addresses a topic of general interest, and necessarily it will not cover every conceptual or substantive area or specific judgment enforcement problem. Among the areas not included here: United States Marshal executions upon federal court judgments;[18] support, alimony or maintenance orders not reduced to money judgments;[19] declaratory judgments; judgments awarding possession of real property or a chattel; judgments directing the sale of real property;[20] equity judgments enforceable by contempt; judgments requiring payment into court or payment by a fiduciary for a wilful default or dereliction of duty; periodic payments or the "structured judgments" of medical and dental malpractice[21] and of personal/property injury and wrongful death judgments.[22]

Also beyond the scope of this chapter but of enormous importance to creditors as they contemplate litigation strategy or are involved in litigation against debtors are the pre-judgment or provisional remedies of

10. *See infra*, § 8.16.
11. *See infra*, § 8.17.
12. *See infra*, § 8.18.
13. *See infra*, § 8.19.
14. *See infra*, § 8.21.
15. *See infra*, §§ 8.24—8.43.
16. *See infra*, § 8.44.
17. *See infra*, § 8.45.
18. 28 U.S.C.A. §§ 2001 *et seq.*

19. *See* Chapter 21 "Domestic Relations," *infra*.

20. CPLR Article 50–A. *See* Chapter 12 "Purchase and Sale of Real Property," *infra*.

21. CPLR Article 50–B. *See* Chapter 29 "Medical Malpractice," *infra*.

22. *See* Chapter 26 "Personal Injury," *infra*.

asset restraint set forth generally in CPLR Article 60, *et seq.* These include: Attachment (Article 62), Injunction (Article 63), Receivership (Article 64), *Lis Pendens* (Article 65) and Liens (*see* New York Lien Law), Replevin (Article 71) and Sequestration (Domestic Relations Law § 233).[23]

§ 8.2 Strategy

More than anything else, *preparation* early in the case and *speed* are the most important factors responsible for a successful outcome to the judgment enforcement process. From a practical perspective, preparation occurs even before you agree to be retained, as you and the potential client attempt to ascertain: whether the matter is worthy of pursuit (*e.g.*, whether, by the time the matter is concluded, the potential judgment debtor will have sufficient assets to satisfy the judgment); whether it is appropriate to seek a provisional remedy at the time of or after commencement of the litigation; or whether it is possible to avoid suit altogether by having the debtor execute a confession of judgment to secure the obligation.

Later, from the moment the money judgment is entered, enforcement, using whatever information you have at your disposal about the debtor's assets, should proceed aggressively, persistently and, above all, with as much alacrity as you can bring to bear. These two guiding principles—preparation and speed—together constitute the most important words of wisdom in this chapter.

No two judgment enforcement matters are the same; so, strictly speaking, there can be no defined strategy applicable to every case. The primary goals are to (a) obtain reliable information about all of the judgment debtor's property and assets and (b) use that information in order to marshal the debtor's property towards the satisfaction of the judgment. No strict order or chronology dictates which judgment enforcement tools or devices must be used, or when; the choices are entirely discretionary and the decision is determined by the particular circumstances of the case. Having said this, however, a general approach may be summarized as follows:

Preliminary investigations. In anticipation of the entry of judgment, carefully review the attorney files and all of the files of the client concerning the debtor. Seek out all materials that provide any insight into the debtor's financial life such as copies of checks, financial statements, loan or other applications, promissory notes, invoices, etc. Attempt to ascertain the existence and location of all real and personal property in which the debtor has an interest, or any other information concerning such property. Review all pleadings, affidavits, interrogato-

---

23. *See* Haig, *et al., Commercial Litigation in New York State Courts* (West 1997) Ch. 14 "Provisional Remedies."

§ 8.2   ENFORCEMENT OF MONEY JUDGMENTS   Ch. 8

ries, deposition transcripts and other litigation materials to find references to financial institutions, creditors of the debtor, or other individuals or entities which may be able to provide leads to further information. Interview the client's credit, financial and sales officers, and other employees with whom the debtor had any dealings. Consider interviewing any other persons who may know the debtor and be familiar with the debtor's financial circumstances.[1]

Outside help. If possible, conduct a credit or other financial search of the debtor. A number of private companies to which you may subscribe can provide credit and other financial reports for individuals and companies. Other companies can provide database access to information concerning the debtor's real property ownership, UCC–1 filings and other kinds of financial information (including the names and addresses of banking institutions with which the debtor has relationships, as well as the nature of those relationships). Pursue other possible sources for the location of assets or information: insurance companies and agents (cash surrender value of policies); other creditors of the debtor; the Board of Elections may supply the address and occupation of a person if furnished with a name and date of birth; the Department of Motor Vehicles can furnish a written abstract and the existence of liens for a fee.

Post-verdict discovery and restraint. After trial or decision but prior to entry of judgment, consider bringing a motion to examine the future judgment debtor and restrain the disposition of assets.[2] To employ this cumbersome procedure effectively, the future judgment creditor must be prepared to show "need" based on an evidentiary demonstration that the debtor may frustrate enforcement of the judgment to be entered by disposing of assets.[3]

Serve restraining notices immediately. Immediately after the judgment is entered, serve restraining notices upon the judgment debtor and upon every other person or entity you believe may owe a debt or obligation to the judgment debtor, or may otherwise be in possession of the debtor's property.[4] This may include service upon all of the banking

---

§ 8.2

1. **CAVEAT:** Because discussion of the debt with others can easily be misconstrued and potentially be the subject of liability under the Fair Credit Reporting Act (15 U.S.C.A. §§ 1681 *et seq.*), the Fair Debt Collection Practices Act (15 U.S.C.A. §§ 1692 *et seq.*), New York State or local consumer protection statutes, and other common law forms of claim, this approach is strongly disfavored. Instead, a subpoena should be used. *See infra,* § 8.23.

2. CPLR 5229.

3. The granting of relief is, of course, discretionary, and because of the high burden of proof, the procedure is used infrequently.

4. **PRACTICE POINTER:** Err, if it be "error" at all, on the side of excess: if the person served does not have the debtor's property or owe a debt at that time, the notice is ineffective. But, to paraphrase Shakespeare, it is better to have served and come up with naught, then never to have restrained at all.

PRACTICE POINTER: Where the judgment debtor is an individual, contemporaneously serve the Notice to Judgment Debtor. *See infra,* § 8.27.

or similar institutions within an arbitrary geographic radius of the debtor.[5] Although the statute provides choices as to the manner of service, personal service usually has a much greater psychological impact upon any recipient.

Subpoenas to the debtor and third parties. If, prior to entry of judgment, sufficient financial information cannot be obtained independent of the judgment debtor or third persons, entry of the judgment gives the right to serve subpoenas for the examination of the debtor and third persons/entities, for documents within their custody or control, or both. Keep a watchful eye on the return dates for the subpoenas and be prepared to follow up promptly if you believe the date will be missed by a witness. As a practical matter, it may be unrealistic to expect every recipient of a subpoena to comply within the statutory deadlines. On the other hand, the success achieved with subpoenas is usually a function of the level of consistent attention given to the process.[6] Where the judgment debtor or witness is recalcitrant, the remedy will be a contempt proceeding.[7]

Prepare for and conduct extensive examinations. Be well prepared for and conduct a "searching" examination of the judgment debtor or witness. Article 52 allows for an extensive examination, permitting the judgment creditor "to compel disclosure of all matter relevant to the satisfaction of the judgment."[8]

Move aggressively to marshal the debtor's property. After property has been located, (a) cause delivery of a property execution or, in appropriate cases, an income execution, to an enforcement officer (sheriff or marshal)[9] and/or (b) bring a motion or commence a special

---

5. Some private companies will "blanket" the institutions in specific areas or counties with restraining notices for a fee.

6. The violation of the statute's time requirement by the recipient of a subpoena remains a violation, regardless of the recipient's "press of business" or otherwise. We do not wish to imply otherwise. But it is improbable that the practitioner will run to the courthouse for relief on the day each subpoenaed witness fails to appear.

PRACTICE POINTER: Assuming appropriate service of the subpoena, attempt to contact the witness by phone shortly before the return date to confirm her appearance. If you agree to adjourn the return date, confirm this, preferably, in a stipulation or, at a minimum, in writing. In either event, the witness should be reminded (a) of the statutory duty imposed by the subpoena, (b) the continuing nature of the subpoena's obligations and (c) that the judgment creditor intends no waiver of any right by consenting to the adjournment.

7. *See infra*, § 8.42.

8. CPLR 5223.

9. **PRACTICE POINTER:** Notwithstanding the existence of the judgment and a statutory framework designed to assist the judgment creditor in locating and liquidating the debtor's property for its satisfaction, the judgment creditor's activities in seeking to "take" the judgment debtor's property necessarily implicate due process and, as such, the procedures used are open to close scrutiny.

Review the execution and other statutes designed to effect the transfer of the debtor's property to assure your, and your enforcement officer's, compliance with each procedural requirement. Generally speaking, because of the courts' due process concerns, such statutes are strictly construed. The prudent exercise of carefully reviewing the statutes ahead of time should minimize the potential for the imposition of a stay of the creditor's activities or even the reversal

§ 8.2   ENFORCEMENT OF MONEY JUDGMENTS   Ch. 8

proceeding for a turnover order where delivery to the sheriff has been refused or the property has been placed beyond reach.[10] Keep an eye on the date by which the execution must be extended beyond the initial 60 day period to avoid a return unsatisfied and concomitant loss of lien priority in the judgment debtor's personal property.[11]

Properly close matters. When the judgment has been satisfied in whole or in part, file the satisfaction-piece and serve the judgment debtor with a copy of the filed instrument. Be sure to file satisfactions in all counties or courts in which the judgment had been filed or transcripted.

§ 8.3 Judgments—Generally

A judgment is defined as the determination of the rights of the parties in an action or special proceeding, and may be either interlocutory[1] or final.[2] The inclusion of findings of fact in a judgment is improper. Rather, the judgment should state that the court has made findings of fact and of law, and the judgment should then decree the relief granted: the decretal sections of the judgment constitute the actual determinations made.[3]

A final judgment is dispositive of all factual and legal issues in the case and judicially settles the matter; accordingly, a final judgment will issue only after all such issues have been decided. The doctrine of *res judicata* applies to a final judgment on the merits.[4] *Res judicata* renders conclusive upon the parties in any subsequent action involving the same cause of action or defense, and applies to any matters actually litigated and to matters that might have been litigated but were not.[5]

---

of much groundwork via the judgment debtor's (or another's) motion for a protective order.

10. See *infra*, §§ 8.39—8.41.

11. See *infra*, § 8.28.

§ 8.3

1. **PRACTICE POINTER:** An interlocutory judgment is one that determines some but not all rights in an action. It is both possible and desirable to obtain a partial judgment upon a part of a cause of action or upon one or more causes of action as to one or more parties. CPLR 5012. Obviously, this will require a dispositive motion in which, *inter alia*, a request is made to sever the claims subject to the motion from the remainder of those in the action. Motions to sever should also be made where there may be several—but not joint—liability. When successfully made early in the case, these motions sometimes yield early, satisfactory resolutions of the entire matter.

2. CPLR 5011. In jurisdictions outside New York, a judgment may be known as a decree.

3. People v. Reinforced Bottle Corp., 176 Misc. 268, 27 N.Y.S.2d 14 (Sup.Ct., N.Y. County, 1941); City Bank Farmers Trust Co. v. Cannon, 265 App.Div. 863, 38 N.Y.S.2d 245 (2d Dep't 1942), mot. for lv. den. 265 App.Div. 862, 38 N.Y.S.2d 370 (1942); Correll v. Correll, 109 N.Y.S.2d 531 (Sup.Ct., N.Y. County, 1951).

4. Gramatan Home Investors Corp. v. Lopez, 46 N.Y.2d 481, 414 N.Y.S.2d 308, 386 N.E.2d 1328 (1979).

5. Reilly v. Reid, 45 N.Y.2d 24, 407 N.Y.S.2d 645, 379 N.E.2d 172 (1978). *See also*, O'Brien v. City of Syracuse, 54 N.Y.2d 353, 445 N.Y.S.2d 687, 429 N.E.2d 1158 (1981) and its companion case, Smith v. Russell Sage College, 54 N.Y.2d 185, 445 N.Y.S.2d 68, 429 N.E.2d 746 (1981). These cases develop a shift in the law: courts will now apply a transactional, pragmatic ap-

A money judgment is an absolute legal obligation to pay and is enforceable for twenty years.[6] A money judgment is expressed in dollars and cents unless the claim was based on another currency, in which case the judgment is expressed in the foreign currency with a conversion into U.S. currency using the exchange rate at the time of entry.[7]

Enforcement of a judgment may begin the moment after it is entered; service of a notice of entry is required only to begin the time in which an appeal may be taken.[8] If an appeal is taken from a judgment directing payment of a sum of money, enforcement is not stayed absent either the giving of an undertaking in the amount of the judgment or a court order.[9]

§ 8.4 Judgments—Methods to Obtain

Generally, there are five methods by which a judgment may be obtained in an original action.

Default Judgment. The first and probably most common method to obtain a judgment is premised upon the default of a party in answering or appearing.[1] When a defendant defaults, he is deemed to have admitted liability. As to damages, where the monetary amount in controversy is liquidated (a sum certain or which can be made certain), the clerk may enter judgment by determining the sum from the body of the complaint, calculating interest on that amount, and adding appropriate costs.[2] In order for the clerk to enter judgment based on a liquidated amount, within one year of the default, the judgment creditor's attorney should submit an affidavit of merits (*i.e.*, the facts constituting the claim,

---

proach to *res judicata*. A cause of action is deemed coterminous with the transaction regardless of the number of theories of recovery asserted in the two cases. Before this, the test was whether "a different judgment in the second [case] would destroy or impair rights or interest as established by the first." Schuylkill Fuel Corp. v. B. & C. Nieberg Realty Corp., 250 N.Y. 304, 307, 165 N.E. 456, 457 (1929). Collateral estoppel applies to different or distinct causes of action and applies to issues rather than whole claims or defenses. *See* Bonde v. General Security Ins. Co. of Canada, 55 Misc.2d 588, 285 N.Y.S.2d 675 (Sup.Ct., Albany County, 1967).

6. CPLR 211(b). *See also*, Reisman v. Independence Realty Corp., 195 Misc. 260, 89 N.Y.S.2d 763, aff'd 277 App.Div. 1020, 100 N.Y.S.2d 407 (1st Dep't 1950) (absolute legal obligation to pay, unaffected by assignment).

CAVEAT: Note that the lien of a judgment extends only for ten years, but may be renewed. *See infra*, § 8.31.

7. Judiciary Law § 27(b).

8. CPLR 5513.

9. CPLR 5519.

§ 8.4

1. PRACTICE POINTER: Simultaneously with or immediately following service of the summons by the process server, be certain to comply with the additional mailing made necessary by CPLR 3215(g)(3) or (4), if applicable. These sections provide that when certain types of service of process have been employed, an additional mailing to the defendant's last known address is required at least twenty (20) days before a judgment will be entered by the clerk. The additional service and affidavit of such service should track the language of the statute. Failure to comply with the additional mailing will unnecessarily delay entry of judgment.

2. CPLR 3215(a). Interest is discussed in *infra*, § 8.6; "taxation" of costs by the clerk is discussed in *infra*, § 8.7.

the default, and the amount due) executed by the party. For this purpose, the allegations of a verified complaint will suffice, as long as an affidavit as to the default is also submitted.[3]

Where the damages alleged in the complaint are not subject to calculation by the clerk, the plaintiff must prove damages to the court (or a referee, if so directed), following application therefor, in an assessment hearing commonly called an "inquest."[4] No findings of fact need be made at the inquest (except in the case of a matrimonial action).[5] At the inquest, damages may be proved by the oral testimony of in-court witnesses or, if the defaulting party does not appear, by executed affidavits.[6]

Judgment After Trial. A judgment may be entered following a trial by the court or by a jury (verdict).[7]

Summary Judgment. Entry of judgment may be based upon a successful motion for summary judgment, including a CPLR 3213 motion for summary judgment in lieu of complaint.[8] Where a decision grants summary judgment and directs settlement of an order or submission of a judgment, diligence is important: The order or judgment to be entered thereon must be submitted for signature within 60 days after the decision was filed. Failure to meet the deadline "shall be deemed an abandonment" unless good cause can be shown.[9]

Confession of Judgment. The fourth method of obtaining judgment is by the defendant's confession of judgment.[10] This is by far the

---

3. CPLR 3215(f). *See infra*, § 8.47.

PRACTICE POINTER: In a complaint based on contract or quasi-contract, be certain to include in the affidavit the date(s) upon which each claim accrued. This will enable the clerk to determine a start date for the accrual of interest. *See infra*, § 8.6. Pre-judgment interest may, of course, be waived.

4. CPLR 3215(b).

PRACTICE POINTER: An attorney's fee is not necessarily unliquidated; if the complaint includes a claim for attorney's fees, those fees may be recoverable upon affidavit. (*See* D. Siegel, *Practice Commentaries*, CPLR C3215:16. However, there appears to be little uniformity among court clerks on this issue, so it would be best to determine the philosophy of the clerk beforehand.) In addition to the affidavit of the party, which should reference the contract provision calling for attorney's fees, the attorney should aver the basis for the claim (*i.e.*, agreement between the parties), describe the attorney's or firm's experience in such cases (*e.g.*, collections matters), detail the precise nature of each of the services performed by the firm and its personnel in connection with the case, set forth the number of hours worked and the hourly rates charged, and state the reasons why the amount sought is fair and reasonable.

5. *Id.*

6. 22 NYCRR § 202.46(b).

7. CPLR 5016.

8. **PRACTICE POINTER:** When the claim is based on an instrument for the payment of money only (*e.g.*, promissory note) or upon a judgment, always consider the use of a CPLR 3213 motion for summary judgment in lieu of complaint. This "motion-action" is usually faster than a plenary action, and the movant can control the hearing date. However, as with any summary judgment motion, should the court find that issues of material fact exist, the motion will be denied and the motion papers will be deemed to be the complaint and answer, respectively, unless the court orders otherwise.

9. 22 NYCRR § 202.48.

10. CPLR 3218.

most efficient method, since it entails none of the incidents of a full blown lawsuit. The confessed judgment may be for money that is due or will become due, or to secure the plaintiff against a contingent liability in behalf of the defendant.[11] The consent to entry of judgment, or the "confession," is evidenced by an affidavit of the debtor which must set forth: (a) a concise statement of the nature of the transaction(s) which caused the debt (whether for money due or to become due, indicating that the amount is or will become justly due or, for a contingent liability, stating the facts constituting the liability and showing that the amount confessed does not exceed the total amount of the liability); (b) the sum for which judgment may be entered; (c) the county in which the judgment debtor resides or authorizes entry; and (d) the judgment debtor's authorization that judgment be entered.[12] The facts constituting the claim should be detailed well enough in the affidavit to give other creditors a sufficient picture of the transaction, in order to permit their investigation of the claim and its validity.[13]

Judgments based on confession must be filed within 3 years of the execution of the supporting affidavit.[14] If the full amount confessed is not yet due, a property execution may issue only to the extent of the sum actually due.[15]

Where the affidavit's terms are satisfied (*i.e.*, where money is due or the contingency had arrived), the judgment debtor may not seek a vacatur of the confessed judgment by motion; he must commence a plenary proceeding to do so.[16] In contrast, other creditors of the judgment debtor may bring a simple motion to vacate the confessed judgment.[17]

Costs in a confessed judgment are limited to $15.[18]

Sister-state judgments based on confession or "cognovit" (the procedure by which the debtor/creditor agreement sets forth the debtor's "warrant of attorney" by which the creditor's attorney confesses judgment on behalf of the debtor) are not automatically entitled to full faith

PRACTICE POINTER: If a payout of a pre-suit claim is negotiated, always attempt to have the original obligation or the settlement obligation secured by the debtor's confession of judgment.

11. CPLR 3218(a).

CAVEAT: In cases in which the debt arises from installment plan purchases of commodities for private use, and is for less than $1,500, a confessed judgment is void and unenforceable where the affidavit was executed prior to the time of default. *See* CPLR 3201.

12. CPLR 3218(a). *See infra*, § 8.48.

13. ILMS Realty Ass'n v. Madden, 174 A.D.2d 603, 571 N.Y.S.2d 310 (2d Dep't 1991); Wood v. Mitchell, 117 N.Y. 439, 22 N.E. 1125 (1889).

14. CPLR 3218(b).

15. CPLR 3218(c). *See infra*, § 8.28.

16. L.R. Dean, Inc. v. International Energy Resources, Inc., 213 A.D.2d 455, 623 N.Y.S.2d 624 (2d Dep't 1995).

17. County Nat. Bank v. Vogt, 28 A.D.2d 793, 280 N.Y.S.2d 1016 (3d Dep't), aff'd 21 N.Y.2d 800, 288 N.Y.S.2d 631, 235 N.E.2d 772 (1968).

18. CPLR 3218(a). In contrast, in fully litigated matters, costs are $200, plus $200 after note of issue, plus $300 after each trial, inquest or assessment of damages. CPLR 8201(1)-(3). *See infra*, § 8.7.

and credit in New York[19] but New York gives its own confessed judgments *res judicata* and collateral estoppel effect.[20]

Failure to Cure Under Stipulation. The fifth method by which judgment is obtained is cousin to the default judgment. Here, there has been a default or other failure to cure under a stipulation. Judgment can be entered where: (a) the parties provide for such entry in the stipulation (*e.g.*, entry without further notice); (b) an action is pending; (c) the amount (including interest, if any) is capable of being liquidated pursuant to the stipulation or is otherwise readily calculable; and (d) the application is accompanied both by an affidavit describing the failure to cure or other default, and the complaint or other statement of the original claim.[21]

§ 8.5 Form of Judgment—Judgment-Roll

The judgment-roll, containing the original basic papers from the court's file, is what is assembled either by the attorney or by the clerk, and filed, when judgment is entered.[1] It includes all matters involving the merits or necessarily affecting the final judgment including the summons, pleadings, admissions, prior judgments, orders, proof of defaults and result of inquest (for default judgments), verdict, appeal decisions and papers on which the appeal was heard, or, in the case of a confessed judgment, the affidavit and a copy of the judgment.[2]

§ 8.6 Form of Judgment—Interest

As the statute makes clear, interest shall be recovered upon awards in breach of contract actions and is computed from the earliest date the cause of action existed.[1] This date must be specified in the verdict, report

---

19. Mallan v. Samowich, 94 A.D.2d 249, 464 N.Y.S.2d 122 (1st Dep't 1983), appeal dism'd 67 N.Y.2d 871, 501 N.Y.S.2d 1029, 492 N.E.2d 795 (1986).

20. *See e.g.*, Rivera v. Blum, 98 Misc.2d 1002, 420 N.Y.S.2d 304 (Sup.Ct., Suffolk County, 1978) (confessed judgments have all the qualities, incidents and attributes of a verdict after trial, including the presumption of validity).

21. CPLR 3215(i)(1).

CAVEAT: Also related to the section on failure to cure under a stipulation is the procedure, set forth in CPLR 5003–a, by which plaintiff tenders to a settling defendant an executed release and stipulation discontinuing the action. If the settling defendant fails to pay all sums due within 21 days of such tender, plaintiff may enter judgment, without notice, for the amount in the release, together with interest on that amount computed from the date of tender. This procedure is clearly risky and has limited usefulness.

§ 8.5

1. CPLR 5017(a). The judgment-roll must state the date and time of filing. *Id.*

2. CPLR 5017(b).

§ 8.6

1. CPLR 5001. Generally, the purpose is to provide full indemnification for a wrongful interference with a property right. De Long Corp. v. Morrison–Knudsen Co., 14 N.Y.2d 346, 251 N.Y.S.2d 657, 200 N.E.2d 557 (1964). It also serves as compensation for delayed payment. *See, e.g.*, Kavares v. Motor Vehicle Acc. Indemnification Corp. 29 A.D.2d 68, 285 N.Y.S.2d 983 (1st Dep't 1967), aff'd 28 N.Y.2d 939, 323 N.Y.S.2d 431, 271 N.E.2d 915 (1971).

or decision.[2] Money judgments bear interest at the rate of 9% per year.[3]

Interest is determined in three phases: (1) from time of accrual of the cause of action until verdict or decision;[4] (2) from verdict or decision until entry of judgment;[5] and (3) from entry of judgment until complete satisfaction of the judgment.[6]

Library References:

West's Key No. Digests, Judgment ⚖=223.

§ 8.7 Form of Judgment—Fees, Costs and Disbursements

In the American judicial system, a judgment is presumed to include certain of the expenses of litigation, but not attorney's fees.[1] The "fees" attributable to the activities of certain judicial and other officers (including sheriffs and County Clerks), as well as the fees incident to certain judicial processes, which may be included in a judgment have been determined by the Legislature.[2]

Perhaps to ameliorate the harshness of the American rule concerning attorney's fees, "costs" are intended to indemnify a party for the

2. CPLR 5001(c).
3. CPLR 5004.
4. CPLR 5001.

The agreement in Astoria Federal Sav. and Loan Ass'n v. Rambalakos, 49 A.D.2d 715, 372 N.Y.S.2d 689 (2d Dep't 1975) required a higher rate of interest "until the principal is fully paid." The case holds that interest in category 1 may accrue at the contract rate until entry of judgment because the contract was merged into the judgment. In Marine Management, Inc. v. Seco Management, Inc., 176 A.D.2d 252, 574 N.Y.S.2d 207 (2d Dep't), aff'd 80 N.Y.2d 886, 587 N.Y.S.2d 900, 600 N.E.2d 627 (1992), the contract's clear, unambiguous and unequivocal expression that interest was to accrue and be collectible at a higher rate until the judgment was satisfied permitted the judgment creditor a recovery at the higher rate.

Note, however, that the court may not permit this form of interest in certain types of actions or on certain claims (e.g., punitive damages). Rocanova v. Equitable Life Assur. Soc. of U.S., 83 N.Y.2d 603, 612 N.Y.S.2d 339, 634 N.E.2d 940 (1994) (demand or request for punitive damages possesses no viability absent its attachment to a substantive cause of action). Interest on punitive damages awards may accrue after the date of the trial court's decision making the award. Delulio v. 320–57 Corp., 99 A.D.2d 253, 472 N.Y.S.2d 379 (1st Dep't 1984).

5. CPLR 5002.

6. CPLR 5003. Satisfaction of judgment, by payment, means that in addition to the amount of the judgment, all interest has been paid. Beneficial Discount Co. of New York, Inc. v. Spike, 91 Misc.2d 733, 398 N.Y.S.2d 651 (Sup.Ct., Yates County, 1977). See infra, § 8.11. Satisfaction may also include an unconditional tender. Meiselman v. Allstate Ins. Co., 197 A.D.2d 561, 602 N.Y.S.2d 659 (2d Dep't 1993).

§ 8.7

1. City of Elmira v. Larry Walter, Inc., 150 A.D.2d 129, 546 N.Y.S.2d 183 (3d Dep't 1989) (counsel fees are not an item of damages, absent statutory authority or a contractual provision).

2. CPLR Article 80 contains the complete list of all such fees. Among those included: witness subpoena and mileage fees (CPLR 8001) (see infra, § 8.23); receiver's commissions (CPLR 8004) (see infra, § 8.38); sheriff's fees on property and income executions (CPLR 8012) (see infra, § 8.28); sheriff's mileage and poundage (CPLR 8012) (see infra, § 8.28); sheriff's expenses (CPLR 8013) (see infra, § 8.28); and County Clerk's fees, including index numbers (CPLR 8016–8022).

expenses of a suit, or otherwise provide some measure of compensation to the attorney or reimbursement to the client.[3] The two kinds of costs which can be included in a judgment are those delineated in the statute and those for which application may be made.[4]

In addition to fees and costs, certain out-of-pocket expenditures have been designated by statute as disbursements[5] which are "taxed" by the clerk. Taxation means that each item is reviewed and examined; the clerk is satisfied that all items are correct and allowable; and all items not supported by an affidavit stating that they have been necessarily incurred and are reasonable in amount have been struck.[6]

Costs may be taxed with or without notice. Where the report of costs (the "bill") is on notice, the adverse party interested in reducing the amount can supply its own bill.[7] Where taxation is *ex parte*, the bill must be served immediately thereafter to permit that party to move to "retax" on five days' notice.[8] Thereafter, application may be made to the court.[9]

The court, in its discretion, may award "additional allowances."[10] Although infrequently granted, there is statutory authority for the exercise of discretion in awarding an additional allowance on a motion relating to the enforcement of a judgment.[11]

Library References:
West's Key No. Digests, Judgment ⟾224.

§ 8.8 Form of Judgment—Entry

A judgment of the court is "entered" when, after being signed by the court or clerk, it is dated, time-stamped and filed by the clerk.[1] "Docketing" of a judgment (considered simultaneous with entry in the

---

3. A.G. Ship Maintenance Corp. v. Lezak, 69 N.Y.2d 1, 511 N.Y.S.2d 216, 503 N.E.2d 681 (1986). See also, Distler, *The Course of Costs of Course*, 46 Cornell L.Q. 76 (1960).

4. CPLR Article 81 sets forth the various circumstances under which costs may be had. These include: an action (CPLR 8101); consolidated, severed or removed [non-federal] actions (CPLR 8104); upon a motion (CPLR 8106); and on an appeal (CPLR 8107).

CPLR Article 82 sets forth the monetary limits of costs in an action (CPLR 8201), on a motion (CPLR 8202) and on appeal (CPLR 8203 and 8204).

5. CPLR 8301(a) reflects a "laundry list" of what disbursements may be included in a judgment.

PRACTICE POINTER: Before submitting a judgment to the clerk, check this section to be sure that all appropriate disbursements are presented for the clerk's taxation. Note that the statute includes a catch-all for "other reasonable and necessary expenses ... according to the course and practice of the court" by law or court order. CPLR 8301(a)(12). The court can also tax as a disbursement the fee for a service performed, even if the fee exceeds the fee usually allowed to a public officer.

6. CPLR 8401.
7. CPLR 8402.
8. CPLR 8403.
9. CPLR 8402.
10. CPLR 8303(a).
11. CPLR 8303(b).

§ 8.8
1. CPLR 5016(a).

supreme or county courts because the clerk is *ex officio* county clerk[2]) is its recordation in certain alphabetized books, and serves as a lien against the real property in which the judgment debtor has an interest in that county.[3] The clerk's role in entering a judgment is purely ministerial and he or she cannot act in any way that is contrary to the precise directions reflected in the court's decision.[4]

Library References:
West's Key No. Digests, Judgment ⊕270–293.

§ 8.9 Form of Judgment—Transcript of Judgment

A transcript of judgment refers to the method by which an inferior court's judgment becomes docketed in the office of the county clerk for purposes of establishing a judgment lien against the real property of the judgment debtor in that county, and/or the method by which a judgment docketed in one county becomes a judgment lien against the debtor's real property in another county.[1] The form of transcript is set forth in Judiciary Law § 255–c (but the clerk may supply it).[2] Where a judgment is transcripted to a second county, that clerk must notify the clerk of the first county of the recordation; the first clerk then makes a notation on her records.[3]

Library References:
West's Key No. Digests, Judgment ⊕290, 291, 292.

§ 8.10 Matters Affecting Judgment—Vacatur

A judgment may be vacated or opened upon a motion premised on such notice as the court may direct (*i.e.*, an Order to Show Cause) by a party or interested person.[1] The motion may be granted in the court's discretion "upon such terms as may be just" on the grounds of (1) excusable default (provided the motion is made within one year of

2. County Law § 525(a).
3. CPLR 5018.
4. Huot v. Dworman, 13 Misc.2d 104, 173 N.Y.S.2d 58 (Sup.Ct., Kings County, 1958), aff'd 8 A.D.2d 829, 190 N.Y.S.2d 202 (2d Dep't 1959).

§ 8.9
1. CPLR 5018(a).
2. A transcript consists of a certification by the clerk (or justice or judge) of the contents of the judgment docket in the clerk's office. It includes the name and address of the judgment creditor; the name and address of the judgment creditor's attorney; the amount of the judgment (damages, costs and total); the court rendering the judgment, including the date and time of docketing; and any change in the status of the judgment (*e.g.*, execution issued or unsatisfied, satisfaction, etc.).

PRACTICE POINTER: When the investigation of the debtor's assets reveals real property in a county other than that in which the judgment was entered, immediately transcript the judgment to the second county to establish the lien of judgment. Failure to do so or delay in doing so may affect the judgment creditor's priority. *See infra*, § 8.33.

3. CPLR 5018(a). Marc v. Pinkard, 133 Misc. 83, 230 N.Y.S. 765 (Mun.Ct., Manhattan, 1928) (clerk is ministerial officer).

§ 8.10
1. CPLR 5015(a).

§ 8.10   ENFORCEMENT OF MONEY JUDGMENTS   Ch. 8

service of a copy of the judgment or order with notice of entry); (2) newly discovered evidence (which, if introduced at trial, would have produced a different result and could not, with reasonable diligence, be obtained at the first trial); (3) fraud, misrepresentation or misconduct of an adverse party; (4) the court's lack of jurisdiction to render the judgment or order; or (5) reversal, modification or vacatur of a prior judgment or order upon which the judgment or order is based.[2] Vacatur of a default judgment may also be effectuated by a stipulation executed by the parties or their attorneys.[3]

It is the public policy of New York that controversies be resolved on their merits; accordingly, courts liberally construe the section relating to vacatur of judgments.[4] In the case of a default judgment, discretion is premised on the movant's provision of a legally cognizable, reasonable excuse for the default and the establishment of a *prima facie* meritorious defense to the action.[5] The court should give balanced consideration to this showing and also to the extent of the delay, the prejudice to the nondefaulting party, and the evidence of intent or lack thereof to deliberately default or abandon the action.[6]

§ 8.11 Matters Affecting Judgment—Satisfaction by Payment or Otherwise

Where a judgment is wholly or partially satisfied, the judgment creditor (or the person entitled to enforce it)[1] must execute and file an acknowledged form of satisfaction-piece which, within ten days of such filing, must also be mailed to the judgment debtor.[2] In the case of a judgment transcripted to other counties, the judgment creditor must file a clerk's certificate in all counties.[3] The judgment creditor who fails to file a satisfaction may face a $100 penalty.[4]

2. CPLR 5015(a).

3. CPLR 5015(b).

4. *See* Myzal v. Mecca, 28 A.D.2d 1022, 283 N.Y.S.2d 785 (3d Dep't 1967).

5. Arred Enterprises Corp. v. Indemnity Ins. Co. of North America, 108 A.D.2d 624, 485 N.Y.S.2d 80 (1st Dep't 1985).

6. *Id.*

§ 8.11

1. *See infra*, § 8.12.

2. CPLR 5020(a). This section says that the instrument shall be filed when satisfaction is received. Presumably, the period between receipt and filing is narrow, but it is not defined by the statute.

CAVEAT: Pursuant to CPLR 5020(b), the authority of the judgment creditor's attorney to execute a satisfaction-piece extends for 10 years; but the attorney may be discharged before then. To avoid an authority problem, the judgment debtor probably should insist that the actual judgment creditor, rather than the creditor's attorney, execute the satisfaction-piece.

3. CPLR 5020(d).

4. CPLR 5020(c). Under the court acts of the inferior courts and pursuant to CPLR 7202, a person aggrieved pursuant to this penalty provision has standing to bring an action to recover the penalty. The judgment debtor can also move the court to direct the clerk to enter a satisfaction on her docket. CPLR 5021(b).

CAVEAT: Although at first glance the amount of the penalty may seem a minor price to pay, considering the ability of credit reporting and investigation agencies to pick up judgment information rapidly, liability for damages resulting from the judgment creditor's failure to timely file a satisfac-

Where a judgment debtor attempts to wholly satisfy by mailing payment to the judgment creditor's last known address, by registered or certified mail, return receipt requested, and the payment is returned as unclaimed or undeliverable, the judgment debtor may deposit the sum with the clerk of the court in the form of a certified check.[5] This procedure serves to cut off further accrual of interest and other enforcement expenses; the clerk notifies any sheriffs involved.[6] Following such tender, the judgment debtor should move the court in which the judgment was entered to require the clerk to enter a notation of satisfaction.[7]

Library References:

West's Key No. Digests, Judgment ⇔874–899.

§ 8.12 Matters Affecting Judgment—Assignment

A judgment may be enforced by another who becomes entitled to enforce it, such as an assignee or one designated by a court order. Such person must file with the clerk of the court in which the judgment was entered (or, in the case of a judgment transcripted from a lower court, the court in which the transcript was filed) the instrument upon which the authority to enforce the judgment is based, acknowledged in the manner of a deed, or a certified copy of the court order granting such authority.[1] The clerk forwards a certificate of change to the clerks of counties in which transcripts have been filed.[2]

Library References:

West's Key No. Digests, Judgment ⇔885.

§ 8.13 Matters Affecting Judgment—Death of Judgment Debtor

A verdict or decision may not be entered as a judgment against a party who has died; the personal representative should be substituted.[1] If following such adjudication the party then dies, judgment may enter against that party in his or her own name.[2]

When a judgment debtor dies, enforcement efforts, in the absence of leave of the appropriate surrogate's court, should be suspended.[3] In only

---

5. CPLR 5020–a.
6. CPLR 5020–a. Notice to the sheriff is effective upon receipt.
7. CPLR 5020–a.

§ 8.12

1. CPLR 5020(c).
2. CPLR 5019(d).

PRACTICE POINTER: Assignees should also immediately notify the judgment debtor of the assignment. Tri City Roofers, Inc. v. Northeastern Indus. Park, 61 N.Y.2d 779, 473 N.Y.S.2d 161, 461 N.E.2d 298 (1984) (actual notice of assignment must be received before duty to pay assignee arises).

§ 8.13

1. CPLR 5016(d); *see also*, CPLR 1015 and CPLR 1021.
2. CPLR 5016(d).
3. CPLR 5208.

one circumstance may an execution be perfected: where it has been issued and levied upon prior to the death.[4] The lien of a judgment against the deceased judgment debtor's real property expires two years after the death or 10 years after the filing of the judgment-roll, whichever is later.[5]

Library References:

West's Key No. Digests, Judgment ⚖12, 798, 800(8), 860.

§ 8.14 Matters Affecting Judgment—Amendment or Correction

Since a judgment is deemed "final" as to the controversies determined,[1] subsequent to entry, a court may not change a substantive provision even where "the equities" would seem to indicate that it should; such changes are possible only by way of motion to vacate or on appeal.[2] Defects or irregularities in judgments that affect no substantial right of a party (*e.g.*, technical, clerical or mathematical errors) do not affect enforcement and may be corrected by the court (or, for certain matters concerning taxation of costs, by the clerk).[3] This power is based on the court's inherent ability to correct its own judgments, exercisable at any time, and is not dependent on statutory authority.[4] Resettlement is the procedure to correct judgments suffering from these types of defects.[5] Correction to refer back to the date the judgment should have been entered (retroactive) may be made by *nunc pro tunc* order.[6]

Library References:

West's Key No. Digests, Judgment ⚖294–335(4).

§ 8.15 Actions on Judgments

Actions on money judgments between the original parties to the judgment need only be maintained in three circumstances. First, an action may be brought for purposes of lien renewal, where 10 years have elapsed since docketing of the judgment (not the date of a subsequent

4. Oysterman's Bank & Trust Co. v. Weeks, 35 A.D.2d 580, 313 N.Y.S.2d 535 (2d Dep't 1970).
5. CPLR 5208.

§ 8.14

1. See *supra*, § 8.3.
2. Empire Produce Co. v. Ring, 225 App. Div. 6, 232 N.Y.S. 82 (4th Dep't 1928).
3. CPLR 5019(a).
4. American Cities Co. v. Stevenson, 187 Misc. 107, 60 N.Y.S.2d 685 (Sup.Ct., N.Y. County, 1946).
5. "Settlement" is the procedure by which the proposed content of an order or judgment is submitted to the court for signature. 22 NYCRR § 202.48. Resettlement is the procedure to correct a judgment for an obvious mistake, irregularity or inadvertence. Allocco v. Rainone, 73 N.Y.S.2d 330 (Sup.Ct., Kings County), aff'd 271 App.Div. 1024, 69 N.Y.S.2d 923, appeal denied 272 App.Div. 816, 72 N.Y.S.2d 264, appeal dism'd 297 N.Y. 583, 74 N.E.2d 555 (1947).

6. Huot v. Dworman, 13 Misc.2d 104, 173 N.Y.S.2d 58 (Sup.Ct., Kings County, 1958), aff'd 8 A.D.2d 829, 190 N.Y.S.2d 202 (2d Dep't 1959).

transcript of judgment).[1] This action may be commenced after nine years and results in a renewal judgment, which picks up precisely where the other ends.[2] As such, the procedure avoids a potential problem where, during a "gap" in lien coverage, another creditor's lien moves up the priority ladder.[3]

An action on a judgment can also be brought when the judgment is by default and the underlying action was served in a manner other than by personal service or service upon an agent.[4] Third, an action on a judgment may be maintained where the court directs.[5]

Library References:
West's Key No. Digests, Judgment ⚖︎900–947.

§ 8.16 Entry of a Foreign Judgment—Sister-State Judgments

In New York, the Uniform Enforcement of Foreign Judgments Act[1] applies to all judgments entitled to full faith and credit, except those obtained by default in appearance or by confession of judgment.[2] If the sister-state judgment is entitled to full faith and credit in New York, it may simply be filed ("registered") here.[3] Even though the presumptive validity of a sister-state judgment may be inquired into by a New York court, its validity may not normally be collaterally attacked.[4]

§ 8.15

1. CPLR 5014(1). Although a money judgment may be enforced for 20 years (see supra, § 8.3), the lien of the judgment against the judgment debtor's real property lasts only 10 years from the date of filing of the judgment-roll. CPLR 5203(a).

2. CPLR 5014. In other words, the judgment is prevented from expiring as a lien. In re Buchardt, 114 B.R. 362 (Bankr. N.D.N.Y.1990).

3. See infra, § 8.31.

4. CPLR 5014(2). The procedure allows a plaintiff, by effecting personal service in the second action, to sue on the earlier judgment and avoid a motion to vacate a default judgment in the earlier action premised on service.

5. CPLR 5014(3). This is the catch-all provision. It provides the court with discretion as to the notice necessary for relief.

§ 8.16

1. CPLR 5408.

2. CPLR 5401. This section embraces "any judgment, decree or order of a court ... entitled to full faith and credit."

However, some cases do discuss appropriate circumstances for straying from the fold. Fiore v. Oakwood Plaza Shopping Center, Inc., 78 N.Y.2d 572, 578 N.Y.S.2d 115, 585 N.E.2d 364 (1991) (procedures employed in Pennsylvania for cognovit judgment comport with due process and, therefore, judgment can be registered here); Mallan v. Samowich, 94 A.D.2d 249, 97 A.D.2d 364, 464 N.Y.S.2d 122 (1st Dep't 1983); appeal dism'd 67 N.Y.2d 871, 501 N.Y.S.2d 1029, 492 N.E.2d 795 (1986) (order entered on notice and consent); Sabrina D. v. Thomas W., 110 Misc.2d 796, 443 N.Y.S.2d 111 (Fam.Ct., Bronx County, 1981) (defendant appeared in action but defaulted at a later date; registration permitted).

3. Nothing in the statute precludes the commencement of a plenary action based on the judgment or a motion for summary judgment in lieu of complaint pursuant to CPLR 3213. In any event, these procedures remain available to enforce any sister-state judgment which is entitled to full faith and credit.

4. Williams v. North Carolina, 325 U.S. 226, 65 S.Ct. 1092, 89 L.Ed. 1577 (1945), rehearing denied 325 U.S. 895, 65 S.Ct.

§ 8.16 ENFORCEMENT OF MONEY JUDGMENTS Ch. 8

To be registered in New York, a sister-state judgment must be filed with a county clerk within 90 days of its authentication.[5] A complete filing[6] consists of the authenticated judgment along with the judgment creditor's affidavit setting forth the judgment debtor's name and last known address and stating that: (a) the judgment was not obtained by an appearance default or confession; (b) the judgment is unsatisfied in whole or in part and is therefore (c) unpaid (setting forth the amount), and (d) enforcement has not been stayed.[7]

The judgment creditor must mail a notice of such filing to the judgment debtor at his last known address within 30 days of registration.[8] As with any New York judgment, enforcement procedures may commence immediately after the filing of the sister-state judgment in New York. However, the proceeds of an execution may not be distributed until 30 days after proof of service of the notice is filed.[9]

If the sister-state judgment has been stayed and, on his application to the New York court the judgment debtor demonstrates this, enforcement here shall also be stayed.[10]

Library References:

West's Key No. Digests, Judgment ⚖︎823.

§ 8.17 Entry of a Foreign Judgment—Federal Court Judgments

A judgment rendered by a federal court in New York may simply be transcripted to the office of the clerk of any New York county.[1] Judg-

1560, 89 L.Ed. 2006 (1945) (Constitution's Full Faith and Credit clause operates with respect to the judgments of courts where subject matter and personal jurisdiction existed); Greschler v. Greschler, 51 N.Y.2d 368, 434 N.Y.S.2d 194, 414 N.E.2d 694 (1980) (where party appeared in first action, in second action she must show fraud in procurement of the judgment or some strong New York policy reason for attacking it).

5. The requirements for proper authentication are set out in CPLR 4540 and 4542.

6. Filing presumes payment of the clerk's fee for an index number. CPLR 5405. That index number and a New York caption should thereafter be used on all enforcement device materials.

7. CPLR 5402(a).

8. CPLR 5403.

9. CPLR 5403. Shine, Julianelle, Karp, Bozelko & Karazin, P.C. v. Rubens, 192 A.D.2d 345, 596 N.Y.S.2d 20 (1st Dep't 1993), appeal dism'd 82 N.Y.2d 778, 604 N.Y.S.2d 548, 624 N.E.2d 685, rearg. denied 82 N.Y.2d 921, 610 N.Y.S.2d 155, 632 N.E.2d 465 (1994), cert. denied 511 U.S. 1142, 114 S.Ct. 2163, 128 L.Ed.2d 887 (1994), rehearing denied 512 U.S. 1270, 115 S.Ct. 12, 129 L.Ed.2d 912 (1994)(failure to mail notice is not jurisdictional defect).

10. CPLR 5404(a). CPLR 5404(b) authorizes a stay "based on other grounds" which, in a proper case, may mean that a stay can issue without the need to post a bond. Pickwick Intern., Inc. v. Tomato Music Co., Ltd. 119 Misc.2d 227, 462 N.Y.S.2d 781 (Sup.Ct., Kings County, 1983).

§ 8.17

1. CPLR 5018(b). The New York transcripting procedure effectively supplants 28 U.S.C.A. § 1962, which makes the judgment of a district court a lien on the property located in the state. United States v. Hodes, 355 F.2d 746 (2d Cir.1966), cert. granted 384 U.S. 968, 86 S.Ct. 1858, 16 L.Ed.2d 680, cert. dism'd 386 U.S. 901, 87 S.Ct. 784, 17 L.Ed.2d 779 (1967).

ments of federal courts outside New York may be entered by obtaining a certified copy of the judgment and filing it with a New York federal district court;[2] thereafter, the transcript may be filed with any county clerk in New York.[3]

Library References:

West's Key No. Digests, Judgment ⚖︎829(1).

§ 8.18 Entry of a Foreign Judgment—Foreign Country Judgments

The Uniform Foreign Country Money–Judgments Recognition Act[1] applies to certain foreign state money judgments that are final, conclusive and enforceable.[2] If an appeal is pending, the debtor may apply to the New York court for a stay of enforcement.[3] Unlike the registration procedure employed for the judgments of sister states, foreign state judgments may be enforced only by means of a plenary action, a motion for summary judgment in lieu of complaint, or an assertion in an existing action as a counterclaim, cross-claim or affirmative defense.[4]

A foreign country judgment *will not* be recognized as conclusive if the foreign country does not provide impartial tribunals or procedures compatible with due process, or if there was no personal jurisdiction in the original court.[5] Personal jurisdiction is established if, among other things, the debtor was served personally, appeared voluntarily or consented to jurisdiction.[6]

A foreign country judgment *need not* be recognized if: there was no subject matter jurisdiction in the foreign court; the defendant did not receive timely notice; the judgment was obtained by fraud or is repugnant to the public policy of New York; the judgment conflicts with another final and conclusive judgment; the proceedings were contrary to the parties' agreement; or, where jurisdiction is based only on personal service, the forum was "seriously inconvenient."[7]

2. 28 U.S.C.A. § 1963.

3. CPLR 5018(b).

CAVEAT: Although a docketed federal court judgment will be accorded much the same effect as a New York judgment, transcripting of a federal court judgment does not give all-purpose jurisdiction to the supreme court. Thus, for example, the docketing of a federal judgment in the county clerk's office does not confer upon the supreme court personal jurisdiction over a defendant. Federal Deposit Ins. Corp. v. Richman, 98 A.D.2d 790, 470 N.Y.S.2d 19 (2d Dep't 1983).

§ 8.18

1. CPLR 5309.

2. CPLR 5402. Generally, foreign states are those other than the United States, its territories and possessions. CPLR 5401(a). Judgments entitled to recognition are those granting or denying recovery of a sum of money other than for a fine, penalty or family support. CPLR 5301(b).

3. CPLR 5306.

4. CPLR 5303.

5. CPLR 5304(a).

6. CPLR 5305.

7. CPLR 5304(b).

§ 8.19 Judgment Enforcement Against Property—Definition of Property

Judgment enforcement is the procedure by which a judgment is satisfied from the property of the judgment debtor. Any analysis, therefore, begins with the nature of "property." In its entirety, CPLR 5201(b) provides:

> A money judgment may be enforced against any property which could be assigned or transferred, whether it consists of a present or future right or interest and whether or not it is vested, unless it is exempt from application to the satisfaction of the judgment. A money judgment entered upon a joint liability of two or more persons may be enforced against individual property of those persons summoned and joint property of such persons with any other persons against whom the judgment is entered.

The myriad nature of property interests cannot be reviewed completely here. Suffice to say that the judgment debtor's property includes all tangible and intangible items (including past due debts or debts that are to become due, wherever incurred).[1] Any property in which the debtor has an interest can be levied upon, regardless of whether the judgment debtor is its owner or merely has a right of possession, and without regard to whether a sheriff can take immediate actual possession of it or not.[2] As a result of the sweeping nature of this definition, all of the following are reachable by judgment creditors: joint tenancies such as bank accounts (the presumption—rebuttable by direct or substantial circumstantial, clear and convincing proof of the living tenants—attaches that each tenant maintains a present unconditional interest in an undivided one half of the monies[3]); tenancies by the entirety (a much more difficult problem because of the nature of potential harm to the non-debtor spouse: under the protective order powers,[4] some courts have held that the judgment debtor's occupancy interest which normally attends the entirety interest is not reachable as a matter of law,[5] with other courts providing a protective order halting a forced sale, albeit providing the creditor with a lien, and permitting the creditor to reach the debtor's interest only upon the sale by both or upon the death of the

---

§ 8.19

1. *See* CPLR 5201(a).

2. M.F. Hickey Co. v. Port of New York Authority, 23 A.D.2d 739, 258 N.Y.S.2d 129 (1st Dep't 1965). Of course, the extent of the debtor's interest, as compared to that of others, must be determined. *See infra*, § 8.45.

3. Denton v. Grumbach, 2 A.D.2d 420, 157 N.Y.S.2d 91 (3d Dep't 1956); Banking Law § 675.

4. CPLR 5240; *see infra*, § 8.44.

5. Berlin v. Herbert, 48 Misc.2d 393, 265 N.Y.S.2d 25 (Dist.Ct., Nassau County, 1965).

non-debtor spouse if he/she predeceases the judgment debtor[6]); an interest as an estate beneficiary; equities of redemption (*e.g.*, any property interest such as an account receivable in which the debtor maintains an interest); interests in cooperative apartments (considered personal property for enforcement purposes, requiring the additional levy procedures for such property);[7] condominiums (considered realty for enforcement purposes so the judgment lien attaches immediately upon entry); and Totten trusts, IRAs and Keogh accounts (where the latter are not pension plans created by the judgment debtor or for the benefit of or in trust for another, the funds are subject to attachment[8]).

On the other hand, some property interests which lack "certainty" may not be reached as a debt or property. Where, for example, the debtor controls the material contingencies affecting a present but unexercised right to receive retirement benefits, the interest may not be reachable.[9] Registered trade names also lack this quality.[10]

§ 8.20 Judgment Enforcement Against Property—Exemptions

It is often and aptly said that the judgment creditor who has properly followed the Article 52 procedures "stands in the shoes" of the judgment debtor. As the practitioner evaluates the various approaches to collection, among the issues to consider are the size of those shoes (*i.e.*, the extent of the debtor's interest in particular items of property), their shine (or value), and whether someone else's feet have been planted in them sooner (*i.e.*, priorities).

Indeed, some "shoes" may not be reached at all by judgment creditors. The exemptions under New York state statutes, certain federal statutes, and those in several unconsolidated laws prevent this, and the practitioner should take pains to promptly notify a judgment debtor who is a natural person of his or her right to claim them.[1] The text of the

---

6. Hammond v. Econo–Car of North Shore, Inc., 71 Misc.2d 546, 336 N.Y.S.2d 493 (Sup.Ct., Nassau County, 1972).

7. State Tax Comm'n. v. Shor, 43 N.Y.2d 151, 400 N.Y.S.2d 805, 371 N.E.2d 523 (1977). Since many entities may have a say in the disposition of shares of the residential cooperative (*e.g.*, cooperative board, lending banks, managing agents, etc.,) the appointment of a receiver to dispose of cooperative shares may be necessary. See *infra*, § 8.37.

8. Abrahams v. New York State Tax Comm'n., 131 Misc.2d 594, 500 N.Y.S.2d 965 (Sup.Ct., Westchester County, 1986).

9. Sochor v. I.B.M. Corp. 60 N.Y.2d 254, 469 N.Y.S.2d 591, 457 N.E.2d 696 (1983). *See also*, Glassman v. Hyder, 28 A.D.2d 974, 283 N.Y.S.2d 419 (1st Dep't 1967), aff'd 23 N.Y.2d 354, 296 N.Y.S.2d 783, 244 N.E.2d 259 (1968) (unmatured rents).

10. Marshak v. Green, 746 F.2d 927 (2d Cir.1984).

§ 8.20

1. The notice must be mailed or personally delivered to the judgment debtor or obligor who is a natural person within 4 days of the service of a restraining notice. CPLR 5222(d). See *infra*, § 8.27. The statute mandates that the notice must be reserved if it has not been served within one year of service of the restraining notice or execution.

§ 8.20　ENFORCEMENT OF MONEY JUDGMENTS　Ch. 8

notice to the judgment debtor is defined in the statute.[2] The section governing provision of notice to the debtor or obligor is specialized: personal delivery or mailing is required. In the case of mailing, the notice must be sent to the defendant's last known residence or, if returned or unknown, to the defendant in care of the defendant's employer in an envelope marked "personal and confidential" and not indicating that it is from an attorney or concerns a judgment.[3]

In addition to the exemptions listed on the notice, other exemptions are separately found in CPLR Article 52, distinguished as personal property exemptions (CPLR 5205) or real property exemptions (CPLR 5206). Exempt personal property includes common household items,[4] causes of action to recover damages for taking or injuring exempt personal property,[5] certain trusts,[6] ninety per cent of the judgment debtor's earnings from personal services,[7] armed forces pay,[8] a farmer's milk money proceeds,[9] residential lease security deposits and deposits for certain utilities used at the debtor's residence,[10] certain medical items[11] and certain life insurance policies.[12]

Listed under the real property exempted from the satisfaction of judgments is the homestead exemption, which is limited to $10,000 above liens and expenses, of property owned and occupied as the debtor's principal residence (unless the judgment was wholly for the purchase price).[13] It also includes a burial plot which conforms to certain, specified conditions.[14]

2. CPLR 5222(e). *See infra,* § 8.49.

PRACTICE POINTER: Because the requirement of CPLR 5222(e) notice is found in other enforcement sections (*e.g.,* property execution under CPLR 5232(c); *see also, infra,* § 8.29), it is probably good practice to arrange for it at the very beginning of the enforcement process.

3. CPLR 5222(d).

4. CPLR 5205(a). Included here are such items as the family bible, a pew or seat in a house of worship, domestic animals and their food, wedding rings and the tools necessary for carrying on the debtor's profession or calling.

5. CPLR 5205(b). Also, the proceeds of the judgment in such actions are exempt for a period of one year.

6. CPLR 5205(c). This section exempts trusts created by or where the trusts have proceeded from persons other than the judgment debtor. Qualified IRA's and I.R.C. 401 programs are included under this definition.

7. CPLR 5205(d)(2). This is the flip side to the 10% portion of a judgment debtor's earnings the creditor may execute upon under an income execution. *See infra,* § 8.34.

8. CPLR 5205(e).

9. CPLR 5205(f).

10. CPLR 5205(g).

11. CPLR 5205(g).

12. CPLR 5205(i).

13. This includes (1) a lot of land with dwelling thereon, (2) shares of stock in a cooperative apartment corporation, (3) a condominium unit, and (4) a mobile home. CPLR 5206.

The homestead exemption is based on the debtor's equity in the property. As long as: the exemption is available, the debtor's equity does not exceed $10,000 (*i.e.,* value or property minus existing liens) and it is occupied as the principle residence, the judgment creditor may not enforce the judgment against that property. If any of these conditions is no longer available to the debtor or his dependents, the judgment creditor may seek to sell the property.

14. A portion must have been actually used for that purpose, it must be less than 1/4th of an acre, and it must contain no building or structure other than as "places of deposit for the dead." CPLR 5206(f).

§ 8.21 Judgment Enforcement Against Property—Property in the Possession of Others

The money judgment can be enforced by proceeding against a person who owes a debt to the judgment debtor or has property in his possession or custody in which the judgment debtor has an interest—a "garnishee."[1] Levying against the proper garnishee is important and is defined, for certain property interests, in the statute: property such as shares in a corporation, interests in a decedent's estate, partnership interests or interests in negotiable instruments.[2] Note also that once the garnishee delivers the property in which the debtor has an interest, the garnishees's obligation is discharged to that extent and the creditor's "hold" is eliminated.[3]

It may be possible to recover property transferred by the debtor or by a garnishee to another by levying on the transferred property (although an enforcement officer may not want to incur liability for wrongful levy when title is in the transferee). In that circumstance, the turnover order procedure discussed in this chapter is tantamount to a plenary action under the Fraudulent Conveyances Article of the Debtor and Creditor Law §§ 270 *et seq.*[4]

Library References:

West's Key No. Digests, Judgment ⟺779, 780, 793.

§ 8.22 Enforcement Against Property—Disclosure of Property

The groundwork investigation for judgment enforcement should commence early on in the case.[1] All materials provided by the client or in its files should be reviewed in an attempt to locate any of the debtor's banks or bank accounts, hard assets of any kind titled to or possessed by him, or any obligations owed to him. All attorney file documents including canceled checks, deposition testimony, and documents produced in discovery by the judgment debtor or third parties should be carefully scrutinized for clues to any entity or person with whom the debtor had business relations.

A number of on-line services may be employed which can provide all manner of valuable information including: skip-tracing facts such as addresses, telephone numbers, relatives and neighbors; public filings of mortgages, liens and UCC information; credit synopses; and various

---

§ 8.21

1. CPLR 105(i).
2. CPLR 5201(c).
3. CPLR 5209. Property acquired after restraint or levy is also subject to delivery to the sheriff. *See, e.g.,* CPLR 5222(b).
4. *See infra,* §§ 8.39—8.41.

§ 8.22

1. *See supra,* § 8.2. During the interval between verdict and entry of judgment, it is possible for the prevailing party to examine an adverse party and restrain his assets. CPLR 5229.

forms of incidental information that may provide "threads" along which the judgment debtor's assets can be traced. Requests for the release of public information may be used during the pendency of litigation without notice, although these may be slow; for example, the Board of Elections will provide the address and occupation of a person if furnished with a name and date of birth, and the Department of Motor Vehicles can furnish a written abstract of the existence of liens.

However, when all of these sources have been exhausted, what can the judgment creditor do?

Library References:
West's Key No. Digests, Execution ⟐373, 385.

§ 8.23 Enforcement Against Property—Disclosure of Property—Subpoenas

CPLR Article 52 expresses an important public policy of this state: Until a judgment is vacated or satisfied, a "judgment creditor may compel disclosure of all matter relevant" to its satisfaction.[1] This policy affords the creditor a complete and searching examination—but only when the object of the disclosure (the witness or the debtor) can be served with the judgment enforcement disclosure device within the State of New York. Note that a witness can be examined simply if the creditor believes that he has relevant information.[2]

The direct method used to obtain information relevant to the satisfaction of a judgment is the subpoena, and CPLR 5224 authorizes three types: testimonial, *duces tecum* and information subpoenas.[3]

Testimonial and Duces Tecum Subpoenas. Service of both types of subpoenas require not less than 10 days' notice (unless a court orders a shorter period).[4] Each subpoena type must be served in the manner of a summons.[5] Service consists of and must be accompanied by (i) a notice of the time and place of the examination or review (to be held during business hours and at a place specified in CPLR 3110);[6] and (ii) traveling

---

§ 8.23

1. CPLR 5223. *See* Leonard v. Wargon, 55 N.Y.S.2d 626, 627 (Sup.Ct., Bronx County, 1945): It is the policy of New York State "to put no obstacle in the path of one seeking to secure the enforcement of a judgment of a court of competent jurisdiction."

2. Oates v. Oates, 33 A.D.2d 133, 306 N.Y.S.2d 108 (1st Dep't 1969). On the other hand, the witness can move for a protective order if he believes he is being subjected to harassment. CPLR 5240; *see infra*, § 8.44.

3. CPLR 5224.

4. CPLR 5224(c).

5. CPLR 2303.

6. CPLR 5224(c).

PRACTICE POINTER: Before enforcing the judgment of an inferior court, you should be certain to review the judgment enforcement rules of those courts. For example, notwithstanding the CPLR procedure discussed in this section, subpoenas for the enforcement of New York City Civil Court judgments are returnable in that court only and the affidavit of service must be filed at least two court days before the return date. Adjournments, and only two are permitted by the rule, are not valid unless they are in writing and received by

expenses and one day's witness fee to anyone other than the judgment debtor.[7] Standard subpoena forms reflect the additional information that is required for all subpoenas (*i.e.*, parties; court, date of entry and amount of judgment; amount due; and the contempt warning).[8] *See infra*, §§ 8.50 and 8.51.[9]

The testimonial examination need not be recorded and transcribed, but the witness must be sworn by the officer before whom the examination will be conducted.[10] Any objections of the witness to the officer shall be noted, but the examination proceeds, with examination and cross-examination as would be permitted in court, subject to the witness's right to secure a protective order.[11] If a transcribed examination is not signed by the witness following submission to him, it may be used as if it had been signed if the officer before whom it is taken certifies that the witness was sworn and the transcription is a true record of the testimony.[12]

A witness may be re-subpoenaed, if necessary. However, leave of court is required before a judgment debtor may be compelled to testify or produce documents within one year of the last such examination.[13]

Inquiries, whether of third persons or of the judgment debtor, into the judgment debtor's property are limited only by "relevance"; appropriate inquiries concern matters relevant to the satisfaction of the judgment.[14] Present and future assets are all subject to examination. Inquiry into past transactions should probably be directed to those which bear a reasonable relationship to the inception of the original obligation[15] or to those in which fraudulent transfers may be suspected.[16] Tax returns—which often refer to current sources of income—can be pro-

---

the witness—evidenced by his acknowledgment on the original—at the time of the adjournment. 22 NYCRR § 208.39. The procedures in the city courts outside New York City (22 NYCRR § 210.39) and the Nassau and Suffolk County District Courts (22 NYCRR § 212.39) are similar.

For subpoenas issued from the inferior courts, if the witness does not reside in, is not regularly employed or does not regularly transact business within the county in which the court issuing the subpoena sits, it should be issued instead from the supreme or county court. CPLR 5221(b).

7. CPLR 2303, 8001(a). If the witness demands his fee for the next day's attendance and is not then paid, he is deemed to be discharged. CPLR 2305(a).

8. *See infra*, §§ 8.49 (Judgment Debtor), 8.50 (Witness).

9. These subpoenas contain restraining notices as well.

10. CPLR 5224(d).

11. CPLR 5224(d).

PRACTICE POINTER: Where an obstreperous or difficult examination is expected, it may be expedient to notice and conduct it at the courthouse. In addition to reserving a room with the clerk, consult as to the availability of a judge to review promptly any objections or problems that might arise from this kind of examination. In this way, all parties are there and additional papers—and delay—may be avoided.

12. CPLR 5224(e).

13. CPLR 5224(f).

14. CPLR 5223.

15. Foremost Ins. Co. v. Facultative Group, Inc., 80 A.D.2d 598, 436 N.Y.S.2d 40 (2d Dep't 1981).

16. Young v. Torelli, 135 A.D.2d 813, 522 N.Y.S.2d 918 (2d Dep't 1987); Raji v.

§ 8.23   ENFORCEMENT OF MONEY JUDGMENTS   Ch. 8

duced even if joint with a non-debtor spouse.[17] A witness must answer all questions concerning a transfer (*e.g.*, good consideration, good faith, etc.). The witness may successfully invoke evidentiary privileges (*e.g.*, attorney/client, husband/wife) in limited circumstances.[18] A court may confer immunity on a witness in accordance with Criminal Procedure Law § 50.20, provided that the district attorney who has an official interest has been provided 24 hours' written notice by the court.[19]

Note that no lien or priority in the judgment debtor's property results from the service of a subpoena.

Disobedience of a subpoena is punishable by contempt proceedings set forth in Article 19 of the Judiciary Law §§ 750 *et seq.*[20]

Information Subpoena. Certainly, the information subpoena is the easiest to use and the subpoena used most frequently. Service of the subpoena and accompanying interrogatories may be in the manner of a summons or by registered or certified mail, return receipt requested.[21] Enclosed should be the original and one copy of the questions, together with a self-addressed, stamped, return envelope.[22] Unlike the other types of subpoenas discussed above, no fee need be tendered. Answers, in writing and under oath, must be returned within seven days after receipt.[23]

§ 8.24   Article 52 Enforcement Devices—Introduction

Referred to in pre-CPLR law as "supplementary proceedings" (*i.e.*, all CPLR Article 52 devices except the property and income executions), each of these enforcement measures has a different purpose or object.

Bank Sepah–Iran, 139 Misc.2d 1026, 529 N.Y.S.2d 420 (Sup.Ct., N.Y. County, 1988).

17. Siemens & Halske Gmbh. v. Gres, 77 Misc.2d 754, 354 N.Y.S.2d 762 (Sup.Ct., N.Y. County, 1973); Leonard v. Wargon, 55 N.Y.S.2d 626 (Sup.Ct., Bronx County, 1945).

18. However, courts will not permit a privilege to shield communications designed to perpetrate frauds upon creditors. G-Fours, Inc. v. Miele, 496 F.2d 809 (2d Cir. 1974).

19. CPLR 5211. Since the goal of the subpoena procedure is to elicit information concerning the judgment debtor's property, little may be accomplished if the debtor or witness refuses to testify because of the potential for self-incrimination. CPLR 5211 provides a way around the impasse. The court must be satisfied that the matter is proper for the conferral of immunity. If compelled to testify pursuant to CPLR 5211 and granted CPL § 50.20 transactional immunity, the witness has complete immunity from prosecution for any crimes disclosed in the course of the testimony. *See* People v. Carlson, 222 App.Div. 54, 225 N.Y.S. 149 (4th Dep't 1927).

20. CPLR 5251. *See infra*, § 8.42.

21. CPLR 5224(a)(3).

22. CPLR 5224(a)(3).

23. *See infra*, § 8.52.

PRACTICE POINTER: Undeniably, this requirement is honored more in the breach than in the main. Indeed, with the mails, you may not receive back the green card certified mail acknowledgment within a week of its receipt by the witness. Larger banks are known especially to contribute to this form of delay because of the enormous volume of information subpoenas they receive, notwithstanding the armies of people they employ whose primary purpose is to address these subpoenas. But none of these factors vitiates the express language of the statute. Accordingly, be sure to maintain a record of the date of receipt by the witness, and follow up aggressively by phone with any errant witness, confirming the discussion in a writing (which may be used in any proceeding that may be necessary later).

There is no order in which the proceedings are required to be used; they may be employed simultaneously. They may be utilized immediately after the entry of judgment, regardless of whether the judgment debtor has been served with notice of entry of the judgment.[1] None of the enforcement measures may be used against the state[2] or deceased persons.[3] Each enforcement measure has peculiar requirements and it is the goal of the following sections of this chapter to illustrate their nature and the procedures for their use.

§ 8.25 Article 52 Enforcement Devices—Restraining Notices—Nature and Use

Although an important tool, the restraining notice is considered a junior remedy among the enforcement proceedings because no lien and no priority in the debtor's personal property is established by its service.[1] The lien of judgment with respect to real property is established when the judgment is docketed in the same county as the property.[2] To establish a lien priority in personal property, the judgment creditor's attorney must deliver an execution to the sheriff who must then levy.[3] Accordingly, the bare restraining notice is always subject to superior rights such as setoff or the right of a transferee who paid fair consideration.[4]

Nonetheless, despite its seeming shortcomings, the restraining notice is frequently the enforcement device used first. Why? The device serves as an "injunction": the recipient is restrained from making any transfer of the judgment debtor's property in his possession except to a sheriff.[5] By its terms, CPLR 5222(b)(which must be recited verbatim, in

§ 8.24

1. Solow v. Bethlehem Steel Corp., 204 A.D.2d 227, 612 N.Y.S.2d 402 (1st Dep't 1994). In the inferior courts, however, service of a copy of the judgment must occur before execution may issue. Where the party appears by attorney, service must be upon the attorney. CPLR 2103(b). Where the party appears but defaults, service must be personal or by certified mail to the address set forth in the appearance. See 22 NYCRR § 208.37 (New York City Civil Court); 22 NYCRR § 210.37 (city courts outside New York City); 22 NYCRR § 212.37 (district courts).

2. CPLR 5207. The statute indicates that these procedures may be not used when the judgment debtor *is* the state. If the state is a garnishee (CPLR 105), all proceedings may be used with two specific exceptions: (a) no judgment may be entered against the state, its officers, agencies or subdivisions in connection with an enforcement proceeding; (b) where an order directs the state to pay money, the order may require payment of monies not claimed by the state. Bankers Trust Co. v. State Dep't of Audit and Control, 28 A.D.2d 272, 284 N.Y.S.2d 594 (3d Dep't 1967).

3. CPLR 5208.

§ 8.25

1. Aspen Industries, Inc. v. Marine Midland Bank, 52 N.Y.2d 575, 439 N.Y.S.2d 316, 421 N.E.2d 808 (1981); *In re* Sullivan, 31 B.R. 125 (Bankr.N.D.N.Y.1983).

2. See infra, § 8.31.

3. See infra, § 8.29.

4. West Harlem Pork Center, Ltd. v. Empire Nat. Bank, 60 A.D.2d 859, 400 N.Y.S.2d 859 (2d Dep't 1978).

5. CPLR 5222(e). Medi–Physics, Inc. v. Community Hospital of Rockland County, 105 Misc.2d 574, 432 N.Y.S.2d 594 (County Ct., Rockland, 1980).

§ 8.25 ENFORCEMENT OF MONEY JUDGMENTS Ch. 8

its entirety, in the restraining notice[6]) forbids the recipient to "make or suffer any sale, assignment or transfer of, or any interference with [property in which the debtor has an interest], or pay over or otherwise dispose of any such debt."[7] Most importantly, the restraining notice requires the recipient to "freeze" or withhold payment of twice the amount of the judgment; once that has been restrained, any additional funds may be used by the garnishee (*i.e.*, notice is ineffective as to these sums). Restraint of twice the judgment amount is a powerful adjunct to enforcement, and occasionally motivates prompt resolution.[8]

When served upon the judgment debtor, the effect of the restraint lasts the remaining life of the judgment (*i.e.*, until vacated or satisfied).[9] When served upon a garnishee, a restraining notice is effective only if, at that time, the garnishee owes a debt or has property of the judgment debtor or in which the judgment debtor has an interest.[10] If this situation exists, the restraining notice will apply to property which is then in and thereafter comes into the possession of the garnishee;[11] if it does not, the restraining notice is entirely ineffective. As to a garnishee, the restraint is effective for one year.[12]

Library References:

West's Key No. Digests, Execution ⟐390.

§ 8.26 Article 52 Enforcement Devices—Restraining Notices—Formal Requirements

The form of restraining notice must specify: all parties to the action, the date of entry of judgment or order, the court in which it was

6. CPLR 5222(a).
7. CPLR 5222(b).
CAVEAT: Note that a restraining notice may not be served upon the debtor's or obligor's employer in an effort to restrain wages or salary due or to become due. CPLR 5222(a). For these purposes, an income execution should be used. *See infra*, § 8.34.
8. **PRACTICE POINTER:** The CPLR prescribes no form of release of a restraining notice; each recipient should advise you what it requires. Generally, an attorney's letter with language indicating that the restraining notice is "vacated, withdrawn and of no further force and effect" should be sufficient.
Although it may appear obvious, the issue of when the practitioner should release the recipient from the effect of the notice is sometimes a problem, especially if the funds restrained are being used to satisfy or par-

tially satisfy the judgment. Use care in drafting stipulations to ensure that the remittances are made payable to the judgment creditor or its attorney, rather than to the judgment debtor, and are in your possession before releasing.
9. CPLR 5222(b). A restraining notice may be served when the subpoena is served. *See, e.g. infra*, §§ 8.50, 8.51.
10. In Zemo Leasing Corp. v. Bank of New York, 158 Misc.2d 991, 602 N.Y.S.2d 503 (Sup.Ct., Rockland County, 1993), the court held that a bank has until close of business on the day after its receipt of the notice to place the hold on the debtor's account. Where banks or persons other than the judgment debtor consent in writing, restraining notices may be served by magnetic tape. CPLR 5222(g).
11. CPLR 5222(b).
12. CPLR 5222(b).

entered,[1] the amount of the judgment and amount remaining due, the names of all parties in whose favor the judgment has been entered as well as those against, CPLR 5222(b) in its entirety, and that disobedience is punishable as a contempt of court.[2] The clerk of the court, the judgment creditor's attorney and a support collection unit are authorized by statute to issue the restraining notice; it must contain an original signature or a copy of the signature of the officer of the court issuing it.[3]

§ 8.27 Article 52 Enforcement Devices—Restraining Notices—Service and Punishment for Disobedience

Service may be personal in the manner of a summons or by registered or certified mail, return receipt requested. Within four days of such service, a copy of the restraining notice must be mailed by first class mail or personally delivered to a judgment debtor or obligor[1] who is a natural person, along with the "Notice to Judgment Debtor or Obligor" if such mailing had not been performed with one year prior to the service of a restraining notice.[2] If mailed, it should be sent to the debtor's residence address or, if undeliverable or unknown, to him in care of his employer in an envelope bearing the legend "personal and confidential" and not indicating on the outside that it comes from an attorney or concerns a judgment.[3]

Disobedience of a restraining notice is punishable by contempt, but whether sanctions will apply is a matter of judicial discretion.[4] In some cases, recovery may be had for actual damages which result from the

---

§ 8.26
1. **PRACTICE POINTER:** This is the court of original entry, not a court to which the judgment has been transcripted.
2. CPLR 5222(a).
3. *See infra*, § 8.53.

In Poughkeepsie Sav. Bank, FSB v. R.S. Paralegal & Recovery Services, Inc., 160 A.D.2d 857, 554 N.Y.S.2d 290 (2d Dep't 1990), the court reversed a decision of the supreme court which held that a conformed signature—"/s/"—on a restraining notice did not meet the requirements of an (albeit, earlier) version of the statute. Subsequently, the statute was changed to comport with the lower court's reasoning.

§ 8.27
1. Several CPLR sections have been amended to bring within the judgment enforcement realm statutorily-defined defaults under certain orders issued by courts for the payment of support, alimony or maintenance. An "obligor" is an individual other than the judgment debtor who, pursuant to court order, is obligated to pay support, alimony or maintenance and whose default has been determined in accordance with income execution provisions. To the extent such orders involve substantive or procedural areas beyond judgment enforcement techniques, they are beyond the scope of this chapter.

2. CPLR 5222(d). *See infra*, § 8.49. For example, in a turnover proceeding based on the restraining notice, the judgment creditor has the burden of proof on the issue of compliance with this section. That proceeding may not be maintained against an individual judgment debtor if there has been no compliance. Chemical Bank v. Flaherty, 121 Misc.2d 509, 468 N.Y.S.2d 315 (Civ.Ct., Queens County, 1983).

3. CPLR 5222(d).

4. CPLR 5251. Dickson v. Ferullo, 96 A.D.2d 745, 465 N.Y.S.2d 328 (4th Dep't 1983).

disobedience of the restraining notice.[5]

§ 8.28 Article 52 Enforcement Devices—Execution

In this and the following sections, the nature and use of the execution will be discussed. An execution (known in some quarters as the "writ of execution") is the formal process issued by the court or an officer thereof evidencing the debt of the judgment debtor to the judgment creditor and commanding the enforcement officer (*i.e.*, sheriff or marshal) to take the property of the former in satisfaction of the debt.[1] In New York practice, the two execution types are governed by two different CPLR sections: the property execution, which directs enforcement efforts toward the real and personal property of the judgment debtor[2], and the income execution, which looks to the debtor's earnings as the wellspring for the satisfaction of the judgment.[3]

An execution is issued by the clerk of the court or by the attorney for the judgment creditor.[4] It directs that the property in which a non-deceased judgment debtor has an interest or debts owed to him are to be levied upon and sold. It specifies the date the judgment or order[5] was entered, the court, the amount of the judgment and remaining amount due, the names of the parties in whose favor and the names of those against whom the judgment was entered, and the last known address of the judgment debtor.[6] Where the execution is based on an order of attachment or a mortgage debt, additional requirements apply.[7]

The enforcement officer must be chosen correctly for the particular court: a city marshal, for example, may not execute upon a supreme court judgment.[8] For judgments issued from supreme or county courts (including the judgments of lower courts transcripted into those courts), issuance of executions is state-wide. That is, inter-county transcripting is not required before an execution may issue to a sheriff in another county.[9]

---

5. *See infra*, § 8.42.

§ 8.28

1. *See, e.g., Black's Law Dictionary* (6th ed. West 1990).

2. CPLR 5230.

3. CPLR 5231. The income execution is discussed *infra*, § 8.34.

4. CPLR 5230(b).

PRACTICE POINTER: The enforcement officer's property execution will be potent and successful only if the practitioner provides a statement describing the nature and the location of specific property. Although the enforcement officer is motivated to levy upon or recover property (both because of his statutory obligation and the "poundage" he can recover), he will not perform "skip trace" or asset location on the judgment creditor's behalf.

5. An "order" means an order directing payment of support, alimony or maintenance. CPLR 5230(e). Treatment of these orders is beyond the scope of this chapter. *See* Borges, *et al., Enforcing Judgments and Collecting Debts in New York* (West 1997) ¶¶ 8:272–8:314.

6. CPLR 5230(a).

7. CPLR 5230(a). *See infra*, § 8.54.

8. Yeh v. Seakan, 119 Misc.2d 681, 464 N.Y.S.2d 627 (Sup.Ct., Oneida County, 1983).

9. **PRACTICE POINTER:** However, it is certainly prudent to transcript the judg-

Because delivery of an execution to the enforcement officer serves to establish the priority date of the creditor's lien in personal property,[10] care should be taken to assure that the time and date of delivery of the execution to the enforcement officer is a definable event.

The judgment creditor's priority in the debtor's personal property is absolutely affected by the required "return" of the execution to the clerk of the court (or support collection unit in the case of a support order) within 60 days after issuance.[11] The purpose of the return is to avoid delays to other judgment creditors. The judgment creditor's attorney must be aware of this time frame and should extend it for 60 days in a writing to the enforcement officer prior to its expiration.[12]

The fee due an enforcement officer for receiving an execution (other than one issued in connection with a small claims court judgment) is fixed by statute.[13] In addition, the sheriff is entitled to mileage fees.[14]

Quite apart from mileage and other incidental fees and expenses, for his services in collecting money pursuant to an execution (or attachment), the sheriff is entitled to a statutory fee award in the nature of a commission.[15] Referred to as poundage, the award generally accrues at the time of levy on the execution or order.[16] Note, therefore, that poundage may be due the sheriff even if there has been (a) a settlement for less than the amount of the judgment or (b) a vacatur of the execution or judgment.[17] For New York City counties, poundage is 5% of the sum collected; in all other counties, it is 5% on the first $250,000 and 3% on the residue.[18] The court may grant the sheriff additional compensation and also can direct a party to pay poundage or additional poundage.[19]

§ 8.29 Article 52 Enforcement Devices—Execution—Property Execution With Regard to Personal Property

From a practical perspective, there are only two categories of personal property that an enforcement officer may levy upon: property that the enforcement officer is capable of taking into possession and property

---

ment for purposes of establishing the judgment lien against the debtor's real property situate in such county.

10. CPLR 5234(b).
11. CPLR 5230(c).
12. CPLR 5230(c).

CAVEAT: Failure to extend the lien results in its loss if the execution is returned unsatisfied. International Ribbon Mills, Ltd. v. Arjan Ribbons, Inc., 36 N.Y.2d 121, 365 N.Y.S.2d 808, 325 N.E.2d 137 (1975). Nothing precludes re-issuance of the execution, but priority may be lost.

13. CPLR 8011.

14. CPLR 8012(a), (d).

PRACTICE POINTER: These fees are payable in advance (i.e., at the time of delivery of the execution to the sheriff). Contact the sheriff's office to obtain the precise amount of the mileage fees, and any other such fees and costs, before forwarding the execution.

15. CPLR 8012.
16. CPLR 8012.
17. CPLR 8012.
18. CPLR 8012.
19. CPLR 8012(c).

§ 8.29   ENFORCEMENT OF MONEY JUDGMENTS   Ch. 8

which, because of its size, nature or location, cannot be taken into custody.[1] In the case of the former, the enforcement officer seizes the judgment debtor's property (but may not interfere with the lawful possession of pledgees or lessees), and then serves a copy of the execution upon the person from whom the property was taken.[2] At the time of the enforcement officer's possession, the lien of the judgment debtor is "perfected." This is the levy by seizure.[3]

Where property cannot be delivered, the enforcement officer acts to perfect the judgment creditor's lien by employing the levy by service, a two step process.[4] First, the enforcement officer serves, as a summons, a copy of the execution upon the judgment debtor or garnishee.[5] As in the restraining notice context, the levy is effective only if, at the time of service, the garnishee owes the judgment debtor or obligor a debt or has possession of property of the debtor or obligor that is not capable of delivery. Assuming the garnishee's possession of such property, the levy will also apply to any of the debtor's property that may subsequently come into the garnishee's possession. The "unperfected" lien created by a levy by service is good until 90 days after service of a copy of the execution.[6]

In order not to lose the lien (*i.e.*, render it void) in a levy by service situation, before expiration of the 90 day period, the second step in the "perfection" process—transfer to the enforcement officer—should occur.[7] However, if it appears that this will not happen within the 90 day period, the judgment creditor should (1) commence a special proceeding for a turnover order against the garnishee or judgment debtor,[8] including a provision in the order to show cause extending the 90 day period, or (2) make a motion to extend the time for some additional period, which the

---

§ 8.29

1. The "levy" occurs when the enforcement officer serves a copy of the execution upon the garnishee. CPLR 5232(a). At this point, the levy may be viewed as a bare lien since it has not been perfected.

CAVEAT: Unless the CPLR 5222(e) Notice To Judgment Debtor or Obligor has been served within one year, the enforcement officer must mail it to the judgment debtor within four days of service of the execution. CPLR 5232(c); *see supra*, § 8.20. Service must be personal or by first class mail. In the case of the latter, it is mailed to the residence address; if undeliverable or returned, it is mailed in care of the place of employment in an envelope marked "personal and confidential" which does not indicate that it concerns a debt or is from an enforcement officer.

PRACTICE POINTER: As you might expect, enforcement officers have little desire or time to perform this function. The attorney for the judgment creditor should undertake this mailing and should so indicate on the execution. *See infra*, § 8.54.

2. CPLR 5232(b).
3. CPLR 5232(b).
4. CPLR 5232(a).
5. **CAVEAT:** Service upon a person designated for service pursuant to CPLR 318 is not good service for this section. CPLR 5232(a).
6. CPLR 5232(a).
7. CPLR 5232(a).
8. If the property is a debt owed the judgment debtor, CPLR 5227 governs. If it is more tangible or concerns the judgment debtor, CPLR 5225 is the section. *See infra*, §§ 8.39—8.41.

court is empowered to extend beyond an additional 90 days.[9] In the levy by service situation, until tender to the enforcement officer or expiration of the lien (if the judgment creditor fails to act), the garnishee is forbidden to transfer the property—except to the enforcement officer or other person as designated by the turnover order.[10]

Library References:

West's Key No. Digests, Execution ⚭20.

§ 8.30 Article 52 Enforcement Devices—Execution—Property Execution With Regard to Personal Property—Sale, Distribution and Priority in Proceeds

Whether by seizure or by service, the enforcement officer's levy results in a sale of the judgment debtor's interest in the personal property, at public auction or as a court directs.[1] The interests are sold, in lots or combinations, in whatever manner the enforcement officer believes will bring the highest price.[2] Notice of such sale must be given by posting at least 6 days before the sale in three public places or, in New York City, notice may be advertised by publication in the auction sections of certain morning newspapers.[3]

After the sale, after no less than 15 days after service of the execution (unless a court orders otherwise), and after the enforcement officer deducts and pays from the proceeds any fees, expenses and applicable taxes, the officer remits the balance, to the extent of the judgment, to the judgment creditor; any excess is paid to the judgment debtor.[4]

Where two or more judgment creditors deliver executions to the same enforcement officer, a priority problems arises. The general rule is that where the two judgment creditors deliver to the same enforcement officer, the execution delivered first in time is satisfied first, followed by the second and so on.[5] Where two or more judgment creditors deliver executions to different enforcement officers who levy in their respective jurisdictions, distribution is (a) to the creditor who first delivered the execution to the levying officer and (b) to those judgment creditors who,

9. Id.
10. Id.

§ 8.30
1. CPLR 5233(a), (c).
2. CPLR 5233(a). If the sheriff believes that the property may not, by law, be sold, he can apply to the court for direction, but must provide the owner with reasonable notice of the application. CPLR 5233(d).

3. CPLR 5233(b).
4. CPLR 5234(a).
5. CPLR 5234(b). Where a judgment creditor and a support collection unit deliver to the same enforcement officer, however, the execution for child support has priority. CPLR 5234(b).

after delivering the execution, made demand upon the second officer, in the order of such demands.[6]

Where a receiver has been appointed or an order of appointment has been extended to include additional creditors by a filed order before levy[7] or a turnover order has been entered,[8] the resolution of the priority problem is different. The rights of these creditors are superior to those of the executing creditor—as long as the officer's delivery, transfer or payment occurs within 60 days of the order.[9] Priority as between creditors who have the benefit of turnover orders is determined in the order of filing of such orders.[10]

Library References:

West's Key No. Digests, Execution ⚖︎213–245, 322–329.

§ 8.31 Article 52 Enforcement Devices—Execution—Property Execution With Regard to Real Property

As we have seen, docketing of a judgment in the office of the clerk of the county in which the judgment debtor has an interest in real property acts immediately to give the judgment creditor a lien on that real property.[1] Although the judgment itself is enforceable for twenty years, the lien of the judgment is only good for ten of those years, measured from the date of the filing of the judgment-roll.[2] When the lien is in issue (*e.g.*, expired), that judgment creditor's execution sale may be in issue as well.[3] A "lien gap" can occur whenever the lien has lapsed, even if only for a brief period.[4]

6. CPLR 5234(b).

CAVEAT: Executions for child support continue to have priority in this scenario as well. *See supra* note 5.

PRACTICE POINTER: Here, again, the judgment creditor who acts quickly secures a possible advantage. A non-levying judgment creditor who receives such notice should immediately cause delivery of a demand to the levying sheriff before the sale in order to share in the proceeds.

7. *See infra*, § 8.37.
8. *See infra*, § 8.39.
9. CPLR 5234(c).
10. CPLR 5234(c).

§ 8.31

1. CPLR 5203(a). *See supra*, § 8.3.
2. CPLR 5235.
3. CPLR 5236(a) cautions that the judgment debtor's interest "which has been levied upon under an execution delivered to the sheriff or which was subject to the lien of the judgment at the time of such delivery shall be sold."

PRACTICE POINTER: The better practice is to avoid the issue altogether. Keep track of the lien and take steps to extend its expiration before it does, in fact, expire.

4. **CAVEAT:** The lien gap provides the opportunity for judgment creditors and others to "slip into" the priority arrangement on the property. Although it is possible to restore some lien protection or create a new lien, the same priority arrangement will not be re-established. Quarant v. Ferrara, 111 Misc.2d 1042, 445 N.Y.S.2d 885 (Sup.Ct., Queens County, 1981) (subsequent *bona fide* purchaser).

PRACTICE POINTER: When the 10 year period will soon expire, deliver an execution to the sheriff before the expiration of the ten year period and immediately move to extend the lien.

Where an execution has been delivered to the enforcement officer before ten years have expired, the potential "lien gap" situation can be ameliorated by a motion seeking an order to extend the lien long enough to complete the execution advertising and sale procedures.[5] If no execution had been delivered and the 10 year period expires, the sheriff may file a notice of levy with the county clerk to create a lien in aid of the sheriff's execution sale, but that lien does not operate as the prior lien of the judgment and is only applicable to property specified in the notice rather than, for example, after-acquired property.[6] It is also possible to create a new lien for the "old" judgment by renewing the judgment.[7]

Library References:
West's Key No. Digests, Execution ⊚=21.

§ 8.32 Article 52 Enforcement Devices—Execution—Property Execution With Regard to Real Property—Notice of Sale of Real Property

The procedures for the execution sale of the real property in which the judgment debtor has an interest are set forth in detail in the statute and must be followed assiduously.[1] The notice of sale, containing the date and time of sale and a description of the property, must be posted at least 56 days and a copy of it published initially between 56 and 63 days, and at three other times (in fourteen successive day periods), before the date of sale.[2]

At least 45 days before the sale date, the judgment creditor must supply the sheriff with a name and address list of all who have an interest in or lien against the property, including the judgment debtor and other judgment creditors.[3] The judgment debtor should be served by the sheriff with a copy of the notice.[4] Each person or entity on the list is served (personal delivery or by certified mail, return receipt requested) by the sheriff at least 30 days prior to the sale date. Any omission to

---

5. CPLR 5203(b). Alternatively, if the judgment creditor had been stayed, the order on this motion may extend the 10 year period, but only as long as the period of the stay. *Id.*

6. CPLR 5235.

7. CPLR 5014(1). *See supra*, § 8.15.

§ 8.32

1. CPLR 5236.

CAVEAT: Within one year after a judicial sale to enforce a judgment, if a substantial right of a party was prejudiced because of a defect in the notice, time or manner of sale requirements, the court may set the sale aside on such terms as may be just.

PRACTICE POINTER: As the person primarily responsible for conducting the execution sale, the enforcement officer can be expected to help guide the practitioner through the process. But such guidance does not substitute for knowledge of what must be done, and when. Monitor the officer's activities at all points.

CAVEAT: The sheriff is not the only person empowered under the statute to sell the property. It may be possible to yield a higher price when the sale is conducted by a receiver. *See infra*, § 8.37.

2. CPLR 5236(b).

3. CPLR 5236(b). Sale may be precluded where the judgment creditor fails to provide the list within 45 days of the sale. Jones v. Knowlton, 199 A.D.2d 871, 606 N.Y.S.2d 355 (3d Dep't 1993).

4. CPLR 5236(c) requires that such service be made as provided for in CPLR 308.

§ 8.32   ENFORCEMENT OF MONEY JUDGMENTS   Ch. 8

provide this notice or any removal of a posted notice does not affect the title of a *bona fide* purchaser who had no notice of such defect.[5]

A non-levying judgment creditor who is notified of the sale (whether because he was included on the name and address list or requested notice of postponements) must deliver a "new" execution to the sheriff prior to the sale to maintain her lien.[6] Further, such creditor must take the appropriate steps to ensure that her execution does not become the victim of an unsatisfied return within the 60 day period.[7]

Unless the sale is ordered delayed or postponed by the sheriff, the sale, by public auction, occurs between the 56th and 63rd days of the first publication of the notice.[8] In no event will a judgment for mortgage debt result in the sale of the property: mortgage foreclosure proceedings are designed for that purpose.[9]

The sheriff, in his discretion, may postpone the sale. Notice of postponement need be served by the sheriff (by personal delivery or by registered/certified mail, return receipt requested) only to those (1) who have served upon the sheriff a request for such notice (also by personal delivery or by registered/certified mail, return receipt requested) received at least five days prior to the postponed date, (2) those who appeared at the time and place set forth in the notice (or at an adjourned date), and (3) to the judgment debtor at his last known address.[10]

Library References:

West's Key No. Digests, Execution ⚖222.

§ 8.33 Article 52 Enforcement Devices—Execution— Property Execution With Regard to Real Property—Distribution of Proceeds of Sale and Conveyance of Title

Following the execution sale, the sheriff deducts and pays fees, expenses and applicable taxes. Distribution is then (unless the court

---

5. CPLR 5236(c).
6. CPLR 5236(e).

CAVEAT: Allow no confusion on this point! Even if the non-levying creditor who received notice has previously delivered an execution to the levying sheriff, another or "new" execution must be delivered to the sheriff prior to the sale to maintain whatever priority the judgment creditor has. The effect of this provision may be illustrated as follows: If the judgment of a creditor who receives notice was recorded earlier than that of the levying creditor, the "new" execution allows the earlier judgment creditor to take sale proceeds ahead of the levying creditor. On the other hand, if a judgment creditor fails to deliver a "new" execution, he will have no interest in the sale proceeds.

7. CPLR 5236(g)(1). The procedures for the extension of the execution are discussed *supra*, § 8.28.

8. CPLR 5236(a).
9. CPLR 5236(b).
10. CPLR 5236(d).

PRACTICE POINTER: When representing a non-levying judgment creditor who receives a notice of sale, remain aware of the proceedings by serving a written request, containing the non-levying creditor's name and address, upon the levying sheriff. You are well advised to serve this notice and the "new" execution at once. See *supra*, note 6.

directs otherwise[1]) to the judgment debtor to the extent of the $10,000 homestead exemption, if applicable;[2] then, with complete satisfaction to one category before moving to the next, to: senior judgment creditors who have delivered executions which have not been returned, in the order their judgments were docketed; the levying judgment creditor; remaining judgment creditors who have delivered executions; and then to the judgment debtor.[3] All other interests senior to the levying creditor remain intact and the property is conveyed subject to them; all junior interests—which now include all other judgment creditors and mortgagees other than purchase money mortgagees[4]—are wiped out.[5]

A thorny issue in execution sales is the amount to be credited to the judgment debtor as a result of the sale. Is it the amount bid at the sale or, as occurs in the mortgage foreclosure context, the fair market value (if higher than the bid)?[6] Rather than "penalize" judgment debtors too harshly, the courts have fashioned inventive remedies under their broad protective order powers.[7]

Although a judicial sale may be set aside within one year,[8] courts will not look into whether the amount paid at an execution sale was adequate.[9] However, some bankruptcy courts, in performing a preference analysis, will determine that the amount paid was not "reasonably equivalent value" and can void the sale if it comes within the ambit of the preference statute.[10]

Within 10 days of the sale, the sheriff's executed deed of the right, title and the interest sold, along with proofs of publication, service and posting of notice, shall be delivered to the purchaser, who may thereafter file the same in the county clerk's office where the property is situate.[11]

If the title in a buyer at an execution sale fails for reasons of irregularity in the sale or if the judgment is vacated, reversed or set aside, the buyer may recover from the judgment creditors who received

§ 8.33

1. Any party, on notice, may request the court to direct the sheriff to dispose of, account for, assign, return or release all or any part of any property or debt, subject to the payment of the sheriff's fees and expense. CPLR 5238.

2. See also, supra, § 8.20. These funds are exempt from execution for one year after payment. CPLR 5206(e).

3. CPLR 5236(g).

4. CPLR 5203(a)(2).

5. See, e.g., Bank Leumi Trust Co. of New York v. Liggett, 115 A.D.2d 378, 496 N.Y.S.2d 14 (1st Dep't 1985).

6. Yellow Creek Hunting Club, Inc. v. Todd Supply, Inc., 145 A.D.2d 679, 535 N.Y.S.2d 222 (3d Dep't 1988) (general policy of reducing mortgage debt by the reasonable or fair market value would seem to apply to a judgment debt).

7. CPLR 5240. See infra, § 8.44.

8. CPLR 2003.

9. Guardian Loan Co., Inc. v. Early, 47 N.Y.2d 515, 419 N.Y.S.2d 56, 392 N.E.2d 1240 (1979). Cf. Pisano v. Tupper, 188 A.D.2d 991, 591 N.Y.S.2d 888 (3d Dep't 1992) (inadequate price "shocks the conscience" of the court and such sales should be set aside).

10. 11 U.S.C.A. § 548. See Matter of Frank, 39 B.R. 166 (Bankr.E.D.N.Y.1984).

11. CPLR 5236(f).

§ 8.33   ENFORCEMENT OF MONEY JUDGMENTS   Ch. 8

the sale proceeds.[12] Such a buyer may also move to have her lien restored, or notations of satisfactions reversed.[13]

Library References:
West's Key No. Digests, Execution ⇔322–329.

§ 8.34   Article 52 Enforcement Devices—Income Execution

If given a choice, most people would not wish to have their financial problems brought to an employer's attention. For this reason, the embarrassment factor behind the income execution, or "continuing levy," may work a powerful enforcement incentive, since its two-step process provides the debtor with notice of the judgment creditor's/enforcement officer's intention to do just that. Under the statutory scheme, the judgment debtor has a "last chance" to comply voluntarily with the income execution.

Like its sibling the property execution, the income execution form specifies the date the judgment or order was entered, the court, the amount of the judgment and remaining amount due, the names of the parties in whose favor and the names of those against whom the judgment was entered, and the last known address of the judgment debtor.[1] In addition, it must contain the name and address of the person from whom the judgment debtor is or will be receiving money, and the amount and frequency of installments. The execution form must contain a notice to commence payment of the installments specified to the sheriff and warning that, on default, the execution will be served upon the person paying the money (e.g., the employer).[2] Finally, it must contain the entire statement set out in CPLR 5231(g).[3]

The first step is accomplished by delivering the income execution to the sheriff of the county in which the debtor resides or where he works. Within 20 days of delivery, the sheriff serves the debtor (in the manner of a summons, or by certified mail, return receipt requested with an additional first class mailing).[4] The debtor then has 20 days in which to pay the defined installments.[5]

If the judgment debtor fails to pay pursuant to the first step or if the sheriff is unable to serve within 20 days of receipt of the execution from the judgment creditor, the second step commences. Now the sheriff will serve the income execution upon the person from whom the debtor is receiving money (in the manner of a summons [except not to an authorized agent for service] or by certified mail, return receipt request-

12. CPLR 5237.
13. Id.

§ 8.34
1. CPLR 5231, citing to CPLR 5230(a).
2. CPLR 5231(a).

3. Id. See infra, § 8.54.
4. CPLR 5231(d). Proof of such service consists of the receipt and a post office certificate of mailing. CPLR 5231(d).
5. CPLR 5231(e).

ed).[6] That person shall then withhold the monies provided for in the execution.[7]

To yield results, the debtor must be receiving earnings[8] which are not exempt[9] and have a weekly disposable income[10] greater than $127.50 or 30 times the present federal minimum hourly wage.[11] If the debtor is subject to a support enforcement order or judgment, and this deduction is greater than 25% of the debtor's disposable earnings, the sheriff may not levy at all.[12]

Priority as between or among judgment creditors who deliver income executions to the sheriff which specify the same obligor is determined by which creditor delivered first.[13] If an execution is returned unsatisfied because the employer is not in the same county as the sheriff and the creditor delivers it within 20 days after return to the proper sheriff, the priority is determined by the date of delivery to the first sheriff.[14] In either case, the first creditor to deliver the income execution to the sheriff is the first to be paid in full.[15]

Finally, it should be noted that the debtor who is discharged, laid off or disciplined (or not hired as an employee) because of the service of an income execution(s) has recourse against that employer.[16] The civil action premised on this claim must be commenced within 90 days of the alleged violation, and the debtor may recover damages of up to six weeks' lost wages and reinstatement (or hiring, in the case of a prospective employee).[17]

Library References:

West's Key No. Digests, Execution ⚖︎420.5; Garnishment ⚖︎7.

§ 8.35 Article 52 Enforcement Devices—Installment Payment Order—Nature and Purpose

Assume that the judgment creditor learns through the use of the

6. CPLR 5231(d).

7. CPLR 5231(f). If the obligor fails to do so, the judgment creditor may commence a proceeding against such person for the accrued installments. National Sur. Corp. v. R.H. Macy & Co., Inc., 116 Misc.2d 780, 455 N.Y.S.2d 1007 (Sup.Ct., N.Y. County, 1982).

8. Earnings are defined in this section as compensation for personal services, including wages, salary, bonus or commission. Also included are periodic payments pursuant to a retirement program or pension plan. CPLR 5231(c)(i).

9. Ninety percent of the earnings of the judgment debtor are exempt, as is the same percentage of income from certain forms of trusts or retirement plans. *See* CPLR 5205(d).

10. Earnings minus those deductions required by law to be made. CPLR 5231(c)(ii).

11. CPLR 5231(b). The statute is expressed in terms of the Fair Labor Standards Act of 1938, rather than the specific amounts in the present text, to accommodate any change made by Congress to the hourly rate.

12. CPLR 5231(b).

13. CPLR 5231(j).

14. CPLR 5231(j).

15. **PRACTICE POINTER:** This is yet another example of the need to act quickly in order to establish judgment enforcement rights.

16. CPLR 5252(1).

17. CPLR 5252(2).

§ 8.35   ENFORCEMENT OF MONEY JUDGMENTS   Ch. 8

disclosure procedures discussed earlier[1] or from any other source that the judgment debtor is receiving or will receive monies above those reachable under the income execution. Is the judgment creditor's "continuing levy" limited to a strict 10% of the debtor's earnings?[2] The short answer is no. The answer requires qualification because, on its motion for an installment payment order, the judgment creditor must demonstrate that the judgment debtor is receiving (or will receive) such monies or that he is attempting to impede the creditor by rendering services without adequate compensation.[3]

The installment payment order remedy can be used in a variety of situations. Circumstances where the debtor is attempting to conceal his true income by receiving "phantom income," or can be shown to be living "comfortably" with no visible means of support, or alleges that he receives a meager salary from a controlled corporation or related person,[4] may subject the debtor to the installment payment order.[5]

The role of the court is to fix the amount of the installment payments to be made to the judgment creditor by considering the debtor's (and his dependents') reasonable requirements, payments required of him or deducted from monies he would receive on account of income executions or wage assignments, the amount due on the judgment and, if the attempt is to impede the judgment debtor by rendering services without adequate compensation, the reasonable value of those services.[6] Once the creditor makes out a *prima facie* entitlement to the relief, the burden shifts to the debtor to establish his and his dependents' requirements, deductions, and other payments he is required to make.[7]

After an installment payment order has been granted, the debtor may seek a modification should his financial circumstances change, including changes to his reasonable requirements or the amount of money he is receiving or will receive.[8] Generally, this is by motion

§ 8.35

1. See supra, §§ 8.22—8.23.
2. See supra, § 8.34 note 9.
3. CPLR 5226. It is possible for the judgment creditor to receive amounts contemporaneously from both an income execution and an installment payment order. See, e.g., Dickens v. Director of Finance of the City of New York, 45 Misc.2d 882, 258 N.Y.S.2d 211 (Sup.Ct., N.Y. County, 1965).

CAVEAT: The installment payment order, by the express language in the statute, applies only to money, not the more general "property."

4. Wirth v. Malter, 11 A.D.2d 614, 201 N.Y.S.2d 528 (3d Dep't 1960) (working for wife); Lackner v. Abrams, 160 Misc. 424, 289 N.Y.S. 1031 (Sup.Ct., N.Y. County, 1936) (same).

5. **PRACTICE POINTER:** In one case, the judgment creditor, using the installment payment order procedure, bypassed all other judgment creditors waiting their turns for income execution. Schwartz v. Goldberg, 58 Misc.2d 308, 295 N.Y.S.2d 245 (Sup.Ct., Bronx County, 1968).

6. CPLR 5226. See Haas v. Reiser, 201 Misc. 234, 237, 105 N.Y.S.2d 98, 102 (Sup. Ct., Nassau County, 1951).

7. See supra, note 3.

8. In re Turner's Estate, 179 Misc. 217, 38 N.Y.S.2d 769 (Surr.Ct., N.Y. County, 1942); Ettinger v. Clayton, 282 App.Div. 876, 124 N.Y.S.2d 469 (2d Dep't 1953).

pursuant to CPLR 5240.[9]

Library References:
West's Key No. Digests, Judgment ⇐875.

§ 8.36 Article 52 Enforcement Devices—Installment Payment Order—Form of Application and Service

The form of application for installment payment order is a noticed motion, served upon the judgment debtor in the manner of a summons or by registered/certified mail, return receipt requested.[1]

§ 8.37 Article 52 Enforcement Devices—Receiver

The court may appoint a receiver and authorize such person to "administer, collect, improve, lease, repair, or sell" property of the debtor in which he has an interest or "to do any other acts designed to satisfy the judgment."[1] It is not uncommon to request the appointment of a receiver where the creditor believes that the public auction of an execution sale won't generate sufficient bids or where leaving the property in the possession of the debtor creates the risk of insolvency or fraud.[2] Appointment is also appropriate where a creditor might wish to act on the claims a debtor may have, because the debtor may have little incentive to do so.[3]

The receiver appointed for the enforcement of a judgment is to be distinguished from the other receiverships authorized under the CPLR. For example, temporary receiverships under CPLR Article 64 result when the movant can establish that "there is danger that the property will be removed from the state, or lost, materially injured or destroyed."[4] No such showing is required here. Yet another type permits a receiver to administer property that was the subject of an underlying action, and carries the court's judgment into effect and/or disposes of that property.[5]

The strongest distinction setting the Article 52 receivership apart from the others authorized in the CPLR is that the post-judgment receiver operates as the creditor's agent, rather than as an officer of the

---

9. See infra, § 8.44.

§ 8.36
1. CPLR 5226.

§ 8.37
1. CPLR 5228(a).
2. United States v. Vulpis, 967 F.2d 734 (2d Cir.1992).
3. For example, where the potential recovery is less than the amount of the judgment. See Vitale v. City of New York, 183 A.D.2d 502, 583 N.Y.S.2d 445 (1st Dep't 1992) (malpractice claim assigned to judgment creditor); In re Kreloff, 65 Misc.2d 692, 319 N.Y.S.2d 51 (Sup.Ct., Bronx County, 1971)(claim for damages beyond that covered by insurance).
4. CPLR 6401(a).
5. CPLR 5106.

court.[6]

§ 8.38 Article 52 Enforcement Devices—Receiver—Application, Appointment and Extension

The court may appoint a receiver upon the motion of a judgment creditor.[1] The judgment creditor moves by order to show cause so that appropriate notice, "as the court may require," to the debtor and other judgment creditors is provided as far as practicable.[2] Upon receipt of such service, another creditor may move, also by order to show cause, to have the receivership also extend to her judgment.[3] Appointment of the receiver and an extension is, of course, premised upon the exercise of the court's discretion.[4]

The order of appointment must specify the specific property to be received, the receiver's duties and the manner of their performance; unless expressly set forth therein, the receiver has no power to hire legal counsel.[5] Post-judgment receivers do take an oath of office, give an undertaking (as fixed by the court in the order making the appointment), are required to maintain written accounts of receipts and expenditures, and are subject to removal at any time.[6]

The receiver is entitled to reimbursement of disbursements necessarily incurred.[7] Moreover, any receiver other than the judgment creditor (whose judgment is presumably being satisfied) may apply to the court to allow a commission of no more than 5% of the sums received and disbursed.[8]

Library References:

West's Key No. Digests, Receivers ⇌29–64.

§ 8.39 Article 52 Enforcement Devices—Turnover Orders for Property or Debts

We have already seen that the sheriff may act to recover identified personal property of the judgment debtor in the debtor's hands or in

6. "He is an instrumentality or weapon of [the judgment] creditor, only." In re Chambers' Will, 169 Misc. 124, 127, 7 N.Y.S.2d 250, 253 (Surr.Ct., Kings County, 1938).

§ 8.38

1. CPLR 5228(a). See also, CPLR 5221(a)(4) to determine the appropriate court.

2. CPLR 5228(a).

PRACTICE POINTER: The order to show cause should also contain a provision giving the receiver priority in the judgment debtor's personal property to be received.

Otherwise, other judgment creditors, upon receipt of service, are in a position to "end-run" the application if, when they receive service of the papers, they deliver an execution to the sheriff who then levies.

3. CPLR 5228(b).

4. Benlian v. Vartabedian, 91 Misc.2d 968, 398 N.Y.S.2d 984 (N.Y.City Civ.Ct., Queens County, 1977).

5. CPLR 5228(a).

6. See CPLR 6402–6405.

7. CPLR 5228(a).

8. CPLR 5228(a).

those of a garnishee. However, if the creditor can establish that other such property exists but has been placed beyond the sheriff's or creditor's reach by either the debtor or the garnishee, the relief to request is commonly called "turnover." The purpose of a turnover (payment or delivery) order is to have the debtor or garnishee directed by the court to pay or deliver such property[1] or to direct such person to execute and deliver any document necessary to accomplish that result.[2] A related situation concerns a debt owed to the judgment debtor: where it is demonstrated that a garnishee is or will become indebted to the judgment debtor, the court may direct the garnishee to pay, to the extent of the judgment, the judgment creditor (rather than the judgment debtor) upon maturity.[3]

§ 8.40 Article 52 Enforcement Devices—Turnover Orders for Property or Debts—Turnover Against the Judgment Debtor

When it is the judgment debtor who holds the property, the procedure is a motion for turnover, served upon the debtor in the manner of a summons or by registered/certified mail, return receipt requested.[1] Entry of the order against the judgment debtor marks the moment of the movant's priority for lien purposes against the personal property in which the debtor has an interest.[2] The order may direct turnover of money to the judgment creditor but, where property is involved, the order will normally direct turnover to the sheriff.[3]

To be successful in a turnover proceeding against a debtor, the judgment creditor must be prepared to clearly establish that the judgment debtor is in possession or custody of money or other personal property in which he has an interest.[4] Failure to obey this order (*i.e.*, refusal or willful neglect) may result in the sanction of contempt.[5]

Library References:

West's Key No. Digests, Execution ⬉400.

§ 8.39
1. CPLR 5225.
2. CPLR 5225(c).
3. CPLR 5227. *See, e.g.,* Freeman v. Freeman, 119 Misc.2d 775, 464 N.Y.S.2d 676 (Sup.Ct., Oneida County, 1983) (earned commissions); City of New York v. Midmanhattan Realty Corp., 119 Misc.2d 968, 464 N.Y.S.2d 938 (Sup.Ct., N.Y. County, 1983) (time deposit in bank).

§ 8.40
1. CPLR 5225(a).
2. CPLR 5234(c).
CAVEAT: The priority is a fragile one. It can be superseded by a judgment creditor who delivers an execution to the sheriff who then levies before the order is entered. CPLR 5234(c). The priority is also subject to that section's 60 day provision ("[w]here delivery, transfer, or payment ...is not completed within sixty days after an order is filed, the judgment creditor who secured the order is divested of priority"). Accordingly, the motion should include a request to have the court direct that the 60 day provision is inapplicable.

3. CPLR 5225(a).
4. CPLR 5225(a).
5. CPLR 5251.

§ 8.41 Article 52 Enforcement Devices—Turnover Orders for Property or Debts—Turnover Against a Garnishee

When turnover is sought against a garnishee or other third person, a special proceeding is required.[1] In a special proceeding, the judgment debtor must be served with notice of the proceeding either in the manner of a summons or by registered/certified mail, return receipt requested.[2] The court may also permit the debtor or an adverse claimant to intervene in the proceeding.[3]

An interesting and important by-product of a special proceeding under CPLR 5225(b) is that it may be employed in lieu of a plenary action to set aside a fraudulent transfer.[4] This is so because the statute specifically authorizes its use "against a person who is the transferee of money or other property from the judgment debtor."[5]

To be successful in a turnover proceeding against a garnishee, the judgment creditor must establish (a) that the judgment debtor has an interest in the property in issue, and (b) that the creditor is entitled to possession of it or (c) that her rights are superior to those of the transferee.[6]

Because the special proceeding against a garnishee for turnover results in a separate judgment, the factors which increased the judgment amount (interest, costs, disbursements) are all pertinent.[7] However, in

§ 8.41

1. *See* CPLR Article 4. The petition, obviously captioned differently than in the underlying action giving rise to the judgment, is served upon the respondent(s) as a summons in an action would be. CPLR 403(c). Following a special proceeding, a judgment, determining the rights of the parties to the proceeding, is entered. CPLR 411.

   PRACTICE POINTER: Before commencing such a special proceeding, consider carefully all garnishees or transferees who should be bound by the judgment for it to afford complete relief—and name all such parties as party respondents. This may avoid a motion to dismiss—and delay—under CPLR 3211(a)(10) or the situation where failure to join renders the judgment ineffective against an "indispensable" party. *See, e.g.*, Kennis v. Sherwood, 82 A.D.2d 847, 439 N.Y.S.2d 962 (2d Dep't 1981).

2. CPLR 5225(b), 5227.

3. *Id.* Pursuant to CPLR 5239, any interested person may commence a special proceeding to determine disputed rights in property. This may also include a trial on the issues. *See infra*, § 8.45.

   Note that the debtor's intervention serves the interests of the garnishee rather than or in contrast to those of the creditor since, if the debtor is not included, he may not be bound by the judgment and can sue the garnishee in a subsequent action. In other words, the judgment may not have *res judicata* effect.

4. Debtor and Creditor Law §§ 270 *et seq*.

5. CPLR 5225(b).

   PRACTICE POINTER: Clearly, this section is also applicable to property transfers in violation of a restraining notice.

6. CPLR 5225(b). Gelbard v. Esses, 96 A.D.2d 573, 465 N.Y.S.2d 264 (2d Dep't 1983).

   CAVEAT: The rights the judgment creditor obtains in the proceeding will be no better than the rights the judgment debtor had in the property. Stuhler v. State, 127 Misc.2d 390, 485 N.Y.S.2d 957 (Sup.Ct., N.Y. County, 1985).

7. *See supra*, §§ 8.6, 8.7.

the case of property, if a party does not dispute the judgment debtor's interest or right to possession or, in the case of indebtedness, does not dispute the indebtedness, costs may not be awarded against such a person.[8]

The remedy for disobedience in failing to obey the judgment directing that property be delivered is contempt.[9] If the judgment directs payment of money, the methods of enforcement set forth in this chapter are all applicable.

Library References:
West's Key No. Digests, Garnishment ⊙=156.

§ 8.42 Article 52 Enforcement Devices—Contempt

The power to punish for contempt is specifically provided to those courts in which a special proceeding for the enforcement of money judgments may be commenced.[1] The contempt punishment in the judgment enforcement realm provides a remedy when there has been a finding of refusal or willful neglect to comply with judicial process (i.e, one issued by the court or by an officer of the court, including the clerk or the judgment creditor's attorney).[2] Such circumstances would include the failure of any person to obey a subpoena,[3] a restraining notice,[4] or a court order.[5] Also punishable as contempt are false swearing on an examination or in answering written questions, and the willful defacing or removal of a posted notice of sale before such sale.[6]

In the judgment enforcement context, the movant seeks civil, rather than criminal, contempt.[7] The civil remedy, enabling a court to punish by fine or imprisonment, is applied where there has been "a neglect or violation of a duty, or other misconduct, by which a right or remedy of a party to a civil action or special proceeding, pending in the court may be defeated, impaired, impeded, or prejudiced."[8]

The application procedure, commenced by order to show cause or notice of motion, requires that the accused show cause why he should not be punished for the alleged offense.[9] The application is noticed, heard

8. CPLR 5225(b), CPLR 5227.
9. CPLR 5104.

§ 8.42
1. CPLR 5210. The courts in which this remedy may be sought are found in CPLR 5221(a).
2. CPLR 5251.
3. CPLR 2308(a).
4. CPLR 5222.
5. For example, a turnover order against the judgment debtor. CPLR 5225(a).
6. CPLR 5251.

7. A complete discussion of the distinctions between civil and criminal contempt is beyond the scope of this chapter. A criminal contempt usually involves egregiously improper conduct such as disorderly, contemptuous or insolent behavior generally directed at a court or its processes. Judiciary Law § 750. Criminal contempt has deterrence as a goal. Frankel v. Frankel, 111 A.D.2d 447, 488 N.Y.S.2d 825 (3d Dep't 1985).

8. Judiciary Law § 753.
9. Judiciary Law § 756.

and determined as a notice of motion would be, but the papers must be served between 10 and 30 days prior to the hearing date.[10] The face page must contain a notice that "the purpose of the hearing is to punish the accused for a contempt of court and that such punishment may consist of fine or imprisonment, or both, according to law"[11] *and* the following legend in at least eight point bold type:[12]

WARNING:
YOUR FAILURE TO APPEAR IN COURT MAY RESULT IN YOUR IMMEDIATE ARREST AND IMPRISONMENT FOR CONTEMPT OF COURT

The rules concerning service of a contempt motion are not easily summarized, and the Judiciary Law offers little clarity.[13] Generally, a party to the underlying action may be served in accordance with CPLR 2103.[14] As to a non-party, the application is a special proceeding, and notice must be served in the manner of a summons.[15]

On the return date, the court must inform the accused of the right to counsel and may appoint counsel if the accused is financially unable.[16] If the accused appears, complies and satisfies the court that he has "at the time" no means, property or income to levy upon, the application will be denied, without prejudice to renewal on the creditor's showing of a change to the accused's financial condition.[17] The motion is addressed to the sound discretion of the court.[18] As such, the accused will usually be provided the opportunity to purge himself of contempt.[19] The court will enter a final order if it determines that the accused committed the offense charged and that it was calculated to, or actually did, defeat,

---

10. Judiciary Law § 756. The provision excepts the provisions governing the arrest of the judgment debtor (CPLR 5250) or if the court orders otherwise.

11. *Id*. If the notice is lacking anywhere in the moving papers, the papers are deficient as a matter of law. Mente v. Wenzel, 192 A.D.2d 862, 596 N.Y.S.2d 520 (3d Dep't 1993), appeal dism'd, lv to appeal dism'd in pt, den. in pt 82 N.Y.2d 843, 606 N.Y.S.2d 593, 627 N.E.2d 514 (1993). However, the accused's contest of the application on the merits without objecting to the notice requirements operates as a waiver of these requirements. Weinreich v. Weinreich, 184 A.D.2d 505, 585 N.Y.S.2d 770 (2d Dep't 1992).

CAVEAT: The notice should stand out or be readily apparent to one reading the papers. Bank Leumi Trust Co. of New York v. Taylor–Cishahayo, 147 Misc.2d 685, 556 N.Y.S.2d 211 (N.Y. City Civ.Ct., Queens County, 1990).

12. *Id. See infra*, § 8.56.

13. Judiciary Law § 761 says that an application for civil contempt "shall be served upon the accused, unless service upon the attorney for the accused be ordered by the court or judge."

14. *See, e.g.*, Quantum Heating Services, Inc. v. Austern, 100 A.D.2d 843, 474 N.Y.S.2d 81 (2d Dep't 1984) (service by mail sufficient).

15. CPLR 403(c).

16. Judiciary Law § 770.

17. Judiciary Law § 770.

18. Garrison Fuel Oil of Long Island, Inc. v. Grippo, 127 Misc.2d 275, 486 N.Y.S.2d 136 (County Ct., Nassau County, 1985).

19. In re Hildreth, 28 A.D.2d 290, 284 N.Y.S.2d 755 (1st Dep't 1967).

impair, impede, or prejudice the rights or remedies of the judgment creditor.[20]

Where the judgment creditor can show actual loss or injury caused by reason of the misconduct, and the case is not one where it is specially prescribed by law, the judgment creditor can recover such damages, as a fine, against the contemnor sufficient to indemnify.[21] Where such damages cannot be shown, a fine of no more than $250 may be imposed in addition to the movant's costs and expenses.[22] Moreover, where a fine is imposed, the order doing so must also include a provision that the offender may purge the contempt within 10 days after personal service of the order upon him, and may include a provision committing the contemnor to prison until the fine, costs and expenses are paid, or until he is discharged.[23] The contemnor may purge by appearing and satisfying the court that he cannot pay the fine or, if the court directs, gives an undertaking conditioned upon payment of the fine, costs and expenses and his appearance and performance of the act for which he is being punished.[24]

Should further relief be necessary, the judgment creditor may submit to the court a certified copy of the order and an affidavit stating that (a) more than 10 days have elapsed since personal service of the order and (b) the fine, costs and expenses have not been paid. The court may then issue a warrant for the offender's arrest, without notice, to be committed or may other another disposition.[25]

Library References:
West's Key No. Digests, Execution ⇔381, 416.

§ 8.43 Article 52 Enforcement Devices—Arrest of the Judgment Debtor

This remedy, premised on the outdated notion of body execution, is as close as the judgment debtor will get to "debtor's prison." Nonetheless, the remedy exists and should be employed where it can be shown that the judgment debtor is about to depart from the state or has kept himself concealed within the state.[1] The purposes of this remedy are to secure the judgment debtor's obeisance to the terms of the restraining

---

20. Judiciary Law § 770.

21. Judiciary Law § 773. See e.g., Kanbar v. Quad Cinema Corp., 151 Misc.2d 439, 581 N.Y.S.2d 260 (App.Term, 1st Dep't 1991), affirmed as mod. 195 A.D.2d 912, 600 N.Y.S.2d 702 (1993). An attorney who had actual notice of a restraining notice to his client was fined $37,000 when the court learned that he, knowing of the restraining notice, did nothing to stop the diversion of funds in that amount by the client.

22. Judiciary Law § 773.

23. Judiciary Law § 773.
PRACTICE POINTER: The order should be served personally upon the contemnor.

24. Judiciary Law § 773.

25. Judiciary Law § 773.

§ 8.43

1. CPLR 5250. The legislative history indicates that the section remains viable when the judgment debtor avoids punishment for the violation of a subpoena simply by evading its service.

notice in the order of arrest and to secure his appearance at an examination.[2] The application may be made *ex parte*, upon an affidavit setting forth the statutory grounds. The court may then issue a warrant to the sheriff, who serves the warrant and papers upon which it is based upon the judgment debtor at the time of the arrest.[3]

In practical terms, other remedies are more efficient than the judgment debtor's arrest. The paucity of case law for this section confirms this conclusion.

Library References:

West's Key No. Digests, Execution ⬅381.

§ 8.44 Protective Orders

In the preceding sections, we have reviewed the full panoply of Article 52's enforcement devices. As compared to the rights afforded judgment creditors under the laws of other states, the New York procedures are relatively potent and simple to employ (*e.g.*, no application to court to commence enforcement). However, recognizing the countervailing interest of the judgment debtor in avoiding abuse, a stop-gap measure provides for the court's issuance of protective orders.[1]

The protective order application is made by the motion of any interested person, upon such notice as the court may require, or by the court, *sua sponte*.[2] Under this provision, the discretionary powers provided to the court are broad, and include the making of orders "denying, limiting, conditioning, regulating, extending or modifying the use" of any enforcement procedure.[3] In addition, the court can itself supervise disclosure proceedings or appoint a referee to do so.[4]

§ 8.45 Proceeding to Determine Adverse Claims

Throughout this chapter, we have discussed the complex priority problems that can occur when one judgment creditor competes against another for the same property in which the judgment debtor has an interest. Moreover, many types of interests may exist against the property both before and after that lien of judgment. Mortgages, purchase money mortgages, mechanic's liens, tax liens, *lis pendens*, UCC–1 security interests and other forms of interest may encumber the property. The teasing apart and ordering of these various interests and the priority of each is the province of the court. The court's jurisdiction should be

2. CPLR 5250.
3. CPLR 5250.

§ 8.44
1. CPLR 5240.
2. CPLR 5240.

3. CPLR 5240.

4. By its terms, CPLR 5240 makes CPLR Section 3104 applicable to judgment enforcement procedures.

engaged prior to the application of the property or debt by the sheriff or receiver to the satisfaction of the judgment.[1]

Although, by definition, the proceeding to determine adverse claims is a special proceeding, it is commenced by any interested person by the filing of a petition which may be served in the manner of a simple notice of motion.[2] Venue is proper either where the property was levied upon or pursuant to the venue provisions of CPLR 5221(a).[3] Any interested person can move to intervene.[4]

The court may vacate the execution or order, vacate the levy, direct the property's disposition and direct the award of damages. Moreover, the court's jurisdiction is plenary for disputed issues of fact; in that instance, it directs the giving of an undertaking by the person holding the property.[5]

Finally, the court can direct that the reasonable expenses of a party, other damages, and an award of attorneys' fees be paid by anyone who is found to have asserted a fraudulent claim.[6]

Library References:

West's Key No. Digests, Execution ⚖=187, 326.

§ 8.46 Forms

Most of the forms that follow contain instructions provided by the author to guide the practitioner in completing them. The forms may be purchased from Julius Blumberg, Inc., New York City 10013, or any of its dealers.

§ 8.45

1. CPLR 5239.

CAVEAT: The courts are not in agreement on the meaning of "prior to the application" language in the statute. Most appear to hold that it means while the property or debt are in the hands of the sheriff or officer. At least one court, using a laches analysis, has held that it refers to the actual distribution of the proceeds. Herman v. Siegmund, 69 A.D.2d 871, 415 N.Y.S.2d 681 (2d Dep't 1979), appeal after remand 102 A.D.2d 810, 476 N.Y.S.2d 590 (1984).

2. CPLR 5239. Cf. CPLR 403(c).

PRACTICE POINTER: Service of the motion upon the judgment debtor and the sheriff or receiver, if applicable, is self-evident. Use an order to show cause to have the court direct upon whom service should be made where the identities of the holders of interests, or of the interests themselves, is unclear.

3. CPLR 5239.

4. CPLR 5239.

5. CPLR 5239.

6. CPLR 5239.

§ 8.47   ENFORCEMENT OF MONEY JUDGMENTS   Ch. 8

§ 8.47 Forms—Statement for Judgment (Default Judgment), Affidavit of Facts Constituting the Claim, the Default and the Amount Due

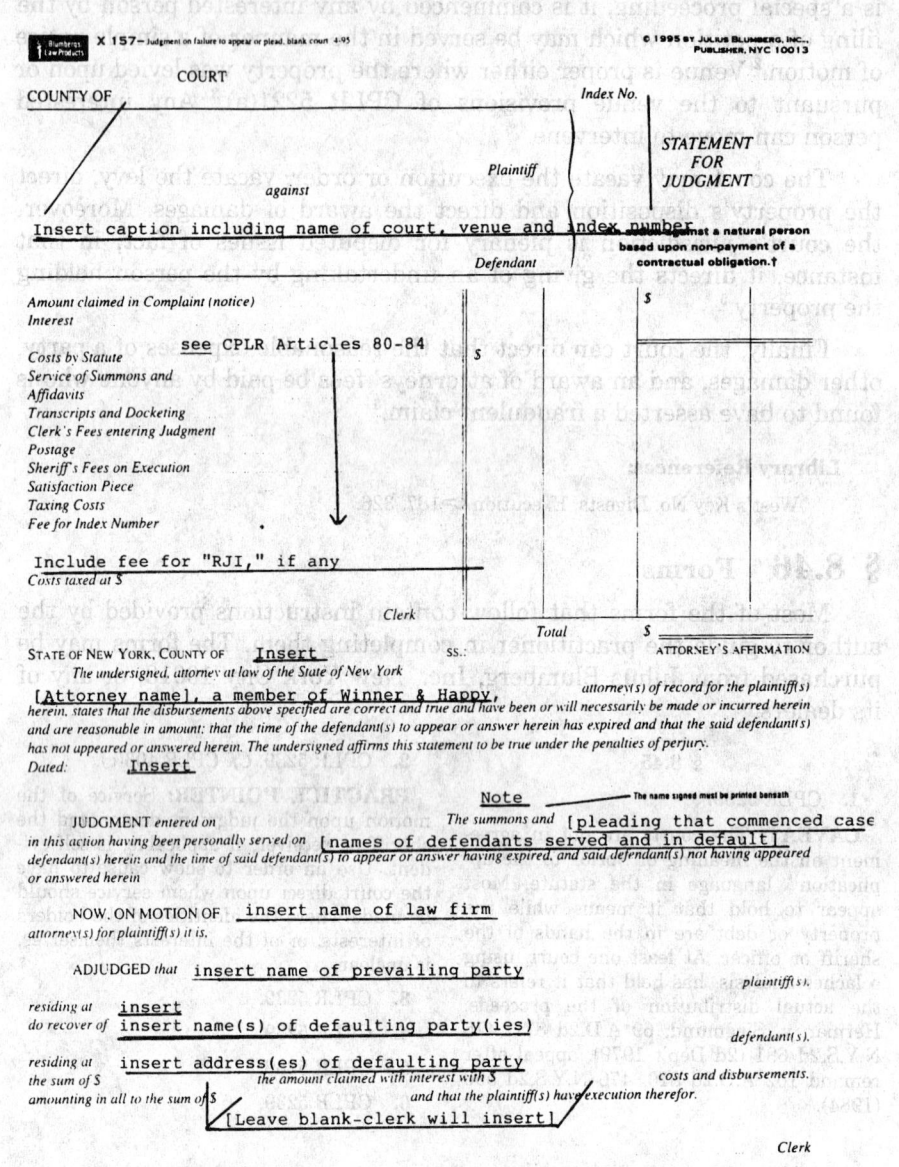

X 157—Judgment on failure to appear or plead, blank court 4/95 © 1995 BY JULIUS BLUMBERG, INC., PUBLISHER, NYC 10013

COURT
COUNTY OF _____   Index No. _____

_____ Plaintiff
                against
Insert caption including name of court, venue and index number   STATEMENT
                                                                                  FOR
                                                                                  JUDGMENT
_____ Defendant   against a natural person based upon non-payment of a contractual obligation.†

Amount claimed in Complaint (notice) $
Interest
                      see CPLR Articles 80-84
Costs by Statute $
Service of Summons and
Affidavits
Transcripts and Docketing
Clerk's Fees entering Judgment
Postage
Sheriff's Fees on Execution
Satisfaction Piece
Taxing Costs
Fee for Index Number

Include fee for "RJI," if any
Costs taxed at $

                                    Clerk
                                                      Total $

STATE OF NEW YORK, COUNTY OF   **Insert**   SS.:   ATTORNEY'S AFFIRMATION
    The undersigned, attorney at law of the State of New York
[Attorney name], a member of Winner & Happy,   attorney(s) of record for the plaintiff(s)
herein, states that the disbursements above specified are correct and true and have been or will necessarily be made or incurred herein and are reasonable in amount; that the time of the defendant(s) to appear or answer herein has expired and that the said defendant(s) has not appeared or answered herein. The undersigned affirms this statement to be true under the penalties of perjury.
Dated: **Insert**

                                                Note ———— The name signed must be printed beneath
JUDGMENT entered on _____   The summons and **[pleading that commenced case**
in this action having been personally served on **[names of defendants served and in default]**
defendant(s) herein and the time of said defendant(s) to appear or answer having expired, and said defendant(s) not having appeared or answered herein.

    NOW, ON MOTION OF   **insert name of law firm**
attorney(s) for plaintiff(s) it is,

    ADJUDGED that   **insert name of prevailing party**   plaintiff(s).
residing at   **insert**
do recover of   **insert name(s) of defaulting party(ies)**   defendant(s).
residing at   **insert address(es) of defaulting party**
the sum of $ _____   the amount claimed with interest with $ _____   costs and disbursements,
amounting in all to the sum of $ _____   and that the plaintiff(s) have execution therefor.
                              [Leave blank-clerk will insert]
                                                                                      Clerk

† A notice of default must be mailed to defendants in an action against a natural person based upon non-payment of a contractual obligation (CPLR 308, as amended).
Delete if inapplicable.
            Forms may be purchased from Julius Blumberg, Inc., New York City
                10013, or any of its dealers. Reproduction prohibited.

Ch. 8 **STATEMENT FOR JUDGMENT** § 8.47

_____ COURT, COUNTY OF _____

Plaintiff(s)	AFFIDAVIT OF FACTS
against	CONSTITUTING THE CLAIM
	THE DEFAULT AND THE
Defendant(s)	AMOUNT DUE

STATE OF NEW YORK, COUNTY OF _____ ss.:

_____ being duly sworn, deposes and says: that the deponent is the plaintiff(s) in the within action; this action was commenced by service of the summons _____ upon defendant(s) and is an action _____

Notice of default (a copy of the summons _____) was mailed to defendant(s) on _____ a date which is at least 20 days prior to entry of this judgment and proof of service thereof is annexed.†

Wherefore deponent demands judgment against the defendant(s) in the sum of $_____ with interest from _____ together with the costs and disbursements of this action.

Sworn to before me on

The name signed must be printed beneath

† Delete if applicable.
* Show basis of venue   *Information pursuant to Section 5018(c) of the Civil Practice Law and Rules*

Residence and trade or profession of Defendant

Residence address of Plaintiff

[Judgment Roll form layout with fields: Index No., Court, County of, Plaintiff(s), against, Defendant(s), Judgment Roll, Attorney(s) for Plaintiff(s), Office and Post Office Address, Amount and interest $, Costs and disbursements $, Filed __ o'clock __ M., at]

Library References:
West's Key No. Digests, Judgment ⇐110, 121, 126.

§ 8.48　ENFORCEMENT OF MONEY JUDGMENTS　Ch. 8

§ 8.48　Forms—Affidavit of Confession of Judgment and Judgment by Confession

Blumberg's Law Products　X 245—Confession of Judgment. Ind. or Corp. Blank Court.　COPYRIGHT 1973 BY JULIUS BLUMBERG, INC., LAW BLANK PUBLISHERS

COURT
COUNTY OF　　　　　　　　　　　　　　　　　Index No.
Insert caption and venue; index number will be assigned on filing

　　　　　　　　　　　　　　　Plaintiff(s)　　　AFFIDAVIT OF
　　　　　　against　　　　　　　　　　　　　CONFESSION OF
　　　　　　　　　　　　　　　　　　　　　　JUDGMENT
　　　　　　　　　　　　　　　Defendant(s)

STATE OF NEW YORK, COUNTY OF　County in which the defendant executes
being duly sworn, deposes and says; that deponent is

† (the　　　　　　of
a　　　　　　corporation and is duly authorized to make this affidavit on behalf of the corporate)
defendant herein.
　　The defendant hereby confesses judgment herein and authorizes entry thereof against defendant in the
sum of $　insert
　　Defendant resides at　insert
in the County of　insert　　　State of　insert　　. Defendant authorizes entry
of judgment in　insert name of county
　　　　　　　　　　　　　　　　County, New York, if said residence address is not in New York State.

　　This confession of judgment is for a debt justly °　　　due to the plaintiff arising from
the following facts:

Set forth a detailed description of the transaction (e.g., origin of the obligation, how the amount was calculated, any contingencies that must be satisfied before entry, etc.)

　　This affidavit, if made in connection with an agreement for the purchase for $1,500.00 or less of any commodities for any use other than a commercial or business use upon any plan of deferred payments whereby the price or cost is payable in two or more installments, was executed subsequent to the time a default occurred in the payment of an installment thereunder.

Sworn to before me this
　　day of　　　　　　19
　　　　　　　　　　　　　　　　　　　　　　— The name signed must be printed beneath
　　　　　　　　　　　　Insert

† Strike out matter in parenthesis if defendant is individual
° Insert words "to become" if debt is not yet due.
°° If in a city court, insert name of court. UCCA §1403.

Forms may be purchased from Julius Blumberg, Inc., New York City 10013, or any of its dealers. Reproduction prohibited.

Ch. 8 CONFESSION OF JUDGMENT § 8.48

```
                    COURT                                    Index No.
COUNTY OF                                                    Address of Plaintiff:
                                                             insert
Insert caption and venue
                                          Plaintiff(s)
              against
                                          Defendant(s)      JUDGMENT BY
                                                            CONFESSION

Amount Confessed   - - - - - - - - - - $
Interest          -                                          $

Costs by Statute  - - CPLR 3218(b) - - - - - 15.00
Transcript -
Fees on Execution
Satisfaction
Filing Fee        - - - - - - - - -
                                       Total        $
```

STATE OF NEW YORK, COUNTY OF insert ATTORNEY'S AFFIRMATION
    The undersigned, attorney at law of the State of New York, affirms that   he is <u>a member of Winner & Happy, the</u> attorney(s) of record for the plaintiff   herein and states that the disbursements above specified are correct and true and have been or will necessarily be made or incurred herein and are reasonable in amount and affirms this statement to be true under the penalties of perjury.

Dated: <u>insert</u>
                              note   —Print Name Beneath Signature

JUDGMENT entered the   day of   19   .
    On filing the foregoing affidavit of Confession of Judgment made by the defendant   herein, sworn to the <u>insert</u>   day of   <u>insert</u>   19   ,
    NOW, ON MOTION OF   WINNER & happy,
attorney(s) for plaintiff   it is
    ADJUDGED that   <u>insert plaintiff's name</u>   plaintiff   ,
residing at   <u>insert plaintiff's address</u>
do recover of   <u>insert name of the defendant</u>   defendant ,
residing at   insert defendant's address
the sum of $ <u>insert</u>   with interest of $ making a total of $
together with $ costs and disbursements, amounting in all to the sum of $
and that the plaintiff   have execution therefor.
                                         clerk will insert
                                         .... Clerk

```
                                    Plaintiff(s)        Defendant(s)
Index No.   COUNTY OF   COURT   Insert caption and venue                    Affidavit and           Insert name of law firm   Insert address and telephone
                                            against                         Judgment by Confession   Attorney(s) for Plaintiff
                                                                                                     Office and Post Office Address
```

Library References:

West's Key No. Digests, Judgment ⚖=51.

235

§ 8.49   ENFORCEMENT OF MONEY JUDGMENTS   Ch. 8

§ 8.49   Forms—Notice to Judgment Debtor [or Obligor]

T 426— Notice to judgment debtors.
CPLR 5222, 2-94

© 1982 BY JULIUS BLUMBERG, INC., PUBLISHER
62 WHITE STREET, NEW YORK, N.Y. 10013

COURT
COUNTY OF _____   Index No. _____

Insert caption including name of court, venue and index number

                                                    Plaintiff
                        against
                                                    Defendant

TO: Insert name of judgment debtor

NOTICE TO JUDGMENT DEBTOR OR OBLIGOR

Money or property belonging to you may have been taken or held in order to satisfy a judgment or order which has been entered against you. Read this carefully.

YOU MAY BE ABLE TO GET YOUR MONEY BACK

State and federal laws prevent certain money or property from being taken to satisfy judgments or orders. Such money or property is said to be "exempt". The following is a partial list of money which may be exempt:

1. Supplemental security income, (SSI);
2. Social security;
3. Public assistance (welfare);
4. Alimony or child support;
5. Unemployment benefits;
6. Disability benefits;
7. Workers' compensation benefits;
8. Public or private pensions; and
9. Veterans benefits.

If you think that any of your money that has been taken or held is exempt, you must act promptly because the money may be applied to the judgment or order. If you claim that any of your money that has been taken or held is exempt, you may contact the person sending this notice.

Also, YOU MAY CONSULT AN ATTORNEY, INCLUDING LEGAL AID IF YOU QUALIFY. The law (New York civil practice law and rules, article four and sections fifty-two hundred thirty-nine and fifty-two hundred forty) provides a procedure for determination of a claim to an exemption.

Dated   Insert

See over: Complete upper portion of
affidavit of service. If it's returned
from the residence address, complete ....
the bottom portion.   *Creditor or Attorney(s) for Judgment Creditor*
                                           Office and Post Office Address

                        Sign and insert name, firm name,
                          address and telephone number

Forms may be purchased from Julius Blumberg, Inc., New York City
10013, or any of its dealers. Reproduction prohibited.

Ch. 8   **NOTICE TO JUDGMENT DEBTOR**   § 8.49

State of New York, County of _____ ss.:

_____ being duly sworn, deposes and says: that deponent is not a party to this action, is over 18 years of age and resides at _____

That on _____, 19___ at _____. M., at _____ deponent served the within Notice to Judgment Debtor to the judgment debtor therein named, by enclosing a copy of the Notice in a postpaid sealed wrapper properly addressed to the judgment debtor

☐ **First Class Mail to Residence**   to the last known residence address at _____ and the deponent deposited the envelope in an official depository under the exclusive care and custody of the United States Postal Service within New York State.

☐ **First Class Mail to Place of Employment**   to the judgment debtor's place of employment at _____

by depositing the envelope in an official depository under the exclusive care and custody of the United States Postal Service within New York State. The envelope bore the legend "personal and confidential" and did not indicate on the outside thereof, by the return address or otherwise, that the communication was from an attorney or concerned a judxgment.

The notice sent to the judgment debtor's residence had been returned.

☐ **First Class Mail to Other Address**   to (address) _____ and by depositing the envelope in an official depository under the exclusive care and custody of the United States within New York State.

The notice sent to the judgment debtor's residence had been returned and neither the residence address or the place of employment of the judgment debtor is known.

☐ **Personal Delivery**   by delivering a copy of the Notice on the judgment debtor personally; deponent knew the person so served to be the person described as the judgment debtor therein.

Sworn to before me on _____

_____
Print name beneath signature

§ 8.50 Forms—Subpoena (*Duces Tecum*) to Take Deposition of Judgment Debtor With Restraining Notice

T 429—Subpoena to take deposition of Judgment Debtor and to produce books and records (duces tecum) with RESTRAINING NOTICE Enforcement of Money Judgment Blank Court 1-95

© 1976 BY JULIUS BLUMBERG, INC., PUBLISHING, NYC 10013

THIS SUBPOENA REQUIRES YOUR PERSONAL APPEARANCE AT THE TIME AND PLACE SPECIFIED. FAILURE TO APPEAR MAY SUBJECT YOU TO FINE AND IMPRISONMENT FOR CONTEMPT OF COURT.

Insert caption, including name of court, venue and index number

Plaintiff

against

Defendant

Index No.

SUBPOENA
(Duces Tecum)
To Take Deposition of
Judgment Debtor
with Restraining Notice

The People of the State of New York

TO Judgment debtor _judgment debtor_ GREETING:
Address: insert

WHEREAS, in an action in the Court of Where was judgment entered?
County of between
  insert names of all parties, as plaintiff(s) and
  insert names of all parties as defendant(s)
who are all the parties named in said action, a judgment was entered on date in favor of
insert name of the party who is the _judgment creditor_ and against
insert name of the party who is the _judgment debtor_
in the amount of $ judgment amount of which $ amount still due together with interest thereon
from date remains due and unpaid; and

WHEREAS, the judgment debtor; resides; is regularly employed; has an office for the regular transaction of business in
person; in insert County.

WE COMMAND YOU to appear and attend before "a notary public"
at what specific location?
on what date? at time M. and at any recessed or adjourned date for the
taking of a deposition under oath upon oral or written questions on all matters relevant to the satisfaction of such judgment;

AND WE FURTHER COMMAND YOU to produce for examination at such time and place the following books, papers
and records:

insert here specific documents

and all other books, papers and records in your possession or control which have or may contain information concerning your
property, income or other means relevant to the satisfaction of the judgment;

TAKE NOTICE that false swearing or failure to comply with this subpoena is punishable as a contempt of court.

RESTRAINING NOTICE: TAKE NOTICE that pursuant to subdivision (b) of Section 5222 of the Civil Practice Law and Rules, which is set forth in full herein, you are hereby forbidden to make or suffer any sale, assignment or transfer of, or any interference with any property in which you have an interest, except as therein provided. Disobedience of this Restraining Notice is punishable as a contempt of court.

Section 5222(b) Effect of restraint; prohibition of transfer; duration. A judgment debtor or obligor served with a restraining notice is forbidden to make or suffer any sale, assignment, transfer or interference with any property in which he or she has an interest, except upon direction of the sheriff or pursuant to an order of the court, until the judgment or order is satisfied or vacated. A restraining notice served upon a person other than the judgment debtor or obligor is effective only if, at the time of service, he or she owes a debt to the judgment debtor or obligor or he or she is in the possession or custody of property in which he or she knows or has reason to believe the judgment debtor or obligor has an interest, or if the judgment creditor or support collection unit has stated in the notice that a specified debt is owed by the person served to the judgment debtor or obligor or that the judgment debtor or obligor has an interest in specified property in the possession or custody of the person served. All property in which the judgment debtor or obligor is known or believed to have an interest then in and thereafter coming into the possession or custody of such a person, including any specified in the notice, and all debts of such a person, including any specified in the notice, then due and thereafter coming due to the judgment debtor or obligor, shall be subject to the notice. Such a person is forbidden to make or suffer any sale, assignment or transfer of, or any interference with, any such property, or pay over or otherwise dispose of any such debt, to any person other than the sheriff or the support collection unit, except upon direction of the sheriff or pursuant to an order of the court, until the expiration of one year after the notice is served upon him or her, or until the judgment or order is satisfied or vacated, whichever event first occurs. A judgment creditor or support collection unit which has specified personal property or debt in a restraining notice shall be liable to the owner of the property or the person to whom the debt is owed, if other than the judgment debtor or obligor, for any damages sustained by reason of the restraint. If a garnishee served with a restraining notice withholds the payment of money belonging or owed to the judgment debtor or obligor in an amount equal to twice the amount due on the judgment or order, the restraining notice is not effective as to other property or money.

Dated: insert
The name signed must be printed beneath

individual or firm name
firm name, address and phone number

Attorney(s) for Judgment Creditor:
Office and Post Office Address:

Forms may be purchased from Julius Blumberg, Inc., New York City
10013, or any of its dealers. Reproduction prohibited.

SUBPOENA (*DUCES TECUM*) § 8.50

AFFIDAVIT OF SERVICE

STATE OF NEW YORK, COUNTY OF _____ SS The undersigned, being duly sworn, deposes and says; deponent is not a party herein, is over 18 years of age and resides at
That on _____ at _____ M., at
deponent served the within subpoena on _____ judgment debtor therein named.

INDIVIDUAL
1. ☐ by delivering a true copy *of each* to said judgment debtor personally; deponent knew the person so served to be the judgment debtor described in the subpoena.

CORPORATION
2. ☐ a _____ corporation, by delivering thereat a true copy *of each* to _____ personally, deponent knew said corporation so served to be the corporate judgment debtor described in the subpoena and knew said individual to be _____ thereof.

SUITABLE AGE PERSON
3. ☐ by delivering thereat a true copy *of each* to _____ a person of suitable age and discretion. Said premises is judgment debtor's—actual place of business—dwelling place—usual place of abode—within

AFFIXING TO DOOR, ETC.
4. ☐ the state.by affixing a true copy *of each* to the door of said premises, which is judgment debtor's—actual place of business—dwelling place—usual place of abode—within the state. Deponent was unable, with due diligence to find judgment debtor or a person of suitable age and discretion thereat, having called there

MAILING TO RESIDENCE USE WITH 3 OR 4
5A. ☐ Within 20 days of such delivery or affixing, deponent enclosed a copy of same in a postpaid envelope properly addressed to judgment debtor at judgment debtor's last known residence, at _____ and deposited said envelope in an official depository under the exclusive care and custody of the U.S. Postal Service within New York State.

MAILING TO BUSINESS USE WITH 3 OR 4
5B. ☐ Within 20 days of such delivery or affixing, deponent enclosed a copy of same in a first class postpaid envelope properly addressed to judgment debtor at judgment debtor's actual place of business, at _____ in an official depository under the exclusive care and custody of the U.S. Postal Service within New York State. The envelope bore the legend "Personal and Confidential" and did not indicate on the outside thereof, by return address or otherwise, that the communication was from an attorney or concerned an action against the judgment debtor.

DESCRIPTION USE WITH 1, 2 OR 3
☐

☐ Male	☐ White Skin	☐ Black Hair	☐ White Hair	☐ 14-20 Yrs.	☐ Under 5'	☐ Under 100 Lbs.
☐ Female	☐ Black Skin	☐ Brown Hair	☐ Balding	☐ 21-35 Yrs.	☐ 5'0"-5'3"	☐ 100-130 Lbs.
	☐ Yellow Skin	☐ Blonde Hair	☐ Mustache	☐ 36-50 Yrs.	☐ 5'4"-5'8"	☐ 131-160 Lbs.
	☐ Brown Skin	☐ Gray Hair	☐ Beard	☐ 51-65 Yrs.	☐ 5'9"-6'0"	☐ 161-200 Lbs.
	☐ Red Skin	☐ Red Hair	☐ Glasses	☐ Over 65 Yrs.	☐ Over 6'	☐ Over 200 Lbs.

Other identifying features: _____

At the time of said service, deponent paid (tendered) in advance $ _____ the authorized traveling expenses and one day's witness fee.

Sworn to before me on _____

Print name beneath signature.

LICENSE NO. _____

Index No. _____
County of _____ Court
_____ Plaintiff(s)
against
_____ Defendant(s)

Subpoena Duces Tecum
To Examine Judgment Debtor
with Restraining Notice

Attorney(s) for Judgment Creditor
Office and Post Office Address

NOTATION OF DEFAULT
The person to be examined, having this day been duly called in open Court - at the office of _____ by _____ at _____ M. and having failed to appear or answer h_____ herein is duly noted.
Dated _____

Notary Public _____ M. respectively default

The name signed must be printed beneath.

Library References:

West's Key No. Digests, Execution ⚖︎373.

§ 8.51 ENFORCEMENT OF MONEY JUDGMENTS Ch. 8

§ 8.51 Forms—Subpoena (*Duces Tecum*) to Take Deposition of Witness With Restraining Notice

X 418—Subpoena to take deposition of witness to produce books and records (duces tecum) with RESTRAINING NOTICE, Enforcement of Money Judgment Blank Court, 8-78
© 1978 BY JULIUS BLUMBERG, INC.
PUBLISHER, NYC 10013

COURT	COUNTY OF
	Index No.
Plaintiff(s)	SUBPOENA (*Duces Tecum*) To Take Deposition of Witness
against	
Defendant(s)	with Restraining Notice

The People of the State of New York

TO witness, GREETING:
Address:
WHEREAS, in an action in the Court of
County of
between:
 as plaintiff(s) and
as defendant(s) who are all the parties named in said action, a judgment was entered on 19
in favor of judgment creditor
and against judgment debtor
in the amount of $ of which $ together with interest thereon from
 19 remains due and unpaid; and WHEREAS, the witness: resides; is regularly employed;
has an office for the regular transaction of business in person; in County.
WE COMMAND YOU to appear and attend before
at
on 19 at M. and at any recessed or adjourned date for the taking of a deposition
under oath upon oral or written questions on all matters relevant to the satisfaction of such judgment.
AND WE FURTHER COMMAND YOU to produce for examination at such time and place the following books, papers and records:

and all other books, papers and records in your possession or control which have or may contain information concerning the property, income or other means of the judgment debtor relevant to the satisfaction of the judgment.
TAKE NOTICE that false swearing or failure to comply with this subpoena is punishable as a contempt of court.
RESTRAINING NOTICE WHEREAS, it appears that you owe a debt to the judgment debtor or are in possession or in custody of property in which the judgment debtor has an interest.

TAKE NOTICE that pursuant to subdivision (b) of Section 5222 of the Civil Practice Law and Rules, which is set forth in full herein, you are hereby forbidden to make or suffer any sale, assignment or transfer of, or any interference with, any such property or pay over or otherwise dispose of any such debt except as therein provided.
TAKE FURTHER NOTICE that this notice also covers all property in which the judgment debtor has an interest hereafter coming into your possession or custody, and all debts hereafter coming due from you to the judgment debtor.

CIVIL PRACTICE LAW AND RULES

Section 5222.b Effect of restraint: prohibition of transfer; duration. A judgment debtor served with a restraining notice is forbidden to make or suffer any sale, assignment, transfer or interference with any property in which he has an interest, except upon direction of the sheriff or pursuant to an order of the court, until the judgment is satisfied or vacated. A restraining notice served upon a person other than the judgment debtor is effective only if, at the time of service, he owes a debt to the judgment debtor or he is in the possession or custody of property in which he knows or has reason to believe the judgment debtor has an interest, or if the judgment creditor has stated in the notice that a specified debt is owed by the person served to the judgment debtor or that the judgment debtor has an interest in specified property in the possession or custody of the person served. All property in which the judgment debtor is known or believed to have an interest then in and thereafter coming into the possession or custody of such a person, including any specified in the notice, and all debts of such a person, including any specified in the notice, then due and thereafter coming due to the judgment debtor, shall be subject to the notice. Such a person is forbidden to make or suffer any sale, assignment or transfer of, or any interference with any such property, or pay over or otherwise dispose of any such debt, to any person other than the sheriff, except upon direction of the sheriff or pursuant to an order of the court, until the expiration of one year after the notice is served upon him, or until the judgment is satisfied or vacated, whichever event first occurs. A judgment creditor who has specified personal property or debt in a restraining notice shall be liable to the owner of the property or the person to whom the debt is owed, if other than the judgment debtor, for any damages sustained by reason of the restraint. If a garnishee served with a restraining notice withholds the payment of money belonging or owed to the judgment debtor in an amount equal to twice the amount due on the judgment, the restraining notice is not effective as to other property or money.

TAKE NOTICE that disobedience of this Restraining Notice is punishable as a contempt of court.
WITNESS, Honorable one of the justices of our said court,
at the court house in the county of the day of 19 .

_____
The name signed must be printed beneath

Attorney(s) for Judgment Creditor(s):
Office and Post Office Address:

space provided if

THIS SUBPOENA REQUIRES YOUR PERSONAL APPEARANCE AT THE TIME AND PLACE SPECIFIED. FAILURE TO APPEAR MAY SUBJECT YOU TO FINE AND IMPRISONMENT FOR CONTEMPT OF COURT.

Forms may be purchased from Julius Blumberg, Inc., New York City 10013, or any of its dealers. Reproduction prohibited.

Ch. 8   **SUBPOENA (*DUCES TECUM*)**   § 8.51

Library References:
West's Key No. Digests, Execution ⚖=385.

§ 8.52 Forms—Information Subpoena

COURT
COUNTY OF _____ Index No. _____

Insert caption, venue and index number

against

Plaintiff

Defendant

INFORMATION SUBPOENA

Re: insert name
Judgment Debtor
Address: insert judgment debtor's address

The People of the State of New York

TO insert name of witness   The person to be examined
Address: insert witness address

GREETING:
WHEREAS, in an action in the name of the court of the State of New York county of insert between insert names of all parties as plaintiff and insert names of all parties as as defendant who are all the parties named in said action, a judgment was entered on insert date in favor of insert name of the judgment creditor and against insert name of the judgment debtor in the amount of $ judgment amount of which $ balance together with interest thereon from date of entry/payment remains due and unpaid; and
WHEREAS, the person to whom this subpoena is directed; resides; is regularly employed; has an office for the regular transaction of business in person; in insert county;

NOW, THEREFORE WE COMMAND YOU, that you answer in writing under oath, separately and fully, each question in the questionnaire accompanying this subpoena. each answer referring to the question to which it responds; and that you return the answers together with the original questions within 7 days after your receipt of the questions and this subpoena.
TAKE NOTICE that false swearing or failure to comply with this subpoena is punishable as a contempt of court.
_____ WITNESS, Honorable _____ one of the justices of our said court, at the court house in the county of _____ the _____ day of _____ .

N.B.: An attorney may issue this subpoena; this section is optional

The name signed must be printed beneath

Name of firm
Attorney(s) for Judgment Creditor:
Office and Post Office Address:
Address

Enclosed: Question form; original and copy. —— Use a form or prepare your own
Prepaid, addressed return envelope.

Forms may be purchased from Julius Blumberg, Inc., New York City 10013, or any of its dealers. Reproduction prohibited.

Ch. 8   INFORMATION SUBPOENA   § 8.52

Library References:

West's Key No. Digests, Execution ⇔390.

§ 8.53 Forms—Restraining Notice to Judgment Debtor

COURT
COUNTY OF _____   Index No. _____

Insert caption, venue and index number

against

Plaintiff

} RESTRAINING NOTICE TO JUDGMENT DEBTOR

Defendant

The People of the State of New York

TO   Insert the name of the   judgment debtor   GREETING:

WHEREAS, in an action in the **name of the** court of **the State of New York or foreign**
county of **insert** between **court if judgment was registered**
insert names of all parties as as plaintiff and
insert names of all parties as as defendant
who are all the parties named in said action, a judgment was entered on **insert date** in favor of
insert name of the judgment creditor and against
insert name of the judgment debtor
in the amount of $ **insert** of which $ **insert** together with interest thereon
from **date of entry/payment** remains due and unpaid;

TAKE NOTICE that pursuant to CPLR §5222(b), which is set forth in full herein, you are hereby forbidden to make or suffer any sale, assignment or transfer of, or any interference with any property in which you have an interest, except as therein provided.

CIVIL PRACTICE LAW AND RULES

Section 5222(b) Effect of restraint: prohibition of transfer; duration. A judgment debtor or obligor served with a restraining notice is forbidden to make or suffer any sale, assignment, transfer or interference with any property in which he or she has an interest, except upon direction of the sheriff or pursuant to an order of the court, until the judgment or order is satisfied or vacated. A restraining notice served upon a person other than the judgment debtor or obligor is effective only if, at the time of service, he or she owes a debt to the judgment debtor or obligor or he or she is in the possession or custody of property in which he or she knows or has reason to believe the judgment debtor or obligor has an interest, or if the judgment creditor or support collection unit has stated in the notice that a specified debt is owed by the person served to the judgment debtor or obligor or that the judgment debtor or obligor has an interest in specified property in the possession or custody of the person served. All property in which the judgment debtor or obligor is known or believed to have an interest then in and thereafter coming into the possession or custody of such a person, including any specified in the notice, and all debts of such a person, including any specified in the notice, then due and thereafter coming due to the judgment debtor or obligor, shall be subject to the notice. Such a person is forbidden to make or suffer any sale, assignment or transfer of, or any interference with, any such property, or pay over or otherwise dispose of any such debt, to any person other than the sheriff or the support collection unit, except upon direction of the sheriff or pursuant to an order of the court, until the expiration of one year after the notice is served upon him or her, or until the judgment or order is satisfied or vacated, whichever event first occurs. A judgment creditor or support collection unit which has specified personal property or debt in a restraining notice shall be liable to the owner of the property or the person to whom the debt is owed, if other than the judgment debtor or obligor, for any damages sustained by reason of the restraint. If a garnishee served with a restraining notice withholds the payment of money belonging or owed to the judgment debtor or obligor in an amount equal to twice the amount due on the judgment or order, the restraining notice is not effective as to other property or money.

TAKE FURTHER NOTICE that disobedience of this Restraining Notice is punishable as a contempt of court.

Dated: **insert**   The name signed must be printed beneath

Insert name and address of firm
Attorney(s) for Judgment Creditor:
Office and Post Office Address:

Forms may be purchased from Julius Blumberg, Inc., New York City 10013, or any of its dealers. Reproduction prohibited.

Ch. 8 RESTRAINING NOTICE TO JUDGMENT DEBTOR § 8.53

SERVICE BY PERSONAL DELIVERY

State of New York, County of   ss.:

being duly sworn, deposes and says: that deponent is not a party to the action, is over 18 years of age and resides at:

That on
at No.

deponent served the within Restraining Notice on

strike out either (a) or (b)

(a) judgment debtor therein named, by delivering a true copy to said judgment debtor personally; deponent knew the person so served to be the person described as said judgment debtor therein.

(b) a   corporation, judgment debtor therein named, by delivering a true copy to   personally,

deponent knew said corporation so served to be the the corporation described in said restraining notice as said judgment debtor and knew said individual to be
thereof.

Sworn to before me on

SERVICE BY REGISTERED OR CERTIFIED MAIL

State of New York, County of   ss.:

being duly sworn, deposes and says: that deponent is not a party to the action, is over 18 years of age and resides at

On
deponent served the within Restraining Notice on

judgment debtor by mailing a copy of same in a securely sealed postpaid wrapper properly addressed to the judgment debtor at

strike out either (a) or (b)

(a) by registered mail, return receipt requested. Deponent delivered said wrapper in the Registry Clerk at a United States post office department within the State of New York, and the requisite fee, and obtained Receipt No.
of such mailing which is attached hereto.

(b) by certified mail, return receipt requested. Deponent deposited said wrapper with the requisite postage and return receipt card affixed in a post office official depository under the care and custody of the United States Postal Service within the State of New York.

Sworn to before me on

Index No.
                                                COURT
COUNTY OF

                                   Plaintiff
          against
                                   Defendant

Restraining Notice
TO JUDGMENT DEBTOR
Enforcement of Money Judgment

Attorney(s) for Judgment Creditor
Office and Post Office Address

245

§ 8.54 ENFORCEMENT OF MONEY JUDGMENTS   Ch. 8

§ 8.54 Forms—Execution

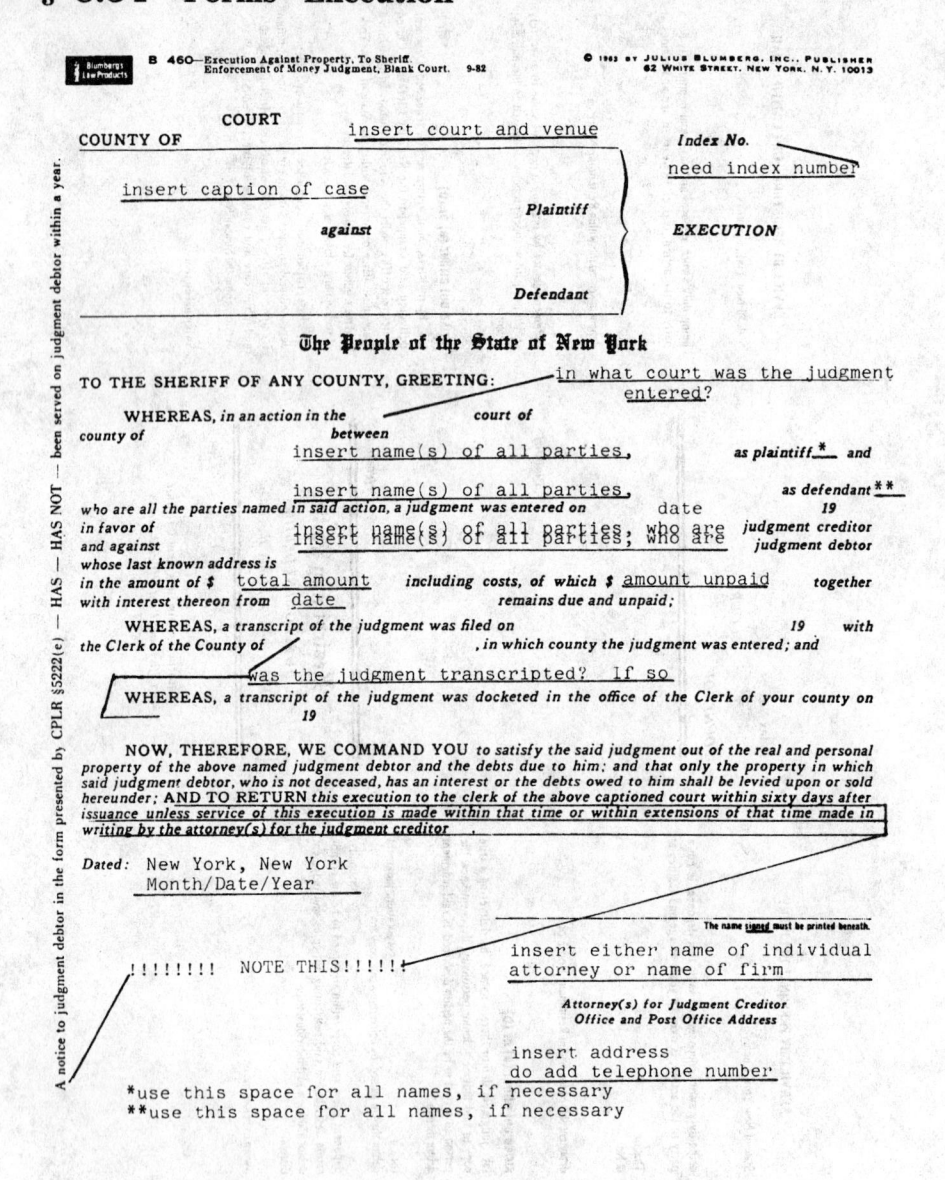

B 460—Execution Against Property, To Sheriff. Enforcement of Money Judgment, Blank Court. 9-82
© 1983 BY JULIUS BLUMBERG, INC., PUBLISHER
62 WHITE STREET, NEW YORK, N.Y. 10013

COURT _insert court and venue_
COUNTY OF

insert caption of case

Plaintiff

against

Defendant

Index No.   _need index number_

EXECUTION

The People of the State of New York

TO THE SHERIFF OF ANY COUNTY, GREETING: _in what court was the judgment entered?_

WHEREAS, *in an action in the* _____ *court of* _____ *county of* _____ *between* _insert name(s) of all parties,_ *as plaintiff* * and _insert name(s) of all parties,_ *as defendant* ** *who are all the parties named in said action, a judgment was entered on* _date_ *19* _____ *in favor of* _insert name(s) of all parties; who are_ *judgment creditor* *and against* *judgment debtor* *whose last known address is* _____ *in the amount of $* _total amount_ *including costs, of which $* _amount unpaid_ *together with interest thereon from* _date_ *remains due and unpaid;*

WHEREAS, *a transcript of the judgment was filed on* _____ *19* _____ *with the Clerk of the County of* _____ *, in which county the judgment was entered; and*

was the judgment transcripted? If so

WHEREAS, *a transcript of the judgment was docketed in the office of the Clerk of your county on* _____ *19*

NOW, THEREFORE, WE COMMAND YOU *to satisfy the said judgment out of the real and personal property of the above named judgment debtor and the debts due to him; and that only the property in which said judgment debtor, who is not deceased, has an interest or the debts owed to him shall be levied upon or sold hereunder; AND TO RETURN this execution to the clerk of the above captioned court within sixty days after issuance unless service of this execution is made within that time or within extensions of that time made in writing by the attorney(s) for the judgment creditor* _____ *.*

Dated: New York, New York
Month/Date/Year

!!!!!!!! NOTE THIS!!!!!!

The name signed must be printed beneath.

insert either name of individual attorney or name of firm

Attorney(s) for Judgment Creditor
Office and Post Office Address

insert address
do add telephone number

*use this space for all names, if necessary
**use this space for all names, if necessary

(left margin: A notice to judgment debtor in the form presented by CPLR §5222(e) — HAS — HAS NOT — been served on judgment debtor within a year.)

Forms may be purchased from Julius Blumberg, Inc., New York City 10013, or any of its dealers. Reproduction prohibited.

Library References:

West's Key No. Digests, Execution ⚖︎59–105.

246

§ 8.55 Forms—Income Execution

T 439—Income Execution CPLR § 5231
Blank C. url, 10-96

insert name and venue of the court   Index No. insert

Judgment Creditor(s)   Insert names

Income Execution

Judgment Debtor(s) (name and last known address)

The People of the State of New York

Insert all information

TO THE ENFORCEMENT OFFICER, GREETING:

The Enforcement Officer is the Sheriff, Marshal of the City or Constable of the Town or Village authorized by law to enforce money executions.

A judgment was entered in the within court in favor of the Judgment Creditor(s) and the particulars are as follows:

Court of Original Entry	Entry Date	Original Amount	Amount Due	Plus Interest From
insert	date	amount	due	date

The Judgment was recovered against insert name of the defendant(s) and transcripted with the Clerk of [if applicable] County on date

This execution is issued against insert name of the judgment debtor whose last known address is insert
whose social security number is [if known]   and who is receiving or will receive $ [if known] for each [if known] pay period from the Employer. "Employer," herein, includes any payor of money to Judgment Debtor. The Employer's name and address is insert all information

You are directed to satisfy the judgment with interest together with your fees and expenses, out of all monies now and hereafter due and owing to the Judgment Debtor from the Employer pursuant to CPLR § 5231.

Directions to Judgment Debtor: You are notified and commanded immediately to start paying to the Enforcement Officer serving a copy of this Income Execution or you installments amounting to 10% (but no more than the Federal limits set forth in I. Limitations on the amount that can be withheld, below) of any and all salary, wages or other income, including any and all overtime earnings, commissions or other irregular compensation received or hereafter to be received from your Employer and to continue paying such installments until the judgment with interest and the fees and expenses of this Income Execution are fully paid and satisfied, and if you fail to do so within 20 days this Income Execution will be served upon the Employer by the Enforcement Officer.

Directions to the Employer: You are commanded to withhold and pay over to the Enforcement Officer serving a copy of this Income Execution on you installments amounting to 10% (but no more than the Federal limits set forth in I. Limitations on the amount that can be withheld, below) of any and all salary, wages or other income, including any and all overtime earnings, commissions or other irregular compensation now or hereafter becoming due to Judgment Debtor until the judgment with interest and the fees and expenses of this Income Execution are fully paid and satisfied.

Dated   insert   The name signed must be printed beneath

Insert name of law firm
Office and Post Office Address
address and
telephone

Important Statement

This income execution directs the withholding of up to 10 percent of the judgment debtor's gross income. In certain cases, however, state or federal law does not permit the withholding of that much of the judgment debtor's gross income. The judgment debtor is referred to New York Civil Practice Law and Rules § 5231 and 15 United States Code § 1671 et seq.

I. Limitations on the amount that can be withheld

A. An income execution for installments from a judgment debtor's gross income cannot exceed ten percent (10%) of the judgment debtor's gross income.

B. If a judgment debtor's weekly disposable earnings are less than thirty (30) times the current federal minimum wage ($4.75* per hour), or $142.50* no deduction can be made from the judgment debtor's earnings under this income execution.

C. A judgment debtor's weekly disposable earnings cannot be reduced below the amount arrived at by multiplying thirty (30) times the current minimum wage ($4.75* per hour), or $142.50* under this income execution.

Forms may be purchased from Julius Blumberg, Inc., New York City 10013, or any of its dealers. Reproduction prohibited.

§ 8.55   ENFORCEMENT OF MONEY JUDGMENTS   Ch. 8

D. If deductions are being made from a judgment debtor's earnings under any orders for alimony, support or maintenance for family members or former spouses, and those deductions equal or exceed twenty-five percent (25%) of the judgment debtor's disposable earnings, no deduction can be made from the judgment debtor's earnings under this income execution.

E. If deductions are being made from a judgment debtor's earnings under any orders for alimony, support or maintenance for family members or former spouses, and those deductions are less than twenty-five percent (25%) of the judgment debtor's disposable earnings, deductions may be made from the judgment debtor's earnings under this income execution. However, the amount arrived at by adding the deductions from earnings made under this execution to the deductions made from earnings under any orders for alimony, support or maintenance for family members or former spouses cannot exceed twenty-five percent (25%) of the judgment debtor's disposable earnings.

NOTE: Nothing in this notice limits the proportion or amount which may be deducted under any order for alimony, support or maintenance for family members or former spouses.

II. Explanation of limitations

Definitions

Disposable Earnings — Disposable earnings are that part of an individual's earnings left after deducting those amounts that are required by law to be withheld (for example, taxes, social security and unemployment insurance, but not deductions for union dues, insurance plans, etc.).

Gross Income — Gross income is salary, wages or other income, including any and all overtime earnings, commissions, and income from trusts, before any deductions are made from such income.

Illustrations regarding earnings:

If disposable earnings is:	Amount to pay or deduct from earnings under this income execution is:
(a) 30 times federal minimum wage ($142.50*) or less	No payment or deduction allowed.
(b) more than 30 times federal minimum wage ($142.50*) and less than 40 times federal minimum wage ($190.00*)	The lesser of: the excess over 30 times the federal minimum wage ($142.50*) in disposable earnings, or 10% of gross earnings.
(c) 40 times the federal minimum wage ($190.00*) or more	The lesser of: 25% of disposable earnings or 10% of gross earnings.

III. Notice: You may be able to challenge this income execution through the procedures provided in CPLR § 5231(i) and CPLR § 5240.

If you think that the amount of your income being deducted under this income execution exceeds the amount permitted by state or federal law, you should act promptly because the money will be applied to the judgment. If you claim that the amount of your income being deducted under this income execution exceeds the amount permitted by state or federal law, you should contact your employer or other person paying your income. Further, YOU MAY CONSULT AN ATTORNEY, INCLUDING LEGAL AID IF YOU QUALIFY. New York State law provides two procedures through which an income execution can be challenged.

CPLR § 5231(i) Modification. At any time, the judgment debtor may make a motion to a court for an order modifying an income execution.

CPLR § 5240 Modification or protective order; supervision of enforcement. At any time, the judgment debtor may make a motion to a court for an order denying, limiting, conditioning, regulating, extending or modifying the use of any post-judgment enforcement procedure, including the use of income executions.

*Based upon $4.75 minimum wage effective October 1, 1996. Minimum wage will increase to $5.15 on September 1, 1997. Recalculate and insert correct figures when the minimum wage changes.

Return (for Sheriff's or Marshal's use only)

☐ Fully satisfied .... 19 ...   ☐ Unsatisfied
☐ Partially satisfied .... 19 ... $ ....

☐ Because I was unable to find the Garnishee (the Employer) within my jurisdiction I returned this Income Execution to Judgment Creditor's Attorney on .... 19 ....

Date and time received: ....
☐ Marshal, City of ....
☐ Sheriff, County of ....
☐ Constable of the ☐ Town ☐ Village of ....

Library References:

West's Key No. Digests, Execution ⚘420.5; Garnishment ⚘7.

§ 8.56 FORMS—Affirmation and Order to Show Cause to Punish Judgment Debtor—Witness For Contempt

SUPREME COURT OF THE STATE OF NEW YORK
COUNTY OF WESTCHESTER

_____)
)
_____,)
) Index No.
                Plaintiff,   )
)
        -against-   ) AFFIRMATION IN
) SUPPORT OF ORDER
) TO SHOW CAUSE
)
_____,)
)
                Defendants.   )

[ATTORNEY], an attorney admitted to practice before the courts of the State of New York, affirms the following to be true under penalties of perjury pursuant to CPLR 2106:

1. I am associated with _____, attorneys for the judgment creditor herein, Judgment Creditor ("Creditor"). I make and respectfully submit this Affirmation in support of Creditor's motion, by Order to Show Cause, why this Court should not find [Witness] in contempt of Court. I have been duly authorized by Creditor to bring this proceeding on his behalf.

2. In accordance with the December 17, 1992 Order of this Court (which was adhered to in this Court's January 20, 1993 Order following defendants' Motion for Reconsideration[1]), judgment was entered against the defendants on December 22, 1992 in the amount of $43,035.12.

3. On February 26, 1993, an Information Subpoena (the "Subpoena"), a copy of which is annexed hereto as Exhibit B, was duly issued from this Court requiring [Witness] to answer in writing under oath certain written questions accompanying the Subpoena relevant to the satisfaction of the judgment referred to in the Subpoena. As set forth in the affidavit of service on the reverse of the Subpoena, the Subpoena was served, together with questions in duplicate, along with a prepaid, self-addressed, return envelope on [Witness] by certified mail, return receipt requested.

§ 8.56
1. Copies of both Orders are annexed hereto as Exhibit A.

4. No answer to the written questions has been received by your affirmant, although more than seven days have elapsed since the date of the witness's receipt thereof, as appears from the Post Office return receipt, a copy of which is annexed hereto as Exhibit C.

5. In lieu of answering the written questions, [*Witness*] forwarded a letter to your affirmant under date of March 2, 1993 in which he "decline[d] to answer the questions asked upon my clients' refusal to waive the attorney-client privilege." In response, your affirmant forwarded a letter under date of March 8, 1993 advising [*Witness*] of Creditor's intention to move before this Court for a finding of contempt since [*Witness*] failed to answer even one of the written questions presented. Copies of both letters are annexed hereto as Exhibit D.

6. By virtue of his failure to answer even one of the questions posed to him, it is clear that the conduct of [*Witness*] was calculated to and actually did defeat, impair, impede and prejudice the rights and remedies of Creditor in that Creditor has been unable obtain information on matters relevant to the satisfaction of the judgment as authorized by law.

7. Further, the cases cited in my March 8 letter (Exhibit D) make it abundantly clear that the attorney client privilege may not be invoked *vis-a-vis* the interrogatories posed to [*Witness*]. His receipt of the letter is established by the facsimile conformation report annexed to the exhibit. Accordingly, the costs of this motion, at a minimum, should be imposed, although sanctions, it is respectfully submitted, is the more appropriate remedy for frivolous conduct.

8. No previous application for the relief requested herein has been made to this or any other Court.

WHEREFORE, your affirmant respectfully requests an Order of this Court requiring [*Witness*] to show cause why he should not be punished for contempt and granting to Creditor such other, further and different relief as to the Court may seem just and proper, together with the costs of this motion.

Dated: New York, New York

_____, 199__

[*ATTORNEY*]

Ch. 8 WITNESS FOR CONTEMPT § 8.56

WARNING:

PLEASE TAKE NOTICE THAT THE PURPOSE OF THIS HEARING IS TO PUNISH THE ACCUSED FOR CONTEMPT OF COURT AND SUCH PUNISHMENT MAY CONSIST OF FINE OR IMPRISONMENT, OR BOTH, ACCORDING TO LAW.

WARNING:

YOUR FAILURE TO APPEAR IN COURT MAY RESULT IN YOUR IMMEDIATE ARREST AND IMPRISONMENT FOR CONTEMPT OF COURT

At an IA Part of the Supreme Court of the State of New York held at the Courthouse, located at _____ Street, _____, New York, on the _____ day of _____, 199__.

PRESENT: HON. _____
               Justice.

_____

     _____,) Index No.

                Plaintiff,) ORDER TO SHOW CAUSE
) WHY [*WITNESS*] SHOULD
       -against-) NOT BE PUNISHED BY
) FINE, IMPRISONMENT, OR
  _____,) BOTH FOR CONTEMPT
) OF COURT
             Defendants.)

_____

Upon reading and filing the annexed Affirmation of [*Attorney*] dated _____, 199__, the exhibits annexed thereto (including the Information Subpoena and affidavit showing due service of both the subpoena and accompanying questions upon [*Witness*]) by which it appears that [*Witness*] failed to comply with said Subpoena;

Now, on motion of [*firm name*], attorneys for the judgment creditor, it is hereby

ORDERED, that [*Witness*] appear before this Court at the Supreme Court of the State of New York, County of _____, Room ___, to be held at the Courthouse, _____ Street, _____, New York, on March __, 19__, at __ a.m./p.m. of that day, or as soon thereafter as counsel may be heard, and show cause why [*Witness*] should not be punished as a contemnor for violation of and noncompliance with the said Information Subpoena in that he failed to answer the questions served with the Information Subpoena and why he should not pay the costs of this motion, and why the judgment creditor should not have such other, further and different relief as may be proper.

Sufficient cause appearing therefor, let personal service of a copy of this Order and the papers upon which it is based on [*Witness*] at _____, _____, New York, on or before _____, 199__ be deemed good and sufficient notice of this application.

ENTER:

_____
J.S.C.

Library References:
West's Key No. Digests, Execution ⟶416.

Chapter 9

BANKRUPTCY

by
Jeffrey L. Tanenbaum
John J. Rapisardi
Jacqueline B. Stuart

Table of Sections

9.1	Scope Note.
9.2	Strategy.
9.3	⎯⎯ Checklist for Representing a Debtor.
9.4	⎯⎯ Checklist for Representing a Creditor.
9.5	Governing Law.
9.6	Nature of Cases Under Each Chapter of the Bankruptcy Code.
9.7	Eligibility to File.
9.8	Commencement of a Case—Voluntary Cases.
9.9	⎯⎯ Involuntary Cases.
9.10	⎯⎯ ⎯⎯ Procedure.
9.11	⎯⎯ Additional Requirements.
9.12	⎯⎯ First–Day Orders.
9.13	Joint Administration.
9.14	Substantive Consolidation.
9.15	Types of Proceedings in Cases Under the Bankruptcy Code.
9.16	⎯⎯ Adversary Proceedings.
9.17	⎯⎯ Contested Matters.
9.18	Jurisdiction of the Bankruptcy Court.
9.19	⎯⎯ Types of Jurisdiction.
9.20	⎯⎯ Case Ancillary to Foreign Proceedings.
9.21	Venue.
9.22	Withdrawal of Reference.
9.23	Abstention.
9.24	Removal.
9.25	Appeals—To District Court and Bankruptcy Appellate Panel From Bankruptcy Court.
9.26	⎯⎯ To Court of Appeals From District Court.
9.27	The Debtor in Possession.
9.28	⎯⎯ Rights, Powers and Duties.
9.29	Employment of Professionals.
9.30	⎯⎯ Compensation.
9.31	⎯⎯ ⎯⎯ Fee Applications.
9.32	U.S. Trustee.
9.33	⎯⎯ Duties Owed by Debtors and Trustees.

BANKRUPTCY Ch. 9

9.34 Bankruptcy Trustee.
9.35 Mediators.
9.36 Creditors.
9.37 ___ Meeting of Creditors.
9.38 ___ ___ Scope of Examination.
9.39 Examinations Under Bankruptcy Rule 2004.
9.40 ___ Notice Requirements.
9.41 ___ Subpoena.
9.42 Right of Parties in Interest to Be Heard.
9.43 Statutory Committees.
9.44 ___ Function and Duties.
9.45 ___ Right to Bring Litigation.
9.46 ___ Fiduciary Duty.
9.47 ___ Removal of Members.
9.48 ___ Organizational Meeting.
9.49 Property of the Estate.
9.50 Automatic Stay.
9.51 ___ Exceptions.
9.52 ___ Obtaining Relief.
9.53 ___ ___ Strategy.
9.54 ___ ___ Hearing.
9.55 ___ ___ Single Asset Real Estate Debtor.
9.56 Adequate Protection.
9.57 ___ Types.
9.58 ___ Strategy.
9.59 ___ Objections and Hearing.
9.60 Use, Sale, or Lease of Property.
9.61 ___ Ordinary Course of Business.
9.62 ___ Outside Ordinary Course of Business.
9.63 ___ Sales Free and Clear of Liens.
9.64 ___ Appeals from Order Authorizing Sale.
9.65 Cash Collateral.
9.66 ___ Strategy.
9.67 ___ Hearing.
9.68 ___ Postpetition Proceeds.
9.69 ___ ___ Security Interests in Rents and Hotel Revenues.
9.70 Abandonment of Property.
9.71 Postpetition Financing.
9.72 ___ Hearing.
9.73 ___ Appeals From Order Authorizing.
9.74 Executory Contracts and Unexpired Leases.
9.75 ___ Strategy.
9.76 ___ Time for Assumption or Rejection.
9.77 ___ Nonresidential Real Property Leases.
9.78 ___ Assumption by the Debtor.
9.79 ___ Assumption and Assignment.
9.80 ___ Exceptions to Assumption and Assignment.
9.81 ___ Rejection by Debtor.
9.82 ___ Damages Arising From Rejection: Debtor as Tenant/Lessee.
9.83 ___ Calculation of Allowed Real Property Lease Rejection Damages.
9.84 ___ Debtor as Landlord/Lessor.

254

Ch. 9 BANKRUPTCY

9.85 ____ Unexpired Personal Property Leases.
9.86 Collective Bargaining Agreements.
9.87 Retired Employees' Insurance Benefits.
9.88 ____ Procedure for Modifying.
9.89 Utility Services.
9.90 Claims Procedures.
9.91 ____ Filing Proofs of Claim or Interest.
9.92 ____ ____ Bar Dates.
9.93 ____ Late–Filed Proofs of Claim.
9.94 ____ Amendment of Proofs of Claim or Interest.
9.95 ____ Withdrawal of Claims.
9.96 ____ Allowance of, and Objections to, Claims or Interests.
9.97 ____ Compromise and Settlement of Claims.
9.98 ____ Allowance of Administrative Expense Claims.
9.99 ____ Secured Claims.
9.100 ____ ____ Bifurcation of Claims.
9.101 ____ ____ Avoidance of Liens.
9.102 ____ Interest on Claims and Charges Against Secured Claims.
9.103 ____ Valuation of Collateral.
9.104 ____ ____ Methods of Valuation.
9.105 ____ Reclamation Claims.
9.106 Priorities.
9.107 Subordination.
9.108 ____ Strategy.
9.109 Setoff.
9.110 ____ Strategy.
9.111 ____ Characteristics of Claims.
9.112 Recoupment.
9.113 The Avoiding Powers.
9.114 ____ Strategy.
9.115 ____ Strong Arm Powers.
9.116 ____ Avoidance of Certain Statutory Liens.
9.117 ____ Preferences.
9.118 ____ Exceptions to the Avoidance of Preferential Transfers.
9.119 ____ Fraudulent Conveyances.
9.120 ____ Liability of Transferee of Avoided Transfer.
9.121 ____ Statute of Limitations and Standing.
9.122 ____ Relation–Back Provision.
9.123 ____ Reclamation.
9.124 Return of Goods by Debtor.
9.125 Exemptions.
9.126 ____ Procedure.
9.127 ____ Objections.
9.128 ____ Lien Avoidance.
9.129 ____ Liens on Exempt Property.
9.130 Reaffirmation of Debts.
9.131 ____ Strategy.
9.132 Protection Against Discriminatory Treatment.
9.133 Tax Considerations.
9.134 Conversion and Dismissal of Cases Under Title 11.
9.135 Effect of Conversion.

255

9.136	Effect of Dismissal.
9.137	Closing and Reopening Cases.
9.138	Chapter 11—Appointment of a Trustee.
9.139	____ Duties of a Trustee.
9.140	____ Appointment of an Examiner.
9.141	____ Duties of an Examiner.
9.142	____ Exclusivity—Right to File a Plan.
9.143	____ ____ Small Businesses.
9.144	____ ____ Strategy: Representing a Debtor.
9.145	____ ____ Strategy: Representing a Creditor.
9.146	____ ____ Appealability of Orders.
9.147	____ Plan.
9.148	____ ____ Mandatory Provisions.
9.149	____ ____ Discretionary Provisions.
9.150	____ ____ Exemption from Securities Registration.
9.151	____ ____ Retention of Jurisdiction by the Court.
9.152	____ Classification of Claims.
9.153	____ ____ Effect on Voting.
9.154	____ ____ Substantially Similar Claims.
9.155	____ ____ Convenience Class.
9.156	____ Recourse and Nonrecourse Claims: The § 1111(b) Election.
9.157	____ ____ Strategy.
9.158	____ Impairment of Claims or Interests.
9.159	____ ____ Rights Are Altered.
9.160	____ ____ Defaults Are Not Cured.
9.161	____ Disclosure and Solicitation.
9.162	____ Acceptance of a Plan.
9.163	____ Prepackaged and Prenegotiated Plans.
9.164	____ Modification of a Plan.
9.165	____ Confirmation.
9.166	____ Cramdown.
9.167	____ Effect of Confirmation.
9.168	____ Discharge.
9.169	____ ____ Limitations.
9.170	____ ____ Release of Nondebtor.
9.171	____ Channelling Injunctions: Asbestos–Related Cases.
9.172	____ Plan Implementation.
9.173	____ Small Business Reorganizations.
9.174	____ Conversion or Dismissal of Cases.
9.175	____ ____ Procedure.
9.176	____ Closing and Reopening Cases.
9.177	Chapter 7—Overview.
9.178	____ Commencement of a Case.
9.179	____ Fees.
9.180	____ Appointment of an Interim Trustee.
9.181	____ Election of a Permanent Trustee.
9.182	____ Duties of a Trustee.
9.183	____ Employment of Professionals.
9.184	____ Creditors' Committee.
9.185	____ Protection Against Discriminatory Treatment.
9.186	____ The Debtor's Statement of Intention.

Ch. 9   BANKRUPTCY

9.187 ____ Exemptions.
9.188 ____ Redemption of Property.
9.189 ____ ____ Procedure.
9.190 ____ Reaffirmation of Debts.
9.191 ____ Abandonment of Property.
9.192 ____ Debtor's Surrender of Property and Records.
9.193 ____ Trustee's Turnover Powers.
9.194 ____ Liability of General Partners.
9.195 ____ Trustee's Operation of the Business.
9.196 ____ Executory Contracts.
9.197 ____ Adversary Proceedings to Avoid Liens and Transfers.
9.198 ____ ____ Statute of Limitations.
9.199 ____ Treatment of Certain Liens.
9.200 ____ Trustee's Sale of Assets.
9.201 ____ Disposition of Property Subject to the Interest of Another.
9.202 ____ Priorities.
9.203 ____ Special Tax Provisions.
9.204 ____ Discharge.
9.205 ____ ____ Exceptions to General Discharge of the Debtor.
9.206 ____ ____ Procedure for Objections to General Discharge of the Debtor.
9.207 ____ ____ Exceptions to Discharge of Particular Debts.
9.208 ____ ____ Procedure for Objections to Discharge of Particular Debts.
9.209 ____ Conversion or Dismissal of Cases.
9.210 ____ ____ Procedure.
9.211 ____ Closing and Reopening Cases.
9.212 Chapter 12—Overview.
9.213 ____ Rights and Powers of Debtor.
9.214 ____ Appointment of a Trustee.
9.215 ____ Duties of a Trustee.
9.216 ____ Automatic Stay.
9.217 ____ Property of the Estate.
9.218 ____ Sales Free of Interests.
9.219 ____ Adequate Protection.
9.220 ____ Exclusivity—Right to File a Plan.
9.221 ____ Plan.
9.222 ____ ____ Mandatory Provisions.
9.223 ____ ____ Discretionary Provisions.
9.224 ____ ____ Modification.
9.225 ____ ____ Confirmation.
9.226 ____ ____ Confirmation: Objections.
9.227 ____ Disbursements.
9.228 ____ Effect of Confirmation.
9.229 ____ Discharge.
9.230 ____ Modification after Confirmation.
9.231 ____ Special Tax Provisions.
9.232 ____ Revocation of Confirmation Order.
9.233 ____ Conversion or Dismissal of Cases.
9.234 ____ ____ Procedure.
9.235 ____ Closing and Reopening Cases.
9.236 Chapter 13—Overview.
9.237 ____ Eligibility.

9.238	____ Rights and Powers of Debtor.
9.239	____ Appointment of a Trustee.
9.240	____ Duties of a Trustee.
9.241	____ Automatic Stay.
9.242	____ ____ Relief.
9.243	____ Property of the Estate.
9.244	____ ____ Use, Sale, or Lease.
9.245	____ Exclusivity—Right to File a Plan.
9.246	____ Plan.
9.247	____ ____ Mandatory Provisions.
9.248	____ ____ Discretionary Provisions.
9.249	____ ____ Discretionary Provisions: Debtor's Principal Residence.
9.250	____ ____ Modification.
9.251	____ ____ Confirmation.
9.252	____ ____ Confirmation: Objections.
9.253	____ ____ Confirmation: Effect.
9.254	____ Payments.
9.255	____ Discharge.
9.256	____ ____ Exceptions.
9.257	____ ____ Objections.
9.258	____ ____ Revocation.
9.259	____ Postconfirmation Modification of a Plan.
9.260	____ Revocation of Confirmation Order.
9.261	____ Conversion or Dismissal of Cases.
9.262	____ ____ Procedure.
9.263	____ Closing and Reopening Cases.
9.264	Procedural Checklist—Commencing a Voluntary Case.
9.265	____ Lists and Schedules to be Filed at the Commencement of a Case Under Chapter 7, 11, 12, or 13.
9.266	____ Commencing an Adversary Proceeding.
9.267	____ Commencing a Contested Matter.
9.268	____ Appeal from an Interlocutory Judgment, Order, or Decree of a Bankruptcy Judge.
9.269	____ Creditor's Motion to Request Relief from the Automatic Stay.
9.270	____ Creditor's Motion to Obtain Adequate Protection.
9.271	____ Debtor's Motion to Use, Sell, or Lease Property of the Estate.
9.272	____ Debtor's Motion to Request Use of Cash Collateral.
9.273	____ Cash Collateral Stipulation.
9.274	____ Debtor's Motion to Obtain Postpetition Financing.
9.275	____ Request to Assume, Reject, or Assign an Executory Contract or Unexpired Nonresidential Real Property Lease.
9.276	____ Debtor's Motion to Reject or Modify a Collective Bargaining Agreement.
9.277	____ Debtor's Motion to Obtain Approval of a Compromise and Settlement of a Claim.
9.278	____ Claiming Exemptions.
9.279	____ Debtor's Motion to Avoid a Judicial Lien or a Nonpossessory, Nonpurchase–Money Security Interest that Impairs Exempt Property.
9.280	____ Debtor's Motion to Obtain Court Approval of a Reaffirmation Agreement.

9.281 ____ Debtor's Motion to Request an Extension of Exclusivity.
9.282 ____ Filing a Chapter 11 Plan and Disclosure Statement.
9.283 ____ Soliciting Acceptance of a Chapter 11 Plan.
9.284 ____ Filing a Chapter 12 or 13 Plan of Debt Adjustment.
9.285 ____ Objection to a Chapter 12 or 13 Plan.
9.286 ____ Debtor's Motion to Request Modification of a Chapter 12 or 13 Plan after Confirmation
9.287 Drafting Checklist—General Rules for all Motions, Applications, and Complaints.
9.288 ____ Complaint in an Adversary Proceeding.
9.289 ____ Motion for Leave to Appeal From an Interlocutory Judgment, Order, or Decree of a Bankruptcy Judge.
9.290 ____ Motion for a Stay of a Bankruptcy Court Judgment or Order Pending Appeal.
9.291 ____ Application of Debtor or Statutory Committee to Retain Professionals.
9.292 ____ Creditor's Motion to Request Relief From the Automatic Stay.
9.293 ____ Creditor's Motion to Obtain Adequate Protection.
9.294 ____ Debtor's Motion to Use, Sell, or Lease Property of the Estate.
9.295 ____ Debtor's Motion to Request Use of Cash Collateral.
9.296 ____ Cash Collateral Stipulation.
9.297 ____ Debtor's Motion to Obtain Postpetition Financing.
9.298 ____ Motion to Assume or Reject an Executory Contract or Unexpired Non-residential Real Property Lease.
9.299 ____ Debtor's Motion to Reject or Modify a Collective Bargaining Agreement (CBA).
9.300 ____ Debtor's Motion to Obtain Approval of a Compromise and Settlement of a Claim.
9.301 ____ Debtor's Motion to Avoid a Judicial Lien or a Nonpossessory, Nonpurchase–Money Security Interest that Impairs Exempt Property.
9.302 ____ Reaffirmation Agreement.
9.303 ____ Debtor's Motion for Approval of a Reaffirmation Agreement.
9.304 ____ Debtor's Motion to Request an Extension of Exclusivity.
9.305 Forms—Notice of Appearance and Demand for Service of Documents.
9.306 ____ Contested Matter—Motion.
9.307 ____ ____ Notice of Motion.
9.308 ____ ____ Proposed Order.
9.309 ____ Adversary Proceeding—Complaint.
9.310 ____ Retention of Professionals—Application.
9.311 ____ ____ Affidavit.
9.312 ____ Plan Provision for Retention of Jurisdiction.

WESTLAW Electronic Research

See WESTLAW Electronic Research Guide preceding the Summary of Contents.

§ 9.1 Scope Note

This chapter provides a basic guide through the substantive and procedural aspects of federal bankruptcy law under chapters 7, 11, 12, and 13 of title 11, commonly known as the Bankruptcy Code.[1] The Bankruptcy Code is a federal statute and is intended to preempt state or other federal laws on the subject of bankruptcy law. However, bankruptcy problems and issues often implicate other disciplines, such as tax, real estate, labor, securities, and environmental law, as well as accounting and financial reporting. In many situations, the rights of parties and the debtor are defined by state law and other federal laws and, in some cases, the goals of the state and federal laws may conflict with the policy goals of the Bankruptcy Code. In such cases, courts frequently have been called upon to decide which competing policy or interest should prevail.

In understanding the interplay of federal bankruptcy law with other areas of the law, one must keep in mind Congress' policy goals in enacting the Bankruptcy Code: (i) equality of distribution among creditors holding claims of equal rank against the debtor and (ii) orderly rehabilitation or liquidation.[2]

Sources of governing law that must be consulted in addition to the Bankruptcy Code are discussed in Section 9.5. In representing a client under financial duress, the initial step must be a consideration of the options that may be available—whether out of court, under state law, or under the federal Bankruptcy Code—in order to assist the client in determining what is the best option. Overall strategy is discussed in Section 9.2 and checklists of issues to consider when representing a debtor or a creditor may be found in Sections 9.3 and 9.4, respectively.

The nature of the relief available and the eligibility requirements for filing under each of chapters 7, 11, 12, and 13 are covered in Sections 9.6–9.7. Many of the restrictions imposed by the Bankruptcy Code as well as the protections it offers to a debtor are applicable under all the chapters of the Bankruptcy Code. The common elements of cases under all chapters of the Code are covered in Sections 9.2–9.137; and, where appropriate, the applicability of particular Code sections to a case under different chapters of the Code is distinguished.

While the Bankruptcy Code offers significant relief to parties burdened by severe financial pressures, one of the prices of that relief is complete financial disclosure. Accordingly, extensive and stringent requirements for disclosure are imposed on any entity upon filing for bankruptcy relief. The process of commencing both voluntary and involuntary cases under the Bankruptcy Code and the various lists, schedules, and "first-day" orders that must be filed are discussed in Sections 9.8–9.12. When more than one related debtor files, counsel and clients should consider whether to seek joint administration for the sake of efficiency and convenience, or even substantive consolidation. Sections 9.13 and 9.14 cover these issues.

§ 9.1
1. 11 U.S.C.A. §§ 101–1330.

2. H.R.Rep.No. 95–595, 95th Cong., 1st Sess. 16, 177–78, 220 (1977).

Any entity that is a debtor under the Bankruptcy Code is subject to the continuous supervision of the bankruptcy court. In that regard, the principal types of court proceedings under the Bankruptcy Code, contested matters and adversary proceedings, are discussed in Sections 9.15–9.17. Jurisdiction of the bankruptcy court and other important procedural matters are covered in Sections 9.18–9.24. Appeals are discussed in Sections 9.25 and 9.26.

In most cases, the individual or entity that seeks relief under the Bankruptcy Code assumes the status of a debtor in possession upon commencement of the case. What this means, and the rights, powers, and duties of the debtor in possession are discussed in Sections 9.27 and 9.28. The debtor's employment of professionals, including counsel, and the provisions regulating their engagement and compensation are covered in Sections 9.29–9.31. A filing under the Bankruptcy Code involves not only the court, but brings a number of other participants into the debtor's affairs. Other possible players—the United States trustee, an operating trustee, an examiner, or mediators, are discussed in Sections 9.32–9.35.

The most important participants in a case under the Bankruptcy Code, in addition to the debtor, are its creditors. The rights of creditors to obtain information from the debtor and to be heard in a title 11 case are discussed in Sections 9.36–9.42. In cases under chapter 7 or 11, the U.S. trustee is generally required to appoint a committee of creditors to represent unsecured creditors in the case. The appointment, functions, and duties of the creditors' committee are covered in Sections 9.43–9.48.

The filing of a case under the Bankruptcy Code creates a bankruptcy estate of all the debtor's legal and equitable interests in property as of that date. This is an important concept because "property of the estate" is subject to administration under the Bankruptcy Code. Property of the estate is discussed in Section 9.49. Use, sale, or lease of property, within and outside of the ordinary course of business, are discussed in Sections 9.60–9.64 and 9.70. Property in which nondebtors also hold an interest—cash collateral and security interests in after-acquired property (postpetition proceeds)—are covered in Sections 9.65–9.69. Protection for a nondebtor's interest in property of the estate is discussed in Sections 9.56–9.59.

Critical to the successful outcome of a filing for reorganization or debt adjustment is the debtor's access to postpetition financing, which is discussed in Sections 9.71–9.73.

One of the fundamental protections of the Bankruptcy Code is the automatic stay that is triggered upon a bankruptcy filing. The automatic stay, exceptions to the stay, and relief from the stay are covered in Sections 9.50–9.55. Another benefit afforded a debtor under the Bankruptcy Code is the right to reject ongoing contracts that are burdensome to the estate. The treatment of such executory contracts and unexpired leases is discussed in Sections 9.74–9.85. Sections 9.86–9.88 deal with issues concerning a debtor's obligations with respect to collective bargaining agreements and retiree benefit plans. The provision concerning the continued supply of utility services to a debtor postpetition is discussed in Section 9.89.

Inasmuch as a case under title 11 is filed because a debtor has liabilities that it is unable to satisfy outside of bankruptcy, the treatment of creditors' claims against the debtor is central to the bankruptcy process. Claims procedures are covered in Sections 9.90–9.105. The allowance of administrative expense claims is discussed in Section 9.98. The treatment of secured claims is discussed in Sections 9.99–9.104, and reclamation claims are discussed in Section 9.105. Since treatment of particular secured claims often is dependent on the value of the collateral securing such claims, valuation is covered in Sections 9.103 and 9.104.

Distributions to creditors should be the result in any case except a no-asset case under title 11. Accordingly, certain provisions that affect distributions to creditors are explained in Sections 9.106–9.112. Since debtors who file for bankruptcy protection rarely have sufficient assets to pay all creditors in full, the Bankruptcy Code establishes an order of priorities in which different types of claims will be satisfied. This is covered in Section 9.106. Sometimes this order of priorities is changed because a claim or claims are subordinated to others. The provision governing subordination of claims and its application are discussed in Sections 9.107 and 9.108. A creditor's ability to exercise a right of setoff is covered in Sections 9.109–9.111, and a discussion of the right of recoupment may be found in Section 9.112.

The various "avoiding powers" under the Bankruptcy Code—that is, the powers to undo certain prepetition transfers of property in which the debtor had an interest that would be valid and enforceable under nonbankruptcy law—are among the most far-reaching powers accorded a debtor or an operating trustee to bring assets back into the bankruptcy estate for the benefit of creditors. The various avoiding powers are the focus of Sections 9.113–9.123. Specifically, the "strong arm clause" is covered in Section 9.115; the avoidance of certain statutory liens is covered in Section 9.116; preferences are covered in Sections 9.117–9.118; and fraudulent conveyances are covered in Section 9.119.

One of the significant benefits that the Bankruptcy Code affords to an individual debtor is the right to exempt certain property from distribution to creditors. Sections 9.125–9.129 discuss the exemptions available in New York and their effect on liens against the debtor's property. Under certain limited circumstances, a debtor may wish to reaffirm an existing debt. Reaffirmation is discussed in Sections 9.130 and 9.131. The benefits of filing under the Bankruptcy Code would be frustrated if the government or quasi-governmental organizations were permitted to discriminate against debtors or former debtors because of their bankruptcy. The Bankruptcy Code's protection against discriminatory treatment is discussed in Section 9.132. Tax considerations are covered in Section 9.133.

Finally, conversion and dismissal of cases and closing and reopening of cases are discussed in Sections 9.134–9.137.

Chapter 11. A detailed examination of chapter 11 is provided before a discussion of the other chapters under the Bankruptcy Code because it is the most inclusive chapter. With very limited exception, anyone eligible to be a debtor under chapter 7, 12, or 13 could be a debtor under chapter 11, while the converse is not true. More importantly, a presentation of the provisions of chapter 11 provides the framework for understanding many of the provisions in chapters 7, 12, and 13. Sections 9.138–9.176 cover chapter 11.

Under certain circumstances, a chapter 11 debtor in possession is replaced by an operating trustee or an examiner is appointed to investigate the debtor. Sections 9.138–9.141 discuss the appointment of a trustee or an examiner and their respective duties.

Sections 9.142–9.167 focus on matters relating to the ultimate goal of chapter 11—filing a plan of reorganization and obtaining its confirmation. The Bankruptcy Code favors the debtor by giving it the exclusive right to file a plan during the initial period of a chapter 11 case. "Exclusivity" is the subject of Sections 9.142–9.146. The provisions that must be included in a plan and those that may be included are described in Sections 9.147–9.151. Chapter 11 requires that claims be grouped in classes, and classification is covered in Sections 9.152–9.157. Since, as noted above, all claims generally cannot be paid in full, the impairment of claims and interests is addressed in Sections 9.158–9.160.

After a debtor has negotiated the terms of its plan with its creditors, it must prepare a "disclosure statement" which provides creditors with information about the plan that the court must determine to be "adequate." Once the court has approved the disclosure statement, the debtor can solicit acceptances of its plan by creditors. Disclosure and solicitation are explained in Section 9.161, and acceptance of a plan is discussed in Section 9.162.

Sometimes a debtor negotiates the terms of its plan with its creditors before filing for protection under the Bankruptcy Code. If the debtor not only negotiates its plan, but also solicits ballots accepting or rejecting the plan before commencing its chapter 11 case. In such cases, the plan is called a "prepackaged" plan. Such prenegotiated and prepackaged plans are discussed in Section 9.163. Modification of a plan is addressed in Section 9.164. Confirmation, both consensual and nonconsensual (cramdown), are covered in Sections 9.165 and 9.166. The effect of confirmation is explained in Section 9.167; discharge is covered in Sections 9.168–9.170; and plan implementation is discussed in Section 9.172. The special provisions affecting small business reorganizations are noted in Section 9.173. Finally, conversion or dismissal of cases under chapter 11 is discussed in Sections 9.174 and 9.175.

Topics that specifically concern chapter 7 are the subject of Sections 9.177–9.211. Chapter 12 is the focus of Sections 9.212–9.235, and chapter 13 the focus of Sections 9.236–9.263. Procedural checklists may be found in Sections 9.264–9.286, drafting checklists in Sections 9.287–9.304, and forms in Sections 9.305–9.312.

See Chapter 7, "Consumer Law," Chapter 8, "Enforcement of Money Judgments," and Chapter 11, "Mortgage Foreclosure," for a discussion of debtor-creditor issues under state law.

§ 9.2 Strategy

When handling a matter where a bankruptcy filing appears to be a possible course of action, the threshold consideration is whether to file under the Bankruptcy Code, and if so, under which chapter. Counsel must assist the client in making this decision based upon careful consideration of the client's problems and a comprehensive analysis of the client's financial circumstances, including the nature and amount of all assets and liabilities, future financial projections, and the dischargeability of the client's debts. Counsel should assist the client in ensuring that no relevant facts have been overlooked.[1] Based on the facts of the particular case, counsel should carefully review with the client the advantages and disadvantages of all the options, including refinancing, an out-of-court restructuring, and remedies available under state law compared to filing under the various chapters of the Bankruptcy Code.[2] Filing a bankruptcy petition offers the following advantages:

- The automatic stay, with limited exceptions, immediately stays all suits against the debtor, all collection efforts by creditors, and precludes a secured creditor from foreclosing on collateral.
- Discharge of prepetition debts affords a reorganized debtor a fresh start.
- A debtor can review its operations and reject burdensome executory contracts or unexpired leases.
- Interest stops accruing on unsecured debt.
- Preferences and fraudulent conveyances may be avoided.
- Security interests may be avoided.

---

§ 9.2

1. An examination of Official Forms 1–4 and 6–8 (*see infra*, § 9.5) as well as the checklists at *infra*, §§ 9.264, 9.265 reveal the breadth of information that should be obtained from a client before filing.

2. *See supra*, Chapter 8, "Enforcement of Money Judgments" and *infra*, Chapter 11, "Mortgage Foreclosure" for discussion of remedies available under state law. For a helpful discussion of whether to file and, if so, under which chapter, *see* Jean Braucher, *Counseling Debtors to Make Their Own Informed Choices—A Question of Professional Responsibility*, 5 Am.Bankr.L.R. 165 (Spring 1997).

- A chapter 12 or 13 debtor has the exclusive right to file a plan for the adjustment of its debts.[3] A chapter 11 debtor has the exclusive right to file a plan for 120 days, but this period may be extended by the court.[4]
- Financing after a chapter 11 filing is more accessible because of the ability to grant the postpetition lender superpriority administrative status, possibly to prime existing liens.[5]

However, there are a number of possible disadvantages to filing for bankruptcy, including:

- Stigma of bankruptcy—difficulty obtaining goods, credit, and employment.
- Constant regulation by the bankruptcy court, requiring substantial time and energy.
- Chapter 11 cases can be expensive—the debtor is responsible not only for paying the fees of its own professionals, but also those of the various creditors' committees.[6]
- A chapter 11 debtor faces the risk of liquidation or appointment of a trustee.
- Certain debts are nondischargeable; moreover, a debtor may be denied a discharge.[7]

The decision by creditors to commence an involuntary case against an individual or corporation must be carefully considered. Typically, the circumstances under which consideration is given to such filing involve a debtor who is known to be in the act of committing fraud or liquidating its assets and preferring payment to certain creditors over others. Under such circumstances, a creditor may desire to file an involuntary petition so that the debtor's transfers fall within the 90–day preference recovery period.[8]

Before a creditor decides whether to join in filing an involuntary petition against a debtor, it should assess whether the debtor's problems

---

3. 11 U.S.C.A. §§ 1221, 1321. *See infra*, §§ 9.220, 9.245.

4. 11 U.S.C.A. § 1121. *See infra*, § 9.142.

5. *See* 11 U.S.C.A. § 364; *see infra*, § 9.71.

6. In addition, a party commencing a case under title 11 is obligated to pay certain fees to the court. The filing fee for a chapter 7 or 13 case is $130, the fee for a chapter 11 case not concerning a railroad is $800, and the fee for a chapter 12 case is $200. 28 U.S.C.A. § 1930(a). A chapter 11 debtor also must pay a quarterly fee to the United States Trustee for deposit in the Treasury for each quarter until the case is closed. The amount of the fee ranges from $250 through $5,000 and depends upon the total amount of disbursements made by the debtor for each quarter. 28 U.S.C.A. § 1930(a)(6).

7. *See infra*, §§ 9.169, 9.205, 9.207, 9.229, 9.256 for a discussion of nondischargeable debts.

8. *See* 11 U.S.C.A. § 547(b)(4); *see infra*, §§ 9.117, 9.118 for a discussion of the recovery of preferential transfers. Moreover, the filing of an involuntary petition does activate application of the automatic stay under Section 362, thereby preventing creditors from taking precipitous action against a debtor's assets.

can be consensually resolved outside of bankruptcy. A debtor's bankruptcy creates great uncertainty for a creditor as to when and how much it ultimately will be paid on its prepetition debts. Moreover, the filing of an involuntary petition involves the potential for sanctions to be assessed against the filing petitioners in the event they fail to demonstrate that (i) the requisite number of petitioning creditors have filed the involuntary petition, (ii) the debtor is generally not paying its debts as they become due, and (iii) the petition was filed in bad faith.[9] Accordingly, although the commencement of an involuntary case is a legitimate threat by creditors and affords leverage in out-of-court negotiations, such action should not be taken lightly.

§ 9.3 Strategy—Checklist for Representing a Debtor

The following are some of the principal issues a practitioner should consider before recommending that a client file for relief under a particular chapter of the Bankruptcy Code:

1. Review the benefits and burdens of filing under the Bankruptcy Code. (*See* § 9.2)

2. Consider what entities should seek relief under each chapter of the Bankruptcy Code. (*See* § 9.7 concerning eligibility for relief)

3. Determine the total amount of assets and liabilities and identify the secured and unsecured creditors.

4. Consider the implications of possible insolvency prior to filing a petition.[1]

5. What is the status of workout negotiations? Are creditors intransigent on certain issues? Will the cramdown provisions of the Bankruptcy Code help? (*See* § 9.166) The decision to file a bankruptcy case should only be made after all possibilities for an out-of-court workout have been carefully considered and dismissed.

6. Are there any state court actions or other threatened actions by creditors that will be stayed under the Bankruptcy Code and, thereby, afford the client protections unavailable absent a bankruptcy filing? (*See* §§ 9.50, 9.51 for a discussion of the automatic stay)

7. Assess the ability of the client to obtain financing outside of bankruptcy.

---

9. See 11 U.S.C.A. § 303(i).

§ 9.3
1. *See, e.g., infra,* §§ 9.113–9.119 discussing avoidance actions.

8. Consider the financing provisions under Section 364 of the Bankruptcy Code. (*See* § 9.71)

9. Were there any significant transfers by the client of its legal or equitable interests in any property within one year of an anticipated filing? Analyze the impact of the filing date in relation to potential preference and fraudulent conveyance actions. (*See infra*, §§ 9.113–9.119 for a discussion of avoidance actions)

10. Will the client benefit from rejecting executory contracts or unexpired leases under the Bankruptcy Code? Will lease damage claims be capped under the Bankruptcy Code? (*See* §§ 9.74–9.85)

11. Ascertain the number of creditors and the amounts and types of claims. Are there unliquidated or contingent claims that will be subject to estimation by the bankruptcy court and, thus, could not readily be settled out of court? (*See* § 502(c) of the Bankruptcy Code)

12. Consider the possible classification of claims and the impact on the ability to confirm a plan. (*See* §§ 9.152–9.162 (chapter 11); §§ 9.225–9.226 (chapter 12); §§ 9.251–9.252 (chapter 13))

13. Consider the impact of the special tax provisions under a chapter 11 plan of reorganization. (*See* 11 U.S.C.A. § 1146(c))

14. *If the client is an operating business entity*, is there a viable business to preserve? A cautious course of action may be to file a chapter 11 reorganization case rather than make the more drastic and final decision to liquidate under chapter 7. Counsel should remember that a corporation may liquidate under a chapter 11 plan through the sale of all or substantially all of its assets, thereby avoiding the potential increased expense of a chapter 7 trustee.[2]

15. *If the client is an individual*, the decision whether to file under chapter 7, 11, or 13 is often dictated by any assets sought to be preserved, as well as the discharge sought to be attained. Consider the following:

    - Is the individual eligible to file under chapter 13? (*See* § 9.237)

    - Does the individual have sufficient disposable income to pay his debts under a chapter 13 plan? If so, chapter 7 is not an option. (*See infra*, § 9.209 note 9)

2. If necessary at a later date, a chapter 11 debtor (with certain exceptions) may convert the case to a case under chapter 7. 11 U.S.C.A. § 1112. In any event, the Bankruptcy Code precludes a liquidating debtor that is not an individual from receiving a discharge. *See* 11 U.S.C.A. §§ 727(a)(1); 1141(d)(3).

- Determine the total amount of assets, exempt and nonexempt, and the amount of disposable income. Does the individual have non-exempt assets that would have to be liquidated under chapter 7? (*See* § 9.125 for a discussion of exemptions)
- Determine the ownership of assets as between the client and spouse. Were there transfers of jointly-held assets before the bankruptcy filing that may be subject to avoidance actions? (*See* §§ 9.113–9.119 for a discussion of avoidance actions)
- Identify dischargeable and non-dischargeable debts. (*See* §§ 9.168–9.169; 9.204–9.205; 9.207; 9.229; 9.255–9.256) Does the client have debts that could not be discharged?[3] Some debts are not dischargeable under chapter 7 but can be discharged under chapter 13. (*See infra*, § 9.255)
- Are challenges to the client's general discharge likely? Has the client filed a prior bankruptcy case within the last six years? (*See* § 9.205)
- Consider whether reaffirmation of certain debts would be in the client's best interest. This may be the case if the client wishes to retain property, such as a car, in chapter 7 or if the debt is likely to be found nondischargeable anyway. (*See infra*, §§ 9.130–131 for a discussion of reaffirmation)

16. *If the client is a partnership*, a bankruptcy filing will trigger the dissolution of the partnership under New York Partnership Law.[4] If all of the partners do not consent to a chapter 11 filing, an involuntary petition is required. (*See infra*, § 9.9)

- Partners may be personally liable for partnership debts.
- The trustee appointed in the case will review all transfers for possible preference or fraudulent conveyance actions against partners.

§ 9.4 Strategy—Checklist for Representing a Creditor

1. Obtain a copy of the debtor's petition.

---

3. Certain debts, *e.g.*, debts for alimony, maintenance, child support, certain taxes, some educational loans, and debts incurred by fraud are not dischargeable. *See* 11 U.S.C.A. §§ 523, 727, 1141(d)(3) for a complete list of nondischargeable debts and circumstances under which debts are nondischargeable. Additionally, the court may dismiss a chapter 7 case filed by an individual debtor whose debts are primarily consumer debts if it finds that granting relief would be a substantial abuse. 11 U.S.C.A. § 707(b).

4. The Second Circuit has held that a partnership that is in dissolution is not eligible to file for chapter 11 relief because it "no longer exists except for the purpose of liquidation" and, therefore, is not an "eligible person." C–TC 9th Avenue Partnership v. Norton Company (In re C–TC 9th Avenue Partnership), 113 F.3d 1304 (2d Cir. 1997).

Ch. 9   CHECKLIST FOR REPRESENTING A CREDITOR   § 9.4

2. Are there multiple debtors whose cases are being jointly administered? (*See* § 9.13)

3. Consider whether filing a notice of appearance to receive all motion papers is advisable. (*See* § 9.36 note 3[1])

4. Has the debtor filed all schedules and lists of creditors? (*See* § 9.11 and checklist § 9.265) Obtain a copy of the schedules. Determine if the client's claim is listed in the schedules and, if so, if the client agrees with the listing in respect to both amount and classification. If the client does not agree with the listing of its claim in the debtor's schedules, it is mandatory that it file a proof of claim before the bar date deadline expires. (*See* § 9.91)

5. Determine the composition of the debtor's creditor body by referring to the schedules of liabilities. Is the client's claim secured by a lien on any of the debtor's assets or is it unsecured; if secured, is it oversecured or undersecured? Who are the secured creditors? Are the secured creditors oversecured or undersecured? (*See* §§ 9.99, 9.100 for information concerning a claim's status)

6. Has the United States trustee appointed the creditors' committee? If it is a chapter 7 case, should a creditors' committee be elected?[2] Consider the client's membership on a creditors' committee. (*See* §§ 9.43–9.45 for a discussion of issues related to the creditors' committee)

7. Does the client hold any monies on account or is the client owed any money by the debtor? Consider the possibilities for an administrative freeze, setoff, recoupment, or reclamation of goods. (*See* §§ 9.109–9.112, 9.105)

8. Is any lien or transfer to the client subject to avoidance as a preference or fraudulent conveyance? (*See* §§ 9.113–9.119 for a discussion of avoidance actions)

9. Determine whether the client should object to the dischargeability of its claim against the debtor or to the debtor's general discharge. (*See* §§ 9.168–9.169, 9.204–9.205, 9.207, 9.229, 9.255–9.256)

10. Consider whether reaffirmation of an individual debtor's obligations to the client would be in the client's best interest. (*See* § 9.130 for a discussion of reaffirmation)

§ 9.4

1. **CAVEAT**: While it may not be necessary to receive all papers, since a creditor should receive notices of any proposed actions that may affect its interest, filing a notice of appearance assures the attorney that he or she will receive any important information concerning the case. If no notice of appearance is filed, important notices will be sent directly to the creditor, and the attorney will be dependent on the client's diligence in passing along information in a timely manner.

2. Only chapter 7 provides for the election of a creditors' committee. *See* 11 U.S.C.A. § 705 and *infra*, § 9.184. Under chapter 11, a creditors' committee is appointed by the U.S. trustee. *See* 11 U.S.C.A. § 1102 and *infra*, § 9.43.

§ 9.4 BANKRUPTCY Ch. 9

11. Has the debtor obtained postpetition financing? (See §§ 9.65–9.66)

12. Monitor the docket for motions regarding sale of assets, retention of professionals, and employee compensation issues. (See §§ 9.60–9.63, 9.29, 9.12)

13. Monitor Section 341 meetings. (See § 9.37)

14. Determine whether the debtor's request for an extension of exclusivity should be opposed. Consider whether there are grounds to shorten exclusivity. (See §§ 9.142–9.145, 9.220)

15. If representing a secured creditor, determine whether there is a reasonable basis for seeking adequate protection of the creditor's secured interest in the debtor's property. (See §§ 9.56–9.58)

16. Determine if relief from the automatic stay is appropriate. (See §§ 9.50–9.55)

17. Determine whether cause exists for the appointment of a trustee or examiner. (See §§ 9.138–9.141, 9.214)

§ 9.5 Governing Law

The United States Constitution grants Congress the exclusive power to establish bankruptcy laws.[1] The bankruptcy laws, as amended from time to time, are codified in title 11 of the United States Code, which is known as the Bankruptcy Code.[2] The most recent revision of the Bankruptcy Code was enacted pursuant to the Bankruptcy Reform Act of 1994.[3] In addition to numerous amendments to the Bankruptcy Code, the Bankruptcy Reform Act of 1994 provided for the creation of a National Bankruptcy Review Commission charged, among other things, with the task of reviewing, improving, and updating the Bankruptcy Code. It is anticipated that after the Commission has completed its work and submitted its report to the President, Congress, and the Chief Justice, the Bankruptcy Code will likely undergo further amendment.

The Federal Rules of Bankruptcy Procedure (the "Bankruptcy Rules"), as promulgated by the United States Supreme Court, establish special procedural rules as well as certain official forms[4] which govern every aspect of practice under the Bankruptcy Code.[5] Certain of the Bankruptcy Rules specifically make the Federal Rules of Civil Procedure applicable to bankruptcy practice, particularly rules in Parts VII and IX

§ 9.5
1. U.S. Constitution, Art. I, § 8, cl. 4.
2. 11 U.S.C.A. §§ 101–1330.
3. Pub.L. 103–394 (1994).
4. **PRACTICE POINTER**: Although the practitioner can obtain printed forms produced by private publishers, he or she should refer to the Official Forms section of a current copy of the Bankruptcy Rules for further guidance. See Official Bankr.Forms, 11 U.S.C.A. Generally, alterations may be used as appropriate and modified to permit economies in their use. Bankr.R. 9009.
5. 28 U.S.C.A. § 2075.

of the Bankruptcy Rules dealing with litigation.[6] The Federal Rules of Evidence apply with regard to any hearing at which proof is offered.[7] Additionally, each federal district has its own local rules which, like the Bankruptcy Rules themselves, should be referred to for specific procedural questions, including an attorney's admission to practice in the bankruptcy court.[8] Within particular districts, there also may be supplemental local rules or standing orders.[9] Individual judges often have rules of chambers which also must be observed.[10]

Library References:

West's Key No. Digests, Bankruptcy ⚙=2002.

§ 9.6 Nature of Cases Under Each Chapter of the Bankruptcy Code

The Bankruptcy Code comprises several chapters that govern different types of debtors. Chapter 7 governs the liquidation of the assets of individuals and companies that are unable to reorganize. Upon the filing of a chapter 7 case, a trustee is appointed and charged with the responsibility of liquidating all of the debtor's non-exempt assets. Chapter 9 deals with the adjustment of debts of municipalities and is not covered herein. Chapter 11 primarily governs corporate reorganizations, but individuals may also file under chapter 11.[1] Chapter 12 provides for the adjustment of the debts of family farmers with regular annual income and is available to family farmers that are corporations or partnerships, as well as to individuals.[2] Chapter 13 governs the adjustment of debts of individuals with regular income.[3] Under chapter 13, an individual debtor may avoid the liquidation of assets; however, there are strict limits on the length of time one may take to pay creditors' claims[4]

---

6. *See, e.g.*, Bankr.R. 7001, Advisory Committee Note.

7. Bankr.R. 9017.

8. *Collier Bankruptcy Practice Guide*, Appendix 2 (Herzog and King, eds., 15th ed.1995) contains the local bankruptcy rules for each of the federal districts in New York.

9. **PRACTICE POINTER**: Contact the bankruptcy clerk in the appropriate federal district to find out if any supplemental rules, amendments, or standing orders have been promulgated.

10. **CAVEAT**: Because bankruptcy practice is subject to several sources of rules, care must be taken to ensure compliance so as to avoid causing prejudice to your client's case.

§ 9.6

1. **PRACTICE POINTER**: Debtors who fail to reorganize successfully under chapter 11 may liquidate under that chapter (11 U.S.C.A. § 1123(b)(4)) or convert to chapter 7. 11 U.S.C.A. § 1112. *See infra*, § 9.7 for a discussion of eligibility to file.

2. *See infra*, § 9.212 discussing the definition of family farmer under the Bankruptcy Code.

3. *See infra*, § 9.237 for a discussion of eligibility to file under chapter 13.

4. A chapter 13 plan may not provide for payments over a period that is longer than 3 years unless the court, for cause, approves a longer period. The court may not approve a period that is longer than 5 years under any circumstance. 11 U.S.C.A. § 1322(c).

§ 9.6

and the ability to affect secured indebtedness.[5]

Chapters 1, 3, and 5 of the Code set forth the general provisions relating to case administration and the debtor's estate. However, while the individual Code sections of these chapters generally apply to each of chapters 7, 9, 11, 12, and 13, in some instances certain sections do not apply in a specific chapter, or do not apply uniformly in all chapters. Section 103 of the Bankruptcy Code explains which of the administrative chapters apply in a case under chapter 7, 9, 11, 12, or 13. Section 102 sets forth rules of construction applicable under title 11.[6]

Library References:

West's Key No. Digests, Bankruptcy ⟿2251, 3481, 3501, 3671, 3701.

§ 9.7 Eligibility to File

Section 109 of the Bankruptcy Code sets forth the eligibility requirements for filing under each chapter of the Code.[1] Those eligible to file under each chapter are:

Chapter 7: Any person,[2] *i.e.*, an individual, partnership, or corporation except a railroad, insurance company, bank, savings and loan association, or similar federally insured institution;

Chapter 11: Any person eligible under chapter 7 except a stockbroker, commodity broker, railroad, or nonbusiness trust;[3]

Chapter 12: A family farmer with regular annual income;[4] and

Chapter 13: An individual or an individual and spouse with regular income (except a stockbroker or a commodity broker) whose noncon-

---

5. Although a chapter 13 plan may modify the rights of holders of secured claims, it may not modify the rights of a creditor whose claim is secured only by the debtor's principal residence. 11 U.S.C.A. § 1322(b)(2). This limitation is intended to prevent potential bankruptcy filings from having a chilling effect on home mortgage lending.

6. **PRACTICE POINTER**: Definitions play a crucial role in interpreting the Bankruptcy Code. Accordingly, practitioners should familiarize themselves with the key definitions in Section 101 and check the definition section as well as the index when referring to any section of the Bankruptcy Code.

§ 9.7

1. Any debtor must reside or have a domicile, place of business, or property in the United States. 11 U.S.C.A. § 109(a).

2. 11 U.S.C.A. § 101(41).

3. **PRACTICE POINTER**: The Second Circuit has held that a partnership in dissolution under New York law, while allowed to continue until the winding up of partnership affairs is complete, is not a "person" for purposes of chapter 11 and, therefore, is ineligible for chapter 11 relief because its restricted capacity is inconsistent with the chapter 11 objective of obtaining a "fresh start." C-TC 9th Ave. Partnership v. Norton Co. (In re C-TC 9th Ave. Partnership), 113 F.3d 1304 (2d Cir.1997).

4. See infra, § 9.212.

tingent, liquidated debts on the date of filing are less than $250,000 (unsecured) and $750,000 (secured).[5]

Other than the eligibility requirements for the various chapters listed above and the filing fees,[6] there are no additional requirements for filing a chapter 7, 11, 12, or 13 petition.[7] Notably, a voluntary chapter 7, 11, 12, or 13 debtor need not demonstrate to the bankruptcy court that it is insolvent.[8] Further, there is no requirement that a voluntary debtor demonstrate in the first instance that it is filing its petition in good faith.[9]

Library References:

West's Key No. Digests, Bankruptcy ⟐2222.1–2233(3).

§ 9.8 Commencement of a Case—Voluntary Cases

Entities that qualify as debtors under chapter 7, 11, 12, or 13,[1] respectively, may commence a voluntary case by filing a petition under the appropriate chapter with the clerk of the Bankruptcy Court.[2] The filing of a voluntary petition under title 11 constitutes the "order for relief" and represents the official commencement of a bankruptcy case.[3]

---

5. *See infra*, § 9.237.

6. The filing fees are as follows: (1) chapter 7 or 13: $130; (2) chapter 11: $800 and (3) chapter 12: $200. 28 U.S.C.A. § 1930(a). Upon application to the court, and upon certain conditions, an individual who is unable to pay the filing fee may obtain court authorization to pay the fee in installments. Bankr.R. 1006(b).

7. However, 11 U.S.C.A. § 109(g) sets certain limitations on filings of an individual or family farmer who has filed previously.

8. The requirement set forth at Section 109(c)(3) of the Code that a municipality be insolvent to qualify as a debtor under chapter 9, which governs municipal bankruptcies, is the only insolvency requirement for becoming a debtor under title 11. 11 U.S.C.A. § 109.

9. **PRACTICE POINTER**: Although there is no requirement that a voluntary debtor prove that it is filing its petition in good faith, a party who opposes the bankruptcy filing may attempt (and perhaps, succeed) in having the case dismissed on the ground that the petition was not filed in good faith. *See, e.g.*, C–TC 9th Ave. Partnership v. Norton Co. (In re C–TC 9th Ave. Partnership), 113 F.3d 1304 (2d Cir.1997); Marsch v. Marsch (In re Marsch), 36 F.3d 825 (9th Cir.1994).

Allegations of bad faith filings are prevalent in chapter 11 cases involving single asset real estate debtors, where petitions are filed on the eve of foreclosure, and where there is little prospect for a successful reorganization. *See, e.g.*, Little Creek Dev. Co. v. Commonwealth Mortgage Corp. (In re Little Creek Dev. Co.), 779 F.2d 1068 (5th Cir.1986); 9281 Shore Rd. Owners Corp. v. Seminole Realty Co. (In re 9281 Shore Rd. Owners Corp.), 187 B.R. 837 (E.D.N.Y.1995). Indeed, recent amendments to the Bankruptcy Code have made it more difficult for the filer of a single asset real estate case to remain in chapter 11 for an extensive period of time. *See* 11 U.S.C.A. § 362(d)(3), which makes it easier for a creditor whose claim is secured by such real estate to have the automatic stay lifted. *See* 11 U.S.C.A. § 101(51B) for the definition of "single asset real estate" and *see infra*, §§ 9.50–9.52, 9.55 for a discussion of the automatic stay and relief therefrom.

§ 9.8

1. *See supra*, § 9.7 and 11 U.S.C.A. § 109 for debtor eligibility for relief under title 11.

2. 11 U.S.C.A. § 301; Bankr.R. 1002(a). *See infra*, § 9.264 for a procedural checklist for commencing a voluntary case.

3. 11 U.S.C.A. § 301.

§ 9.8   BANKRUPTCY   Ch. 9

It is important because it triggers the automatic stay[4] and the running of certain time limits.[5]

Library References:

West's Key No. Digests, Bankruptcy ⚖︎2257.

§ 9.9   Commencement of a Case—Involuntary Cases

An involuntary case may be commenced only under chapter 7 or 11 against entities that are entitled to file under those chapters.[1] A petition for the commencement of an involuntary chapter 7 or 11 case may be filed by:

- Three or more holders of undisputed, noncontingent claims that aggregate at least $10,000 more than the value of any liens securing such claims;[2]

- One or more holders of claims that aggregate at least $10,000 (excluding any employee or insider of the debtor and any transferee of an avoidable transfer),[3] if there are fewer than twelve such claim holders;

- Fewer than all the general partners if the person is a partnership; or by a general partner in such partnership if all the general partners have filed their own bankruptcy petitions; or the trustee of a general partner; or a holder of a claim against the partnership.[4]

Library References:

West's Key No. Digests, Bankruptcy ⚖︎2290.1.

§ 9.10   Commencement of a Case—Involuntary Cases— Procedure

A petitioning creditor must pay the filing fee of $130 in a chapter 7

---

4. See 11 U.S.C.A. § 362 and discussion of the automatic stay *infra*, §§ 9.50–9.55.

5. **CAVEAT**: There are numerous time limits in bankruptcy practice, and failure to comply with them can be fatal to the client's interests. Accordingly, counsel must exercise great care to ensure that proper representation is provided. *See* Appendix C in Berk and Jensen–Conklin, *Consumer Bankruptcy* (1989) for a helpful list of time limits. However, counsel must check the appropriate sections of a current copy of the Bankruptcy Code and Rules to make certain that the relevant time limit has not been amended. The applicable Local Rules also must be consulted for additional time limits. *See* Bankruptcy Rule 9006 and 11 U.S.C.A. § 108 for computation of time and other information governing application of time periods under the Bankruptcy Code.

§ 9.9

1. 11 U.S.C.A. § 303(a).

2. The joinder of an indenture trustee to an involuntary bankruptcy petition does not extinguish the claims of the underlying debenture holders for purposes of satisfying the three petitioning creditor requirement of § 303(b) of the Bankruptcy Code. Grey v. Federated Group, Inc. (In re Federated Group, Inc.), 107 F.3d 730 (9th Cir.1997).

3. *See infra*, §§ 9.113–9.119 for a discussion of avoidable transfers.

4. 11 U.S.C.A. § 303.

case or $800 in a chapter 11 case.[1] Upon the filing of an involuntary petition, the clerk of the Bankruptcy Court will issue a summons for service. The summons should be served on the debtor with a copy of the petition in the same manner as service of a summons and complaint in an adversary proceeding.[2]

Defenses and objections to the petition are governed by Rule 12 of the Federal Rules of Civil Procedure and must be filed and served within 20 days after service of the summons. If service is by publication, the court will prescribe the time for filing and serving the response.[3]

An involuntary case does not automatically commence upon the filing of an involuntary petition.[4] If no pleading is filed in response to the summons within 20 days after it has been served, the court, on the next day, or shortly thereafter, will enter an order for the relief requested in the petition.[5] If the debtor requests that the case be converted to a voluntary case, the court will grant the order for relief.[6] If the debtor contests that the petition was filed by fewer than 3 creditors although 12 or more exist, the debtor must file a list of all creditors with addresses and a brief statement of the nature and amount of such creditors' claims.[7] If the answer controverts the involuntary petition on other grounds, the court will determine if the relief should be granted based upon: (1) whether the debtor is generally not paying its debts as they become due unless such debts are subject to a *bona fide* dispute,[8] or (2) whether within 120 days before the filing, a custodian other than a trustee, receiver, or agent appointed to enforce a lien, was appointed or took possession.[9]

§ 9.11 Commencement of a Case—Additional Requirements

Numerous lists, schedules, and statements must be filed at the

§ 9.10

1. 28 U.S.C.A. § 1930(a).

2. Bankr.R. 1010; *see* Bankr.R. 7004. See infra, § 9.16 for a discussion of adversary proceedings.

3. Bankr.R. 1011(b).

4. **PRACTICE POINTER**: A debtor who is the subject of an involuntary petition may continue to operate its business and may use, acquire, or dispose of property as if an involuntary case had not been filed against it until the order for relief is entered. 11 U.S.C.A. § 303(f). This is so even though a debtor's use or sale of its property is limited under Section 363 once the order for relief has been entered. *See infra,* §§ 9.60–9.70 for a discussion of the debtor's use, sale, or lease of its property.

5. Bankr.R. 1013(b), 1011(b).

6. Frequently, a debtor in an involuntary chapter 7 case will have the court convert the case to a voluntary chapter 11 case. *See, e.g.,* In re Williams, 188 B.R. 331 (E.D.N.Y.1995); In re Rundlett, 153 B.R. 126 (S.D.N.Y.1993). A chapter 7 debtor has "one absolute right of conversion of a liquidation case to a reorganization or individual repayment plan case.... The policy of the provision is that the debtor should always be given the opportunity to repay his debts." H.R.Rep.No. 95–595, 95th Cong., 1st Sess. 380 (1977).

7. Bankr.R. 1003(b).

8. *See* In re Busick, 831 F.2d 745 (7th Cir.1987) (a *bona fide* dispute is present if there is an objective basis for either a factual or legal dispute as to the validity of a debt).

9. 11 U.S.C.A. § 303(h).

§ 9.11

commencement of a case under title 11.[1] The petition, all lists, schedules, statements, and any amendments must be verified or contain an unsworn declaration.[2] The debtor can obtain an extension of time for filing the lists, schedules, and statements only on notice and motion for "cause."[3] At any time before the case is closed, the debtor may amend a voluntary petition, list, schedule, or statement as of right by giving notice to the trustee and any entity affected thereby.[4] In large chapter 11 cases, additional time to complete the schedules is generally requested based on the sheer number of the debtor's obligations and the time required to locate and itemize each one.

§ 9.12 Commencement of a Case—First–Day Orders

In cases where the debtor will be operating its property under the Bankruptcy Code, a variety of motions may be filed at the commencement of the case to ensure a smooth transition to operation under the Bankruptcy Code. The following are some examples:

1. Authorization pursuant to 11 U.S.C.A. § 327 to retain bankruptcy counsel and any other professionals who may be needed. This is essential at the outset of any case under title 11.[1]

2. Authorization pursuant to 11 U.S.C.A. § 105(a) to continue using prepetition business forms and bank accounts (with a designation of the debtor's status under the Bankruptcy Code).

3. For business debtors, authorization to pay prepetition wages, salaries, and employee benefits pursuant to 11 U.S.C.A. §§ 363(b) and 105(a).

§ 9.13 Joint Administration

A debtor that has subsidiaries or related entities may, at the onset of the bankruptcies, move in the bankruptcy court for procedural consolidation of the cases.[1] Procedural consolidation is done solely to facilitate the administration of the various cases and does not affect the underlying

---

§ 9.11

1. See infra, § 9.265 for a procedural checklist of the documents that must be filed.
2. Official Form 6. Bankr.R. 1008.
3. Bankr.R. 1007(a)(4), (c).
4. Bankr.R. 1009(a).

§ 9.12

1. **CAVEAT**: Courts have refused to compensate professionals for services rendered and have ordered disgorgement of fees awarded if counsel was not properly retained at the commencement of the case or if disclosure of the professional's connections with the debtor, creditors, any other party in interest, and their attorneys and accountants required by Bankr.R. 2014 was subsequently found to be deficient. See, e.g., Futuronics Corp. v. Arutt, Nachamie & Benjamin (In re Futuronics Corp.), 655 F.2d 463 (2d Cir.1981), cert. denied 455 U.S. 941, 102 S.Ct. 1435, 71 L.Ed.2d 653 (1982); Michel v. Federated Dept. Stores, Inc. (In re Federated Dept. Stores, Inc.), 44 F.3d 1310 (6th Cir.1995). See infra, § 9.29 for a discussion of the requirements and procedure for retention of professionals.

§ 9.13

1. Bankr.R. 1015.

relationship between the related debtor parties. The related debtors may administer their cases pursuant to a single docket, and a uniform caption will appear on each pleading filed in any of the procedurally consolidated cases.

Library References:

West's Key No. Digests, Bankruptcy ⚖︎2311.

§ 9.14 Substantive Consolidation

The equitable doctrine of substantive consolidation permits a bankruptcy court in a case involving one or more related corporate entities to disregard the separateness of the corporate entities and to consolidate and pool the entities' assets and liabilities and treat them as though held and incurred by one entity. A court will invoke its broad equitable powers to order substantive consolidation only after review of the particular facts of a case and consideration of the guidelines gleaned from case law.[1]

Library References:

West's Key No. Digests, Bankruptcy ⚖︎2084.1.

§ 9.15 Types of Proceedings in Cases Under the Bankruptcy Code

There are two types of proceedings under the Bankruptcy Code, namely, adversary proceedings and contested matters. They are controlled by different procedural rules and requirements.[1]

§ 9.14

1. In the Second Circuit, courts apply a standard established in Union Savings Bank v. Augie/Restivo Baking Co., Ltd. (In re Augie/Restivo Baking Co., Ltd.), 860 F.2d 515, 518 (2d Cir.1988). Under this standard, substantive consolidation is appropriate when *either* (i) creditors dealt with the entities as a single economic unit and did not rely on their separate identity in extending credit, *or* (ii) the affairs of the debtors are so intertwined that consolidation will benefit all creditors.

The District Court for the Southern District of New York has held that in order to permit a meaningful appellate review of the denial of a request for substantive consolidation, the bankruptcy court must make express factual findings on each of the two alternative tests. In re 599 Consumer Electronics, Inc., 195 B.R. 244 (S.D.N.Y.1996).

§ 9.15

1. The concept of "after notice and a hearing" (or a similar phrase) is central to the Bankruptcy Code and recurs throughout the Code. As explained in Section 102 of the Code, it means "after such notice as is appropriate in the particular circumstances, and such opportunity for a hearing as is appropriate in the particular circumstances." 11 U.S.C.A. § 102(1)(A). The notice is prescribed by the Bankruptcy Rules or, in circumstances that the Rules do not cover, by the court. A hearing will not be necessary in every instance. If notice is given properly and there is no timely objection to the proposed action, it may proceed without court approval. 11 U.S.C.A. § 102(1)(B)(i). Or, if there is insufficient time for a hearing before an act must be done, it may be authorized by the court without a hearing. 11 U.S.C.A. § 102(1)(B)(ii). The flexibility of the requirement for a hearing is intended to permit the courts to dispense with hearings when speed is essential. H.R.Rep.No. 95–595, 95th Cong., 1st Sess. 315 (1977); S.Rep.No. 95–989, 95th Cong., 2d Sess. 27 (1978). Bankruptcy Rule 2002 prescribes

§ 9.16 Types of Proceedings in Cases Under the Bankruptcy Code—Adversary Proceedings

Adversary proceedings are akin to civil actions in a federal district court and are commenced by the filing of a complaint.[1] With certain exceptions, an adversary proceeding is a proceeding to: (1) recover money or property; (2) determine the validity, priority, or extent of a lien or other interest in property; (3) obtain approval pursuant to Section 363(h) of the Bankruptcy Code for the sale of the interest of the estate or of a co-owner in property; (4) object to, or revoke a discharge; (5) revoke an order of confirmation of a chapter 11, 12, or 13 plan; (6) determine the dischargeability of a debt; (7) obtain an injunction or other equitable relief; (8) subordinate any allowed claim or interest, except when subordination is provided in a chapter 9, 11, 12, or 13 plan; (9) obtain a declaratory judgment relating to any of the foregoing; or (10) determine a claim or cause of action removed pursuant to 28 U.S.C.A. § 1452.[2] A filing fee may be required for an adversary proceeding.[3] The bankruptcy rules governing adversary proceedings either incorporate or are adaptations of most of the Federal Rules of Civil Procedure.[4]

Library References:
West's Key No. Digests, Bankruptcy ⚞2156.

§ 9.17 Types of Proceedings in Cases Under the Bankruptcy Code—Contested Matters

Contested matters include all matters that do not fall within Bankruptcy Rule 7001's definition of an adversary proceeding.[1] Contested the method and manner of notice to creditors and other parties in interest. Bankruptcy Rule 9006 prescribes the computation of time for notice purposes and those circumstances under which time periods may be enlarged or reduced by the court. Reference should also be made to local rules for notice requirements.

§ 9.16

1. See infra, § 9.266 for a procedural checklist for commencing an adversary proceeding, § 9.287 for a drafting checklist outlining general requirements for pleadings in cases under the Bankruptcy Code, and § 9.309 for a sample form of a complaint to commence an adversary proceeding.

2. Bankr.R. 7001.

CAVEAT: In addition to the general docket for the overall bankruptcy case, there is also a specific docket for each adversary proceeding. The adversary proceeding docket must be consulted on a regular basis to avoid missing the entry of an order because the date of the entry of the order on that docket may have important consequences. For example, the time to appeal an order starts to run upon the date of the entry of an order on the adversary proceeding docket.

3. 28 U.S.C.A. §§ 1930, 1914(a).

4. Most of the rules in Part VII of the Bankruptcy Rules (governing adversary proceedings) have a comparable rule in the Federal Rules of Civil Procedure. Furthermore, pursuant to Bankruptcy Rule 7002, "[w]henever a Federal Rule of Civil Procedure applicable to adversary proceedings makes reference to another Federal Rule of Civil Procedure, the reference shall be read as a reference to the Federal Rule of Civil Procedure as modified in this part VII."

§ 9.17

1. See supra, § 9.16. See infra, § 9.267 for a procedural checklist for commencing a contested matter, § 9.287 for a drafting checklist outlining general requirements for

matters include motions seeking: relief from the automatic stay,[2] adequate protection of a secured creditor's interest in property of the estate,[3] the assumption or rejection of leases and executory contracts,[4] approval of the sale or use of property outside the ordinary course of business,[5] and extension of the exclusive period for filing a plan of reorganization.[6] These proceedings are governed by Bankruptcy Rule 9014, which provides that in a contested matter, relief must be requested by motion, and reasonable notice and opportunity for a hearing must be afforded the party against whom relief is sought.[7] A filing fee may be required for certain contested matters.[8]

Library References:
West's Key No. Digests, Bankruptcy ⚖2156.

§ 9.18 Jurisdiction of the Bankruptcy Court

Bankruptcy judges do not have jurisdiction to enter final judgments on all proceedings that arise during the course of a bankruptcy case. Rather, in so-called "non-core" proceedings,[1] bankruptcy judges may only issue proposed findings of fact and conclusions of law that are subject to *de novo* review by the district court. This is because bankruptcy judges are appointed to courts created by Congress pursuant to its powers under Article I of the Constitution and may not exercise the full judicial power of the United States, as do federal district court judges who are appointed to courts created by Congress pursuant to its powers under Article III of the United States Constitution.[2]

pleadings in cases under the Bankruptcy Code, and §§ 9.306–9.308 for sample motion papers to commence a contested matter.

2. See infra, § 9.52.

3. See infra, § 9.56.

4. See infra, § 9.74.

5. See infra, § 9.62.

6. See infra, § 9.142.

7. Counsel should consult Bankruptcy Rule 2002 as well as the local rules to ascertain the notice requirements. Bankruptcy Rule 9006 determines the computation of time for notice purposes. Several specific rules from Part VII of the Bankruptcy Rules are listed in Bankruptcy Rule 9014 as also applying to contested matters; additionally, the court may direct that one or more of the other rules in Part VII shall apply. Note that Bankruptcy Rule 9013 requires that a "motion shall state with particularity the grounds therefor, and shall set forth the relief or order sought." See infra, § 9.287 for a drafting checklist of general rules for all motions.

8. 28 U.S.C.A. §§ 1930, 1914(a).

§ 9.18

1. See infra, § 9.19.

2. See 28 U.S.C.A. § 157; Northern Pipeline Construction Co. v. Marathon Pipe-line Co., 458 U.S. 50, 102 S.Ct. 2858, 73 L.Ed.2d 598 (1982). Although the Eleventh Amendment to the U.S. Constitution deprives the federal courts of jurisdiction over nonconsenting state governmental units, until recently bankruptcy courts nevertheless exercised limited jurisdiction over states in reliance on the authority of the Bankruptcy Code, which Congress enacted pursuant to the powers granted it under the Bankruptcy Clause of Article I of the Constitution. Section 106 of the Bankruptcy Code, which was significantly expanded by the Bankruptcy Reform Act of 1994, deems sovereign immunity to be waived by governmental units in a number of contexts, including many core matters of bankruptcy administration and adjudication of defenses to claims filed against the estate. 11 U.S.C.A. § 106.

§ 9.18   BANKRUPTCY   Ch. 9

Section 105(a) of the Bankruptcy Code provides a bankruptcy judge with broad equitable powers to issue any order or judgment "that is necessary or appropriate" to carry out the provisions of title 11.[3] However, Section 105(a) does not empower the court to create a cause of action otherwise unavailable under the Code, and a bankruptcy judge may not rely on Section 105(a) to contravene a specific Code provision.[4]

The jurisdiction of federal courts over the claims of and actions by state governmental units in bankruptcy cases is now a hotly contested issue as a result of decisions made by the United States Supreme Court in 1996. In Seminole Tribe of Florida v. Florida, ___ U.S. ___, 116 S.Ct. 1114, 134 L.Ed.2d 252 (1996), the Court held that the Eleventh Amendment was enacted, *inter alia*, to avoid "the indignity of subjecting a State to the coercive process of judicial tribunals at the instance of private parties." 116 S.Ct. at 1124. The Court ruled that Congress has the power to abrogate the sovereign immunity of the states only under the authority of the Fourteenth Amendment. Following the decision in Seminole Tribe, which did not concern bankruptcy, the Supreme Court quickly made clear that its decision in Seminole Tribe was equally applicable in the bankruptcy context. In Ohio Agricultural Commodity Depositors' Fund v. Mahern, ___ U.S. ___, 116 S.Ct. 1411, 134 L.Ed.2d 537 (1996), a bankruptcy trustee sought to recover, pursuant to § 547 of the Bankruptcy Code, an alleged preferential transfer from an arm of the State of Ohio. The Seventh Circuit had held that Congress can abrogate the states' Eleventh Amendment immunity when it acts pursuant to the plenary powers granted it under Article I of the Constitution. However, the Supreme Court vacated the decision and remanded the case to the Seventh Circuit for further consideration in light of Seminole. These decisions will create significant difficulties in adjudicating matters involving sovereign states in bankruptcy cases.

For example, in the only circuit court decision to date implementing Seminole in the bankruptcy context, the Fourth Circuit has concluded that Congress lacked the power to abrogate the states' sovereign immunity by means of Bankruptcy Code section 106. Schlossberg v. State of Maryland (In re Creative Goldsmiths of Washington, D.C.), 119 F.3d 1140 (4th Cir.1997). In Creative Goldsmiths, the Fourth Circuit held that because the Supreme Court's holding in Seminole extended to restrict all federal jurisdiction over the states based on Article I powers, Congress had no authority to abrogate state sovereign immunity in federal courts. Therefore, its enactment of 11 U.S.C.A. § 106 was unconstitutional and ineffective. *Id.* at 1147. In the absence of constitutional authorization, the Fourth Circuit found that "it lies solely within a state's sovereign power to waive its immunity voluntarily and to consent to federal jurisdiction." *Id.* The Fourth Circuit stated that in order to waive its sovereign immunity to suit in a particular context, a state's consent to be sued must be clearly intended by a statute or constitutional provision and it must be implemented by a state officer acting properly under that law. *Id.* at 1148.

3. In fact, the United States Supreme Court reversed a decision of the United States Court of Appeals for the Fifth Circuit and made clear that where a bankruptcy court has jurisdiction—even if its jurisdiction is based on the statutory language of "arising in or related to cases under title 11" (*see infra*, § 9.19)—a bankruptcy court's decision must be accorded respect and may not be avoided or challenged by a collateral attack in another jurisdiction. Celotex Corp. v. Edwards, 514 U.S. 300, 115 S.Ct. 1493, 131 L.Ed.2d 403 (1995).

4. Bankruptcy Rule 9020(a) provides that "[c]ontempt committed in the presence of a bankruptcy judge may be determined summarily by a bankruptcy judge." Bankruptcy Rule 9020(b) provides that contempt committed in a case or proceeding pending before a bankruptcy judge, out of the presence of such judge, "may be determined by the bankruptcy judge only after a hearing on notice." However, the Advisory Committee Note to the 1987 Amendment states that "this rule, as amended, recognizes that bankruptcy judges may not have the power to punish for contempt."

Several lower federal courts in New York have relied on Bankruptcy Rule 9020 and Section 105(a) of the Bankruptcy Code in holding that a bankruptcy court has the power to impose penalties for contempt. *See* Bartel v. Shugrue (In re Ionosphere Clubs, Inc.), 171 B.R. 18, 21 (S.D.N.Y.1994); Federation of Puerto Rican Orgs. of Brownsville, Inc. v. Howe, 157 B.R. 206, 211

Section 105(d) of the Bankruptcy Code, which was one of the amendments to the Code enacted in 1994, authorizes bankruptcy judges (either on their own volition or on motion of any party in interest) to hold status conferences regarding any case or proceeding after notice to parties in interest. The conferences, which are essentially a meeting of the debtor's creditors in the presence of the judge, are intended to expedite the case. The court may issue certain orders at these conferences even though the conferences lack the protections and procedures of formal hearings.

The 1994 amendments authorize a bankruptcy judge to conduct jury trials in core proceedings[5] if that judge is "specially designated" by the district court to exercise such jurisdiction and if all parties to the proceeding consent.[6]

(E.D.N.Y.1993); Balaber-Strauss v. Markowitz (In re Frankel), 192 B.R. 623, 629-30 (Bankr.S.D.N.Y.1996) (and cases cited therein).

The bankruptcy court for the Southern District of New York has articulated the following as the appropriate standard for finding a party in civil contempt:

> A court's inherent power to hold a party in civil contempt may be exercised only when (1) the order the party allegedly failed to comply with is clear and unambiguous, (2) the proof of noncompliance is clear and convincing, and (3) the party has not diligently attempted in a reasonable manner to comply.

Frankel, 192 B.R. at 627-28 (citing New York State Nat'l Org. for Women v. Terry, 886 F.2d 1339, 1351 (2d Cir.1989), cert. denied 495 U.S. 947, 110 S.Ct. 2206, 109 L.Ed.2d 532 (1990)). Although the party alleging contempt has the initial burden of proof,

> once the breach of a court order has been demonstrated, the burden must shift to the breaching party to establish as an affirmative defense that he was incapable of compliance through no fault of his own and despite diligent efforts to comply. The burden is on "the alleged contemnor [to] clearly establish[] his inability to comply with the terms of the order."

Frankel, 192 B.R. at 628 (citing Huber v. Marine Midland Bank, 51 F.3d 5, 10 (2d Cir.1995)).

The majority of the circuit courts of appeals that have considered whether a bankruptcy court has the authority to issue criminal contempt orders have concluded that a bankruptcy court does not have such authority. The Ninth Circuit has held that a bankruptcy court seeking issuance of a criminal contempt order must certify facts to the district court for *de novo* review. Plastiras v. Idell (In re Sequoia Auto Brokers, Ltd.), 827 F.2d 1281 (9th Cir.1987). The Fifth Circuit has stated that a bankruptcy court lacks the power to hear and determine criminal contempts, at least as to contempts not committed in (or near) its presence. Rather, the hearings and determination of such contempt prosecution must be by and before the district court. See Griffith v. Oles (In re Hipp, Inc.), 895 F.2d 1503, 1509 (5th Cir.1990), appeal after remand 5 F.3d 109 (5th Cir.1993). Although the Eighth Circuit has held that a bankruptcy court order holding a party in criminal contempt did not violate Article III of the Constitution, the bankruptcy court explicitly made the order reviewable *de novo* by the district court. Brown v. Ramsay (In re Ragar), 3 F.3d 1174 (8th Cir.1993).

The Second Circuit has held that a *district court* may punish for criminal contempt a violation of an order of a bankruptcy court. United States v. Guariglia, 962 F.2d 160, 162 (2d Cir.1992). Although the Second Circuit has not been required to resolve the issue of whether the bankruptcy court itself could make such a ruling, the court stated that "there is a serious question as to whether the bankruptcy court would have had the authority to punish [the alleged contemnor] for criminal contempt of its Order." Id. at 163.

5. See infra, § 9.19 for a discussion of core proceedings.

6. 28 U.S.C.A. § 157(e).

§ 9.19 Jurisdiction of the Bankruptcy Court—Types of Jurisdiction

A distinction must be made between a bankruptcy "case" and a bankruptcy "proceeding." The bankruptcy case is the overall matter pending in the bankruptcy court—the entire process of reorganizing or liquidating a debtor's estate. The individual controversies that arise during the bankruptcy case are "proceedings." The district court has exclusive jurisdiction over the bankruptcy case as a whole pursuant to 28 U.S.C.A. § 1334(a). Under 28 U.S.C.A. § 1334(b), however, the district court has only concurrent jurisdiction over the individual civil proceedings "arising under" the Bankruptcy Code, or "arising in" or "related to" a bankruptcy case.[1]

Under 28 U.S.C.A. § 151, the bankruptcy court constitutes a unit of the district court. Section 157(a) of title 28 gives the federal district court the power to refer all bankruptcy cases and proceedings to the bankruptcy court. Therefore, most district courts have a standing general order to refer all bankruptcy cases to the bankruptcy court. Even though the district court has referred the entire bankruptcy case to the bankruptcy court, pursuant to 28 U.S.C.A. § 157(b)(1), bankruptcy courts may enter final judgments only in so-called "core" proceedings. Bankruptcy courts may not enter final judgments in "non-core" or "related to" proceedings without the consent of the parties.[2] Therefore,

---

§ 9.19

1. See 28 U.S.C.A. § 1409 for venue of proceedings arising under title 11 or arising in or related to cases under title 11. See also, 11 U.S.C.A. § 305 setting forth the circumstances under which a court may dismiss a case or suspend all proceedings in a case under title 11.

2. **PRACTICE POINTER**: A "non-core" or "related to" proceeding may be converted into a "core" proceeding where a party submits itself to the jurisdiction of the court. Accordingly, where a debtor commences a "non-core" or a "related to" proceeding against a third party, such third party must consider the ramifications of participating in the title 11 process by filing a claim against the debtor's estate, and the concomitant potential submission to the jurisdiction of the court.

PRACTICE POINTER: The Second Circuit has held that by filing a proof of claim, a creditor submits itself to the bankruptcy court's equitable jurisdiction and waives its right to a jury trial with respect to a determination of that claim. See, e.g., S.G. Phillips Constructors, Inc. v. City of Burlington (In re City of Burlington), 45 F.3d 702 (2d Cir.1995) (relying on Supreme Court decisions such as Langenkamp v. Culp, 498 U.S. 42, 111 S.Ct. 330, 112 L.Ed.2d 343 (1990)), rehearing denied 498 U.S. 1043, 111 S.Ct. 721, 112 L.Ed. 2d 709 (1991); In re Leslie Fay Cos., Inc., 181 B.R. 156 (Bankr. S.D.N.Y.1995). Note, however, that the Second Circuit also has held that the filing of a proof of claim does not automatically waive the right to a jury trial as to all disputes between the debtor and the claimant. Rather, in order for the filing of a proof of claim to constitute waiver of a jury trial, the dispute must be part of the claims allowance process or affect the hierarchical ordering of creditors' claims. See Germain v. Connecticut Nat'l Bank, 988 F.2d 1323 (2d Cir.1993); Hassett v. BancOhio Nat'l Bank (In re CIS Corp.), 172 B.R. 748 (S.D.N.Y. 1994).

Other circuit courts, however, have determined that in filing a proof of claim, the claimant waives its rights to a jury trial with respect to all disputes with the debtor vital to the process of allowance and disallowance of claims, including the power to inquire into the validity of its claim. See, e.g., Benedor Corp. v. Conejo Enter., Inc. (In re Conejo Enter., Inc.), 96 F.3d 346 (9th Cir.1996).

whether a matter is deemed "core" or "non-core" directly affects the bankruptcy court's jurisdiction to determine a proceeding.[3]

In general, core proceedings are those proceedings "arising under title 11" or "arising in a case under title 11." The phrase "arising under title 11" describes those proceedings that involve a cause of action created or determined by a statutory provision of title 11. "Arising in" proceedings are not based on any right expressly created by title 11, but would have no existence outside the bankruptcy.[4]

Proceedings that are only "related to" a case under title 11 are considered "non-core" proceedings and are governed by 28 U.S.C.A. § 157(c). Although a bankruptcy judge may hear a non-core proceeding that is related to a case under title 11, in those proceedings the judge may only submit "proposed findings of fact and conclusions of law to the district court, and any final order or judgment shall be entered by the district judge after considering the bankruptcy judge's proposed findings and conclusions and after reviewing *de novo* those matters to which any party has timely and specifically objected."[5]

A proceeding is entitled to "related to" jurisdiction if "the outcome of that proceeding could conceivably have any effect on the estate being administered in bankruptcy."[6] Thus, a proceeding is "related to bankruptcy if the outcome could alter the debtor's rights, liabilities, options, or freedom of action (either positively or negatively) and which in any way impacts upon the handling and administration of the bankrupt estate."[7] Therefore, the proceeding need not necessarily directly involve the debtor or the debtor's property.[8]

---

3. The parties may consent to the bankruptcy court's hearing and determining a non-core proceeding pursuant to 28 U.S.C.A. § 157(c)(2).

4. *See* Wood v. Wood (In re Wood), 825 F.2d 90, 96–97 (5th Cir.1987).

PRACTICE POINTER: In the interest of justice, or in the interest of comity with state courts or respect for state law, a district court may abstain from hearing a proceeding arising under title 11 or arising in or related to a case under title 11. 28 U.S.C.A. § 1334(c). *See infra*, § 9.23 discussing abstention.

5. 28 U.S.C.A. § 157(c)(1). If all the parties to the proceeding consent, the district court may refer a proceeding related to a case under title 11 to a bankruptcy judge to hear, determine, and enter appropriate orders and judgments. 28 U.S.C.A. § 157(c)(2).

6. *See, e.g.*, In re Turner, 724 F.2d 338, 340–41 (2d Cir.1983). The best-known expression of this test was in Pacor, Inc. v. Higgins, 743 F.2d 984, 994 (3d Cir.1984).

The Supreme Court expressed its approval of the test articulated in Pacor. *See* Celotex Corp. v. Edwards, 514 U.S. 300, 115 S.Ct. 1493, 131 L.Ed.2d 403 (1995).

7. Pacor, Inc. v. Higgins, 743 F.2d 984, 994 (3d Cir.1984).

8. For example, in the mass tort chapter 11 case of the Dow Corning Corporation, the Sixth Circuit held that under 28 U.S.C.A. § 1334(b), the district court in which the debtor's case is pending has "related to" subject matter jurisdiction over the tens of thousands of personal injury claims pending against *nondebtor* defendants, and could transfer the claims removed from state courts or filed in other federal courts pursuant to 28 U.S.C.A § 157(b)(5). In re Dow Corning Corp., 86 F.3d 482 (6th Cir.1996), cert. denied ___ U.S. ___, 117 S.Ct. 718, 136 L.Ed.2d 636 (1997). The court agreed with the nondebtors who argued that the district court had "related to" jurisdiction over the personal injury claims because (i) the contingent claims for contribution and indemnification

§ 9.19

Library References:

West's Key No. Digests, Bankruptcy ⚖︎2043(1)–2043(3).

§ 9.20 Jurisdiction of the Bankruptcy Court—Case Ancillary to Foreign Proceedings

A voluntary case ancillary to a foreign proceeding[1] may be commenced by the filing of a petition by the duly selected representative of the estate[2] in the foreign proceeding.[3] The filing of an ancillary petition does not commence a full bankruptcy case. Instead, it prevents piecemeal distribution of a foreign debtor's assets in the U.S. by local creditors when a bankruptcy case is pending in a foreign jurisdiction, and it enables the court to provide other appropriate relief.[4] The eligibility requirements of Section 109 of the Code do not apply so long as the foreign debtor is eligible to be the subject of a foreign proceeding under the laws of its home jurisdiction.[5]

Library References:

West's Key No. Digests, Bankruptcy ⚖︎2341.

§ 9.21 Venue

The proper venues for commencing a case under title 11 include the district court for the district in which the domicile, residence, principal place of business in the United States, or principal assets in the United States, of the debtor have been located for the 180 days (or the longest portion thereof) immediately preceding the filing of the petition. A case under title 11 also may be commenced in the district court for the district "in which there is pending a case under title 11 concerning such

by or against the debtor, (ii) the jointly held insurance policies between the debtor and the nondebtor manufacturers, (iii) the potential collateral estoppel effect and increased exposure to liability, and (iv) the burden of continued litigation in tens of thousands of cases, could conceivably affect the reorganization of the debtor. *Id.*

§ 9.20

1. A "foreign proceeding" is a "proceeding, whether judicial or administrative and whether or not under bankruptcy law, in a foreign country in which the debtor's domicile, residence, principal place of business, or principal assets were located at the commencement of such proceeding, for the purpose of liquidating an estate, adjusting debts by composition, extension, or discharge, or effecting a reorganization." 11 U.S.C.A. § 101(23).

2. *See* 11 U.S.C.A. § 101(24).

3. 11 U.S.C.A. § 304(a).

4. H.R.Rep.No. 95–595, 95th Cong., 1st Sess. 324–25 (1977); S.Rep.No. 95–989, 95th Cong., 2d Sess. 35 (1978). *See* Victrix Steamship Co., S.A. v. Salen Dry Cargo A.B., 825 F.2d 709, 713–14 (2d Cir.1987); Cunard Steamship Co. Ltd. v. Salen Reefer Servs. A.B., 773 F.2d 452, 454–55 (2d Cir. 1985). An ancillary case under Section 304 is "a somewhat amorphous vehicle whose shape can be ascertained only in reference to the specific type of relief sought in each case." In re Brierley, 145 B.R. 151, 155 (Bankr.S.D.N.Y.1992).

5. In re Brierley, 145 B.R. 151, 159 (Bankr.S.D.N.Y.1992) (foreign debtor in an ancillary proceeding is not a debtor in a case under title 11, but a debtor only under foreign law).

person's affiliate, general partner, or partnership."[1]

With certain exceptions, a bankruptcy proceeding may be commenced in the district court in which the underlying bankruptcy case itself is pending.[2] However, if a debtor or trustee seeks to recover a money judgment of, or property worth less than $1,000, or a consumer debt of less than $5,000, the proceeding can be commenced only in the district court for the district in which the defendant resides.[3]

On motion and after a hearing, a district court may transfer a case or proceeding under title 11 to a district court for another district in the interest of justice or for the convenience of the parties.[4]

Library References:
   West's Key No. Digests, Bankruptcy ⇐2081, 2082.

§ 9.22 Withdrawal of Reference

The district court can "withdraw" its "reference" of a particular case or proceeding (*i.e.*, revoke its prior automatic referral of the matter to the bankruptcy court) if the matter involves issues that should or must be adjudicated by an Article III court.[1] Withdrawal of the reference may be required under certain circumstances, or a district court may at its discretion determine to withdraw the reference of the case or proceeding for cause shown.

In general, there are three conditions that must be met to justify mandatory withdrawal.[2] First, the entity moving for withdrawal of the reference must be a party. Second, the motion to withdraw the reference must be timely. Third, the resolution of the proceedings must require consideration of both the Bankruptcy Code and non-bankruptcy federal law "regulating interstate commerce."[3] Once this standard for mandatory withdrawal has been met, a district court does not have discretion to deny a motion for withdrawal.[4]

The meaning of the statutory provision compelling withdrawal of the reference if resolution of the matter requires "consideration of both

---

§ 9.21

1. 28 U.S.C.A. § 1408.

2. *See supra*, § 9.19 explaining the distinction between a bankruptcy case and a bankruptcy proceeding.

3. 28 U.S.C.A. § 1409(b).

4. Bankr.R. 7087; 28 U.S.C.A. § 1412.

§ 9.22

1. For example, in one case, the district court withdrew the reference of the case to the bankruptcy court, "re-referred" the core portions of the case to the bankruptcy court, and ordered that the non-referred portions of the case were to be administered jointly by the district court and the bankruptcy court. *See* The Drexel Burnham Lambert Group, Inc. v. Vigilant Ins. Co., 130 B.R. 405, 406 (S.D.N.Y.1991), on remand 157 Misc.2d 198, 595 N.Y.S.2d 99 (1993).

2. *See* In re Texaco, 84 B.R. 911 (S.D.N.Y.1988).

3. A motion for withdrawal of a case or proceeding must be heard by a district court judge. Bankr.R. 5011(a).

4. In re Combustion Equip. Assocs., Inc., 67 B.R. 709 (S.D.N.Y.1986).

title 11 and other laws of the United States regulating organizations or activities affecting interstate commerce"[5] is subject to much debate among the courts, and courts have utilized two approaches in applying this requirement. Certain courts have applied a "strict" construction of Section 157(d), concluding that "withdrawal is mandatory when the proceeding requires resolution of title 11 and non-bankruptcy code federal law statutes, regardless of the substantiality of the legal questions presented."[6] The emerging trend, however, appears to be a more "liberal" construction, mandating withdrawal only "if resolution of the issues requires 'substantial and material consideration' of non-bankruptcy code statutes."[7]

Section 157(d) further provides for the "discretionary" withdrawal of the reference of any case or proceeding even if the case is one that could properly be heard in the bankruptcy court. Permissive withdrawal of the reference may occur for "cause shown," and the standard for permissive withdrawal is flexible.[8] There are a number of factors which should be considered in determining whether to exercise such "permissive withdrawal," including whether the proceeding is a core or a non-core proceeding, whether one of the parties has demanded or is entitled to a jury trial, judicial economy, prevention of forum shopping, uniformity in the administration of bankruptcy law, and expertise of the court.

Note, however, that certain courts have held that the presence of a jury demand and the non-core nature of the proceeding alone do not constitute "cause" to immediately withdraw the reference to the bankruptcy court. Rather, courts may focus on the status of the case—in particular, whether the case is ready for trial—in determining what is the most efficient use of judicial resources. These courts frequently wait to withdraw the reference until the case is actually ready to go to the jury, and allow the bankruptcy court to preside over pretrial matters.[9]

Library References:
West's Key No. Digests, Bankruptcy ⚖2103.

§ 9.23 Abstention

A party also may move that the bankruptcy court abstain from

---

5. 28 U.S.C.A. § 157(d).

6. *See* In re American Body Armor & Equip., Inc., 155 B.R. 588, 590 (M.D.Fla. 1993).

7. *See* In re Mahlmann, 149 B.R. 866, 870 (N.D.Ill.1993) (Section 157(d) requires "significant interpretation" rather than "simple application" of non-Bankruptcy Code statutes).

8. *See* American Community Servs., Inc. v. Wright Marketing, Inc. (In re American Community Servs., Inc.), 86 B.R. 681, 686 (D.Utah 1988) ("permissive withdrawal of the reference is within the sound discretion of the court and predicated upon 'cause' shown on a case by case basis").

9. *See* In re Orion Pictures Corp., 4 F.3d 1095 (2d Cir.1993), cert. dismissed 511 U.S. 1026, 114 S.Ct. 1418, 128 L.Ed.2d 88 (1994); Times Circle East, Inc. v. Edward Isaacs & Co. (In re Times Circle East), No. 94 B 455593 (TLB), 1995 WL 489551 (S.D.N.Y.1995).

hearing a particular proceeding.[1] Abstention may be either mandatory or discretionary. The mandatory abstention requirements are contained in 28 U.S.C.A. § 1334(c)(2).[2] A decision to abstain or not to abstain, other than a mandatory decision to abstain, is not reviewable on appeal.[3]

Library References:

West's Key No. Digests, Federal Courts ⇐47.1.

§ 9.24 Removal

A party may remove any claim or cause of action to the district court for the district wherein a civil action other than a proceeding before the United States Tax Court or a civil action by a governmental unit to enforce such governmental unit's police or regulatory power is pending, if such district court has jurisdiction of such claim or cause of action under 28 U.S.C.A. § 1334.[1] Bankruptcy Rule 9027(a)(2) governs the timing for seeking to remove a state court action.[2]

Library References:

West's Key No. Digests, Bankruptcy ⇐2086.1–2091.

§ 9.25 Appeals—To District Court and Bankruptcy Appellate Panel From Bankruptcy Court

The district courts have jurisdiction to hear appeals from final judgments, orders, and decrees, and, with leave of the court, from interlocutory orders and decrees of bankruptcy judges.[1] The Bankruptcy Reform Act of 1994 provides for the establishment in each judicial circuit of a bankruptcy appellate panel, composed of sitting bankruptcy judges, to serve in place of the district court in reviewing bankruptcy court decisions.[2] A three-judge Bankruptcy Appellate Panel will hear and

§ 9.23

1. 28 U.S.C.A. § 1334(c).

2. *See* In re Republic Reader's Service, Inc., 81 B.R. 422, 429 (Bankr.S.D.Tex.1987) for factors that a court should consider in determining whether to exercise discretionary abstention.

A motion for abstention pursuant to § 28 U.S.C.A. § 1334(c) is governed by Bankruptcy Rule 9014 and must be served on the parties to the proceeding. Bankr.R.5011.

3. 28 U.S.C.A. § 1334(d).

§ 9.24

1. 28 U.S.C.A. § 1452.

2. **PRACTICE POINTER**: A debtor, especially a larger debtor who is a party to a number of state court actions, should consider moving in the bankruptcy court for an extension of the time period in which to remove the state court actions to the appropriate district court.

§ 9.25

1. 28 U.S.C.A. § 158(a). *See infra*, § 9.268 for a procedural checklist for filing an appeal from an interlocutory judgment, order, or decree.

PRACTICE POINTER: Counsel should refer with care to Part VIII of the Bankruptcy Rules for the detailed procedural requirements governing appeals. The summary herein concerning appellate procedure is not intended to be exhaustive.

2. *See* 28 U.S.C.A. § 158(b), (c). The Judicial Council of the Second Circuit has established a Bankruptcy Appellate Panel (BAP) Service effective July 1, 1996. Its jurisdiction extends to Vermont, the Northern District of New York, and Connecticut,

determine, with the consent of all parties, any appeals which formerly would have been heard by a district court.[3]

In general, pursuant to F.R.C.P. 62, which applies in adversary proceedings, actions to enforce a judgment are stayed for a period of ten days from entry of an order. However, in addition to the exceptions to the rule listed in F.R.C.P. 62(a), Bankruptcy Rule 7062 excepts from the 10–day stay of enforcement orders that:

- Grant relief from the automatic stay provided by Section 362, 1201, or 1301;
- Authorize or prohibit the use of cash collateral;
- Authorize the use, sale, or lease of property of the estate under Section 363;
- Authorize the extension of credit under Section 364; and
- Authorize the assumption or rejection of an executory contract or unexpired lease under Section 365.

A notice of appeal must be filed with the clerk of the bankruptcy court within ten days of entry of a final judgment or decree.[4] The bankruptcy judge may extend the time for filing the notice of appeal by any party for an additional 20–day period.[5] However, the motion to extend the time to file a notice of appeal must be made within the initial 10–day period, except that a request made no more than 20 days after the expiration of the time for filing a notice of appeal may be granted upon a showing of excusable neglect if the judgment, order, or decree appealed from does not authorize the sale of any property or the obtaining of credit or the incurring of debt under Section 364 of the Bankruptcy Code, or is not a judgment or order approving a disclosure statement, confirming a plan, dismissing a case, or converting the case to a case under another chapter of the Code.

An appeal from an interlocutory judgment, order, or decree of a bankruptcy judge is to be taken by filing a notice of appeal accompanied by a motion for leave to appeal prepared in accordance with Bankruptcy Rule 8003 and with proof of service in accordance with Bankruptcy Rule 8008. Within 10 days after service of a motion for leave to appeal, an adverse party may file an answer in opposition.[6]

but will not extend initially to the Eastern District of New York, the Western District of New York, and the Southern District of New York. It is anticipated that the service will be extended to the three remaining districts after an initial period. The BAP will hear appeals initiated on or after July 1, 1996 in cases filed on or after October 22, 1994.

3. 28 U.S.C.A. § 158(b)(1).

4. Bankr.R. 8001(a), 8002(a). If a notice of appeal is mistakenly filed with the district court or the bankruptcy appellate panel, the clerk of the district court or the clerk of the bankruptcy appellate panel is required to note the date it was received and transmit the notice to the clerk of the bankruptcy court. It will be deemed filed with the clerk of the bankruptcy court on the date noted. Bankr.R. 8002(a).

5. Bankr.R. 8002(c).

6. Bankr.R. 8003(a).

Only parties that satisfy the "persons aggrieved" standard have standing to appeal a decision in a bankruptcy case. A "person aggrieved" has been defined as a person whose "rights or interests are 'directly affected pecuniarily' by the order or decree of the bankruptcy court."[7]

Whether a proceeding constitutes a core or a non-core matter determines the district court's standard of review on an appeal of a bankruptcy court decision. The bankruptcy court's findings of fact and conclusions of law in non-core matters are both subject to *de novo* review by the district court.[8] In core matters a district court reviews the bankruptcy court's conclusions of law *de novo*, but reviews the bankruptcy court's findings of facts under the more deferential "clearly erroneous" standard.[9]

A party also may file a motion for a stay of a judgment or order of the bankruptcy judge pending appeal.[10] A party may seek a stay in order to prevent an order (such as an order confirming a plan of reorganization) from becoming substantially consummated prior to the time the district court rules on the appeal. If it is not stayed, an appeal of the bankruptcy court order may become moot by the time the district court rules on the appeal.[11]

---

7. "A person who seeks to appeal an order of the bankruptcy court must be 'directly and adversely affected pecuniarily' by it." Kane v. Johns–Manville Corp. (In re Johns–Manville Corp.), 843 F.2d 636, 641 (2d Cir.1988), citing Cosmopolitan Aviation Corp. v. New York State Dep't of Transp. (In re Cosmopolitan Aviation Corp.), 763 F.2d 507, 513 (2d Cir.), cert. denied 474 U.S. 1032, 106 S.Ct. 593, 88 L.Ed.2d 573 (1985). *See* General Motors Acceptance Corp. v. Dykes (In re Dykes), 10 F.3d 184, 187 (3d Cir.1993) ("Litigants are 'persons aggrieved' if the order diminishes their property, increases their burdens, or impairs their rights").

8. 28 U.S.C.A. § 158(c).

9. Bankr.R. 8013. The Second Circuit has stated that an unreviewed decision of a district court should not have a binding effect on a bankruptcy court. Robb v. New York Joint Board, Amalgamated Clothing Workers of America, 506 F.2d 1246, 1247 (2d Cir.1974).

10. Bankr.R. 8005. *See infra*, § 9.268 for a procedural checklist and § 9.290 for a drafting checklist for a stay pending appeal.

11. **PRACTICE POINTER**: From the debtor's perspective, it is wise to move expeditiously to implement the authorization granted under certain court orders. For example, when a debtor is authorized to sell property pursuant to Section 363 of the Bankruptcy Code, an alleged aggrieved party may not obtain reversal or modification of such authorization on appeal unless the sale is stayed pending appeal. *See* 11 U.S.C.A. § 363(m). *See infra*, § 9.64 note 1 for discussion of a case demonstrating the importance of obtaining a stay pending appeal of an order authorizing the sale of property of the debtor's estate. Accordingly, it behooves a debtor to act promptly to close such a transaction upon receiving authorization to do so.

In cases wherein an appeal of an order confirming a plan of reorganization has been filed, courts frequently have found that effective appellate relief from a plan confirmation order is impracticable or inequitable because non-appealing parties have relied on transactions that have been substantially consummated after plan confirmation. Under such circumstances, courts may decline to grant relief based upon mootness. *See, e.g.*, Resolution Trust Corp. v. Best Prods. Co. (In re Best Prods. Co.), 177 B.R. 791 (S.D.N.Y.1995), aff'd 68 F.3d 26 (2d Cir.1995). However, the Second Circuit has held that substantial consummation of a plan of reorganization does not *necessarily* moot a creditor's appeal of its treatment under a confirmed plan of reorganization. In re Chateaugay Corp., 10 F.3d 944 (2d Cir.1993).

§ 9.26 Appeals—To Court of Appeals From District Court

The federal courts of appeals have jurisdiction of appeals from all *final* decisions, judgments, orders, and decrees entered by district courts in bankruptcy cases.[1] Although no *right* of appeal lies from an interlocutory order of the district court under 28 U.S.C.A. § 158(d), a party may move to certify an interlocutory appeal to the circuit court under 28 U.S.C.A. § 1292(b).[2] To obtain appellate review under Section 1292(b), both the district court and the circuit court must agree that the issue should be certified for appeal:

> When a district judge, in making in a civil action an order not otherwise appealable under this section, shall be of the opinion that such order involves a controlling question of law as to which there is substantial ground for difference of opinion and that an immediate appeal from the order may materially advance the ultimate termination of the litigation, he shall so state in writing in such order. The Court of Appeals which would have jurisdiction of an appeal of such action may thereupon, in its discretion, permit an appeal to be taken from such order, if application is made to it within ten days after the entry of the order.[3]

Thus, certification lies principally within the discretion of the district court judge.[4]

Library References:

West's Key No. Digests, Bankruptcy ⇌3761.

§ 9.27 The Debtor in Possession

Upon the filing of a voluntary petition in a chapter 11 or 12 case, or upon the entry of an order for relief in an involuntary chapter 11 case, the individual or entity that is the subject of the bankruptcy petition assumes the status of a debtor in possession.[1] A debtor in possession does

---

§ 9.26

1. 28 U.S.C.A. § 158(d).

   PRACTICE POINTER: Counsel should refer to Part VIII of the Bankruptcy Rules for procedural requirements governing appeals.

2. *See* Connecticut Nat'l Bank v. Germain, 503 U.S. 249, 112 S.Ct. 1146, 117 L.Ed.2d 391 (1992) ("so long as a party to a proceeding or case in bankruptcy meets the conditions imposed by § 1292, a court of appeals may rely on that statute as a basis for jurisdiction" to hear an interlocutory appeal).

3. 28 U.S.C.A. § 1292(b).

4. J. Moore, *Moore's Federal Practice* ¶ 110.22[3], at 277–78 (2d ed.1995).

§ 9.27

1. *See* 11 U.S.C.A. § 1101(1). The debtor in possession is frequently referred to by its acronym, DIP.

not become a legal entity separate from the prepetition debtor.[2] The Supreme Court has held that it is "sensible to view" the debtor in possession as the same "entity" which existed prior to the bankruptcy filing but empowered with certain duties and responsibilities under the Bankruptcy Code.[3] A debtor in possession retains possession of all the debtor's property and business and is vested with fiduciary duties to creditors and equity security holders.[4] In cases under chapter 11, 12, or 13, the debtor remains in possession of its property during the pendency of the case unless the court orders the appointment of a trustee.[5] If a trustee is serving in a chapter 7, 12, or 13 case that is subsequently converted to chapter 11, the conversion terminates the trustee's tenure.[6]

Library References:
West's Key No. Digests, Bankruptcy ⇐3622.

§ 9.28 The Debtor in Possession—Rights, Powers and Duties

The debtor in possession in a chapter 11 or 12 case is vested with all the powers and duties of a trustee appointed in a chapter 11 case, as described below, except for the investigative duties delegated to a trustee.[1] With respect to the use, sale, or lease of its property, a debtor under chapter 13 is vested with the identical rights and powers, and is subject to the same limitations, as a trustee under chapters 7, 11, or 12.[2] Chapter 13 does not specifically grant or deny a debtor the trustee's power to pursue avoidance actions,[3] and courts are divided on whether a chapter 13 debtor may exercise such powers.[4] The debtor in possession is authorized to continue to operate its business unless the court, after notice and a hearing, upon request of a party in interest, orders otherwise.[5] The debtor in possession and its officers and directors bear the

---

2. NLRB v. Bildisco and Bildisco, 465 U.S. 513, 528, 104 S.Ct. 1188, 1197, 79 L.Ed.2d 482 (1984).

3. *Id.*

4. *See* H. Miller, *Corporate Governance in Chapter 11*, 23 Seton Hall L.Rev.1467 (1993).

5. 11 U.S.C.A. §§ 1101, 1107(a), 1203, 1304.

6. 11 U.S.C.A. § 348(e).

§ 9.28

1. 11 U.S.C.A. §§ 1107(a), 1203. Accordingly, references in the Bankruptcy Code to the trustee should be understood to be references to the debtor in possession. 124 Cong.Rec. H 11,102 (Sept. 28, 1978); S 17,419 (Oct. 6, 1978).

2. 11 U.S.C.A. §§ 1303, 1304.

3. *See infra,* §§ 9.113–9.119 for a discussion of avoidance actions.

4. *Compare* In re Pruitt, 72 B.R. 436, 438 (Bankr.E.D.N.Y.1987) (chapter 13 debtor has power to avoid fraudulent transfers under section 548 of the Bankruptcy Code) and In re Ottaviano, 68 B.R. 238, 240 (Bankr.D.Conn.1986) ("I ... accept the majority view that a chapter 13 debtor has standing to bring [avoidance] actions.") with In re Walls, 17 B.R. 701, 704 (Bankr. S.D.W.Va.1982) (chapter 7 debtor does not have the exclusive right to use the trustee's avoiding powers) and In re Mast, 79 B.R. 981, 982 (Bankr.W.D.Mich.1987) ("those cases which hold the Chapter 13 debtor lacks the power to unilaterally set aside avoidable transfers are better reasoned and more persuasive than those cases decided to the contrary").

5. 11 U.S.C.A. § 1108.

§ 9.28 BANKRUPTCY Ch. 9

same fiduciary duties to creditors and stockholders of the debtor as does a trustee in bankruptcy.[6]

Library References:

West's Key No. Digests, Bankruptcy ⚖3622.

§ 9.29 Employment of Professionals

A debtor in possession or trustee is permitted to employ attorneys, accountants, appraisers, auctioneers, or other professional persons,[1] with prior court approval,[2] provided such persons (1) do not hold or represent any interest adverse to the estate, and (2) are disinterested.[3] A statutory committee appointed in a debtor's chapter 11 case also may employ attorneys, accountants, or other agents to represent or perform services for them.[4] Such professionals also are subject to the requirements of Section 327(a).[5] Once an attorney or other professional is retained, any other members, partners, or regular associates of his or her firm may act in the case without further court approval.[6]

A "disinterested person" means a person who (1) is not a creditor,[7] an equity security holder, or an insider,[8] (2) is not and was not an

---

6. Commodity Futures Trading Comm'n v. Weintraub, 471 U.S. 343, 355, 105 S.Ct. 1986, 1994, 85 L.Ed.2d 372 (1985), citing Wolf v. Weinstein, 372 U.S. 633, 649–52, 83 S.Ct. 969, 979–81, 10 L.Ed.2d 33 (1963). In dicta, the Second Circuit has left open the question of whether an insolvent debtor has any duties to stockholders, since stockholders would have no equity in an insolvent company and, therefore, would no longer be real parties in interest. Manville Corp. v. The Equity Security Holders Committee (In re Johns–Manville Corp.), 801 F.2d 60, 65 note 6 (2d Cir.1986).

CAVEAT: The officers and directors of a debtor in possession may, like a trustee, be required to waive attorney-client privilege in order to uphold fiduciary duties to creditors and shareholders. Commodity Futures Trading Comm'n v. Weintraub, 471 U.S. 343, 355–56, 105 S.Ct. 1986, 1994–95, 85 L.Ed.2d 372 (1985).

§ 9.29

1. "For the purposes of section 327(a), 'professional person' is limited to persons in those occupations which play a central role in the administration of the debtor proceeding. Court approval is required for the retention of attorneys, accountants, appraisers, auctioneers and persons in other professions intimately involved in the administration of the debtor's estate." In re Seatrain Lines, Inc., 13 B.R. 980, 981 (Bankr.S.D.N.Y.1981).

2. The United States trustee is responsible for monitoring and overseeing the appointment and compensation of professionals retained by debtors or statutory committees in cases under the Bankruptcy Code. 28 U.S.C.A. § 586(a)(3)(A) and (H).

CAVEAT: Counsel should file an application for retention when the case is commenced; failure to obtain court approval may result in forfeiture of fees. See infra, § 9.291 for a drafting checklist for an application of a professional for retention and §§ 9.310–9.311 for a sample application for retention and attorney's affidavit.

3. 11 U.S.C.A. § 327(a).

4. 11 U.S.C.A. § 1103(a).

5. In re Caldor, Inc., 193 B.R. 165 (Bankr.S.D.N.Y.1996).

6. Bankr.R. 2014(b).

7. CAVEAT: A professional who is owed money by the debtor when the case is filed is a creditor of the debtor and, therefore, may be ineligible for retention for failure to be disinterested.

8. 11 U.S.C.A. § 101(14)(A). An "insider" is defined at 11 U.S.C.A. § 101(31) and includes such persons as relatives, partners, officers, directors, and persons in control of the debtor.

investment banker for any outstanding security of the debtor,[9] (3) has not been, within three years before the date of the filing of the petition, an investment banker for a security of the debtor, or an attorney for such investment banker in connection with the offer, sale, or issuance of a security of the debtor,[10] and (4) is not and was not a director, officer, or employee of the debtor or the debtor's investment banker within two years of the filing of the petition,[11] and who does not hold "an interest materially adverse to the interest of the estate or of any class of creditors or equity security holders, by reason of any direct or indirect relationship to, connection with, or interest in the debtor or an investment banker [as described above]."[12] Although the term "interest adverse" is not defined in the Bankruptcy Code, courts have interpreted it to mean "a competing economic interest tending to diminish estate values or to create a potential or actual dispute in which the estate is a rival claimant."[13] In other words, a professional has a disqualifying conflict if there is a meaningful incentive to act differently than he or she would act without that conflict.[14]

Section 327(e) provides that "for a specified special purpose," other than to represent the trustee or debtor in conducting the case, the trustee or debtor may employ an attorney who has represented the debtor prepetition if it is in the best interest of the estate, and the attorney does not hold any interest adverse to the estate with respect to the matter on which such attorney is to be employed.[15]

Although a person is not disqualified for employment solely because he or she previously was employed by or represented a creditor, the bankruptcy court is empowered to disqualify a professional from employment by the trustee or the debtor in possession if another creditor or the

---

9. 11 U.S.C.A. § 101(14)(B).

10. 11 U.S.C.A. § 101(14)(C).

11. 11 U.S.C.A. § 101(14)(D).

12. 11 U.S.C.A. § 101(14)(E).

13. In re Caldor, 193 B.R. 165, 171 (Bankr.S.D.N.Y.1996), citing In re TWI Int'l, Inc. v. Vanguard Oil & Serv. Co., 162 B.R. 672, 675 (S.D.N.Y.1994).

14. Id., citing In re Leslie Fay Cos., Inc., 175 B.R. 525, 533 (Bankr.S.D.N.Y.1994). See also In re CF Holding Corp., 164 B.R. 799 (Bankr.D.Conn.1994) (adverse interest means an interest that would tend to decrease the value of the estate or a predisposition or bias against the estate).

15. 11 U.S.C.A. § 327(e). This provision enables the debtor to employ as "special counsel" an attorney who has represented the debtor prepetition even if the attorney is not disinterested (that is, even if the attorney is owed money by the debtor and, therefore, is a creditor) as long as the attorney holds no interest adverse to the interests of the estate. The provision is intended to permit the debtor to retain the benefit of the special knowledge that an attorney has acquired in representing the debtor in a particular special matter. "The subsection will most likely be used when the debtor is involved in complex litigation, and changing attorneys in the middle of the case after the bankruptcy case has commenced would be detrimental to the progress of that other litigation." H.R.Rep.No. 95-595, 95th Cong., 1st Sess. 328 (1977); see S.Rep.No. 95-989, 95th Cong., 2d Sess. 38 (1978).

CAVEAT: Special counsel retained pursuant to § 327(e) may not assist in "conducting the case," that is, in matters related to the normal administration of a case, such as plan negotiation and formulation, examining the validity of claims or liens, or pursuing avoidance actions. Compensation for special counsel will only be authorized for professional services directly related to the limited scope of retention.

§ 9.29   BANKRUPTCY   Ch. 9

U.S. trustee objects, and the court finds that such employment would create an actual conflict of interest based on the professional's prior employment by or representation of a creditor.[16]

A debtor in possession, trustee, or statutory committee appointed in the case must file an application and transmit a copy to the U.S. trustee to retain each professional required in the case.[17] Pursuant to Bankruptcy Rule 2014(a), an affidavit of the professional seeking to be retained must be filed with the application for retention. The affidavit must disclose all of the professional's connections with the debtor, creditors, any other party in interest, and their respective attorneys and accountants, the U.S. trustee, and any employee in the office of the U.S. trustee. Bankruptcy Rule 2014(a) serves to ensure that prospective professionals avoid even the most remote appearance of a conflict of interest, regardless of the integrity or reputation of the professional in question.[18] Thus, Bankruptcy Rule 2014 is intended to provide the court with information necessary to determine whether employment is in the best interest of the estate. Failure to disclose any fact that may influence the court's decision in this regard may result in a later determination that disclosure was inadequate, and sanctions (ranging from disgorgement of fees to disqualification to both) may be imposed.[19]

Library References:
West's Key No. Digests, Bankruptcy ⇒3029.1, 3030.

§ 9.30   Employment of Professionals—Compensation

Professionals such as attorneys or financial advisors may be retained by the trustee or a committee appointed under the Bankruptcy Code

---

16. 11 U.S.C.A. § 327(c). *See* In re Caldor, Inc., 193 B.R. 165 (Bankr.S.D.N.Y. 1996) (no impermissible conflict of interest existed where a law firm that sought authorization to represent a creditors' committee was simultaneously representing the creditors' committee in a separate case filed by the debtor's direct competitor).

CAVEAT: The remedy for failure to disclose a conflict of interest includes disallowance or disgorgement of fees. *See* 11 U.S.C.A. § 328 and In re Kliegl Bros. Universal Elec. Stage Lighting Co., 189 B.R. 874 (Bankr.E.D.N.Y.1995).

17. *See* 11 U.S.C.A. § 327(a); Bankr.R. 2014(a). *See infra*, § 9.291 for a drafting checklist for an application of a professional for retention and §§ 9.310–9.311 for a sample application for retention and attorney's affidavit.

PRACTICE POINTER: If a professional whose retention requires court approval performs services without having first obtained such approval, he or she may seek to obtain subsequent approval *"nunc pro tunc"* by filing an application and the professional's affidavit. However, the court may require a showing of excusable neglect. *See, e.g.,* In re 245 Assocs., LLC, 188 B.R. 743 (Bankr.S.D.N.Y.1995). It is strongly recommended that counsel timely file an application for retention rather than proceed with representation before obtaining court approval.

18. In re Bellevue Place Associates, 171 B.R. 615, 625–26 (Bankr.N.D.Ill.1994).

19. Section 328(c) of the Bankruptcy Code authorizes the court to deny the allowance of compensation and reimbursement of expenses if the court later determines that the professional retained was not disinterested or held an interest adverse to the interest of the estate. *See, e.g.,* In re Leslie Fay Cos., Inc., 175 B.R. 525 (Bankr.S.D.N.Y.1994).

with the court's approval on terms that are reasonable, including a retainer, payment on an hourly basis, or a contingent fee basis.[1] The court has the power to change the terms of such retention following the conclusion of a professional's employment if the terms and conditions prove to have been "improvident in the light of developments not capable of being anticipated at the time of the fixing of such terms and conditions."[2] The court also may deny compensation for services and reimbursement of expenses of a retained professional if, during the period of employment, the professional is not disinterested or represents or holds an interest adverse to the estate with respect to matters on which such person is employed.[3]

If a trustee appointed by the court also serves as an attorney or accountant for the estate and has been retained under Section 327(d) of the Bankruptcy Code, the court may permit compensation for the trustee's services as an attorney or accountant only to the extent that such services were performed for the estate and not with respect to those duties of the trustee that are generally performed without the assistance of an attorney or an accountant.[4]

Professionals retained under Section 327 may not agree to share with another person, nor may they so share, any of their permitted compensation or reimbursement, or any compensation or reimbursement received by another person, except among members, partners, or regular associates in their professional association, corporation, firm, or partnership.[5] However, an attorney for a creditor who files an involuntary petition may share compensation or reimbursement received under Section 503 with any other attorney contributing to such services rendered or expenses incurred.[6]

Library References:

West's Key No. Digests, Bankruptcy ⚖3151–3205.

§ 9.31 Employment of Professionals—Compensation—Fee Applications

Reimbursement of expenses and payment of fees to an attorney, accountant, or other professional person retained in a chapter 7, 11, 12, or 13 case are subject to court approval, after notice to parties in interest and the U.S. trustee and a hearing.[1] Professionals may file an application

§ 9.30
1. 11 U.S.C.A. § 328(a).
2. 11 U.S.C.A. § 328(a).
3. 11 U.S.C.A. § 328(c).
4. 11 U.S.C.A. § 328(b).
5. 11 U.S.C.A. § 504.
6. 11 U.S.C.A. § 504.

§ 9.31
1. 11 U.S.C.A. § 330(a)(1).

CAVEAT: The Executive Office for United States Trustees promulgates Guidelines for Reviewing Applications for Compensation and Reimbursement of Expenses Filed under 11 U.S.C.A. § 330. The guidelines set forth extensive, detailed requirements for fee applications, including the narrative in-

§ 9.31

pursuant to Bankruptcy Rule 2016 seeking court authorization for the debtor to pay such fees and expenses. Retained professionals may seek interim payment by filing an interim fee application not more than once every 120 days after the order for relief in a case, or more often if the court permits.[2]

An application for compensation for services rendered and for reimbursement of expenses incurred must include a detailed statement of the following: (1) the services rendered, the time expended, and the expenses incurred, (2) the amounts requested, (3) payments made or promised for services rendered or to be rendered and the sources of such compensation, and (4) whether such payments have been shared, and whether an agreement exists for sharing of compensation, except with respect to intrafirm sharing.[3]

Professional persons retained by the debtor following court approval are entitled only to reasonable compensation and reimbursement for actual, necessary services and expenses.[4] Reasonable compensation is based upon the nature, extent, and value of services rendered, determined by weighing numerous factors including: (1) the time spent,[5] (2) the rate of charges,[6] (3) whether the services rendered were necessary or beneficial to the estate and the completion of the case,[7] (4) whether the services rendered were performed in a reasonable time, considering the complexity, importance, and nature of the issues or tasks addressed,[8] and (5) whether the compensation requested is reasonable based upon the compensation customarily charged in nonbankruptcy cases by comparably skilled practitioners.[9]

---

formation that must be included, the contents and a sample of the format for a summary cover sheet, the form in which itemized time records must be submitted, including a list of suggested project categories, and information concerning allowable reimbursable expenses. In addition to these guidelines, the applicable local rules, judge's practice rules, and guidelines issued by the local U.S. trustee must be strictly observed. It is strongly recommended that counsel for a debtor, trustee, or statutory committee familiarize themselves, their colleagues, and support personnel with these requirements *before* commencing work on a title 11 matter to ensure that records are properly kept from the start so as to make possible compliance with the requirements for fee applications.

2. 11 U.S.C.A. § 331. *See supra*, §§ 9.8, 9.10 for a discussion of the order for relief in voluntary and involuntary cases, respectively.

3. Bank.R. 2016(a).
4. 11 U.S.C.A. § 330(a)(1).
5. 11 U.S.C.A. § 330(a)(3)(A).
6. 11 U.S.C.A. § 330(a)(3)(B).
7. 11 U.S.C.A. § 330(a)(3)(C).
8. 11 U.S.C.A. § 330(a)(3)(D).
9. 11 U.S.C.A. § 330(a)(3)(E). The court will not allow compensation for unnecessary duplication of services or for services that were not reasonably likely to benefit the debtor's estate or necessary for the administration of the case. 11 U.S.C.A. § 330(a)(4)(A). In a case of an individual debtor under chapter 12 or 13, the court may allow reasonable compensation to the debtor's attorney for representing the interest of the debtor in connection with the case based on the benefit and necessity of services to the debtor and on the other factors described in § 330. 11 U.S.C.A. § 330(a)(4)(B).

In addition to the debtor's professionals, other professionals who act on behalf of creditors and other parties in interest may recover fees if their services result in a "substantial contribution" to the debtor's estate.[10]

Library References:

West's Key No. Digests, Bankruptcy ⟺3203(1)–3203(7).

§ 9.32 U.S. Trustee

The office of the U.S. trustee was created by Congress as part of a test pilot program under the Bankruptcy Code originally enacted in 1978. In 1986 the U.S. trustee program was made permanent in all districts throughout the United States. The Office of U.S. trustee is a division within the Department of Justice. The duties of the U.S. trustee include:

1. Establish, maintain and supervise a panel of trustees that are eligible and available to serve as trustees in chapter 7 cases;

2. Serve as and perform the duties of the trustee in a case when required; and

3. Supervise the administration of cases and trustees in cases under chapter 7, 12, or 13 whenever the U.S. trustee considers it to be appropriate, including overseeing the retention and compensation of professionals retained in bankruptcy cases.[1]

Library References:

West's Key No. Digests, Bankruptcy ⟺3001.

§ 9.33 U.S. Trustee—Duties Owed by Debtors and Trustees

Debtors in possession or trustees appointed in cases under the Bankruptcy Code are required to fulfill certain obligations to enable the U.S. trustee to better perform his or her statutory duties.[1] The following

---

10. See 11 U.S.C.A. § 503(b); Trade Creditor Group v. L.J. Hooker Corp., Inc. (In re L.J. Hooker Corp., Inc.), 188 B.R. 117 (S.D.N.Y.1995) (creditors' group and its attorneys were denied compensation for substantial contribution where efforts of the committee benefitted only one creditor group); In re Best Prods. Co., Inc., 173 B.R. 862 (Bankr.S.D.N.Y.1994) (creditors acting in their own self interest were not entitled to compensation for substantial contribution); In re Alert Holdings, Inc., 157 B.R. 753 (Bankr.S.D.N.Y.1993), affirmed 104 F.3d 349 (2d Cir.1996) (the substantial contribution doctrine should be limited to control "mushrooming" administrative expenses).

§ 9.32

1. 28 U.S.C.A. § 586.

§ 9.33

1. See 28 U.S.C.A. § 586 for duties of the U.S. trustee.

§ 9.33   BANKRUPTCY   Ch. 9

obligations are owed by debtors in possession or trustees to the U.S. trustee:[2]

1. *Inventory of Property.* In a chapter 7 case, in a chapter 11 case (if the court directs), in a chapter 12 case, and in a chapter 13 case when the debtor is engaged in business, the trustee or debtor in possession is required to file and transmit to the U.S. trustee a complete inventory of the property of the debtor within 30 days after qualifying as a debtor in possession or a trustee.[3]

2. *Record-Keeping.* In any case under chapter 7, 11, 12, or 13, the debtor in possession or the trustee must keep a record of receipts and the disposition of all money and property.[4]

3. *Notice of the Case.* In any case under chapter 7, 11, 12, or 13, except for a chapter 13 case when the debtor is not engaged in business, as soon as possible after commencement of the case, the debtor or the trustee must give notice of the case to every entity known to be holding money or property subject to withdrawal, including banks, utilities, landlords with deposits, and insurance companies that have issued a policy with a cash surrender value payable to the debtor.[5]

4. *Quarterly Fees.* In a chapter 11 case, the trustee or debtor in possession is required to pay a quarterly fee to the U.S. trustee until the case is closed.[6] The fees payable to the U.S. trustee escalate as disbursements made by the estate increase.[7] On or before the last day of the month after each calendar quarter until a case is closed, the debtor or trustee must file and transmit to the U.S. trustee a statement of the disbursements made during the calendar quarter and a statement showing the fee paid during the quarter related to such disbursements, as required pursuant to 28 U.S.C.A. § 1930(a)(6).[8]

2. CAVEAT: Additionally, counsel must obtain and comply with all guidelines issued by the U.S. trustee. Such guidelines set forth certain operating procedures and reporting requirements.

3. Bankr.R. 2015(a)(1), 2015(b), 2015(c)(1).

4. Bankr.R. 2015(a)(2), 2015(b), 2015(c).

5. Bankr.R. 2015(a)(4), 2015(b), 2015(c)(1).

6. 28 U.S.C.A. § 1930(a)(6).

PRACTICE POINTER: Until the passage of H.R.2880 in February 1995, quarterly fees were payable only until the plan was confirmed or the case was converted or dismissed, whichever occurred first. The amendment is intended to make quarterly fees payable in both new cases and cases in which the plan of reorganization has been confirmed but the case is not yet closed. Conference Rep.No. 104-378 (Dec. 1, 1995). The extension of the requirement that fees be paid until the case is closed could cause a significant drain on a debtor's resources. Accordingly, counsel should seek to close cases expeditiously, subject to the court's retention of jurisdiction for discrete purposes.

7. 28 U.S.C.A. § 1930(a)(6).

8. Bankr.R. 2015(a)(5).

5. *Periodic Reports.* If the debtor's business is authorized to be operated in any case under chapter 7, 11, 12, or 13, the trustee or debtor in possession must file and transmit to the U.S. trustee a summary of business operations, including a statement of disbursements made during the calendar quarter.[9]

6. *Transmission of Reports.* In a chapter 11 case, the court may direct that copies or summaries of annual and other reports issued by the debtor be published and mailed to creditors, equity security holders, and indenture trustees. Each report mailed or published also must be transmitted to the U.S. trustee.[10]

Library References:

West's Key No. Digests, Bankruptcy ⟜3008.1, 3022.

§ 9.34 Bankruptcy Trustee

In all cases under chapter 7, a trustee is appointed to take possession of all of the debtor's assets.[1] In most cases under chapter 11, 12, or 13, the debtor retains possession of its assets. However, a trustee may be appointed in a case under chapter 11 if cause is shown to remove the debtor as debtor in possession.[2] While a debtor under chapter 12 or 13 normally retains possession of its assets, a trustee may be appointed in such cases to perform limited duties.[3]

Library References:

West's Key No. Digests, Bankruptcy ⟜3001.

§ 9.35 Mediators

Some bankruptcy courts have appointed mediators in an alternative dispute resolution process pursuant to 11 U.S.C.A. § 105(a).[1]

---

9. Bankr.R. 2015(a)(3), 2015(b), 2015(c)(1), 11 U.S.C.A. § 704(8). This also must be filed with the appropriate taxing authority. 11 U.S.C.A. § 704(8).

10. Bankr.R. 2015(d).

§ 9.34

1. 11 U.S.C.A. § 701. See infra, §§ 9.180–9.182 for a more detailed discussion of a chapter 7 trustee.

2. 11 U.S.C.A. § 1104. See infra, §§ 9.138–9.139 for a more detailed discussion of a chapter 11 trustee.

3. See 11 U.S.C.A. §§ 1202, 1302 and see infra, §§ 9.214–9.215 and 9.239–9.240, respectively, for a discussion of a chapter 12 or 13 trustee.

§ 9.35

1. For example, the Bankruptcy Court for the Southern District of New York has issued a General Order re Adoption of Procedures Governing Mediation Matters and Adversary Proceedings (Bankr.S.D.N.Y. Nov. 10, 1993), as amended by Amended General Order re Adoption of Procedures Governing Mediation of Matters in Bankruptcy Cases and Adversary Proceedings (Bankr.S.D.N.Y. Jan. 17, 1995). The standing order in the Southern District permits the court to refer any disputes to mediation upon its own motion or upon motion of a party in interest or the U.S. trustee. The order sets forth detailed requirements regulating the mediation process.

§ 9.36 Creditors

Any person who holds a "claim" against the debtor is a creditor of the debtor.[1] "Claim" is defined under the Bankruptcy Code as a "right to payment, whether or not such right is reduced to judgment, liquidated, unliquidated, fixed, contingent, matured, unmatured, disputed, undisputed, legal, equitable, secured, or unsecured," as well as a right to an equitable remedy for breach of performance that gives rise to a right to payment.[2] The legislative history states that Congress, by "this broadest possible definition ... contemplates that all legal obligations of the debtor, no matter how remote or contingent, will be able to be dealt with in the bankruptcy case. It permits the broadest possible relief in the bankruptcy court."[3]

Any person who holds (i) a share in a corporation, whether or not it is transferable or is denominated "stock;" (ii) a partnership interest; or (iii) a warrant or right (other than a right to convert) to buy, sell, or subscribe to an interest in a corporation or partnership, is an "equity security holder" of the debtor.[4] Unless otherwise specified, equity security holders are governed by the same Code sections and Bankruptcy Rules as creditors.

Library References:
West's Key No. Digests, Bankruptcy ⟜3024.

§ 9.37 Creditors—Meeting of Creditors

Pursuant to Section 341(a) of the Bankruptcy Code, the U.S. trustee is obligated, within a reasonable time after the order for relief is entered, to convene and preside at a meeting of creditors.[1] In a chapter 7 or 11 case, the U.S. trustee must hold the meeting of creditors no earlier than

---

§ 9.36

1. A person may become a creditor of a debtor by becoming the assignee or the purchaser of a claim against the debtor. See infra, § 9.91 note 1 discussing the claim of a transferee claim holder.

2. 11 U.S.C.A. § 101(5).

3. H.R. Rep. No. 95–595, 95th Cong., 1st Sess. 309 (1977); S.Rep. No. 95–989, 95th Cong., 2d Sess. 21 (1978).

PRACTICE POINTER: In cases under title 11, with the exception of certain key events such as commencement of a case, the meeting of creditors, the bar date for filing proofs of claim, and the hearings on adequacy of the disclosure statement and modification or confirmation of a plan, the court generally will not require that notice of proposed actions be sent to all creditors. (See supra, § 9.15 note 1 for a discussion of the Bankruptcy Code's flexible concept of notice.) While the court will require that notice be sent to any creditor whose claim or collateral will be directly affected by a proposed action, counsel representing certain creditors, particularly those who hold very large claims, may wish to receive notice of all actions and events requiring notice to all creditors who request notice under Bankruptcy Rule 2002(i). Accordingly, counsel who wish to receive all such notices must file a Notice of Appearance and request for such notices pursuant to Bankruptcy Rule 2002(i). See infra, § 9.305 for a sample form of a Notice of Appearance.

4. 11 U.S.C.A. § 101(16), 101(17).

§ 9.37

1. 11 U.S.C.A. § 341. The U.S. trustee may also convene a meeting of equity security holders. 11 U.S.C.A. § 341(b); Bankr.R. 2003(2).

20 days and no later than 40 days after the order for relief is entered. In a chapter 12 case, the U.S. trustee must hold the meeting of creditors between 20 and 35 days after the order for relief is entered. In a chapter 13 case, the U.S. trustee must hold the meeting of creditors between 20 and 50 days after entry of the order for relief.[2] The bankruptcy court is precluded from attending any meeting of creditors, and the U.S. trustee presides over the meeting.[3]

Library References:
West's Key No. Digests, Bankruptcy ⇔3024.

§ 9.38 Creditors—Meeting of Creditors—Scope of Examination

The debtor must appear at the meeting of creditors and submit to examination under oath by creditors, indenture trustees, any trustee or examiner in the case, or the U.S. trustee.[1] The purpose of the examination is to enable creditors and the trustee to determine if any assets have been disposed of improperly or concealed, or if there are any grounds for objection to discharge. The scope of the examination is intended to extend "only to the debtor's acts, conduct, or property, or any matter that may affect the administration of the estate or the debtor's right to a discharge."[2]

Library References:
West's Key No. Digests, Bankruptcy ⇔3040.1–3048.

§ 9.39 Examinations Under Bankruptcy Rule 2004

The debtor or any other party may also be examined by order of the court on motion by any party in interest pursuant to Bankruptcy Rule 2004. The scope of examination under Bankruptcy Rule 2004 extends to the acts, conduct, or property, or to the liabilities and financial condition, of the debtor, or to the debtor's right to a discharge, or to any matter relevant to the case or the formulation of a plan, including the operation of the debtor's business and the source of any money or property to be acquired for purposes of consummating the plan.[1] The primary function of Bankruptcy Rule 2004 examinations is to allow inquiry into the existence of assets of the debtor that may be collected and distributed to

---

2. Bankr.R. 2003(a). If there is an appeal from or a motion to vacate the order for relief, or if there is a motion to dismiss the case, the U.S. trustee may set a later date for the meeting of creditors. If the U.S. trustee determines to hold the meeting at a place not regularly staffed by the U.S. trustee or designates an assistant to preside at the meeting, the meeting may be held between 20 and 60 days after the order for relief is entered. Bankr.R. 2003(a).

3. 11 U.S.C.A. § 341(c).

§ 9.38

1. 11 U.S.C.A. § 343.

2. H.R.Rep.No. 95–595, 95th Cong., 1st Sess. 332 (1977); *see* S.Rep.No. 95–989, 95th Cong., 2d Sess. 43 (1978).

§ 9.39

1. Bankr.R. 2004(b).

§ 9.39   BANKRUPTCY   Ch. 9

creditors of the estate.[2] Consequently, the scope of examination under Bankruptcy Rule 2004 is extremely broad.[3]

Library References:
West's Key No. Digests, Bankruptcy ⇐3040.1–3048.

§ 9.40   Examinations Under Bankruptcy Rule 2004—Notice Requirements

A Bankruptcy Rule 2004 examination is commenced by a written or oral motion to the bankruptcy court requesting authority to conduct the examination and identifying the person to be examined and the purpose of the examination. The motion may be made on an *ex parte* basis or on notice.[1] Generally, when an examination of the debtor is requested, courts will enter an order authorizing such an examination, on an *ex parte* basis or otherwise, without placing a heavy burden of proof on the movant.[2] The burden on the movant is more stringent when the party to be examined is not the debtor. The inquiry to be made of nondebtor parties generally must be related to the actions and property of the debtor. It requires the movant to demonstrate that good cause exists and that all reasonable alternatives for obtaining the required information have been explored.[3]

Library References:
West's Key No. Digests, Bankruptcy ⇐3041.

§ 9.41   Examinations Under Bankruptcy Rule 2004—Subpoena

The bankruptcy court may, if necessary, authorize the issuance of a

---

2. *See* Freeman v. Seligson, 405 F.2d 1326, 1333 (D.C.Cir.1968).

3. *See* In re Drexel Burnham Lambert Group, Inc., 112 B.R. 584 (Bankr.S.D.N.Y. 1990) (the history of Bankruptcy Rule 2004 indicates that its scope is meant to be broader than the scope of discovery under the Federal Rules of Civil Procedure); In re Johns–Manville Corp., 42 B.R. 362, 364 (S.D.N.Y.1984) (Bankruptcy Rule 2004 "contemplates a broad and far-reaching inquiry, even a 'fishing expedition,' *see* In re Frigitemp Corp., 15 B.R. 263, 264 n. 3 (Bankr.S.D.N.Y.1981), and that creditors and third parties, as well as the debtor, may be examined"); In re Wilcher, 56 B.R. 428, 433 (Bankr.N.D.Ill.1985); In re Mittco, Inc., 44 B.R. 35, 36 (Bankr.E.D.Wis.1984); In re Vantage Petroleum Corp., 34 B.R. 650 (Bankr.E.D.N.Y.1983).

§ 9.40

1. Bankr.R. 2004(a), Advisory Committee Note.

2. *See* In re Kreiss, 46 B.R. 164, 165 (E.D.N.Y.1985) ("Upon the issuance of an order granting [a Rule 2004] examination request, the examinee may move to vacate the order."); In re GHR Energy Corp., 35 B.R. 534, 535 (Bankr.D.Mass.1983) ("Often times when an application appears proper on its face, it will be allowed. It is only when an objection is filed that the Court has an opportunity to fully investigate the purpose behind the examination.").

3. *See* Keene Corp. v. Johns–Manville Corp. (In re Johns–Manville Corp.), 42 B.R. 362 (S.D.N.Y.1984) (the examination of the debtor's competitor under Bankruptcy Rule 2004 must be limited to the debtor's affairs); Freeman v. Seligson, 405 F.2d 1326 (D.C.Cir.1968) (before ordering an examination of a nondebtor under Bankruptcy Rule 2004, a court should make "a determination of good cause" which requires that all reasonable alternatives for obtaining information have been explored).

subpoena to compel attendance at a Bankruptcy Rule 2004 examination.[1] The issuance of a subpoena generally will only be appropriate in connection with the proposed examination of a nondebtor party, as the debtor is required to appear and submit to examination under oath at the meeting of creditors.[2]

Library References:

West's Key No. Digests, Bankruptcy ⟐3043.

§ 9.42 Right of Parties in Interest to Be Heard

Pursuant to Section 1109(b) of the Bankruptcy Code, any "party in interest," including the debtor, the trustee, a creditors' committee, an equity security holder, or an indenture trustee, may raise, appear, and be heard on any issue in a case under chapter 11 of the Bankruptcy Code.[1] The list of parties in interest set forth in Section 1109(b) is not exclusive. In a case under any chapter of the Bankruptcy Code, the court may permit any interested party to intervene generally or with respect to a specified matter.[2]

The Bankruptcy Code and Bankruptcy Rules also provide for the participation of other specific parties in cases under the Bankruptcy Code, subject to certain limitations:

- In a chapter 11 case, the Securities and Exchange Commission may raise, appear, and be heard on any issue, but may not appeal from any judgment or order of the court.[3]

- The U.S. trustee may raise, appear, and be heard on any issue in any case under title 11, but may not file a plan of reorganization.[4]

§ 9.41
1. Bankr.R. 2004(c). The requirements for obtaining a subpoena are set forth in Bankr.R. 9016, which incorporates Rule 45 of the Federal Rules of Civil Procedure.
2. 11 U.S.C.A. § 343; Bankr.R. 2004(c), Advisory Committee Note.

§ 9.42
1. 11 U.S.C.A. § 1109(b); Bankr.R. 2018(a).

CAVEAT: Although the creditors' committee generally may appear and be heard on any issue in a case under chapter 11 of the Bankruptcy Code, the same may not hold true for an adversary proceeding arising in or related to a chapter 11 case. See In re Charter Co., 50 B.R. 57, 60 (W.D.Tex. 1985).

When a debtor fails to assert claims that it is entitled to assert on behalf of a bankruptcy estate, a bankruptcy court may authorize a creditors' committee to stand in the shoes of the debtor to assert such claims. However, a creditors' committee standing in the debtor's shoes can only assert claims that the debtor is entitled to assert. Thus, a creditors' committee cannot exercise the debtor's powers to assert claims that belong to the creditors *qua* creditors. In re The Mediators, Inc., 105 F.3d 822 (2d Cir.1997) (The creditors' committee lacked standing to bring a claim against third parties for aiding and abetting the debtor's breach of its fiduciary duties to creditors because the debtor could not recover on a claim of aiding and abetting its own fraudulent conduct.).

2. Bankr.R. 2018(a).
3. 11 U.S.C.A. § 1129(a).
4. 11 U.S.C.A. § 307.

§ 9.42 BANKRUPTCY Ch. 9

- In a case under chapter 7, 11, 12, or 13, the state Attorney General may intervene on behalf of consumer creditors if the court determines that such intervention is in "the public interest." The state Attorney General may not, however, appeal any judgment or order of the court.[5]

- In a chapter 11 or 12 case, a labor union or employees' association has the right to be heard on the economic soundness of a plan that affects the interest of employees, but, unless otherwise permitted by law, may not appeal any judgment or order relating to the plan.[6]

Library References:

West's Key No. Digests, Bankruptcy ⇌2204.1–2206.

§ 9.43 Statutory Committees

In a chapter 11 case, the U.S. trustee is required to appoint a committee of creditors holding unsecured claims as soon as practicable after the order for relief is entered.[1] If, prior to the commencement of a chapter 11 case, the debtor's creditors organized a creditors' committee, such committee may be appointed to serve as the statutory creditors' committee provided that it was fairly chosen and is representative of the different kinds of claims to be represented.[2] Generally, the appointment of a creditors' committee is mandatory in a case under chapter 11.[3] However, in a case in which the debtor is a "small business,"[4] the court may, upon request of a party in interest, for cause shown, order that a creditors' committee not be appointed.[5]

Typically, the creditors' committee will consist of the creditors (willing to serve) that hold the seven largest unsecured claims against the debtor.[6] There is, however, no statutory bar to having more or fewer

---

5. Bankr.R. 2018(b).
6. Bankr.R. 2018(d).

§ 9.43

1. 11 U.S.C.A. § 1102(a)(1). In voluntary cases under chapter 11, the order for relief occurs on the date of filing of the chapter 11 petition. 11 U.S.C.A. § 301. In involuntary cases under chapter 11, entry of the order for relief may, if the petition is challenged, occur days, weeks, or months after the filing date. See 11 U.S.C.A. § 303(h). See supra, § 9.10 for a discussion of involuntary petitions.

See infra, § 9.184 for a discussion of the election of a creditors' committee in a chapter 7 case. There is no provision under chapter 12 or 13 for the appointment of a creditors' committee.

2. 11 U.S.C.A. § 1102(b)(1).

3. See infra, § 9.184 for a discussion of the creditors' committee in a chapter 7 case. There is no provision in chapter 12 or 13 for the appointment or election of a statutory committee.

4. "Small business" is defined as "a person engaged in commercial or business activities (but does not include a person whose primary activity is the business of owning or operating real property and activities incidental thereto) whose aggregate noncontingent liquidated secured and unsecured debts as of the date of the petition do not exceed $2,000,000." 11 U.S.C.A. § 101(51C).

5. 11 U.S.C.A. § 1102(a)(3).

6. 11 U.S.C.A. § 1102.

than seven creditors on the committee.[7] In commercial cases, the creditors' committee usually consists of trade creditors and lending institutions. The U.S. trustee may, in its discretion, appoint additional committees of creditors or equity security holders as it deems appropriate.[8] In addition, upon request of a party in interest, the bankruptcy court may order the appointment of additional committees if necessary to ensure adequate representation.[9] In the event the court orders the appointment of an additional committee, the U.S. trustee is required to make the appointment.[10]

Although unsecured creditor status is a prerequisite for membership on the creditors' committee, it is not in and of itself sufficient. An unsecured creditor also must be a "person" as defined in the Bankruptcy Code.[11] Because most governmental entities are excluded from the definition of "person" under the Bankruptcy Code, they may not serve as official members of the creditors' committee or other statutory committees.[12] Government entities barred from serving may, however, serve as *ex officio* members of the creditors' committee or other statutory committees.[13] The Bankruptcy Code does not explicitly provide that lack of

7. PRACTICE POINTER: Requests for a change in the size or membership of a statutory committee that has been appointed should be directed to the U.S. trustee. Should the trustee refuse to honor such a request, a creditor must seek relief from the bankruptcy court. In re Texaco, 79 B.R. 560 (Bankr.S.D.N.Y.1987).

8. 11 U.S.C.A. § 1102(a)(1).

9. A committee of equity security holders, for example, may be appropriate where the debtor is not insolvent and equity security holders would have difficulty protecting their interests individually. See In re White Motor Credit Corp., 27 B.R. 554 (Bankr. N.D. Ohio 1982); In re Emons Indus. Inc., 50 B.R. 692 (Bankr.S.D.N.Y.1985). Other types of committees that may be appropriate include a trade creditors' committee, a secured creditors' committee, and an employees' committee. However, a court will be reluctant to authorize the appointment of any additional committees, with the concomitant expense to the debtor's estate, unless the benefits of doing so outweigh the additional costs. In re Johns–Manville Corp., 68 B.R. 155 (S.D.N.Y.1986), appeal dismissed 824 F.2d 176 (2d Cir.1987).

The party seeking the appointment of an additional committee has the burden of demonstrating that it is not adequately represented. However, once this burden is met, the burden shifts to the opponent of the committee to demonstrate that the costs of such committee outweigh the need for adequate representation and cannot be alleviated in other ways. See In re Beker Indus. Corp., 55 B.R. 945, 949 (Bankr.S.D.N.Y. 1985).

10. 11 U.S.C.A. § 1102(a)(2).

PRACTICE POINTER: Creditors may form an unofficial committee to deal with the debtor. However, unlike an official committee, the administrative costs of such a committee (*i.e.*, costs of professional fees and expenses) cannot be recovered from the estate unless the applicant can demonstrate that it made a substantial contribution *to the estate* by rendering the services for which compensation is sought. 11 U.S.C.A. § 503(b)(3)(D).

11. See 11 U.S.C.A. § 101(41).

12. The Bankruptcy Reform Act of 1994 amended the definition of person for purposes of Section 1102, thereby including such entities as the Federal Deposit Insurance Corporation, the Resolution Trust Corporation, the Pension Benefit Guaranty Corporation, and state employee pension funds as persons eligible to serve on statutory committees. See 11 U.S.C.A. §§ 101(41), 1102(b)(1).

13. See In re New Valley Corp., 168 B.R. 73, 75 (Bankr.D.N.J.1994) (Pension Benefit Guaranty Corporation served as an *ex officio* member of the creditors' committee in a chapter 11 case); *see also* In re Gates Eng'g Co., 104 B.R. 653, 654 (Bankr. D.Del.1989) (the appointment of a governmental entities committee was unwarranted

disinterestedness or insider status automatically precludes a creditor from serving on a statutory committee.[14] Even potential conflicts of interest with either the debtor or other unsecured creditors do not automatically preclude committee membership. Indeed, courts have held that insiders of the debtor, competitors of the debtor, and partially secured creditors may serve on statutory committees, so long as no fiduciary duty is violated and no actual conflict exists.[15]

Library References:
West's Key No. Digests, Bankruptcy ⚖3024.

§ 9.44 Statutory Committees—Function and Duties

The appointment of a statutory committee under Section 1102 of the Bankruptcy Code is intended to ensure that in a chapter 11 case, a body will be formed to represent and protect the interests of unsecured creditors, supervise the debtor or trustee, and serve as the primary negotiating body for the formulation of a plan of reorganization.[1] Specifically, the committee may, in addition to meeting with the trustee or debtor in possession,[2] investigate the debtor,[3] participate in the formulation of a plan and advise its constituents as to the committee's recommendations on a proposed plan,[4] request the appointment of a trustee or examiner,[5] and perform other services in the interest of its constituents.[6] A statutory committee is a party in interest with the right to appear and be heard on all issues in a chapter 11 case.[7]

Without a statutory committee, a debtor would have to deal with its creditors on an individual basis, making the reorganization process more

where the state of Tennessee served as an *ex officio* member of the warranty claimants' committee).

14. *See* In re First RepublicBank Corp., 95 B.R. 58, 61 (Bankr.N.D.Tex.1988) ("The Bankruptcy Code does not expressly prohibit a person from serving on a committee because of a lack of disinterestedness or even insider status."); compare 11 U.S.C.A. § 1102(a) *with* 11 U.S.C.A. § 327(a).

15. *See* In re Seaescape Cruises, Ltd., 131 B.R. 241 (Bankr.S.D.Fla.1991); In re Map Int'l, Inc., 105 B.R. 5 (Bankr.E.D.Pa. 1989); In re Vermont Real Estate Inv. Trust, 20 B.R. 33 (Bankr.D.Vt.1982).

§ 9.44

1. H.R.Rep.No. 95–595, 95th Cong., 1st Sess. 401 (1977).

2. 11 U.S.C.A. § 1103(c)(1).

3. 11 U.S.C.A. § 1103(c)(2).

4. 11 U.S.C.A. § 1103(c)(3).

5. 11 U.S.C.A. § 1103(c)(4). *See infra*, § 9.138 for a discussion of the requirements for the appointment of a trustee and *infra*, § 9.140 for a discussion of the requirements for the appointment of an examiner.

6. 11 U.S.C.A. § 1103(c)(5).

7. 11 U.S.C.A. § 1109(b). *See* Louisiana World Exposition v. Federal Ins. Co., 858 F.2d 233 (5th Cir.1988), reh'g denied (en banc) 864 F.2d 1147 (5th Cir.1989).

PRACTICE POINTER: In light of the extensive powers the Bankruptcy Code accords to a statutory committee to monitor and investigate the acts of the debtor, counsel for either a debtor or a creditors' committee should seek to establish a cooperative working relationship early in the case to minimize the drain on the estate of unnecessary litigation.

CAVEAT: A debtor that is unable to work effectively with its creditors is more likely to be subject to creditors' attempts to terminate the debtor's exclusivity (*see infra*, §§ 9.142–9.145) or have the court appoint a trustee, thereby ousting the debtor from control (*see infra*, §§ 9.138–9.139).

difficult for the debtor and creditors alike. Moreover, there would be no body to oversee the debtor's activities and ensure that the creditors' interests are protected.

Library References:
West's Key No. Digests, Bankruptcy ⚖3024.

§ 9.45 Statutory Committees—Right to Bring Litigation

Under certain circumstances, a statutory committee may desire to bring an action, including a preference or fraudulent conveyance action,[1] against a third party on behalf of the debtor in possession for the benefit of the estate. Because such an action by the committee may encroach upon the responsibilities and leverage of the debtor in possession, the statutory committee will generally be permitted to bring such actions only in circumstances where the debtor in possession has unjustifiably or unreasonably refused to do so.[2] In evaluating whether the committee may bring an action, a court must determine that the cause of action is colorable and that, from the perspective of the estate, the potential benefits of bringing the action outweigh its costs.

Library References:
West's Key No. Digests, Bankruptcy ⚖3024.

§ 9.46 Statutory Committees—Fiduciary Duty

The members of a committee in a case under chapter 11 owe a fiduciary duty to those creditors or interest holders whom they represent.[1] The fiduciary duties of members of a committee have generally not

---

§ 9.45

1. *See infra*, §§ 9.117, 9.119, respectively, for a discussion of preference and fraudulent conveyance actions.

2. *See* In re STN Enterprises, 779 F.2d 901 (2d Cir.1985).

PRACTICE POINTER: The debtor in possession's consent to the committee's bringing of a specific action may obviate the need for the committee to demonstrate to the court that the debtor in possession unjustifiably or unreasonably refused to bring the action. *See* In re Jermoo's Inc., 38 B.R. 197 (Bankr.W.D.Wis.1984) (a creditors' committee had standing to prosecute a fraudulent conveyance where the debtor ratified the creditors' committee's complaint).

Counsel should bear in mind that the creditors' committee cannot stand in the debtor's shoes to bring an action that rightfully belongs to creditors, not the debtor. For example, in The Mediators, Inc. v. Manney (In re The Mediators, Inc.), 105 F.3d 822 (2d Cir.1997), the creditors' committee sought to stand in the shoes of the debtor to recover from third parties for aiding and abetting the debtor in a fraudulent transfer of assets. The Second Circuit explained that the creditors' committee, standing in the shoes of the debtor, could only bring an action that the debtor could bring. Since the debtor could not bring an action against the third parties for aiding and abetting its own breach of fiduciary duties, the committee could not bring the action on behalf of the debtor. Thus, the claims were owned by the creditors as creditors, and a trustee (or the creditors' committee standing in the shoes of a trustee) could not bring such an action.

§ 9.46

1. *See* In re Map Int'l, Inc., 105 B.R. 5, 6 (Bankr.E.D.Pa.1989) ("[M]embers of a creditors' committee are obligated to act in

been extended to the estate or parties other than the creditor's constituents.[2]

Library References:

West's Key No. Digests, Bankruptcy ⚍3024.

§ 9.47 Statutory Committees—Removal of Members

The primary ground for removing a committee member is a breach of fiduciary duty. Prior to 1986, the bankruptcy court had the authority, pursuant to former Section 1102(c) of the Bankruptcy Code (now repealed), to remove members of the creditors' committee. Although the repeal of section 1102(c) in 1986 left uncertainty in the law, the majority rule appears to be that requests for removal of a member from a committee should first be addressed to the U.S. trustee, rather than to the bankruptcy court.[1] However, courts have held that if the U.S. trustee refuses to effectuate such changes in committee membership, a party may apply to the bankruptcy court for relief.[2]

a fiduciary capacity and may not use their positions . . . to advance only their individual interests."); In re REA Holding Corp., 8 B.R. 75, 81 (Bankr.S.D.N.Y.1980) ("Those who serve on a creditors' committee owe a fiduciary duty to all creditors which they fulfill by advising creditors of their rights and of the proper course of action in the bankruptcy proceeding.").

For an interesting discussion of the conflicts between self-interest and fiduciary duty inherent in creditors' committees, see Carl A. Eklund & Lynn W. Roberts, *The Problem with Creditors' Committees in Chapter 11: How to Manage the Inherent Conflicts without Loss of Function*, 5 Am. Bankr.Inst.L.R. 129 (Spring 1997).

PRACTICE POINTER: As a consequence of the fiduciary duty owed to their constituent creditors, committee members' dealings with the debtor will be scrutinized when a group to which the committee member belongs speculates in securities of the debtor. *See* In re Allegheny Int'l, Inc., 100 B.R. 241 (Bankr.W.D.Pa.1988). Nonetheless, one court has held that committee members may trade in securities of the debtor if appropriate procedural mechanisms are put in place to ensure that such speculation or trading is not based on inside information obtained from the debtor. *See* In re Federated Dept. Stores, Inc., No. 1-90-00130, 1991 WL 79143 (Bankr.S.D.Ohio 1991).

2. *See* Woods v. City Nat'l Bank & Trust Co., 312 U.S. 262, 268–69, 61 S.Ct. 493, 497, 85 L.Ed. 820 (1941); In re Johns-Manville Corp., 60 B.R. 842, 853–54 note 22 (S.D.N.Y.1986), rev'd on other grounds 801 F.2d 60 (2d Cir.1986); *but see* In re Tucker Freight Lines, Inc., 62 B.R. 213 (Bankr. W.D.Mich.1986) (holding committee members to a "concurrent fiduciary duty to all the unsecured creditors").

§ 9.47

1. *See* In re Dow Corning Corp., 212 B.R. 258, 263 (E.D.Mich.1997) (Section 1102(a)(1) does not give the bankruptcy court a role in the appointment or modification of creditor committees; therefore, the bankruptcy court's *sua sponte* removal of committee members and direction to the U.S. trustee to appoint new members was outside the scope of the court's authority.); In re Wheeler Technology, Inc., 139 B.R. 235, 238–39 (9th Cir.BAP 1992) (the court could not remove a committee member for violation of the automatic stay); In re Hills Stores Co., 137 B.R. 4, 8 (Bankr.S.D.N.Y. 1992) (the statute no longer permits the court to add or remove members of committees); In re Drexel Burnham Lambert Group, Inc., 118 B.R. 209 (Bankr.S.D.N.Y. 1990) (Congress vested only the U.S. trustee with authority to select committee members).

2. *See* In re House of Fabrics, Inc., 27 Bankr.Ct.Dec. (CRR) 742 (Bankr.C.D.Cal. 1995); In re McLean Indus., Inc., 70 B.R. 852 (Bankr.S.D.N.Y.1987); In re Texaco Inc., 79 B.R. 560, 565–66 (Bankr.S.D.N.Y. 1987).

§ 9.48 Statutory Committees—Organizational Meeting

Under Section 1102(a)(1) of the Bankruptcy Code, the U.S. trustee must appoint a committee of unsecured creditors "as soon as practicable after the order for relief under chapter 11," except in a small business case where the court, for cause, orders that a committee of creditors not be appointed.[1] Section 1103 of the Bankruptcy Code requires an organizational meeting for each statutory committee appointed under Section 1102. If a majority of committee members is present, the committee may select and authorize the employment of one or more attorneys, accountants, or other agents, subject to court approval.[2] An attorney or accountant employed by the creditors' committee may not represent any other entity having an adverse interest in the chapter 11 case.[3] Representation of one or more creditors of the same class as represented by the committee does not *per se* constitute the representation of an adverse interest.[4]

Library References:
West's Key No. Digests, Bankruptcy ⚖3024.

§ 9.49 Property of the Estate

The commencement of a voluntary or involuntary case under chapter 7, 11, 12, or 13 creates an estate that includes all the debtor's legal or equitable interests in property, both tangible and intangible, wherever located and by whomever held, as of the commencement of the case.[1] The

---

§ 9.48

1. 11 U.S.C.A. § 1102(a)(1), (3).

2. *See supra*, § 9.29 for a discussion of retention of professionals.

CAVEAT: Notwithstanding the language of section 1103(a) of the Bankruptcy Code, cause must be shown to appoint more than one attorney. *See* H.R. No. 95–595, 95th Cong., 1st Sess. 402 (1977).

3. 11 U.S.C.A. § 1103(b).

4. 11 U.S.C.A. § 1103(b). The interests of creditors' committees in separate, unrelated cases filed by direct competitors has been found "not adverse." Accordingly, representation of such committees simultaneously has been permitted. *See* In re Caldor, Inc., 193 B.R. 165 (Bankr.S.D.N.Y. 1996).

§ 9.49

1. 11 U.S.C.A. § 541(a). United States v. Whiting Pools, Inc., 462 U.S. 198, 103 S.Ct. 2309, 76 L.Ed.2d 515 (1983).

PRACTICE POINTER: Section 541(c)(2) of the Bankruptcy Code excludes from property of the estate any beneficial interest of the debtor in a trust that is subject to a restriction on transfer that is enforceable under applicable nonbankruptcy law. Thus, the provision excludes from property of the estate a debtor's interest in a spendthrift trust that is protected from creditors under applicable nonbankruptcy law. Patterson v. Shumate, 504 U.S. 753, 762, 112 S.Ct. 2242, 2248, 119 L.Ed.2d 519 (1992) citing H.R.Rep. 95–595, 95th Cong., 1st Sess. 176 (1977).

Whether or not IRA accounts are found to be property of the estate generally depends on whether or not they satisfy the requirements for qualified retirement plans under 26 U.S.C.A. § 401(a) of the Internal Revenue Code, which contains an anti-alienation provision. Commonly, an IRA is subject to complete control by its creator, who can withdraw the entire amount of the

broad definition of "property of the estate" authorizes the bankruptcy court to administer all of the debtor's property, no matter how limited or tangential the debtor's interest therein. Nonetheless, the existence or nature of the debtor's interest in property generally is governed by applicable state law.[2]

In general, the estate acquires no greater interest in property than that held by the debtor as of the commencement of the case. However, the estate includes certain additional property such as property recovered by the trustee or debtor in possession from third parties under the avoiding powers,[3] property acquired by the debtor within 180 days after the commencement of the case, and proceeds, products, rents, or profits derived from property of the estate, except services performed by an individual debtor after the commencement of the case.[4] Property of the debtor's estate also includes all claims or causes of action owned by the

---

IRA deposits with the only penalty being the imposition of a tax penalty. Accordingly, such accounts are not spendthrift trusts, and courts find such IRAs to be property of the estate that is not exempt from distribution under the Bankruptcy Code. *See, e.g.,* Smith v. The Affinity Group, Inc. (In re Morgan), 145 B.R. 760, 763 (Bankr. N.D.N.Y.1992); In re Kramer, 128 B.R. 707 (Bankr.E.D.N.Y.1991).

Debtor & Creditor Law § 282, which sets forth exemptions provided under New York law, affords spendthrift trusts a source of protection from creditors in addition to the exclusion under Section 541(c)(2). Section 282 provides that a debtor may exempt from property of the estate the exemptions allowed pursuant to CPLR 5205, which incorporates by reference the anti-alienation provision contained in Section 401 of the Internal Revenue Code. CPLR 5205(c)(2) and (3) provide that:

[A]ll trusts, custodial accounts, annuities, insurance contracts, monies, assets or interests established as part of, and all payments from, either any trust or plan, which is qualified as an individual retirement account under section four hundred eight [sic] of the United States Internal Revenue Code of 1986, as amended, or a Keogh (HR–10), retirement or other plan established by a corporation, which is qualified under section 401 of the United States Internal Revenue Code of 1986, as amended, or created as a result of rollovers from such plans pursuant to Sections 402(a)(5), 403(a)(4) or 408(d)(3) of the Internal Revenue Code of 1986, as amended ... shall be conclusively presumed to be spendthrift trusts under this section and the common law of the state of New York for all purposes, including ... all cases arising under or related to a case arising under ... the United States Bankruptcy Code.

Accordingly, retirement annuities that satisfy the anti-alienation requirement or an IRA created as a result of a rollover from a qualified plan have been found to be excluded from property of the estate. In re Bennett, 185 B.R. 4, 6 (Bankr.E.D.N.Y.1995); In re Morgan, 145 B.R. 760, 762 (Bankr. N.D.N.Y.1992).

2. *See* Butner v. United States, 440 U.S. 48, 55, 99 S.Ct. 914, 918, 59 L.Ed.2d 136 (1979).

3. 11 U.S.C.A. § 541(a)(3). *See infra,* §§ 9.113–9.119 for a discussion of the avoiding powers that may be employed by a debtor or trustee to recover property of the estate.

4. 11 U.S.C.A. § 541(a). Although Section 541(a)(6) specifically excludes from property of the estate "earnings from services performed by an individual debtor after the commencement of the case," the Fourth Circuit has held that postpetition payments received by a debtor pursuant to a prepetition noncompetition agreement are not earnings from "*services performed* by the debtor after the commencement of the case." Instead, the court found that the payments were inextricably rooted in the debtor's prepetition activities and were proceeds that flowed from the prepetition assets. Accordingly, they were included in the debtor's estate. In re Andrews, 80 F.3d 906 (4th Cir.1996).

debtor as of the petition date.[5] The debtor in possession or trustee may bring all such actions provided the pursuit of such claims, on balance, benefits the estate. Additionally, the estate created under chapter 12 or 13 includes all property acquired by the debtor after the commencement of the case and earnings derived from services performed by the debtor after the commencement of the case.[6]

Library References:
West's Key No. Digests, Bankruptcy ⚿2531–2559.

§ 9.50 Automatic Stay

The filing of a voluntary or involuntary bankruptcy petition invokes an automatic stay, which enjoins the commencement or continuation of virtually all acts or actions against the debtor and to recover property of the estate.[1] Section 362(a) prohibits the enforcement of prepetition judgments, any act to obtain possession or exercise control over property of the estate, any act to create, perfect, or enforce any lien against property of the estate, and any act to collect, assess, or recover prepetition claims against the debtor.[2]

Library References:
West's Key No. Digests, Bankruptcy ⚿2391–2443.

§ 9.51 Automatic Stay—Exceptions

Under Section 362(b) of the Bankruptcy Code, 18 specific acts are excepted from the automatic stay provisions of Section 362(a). They include criminal actions against the debtor, collections of alimony, maintenance, or support from property that is not property of the estate, acts to perfect an interest in property that could have been perfected under applicable non-bankruptcy law, and actions or proceedings to enforce the government's police or regulatory power.[1]

§ 9.52 Automatic Stay—Obtaining Relief

Since the automatic stay is one of the fundamental protections provided by the Bankruptcy Code, a court will not readily grant relief from the stay unless the creditor can make a strong showing of cause.[1] The Bankruptcy Code lists only three specific grounds for stay relief. The first is the lack of adequate protection of a creditor's interest in property

---

5. 11 U.S.C.A. § 541(a).
6. 11 U.S.C.A. §§ 1207, 1306.

§ 9.50

1. 11 U.S.C.A. § 362(a).
2. See 11 U.S.C.A. § 362(a) for an inclusive list. The Bankruptcy Code's encompassing definition of the term "claim," set forth in Section 101(5), is discussed *supra*, § 9.36.

§ 9.51

1. See 11 U.S.C.A. § 362(b) for the list of all exceptions to the stay.

§ 9.52

1. See *infra*, §§ 9.269, 9.292 for procedural and drafting checklists for a motion to obtain relief from the automatic stay.

§ 9.52   BANKRUPTCY   Ch. 9

of the estate.[2] The second ground for relief from the stay of an act against property requires (i) that the debtor not have any equity in such property *and* (ii) that the property not be necessary to an effective reorganization.[3] The third specific ground for stay relief concerns only single asset real estate cases.[4] Stay relief based on other grounds not specifically mentioned in the Code must be for "cause."[5] Unfortunately, the Bankruptcy Code does not define cause, and the decision lies within the discretion of the bankruptcy court.[6] When continuation of the stay imposes a hardship on a creditor while lifting the stay does not prejudice the debtor or the bankruptcy estate, courts have granted stay relief under the Bankruptcy Code and the former Bankruptcy Act.[7] Thus, stay relief may be granted when the action to be permitted concerns the rights of third parties and does not interfere with or impact the bankruptcy case; for example, a divorce or child custody action, a probate proceeding in which the debtor is the executor or administrator, or a proceeding in which the debtor is a fiduciary.[8] Claims covered by insurance or indemnity also fall within this category.[9]

Library References:
West's Key No. Digests, Bankruptcy ⚖=2421–2443.

§ 9.53   Automatic Stay—Obtaining Relief—Strategy

Because one of the fundamental protections afforded debtors upon the filing of a petition under the Bankruptcy Code is the invocation of the automatic stay, courts are hesitant to deprive the debtor of such

---

2. 11 U.S.C.A. § 362(d)(1). *See infra*, § 9.56 for a discussion of adequate protection.

3. 11 U.S.C.A. § 362(d)(2).

4. *See infra*, § 9.55 for a discussion of stay relief in single asset real estate cases.

5. 11 U.S.C.A. § 362(d)(1).

6. Sonnax Indus., Inc. v. Tri Component Products Corp. (In re Sonnax Indus., Inc.), 907 F.2d 1280 (2d Cir.1990); Foust v. Munson Steamship Lines, 299 U.S. 77, 83, 57 S.Ct. 90, 93, 81 L.Ed. 49 (1936). As courts of equity, bankruptcy courts' stay relief decisions must be consonant with equitable considerations. Matthews v. Rosene, 739 F.2d 249 (7th Cir.1984). *See* In re Curtis, 40 B.R. 795 (Bankr.D.Utah 1984) for a list of factors that courts may consider in deciding whether litigation should be permitted to proceed in another forum.

It is generally recognized that a bankruptcy court's wide latitude to grant relief from the automatic stay includes the power to grant retroactive relief under Section 362(d), thereby ratifying a postpetition action that otherwise would have been a violation of the automatic stay. *See, e.g.*, Schwartz v. United States (In re Schwartz), 954 F.2d 569 (9th Cir.1992). However, case law acknowledges that such relief should be granted sparingly. *See, e.g.*, Soares v. Brockton Credit Union (In re Soares), 107 F.3d 969 (1st Cir.1997); Weltman v. Independence Savs. Bank, Bankr.L.Rep. ¶ 73,513, 1990 WL 96087 (S.D.N.Y.1990); In re Ellinwood, 206 B.R. 300 (Bankr.W.D.N.Y.1997); Massachusetts Mutual Life Ins. Co. v. Columbus Broadway Marble Corp. (In re Columbus Broadway Marble Corp.), 84 B.R. 322 (Bankr.E.D.N.Y.1988).

7. *See, e.g.*, Foust v. Munson Steamship Lines, 299 U.S. 77, 84, 87, 57 S.Ct. 90, 94, 95, 81 L.Ed. 49 (1936); In re Holtkamp, 669 F.2d 505, 508–09 (7th Cir.1982), In re Adolf Gobel, Inc., 89 F.2d 171, 172 (2d Cir.1937).

8. H.R.Rep.No. 95–595, 95th Cong., 1st Sess. 343–4 (1977); S.Rep.No. 95–989, 95th Cong., 2d Sess. 52–53 (1978).

9. *See* Foust v. Munson Steamship Lines, 299 U.S. at 84, 87, 57 S.Ct. at 94, 95, 81 L.Ed. 49; In re Holtkamp, 669 F.2d at 508–09; In re Adolf Gobel, Inc., 89 F.2d at 172.

protection during the early stages of a bankruptcy case without affording it an opportunity to reorganize. Consequently, a creditor must not expect immediate satisfaction when seeking to obtain relief from the automatic stay in order to proceed to enforce rights against its collateral.[1] Nevertheless, it is important that a creditor take all steps necessary to protect the value of its collateral upon the filing of a case.

If a creditor's collateral is declining in value during the course of the case, a creditor is entitled to be "adequately protected" from the diminution in such value.[2] As will be discussed below, the Bankruptcy Court is charged with the responsibility of protecting the creditor's rights while affording the debtor an opportunity to use the creditor's property. If a creditor does not receive relief from the automatic stay, a Bankruptcy Court should fashion an appropriate remedy to assure that a creditor's collateral value is preserved. One significant reason for taking prompt action in seeking relief from the automatic stay or adequate protection is that under Section 507(b) of the Bankruptcy Code, a creditor is afforded a superpriority administrative claim with priority over all other administrative claims to the extent that protection afforded by the court under Sections 362, 363, or 364 of the Bankruptcy Code proves to be inadequate.[3] Accordingly, by taking early steps to seek relief from the stay or adequate protection, a creditor places itself in a position, at the very least, to argue for such administrative priority in the future.[4]

Frequently, a request for relief from the stay is accompanied by an alternative request for adequate protection so that the creditor's interest

§ 9.53

1. **PRACTICE POINTER**: If the party seeking stay relief can demonstrate immediate and irreparable injury, the court may grant *ex parte* relief from the automatic stay. See *infra*, § 9.54 notes 3–4 and accompanying text.

2. 11 U.S.C.A. § 362(d). See *infra*, §§ 9.56–9.57 for a discussion of adequate protection.

3. 11 U.S.C.A. § 507(b).

4. **PRACTICE POINTER**: Even if a bankruptcy court finds that a secured creditor is adequately protected by virtue of a sufficient equity cushion, if the value of the collateral subsequently declines, the secured creditor's claim for the deficiency amount between the value of its collateral and the amount of its secured claim may not be accorded superpriority status. That is, the secured creditor may have to demonstrate that the debtor's estate derived an actual benefit from use of the collateral, thereby entitling the secured creditor to a superpriority claim for the deficiency amount caused by the decline in the collateral value. Ford Motor Credit Co. v. Dobbins, 35 F.3d 860 (4th Cir.1994).

CAVEAT: A creditor should be forewarned that in seeking relief from the automatic stay, it is often necessary to demonstrate that the debtor has no equity in the subject property and the property is not necessary for an effective reorganization. 11 U.S.C.A. § 362(d)(2). In meeting that burden, a creditor is obligated to demonstrate a value for the property which is less than the amount of its debt. In making its case, a creditor may (but will not necessarily) be bound in the future by the value it places on its collateral. If a creditor argues that it is "undersecured," it will not be entitled to the accrual of interest on its claim postpetition. See 11 U.S.C.A. § 506(b). Moreover, its claim may be bifurcated as part of the chapter 11 plan process into a secured and unsecured claim, and it may receive less than full value on either or both of these claims. See *infra*, § 9.100 for a discussion of the bifurcation of a secured creditor's claim. Accordingly, there are risks inherent in seeking early relief from the stay and thereby taking positions on valuation.

will be protected if the court denies relief from the stay.[5] The type of relief requested will depend upon the nature of the creditor's collateral, and counsel should keep in mind that often, a creditor's interests are protected best by working with the debtor to find a negotiated solution enabling it to remain in business.

Where the collateral is real property, a request for relief from the automatic stay frequently takes the form of a request to proceed with a foreclosure action under state law.[6] A court is unlikely to grant such drastic relief if it is early in the case, when the debtor has not had substantial time to attempt to refinance or sell the property, or if the value of the property is stable or increasing. On the other hand, if the debtor has previously sought relief under title 11 or a receiver was appointed under state law, or if the debtor had obtained significant prebankruptcy relief, such as an injunction, without successful rehabilitation, a court is likely to be more sympathetic to the creditor. A debtor defending against stay relief litigation should prevent deterioration of the secured creditor's interest by remaining current on payments of taxes and interest.

When real property produces rental income, the creditor may seek to modify the automatic stay to sequester the rents unless its interest in the rents is already perfected.[7] Or, in a separate adversary proceeding, it may seek an injunction to restrict the use of the rents to the direct expenses of the property, thereby preventing their dissipation for nonessential or general administrative purposes.

Lessors of equipment or creditors who are secured by interests in inventory may seek stay relief to obtain possession of the collateral and proceed with liquidation under state law. However, lenders should consider whether immediate liquidation would be preferable to the debtor's continued operation. It may be advisable, instead, to file a motion pursuant to Section 363(e) of the Code and Bankruptcy Rule 4001 to condition or restrict the use of the collateral.

A creditor whose claim is covered by insurance may seek stay relief to proceed with state court litigation up to the point of judgment, since recovery from an insurer will not affect the debtor's estate.[8] If a creditor seeks stay relief to proceed with litigation that had been commenced prepetition, the court may be influenced by such factors as how far the

---

5. *See infra*, § 9.56 for a discussion of adequate protection.

6. *See infra*, Chapter 11, "Mortgage Foreclosure."

7. PRACTICE POINTER: Perfection of an interest in rents is governed by state law; however, the Bankruptcy Reform Act of 1994, which applies to cases filed on or after October 22, 1994, provides an exception to state law perfection requirements under certain circumstances. *See infra*, § 9.69 for a discussion of the perfection of a postpetition interest in rents.

8. *See* Foust v. Munson Steamship Lines, 299 U.S. 77, 84, 87, 57 S.Ct. 90, 94, 95, 81 L.Ed. 49 (1936); In re Holtkamp, 669 F.2d 505, 508–09 (7th Cir.1982); In re Adolf Gobel, Inc., 89 F.2d 171, 172 (2d Cir.1937).

litigation had advanced prepetition and whether permitting the litigation will open the floodgates for numerous other actions.[9]

A creditor who also is indebted to the debtor for a claim that is subject to setoff may request relief from the stay to set off its debt. However, a debtor may be able to defeat such a request by showing that the amount subject to setoff is necessary to an effective reorganization.[10] Indeed, a debtor may request court authorization to use such "cash collateral" pursuant to Section 363(c)(2) of the Code.[11] In this event, the creditor should ensure that any authorization to use its cash collateral must preserve its right of setoff and provide adequate protection for the use of its cash collateral.[12]

With respect to acts against property of the estate, the stay automatically terminates 30 days after a party files a motion requesting relief from the stay unless the court determines, after notice and a hearing, to continue the stay.[13]

§ 9.54 Automatic Stay—Obtaining Relief—Hearing

The Bankruptcy Code requires that any hearing on a motion requesting relief from the stay must be held within 30 days after the filing of the motion requesting relief.[1] The hearing may be a preliminary hearing, or the preliminary and final hearings may be consolidated. If a preliminary hearing is held, the court may continue the stay pending the conclusion of the final hearing if it determines at the preliminary hearing that there is a reasonable likelihood that the party opposing stay relief will prevail at a final hearing. If the hearings are not consolidated, the final hearing must be concluded within 30 days after the conclusion of the preliminary hearing unless the 30-day period is extended with the consent of the parties or for a specific time which the court finds is required by compelling circumstances.[2]

If the party seeking stay relief can demonstrate immediate and irreparable injury, the court may grant *ex parte* relief from the automatic stay.[3] The standard for such relief is the same as the standard for

---

9. *See* Sonnax Indus., Inc. v. Tri Component Products Corp. (In re Sonnax Indus., Inc.), 907 F.2d 1280 (2d Cir.1990).

10. 11 U.S.C.A. § 362(d)(2)(B).

11. *See infra*, § 9.65 for a discussion of the debtor's use of cash collateral.

12. *See infra*, § 9.56 for a discussion of adequate protection.

13. 11 U.S.C.A. § 362(e).

§ 9.54

1. **CAVEAT**: The legislative history states that this hearing is not the appropriate time to raise "other issues, such as counterclaims against the creditor on largely unrelated matters." 124 Cong.Rec. H 11,092–3 (Sept. 28, 1978).

2. 11 U.S.C.A. § 362(e). The timing requirements are intended to prevent unjustified postponement of final action. However, property frequently will have to be valued to determine whether the debtor has equity in such property or whether the creditor lacks adequate protection, and completion of the appraisals by both parties' appraisers may be difficult within the prescribed period.

3. 11 U.S.C.A. § 362(f); Bankr.R. 4001(a)(2).

granting a preliminary injunction.[4]

Library References:

West's Key No. Digests, Bankruptcy ⟸2440.

§ 9.55 Automatic Stay—Obtaining Relief—Single Asset Real Estate Debtor

The Bankruptcy Code allows a creditor to seek a court order modifying or terminating the automatic stay in single asset real estate cases,[1] wherein the court must grant relief from the automatic stay within 90 days after the commencement of the case (unless extended by the court for cause)[2] unless (a) the debtor files a plan of reorganization that has a reasonable possibility of being confirmed within a reasonable time, or (b) the debtor makes monthly payments to the secured creditor equal to interest at a current fair market rate on the value of such creditor's interest in the property.[3]

§ 9.56 Adequate Protection

By requiring a debtor to afford "adequate protection" to a lender's security interest in property of the estate, the Bankruptcy Code seeks to protect lenders against three types of risks that may occur.[1] First, at the commencement of a bankruptcy case, the automatic stay[2] immediately suspends or eliminates a lender's state-law remedies with respect to its secured interest in the debtor's property even though the value of that property may decline during the bankruptcy case. Second, a debtor may seek to use the property in which the lender has a security interest, such

---

4. In re Wildcat Construction Co., 57 B.R. 981 (Bankr.D.Vt.1986). In the Second Circuit, this standard is well established. The applicant seeking such relief must show that he "is likely to suffer irreparable injury if [such] relief is denied [and] there is either (1) a likelihood of success on the merits or (2) sufficiently serious questions going to the merits to make them a fair ground for litigation, with a balance of hardships tipping decidedly in the [applicant's] favor." *Id*. citing In re Feit & Drexler, 760 F.2d 406, 415 (2d Cir.1985).

§ 9.55

1. "Single asset real estate" is defined as "real property constituting a single property or a project, other than residential real property with fewer than 4 residential units, which generates substantially all of the gross income of a debtor and on which no substantial business is being conducted by a debtor other than the business of operating the real property and activities incidental thereto having aggregate noncontingent, liquidated secured debts in an amount no more than $4,000,000." 11 U.S.C.A. § 101(51B).

2. **CAVEAT**: At this writing, there is no case law determining what may suffice as "cause" for a court to extend the 90-day period.

3. 11 U.S.C.A. § 362(d)(3). By enacting this provision, the Bankruptcy Reform Act of 1994 created an exception for single asset debtors from the rule that prohibits undersecured creditors from receiving interest payments. *See infra*, § 9.102 and *infra*, § 9.58 note 1 and accompanying text discussing the circumstances under which creditors may receive interest.

§ 9.56

1. *See* 11 U.S.C.A. § 361.

2. *See supra*, § 9.50 for a discussion of the automatic stay.

as by seeking to use cash collateral.[3] Third, a debtor may seek to obtain postpetition financing that is secured by a "priming" lien—that is, a senior or equal lien on the property that serves as collateral for the prepetition secured creditor.[4] Under any of these circumstances, adequate protection seeks to ensure that the value of a lender's interest in property is maintained throughout the case and that the lender retains the value of its bargained-for rights to the fullest extent possible.[5]

Library References:
West's Key No. Digests, Bankruptcy ⇒2430.1–2434, 3065, 3073.

§ 9.57 Adequate Protection—Types

The Bankruptcy Code suggests three principal means of furnishing adequate protection: periodic cash payments, additional or replacement liens, and such other forms of adequate protection as will afford the creditor the "indubitable equivalent" of its interest.[1] The "indubitable equivalent" method permits debtors to offer a variety of credit enhancements developed on a case-by-case basis, such as collateralized guarantees, as a form of adequate protection to offset the projected decline in security value.

§ 9.58 Adequate Protection—Strategy

Valuation of the collateral and its projected value in the future obviously is central to the question of whether or not a creditor is entitled to adequate protection. It may be in the best interests of a debtor to demonstrate the highest possible value for a secured creditor's collateral in order to have the court find a sufficient equity cushion (the excess of the value of the collateral over the secured creditor's interest in the collateral) or the debtor may wish to demonstrate that the value of the collateral is not declining in order to forestall the need for adequate protection or relief from the automatic stay. The secured creditor, by contrast, would want to demonstrate the lowest possible value for its collateral or that the collateral is declining in value to establish that it lacks adequate protection (*i.e.*, its interest in the collateral is greater than the value of the collateral) and prove that it is entitled to receive

---

3. *See infra*, §§ 9.60–9.65 for a discussion of the use, sale, or lease of property of the estate, including the use of cash collateral.

4. *See infra*, § 9.71 for a discussion of priming liens.

5. *See infra*, §§ 9.270, 9.293 for procedural and drafting checklists for a motion seeking adequate protection.

CAVEAT: A secured creditor may lose its right to adequate protection if it fails to timely seek adequate protection. *See* In re Best Products Co., 138 B.R. 155 (Bankr. S.D.N.Y.), aff'd 149 B.R. 346 (S.D.N.Y.1992) (creditor that failed to move for adequate protection until after it obtained possession of the property is not entitled to adequate protection to compensate for the deterioration in value during the chapter 11 case).

§ 9.57

1. 11 U.S.C.A. § 361. The term "indubitable equivalent" derives from a decision by Judge Learned Hand. In re Murel Holding Corp., 75 F.2d 941 (2d Cir.1935).

§ 9.58 BANKRUPTCY Ch. 9

additional protection or obtain relief from the stay to foreclose on its collateral.[1]

Ironically, a debtor that argues for a high collateral value will subsequently be faced with a larger secured claim, possibly including postpetition interest (which accrues only on oversecured claims) that it must address in its reorganization. In contrast, a creditor that argues it is undersecured will not be able—absent a significant change in circumstances—to seek postpetition interest on its claim.[2]

§ 9.59 Adequate Protection—Objections and Hearing

Unless the court fixes a different time, objections to a motion for adequate protection may be filed within 15 days after the notice of motion is mailed.[1] If no objection is filed, the court may act on the motion without a hearing. If an objection is filed, a hearing will be held on no less than 5 days' notice to all parties in interest.[2]

§ 9.60 Use, Sale, or Lease of Property

Section 363 of the Bankruptcy Code governs the use, sale, or lease of property of the estate during the administration of the case and the rights of third parties that have interests in such property.[1] In general, and as described below, the use, sale, or lease of property may occur within or outside of the ordinary course of the debtor's business, may depend upon the provision of adequate protection, may require notice and a hearing, and may impact upon the automatic stay.[2] In chapter 11, 12, or 13 cases, or after court authorization to continue the debtor's

§ 9.58

1. *See supra*, § 9.53 note 4 CAVEAT, which also is applicable with respect to valuations in adequate protection proceedings.

2. The United States Supreme Court has held that an undersecured creditor is not entitled to receive postpetition interest as compensation for a delay in foreclosing on its collateral due to the imposition of the automatic stay. United Sav. Ass'n v. Timbers of Inwood Forest Assocs., Ltd. (In re Timbers of Inwood Forest Assocs., Ltd.), 484 U.S. 365, 108 S.Ct. 626, 98 L.Ed.2d 740 (1988). This decision has generally been interpreted as precluding payment of postpetition interest to undersecured creditors. Oversecured creditors are entitled to interest on their claims. 11 U.S.C.A. § 506(b). Such interest, however, cannot be paid until the later of the plan's confirmation or its effective date. United Sav. Ass'n of Texas v. Timbers of Inwood Forest Assocs., Ltd. (In re Timbers of Inwood Forest Assocs., Ltd.), 793 F.2d 1380, 1381, 1407 (5th Cir.1986), on reh'g 808 F.2d 363 (5th Cir.1987)(en banc), aff'd 484 U.S. 365, 108 S.Ct. 626, 98 L.Ed.2d 740 (1988).

§ 9.59

1. Bankr.R. 4001(d)(2).
2. Bankr.R. 4001(d)(3).

§ 9.60

1. *See infra*, §§ 9.271, 9.294 for procedural and drafting checklists for motions to use, sell, or lease property of the estate.

2. **CAVEAT**: Section 363(n) of the Bankruptcy Code authorizes a trustee to avoid a sale of estate property if the sale price was controlled by an agreement among potential bidders. Accordingly, a party who wishes to purchase assets of a debtor should refrain from entering into secret side deals or agreements with other interested bidders that may be viewed as attempting to eliminate competitive bidding or otherwise control the sale price of the debtor's assets. In re New York Trap Rock Corp., Lone Star Indus., Inc., 42 F.3d 747 (2d Cir.1994).

business in a chapter 7 case, the debtor may use, sell, or lease property of the estate in the "ordinary course of business" without notice, a hearing, and a court order.[3]

Library References:

West's Key No. Digests, Bankruptcy ⊙⟶3067.1–3088.

§ 9.61 Use, Sale, or Lease of Property—Ordinary Course of Business

Although the Bankruptcy Code does not define "ordinary course of business," case law has developed two tests that courts apply to any transaction to determine whether or not it is within the ordinary course of business.[1] The "horizontal" or industry-wide test examines the transaction from an industry-wide perspective to determine if it is of the sort that is commonly undertaken by companies in the debtor's business. The "vertical test," sometimes called the "creditor's expectation test," examines the transaction from the perspective of a hypothetical creditor to determine whether the transaction subjects the creditor to an economic risk of a different nature than those the creditor accepted when it decided to extend credit.[2] Accordingly, application of the vertical test requires the court to compare the debtor's prepetition business practices and conduct with its postpetition conduct.[3]

Library References:

West's Key No. Digests, Bankruptcy ⊙⟶3025.1.

§ 9.62 Use, Sale, or Lease of Property—Outside Ordinary Course of Business

When either the proposed use, sale, or lease of property is not in the ordinary course of business or the debtor's business is not authorized to be operated (*i.e.*, in a typical chapter 7 case), the trustee or debtor in possession may only use, sell, or lease property after notice and a hearing.[1] Sales that are not in the ordinary course of business may be

---

3. 11 U.S.C.A. § 363(c)(1).

§ 9.61

1. *See, e.g.*, In re Johns–Manville Corp., 60 B.R. 612, 616–17 (Bankr.S.D.N.Y.1986); B. Weintraub & A. Resnick, *The Meaning of "Ordinary Course of Business" Under the Bankruptcy Code—Vertical and Horizontal Analysis*, 19 UCC L.J. 364 (1987).

2. *Id.*

3. The "ordinary course of business" standard is not defined so narrowly that changes between prepetition and postpetition activities are *per se* evidence of activities outside the ordinary course of business. Instead, courts attempt to allow a debtor sufficient flexibility to run its business. *See* In re Johns–Manville Corp., 60 B.R. 612, 617 (Bankr.S.D.N.Y.1986).

§ 9.62

1. 11 U.S.C.A. § 363(b)(1); Bankr.R. 6004(f)(1). For example, where a debtor/physician cancelled malpractice insurance without notice and a hearing pursuant to 11 U.S.C.A. § 363(b)(1), the Second Circuit found the cancellation was void because it constituted use of estate property beyond the ordinary course of business without the required notice and a hearing. Accordingly, the policy remained property of the estate when the case was converted

§ 9.62 BANKRUPTCY Ch. 9

conducted by private sale or by public auction.[2] On request of an entity that has an interest in property used, sold, or leased, or proposed to be used, sold, or leased (including property that is subject to an unexpired lease of personal property), the court, with or without a hearing, may prohibit or condition such use, sale, or lease as is necessary to provide adequate protection of the creditor's interest in the property.[3]

Major asset sales outside the ordinary course of business may determine issues that would otherwise be determined by a plan of reorganization. Consequently, courts will carefully scrutinize a sale of assets outside the ordinary course of business before the confirmation of a plan of reorganization to ensure that such a sale does not represent an attempt by the debtor to evade Bankruptcy Code requirements for adequate disclosure and plan confirmation. Courts generally require the debtor to demonstrate some articulated business justification for such a sale.[4]

Library References:

West's Key No. Digests, Bankruptcy ⟐3069.

§ 9.63 Use, Sale, or Lease of Property—Sales Free and Clear of Liens

The debtor may sell property of the estate free and clear of all interests in such property, including liens, if one of the following

from chapter 11 to chapter 7, and the chapter 7 trustee was able to exercise the option timely to purchase additional coverage on behalf of the bankruptcy estate. Medical Malpractice Ins. Assoc. v. Hirsch (In re Lavigne), 114 F.3d 379 (2d Cir.1997).

2. Bankr.R. 6004(f).

3. 11 U.S.C.A. § 363(e). See supra, § 9.56 for a discussion of adequate protection of a creditor's interest in property.

4. Committee of Equity Security Holders v. Lionel Corp. (In re Lionel Corp.), 722 F.2d 1063 (2d Cir.1983); see, e.g., Stephens Indus., Inc. v. McClung, 789 F.2d 386 (6th Cir.1986) (sale of radio station approved because trustee could not operate at a profit or meet expenses and FCC licenses would be lost if station ceased operating for an extended period).

In negotiating the purchase of assets, a prospective purchaser sometimes requires that the agreement include a provision for a break-up fee. A break-up fee is a payment of a fee by the seller to the prospective purchaser if, through no fault of the initial purchaser, the target company accepts a bid offered by a subsequent bidder. The break-up fee generally is intended to compensate the original purchaser for the expenses it incurred in developing an acceptable offer. Most courts and practitioners have recognized the United States District Court for the Southern District of New York's decision in In re Integrated Resources as the leading case on the propriety of break-up fees in bankruptcy cases. In determining whether the proposed arrangement would be permissible under the business judgment rule, the court concluded that such fees were permissible if the answer to three questions was negative: (1) Was the relationship of the parties who negotiated the break-up fee tainted by self-dealing or manipulation? (2) Did the fee hamper, rather than encourage, additional bidding? (3) Was the amount of the fee unreasonable relative to the proposed purchase price? In re Integrated Resources, Inc., 147 B.R. 650 (S.D.N.Y.1992), appeal dismissed 3 F.3d 49 (2d Cir.1993).

conditions is met:[1]

(i) Applicable non-bankruptcy law permits the sale free and clear of interests;

(ii) Entities with an interest in such property consent;

(iii) The interest is a lien and the sale price is greater than the value of all liens on the subject property;

(iv) The interest is the subject of a *bona fide* dispute; or

(v) Entities with an interest could be compelled in a legal or equitable proceeding to accept a money satisfaction in lieu of their interests.[2]

To enable a family farmer to scale down its operations under chapter 12, a chapter 12 trustee or debtor in possession may sell farmland and farm equipment free and clear of interests, including liens, without having to satisfy any of the conditions listed in the preceding paragraph.[3] Upon consummation of the sale, in cases under chapter 7, 11, 12, or 13, interests in the property will generally attach to the proceeds of sales.[4]

Library References:

West's Key No. Digests, Bankruptcy ⚬=3073.

§ 9.63

1. *See infra*, §§ 9.271, 9.294 for procedural and drafting checklists for a motion to use, sell, or lease property of the estate.

CAVEAT: If a buyer of a business's assets maintains and operates substantially the same business, it may become responsible for environmental clean-up liabilities of the purchased business under the Comprehensive Environmental Response, Compensation, and Liability Act ("CERCLA") notwithstanding its express disclaimer of responsibility for any liabilities. The Second Circuit has adopted the "continuity of enterprise" or "substantial continuity" test to determine whether a successor entity is a "mere continuation" of the predecessor entity. B.F. Goodrich v. Betkoski, 99 F.3d 505 (2d Cir.1996). Under this test, successor liability may be imposed if the successor maintains the same business, with the same employees, doing the same jobs under the same supervisors, working conditions, and production processes, and produces the same products for the same customers. Identity of stock, stockholders, and directors between the predecessor and the successor entities is not required. *Id.* at 519. This potential liability is of particular concern when assets are acquired from an insolvent business that may be unable to indemnify the purchaser for liability that accrued before the date of purchase.

2. 11 U.S.C.A. § 363(f).

3. 11 U.S.C.A. § 1206.

PRACTICE POINTER: In the context of sales of estate property, other provisions of the Bankruptcy Code may be relevant in chapter 7 and 11 cases involving individual debtors, or in cases under chapters 12 and 13. *See, e.g.*, 11 U.S.C.A. § 363(g) (sale free and clear of dower or curtesy rights); 11 U.S.C.A. § 363(h) (sale free and clear of the interest of a co-owner); 11 U.S.C.A. § 522(b) (the effect of federal or state-law exemptions upon the sale of debtor's residential real property).

4. 11 U.S.C.A. § 363(a). The proceeds thereafter become cash collateral, and the further disposition of such proceeds is governed by 11 U.S.C.A. § 363(c). *See infra*, § 9.65 for a discussion of cash collateral.

§ 9.64 Use, Sale, or Lease of Property—Appeals From Order Authorizing Sale

Section 363(m) of the Bankruptcy Code protects "good faith" purchasers or lessees of estate assets by providing that the reversal or modification on appeal of an authorization to sell or lease property does not affect the validity of the sale or lease to a "good faith" purchaser.[1]

Library References:
West's Key No. Digests, Bankruptcy ⊙=3776.5(5).

§ 9.65 Cash Collateral

Cash and cash equivalents that constitute a secured lender's collateral or the proceeds derived therefrom are referred to as "cash collateral" under the Bankruptcy Code.[1] The Bankruptcy Code offers greater protection to parties with an interest in cash collateral than to parties with an interest in non-cash collateral due to the inherent risk of dissipation of such liquid assets during the course of the case.[2]

Unlike non-cash collateral, which a trustee or debtor in possession may use, sell, or lease in the ordinary course of business without notice and a hearing,[3] cash collateral may not be used, sold, or otherwise disposed of, either in or outside the ordinary course of business,[4] without the consent of the entity whose claim is secured by the cash collateral, unless the debtor obtains court approval after notice and a hearing.[5]

---

§ 9.64

1. 11 U.S.C.A. § 363(m).

CAVEAT: Pursuant to § 363(m) of the Bankruptcy Code, unless an objecting party has obtained a stay blocking a sale pending appeal, an order approving the sale of a debtor's assets is final and unappealable except on the limited issue of whether the sale was made to a good faith purchaser. Indeed, the Second Circuit has concluded that an appellate court lacks jurisdiction to review an unstayed sale order except on this limited issue. Licensing by Paolo, Inc. v. Sinatra (In re Paolo Gucci), 105 F.3d 837 (2d Cir.1997). Accordingly, any party objecting to a sale of a debtor's assets must act immediately to obtain an emergency hearing seeking an interim stay before its substantive rights are extinguished upon consummation of the sale.

§ 9.65

1. Cash collateral is defined generally as "cash, negotiable instruments, documents of title, securities, deposit accounts, or other cash equivalents whenever acquired in which the estate and another entity have an interest and includes the proceeds, products, offspring, rents, or profits of property and the fees, charges, accounts or other payments for the use or occupancy of rooms and other public facilities in hotels, motels, or other lodging properties...." 11 U.S.C.A. § 363(a).

2. See In re Cropper Co., 35 B.R. 625, 633 (Bankr.M.D.Ga.1983) (cash collateral requires special protection because it "is the most likely form of collateral to be consumed in the reorganization process [and] is subject to change on a daily basis").

3. 11 U.S.C.A. § 363(c)(1).

4. See supra, § 9.61 for a discussion of the meaning of "ordinary course of business" under the Bankruptcy Code.

5. 11 U.S.C.A. § 363(c)(2). The concept of "notice and a hearing," is flexible and in certain circumstances may allow for abbreviated notice and/or, if not timely requested by a party in interest that has been given notice, no hearing at all. See supra, § 9.15 note 1 for a more detailed discussion of the concept of notice and a hearing.

See infra, §§ 9.272, 9.295 for procedural and drafting checklists for a motion to use cash collateral.

Library References:
West's Key No. Digests, Bankruptcy ⟐3082.1–3084.

§ 9.66 Cash Collateral—Strategy

Because a bankruptcy filing prohibits the debtor from using cash collateral without consent, it constricts a debtor's normal business operations. Consequently, at the outset of a bankruptcy case or, when possible, before filing, a debtor will have to arrange for the financing of its postpetition operation by obtaining the use of cash collateral consensually or by court order, or by obtaining new financing. Since the debtor's continued operation—to facilitate a restructuring or even an orderly liquidation—is likely to be in the creditor's best interest, and use of a creditor's cash collateral may be essential for the debtor to continue operating, it may be in the creditor's interest to negotiate with the debtor a stipulation governing the debtor's consensual use of cash collateral (a cash collateral stipulation).[1] A creditor may be able to obtain more favorable terms in a consensual agreement than in a court order resolving litigation over use of cash collateral.

A cash collateral stipulation generally provides for:

- The permitted uses of the collateral;[2]

- Maintenance of a segregated bank account containing the cash collateral and any proceeds, products, or profits of the creditor's collateral;

- Agreed upon means of monitoring use of the collateral, such as a business plan, periodic budgets, and financial reports;

- The adequate protection to be provided;

- A reservation of the creditor's rights under the documents that gave rise to the secured claim or assurance that the value of the collateral will be preserved; and

- A waiver by the debtor of the automatic stay in the event of a default under the cash collateral stipulation, thereby enabling the creditor to proceed with its nonbankruptcy remedies.

In addition, cash collateral stipulations frequently include a provision acknowledging that expenses authorized by the stipulation are reason-

PRACTICE POINTER: Although the form of consent required under Section 363(c)(2)(A) is not specified, caution dictates that prior *written* consent be obtained from each party with an interest in the cash collateral.

§ 9.66

1. See *infra*, §§ 9.272, 9.295 for procedural and drafting checklists for a motion to use cash collateral and see *infra*, §§ 9.273, 9.296 for procedural and drafting checklists for a cash collateral stipulation.

2. **PRACTICE POINTER**: Where the collateral produces cash proceeds, such as rents from real estate, the creditor should ensure that any excess proceeds that are not needed for operation of the property are used only for acceptable purposes such as reasonable, necessary maintenance of the property or are paid to the creditor.

§ 9.66 BANKRUPTCY Ch. 9

able and necessary expenses to maintain and preserve the value of the collateral for the benefit of the secured creditor. Such a provision permits the uncontested deduction of these expenses from the net allowed value of the collateral pursuant to 11 U.S.C.A. § 506(c).[3]

If a creditor finds that the debtor is using its cash collateral without authorization, and a phone request to the debtor's counsel does not bring immediate results, the creditor should request a temporary restraining order and file a motion pursuant to Section 363(e) of the Bankruptcy Code and Bankruptcy Rule 4001(a)(1), requesting the court to prohibit or condition the debtor's use of its cash collateral. A debtor's counsel should educate the debtor to ensure that it does not make unauthorized use of cash collateral.

Sometimes there is uncertainty as to whether the creditor has an interest in the debtor's property that qualifies as cash collateral, and this question must be resolved by the court. This is common, for example, when a mortgage on real property includes an assignment of rents provision. If the mortgagee's interest in the rents is a conditional assignment, rather than an absolute assignment, and all steps necessary to perfect that interest under state law were not taken prepetition, the mortgagee may not have a "cash collateral" interest in the rents because the automatic stay prohibits the mortgagee from perfecting its interest in the rents postpetition.[4]

§ 9.67 Cash Collateral—Hearing

The court may not commence a final hearing on a motion to use cash collateral earlier than 15 days after service of the motion; however, upon request of the debtor, the court may conduct a preliminary hearing

---

3. *See infra*, § 9.102 for a discussion of charges against the value of a secured creditor's collateral.

4. However, with respect to cases filed on or after October 22, 1994, *see infra*, § 9.69, which discusses the effect of the 1994 amendments to the Bankruptcy Code.

PRACTICE POINTER: Some courts have held that a debtor's interest in rents and, therefore, its ability to use the rents as cash collateral, were cut off on the debtor's prepetition default because an assignment of rents was held to be an absolute assignment which conveyed all right in the rents to the mortgagee. *See, e.g.*, First Fidelity Bank, N.A. v. Jason Realty, L.P. (In re Jason Realty, L.P.), 59 F.3d 423 (3d Cir. 1995), reh'g denied; Commerce Bank v. Mountain View Village, Inc., 5 F.3d 34 (3d Cir.1993); 641 Avenue of the Americas, L.P. v. 641 Assocs., Ltd., 189 B.R. 583 (S.D.N.Y. 1995) (lender was entitled to the rents because it had taken all steps required under state law to obtain an enforceable interest in rents); Credit Lyonnais v. Getty Square Assocs., 876 F.Supp. 517 (S.D.N.Y.1995) (assignment of rents was found to be an absolute assignment that entitled the mortgage lender to all rents from the date of the mortgagor's default). Accordingly, a creditor's counsel should argue that an assignment of rents was intended to be an absolute assignment and that all right in the rents has been conveyed to the creditor or, if this is not a well-founded argument, a creditor's counsel should argue that the creditor has an interest in the rents sufficient to treat the rents as the creditor's cash collateral. On the other hand, a debtor's counsel should argue that an assignment of rents is merely additional security that does not constitute cash collateral. *See* John J. Rapisardi and Elliot L. Hurwitz, *The Mortgagee's Right to Rents After Default: An Unsettled Controversy*, 6 J.Bankr.L. & Prac. 331 (May/June 1997).

within such 15-day period.[1] At the preliminary hearing, the court may authorize the use of cash collateral only if there is a reasonable likelihood that the trustee or debtor in possession will prevail at a final hearing[2] and only in an amount necessary to avoid immediate and irreparable harm to the estate pending such final hearing.[3]

Library References:
West's Key No. Digests, Bankruptcy ⊗3084.

§ 9.68 Cash Collateral—Postpetition Proceeds

Agreements between debtors and lenders often contain clauses that provide lenders security interests in some or all after-acquired property of the debtor. Although this form of security interest is valid under state law, under the Bankruptcy Code a security interest in after-acquired property generally may not extend to property that is acquired by the estate or the debtor after the commencement of the case.[1] This general rule does not apply to security interests in after-acquired "proceeds, product, offspring or profits" of property of the estate, which continue to be valid under the Bankruptcy Code.[2]

Library References:
West's Key No. Digests, Bankruptcy ⊗2573.

§ 9.69 Cash Collateral—Postpetition Proceeds—Security Interests in Rents and Hotel Revenues

As a general rule, perfection of an interest in rents is governed by state law; however, the Bankruptcy Reform Act of 1994 provides an exception to state law perfection requirements under certain circumstances.[1] When a secured creditor holds a security interest in an underlying lease or mortgage that has been properly perfected under state law, and that security agreement extends to rents or to receipts from lodging properties, in many states including New York, after a default, the lender may not *enforce* its security interest in the rents without taking additional action required under state law.[2] Typically, this additional action includes taking possession of the mortgaged premises, having a receiver appointed, having a state court order issued to sequester the rents, or foreclosing on the mortgaged property.[3] When a bankruptcy

---

§ 9.67
1. Bankr.R. 4001(b)(2).
2. 11 U.S.C.A. § 363(c)(3).
3. Bankr.R. 4001(b)(2).

§ 9.68
1. 11 U.S.C.A. § 552(a).
2. 11 U.S.C.A. § 552(b).

§ 9.69
1. The Bankruptcy Reform Act of 1994 applies to cases filed on or after October 22, 1994.
2. *See* In re Vienna Park Properties, 976 F.2d 106 (2d Cir.1992).
3. *See, e.g.*, 641 Avenue of the Americas L.P. v. 641 Assocs., Ltd., 189 B.R. 583, 591 (S.D.N.Y.1995); In re Northport Marina As-

case is filed and the automatic stay takes effect, a lender is precluded from taking such steps to enforce its security interest in rents.[4] Accordingly, even where a lender has had a prepetition, perfected security interest in a lease or mortgage that extended to rents, courts frequently have held that the lender is not entitled to have the rents treated as cash collateral in a bankruptcy case because the lender has not taken the additional steps required under state law to "perfect" (*i.e.*, enforce) its interest in the rents.[5]

In order to solve this perfection problem, the 1994 amendments to the Bankruptcy Code provide that when an underlying security agreement that extends to rents or to receipts from lodging properties is valid, enforceable, and perfected before a bankruptcy filing, it automatically results in a valid, enforceable, and perfected security interest in the rents or hotel receipts after the filing (except to the extent that the court orders otherwise based on the equities of the case).[6] This provision is intended to establish uniform treatment of security interests in postpetition rents in bankruptcy cases by focusing on the validity, enforceability, and perfection of the underlying security interest, instead of the varying state-law perfection procedures concerning rents.[7] It permits the rents to be treated as the secured lender's cash collateral.[8] Accordingly, the trustee or debtor must segregate such rents and is prohibited from using them without the consent of the secured lender or court authorization.[9]

The second change affecting postpetition rents made by the Bankruptcy Reform Act of 1994 was to clarify the treatment in bankruptcy of the fees, charges, accounts, or other payments for the use or occupancy of rooms and other public facilities in hotels, motels, or other lodging properties. Before the amendment, there was considerable divergence in opinion among the courts as to whether such revenue fell within the purview of Section 552 of the Code as postpetition proceeds that are subject to prepetition security interests. Many courts held that revenues from lodging facilities were not "rents" but, rather, personalty under

---

socs., 136 B.R. 911, 916–17 (Bankr.E.D.N.Y. 1992).

4. *See* 11 U.S.C.A. § 362(a)(4).

5. *See, e.g.*, In re Multi–Group III L.P., 99 B.R. 5 (Bankr.D.Ariz.1989); In re Association Center L.P., 87 B.R. 142 (Bankr. W.D.Wash.1988).

6. 11 U.S.C.A. § 552(b)(2).

7. 140 Cong.Rec. H 10,768 (Oct. 4, 1994).

8. **PRACTICE POINTER**: Although the Bankruptcy Reform Act of 1994 applies only to cases commenced on or after October 22, 1994, New York courts have held that a perfected (*i.e.*, recorded) security interest in rents is entitled to protection as cash collateral even if the lender did not take the necessary steps to *enforce* its security interest. In re Vienna Park Properties, 976 F.2d 106, 113 (2d Cir.1992); In re Carmania Corp., 154 B.R. 160, 164 (S.D.N.Y. 1993).

See infra, § 9.102 note 4 for reference to cases dealing with the controversy concerning whether postpetition rents paid to undersecured creditors should be applied to the secured or the unsecured portion of their claim.

9. 11 U.S.C.A. § 363(c)(2).

applicable state law.[10] The amendment makes clear that revenues from lodging facilities are, indeed, revenues that are subject to prepetition security interests and, therefore, are to be accorded treatment as cash collateral.[11]

However, the rights of lenders remain circumscribed to protect the competing interests of debtors and their employees. As noted above, courts are given the power to limit creditors' rights in postpetition proceeds "based on the equities of the case."[12] This provision is intended to prevent secured creditors from obtaining undeserved windfalls and to afford the courts broad discretion to balance the interests of secured creditors against the strong public policies that favor rehabilitation of debtors, preservation of going-concern values, and continuation of jobs.[13] The rights of secured creditors in postpetition proceeds also are expressly subject to other sections of the Bankruptcy Code which further circumscribe such rights. The list includes: Section 363, which permits the debtor to use cash collateral, with certain restrictions;[14] Section 506(c), which permits operating expenses to be charged against pledged revenues;[15] Section 522, which permits an individual debtor to exempt certain property from the bankruptcy estate;[16] and Sections 544, 545, 547, and 548, which give the debtor powers to avoid certain transfers and liens.[17]

Library References:

West's Key No. Digests, Bankruptcy ⇒2578.

§ 9.70 Abandonment of Property

Section 554 of the Bankruptcy Code, which applies in cases under chapters 7, 11, 12, and 13, authorizes the trustee or debtor in possession or any party in interest, after notice and a hearing, to abandon property of the estate that is burdensome or of inconsequential value and benefit to the estate.[1] If the trustee or debtor in possession determines to

---

10. *See, e.g.*, In re Shore Haven Motor Inn, Inc., 124 B.R. 617 (Bankr.S.D.Fla. 1991); In re Kearney Hotel Partners, 92 B.R. 95 (Bankr.S.D.N.Y.1988) (interpreting Nebraska law).

11. 140 Cong.Rec. H 10,768 (Oct. 4, 1994).

12. 11 U.S.C.A. § 552(b)(1).

13. 140 Cong.Rec. H 10,768 (Oct. 4, 1994).

14. *See supra*, § 9.65 for a discussion of the debtor's use of cash collateral.

15. *See infra*, § 9.102 for a discussion of the charges permitted against a secured creditor's collateral.

16. *See infra*, § 9.125 for a discussion of exemptions.

17. *See infra*, §§ 9.113–9.119 for a discussion of the trustee's or debtor's avoiding powers.

§ 9.70

1. 11 U.S.C.A. § 554.

CAVEAT: The Supreme Court has held that, notwithstanding Section 554 of the Bankruptcy Code, property of the estate may not be abandoned in violation of a state statute or regulation that is reasonably designed to protect the public health or safety from identified hazards. Midlantic Nat'l Bank v. New Jersey Dep't of Environmental Protection (In re Quanta Resources), 474 U.S. 494, 507, 106 S.Ct. 755, 762, 88 L.Ed.2d 859 (1986).

abandon property of the estate, it must give notice thereof to the United States trustee, all creditors, indenture trustees, and committees elected or appointed under the Bankruptcy Code.[2] If a timely objection—within 15 days of mailing of notice or within time fixed by the court—is made by one of such parties, the court must hold a hearing to determine whether or not to approve the proposed abandonment.[3] A party in interest may file and serve a motion requiring the trustee or debtor in possession to abandon property of the estate.[4] A motion to abandon property or to compel the abandonment of property must be filed in accordance with the requirements for a contested matter under Bankruptcy Rule 9014.[5]

Library References:
West's Key No. Digests, Bankruptcy ⊙⇒3131–3137.

§ 9.71 Postpetition Financing

Section 364 of the Bankruptcy Code, which applies in cases under chapters 7, 11, 12, and 13, allows a trustee, debtor in possession, or debtor that is authorized to operate the business of the debtor to obtain postpetition financing of its business operations during the pendency of the case.[1] The debtor in possession or a trustee that is authorized to operate the debtor's business may obtain unsecured credit and incur unsecured debt in the ordinary course of business.[2] Unsecured debt incurred in the ordinary course of business is allowable under Section 503(b)(1) of the Code as an administrative expense.[3] Similarly, the debtor or the trustee may obtain unsecured credit or incur unsecured debt outside the ordinary course of business[4] that is allowable under Section 503(b)(1) of the Code as an administrative expense, provided the court so authorizes after notice and a hearing.[5]

If the debtor can demonstrate that it is unable to obtain postpetition financing on an unsecured basis as an administrative expense, it may obtain credit by granting a lender: (i) priority over any or all administra-

---

2. 11 U.S.C.A. § 554(a); Bankr.R. 6007(a).

3. Bankr.R. 6007(a).

4. 11 U.S.C.A. § 554(b); Bankr.R. 6007(b).

5. *See supra*, § 9.17 for a discussion of contested matters pursuant to Bankruptcy Rule 9014 and *see infra*, § 9.267 for a procedural checklist for commencing a contested matter and §§ 9.306–9.308 for sample pleadings to commence a contested matter. *See also* Bankr.R. 7001(1) (proceeding to compel debtor to abandon property under section 554 of the Bankruptcy Code is not an adversary proceeding governed by Bankruptcy Rule 7001).

§ 9.71

1. *See infra*, §§ 9.274, 9.297 for procedural and drafting checklists for a motion to obtain postpetition financing.

2. *See supra*, § 9.61 discussing the meaning of "ordinary course of business" under the Bankruptcy Code.

3. 11 U.S.C.A. § 364(a). *See infra*, § 9.98 discussing administrative expense claims.

4. *See supra*, § 9.62 discussing transactions that are outside the ordinary course of business.

5. 11 U.S.C.A. § 364(b).

tive claims of the kind specified in Sections 503(b) or 507(b) of the Code; (ii) a lien on unencumbered assets; or (iii) a junior lien on property that already is subject to a lien.[6] Finally, if a debtor is unable to obtain postpetition financing on the foregoing terms, it is allowed to offer the postpetition lender a lien on encumbered property that is equal or senior to existing liens—a "priming" lien.[7] Because this option is considered the most disruptive of prepetition creditors' interests, the Bankruptcy Code requires that affected lienholders be provided "adequate protection" of their liens if such liens are to be primed.[8] If a debtor gives a creditor adequate protection of a secured claim and the adequate protection proves insufficient, that creditor's deficiency claim is entitled to superpriority, that is, priority over every other allowable claim entitled to administrative expense priority.[9]

Where a debtor was unable to obtain needed financing on less onerous terms, the Second Circuit has permitted financing transactions providing for "forward cross-collateralization," that is, granting a lender a lien on postpetition collateral to secure an outstanding prepetition debt, provided notice is given to the secured creditor whose lien is being primed.[10] While such forward cross-collateralization is not expressly permitted by the Bankruptcy Code, courts have authorized a financing order containing such forward cross-collateralization when not excessive and when the debtor lacked other financing options, provided there was adequate notice and a hearing.[11]

6. 11 U.S.C.A. § 364(c).

7. 11 U.S.C.A. § 364(d).

8. 11 U.S.C.A. § 364(d)(1)(B). See supra, § 9.56 for a discussion of adequate protection.

9. 11 U.S.C.A. § 507(b).

CAVEAT: The secured creditor may still have to prove that the debtor derived a benefit from the use of the collateral. See supra, § 9.53 note 4.

CAVEAT: Although professional fees are entitled to administrative priority in cases under title 11, such fees cannot be accorded priority over the claim of a lender who has extended credit under Section 364(c) unless the lender *consented* to the payment of such fees or the professional can demonstrate that its services benefited that lender rather than the debtor or other creditors. General Electric Credit Corp. v. Levin & Weintraub (In re Flagstaff Foodservice Corp.), 739 F.2d 73, 75 (2d Cir.1984). Inasmuch as such demonstration by the professional would be a difficult burden, a debtor's counsel should seek to negotiate a "carve out" which will provide for the payment of the debtor's professional fees up to an agreed limit before payment to the lender in the event of a liquidation.

10. Otte v. Manufacturers Hanover Commercial Corp. (In re Texlon Corp.), 596 F.2d 1092 (2d Cir.1979).

11. Id. See also In re Beker Industries Corp., 58 B.R. 725, 742 (Bankr.S.D.N.Y. 1986). The court in Beker Industries concluded that so long as (a) there was no injury to, or objection from, the unsecured creditors that could be adversely affected by the cross-collateralization, and (b) proper notice and a hearing was given, such forward cross-collateralization was permitted. *Accord* In re Vanguard Diversified, Inc., 31 B.R. 364, 366–67 (Bankr.E.D.N.Y.1983). The court in Vanguard noted that because cross-collateralization accords preferential treatment to the claims of the financing party, it is a device that ought to be utilized as a last resort only when the debtor is otherwise unable to obtain needed financing on less onerous terms. *Id.* at 366. Accordingly, before granting cross-collateralization, the court required the debtor in possession to demonstrate that:

(1) Absent the proposed financing, the debtor in possession's business operations would not survive;

§ 9.72 Postpetition Financing—Hearing

A final hearing on a motion for postpetition financing is prohibited earlier than 15 days after service of the motion; however, upon request of the debtor, the court may conduct a preliminary hearing within such 15-day period.[1] The court may authorize credit at the preliminary hearing only to the extent necessary to avoid immediate and irreparable harm to the estate pending a final hearing.[2]

Library References:

West's Key No. Digests, Bankruptcy ⟐3038.

§ 9.73 Postpetition Financing—Appeals From Order Authorizing

When an order approving postpetition financing is entered, the reversal or modification on appeal of such order does not affect the validity of the extension of credit or the liens afforded to a lender that has extended credit in good faith, even though the lender knew of the pendency of the appeal.[1] However, to the extent financing is not entered into in good faith, the incurrence of such debt may be subject to modification or reversal on appeal.[2]

(2) The debtor in possession was unable to obtain alternative financing on acceptable terms;

(3) The proposed lender would not accede to less preferential terms; and

(4) The proposed financing was in the best interests of the general creditor body. *Id.*

Other courts have followed this four-prong analysis. *See, e.g.,* In re Roblin Industries, Inc., 52 B.R. 241, 244 (Bankr.W.D.N.Y. 1985); In re Antico Mfg. Co., Inc., 31 B.R. 103, 105 (Bankr.E.D.N.Y.1983).

CAVEAT: Although the Sixth and Ninth Circuits also have permitted cross-collateralization, the Eleventh Circuit has held that this method of obtaining financing is *per se* impermissible. Shapiro v. Saybrook Mfg. Co. (In re Saybrook Mfg. Co.), 963 F.2d 1490 (11th Cir.1992).

§ 9.72

1. Bankr.R. 4001(c)(2).

2. *Id.* A chapter 11 debtor can satisfy the irreparable harm test by demonstrating a risk of losing its business absent postpetition financing. In re Ames Dept. Stores, Inc., 115 B.R. 34 (Bankr.S.D.N.Y.1990).

§ 9.73

1. 11 U.S.C.A. § 364(e).

CAVEAT: A lender may not be accorded protection from an appeal unless the bankruptcy court makes an explicit finding when the loan is authorized that the lender has acted in good faith. *See* In re Revco DS, Inc., 901 F.2d 1359 (6th Cir.1990).

2. *See* 11 U.S.C.A. § 364(e). However, the Third Circuit has held that a court reviewing an appeal from an order authorizing a debtor to obtain postpetition financing may reverse or modify such an order even if the appellant failed to obtain a stay pending appeal as long as the court could fashion relief without disturbing the superpriority status of the postpetition lender's lien. RTC v. Sweeland Dev. Group, Inc. (In re Sweeland Dev. Group), 16 F.3d 552 (3d Cir.1994) (court could prohibit disbursement of funds that were not yet disbursed under approved postpetition financing).

§ 9.74 Executory Contracts and Unexpired Leases

Upon commencement of a bankruptcy case, the debtor will likely be a party to various executory contracts and unexpired leases. Although the term "executory contract" is not defined in the Bankruptcy Code, it is generally held to encompass contracts in which performance remains due to some extent on both sides.[1] To enable the debtor to be relieved of burdensome contracts or to enjoy beneficial ones, Section 365 of the Bankruptcy Code authorizes a debtor, subject to the approval of the bankruptcy court, to assume or reject any executory contract or unexpired lease.[2] Section 365 applies only to executory contracts and leases that have not expired or been terminated before the commencement of the bankruptcy case. Once an agreement has expired or has been terminated under applicable state law, it is no longer executory, and the debtor retains no interest capable of assumption or rejection.[3]

§ 9.74

1. See NLRB v. Bildisco and Bildisco, 465 U.S. 513, 522 n. 6, 104 S.Ct. 1188, 1194 n. 6, 79 L.Ed.2d 482 (1984). The legislative history regarding this section states that "[t]hough there is no precise definition of what contracts are executory, it generally includes contracts on which performance remains due to some extent on both sides." H.R.Rep.No. 95–595, 95th Cong., 1st Sess. 347 (1977); S.Rep.No. 95–989, 95th Cong., 2d Sess. 58 (1978). See also V. Countryman, *Executory Contracts in Bankruptcy*, 57 Minn.L.Rev. 439, 460 (1973) (defining an executory contract as a "contract under which the obligation of both the bankrupt and the other party to the contract are so far unperformed that the failure of either to complete performance would constitute a material breach excusing the performance of the other"). A New York bankruptcy court recently concluded that the Countryman definition is too restrictive and adopted the legislative history definition to find that an option agreement is an executory contract that is therefore subject to rejection. In re Riodizio, Inc., 204 B.R. 417 (Bankr.S.D.N.Y.1997).

Licenses for the right to use intellectual property may be executory contracts, and § 365(n) of the Bankruptcy Code deals with the licensee's rights if a debtor/licensor of a right to intellectual property rejects such a contract. 11 U.S.C.A. § 365(n). See 3 Collier on Bankruptcy ¶ 365.14 (L.King, ed., 15th Ed.1996) for a good discussion of § 365(n).

CAVEAT: Certain courts eschew the foregoing definitions of an executory contract and instead use a results-oriented approach. Specifically, if treatment of a contract as executory will yield a result consistent with the policies underlying the Bankruptcy Code, the contract will be found executory. See, e.g., In re Becknell & Crace Coal Co., 761 F.2d 319 (6th Cir. 1985); Cohen v. The Drexel Burnham Lambert Group, Inc. (In re The Drexel Burnham Lambert Group, Inc.), 138 B.R. 687 (Bankr.S.D.N.Y.1992).

2. See infra, §§ 9.275, 9.298 for procedural and drafting checklists for a motion to assume or reject an executory contract or unexpired lease. See infra, § 9.79 for a discussion of the conditions that a debtor must satisfy before a court will authorize assumption of an executory contract or unexpired lease.

3. See In re B–K of Kansas, Inc., 69 B.R. 812 (Bankr.D.Kan.1987).

PRACTICE POINTER: There is some uncertainty as to the proper procedure for resolving a dispute concerning an executory contract that a debtor wishes to assume. The Second Circuit has ruled that a bankruptcy court erred in determining a dispute regarding an alleged default under a prepetition contract during the course of a hearing on the debtor's request to assume the contract. Orion Pictures Corp. v. Showtime Networks, Inc., 4 F.3d 1095 (2d Cir.1993), cert. dismissed 511 U.S. 1026, 114 S.Ct. 1418, 128 L.Ed.2d 88 (1994). However, only four months earlier, the Second Circuit had concluded that a bankruptcy court had erred by authorizing a debtor to assume a lease without first determining whether the debtor's alleged prepetition default had terminated the lease before the bankruptcy filing. Hart Envtl. Mgmt. Corp. v. Sanshoe Worldwide Corp. (In re Sanshoe Worldwide

§ 9.74

Any provision in an executory contract, unexpired lease, or applicable nonbankruptcy law intended to terminate or modify such a contract or lease or any rights thereunder that is conditioned solely on the insolvency or financial condition of the debtor or the commencement of a case under title 11 is unenforceable under the Bankruptcy Code.[4]

Library References:

West's Key No. Digests, Bankruptcy ⇐3101–3117.

§ 9.75 Executory Contracts and Unexpired Leases—Strategy

From a debtor's perspective, there are two primary rules that should be followed when contemplating the assumption or rejection of executory contracts or unexpired leases. First, to the extent that prior to the filing of a petition, a debtor has determined which of its executory contracts and unexpired leases are burdensome and of little or no value upon assignment, a motion to reject such contracts and unexpired leases should be filed immediately upon the filing of the petition. Section 365(d)(3) of the Bankruptcy Code requires that a debtor timely perform all the obligations under any unexpired lease of nonresidential real property that arise from the time of the order for relief until such lease is assumed or rejected. Thus, prompt rejection of undesirable leases enables a debtor to avoid the incurrence of administrative expense claims postpetition, as well as the unnecessary expense of litigating with parties to such contracts.

Second, to the extent that a debtor requires additional time to determine its viable "core" business and, therefore, those executory contracts or unexpired leases that it may desire to assume and/or assign, a debtor should attempt to obtain as much time as possible in order to make such a decision. Typically, courts will grant debtors additional time within which to determine whether to assume or reject executory contracts or unexpired leases so long as the nondebtor parties to such contracts or leases are not harmed in the process. In seeking additional time to assume or reject, debtors should be cognizant of the fact that they will be required to pay postpetition amounts due and owing under the contracts and leases as administrative expense claims; however, in consideration for incurring such costs, debtors avoid prematurely assum-

Corp.), 993 F.2d 300 (2d Cir.1993). Given these seemingly conflicting decisions, the prudent course of action would be to file an adversary proceeding to resolve separately any contract disputes concerning an executory contract as soon as the debtor determines that it wishes to assume the contract and before it files a motion to assume such a contract under Section 365.

4. 11 U.S.C.A. § 365(e)(1). These unenforceable provisions that are intended to terminate a contract upon a bankruptcy filing or similar financial condition are known as *"ipso facto"* clauses.

ing such contracts and leases and, thereby, converting all obligations thereunder into administrative claims.[1]

From a creditor's perspective, upon the filing of a case under the Bankruptcy Code, consideration should be given to immediately moving before the bankruptcy court for an order directing the debtor to assume or reject its unexpired leases or other executory contracts. Such a motion should be brought, in particular, if the debtor fails to pay any of its postpetition obligations and the creditor has an alternative lessee desirous of leasing the subject property. Although such a motion may likely be denied in the early stages of a case, often the court will place the debtor under time constraints within which to make a decision to assume or reject, which may benefit the nondebtor party.

§ 9.76 Executory Contracts and Unexpired Leases—Time for Assumption or Rejection

In chapter 7 cases, each executory contract and unexpired lease of the debtor is deemed rejected unless the trustee assumes it within 60 days after the order for relief, or within such additional time as the court, for cause, directs before the expiration of the 60-day period.[1] The debtor in a chapter 11, 12, or 13 case may assume or reject an executory contract or unexpired lease, except a lease of nonresidential real property, at any time prior to the confirmation of a plan. However, a party to the executory contract or unexpired lease may request the bankruptcy court, for cause, to order the debtor to assume or reject within a more limited period of time.[2] Assumption or rejection also may be provided for

---

§ 9.75

1. The Second Circuit has confirmed that once a lease has been assumed in a bankruptcy case, all claims for future rents arising under that lease are entitled to administrative expense status and are not subject to the cap on such damages under 11 U.S.C.A. § 502(b)(6), regardless of whether the assumed lease is rejected subsequently. Nostas Assocs. v. Costich (In re Klein Sleep Prods., Inc.), 78 F.3d 18 (2d Cir.1996). However, a New York bankruptcy court has held that when a debtor files a second chapter 11 case after a failed reorganization, lease rejection claims arising from leases that the debtor rejected without first assuming in the debtor's second chapter 11 case are not entitled to administrative priority on the ground that the debtor had assumed those leases in its prior chapter 11 case. In re Jamesway Corp., 202 B.R. 697 (Bankr.S.D.N.Y.1996). The court in Jamesway reasoned that the decision in Klein Sleep was inapplicable because in Klein Sleep, the leases were first assumed and then rejected in the same bankruptcy case. In contrast, the court found that the debtor in the first Jamesway case was a separate and distinct legal entity from the debtor in the second case, and the bankruptcy estate created on the commencement of the first case was separate and distinct from the estate created on the commencement of the second case. *Id.* at 701. *See infra*, § 9.98 for a discussion of administrative expense claims and *see infra*, § 9.83 for a discussion of the cap on lease rejection damages.

§ 9.76

1. 11 U.S.C.A. § 365(d)(1).
2. 11 U.S.C.A. § 365(d)(2).

PRACTICE POINTER: Once the time for a debtor to assume or reject an executory contract or unexpired lease is placed at issue, courts generally will grant the debtor a "reasonable" time to decide whether to assume or reject.

in a chapter 11, 12, or 13 plan.³

Library References:

West's Key No. Digests, Bankruptcy ⇒3103(1)–3103.2.

§ 9.77 Executory Contracts and Unexpired Leases—Nonresidential Real Property Leases

Unexpired leases of nonresidential real property in a chapter 11, 12, or 13 case are treated in the same manner as all executory contracts and unexpired leases in chapter 7 cases and are deemed rejected 60 days after the order for relief unless the court, for cause, extends the 60–day period prior to its expiration.¹ During the postpetition period prior to the assumption or rejection of a lease, landlords under unexpired leases of nonresidential real property are entitled to receive the rent provided in the lease even if it is more than the fair market value of the property.²

3. 11 U.S.C.A. §§ 1123(b)(2), 1222(b)(6), 1322(b)(7).

§ 9.77

1. 11 U.S.C.A. § 365(d)(4). The language of the statute is somewhat unclear as to whether a debtor satisfies the 60–day time limit to extend the time to assume a lease merely by filing a motion requesting an extension of the 60–day period before its expiration. When the statute was first enacted, some courts held that a lease was deemed rejected, even if a request for an extension had been filed within the 60–day period, if the court had not entered an order for such extension before the expiration of the 60 days. Additionally, some courts, after granting an extension of time within the initial 60–day postpetition period, interpreted the statute to preclude the granting of any additional extension of time after the termination of the initial 60–day period. Subsequent and better-reasoned decisions hold that a court may grant an extension of the 60–day period as long as the debtor or trustee files a motion requesting an extension before the expiration of the 60–day period. Moreover, courts will grant additional extensions for cause, provided that the motions requesting such extensions are filed before the expiration of the extended time. See, e.g., In re Channel Home Centers, Inc., 989 F.2d 682 (3d Cir. 1993), cert. denied 510 U.S. 865, 114 S.Ct. 184, 126 L.Ed.2d 143 (1993); In re American Healthcare Management, Inc., 900 F.2d 827 (5th Cir.1990); In re Victoria Station, Inc., 875 F.2d 1380 (9th Cir.1989); Tigr Restaurant, Inc. v. Rouse S.I. Shopping Center, Inc., 79 B.R. 954 (E.D.N.Y.1987).

Although the Bankruptcy Code requires the debtor to pay postpetition rents timely as administrative expenses, many courts will allow a debtor to defer performance of this obligation if there is a substantial likelihood that insufficient funds will be available to pay all administrative priority claims in full. Consequently, it is not uncommon for a debtor to be permitted to continue to occupy leased premises during the period before a final decision is made to assume or reject a lease without keeping postpetition rent current. A request for an extension of the 60–day period may be particularly troubling to landlords when a debtor is in default of postpetition rent. However, the Second Circuit has held that a bankruptcy court may not deny an extension of the 60–day deadline on the exclusive ground that the debtor has not brought rents current. It held that any decision must be premised on proper standards, including the following non-exclusive list of relevant factors: (1) whether the debtor was paying rent; (2) whether the debtor's occupation of the premises could damage the landlord beyond the compensation afforded under the Bankruptcy Code; (3) whether the lease is an important asset of the debtor's estate; (4) whether the debtor has had sufficient time to formulate a plan of reorganization; (5) the size and complexity of the debtor's case; (6) the number of leases that the debtor must evaluate; and (7) the need for judicial determination of whether the lease, in fact, exists. South Street Seaport Limited Partnership v. Burger Boys, Inc. (In re Burger Boys, Inc.), 94 F.3d 755 (2d Cir.1996).

2. 11 U.S.C.A. § 365(d)(3).

§ 9.78 Executory Contracts and Unexpired Leases—Assumption by the Debtor

Section 365 requires court approval for the assumption of an executory contract or unexpired lease. Generally, when a trustee or debtor in possession applies for an order approving its assumption of an executory contract or unexpired lease, its business judgment is the determinative factor.[1] Because assumption usually does not prejudice the nondebtor party to the contract (provided the debtor cures all defaults and gives adequate assurance of future performance), the court must ascertain only whether the future benefits accruing to the debtor under the contract or lease outweigh the costs to the debtor associated with assuming the contract or lease.

§ 9.79 Executory Contracts and Unexpired Leases—Assumption and Assignment

The Bankruptcy Code expressly renders unenforceable certain anti-assignment clauses and other contract termination clauses and enables the debtor to assume and assign certain valuable executory contracts or unexpired leases otherwise unassignable under nonbankruptcy law.[1] However, the debtor may only assume an executory contract or unexpired lease if the debtor fulfills three preconditions:

(1) It cures any default or provides adequate assurance that it will promptly do so;[2]

(2) It compensates the nondebtor party for any pecuniary loss resulting from a default, or provides adequate assurance that it will promptly do so; and

(3) It gives adequate assurance of future performance under the lease.[3]

Additionally, the debtor must demonstrate that any assignee will provide adequate assurance of future performance, regardless of whether there has been a default in the executory contract or unexpired lease.[4] This means that the debtor must demonstrate that the assignee has sufficient financial means and stability to provide adequate assurance of its full performance in the future. This may include the provision of a bond, guaranty, or other additional security. The debtor/assignor is

PRACTICE POINTER: Consequently, a debtor's counsel should encourage a decision on the assumption or rejection of nonresidential real property leases as early in the case as possible.

§ 9.78

1. *See* NLRB v. Bildisco and Bildisco, 465 U.S. 513, 104 S.Ct. 1188, 79 L.Ed.2d 482 (1984); In re Minges, 602 F.2d 38 (2d Cir.1979).

§ 9.79

1. 11 U.S.C.A. § 365(f).

2. *See infra*, § 9.248 note 4 for a discussion of the meaning of "curing defaults" under the Bankruptcy Code.

3. 11 U.S.C.A. § 365(b)(1).

4. 11 U.S.C.A. § 365(f)(2).

§ 9.79   **BANKRUPTCY**   Ch. 9

released from any and all liability resulting from a breach of the executory contract or unexpired lease that arises after the assignment.[5]

Library References:
West's Key No. Digests, Bankruptcy ⇐3102.1.

§ 9.80   Executory Contracts and Unexpired Leases—Exceptions to Assumption and Assignment

The Bankruptcy Code prohibits a debtor from assuming or assigning an executory contract or unexpired lease if otherwise applicable non-bankruptcy law excuses the other party to the contract or lease from accepting performance from, or rendering performance to, an entity other than the debtor under the contract or lease (for example, personal service contracts) unless the other party consents to the assumption or assignment.[1] Contracts to make a loan or extend financial accommodations to the debtor may not be assumed or assigned.[2]

Library References:
West's Key No. Digests, Bankruptcy ⇐3105.1–3108.

§ 9.81   Executory Contracts and Unexpired Leases—Rejection by Debtor

Courts generally will grant a debtor's motion to reject an executory contract or unexpired lease if rejection is based on the debtor's business judgment and if rejection will benefit the debtor's estate.[1] However, the court may disapprove rejection of a contract or lease on equitable grounds.[2] Accordingly, a debtor should estimate the damage claims arising from a contract or lease rejection as well as the potential benefits to the estate (including the possible limitation on the total amount of damages that may be claimed under the Bankruptcy Code)[3] in order to

---

5. 11 U.S.C.A. § 365(k).

§ 9.80

1. 11 U.S.C.A. § 365(c). *See* In re Wills Motors, Inc., 133 B.R. 303 (Bankr. S.D.N.Y.), aff'd 134 B.R. 124 (S.D.N.Y. 1991); In re Yachthaven Restaurant, 103 B.R. 68 (Bankr.E.D.N.Y.1989); Delightful Music Ltd. v. Taylor (In re Taylor), 913 F.2d 102 (3d Cir.1990).

2. 11 U.S.C.A. § 365(c). In essence, Section 365(c) prohibits a debtor from forcing a lender to continue to provide financing once the debtor has commenced a case under the Bankruptcy Code. *See supra*, § 9.71 for a discussion of obtaining credit.

§ 9.81

1. NLRB v. Bildisco & Bildisco, 465 U.S. 513, 523, 104 S.Ct. 1188, 1194, 79 L.Ed.2d 482 (1984); In re Minges, 602 F.2d 38 (2d Cir.1979).

2. *See, e.g.*, In re Chinichian, 784 F.2d 1440 (9th Cir.1986).

3. The maximum allowable claim of an employee arising from the termination of an employment contract is limited to the compensation provided under such contract, without acceleration, for one year following the earlier of the petition date or the date on which employment was terminated (by either party) plus any unpaid compensation due under the contract, without acceleration, on the earlier of such dates. 11 U.S.C.A. § 502(b)(7). Courts have uniformly held that the limitation on employee termination claims mandated under Section 502(b)(7) of the Bankruptcy Code applies to employee claims that arise after the debt-

enable the court to weigh them against the prejudice to the nondebtor party.

§ 9.82 Executory Contracts and Unexpired Leases—Damages Arising From Rejection: Debtor as Tenant/Lessee

The rejection by the debtor of an executory contract or unexpired lease of real property has the effect of a breach of the contract or lease immediately before the date the bankruptcy petition is filed (the petition date) and entitles the nondebtor party to assert a claim against the debtor's bankruptcy estate for damages arising from the breach.[1]

Damages arising from a lease rejection should be calculated in accordance with the usual procedures for determining damages arising from the rejection of a lease, pursuant to the lease provisions and applicable state law. The notion behind the calculation of damages under state law is that the landlord/lessor should be made whole by receiving the benefit of the bargain under the lease.[2]

Library References:

West's Key No. Digests, Bankruptcy ⟸2834.

or's bankruptcy filing. The Third Circuit, the only circuit court of appeals to have addressed the issue to date, has held that the Section 502(b)(7) cap is not limited to executory contracts, but also applies to prepetition employee termination claims. The Third Circuit stated that Section 502(b)(7) does not require any nexus between an employee's termination and the debtor's bankruptcy; nor does it preclude application to terminations that are remote in time from the commencement of the bankruptcy case or that were reduced to judgment before commencement of the bankruptcy case. Anthony v. Interform Corp., 96 F.3d 692 (3d Cir.1996). In Anthony, the employee's wrongful termination claim was reduced to judgment in state court approximately four years before the employer's bankruptcy filing. Nevertheless, the Third Circuit held that the Bankruptcy Code caps such a claim, regardless of the claimant's asserted or actual right to damages under state law. Id. See infra, § 9.83 discussing the Bankruptcy Code's cap on damages arising from the rejection of a real property lease.

PRACTICE POINTER: The First Circuit has held that a debtor's rejection of a nonresidential real property lease does not take effect until the court has approved the lease rejection. Accordingly, the court held that the landlord was entitled to administrative rent from the date the bankruptcy petition was filed until the date rejection became effective on court approval. Thinking Machs. Corp. v. Mellon Fin. Servs. Corp. (In re Thinking Machs. Corp.), 67 F.3d 1021 (1st Cir.1995). The First Circuit, which is the only court of appeals to have addressed this issue to date, took the position of the majority of lower courts that have considered the question. There are a small number of lower courts that have held that a debtor's lease rejection is effective on the date the lease rejection motion is filed and that court approval, required by 11 U.S.C.A. § 365(a), is a condition subsequent to effective rejection of a nonresidential lease. See, e.g., In re Joseph C. Spiess Co., 145 B.R. 597 (Bankr.N.D.Ill.1992).

§ 9.82

1. 11 U.S.C.A. § 365(g)(1). See Finkelstein and Ferrara, *Landlord and Tenant Practice in New York* (West 1997) Ch. 20 "Bankruptcy."

2. However, certain claims are limited under the Bankruptcy Code. See supra, § 9.81 note 3, discussing the cap on claims arising from the termination of an employment agreement and see infra, § 9.83, discussing the cap on claims arising from the rejection of a real-property lease.

§ 9.83 Executory Contracts and Unexpired Leases— Calculation of Allowed Real Property Lease Rejection Damages

The Bankruptcy Code caps the damages allowable to a lessor of the debtor under a real property lease to prevent a claim so large (based on a long-term lease) as to preclude other general unsecured creditors from recovering a distribution from the estate.[1] The following worksheet sets forth the steps to calculate damages under the Bankruptcy Code's cap.

Section 502(b)(6) Worksheet

A. $_____ Rent for the first year following the earlier of the petition date or the date the lessee surrenders or the lessor repossesses the property.

B. $_____ To calculate this dollar amount, (i) some courts calculate 15% × the aggregate dollar amount remaining under the lease; (ii) other courts first calculate 15% × the time remaining under the lease and then calculate the rent for this period of time following the bankruptcy filing.[2]

C. $_____ Dollar amount of rent for three years following the petition date.

D. $_____ Take the lesser of B and C.

E. $_____ Take the greater of A and D.

F. $_____ Unpaid rent due under the lease (as of the petition date).

G. $_____ Add E and F; this represents the damage cap imposed by Section 502(b)(6).

H. $_____ Calculate the present value of actual damages under state law (after commercially reasonable mitigation, if required by the lease or the court).

I. $_____ Take the lesser of G and H. This is the landlord's allowed claim for damages arising from the debtor-tenant's lease rejection. It does not include postpetition-prerejection unpaid

---

§ 9.83

1. 11 U.S.C.A. § 502(b)(6).

2. **PRACTICE POINTER**: The issue of how the 15% factor should be applied (*see* Step B in the worksheet) has been a source of considerable controversy. *Compare* Wolf Partnership v. Monheit (In re Ames Dep't Stores, Inc.), 173 B.R. 80 (S.D.N.Y.1994) and In re Gantos, 176 B.R. 793 (W.D.Mich. 1995) (15% is multiplied by the aggregate amount of rent left to be paid under the lease) *with* In re Iron–Oak Supply Corp., 169 B.R. 414 (Bankr.E.D.Cal.1994) (15% should be multiplied by the amount of time remaining under the lease and the rent calculated for that period following the bankruptcy filing). If there is no rent escalation clause in the lease, the damage cap is the same no matter which calculation method is used. However, if the lease provides for rent escalation over time, the damage cap will be larger if the 15% is multiplied by the *rent* remaining under the lease rather than the amount of *time* remaining under the lease.

rent, which may be entitled to administrative priority. If accorded administrative priority, postpetition-prerejection rent would have to be paid in full according to the lease terms.

Library References:
West's Key No. Digests, Bankruptcy ⇔2834.

§ 9.84 Executory Contracts and Unexpired Leases—Debtor as Landlord/Lessor

Under the Bankruptcy Code, when a lessee is in possession of leased real property under which the debtor is the landlord/lessor, the lessee may elect to remain in possession for the remainder of the lease term, including any renewals or extensions, notwithstanding the rejection of the lease by the lessor.[1] The Bankruptcy Reform Act of 1994 clarified that the nondebtor lessee's rights are not limited to possession, but include "rights such as those relating to the amount and timing of payment of rent and other amounts payable by the lessee and any rights of use, possession, quiet enjoyment, subletting, assignment, or hypothecation" that are appurtenant to the real property.[2] Moreover, "lessee" is defined to include "any successor, assign, or mortgagee permitted under the terms" of the lease.[3] Under such circumstances, the lessee must pay the rent provided under the lease, but has a right of offset against the debtor for any damages incurred as a result of the nonperformance of any of the debtor's obligations under the lease. The lessee, however, forfeits the right to assert any other claims against the debtor's estate.[4] Alternatively, if the lessee does not wish to remain in possession, it has the right to treat the lease as terminated, vacate the premises, and assert a prepetition claim for damages.[5]

Library References:
West's Key No. Digests, Bankruptcy ⇔3101.

§ 9.85 Executory Contracts and Unexpired Leases—Unexpired Personal Property Leases

The 1994 Amendments to the Bankruptcy Code added a subsection to Section 365 which provides similar, although not as extensive, protec-

§ 9.84
1. 11 U.S.C.A. § 365(h).
2. 11 U.S.C.A. § 365(h)(1)(A)(ii).
3. 11 U.S.C.A. § 365(h)(1)(D).
4. 11 U.S.C.A. § 365(h)(1).
5. 11 U.S.C.A. § 365(h)(1)(A)(i).

PRACTICE POINTER: The 1994 amendments to the Bankruptcy Code should give some comfort to a leasehold mortgagee when a debtor/landlord rejects the lease of a mortgagor/lessee. Under the new provisions, and based on the broad definition of "lessee" discussed above, the rejection of a lease by a debtor/landlord should not result in the extinguishment of the mortgagee's security interest in the leasehold but, rather, should permit the mortgagee to exercise its rights and remedies upon such debtor's determination to reject. The case law in this area will be developing, and attorneys representing leasehold mortgagees should be cognizant of such developments.

tions for lessors of personal property as the rest of Section 365 provides to lessors of real property.[1] Generally, a debtor is required to perform all obligations first arising from or under an unexpired lease of personal property on or after the sixtieth day following the commencement of the case until the lease is assumed or rejected. The bankruptcy court may, however, suspend the debtor's duty to timely perform its obligations based on the equities of the case.

§ 9.86 Collective Bargaining Agreements

Although collective bargaining agreements[1] are considered executory contracts subject to assumption or rejection, Section 365 of the Code, which deals with executory contracts, is inapplicable for purposes of rejection by the debtor.[2] In 1984, Congress enacted Section 1113, which specifically sets forth the conditions that must be satisfied before a debtor can reject or modify a collective bargaining agreement.[3] Before rejecting or modifying a collective bargaining agreement, the debtor must:

1. Make a proposal to the employee's representative (usually a labor union)[4] based on the most complete and reliable information available, stating the modifications in employee benefits and protections necessary to permit reorganization and to assure that all creditors, the debtor, and affected parties are treated fairly and equitably.[5]

2. Provide the employee representative with all relevant information necessary to evaluate the proposal.[6]

3. Meet at reasonable times with the employee representative in a good faith[7] effort to reach a mutually satisfactory modification following submission of the proposal and a hearing (which must be set no later than 14 days after the motion is filed).[8]

§ 9.85

1. 11 U.S.C.A. § 365(d)(10).

§ 9.86

1. See infra, Chapter 17, "Employment Law."

2. Collective bargaining agreements can be assumed under Section 365 of the Code, subject to the same requirements as other executory contracts. See supra, § 9.74 for a discussion of executory contracts and see supra, §§ 9.76, 9.78 for a discussion of their assumption by the debtor.

3. See infra, §§ 9.276, 9.299 for procedural and drafting checklists for rejecting or modifying a collective bargaining agreement.

4. Unions, as parties to a collective bargaining agreement, have standing to assert claims against an estate on behalf of their membership and those employees benefiting from the collective bargaining agreement.

5. 11 U.S.C.A. § 1113(b)(1)(A). See Century Brass Prods., Inc. v. UAW Local 1604 (In re Century Brass Prods., Inc.), 795 F.2d 265, 273 (2d Cir.1986), cert. denied 479 U.S. 949, 107 S.Ct. 433, 93 L.Ed.2d 383 (1986).

6. 11 U.S.C.A. § 1113(b)(1)(B).

7. See In re GCI, Inc., 131 B.R. 685 (Bankr.N.D.Ind.1991).

8. 11 U.S.C.A. § 1113(b)(2).

The bankruptcy court will authorize rejection of a collective bargaining agreement if (1) the debtor satisfies the procedural requirements listed above, (2) the employee representative refuses to accept the proposal without "good cause,"[9] and (3) "the balance of the equities clearly favors rejection of the collective bargaining agreement."[10]

It has been held that a postpetition modification of a collective bargaining agreement that contains provisions that are outside the ordinary course of business,[11] even if consensual, is unenforceable unless the debtor has complied with the Bankruptcy Code's notice and hearing requirements for transactions outside the ordinary course of business.[12]

Although the debtor may not unilaterally terminate or alter any provision of a collective bargaining agreement without complying with the provisions of Section 1113 of the Bankruptcy Code, as listed above in this section, the debtor may seek interim relief (after notice and a hearing) if such relief is essential to the continuation of the debtor's business and will avoid irreparable damage to the estate.[13]

Even if a debtor satisfies the requirements of Section 1113 and obtains bankruptcy court authorization to reject its collective bargaining agreement, the union remains the exclusive bargaining representative for the employees, and the debtor must negotiate with the union pursuant to the National Labor Relations Act.[14] In addition, employees retain their right to resign or strike if the changes imposed by the debtor are unacceptable to them.[15]

Library References:

West's Key No. Digests, Bankruptcy ⇐3101, 3108, 3113.

§ 9.87 Retired Employees' Insurance Benefits

Section 1114 requires a debtor or trustee to timely pay any health care and similar benefits owing to retired employees under any prepeti-

---

9. New York Typographical Union No. 6 v. Maxwell Newspapers, Inc. (In re Maxwell Newspapers, Inc.), 981 F.2d 85 (2d Cir. 1992) (analyzing meaning of "good cause" under Section 1113(c)).

10. 11 U.S.C.A. § 1113(c). See In re Texas Sheet Metals, Inc., 90 B.R. 260 (Bankr.S.D.Tex.1988) (listing six considerations in balancing the equities).

11. See infra, § 9.62 for a discussion of what constitutes transactions that are outside the ordinary course of business under the Bankruptcy Code.

12. In re Leslie Fay Cos., 168 B.R. 294 (Bankr.S.D.N.Y.1994).

13. 11 U.S.C.A. § 1113(e).

14. See In re Century Brass Products, Inc., 795 F.2d 265 (2d Cir.1986); In re Salt Creek Freightways, 47 B.R. 835 (Bankr. D.Wyo.1985). See infra, Chapter 17, "Employment Law."

15. In re Royal Composing Room, Inc., 62 B.R. 403, 15 C.B.C.2d 1, 3 (Bankr. S.D.N.Y.1986), aff'd 78 B.R.671 (S.D.N.Y. 1987), aff'd 848 F.2d 345 (2d Cir.1988), cert. denied 489 U.S. 1078, 109 S.Ct. 1529, 103 L.Ed.2d 834.

tion plan, fund, or program,[1] and prohibits modification of such benefits without a court order. Section 1114 establishes a procedural structure similar to the one governing modification of collective bargaining agreements under Section 1113.[2] Thus, management and the retirees' representatives (generally labor unions) must negotiate before a debtor can seek court authorization to modify or reject a prepetition plan covering retiree health insurance benefits.[3]

If the debtor complies with the procedure described in Section 1114, the court must authorize the proposal if it has found that the employees' authorized representative refused to accept the proposal without good cause and the proposal is "clearly favored" by the balance of the equities.[4] As with Section 1113, after notice and a hearing, the debtor in possession may seek an interim order implementing modifications if it is essential to the continuation of the debtor's business or will avoid irreparable injury to the estate.[5]

Library References:
West's Key No. Digests, Bankruptcy ⟸2961, 3113.

§ 9.88 Retired Employees' Insurance Benefits—Procedure for Modifying

The procedure for notice and a hearing is the same as the procedure for rejecting a collective bargaining agreement.[1] If the court does not rule on the application within 90 days of the commencement of the hearing or any additional time agreed to between the parties, the debtor may implement the proposed modifications pending the court's ruling.[2]

Claims for damages for loss of retiree benefits are calculated in accordance with nonbankruptcy law. Such claims are not limited by Section 502(b)(7), which limits the claim of an employee for damages resulting from the termination of an employment contract.[3]

§ 9.89 Utility Services

Following the filing of a petition under the Bankruptcy Code, suppliers generally are not obligated to continue doing business with the

---

§ 9.87

1. Since the Bankruptcy Code does not define the words, "plan, fund, or program," courts have defined these terms by reference to the federal statute that protects employee rights to retirement benefits—the Employee Retirement Income Security Act ("ERISA"). *See, e.g.,* Nagy v. Riblet Prods. Corp., 79 F.3d 572, 574 (7th Cir.1996); In re New York Trap Rock Corp., 126 B.R. 19, 22 (Bankr.S.D.N.Y.1991). *See also infra,* Chapter 17, "Employment Law."

2. *See supra,* § 9.86.

3. *See* 11 U.S.C.A. § 1114 for a detailed description of the required procedure. Generally, Section 1114 does not apply to retirees or their dependents whose gross income for the 12 months preceding the bankruptcy filing equals or exceeds $250,000.

4. 11 U.S.C.A. § 1114(g).

5. 11 U.S.C.A. § 1114(h).

§ 9.88

1. *See supra,* § 9.86.

2. 11 U.S.C.A. § 1114(k)(2).

3. 11 U.S.C.A. § 1114(j).

debtor in possession. However, the Bankruptcy Code protects the debtor from the sudden cut-off of utility services[1] because these services, which generally are essential for survival, frequently are monopolistic services that are not readily available from another vendor. For 20 days after the petition date, Section 366 of the Code prohibits a utility from altering, refusing, or discontinuing service to a debtor due to the commencement of a case under title 11 or an unpaid prepetition obligation. Within the 20-day period the debtor must provide "adequate assurance of payment"[2] in the form of a deposit or other security.[3] However, on request of a party in interest and after notice and a hearing, the court may order reasonable modification of the deposit or other security necessary to provide adequate assurance of payment.[4]

Library References:
West's Key No. Digests, Bankruptcy ⚖︎2481, 2482.

§ 9.90 Claims Procedures

As explained *supra*, § 9.36, any entity that holds a claim against the debtor's estate is a creditor whose rights are protected under the Bankruptcy Code. However, the Bankruptcy Code's protection of creditors' rights often requires creditors to take affirmative action. Filing a proof of claim in the debtor's bankruptcy case is the basic action necessary to protect a claim against the debtor's estate.[1]

§ 9.89

1. **PRACTICE POINTER**: For purposes of practice under the Bankruptcy Code, providers of such services as telephone and telecommunications generally are treated as "utilities" in addition to gas, electric, and water companies.

2. *See* In re Keydata Corp., 12 B.R. 156 (1st Cir.BAP1981) ("Adequate assurance of payment" does not require an absolute guarantee of payment so long as the utility is protected from an unreasonable risk of nonpayment). The Second Circuit has held that when the safeguards otherwise available under the Bankruptcy Code provide a utility with adequate assurance of payment pursuant to Section 366(b), a bankruptcy court need not require that any additional safeguards be provided. Virginia Electric & Power Co. v. Caldor (In re Caldor), 117 F.3d 646 (2d Cir.1997). The court noted that in this case, the safeguards that had been provided under the Code were: (i) administrative expense priority for the utilities' claims; (ii) an expedited procedure for relief in the event of the debtors' default; and (iii) an order requiring the debtors to convey their monthly operating statements to the utilities. *Id.* at 647. Moreover, the court may extend the protection of Section 366 to the confirmation date, as it did in Caldor.

3. 11 U.S.C.A. § 366(b). A utility holding a prepetition deposit may recoup its prepetition debt against the deposit and seek a postpetition deposit as adequate assurance of future performance. *See* In re Norsal Industries, Inc., 147 B.R. 85 (Bankr. E.D.N.Y.1992).

4. 11 U.S.C.A. § 366(b).

PRACTICE POINTER: In a case involving numerous utilities, such as apartment properties or retail locations, onerous utility deposits could make operation and reorganization impossible. Accordingly, the practitioner should prepare in advance for negotiations with utilities and, alternatively, prepare motions for (i) an extension of the 20-day period to provide adequate assurance and (ii) waiver or modification of deposit requirements.

§ 9.90

1. **CAVEAT**: The Second Circuit has held that by filing a proof of claim, a creditor submits itself to the bankruptcy court's equitable jurisdiction and waives its right to

§ 9.90   BANKRUPTCY   Ch. 9

Library References:
West's Key No. Digests, Bankruptcy ⟐2891–2933.

§ 9.91 Claims Procedures—Filing Proofs of Claim or Interest

A proof of claim is a written statement of the creditor's claim and should conform substantially to Official Form 10.[1] A proof of claim for a secured claim must include the original or a duplicate of written evidence of the claim and evidence of its perfection.[2] A proof of claim or interest must be filed with the clerk in the district where the case is pending, or the judge may permit filing with the judge.[3] No filing fee is required.

A debtor under chapter 7, 11, 12, or 13 is required pursuant to Section 521(1) of the Bankruptcy Code to file a schedule of liabilities[4] which provides *prima facie* evidence of the amount and validity of the debtor's obligations. A proof of claim is "deemed filed" under Section 501 of the Bankruptcy Code for any claim or interest that appears in the schedules filed in accordance with Section 521(1) or Section 1106(a)(2) of the Bankruptcy Code except a claim or interest that is scheduled as disputed, contingent, or unliquidated.[5] If the creditor in a chapter 7, 11, 12, or 13 case agrees with the scheduled amount of its claim, it is not obligated to file a proof of claim. But, if the debtor fails to schedule an obligation, includes a dollar amount or classification that the creditor contests, or schedules a debt as disputed, contingent, or unliquidated, a creditor must file a proof of claim or interest to put the debtor in possession or trustee on notice of the existence of the obligation in the amount the creditor believes is correct.[6] By filing a proof of claim, the creditor supersedes the debtor's schedules.[7] The proof of claim is *prima*

a jury trial with respect to a determination of that claim. *See supra* § 9.19 note 2.

§ 9.91

1. Bankr.R. 3001(a). *See supra*, § 9.5 and note 3 for a discussion of Official Forms. Bankruptcy Rule 3001(e) sets forth the requirements and procedure for filing a proof of claim that has been acquired by transfer from the original claim holder. *See infra*, § 9.162 note 3 for a discussion of the treatment of transferred claims in the plan acceptance process.

PRACTICE POINTER: Some courts have accepted an "informal proof of claim," but a document purporting to evidence such claim must (1) have been timely filed with the bankruptcy court and have become part of the judicial record, (2) state the existence and nature of the debt, (3) state the amount of the claim against the estate, and (4) evidence the creditor's intent to hold the debtor liable for the debt. Houbigant, Inc. v. ACB Mercantile, Inc. (In re Houbigant, Inc.), 190 B.R. 185 (Bankr.S.D.N.Y.1995).

2. Bankr.R. 3001(c), (d).

3. Bankr.R. 5005.

CAVEAT: Counsel for a creditor should create a filing tickler to ensure that a proof of claim is filed timely. Failure to file timely generally results in the disallowance and discharge of the claim. *See infra*, §§ 9.92–9.93 for a discussion of bar dates and late-filed proofs of claim.

4. *See infra*, § 9.265 for a checklist of the schedules that a debtor must file.

5. 11 U.S.C.A. § 1111(a); Bankr.R. 3003(b)(1).

6. 11 U.S.C.A. § 501; Bankr.R. 3002(a), 3003(c)(2).

7. Bankr.R. 3003(c)(4).

facie evidence of the validity and amount of the claim[8] and will be the basis of the estate's distribution to the creditor unless the debtor objects to the proof of claim. If a creditor fails to timely file a proof of claim and has received proper notice of the last date to file claims (the "bar date"),[9] the creditor's claim is forever barred and, upon confirmation of the debtor's case, discharged.[10]

If a creditor fails to file a timely proof of claim, an entity other than the creditor may file a proof of claim on behalf of that creditor.[11] In order to effectively discharge a claim, a debtor or trustee may file a proof of claim on behalf of a creditor within 30 days after the expiration of the time for filing claims.[12]

Proofs of claim evidence *prepetition* obligations of the debtor. However, the Bankruptcy Code provides that certain obligations that arise *postpetition* are treated as if they had arisen prepetition. A proof of claim may be filed to preserve these obligations, which will be treated as if they had arisen prepetition. These include:

1. Reimbursement or contribution claims against the debtor that become fixed after the commencement of the case.[13]
2. Claims that arose in an involuntary bankruptcy prior to the entry of the order for relief, so called "involuntary gap claims."[14]
3. Claims for damages arising from rejection of an executory contract or unexpired lease.[15]
4. Claims based on the recovery of property.[16]
5. Claims based on a creditor's right to offset a mutual debt.[17]
6. Claims by governmental units for certain taxes.[18]

Library References:

West's Key No. Digests, Bankruptcy ⚖︎2891–2896.

§ 9.92 Claims Procedures—Filing Proofs of Claim or Interest—Bar Dates

The bar date is the last date to file a proof of claim or interest. In a chapter 11 case, the bar date is established upon application of the

---

8. Bankr.R. 3001(f).
9. *See infra*, § 9.92, discussing the bar date.
10. 11 U.S.C.A. §§ 502(b)(9), 1141(d), 1228(c), 1328(c). An entity that is liable to a creditor with the debtor, or that has secured such creditor, also may file a proof of such claim. 11 U.S.C.A. § 501(b); Bankr.R. 3005.
11. Bankr.R. 3001(b).
12. 11 U.S.C.A. § 501(c); Bankr.R. 3004.
13. 11 U.S.C.A. §§ 501(d), 502(e).
14. 11 U.S.C.A. §§ 501(d), 502(f).
15. 11 U.S.C.A. §§ 501(d), 502(g).
16. 11 U.S.C.A. §§ 501(d), 502(h).
17. 11 U.S.C.A. §§ 501(d), 502(h), 553.
18. 11 U.S.C.A. §§ 501(d), 502(i).

§ 9.92   BANKRUPTCY   Ch. 9

debtor and may be extended for "cause shown."[1] In a chapter 7, 12, or 13 case, a creditor holding a claim must file a proof of claim or interest within 90 days after the first date set for the meeting of creditors under § 341(a) of the Bankruptcy Code.[2] Additional time for filing is allowed under chapters 7, 11, 12, or 13 for certain exceptions which include the following:[3]

- An unsecured claim that arises or becomes allowable as a result of a judgment may be filed within 30 days after the judgment becomes final.[4]

- A claim arising from the rejection of an executory contract or unexpired lease may be filed within such time as the court may direct.[5]

- In a chapter 7 liquidation case where a notice of insufficient assets to pay a dividend was sent previously, a claim may be filed within 90 days after the mailing of a notice that payment of a dividend appears possible.[6]

Library References:

West's Key No. Digests, Bankruptcy ⟸2897.1–2900(2).

§ 9.93   Claims Procedures—Late–Filed Proofs of Claim

The bar date is very important to the debtor in a case under chapter 11, 12, or 13 because it enables the debtor to ascertain with certainty the full extent of its liabilities so that it can formulate its plan of reorganization or debt adjustment.[1] In chapter 7 cases, the bar date also is important because it allows the trustee to determine the scope of claims against the estate.

Prior to the enactment of the Bankruptcy Reform Act of 1994, there was no provision in the Bankruptcy Code that expressly defined the treatment to be accorded late-filed claims. Some courts concluded that a failure to file a timely proof of claim was not a ground for disallowing such claim.[2] Section 502(b)(9) was added to the Code in 1994 to disallow late-filed claims that are not specifically allowed pursuant to some other

---

§ 9.92

1. Bankr.R. 3003(c)(3).
2. Bankr.R. 3002(c). See supra, § 9.37 for a discussion of the meeting of creditors.
3. See Bankruptcy Rule 3002(c), 3003(c)(3) for the complete list of exceptions. See also Bankruptcy Rule 9006(b)(1), which empowers the court, for cause shown, to enlarge the time within which an act may be done if the request therefor is made before the expiration of the prescribed period.
4. Bankr.R. 3002(c)(3), 3003(c)(3).
5. Bankr.R. 3002(c)(4), 3003(c)(3).
6. Bankr.R. 3002(c)(5).

§ 9.93

1. See In re Best Products Co., Inc., 140 B.R. 353, 357 (Bankr.S.D.N.Y.1992).
2. See, e.g., In re Hausladen, 146 B.R. 557 (Bankr.D.Minn.1992).

Code section.[3] However, to protect the payment of priority claims under chapter 7, Section 726(a)(1) was amended to permit payment of a late-filed priority claim as long as distribution has not commenced.[4] Unchanged is the Code provision stating that a late-filed proof of claim is not allowed unless (i) the creditor holding such a claim had neither notice nor actual knowledge of the case in time to file a timely proof of claim,[5] or (ii) in a chapter 7 case, such a claim is filed in time to permit payment.[6]

Even before the enactment of the provision restricting tardily-filed claims, courts looked with disfavor on creditors' attempts to file proofs of claim after the bar date. In chapter 11 cases, creditors that failed to file timely proofs of claim or interest sometimes have obtained additional time to file such claims if they could establish "excusable neglect."[7] Proper notice is essential to the enforcement of the bar date; indeed, the Supreme Court decision permitting the filing of a late claim based on the creditor's "excusable neglect" was grounded on a defect in the form of notice.[8]

Creditors under chapter 7, 12, or 13 may not file late claims except under limited circumstances specified in Bankruptcy Rule 3002(c).[9] In addition, as noted above, a creditor in a chapter 7 case may not file a late claim unless such claim is filed in time to permit payment.[10]

Library References:
West's Key No. Digests, Bankruptcy ⚭2900(1)–2900(2).

§ 9.94 Claims Procedures—Amendment of Proofs of Claim or Interest

Amendments to a proof of claim or interest may be filed freely before the bar date. After the bar date, courts generally permit creditors to amend filed proofs of claim if the amendment is intended to cure a defect in the claim as originally filed, or if it is intended to describe the claim with greater particularity, or plead a new theory of recovery on the

---

3. The amendments to the Bankruptcy Code enacted by the Bankruptcy Reform Act of 1994 apply to all cases filed on or after October 22, 1994. An exception was carved out to provide that a claim of a governmental unit is timely filed if it is filed before 180 days after the date of the order for relief or such later time as the Bankruptcy Rules may provide. 11 U.S.C.A. § 502(b)(9).

4. Previously, the Second Circuit had held that "the scheme set forth in § 726(a) imposes no threshold requirement of timely filing for a claim to be 'allowed' and thus eligible for payment." In re Vecchio, 20 F.3d 555, 558 (2d Cir.1994).

5. 11 U.S.C.A. §§ 502(b)(9), 726(a)(2)(C)(i).

6. 11 U.S.C.A. § 726(a)(2)(C)(ii); Bankr.R. 3002(c)(6).

7. Bankr.R. 9006(b)(1). See Pioneer Investment Services Co. v. Brunswick Associates Limited Partnership, 507 U.S. 380, 113 S.Ct. 1489, 123 L.Ed.2d 74 (1993).

8. Id.

9. Bankr.R. 9006(b)(3). See supra, § 9.92 for a list of the principal exceptions specified in Bankruptcy Rule 3002(c).

10. 11 U.S.C.A. § 726(a)(2)(C)(ii); Bankr.R. 3002(c)(6).

§ 9.94 BANKRUPTCY Ch. 9

facts set forth in the original claim.[1] However, courts carefully scrutinize amendments filed after the bar date to ensure that any alleged amendment is not actually an attempt to file an entirely new claim. First they determine whether there was a timely assertion of a similar claim or demand evidencing the creditor's intention to hold the estate liable. Then they determine whether it would be equitable to all parties to allow the amendment.[2]

Library References:

West's Key No. Digests, Bankruptcy ⚖=2903.

§ 9.95 Claims Procedures—Withdrawal of Claims

A creditor may withdraw a claim as of right by filing a notice of withdrawal. A creditor loses that right once an objection has been filed or a complaint has been filed against the creditor in an adversary proceeding, or the creditor has voted to accept or reject a plan of reorganization or has participated in a significant fashion in the case. Once any of those events has occurred, a creditor must obtain court approval in order to withdraw its claim. A creditor's withdrawal of a claim also acts to withdraw any vote that the creditor has filed to accept or reject a plan.[1]

Library References:

West's Key No. Digests, Bankruptcy ⚖=2903.

§ 9.96 Claims Procedures—Allowance of, and Objections to, Claims or Interests

A claim or interest is deemed allowed for purposes of voting and distribution unless a party in interest objects.[1] The presumption of validity may be overcome by an objecting party only if it offers evidence of equally probative value.[2] Although the existence of the claim is determined in accordance with applicable nonbankruptcy law, the allowance or disallowance of a claim is determined under federal bankruptcy law.[3]

An objection to the allowance of a claim must be in writing and filed with the court. A copy of the objection with notice of the hearing must be mailed or delivered to the claimant, the debtor or debtor in possession,

---

§ 9.94

1. *See, e.g.,* In re Integrated Resources, Inc., 157 B.R. 66, 70 (S.D.N.Y.1993).

2. *See id.* for a list of factors that courts consider when balancing the equities of permitting an amendment after the bar date.

§ 9.95

1. Bankr.R. 3006.

§ 9.96

1. 11 U.S.C.A. § 502(a).

2. *See* In re Allegheny Int'l, Inc., 954 F.2d 167 (3d Cir.1992) (discusses burden shifting).

3. 11 U.S.C.A. § 502.

and the trustee at least 30 days before the hearing.[4] Since filing an objection has the effect of disenfranchising a creditor, prior to the determination of the validity of the claim at the claims objection hearing, after notice and a hearing, the court may temporarily allow the claim in an amount which the court deems proper for purposes of voting to accept or reject a plan.[5]

Library References:
West's Key No. Digests, Bankruptcy ⚖︎2921–2933.

§ 9.97 Claims Procedures—Compromise and Settlement of Claims

After the debtor's counsel has filed an objection to disputed claims, it is common practice, in the interests of efficient and economical administration, for the debtor's counsel to negotiate with counsel for creditors on behalf of their respective clients in an attempt to compromise and settle such claims. If a consensual agreement can be reached, the compromise and settlement of disputed claims must be approved by the court.[1]

A court's determination as to whether to approve a debtor's request to enter into a settlement will be guided by the fairness and reasonableness of the settlement.[2] A bankruptcy court will consider the probability of success were the debtor to litigate the claim, as well as the complexity, expense, and delay of litigation.[3] The standard for approving a settlement is whether it is in the best interest of the estate and its creditors.[4]

Library References:
West's Key No. Digests, Bankruptcy ⚖︎3032.1.

§ 9.98 Claims Procedures—Allowance of Administrative Expense Claims

To foster the reorganization of the debtor, the Bankruptcy Code accords to entities and individuals that choose to do business with a debtor in possession or trustee an administrative expense priority for amounts provided to the debtor for the actual, necessary costs and

4. Bankr.R. 3007.
5. Bankr.R. 3018(a).

§ 9.97

1. Bankr.R. 9019. *See infra*, §§ 9.277, 9.300 for procedural and drafting checklists for filing a compromise and settlement of a claim.
2. Protective Comm. for Independent Stockholders of TMT Trailer Ferry Inc. v. Anderson, 390 U.S. 414, 88 S.Ct. 1157, 20 L.Ed.2d 1 (1968); In re W.T.Grant Co., 699 F.2d 599, 608 (2d Cir.), cert. denied sub.

nom Cosoff v. Rodman, 464 U.S. 822, 104 S.Ct. 89, 78 L.Ed.2d 97 (1983).

3. *See, e.g.*, In re Crowthers McCall Pattern, Inc., 120 B.R. 279 (Bankr.S.D.N.Y. 1990).

4. The Supreme Court established guidelines for approval of settlements in Protective Comm. for Independent Stockholders of TMT Trailer Ferry, Inc. v. Anderson, 390 U.S. 414, 88 S.Ct. 1157, 20 L.Ed.2d 1 (1968).

§ 9.98   BANKRUPTCY   Ch. 9

expenses of preserving the estate.[1] Administrative priority means that such claims are paid in full from the estate's unencumbered assets. For a chapter 11 debtor, ordinary course of business[2] obligations comprise a significant portion of the debtor's administrative claims.[3] These amounts include wages, salaries, or commissions for services rendered after the commencement of the case, as well as certain taxes. Administrative expense claims are permitted in respect of actual, necessary expenses incurred by certain creditors such as:[4]

1. Creditors that file an involuntary petition;[5]
2. Creditors, indenture trustees, equity security holders, or a committee representing creditors or equity security holders other than one appointed under the Bankruptcy Code who make a "substantial contribution" in a chapter 11 case;[6]
3. Members of committees appointed under the Bankruptcy Code if expenses incurred were in the performance of committee duties;[7]
4. Attorneys or accountants of parties such as those listed above, based upon the time, nature, extent, and value of services rendered, subject to court approval.[8]

Additionally, compensation and reimbursement awarded to a trustee, examiner, professional person, or attorney under § 330(a) is entitled to administrative expense status.[9]

In a chapter 11 case, a debtor in possession or trustee may request the court to set an administrative bar date to determine the dollar amount of administrative claims for purposes of a plan of reorganization. During the pendency of the case, creditors providing goods and services generally receive payment in accordance with ordinary business terms. Other creditors holding administrative claims may timely file requests for payment of such claims or they may tardily file requests if they are permitted to do so by the court for "cause."[10]

§ 9.98
1. 11 U.S.C.A. § 503(b)(1)(A).
CAVEAT: This rule does not apply to the debtor's professionals, whose retention, compensation, and expense reimbursement must receive court authorization. 11 U.S.C.A. §§ 327, 328, 330; Bankr.R. 2014, 2016. See supra, §§ 9.29–9.30 for a discussion of retention and compensation of professionals.
2. See supra, § 9.61 for a discussion of the meaning of "ordinary course of business" under the Bankruptcy Code.
3. See supra, § 9.71 for a discussion of administrative expense priority accorded in connection with postpetition financing.
4. See 11 U.S.C.A. § 503(b) for a complete list of creditors whose claims are accorded administrative expense priority.
5. 11 U.S.C.A. § 503(b)(3)(A).
6. 11 U.S.C.A. § 503(b)(3)(D).
7. 11 U.S.C.A. § 503(b)(3)(F).
8. 11 U.S.C.A. § 503(b)(4). See supra, § 9.30 for a discussion of compensation of professionals retained in cases under title 11.
9. 11 U.S.C.A. § 503(b)(2).
10. 11 U.S.C.A. § 503(a).

Library References:
West's Key No. Digests, Bankruptcy ⚖︎2871–2879.

§ 9.99 Claims Procedures—Secured Claims

Under nonbankruptcy law, a creditor with a lien on assets may foreclose on the collateral in satisfaction of its obligation. From the commencement of a case under chapter 7, 11, 12, or 13, however, the automatic stay[1] prevents the secured creditor from taking any action to improve its position or foreclose on its collateral. But, if the creditor can establish "cause," including a lack of adequate protection of its interest in the collateral,[2] the creditor may seek to lift or modify the automatic stay[3] for the purpose of foreclosing or obtaining the collateral and seeking immediate payment.

The debtor is prohibited by Section 363(c)(2) of the Bankruptcy Code from using a creditor's cash collateral without the consent of the creditor or court authorization after notice and a hearing.[4]

Library References:
West's Key No. Digests, Bankruptcy ⚖︎2851–2855.

§ 9.100 Claims Procedures—Secured Claims—Bifurcation of Claims

When the amount of a creditor's claim exceeds the value of the property upon which the creditor has a lien, the claim is undersecured. In that case, Section 506(a) of the Bankruptcy Code bifurcates the secured creditor's claim into two portions—a claim that is deemed secured to the extent of the value of the collateral, and a claim that is deemed unsecured (a deficiency claim) to the extent of the amount of the claim that exceeds the value of the collateral.[1] For example, if a creditor holds a $1 million claim that is secured by a lien on property of the debtor that is valued at $750,000, pursuant to Section 506(a), the lender will hold a $750,000 secured claim and a $250,000 unsecured deficiency claim.[2]

§ 9.99

1. See supra, § 9.50 for a discussion of the automatic stay.

2. See supra, § 9.56 for a discussion of adequate protection.

3. See supra, § 9.52 for a discussion of relief from the automatic stay.

4. See supra, §§ 9.65–9.66 for a discussion of cash collateral and the strategic considerations related to its use.

§ 9.100

1. 11 U.S.C.A. § 506(a). See infra, § 9.157 for a discussion of the role that can be played by the holder of a sizable deficiency claim in the plan confirmation process.

2. **PRACTICE POINTER**: In chapter 11 cases, 11 U.S.C.A. § 1111(b) establishes a general rule that a nonrecourse secured claim will be treated as a recourse claim whether or not the claim is nonrecourse by agreement or applicable law. Accordingly, an undersecured creditor has recourse to the debtor with respect to its deficiency claim. Alternatively, Section 1111(b) permits a class of secured claim holders to elect to have the claims in such class treated as secured to the full extent of the claims rather than to the extent of the value of the

§ 9.100   BANKRUPTCY   Ch. 9

Library References:
West's Key No. Digests, Bankruptcy ⚭2852.

§ 9.101 Claims Procedures—Secured Claims—Avoidance of Liens

"Lien stripping" refers to the use of a Bankruptcy Code provision that permits the debtor or trustee to void a creditor's lien to the extent it does not secure an "allowed secured claim." Specifically, Section 506(d) of the Code voids a creditor's lien securing a claim which is *not an allowed secured claim* under the Bankruptcy Code unless the claim was only disallowed because:

(1) It has not yet matured pursuant to Section 502(b)(5);

(2) It is a claim of a codebtor, surety, or guarantor for reimbursement or contribution that has not been paid in full and is disallowed pursuant to Section 502(e); or

(3) No entity has filed a proof of claim with respect to such claim under Section 501 of the Code.

Lien stripping permits a debtor to retain the property securing an undersecured claim and "strip" the lien; that is, the debtor's obligation is reduced from the full amount of the lien to the amount of the collateral value. Consequently, the creditor will be deprived of the benefit of its prebankruptcy bargain—the realization of any potential increase in the value of the collateral up to the point of foreclosure.

The Supreme Court, in *Dewsnup v. Timm*,[1] a chapter 7 case, specifically held that Section 506(d) does not permit a mortgagee's lien to be "stripped down" to the value of the collateral as determined pursuant to its bifurcation under Section 506(a).[2] In other words, a lien cannot be voided merely because a portion of the claim is deemed unsecured pursuant to Section 506(a).[3] Instead, in *Dewsnup*, the Supreme Court stated that a lien can be voided by operation of Section 506(d) of the Code only if the underlying claim is *not allowed*.[4]

---

collateral under Section 506(a). Because the claims of creditors who make the election under Section 1111(b) of the Code are treated as fully secured, such creditors no longer hold deficiency claims. Consequently, claims in the electing class are not subject to potential lien stripping. See *infra*, § 9.101 discussing lien stripping and § 9.156 discussing Section 1111(b) of the Bankruptcy Code.

§ 9.101

1. 502 U.S. 410, 417, 112 S.Ct. 773, 778, 116 L.Ed.2d 903 (1992).

2. *Id*.

3. *Id*. at 415–17, 112 S.Ct. at 777–78.

4. *Id*. at 415–17, 112 S.Ct. at 777–78. This interpretation is supported by the legislative history, which states, "if a party in interest requests the court to determine and allow or disallow the claim secured by the lien under Section 502 and the claim is not allowed, then the lien is void to the extent that the claim is not allowed." H.R.Rep. 95–595, 95th Cong., 1st Sess. 357 (1977).

The Supreme Court stated that liens securing allowed claims survive bankruptcy *in rem*, even if the debtor's *in personam* liability is extinguished by a bankruptcy discharge. *Id*. at 418, 112 S.Ct at 778. Thus, the long-established principle that liens

The Supreme Court's decision in *Dewsnup* clearly held that lien stripping cannot be applied in a chapter 7 case to strip down a mortgagee's consensual lien.[5] Moreover, the Bankruptcy Code prohibits a plan under chapter 11 or 13 from modifying a mortgagee's claim secured only by a security interest in real property that is the debtor's principal residence, regardless of whether or not it is undersecured.[6]

Notwithstanding the Supreme Court's decision in *Dewsnup*, the Court noted that it based its decision on the case before it and "would allow other facts to await their legal resolution on another day."[7] Consequently, some courts have held that the decision does not apply to the facts of other cases and have permitted lien stripping.[8]

Library References:

West's Key No. Digests, Bankruptcy ⚖︎2571–2585.

§ 9.102 Claims Procedures—Interest on Claims and Charges Against Secured Claims

Interest that is unmatured at the petition date is not allowable under the Bankruptcy Code.[1] In general, a creditor's right to interest on its claim depends on whether the creditor is undersecured or oversecured. If a creditor's claim exceeds the value of the property upon which the creditor has a lien, the claim is undersecured. Conversely, if a creditor's total claim (including principal, accrued prepetition interest,

pass through bankruptcy unaffected remains valid. This is further supported by the legislative history of § 506 of the Bankruptcy Code. "Subsection (d) permits liens to pass through the bankruptcy case unaffected." H.R.Rep. 95-595, 95th Cong., 1st Sess. 357 (1977).

CAVEAT: There still is considerable controversy concerning whether or not a lien survives bankruptcy unaffected under certain circumstances due to differing views of the interpretation of Sections 506(d)(2) and 1141(c) of the Code (concerning the effect of plan confirmation). The Seventh Circuit has held that when a chapter 11 plan of reorganization is silent as to the treatment of a lien and the secured creditor participated in the debtor's case, the lien is extinguished when the plan becomes effective. In re Penrod, 50 F.3d 459 (7th Cir.1995).

5. Dewsnup v. Timm, 502 U.S. 410, 112 S.Ct. 773, 116 L.Ed.2d 903 (1992).

6. 11 U.S.C.A. §§ 1123(b)(5); 1322(b)(2). The prohibition in chapter 11 cases was enacted pursuant to the Bankruptcy Reform Act of 1994 and applies to cases commenced on or after October 22, 1994. See Nobelman v. American Sav. Bank, 508 U.S. 324, 113 S.Ct. 2106, 124 L.Ed.2d 228 (1993) (interpreting 11 U.S.C.A. § 1322(b)(2) to prohibit lien stripping in a chapter 13 case with respect to a lien on the debtors' principal residence). While this prohibition against lien stripping in 11 U.S.C.A. §§ 1123(b)(5) and 1322(b)(2) appears to be at odds with the rehabilitative policy underlying chapters 11 and 13, it serves an interest which Congress finds overriding—encouraging the banking industry to make home loans.

7. Dewsnup, 502 U.S. at 416–17, 112 S.Ct. at 777–78.

8. *See, e.g.,* Howard v. National Westminster Bank, U.S.A. (In re Howard), 184 B.R. 644 (Bankr.E.D.N.Y.1995) (permitting a debtor in a chapter 7 case to void a bank's wholly unsecured judgment lien); In re 680 Fifth Ave. Assocs., 156 B.R. 726 (Bankr. S.D.N.Y.1993), aff'd 169 B.R. 22 (S.D.N.Y. 1993), aff'd 29 F.3d 95 (2d Cir.1994) (recognizing the debtor's ability to strip liens in a chapter 11 case).

§ 9.102

1. 11 U.S.C.A. § 502(b)(2).

and other charges) is less than the value of the property upon which the creditor has a lien, the claim is oversecured.[2]

Undersecured creditors are not entitled to receive postpetition interest on their collateral, nor may they receive compensation or "adequate protection" for "lost opportunity costs" that result from the imposition of the automatic stay.[3] Payment of "lost opportunity costs" would be tantamount to payment of unmatured interest, which is prohibited. However, undersecured creditors may receive periodic adequate protection payments,[4] often measured by the contractual interest rate, if the value of their collateral is declining or the threat of decline is imminent.[5]

Oversecured creditors are entitled to (i) interest on their claims[6] and (ii) any reasonable fees, costs, or charges that may be provided for under the agreement that gave rise to the claim.[7] However, secured claims are subject to recovery by the trustee or debtor of the reasonable, necessary costs and expenses of preserving or disposing of the collateral to the extent the secured creditor benefited.[8] While some interested parties have attempted to construe Section 506(c) broadly, courts generally have limited charges against a creditor's collateral to such expenses as fees for appraisal, auctioneers, advertising, marketing, moving, storage, maintenance, and repairs.[9] In the context of chapter 11, interest on oversecured

2. The value of the collateral that exceeds the amount of the creditor's claim against the debtor is called the "equity cushion."

3. United Sav. Assoc. v. Timbers of Inwood Forest Assocs., Ltd. (In re Timbers of Inwood Forest Assocs., Ltd.), 484 U.S. 365, 108 S.Ct. 626, 98 L.Ed.2d 740 (1988).

4. **PRACTICE POINTER**: A controversy remains as to whether postpetition rent payments should be applied to the secured or the unsecured portion of an undersecured creditor's claim. For a discussion of this issue, see In re 354 East 66th Street Realty Corp., 177 B.R. 776 (Bankr. E.D.N.Y.1995); In re Union Meeting Partners, 178 B.R. 664 (Bankr.E.D.Pa.1995); In re Kalian, 169 B.R. 503 (Bankr.D.R.I.1994); Confederation Life Ins. Co. v. Beau Rivage Ltd., 126 B.R. 632 (N.D.Ga.1991).

5. See LNC Investments, Inc. v. First Fidelity Bank, No. 92 Civ. 7584 (MBM), 1995 WL 231322 (S.D.N.Y. 1995). See supra, § 9.56 for a discussion of adequate protection.

6. United States v. Ron Pair Enters., Inc., 489 U.S. 235, 109 S.Ct. 1026, 103 L.Ed.2d 290 (1989). When a creditor becomes oversecured during the course of a case, interest begins to accrue to the extent the creditor is oversecured at the point in time when the creditor becomes oversecured. Financial Security Assurance, Inc. v. T–H New Orleans Limited Partnership (In re T–H New Orleans Limited Partnership), 116 F.3d 790, 798 (5th Cir.1997). This may occur if the value of the creditor's collateral is increasing and/or the creditor's allowed claim is reduced by cash collateral payments.

7. 11 U.S.C.A. § 506(b); 489 U.S. at 241, 109 S.Ct. at 1030.

8. 11 U.S.C.A. § 506(c).

9. **PRACTICE POINTER**: Nevertheless, there is frequent litigation over this issue, and counsel should check the most recent applicable case law. See, e.g., In re Comband Technologies, Inc., 69 F.3d 532 (4th Cir.1995) (secured creditor's collateral surcharged for expenses incurred in preserving the going-concern value of a business because its assets, consisting of intellectual property, could lose all value if the business ceased to operate); Precision Steel Shearing, Inc. v. Fremont Financial Corp. (In re Visual Indus., Inc.), 57 F.3d 321 (3d Cir.1995) (absent a "direct benefit" to the secured creditor, collateral was not surcharged for the costs of a trade creditor whose postpetition supply of raw materials to the debtor enabled the debtor to continue operating and, therefore, reduce the secured creditor's claim by nearly $1 million); In re C.S.Assocs., 29 F.3d 903 (3d Cir.1994)

claims may accrue up to the point that the total amount of principal and accrued interest equals the value of the collateral. Such interest cannot be paid periodically during the bankruptcy case, but must await confirmation or completion of the reorganization.[10]

Library References:
West's Key No. Digests, Bankruptcy ⟸2835.1–2836.

§ 9.103   Claims Procedures—Valuation of Collateral

At some point in the case, a secured creditor's collateral will have to be valued at a hearing or by assent. A party in interest may request a valuation hearing on notice to the holder of the secured claim and others, as directed by the court. At the hearing, the court may determine the value of the claim secured by a lien on property in which the estate has an interest.[1] The Bankruptcy Code merely states that value should be "determined in light of the purpose of the valuation and of the proposed disposition or use" of the property.[2]

Among the numerous purposes that a court may have for valuing the property securing a creditor's claim are whether:

- To continue, modify or terminate the automatic stay or the use of cash collateral based on the ability of the debtor to provide adequate protection of the creditor's interest in the debtor's property;
- To permit a proposed sale of collateral under Section 363(b);
- To prime a lien on an existing security interest as a result of a postpetition financing under Section 364;
- To permit a "cramdown" of a creditor's claim;

(secured creditor's collateral was not surcharged for unpaid, postpetition municipal real property taxes because the general services provided by the municipality did not confer a direct benefit on the secured creditor); General Electric Credit Corp. v. Levin & Weintraub (In re Flagstaff Foodservice Corp.), 739 F.2d 73 (2d Cir.1984) (holder of secured claim who consents to expenses and services incurred for the preservation of the secured collateral is responsible for payment of such expenses).

10. Orix Credit Alliance, Inc. v. Delta Resources, Inc. (In re Delta Resources, Inc.), 54 F.3d 722 (11th Cir.), cert. denied ___ U.S. ___, 116 S.Ct. 488, 133 L.Ed.2d 415 (1995).

§ 9.103
1. Bankr.R. 3012.
2. 11 U.S.C.A. § 506(a).

PRACTICE POINTER: A debtor ordinarily would seek a high valuation for automatic stay litigation and a relatively low valuation for cramdown purposes; whereas, a creditor would seek to establish the converse. However, barring a dramatic change in the value of collateral, a court may be unwilling to alter a valuation that has been determined for another purpose. Accordingly, debtors and creditors alike must consider their overall strategy before any hearing on valuation. See supra, § 9.53 note 4 CAVEAT.

A creditor should not wait until the end of a case to have the value of its collateral determined. The burden is on the creditor to have the value established. See Financial Security Assurance, Inc. v. T–H New Orleans Limited Partnership (In re T–H New Orleans Limited Partnership), 116 F.3d 790, 798 (5th Cir.1997).

- To avoid an allegedly preferential transfer due to unsecured status;
- To bifurcate and value an undersecured claim for purposes of Section 506(b);
- A creditor's claim has been impaired pursuant to Section 1124; and
- A creditor is receiving more under a chapter 11, 12, or 13 plan than through a hypothetical liquidation (the "best interest of creditors" test).[3]

Library References:

West's Key No. Digests, Bankruptcy ⚖2852.

§ 9.104 Claims Procedures—Valuation of Collateral—Methods of Valuation

There are at least six distinct standards for valuing property that secures a security interest in a title 11 case: (1) retail value, (2) wholesale value, (3) forced sale value, (4) liquidation value, (5) going concern value, and (6) reorganization value.[1] As noted above,[2] the method of valuation selected should be "determined in light of the purpose of the valuation and of the proposed disposition or use" of the property. Thus, a valuation for one purpose will not necessarily control for another purpose because considerations relevant to valuation vary, depending on the purpose of the valuation.[3] Moreover, the value of particular collateral may change during the course of a bankruptcy case.

§ 9.105 Claims Procedures—Reclamation Claims

Absent a bankruptcy filing, state law grants the right to reclaim goods to a seller who discovers that a buyer has received goods on credit while the buyer was insolvent, provided the goods have not been resold in the ordinary course of the buyer's business.[1] Under the UCC, the seller must make a written demand for reclamation before 10 days after the debtor's receipt of the goods. The 10-day period does not apply if the

---

3. See J. Queenan, Jr., *Standards for Valuation of Security Interests in Chapter 11*, 92 Comm.L.J. 18 (1987).

§ 9.104

1. See id.; C. Fortgang & T. Mayer, *Valuation in Bankruptcy*, 32 UCLA L.Rev. 1061 (1985).

2. See supra, § 9.103; 11 U.S.C.A. § 506(a).

3. To understand this concept, it may be helpful to read the discussion in Associates Commercial Corp. v. Rash (In re Rash), 90 F.3d 1036, 1045–46 (5th Cir.1996), rev'd, ___ U.S. ___, 117 S.Ct. 1879, 138 L.Ed.2d 148, (1997). See infra, § 9.251 note 3 for a discussion of the decision in Rash and the different methods of valuing a secured creditor's collateral for purposes of confirming a cramdown plan under chapter 11, 12, or 13.

§ 9.105

1. See UCC § 2–702.

seller received written misrepresentations of solvency within three months before delivery.[2]

Section 546(c) of the Bankruptcy Code incorporates nonbankruptcy law and preserves the right of a seller of goods who has sold goods to the debtor in the ordinary course of the seller's business to reclaim such goods if the debtor received the goods while insolvent.[3] If the 10-day period expires after the commencement of the case, the seller has until 20 days after receipt of the goods by the debtor to demand reclamation.[4] The bankruptcy court may deny reclamation if it grants the seller an administrative priority for its claim under Section 503(b) of the Code or secures the claim with a lien on debtor assets.[5]

Several courts have held that a prior perfected security interest in the debtor's inventory is superior to a vendor's right of reclamation. These courts have equated the rights of a secured creditor with those of a good faith purchaser, and a seller's right to reclaim is subject to the rights of a good faith purchaser.[6] Some courts have held that the security interest in a debtor's property completely extinguishes a vendor's reclamation rights, so that the vendor is not entitled to a substituted administrative expense claim.[7] However, other courts have held that these reclamation rights are not completely extinguished; instead, after the secured creditors' superior interests have been satisfied or released, the reclaiming seller either would retain a priority interest in any remaining goods and in any surplus proceeds from the secured creditors' foreclosure sale, or would be entitled to an administrative expense claim.[8]

2. *Id.*

PRACTICE POINTER: A supplier who deals regularly with retailers and becomes aware of any financial problems relating to a company should be poised to transmit timely the required reclamation notice in order to preserve its claim. Moreover, a debtor in a bankruptcy case, prior to accepting the validity of any reclamation claim, should scrutinize all the conditions required for a valid claim, including the existence of the subject goods, their content, their continued possession by the debtor on the date the reclamation demand is received, and the timing of delivery.

3. 11 U.S.C.A. § 546(c).

4. 11 U.S.C.A. § 546(c)(1).

5. 11 U.S.C.A. § 546(c)(2).

PRACTICE POINTER: A creditor who demands an administrative priority claim in lieu of reclamation must be able to prove the value of its goods in the debtor's possession at the time the debtor receives the reclamation demand. In re Adventist Living Centers, Inc., 52 F.3d 159 (7th Cir.1995).

CAVEAT: An administrative claim may satisfy the requirements of § 546(c) of the Code even if it ultimately proves worthless due to the bankruptcy estate's insufficient assets. In re Reliable Drug Stores, Inc., 70 F.3d 948 (7th Cir.1995).

6. *See* UCC § 2-702(3); Pester Refining Co. v. Ethyl Corp. (In re Pester Refining Co.), 964 F.2d 842 (8th Cir.1992); In re Samuels & Co., Inc., 526 F.2d 1238 (5th Cir.1976) (en banc), cert. denied sub. nom Stowers v. Mahon, 429 U.S. 834, 97 S.Ct. 98, 50 L.Ed.2d 99 (1976).

7. *See* In re Shattuc Cable Corp., 138 B.R. 557 (Bankr.N.D.Ill.1992); In re Lawrence Paperboard Corp., 52 B.R. 907, 911 (Bankr.D.Mass.1985) ("If a seller does not have a valid right of reclamation under the UCC, there is no legal basis for granting administrative status").

8. *See* In re Pester Refining Co., 964 F.2d 842 (8th Cir.1992). Notably, the Seventh Circuit recently disapproved the bankruptcy court holdings in Shattuc Cable and Lawrence Paperboard that a reclamation

§ 9.105

Library References:

West's Key No. Digests, Bankruptcy ⚖2741–2745.

§ 9.106 Priorities

The Bankruptcy Code specifies the kinds of claims that are entitled to priority in distribution, and the order of the priority. After payment of all secured claims, setoffs[1] and recoupments,[2] distributions are made for any court fees and charges assessed against the estate under chapter 123 of title 28 of the U.S. Code and to holders of administrative expense claims in the following order of priority:

- "Superpriority" claims of creditors resulting from an order authorizing the granting of postpetition loans to the debtor in possession if the debtor is unable to obtain credit as an ordinary administrative expense.[3] Such claims prime all other priority claims, including any superpriority claim accorded pursuant to Section 507(b) of the Bankruptcy Code for failure of adequate protection; and

- "Superpriority" claims accorded priority under Section 507(b) of the Code for failure of adequate protection under Sections 362, 363, or 364(d) of the Bankruptcy Code.[4] Such "superpriority" claims are primed only by claims arising from the granting of court-authorized postpetition loans, as described above.

After payment is made on account of the priority claims listed above, remaining expenses and claims are paid in accordance with the priorities set forth in Section 507 of the Bankruptcy Code, as follows:

- **First Priority:** Claims for postpetition administrative expenses of the estate, including the actual, necessary expenses of preserving the estate and compensation and reimbursement of retained professionals;[5]

- **Second Priority:** Claims of "gap creditors" who extended credit during the period following the filing of an involuntary petition and the earlier of the date of the entry of the order for relief or the appointment of a trustee;[6]

- **Third Priority:** Claims limited to $4,000 for each individual or corporation for wages, salaries, and commissions, including vacation, severance, and sick leave earned the earlier of 90 days before

claimant is not entitled to an administrative expense claim. *See* In re Reliable Drug Stores, Inc., 70 F.3d 948, 950 (7th Cir.1995) ("If senior secured lenders can be satisfied from the inventory, a reclamation claimant also can be satisfied from the residue. A reclamation claim is 'subject to' the interests of good faith purchasers under UCC 2–702(3) but is not extinguished by them.") (citing In re Pester Refining Co.).

§ 9.106

1. *See infra*, § 9.109.
2. *See infra*, § 9.112.
3. 11 U.S.C.A. § 364(c)(1).
4. 11 U.S.C.A. § 507(b).
5. 11 U.S.C.A. §§ 503(b), 507(a)(1).
6. 11 U.S.C.A. §§ 502(f), 507(a)(2).

the commencement of the case or the date of the cessation of the debtor's business.[7] The priority includes sales commissions earned by an individual or corporation with only one employee acting as an independent contractor if in the sale of goods or services for the debtor in the ordinary course of the debtor's business if, during the preceding 12 months, at least 75% of the individual's earnings as an independent contractor were earned from the debtor;[8]

- **Fourth Priority:** Claims for contributions to an employee benefit plan arising from services within 180 days before the petition date to the extent of $4,000 per covered employee less the amount paid to each employee pursuant to the third priority;[9]
- **Fifth Priority:** Claims up to $4,000 per individual of persons engaged in grain raising or production or engaged as United States fishermen;[10]
- **Sixth Priority:** Claims of individuals up to $1,800 for prepetition deposits of money in connection with the purchase, lease, or rental of property, or the purchase of services for personal, family, or household use;[11]
- **Seventh Priority:** Claims of a spouse, former spouse, or child for alimony, maintenance, or support in connection with a separation agreement, divorce decree, or court order;[12]
- **Eighth Priority:** Claims of governmental units for certain specified taxes;[13]
- **Ninth Priority:** Claims based upon any commitment by the debtor to a federal depository institution or regulatory agency to maintain the capital of an insured depository institution.[14]

Library References:
West's Key No. Digests, Bankruptcy ⚖2951–2972.

§ 9.107 Subordination

The Bankruptcy Code provides for the subordination of one claim or interest to some or all other claims or interests under the following circumstances:

---

7. **PRACTICE POINTER:** In cases under chapter 11, a debtor in possession generally will seek court authorization at the commencement of the case to make payment to its employees of prepetition priority and nonpriority wages, salaries, and commissions, and to maintain its prepetition compensation packages, including the carrying over of earned, but unused vacation days and accrued severance obligations. The same rationale for such requests is embodied in the granting of the priority; that is, preventing the loss of employees and employee morale and encouraging employees to continue assisting in the reorganization of the debtor.

8. 11 U.S.C.A. § 507(a)(3).
9. 11 U.S.C.A. § 507(a)(4).
10. 11 U.S.C.A. § 507(a)(5).
11. 11 U.S.C.A. § 507(a)(6).
12. 11 U.S.C.A. § 507(a)(7).
13. 11 U.S.C.A. § 507(a)(8).
14. 11 U.S.C.A. § 507(a)(9).

§ 9.107   BANKRUPTCY   Ch. 9

1. *Co-Debtor Claims.* The claim of a co-debtor or a surety is subordinated to the claim of an entity that is liable with the debtor on, or that has secured, such creditor's claim, until such creditor's claim is paid in full.[1] The purpose of the foregoing rule is to prevent a party who is secondarily liable with the debtor from competing with the obligee for payment from the debtor's estate.

2. *Consensual subordination agreements.* Subordination agreements[2] are enforceable in cases filed under the Bankruptcy Code to the same extent as under nonbankruptcy law and entitle "senior" debt holders to separate classification for purposes of voting and distribution.[3] Typically, where subordinated debt exists, the debtor's plan of reorganization will classify unsecured creditor claims into separate classes as follows: Class A, comprised of unsecured trade debt; Class B, comprised of subordinated debt holders who have agreed to subordinate their claims; and Class C, comprised of the senior creditors to whom the creditors of Class B have subordinated their claims. Distributions under a plan of reorganization must comply with the "fair and equitable rule"[4] and must not "unfairly discriminate."[5]

3. *Rescission Claims.*[6] A claim arising from the rescission of a purchase or sale of the debtor's security or for damages arising from the purchase or sale of such security must be subordinated to all claims or interests that are senior or equal to the claim or interest represented by the security.[7] If a claim arises from the sale of common stock, it will have the same priority as common stock.[8] If a claim arises from a debt instrument, it will be deemed a general unsecured claim.[9]

4. *Equitable Subordination.* The court has broad power under the principles of equitable subordination to subordinate all or part of an allowed claim or interest to others and to avoid a lien

---

§ 9.107

1. 11 U.S.C.A. § 509(c).

2. Subordination agreements generally are embodied in debt indentures which provide that purchasers of subordinated or "junior" debt agree to permit "senior" debt to receive payments otherwise payable to "junior" debt if an event of default is triggered in the "senior" debt.

3. 11 U.S.C.A. § 510(a); see 11 U.S.C.A. § 1122(a) and *infra*, §§ 9.152–9.153 for a discussion of classification claims.

4. See 11 U.S.C.A. § 1129(b)(2).

5. See 11 U.S.C.A. § 1129(b)(1).

6. See 11 U.S.C.A. § 510(b).

7. These claims are automatically subordinated because the stockholders, not general creditors, have taken the risk of an unlawful issuance of securities and have accepted a position junior to that of general creditors in exchange for the benefit of potentially receiving profits from the enterprise. Section 510(b) of the Code is intended to prevent stockholders from improving the status of their claims to that of general unsecured claims.

8. 11 U.S.C.A. § 510(b).

9. H.R.Rep.No. 95–595, 95th Cong., 1st Sess. 359 (1977); S.Rep.No. 95–989, 95th Cong., 2d Sess. 74 (1978).

securing a subordinated claim.[10] Three conditions generally must be present to invoke equitable subordination: (1) the claimant must have been engaged in some type of inequitable conduct; (2) such misconduct must have resulted in injury to creditors of the debtor or conferred an unfair advantage on the claimant; and (3) subordination must be consistent with the provisions of the Bankruptcy Code.[11] Some courts have identified three categories of inequitable conduct: (i) fraud, illegality, and breach of fiduciary duty; (ii) substitution of debt for capital when a company is undercapitalized; and (iii) the claimant's use of the debtor as its alter ego instrumentality.[12]

Misconduct. The level of misconduct that is required to justify subordination of claims of non-insiders of the debtor[13] sometimes has been described as "egregious conduct," rather than merely "inequitable conduct."[14] However, even a creditor who is not an insider may be subject to the more inclusive "inequitable conduct" standard if it exerts control over the debtor to the detriment of the debtor or other creditors.[15] Furthermore, the inequitable conduct need not be related to the acquisition or assertion of the claim sought to be subordinated.[16] All or part of a claim (secured or unsecured) may be subordinated to all or part of another claim or claims. However, claims should be subordinated only to the extent necessary to offset actual injury caused to the debtor and creditors by the inequitable conduct.[17]

---

10. 11 U.S.C.A. § 510(c). "The bankruptcy courts have exercised these equitable powers in passing on a wide range of problems arising out of the administration of bankrupt estates. They have been invoked to the end that fraud will not prevail, that substance will not give way to form, that technical considerations will not prevent substantial justice from being done." Pepper v. Litton, 308 U.S. 295, 304–05, 60 S.Ct. 238, 244, 84 L.Ed. 281 (1939) (citation omitted).

11. See, e.g., In re Baker & Getty Fin. Servs., Inc., 974 F.2d 712, 718 (6th Cir. 1992); In re Giorgio, 862 F.2d 933 (1st Cir.1988); Benjamin v. Diamond (In re Mobile Steel Co.), 563 F.2d 692, 700 (5th Cir. 1977). See Bienenstock, *Bankruptcy Reorganization* 638–55 (1987 & Supp.1989) for a discussion of the circumstances under which equitable subordination may be invoked.

12. See, e.g., Wilson v. Huffman (In re Missionary Baptist Found.), 712 F.2d 206, 212 (5th Cir.1983); 9281 Shore Rd. Owners Corp. v. Seminole Realty Co. (In re 9281 Shore Rd. Owners Corp.), 187 B.R. 837 (Bankr.E.D.N.Y.1995).

13. The relationships that are included as an "insider" for individual, partnership, and corporate debtors are listed at 11 U.S.C.A. § 101(31) and include such relationships as relatives, officers and directors, and persons in control of a debtor.

14. See, e.g., In re W.T. Grant Co., 4 B.R. 53, 74–75 (Bankr.S.D.N.Y.1980), aff'd 20 B.R. 186 (S.D.N.Y.1982), aff'd 699 F.2d 599 (2d Cir.1983).

15. See In re Clark Pipe and Supply Co., 893 F.2d 693, 699–703 (5th Cir.1990) (creditor may properly enforce its remedies under its agreements with the debtor provided it does not exercise such control over the debtor as to have taken over the debtor's decision-making capacity); In re Teltronics Services, Inc., 29 B.R. 139, 168–72 (Bankr. E.D.N.Y.1983) (standards governing equitable subordination). See A. DeNatale & P. Abram, *The Doctrine of Equitable Subordination as Applied to Nonmanagement Creditors*, 40 Bus. Lawyer 417 (2/85).

16. Machinery Rental, Inc. v. Herpel (In re Multiponics, Inc.), 622 F.2d 709 (5th Cir.1980).

17. See, e.g., Benjamin v. Diamond (In re Mobile Steel Corp.), 563 F.2d 692 (5th Cir.1977).

So long as creditors do not overreach the bounds of normal conduct to protect their interests, they need not fear that their claims will be subordinated under the Bankruptcy Code's equitable subordination provision. Thus, when a borrower becomes financially troubled, a lender may obtain collateral security, closely monitor the borrower's business, and use its bargaining power to oppose a debtor's sale of assets to raise funds to satisfy subordinated debt.[18] Nor can a lender's claim be subordinated because of the lender's refusal to advance additional funds if the lender's refusal to advance such funds complies with the loan agreement.[19]

Inequitable Conduct Requirement May Not Be Absolute. Although the classic ground for subordination of a creditor's claim requires inequitable conduct by the creditor to the detriment of other creditors, this has not been the sole basis for subordination of claims. Courts also have subordinated claims for penalties or punitive damages because such claims are intended to punish the wrongdoer and deter future wrongful conduct. The rationale for subordination of such claims is that in bankruptcy, the payment of such claims by the bankruptcy estate does not serve its intended purpose but, instead, has the effect of forcing other creditors, who are innocent third parties, to pay for the debtor's wrongdoing. Accordingly, courts have invoked the principle of equitable subordination to prevent prepetition claims for penalties or punitive damages from sharing equally with other general unsecured claims.[20]

While the Supreme Court has not addressed the question of whether inequitable conduct is required to equitably subordinate claims, it has reversed decisions which have permitted equitable subordination of tax penalties based solely upon the nature of such claims.[21]

---

18. *See* Cosoff v. Rodman (In re W.T. Grant Co.), 699 F.2d 599, 609–10 (2d Cir. 1983), cert. denied 464 U.S. 822, 104 S.Ct. 89, 78 L.Ed.2d 97 (1983).

19. Pan Am Corp. v. Delta Air Lines, Inc., 175 B.R. 438 (S.D.N.Y.1994).

20. *See, e.g.,* In re Virtual Network Servs. Corp., 902 F.2d 1246 (7th Cir.1990)(subordination of nonpecuniary loss tax penalties); Novak v. Callahan (In re GAC Corp.), 681 F.2d 1295 (11th Cir.1982) (subordination of punitive damages claims for violation of securities laws); In re Colin, 44 B.R. 806 (Bankr.S.D.N.Y.1984) (subordination of punitive damages claims for wrongful acts by the debtor in his capacity as corporate director).

21. The United States Supreme Court reversed a decision that had permitted the equitable subordination of claims of the IRS for postpetition, nonpecuniary loss tax penalties without any finding of inequitable conduct by the IRS. United States v. Noland, ___ U.S. ___, 116 S.Ct. 1524, 134 L.Ed.2d 748 (1996), reversing United States v. Noland (In re First Truck Lines, Inc.), 48 F.3d 210 (6th Cir.1995). The Supreme Court held that a bankruptcy court cannot equitably subordinate claims *on a categorical basis* in derogation of Congress's scheme of priorities. While the Court acknowledged that " 'principles of equitable subordination' may allow a bankruptcy court to reorder a tax penalty in a given

The Seventh Circuit is the only circuit court of appeals that has extended the court's power to authorize equitable subordination of claims beyond the limits of the circumstances described above.[22]

case," it stated that exceptions to the general rule are permitted when they are "justified by particular facts." 116 S.Ct. at 1525. It strongly criticized the Sixth Circuit's conclusion that "postpetition, nonpecuniary loss penalty claims" are "susceptible to subordination" *by their very nature*. *Id*. at 1527, citing In re First Truck Lines, 48 F.3d 210, 218.

The Supreme Court also reversed a decision of the Tenth Circuit Court of Appeals that had permitted the equitable subordination pursuant to 11 U.S.C.A. § 510(c) of a claim for which the IRS claimed priority status as an excise tax under Section 507(a)(7)(E) of the Bankruptcy Code. United States v. Reorganized CF & I Fabricators, ___ U.S. ___, 116 S.Ct. 2106, 135 L.Ed.2d 506 (1996). The Supreme Court affirmed the conclusion of the lower courts that an excise tax liability arising from the failure to make a required pension plan contribution is a nonpecuniary loss penalty rather than an excise tax and, thus, is not entitled to tax priority under Section 507(a)(7)(E) of the Bankruptcy Code. Accordingly, the Court held that the claim is an ordinary, unsecured claim.

The Court reversed the lower courts' holding that the IRS claim could be equitably subordinated to other general unsecured claims pursuant to Section 510(c) of the Bankruptcy Code when the subordination was simply a "categorical reordering of priorities" based only on the nature of the claim. 116 S.Ct. at 2115.

The Bankruptcy Code provision governing the priority of *prepetition* tax penalties accords priority status over other general unsecured claims only to tax penalties compensating a taxing authority for actual pecuniary loss. Thus, nonpecuniary loss penalty claims are not entitled to priority. In contrast, the claims which the Sixth Circuit subordinated in *First Truck Lines* were accorded priority as administrative expenses under Section 503(b)(1) of the Bankruptcy Code because they arose *postpetition*. Since the claims in First Truck Lines were accorded administrative priority because they arose postpetition, the Supreme Court's decision in that case was based on facts that differed from prior circuit court decisions in which *prepetition* (low priority) tax penalty claims had been subordinated without a finding of inequitable conduct by the claimants. It was not entirely clear from the decision in First Truck Lines to what extent it was restricted to the facts of that case.

Because the Court's subsequent decision in CF & I Fabricators concerns a prepetition claim, it is now clear that the decision in First Truck Lines applies to prepetition, as well as postpetition claims. Thus, the decision in CF & I clarifies that the Supreme Court will find any equitable subordination under Section 510(c) based on nothing more than the characteristics of the claims to be an improper derogation of the Bankruptcy Code's scheme of priorities, whether the subordination moves the claim from a higher to a lower priority class, as in First Truck Lines, or subordinates the claim within the same class, as in CF & I Fabricators.

22. In re Envirodyne Indus., Inc., 79 F.3d 579 (7th Cir.1996), cert. denied ___ U.S. ___, 117 S.Ct. 77, 136 L.Ed.2d 65 (1996). The Seventh Circuit stated that "§ 510(c) authorizes courts to equitably subordinate claims to other claims on a case-by-case basis without requiring in every instance inequitable conduct on the part of the creditor claiming parity among other unsecured general creditors." *Id*. at 581. Instead, the Seventh Circuit stated that a "flexible approach ... makes sense in light of the Bankruptcy Code's primary goal of equality of distribution and the fluid concept of equity at the heart of Section 510(c) subordination." *Id*. at 582.

In Envirodyne, the defendants failed to tender shares of stock in a corporation entering a shortform merger under Delaware law. The stock of the non-tendering shareholders was canceled, and their equity interest was converted into debt. They were entitled to redeem their canceled shares for a specified dollar amount without interest. The defendants failed to redeem their canceled shares for over 3 years after the merger.

After the company filed under chapter 11, the bankruptcy court equitably subordinated the claims of the defendants to the claims of other general unsecured creditors, and the district court affirmed. The Seventh Circuit affirmed, reasoning that although the defendants were creditors, their claims were "in substance, based on equity

§ 9.107

Standing. The debtor or trustee is the proper party to commence an action seeking equitable subordination.[23] A creditor who wishes to seek subordination of another creditor's claim should request the trustee or debtor to take such action. If the trustee or debtor refuses, the creditor should seek bankruptcy court authorization to seek equitable subordination.[24] Except when subordination is provided in a chapter 11, 12, or 13 plan, a creditor's action for equitable subordination is an adversary proceeding and must be commenced by a complaint pursuant to Bankruptcy Rule 7001(8).[25]

Library References:

West's Key No. Digests, Bankruptcy ⚖2967.1–2972.

§ 9.108 Subordination—Strategy

In representing a debtor, it may be necessary to determine if any creditor claims may be subordinated to other claims of equal priority. Such subordination may be consensual by and between the creditor and debtor prior to bankruptcy. On the other hand, subordination may be imposed upon a creditor as a matter of equity if it can be demonstrated

---

interests." *Id.* at 583. It stated, "the fact that Delaware law converted Defendants' surviving interest into debt rather than equity does not change our analysis. The form of the transaction does not alter the origin and nature of Defendants' claims as essentially equity interests." *Id.*

Based on the Supreme Court's reversal of the Sixth Circuit's decision in First Truck Lines and its reversal of the Tenth Circuit's decision in CF & I Fabricators, discussed *supra*, note 21, it is very doubtful that the Seventh Circuit's decision in Envirodyne was decided correctly. It could be argued that the subordination of the Envirodyne defendants' claims because of their derivation from equity interests was subordination based on a categorical characterization of the nature of the claims and, thus, the kind of action prohibited by the Supreme Court.

23. *See, e.g.,* In re Lockwood, 14 B.R. 374, 381 (Bankr.E.D.N.Y.1981). *But see* In re Vitreous Steel Prods. Co., 911 F.2d 1223, 1231 (7th Cir.1990) (Individual creditor has standing to pursue subordination action because individual creditor may have an interest in subordination apart from interests of the estate as a whole).

24. *See, e.g.,* In re Parker Montana Co., 47 B.R. 419, 421 (D.Mont.1985).

CAVEAT: Counsel should carefully review the relevant facts and applicable law before seeking equitable subordination of a claim. Bankruptcy Rule 9011, the counterpart of F.R.C.P. 11, will subject counsel to sanctions if any pleading is not "well grounded in fact" and "warranted by existing law or a good faith argument for the extension, modification, or reversal of existing law." Courts have held that "an objection on equitable grounds cannot be merely formal, but rather must contain some substantial factual basis to support its allegation of impropriety." *See, e.g.,* Wilson v. Huffman (In re Missionary Baptist Found.), 712 F.2d 206, 213 (5th Cir.1983).

PRACTICE POINTER: The Bankruptcy Code entitles an oversecured lender to recover its reasonable fees, costs, and other charges provided for under the loan documents up to the value of the lender's collateral. 11 U.S.C.A. § 506(b). Accordingly, if a loan agreement so provides, a lender may recover any reasonable expenses it incurs to protect and maintain the value of its collateral, including the costs of defending against an adversary proceeding to equitably subordinate the lender's claims. Manufacturers Nat'l Bank v. Auto Specialties Mfg. Co. (In re Auto Specialties Mfg. Co.), 18 F.3d 358 (6th Cir.1994).

25. *See supra,* § 9.16 for a discussion of adversary proceedings and *see infra,* §§ 9.266, 9.288 for procedural and drafting checklists for commencing an adversary proceeding.

that the creditor engaged in inequitable conduct. The debtor will bear the burden of establishing the elements for equitable subordination of a creditor's claim. In most cases, a non-insider creditor's claim will be difficult to subordinate unless it can be established that it exercised undue influence over the debtor's operations.

In representing subordinated debtholders when there is little or no value available from the debtor's assets to pay this junior class under a plan of reorganization, it is common strategy to adopt an aggressive posture in the debtor's chapter 11 case. For example, the subordinated debtholders can seek to have a committee appointed in the debtor's case representing their class of claims and challenge the administrative expenses of the debtor's professionals and any unsecured creditors' committee representing the senior class. Moreover, they can seek to propose a plan of reorganization that will preserve or create value for distribution to the subordinated class.[1]

§ 9.109 Setoff

The Bankruptcy Code *preserves* a creditor's nonbankruptcy *right* of setoff in bankruptcy cases, with certain limitations, if mutual debts of the debtor and a creditor arose prepetition.[1] However, *exercise* of the right of setoff is subject to the automatic stay,[2] which must be lifted before a setoff may be exercised.[3]

§ 9.108

1. CAVEAT: Creditors and their counsel who attempt to create value on behalf of the subordinated class should bear in mind that courts will enforce the intent of subordination agreements unless senior creditors consent. *See, e.g.*, In re Envirodyne Indus., 161 B.R. 440 (Bankr.N.D.Ill.1993).

§ 9.109

1. 11 U.S.C.A. § 553. Mutuality generally requires that the two debts be owing and owed to the same two parties.

CAVEAT: The right of setoff can be waived by conduct that is inconsistent with the exercise of that right. For example, a creditor's agreement to settle a claim without expressly preserving the right of setoff in the settlement agreement may be construed as an act that is incompatible with the right of setoff and, thus, a waiver of such right. In re Holder, 182 B.R. 770 (Bankr.M.D.Tenn.1995).

PRACTICE POINTER: A creditor who believes it may have a setoff right against the debtor should take care to preserve that right by asserting it early in the case. Several opportunities to do so arise in a bankruptcy case. First, in its proof of claim, a creditor must certify that it has taken all setoffs into account in the calculation of its claim. The creditor should attach to its proof of claim a brief explanation of the circumstances evidencing its setoff right. A creditor may also protect its setoff right by objecting to any motion dealing with the creditor's claim or the debt to be set off unless its setoff rights are recognized. As noted in the text, a creditor also may seek to lift the automatic stay to exercise its setoff right or seek adequate protection of the amount subject to setoff. If a proposed plan is silent as to the creditor's setoff rights, the creditor can object to confirmation of the plan.

2. *See supra*, § 9.50 for a discussion of the automatic stay.

3. 11 U.S.C.A. § 362(a)(7). *See supra*, § 9.52 for a discussion of relief from the automatic stay and *see infra*, §§ 9.269, 9.292 for procedural and drafting checklists for a motion to lift the automatic stay.

PRACTICE POINTER: The United States Supreme Court has ruled that a *temporary* administrative hold on funds in a debtor's account in order to preserve the right of setoff while the creditor seeks relief from the stay to exercise its setoff right does not constitute an exercise of the right

§ 9.109   BANKRUPTCY   Ch. 9

The right of setoff is particularly valuable in a bankruptcy case because it may enable the creditor to receive more than it would otherwise receive.[4] Under Section 506(a) of the Bankruptcy Code, an allowed claim that is subject to the right of setoff is a secured claim to the extent of the amount subject to setoff. Thus, a creditor with such a claim may seek relief from the automatic stay[5] to exercise its right of setoff or adequate protection[6] (and a superpriority administrative claim if such protection proves to be inadequate).[7]

Library References:

West's Key No. Digests, Bankruptcy ⟬2671–2680.

§ 9.110   Setoff—Strategy

In determining whether a right of setoff exists, counsel may find that the creditor's claim is limited by operation of the Bankruptcy Code.[1] If counsel determines that the creditor can exercise a right of setoff against the debtor, it can only do so after it obtains bankruptcy court approval. If the creditor fails to obtain court approval prior to exercising its right of setoff, it runs the risk of having sanctions imposed.

If counsel determines that the creditor has no right of setoff, it should determine if the creditor qualifies to assert the equitable remedy of recoupment, which may not be subject to the same restrictions as setoff under the Bankruptcy Code.[2]

§ 9.111   Setoff—Characteristics of Claims

In order for a claim to be eligible for setoff, it must bear the following characteristics:

- The debt must be mutual, *i.e.*, the debt must be in the same right between the same parties standing in the same capacity.[1] For

---

of setoff and, therefore, a violation of the automatic stay. Citizens Bank v. Strumpf, 516 U.S. 16, 116 S.Ct. 286, 133 L.Ed.2d 258 (1995).

4. For example, assume that a debtor owes a supplier $10,000 for delivered merchandise, while the supplier owes the debtor $8,000 from a previous overpayment. Assume, further, that the debtor has assets sufficient to provide only a 10 percent distribution to unsecured creditors. The supplier who holds an $8,000 setoff right will, in effect, receive $8,000 from the setoff plus a 10 percent distribution on the remaining $2,000 claim, for a total recovery of $8,200. Another supplier, who also holds a $10,000 claim against the debtor but has no right of setoff, would receive only 10 percent of $10,000, or a total recovery of $1,000.

5. *See supra*, § 9.52 for a discussion of relief from the stay.

6. *See supra*, § 9.56 for a discussion of adequate protection.

7. *See supra*, § 9.53 for a discussion of acquiring superpriority administrative claim status upon the failure of adequate protection.

§ 9.110

1. *See* 11 U.S.C.A. § 553; *see infra*, § 9.111.

2. *See infra*, § 9.112 for a discussion of recoupment.

§ 9.111

1. The circuit courts are split as to whether different agencies of the U.S. government are the same creditor for purposes

Ch. 9   **SETOFF—CHARACTERISTICS OF CLAIMS**   **§ 9.111**

example, the debt of a lender to a debtor arising out of a deposit account maintained by the debtor with the lender may not be offset against the debt of the debtor to a separate corporate affiliate of the lender because the debt is not owed directly to the lender. The requirement that debts be mutual does not mean that the debts must arise out of the same transaction or even the same type of transaction.[2]

- Both debts must arise prior to the filing of the petition, *i.e.*, postpetition claims cannot be set off against prepetition claims.

- The claim of the creditor against the debtor must be allowable under Section 502 of the Bankruptcy Code.[3]

A timely proof of claim need not be filed to assert a setoff right.[4] Moreover, the right of setoff survives a bankruptcy court's discharge of the debtor's debts.[5]

A creditor cannot exercise a setoff against its indebtedness to the debtor if any of the following applies:

- Its claim against the debtor was transferred to the creditor (i) after commencement of a case under title 11[6] or (ii) within 90 days preceding the filing of the bankruptcy petition if the debtor was insolvent[7] (there is a rebuttable presumption that the debtor was insolvent for 90 days prepetition);[8]

- The debt owed by the debtor to the creditor (i) was incurred within 90 days preceding the filing of the debtor's bankruptcy petition, (ii) while the debtor was insolvent, and (iii) for the purpose of obtaining a right of setoff;[9] or

---

of Section 553. *Compare* HAL, Inc. v. United States (In re HAL, Inc.), 196 B.R. 159 (Bankr.9th Cir.1996), affirmed 122 F.3d 851 (9th Cir.1997) (all governmental agencies constitute a single creditor) and (In re Doe, 58 F.3d 494 (9th Cir.1995)) (same) *with* In re Turner, 59 F.3d 1041 (10th Cir.1995) (different federal agencies are different creditors).

The Second Circuit has concluded that a common law right exists that allows government agencies to set off nontax liabilities against tax refunds. Thus, the Second Circuit has concluded that different agencies are the same creditor for purposes of setoff. The Aetna Casualty & Surety Co. v. LTV Steel Co. (In re Chateaugay Corp.), 94 F.3d 772 (2d Cir.1996).

2. *See, e.g.*, Vaughan v. Resolution Trust Corp. (In re Lease-Sea, Inc.), 140 B.R. 182, 184 (Bankr.N.D. Ohio 1992); In re Defense Servs., 104 B.R. 481, 484 (Bankr. S.D.Fla.1989).

3. *See* Section 502(b) of the Bankruptcy Code for grounds for disallowance of a claim.

4. Davidovich v. Welton (In re Davidovich), 901 F.2d 1533, 1538–39 (10th Cir. 1990).

5. *Id.* at 1539; Carolco Television, Inc. v. National Broadcasting Co. (In re DeLaurentiis Entertainment Group, Inc.), 963 F.2d 1269, 1276 (9th Cir.), cert. denied 506 U.S. 918, 113 S.Ct. 330, 121 L.Ed.2d 249 (1992); Friedlander v. Doherty, 851 F.Supp. 515, 518 (N.D.N.Y.1994).

6. 11 U.S.C.A. § 553(a)(2)(A).

7. 11 U.S.C.A. § 553(a)(2)(B).

8. 11 U.S.C.A. § 553(c).

9. 11 U.S.C.A. § 553(a)(3).

§ 9.111 BANKRUPTCY Ch. 9

- The property against which the setoff would be exercised is exempt from the debtor's estate.[10]

A trustee or debtor may recover from a creditor who has exercised a right of setoff on or within 90 days prepetition any amount offset which represents an improvement in the creditor's position between the date of setoff and 90 days prepetition. If the amount available for setoff becomes insufficient during the 90–day period, the creditor's improvement in position is measured from the first date during the 90–day period on which the amount available for setoff became insufficient to offset the creditor's claim.[11]

§ 9.112 Recoupment[1]

When a debtor and creditor have mutual claims *arising from the same transaction*,[2] the doctrine of recoupment permits the settlement of the mutual claims in a single transaction within the claims adjustment process.[3] That is, the claims owed by the debtor to the creditor can be reduced by the amount of the claims owed by the creditor to the debtor as long as the mutual claims arise from the same transaction. Thus, recoupment is essentially a defense to a debtor's claim against a creditor and is simply a matter of determining the correct amount of a liability. There is no independent claim to be set off. Accordingly, recoupment is not a claim and gives no right to actual payment.[4]

When setoff is unavailable because the creditor's obligations were incurred postpetition, some courts will permit a creditor to apply prepetition obligations of a debtor against the creditor's *postpetition* obligations to such debtor under the doctrine of recoupment—provided the obligations arose from the same transaction. Recoupment is an equitable doctrine distinct from setoff. It is grounded in the principle that it is

---

10. See 11 U.S.C.A. § 522(c); see infra, § 9.125 for a discussion of exempt property.

11. 11 U.S.C.A. § 553(b). For example, on the 90th day prior to the filing of the petition, a debtor owes the bank $10,000 and has $5,000 in a deposit account with the bank. The "insufficiency" on that date equals $5,000. Ten days before the bankruptcy filing, the debtor still owes the bank $10,000, but the amount held by the bank on deposit for the debtor's account increases from $5,000 to $7,000, thereby reducing the amount of the insufficiency to $3,000. Thus, the bank improves its position by $2,000, which amount may be recovered by the trustee or debtor.

§ 9.112

1. There is no Bankruptcy Code provision for recoupment. It arose as an equitable rule to avoid having two separate actions concerning the same transaction.

2. For a discussion of what constitutes the same transaction for purposes of recoupment, see Moore v. New York Cotton Exchange, 270 U.S. 593, 610, 46 S.Ct. 367, 371, 70 L.Ed. 750 (1926) quoted in Newbery Corp. v. Fireman's Fund Ins. Co., 95 F.3d 1392, 1402 (9th Cir.1996) (a transaction "may comprehend a series of many occurrences, depending not so much upon the immediateness of their connection as upon their logical relationship").

3. See, e.g., Mercy Hospital v. New York State Dept. of Social Servs., 171 B.R. 490, 496 (N.D.N.Y.1994); Integrated Resources, Inc. v. Ameritrust Co. Nat'l Assoc. (In re Integrated Resources, Inc.), 157 B.R. 66, 73 (S.D.N.Y.1993). See supra, §§ 9.96–9.97 for a discussion of the claims adjustment process.

4. Mercy Hospital, 171 B.R. at 494 citing Mullen v. United States, 696 F.2d 470, 471 (6th Cir.1983).

inequitable to require a creditor to make full payment on its obligations despite the existence of a valid defense based on the debtor's obligation in the same transaction.[5]

Library References:
West's Key No. Digests, Bankruptcy ⇔2671.

§ 9.113 The Avoiding Powers

In any case under chapter 7, 11, 12, or 13, the debtor or the trustee, if one has been appointed, has a fiduciary duty to locate the debtor's assets, including claims and causes of action, and to return those assets to the estate for the benefit of creditors. Among the most powerful tools provided to the trustee or debtor in possession to accomplish this task are the avoiding powers, which limit the preferred status of certain creditors and avoid certain transfers which would be valid and enforceable under nonbankruptcy law. To reinforce the avoiding powers, the Bankruptcy Code requires the court to disallow any claim of a creditor from whom property is recoverable under the avoiding powers unless the creditor has returned the recoverable property for the benefit of the debtor's estate.[1] A debtor or trustee's action to exercise any of the avoiding powers, including the avoidance of a preference or a fraudulent conveyance, is an adversary proceeding governed by Parts VII and IX of the Bankruptcy Rules.[2]

§ 9.114 The Avoiding Powers—Strategy

The most significant avoiding power granted to a trustee or debtor in possession is the ability to avoid a creditor's lien that was not properly perfected before the bankruptcy filing. Prepetition secured creditors in chapter 11 reorganization cases that are requested to extend postpetition financing to debtors often will insist that the debtor waive its avoiding powers with respect to a potential challenge to the secured creditor's

---

5. *See* In re The Drexel Burnham Lambert Group Inc., 113 B.R. 830 (Bankr. S.D.N.Y.1990). In Drexel, the court explains the origins in equity of the doctrine of recoupment but rejects the netting out of pre- and postpetition claims because prepetition claims generally are not paid 100 cents on the dollar in bankruptcy, whereas postpetition claims are given administrative priority and, thus, are paid in full. Accordingly, allowing the netting out of postpetition obligations against prepetition claims would effectively prime all other unsecured creditors. *Id.* at 855. *See also* H. Buschman, *Benefits and Burdens: Post–Petition Performance of Unassumed Executory Contracts*, 5 Bank.Dev.J. 341 (1988) and J. Wynn, *Freeze and Recoupment: Methods for Circumventing the Automatic Stay?*, 5 Bank.Dev.J. 85 (1987) (both questioning the equity of allowing recoupment of postpetition obligations against prepetition claims). *But see* In re Yonkers Hamilton Sanitarium, Inc., 34 B.R. 385, 387–88 (S.D.N.Y.1983) and cases cited *supra*, note 2, permitting recoupment or acknowledging its permissibility within narrowly defined limits.

§ 9.113

1. 11 U.S.C.A. § 502(d)(1); In re McLean Indus., 184 B.R. 10 (Bankr.S.D.N.Y. 1995), affirmed 196 B.R. 670 (S.D.N.Y. 1996).

2. *See supra*, § 9.16 for a discussion of adversary proceedings.

prepetition lien. The debtor in possession, as a fiduciary of its estate, prior to waiving such claim, should make sure that the secured creditor's lien has been properly perfected and is not subject to challenge. Even so, the bankruptcy court may not allow the waiver of the debtor's ability to challenge the secured creditor's lien until the statutory committee of unsecured creditors[1] has been appointed and has had an opportunity to perform due diligence.

§ 9.115 The Avoiding Powers—Strong Arm Powers

Section 544 of the Bankruptcy Code, known as the "strong arm clause," gives the debtor in possession or the trustee special hypothetical status to defeat the status of certain creditors. Whether or not such a creditor actually exists, Section 544 gives the estate's representative the rights and powers of:

1. A creditor on a simple contract who, at the commencement of the case, extends credit and obtains a judicial lien on all of the debtor's property.[1] Thus, the trustee can avoid for the benefit of the estate any unperfected prepetition security interests granted by the debtor. However, the rights and powers of the trustee under this section are subject to any applicable nonbankruptcy law that permits a creditor to perfect his lien against an intervening interest holder.[2] For example, the Uniform Commercial Code provides that a purchase money security interest which is perfected within 10 days after delivery of the goods takes priority over the rights of a creditor who obtains a lien between the time of delivery of the goods and the time of perfection of the purchase money security interest.[3] Accordingly, a purchase money security interest holder can perfect its security interest after a debtor's bankruptcy filing but within ten days after delivery. Such perfection will defeat the "hypothetical judicial lien creditor" who obtained the lien on the date of bankruptcy.

2. A creditor on a simple contract who, at the commencement of the case, extends credit and obtains a writ of execution against the property of the debtor that was returned unsatisfied.[4]

3. A *bona fide* purchaser of real property (other than fixtures) as of the commencement of the case if applicable state law permits a transfer to be perfected against a bona fide purchaser.[5] Thus, the trustee or debtor in possession can avoid prepetition unrecorded transfers of real property.

§ 9.114
1. *See supra*, § 9.43 for a discussion of statutory committees.

§ 9.115
1. 11 U.S.C.A. § 544(a)(1).
2. 11 U.S.C.A. § 546(b)(1).
3. UCC § 9–301(2).
4. 11 U.S.C.A. § 544(a)(2).
5. 11 U.S.C.A. § 544(a)(3).

In addition, the strong arm clause gives the trustee or debtor in possession the right to avoid any transfer that an actual unsecured creditor with an allowable claim in the case would be able to void under applicable nonbankruptcy law,[6] *i.e.*, New York's Fraudulent Conveyances Statute.[7]

Library References:

West's Key No. Digests, Bankruptcy ⟸2571–2588, 2701–2706.

§ 9.116 The Avoiding Powers—Avoidance of Certain Statutory Liens

The trustee or debtor in possession may avoid statutory liens on property of the debtor's estate that become effective on the debtor's bankruptcy or insolvency and liens that were not perfected or enforceable against a hypothetical *bona fide* purchaser at the commencement of the case.[1] In addition, a lien for rent or distress for rent is voidable whether it is a statutory or common law lien.[2]

Library References:

West's Key No. Digests, Bankruptcy ⟸2580.1–2585.

§ 9.117 The Avoiding Powers—Preferences

To prevent the debtor from according preferential treatment to certain creditors over others, the Bankruptcy Code gives to the trustee or debtor in possession the power to avoid preferential transfers—*i.e.*, certain transfers of property of the debtor's estate that were made during the period immediately preceding a filing under the Bankruptcy Code. By avoiding such transfers, the trustee or debtor in possession can recover the transferred property for the benefit of the estate's creditors. This power to avoid preferential transfers is intended to promote the two important policy goals that underlie federal bankruptcy law. First, it helps to effectuate equality of distribution to similarly situated creditors. Second, it deters creditors from a prepetition "race to the courthouse" to dismember the debtor and, thus, fosters an environment in which the debtor can seek to work its way out of its financial difficulties through cooperation among all its creditors.

6. 11 U.S.C.A. § 544(b).

PRACTICE POINTER: Since the rights that can be asserted pursuant to Section 544(b) of the Code are those of an actual unsecured creditor in the case, they are subject to any defenses available against such a creditor.

7. Debtor and Creditor Law, Art. 10. *See* Chapter 8, "Enforcement of Money Judgments," *supra*.

§ 9.116

1. 11 U.S.C.A. § 545. *See* 11 U.S.C.A. § 545 for the detailed list of circumstances under which a statutory lien can be avoided.

2. 11 U.S.C.A. § 545(3),(4).

§ 9.117

To be a preference, a transfer[1] of an interest of the debtor in property must be:

1. To or for the benefit of a creditor;[2]
2. On account of an antecedent debt;[3]

§ 9.117

1. A transfer is defined as "every mode, direct or indirect, absolute or conditional, voluntary or involuntary, of disposing of or parting with property or with an interest in property, including retention of title as a security interest and foreclosure of the debtor's equity of redemption." 11 U.S.C.A. § 101(54).

A transfer is not made until the debtor acquires rights in the transferred property. 11 U.S.C.A. § 547(e)(3). That is, for purposes of Section 547, a transfer is not deemed to occur when the transaction is completed and irrevocable between the debtor and the transferee. It is not a "transfer" for preference purposes until it is perfected against third parties. For preference purposes, a transfer is made (1) at the time it takes effect between the parties if such transfer is perfected within 10 days after the time of transfer, (2) at the time such transfer is perfected if the transfer is perfected after such 10-day period, or (3) immediately before the petition date if the transfer is not perfected at the later of the commencement of the case or 10 days after the transfer takes effect. 11 U.S.C.A. § 547(e)(2).

Different rules have developed concerning when a payment made by check is considered to be a transfer for preference purposes depending on whether (i) the debtor or trustee is seeking to make a *prima facie* case that a transfer has occurred within the preference period (see Section 547(b), enumerating the five elements required for a preference) or (ii) a creditor is seeking to prove that one of the *defenses* to preferential transfers is applicable (see Section 547(c), listing the exceptions to a voidable preference).

For purposes of determining whether a transfer made by check falls within the preference period (*i.e.*, whether it satisfies Section 547(b)), the Supreme Court has ruled that the date upon which the drawee bank *honors* the check is the date of transfer. Barnhill v. Johnson, 503 U.S. 393, 399, 112 S.Ct. 1386, 1390, 118 L.Ed.2d 39 (1992). The Supreme Court's rationale is based on the fact that until the moment of honor, the debtor retains full control over the funds in the account, and a variety of actions by third parties can occur that would result in the check's being dishonored. *Id.* at 401, 112 S.Ct. at 1391.

However, for purposes of determining whether any of the *defenses* against a preference is applicable (*i.e.*, Section 547(c)), prior to the Supreme Court's decision (and in accordance with the legislative history), the five circuit courts of appeals that had considered this issue (the First, Fourth, Fifth, Ninth, and Tenth Circuits) were unanimous in concluding that the date of delivery is the date of transfer of payments by check. See Barnhill v. Johnson, *supra*, 503 U.S. at 402, 112 S.Ct. at 1391, for a list of the circuit court decisions, and *see, e.g.*, Braniff Airways, Inc. v. Midwest Corp., 873 F.2d 805, 807 (5th Cir.1989). Moreover, the Supreme Court in Barnhill noted that its decision expressed no view on this issue (*i.e.*, what rule should determine when payment by check constitutes a transfer for purposes of Section 547(c)). At this writing, no circuit courts have adopted the Supreme Court's rule governing Section 547(b) for purposes of Section 547(c).

Although the Second Circuit has *not* ruled on this issue, the Bankruptcy Court for the Southern District of New York has ruled that for purposes of Section 547(c) (defense against a preferential transfer), a payment by check constitutes a transfer on the date of delivery, provided that the check is presented within a reasonable period of time—approximately 30 days—and is not dishonored. *See, e.g.*, Young v. Continental Worsteds, Inc. (In re Wingspread), 120 B.R. 8, 10 (Bankr.S.D.N.Y.1990) and cases cited therein. The court noted that this rule is supported by the legislative history and is consistent with the policy goal of encouraging creditors to continue to deal with failing companies because it relieves their fear that any payment made by the debtor could be avoided later. *Id.*

2. 11 U.S.C.A. § 547(b)(1). See supra, § 9.36 for a discussion of who is a creditor under the Bankruptcy Code.

3. 11 U.S.C.A. § 547(b)(2). Although the Bankruptcy Code does not define "antecedent debt," the courts have defined "ante-

3. Made while the debtor was insolvent;[4]
4. Made within 90 days before the petition date[5] (one year if the transferee was an insider);[6] and
5. More than the transferee would receive in a chapter 7 case if the transfer had not been made.[7]

Library References:
West's Key No. Digests, Bankruptcy ⬚2601–2623.

§ 9.118 The Avoiding Powers—Exceptions to the Avoidance of Preferential Transfers

Although avoidance of preferential transfers deters last-minute payments that benefit certain creditors at the expense of others, the Bankruptcy Code permits preferential payments to certain creditors in order to assist distressed businesses, maintain going concern values, and

cedent debt" as a debt incurred prior to the relevant transfer. A debt is incurred when the debtor first becomes legally obligated to pay. *See, e.g.*, Pereira v. Lehigh Sav. Bank (In re Artha Mgmt., Inc.), 174 B.R. 671 (Bankr.S.D.N.Y.1994). Thus, the incurrence of debt often depends on the nature of the performance required and the process of delivery. In accordance with applicable UCC provisions, a debt is incurred not when a contract is signed, but when the goods are shipped. Nolden v. Van Dyke Seed Co. (In re Gold Coast Seed Co.), 751 F.2d 1118, 1119 (9th Cir.1985). When performance is divisible or ongoing, the debt is incurred incrementally on receipt of services. Scherling v. Texaco Int'l Trade, Inc. (In re Transpacific Carriers Corp.), 50 B.R. 649, 652 (Bankr.S.D.N.Y.1985). Similarly, the obligation to pay rent generally is deemed to arise on the dates rent is due under the lease, not when the lease was signed. *See, e.g.*, Child World, Inc. v. Service Merchandise Co. (In re Child World, Inc.), 173 B.R. 473, 476 (Bankr.S.D.N.Y.1994). *But see* Pereira, 174 B.R. at 678 (interest payments on a loan were found to be antecedent debt because the debtor became obligated to pay them when it entered into the loan agreement) and Fisher v. New York City Dept. of Housing Preservation and Dev. (In re Pan Trading Corp.), 125 B.R. 869, 875 (Bankr. S.D.N.Y.1991), (installment payments on a settlement agreement were found to be antecedent debt because the obligation to pay them was incurred when the parties signed the consent order).

Frequently, whether or not a payment is made on account of antecedent debt depends on whether or not it is found to be in the "ordinary course of business." *See supra*, § 9.61 for a discussion of "ordinary course of business" under the Bankruptcy Code.

4. 11 U.S.C.A. § 547(b)(3). The debtor is presumed insolvent on and during the 90 days preceding the petition date. 11 U.S.C.A. § 547(f). This presumption is rebuttable. If a creditor introduces evidence that the debtor was not insolvent at the time of the transfer, the trustee or debtor in possession must satisfy its burden of proof of insolvency by a preponderance of the evidence. *See* Roblin Indus., Inc. v. Ford Motor Co. (In re Roblin Indus., Inc.), 78 F.3d 30, 34 (2d Cir.1996). Insolvency is defined in the Bankruptcy Code as the financial condition such that an entity's liabilities are greater than all of the entity's property, at a fair valuation. 11 U.S.C.A. § 101(32). In the context of a going concern, fair valuation is the fair market price that could be obtained for the debtor's assets if sold in a prudent manner within a reasonable period of time. *See* Rubin v. Manufacturers Hanover Trust Co., 661 F.2d 979, 995 (2d Cir.1981). The issue of insolvency is a question of fact, and a bankruptcy court's findings of fact cannot be set aside unless clearly erroneous. Roblin, 78 F.3d at 35.

5. 11 U.S.C.A. § 547(b)(4)(A).

6. 11 U.S.C.A. § 547(b)(4)(B). *See* 11 U.S.C.A. § 101(31) and *supra*, § 9.29 note 8 for the Bankruptcy Code's definition of insider.

7. 11 U.S.C.A. § 547(b)(5).

§ 9.118 BANKRUPTCY Ch. 9

perhaps avoid a bankruptcy filing. To that end, the following are exceptions to the avoidance of otherwise preferential transfers:[1]

1. *Contemporaneous Exchange For New Value*: A transfer is excepted to the extent it was intended by the debtor and creditor to be a contemporaneous exchange which brings new value[2] to the estate, and is in fact a substantially contemporaneous exchange.[3] The exception is intended to protect transfers that are not on account of antecedent debt.

2. *Ordinary Course of Business*:[4] A transfer is excepted to the extent the transferee can prove: (a) the payment was made on account of *debt incurred* in the ordinary course of business of the debtor and the transferee,[5] (b) the *payment*, itself, was made in the ordinary course of business of both parties,[6] and (c) the

§ 9.118

1. See supra, § 9.117 note 1 for a discussion of when a payment by check constitutes a transfer for purposes of Section 547(c) (*i.e.*, whether any of the *defenses* against a preference is applicable).

2. "New value" includes "money or money's worth in goods, services, or new credit or release" of a prior transfer. It does not include substituting a new obligation for an old one. 11 U.S.C.A. § 547(a)(2).

3. 11 U.S.C.A. § 547(c)(1).

PRACTICE POINTER: Courts will examine the facts of the case to ensure that the parties *intended* the exchange to be contemporaneous, and the exchange is *in fact*, substantially contemporaneous. The crucial factor in determining if the transfer was contemporaneous is whether the transfer was made to pay a *preexisting* debt.

A transfer made by check is "intended to be contemporaneous" if the check is presented for payment in the normal course of affairs, which the Uniform Commercial Code specifies as 30 days (UCC § 3–503(2)(a)). H.R.Rep.No. 95–595, 95th Cong., 1st Sess. 373 (1977).

4. The legislative history of the "ordinary course" exception states:

The purpose of this exception is to leave undisturbed normal financial relations, because it does not detract from the general policy preference section to discourage unusual action by either the debtor or his creditors during the debtor's slide into bankruptcy.

S.Rep.No.989, 95th Cong., 2d Sess. 88 (1978), H.R.Rep.No.595, 95th Cong., 1st Sess. 373 (1977). In other words, the exception is intended to benefit all creditors by protecting payments received by those creditors who continue to carry on ordinary business with the debtor and, thereby, promote the debtor's ability to continue in business.

PRACTICE POINTER: Numerous factors are considered by courts in determining whether a transfer is in the ordinary course of the relationship between the debtor and the particular creditor, including the timing, the amount and manner of payment, and the circumstances under which the transfer was made. See Official Committee of Unsecured Creditors v. Vardi Stonehouse, Inc. (In re Faleck & Margolies, Inc.), 153 B.R. 123, 125 (S.D.N.Y.1993).

5. 11 U.S.C.A. § 547(c)(2)(A).

6. 11 U.S.C.A. § 547(c)(2)(B). This requirement compares the transfer to the past course of dealings between the debtor and the particular transferee. Even if the debtor's business transactions were irregular, if they "were the standard course of dealing between the parties, they shall be considered as within the ordinary course of business under section 547(c)(2)." Yurika Foods Corp. v. United Parcel Service (In re Yurika Foods Corp.), 888 F.2d 42, 44 (6th Cir.1989) (quoting In re Fulghum Constr. Corp., 872 F.2d 739, 743 (6th Cir.1989)).

Late payments do not necessarily demonstrate a lack of ordinary course dealings. In fact, late payments during the preference period consistent with a prior history of late payments demonstrate that the parties are continuing to act in the ordinary course of business between them. *Compare* Sapir v. Green Forest Lumber Ltd. (In re Ajayem Lumber Corp.), 145 B.R. 813 (Bankr. S.D.N.Y.1992) (Payments fell within the or-

Ch. 9   EXCEPTIONS TO AVOIDANCE OF TRANSFERS § 9.118

payment was made according to ordinary business terms.[7]

3. *Purchase Money Security Interest In Newly Acquired Property*: A transfer is excepted to the extent that it creates a security interest in property the debtor acquired with new value given by the transferee at or after the signing of the security agreement for the purpose of enabling the debtor to acquire the property subject to the security interest. The security interest must be perfected on or before 20 days after the debtor received possession of the property.[8]

4. *Subsequent New Value*: If, after receiving a preferential transfer, a creditor gives new value to or for the benefit of the debtor (that is not secured by an otherwise unavoidable security interest), the preferential transfer will not be voidable to the extent of the amount of the new value.[9] Thus, this exception allows credit for any subsequent advances of new value by a creditor who has received a preferential transfer. It is aimed at ensuring fairness toward a creditor with a running account.

---

dinary course of business exception even though they were made later than past transactions between the parties when (i) they were made no later than payments to other creditors and (ii) they were not made as a result of the creditor's suspending trading with the debtors or after a phone call to the debtors) *with* In re Faleck & Margolies, Inc., 153 B.R. 123 (S.D.N.Y. 1993) (Payments on promissory notes issued on account of overdue invoices fell outside the ordinary course of business exception when the debtor normally made late payments on invoices but normally made timely payments on promissory notes issued on account of overdue invoices). "A late payment is considered ordinary if it is within the pattern of payments between the parties." Miller v. Perini Corp. (In re A.J. Lane & Co., Inc., 164 B.R. 409, 414 (Bankr. D.Mass.1994) (compiling cases)).

7. 11 U.S.C.A. § 547(c)(2)(C). This requirement compares the transfer to the course of dealings that is ordinary in the pertinent industry.

PRACTICE POINTER: The Second Circuit has joined the great majority of circuit courts that have held that an objective standard should be applied to determine whether a prepetition transfer satisfies the third prong of the "ordinary course of business" exception to the preference rules. Lawson v. Ford Motor Co. (In re Roblin Indus., Inc.), 78 F.3d 30 (2d Cir.1996). Thus, "ordinary business terms" must not be unusual when compared with the range of terms prevailing in the particular industry. Moreover, the Second Circuit rejected "a rule that payments made pursuant to debt restructuring agreements, even when the debt is in default, can never be made according to ordinary business terms as a matter of law." *Id*. at 11. Instead, the Second Circuit stated:

> To apply properly the § 547(c)(2)(C) standard, "ordinary business terms" must include those terms employed by similarly situated debtors and creditors facing the same or similar problems. If the terms in question are ordinary for industry participants under financial distress, then that is ordinary for the industry.

Id.

PRACTICE POINTER: The Supreme Court has determined that payments on long-term debt, as well as payments on short-term debt, may qualify for the ordinary course of business exception to the trustee's power to avoid preferential transfers. Union Bank v. Wolas, 502 U.S. 151, 112 S.Ct. 527, 116 L.Ed.2d 514 (1991).

8. 11 U.S.C.A. § 547(c)(3).

9. 11 U.S.C.A. § 547(c)(4).

§ 9.118   BANKRUPTCY   Ch. 9

5. *Security Interest in Inventory or Receivables*:[10] A transfer that creates a perfected security interest in inventory or a receivable, or the proceeds of either, is excepted to the extent that it does not improve the relative position of the transferee compared to its position 90 days before the bankruptcy filing (one year for insiders). If new value was first given after 90 days prepetition, the date on which new value was first given under the security agreement substitutes for the 90-day point.[11]

6. *Unavoidable Statutory Liens*: A transfer that is the fixing of a statutory lien that is not avoidable under 11 U.S.C.A. § 545 is excepted.[12]

7. *Alimony, Maintenance, and Child Support*: A transfer of a *bona fide* payment of a debt to a spouse or child that is actually for alimony, maintenance, or support in connection with a separation agreement, divorce decree, or other court order is excepted unless it is assigned to a third party.[13]

8. *Individual Debtor's Consumer Debt*: In the case of an individual debtor with primarily consumer debts, a transfer in aggregate value of less than $600 is excepted.[14]

Library References:

West's Key No. Digests, Bankruptcy ⇐2613(1)–2618.

§ 9.119 The Avoiding Powers—Fraudulent Conveyances

Fraudulent conveyances may be avoided by the trustee or debtor in possession using federal bankruptcy law pursuant to 11 U.S.C.A. § 548, or by using state fraudulent conveyance laws pursuant to 11 U.S.C.A. § 544(b). Under the federal scheme, a transfer that occurs within one year before the filing of a petition may be subject to avoidance as a fraudulent conveyance based on a theory of either intentional or constructive fraud.[1]

Intentional Fraud. Any transfer or obligation made with actual intent to hinder, delay, or defraud present or future creditors is consid-

---

10. Inventory and receivables are defined at 11 U.S.C.A. § 547(a).
11. 11 U.S.C.A. § 547(c)(5).
12. 11 U.S.C.A. § 547(c)(6). *See supra*, § 9.116 for a discussion of the avoidance of certain statutory liens.
13. 11 U.S.C.A. § 547(c)(7).
14. 11 U.S.C.A. § 547(c)(8).

§ 9.119
1. 11 U.S.C.A. § 548(a).

PRACTICE POINTER: If a voidable fraudulent conveyance occurred more than one year before the bankruptcy filing, it will be advantageous for a debtor or trustee to pursue an avoidance action under Section 544(b) of the Code to obtain the benefit of the New York State 6–year Statute of Limitations which applies to fraud. *See* CPLR 213(8).

ered an intentional fraud. Since direct evidence of intentional fraud is generally unavailable, courts consider indicia, or "badges," of fraud.[2]

Constructive Fraud. Constructive fraud includes any transfer or obligation for which the debtor received less than reasonably equivalent value in exchange,[3] and any of the following: (i) the debtor was insolvent[4] at the time of the transfer or was rendered insolvent thereby, (ii) the remaining property following the transfer was unreasonably small capital, or (iii) it was intended or anticipated that the debtor would incur debt that would be beyond its ability to pay as it matured.[5]

Library References:

West's Key No. Digests, Bankruptcy ⊙2641–2651.

§ 9.120 The Avoiding Powers—Liability of Transferee of Avoided Transfer

If a transfer is avoided pursuant to the Bankruptcy Code, the trustee or debtor in possession has one year from the avoidance of the transfer, or until the case is closed or dismissed, whichever is earlier, in which to recover such property (or its value) for the benefit of the estate from either the initial transferee or the entity for whose benefit the initial transfer was made, or from subsequent transferees of the initial transfer.[1] A safe harbor is provided to subsequent transferees provided they take for value, in good faith, and without knowledge of the voidabil-

---

2. 11 U.S.C.A. § 548(a)(1). *See, e.g.,* Max Sugarman Funeral Home, Inc. v. A.D.B. Investors, 926 F.2d 1248 (1st Cir. 1991).

3. *See* BFP v. Resolution Trust Corp., 511 U.S. 531, 540, 114 S.Ct. 1757, 128 L.Ed.2d 556 (1994), reh'g denied 512 U.S. 1247, 114 S.Ct. 2771, 129 L.Ed.2d 884 (1994) (the price that is actually received at a real estate foreclosure sale is "reasonably equivalent value," and a court-made rule that defined "reasonably equivalent value" to mean 70% of fair market value constitutes a "policy determination[n] that the Bankruptcy Code gives us no apparent authority to make.") For a discussion of what constitutes reasonably equivalent value, *see, e.g.,* Mellon Bank, N.A. v. The Official Committee of Unsecured Creditors of R.M.L., Inc. (In re R.M.L., Inc.), 92 F.3d 139 (3d Cir.1996); Interpool Ltd. v. Patterson v. RMC Holdings L.P., 890 F.Supp. 259 (S.D.N.Y.1995); In re Davis, 169 B.R. 285 (E.D.N.Y.1994). In In re R.M.L., the United States Court of Appeals for the Third Circuit held that commitment fees paid to a lender on a prepetition loan that did not close were recoverable as fraudulent transfers under Section 548(a)(2) of the Bankruptcy Code because the lender failed to give the debtor "reasonably equivalent value" in exchange for the commitment fees. The Third Circuit acknowledged that the mere "opportunity" to receive an economic benefit in the future constitutes "value" under the Bankruptcy Code. Although the Third Circuit concluded that some value had been conferred on the debtor, it ruled that the detailed factual record demonstrated that the chances of the loan closing were "negligible" and so "remote" that the payment of substantial fees to the lender did not confer "reasonably equivalent value" on the debtor. *Id.* at 148. *See* John J. Rapisardi, *Commitment Fees Paid to Lenders May Be Recoverable as Fraudulent Transfers*, N.Y.L.J., 3/20/97, p.1 for a more detailed discussion of this decision.

4. Insolvency is determined using a balance sheet method. *See* 11 U.S.C.A. § 101(32).

5. 11 U.S.C.A. § 548(a)(2).

§ 9.120

1. 11 U.S.C.A. § 550(a), (f).

§ 9.120

ity of the transfer.[2] Any good faith transferee from whom the trustee may recover the property is entitled to retain a lien on the property recovered to secure the lesser of (i) the costs of any improvements[3] made by that transferee to such property after the transfer (minus any profit realized from the property), or (ii) any increase in the value of the property as a result of such improvements.[4]

A trustee cannot recover a preference avoided during the one-year preference period for insiders from a transferee that was not an insider. Thus, a payment to a non-insider creditor that benefits an insider-guarantor, such as one of the debtor's principals, is not subject to the one-year preference period for insiders.[5]

Library References:

West's Key No. Digests, Bankruptcy ⊶2701.

§ 9.121 The Avoiding Powers—Statute of Limitations and Standing

Any action to avoid a transfer pursuant to the Bankruptcy Code must be commenced before the later of (a) two years after the entry of the order for relief or (b) if a trustee is elected or appointed in a chapter 7, 11, 12, or 13 case within two years from the entry of the order for relief, any avoidance actions must be commenced within one year after the appointment or election of the first trustee unless the case is closed or dismissed before that time.[1] An avoidance action can only be commenced by a trustee or debtor in possession, or if such entity unreasonably refuses, by a creditors' committee, a representative appointed by the

---

2. 11 U.S.C.A. § 550(b).

3. "Improvement" includes any additions or repairs, payment of any tax on the property, payment of any debt secured by a lien on the property that is superior or equal to the trustee's rights, and preservation of the property. 11 U.S.C.A. § 550(e)(2).

4. 11 U.S.C.A. § 550(e)(1).

5. 11 U.S.C.A. § 550(c). This subsection was enacted as part of the Bankruptcy Reform Act of 1994 to overrule Levit v. Ingersoll Rand Financial Corp. (In re V.N. Deprizio Constr. Co.), 874 F.2d 1186 (7th Cir. 1989), and its progeny (permitting recovery of preferences avoided under the one-year preference period for insiders from non-insider initial transferees if the transfers benefited an insider).

§ 9.121

1. 11 U.S.C.A. § 546(a). This Statute of Limitations applies to any action or proceeding under Sections 544 (strong arm powers), 545 (statutory liens), 547 (preferences), 548 (fraudulent conveyances), or 553 (setoffs).

Due to the ambiguity of Section 546(a) before the 1994 amendments to the Bankruptcy Code, there was considerable controversy among lower courts as to whether the Statute of Limitations set forth in that section applied to debtors in possession as well as trustees. Although cases that were filed before October 22, 1994 are not subject to the amendments, the Second Circuit had held that the 2-year Statute of Limitations applies not only to trustees, but to debtors in possession, and it begins to run when the debtor files its petition and becomes a debtor in possession under Section 1101. U.S. Brass & Copper Co. v. Caplan (In re Century Brass Prods., Inc.), 22 F.3d 37 (2d Cir. 1994).

court, or a creditor authorized by the court.[2] Recovery is permitted only if it is for the benefit of the estate.[3]

Library References:

West's Key No. Digests, Bankruptcy ⟐2722, 2723.

§ 9.122 The Avoiding Powers—Relation–Back Provision

The activation of the automatic stay upon a bankruptcy filing normally would preclude a creditor from perfecting a lien postpetition on a prepetition security interest. Since the debtor or trustee can invoke the avoiding powers to avoid liens that are unperfected as of the petition date, such liens would be subject to avoidance. However, Section 546(b)(1) of the Bankruptcy Code defers to any relation-back provisions that would have been applicable absent the filing under the Bankruptcy Code. Thus, if the relation-back provisions of any otherwise applicable nonbankruptcy law would have enabled a transferee to perfect, maintain, or continue a lien on the debtor's property after the petition date that would be enforceable against an entity that acquired rights in the property before the date of perfection, the lien of such a transferee cannot be avoided by the trustee or debtor in possession under Sections 544, 545, or 549 of the Bankruptcy Code.[1] In addition, if such nonbankruptcy law requires any action to perfect or continue perfection that was not commenced before the petition date, the interest in property is deemed perfected by notice given within the time fixed under applicable nonbankruptcy law.[2]

Library References:

West's Key No. Digests, Bankruptcy ⟐2722.

2. *See* The Gibson Group, Inc. v. J.D. Irving (In re Gibson Group), 66 F.3d 1436 (6th Cir.1995); In re STN Enterprises, 779 F.2d 901 (2d Cir.1985); Wellman v. Wellman, 933 F.2d 215 (4th Cir.), cert. denied 502 U.S. 925, 112 S.Ct. 339, 116 L.Ed.2d 279 (1991).

3. 11 U.S.C.A. § 550(a). Wellman v. Wellman, 933 F.2d 215, 218 (4th Cir.1991), cert. denied 502 U.S. 925, 112 S.Ct. 339, 116 L.Ed.2d 279 (1991) (debtor provided non-recourse notes to certain creditors payable from proceeds of Section 548 action; debtor could not maintain such action because no benefit to estate); Whiteford Plastics Co. v. Chase National Bank, 179 F.2d 582, 584 (2d Cir.1950).

§ 9.122

1. 11 U.S.C.A. § 546(b)(1). Section 544 is the strong arm clause, described *supra*, § 9.115; Section 545 provides for the avoidance of certain statutory liens, discussed *supra*, § 9.116; and Section 549 provides for the avoidance of certain postpetition transactions.

For example, pursuant to Section 546(b)(1) of the Bankruptcy Code, the Second Circuit has permitted a mechanic's lienholder to complete certain steps required by state law to continue perfection of its mechanic's lien against the debtor's property after the debtor had filed for bankruptcy protection. Klein v. Civale & Trovato, Inc. (In re The Lionel Corp.), 29 F.3d 88 (2d Cir.1994).

2. 11 U.S.C.A. § 546(b)(2). The provision allowing secured creditors to perform postpetition actions to maintain the perfection of prepetition security interests was added pursuant to the Bankruptcy Reform Act of 1994.

§ 9.123 The Avoiding Powers—Reclamation

A seller's nonbankruptcy right to reclaim goods shipped to an insolvent debtor is preserved under the Bankruptcy Code.[1] A debtor's or trustee's avoiding powers pursuant to Sections 544(a), 545, 547, and 549 are subject to a seller's statutory or common law reclamation rights.[2]

Library References:

West's Key No. Digests, Bankruptcy ⚖︎2741–2745.

§ 9.124 Return of Goods by Debtor

In a chapter 11 case, if the trustee or debtor in possession files a motion within 120 days of the commencement date, after notice and a hearing, the court may authorize the debtor, with the consent of the creditor, to return to the creditor goods shipped prior to the commencement of the case for setoff against such creditor's prepetition claim if the return of such goods is in the best interests of the estate.[1]

§ 9.125 Exemptions

To facilitate the Bankruptcy Code's "fresh start" policy, an individual debtor in a chapter 7, 11, 12, or 13 case may exempt certain property from liability as part of the bankruptcy estate.[1] The Bankruptcy Code permits an individual debtor to choose between alternative exemption systems: (1) the exemptions specifically provided under Section 522(d) of the Bankruptcy Code (unless applicable state law does not so authorize) or (2) the exemptions provided under federal law other than the Bankruptcy Code plus the exemptions provided under state or local law where the debtor is domiciled.[2] Since New York law specifically prohibits election of the Bankruptcy Code exemptions, debtors domiciled in New York are limited to the second alternative.[3] In a joint case, each debtor can exempt the full amount in each category of exemptions.[4] Moreover, a debtor can legally convert nonexempt property into exempt property before filing.[5] The property claimed as exempt is exempt unless a party in interest objects.[6]

New York law permits exemption of:

§ 9.123
1. 11 U.S.C.A. § 546(c). See supra, § 9.105 for a discussion of a seller's reclamation rights.
2. 11 U.S.C.A. § 546(c).

§ 9.124
1. 11 U.S.C.A. § 546(g).

§ 9.125
1. See infra, § 9.278 for a procedural checklist for claiming exemptions.

2. 11 U.S.C.A. § 522(b).
3. Debtor and Creditor Law § 284.
4. 11 U.S.C.A. § 522(m).
5. H.R.Rep.No. 595, 95th Cong., 1st Sess. 360–61 (1977).
6. 11 U.S.C.A. § 522(l). See infra, § 9.127 for a discussion of objections to exemptions.

- Certain specified personal property,[7] generally limited to an aggregate amount of $5,000;[8]

- Certain real property,[9] the principal item of which is a "homestead" exemption of $10,000,[10] or the contingent alternative exemption;[11]

- Insurance policies and annuity contracts and their proceeds;[12] and

- Specified additional exemptions.[13]

In addition, numerous other exemptions are available under New York law, including:[14]

- Police and firemen's retirement benefits;[15]

- Police pensions;[16]

- Shares, dues, and dividends from shares in savings and loan associations to a maximum of $600;[17]

- State employees' retirement benefits;[18]

- Teachers' pension, annuity, and retirement allowance;[19]

- Workers' compensation and disability benefits.[20]

In accordance with Section 522(b)(2)(A) of the Bankruptcy Code, individual debtors claiming exemptions under state or local law also are entitled to any exemptions available under federal law other than Section 522(d) of the Bankruptcy Code. Such exemptions include:

- Foreign Service Retirement and Disability payments;[21]

- Injury or death compensation payments from war risk hazards;[22]

- Wages of fishermen, seamen, and apprentices;[23]

- Civil service retirement benefits;[24]

7. CPLR 5205.
8. Debtor and Creditor Law § 283(1).
9. CPLR 5206.
10. The exemption applies only to real property "owned and occupied as a principal residence." Residences other than a principal residence are not entitled to any exemption. The exemption does not apply upon the foreclosure of a mortgage or a mechanic's lien. CPLR 5206, *Supplementary Practice Commentaries*, C5206:1.
11. Debtor and Creditor Law § 283(2).
12. Insurance Law § 3212.
13. Debtor and Creditor Law § 282.
14. *See supra,* § 9.49 note 1 for a discussion of the treatment of Individual Retirement Accounts under the Bankruptcy Code.
15. Retirement and Social Security Law § 410.
16. Unconsolidated Laws § 934.
17. Banking Law § 407.
18. Retirement and Social Security Law § 110.
19. Education Law § 524.
20. Workers' Compensation Law §§ 33, 218.
21. 22 U.S.C.A. § 4060.
22. 42 U.S.C.A. § 1717.
23. 46 U.S.C.A. § 601.
24. 5 U.S.C.A. §§ 729, 2265.

§ 9.125   BANKRUPTCY   Ch. 9

- Longshoremen's and Harbor Workers' Compensation Act death and disability benefits;[25]
- Railroad Retirement Act annuities and pensions;[26]
- Veterans' benefits;[27]
- Special pensions paid to winners of the Congressional Medal of Honor;[28] and
- Federal homestead lands on debts contracted before issuance of the patent.[29]

An individual debtor also may exempt any interest in property in which it has an interest as a tenant by the entirety or joint tenant to the extent that such interest would be exempt under applicable nonbankruptcy law.[30]

To protect the debtor's fresh start, a debtor's waiver of an exemption generally is unenforceable.[31] The Bankruptcy Code also permits a debtor to avoid (i) certain judicial liens on property to the extent the property could have been exempted absent the lien and (ii) nonpurchase-money security interests in certain household goods.[32] The debtor also can avoid certain transfers of property of the debtor or recover a setoff to the extent that the debtor could have exempted such property if the trustee had avoided the transfer.[33] Certain property that the trustee recovers on behalf of the estate may be exempted to the extent that the debtor could have exempted such property if it had not been transferred.[34]

Library References:

West's Key No. Digests, Bankruptcy ⌐2761–2802.

§ 9.126   Exemptions—Procedure

The debtor must list the property claimed as exempt and the statutory basis for such claim on Schedule C of Official Form 6,[1] the schedule of assets required to be filed by Bankruptcy Rule 1007.[2] If the debtor fails to claim exemptions or file the schedule within the time

25. 33 U.S.C.A. § 916.
26. 45 U.S.C.A. § 228(L).
27. 38 U.S.C.A. §§ 770(g), 3101.
28. 38 U.S.C.A. § 3101.
29. 43 U.S.C.A. § 175.
30. 11 U.S.C.A. § 522(b)(2)(B).
31. 11 U.S.C.A. § 522(e).
32. 11 U.S.C.A. § 522(f)(1).
33. 11 U.S.C.A. § 522(h).
34. 11 U.S.C.A. § 522(g).

§ 9.126

1. See supra, § 9.5 and note 3 discussing official forms.

2. See 11 U.S.C.A. § 522(*l*) and Bankr.R. 4003(a). See supra, § 9.11 for a discussion of the schedules required to be filed under Bankruptcy Rule 1007. See infra, § 9.265 for a procedural checklist of the lists and schedules that must be filed at the commencement of a case under title 11 and the deadlines for such filings.

specified in Bankruptcy Rule 1007, a dependent of the debtor may file the list within 30 days thereafter.[3] The property claimed as exempt is exempt unless a party in interest objects.[4]

Library References:

West's Key No. Digests, Bankruptcy ⚖2794.1–2802.

§ 9.127 Exemptions—Objections

Unless the court permits additional time, the trustee or any creditor can file objections to the claimed exemptions within 30 days following the conclusion of the meeting of creditors required under Section 341 of the Bankruptcy Code[1] or the filing of any amendment to the exemption list or supplemental schedules.[2] Copies of the objections must be delivered or mailed to the trustee, the person filing the list, and the attorney for such person.[3] The objecting party bears the burden of proving that the exemptions are not properly claimed.[4] The court will determine the issues raised by the objections after a hearing on notice.[5]

Library References:

West's Key No. Digests, Bankruptcy ⚖2799.1–2802.

§ 9.128 Exemptions—Lien Avoidance

To protect an individual debtor's fresh start, the Bankruptcy Code allows an individual to protect *exempt property* by avoiding the fixing of certain liens on the debtor's property to the extent that such liens impair an exemption to which the debtor would otherwise be entitled.[1] This lien avoidance power applies to: (1) a judicial lien,[2] other than a judicial lien

---

3. 11 U.S.C.A. § 522(*l*); Bankr.R. 4003(a).

4. 11 U.S.C.A. § 522(*l*).

§ 9.127

1. *See supra*, § 9.37 for a discussion of the meeting of creditors.

2. Bankr.R. 4003(b).

CAVEAT: The United States Supreme Court has held that no exception may be implied to the 30-day deadline for the filing of objections to the debtor's claim of exemptions, even if the debtor had no colorable basis for claiming the exemption. Taylor v. Freeland & Kronz, 503 U.S. 638, 643–45, 112 S.Ct. 1644, 1648–49, 118 L.Ed.2d 280 (1992), cited in In re Chalasani, 92 F.3d 1300 (2d Cir. 1996). The Supreme Court noted that although adherence to bar dates may produce unwelcome results in some cases, their observance by the bankruptcy bar and their enforcement by the courts have the salutary result of bringing finality to bankruptcy proceedings. 503 U.S. at 644, 112 S.Ct. at 1648.

3. Bankr.R. 4003(b).

4. Bankr.R. 4003(c).

5. Bankr.R. 4003(c).

§ 9.128

1. 11 U.S.C.A. § 522(f).

2. "'Judicial lien' means lien obtained by judgment, levy, sequestration, or other legal or equitable process or proceeding." 11 U.S.C.A. § 101(36). Thus, the lien avoidance power granted by Section 522(f) does not apply to statutory liens (defined in Section 101(53)) or security interests, *i.e.*, consensual liens (defined in Section 101(51)).

§ 9.128   BANKRUPTCY   Ch. 9

that secures a debt to a spouse or child for alimony, maintenance, or support in connection with a separation agreement, divorce decree, or other court order (provided such debt is not assigned to another entity voluntarily or involuntarily), or (2) a nonpossessory, nonpurchase-money security interest in household furnishings and goods, clothing, and other personal items as well as tools of the trade and prescribed health aids not exceeding $5,000.[3]

For purposes of Section 522(f) of the Code, except for a judgment arising out of a mortgage foreclosure,[4] a lien is considered to impair an exemption to the extent that the sum of (a) the challenged lien(s), (b) all other liens on the property, and (c) the amount of the exemption that the debtor could claim if there were no liens on the property, exceeds the value that the debtor's interest in the property would have in the absence of any liens.[5] For example, a debtor owns a home with a fair market value of $125,000 on the petition date, subject to a mortgage of $100,000. He can assert a $10,000 homestead exemption.[6] The home is encumbered by judicial liens filed in the following order: (i) $6,000, (ii) $20,000, and (iii) $110,000. Thus, the total amount of challenged liens is $136,000. The sum of (a) the challenged liens, (b) all other liens, and (c) the amount of the exemption that could be claimed if there were no liens on the property, equals $246,000. This sum exceeds by $121,000 the value that the debtor's interest in the property would have in the absence of any liens ($246,000 - $125,000 = $121,000). The $121,000 is considered to be the amount of the impairment. Therefore, the third lien can be avoided entirely ($121,000 - $110,000 = $11,000). The second lien can be avoided to the extent of $11,000, leaving a surviving lien of $9,000 ($20,000 - $11,000 = $9,000). The first lien cannot be avoided.

A proceeding by an individual debtor to avoid a lien on exempt property is a contested matter commenced by motion in accordance with Bankruptcy Rule 9014.[7] Therefore, a creditor must be afforded reasonable notice and an opportunity for a hearing.[8]

Library References:

West's Key No. Digests, Bankruptcy ⚖︎2784.1-2793.

3. 11 U.S.C.A. § 522(f); Debtor and Creditor Law § 283(1).

4. 11 U.S.C.A. § 522(f)(2)(C).

5. 11 U.S.C.A. § 522(f)(2). To compute the debtor's equity for purposes of Section 522, "value" is the fair market value as of the petition date. Property that becomes property of the estate postpetition is valued as of the date it becomes property of the estate. 11 U.S.C.A. § 522(a)(2). When property is subject to more than one lien, a lien that has been avoided is not included in this calculation with respect to other liens. 11 U.S.C.A. § 522 (f)(2)(B).

6. CPLR 5206. See supra, § 9.125 for a list of allowed exemptions.

7. Bankr.R. 4003(d). See supra, § 9.17 for a discussion of contested matters.

8. Bankr.R. 9014.

§ 9.129 Exemptions—Liens on Exempt Property

Liens that are unavoidable under the Bankruptcy Code[1] remain valid against exempt property. Thus the right to claim exemptions does not protect property against valid unavoidable liens.[2] Property that is partially subject to a lien may be exempt to the extent of the unencumbered portion of the property. The remainder of the property subject to the lien is treated as secured property in the bankruptcy case. Thus, the debtor's discharge will not extinguish an unavoidable lien on the debtor's property; it will only extinguish the debtor's personal liability. Consequently, under New York law, if it is not established to the satisfaction of the state court in which a judgment against a debtor is docketed that a lien on a former debtor's real property was invalidated or surrendered in the bankruptcy proceedings (or set aside in an action brought in state court by a trustee or receiver), a qualified discharge will be marked on the docket of judgment.[3] This puts title searchers on notice that judgment liens may still exist.

Liens that the trustee can avoid under Sections 544, 545, 547, 548, 549, and 724(a)[4] of the Bankruptcy Code are rendered ineffective not only against property remaining in the debtor's estate for the benefit of creditors, but also against property that the debtor may exempt from liability.[5] Accordingly, the debtor may exempt property recovered under the trustee's avoidance powers if such property could have been exempted had it not been transferred unless:

- The debtor's transfer was *voluntary*;[6] or
- The debtor concealed such property.[7]

Library References:
West's Key No. Digests, Bankruptcy ⟲2784.4(1)–2793.

§ 9.130 Reaffirmation of Debts

Under certain limited circumstances, for example, if an individual debtor wishes to retain possession of an automobile held as security for a

---

§ 9.129

1. Certain liens, such as certain tax liens and certain statutory liens, are not avoidable under the Bankruptcy Code.

2. 11 U.S.C.A. § 522(c)(2). See Johnson v. Home State Bank, 501 U.S. 78, 82–84, 111 S.Ct. 2150, 115 L.Ed.2d 66 (1991) (unavoided liens survive bankruptcy and can be enforced against the debtor's property pursuant to applicable state law after the bankruptcy case is closed).

3. Debtor and Creditor Law § 150.4.

4. Section 544, the "strong arm" clause, is discussed *supra*, § 9.115; Section 545, avoidance of statutory liens, is discussed *supra*, § 9.116; Section 547, avoidance of preferential transfers, is discussed *supra*, § 9.117; Section 548, avoidance of fraudulent conveyances, is discussed *supra*, § 9.119. Section 549 provides for the avoidance of certain postpetition transfers. Section 724(a) empowers a chapter 7 trustee to avoid a lien securing a claim for a "fine, penalty, or forfeiture, or for multiple, exemplary, or punitive damages, arising before the earlier of the order for relief or the appointment of a trustee" that is not compensation for an actual pecuniary loss.

5. 11 U.S.C.A. § 522(c).

6. 11 U.S.C.A. § 522(g)(1)(A).

7. 11 U.S.C.A. § 522(g)(1)(B).

debt, it may be advantageous for the debtor to enter into a reaffirmation agreement, thereby committing to repay a debt that would otherwise be dischargeable. The Bankruptcy Code permits a debtor under chapter 7, 11, 12, or 13 to enter such an agreement, providing that it satisfies the requirements of the Bankruptcy Code,[1] which are intended to protect the debtor from coercion by creditors.

Section 524 of the Code permits a debtor to reaffirm and agree to pay a debt that is dischargeable.[2] Because reaffirmation of an otherwise dischargeable debt may not be in the best interests of the debtor, the Bankruptcy Code affords extensive safeguards that the courts strictly enforce to protect a debtor from coercion or deceptive practices by creditors attempting to evade the effect of a discharge.[3] A reaffirmation agreement is enforceable only to the extent that it would be enforceable under applicable nonbankruptcy law,[4] and only if:

(1) *Made Prior to Discharge*. The reaffirmation agreement must be made or entered into in writing prior to the granting of a discharge under Section 727 of the Bankruptcy Code.[5]

(2) *Clear and Conspicuous Statement: Rescission Possible*. The reaffirmation agreement must contain a clear and conspicuous statement advising the debtor that it may be rescinded by the debtor at any time prior to discharge or within 60 days after it has been filed with the court, whichever is later, by giving notice of rescission to the nondebtor party to the agreement.[6]

(3) *Clear and Conspicuous Statement: Agreement Is Not Required*. The reaffirmation agreement must contain a clear and conspicuous statement advising the debtor that the reaffirmation agreement is not required under title 11, nonbankruptcy law, or under any agreement not in accordance with the provisions of Section 524(c).[7]

(4) *Filed*. The reaffirmation agreement must be filed with the court.

§ 9.130

1. 11 U.S.C.A. § 524(c), (d).

2. 11 U.S.C.A. § 524(c), (d). Section 524 applies to cases under chapters 7, 11, 12, and 13. *See infra*, § 9.302 for a drafting checklist for a reaffirmation agreement and *see infra*, §§ 9.280, 9.303, respectively, for procedural and drafting checklists for a motion requesting approval of a reaffirmation agreement.

3. *See, e.g.*, Republic Bank v. Getzoff (In re Getzoff), 180 B.R. 572 (9th Cir.BAP 1995); In re Johnson, 148 B.R. 532 (Bankr. N.D.Ill.1992); Lindale National Bank v. Artzt (In re Artzt), 145 B.R. 866 (Bankr. E.D.Tex.1992).

4. 11 U.S.C.A. § 524(c).

5. 11 U.S.C.A. § 524(c)(1). *See, e.g.*, In re Eccleston, 70 B.R. 210 (Bankr.N.D.N.Y. 1986) (reaffirmation agreement entered into after discharge held unenforceable).

6. 11 U.S.C.A. § 524(c)(2)(A). *See, e.g.*, In re Noble, 182 B.R. 854 (Bankr. W.D.Wash.1995); In re Perryman, 111 B.R. 227 (Bankr.E.D.Ark.1990) (reaffirmation agreement that did not include statement advising debtor that it could be rescinded at any time prior to discharge or within 60 days after it was filed with the court held unenforceable).

7. 11 U.S.C.A. § 524(c)(2)(B).

(5) *Court Hearing.* If an individual debtor was represented by an attorney, no court approval is required if the reaffirmation agreement is accompanied by a declaration or affidavit of such attorney stating that: (a) the debtor was fully informed and made the agreement voluntarily;[8] (b) the agreement does not impose an undue hardship on the debtor or a dependent of the debtor; and (c) the attorney fully informed the debtor of the legal consequences of a reaffirmation agreement and any default thereunder.[9] If an individual debtor was not represented by an attorney during the negotiation of the reaffirmation agreement, or if the attorney declines to sign the declaration or affidavit, the court must conduct a hearing at which the debtor must appear.[10] At the hearing, the court will inform the debtor that such an agreement is not required. The court also will inform the debtor of the legal consequences of a reaffirmation agreement and any default thereunder. If the consideration for the reaffirmation is based in whole or in part on a consumer debt that is not secured by real property of the debtor, then at the hearing the court must also approve the agreement as (a) not imposing an undue hardship on the debtor or a dependent of the debtor and (b) in the best interest of the debtor.[11]

(6) *Rescission.* The reaffirmation agreement is enforceable only if the debtor has not rescinded the agreement at any time prior to discharge or within 60 days after such agreement has been filed with the court, whichever occurs later, by giving notice of rescission to the holder of such claim.[12]

Library References:

West's Key No. Digests, Bankruptcy ⇔3415.1–3417.

8. Some courts have held that a reaffirmation agreement requires the voluntary consent of both parties. *See, e.g.,* In re Schmidt, 64 B.R. 226 (Bankr.S.D.Ind.1986).

9. 11 U.S.C.A. § 524(c)(3).

10. A hearing was mandatory in all cases filed before October 22, 1994 in which the debtor wished to execute a reaffirmation agreement. Pursuant to the Bankruptcy Reform Act of 1994, for cases filed on or after that date, a hearing is required only if the debtor was not represented by an attorney during the negotiation of the reaffirmation agreement or if the attorney declines to sign the declaration or affidavit. 11 U.S.C.A. § 524(d).

11. 11 U.S.C.A. § 524(c)(6), (d). The court hearing required pursuant to Section 524(d) of the Bankruptcy Code must be held not more than 30 days following the entry of an order granting or denying a discharge (or confirming a plan in a chapter 11 case concerning an individual debtor) and on not less than 10 days notice to the debtor and the trustee. The motion for approval of a reaffirmation agreement must be filed before or at such hearing. Bankr.R. 4008.

CAVEAT: Many courts will not accept a reaffirmation agreement for filing after the discharge date.

See Bankr.R. 4004 and 4008 for additional information concerning the requirements and procedure for obtaining approval of a reaffirmation agreement.

12. 11 U.S.C.A. § 524(c)(4).

§ 9.131 Reaffirmation of Debts—Strategy

While both the court and debtors' attorneys generally dislike reaffirmation agreements because of the risk of personal liability which they impose on a debtor,[1] such an agreement may be the debtor's best alternative if a well-founded case for nondischargeability may be anticipated. Under such circumstances, a debtor may be best served by negotiation of a reaffirmation agreement in a reduced amount. However, a debtor should never enter into a reaffirmation agreement merely because he or she wishes to pay the debt. Nothing in the Bankruptcy Code precludes a debtor from repaying a debt voluntarily after it has been discharged,[2] and voluntary repayment does not expose the debtor to personal liability nor deprive the debtor of the benefits of a discharge, as does a reaffirmation agreement.

From a creditor's point of view, it may be beneficial to negotiate a reaffirmation agreement, even in an amount that is less than the amount of the debt, to settle a potentially protracted dischargeability proceeding.[3] Negotiation of such an agreement avoids the uncertainty

---

§ 9.131

1. **CAVEAT**: The risk to the debtor is that a reaffirmation agreement *personally obligates the debtor to pay* the otherwise dischargeable debt and *any deficiency* that could result from a repossession and sale of collateral upon a default.

A creditor must take care to make sure that any reaffirmation agreement entered into with the debtor is filed with the court and that a hearing is held, if required. The local rules of some bankruptcy courts require the debtor to request a hearing, if required, when the reaffirmation agreement is filed.

Furthermore, the creditor must refrain from any actions that could be construed as putting pressure on the debtor to enter into such an agreement; however, courts may differ as to what constitutes coercion. *Compare* In re Duke, 79 F.3d 43 (7th Cir.1996) (nonthreatening letter to the debtor concerning reaffirmation is not coercive); Brown v. Pennsylvania State Employees Credit Union, 851 F.2d 81 (3d Cir.1988) (mildly worded letter informing debtor that she would be barred from membership in credit union if she did not reaffirm did not violate Bankruptcy Code even though letter was sent directly to debtor who was represented by counsel) *with* In re Flynn, 143 B.R. 798 (Bankr.D.R.I.1992) (damages imposed on creditor for violation of the automatic stay where creditor made direct contact with debtor represented by counsel for the purpose of obtaining a reaffirmation).

2. *See* 11 U.S.C.A. § 524(f).

3. **CAVEAT**: A court may find that a reaffirmation agreement that merely suggests that there might be a nondischargeability action with respect to the debt in question is coercive if there is no factual basis for nondischargeability. For example, where a retailer's form reaffirmation agreement stated "debtor wishes either to retain the property securing the account balance, to settle creditor's claim of nondischargeability under § 523, and/or to continue to use the [retailer's] Charge Account by reaffirming said debt and security agreement," the court found that if no nondischargeability claim had been made, this language was intended in bad faith to induce the debtor to reaffirm. Accordingly, the court held that the agreement was a violation of Bankruptcy Rule 9011 and authorized the imposition of sanctions. *See* In re Latanowich, 207 B.R. 326, 331 (Bankr.D.Mass.1997) (discussing In re Iappini, 192 B.R. 8 (Bankr.D.Mass. 1995).

However, when a valid nondischargeability action has been commenced and settled by means of a reaffirmation agreement, a creditor should not dismiss the nondischargeability claim until the reaffirmation agreement becomes legal and binding and the time period during which the debtor may rescind has expired. *See infra*,

and costs of litigation and achieves a result that is comparable to a judgment of nondischargeability, although the reaffirmed amount will probably be less than the original debt.

§ 9.132 Protection Against Discriminatory Treatment

To protect persons who have been or are debtors under the Bankruptcy Code and associates of such persons, Section 525 of the Bankruptcy Code prohibits discriminatory treatment by governmental units against such persons solely because they (i) have been or are a bankrupt or debtor; (ii) have been insolvent before the commencement of the case or during the case but before the granting or denial of a discharge; or (iii) have not paid a dischargeable debt.[1] The prohibition applies only to discrimination based solely on bankruptcy or insolvency and does not preclude consideration of other financial factors such as future financial responsibility or ability; nor does it prohibit the imposition of financial requirements such as net capital rules, as long as they are applied in a nondiscriminatory manner.[2]

Section 525 provides that a governmental unit[3] may not deny, revoke, suspend, or refuse renewal of a license, permit, charter, franchise, or similar grant; nor may it discriminate against debtors and their associates with respect to employment.[4] Moreover, the provision prohibits private employers from discriminating against persons protected under the provision with respect to employment for the reasons enumerated in the preceding paragraph.[5]

In addition, the 1994 amendments to the Bankruptcy Code prohibit a governmental unit that operates a student grant or loan program from denying a student grant, loan, loan guarantee, or loan insurance to a person protected under the provision for the reasons enumerated above.[6]

Library References:
West's Key No. Digests, Bankruptcy ⚖2363.1–2374.

§ 9.133 Tax Considerations

Section 346 of the Bankruptcy Code creates special tax provisions which apply to cases under title 11 "notwithstanding any State or local

---

§§ 9.204–9.208 for a discussion of discharge under chapter 7 of the Bankruptcy Code.

§ 9.132

1. 11 U.S.C.A. § 525(a). *See* Perez v. Campbell, 402 U.S. 637, 91 S.Ct. 1704, 29 L.Ed.2d 233 (1971).

2. H.R.No. 95–595, 95th Cong., 1st Sess. 366–67 (1977); S.R.No. 95–989, 95th Cong., 2d Sess. 81 (1978). The legislative history reveals that the provision is intended to be developed to prohibit other forms of discrimination, particularly by governmental or quasi-governmental organizations such as bar or medical associations or trade unions. *Id.*

3. "Governmental unit" is defined at 11 U.S.C.A. § 101(27). It includes the United States and any department, agency, or instrumentality thereof (except a U.S. trustee serving as a trustee in a case under the Bankruptcy Code), any state, commonwealth, municipality, or similar entity.

4. 11 U.S.C.A. § 525(a).

5. 11 U.S.C.A. § 525(b).

6. 11 U.S.C.A. § 525(c). For purposes of this section, "student loan program" means the program operated under part B, D, or E of title IV of the Higher Education Act of 1965 or a similar program operated under state or local law. 11 U.S.C.A. § 525(c)(2).

law imposing a tax, but subject to the Internal Revenue Code of 1986."[1] For example, in an individual's chapter 11 case, any income of the estate may be taxed under a state or local income tax "only to the estate, and may not be taxed to such individual."[2] If such individual is a partner in a partnership, the tax attributes of the partnership may be distributed to the partner's estate rather than to the partner.[3] However, the commencement of a case of a corporation or a partnership does not effect a change in the status of such corporation or partnership for the purpose of any state or local income tax, as any income of the estate in such case may be taxed only as though such case had not been commenced.[4] In addition, the debtor or trustee, as is applicable, must withhold from any payment of wages, salaries, commissions, or other payments, or collect any amount required to be withheld or collected under applicable state or local law, and pay such withheld or collected tax to the appropriate governmental unit.[5]

§ 9.134 Conversion and Dismissal of Cases Under Title 11

Several sections of the Bankruptcy Code provide for converting a case from one chapter to another, or for dismissing a case entirely.[1] Conversion may be desirable under a variety of circumstances. For example, a party against whom an involuntary chapter 7 petition has been filed may convert the case to a voluntary chapter 11 rather than oppose the involuntary petition. Similarly, circumstances may change during the course of a debtor's chapter 7 case which enable the debtor to repay its debts without having to liquidate, making a conversion to chapter 11 or 13 desirable. At the opposite end of the spectrum, a party who has been attempting to reorganize under chapter 11, 12, or 13 may realize that such attempts are futile, and the most prudent course may be to convert the case to a chapter 7 liquidation.

Library References:

West's Key No. Digests, Bankruptcy ⟐3591(1)–3594.

§ 9.133

1. 11 U.S.C.A. § 346(a).
2. 11 U.S.C.A. § 346(b)(1).
3. 11 U.S.C.A. § 346(b)(1).
4. 11 U.S.C.A. § 346(c)(1).
5. 11 U.S.C.A. § 346(f). The United States Supreme Court has held that a chapter 11 trustee, appointed pursuant to a confirmed plan to liquidate the debtor's property that had been placed in a trust, had a duty to file tax returns and pay taxes on the gain realized from the sale of real estate, as the corporate debtor would have been required to do if it had retained the property. In addition, the Court held that as fiduciary of the trust holding the property, the trustee also had to file returns and pay taxes on the income that was attributable to the individual debtor's property. Holywell Corp. v. Smith, 503 U.S. 47, 112 S.Ct. 1021, 117 L.Ed.2d 196 (1992), on remand 965 F.2d 994 (11th Cir.1992).

§ 9.134

1. *See* 11 U.S.C.A. §§ 706, 1112, 1208, 1307. For a discussion of conversion or dismissal of a case under a specific chapter of the Bankruptcy Code, *see infra*, § 9.209 for a case under chapter 7; *infra*, § 9.174 for a case under chapter 11; *infra*, § 9.233 for a case under chapter 12; and *infra*, § 9.261 for a case under chapter 13.

§ 9.135 Effect of Conversion

The conversion of a case from a case under one chapter of the Bankruptcy Code to a case under another chapter of the Bankruptcy Code raises the issue as to the expiration of certain time limits that existed before the conversion of the case. Section 348(a) of the Bankruptcy Code provides that conversion constitutes an order for relief under the chapter to which the case is converted.[1] It generally does not change the petition date or the date of the commencement of the case or the order for relief.[2] For example, if a chapter 11 case is converted to a chapter 7 case, the petition date or the date of the order for relief in the chapter 7 case will be deemed to be the date the chapter 11 petition was filed.[3] However, the time the trustee or debtor in possession has under Section 365(d) to assume or reject an executory contract or unexpired lease[4] begins anew as if the conversion order were the order for relief.[5] For example, if a case is converted from chapter 11 to chapter 7, the 60-day period during which the trustee may assume or reject an executory contract or unexpired lease runs from the conversion date. This provision is intended to afford a new trustee an opportunity to become familiar with the case before having to make decisions concerning assumption or rejection of contracts or leases.

With the exception of claims accorded administrative expense status under Section 503(b),[6] a claim against the estate or the debtor that arises postpetition but before conversion to a chapter 7 case from a chapter 11, 12, or 13 case is treated as a claim that arose before the filing of the petition, *i.e.*, a prepetition claim.[7] When a case under chapter 13 is converted to a case under another chapter, property of the estate in the converted case consists of the property of the chapter 13 estate as of the petition date that remains in the possession or under the control of the debtor on the date of conversion, and valuations of property and of allowed secured claims in the chapter 13 case apply in the converted

---

§ 9.135

1. 11 U.S.C.A. § 348(a). See *supra*, §§ 9.8, 9.10, respectively, for a discussion of the order for relief in voluntary and involuntary cases.

2. 11 U.S.C.A. § 348(a). See Bankr.R. 1019, which governs conversion of cases under chapter 11, 12, or 13 to cases under chapter 7.

3. This is significant because it affects the calculation of certain time periods such as the 90-day prepetition period during which transfers by the debtor may be found to be avoidable preferences. See *supra*, §§ 9.115–9.119.

4. See *supra*, §§ 9.74–9.81 for a discussion of assumption and rejection of executory contracts and unexpired leases.

5. 11 U.S.C.A. § 348(c).

6. See *supra*, § 9.98 for a discussion of administrative expense claims.

7. 11 U.S.C.A. § 348(d). Some examples of the kinds of claims that would fall in this category are claims that arise under (i) Section 502(f) (involuntary gap claims, discussed *infra*, § 9.148 note 3), (ii) Section 502(g) (claims arising from the rejection of an executory contract or unexpired contract that has not been assumed, discussed *supra*, § 9.82), and (iii) Section 502(i) (claims for taxes entitled to priority under Section 507(a)(8) that do not arise until the postpetition period).

§ 9.135

case, with allowed secured claims reduced to the extent that they have been paid in accordance with the chapter 13 plan.[8]

Library References:

West's Key No. Digests, Bankruptcy ⚖︎3594.

§ 9.136 Effect of Dismissal

Unless the court orders otherwise for cause, the dismissal of a case is without prejudice. Dismissal does not bar a debtor from receiving a discharge in a later case unless the debtor received a discharge in the dismissed case.[1]

In general, dismissal of a case has the effect of restoring all property rights to their prepetition status. Thus, dismissal:

- Reinstates proceedings or custodianships that were superseded by the bankruptcy case;
- Reinstates avoided transfers;
- Reinstates voided liens;
- Vacates any order, judgment, or transfer ordered as a result of the avoidance of a transfer; and
- Revests property of the estate in the entity in which it was vested immediately before commencement of the case.[2]

Library References:

West's Key No. Digests, Bankruptcy ⚖︎3594.

§ 9.137 Closing and Reopening Cases

The court will close the case after an estate is fully administered and the court has discharged the trustee.[1] However, the case may be reopened on motion of the debtor or other party in interest to administer assets, to accord relief to the debtor, or for other cause.[2]

---

8. 11 U.S.C.A. § 348(f)(1). However, if the case has been converted in bad faith, property in the converted case consists of property of the estate at the conversion date. 11 U.S.C.A. § 348(f)(2). Since property of the estate under chapter 13, but not under chapter 7, includes property that has been acquired postpetition, the effect of this provision is to penalize a debtor who converts a case from chapter 13 to chapter 7 in bad faith. This is so because property acquired postpetition and held at the conversion date will be included in the chapter 7 case and thus, will be subject to liquidation for the benefit of creditors.

§ 9.136

1. 11 U.S.C.A. § 349(a).
2. 11 U.S.C.A. § 349(b).

§ 9.137

1. 11 U.S.C.A. § 350(a).
2. 11 U.S.C.A. § 350(b); Bankr.R. 5010. In addition, Rule 9024 exempts motions to reopen cases from the one-year limitation of F.R.C.P. 60(b). *See supra*, § 9.33 note 6 regarding the desirability of closing cases expeditiously to avoid the incurrence of additional fees under 28 U.S.C.A. § 1930(a).

§ 9.138 Chapter 11—Appointment of a Trustee

Any party in interest or the U.S. trustee may seek the appointment of a chapter 11 operating trustee, provided such party or U.S. trustee establishes by clear and convincing evidence[1] "cause," including fraud, dishonesty, incompetence, or gross mismanagement of the affairs of the debtor,[2] or that such appointment would be in the interests of creditors and other interest holders.[3] There are few situations where grounds will exist for the appointment of a trustee under the interests of creditors' test where "cause" for such appointment does not otherwise exist.[4] "Cause" also may include inadequate financial disclosure, failure to respond to data requests, inaccurate and unreliable record-keeping, removal of property, improper preferential treatment of the debtor's affiliates, and breach of the debtor's fiduciary duties.[5] If a trustee is appointed in a chapter 11 case, the trustee is vested with authority to operate the debtor's business.[6]

If a party in interest or the U.S. trustee has filed a motion requesting the appointment of a trustee in a chapter 11 case and the court has ordered such appointment, the U.S. trustee, after consultation with parties in interest, and subject to the court's approval, will appoint one disinterested person other than the U.S. trustee to serve as trustee[7] unless a party in interest requests that the trustee be elected by creditors. Within 30 days after the court has ordered the appointment of a trustee, a party in interest may request the U.S. trustee to convene a meeting of creditors for the purpose of electing one disinterested person to serve as trustee. If such a request is made of the U.S. trustee, a trustee will be elected according to the same procedures as are provided for the election of a chapter 7 trustee.[8] At any time before confirmation

---

§ 9.138

1. *See* In re Cardinal Industries, Inc., 109 B.R. 755, 765 (Bankr.S.D.Ohio 1990); In re Mako, Inc., 102 B.R. 809, 811–12 (Bankr.E.D.Okla.1988); In re St. Louis Globe–Democrat, Inc., 63 B.R. 131, 138 (Bankr.E.D.Mo.1985); In re General Oil Distribs., Inc., 42 B.R. 402, 408 (Bankr. E.D.N.Y.1984).

2. 11 U.S.C.A. § 1104(a)(1).

3. 11 U.S.C.A. § 1104(a)(2). For the provisions concerning a trustee in any case under title 11, *see* the following sections of the Bankruptcy Code: eligibility to serve as a trustee, 11 U.S.C.A. § 321; qualification of a trustee, 11 U.S.C.A. § 322; role and capacity of a trustee, 11 U.S.C.A. § 323; removal of a trustee or examiner, 11 U.S.C.A. § 324; effect of vacancy, 11 U.S.C.A. § 325; limitation on the compensation of a trustee, 11 U.S.C.A. § 326.

4. *See* 5 *Collier on Bankruptcy* ¶ 1104.01[d], at 1104–24 (L. King, ed., 15th ed. 1989).

5. *See, e.g.*, In re Sharon Steel Corp., 871 F.2d 1217, 1228–29 (3d Cir.1989).

6. 11 U.S.C.A. § 1108.

7. 11 U.S.C.A. § 1104(d).

8. 11 U.S.C.A. § 1104(b). *See* 11 U.S.C.A. § 702 for the provision governing the election of a trustee in a chapter 7 case and *see infra*, § 9.181 for a brief discussion of the election of a trustee. *See infra*, §§ 9.214, 9.239, respectively, for discussions of the appointment of a trustee in chapters 12 or 13.

§ 9.138   BANKRUPTCY   Ch. 9

of a plan, on request of a party in interest or the U.S. trustee, and after notice and a hearing, the court may terminate the trustee's appointment and restore the debtor to possession and management of the property of the estate and of the operation of the debtor's business.[9]

Library References:
West's Key No. Digests, Bankruptcy ⊘3623.1–3626.

§ 9.139   Chapter 11—Duties of a Trustee

A chapter 11 trustee replaces management of the debtor. The trustee operates the debtor's business and manages its properties as a fiduciary for the estate, its creditors and, if a possibility exists that the debtor's estate is or will be solvent, for equity security holders.[1] A chapter 11 trustee must:

1. Be accountable for all property received;[2]
2. If beneficial, examine proofs of claims and object to the allowance of improper claims;[3]
3. Furnish information concerning the estate and the estate's administration if requested by a party in interest;[4]
4. File periodic reports and summaries of the debtor's operations, including a statement of receipts and disbursements, with copies to the U.S. trustee;[5]
5. Make a final report and file a final account of the administration of the estate with the court and with the U.S. trustee;[6]
6. If the debtor has not done so, file the list of creditors, schedule of assets and liabilities, schedules of current income and expen-

---

9. 11 U.S.C.A. § 1105.

§ 9.139

1. In re Delta Petroleum (P.R.), Ltd., 193 B.R. 99, 110 (D.P.R.1996) ("A chapter 11 trustee is a fiduciary of the estate, pursuant to 11 U.S.C. § 1106") (citing Commodity Futures Trading Comm'n v. Weintraub, 471 U.S. 343, 105 S.Ct. 1986, 85 L.Ed.2d 372 (1985); Mosser v. Darrow, 341 U.S. 267, 71 S.Ct. 680, 95 L.Ed. 927 (1951); 5 *Collier on Bankruptcy*, ¶ 1106.01 [b], at 1106–7 to 1106–8 (L. King, ed., 15th ed. 1994) ("In addition to those duties specified in the Bankruptcy Act, the reorganization trustee is a fiduciary who has an obligation to treat all parties in a reorganization case fairly")).

2. 11 U.S.C.A. §§ 1106(a)(1), 704(2). Section 345 of the Bankruptcy Code governs the trustee's or debtor's management of the money of an estate under title 11. It permits the trustee to deposit or invest estate funds in a manner that will yield the maximum reasonable return on such money, taking into account the safety of the funds. For any deposit or investment that is not backed by the full faith and credit of the United States, unless the court for cause orders otherwise, the trustee or debtor must obtain from the entity with which the funds are invested a bond in favor of the United States secured by an approved corporate surety and conditioned on a proper accounting. Alternatively, the trustee may require the deposit of securities of a kind specified in 31 U.S.C.A. § 9303 governing the posting of security by banks that receive public moneys on deposit.

3. 11 U.S.C.A. §§ 1106(a)(1), 704(5).
4. 11 U.S.C.A. §§ 1106(a)(1), 704(7).
5. 11 U.S.C.A. §§ 1106(a)(1), 704(8).
6. 11 U.S.C.A. §§ 1106(a)(1), 704(9).

ditures, and a statement of the debtor's financial affairs;[7]

7. Investigate the acts, conduct, and financial condition of the debtor and the desirability of continuing the operations of the debtor's business, and any matter relevant to the case or to the formulation of a chapter 11 plan;[8]

8. File as soon as possible a statement of the results of any investigation and send a copy or a summary to the statutory committees appointed in the case and to any indenture trustee;[9]

9. File as soon as possible a chapter 11 plan, or a report of why a plan will not be filed, or recommend conversion to chapter 7, 12, or 13, or dismissal of the case;[10]

10. Provide relevant tax information to the taxing authority;[11] and

11. Following confirmation, file any reports necessary or requested by the court.[12]

Library References:

West's Key No. Digests, Bankruptcy ⟺3008.1–3009.

§ 9.140 Chapter 11—Appointment of an Examiner

If the court does not order the appointment of a trustee in a chapter 11 case, upon the request of a party in interest or the U.S. trustee at any time prior to confirmation, the court must order the appointment of an examiner to investigate allegations of fraud, dishonesty, incompetence, misconduct, mismanagement, or irregularity in the management of the debtor's affairs by current management before or after the commencement of the case provided the movant establishes (1) that such appointment is in the interests of creditors, equity security holders, and other interests of the estate,[1] or (2) that the debtor's fixed, liquidated, unsecured debts, other than debts for goods, services, or taxes, or amounts owed to insiders, exceed $5 million.[2] Appointment of an examiner per-

7. 11 U.S.C.A. §§ 1106(a)(2), 521(1).
8. 11 U.S.C.A. § 1106(a)(3).
9. 11 U.S.C.A. § 1106(a)(4).
10. 11 U.S.C.A. § 1106(a)(5).
11. 11 U.S.C.A. § 1106(a)(6).
12. 11 U.S.C.A. § 1106(a)(7).

§ 9.140

1. 11 U.S.C.A. § 1104(c).
2. 11 U.S.C.A. § 1104(c)(2). See In re Revco D.S., Inc., 898 F.2d 498 (6th Cir. 1990) (when the statutory requirements of § 1104(b)(2) [now (c)(2)] are present, the court has no discretion but to order the appointment of an examiner; the statute is clear on its face). But, it has been held that when a debtor's fixed, liquidated, unsecured debts, other than debts for goods, services or taxes, or debts owing to an insider, exceeded $5,000,000, the appointment of an examiner was not required. In re Shelter Resources Corp., 35 B.R. 304 (Bankr. N.D.Ohio 1983) (the court found that the appointment of an examiner would unduly delay the administration of the debtor's estate and most likely would cause the debtor's estate to incur unnecessary costs and expenses); In re GHR Cos., Inc., 43 B.R. 165, 11 C.B.C.2d 604 (Bankr.D.Mass.1984) (the court denied a request for mandatory appointment of an examiner for a privately held company).

mits investigation of the debtor's affairs without stripping it of its status as debtor in possession and without exercising the administrative and management powers of a trustee.[3] If the court orders the appointment of an examiner, then the U.S. trustee, after consultation with parties in interest and subject to the court's approval, must appoint one disinterested person[4] to serve as examiner.[5]

Library References:

West's Key No. Digests, Bankruptcy ⇐3623.1–3626.

§ 9.141   Chapter 11—Duties of an Examiner

Unless the court requests otherwise, the services provided by an examiner appointed in a chapter 11 case are limited to the following duties:

1. Investigate the acts, conduct, and financial condition of the debtor, the operation of the debtor's business and the desirability of continuing such business, and any matter relevant to the case or to the formulation of a chapter 11 plan;[1]

2. File as soon as possible a statement of the results of any investigation, including any facts pertaining to fraud, dishonesty, incompetence, misconduct, or mismanagement, and send a copy or a summary to the statutory committees appointed in the case and any indenture trustee;[2] and

3. Perform any other duties of a trustee that the court orders the debtor in possession not to perform, except to the extent the court orders otherwise.[3]

Library References:

West's Key No. Digests, Bankruptcy ⇐3627.

§ 9.142   Chapter 11—Exclusivity—Right to File a Plan

The paramount objective of a chapter 11 case is the formulation and confirmation of a plan of reorganization. The Bankruptcy Code favors the debtor by providing it with the exclusive right to file a plan during the first 120 days of the case and, if the plan is filed within such period,

---

3. See In re Olympia & York Realty Corp., Nos. 92 B 42698–700 and 42702 (JLG) (Bankr.S.D.N.Y. May 28, 1993) (approving the appointment of an examiner); In re Maxwell Comm. Corp., No. 91 B 15741 (Bankr.S.D.N.Y. Dec. 20, 1991) (same).

4. See 11 U.S.C.A. § 101(14) and *supra*, § 9.29 for the definition of "disinterested person" under the Bankruptcy Code.

5. 11 U.S.C.A. § 1104(d).

§ 9.141
1. 11 U.S.C.A. § 1106(a)(3), (b).
2. 11 U.S.C.A. § 1106(a)(4), (b).
3. 11 U.S.C.A. § 1106(b).

to solicit acceptances during the first 180 days of the case.[1] Parties in interest, other than the debtor, may file a plan if and only if (i) a trustee has been appointed in the case; (ii) the debtor has not filed a plan before 120 days after the order for relief; or (iii) the debtor has not filed a plan that has been accepted before 180 days after the order for relief by each class of claims or interests which is impaired under the plan.[2]

Notwithstanding the foregoing, on the request of a party in interest, the court may, for "cause," increase or reduce the debtor's 120–day and 180–day exclusivity periods.[3] In order to increase the exclusivity periods, the debtor should request an extension prior to the expiration of its exclusivity.[4] In determining whether a debtor has established cause for an extension of its exclusivity periods, courts look to: (i) the time that has elapsed since filing, (ii) the size and complexity of the case; (iii) the nature of the debtor's business; (iv) the progress made by the debtor toward formulating a plan; (v) the debtor's motive in requesting an extension; (vi) the possibility that an extension will harm creditors; (vii) the postpetition conduct of creditors; and (viii) the debtor's prospects for filing a viable plan if the extension is granted.[5]

Library References:

West's Key No. Digests, Bankruptcy ⚖3534.

§ 9.143 Chapter 11—Exclusivity—Small Businesses

To expedite small business reorganizations, the Bankruptcy Reform Act of 1994 amended the Bankruptcy Code to provide that in a case in which the debtor is a small business and elects to be considered a small business, the debtor enjoys the exclusive right to file a plan for the first

---

§ 9.142

1. 11 U.S.C.A. § 1121(b), 1121(c)(3). Section 1121(a) of the Bankruptcy Code provides the debtor with the option of filing a plan contemporaneously with the petition commencing a voluntary case.

2. 11 U.S.C.A. § 1121(c).

3. 11 U.S.C.A. § 1121(d).

4. *See* In re Cramer, Inc., 105 B.R. 433 (Bankr.W.D.Tenn.1989) (the court may not increase exclusivity if the request is made after the expiration of exclusivity).

PRACTICE POINTER: Due to conflicting authority concerning whether an extension of the 120–day period for filing a plan automatically extends the 180–day period for soliciting acceptances of a plan, a debtor is well advised to seek an extension of both exclusivity periods. *Compare* In re Trainer's, Inc., 17 B.R. 246 (Bankr.E.D.Pa.1982) (extension of 120–day period does not automatically extend 180–day period) *with* In re United Press Int'l, Inc., 60 B.R. 265 (Bankr. D.Colo.1986) (extension of 120–day period automatically extends 180–day period).

5. *See* In re Crescent Mfg. Co., 122 B.R. 979 (Bankr.N.D.Ohio 1990); In re Washington–St. Tammany Elec. Coop., Inc., 97 B.R. 852 (E.D.La.1989); In re Public Serv. Co. of New Hampshire, 88 B.R. 521 (Bankr. D.N.H.1988); In re McLean Indus., 87 B.R. 830 (Bankr.S.D.N.Y.1987); In re Texaco Inc., 76 B.R. 322 (Bankr.S.D.N.Y.1987); In re Southwest Oil Co., 84 B.R. 448 (Bankr. W.D.Tex.1987); In re Sharon Steel Corp., 78 B.R. 762 (Bankr.W.D.Pa.1987).

See infra, §§ 9.281, 9.304 for procedural and drafting checklists for a debtor's motion to extend exclusivity.

§ 9.143 BANKRUPTCY Ch. 9

100 days after the order for relief is entered.[1] All plans must be filed within 160 days after the order for relief is entered.[2] Nonetheless, as in traditional chapter 11 cases, the court may reduce the 100–day or 160–day exclusivity periods for cause on the request of a party in interest made within the respective 100–day or 160–day period. In the case of a small business, however, the legal standard for increasing the 100–day period is no longer "cause." Rather, the debtor must demonstrate that the need for an increase is caused by "circumstances for which the debtor should not be held accountable."[3] There is no provision for increasing the 160–day period within which a party in interest may file a plan.[4]

§ 9.144 Chapter 11—Exclusivity—Strategy: Representing a Debtor

For the debtor, maintaining the exclusive right to file a plan will often be paramount to the future success of its business. Consequently, if the debtor is unable to propose a plan within the initial 120–day exclusivity period, within that period, it should seek an extension of such period and the concurrent 180–day period for soliciting acceptances. Although the court has an independent obligation to determine whether cause exists to extend exclusivity, in general, the fewer objections interposed by creditors and other parties in interest to such motion, the more likely a court is to extend exclusivity. Thus, the debtor should, to the extent practicable, promote amicable relations with the statutory committees and other key constituencies by, among other things, keeping them informed as to progress on a plan, providing them with the business plan and other financial reports, negotiating with and seeking their input in formulating the plan, resolving outstanding claims and legal issues as soon as practicable, and taking those steps necessary to improve the financial performance of the debtor's business.

§ 9.145 Chapter 11—Exclusivity—Strategy: Representing a Creditor

Although a creditor may be interested in proposing its own plan of reorganization at the outset of a case under chapter 11, it is extremely difficult for a creditor to demonstrate "cause" to reduce or terminate the debtor's initial statutory 120–day exclusivity period.[1] Depending on the

§ 9.143

1. 11 U.S.C.A. § 1121(e)(1). *See supra*, § 9.43 note 4 for the definition of "small business" under the Bankruptcy Code.
2. 11 U.S.C.A. § 1121(e)(2).
3. 11 U.S.C.A. § 1121(e)(3).
4. 11 U.S.C.A. § 1121(e)(3).

§ 9.145

1. *See* In re Interco, Inc., 137 B.R. 999 (Bankr.E.D.Mo.1992) (the party requesting immediate termination of the exclusivity period, as originally authorized by statute or as it may have been extended by the court, bears a heavy burden where the evidence established that the debtors were

facts of the case—e.g., the debtor's progress in proposing a plan, the debtor's relationship with creditors, the size and complexity of the case—a creditor or creditors' committee may or may not be able to terminate subsequent exclusivity periods or defeat the debtor's proposed extension of its exclusivity periods. A careful analysis of case law should allow the creditor to predict with a fair degree of accuracy whether the facts in its chapter 11 case suffice to demonstrate cause to terminate or defeat a proposed extension of exclusivity. Moreover, a creditor should be able to use the threat of seeking to terminate, or opposing, an extension of exclusivity as leverage in plan negotiations.

§ 9.146 Chapter 11—Exclusivity—Appealability of Orders

As a consequence of the Bankruptcy Reform Act of 1994, district courts now have jurisdiction to hear appeals as of right from interlocutory orders issued under Section 1121(d) of the Bankruptcy Code increasing or decreasing the debtor's exclusivity periods.[1] This amendment effectuates a marked change from the prior law, which required that a party seeking appeal of an order increasing or decreasing a debtor's exclusivity periods seek leave of the district court in order to pursue its appeal.

Library References:

West's Key No. Digests, Bankruptcy ⚖3766.1–3768.

§ 9.147 Chapter 11—Plan

The Bankruptcy Code specifies a list of requirements that must be satisfied for a chapter 11 plan to be confirmable.[1] In addition to the mandatory requirements set forth in Section 1123(a), a list of provisions that may be included in a plan is set forth in Section 1123(b) of the Code.

Library References:

West's Key No. Digests, Bankruptcy ⚖3531–3570.

§ 9.148 Chapter 11—Plan—Mandatory Provisions

A chapter 11 plan must do the following:

making good faith progress toward reorganization).

§ 9.146
1. 28 U.S.C.A. § 158(a)(2).

§ 9.147
1. 11 U.S.C.A. § 1123(a).

CAVEAT: The practitioner should review a draft plan with care to ensure that all mandatory requirements have been satisfied. Failure to satisfy any of the mandatory requirements will be grounds for objection to the plan by any party in interest, and a bankruptcy judge generally will deny confirmation of a plan that fails to meet the requirements of Section 1123 of the Code.

§ 9.148 BANKRUPTCY Ch. 9

1. *Designate Classes of Claims and Interests.* A plan must designate classes of claims and interests,[1] other than claims for costs of administration,[2] "involuntary gap" claims,[3] and priority tax claims.[4]

2. *Specify Unimpaired Classes.* A plan must specify any class that is not impaired under the plan.[5] A plan that fails to specify unimpaired classes as required by Section 1123(a)(2) does not comply with chapter 11, as required by Section 1129(a)(1).[6]

3. *Specify Treatment of Impaired Classes.* A plan must specify the treatment of any class that is impaired under the plan.[7]

4. *Provide Same Treatment for Claims Within a Class.* A plan must provide the same treatment for claims within a particular class, unless the holder of a particular claim or interest otherwise agrees to less favorable treatment.[8]

5. *Provide for Plan Implementation.* A plan must provide adequate means for implementation of the plan,[9] which may include:

   • Retention by the debtor of all or part of the property of the estate;

   • Transfer of all or any part of the property of the estate to one or more entities (whether organized preconfirmation or postconfirmation);

§ 9.148

1. 11 U.S.C.A. § 1123(a)(1). See infra, §§ 9.152–9.154 for a discussion of the classification of claims and interests and its effect on voting to accept or reject a plan of reorganization.

2. 11 U.S.C.A. § 507(a)(1).

3. 11 U.S.C.A. § 507(a)(2). "Involuntary gap" claims are claims that arise in the ordinary course of the debtor's business or financial affairs during the period between the time an involuntary petition is filed and the time the order for relief is entered.

4. 11 U.S.C.A. § 507(a)(7). *But see* In re Eagle Bus Mfg., Inc., 134 B.R. 584 (Bankr. S.D.Tex.1991) (administrative and priority tax claims were not required to be classified in order for the chapter 11 plan to satisfy the statutory requirement that the plan designate classes of claims and interests).

5. 11 U.S.C.A. § 1123(a)(2). *See* In re Eagle Bus Mfg., Inc., 134 B.R. at 596.

6. *See* In re Polytherm Indus., Inc., 33 B.R. 823, 829 (W.D.Wis.1983).

7. 11 U.S.C.A. § 1123(a)(3). *See infra,* §§ 9.158–9.160 for discussion of impairment of claims.

8. 11 U.S.C.A. § 1123(a)(4). Some courts have not strictly enforced this requirement. *See* In re AOV Indus., 792 F.2d 1140, 1152 (D.C.Cir.1986) (Section 1123(a)(4) leaves parties and courts some flexibility in providing unequal treatment among claims, particularly when faced with a complex reorganization); In re General Homes Corp., 134 B.R. 853 (Bankr.S.D.Tex. 1991) (one rationale which will support a separate classification is the demonstrated economic need to treat certain otherwise similar claims differently); In re Eagle Bus Mfg., Inc., 134 B.R. 584, 596 (Bankr. S.D.Tex.1991); In re Monroe Well Serv., Inc., 80 B.R. 324, 335 (E.D.Pa.1987) ("equality of treatment thus becomes a matter of degree, not one of mathematical exactitude"); In re Furlow, 70 B.R. 973, 978 (Bankr.E.D.Pa.1987) (different treatment is permissible "if the debtor is able to prove a reasonable basis for the degree of discrimination contemplated by the Plan"); *but see* In re MCorp Fin., Inc., 137 B.R. 219 (Bankr.S.D.Tex.1992) (a chapter 11 plan which did not provide the same treatment for each claim or interest of a particular class, without consent of disfavored creditors, could not be confirmed).

9. 11 U.S.C.A. § 1123(a)(5).

- Merger or consolidation of the debtor with one or more persons;
- Sale of all or part of the property of the estate, either subject to or free of any lien, or the distribution of all or part of the property of the estate among those having an interest therein;
- Satisfaction or modification of any lien;
- Cancellation or modification of any indenture or similar instrument;
- Curing or waiving of any default;
- Extension of a maturity date or a change in an interest rate or other term of outstanding securities;
- Amendment of the debtor's charter; or
- Issuance of securities of the debtor or the debtor's successor under the plan.

6. *Prohibit Issuance of Nonvoting Equity Securities.* The plan must provide for the inclusion in a corporate debtor's (or its successor's) charter of incorporation a provision prohibiting the issuance of nonvoting equity securities, and providing an appropriate distribution of voting power among classes of securities possessing voting power.[10]

7. *Provide for Selection of Officers.* The plan must contain only provisions that are consistent with the interests of creditors and equity security holders and with public policy regarding the manner of selection of any officer, director, or trustee and any successors thereto.[11]

8. *Corollary Provision—Plan Implementation.* Section 1142 of the Bankruptcy Code provides that the debtor (or its successor) must carry out the plan "[n]otwithstanding any otherwise applicable nonbankruptcy law, rule, or regulation relating to financial condition."[12]

---

10. 11 U.S.C.A. § 1123(a)(6). This provision is intended to prevent creditors who must accept equity securities of the debtor from being deprived of voting power and an equitable share of control over the company. *See* Hillis Motors, Inc. v. Hawaii Automobile Dealers' Assoc., 997 F.2d 581, 593 note 22 (9th Cir.1983).

PRACTICE POINTER: Notwithstanding section 1123(a)(6), pursuant to a plan, existing equity securities may be stripped of voting rights. *See* In re Acequia, Inc., 787 F.2d 1352, 1361 (9th Cir.1986); In re Texaco Inc., 81 B.R. 806, 813 (Bankr.S.D.N.Y. 1988).

11. 11 U.S.C.A. § 1123(a)(7).

12. 11 U.S.C.A. § 1142(a). This provision is intended to prevent any party from frustrating implementation of the plan by invoking a nonbankruptcy law concerning financial condition. *See* 8 Collier on Bankruptcy ¶ 1142.02[1], at 1142–2 (L.King, ed., 15th ed.rev.1997).

§ 9.149 Chapter 11—Plan—Discretionary Provisions

The Bankruptcy Code specifically provides that a plan may:

1. *Impair or Not Impair Claims.* A plan may impair or leave unimpaired any class of claims, secured or unsecured, or a class of interests.[1]

2. *Provide for Treatment of Executory Contracts.* Subject to section 365, a plan may provide for the assumption, rejection, or assignment of any executory contract or unexpired lease of the debtor not previously rejected under § 365 of the Code.[2]

3. *Provide for Settlement of Claims.* A plan may provide for the settlement or adjustment of any claim or interest belonging to the debtor or to the estate, or the retention and enforcement by the debtor or trustee of any such claim or interest.[3]

4. *Provide for Sale of Estate Property.* A plan may provide for the sale of all or substantially all of the property of the estate, and the distribution of the proceeds among holders of claims or interests.[4]

5. *Include Other Provisions.* A plan may include any other appropriate provision not inconsistent with the applicable provisions of chapter 11.[5]

§ 9.150 Chapter 11—Plan—Exemption From Securities Registration

In order to facilitate the issuance of new securities, including debt instruments and equity in a plan of reorganization, Section 1145 of the Bankruptcy Code provides a limited safe harbor exemption from the

---

§ 9.149

1. 11 U.S.C.A. § 1123(b)(1).
2. 11 U.S.C.A. § 1123(b)(2).

PRACTICE POINTER: If a debtor wishes to reject executory contracts pursuant to a plan of reorganization, many courts will require the debtor to send a notice of rejection to those parties affected by the rejection, thereby affording them an opportunity to file a proof of claim for the damages arising from the rejection. Pursuant to Bankruptcy Rule 3002(c)(4), a date will be set by the court to provide for the filing of claims arising from the rejection.

See supra, §§ 9.74–9.81 for a discussion of the assumption, rejection, or assignment of executory contracts and unexpired leases, which are governed by Section 365 of the Bankruptcy Code.

3. 11 U.S.C.A. § 1123(b)(3). See In re Drexel Burnham Lambert Group, Inc., 138 B.R. 723 (Bankr.S.D.N.Y.1992) (the approval of a chapter 11 plan requires the court to inquire into the reasonableness of the proposed settlement, *i.e.*, whether the settlement falls below the lowest point in the range of reasonableness). The plan proponent must be prepared to introduce into evidence at the confirmation hearing facts that will support the compromise and settlement of claims as set forth in the plan.

4. 11 U.S.C.A. § 1123(b)(4). By contemplating the sale of all or substantially all of the property of the estate and the distribution of the proceeds, Section 1123(b)(4) provides for liquidating chapter 11 plans. See In re Coastal Equities, Inc., 33 B.R. 898, 904 (Bankr.S.D.Cal.1983); In re L.N. Scott Co., 13 B.R. 387 (Bankr.E.D.Pa.1981); In re WFDR, Inc., 10 B.R. 109 (Bankr.N.D.Ga. 1981).

5. 11 U.S.C.A. § 1123(b)(5).

securities laws for securities issued under a plan of reorganization and for certain other securities.[1]

§ 9.151 Chapter 11—Plan—Retention of Jurisdiction by the Court

The debtor's counsel should include a provision in the plan of reorganization specifically providing that the bankruptcy court retains jurisdiction after confirmation of a chapter 11 plan. This provision should be predicated upon (i) the court's power, pursuant to Section 105 of the Bankruptcy Code, to issue any order, process, or judgment necessary or appropriate to carry out the provisions of the Bankruptcy Code,[1] and (ii) the court's power, pursuant to Section 1142 of the Bankruptcy Code, to direct the debtor to execute or deliver any instruments required to effect a transfer of property under a plan, and to perform any other act necessary in connection with the implementation and consummation of the plan.[2]

§ 9.152 Chapter 11—Classification of Claims

The classification of claims and equity interests has a direct impact upon distributions to be made to creditors and interest holders under a chapter 11 plan. Pursuant to Section 1122(a) of the Bankruptcy Code, a plan proponent may place a claim or interest in a particular class only if it is substantially similar to other claims or interests in the class.[1] Each claim or interest within a class must be afforded the same treatment, unless a claim holder or interest holder agrees to less favorable treatment.[2] A chapter 11 plan generally affords different treatment to each class of claims and interests.

Library References:
West's Key No. Digests, Bankruptcy ⚖3550.

§ 9.153 Chapter 11—Classification of Claims—Effect on Voting

Classification also significantly affects the outcome of voting on the acceptance or rejection of the plan. After approval of a disclosure statement and the solicitation of votes by the plan proponent,[1] the holders of claims or interests in each impaired class may vote to accept

§ 9.150
1. 11 U.S.C.A. § 1145. See H.R.Rep.No. 95-595, 95th Cong., 1st Sess. 419 (1977).

§ 9.151
1. 11 U.S.C.A. § 105(a).
2. 11 U.S.C.A. § 1142. See infra, § 9.312 for an example of a plan provision for retention of jurisdiction by the bankruptcy court.

§ 9.152
1. 11 U.S.C.A. § 1122(a).
2. 11 U.S.C.A. § 1123(a)(4).

§ 9.153
1. See infra, § 9.161.

§ 9.153   BANKRUPTCY   Ch. 9

or reject the plan.[2] Acceptance by the holders of more than one-half in number and at least two-thirds in amount of the claims, or by the holders of at least two-thirds in amount of the interests, actually voted in each impaired class, constitutes acceptance by the class and binds dissident claim holders or interest holders.[3] As a consequence of this voting mechanism, and because the Bankruptcy Code requires the affirmative acceptance of the plan by at least one class of impaired claims (excluding the votes of any insiders),[4] there is an incentive for a plan proponent to "gerrymander" the membership of certain classes under the plan to ensure that at least one class of impaired claims votes to accept the plan.[5] If a class of claims or interests is improperly classified pursuant to Section 1122 of the Bankruptcy Code, then, notwithstanding acceptance by the required majority within the class, a claim holder or interest holder in the affected class may object to confirmation of the plan on the ground that the plan fails to comply with the provisions of title 11.[6]

Library References:
West's Key No. Digests, Bankruptcy ⟜3544.

§ 9.154   Chapter 11—Classification of Claims—Substantially Similar Claims

Pursuant to Section 1122(a) of the Bankruptcy Code, a plan may place a claim or an interest in a particular class only if such claim or interest is "substantially similar" to other claims or interests in the class.[1] Thus, secured and unsecured claims cannot be placed in the same class because the rights that secured creditors have against specific collateral distinguish their claims from unsecured claims.[2] Similarly, claims and equity interests cannot be placed in the same class because they represent disparate legal relationships with the debtor.

As a general rule, a plan proponent cannot separately classify similarly situated creditors for the sole purpose of creating an accepting impaired class of claimants required for confirmation under Section 1129 of the Bankruptcy Code.[3] Section 1122(a), however, does not automati-

---

2. 11 U.S.C.A. § 1126(a). Classes whose claims are unimpaired are presumed to have accepted the plan. 11 U.S.C.A. § 1126(f). Classes of claims that do not receive or retain any property under the plan are deemed to have rejected the plan. 11 U.S.C.A. § 1126(g). Accordingly, members of such classes are not entitled to vote to accept or reject the plan. 11 U.S.C.A. § 1126(f), (g).

3. 11 U.S.C.A. § 1126(c), (d).

4. 11 U.S.C.A. § 1129(a)(10).

5. *See infra*, §§ 9.165–9.166 for a discussion of the requirements for confirmation of a plan.

6. 11 U.S.C.A. § 1129(a)(1).

§ 9.154

1. 11 U.S.C.A. § 1122(a).

2. *See, e.g.,* In re Sullivan, 26 B.R. 677 (Bankr.W.D.N.Y.1982) (secured and unsecured tax claims must be separately classified).

3. *See, e.g.,* In re Lumber Exch. Bldg. Ltd., Partnership, 968 F.2d 647, 649 (8th

cally preclude separate classification of similar claims. Indeed, there is considerable authority for the proposition that, pursuant to Section 1122(a), a plan proponent may classify similar claims separately if each such classification is reasonable and rationally related to the efficacy of the proposed plan. For example, separate classification of trade creditors from other unsecured creditors has been approved as rational due to the debtor's need to foster a continuing business relationship with trade creditors.[4]

Library References:

West's Key No. Digests, Bankruptcy ⟐3552.

§ 9.155 Chapter 11—Classification of Claims—Convenience Class

Pursuant to Section 1122(b) of the Bankruptcy Code, a plan may designate a separate class of claims consisting of every unsecured claim that is less than or reduced to an amount that the court approves as reasonable and necessary for administrative convenience.[1] In practical terms, Section 1122(b) allows a plan proponent to designate a separate class of all unsecured claims below a certain dollar amount and permits creditors with larger claims to voluntarily reduce their claims to that amount. The creation of such a convenience class allows the plan proponent to offer full or partial cash payments to small creditors as an incentive to accept the plan without making the plan unfairly discriminatory to other creditors.[2]

Library References:

West's Key No. Digests, Bankruptcy ⟐3550.

§ 9.156 Chapter 11—Recourse and Nonrecourse Claims: The § 1111(b) Election

Section 1111(b) of the Bankruptcy Code states the general rule that in chapter 11 cases, an undersecured claim is treated as a recourse claim

Cir.1992); In re Bryson Properties, XVIII, 961 F.2d 496, 502 (4th Cir.1992), cert. denied 506 U.S. 866, 113 S.Ct. 191, 121 L.Ed. 2d 134 (1992); In re Greystone III Joint Venture, 995 F.2d 1274, 1279 (5th Cir. 1991), cert. denied 506 U.S. 821, 113 S.Ct. 72, 121 L.Ed.2d 37 (1992); Hanson v. First Bank of South Dakota, N.A., 828 F.2d 1310, 1313 (8th Cir.1987); In re Boston Post Road Ltd. Partnership, 145 B.R. 745, 748 (Bankr. D.Conn.1992), aff'd 21 F.3d 477 (2d Cir. 1994), cert. denied 513 U.S. 1109, 115 S.Ct. 897, 130 L.Ed.2d 782 (1995).

4. *See* In re Richard Buick, Inc., 126 B.R. 840 (Bankr.E.D.Pa.1991); In re AG Consultants Grain Division, Inc., 77 B.R. 665 (Bankr.N.D.Ind.1987); *see also* In re U.S.Truck Co., 42 B.R. 790 (Bankr. E.D.Mich.1984) (a plan proponent could separately classify a labor union's unsecured claims from other unsecured claims); In re Chateaugay Corp., 155 B.R. 625 (Bankr.S.D.N.Y.1993) (a plan proponent could separately classify individual workers' compensation claims from insurance companies' subrogated compensation claims).

§ 9.155

1. 11 U.S.C.A. § 1122(b).

2. *See* In re Realty Assocs., 53 F.Supp. 1010 (E.D.N.Y.1943).

regardless of whether the claim is a recourse claim under applicable nonbankruptcy law.[1] The recourse is embodied in the deficiency claim[2] against the debtor's assets.

Creditors with nonrecourse claims under nonbankruptcy law do not receive this benefit if the property is sold under Section 363 of the Bankruptcy Code or is to be sold pursuant to a plan of reorganization.[3] However, if the property is sold under Section 363(b) of the Bankruptcy Code, the creditor may bid at the sale, and if successful, offset the amount of its claim against the purchase price of the property.[4]

If the debtor will retain the lienholder's collateral under its plan of reorganization, an undersecured creditor may elect, under Section 1111(b)(2), to terminate its recourse status and have its claim secured in its entire allowed amount rather than bifurcated under Section 506(a) of the Code. If the Section 1111(b)(2) election applies, a creditor is entitled to have the entire amount of the related debt secured by a lien even if the value of the collateral is less than the amount of the debt. The plan must provide for payments, either present or deferred, of a principal face amount equal to the amount of the debt and of a present value, as of the effective date of the plan, equal to the value of the collateral.[5] The electing claim holder, instead of the debtor, receives the benefit of the enhanced value if the collateral appreciates in value.

If the secured claim is part of a class with other secured claims,[6] the election under Section 1111(b)(2) must be approved by two-thirds in amount and more than half in number of allowed claims within the class.[7] A class may make such an election only if the collateral is not of inconsequential value or the claimant had recourse against the debtor and the asset was not sold under Section 363 of the Code or is not to be

§ 9.156

1. A recourse creditor has the right to look to a debtor's other assets to seek payment of any deficiency between the value of its collateral and the amount of the debt it is owed. A nonrecourse creditor has the right to look only to its collateral for the payment of its debt; it has no right to seek payment of any deficiency from a debtor's other assets.

PRACTICE POINTER: The Second Circuit has ruled that an undersecured lienholder is entitled to the benefits of Section 1111(b) of the Code whether or not it is in direct contractual privity with the debtor. 680 Fifth Ave. Assocs. v. The Mutual Benefit Life Ins. Co. (In re 680 Fifth Ave. Assocs.), 29 F.3d 95 (2d Cir.1994) (mortgagee was entitled to the benefits of Section 1111(b) even though the debtor did not contractually assume the mortgage or execute a debt instrument in favor of the mortgagee when it acquired the property subject to the mortgage).

2. See 11 U.S.C.A. § 506(a); see supra, § 9.100 regarding the bifurcation of secured claims.

3. 11 U.S.C.A. § 1111(b)(1)(A)(ii).

4. 11 U.S.C.A. § 363(k). This is commonly called "bidding in" a claim.

5. 11 U.S.C.A. § 1129(a)(7)(B), 1129(b)(2)(A)(i)(II). See In re 222 Liberty Assocs., 108 B.R. 971, 993 (Bankr.E.D.Pa. 1990); 124 Cong.Rec. H 11,103 (Sept. 28, 1978); S 17,420 (Oct. 6, 1978).

6. Normally, each secured claim is separately classified. In re Sullivan, 26 B.R. 677 (Bankr.W.D.N.Y.1982). See supra, § 9.152 for a discussion of classification of claims.

7. 11 U.S.C.A. § 1111(b)(1)(A)(i).

sold under the plan.[8] A class of creditors qualified to make the election under Section 1111(b)(2) in a chapter 11 case may do so at the disclosure statement hearing[9] or at any time before the disclosure statement hearing by a signed writing. The court may grant additional time. The election is binding on all class members.[10]

Library References:

West's Key No. Digests, Bankruptcy ⚷2852.

§ 9.157 Chapter 11—Recourse and Nonrecourse Claims: The § 1111(b) Election—Strategy

A creditor who makes the Section 1111(b)(2) election forfeits its deficiency claim and the attendant right to vote[1] its deficiency claim in the class of general unsecured creditors. If, absent the Section 1111(b)(2) election, a creditor would have a large deficiency claim compared to the aggregate amount of general unsecured claims against the debtor, the creditor might be able to control the vote of the class of general unsecured creditors. This is important because at least one class of impaired claims[2] must vote to accept a chapter 11 plan in order for it to be confirmed on a cramdown (nonconsensual), rather than a consensual basis.[3] Since the class of unsecured creditors most often is intended under a plan to be the impaired class that accepts the plan, control of the vote of that class may give a creditor effective control over the entire process of plan acceptance. Thus, the creditor's ability to control the process of plan acceptance could outweigh the benefit of having its claim fully secured.[4]

On the other hand, a secured creditor might make the Section 1111(b)(2) election if (i) its deficiency claim will be too small to control

---

8. 11 U.S.C.A. § 1111(b)(1)(B).

9. *See infra*, § 9.161 for a discussion of the disclosure statement.

10. Bankr.R. 3014.

§ 9.157

1. *See infra*, § 9.162 for a discussion of voting on a plan.

2. *See infra*, §§ 9.158–9.160 for a discussion of impaired claims.

3. 11 U.S.C.A. § 1129(b)(1), 1129(a)(8). *See infra*, §§ 9.162, 9.166, respectively, for a discussion of the procedure for acceptance of a plan of reorganization on a consensual or nonconsensual basis.

4. The reason a creditor with a large deficiency claim may be able to control the plan acceptance process is that the majority of circuit courts of appeals (the Second, Third, Fourth, Fifth, and Eighth Circuits) have held that an unsecured deficiency claim is similar to other general unsecured claims and, therefore, cannot be placed in a separate class of claims in a plan of reorganization solely to achieve plan confirmation. *See, e.g.*, In re Boston Post Rd. L.P., 21 F.3d 477 (2d Cir.1994), cert. denied 513 U.S. 1109, 115 S.Ct. 897, 130 L.Ed.2d 782 (1995). Until recently, debtors frequently sought to classify a large mortgage deficiency claim separately from other general unsecured claims and provide acceptable treatment to the separate class of general unsecured claims solely to create one accepting class of impaired claims, thereby making cramdown possible. *See, e.g.*, In re D & W Realty Corp., 156 B.R. 140 (Bankr. S.D.N.Y.1993), rev'd by 165 B.R. 127 (S.D.N.Y.1994). However, the majority of circuit courts has now held that separate classification of a deficiency claim is imper-

§ 9.157   BANKRUPTCY   Ch. 9

the vote of the class of general unsecured claims; or (ii) the distribution under the plan is anticipated to be insignificant; or (iii) there is a likelihood that both the collateral will appreciate in value and the debtor will default on its obligations under the plan, thereby potentially enabling the creditor to realize the full amount of its claim from the collateral. By making the Section 1111(b)(2) election, the creditor can prevent the debtor from cashing out the creditor based upon the appraised value of its collateral rather than the full amount of its claim.[5]

§ 9.158   Chapter 11—Impairment of Claims or Interests

A creditor may only vote on a plan of reorganization if its claim is considered "impaired" under the plan because members of a class that is not impaired under a plan "are conclusively presumed to have accepted the plan."[1] The rationale behind this rule is that if a claimant's interests are unimpaired by a proposed plan, that claimant should not be able to object to the treatment of claims of other creditors under the plan. Whether a class of creditors is impaired has a particular significance in a "cramdown" setting because a plan proponent may only "cram down" a plan of reorganization over a dissenting class of creditors if at least one impaired class has voted in favor of the plan.[2]

Section 1124 of the Bankruptcy Code provides that a claim is impaired unless the plan of reorganization (1) leaves unaltered the legal, equitable, and contractual rights of the holder or (2) cures prior defaults, reinstates the maturity of the claim or interest as it existed prior to default, and compensates the holder for damages resulting from a reasonable reliance on a right to receive accelerated payments.[3] Some courts have held that if a creditor is impaired, even in the "slightest fashion," it is entitled to vote on plan confirmation.[4]

missible absent a legitimate business reason.

5. PRACTICE POINTER: To effect a cramdown on a secured creditor that makes the Section 1111(b) election, either that creditor must: (i) be accorded a claim equal to the full amount of its claim, but with deferred cash payments having a present value equal only to the value of its collateral interest or, if the "indubitable equivalent" is to be paid, (ii) receive a payment equal to the full amount of its claim. *See* In re 222 Liberty Assocs., 108 B.R. 971 (Bankr.E.D.Pa.1990). *Cf.* In re Montgomery Court Apartments, 141 B.R. 324 (Bankr. S.D.Ohio 1992).

§ 9.158

1. 11 U.S.C.A. § 1126(f).

2. 11 U.S.C.A. § 1129(a)(10), 1129(b)(1). *See infra,* § 9.166 for a discussion of cramdown.

3. 11 U.S.C.A. § 1124.

PRACTICE POINTER: Although an entire outstanding loan may have been accelerated by a default, reinstatement of the debt cures the default and deaccelerates the debt. Since curing a default takes care of the triggering event and returns the indebtedness to pre-default conditions, interest must be paid only on loan payments that came due and were unpaid during the course of the chapter 11 case, not on the entire principal. Official Committee of Manville Forest Prods. Corp. v. Manville Forest Prods. Corp. (In re Manville Forest Prods. Corp.), 60 B.R. 403 (S.D.N.Y.1986).

4. *See, e.g.,* In re American Solar King Corp., 90 B.R. 808 (Bankr.W.D.Tex.1988). *See also infra,* § 9.160 note 6 for a discussion of a decision on what constitutes impairment.

A plan is required to specify which classes of claims or interests are not impaired.[5] However, statements by a debtor that a class is not impaired are not dispositive. If a proposed plan specifies that a particular class is not impaired, that class may contest the issue of impairment.[6] A creditor or a class of creditors may assert that it is improperly treated as unimpaired by filing an objection to confirmation and arguing the issue of impairment at the confirmation hearing.[7]

Library References:

West's Key No. Digests, Bankruptcy ⊕=3551.

§ 9.159 Chapter 11—Impairment of Claims or Interests—Rights Are Altered

A claim or interest is impaired if the legal, equitable, or contractual rights of the holder are altered under the plan.[1] Courts have ruled that a plan impairs the rights of a creditor if it:

- Surrenders excess collateral;[2]
- Cancels a guarantee;[3]
- Modifies shareholder voting rights;[4] or
- Pays employees' wages in goods, rather than cash.[5]

However, a creditor's claim need not be materially and adversely affected in order to be considered impaired under Section 1124 of the Code. Indeed, courts have found impairment where the pertinent alteration resulted in the improvement of the holder's economic interest.[6]

---

5. 11 U.S.C.A. § 1123(a)(2). A plan which fails to specify unimpaired classes as required by Section 1123(a)(2) does not comply with chapter 11 and, therefore, fails to satisfy the requirements for confirmation pursuant to Section 1129(a)(1). See In re Polytherm Indus., Inc., 33 B.R. 823, 829 (W.D.Wis.1983). See also In re Drexel Burnham Lambert Group, Inc., 138 B.R. 723, 767 (Bankr.S.D.N.Y.1992) ("In accordance with § 1123(a)(2) ... the Plan specifies the impaired and unimpaired classes").

6. See, e.g., In re Jeppson, 66 B.R. 269, 294 note 179 (Bankr.D.Utah 1986).

7. In re Otero Mills, Inc., 31 B.R. 185 (Bankr.D.N.M.1983); In re Forrest Hills Assocs., Ltd., 18 B.R. 104 (Bankr.D.Del.1982). In addition to filing an objection to confirmation, a creditor wishing to contest the issue of impairment also may solicit rejections of the plan after the disclosure statement has been approved by the court. Forrest Hills Assocs., 18 B.R. 104. See infra, § 9.161 for a discussion of the disclosure statement and solicitation.

§ 9.159

1. 11 U.S.C.A. § 1124(1).

2. In re Sacred Heart Hospital, 182 B.R. 413, 424 (Bankr.E.D.Pa.1995) ("Although a secured creditor can be forced to take back its collateral in full payment of its claim ... such treatment most certainly impairs the secured claim.").

3. In re Eller Bros., Inc., 53 B.R. 10, 12 (Bankr.M.D.Tenn.1985).

4. In re Acequia, Inc., 787 F.2d 1352, 1361 (9th Cir.1986).

5. In re Wilhelm, 101 B.R. 120 (Bankr.W.D.Mo.1989) (a wage claim was impaired under a plan which proposed to satisfy part of the claim through transfer of a motor vehicle).

6. See, e.g., id.; In re Witt, 60 B.R. 556 (Bankr.N.D.Iowa 1986).

§ 9.160 Chapter 11—Impairment of Claims or Interests—Defaults Are Not Cured

A claim or interest is impaired if the plan does not cure all prepetition and postpetition defaults under the contract except those that are considered *"ipso facto"* or "bankruptcy clause" defaults.[1] The weight of authority is that, notwithstanding a judgment of foreclosure, a mortgage can be unimpaired if restored to its position on the eve of acceleration, *i.e.*, the claimant's rights under the contract, and not the judgment, are the rights to which Section 1124 applies.[2] Accordingly, defaults may be cured up to the point of a foreclosure sale. For creditors to be unimpaired, defaults are to be cured by the effective date of the plan, and a class will be impaired if the debtor takes too long to cure defaults. Some courts, however, have held that legal rights are altered and a claim impaired when a creditor has obtained a foreclosure judgment and, through an attempted reinstatement, is forced to forego payment of the judgment.[3]

In addition, the plan must reinstate the original maturity date and predefault interest rate of the obligation. Therefore, a claim is impaired if the obligation is not reinstated exactly according to its terms.[4]

Before it was repealed pursuant to the Bankruptcy Reform Act of 1994, Section 1124(3) had provided that a class of claims was unimpaired with respect to each claim of such class if, on the effective date of a plan of reorganization, the holder of such claim received cash equal to the "allowed amount of such claim."[5] Section 213(d) of the Bankruptcy Reform Act of 1994 deleted Subsection 1124(3), so full payment of an allowed claim no longer will render the claim unimpaired. This change is intended to permit creditors who are paid in full on the effective date of a plan, but who are not paid postpetition interest, to vote against the plan. Should such a class of creditors vote to reject a plan, such plan could not be confirmed consensually and would have to be shown to be "fair and equitable" under Section 1129(b) in order to be "crammed down." Additionally, since the creditors are impaired, the debtor also would have to demonstrate that such creditors were receiving at least as

---

§ 9.160

1. *See supra*, § 9.74 and note 4 and accompanying text for a discussion of *ipso facto* clauses. *See infra*, § 9.248 note 4 for a discussion of the meaning of "curing defaults" under the Bankruptcy Code.

2. In re Madison Hotel Assoc., 749 F.2d 410 (7th Cir.1984) (Section 1124(2) used to reverse an order of foreclosure under applicable state law); In re Taddeo, 685 F.2d 24 (2d Cir.1982) (chapter 13 case); *but cf.* In re DeSeno, 17 F.3d 642 (3d Cir.1994) (entry of a foreclosure judgment terminated chapter 11 debtor's right to cure default in the mortgage).

3. *See* In re Celeste Court Apartments, Inc., 47 B.R. 470 (D.Del.1985); In re St. Peter's School, 16 B.R. 404 (Bankr.S.D.N.Y. 1982).

4. *See* 11 U.S.C.A. § 1124(2)(B) and *see* In re B & B West 164th Street Corp., 147 B.R. 832 (Bankr.E.D.N.Y.1992); In re Block Shim Dev. Co.-Irving, 118 B.R. 450 (N.D.Tex.1990), aff'd 939 F.2d 289 (5th Cir. 1991).

5. 11 U.S.C.A. § 1124(3) (repealed).

much as such creditors would receive in a chapter 7 liquidation pursuant to 11 U.S.C.A. § 1129(a)(7).[6]

§ 9.161 Chapter 11—Disclosure and Solicitation

Once the debtor has drafted a proposed chapter 11 plan of reorganization and is ready to file the plan with the court, it must also file a disclosure statement with the plan or within a time fixed by the court.[1] Prior to distributing the plan, disclosure statement, and related material to the creditors for solicitation of acceptances, the debtor must obtain bankruptcy court approval of any materials to be distributed, including a disclosure statement which details, among other things, how the various classes will be treated under the proposed plan.[2] Following the filing of a disclosure statement, the court must hold a hearing on not less than twenty-five days notice to the debtor, creditors, equity security holders, and other parties in interest, to consider the disclosure statement and any objections or modifications thereto. The court will enter an order establishing a date for the hearing and may fix a deadline for filing objections to the disclosure statement.[3]

Pursuant to Section 1125 of the Bankruptcy Code, a debtor must provide its impaired creditors with "adequate information" regarding the debtor's proposed plan of reorganization. In that regard, Section 1125(a)(1) provides:

> "[A]dequate information" means information of a kind, and in sufficient detail, as far as is reasonably practicable in light of the nature and history of the debtor and the condition of the debtor's books and records, that would enable a hypothetical reasonable investor typical of holders of claims or interests of the relevant class to make an informed judgment about the plan....[4]

Thus, the debtor's disclosure statement must, as a whole, provide information that is "reasonably practicable" to permit an "informed

---

6. 140 Cong.Rec.H 10,768 (Oct. 4, 1994). The repeal of Section 1124(3) was intended to overrule In re New Valley Corp., 168 B.R. 73 (Bankr.D.N.J.1994), in which unsecured creditors were denied postpetition interest on their allowed claims *even though the debtor was solvent*. In that case, the court found that the creditors were unimpaired under Section 1124(3) and, consequently, could not vote to accept or reject the plan.

In the first published decision discussing the ramifications of this change in the Code, a bankruptcy court in Georgia concluded that a class of creditors who were to receive 95% of their allowed claims (and could have received 100% by the payment of only $154.33 more) were an impaired class that could constitute the accepting impaired class for purposes of cramdown even though the court made no finding as to the solvency or insolvency of the debtor. Equitable Life Ins. Co. v. Atlanta–Stewart Partners (In re Atlanta–Stewart Partners), 193 B.R. 79 (Bankr.N.D.Ga.1996). *See infra*, § 9.166 for a discussion of the requirements for cramdown.

§ 9.161

1. *See* Bankr.R. 3016(c).

2. *See* 11 U.S.C.A. § 1125; Bankr.R. 3016(c); *see infra*, § 9.282 for a procedural checklist for filing a plan and disclosure statement.

3. *See* Bankr.R. 3017.

4. 11 U.S.C.A. § 1125(a)(1).

§ 9.161

judgment" by impaired creditors entitled to vote on the plan of reorganization.[5]

The bankruptcy court has broad discretion in examining the adequacy of the information contained in a disclosure statement. This grant of discretion was intended to facilitate effective reorganization of a debtor in the broad range of businesses in which chapter 11 debtors engage, and the broad range of circumstances that accompany chapter 11 cases.[6] Accordingly, the determination of whether a disclosure statement contains adequate information is to be made on a case-by-case basis, focusing on the unique facts and circumstances of each case.[7] A disclosure statement generally contains the following types of information:

(a) The circumstances that gave rise to the filing of the bankruptcy petition;

(b) A complete description of the available assets and their value;

(c) The anticipated future of the debtor;

(d) The source of the information provided in the disclosure statement;

(e) A disclaimer, which typically indicates that no statements or information concerning the debtor or its assets or securities are authorized other than those set forth in the disclosure statement;

(f) The condition and performance of the debtor while in chapter 11;

(g) Information regarding claims against the estate;

---

5. CAVEAT: Note that the securities laws and any other applicable non-bankruptcy law are generally inapplicable in determining whether a disclosure statement contains adequate information; nonetheless, agencies or other officials administering securities laws may be heard on the issue of whether a disclosure statement contains adequate information. See 11 U.S.C.A. § 1125(d); In re H.B. Michelson, 141 B.R. 715, 718 (Bankr.E.D.Cal.1992). However, "such an agency or official [e.g., the SEC] may not appeal from, or otherwise seek review of, an order approving a disclosure statement." 11 U.S.C.A. § 1125(d). Nevertheless, such an agency or official "may join in an appeal by a true party in interest." H.Rep.No.95–595, 95th Cong., 1st Sess. 408 (1977).

6. "In reorganization cases, there is frequently great uncertainty. Therefore the need for flexibility is greatest." H.Rep. No.95–595, 95th Cong., 1st Sess. 408 (1977).

7. PRACTICE POINTER: Courts are averse to entertain any collateral attacks against an approved disclosure statement or a confirmed plan if the proponents of such attacks had the opportunity to be heard earlier in the case. See, e.g., Kaufman v. Public Serv. Co. (In re Public Serv. Co.), 43 F.3d 763 (1st Cir.1995), cert. denied 514 U.S. 1108, 115 S.Ct. 1959, 131 L.Ed.2d 850 (1995); Jacobson v. AEG Capital Corp., 50 F.3d 1493 (9th Cir.1995). Accordingly, creditors or equity interest holders who oppose approval of a disclosure statement or confirmation of a plan must conduct sufficient due diligence before the hearing and raise all objections at such hearing, since they probably will be barred from doing so subsequently. Likewise, plan proponents who intend to rely for protection from claims which may be asserted in the future on a bankruptcy court order approving a disclosure statement or confirming a plan should ensure that the debtor provides notice of the court proceedings and an opportunity to be heard to any party that may reasonably have an interest in or a claim against the debtor.

(h) A liquidation analysis setting forth the estimated return that creditors would receive under chapter 7;

(i) The accounting and valuation methods used to produce the financial information in the disclosure statement;

(j) Information regarding the future management of the debtor, including the amount of compensation to be paid to any insiders, directors, and/or officers of the debtor;

(k) A summary of the plan of reorganization, including a description of each class of claims or interests and a statement indicating whether or not such class is impaired under the plan, as well as a projection of the percentage recovery anticipated for each class under the plan;

(*l*) An estimate of all administrative expenses, including attorneys' fees and accountants' fees;

(m) The collectibility of any accounts receivable;

(n) Any financial information, valuations, or *pro forma* projections that would be relevant to creditors' determinations of whether to accept or reject the plan;

(o) Information relevant to the risks being taken by the creditors and interest holders;

(p) The actual or projected value that can be obtained from avoidable transfers;

(q) The existence, likelihood, and possible success of nonbankruptcy litigation;

(r) The tax consequences of the plan;

(s) The relationship of the debtor with its affiliates; and

(t) Identification of those facts favoring the settlement of claims being implemented by the plan.[8]

Notably, however, the bankruptcy court need not conduct a valuation of the debtor or an appraisal of the debtor's assets before approving a disclosure statement.[9]

It is well-established that a party objecting to a disclosure statement may only object to the adequacy of information provided for the claimant's particular class. Accordingly, a party lacks standing to object to the adequacy of information provided for a different class.[10]

Obtaining the bankruptcy court's approval of the disclosure statement is crucial because such approval is required before the plan

---

8. *See, e.g.*, In re Scioto Valley Mortgage Co., 88 B.R. 168, 170–71 (Bankr.S.D.Ohio 1988).

9. 11 U.S.C.A. § 1125(b).

10. *See* In re Scioto Valley Mortgage Co., 88 B.R. at 171; In re Adana Mortgage Bankers, Inc., 14 B.R. 29, 30 (Bankr. N.D.Ga.1981). *See also* In re Snyder, 56 B.R. 1007, 1010–11 (N.D.Ind.1986).

§ 9.161 BANKRUPTCY Ch. 9

proponent may solicit votes on a proposed plan.[11] Accordingly, the hearing on the disclosure statement "will be one of, if not the major procedural hearing in a reorganization case."[12]

Once the bankruptcy court approves the disclosure statement, the court must fix a time within which the holders of claims and interests may accept or reject the plan and may fix a date for the hearing on confirmation.[13] Bankruptcy Rule 3017(d) requires the debtor in possession, trustee, plan proponent, or clerk to mail to all creditors and equity security holders (and in a chapter 11 reorganization case, the U.S. trustee) a copy of the plan or a court-approved summary, the court-approved disclosure statement, notices of the time within which acceptances and rejections of the plan may be filed, and such other information as the court may direct.[14] At the disclosure statement hearing, the bankruptcy court also must consider procedures for transmitting the above-described documents and information to beneficial holders of stock, bonds, debentures, notes, and other securities.[15]

Library References:
West's Key No. Digests, Bankruptcy ⚖3539.1–3540.

§ 9.162 Chapter 11—Acceptance of a Plan

Section 1126 of the Bankruptcy Code establishes the methods for determining whether or not a class of creditors has voted to accept a proposed plan.[1] A class of claims has accepted a plan if such plan has been accepted by creditors that hold at least two-thirds in amount and more than one-half in number of the allowed claims of such class that have voted on the plan.[2] Notably, the two-thirds and one-half requirements are computed based on a denominator that equals the amount or number of claims that have actually been voted for or against the plan, rather than the total number and amount of claims in the class.[3] Two-

---

11. 11 U.S.C.A. § 1125(b).

12. See H.R.Rep.No.95–595, 95th Cong., 1st Sess. 227 (1977).

13. Bankr.R. 3017.

PRACTICE POINTER: In a case in which the debtor is a small business, the hearing on the disclosure statement may be combined with the hearing on confirmation of a plan. 11 U.S.C.A. § 1125(f)(3). See infra, § 9.173 for a discussion of small business reorganizations.

PRACTICE POINTER: Note that Section 1125(c) of the Bankruptcy Code provides that although the same disclosure statement shall be transmitted to each holder of a claim or interest of a particular class, "there may be transmitted different disclosure statements, differing in amount, detail, or kind of information, as between classes." 11 U.S.C.A. § 1125(c).

14. See infra, § 9.283 for a procedural checklist for solicitation of votes on a plan.

15. Bankr.R. 3017(e).

§ 9.162

1. See infra, § 9.163 for a discussion of prepackaged plans and the requirements for acceptance of such plans.

2. 11 U.S.C.A. § 1126(c). The double count by amount and number is intended to prevent a few large creditors from controlling the vote of a class.

3. See H.R.Rep.No.95–595, 95th Cong., 1st Sess. 410 (1977).

PRACTICE POINTER: There is some uncertainty concerning whether a purchas-

thirds in amount is required for acceptance of a plan by a class of interests.[4]

For cause shown, the court, after notice and a hearing, may permit a creditor or equity security holder to change or withdraw an acceptance or rejection.[5] If an objection has been filed against a claim or interest, the holder of such claim or interest will not be allowed to vote such claim or interest unless the court, after notice and a hearing, temporarily allows the claim or interest in an amount which the court deems proper for the purpose of accepting or rejecting a plan.[6]

An acceptance or rejection must be in writing. It must identify the plan or plans accepted or rejected; it must be signed by the creditor or equity security holder or an authorized agent; and it must conform to the appropriate Official Form. If more than one plan is transmitted pursuant to Bankruptcy Rule 3017, an acceptance or rejection may be filed by each creditor or equity security holder for any number of plans transmitted. If acceptances are filed for more than one plan, the creditor or equity security holder may indicate a preference or preferences among the plans so accepted.[7]

Section 1126(e) provides a means for challenging a vote that was not cast in good faith. On request of a party in interest and after notice and a hearing, the court may designate any entity whose acceptance or rejection was not in good faith, or was not solicited or procured in good faith.[8] The votes of any entities so designated are excluded from the tally of votes for acceptance or rejection of the plan.[9] For example, a plan proponent may seek to challenge a vote to reject a proposed plan as being in bad faith when the rejecting creditor is a business competitor and has an ulterior motive of destroying the debtor's business to further its own business interests.[10]

---

er of claims is entitled to a separate vote to accept or reject a plan for each claim purchased, or merely a single vote for all claims in a particular class. It is generally accepted that for purposes of counting votes, the vote of a holder of two or more publicly traded debentures counts as a single vote in a class comprised of such debentures. However, where acquired claims evidence separate obligations arising from separate, unrelated transactions, courts have held that the acquirer of such claims is entitled to one vote for each claim held. In re Concord Square Apts., 174 B.R. 71 (Bankr.S.D.Ohio 1994); In re Gilbert, 104 B.R. 206 (Bankr.W.D.Mo. 1989). The Ninth Circuit has noted that 11 U.S.C.A. § 1126(c) speaks in terms of the numbers of claims, not the number of creditors. Accordingly, it has concluded that a creditor with multiple claims is entitled to a voting right for each claim it holds. Figter Ltd. v. Teachers Ins. & Annuity Assoc. (In re Figter Ltd.), 118 F.3d 635, at 640 (9th Cir. 1997) citing Gilbert, 104 B.R. at 211 and Concord Square Apts., 174 B.R. at 74.

4. 11 U.S.C.A. § 1126(d).

5. Bankr.R. 3018.

6. Bankr.R. 3018(a).

7. Bankr.R. 3018(c).

8. 11 U.S.C.A. § 1126(e).

9. 11 U.S.C.A. § 1126(c), (d).

10. For example, in a case in the Southern District of New York, a secured creditor purchased claims for the avowed purpose of defeating plan confirmation after the court denied the creditor's motion to dismiss the case. The court found there was sufficient evidence in the record to question whether the creditor's opposition to the debtor's plan was in bad faith, "without regard to the treatment of its claim, but instead, to

§ 9.162   BANKRUPTCY   Ch. 9

As discussed above,[11] unimpaired classes and each holder of a claim or interest in such class are conclusively presumed to have accepted the plan.[12] Correspondingly, a class is deemed to have rejected a plan if the plan provides that the class members are not entitled to receive or retain any property under the plan on account of such claims or interests.[13] A vote may be changed if the change is approved by the court for cause after notice and a hearing.[14]

Library References:

West's Key No. Digests, Bankruptcy ⊙=3541.1–3547.

§ 9.163   Chapter 11—Prepackaged and Prenegotiated Plans

The Bankruptcy Code permits a party in financial distress to negotiate a plan of reorganization with its creditors and to solicit the approval of such a plan before filing a petition to commence a case, providing the party complies with any applicable nonbankruptcy law, rule, or regulation governing the adequacy of disclosure or, if there is no such regulation, with the disclosure requirements under Section 1125(a) of the Bankruptcy Code.[1] If the requisite number of creditors approve the plan (the requirements are the same as for a regular chapter 11 plan),[2] the

achieve some benefit or goal inconsistent with interests of the estate and its creditors." Consequently, the court overruled the creditor's objections to the debtor's disclosure statement and raised the question of whether the court should designate the secured creditor's vote. In re Dune Deck Owners Corp., 175 B.R. 839, 845 (Bankr. S.D.N.Y.1995). *See also* In re Applegate Property, Ltd., 133 B.R. 827 (Bankr. W.D.Tex.1991) (an insider's purchase of claims in order to ensure confirmation of a debtor's proposed chapter 11 plan and defeat a creditor's competing plan warranted disallowance of votes cast by the insider against the creditor's plan on the ground that they were neither acquired nor voted in good faith; the argument that claims were purchased only to prevent the creditor from doing the same was rejected); In re Allegheny Int'l, Inc., 118 B.R. 282 (Bankr. W.D.Pa.1990) (blocking votes were disqualified under Section 1126(e) as having been acquired in bad faith when a noncreditor intending to take over the company acquired claims, proposed plans, and acquired more claims to block confirmation of the debtor's plan). However, when an existing creditor purchases additional claims for the purpose of protecting its own existing claim, "not to secure some untoward advantage over other creditors" or for some ulterior motive, courts will not attribute bad faith to the purchase of claims to control a class vote. Figter Ltd. 118 F.3d at 638 citing Gilbert, 104 B.R. at 217. Thus, courts generally will not designate a ballot as having been cast in bad faith without evidence that the creditor acquired the claim for an improper purpose. *See, e.g.,* In re Stanley, 185 B.R. 417, 430 (Bankr.D.Conn.1995).

11. *See supra,* § 9.158.

12. 11 U.S.C.A. § 1126(f).

13. 11 U.S.C.A. § 1126(g).

14. Bankr.R. 3018(a).

§ 9.163

1. 11 U.S.C.A. § 1126(b).

2. *See* 11 U.S.C.A. § 1126; *see supra,* § 9.162. Bankruptcy Rule 3018(b) provides in pertinent part:

A holder of a claim or interest who has accepted or rejected a plan before the commencement of the case under the Code shall not be deemed to have accepted or rejected the plan if the court finds after notice and hearing that the plan was not transmitted to substantially all creditors and equity security holders of the same class, that an unreasonably short time was prescribed for such creditors and equity security holders to accept

debtor can file its petition commencing the case with a confirmable plan in hand, thereby substantially shortening the chapter 11 process. If the debtor solicits acceptances before filing its petition and files its accepted plan at the time it files its petition, the plan is called a prepackaged plan. If the debtor has negotiated the terms of a plan but wishes to commence a chapter 11 case before soliciting votes, the plan is termed a prenegotiated plan.

Prepackaged plans minimize the time and expense of operating under the constraints of the Bankruptcy Code because the most difficult and time-consuming aspects of a chapter 11 case—negotiating and gaining acceptance of a plan—have been completed before the case begins. However, such plans are not well-suited for most debtors. Even if the debtor has negotiated the terms of a reorganization plan, the debtor may be best served by commencing a chapter 11 case before soliciting votes on the plan (*i.e.*, filing a prenegotiated plan) if any of the following circumstances exist:

- Court approval of the adequacy of the debtor's disclosure statement appears necessary to avoid the expense of possibly having to resolicit votes on the plan. This may be the case if a vocal or litigious group of minority creditors is likely to challenge a prepackaged plan.

- A chapter 11 proceeding is necessary to resolve claims and disputes effectively and efficiently.

- Where a debtor has issued publicly traded securities or claims against it are being traded, a chapter 11 filing can provide the procedure for fixing its creditor constituency so that votes can be solicited effectively.

If any of the following conditions are applicable, the debtor would be better served by commencing a regular case under chapter 11:

- The debtor requires the protection of the automatic stay. This is so if a creditor has a present right to foreclose or institute other disruptive legal proceedings.

- The debtor needs to improve operating cash flow. If restructuring is necessary to improve cash flow, filing under chapter 11 permits the debtor to:

    1. Reject unfavorable executory contracts or leases.[3]
    2. Obtain cheaper working capital financing by using the superpriority provisions of the Bankruptcy Code.[4]

---

or reject the plan, or that the solicitation was not in compliance with Section 1126(b) of the Code.

[3] *See* 11 U.S.C.A. § 365; *see supra*, § 9.81.

[4] *See* 11 U.S.C.A. § 364; *see supra*, § 9.71.

3. Obtain the benefit of a moratorium on accrual of interest on unsecured debt.[5]
4. Modify or reject burdensome collective bargaining agreements.[6]
5. Modify retirement benefit obligations.[7]

- The debtor has unliquidated, contingent, or unknown claims that must be dealt with in order to reorganize successfully. In this situation, the chapter 11 process will enable the debtor to estimate claims,[8] litigate or settle claims, and establish a bar date to cut off claims.[9]

- The debtor wishes to pursue fraudulent conveyance litigation.[10] The Bankruptcy Code enables the debtor to maximize its interests in such litigation, which would be controlled by creditors outside of bankruptcy.

§ 9.164 Chapter 11—Modification of a Plan

After it distributes a proposed plan to creditors, a plan proponent may find it necessary to make changes to the plan. The proponent, however, may wish to avoid sending creditors a new disclosure statement that reflects the modification, or to resolicit votes that already have been cast by creditors in favor of the plan. There are two operative provisions that must be considered: Section 1127 of the Bankruptcy Code and Bankruptcy Rule 3019. Section 1127(a) of the Bankruptcy Code provides that a plan proponent may modify the plan at any time *before* confirmation so long as the plan as modified continues to meet the requirements of Section 1122 (proper classification of claims) and Section 1123 (specifying the mandatory and discretionary elements of a plan).[1] The modified plan also must satisfy the "adequate information" requirements of Section 1125.[2] After the plan proponent files a modification of the plan with the court, the plan as modified becomes the plan.[3]

The Bankruptcy Code provision suggests that a hearing is not necessary if the proposed modification meets the requirements of Sections 1122, 1123, and 1125, and the modified plan is filed before confirmation. However, Bankruptcy Rule 3019 provides that if a proposed modification is filed *after acceptance* but *before confirmation*, a

---

5. See 11 U.S.C.A. § 502; see supra, § 9.102.

6. See 11 U.S.C.A. § 1113; see supra, § 9.86.

7. See 11 U.S.C.A. § 1114; see supra, § 9.87.

8. See 11 U.S.C.A. § 502(c).

9. See Bankr.R. 3003(c)(3); see supra, § 9.92.

10. See 11 U.S.C.A. § 548; see supra, § 9.119.

§ 9.164

1. 11 U.S.C.A. § 1127(a). Practitioners should also consult the applicable local Bankruptcy Rules.

2. 11 U.S.C.A. § 1127(c).

3. 11 U.S.C.A. § 1127(a).

hearing is necessary, and the court must find that the proposed modification does not adversely change the treatment of any creditor or equity security holder who has not accepted in writing the modification.

In accordance with Bankruptcy Rule 3019, if the court determines, after a hearing on notice to the trustee, to any committee appointed under the Code, and to any other entity designated by the court, that the proposed modification does not "adversely change the treatment of the claim of any creditor or the interest of any equity security holder who has not accepted in writing the modification, it shall be deemed accepted by all creditors and equity security holders who have previously accepted the plan." Any holder of a claim or interest that has accepted or rejected a plan is deemed to have accepted or rejected, as the case may be, the modified plan unless such holder changes its previous acceptance or rejection within the time fixed by the court.[4] Pursuant to Section 1127(b) of the Bankruptcy Code, the plan proponent may modify a plan *after* confirmation but before substantial consummation[5] if: (i) the modified plan continues to meet the requirements of Sections 1122 and 1123; (ii) the court finds that circumstances warrant such modification; and (iii) the court, after notice and a hearing, confirms the modified plan.[6]

Library References:

West's Key No. Digests, Bankruptcy ⇐3569.

§ 9.165 Chapter 11—Confirmation

The bankruptcy court will confirm a plan only if all of the requirements enumerated under Section 1129(a) of the Bankruptcy Code are met:

1. *Plan Complies with Title 11*. The plan must comply with all applicable provisions of title 11;[1]

2. *Plan Proponent Complies with Title 11*. The plan proponent must comply with all of the applicable provisions of title 11 (*e.g.*, complying with the disclosure requirements when soliciting acceptance of its plan);[2]

3. *Good Faith*. The plan must have been proposed in good faith and not by any means forbidden by law;[3]

4. *Certain Payments Must Be Subject to Court Approval as Reasonable*. Any payment made or to be made by the plan propo-

---

4. 11 U.S.C.A. § 1127(d).

5. *See infra*, § 9.172 for a discussion of substantial consummation.

6. 11 U.S.C.A. § 1127(b).

§ 9.165

1. 11 U.S.C.A. § 1129(a)(1).
2. 11 U.S.C.A. § 1129(a)(2).
3. 11 U.S.C.A. § 1129(a)(3).

§ 9.165 BANKRUPTCY Ch. 9

nent, by the debtor, or by a person issuing securities or acquiring property under the plan, for services or for costs and expenses in connection with the case or the plan must be found reasonable by the court;[4]

5. *Identity of Directors, Officers, and Insiders Must Be Disclosed.* The debtor must disclose the identity and affiliations of any individual proposed to serve postconfirmation as a director, officer, voting trustee, successor, or affiliate of the debtor. The proponent also must disclose the identity and compensation of any insider who will be employed or retained by the reorganized debtor. Such employment must be consistent with the interests of creditors and equity security holders and with public policy;[5]

6. *Rate Approvals.* Any governmental regulatory commission with jurisdiction over the rates of the debtor must have approved any rate change provided for in the plan or such rate change may be expressly conditioned on such approval;[6]

7. *Protection Afforded the Dissenting Members of an Impaired Accepting Class.* In each impaired class, each holder (i) must have accepted the plan; or (ii) will receive or retain under the plan on account of such claim or interest, property of a value, as of the effective date of the plan, that is not less than the amount such holder would receive or retain if the debtor were liquidated under chapter 7. This requirement, known as the "best interest of creditors" test, is applicable to secured and unsecured creditors alike;[7]

8. *Acceptance or Non–Impairment.* In order for a plan to be confirmed on a consensual basis, every impaired class must have accepted the plan,[8] and all other requirements under 11 U.S.C.A. § 1129(a) must be met. However, as noted below under number 10, as long as one impaired class has accepted the plan, the plan may be confirmed on a nonconsensual or "cramdown" basis under 11 U.S.C.A. § 1129(b);[9]

9. *Mandatory Treatment of Certain Priority Claims.* Unless the holder of a particular claim has agreed to different treatment, the plan must provide to holders of:

4. 11 U.S.C.A. § 1129(a)(4). This is to ensure that holders of claims or interests are aware of facts which might affect their voting on a plan, such as postpetition claims for services or payments to certain creditors outside the framework of the plan.

5. 11 U.S.C.A. § 1129(a)(5).

6. 11 U.S.C.A. § 1129(a)(6).

7. 11 U.S.C.A. § 1129(a)(7)(A).

8. 11 U.S.C.A. § 1129(a)(8).

9. *See infra,* § 9.166 for a discussion of cramdown.

a. *Administrative*[10] and *"involuntary gap" claims*:[11] On the effective date of the plan, full cash payment equal to the allowed amount of their claims;[12]

b. *Wage priority*,[13] *employee benefit contribution*,[14] *grain and fish reclamation*,[15] and *consumer deposit priority claims*:[16]

   (i) *If their class accepts the plan*: deferred cash payments of a value, as of the effective date of the plan, equal to the allowed amount of such claims;[17] or

   (ii) *If their class rejects the plan*: cash on the effective date of the plan equal to the allowed amount of such claims;[18]

c. *Priority tax claims*: Deferred cash payments over a period not exceeding six years after the date of assessment of the claim, such payments to have a value as of the effective date of the plan equal to the allowed amount of such claim;[19]

10. *Minimum of One Class Must Accept the Plan*: If a class of claims is impaired under the plan, at least one class of impaired claims must have accepted the plan, excluding acceptance votes by any insider.[20] This provision makes available a "cramdown" procedure;[21]

11. *Feasibility Standard*: Unless the plan contemplates a liquidation of the debtor, the court must determine that its implementation is not likely to result in a liquidation or the need for further reorganization of the debtor or any successor to the debtor under the plan.[22] In determining feasibility, a proposed

---

10. See 11 U.S.C.A. § 507(a)(1); *see supra*, § 9.98 for a discussion of administrative claims.

11. See 11 U.S.C.A. § 507(a)(2); *see supra*, § 9.91 for a description of involuntary gap claims.

12. 11 U.S.C.A. § 1129(a)(9)(A).

13. See 11 U.S.C.A. § 507(a)(3).

14. See 11 U.S.C.A. § 507(a)(4).

15. See 11 U.S.C.A. § 507(a)(5).

16. See 11 U.S.C.A. § 507(a)(6).

17. 11 U.S.C.A. § 1129(a)(9)(B)(i).

18. 11 U.S.C.A. § 1129(a)(9)(B)(ii).

19. 11 U.S.C.A. § 1129(a)(9)(C).

20. 11 U.S.C.A. § 1129(a)(10). See 11 U.S.C.A. § 101(31) for the definition of "insider" and *see supra*, § 9.29 note 8 for a brief description of "insider" under the Bankruptcy Code.

CAVEAT: Votes by corporations related to the debtor are excluded as insider votes. In re Featherworks Corp., 25 B.R. 634 (Bankr.E.D.N.Y.1982), aff'd 36 B.R. 460 (E.D.N.Y.1984). So are votes by certain shareholders. In re Future Energy Corp., 83 B.R. 470 (Bankr.S.D.Ohio 1988). One court has held that unsecured creditor claims that were purchased by an insider were insider claims and should be disregarded in determining the vote of an impaired class. In re Applegate Property, 133 B.R. 827 (Bankr.W.D.Tex.1991).

21. *See infra*, § 9.166 for a discussion of cramdown.

22. 11 U.S.C.A. § 1129(a)(11).

plan should be scrutinized carefully to determine whether it offers a reasonable prospect of success and is workable;[23]

12. *Payment of Fees*: The debtor must have paid all bankruptcy fees and costs required under 28 U.S.C.A. § 1930, including filing fees and quarterly fees payable to the office of the United States trustee, or the plan must provide for payment of such fees on the effective date;[24]

13. *Continuation of Retiree Benefits*: The plan must provide for the continuation after its effective date of payment of all retiree benefits[25] for the duration of the period the debtor has obligated itself to provide such benefits.[26]

Library References:

West's Key No. Digests, Bankruptcy ⊕3566.1–3568(3).

§ 9.166 Chapter 11—Cramdown

The Bankruptcy Code also provides a means for confirming a plan even when a class of creditors has voted to reject a plan. Section 1129(b) allows for a plan proponent to "cram down" a plan on a dissenting class of creditors, provided that certain safeguards are satisfied. Thus, even if all impaired classes do not accept the plan, as required for confirmation on a consensual basis,[1] a proponent may nonetheless obtain confirmation if all of the other requirements under Section 1129(a)[2] are satisfied and (1) the proponent requests the court to confirm its plan; (2) at least one impaired class accepts the plan; (3) the plan does not discriminate unfairly against non-accepting impaired classes; and (4) the plan is fair and equitable to non-accepting impaired classes.[3]

In essence, a plan does not "discriminate unfairly" with respect to a dissenting class if the plan treats such class in a manner consistent with the treatment of other classes, based on their relative priority. Because the satisfaction of this requirement depends on the treatment of the dissenting class *relative* to the treatment of other classes, it must be viewed from the perspective of the dissenting class whose treatment is at

---

23. See In re Johns–Manville, 68 B.R. 618, 635 (Bankr.S.D.N.Y.1986), aff'd 78 B.R. 407, aff'd sub nom. Kane v. Johns–Manville Corp., 843 F.2d 636 (2d Cir.1988); In re Merrimack Valley Oil Co., 32 B.R. 485, 488 (Bankr.D.Mass.1983); In re Nite Lite Inns, 17 B.R. 367 (Bankr.S.D.Cal. 1982).

24. 11 U.S.C.A. § 1129(a)(12).

25. The term "retiree benefits" is defined at 11 U.S.C.A. § 1114(a). The level of benefits to be paid may only be modified by agreement of the authorized representative of the recipients or by court order. 11 U.S.C.A. § 1114(e)(1)(B) or (g). *See supra*, § 9.87.

26. 11 U.S.C.A. § 1129(a)(12).

§ 9.166

1. *See* 11 U.S.C.A. § 1129(a)(8).

2. *See supra*, § 9.165 for a discussion of the requirements for consensual confirmation set forth at Section 1129(a).

3. 11 U.S.C.A. § 1129(b)(1).

issue.[4] Some courts hold that claims of similar legal character must all be treated alike except in situations when equitable subordination or administrative convenience applies. Other courts have held that for discriminatory treatment of claims to be fair, four tests must be satisfied: (i) there is a reasonable basis for discriminating, (ii) the debtor cannot consummate the plan without discrimination, (iii) the discrimination is proposed in good faith, and (iv) the degree of discrimination is in direct proportion to its rationale.[5]

The fair and equitable test is intended to ensure that relative priorities of payment are preserved by mandating that no junior class or interest may receive anything under a plan unless all dissenting senior classes have been paid in full.[6] For a plan to be "fair and equitable," senior creditors must be paid in full before junior creditors receive any distributions, and unsecured and undersecured creditors' claims must be fully paid before equity holders may participate in any recovery. This requirement is known as the "absolute priority" rule.

The minimal requirements for determining whether a plan is "fair and equitable" are set forth in Section 1129(b)(2).[7] To be fair and equitable to a dissenting class of secured creditors, the Code requires that the creditors (i) retain the liens securing their claims and receive deferred cash payments with a present value as of the effective date of the plan equal to at least the value of the liens;[8] or (ii) if the debtor sells

4. To understand the requirement that a plan not "discriminate unfairly," counsel should read the explanation and examples contained in the House report interpreting that requirement. *See* H.R.Rep.No. 95–595, 95th Cong., 1st Sess. 416–17 (1977).

5. *See, e.g.*, In re Buttonwood Partners, Ltd., 111 B.R. 57 (Bankr.S.D.N.Y.1990).

6. 11 U.S.C.A. § 1129(b)(2).

7. **CAVEAT:** Although a plan which does not meet the standards set forth in Section 1129(b)(2) cannot be "fair and equitable," the Fifth Circuit has held that "technical compliance with all the requirements in § 1129(b)(2) does not assure that a plan is 'fair and equitable.'" In re D & F Constr. Inc., 865 F.2d 673, 675 (5th Cir.1989). Rather, a court "must consider the entire plan in the context of the rights of the creditors under state law and the particular facts and circumstances when determining whether a plan is 'fair and equitable.'" *Id. See also* In re Cellular Information Sys., Inc., 171 B.R. 926, 937 (Bankr.S.D.N.Y.1994) (quoting the Fifth Circuit's statement that "technical compliance with all the requirements in § 1129(b)(2) does not assure that the plan is 'fair and equitable'").

8. *See infra*, § 9.251 note 3 for a detailed discussion of the divergent circuit court decisions and the Supreme Court's ruling concerning the valuation of a secured creditor's collateral for purposes of confirming a cramdown plan.

To ensure that a creditor will receive payments equal to the present value of its claim, the payments must reflect the time value of money. In other words, the stream of payments must include interest at an appropriate rate to compensate the secured creditor for the delay in receiving the principal amount that it would have received upon confirmation if the collateral had been liquidated. Thus, for a cramdown plan to be confirmable, the Bankruptcy Code seeks to put a secured creditor in the same economic position that it would have been in if it had been allowed to foreclose on its collateral or if the debtor had surrendered the collateral to the creditor on the effective date of the plan.

A split among the circuit courts of appeals has developed concerning the proper determination of the rate of interest that will provide a creditor with the present value of its allowed claim. All the circuit courts that have addressed the issue have

§ 9.166 BANKRUPTCY Ch. 9

secured property free and clear of the liens thereon, the liens must attach to the proceeds of the sale, and the proceeds must satisfy the requirements of (i) or (iii); or (iii) the creditors may receive the "indubitable equivalent" of the value of their liens.[9] The term "indubitable equivalent" represents a codification of prior case law,[10] and usually involves a highly fact-specific inquiry by which the court must value both the claim and what is proffered in exchange.

To be fair and equitable to a dissenting class of unsecured creditors, that is, to satisfy the "absolute priority rule," a plan must either allow the creditors to receive or retain property equal to the allowed amount of their claims, that is, a distribution equal to 100% of their claims (with interest if payment is deferred); or provide that no holder junior to the affected class receives or retains anything of value under the plan.[11]

---

concluded that the creditor is entitled to the market rate of interest. However, the different approaches to determining the market rate produce claim treatment that is far from uniform.

The Second Circuit has held that the "market rate" of interest "should be fixed at the rate on a United States Treasury instrument with a maturity equivalent to the repayment schedule under the debtor's reorganization plan." General Motors Acceptance Corp. v. Valenti (*In re Valenti*), 105 F.3d 55, 64 (2d Cir.1997). The court noted that the value of a creditor's claim should not include any degree of profit, but held that the interest rate should include a premium to reflect the risk to the creditor of receiving deferred payments. The court held that a risk premium of from one to three percent is reasonable, but it left it to the bankruptcy court to determine the actual rate, depending on the circumstances of the debtor, including prior credit history and the viability of the reorganization plan. *Id.*

The "T-bill" rate adopted by the Second Circuit to satisfy the Bankruptcy Code's present value requirement will result in a smaller allowed claim for a secured creditor than would result in the majority of other circuits. The Second Circuit explicitly rejected the approach adopted by the majority of circuit courts, the "forced loan" approach. Under that approach, which analogizes the cramdown of a secured creditor to a forced loan, the creditor can only be placed in the same position it would have been in but for the cramdown if it is compensated at the prevailing market rate for a loan of a similar character, amount, and duration, considering the quality of the security and the risk of subsequent default.

See, e.g., Koopmans v. Farm Credit Services, 102 F.3d 874 (7th Cir.1996); General Motors Acceptance Corp. v. Jones, 999 F.2d 63 (3d Cir.1993).

9. 11 U.S.C.A. § 1129(b)(2)(A)(iii).

10. *See supra*, § 9.57 note 1 for the origin of the term.

11. **PRACTICE POINTER**: The absolute priority rule applies only to dissenting classes. Therefore, if only the junior class dissents, and there is no intermediate dissenting class, the plan still may satisfy the absolute priority rule.

CAVEAT: Prior to the enactment of the Bankruptcy Code, a judicial rule called the "new value exception" developed under the former Bankruptcy Act. The exception permitted a debtor's shareholders or partners to make a contribution of new capital as part of a plan of reorganization and, in exchange, retain some or all of the ownership interest in the reorganized entity even though some creditors would not be repaid in full under the plan. Ordinarily, without application of the new value exception, the Bankruptcy Code's "absolute priority rule" would prevent equity holders from retaining any interest in a reorganized company if under the plan of reorganization creditors do not receive a distribution equal to 100% of their claims (with interest if payment is deferred). This is because the "absolute priority rule" can only be satisfied if no distribution under the plan or participation right in the reorganized entity is accorded to any creditors or equity holders on account of their claims if those claims are junior to a class of dissenting creditors who are not being paid in full on the plan's effective date. *See* 11 U.S.C.A. § 1129(b)(2)(B)(ii).

Courts generally will not allow a plan proponent to artificially create an impaired class that will vote to accept a plan solely to be able to impose a cramdown. The majority of the circuit courts that have addressed the issue have prohibited attempts to separately classify similarly situated claims without a legitimate business reason, holding that separate classification to gerrymander an affirmative vote is impermissible.[12]

A party who wishes to object to confirmation must follow the procedures established under Bankruptcy Rule 3020(b)(1). The rule provides that any objections to a plan must be filed and served on the debtor, the trustee, the plan proponent, any statutory committee that has been appointed, and any other entity designated by the court, within a period fixed by the court. Only parties who are directly and adversely affected by a plan have standing to object to confirmation based upon those provisions that directly affect their interests.[13] If no objection is filed, the court may find, without taking proof, that the plan has been proposed in good faith and not by any means forbidden by law.[14]

The so-called "new value exception" provides that equity holders may retain an interest under a plan if they offer value that is (1) new, (2) substantial, (3) money or money's worth, (4) necessary for a successful reorganization, and (5) reasonably equivalent to the value or interest received. Because the exception was expressly authorized under the Bankruptcy Act, but is not codified under the present Bankruptcy Code, courts are divided as to whether or not the "new value exception" has survived the enactment of the Bankruptcy Code. However, the majority of courts that have ruled on the issue have held that the exception has survived.

The Ninth Circuit, which is the only court of appeals that has addressed the issue, has affirmed the continued existence of the new value exception under the Bankruptcy Code. In re Bonner Mall Partnership, 2 F.3d 899 (9th Cir.1993), cert. granted sub nom. U.S. Bancorp Mortg. Co. v. Bonner Mall Partnership, 510 U.S. 1039, 114 S.Ct. 681, 126 L.Ed.2d 648 (1994), motion to vacate denied and appeal dismissed 513 U.S. 18, 115 S.Ct. 386, 130 L.Ed.2d 233 (1994). The *Bonner Mall* case was due to be heard by the Supreme Court on *certiorari* but was rendered moot when the parties settled. Nevertheless, the Supreme Court refused to vacate the Ninth Circuit's decision, stating, "Judicial precedents are presumptively correct and valuable to the legal community as a whole." 513 U.S. at 25, 115 S.Ct. at 392.

The District Court for the Southern District of New York has held that a debtor must demonstrate that there was a diligent search for alternate sources of funding and that the opportunity to invest was exposed to the market before the court can find that a capital contribution *by former equity holders* was "necessary" for a successful reorganization. BT/SAP Pool C Assocs., L.P. v. Coltex Loop Central Three Partners, L.P., 203 B.R. 527 (S.D.N.Y.1996).

12. *See, e.g.*, Boston Post Road Ltd. Partnership v. F.D.I.C. (In re Boston Post Road Ltd. Partnership), 21 F.3d 477 (2d Cir.1994), cert. denied 513 U.S. 1109, 115 S.Ct. 897, 130 L.Ed.2d 782 (1995); Phoenix Mut. Life Ins. Co. v. Greystone III Joint Venture (In re Greystone III Joint Venture), 995 F.2d 1274 (5th Cir.1991), cert. denied 506 U.S. 821, 113 S.Ct. 72, 121 L.Ed.2d 37 (1992).

CAVEAT: The issue of what constitutes impairment may have to be redetermined based on the 1994 amendments to the Bankruptcy Code. *See supra*, § 9.160 note 6 for reference to a case that has addressed this issue.

13. In re Johns–Manville Corp., 68 B.R. 618, 623–24 (Bankr.S.D.N.Y.1986), aff'd 78 B.R. 407 (S.D.N.Y.1987), aff'd 843 F.2d 636 (2d Cir.1988).

14. Bankr.R. 3020(b)(2).

Library References:

West's Key No. Digests, Bankruptcy ⚖3563.1–3565.

§ 9.167 Chapter 11—Effect of Confirmation

The provisions of a confirmed plan bind the debtor, as well as any entity issuing securities under the plan, any entity acquiring property under the plan, and any creditor, equity security holder, or general partner of, the debtor, whether or not the claim or interest of such person is impaired under the plan and whether or not such person has accepted the plan.[1] Accordingly, a debtor will be equitably estopped from attacking the validity of a plan which it proposed, or for which it sought confirmation, or from which it derived substantial benefits.[2] The confirmation of a plan vests all the property of the estate in the reorganized debtor unless otherwise provided in the plan or in the order confirming the plan.[3] This section enables a debtor to include language in the plan and the order confirming the plan which authorizes the bankruptcy court to retain limited jurisdiction over matters that may need to be addressed after confirmation. In addition, a plan and confirmation order may specifically provide for bankruptcy court jurisdiction over actions pending at the time of confirmation and any assets recovered as a result of these actions. Section 1141 further provides that, except as otherwise provided in the plan or in the order confirming the plan, the property dealt with by the plan is free and clear of all claims and interests of creditors, equity security holders, and of general partners in the debtor.[4]

§ 9.167

1. 11 U.S.C.A. § 1141(a).

2. **CAVEAT**: A confirmed plan is accorded *res judicata* effect with respect to all matters relevant to confirmation. Stoll v. Gottlieb, 305 U.S. 165, 59 S.Ct. 134, 83 L.Ed. 104 (1938), reh'g denied 305 U.S. 675, 59 S.Ct. 250, 83 L.Ed. 437 (1938) (an order confirming a plan of reorganization that cancelled a personal guaranty of the debtor's bonds held *res judicata* even though the bankruptcy court had lacked subject matter jurisdiction to release the guaranty); Republic Supply Co. v. Shoaf, 815 F.2d 1046 (5th Cir.1987) (the doctrine of *res judicata* barred a creditor's suit against a nondebtor third party to enforce a guaranty that was released under a confirmed reorganization plan); In re Henderberg, 108 B.R. 407 (Bankr.N.D.N.Y.1989) (a confirmation order is accorded *res judicata* effect with respect to all matters relevant to confirmation, whether raised or not; therefore, it is binding on all creditors who had notice, including local taxing authorities whose prepetition tax liens were extinguished under the plan); In re Penn–Dixie Indus., 32 B.R. 173 (Bankr.S.D.N.Y.1983) (the doctrine of *res judicata* barred a motion by taxing authorities to amend a tax order incorporated in the confirmed plan).

3. 11 U.S.C.A. § 1141(b).

4. 11 U.S.C.A. § 1141(c).

CAVEAT: Courts are divided as to whether a prepetition lien is preserved where a plan or confirmation order does not explicitly provide for that result. *Compare* In re Penrod, 50 F.3d 459, 462–63 (7th Cir.1995) (where a plan of reorganization provides for the payment of a secured creditor's claim but does not say whether the lien is extinguished, the default rule is "extinction"), *with* Cen–Pen Corp. v. Hanson, 58 F.3d 89 (4th Cir.1995) (in a chapter 13 case, the debtor could not invalidate a lien merely by providing that the lien of a creditor who did not file a proof of claim would be voided upon confirmation of the plan). *See also* J. Rapisardi, *Attention Lenders: Liens May Not Be As Secure As You Thought*, N.Y.L.J., 7/24/95, p.1, col.1. (analyzing In re Penrod).

Library References:

West's Key No. Digests, Bankruptcy ⟸3568(1)–3568(3).

§ 9.168 Chapter 11—Discharge

A fundamental goal of the Bankruptcy Code is to provide a debtor with a "fresh start" upon emerging from bankruptcy or reorganization. Integral to such objective is the bankruptcy discharge of prebankruptcy debts and liabilities in accordance with the Bankruptcy Code. A discharge is generally obtained upon confirmation of a chapter 11 plan and the occurrence of the "effective date" of such plan. Subject to certain exceptions, Section 1141(d) discharges the debtor from any liability on claims that arose prior to confirmation of the plan, including those traceable to a tax claim, or to the rejection of executory contracts or unexpired leases, or to the recovery of property.[1]

Each chapter of the Bankruptcy Code includes a provision that specifically concerns discharge under that chapter. In addition, the Bankruptcy Code includes certain sections that govern exceptions to discharge[2] and the effect of a discharge under any chapter of the Code. Section 524 of the Bankruptcy Code, applicable to all chapters of the Code, sets forth detailed provisions concerning the effect of a discharge. Among other things, it provides that a discharge voids any judgment to the extent that it is a determination of a debtor's personal liability for a prepetition debt.[3] It also enjoins any action to collect, recover, or offset any discharged debt as a personal liability of the debtor.[4] In addition, Section 525 of the Bankruptcy Code promotes the policy goal of affording a debtor a "fresh start" by prohibiting governmental units and private employers from engaging in certain forms of discriminatory treatment against a person solely because of bankruptcy, insolvency, or nonpayment of a discharged or dischargeable debt.[5]

Library References:

West's Key No. Digests, Bankruptcy ⟸3568(3).

§ 9.169 Chapter 11—Discharge—Limitations

The confirmation of a plan does not discharge an individual debtor from nondischargeable debts under Section 523, including certain taxes, unscheduled debts, child support, fines, debts arising from fraud, and debts arising from certain judgments.[1] Moreover, the confirmation of a

---

§ 9.168

1. 11 U.S.C.A. § 1141(d)(1)(A).
2. *See* 11 U.S.C.A. § 523 and *infra*, § 9.169.
3. 11 U.S.C.A. § 524(a)(1).
4. 11 U.S.C.A. § 524(a)(2).
5. 11 U.S.C.A. § 525. *See supra*, § 9.132 for a discussion of this provision.

§ 9.169

1. 11 U.S.C.A. § 1141(d)(2). *See infra*, § 9.207 for a discussion of debts that are excepted from discharge under 11 U.S.C.A. § 523.

§ 9.169　　　　　　　　　　BANKRUPTCY　　　　　　　　　　Ch. 9

plan will not discharge a debtor if (i) the plan is a liquidating plan, (ii) the debtor does not engage in business after consummation of a plan, and (iii) the debtor would be denied a discharge under Section 727(a)[2] if the case were a case under chapter 7.[3]

Additionally, due process requires the providing of reasonable notice to those parties whose claims are to be discharged. Thus, an issue arises as to whether the claims may be discharged of creditors who did not receive actual notice of the deadline for filing claims (the bar date). The general rule is that claimants known to the debtor to be actual or potential claimants are entitled to actual notice of the bar date. If actual notice is not given to such claimants, due process is not satisfied, and the claims of the creditors will not be discharged upon confirmation. However, claimants who could not be personally identified with reasonable effort are not entitled to actual personal notice of the bar date but are, instead, merely entitled to notice which was reasonably calculated, under all the circumstances, to apprise them of the pendency of the action and to afford them an opportunity to present their objections (*i.e.*, notice by publication). Thus, the claims of claimants who do not file proofs of claim may be discharged.[4] Courts also have considered whether claims that are based on events occurring or contracts entered into prior to the filing of a petition under chapter 11, but which do not become manifest until after the confirmation date, may be discharged. Certain courts have held that such future claims may not be discharged in a bankruptcy proceeding.[5]

In addition to the limits on dischargeable debts, Section 523 lists a number of specific types of debts which are nondischargeable, including debts:[6] for certain taxes or customs duties; that were obtained by false pretenses, a false representation, or actual fraud; for alimony, child support, or debts assumed in the context of a divorce or separation

---

2. That is, the debtor is not an individual or has committed an act that denies discharge.

3. 11 U.S.C.A. § 1141(d)(3).

4. *See* Texaco Inc. v. Sanders (In re Texaco Inc.), 182 B.R. 937 (Bankr.S.D.N.Y. 1995).

5. *See* Lemelle v. Universal Mfg. Corp., 18 F.3d 1268 (5th Cir.1994); Waterman Steamship Corp. v. Aguiar (In re Waterman Steamship Corp.), 157 B.R. 220 (S.D.N.Y. 1993), on remand 200 B.R. 770 (Bankr. S.D.N.Y.1996). *But see* In re Fairchild Aircraft Corp., 184 B.R. 910 (Bankr.W.D.Tex. 1995) (declining to discharge claims that would have been future claims at the time of plan confirmation but holding that future claims could have been discharged if the debtor had provided potential future claimants with adequate notice and a means for filing claims against the estate). However, in a case where a legal representative was appointed to represent future claimants and filed a proof of claim on their behalf, the Eleventh Circuit found that the scope of a bankruptcy "claim" could not extend to unidentified and unidentifiable individuals with no discernible preconfirmation relationship with the debtor. Epstein v. Official Comm. of Unsecured Creditors of the Estate of Piper Aircraft Corp., 58 F.3d 1573 (11th Cir.1995).

6. *See* 11 U.S.C.A. § 523 for the complete list of debts excepted from discharge under this section.

agreement;[7] for wilful and malicious injury; for a fine, penalty, or forfeiture payable to a governmental unit; for student loans made, insured, or guaranteed by the government; or for death or personal injury claims arising from the debtor's driving while intoxicated.

In a chapter 7, 11, or 12 case, the deadline for filing a complaint under Section 523(c) to determine the dischargeability of a particular debt is 60 days after the first date set for the meeting of creditors held pursuant to Section 341 of the Bankruptcy Code.[8] In any case under title 11, the court must give all creditors not less than 30 days notice.[9] A creditor's complaint objecting to the discharge of a particular claim is an adversary proceeding under Bankruptcy Rule 7001.[10]

In a chapter 11 case, a complaint objecting to the debtor's discharge under Section 727(a) of the Bankruptcy Code must be filed not later than the first date set for the hearing on confirmation. Not less than 25 days notice must be given to the U.S. trustee, all creditors on the list created pursuant to Bankruptcy Rule 2002, and to the trustee and the trustee's attorney.[11]

§ 9.170 Chapter 11—Discharge—Release of Nondebtor

Section 524(e) of the Bankruptcy Code provides that "discharge of a debt of the debtor does not affect the liability of any other entity on, or the property of any other entity for, such debt."[1] Additionally, a number of decisions have held that Section 524(e) of the Bankruptcy Code (or its predecessor, Section 16 of the former Bankruptcy Act of 1898) prohibits the bankruptcy court from either authorizing the release of a nondebtor party or permanently enjoining suits against a nondebtor.[2] However, the Bankruptcy Code does not specifically preclude the possibility of effecting the release of claims against third parties as part of a bankruptcy

---

7. See 11 U.S.C.A. § 523(a)(15). See generally Scheinkman, New York Law of Domestic Relations, (West 1997) Ch. 26, "Impact of Bankruptcy upon Matrimonial Law."

8. Bankr.R. 4007(c). On motion of a party in interest after a hearing on notice, the court, for cause, and before the time has expired, may extend the time to file complaints to determine dischargeability. Id. See supra, § 9.37 for a discussion of the meeting of creditors.

9. Bankr.R. 4007(c).

10. See supra, § 9.16 for a discussion of adversary proceedings, and infra, §§ 9.266, 9.288 for procedural and drafting checklists for the commencement of an adversary proceeding.

11. Bankr.R. 4004(a).

§ 9.170

1. 11 U.S.C.A. § 524(e).

2. See, e.g., Resorts International, Inc. v. Lowenschuss (In re Lowenschuss), 67 F.3d 1394, 1401 (9th Cir.1995), cert. denied ___ U.S. ___, 116 S.Ct. 2497, 135 L.Ed.2d 189 (1996). Landsing Diversified Properties–II v. First Nat'l Bank and Trust Co. (In re Western Real Estate Fund, Inc.), 922 F.2d 592, 601–02 (10th Cir.1990), modified, sub nom. Abel v. West, 932 F.2d 898 (10th Cir.1991); Underhill v. Royal, 769 F.2d 1426 (9th Cir.1985); Union Carbide Corp. v. Newboles, 686 F.2d 593 (7th Cir.1982); In re Consolidated Motor Inns, 666 F.2d 189, 191 (5th Cir.1982) (en banc), cert. denied sub nom. Consolidated Motor Inns v. BVA Credit Corp., 457 U.S. 1140, 102 S.Ct. 2973, 73 L.Ed.2d 1359 (1982).

case, particularly a reorganization case. Thus, several decisions have interpreted the lack of any express prohibition against releasing non-debtor third parties in Section 524(e) as meaning that releases and/or injunctions are not *per se* prohibited. Some of the factors that courts consider in granting third-party releases and/or injunctions are:

- The non-debtor third party has provided specific consideration in exchange for a release/injunction (by, for example, contributing value to the debtor's reorganization);[3]

- The affected creditors have explicitly consented to the release/injunction;[4]

- The plans provided options pursuant to which a creditor could elect to receive additional consideration on its claim in exchange for releasing the non-debtor parties;[5] and

- The release/injunction is essential to the likelihood of success of the debtor's reorganization.[6]

§ 9.171 Chapter 11—Channelling Injunctions: Asbestos–Related Cases

The Bankruptcy Reform Act of 1994 added Section 524(g) to the Bankruptcy Code. The amendment establishes a procedure, modeled on the trust/injunction and channeling order used in the Johns–Manville case for dealing with future personal injury claims against a chapter 11 debtor based on exposure to asbestos-containing products. The provision provides that present claimants cannot be bound by a trust/injunction unless the following requirements are met: the trust must have the capability of owning a majority of the shares of the debtor or its parent or a subsidiary; the debtor must prove that it is likely to be subject to substantial future asbestos claims, the number of which cannot be easily predicted, and the trust is needed to deal equitably with present and

---

3. *See* In re Master Mortgage Investment Fund, Inc., 168 B.R. 930 (Bankr. W.D.Mo.1994); In re Resorts Int'l, Inc., 145 B.R. 412 (Bankr.D.N.J.1990); In re AOV Indus., Inc., 792 F.2d 1140 (D.C.Cir.1986).

4. *See, e.g.,* In re Specialty Equipment Cos., Inc., 3 F.3d 1043, 1047 (7th Cir.1993); In re Resorts Int'l, Inc., 145 B.R. 412 (Bankr.D.N.J.1990). *Cf.* In re West Coast Video Enters., Inc., 174 B.R. 906, 911 (Bankr.E.D.Pa.1994) (a provision in the debtor's plan which purported to release nondebtor principals could not be enforced against those parties who did not affirmatively agree to the releases); In re Market Square Inn, Inc., 163 B.R. 64, 66–68 (Bankr.W.D.Pa.1994) (the debtor's president/sole shareholder could not be compelled by the terms of a plan proposed by the debtor's lessor to involuntarily relinquish his causes of action against the nondebtor plan proponent).

5. *See* In re Monroe Well Service, Inc., 80 B.R. 324, 329 (Bankr.E.D.Pa.1987).

6. *See* In re A.H. Robins, 880 F.2d 694 (4th Cir.), cert. denied 493 U.S. 959, 110 S.Ct. 376, 107 L.Ed.2d 362 (1989); MacArthur Co. v. Johns–Manville Corp., 837 F.2d 89 (2d Cir.1988), cert. denied 488 U.S. 868, 109 S.Ct. 176, 102 L.Ed.2d 145 (1988); LTV Corp. v. Aetna Casualty and Surety Co. (In re Chateaugay Corp.), 167 B.R. 776, 780 (S.D.N.Y.1994); In re The Drexel Burnham Lambert Group Inc., 138 B.R. 723, 754 (Bankr.S.D.N.Y.1992).

future claims.[1] A separate creditor class comprised of those creditors with present claims must vote by a 75 percent margin to approve the plan. The amendment further provides that in order for future claimants to be bound by a trust/injunction, the trust must be structured so that it operates in a manner necessary to give reasonable assurance that it will value, and be able to pay, similar present and future claims in substantially the same manner.[2]

Library References:

West's Key No. Digests, Bankruptcy ⇔3570.

§ 9.172 Chapter 11—Plan Implementation

Upon confirmation and the effective date of the plan, the plan proponent must begin the process of plan implementation. Section 1101(2) defines "substantial consummation" of a plan as the

(A) Transfer of all or substantially all of the property proposed by the plan to be transferred;

(B) Assumption by the debtor or by the debtor's successor under the plan of the business or of the management of all or substantially all of the property dealt with by the plan; and

(C) Commencement of distribution under the plan.

Upon substantial consummation of the plan, challenges to aspects of the plan may be dismissed as moot.[1]

Library References:

West's Key No. Digests, Bankruptcy ⇔3570.

§ 9.173 Chapter 11—Small Business Reorganizations

Under Section 1121(e) of the Bankruptcy Code, which was added pursuant to the 1994 amendments to the Bankruptcy Code, in a case in which the debtor is a small business and elects to be considered a small business, only the debtor may file a plan until after 100 days following the entry of the order for relief, subject to extension "if the debtor shows that the need for an increase is caused by circumstances for which the debtor should not be held accountable," and subject to contraction if a party in interest demonstrates "cause."[1] A "small business" is defined as

§ 9.171
1. 11 U.S.C.A. § 524(g)(1)(B).
2. 11 U.S.C.A. § 524(g)(2)(B)(ii)(V).

§ 9.172
1. *See supra*, § 9.25 note 9 for a discussion of appeals of plans after substantial consummation.

§ 9.173
1. 11 U.S.C.A. § 1121(e). Bankruptcy Rule 1020 requires a debtor to make a written statement of election for treatment as a small business within 60 days after entry of the order for relief.

§ 9.173   BANKRUPTCY   Ch. 9

a person (including an individual or a corporation) "engaged in commercial or business activities (but does not include a person whose primary activity is the business of owning or operating real property and activities incidental thereto) whose aggregate noncontingent liquidated secured and unsecured debts as of the date of the petition do not exceed $2,000,000."[2]

Prior to the 1994 amendments, no distinction existed between small business debtors and other debtors. Small business debtors had the same 120-day exclusive period and the same standard of proof for extension or contraction of exclusivity as other debtors. The purpose of the new section is to permit an expedited and less expensive procedure for reorganizing a small business in chapter 11. However, this amendment applies only to those small businesses which elect to be treated as such. If the small business option is elected, the standard of proof for debtors in extending exclusivity appears to be much more stringent than the "cause" requirement for other debtors.

Additionally, under the 1994 amendments, the court may order that a creditors' committee not be appointed in the case of a small business if a party in interest so requests and the court finds there is cause.[3]

The 1994 amendments also added Section 1125(f) to the Bankruptcy Code. This section provides that a debtor that has elected under Section 1121(e) to be considered a small business may solicit acceptances of a proposed plan on a "conditionally approved" disclosure statement which provides adequate information to each holder of a claim or interest whose vote the debtor is soliciting. The conditionally approved disclosure statement must be mailed at least ten days prior to the hearing on confirmation, which hearing may be combined with a hearing on approval of the disclosure statement.[4]

§ 9.174   Chapter 11—Conversion or Dismissal of Cases

A chapter 11 debtor has the right to convert its case to chapter 7 unless (1) the debtor is not a debtor in possession, (2) the debtor's case was originally commenced as an involuntary chapter 11 case, or (3) the case was converted to chapter 11 other than on the debtor's request.[1] The court does not have discretion to deny the debtor's Section 1112(a) motion to convert even if such denial would be in the best interests of creditors.[2] Rather, Section 1112(a) "by its terms, gives the debtor an absolute right to convert, unless the case is governed by one of the

---

2. 11 U.S.C.A. § 101(51)(C).
3. 11 U.S.C.A. § 1102(a)(3).
4. 11 U.S.C.A. § 1125(f)(3).

§ 9.174

1. 11 U.S.C.A. § 1112(a).

2. **CAVEAT**: The court may not convert a chapter 11 case to a chapter 7 case if the debtor is a farmer or a corporation that is not a moneyed, business, or commercial corporation unless the debtor requests such conversion. 11 U.S.C.A. § 1112(c).

enumerated exceptions."[3] A case may not be converted to another chapter unless the debtor may be a debtor under such chapter.[4]

A party in interest also may request that the court, for cause, either (1) convert a chapter 11 case to a chapter 7 liquidation or (2) dismiss the case in its entirety, whichever is in the best interest of creditors and the estate.[5] The purpose of this provision is "not to test a debtor's good faith; it is to provide relief where the debtor's efforts, however heroic, have proven inadequate to the task of reorganizing his affairs effectively within a reasonable amount of time."[6] In light of Congress's determination that it is better to reorganize than terminate a business when possible, "a court should resolve doubts in favor of the debtor in deciding a § 1112(b) motion."[7] Furthermore, the burden of proof in an Section 1112(b) motion is "squarely upon the moving party."[8]

A bankruptcy court has wide discretion to make an appropriate disposition of the case when a party in interest requests.[9] Section 1112(b) lists certain factors that may constitute cause for either conversion or dismissal upon motion of an interested party. These factors include, among others:

1. Continuing loss or diminution of the estate and absence of a reasonable likelihood of rehabilitation;
2. Inability to effectuate a plan;
3. Unreasonable delay by the debtor that is prejudicial to creditors;
4. Failure to propose a plan within the time fixed by the court;
5. Denial of confirmation of every proposed plan and denial of a request made for additional time for filing another plan;
6. Revocation of an order of confirmation and denial of confirmation of another plan;
7. Inability to effectuate substantial consummation of a confirmed plan; and
8. Material default with respect to a confirmed plan.

---

3. In re Dieckhaus Stationers of King of Prussia, Inc., 73 B.R. 969, 970 (Bankr. E.D.Pa.1987).

CAVEAT: Once a plan of reorganization is confirmed, the debtor loses its status as a debtor in possession and, therefore, is no longer entitled to an automatic conversion under Section 1112(a). See In re T.S.P. Industries, Inc., 120 B.R. 107, 109 (Bankr. N.D.Ill.1990); In re Marill Alarm Systems, Inc., 100 B.R. 606, 607 (Bankr.S.D.Fla. 1989).

4. 11 U.S.C.A. § 1112(f).

5. 11 U.S.C.A. § 1112(b).

6. In re Tiana Queen Motel, Inc., 749 F.2d 146, 152 (2d Cir.1984), cert. denied 471 U.S. 1138, 105 S.Ct. 2681, 86 L.Ed.2d 699 (1985). "The essential command of § 1112(b) is that the court and all parties concerned be placed on notice of the nature of the motion and the identity of the movant." Id. at 149.

7. In re Smith, 77 B.R. 496, 499 (Bankr. E.D.Pa.1987).

8. Id.

9. See H.Rep.No. 95-595, 95th Cong., 1st Sess. 405 (1977).

§ 9.174   BANKRUPTCY   Ch. 9

However, this list is not exhaustive, and the Bankruptcy Code affords a bankruptcy court wide discretion to determine if cause exists.[10]

Several courts have cautioned against converting or dismissing "reflexively" whenever cause may exist, as Section 1112(b) requires that conversion from a chapter 11 reorganization to a chapter 7 liquidation be in the "best interests of creditors and the estate." The best interests test requires that the court compare the creditors' interests in bankruptcy with those they would have under state law.[11]

Additionally, the court, on request of the U.S. trustee, may dismiss or convert a chapter 11 case to a chapter 7 liquidation, whichever is in the best interest of creditors and the estate, if a voluntary chapter 11 debtor fails to file, within 15 days after the filing of the petition commencing the case (or such additional time as the court may allow), the list of creditors, schedule of assets and liabilities, and statement of financial affairs required by Section 521(1) of the Bankruptcy Code.[12]

The court also may convert a chapter 11 case to a case under either chapter 12 or 13, but only if (1) the debtor requests such conversion; (2) the debtor has not been discharged; and (3) if the debtor requests conversion to chapter 12, such conversion is equitable.[13]

Library References:

West's Key No. Digests, Bankruptcy ⟜3591(1)–3594.

§ 9.175   Chapter 11—Conversion or Dismissal of Cases—Procedure

Bankruptcy Rule 1017(d) provides that a proceeding to dismiss or convert a case to another chapter that is brought by a party in interest is a contested matter governed by Bankruptcy Rule 9014. A motion to dismiss or convert brought by the debtor must be filed and served as

---

10. In re Tornheim, 181 B.R. 161, 163 (Bankr.S.D.N.Y.1995), appeal dismissed No. 95 Civ. 8474 (PKL), 1996 WL 79333 (S.D.N.Y.1996).

11. See In re Continental Holdings, Inc., 170 B.R. 919, 927 (Bankr.N.D.Ohio 1994). See also In re Clark, No. 95 C 2773, 1995 WL 495951, *4 (N.D.Ill.1995) (holding that determining best interests "implies a balancing test to be applied, with the final determination a matter for the discretion of the bankruptcy court"; moreover, "best interests" need not be best interests of every creditor, as "[t]he interest of a single creditor with a large enough claim will suffice").

CAVEAT: The practitioner should also consider the interaction of Section 105(a) with Section 1112(b). As one court has noted, Section 105(a) "overrides the requirement of § 1112(b) that a party in interest ... request a dismissal or conversion, and allows the court to act on its own initiative to order such a remedy for cause." In re Pedro Abich, Inc., 165 B.R. 5, 8 (D.P.R. 1994). However, "the power of the court to act *sua sponte* should be used sparingly and only in emergency situations." See S.Rep. No. 95-989, 95th Cong., 2d Sess. 117 (1978).

12. 11 U.S.C.A. § 1112(e).

13. 11 U.S.C.A. § 1112(d). This section prohibits a conversion of a chapter 11 case to a chapter 12 or 13 case without the debtor's consent because an involuntary chapter 12 or 13 case is not permitted. See 11 U.S.C.A. § 303(a).

required by Bankruptcy Rule 9013.[1] The hearing on the dismissal of the case or the conversion of the case to another chapter requires no less than 20 days notice by mail.[2] Bankruptcy Rule 1019 establishes the procedural effects of the conversion of a chapter 11, 12, or 13 case to a chapter 7 liquidation. For example, all claims actually filed by a creditor in the superseded case will be deemed filed in the chapter 7 case.[3] However, any claim that was not *actually filed* in the superseded case must be filed in the chapter 7 case.[4] The rule is "not intended to invalidate any action taken in the superseded case before its conversion to chapter 7."[5]

§ 9.176 Chapter 11—Closing and Reopening Cases

The court will close the case after an estate is fully administered and the court has discharged the trustee or debtor in possession.[1] However, the case may be reopened on motion of the debtor or other party in interest to administer assets, to accord relief to the debtor, or for other cause.[2]

Library References:
West's Key No. Digests, Bankruptcy ⇔3441–3445.

§ 9.177 Chapter 7—Overview[1]

Chapter 7 of the Bankruptcy Code has two primary goals. First, it provides creditors with an equitable share of the debtor's nonexempt assets. Second, it grants individual debtors[2] a fresh start by discharging certain debts so that a debtor may begin a new financial life. Unlike chapter 11 of the Bankruptcy Code, which is primarily concerned with the debtor's rehabilitation as an operating entity, chapter 7 of the Bankruptcy Code focuses on an expeditious liquidation of the debtor's assets and a prompt distribution of the proceeds of the assets to the

§ 9.175

1. Bankr.R. 1017(d).
2. Bankr.R. 2002(a)(4).
3. Bankr.R. 1019(3).
4. Bankr.R. 1019(3).
5. *See* Bankr.R. 1019, Advisory Committee Note.

§ 9.176

1. 11 U.S.C.A. § 350(a).
2. 11 U.S.C.A. § 350(b); Bankr.R. 5010. In addition, Rule 9024 exempts motions to reopen cases from the one-year limitation of F.R.C.P. 60(b). *See supra*, § 9.33 note 6 regarding the desirability of closing cases expeditiously to avoid the incurrence of additional fees under 28 U.S.C.A. § 1930(a).

§ 9.177

1. Much of the information covered in the preceding sections of this chapter is applicable to chapter 7 and is not repeated in this portion of the chapter. For topics of particular interest, refer to the *Table of Sections*, and particularly to §§ 9.1–9.137, *supra*, which are applicable to all chapters under the Bankruptcy Code unless otherwise noted. Subchapter III of chapter 7, which deals with stockbroker liquidation, and subchapter IV, which deals with commodity broker liquidation, are not covered herein.

2. Only individual debtors are eligible for discharge under chapter 7. Corporate debtors are not eligible for discharge under chapter 7. 11 U.S.C.A. § 727(a)(1), 1141(d)(3)(C).

§ 9.177   **BANKRUPTCY**   Ch. 9

debtor's creditors. Under chapter 7, a trustee is appointed to take possession of the debtor's assets, sell all non-exempt assets, and distribute the proceeds to creditors in accordance with the distribution scheme established under the Bankruptcy Code.[3] The remaining unpaid debts are then discharged.[4] *See supra*, § 9.7 for a discussion of eligibility to file.[5]

§ 9.178   Chapter 7—Commencement of a Case

The commencement of a voluntary or involuntary case under chapter 7 is discussed *supra*, §§ 9.8–9.12. Counsel also should refer to §§ 9.2–9.5 *supra*, containing a discussion of overall strategy, checklists for representing a debtor or creditor, and governing law.

In general, the same papers must be filed to commence a case under chapter 7 as described for the commencement of a case under chapter 11.[1]

Library References:

West's Key No. Digests, Bankruptcy ⚖=2202.

§ 9.179   Chapter 7—Fees

Pursuant to 28 U.S.C.A. § 1930, the filing fee for a chapter 7 case is $160. For an individual debtor's chapter 7 case, this filing fee may be paid in installments[1] or may be waived in certain districts if the bankruptcy court determines that the debtor clearly lacks the ability to pay the filing fee.[2]

---

3. *See* 11 U.S.C.A. §§ 725, 726, 507; *see supra*, § 9.106.

4. There are, however, exceptions to discharge, and certain debts are nondischargeable. *See infra*, §§ 9.205, 9.207 for a discussion of exceptions to discharge.

5. **CAVEAT**: Note that Section 109(g) of the Bankruptcy Code specifically prohibits an individual (or a family farmer) from filing under the Bankruptcy Code if such person has been a debtor in a case pending under title 11 at any time in the preceding 180 days if that case was dismissed for willful failure of the debtor to abide by court orders or properly prosecute the case, or if the debtor requested and obtained the voluntary dismissal of the case following the filing of a request for relief from the automatic stay.

§ 9.178

1. *See infra*, § 9.264 for a procedural checklist for commencing a voluntary case and § 9.265 for a checklist of the lists and schedules that must be filed at the commencement of a case.

§ 9.179

1. Official Form 3 provides the form of the application and order to pay the filing fee in installments. *See* Bankruptcy Rule 1006 for requirements and limitations imposed on an individual who wishes to apply for permission to pay the filing fee in installments.

CAVEAT: An individual applying for permission to pay the filing fee in installments may not have paid any money or transferred any property to an attorney for services in connection with the case. Bankr.R. 1006(b)(1). Nor may an attorney or any other person who provides services to the debtor in connection with the case receive payment of any fees until the filing fee has been fully paid. Bankr.R. 1006(b)(3).

2. *See* Departments of Commerce, Justice, and State, the Judiciary, and Related Agencies Appropriations Act, 1994, Pub. L.No. 103–121, 107 Stat. 1153, 1165.

§ 9.180 Chapter 7—Appointment of an Interim Trustee

Promptly after an order for relief is entered,[1] the United States trustee is required to appoint one disinterested person from a panel of trustees established under 28 U.S.C.A. § 586(a)(1) to serve as interim trustee.[2] The interim trustee serves as a caretaker and is expected to do little more than protect the assets of the estate and ensure continuity of estate administration until the first meeting of creditors.[3]

Library References:
West's Key No. Digests, Bankruptcy ⊛3002.

§ 9.181 Chapter 7—Election of a Permanent Trustee

Shortly after the chapter 7 case is commenced, creditors meet pursuant to Section 341 of the Bankruptcy Code.[1] At the Section 341 meeting, the U.S. trustee orally examines the debtor under oath to ensure, among other things, that the chapter 7 debtor is aware of the consequences of seeking a discharge and of reaffirming its debts.[2] Additionally, at the Section 341 meeting, creditors may elect a permanent trustee if the election of a trustee is requested by creditors.[3] In the absence of an election by creditors, the interim trustee is automatically appointed permanent trustee at the first Section 341 meeting.[4]

---

§ 9.180

1. See supra, §§ 9.8, 9.10 for discussions of the order for relief in voluntary and involuntary cases, respectively.

2. 11 U.S.C.A. § 701(a)(1).

3. Weinman v. Hamilton Properties Corp. (In re Hamilton), 186 B.R. 991, 1004 (Bankr.D.Colo.1995). As one court noted, the interim trustee will have little involvement in the complex matters of a liquidation case, and should take "little" affirmative action until after the election or designation of a permanent trustee. Fitzgerald v. Bertram (In re Killian Constr. Co.), 24 B.R. 848, 849 (Bankr.D. Idaho 1982).

§ 9.181

1. See supra, § 9.37 for a discussion of the meeting of creditors.

2. **PRACTICE POINTER**: Statements under oath include statements in documents, such as the schedules and statement of financial affairs filed under the penalty of perjury, and statements that falsely value assets. As one court noted, creditors are entitled to a "truthful" statement of the debtor's financial condition. Montey Corp. v. Maletta (In re Maletta), 159 B.R. 108, 112 (Bankr.D.Conn.1993).

3. See 11 U.S.C.A. § 702 for the provision governing the election of a trustee. A creditor may vote for a trustee if such creditor (i) holds an allowable, undisputed, fixed, liquidated, unsecured claim entitled to distribution under Section 726(a)(2), (3), or (4) or under Section 752(a), 766(h) or (i); (ii) does not have an interest materially adverse to the interest of creditors entitled to such distribution, other than an equity interest that is insubstantial in relation to such creditor's interest as a creditor; and (iii) is not an insider. 11 U.S.C.A. § 702(a).

4. 11 U.S.C.A. § 702(d).

PRACTICE POINTER: For purposes of determining when a trustee becomes permanent, the Section 341 meeting is considered to have been actually held when the debtor submits to an examination under oath. See Kroh v. T.R.M. Mfg. (In re Conco Bldg. Supplies), 102 B.R. 190, 191–92 (9th Cir.BAP 1989); In re Fort Worth Campbell & Assocs., 182 B.R. 748 (Bankr.N.D.Tex.

§ 9.182 Chapter 7—Duties of a Trustee

Section 704 of the Bankruptcy Code enumerates the duties of the trustee.[1] In a chapter 7 case, they include items 1 through 5 listed *supra*, § 9.139 and the following:

1. Collect and reduce to money the debtor's property, and close the estate as expeditiously as is compatible with the best interests of parties in interest;[2]

2. Ensure that the debtor complies with its stated intentions as to the retention or surrender of property if the debtor is an individual with scheduled liabilities which include consumer debts which are secured by property of the estate;[3]

3. Investigate the financial affairs of the debtor;[4]

4. If a purpose would be served, examine proofs of claim and object to the allowance of any claim that is improper;[5]

5. If the debtor's business is authorized to be operated, file with the court and transmit to the U.S. trustee and any pertinent taxing authority periodic reports and summaries of the business operations, including a statement of receipts and disbursements, and any other information required by the court or the U.S. trustee;[6] and

6. Oppose the discharge of the debtor, if advisable.[7]

As noted above, prime among the trustee's duties is the obligation to gather the assets of the debtor's estate expeditiously and convert those assets into cash. The means by which the trustee gathers estate assets include: (1) voluntary surrender of estate property by the debtor and third parties,[8] (2) surrender of property to the trustee pursuant to orders for turnover,[9] and (3) adversary proceedings to recover certain liens and transfers.[10]

Some of this property will be turned over to the debtor as exempt. Some will be subject to valid liens and, therefore, used to satisfy the

---

1995); Grella v. Zimmerman (In re Art & Co., Inc.), 179 B.R. 757, 761 (Bankr.D.Mass. 1995).

§ 9.182
1. *See supra*, § 9.139 for a discussion of the trustee's duties.
2. 11 U.S.C.A. § 704(1).
3. 11 U.S.C.A. § 704(3).
4. 11 U.S.C.A. § 704(4).
5. 11 U.S.C.A. § 704(5).
6. 11 U.S.C.A. § 704(8).
7. 11 U.S.C.A. § 704(6).
8. *See infra*, § 9.192 for a discussion of the surrender of estate property.
9. *See infra*, § 9.193 for a discussion of the trustee's turnover powers.
10. *See* 11 U.S.C.A. §§ 506(d), 544–545, 547–549; *see supra*, §§ 9.113–9.119.

secured creditors' claims. The remaining property will be liquidated and reduced to cash proceeds. These cash proceeds will be distributed to the unsecured creditors in accordance with the Bankruptcy Code's priority scheme.[11]

Library References:

West's Key No. Digests, Bankruptcy ⟲3008.1–3009.

§ 9.183 Chapter 7—Employment of Professionals

A detailed discussion of the employment and compensation of professionals is set forth in §§ 9.29–9.30, *supra*.

Library References:

West's Key No. Digests, Bankruptcy ⟲3029.1–3030.

§ 9.184 Chapter 7—Creditors' Committee

At the meeting of creditors held pursuant to Section 341(a) of the Bankruptcy Code,[1] the creditors who are eligible to vote for a trustee[2] may elect a committee of no fewer than three and no more than 11 creditors, each of whom holds an allowable, unsecured claim of a kind entitled to distribution under Section 726(a)(2) of the Bankruptcy Code.[3] The creditors' committee may consult with the chapter 7 trustee or the U.S. trustee concerning the administration of the estate, make recommendations concerning the performance of the trustee's duties, and submit to the court or the U.S. trustee any question affecting the estate's administration.[4]

Library References:

West's Key No. Digests, Bankruptcy ⟲3024.

§ 9.185 Chapter 7—Protection Against Discriminatory Treatment

The Bankruptcy Code affords a person who is or has been a debtor under any chapter of the Bankruptcy Code certain protection against discriminatory treatment by a governmental unit or a private employer solely because of being a debtor or being insolvent before the bankruptcy case, or during the case but before obtaining a discharge, or because of

---

11. See 11 U.S.C.A. §§ 725, 726; see supra, § 9.106.

§ 9.184

1. See supra, § 9.37.

2. See supra, § 9.181 note 3 for a description of creditors eligible to vote for a trustee and a creditors' committee.

3. 11 U.S.C.A. § 705(a). See infra, § 9.202 for a discussion of the claims entitled to distribution under Section 726.

4. 11 U.S.C.A. § 705(b).

§ 9.185　　　　　　　　BANKRUPTCY　　　　　　　　Ch. 9

not paying a debt that was discharged in a bankruptcy case.[1]

Library References:
West's Key No. Digests, Bankruptcy ⚖2363.1–2374.

§ 9.186　Chapter 7—The Debtor's Statement of Intention

Section 521(2)(A) of the Bankruptcy Code requires an individual chapter 7 debtor who has scheduled secured consumer debts to file with the clerk of the bankruptcy court a statement of intention with respect to the collateral securing such consumer debts. The statement must specify which of the assets the debtor will retain and which the debtor will abandon;[1] which property will be claimed as exempt,[2] as well as the debtor's intention to redeem[3] or reaffirm[4] the debts secured by such property.[5] This statement of intention must be filed by the earlier of (i) 30 days after the filing of the petition, or (ii) the first meeting of creditors pursuant to Section 341 of the Bankruptcy Code.[6] The debtor is required to perform in accordance with its stated intentions within 45 days of the filing of its statement of intention.[7] However, the purpose of the statement is to ease the burden on creditors by giving them early notice of the debtor's intentions.[8] The statement may be amended within the 45-day period if the debtor's intentions change.[9] Moreover, the filing of the statement of intention is not intended to alter or circumscribe the debtor's rights with respect to the property included in the statement.[10] Thus, the debtor can decide, for example, to redeem or exempt property after the statement has been filed.

As a consequence of the apparently mandatory language of Section 521(2)(A), the courts have split concerning whether the debtor's options are limited to the acts that are mentioned in Section 521(2)(A); that is, whether the debtor *must* either abandon, redeem, or reaffirm the debt which is secured by property of the estate. In certain jurisdictions, abandonment, redemption, or reaffirmation are the debtor's sole options. In other jurisdictions, however, the debtor may not be required to

---

§ 9.185

1. 11 U.S.C.A. § 525. See supra, § 9.132 for a more detailed discussion of the protection against discriminatory treatment.

§ 9.186

1. See supra, § 9.70 for a discussion of abandonment of property of the debtor's estate.

2. See supra, § 9.125 for a discussion of exemptions.

3. See infra, §§ 9.188–9.189 for a discussion of the debtor's redemption of property.

4. See infra, § 9.190 for a discussion of reaffirmation of debts.

5. The statement of intention should be filed in the form of Official Form 8. See supra, § 9.5 and note 3 and accompanying text for a discussion of official forms.

6. 11 U.S.C.A. § 521(2)(A). See supra, § 9.37 for a discussion of the meeting of creditors.

7. 11 U.S.C.A. § 521(2)(B).

8. See 3 *Collier on Bankruptcy* ¶ 521.09A[5] (L. King, ed., 15th ed. 1996).

9. Bankr.R. 1009(b).

10. 11 U.S.C.A. § 521(2)(C).

abandon, reaffirm, or redeem in circumstances where it has not defaulted on payments to a creditor holding a security interest in such property. Instead, the nondefaulting debtor may continue to pay the debt according to its terms.[11] As a consequence of the split in authority, counsel should consult the case law of the applicable jurisdiction before advising a client as to its options for dealing with estate property that secures consumer debts.

Library References:

West's Key No. Digests, Bankruptcy ⇐3022.

§ 9.187 Chapter 7—Exemptions

The same exemptions apply to an individual debtor under each chapter of the Bankruptcy Code.[1]

Library References:

West's Key No. Digests, Bankruptcy ⇐2761–2802.

§ 9.188 Chapter 7—Redemption of Property

The Bankruptcy Code authorizes an individual debtor to redeem tangible personal property intended primarily for personal, family, or household use from a lien securing a dischargeable consumer debt if such property is exempt[1] or has been abandoned pursuant to Section 554 of the Bankruptcy Code.[2] The debtor may redeem such property by paying the lienholder the amount of the allowed claim that is secured by the lien. Because Section 722 of the Bankruptcy Code refers only to "individual" debtors, partnership and corporate debtors are excluded. The right of redemption is personal to the debtor and cannot be waived[3]

---

11. *Cf.* In re Taylor, 3 F.3d 1512 (11th Cir.1993) (pursuant to Section 521(2)(A) of the Bankruptcy Code, debtor must either negotiate a reaffirmation agreement, redeem, or surrender the property; even if it has not defaulted, the debtor may not retain secured property absent redemption or reaffirmation) *with* In re Belanger, 962 F.2d 345 (4th Cir.1992) (Section 521(2)(A) of the Bankruptcy Code does not require debtor to choose one of the non-exclusive options listed therein concerning the debtor's treatment of property secured by consumer debts; rather, if the debtor has not defaulted, it may retain the collateral without redemption or reaffirmation by keeping payments current) *and* In re Boodrow, 192 B.R. 57 (Bankr.N.D.N.Y.1995), affirmed 197 B.R. 409 (N.D.N.Y.1996), aff'd 126 F.3d 43, (2d Cir.1997) (adopting holding in Belanger).

§ 9.187

1. For a detailed discussion of exemptions, *see supra*, § 9.125.

§ 9.188

1. *See supra*, § 9.125 for a discussion of the exemptions available under New York law. *See, e.g.,* In re Zaicek, 29 B.R. 31 (Bankr.W.D.Ky.1983) (debtor could not redeem mobile home that was not exempt property under state law).

2. 11 U.S.C.A. § 722. *See, e.g.,* In re Schweitzer, 19 B.R. 860, 862 (Bankr. E.D.N.Y.1982). *See supra*, § 9.70 for a discussion of the abandonment of property of the estate.

3. H.R.Rep.No. 95–595, 95th Cong., 1st Sess. 381 (1977).

§ 9.188   BANKRUPTCY   Ch. 9

or assigned.[4]

The right to redeem extends to the entire property, not just the debtor's exempt interest in it. Thus, the debtor can eliminate the security interest and redeem the entire property by paying the lienholder the amount of the allowed claim secured by the lien or the fair market value of the property, whichever is less.[5] For example, if an individual debtor owns an automobile valued at $3,000, subject to a $1,800 lien, and uses such automobile for personal or family purposes, the debtor may pay the lienholder $1,800 and redeem the entire automobile as long as the individual debtor's interest therein ($1,200) is exempt.[6]

Library References:

West's Key No. Digests, Bankruptcy ⚛3034.

§ 9.189   Chapter 7—Redemption of Property—Procedure

If the debtor and the lienholder agree on the amount of the allowed secured claim in respect of a lien securing a dischargeable consumer debt, the debtor may redeem the property by paying the agreed amount to the lienholder in exchange for a release or satisfaction of the lien without the necessity of filing a motion. If, however, the allowable amount of the secured claim or any aspect of the redemption is subject to dispute, the debtor must file a motion in accordance with the requirements for a contested matter under Bankruptcy Rule 9014 seeking court authorization of redemption.[1] The debtor's motion to redeem should be filed within 45 days after the debtor files the required statement of intention regarding the retention or surrender of property securing consumer debts.[2] On a finding of cause, the court may grant an extension of the 45-day period for filing a redemption motion. After reasonable notice to the lienholder and a hearing, the court may authorize the redemption of property from a lien or from a sale to enforce a lien in accordance with applicable law.[3]

---

4. S.Rep.No. 95–989, 95th Cong., 2d Sess. 95 (1978).

5. Id.

6. See H.R.Rep.No. 95–595, 95th Cong., 1st Sess. 381 (1977). See, e.g., In re Fitzgerald, 20 B.R. 27 (Bankr.N.D.N.Y.1982) (debtor entitled to redeem automobile used for family purposes by paying amount of allowed secured claim where debtor's interest in automobile was exempted).

PRACTICE POINTER: The debtor must make a lump-sum payment to redeem property unless the creditor agrees to another arrangement. See, e.g., In re Schweitzer, 19 B.R. 860 (Bankr.E.D.N.Y.1982) (holding that redemption payment must be made in lump sum).

§ 9.189

1. Bankr.R. 6008. See infra, § 9.267 for a procedural checklist for commencing a contested matter pursuant to Bankruptcy Rule 9014.

2. 11 U.S.C.A. § 521(2)(B). See supra, § 9.186 for a discussion of the debtor's statement of intention.

3. Bankr.R. 6008.

§ 9.190 Chapter 7—Reaffirmation of Debts

Under certain limited circumstances, the Bankruptcy Code permits a debtor to reaffirm and agree to pay a debt that is dischargeable.[1]

Library References:

West's Key No. Digests, Bankruptcy ⇔3415.1–3417.

§ 9.191 Chapter 7—Abandonment of Property

Section 554 of the Bankruptcy Code, which applies in cases under chapters 7, 11, 12, and 13 of the Bankruptcy Code, authorizes the trustee or debtor in possession or any party in interest, after notice and a hearing, to abandon property of the estate that is burdensome or of inconsequential value and benefit to the estate.[1]

Library References:

West's Key No. Digests, Bankruptcy ⇔3131–3137.

§ 9.192 Chapter 7—Debtor's Surrender of Property and Records

A chapter 7 debtor generally is required to surrender to the trustee all property of its estate and all of its books, records, and other information relating to its property.[1] If the debtor fails to comply with these turnover requirements, the bankruptcy court may deny the chapter 7 debtor its discharge or dismiss the debtor's chapter 7 case.

Library References:

West's Key No. Digests, Bankruptcy ⇔3022, 3285.

§ 9.193 Chapter 7—Trustee's Turnover Powers

With certain exceptions, an entity in possession, custody, or control of a debtor's property must deliver that property (or the value thereof) to the trustee, unless such property is of inconsequential value or benefit to

---

§ 9.190

1. 11 U.S.C.A. § 524(c), (d). See supra, § 9.130 for a more detailed discussion of reaffirmation. See infra, § 9.302 for a drafting checklist for a reaffirmation agreement and see infra, §§ 9.280, 9.303, respectively, for procedural and drafting checklists for a motion for approval of a reaffirmation agreement.

§ 9.191

1. See supra, § 9.70 for a discussion of the abandonment of property of the debtor's estate.

§ 9.192

1. 11 U.S.C.A. § 521(4). This generally is not interpreted to mean that actual physical delivery of estate property is required, but that constructive delivery is made when the case is commenced. See In re Figueira, 163 B.R. 192, 194 (Bankr.D.Kan.1993).

§ 9.193 BANKRUPTCY Ch. 9

the debtor's estate.[1] In addition, any entity that owes a debt to the debtor that is matured, payable on demand, or payable on order, must pay that amount to the trustee.[2] The trustee may issue turnover orders to require payment of debt that is payable to the estate except to the extent such debt may be offset against a claim against the debtor pursuant to Section 553 of the Bankruptcy Code.[3] Section 542 of the Bankruptcy Code does not require that the debtor have a possessory interest in the property for the turnover provisions of the Bankruptcy Code to be applicable.[4]

Library References:
West's Key No. Digests, Bankruptcy ⟺3063.1–3066(6).

§ 9.194 Chapter 7—Liability of General Partners

When a partnership files for relief under chapter 7 of the Bankruptcy Code, the trustee may seek contributions from the general partners. Section 723 of the Bankruptcy Code permits the trustee in a partnership liquidation to satisfy a deficiency claim from the assets of the debtor partnership's noncreditor general partners who are co-liable on estate debts.[1] Bear in mind, however, that Section 723(a) affords the trustee a claim against the nondebtor partners only to the extent necessary to pay the estate's deficiency claim, not to the extent necessary to pay interest on the claim.[2]

Library References:
West's Key No. Digests, Bankruptcy ⟺2559.

§ 9.195 Chapter 7—Trustee's Operation of the Business

In general, chapter 7 of the Bankruptcy Code contemplates the prompt closure of the debtor's business or affairs and the expeditious

However, if the trustee demands physical surrender of property, the debtor should comply promptly.

§ 9.193
1. 11 U.S.C.A. § 542(a).
2. 11 U.S.C.A. § 542(b).
3. 11 U.S.C.A. § 542(b). See supra, § 9.109 for a discussion of a creditor's right of setoff.
4. For example, a promissory note pledged to, and in the possession of, a creditor prior to a default by the debtor is property of the debtor's estate subject to the turnover provisions of Section 542(a). Leeling v. Smith (In re Leeling), 129 B.R. 637 (Bankr.D.Colo.1991).

§ 9.194
1. See 11 U.S.C.A. § 723; Coan v. Bernier (In re Bernier), 176 B.R. 976, 986 (Bankr.D.Conn.1995). At least one court has intimated that the trustee can utilize Section 723(a) to try to hold limited partners who act like general partners liable to the estate to satisfy any deficiency, notwithstanding that the question of whether a limited partner is personally liable on a claim is determined not by the Bankruptcy Code, but by relevant state partnership law. See Marshack v. Mesa Valley Farms, L.P. (In re Ridge II), 158 B.R. 1016, 1022–23 (Bankr.C.D.Cal.1993).

2. **PRACTICE POINTER**: A trustee's action brought under Section 723 to recover deficiencies from the debtor's general and limited partners is not subject to the Statute of Limitations prescribed in Section 546(a).

liquidation of the debtor's non-exempt assets for distribution to creditors. However, in certain limited circumstances (such as where the sale of a business as a going concern would fetch more in either a private or public sale than the sale of a business which had ceased operation), the trustee, with court approval, may operate the business for a limited period of time.[1] That is, if the continued operation of the debtor's business by the trustee is in the best interest of the estate and consistent with the orderly liquidation of the estate, the trustee may operate the business for a limited time.[2]

Often, the chapter 7 trustee requests permission to continue operating the debtor's business because potential purchasers of the business feel that a cessation in the operation of the debtor's business, however temporary, will diminish the enterprise value. Consequently, chapter 7 trustees often seek to operate the business with an eye toward the private sale of the business pursuant to Section 363 of the Bankruptcy Code.[3]

Library References:

West's Key No. Digests, Bankruptcy ⟬3025.1.

§ 9.196 Chapter 7—Executory Contracts

In a chapter 7 case, if the trustee does not assume or reject an executory contract[1] or unexpired lease of residential or nonresidential real or personal property within 60 days after entry of an order for relief,[2] or within such additional time as the bankruptcy court permits, then such contract or unexpired lease of residential or nonresidential real or personal property is deemed rejected by operation of law.[3] The purpose of allowing the trustee to reject executory contracts is to relieve the estate of burdensome obligations and to effect a breach of contract that will allow the injured party to file a claim.[4]

Library References:

West's Key No. Digests, Bankruptcy ⟬3101–3117.

§ 9.195

1. 11 U.S.C.A. § 721.
2. *See, e.g.*, In re Sher–Del Foods, Inc., 186 B.R. 358, 363 (Bankr.W.D.N.Y.1995).
PRACTICE POINTER: The trustee must obtain court authorization prior to operating the debtor's business.
3. *See supra*, §§ 9.60–9.61 for a discussion of the sale of the debtor's property.

§ 9.196

1. *See supra*, § 9.74 for a more detailed discussion of executory contracts.

2. *See supra*, §§ 9.8, 9.10 for discussions of the order for relief in voluntary and involuntary cases, respectively.

3. 11 U.S.C.A. § 365(d)(1), 365(d)(4). In a case under any other chapter under title 11, this rule applies only to an unexpired lease of nonresidential real property. 11 U.S.C.A. § 365(d)(4).

4. *See supra*, §§ 9.90–9.92 for a discussion of the filing of proofs of claim or interest.

§ 9.197 Chapter 7—Adversary Proceedings to Avoid Liens and Transfers

A detailed discussion of the trustee's powers to commence adversary proceedings to avoid liens and transfers of property is set forth above.[1]

Library References:

West's Key No. Digests, Bankruptcy ⚖2721–2729.

§ 9.198 Chapter 7—Adversary Proceedings to Avoid Liens and Transfers—Statute of Limitations

Section 546(a) of the Bankruptcy Code provides the Statute of Limitations for the commencement of avoidance actions by the trustee. The trustee must commence all avoidance actions before the later of: (a) two years after entry of the order for relief, or (b) one year after the appointment or election of the first trustee under Section 702 of the Bankruptcy Code, if such appointment or election occurs before the expiration of the two years noted above; or by the time the case is closed or dismissed, if this occurs before the running of the above-described period.[1]

§ 9.197

1. *See supra*, §§ 9.113–9.119.

CAVEAT: A debtor under chapter 7 may not "strip down" liens against its property. *See supra*, § 9.101 discussing the Supreme Court's decision in Dewsnup v. Timm, 502 U.S. 410, 112 S.Ct. 773, 116 L.Ed.2d 903 (1992).

§ 9.198

1. **CAVEAT**: Prior to Congress's enactment of the Bankruptcy Reform Act of 1994, Section 546(a) simply provided for a two-year Statute of Limitations which commenced upon the earlier of (a) the appointment of a trustee under Sections 702, 1104, etc., or (b) the time the case was closed or dismissed. This language led to a dichotomy in the case law with respect to whether the phrase "appointment of a trustee under section 702" referred to the United States trustee's appointment of the interim trustee, or the later appointment of a permanent trustee. While a scant minority of courts has held that the limitations period commenced upon the appointment of the interim trustee, *see, e.g.*, Clark Oil and Trading Co. v. Haberbush (In re Sahuaro Petroleum), 170 B.R. 689 (Bankr.C.D.Cal.1994), the overwhelming majority of courts that considered the issue determined that the limitations period began to run on the date the trustee was designated permanent trustee. *See, e.g.*, In re Ted A. Petras Furs, Inc., 172 B.R. 170, 175–76 (Bankr.E.D.N.Y. 1994) (it is the trustee's election as "permanent trustee" and not "interim trustee" that triggers Section 546(a)), appeal dismissed 100 F.3d 943 (2d Cir. 1996); In re North American Dealer Group, 62 B.R. 423 (Bankr.E.D.N.Y.1986) (same); In re Black & Geddes, 35 B.R. 827 (Bankr.S.D.N.Y.1983) (same); Grella v. Zimmerman (In re Art & Co., Inc.), 179 B.R. 757, 761 (Bankr.D.Mass. 1995); In re Goetz, 175 B.R. 743 (Bankr. C.D.Cal.1994); Martino v. Assco Assocs., Inc. (In re SSS Enters., Inc.), 145 B.R. 915 (Bankr.N.D.Ill.1992).

While Section 546(a) in its present form may have ended this interpretive debate, the careful practitioner should take note of whether the bankruptcy case in question was commenced after the enactment of the Bankruptcy Reform Act of 1994 (October 22, 1994), since the amendments apply only to cases commenced after the date of enactment. If the case was already pending, the practitioner should take note of this dichotomy in the case law and recognize what opinions, if any, have emanated in the relevant jurisdiction.

A second, related issue involved the question of whether the Statute of Limitations

A majority of bankruptcy courts also have concluded that the Statute of Limitations prescribed in Section 546(c) of the Bankruptcy Code is a true Statute of Limitations, not a grant of jurisdiction and, therefore, can be extended or waived, and is subject to the doctrine of equitable estoppel.[2]

Library References:

West's Key No. Digests, Bankruptcy ⟸2722.

§ 9.199 Chapter 7—Treatment of Certain Liens[1]

The Bankruptcy Code authorizes a chapter 7 trustee to avoid a lien that secures a fine, penalty, forfeiture, or punitive or similar damages to the extent the claim secured by such lien is not compensation for actual pecuniary loss.[2]

In addition, even though tax claims may be properly secured, the Bankruptcy Code subordinates tax liens on real and personal property to the payment of unsecured claims that have a higher priority than unsecured tax claims.[3] This means that claims with a higher priority than unsecured tax claims may be satisfied from the amount that

---

period under former Section 546(a) began to run anew following the conversion of a chapter 11 case to a chapter 7 case and the replacement of the chapter 11 trustee with a chapter 7 trustee. The United States Courts of Appeals that have considered the issue have all concluded that the limitations period under former Section 546(a) does not begin to run again. *See* Jobin v. Boryla (In re M & L Business Machine Co., Inc.), 75 F.3d 586 (10th Cir. 1996); McCuskey v. Central Trailer Services, Ltd., 37 F.3d 1329, 1332 (8th Cir.1994); Ford v. Union Bank (In re San Joaquin Roast Beef), 7 F.3d 1413 (9th Cir.1993). However, the lower courts have divided on the issue.

Yet a third, related issue centered on whether the Statute of Limitations began to run anew if a chapter 11 case under the control of a debtor in possession (that is, operated without a chapter 11 trustee) was converted to a chapter 7 case. Although several courts had concluded that the two-year Statute of Limitations indeed began running anew upon the appointment of the first statutory trustee following a debtor in possession, the Court of Appeals for the Second Circuit held that the 2-year Statute of Limitations applies to debtors in possession as well as trustees. *See* U.S. Brass & Copper Co. v. Caplan (In re Century Brass Prods., Inc.) 22 F.3d 37 (2d Cir.1994). Accordingly, the 2-year statute would not begin to run again upon conversion of the chapter 11 case to a chapter 7 case and the appointment of a chapter 7 trustee. That is, the 2-year period would have run from the filing of the chapter 11 petition. For cases filed on or after October 22, 1994, this issue has been settled by the Bankruptcy Reform Act, as set forth in the text to which this footnote relates.

2. *See, e.g.*, The Mediators, Inc. v. Manney (In re The Mediators, Inc.), 190 B.R. 515, 524 (S.D.N.Y.1995), affirmed 105 F.3d 822 (2d Cir.1997) (equitable tolling may be available to a plaintiff seeking to recover fraudulent transfer); In re Smith, 190 B.R. 753, 757 (Bankr.E.D.N.Y.1996) (equitable tolling may be applied to Section 546(c)); Metzeler v. Bouchard (In re Metzeler), 66 B.R. 977, 980 (Bankr.S.D.N.Y.1986) (same); In re Shape, 138 B.R. 334, 337 (Bankr. D.Me.1992) (Section 546(a) is a true Statute of Limitations and, therefore, may be extended by agreement of the parties).

§ 9.199

1. *See supra* §§ 9.128–9.129 for a discussion of the treatment of liens on exempt property. *See supra*, § 9.101 for a discussion of lien stripping, that is, avoidance of liens to the extent they secure claims that exceed the value of the property.

2. 11 U.S.C.A. § 724(a).

3. 11 U.S.C.A. § 724(b).

§ 9.199

otherwise would have been applied to the tax lien. Thus, the order of distribution of property subject to a tax lien is:[4]

First. To holders of liens senior to the tax lien;

Second. To holders of claims entitled to priority under Sections 507(a)(1), (2), (3), (4), (5), (6), and (7) to the extent of the amount of the allowed tax claim that is secured by the tax lien;

Third. To the extent that the amount of the allowed tax claim secured by the tax lien exceeds the amount distributed to priority claimants under the second priority above, such excess is distributed to the holder of the tax lien;

Fourth. To satisfy claims of junior lienholders;

Fifth. To the holder of the tax lien to the extent it was not fully paid above under the third priority;

Sixth. To the estate.

Library References:

West's Key No. Digests, Bankruptcy ⇐2580.1–2585.

§ 9.200 Chapter 7—Trustee's Sale of Assets

As discussed above,[1] prime among the trustee's duties is to gather the assets of the estate expeditiously and convert those assets to cash.[2] The mechanism by which the trustee converts the assets to cash is through a sale, whether that sale be private or public. Although the Bankruptcy Code expresses no preference between private and public sales, trustees generally prefer to use public sales whenever possible because public sales enable the trustee to liquidate estate assets quickly and with a high degree of visibility. However, if the estate property is unusual in nature or has a substantial market value, a trustee may determine that a private sale is in the best interests of the estate.[3]

All sales of property, whether public auctions or private sales, are governed by Section 363 of the Bankruptcy Code and Bankruptcy Rule 6004.[4] The trustee may sell estate property "after notice and a hearing," and may, under certain circumstances, sell estate property free and clear of all liens and other interests.[5] Timing and notice requirements for any such sale are governed by Bankruptcy Rule 2002.

---

4. *Id.*

§ 9.200

1. *See supra,* § 9.182.
2. 11 U.S.C.A. § 704.
3. **PRACTICE POINTER**: Competing purchasers may appear at a hearing on a proposed private sale and turn a negotiated private sale into a public auction.

4. *See supra,* §§ 9.60–9.63 for a discussion of the sale of the estate's assets.

5. 11 U.S.C.A. § 363(f). *See, e.g.,* Yadkin Valley Bank v. Northwestern Bank (In re Hutchinson), 132 B.R. 827, 836 (Bankr. M.D.N.C.1991), aff'd in part and remanded 5 F.3d 750 (4th Cir.1993).

Bankruptcy Rule 2002(a) requires the trustee to provide at least 20 days notice by mail of a proposed asset sale to all parties in interest. This includes all creditors, the debtor, any prospective purchasers, the United States trustee, and others where applicable.[6] The notice must include the time and place of a public sale, the terms and conditions of a private sale, and the time fixed for filing objections thereto. The notice is considered sufficient if it generally describes the property to be sold.[7] The bankruptcy court may order the trustee to notice the sale by publication if notice by mail is impracticable or if the court finds that notice by publication is desirable to supplement the notice by mail. The bankruptcy court has wide discretion to determine when notice can be altered, limited, or denied to creditors.[8]

Library References:

West's Key No. Digests, Bankruptcy ⇌3067.1–3084.

§ 9.201 Chapter 7—Disposition of Property Subject to the Interest of Another

Before the final distribution of property of the estate, the trustee, after notice and a hearing, must dispose of any property in which an entity other than the estate has an interest.[1] This provision is intended "to ensure that collateral or its proceeds is returned to the proper secured creditor, that consigned or bailed goods are returned to the consignor or bailor, and so on."[2]

Library References:

West's Key No. Digests, Bankruptcy ⇌3068.

§ 9.202 Chapter 7—Priorities

Pursuant to Section 726 of the Bankruptcy Code, property of the estate in a chapter 7 liquidation must be distributed to holders of claims according to the following order of priorities:[1]

6. PRACTICE POINTER: If a statutory committee of creditors or equity security holders is serving in a chapter 7 case, the bankruptcy court may enter an order limiting the mailing of sale notices to such committees and the other creditors and equity security holders who have filed a request for all notices pursuant to Bankruptcy Rule 2002. See Bankr.R. 9006 for information concerning the computation, enlargement, and reduction of time periods under the Bankruptcy Code. For a more detailed discussion of asset sales, see generally *Representing Purchasers of Assets from Bankruptcy Estates*, 20 Colo.Law. 2259 (November 1991).

7. United States v. Goodstein, 883 F.2d 1362, 1366 (7th Cir.1989), cert. denied 494 U.S. 1007, 110 S.Ct. 1305, 108 L.Ed.2d 481 (1990).

8. Bankr.R. 2002(m).

§ 9.201

1. 11 U.S.C.A. § 725.

2. H.R.Rep.No. 95–595, 95th Cong., 1st Sess. 382–83 (1977); S.Rep.No. 95–989, 95th Cong., 2d Sess. 96 (1978).

§ 9.202

1. For cases previously filed under another chapter of the Bankruptcy Code and converted to chapter 7, see infra, § 9.209 for a discussion of the effects of conversion.

First Priority. Claims in the order specified in Section 507 of the Bankruptcy Code.[2] Payment will be made on first priority claims if proof of such claims was timely filed under Section 501 of the Code or if proof of such claims was tardily filed before the date when the trustee commences distribution;[3]

Second Priority. Claims of general unsecured creditors excluding priority creditors, creditors that hold certain late filed claims,[4] and creditors whose claims are for any fine, penalty, punitive, or similar damages that are not compensation for an actual pecuniary loss;

Third Priority. Tardily filed allowed, unsecured claims that do not qualify for distribution under the second priority;

Fourth Priority. Any allowed, secured or unsecured claims for any fine, penalty, punitive, or similar damages arising before the earlier of the order for relief or the appointment of a trustee, to the extent such claims are not compensation for actual pecuniary loss;

Fifth Priority. Claims for interest at the legal rate from the petition date on any claims paid under the first through fourth priorities above;

Sixth Priority. To the debtor.

If there are insufficient funds to pay the holders of claims of a particular class in full, payment must be made on a *pro rata* basis to holders of claims within such class.[5] In a case that has been converted to chapter 7 from a case under another chapter of the Bankruptcy Code, the administrative expenses of the chapter 7 case receive priority in payment over the administrative expenses of the preceding case under another chapter of the Code.[6]

Library References:

West's Key No. Digests, Bankruptcy ⚖=2951–2972.

§ 9.203 Chapter 7—Special Tax Provisions

For purposes of state or local income tax, the taxable year of an individual debtor under chapter 7 terminates on the date of the order for relief.[1] If an individual or corporate debtor under chapter 7 has net taxable income at the close of the case, the trustee must file an income

---

2. See supra, § 9.106 for a list of the priorities set forth in 11 U.S.C.A. § 507.

3. 11 U.S.C.A. § 726(a)(1).

4. Holders of tardily filed claims may be paid under the second priority if the tardiness was due to lack of notice or knowledge of the case, providing the claim is filed in time to permit its payment. 11 U.S.C.A. § 726(a)(2)(C).

5. 11 U.S.C.A. § 726(b).

6. *Id. See supra*, § 9.98 for a discussion of administrative expense claims.

§ 9.203

1. 11 U.S.C.A. § 728(a). If the case originally was filed under chapter 11 or 12, the individual debtor's taxable year ended when the estate first became a separate taxable entity. *See supra*, §§ 9.8, 9.10 for discussions of the order for relief in voluntary and involuntary cases, respectively.

tax return for each year during which the case was pending after the order for relief.[2] If chapter 7 cases of a partnership and a partner in such partnership are both pending, and an income tax liability arose from the inclusion of undistributed earnings in the partner's taxable income, the court is required to disallow the tax claim against the partner's estate and to allow the tax claim against the partnership estate.[3]

§ 9.204 Chapter 7—Discharge[1]

Section 727(b), which governs discharge in chapter 7 cases, discharges all debts (listed or unlisted) other than debts specifically excepted from discharge. Section 727(a) lists 9 grounds for denial of a general discharge.[2]

Library References:
West's Key No. Digests, Bankruptcy ⚖3251–3423.

§ 9.205 Chapter 7—Discharge—Exceptions to General Discharge of the Debtor

The specific grounds for denial of a discharge pursuant to Section 727(a) are as follows:

1. *Debtor is not an individual.* Partnerships and corporations cannot be granted a discharge under chapter 7;[1]

2. *Fraudulent Transfer or Concealment.* The debtor, with intent to hinder, delay, or defraud a creditor or officer of the estate, has transferred, removed, destroyed, mutilated, or concealed property of the debtor (or permitted or caused it to occur) within one year prior to the petition date, or property of the estate after the petition date;[2]

---

2. 11 U.S.C.A. § 728(b).

3. 11. U.S.C.A. § 728(c). Section 723(c) permits the partnership trustee to assert any unsatisfied tax claims against the partner's estate.

§ 9.204

1. *See also* 11 U.S.C.A. §§ 523, 524, and 727; *see supra* §§ 9.168–9.170 for additional information concerning discharge and exceptions to discharge.

2. *See supra*, §§ 9.168–9.169 for a discussion of the effect of a discharge and other general information which also is relevant to chapter 7.

§ 9.205

1. 11 U.S.C.A. § 727(a)(1). *See* National Labor Relations Bd. v. Better Bldg. Supply Corp., 837 F.2d 377 (9th Cir.1988).

2. 11 U.S.C.A. § 727(a)(2).

CAVEAT: A creditor filing a motion opposing discharge pursuant to Section 727(a)(2) of the Bankruptcy Code must demonstrate actual intent to hinder, defraud, or delay; actual intent may be demonstrated by circumstantial and inferential evidence. Constructive intent cannot be the basis for the denial of discharge under such section. *See, e.g.,* In re Glaser, 49 B.R. 1015 (Bankr.S.D.N.Y.1985); In re Marcus, 45 B.R. 338 (Bankr.S.D.N.Y.1984).

CAVEAT: There is a split in authority concerning whether, for purposes of Section 727(a)(2) of the Bankruptcy Code, the transfer of a deed, security interest, mortgage, or other instrument occurs at the moment of transfer or upon recordation. *Compare* In re Rubin, 12 B.R. 436 (Bankr. S.D.N.Y.1981) (transfer of deed not considered a complete transfer for purposes of

§ 9.205   BANKRUPTCY   Ch. 9

3. *Destruction or Falsification of Records.* The debtor has concealed, destroyed, mutilated, falsified, or failed to keep or preserve books, documents, records, and papers from which the debtor's financial condition or business transactions might be ascertained unless such failure to act was justified under the circumstances of the case;[3]
4. *False Oath, Account, or Claim.* The debtor has, in connection with the case, knowingly and fraudulently, (a) made a false oath or account, (b) presented or used a false claim, (c) given, offered, received, or attempted to obtain money, property, or advantage (or a promise thereof), for acting or forbearing to act, or (d) withheld from an officer of the estate entitled to possession, any recorded information, including books, documents, records, and papers relating to the debtor's property or financial affairs;[4]
5. *Failure to Explain Loss or Deficiency of Assets.* The debtor has failed to explain satisfactorily any loss of assets or deficiency of assets to meet the debtor's liabilities;[5]
6. *Refusal to Obey Court Order.* The debtor has refused in the case to (a) obey any lawful order of the court, other than an order to respond to a material question or testify, or (b) respond to a material question approved by the court after

barring discharge until perfection by recordation) *with* In re Kock, 20 B.R. 453 (Bankr.D.Neb.1982) (for purposes of discharge, transfer of mortgage occurred when debtor transferred mortgage to mortgagee, not when mortgagee perfected its interest by filing).

PRACTICE POINTER: In analyzing transfers under Section 727(a)(2), the practitioner must be cognizant of the extremely broad definition of "transfer" under Section 101(54) of the Bankruptcy Code. *See* 11 U.S.C.A. § 101(54); *see supra*, § 9.117 note 1.

3. 11 U.S.C.A. § 727(a)(3).

PRACTICE POINTER: The debtor's failure to keep or preserve books and records need not be intentional to support an objection to discharge pursuant to 11 U.S.C.A. § 727(a)(3). *See* In re Frommann, 153 B.R. 113 (Bankr.E.D.N.Y.1993).

4. 11 U.S.C.A. § 727(a)(4).

PRACTICE POINTER: One common example of a false oath and/or a concealment under Section 727(a)(4) of the Bankruptcy Code arises in circumstances where the debtor declares that its schedules of assets and liabilities are true and correct, but knowingly and fraudulently omits property therefrom. Counsel must instruct the debtor to include all known assets and liabilities in the schedules. *See* In re Sicari, 187 B.R. 861, 880 (Bankr.S.D.N.Y.1994) ("A material omission from a debtor's sworn statement of affairs or schedules presents grounds for denying a discharge under 11 U.S.C. § 727(a)(4)(A)."). *But see* In re Espino, 806 F.2d 1001 (11th Cir.1986) (failure by debtors to list contingent guaranty of corporate debt was insufficient to warrant denial of discharge absent sufficient evidence of intent to defraud).

CAVEAT: Counsel will be held liable for assisting a debtor in committing bankruptcy fraud. *See* United States v. Dolan, 120 F.3d 856 (8th Cir.1997) (debtor's attorney sentenced to 2 years imprisonment followed by 3 years of supervision for conviction on conspiracy to commit bankruptcy fraud and aiding and abetting in the concealment of property of a bankruptcy estate).

5. 11 U.S.C.A. § 727(a)(5).

CAVEAT: Section 727(a)(5) of the Bankruptcy Code does not require a demonstration of fraudulent intent to deny a debtor's discharge on the ground that the debtor failed to adequately explain the loss of as-

Ch. 9   PROCEDURE: OBJECTIONS TO DISCHARGE   § 9.206

having been granted immunity or after improperly invoking the constitutional privilege against self-incrimination;[6]

7. *Conduct in Bankruptcy Case of an Insider.* The debtor has, within one year before the petition date, or at any time during the case, committed any act listed above in paragraphs 2–6 in connection with the bankruptcy case of an insider of the debtor;[7]

8. *Prior Chapter 7 or 11 Discharge.* The debtor has been granted a discharge under chapter 7 or 11 of the Bankruptcy Code in a case commenced within six years before the petition date;[8]

9. *Prior Chapter 12 or 13 Discharge.* The debtor has been granted a discharge under chapter 12 or 13 of the Bankruptcy Code in a case commenced within six years before the petition date, unless payments under the plan in such prior case totalled 100% of the allowed unsecured claims in such case; or 70% of the allowed unsecured claims were paid under the plan and the plan was proposed in good faith and was the debtor's best effort;[9]

10. *Written Waiver.* The court has approved a written waiver of discharge executed by the debtor after the order for relief was entered.[10]

Library References:

West's Key No. Digests, Bankruptcy ⇌3271–3290.

§ 9.206   Chapter 7—Discharge—Procedure for Objections to General Discharge of the Debtor

The trustee, a creditor, or the United States trustee may object to the granting of a discharge on the grounds set forth in Section 727(a) of the Bankruptcy Code, described above.[1] In addition, as a safeguard against collusion between debtors and creditors in chapter 7, upon the request of a party in interest, the court may order the trustee to examine

sets. *See* In re Lorenzato, 147 B.R. 346 (Bankr.S.D.N.Y.1992).

6. 11 U.S.C.A. § 727(a)(6). *See* In re Minton Group, Inc., 43 B.R. 705 (Bankr. S.D.N.Y.1984) (if a debtor is granted immunity and thereafter refuses to testify based upon the privilege against self-incrimination, such debtor's discharge may be denied under Section 727(a)(6) of the Bankruptcy Code).

7. 11 U.S.C.A. § 727(a)(7). Section 727(a)(7) of the Bankruptcy Code provides that the debtor's prohibited actions in the bankruptcy case of an "insider" will result in denial of discharge to the debtor. *See* In re Jacobe, 116 B.R. 463 (Bankr.E.D.Va. 1990); 11 U.S.C.A. § 101(31) (definition of "insider").

8. 11 U.S.C.A. § 727(a)(8). *See* In re Mendoza, 16 B.R. 990, 993 (Bankr.S.D.Cal. 1982) ("The purpose of this six year provision is to prevent the creation of a class of habitual debtors, who would rid themselves of their debts by going through bankruptcy every time they find themselves unable to pay their debts.").

9. 11 U.S.C.A. § 727(a)(9).

10. 11 U.S.C.A. § 727(a)(10).

§ 9.206

1. 11 U.S.C.A. § 727(c)(1). *See supra,* § 9.205.

453

§ 9.206

the acts and conduct of the debtor to determine whether a ground exists for denial of discharge.[2]

Further, the trustee, a creditor, or the United States trustee also may request a revocation of discharge *after* the court has granted such discharge, as follows: (i) within one year after the granting of a discharge, if the discharge was obtained through the fraud of the debtor, which fraud was unknown to the requesting party until after the discharge was granted, or (ii) before the later of one year after the granting of a discharge and the date that the case is closed, if the debtor acquired property that is property of the estate (or became entitled to acquire such property) and knowingly and fraudulently failed to report such acquisition (or entitlement) or to deliver or surrender such property to the trustee.[3]

Objections to discharge (and requests for revocation of discharge) must be brought by adversary proceeding under the Bankruptcy Rules.[4] The complaint in support of an objection to discharge must be filed not later than 60 days following the first date set for the meeting of creditors unless the court grants an extension for cause.[5] Not less than 25 days notice must be given to the U.S. trustee, all creditors on the list created pursuant to Bankruptcy Rule 2002, and to the trustee and the trustee's attorney.[6] Upon the expiration of the time for filing a complaint objecting to discharge and the expiration of the time fixed for filing a motion to dismiss the case (also 60 days after the first meeting of creditors, unless extended for cause), the bankruptcy court must grant a discharge to the debtor unless: (i) the debtor is not an individual, (ii) a complaint objecting to the discharge has been filed, (iii) the debtor has filed a written waiver of discharge pursuant to Section 727(a)(10) of the Bankruptcy Code, or (iv) a motion to dismiss the case under Bankruptcy Rule 1017(e) is pending.[7]

---

2. 11 U.S.C.A. § 727(c)(2).

3. 11 U.S.C.A. § 727(d), (e).

4. Bankr.R. 4004(d); Bankr.R. 7001(4). See *infra*, § 9.266 for a procedural checklist for commencing an adversary proceeding.

5. Bankr.R. 4004(a), (b). See Bankr.R. 9006 for information concerning the computation, enlargement, and reduction of time periods under the Bankruptcy Code. See *supra*, § 9.37 for a discussion of the meeting of creditors.

PRACTICE POINTER: If the creditor requires additional time to file a complaint objecting to discharge, such as in circumstances where the creditor is negotiating with the debtor regarding its claim, the creditor should file its motion in connection therewith within the 60-day period set forth in Bankruptcy Rule 4004 and prior to any bar date that may have been established by the court. See In re Horton, 149 B.R. 49 (Bankr.S.D.N.Y.1992) (the bankruptcy court does not have discretion to grant a motion to extend time to file a complaint objecting to discharge where the motion was filed after the bar date); In re Webb, 157 B.R. 614 (Bankr.N.D.Ohio 1993) (objection to discharge filed more than 60 days after the first date set for the meeting of creditors would not be entertained where no extension of time to file such objection had been sought).

6. Bankr.R. 4004(a).

7. Bankr.R. 4004(c). The court may, upon motion of the debtor, defer entry of an order granting discharge for 30 days, or on a motion made within such 30-day period, for a longer period. *Id*. Generally, the purpose of such deferral will be to allow the debtor time to negotiate and consummate

§ 9.207 Chapter 7—Discharge—Exceptions to Discharge of Particular Debts

The general discharge granted to individual debtors under Section 727(b) is also specifically subject to Section 523 of the Bankruptcy Code, which lists 16 categories of nondischargeable debts.[1] Thus, Section 727(a) of the Bankruptcy Code enables a creditor to object to the granting of a general discharge to a chapter 7 debtor, thereby seeking to render all debts of such a debtor nondischargeable; whereas Section 523 of the Bankruptcy Code provides a means by which a creditor may object to the discharge of certain specific debts of an individual debtor. While some of the categories of debts listed in Section 523(a) are unconditionally nondischargeable, subsections (b) and (c) set forth certain limitations and conditions on nondischargeability. Under Section 523(b), certain non-fraud debts that were excepted from discharge in a prior bankruptcy case are dischargeable in a subsequent case unless they specifically are nondischargeable in the subsequent case.[2]

Section 523(a)(3) bars the discharge of any debts that the debtor has not scheduled in time to permit timely filing by a creditor of a proof of claim and a dischargeability complaint unless the creditor had notice or actual knowledge of the case in time to protect its rights by such timely filing. In many no-asset chapter 7 cases, however, no deadline to file a proof of claim is established.[3] In those cases, the debtor's failure to schedule a debt will not prevent a discharge under Section 727(b) of a claim that is not a fraud claim even if it was never listed.[4]

---

reaffirmation agreements, which may only be entered into prior to entry of the discharge order. 11 U.S.C.A. § 524. See Bankr.R. 4004, Advisory Committee Note. See also, supra, § 9.130 for a discussion of reaffirmation agreements pursuant to Section 524 of the Bankruptcy Code.

§ 9.207
1. PRACTICE POINTER: Bear in mind that Section 523 applies to cases under chapters 7, 11, 12, and 13.
2. See, e.g., In re Chaffin, 816 F.2d 1070 (5th Cir.1987) (filing of chapter 13 petition to discharge a claim that had been held nondischargeable in debtor's prior case was not sufficient cause to find that debtor's subsequent chapter 13 plan had been proposed in bad faith); In re Lilley, 185 B.R. 489 (E.D.Pa.1995), reversed 91 F.3d 491 (3d Cir.1996) (same); Nolan v. United States (In re Nolan), 205 B.R. 885 (Bankr. M.D.Tenn.1997) (certain tax claims were dischargeable in debtor's chapter 7 case because they were outside the 3-year "look back" period for nondischargeability and were held not extended or tolled by reason of debtor's prior chapter 7 case).

3. Although Bankruptcy Rule 3002 provides that a proof of claim in a chapter 7 case is timely filed if it is filed no later than 90 days after the first date for the meeting of creditors under 11 U.S.C.A. § 341(a) (see supra, § 9.37), Bankruptcy Rule 2002(e) provides an exception to this general rule. In cases where there are no assets from which distributions to creditors can be made, the notice of the meeting of creditors may include a statement to this effect and a statement that it is unnecessary to file proofs of claim. Bankr.R. 2002(e).

4. Judd v. Wolfe, 78 F.3d 110 (3d Cir. 1996); Beezley v. California Land Title Co. (In re Beezley), 994 F.2d 1433 (9th Cir. 1993); but see In re Grant, 160 B.R. 839 (Bankr.S.D.Cal.1993) (reconsideration granted more than one year after discharge

§ 9.207 BANKRUPTCY Ch. 9

Library References:

West's Key No. Digests, Bankruptcy ⚖3341–3362.

§ 9.208 Chapter 7—Discharge—Procedure for Objections to Discharge of Particular Debts

Objections to the discharge of a particular debt pursuant to Section 523 of the Bankruptcy Code, like an objection to a general discharge pursuant to Section 727, must be brought by an adversary proceeding under the Bankruptcy Rules.[1] The debtor or any creditor may file a complaint to obtain a determination of the dischargeability of any debt.[2]

If an omitted debt is a claim of a kind specified under Section 523(a)(2) (for money, property, services, or credit obtained by false pretenses, false representation, or fraud),[3] Section 523(a)(4) (for fraud or where the discharged debt arguably fell within the scope of Section 523(a)(2), (4), or (6)).

§ 9.208

1. Bankr.R. 4007(e); Bankr.R. 7001(6). See infra, § 9.266 for a procedural checklist for commencing an adversary proceeding.

2. Bankr.R. 4007(a).

PRACTICE POINTER: If a chapter 7 debtor anticipates that a creditor may object to the dischargeability of a significant debt, under Bankruptcy Rule 4007, it may file a complaint seeking a determination of the dischargeability of such debt early in the case. If the court determines that the debt is not dischargeable, the debtor may consider entering into a reaffirmation agreement with the creditor or converting the case to one under chapter 13 of the Bankruptcy Code. See 11 U.S.C.A. § 524(c). See supra, §§ 9.130–9.131 for a discussion of reaffirmation and the very important caveats relating thereto. See infra, §§ 9.255–9.256 for a discussion of the discharge provisions under chapter 13 of the Bankruptcy Code.

3. **PRACTICE POINTER**: Section 523(a)(2)(A) excepts from discharge the debt of an individual for money, property, services, or credit to the extent such debt was obtained by false pretenses, false representation, or actual fraud (other than a statement concerning the debtor's or an insider's financial condition). The Supreme Court has held that the degree of reliance required for Section 523(a)(2)(A) to be applicable is "justifiable reliance," not the more demanding standard of "reasonable reliance" that is specifically required under Section 523(a)(2)(B). Field v. Mans, 516 U.S. 59, 116 S.Ct. 437, 133 L.Ed.2d 351 (1995). The Court explained that a person is justified in relying on a representation of fact unless the facts within his immediate observation at the time the representation is made serve as a warning that he is being deceived.

In contrast, a creditor who seeks to except a debt from discharge pursuant to Section 523(a)(2)(B) (use of a written statement concerning the debtor's or an insider's financial condition) must have established procedures that will evidence the reasonable reliance required under the statute. For example, the Eighth Circuit rejected a bank's attempt to deny a discharge of a debt owed to it because the court found that the bank failed to prove that it had relied on the false information provided by the borrower when it extended the credit, or if it had relied on the false information, its reliance had not been reasonable under the circumstances of the case. First National Bank v. Pontow, 111 F.3d 604 (8th Cir.1997).

The Ninth Circuit has issued three decisions concerning the standards for determining when a debtor has committed actual fraud with respect to credit card charges. While the Ninth Circuit endorsed applying a "totality of the circumstances" standard, it focused its attention on the debtor's subjective intent at the time of each transaction; that is, whether or not the debtor had intended to escape his debt through bankruptcy at the time the debts were incurred. See American Express Travel Related Services v. Hashemi (In re Hashemi), 104 F.3d 1122 (9th Cir.1996), cert. denied ___ U.S. ___, 117 S.Ct. 1824, 137 L.Ed.2d 1031 (1997); Citibank, N.A. v. Eashai (In re

defalcation while acting in a fiduciary capacity, embezzlement, or larceny), Section 523(a)(6) (for willful and malicious injury to another or another's property), or Section 523(a)(15) (certain debts incurred by the debtor in the course of a divorce or separation), then Section 523(c)(1) requires a creditor who is owed such a debt to initiate proceedings requesting the bankruptcy court to determine the dischargeability of the debt. Such debts may be challenged as nondischargeable only in the bankruptcy court, upon request of the creditor to whom the debt is owed, by complaint filed not later than 60 days following the first date set for the meeting of creditors, or such later time as the court determines for cause.[4] If the creditor fails to act within the 60-day period or such extended period as is approved by the court, the debt will be discharged unless the creditor had no notice or actual knowledge of the case in time to permit a timely request for a determination as to dischargeability.[5]

In contrast to the debts referred to in Section 523(c)(1) of the Bankruptcy Code, described in the preceding paragraph, a complaint to obtain a determination of the dischargeability of the remaining "nondischargeable" debts referenced in Section 523(a) of the Bankruptcy Code may be filed at any time, including after the chapter 7 case has been closed.[6]

Under Bankruptcy Rule 9021, a judgment in an adversary proceeding is effective when it is entered on the docket pursuant to Bankruptcy Rule 5003.[7] Nevertheless, a debtor may move for deferral of the entry of an order granting a discharge for 30 days and, on motion within such period, the court may defer entry of an order to a date certain.[8] This rule is intended to permit the debtor to enter into a reaffirmation agreement. Since reaffirmation agreements are enforceable only if they are made before the granting of a discharge,[9] the deferral of entry of an order

Eashai), 87 F.3d 1082 (9th Cir.1996); Anastas v. American Savings Bank (In re Anastas), 94 F.3d 1280 (9th Cir.1996).

4. 11 U.S.C.A. § 523(c)(1); Bankr.R. 4007(c). See supra, § 9.37 for a discussion of the meeting of creditors.

5. Section 523(c)(2) limits the applicability of Section 523(c)(1) with respect to certain federal regulatory agencies.

See Bankruptcy Rules 4004, 4005, and 4007 for the procedure governing complaints to obtain a determination of the dischargeability of a debt. See supra, §§ 9.204–9.205, 9.207 for additional information concerning discharge.

PRACTICE POINTER: Because many of the grounds for objection to discharge arise as a consequence of actions taken by the debtor prior to filing the chapter 7 petition, counsel must carefully examine the debtor before filing the petition to determine if grounds for the denial of a discharge exist. If grounds for the denial of a discharge exist, chapter 7 may not be a realistic alternative. Moreover, counsel must caution the debtor to prevent the debtor from taking actions after the filing of the petition that would provide grounds for the denial of a discharge.

6. Bankr.R. 4007(b).

7. After the court grants a discharge, a discharge order in the form of Official Form 18 should be submitted for entry.

8. Bankr.R. 4004(c).

9. See 11 U.S.C.A. § 524(c)(1). See supra, §§ 9.130–9.131 for a discussion of reaffirmation and the very important caveats relating thereto.

§ 9.208   BANKRUPTCY   Ch. 9

granting a discharge affords the debtor an opportunity to execute a reaffirmation agreement as part of a settlement.

Library References:
West's Key No. Digests, Bankruptcy ⟜3381–3423.

§ 9.209   Chapter 7—Conversion or Dismissal of Cases[1]

A chapter 7 debtor has a one-time absolute right to convert its liquidation case to a reorganization or repayment plan case under chapter 11, 12, or 13 at any time; however, if the case was previously converted from chapter 11 or 13 to chapter 7, then the debtor no longer has an absolute right to reconvert the case back to chapter 11 or 13.[2] The policy allowing conversion is that "the debtor should always be given the opportunity to repay his debts" without having to liquidate.[3] Any waiver of the right to convert a chapter 7 case is unenforceable.[4] Although the court may grant the request by a party in interest to convert a chapter 7 case to a chapter 11 case at any time,[5] the court may not convert a chapter 7 case to a chapter 12 or 13 case unless the debtor requests such conversion.[6] The court may only convert the case to another chapter if the debtor is eligible to be a debtor under such chapter.[7]

The court may dismiss a chapter 7 case after notice and a hearing for cause, including:

1. Unreasonable delay by the debtor that is prejudicial to creditors;
2. Nonpayment of any required fees or charges required under chapter 123 of title 28; or
3. Failure of a debtor in a voluntary case, within 15 days after the filing of the petition commencing the case (or such additional time as the court may allow), to file the list of creditors, schedule of assets and liabilities, and statement of financial affairs required by § 521(1) of the Bankruptcy Code.[8]

In addition, the court, on its own motion or on a motion by the U.S. trustee, but not at the request or suggestion of any party in interest,

---

§ 9.209

1. Conversion and dismissal are governed by Bankruptcy Rule 1017. See supra, § 9.174 for a brief general discussion of conversion or dismissal of cases under title 11.

2. 11 U.S.C.A. § 706(a).

3. See H.Rep.No. 95–595, 95th Cong., 1st Sess. 380 (1977).

4. 11 U.S.C.A. § 706(a).

5. 11 U.S.C.A. § 706(b). The "decision whether to convert is left to the sound discretion of the court, based on what will most inure to the benefit of all parties in interest." See 124 Cong.Rec.H 11,098 (Sept. 28, 1978); S 17,414 (Oct. 6, 1978).

6. 11 U.S.C.A. § 706(c). This subsection is part of the prohibition against involuntary chapter 12 or 13 cases. See H.Rep.No. 95–595, 95th Cong., 1st Sess. 380 (1977); S.Rep.No. 95–989, 95th Cong., 2d Sess. 94 (1978).

7. 11 U.S.C.A. § 706(d).

8. 11 U.S.C.A. § 707(a). Dismissal for failure to file the required lists and schedules may only be on motion by the U.S. trustee. 11 U.S.C.A. § 707(a)(3).

458

may dismiss the case of an individual chapter 7 debtor whose debts are "primarily consumer debts" if it finds that granting relief under chapter 7 "would be a substantial abuse" of the provisions of that chapter.[9] If the debtor requests dismissal of its chapter 7 case, there is a presumption in favor of granting the relief requested by the debtor.[10]

Library References:

West's Key No. Digests, Bankruptcy ⟸2259.1–2264(3), 2331–2332.

§ 9.210 Chapter 7—Conversion or Dismissal of Cases—Procedure

Bankruptcy Rule 1017(d) provides that a proceeding that is brought by a party in interest to dismiss or convert a case to another chapter is a contested matter governed by Bankruptcy Rule 9014. A motion to dismiss or convert brought by the debtor must be filed and served as required by Bankruptcy Rule 9013.[1] The hearing on the dismissal of the case or the conversion of the case to another chapter requires no less than 20 days notice by mail (unless the hearing is pursuant to Section 707(b) of the Bankruptcy Code).[2] Section 348 of the Bankruptcy Code

---

9. 11 U.S.C.A. § 707(b). To prevent the use of chapter 7 relief by debtors who are not needy, Congress added Section 707(b) to the Bankruptcy Code in 1984. Section 707(b) provides:

After notice and a hearing, the court, on its own motion or on a motion by the United States trustee, but not at the request or suggestion of any party in interest, may dismiss a case filed by an individual debtor under this chapter whose debts are primarily consumer debts if it finds that the granting of relief would be a substantial abuse of the provisions of this chapter. There shall be a presumption in favor of granting the relief requested by the debtor.

By denying relief to debtors who are not needy, this subsection was intended to promote fairness to creditors and increase the availability of consumer credit. The Bankruptcy Code defines "consumer debt" as "debt incurred by an individual primarily for a personal, family, or household purpose." 11 U.S.C.A. § 101(8). A chapter 7 debtor's "ability to fund a chapter 13 plan 'is the primary factor to be considered in determining whether granting relief would be substantial abuse.'" Stuart v. Koch (In re Koch), 109 F.3d 1285, 1285 (8th Cir. 1997) (citation omitted); Zolg v. Kelly (In re Kelly), 841 F.2d 908 (9th Cir.1988); In re Edwards, 50 B.R. 933 (Bankr.S.D.N.Y. 1985). A court in New York has noted that "the debtor's future ability to pay is the proper focus" of a court's determination under section 707(b) inasmuch as that subsection of the Code is intended to deal with the "perceived abuse of a debtor presently insolvent but whose immediate future income would permit payment of his debts over a reasonable time period." Edwards, 50 B.R. at 938. Accordingly, a debtor who can pay his debts within a period of three to five years should file under chapter 13 or should not seek to avail himself of bankruptcy relief.

PRACTICE POINTER: In calculating disposable future income for purposes of ascertaining whether a debtor will be able to fund a chapter 13 plan, *postpetition* income that would otherwise be exempt from the claims of creditors under state law is income, the disposable portion of which must be paid to unsecured creditors. Koch, 109 F.3d at 1289. *See infra*, § 9.252 note 2 for additional cases.

10. 11 U.S.C.A. § 707(b).

§ 9.210

1. Bankr.R. 1017(d). A fee of $400 is required for converting a case under chapter 7 to a case under chapter 11 on the request of a debtor. 28 U.S.C.A. § 1930(a).

2. Bankr.R. 2002(a)(5). *See supra*, § 9.209 note 9 for a discussion of Section 707(b) of the Bankruptcy Code. See Bankruptcy Rule 9006 for information

and Bankruptcy Rule 1019 establish the effects of the conversion of a chapter 11, 12, or 13 case to a chapter 7 liquidation. For example, all claims actually filed by a creditor in the superseded case will be deemed filed in the chapter 7 case.[3] The rule is not intended to invalidate any action taken in the superseded case before its conversion to chapter 7.[4]

§ 9.211 Chapter 7—Closing and Reopening Cases

The court will close the case after an estate is fully administered and the court has discharged the trustee.[1] However, the case may be reopened on motion of the debtor or other party in interest to administer assets, to accord relief to the debtor, or for other cause.[2]

Library References:

West's Key No. Digests, Bankruptcy ⚖=3441–3445.

§ 9.212 Chapter 12—Overview[1]

Chapter 12 of the Bankruptcy Code, entitled Adjustment of Debts of a Family Farmer With Regular Annual Income, is designed to provide an expedited means for troubled farmers to restructure their debts without having to lose their farms. Only a family farmer with regular annual income may be a debtor under chapter 12.[2] The Bankruptcy Code includes alternative definitions for the term "family farmer," depending on whether the debtor is, on the one hand, an individual or individual and spouse or, on the other hand, a corporation or partnership. Thus, "family farmer" means an individual or individual and spouse engaged in a farming operation[3] who received more than 50% of their gross income from such farming operation during the taxable year preceding the taxable year in which the case was filed. Alternatively, "family farmer" means a corporation (whose stock, if any, is not publicly traded)

---

concerning the computation, enlargement, and reduction of time periods under the Bankruptcy Code.

3. Bankr.R. 1019(3).

4. *See* Bankr.R. 1019, Advisory Committee Note.

§ 9.211

1. 11 U.S.C.A. § 350(a).

2. 11 U.S.C.A. § 350(b); Bankr.R. 5010. In addition, Rule 9024 exempts motions to reopen cases from the one-year limitation of F.R.C.P. 60(b). *See supra,* § 9.33 note 6 regarding the desirability of closing cases expeditiously to avoid the incurrence of additional fees under 28 U.S.C.A. § 1930(a).

§ 9.212

1. Much of the information covered in the preceding sections of this chapter is applicable to chapter 12 and is not repeated in this portion of the chapter. For topics of particular interest, refer to the *Table of Sections*, and particularly §§ 9.1–9.137, which are applicable to all chapters under the Bankruptcy Code unless otherwise noted.

2. 11 U.S.C.A. § 109(f).

3. The Bankruptcy Code defines "farming operation" as including "farming, tillage of the soil, dairy farming, ranching, production or raising of crops, poultry, or livestock, and production of poultry or livestock products in an unmanufactured state." 11 U.S.C.A. § 101(21).

or partnership in which more than 50% of the outstanding equity is held by one family or one family and the relatives of such family, and such family or relatives conduct the farming operation. More than 80% of the value of the assets of a family farmer partnership or corporation must consist of assets related to the farming operation. In addition, for any form of family farmer to seek relief under chapter 12, its aggregate debts may not exceed $1,500,000 and, on the date the case is filed, not less than 80% of the aggregate noncontingent, liquidated debts (excluding a debt for one principal residence, unless such debt arises out of a farming operation) must arise out of the farming operation owned or operated by the debtor.[4] A "family farmer with regular annual income" is defined as a family farmer whose annual income "is sufficiently stable and regular to enable such family farmer to make payments under chapter 12" of the Bankruptcy Code.[5]

Notably, chapter 12 is to be repealed effective October 1, 1998. However, even if the date of repeal is not extended, as it has been in the past, all cases commenced under chapter 12 before that date and all matters and proceedings in or relating to such cases, must be conducted and determined under chapter 12 following the date of repeal, as if it had not been repealed.[6]

Library References:

West's Key No. Digests, Bankruptcy ⇌3671–3674.

§ 9.213 Chapter 12—Rights and Powers of Debtor

Unless modified by the court, a debtor in possession under chapter 12 has all the rights, other than the right to compensation, all the powers, including operating the debtor's farm, and performs all the duties, except the investigative duties, of a trustee under chapter 11.[1]

Library References:

West's Key No. Digests, Bankruptcy ⇌3672.

§ 9.214 Chapter 12—Appointment of a Trustee

If the United States trustee in a district has appointed an individual to serve as standing trustee in chapter 12 cases, and if that individual qualifies to serve as a trustee pursuant to Section 322 of the Bankruptcy Code, then that individual serves as trustee in any chapter 12 case filed

4. 11 U.S.C.A. § 101(18).
5. 11 U.S.C.A. § 101(19).
6. See Pub.L. 99–554, Title III, § 302(f), Oct. 27, 1986, 100 Stat. 3124, as amended by Pub.L. 103–65, § 1, Aug. 6, 1993, 107 Stat. 311.

§ 9.213
1. 11 U.S.C.A. § 1203. See supra, § 9.139 for a discussion of the rights, powers, and duties of a trustee under chapter 11.

§ 9.214 BANKRUPTCY Ch. 9

in the district. If no standing trustee has been appointed, the United States trustee may appoint a disinterested person to serve as trustee, or the United States trustee may serve in that capacity if necessary.[1] Otherwise, the debtor may serve as debtor in possession[2] and must perform all the duties of a trustee, including operating its farm.[3] If a party in interest demonstrates that there is cause (such as fraud, dishonesty, incompetence, or gross mismanagement of the debtor's affairs) for removal of the debtor as debtor in possession, the court will remove the debtor from being a debtor in possession.[4]

Library References:

West's Key No. Digests, Bankruptcy ⚖3672.

§ 9.215 Chapter 12—Duties of a Trustee

The chapter 12 trustee performs the duties of a chapter 7 trustee described *supra*, § 9.182, except for (1) collecting and reducing to money the debtor's property,[1] (2) investigating the debtor's financial affairs,[2] and (3) if the debtor's business is authorized to be operated, filing periodic reports and summaries of the debtor's operations, including a statement of receipts and disbursements.[3] In addition, a chapter 12 trustee is required to:

1. Appear and be heard at any meeting concerning confirmation or modification of a confirmed plan, or the value of property subject to a lien,[4] and the sale of estate property;[5]

2. Ensure that the debtor commences making timely payments under its plan;[6]

3. If the debtor is engaged in business, perform those duties of a chapter 11 trustee listed as numbers 7 and 8 *supra*, § 9.139.[7]

If a chapter 12 debtor ceases to be a debtor in possession, the trustee must perform certain additional duties set forth at 11 U.S.C.A. § 1202(b)(5).

Library References:

West's Key No. Digests, Bankruptcy ⚖3008.1–3009.

§ 9.214

1. 11 U.S.C.A. § 1202. See 28 U.S.C.A. § 586(e) for provisions governing the compensation of a chapter 12 or 13 trustee.

2. *See supra*, § 9.27 for a description of the debtor in possession.

3. 11 U.S.C.A. § 1203.

4. 11 U.S.C.A. § 1204.

§ 9.215

1. 11 U.S.C.A. §§ 1202(b)(1), 704(1).
2. 11 U.S.C.A. §§ 1202(b)(1), 704(4).
3. 11 U.S.C.A. §§ 1202(b)(1), 704(8).
4. 11 U.S.C.A. § 1202(b)(3).
5. 11 U.S.C.A. § 1202(b)(3)(D).
6. 11 U.S.C.A. § 1202(b)(4).
7. 11 U.S.C.A. § 1202(b)(2).

§ 9.216 Chapter 12—Automatic Stay

The automatic stay available to the debtor under chapter 12 is expanded to also stay actions against any individual that is jointly liable with the debtor on a consumer debt or that secured such debt.[1] Accordingly, after the order for relief is granted,[2] a creditor may not act to collect a consumer debt of the debtor from any individual that is also liable on the debt, or that secured such debt. This rule is not absolute, however, as it does not apply if the codebtor became liable on or secured the debt in the ordinary course of the codebtor's business, or if the case is closed, dismissed, or converted to a chapter 7 liquidation.[3] Moreover, a creditor may obtain relief from the stay with respect to the codebtor to the extent that (i) the codebtor received the consideration for the claim held by the creditor; (ii) the debtor's proposed plan does not propose to pay such claim; or (iii) the creditor's interest would be "irreparably harmed" by continuation of the stay.[4] Significantly, the stay will be terminated 20 days after a creditor moves for relief from the stay to proceed against a codebtor, unless the debtor or the affected codebtor files a written objection to the lift-stay motion.[5]

Section 1201 of the Bankruptcy Code is "designed to protect a debtor ... by insulating him from indirect pressures from his creditors exerted through friends or relatives that may have cosigned an obligation of the debtor."[6] The legislative history explains that the protection is limited, so that the creditor will not lose the benefit of the bargain it made for a cosigner. "The creditor is simply required to share with other creditors to the extent that the debtor will repay him under the ... plan. The creditor is delayed, but his substantive rights are not affected."[7]

Library References:
West's Key No. Digests, Bankruptcy ⌬2391-2443.

§ 9.217 Chapter 12—Property of the Estate

Section 1207 defines property of the chapter 12 debtor's estate. In addition to the property of the estate specified in Section 541,[1] a chapter

---

§ 9.216

1. 11 U.S.C.A. § 1201. Consumer debt is defined as "debt incurred by an individual primarily for a personal, family, or household purpose." 11 U.S.C.A. § 101(8). A creditor is not stayed from presenting a negotiable instrument or from giving notice of dishonor of such an instrument. 11 U.S.C.A. § 1201(b).

2. See supra, § 9.8 for a discussion of the order of relief.

3. 11 U.S.C.A. § 1201(a). See supra, § 9.61 for a discussion of what constitutes the "ordinary course of business" under the Bankruptcy Code.

4. 11 U.S.C.A. § 1201(c).

5. 11 U.S.C.A. § 1201(d).

6. H.R.Rep. 95-595, 95th Cong., 1st Sess. 426 (1977).

7. Id.

§ 9.217

1. See supra, § 9.49 for a discussion of property of the estate under the Bankruptcy Code, in general.

§ 9.217 BANKRUPTCY Ch. 9

12 debtor's estate also includes all property that the chapter 12 debtor acquires *after* the commencement of the case as well as the earnings the debtor makes from services performed postpetition.[2] This contrasts with the situation in a chapter 7 or 11 case, where property of the estate is defined as of the commencement of the case. Moreover, the chapter 12 debtor remains in possession of all property of the estate unless the court orders for cause, pursuant to Section 1204, that the debtor will not be a debtor in possession.[3]

Library References:

West's Key No. Digests, Bankruptcy ⊕2531–2559.

§ 9.218 Chapter 12—Sales Free of Interests

Chapter 12 provides an additional benefit to debtors by allowing them to "scale down their operations" through the sale of unnecessary farmland and farm equipment "free and clear of any interests."[1] Section 1206 modifies Section 363(f) of the Code by allowing the debtor, after notice and a hearing, but without satisfying the requirements set forth in Section 363(f) to sell farmland or farm equipment under Section 363(b) and (c)[2] free and clear of any interest in such property of an entity other than the estate. Thus, Section 1206 allows the debtor to sell assets not needed for the reorganization without the consent of secured creditors, subject to the approval of the court. The proceeds of such sale, however, are subject to whatever interests previously encumbered the property at issue.[3]

Library References:

West's Key No. Digests, Bankruptcy ⊕3073.

§ 9.219 Chapter 12—Adequate Protection

In addition to the authorization to sell farmland and farm equipment free and clear of any interests in such property of an entity other than the estate, as described *supra*, § 9.218, chapter 12 contains additional features which may impact the debtor's secured creditors in ways that would not occur in a chapter 7 or 11 case. For example, Section 361 of the Code, which describes how adequate protection may be provided in cases under other chapters of the Bankruptcy Code, does not apply in a

---

2. 11 U.S.C.A. § 1207(a). The definition of property of the estate under chapter 13 parallels the inclusive definition of property of the estate under chapter 12. *See* 11 U.S.C.A. § 1306(a).

3. 11 U.S.C.A. § 1207(b).

§ 9.218

1. Joint Explanatory Statement of the Comm. of Conference for the 1986 Act.

2. *See supra*, §§ 9.60–9.63 for a discussion of the sale of a debtor's property pursuant to 11 U.S.C.A. § 363.

3. 11 U.S.C.A. § 1206.

case under chapter 12.[1] Rather, when a secured creditor requires adequate protection of its interest in estate property in a chapter 12 case,[2] such adequate protection may be provided by:

1. Requiring the debtor to make a cash payment or periodic cash payments to the extent that the automatic stay, use, sale, or lease of, or any grant of a lien on the encumbered property, results in a decrease in the value of property securing the creditor's claim or ownership interest in property;

2. Giving the creditor an additional or replacement lien to the extent that the automatic stay, use, sale, lease, or grant of a lien results in a decrease in the value of property securing the creditor's claim or ownership interest in property;

3. Paying to the creditor for the use of farmland the reasonable rent customary in the community where the property is located, based upon the rental value, net income, and earning capacity of the property; or

4. Granting such other relief, other than entitling the creditor to administrative expense priority, as will adequately protect the value of the property securing the creditor's claim or ownership interest in property.[3]

Library References:

West's Key No. Digests, Bankruptcy ⟲2430.1–2434, 3062, 3065, 3073.

§ 9.220 Chapter 12—Exclusivity—Right to File a Plan

The debtor in a chapter 12 case is the sole party with authority to file a plan of debt adjustment.[1] The debtor may file a chapter 12 plan either with the petition,[2] or no later than 90 days after the order for relief is granted; however, the court may extend this period if the need for an extension "is attributable to circumstances for which the debtor

§ 9.219

1. 11 U.S.C.A. § 1205(a). See supra, § 9.56 for a discussion of adequate protection under the other chapters of the Bankruptcy Code.

PRACTICE POINTER: In practice, there is much less need for a creditor to seek adequate protection under chapter 12 than there is under chapter 11 because of the relatively short time period between commencement of the case and confirmation of a plan. (When adequate protection is required, it is only required until a plan is confirmed.) Under chapter 12, Section 1221 requires that a plan be filed within 90 days after entry of the order for relief. Pursuant to Section 1224, under chapter 12, a confirmation hearing is required no later than 45 days after the plan was filed. In contrast, under chapter 11 a long period of time sometimes elapses between commencement of the case and the time a plan is confirmed because debtors frequently obtain extensions of their exclusive periods to file a plan and obtain acceptance thereof.

2. See supra, § 9.56 for a description of the circumstances under which adequate protection is required.

3. 11 U.S.C.A. § 1205(b).

§ 9.220

1. 11 U.S.C.A. § 1221. See infra, § 9.284 for a procedural checklist for filing a chapter 12 plan of debt adjustment.

2. Bankr.R. 3015(a).

§ 9.220   BANKRUPTCY   Ch. 9

should not justly be held accountable.'"[3] If the debtor fails to file a plan timely, a party may move to dismiss the case,[4] but may move for conversion to a chapter 7 case only on a showing that the debtor has committed fraud in connection with the case.[5]

Library References:

West's Key No. Digests, Bankruptcy ⇐3681.

§ 9.221   Chapter 12—Plan

Section 1222 of the Bankruptcy Code sets forth the mandatory and discretionary provisions of a chapter 12 plan.

Library References:

West's Key No. Digests, Bankruptcy ⇐3681.

§ 9.222   Chapter 12—Plan—Mandatory Provisions

A chapter 12 plan must provide:

1. That the debtor submits all or such portion of its future earnings or other future income as is necessary for the execution of the plan;[1]

2. For the full payment, in deferred cash payments, of all claims entitled to priority under § 507[2] unless the holder of a particular claim agrees to a different treatment for its claim; and

3. The same treatment for each claim or interest within a particular class, to the extent that the plan classifies claims and interests, unless the holder of a particular claim agrees to a different treatment for its claim.[3]

§ 9.223   Chapter 12—Plan—Discretionary Provisions

In addition, a chapter 12 plan may:[1]

1. Designate a class or classes of unsecured claims, but may not

---

3. 11 U.S.C.A. § 1221.
4. 11 U.S.C.A. § 1208(c)(3).
5. 11 U.S.C.A. § 1208(d).

§ 9.222

1. Generally, the debtor will commit all funds in excess of its operating and living expenses to payments under the plan.
2. See supra, § 9.106 for a discussion of priorities under 11 U.S.C.A. § 507.

PRACTICE POINTER: This provision affords a farmer-debtor a significant advantage for filing under chapter 12 rather than under chapter 11. Under chapter 12, even priority claims can be satisfied by deferred payments over the life of the plan; whereas under chapter 11, certain priority claims must be paid in full in cash on the effective date of the plan.

3. 11 U.S.C.A. § 1222(a). See supra, § 9.152 for a discussion of classification of claims.

§ 9.223

1. The list of discretionary provisions is set forth at 11 U.S.C.A. § 1222(b).

discriminate unfairly against any such class.[2] However, if another individual is also liable with the debtor on a consumer debt, the plan may treat a claim for such consumer debt differently from other unsecured claims;[3]

2. Modify the rights of secured or unsecured creditors, or leave these creditors' rights unaffected;[4]

3. Provide for the curing or waiving of any default;[5]

4. Provide for payments on any unsecured claim to be made concurrently with payments on any other claim, either secured or unsecured;[6]

5. Provide for the curing of any default within a reasonable time and maintenance of payments while the case is pending on any claim (secured or unsecured) on which the last payment is due after the date on which the final payment under the plan is due;

6. Subject to Section 365, provide for the assumption, rejection, or assignment of any executory contract or unexpired lease of the debtor not previously rejected;[7]

7. Provide for the payment of all or part of a claim against the debtor from property of the estate or property of the debtor;

8. Provide for the sale of all or any part of the property of the estate, or the distribution of all or any part of the property of the estate among those having an interest in such property;

9. Provide for payment of allowed secured claims in accordance with the requirements of Section 1225(a)(5) over a period not

---

2. 11 U.S.C.A. § 1222(b)(1). As in chapter 11, a claim may be placed in a particular class only if it is substantially similar to the other claims in such class. *Id. See supra,* §§ 9.152, 9.154–9.155 for a discussion of classification of claims.

3. 11 U.S.C.A. § 1222(b)(1).

4. 11 U.S.C.A. § 1222(b)(2). This provision enables a chapter 12 debtor to alter the rights of all creditors, including those of a mortgagee of the debtor's residence. This contrasts with the rights of a debtor under chapter 11 or 13, who is prohibited from altering debts secured only by the debtor's principal residence. *See* 11 U.S.C.A. §§ 1123(b)(5), 1322(b)(2) and the discussion of lien stripping *supra,* § 9.101.

5. If a plan proposes to cure a default, the amount necessary to do so will be determined in accordance with the underlying agreement and applicable nonbankruptcy law. 11 U.S.C.A. § 1222(d). This provision was added by the Bankruptcy Reform Act of 1994 and is applicable only to agreements entered into after October 22, 1994. It is intended to overrule Rake v. Wade, 508 U.S. 464, 113 S.Ct. 2187, 124 L.Ed.2d 424 (1993), which required a chapter 13 debtor who wished to cure a default and reinstate a mortgage to pay interest on the mortgage arrearages even though interest was not required under the mortgage agreement or applicable state law.

6. 11 U.S.C.A. § 1222(b)(4).

PRACTICE POINTER: Pursuant to this provision, neither priority nor secured claims must be paid before unsecured claims. This is a very significant difference from chapter 11, which accords priority in payment to secured claims and unsecured priority claims.

7. *See supra,* §§ 9.74–9.81 for a discussion of the assumption, rejection, or assignment of executory contracts and unexpired leases.

§ 9.223   **BANKRUPTCY**   Ch. 9

longer than three years, except for cause shown, but in any event, not longer than five years;

10. Provide for the vesting of property of the estate in the debtor, or in any other entity, upon confirmation or at a later time;

11. Include any other appropriate provision not inconsistent with title 11;[8] and

12. Other than the fifth and ninth discretionary provisions listed above, the plan may not provide for payments over a period longer than three years unless the court for cause approves a longer period, which period may not be longer than five years.[9]

§ 9.224   Chapter 12—Plan—Modification

The debtor may modify the proposed plan at any time before confirmation without court approval so long as the modified plan continues to satisfy the requirements of Section 1222 of the Code.[1] If the holder of a secured claim has voted either to accept or reject the plan prior to the modification, that vote will continue in effect after the modification unless (i) the modification provides for a change in rights from the prior plan, and (ii) the holder changes its previous vote.[2]

§ 9.225   Chapter 12—Plan—Confirmation

After expedited notice, the court will hold a hearing on confirmation of a proposed chapter 12 plan.[1] The hearing must be concluded not later than 45 days after the filing of the plan unless there is cause to extend this period.[2] The court will confirm the plan if:

1. The plan complies with the provisions of chapter 12 and the other applicable provisions of the Bankruptcy Code;

2. All required fees, charges, and amounts are paid before confirmation;

3. The plan has been proposed in good faith and not by any means forbidden by law;

4. The value, as of the effective date of the plan, of property to be distributed under the plan on account of each allowed unsecured claim is not less than the amount that would be paid on such claim if the debtor were liquidated under chapter 7;

---

8. 11 U.S.C.A. § 1222(b).
9. 11 U.S.C.A. § 1222(c).

§ 9.224
1. 11 U.S.C.A. § 1223(a); Bankr.R. 3015.
2. 11 U.S.C.A. § 1223(c). Any objections to the modification of a chapter 12 plan are governed by Bankruptcy Rule 9014. Bankr.R. 3015.

§ 9.225
1. 11 U.S.C.A. § 1224.
2. 11 U.S.C.A. § 1224.

5. The holder of each allowed secured claim provided for by the plan has accepted the plan or either:

   (a) the plan provides both that the secured creditor retain its lien, and the value (as of the effective date) of property to be distributed under the plan on account of such claim is not less than the allowed amount of the claim,[3] or

   (b) the plan provides for the surrender to the secured creditor of the property securing the claim; and

6. The debtor will be able to make all payments under and comply with the plan.[4]

§ 9.226 Chapter 12—Plan—Confirmation: Objections

If the trustee or the holder of an allowed unsecured claim objects to confirmation,[1] the court may not approve the plan unless, as of the effective date, either:

1. The value of the property to be distributed under the plan on account of such claim is not less than the amount of such claim; or

2. The plan provides that all of the debtor's projected disposable income to be received in the three-year period (or such longer period as the court may approve pursuant to Section 1222(c))[2] beginning on the date of the first payment due under the plan, will be applied to make payments under the plan.[3]

"Disposable income" in this context means income received by the debtor which is not reasonably necessary to be expended either for the maintenance or support of the debtor or the debtor's dependents, or for the payment of expenditures necessary for the continuation, preservation, and operation of the debtor's business.[4] Notably, after confirmation, the court may order any entity from whom the debtor receives income to pay all or part of such income to the trustee appointed in the debtor's chapter 12 case, if any.[5]

Any objection to confirmation must be filed before confirmation.[6] If no objection is timely filed, the court may determine that the plan has

---

3. See infra, § 9.251 note 3 for a discussion of valuing a secured creditor's collateral for purposes of confirming a cramdown plan and see supra, § 9.166 note 8 for a discussion of calculating present value.

4. 11 U.S.C.A. § 1225(a).

§ 9.226

1. See infra, § 9.285 for a procedural checklist for objecting to a chapter 12 plan.

2. See supra, § 9.223 for a description of Section 1222(c).

3. 11 U.S.C.A. § 1225(b)(1).

4. 11 U.S.C.A. § 1225(b)(2).

5. 11 U.S.C.A. § 1225(c).

6. Bankr.R. 3015(f).

been proposed in good faith and not by any means forbidden by law without receiving evidence on these issues.[7]

§ 9.227 Chapter 12—Disbursements

If a trustee is appointed in the debtor's chapter 12 case, the trustee must retain all payments and funds it receives until confirmation or denial of confirmation of the plan. Unless the plan or confirmation order provides otherwise, the chapter 12 trustee is the disbursing agent for the plan. If the plan is confirmed, the trustee must distribute payments in accordance with the terms of the confirmed plan. If the plan is not confirmed, the trustee must return any such payments to the debtor, after deducting any unpaid allowed administrative claims and any fees owed to a standing trustee. If the plan is confirmed, before making payments to creditors, the trustee must make those deductions described in the preceding sentence as well as any fees and charges assessed against the estate under chapter 123 of title 28.[1]

Library References:

West's Key No. Digests, Bankruptcy ⬅3685.

§ 9.228 Chapter 12—Effect of Confirmation

With the exception of those debts for which a chapter 12 debtor will be unable to obtain a discharge,[1] the confirmed plan binds the debtor, each creditor, each equity security holder, and each general partner in the debtor, whether or not the claim of such party is provided for by the plan, and whether or not such party has objected to, accepted, or rejected the plan.[2] In addition, except as otherwise provided in the plan or the confirmation order, the confirmation of a plan vests all property of the estate in the debtor.[3] The property so vesting in the debtor will be free and clear of any claim or interest of any creditor provided for by the plan.[4] Accordingly, family farmers may provide in their plans for post-confirmation financing secured by assets that have revested in the debtor. The debtor also may use unencumbered revested property to

---

7. Bankr.R. 3015(f).

§ 9.227

1. 11 U.S.C.A. § 1226.

§ 9.228

1. *See infra,* § 9.229 for a discussion of discharge and nondischargeable debts under chapter 12.

2. 11 U.S.C.A. § 1227(a).

PRACTICE POINTER: The order of confirmation is *res judicata* and not subject to collateral attack. 5 *Collier on Bankruptcy* ¶ 1227.01 (L. King, ed., 15th ed. 1996). *See supra,* § 9.167. Accordingly, if a creditor has notice of the plan, it will not be able to challenge the terms of a plan after confirmation. Therefore, a creditor must strenuously object to confirmation of objectionable provisions of a plan or else risk the chance that any subsequent action relating thereto will be barred.

3. 11 U.S.C.A. § 1227(b).

4. 11 U.S.C.A. § 1227(c).

secure post-confirmation credit.[5]

Library References:

West's Key No. Digests, Bankruptcy ⇐3683.1.

§ 9.229 Chapter 12—Discharge

Section 1228, which should be read in conjunction with the general discharge provision of the Bankruptcy Code, § 524,[1] specifies the types of debts discharged in a chapter 12 case and the conditions of such discharge. As soon as practicable after completion by a chapter 12 debtor of all payments under a confirmed plan (excluding payment of certain long-term debts and payment to creditors who are to receive property of the estate), the court will grant the debtor a discharge for all allowed and disallowed debts provided for by the plan.[2] This type of discharge has been referred to as a "full-compliance" discharge.[3] Alternatively, the court may grant a discharge to a debtor that has not completed payments under the plan if (i) the debtor's failure to make such payments is "due to circumstances for which the debtor should not justly be held accountable," (ii) the value, as of the effective date of the plan, of property actually distributed under the plan on account of each allowed unsecured claim is not less than the amount that would have been paid on such claim if the debtor were liquidated under chapter 7, and (iii) modification of the plan is not "practicable."[4] This type of discharge has been referred to as a "hardship discharge."[5] Debts provided for under Section 1222(b)(5) (long-term debts on which the last payment is due after the final payment under the plan) or Section 1222(b)(10) (debts to claimants who are to receive property of the estate) are not discharged under either a full-compliance discharge or a hardship discharge. In addition, debts that are excepted from discharge under Section 523(a) of the Bankruptcy Code also are excepted from discharge under Section 1228.[6] On the request of a party in interest, the court may revoke the discharge within one year after it is granted if the discharge was obtained by the debtor through fraud, and the party seeking revocation did not know of such fraud until after the discharge was granted.[7]

5. *See* Joint Explanatory Statement of the Committee of Conference for the 1986 Act.

§ 9.229

1. *See supra,* § 9.168 for a discussion of the effect of a discharge under Section 524.

2. 11 U.S.C.A. § 1228(a).

3. *See* 5 *Collier on Bankruptcy* ¶ 1228.01 (L. King, ed., 15th ed. 1996).

4. 11 U.S.C.A. § 1228(b).

5. *See* 5 *Collier on Bankruptcy* ¶ 1228.01 (L. King, ed., 15th ed. 1996).

6. 11 U.S.C.A. § 1228(a)(1), (2) and (c). *See supra,* § 9.207 for a discussion of debts excepted from discharge under 11 U.S.C.A. § 523. The requirements governing time for filing a complaint to determine the dischargeability of debts under Section 523(c) are the same for chapter 12 as they are for chapter 7 or 11. Bankr.R. 4007. *See supra,* § 9.208 for a discussion of such time limits.

7. 11 U.S.C.A. § 1228(d).

§ 9.230 Chapter 12—Modification After Confirmation

After confirmation of the plan, but before the completion of payments thereunder, the plan still may be modified at the request of the debtor, the trustee, or the holder of an allowed unsecured claim in order to:

1. Increase or reduce the amount of payments on claims of a particular class provided for by the plan;
2. Extend or reduce the time for such payments; or
3. Alter the amount of the distribution to a creditor whose claim is provided for by the plan to the extent necessary to take account of any payment on such claim other than under the plan.[1] For example, if a nondebtor third party pays a portion of a creditor's claim, the plan may be modified by reducing the amount of distribution to that creditor.

The modified plan still must satisfy the requirements set forth in the Bankruptcy Code.[2] A modified plan may not provide for payments over a period that expires more than three years after the time the first payment under the original confirmed plan was due unless the court, for cause, approves a longer period, which period may not be longer than five years after such time.[3]

Any objection to a proposed modification is governed by Bankruptcy Rule 9014 and must be filed with the court, served on the debtor, the trustee, and any other party designated by the court, and transmitted to the U.S. trustee.[4]

Library References:
West's Key No. Digests, Bankruptcy ⇐3684.

§ 9.231 Chapter 12—Special Tax Provisions

For the purpose of any state or local (but not federal) income tax, the tax year of an individual debtor ends on the date the order for relief was entered in the chapter 12 case (or on the date of the order for relief under chapter 7 if the case originally was filed under chapter 7.)[1] The chapter 12 trustee must file income tax returns for the estate of an

---

§ 9.230

1. 11 U.S.C.A. § 1229(a). *See infra*, § 9.286 for a procedural checklist for modifying a chapter 12 or 13 plan after confirmation.

2. 11 U.S.C.A. § 1229(b)(1). Specifically, the modified plan must meet the requirements of Sections 1222(a) and (b), 1223(c), and 1225(a).

3. 11 U.S.C.A. § 1229(c).

4. Bankr.R. 3015(g).

§ 9.231

1. 11 U.S.C.A. § 1231(a).

individual chapter 12 debtor for each taxable period during which the case is pending, but not for a family farmer that is a corporation or a partnership.[2] The issuance, transfer, or exchange of a security pursuant to a confirmed chapter 12 plan may not be subjected to a stamp tax or other similar tax.[3] Lastly, the court may authorize the plan proponent to request a determination, limited to questions of law, by a state or local government charged with tax collection, of the tax effects of the chapter 12 plan under Section 346 of the Bankruptcy Code and under the law imposing the tax. If there is a controversy between the debtor and the taxing authority, the court is empowered to adjudicate.[4]

§ 9.232   Chapter 12—Revocation of Confirmation Order

On request of a party in interest at any time within 180 days after the entry of the confirmation order, the bankruptcy court, after notice and a hearing, may revoke the confirmation order if such order was procured by fraud.[1] If the court revokes the confirmation order, the court can dismiss the case, convert it to a chapter 7 liquidation, or permit the debtor to propose a modification of the plan pursuant to Section 1229 of the Code.[2]

Library References:
West's Key No. Digests, Bankruptcy ⇔3684.

§ 9.233   Chapter 12—Conversion or Dismissal of Cases

A debtor may convert a chapter 12 case to a chapter 7 liquidation at any time, and any waiver of the right to convert is unenforceable.[1] Similarly, the court must dismiss the case if the debtor so requests, provided that the case has not been converted under Section 706 or 1112. Any waiver of the right to dismiss also is unenforceable.[2]

In addition, upon the request of a party in interest, and after notice and a hearing, the court may dismiss a chapter 12 case for cause, including:

1. Unreasonable delay by the debtor that is prejudicial to creditors;
2. Nonpayment of any fees and charges required under chapter 123 of title 28;
3. Failure to file a plan timely;

2. 11 U.S.C.A. § 1231(b).
3. 11 U.S.C.A. § 1231(c).
4. 11 U.S.C.A. § 1231(d).

§ 9.232
1. 11 U.S.C.A. § 1230. A request for revocation of a confirmation order is an adversary proceeding, governed by Part VII of the Bankruptcy Rules. See supra, § 9.16 for a discussion of adversary proceedings.
2. 11 U.S.C.A. § 1230(b).

§ 9.233
1. 11 U.S.C.A. § 1208(a).
2. 11 U.S.C.A. § 1208(b).

§ 9.233   BANKRUPTCY   Ch. 9

4. Failure to commence making timely payments required by a confirmed plan;
5. Denial of confirmation of a plan and denial of a request for additional time for filing another plan;
6. Material default with respect to a confirmed plan;
7. Revocation of the order of confirmation and denial of modification;
8. Termination of a confirmed plan by an occurrence specified in the plan; or
9. Continuing loss to or diminution of the estate and absence of a reasonable likelihood of rehabilitation.[3]

Additionally, on request of a party in interest, and after notice and a hearing, the court may dismiss a chapter 12 case or convert it to a chapter 7 liquidation on a showing that the debtor committed fraud in connection with the case.[4]

Library References:

West's Key No. Digests, Bankruptcy ⇐3673.

§ 9.234   Chapter 12—Conversion or Dismissal of Cases—Procedure

Bankruptcy Rule 1017(d) provides that a proceeding to dismiss or convert a case to another chapter that is brought by a party in interest is a contested matter governed by Bankruptcy Rule 9014. A motion to dismiss or convert brought by the debtor must be filed and served as required by Bankruptcy Rule 9013.[1] The hearing on the dismissal of the case or the conversion of the case to another chapter requires no less than 20 days notice by mail.[2] Section 348 of the Bankruptcy Code and Bankruptcy Rule 1019 establish the effects of the conversion of a chapter 11, 12, or 13 case to a chapter 7 liquidation. For example, all claims actually filed by a creditor in the superseded case will be deemed filed in the chapter 7 case.[3] The "rule is not intended to invalidate any action taken in the superseded case before its conversion to chapter 7."[4]

§ 9.235   Chapter 12—Closing and Reopening Cases

The court will close the case after an estate is fully administered and the court has discharged the trustee.[1] However, the case may be re-

3. 11 U.S.C.A. § 1208(c).
4. 11 U.S.C.A. § 1208(d).

§ 9.234
1. Bankr.R. 1017(d).
2. Bankr.R. 2002(a)(5).
3. Bankr.R. 1019(3).

4. See Bankr.R. 1019, Advisory Committee Note.

§ 9.235
1. 11 U.S.C.A. § 350(a).

opened on motion of the debtor or other party in interest to administer assets, to accord relief to the debtor, or for other cause.[2]

Library References:

West's Key No. Digests, Bankruptcy ⋘3441–3445.

§ 9.236 Chapter 13—Overview

Chapter 13 is titled the Adjustment of Debts of an Individual with Regular Income. An "individual with regular income" is defined as "an individual whose income is sufficiently stable and regular to enable such individual to make payments under chapter 13," other than a stockbroker or a commodity broker.[1]

Chapter 13 is primarily designed to help an individual with a stable income who is overburdened with consumer debt to restructure such debts without having to liquidate his or her assets. The goal of chapter 13 is to help an individual develop a plan to repay his debts out of future wages over a period of three to five years.

As is the case with chapter 12, chapter 13 is designed to provide a quicker and less expensive means of reorganization than a chapter 11 case. Thus, chapter 13 offers a debtor many benefits which are not available to a chapter 7 or 11 debtor.

Library References:

West's Key No. Digests, Bankruptcy ⋘3701–3718(10).

§ 9.237 Chapter 13—Eligibility

An individual may be a debtor under chapter 13 only if he or she has a regular income and has noncontingent, liquidated debts on the date of filing of less than $250,000 (unsecured) and $750,000 (secured). An individual with regular income and such individual's spouse, except a stockbroker or commodity broker, that owe, on the date of filing, noncontingent, liquidated, unsecured debts that aggregate less than $250,000 and noncontingent, liquidated, secured debts of less than $750,000 may be a debtor under chapter 13.[1] A debtor that is self-employed and incurs trade credit in the production of income from such business is a "debtor engaged in business" and may file under chapter 13 if the debt limits described above are not exceeded.[2]

2. 11 U.S.C.A. § 350(b); Bankr.R. 5010. In addition, Rule 9024 exempts motions to reopen cases from the one-year limitation of F.R.C.P. 60(b). *See supra*, § 9.33 note 6 regarding the desirability of closing cases expeditiously to avoid the incurrence of additional fees under 28 U.S.C.A. § 1930(a).

§ 9.236
1. 11 U.S.C.A. § 101(30).

§ 9.237
1. 11 U.S.C.A. § 109(e).
2. 11 U.S.C.A. § 1304(a). A debtor engaged in business may continue to operate his or her business subject to the limitations and duties set forth in 11 U.S.C.A. § 1304(b), (c).

§ 9.237 BANKRUPTCY Ch. 9

Library References:

West's Key No. Digests, Bankruptcy ⚖︎2233(1)–2233(3).

§ 9.238 Chapter 13—Rights and Powers of Debtor

Subject to any limitations on a trustee under chapter 13, a debtor under chapter 13 has, exclusive of the trustee, the same rights and powers as a liquidation trustee with respect to the use, sale, or lease of property outside the ordinary course of business.[1]

Library References:

West's Key No. Digests, Bankruptcy ⚖︎3703.

§ 9.239 Chapter 13—Appointment of a Trustee

If the United States trustee in a district has appointed an individual to serve as standing trustee in chapter 13 cases, and if that individual qualifies to serve as a trustee pursuant to § 322 of the Bankruptcy Code, then that individual serves as trustee in any chapter 13 case filed in the district. If no standing trustee has been appointed, the United States trustee may appoint a disinterested person to serve as trustee, or the United States trustee may serve in that capacity if necessary.[1]

Library References:

West's Key No. Digests, Bankruptcy ⚖︎3703.

§ 9.240 Chapter 13—Duties of a Trustee

The chapter 13 trustee performs the same duties as a chapter 12 trustee[1] except that a chapter 13 trustee is not required to appear and be heard at any hearing that concerns the sale of estate property.[2] In addition, a chapter 13 trustee must advise the debtor, other than on legal matters, and assist the debtor to perform under the plan.[3]

Library References:

West's Key No. Digests, Bankruptcy ⚖︎3008.1–3009.

§ 9.241 Chapter 13—Automatic Stay

Chapter 13, like chapter 12, extends the automatic stay to nondebtors by providing that after the order for relief is granted, a creditor may

§ 9.238

1. See 11 U.S.C.A. §§ 1303, 363(b), (d), (e), (f), and (*l*).

§ 9.239

1. 11 U.S.C.A. § 1302.

§ 9.240

1. 11 U.S.C.A. § 1302(b). See supra, § 9.215 for a discussion of the duties of a chapter 12 trustee. See 28 U.S.C.A. § 586(e) for provisions governing the compensation of a chapter 12 or 13 trustee.

2. Compare 11 U.S.C.A. § 1302(b)(2) with 11 U.S.C.A. § 1202(b)(3)(D). See also 11 U.S.C.A. § 1303 (giving the debtor rights and powers, exclusive of the trustee, to use, sell, or lease property of the estate outside the ordinary course of business).

3. 11 U.S.C.A. § 1302(b)(4).

not act to collect a *consumer* debt[1] of the chapter 13 debtor from any *individual* that is also liable on the debt with the debtor or that secured such debt.[2] The automatic stay does not prohibit actions against a codebtor if the codebtor became liable or secured such debt in the ordinary course of the codebtor's business, or if the case is closed, dismissed, or converted to a case under chapter 7 or chapter 11.[3] The purpose of extending the stay to nondebtors is the same in chapter 13 as in chapter 12, to protect the debtor from pressures exerted by creditors through codebtors.[4]

Since the extension of the automatic stay to codebtors pertains only to consumer debt, certain debts, such as debts incurred in the ordinary course of the codebtor's business, are not subject to the stay of acts against a codebtor.[5] Moreover, a creditor has the right to seek payment from a codebtor on consumer debt if the debtor fails to make payments when due under the terms of the debtor's payment plan.[6]

Library References:

West's Key No. Digests, Bankruptcy ⇐2391–2443.

§ 9.242 Chapter 13—Automatic Stay—Relief

The Bankruptcy Code requires the court to grant relief from the stay against codebtors upon the request of a party in interest and after notice and a hearing to the extent that:

1. The codebtor received the consideration for the claim held by the creditor; that is, the debtor is actually the codebtor;
2. The debtor's chapter 13 plan fails to provide for the payment of the claim; or
3. The creditor's interest would be irreparably harmed by continuation of the stay.[1]

Library References:

West's Key No. Digests, Bankruptcy ⇐2421–2443.

§ 9.243 Chapter 13—Property of the Estate

As in chapter 12, chapter 13 also defines property of the debtor's estate to include all property that the debtor acquires *after* the com-

§ 9.241

1. Consumer debt is defined as "debt incurred by an individual primarily for a personal, family, or household purpose." 11 U.S.C.A. § 101(8).
2. 11 U.S.C.A. § 1301.
3. 11 U.S.C.A. § 1301(a).
4. *See supra*, § 9.216.

5. 11 U.S.C.A. § 1301(a)(1). A creditor is not stayed from presenting a negotiable instrument or from giving notice of dishonor of such an instrument. 11 U.S.C.A. § 1301(b).
6. S.Rep.No. 95–989, 95th Cong., 2d Sess. 138(1978).

§ 9.242

1. 11 U.S.C.A. § 1301(c).

§ 9.243   **BANKRUPTCY**   Ch. 9

mencement of the case and the earnings the debtor makes from services performed postpetition, as well as the property specified in Section 541.[1]

Library References:

West's Key No. Digests, Bankruptcy ⇐2531–2559.

§ 9.244   Chapter 13—Property of the Estate—Use, Sale, or Lease

With regard to the use, sale, or lease of property of the estate, a chapter 13 debtor has the same rights and powers and is subject to the same limitations in their exercise as a chapter 7 trustee.[1] Thus, a chapter 13 debtor may:

1. Use, sell, or lease property of the estate other than in the ordinary course of business pursuant to Section 363(b) of the Code, to the extent not inconsistent with provisions of the automatic stay set forth in Section 362(c), (d), (e), or (f) of the Code;

2. Sell property free and clear of any interest of another in such property pursuant to the conditions prescribed in Section 363(f); and

3. Use, sell, or lease property of the estate notwithstanding any contractual provisions conditioned on the insolvency or financial condition of the debtor pursuant to Section 363(*l*).

Pursuant to Section 363(e), on the request of an entity with an interest in property used, sold, or leased, or proposed to be used, sold, or leased, the court will prohibit or condition such action as is necessary to provide adequate protection of the nondebtor's interest.[2] The rights and powers accorded a chapter 13 debtor to use, sell, or lease property of the estate pursuant to Section 1303 are given exclusively to the debtor and may not be exercised by the chapter 13 trustee.[3]

Library References:

West's Key No. Digests, Bankruptcy ⇐3061–3088.

§ 9.245   Chapter 13—Exclusivity—Right to File a Plan

A chapter 13 debtor has the exclusive right to propose and file a repayment plan, and is required to file the plan either at the same time

---

§ 9.243

1. 11 U.S.C.A. § 1306(a). See supra, § 9.49 for a discussion of property of the estate under Section 541.

§ 9.244

1. 11 U.S.C.A. § 1303. See supra, §§ 9.60–9.63 discussing the use, sale, or lease of estate property under Section 363 of the Bankruptcy Code.

2. See supra, § 9.56 for a discussion of adequate protection.

3. See 11 U.S.C.A. § 1303. 124 Cong. Rec.H 11,106 (Sept. 28, 1978); S 17,423 (Oct.6, 1978).

it files the petition or within 15 days thereafter.[1]

§ 9.246 Chapter 13—Plan

Chapter 13 is designed to serve "as a flexible vehicle for the repayment of part or all of the allowed claims of the debtor. Section 1322 emphasizes that purpose by fixing a minimum of mandatory plan provisions."[1]

Library References:
West's Key No. Digests, Bankruptcy ⇐3704.1–3715(14).

§ 9.247 Chapter 13—Plan—Mandatory Provisions

As in chapter 12, the proposed chapter 13 plan must provide:

1. For the submission of all or such portion of future earnings or other future income of the debtor to the supervision and control of the trustee as is necessary for the execution of the plan;[1]
2. For the full payment, in deferred cash payments, of all claims entitled to priority under Section 507,[2] unless the holder of a particular claim agrees to a different treatment for its claim;[3] and
3. The same treatment for each claim within a particular class if the plan classifies claims.[4]

§ 9.248 Chapter 13—Plan—Discretionary Provisions

In addition, the chapter 13 plan may:

1. Designate a class or classes of unsecured claims, but may not discriminate unfairly against any such class.[1] However, if another individual is also liable with the debtor on consumer debt, the plan may treat a claim for such consumer debt differently from other unsecured claims;[2]
2. Modify the rights of holders of unsecured or secured claims, other than a claim secured only by the debtor's principal

---

§ 9.245

1. 11 U.S.C.A. § 1321; Bankr.R. 3015(b). See infra, § 9.284 for a procedural checklist for filing a chapter 12 or 13 plan of debt adjustment.

§ 9.246

1. S.Rep.No. 95–989, 95th Cong., 2d Sess. 141 (1978).

§ 9.247

1. 11 U.S.C.A. § 1322(a)(1).
2. See supra, § 9.106 for a discussion of priorities under 11 U.S.C.A. § 507.

3. 11 U.S.C.A. § 1322(a)(2).
4. 11 U.S.C.A. § 1322(a)(3). See supra, § 9.152 for a discussion of classification of claims.

§ 9.248

1. 11 U.S.C.A. § 1322(b)(1). As in chapter 11, a claim may be placed in a particular class only if it is substantially similar to the other claims in such class. Id. See supra, §§ 9.152, 9.154–9.155 for a discussion of classification of claims.
2. 11 U.S.C.A. § 1322(b)(1).

§ 9.248

residence, or leave unaffected the rights of holders of any class of claims;[3]

3. Provide for the curing or waiving of any default;[4]

4. Provide for payments on any unsecured claim to be made concurrently with payments on any other claim (either secured or unsecured);[5]

5. Notwithstanding the restriction of Section 1322(b)(2) concerning the modification of security interests in the debtor's principal residence, provide for the curing of any default within a reasonable time and maintenance of payments while the case is pending on any claim (secured or unsecured) on which the last payment is due after the date on which the final payment under the plan is due;[6]

3. 11 U.S.C.A. § 1322(b)(2). This provision makes clear that a claim secured solely by a security interest in real property that is the debtor's principal residence may not be modified. See supra, § 9.101 for a discussion of lien stripping and the prohibition against stripping down a lien securing a mortgagee's claim secured only by a security interest in real property that is the debtor's principal residence.

CAVEAT: The First Circuit has held that the lien stripping prohibition of Section 1322(b)(2) does not apply in the case of a multi-unit property in which one of the units is the debtor's principal residence when the secured creditor's lien also extends to other income-producing property. Lomas Mortgage, Inc. v. Louis, 82 F.3d 1 (1st Cir.1996) (debtor and his nondebtor brother were co-owners of a three-unit residence in which the third unit was rented to tenants). No other circuit courts have addressed this issue as of this writing. However, a bankruptcy court in New York has declined to adopt the *per se* rule formulated by the First Circuit. Brunson v. Wendover Funding, Inc. (In re Brunson), 201 B.R. 351 (Bankr. W.D.N.Y. 1996).

While recognizing that the Bankruptcy Code's antimodification provisions were not intended to extend to cases involving large apartment complexes simply because the debtor lived in one of the units, the court concluded that a case-by-case approach is necessary to determine whether the antimodification provision is applicable when the debtor's principal residence is in a mixed-use property. The court stated that the requisite analysis must consider the totality of the factors to determine the predominant character of the transaction and what the lender bargained to be within the scope of its lien. If the transaction was viewed by the parties as predominantly a residential loan transaction, the antimodification provision should apply. If it was viewed by the parties as predominantly a commercial loan transaction, a stripdown of the lien will be possible. *Id.*

4. 11 U.S.C.A. § 1322(b)(3). "Curing a default commonly means taking care of the triggering event and returning to pre-default conditions. The consequences are thus nullified. This is the concept of 'cure' used throughout the Bankruptcy Code." In re Taddeo, 685 F.2d 24, 26 (2d Cir.1982). Accordingly, the Second Circuit concluded that "[w]hen Congress empowered Chapter 13 debtors to 'cure defaults,' we think Congress intended to allow mortgagors to 'deaccelerate' their mortgage and reinstate its original payment schedule." *Id.* However, the Ninth Circuit has held that where a nonmonetary default constitutes a historical fact, by definition, it cannot be cured. Accordingly, under the Ninth Circuit's decision, an executory contract under which such a default has occurred cannot be assumed. Claremont Acquisition Corp. v. General Motors Corp. (In re Claremont Acquisition Corp.), 113 F.3d 1029 (9th Cir.1997) (the debtor's failure to operate an automobile dealership for two weeks preceding the bankruptcy filing constituted an incurable default under the franchise agreement that precluded the debtor from assuming and assigning its franchise agreement). Whether the logic of this case will be adopted in other circuits remains to be seen.

5. 11 U.S.C.A. § 1322(b)(4). *See supra*,

6. 11 U.S.C.A. § 1322(b)(5). *See infra*, § 9.249 for a more detailed discussion of this provision.§ 9.223 note 6, discussing the parallel provision under chapter 12.

6. Provide for the payment of all or any part of any claim allowed under Section 1305 of the Bankruptcy Code (which section provides that a proof of claim may be filed for taxes that become payable to a governmental unit while the case is pending, or for a consumer debt that arises after the date of the order of relief and that is for property or services necessary for the debtor's performance under the plan—*e.g.*, medical bills or auto repairs to enable the debtor to get to work);[7]

7. Subject to Section 365, provide for the assumption, rejection or assignment of any executory contract or unexpired lease of the debtor not previously rejected;[8]

8. Provide for the payment of all or part of a claim against the debtor from property of the estate or property of the debtor;[9]

9. Provide for the vesting of property of the estate in the debtor or in any other entity upon confirmation or at a later time;[10] and

10. Include any other appropriate provision not inconsistent with title 11.[11]

The plan may not provide for payments over a period longer than three years unless the court, for cause, approves a longer period, which may not be longer than five years.[12]

§ 9.249 Chapter 13—Plan—Discretionary Provisions: Debtor's Principal Residence

Section 1322(b)(2) of the Bankruptcy Code prohibits the modification of a creditor's claim that is secured *only* by real property that is the debtor's principal residence. Moreover, the United States Supreme Court has held that Section 1322(b)(2) applies not only to the secured portion of a creditor's claim against a debtor's principal residence, but to the entire right to payment.[1] Thus, an undersecured claim that is partially secured by a debtor's principal residence cannot be bifurcated and

---

7. 11 U.S.C.A. § 1322(b)(6). This provision permits the filing and allowance of certain *postpetition* claims. It permits the treatment of such claims as *prepetition* claims. See 11 U.S.C.A. § 1305(b).

8. 11 U.S.C.A. § 1322(b)(7). See supra, §§ 9.74–9.81 for a discussion of the assumption, rejection, or assignment of executory contracts and unexpired leases.

9. 11 U.S.C.A. § 1322(b)(8).
10. 11 U.S.C.A. § 1322(b)(9).
11. 11 U.S.C.A. § 1322(b)(10).
12. 11 U.S.C.A. § 1322(d).

§ 9.249

1. Nobelman v. American Sav. Bank, 508 U.S. 324, 113 S.Ct. 2106, 124 L.Ed.2d 228 (1993).

stripped down to the value of the collateral.[2]

Despite the antimodification provision of Section 1322(b)(2), the Bankruptcy Code permits a debtor to cure defaults in mortgages pursuant to Section 1322(b)(5). The Second Circuit has noted that Congress intended to protect home mortgages from modification, not from cure.[3] The Second Circuit has explained that a debtor may cure defaults and maintain payments under Section 1322(b)(5) without modifying claims and, therefore, without contravening the antimodification provision.[4] Thus, despite the prohibition of Section 1322(b)(2) against modifying a security interest secured solely by the debtor's principal residence, Section 1322(b)(5) permits a debtor to cure defaults under a home mortgage within a reasonable time.[5] The provision allows a chapter 13 debtor to decelerate a mortgage, cure arrearages during the period of the payment plan, and continue payments according to the original terms of the mortgage, including a mortgage under which the final payment extends beyond the term of the debtor's chapter 13 payment plan.[6]

A default with respect to, or which gave rise to, a lien on the debtor's principal residence may be cured until such residence is sold at a foreclosure sale that is conducted in accordance with applicable nonbankruptcy law.[7] This provision, which was added to the Bankruptcy Code pursuant to the Bankruptcy Reform Act of 1994 and, therefore, applies to cases filed on or after October 22, 1994, "safeguards a debtor's rights in a chapter 13 case by allowing the debtor to cure home mortgage defaults at least through completion of a foreclosure sale under applicable nonbankruptcy law."[8]

To cure prepetition defaults under home mortgages, whether the mortgage is oversecured, undersecured, or wholly unsecured, New York courts require that chapter 13 plans provide for the repayment of prepetition arrearages over the term of the payment plan together with "a present value factor equal to the New York State judgment interest rate until the arrearages are paid in full."[9] Pursuant to the Bankruptcy

---

2. See supra, §§ 9.100–9.101 for a discussion of bifurcation of claims and lien stripping.

3. In re Taddeo, 685 F.2d 24, 27 (2d Cir.1982).

4. Id.

5. The Bankruptcy Code has left to the courts the determination of what is a reasonable time. A number of courts have concluded that Section 1322(d) of the Bankruptcy Code requires that the repayment of any claim modified pursuant to Section 1322(b) must be completed within three years unless the court, for cause, extends the payment period to a maximum of five years. See, e.g., In re Javarone, 181 B.R. 151, 154–55 (Bankr.N.D.N.Y.1995).

6. See, e.g., In re Hardware, 189 B.R. 273 (Bankr.E.D.N.Y.1995); In re Callahan, 158 B.R. 898 (Bankr.W.D.N.Y.1993). Debtors will not be discharged from debts that come due after the term of the chapter 13 plan. See 11 U.S.C.A. § 1328(c)(1).

7. 11 U.S.C.A. § 1322(c)(1).

8. See 140 Cong.Rec.H 10,769 (Oct. 4, 1994). "[I]f state law provides the debtor more extensive 'cure' rights (through, for example, some later redemption period), the debtor would continue to enjoy such rights in bankruptcy." Id.

9. See In re Neverla, 194 B.R. 547 (Bankr.W.D.N.Y.1996); In re Hardware, 189 B.R. 273 (Bankr.E.D.N.Y.1995) (mortgagee entitled to interest at New York judgment

Reform Act of 1994, if a plan requires the payment of arrearages, the liability for interest to cure the default will be determined in accordance with the underlying agreement and applicable nonbankruptcy law.[10] This provision was enacted to overrule a U.S. Supreme Court decision that required the payment of interest on mortgage arrearages when the chapter 13 debtor attempted to cure the default and reinstate the mortgage, even if such interest was not provided for in the agreement and was not required by state law.[11] In enacting Section 1322(e), Congress sought to prevent a secured creditor from achieving a windfall at the expense of unsecured creditors by obtaining interest on interest and other charges.[12]

The Bankruptcy Reform Act of 1994 also created one exception to the prohibition of Section 1322(b)(2) against modifying a claim secured only by real property that is the debtor's principal residence. The exception provides that if the last payment on the original payment schedule for such a mortgage is due before the date on which the final payment under the plan is due, the plan may provide for the payment of the claim modified pursuant to the terms of Section 1325(a)(5), that is, in the same manner as any other allowed secured claim provided for by the plan.[13]

Library References:
West's Key No. Digests, Bankruptcy ⟶3708(9).

§ 9.250 Chapter 13—Plan—Modification

A chapter 13 debtor may modify a proposed plan at any time before confirmation without court approval, so long as the modified plan

rate not only on the arrears, but also on the mortgagee's claim for late charges, foreclosure fees, and disbursements which became due under the terms of the mortgage); In re Callahan, 158 B.R. 898 (Bankr.W.D.N.Y. 1993). The New York judgment rate is 9%.

Section 1325(a)(5)(B)(ii) of the Bankruptcy Code requires that a secured creditor be paid an amount equal to the present value of the allowed claim as of the effective date of the plan unless the debtor surrenders the property securing the claim to the creditor.

10. 11 U.S.C.A. § 1322(e). This provision is applicable only to agreements (including refinancing agreements) entered into after October 22, 1994. See 140 Cong. Rec.H 10,770 (Oct. 4, 1994).

11. See Rake v. Wade, 508 U.S. 464, 113 S.Ct. 2187, 124 L.Ed.2d 424 (1993). In Rake v. Wade, the Supreme Court had held that in order for debtors to cure the defaults on their mortgages, the Bankruptcy Code required them to pay interest on the mortgage arrearages even though state law prohibited interest on interest, and the underlying agreement between the parties did not contemplate such payments. The Supreme Court's decision in this case had the effect of providing a windfall to secured creditors at the expense of unsecured creditors by requiring the debtors to pay most of their income to satisfy the secured creditors' claims, including interest on interest and interest on late charges and other fees.

12. 140 Cong.Rec. H 10,770 (Oct. 4, 1994).

13. 11 U.S.C.A. § 1322(c)(2). This provision would afford relief to debtors with short-term mortgages, which often bear high rates of interest, and to debtors who are near the end of the term of a long-term mortgage and, thus, may otherwise risk the loss of their accumulated equity. *Collier on Bankruptcy* ¶ 1322.14B (L. King, ed., 15th ed. 1996).

§ 9.250   BANKRUPTCY   Ch. 9

continues to satisfy the requirements of Section 1322.[1] If the holder of a secured claim has voted either to accept or reject the plan prior to the modification, that vote will continue in effect after the modification, unless (i) the modification provides for a change in rights from the prior plan, and (ii) the holder changes its previous vote.[2]

Library References:

West's Key No. Digests, Bankruptcy ⇔3713.

§ 9.251   Chapter 13—Plan—Confirmation

After notice to all parties in interest, the court must hold a hearing on confirmation of the plan. A party in interest may object to confirmation.[1] The court must confirm the plan if the following requirements are met:

1. The plan complies with the provisions of chapter 13 and the other applicable provisions of the Bankruptcy Code;
2. All required fees, charges, or amounts required under chapter 123 of title 28 or by the plan are paid before confirmation;
3. The plan has been proposed in good faith and not by any means forbidden by law;
4. The value, as of the effective date of the plan, of property to be distributed under the plan on account of each allowed unsecured claim is not less than the amount that would be paid on such claim if the debtor's estate were liquidated under chapter 7 on such date;[2]
5. The holder of each allowed secured claim has accepted the plan, or one of the following two alternate methods of treating the claim of a secured creditor who has not accepted the plan is satisfied:

   (a) the plan provides both that the holder of such claim retains the lien securing the claim, and the value (as of the effective date of the plan) of property to be distributed under the plan on account of such claim is not less than the allowed amount of the claim,[3] or

§ 9.250
1. 11 U.S.C.A. § 1323(a). See supra, §§ 9.247–9.248.
2. 11 U.S.C.A. § 1323.

§ 9.251
1. 11 U.S.C.A. § 1324. See infra, § 9.252.
2. 11 U.S.C.A. § 1325(a)(4). This provision is known as the "best interest of creditors test" under chapter 13. See H.R.Rep. No. 95–595, 95th Cong., 1st Sess. 430 (1977). Thus, confirmation of a chapter 13 plan does not require the acceptance of the plan by unsecured creditors.

3. **PRACTICE POINTER:** In chapter 11, 12, or 13 cases, when the debtor intends to retain property subject to a lien, the valuation of the property securing the lien determines the allowed amount of the claim and, therefore, is of critical importance to both the debtor and the creditor. Since Section 506(a) of the Bankruptcy Code, which governs the valuation of collateral, does not

specify the standard to be used in determining the value of the collateral securing a creditor's interest, courts have differed in determining the appropriate standard. In essence the question is whether the collateral value of property to be retained by the debtor in a cramdown plan of reorganization should be determined at a hypothetical wholesale value, the retail value, or some other value.

Depending upon the timing in the case, a secured creditor may attempt to maximize the value of its collateral by requesting that the court adopt the fair market value of the collateral, since fair market value is higher than wholesale value. Thus, fair market valuation usually increases the secured part of the claim and reduces the part of the claim classified as an unsecured deficiency claim. (*See supra*, § 9.100, discussing bifurcation of secured claims.) A higher valuation of the collateral will increase a secured creditor's leverage because it will be more difficult for the debtor to pay the secured debt and, thus, have a confirmable plan. Naturally, the debtor usually will urge the court to adopt the lower wholesale value.

Because the circuit courts have diverged in determining the appropriate method of valuation of collateral in the context of cramdown plans, the Supreme Court has addressed this issue in Associates Commercial Corp. v. Rash (In re Rash), __ U.S. __, 117 S.Ct. 1879, 138 L.Ed.2d 148 (1997) rev'g 90 F.3d 1036 (5th Cir.1996). In Rash, the debtors' chapter 13 plan treated the creditor's secured claim under the cramdown provision of § 1325(a)(5)(B) of the Bankruptcy Code. Under the confirmed plan, the debtors would retain the collateral securing the creditor's lien—a tractor truck—and pay the creditor the amount of its secured claim, that is, the value of the truck. The bankruptcy court determined that the value of the truck for cramdown purposes was the amount the creditor would realize if it exercised its remedies under state law, that is, if the creditor regained possession of the truck and sold it in accordance with the security agreement. The bankruptcy court concluded that this amount was the truck's wholesale price. In an *en banc* decision, the Fifth Circuit affirmed.

The Supreme Court reversed and held that for the purpose of a debtor's proposed chapter 13 cramdown plan pursuant to Section 1325(a)(5)(B) of the Bankruptcy Code, the appropriate standard of valuation for a secured creditor's collateral is the replacement value, which the Court defined as "the price a willing buyer in the debtor's trade, business, or situation would pay a willing seller to obtain property of like age and condition." *Id.* at __, 117 S.Ct. at 1884 note 2. The Supreme Court based its decision on its interpretation of the first two sentences of 11 U.S.C.A. § 506(a). The Court concluded that "the 'proposed disposition or use' of the collateral [by the debtor] is of paramount importance to the valuation question." *Id.* at __, 117 S.Ct. at 1884.

Since Section 506(a) applies to chapters 7, 11, 12, and 13, the precedential effect of the Supreme Court's decision cannot be limited to chapter 13 cases. However, the Court left the door open for litigation over the appropriate value in cases with different factual circumstances because it noted that "[w]hether replacement value is the equivalent of retail value, wholesale value, or some other value will depend on the type of debtor and the nature of the property." *Id.* at __, 117 S.Ct. at 1886 note 6.

Prior to the Supreme Court's decision, the 1st, 4th, 6th, 8th, and 9th Circuits had held that the value of the collateral in a cramdown should be fair market or retail value. *See, e.g.*, Taffi v. United States (In re Taffi), 96 F.3d 1190 (9th Cir.1996) (en banc), cert. denied, __ U.S. __, 117 S.Ct. 2478, 138 L.Ed.2d 987 (1997) (a chapter 13 case), and Winthrop Old Farm Nurseries, Inc. v. New Bedford Inst. for Savs. (In re Winthrop Old Farm Nurseries, Inc.), 50 F.3d 72 (1st Cir.1995) (a chapter 11 case), both favorably cited by the Supreme Court, which equated the fair market standard in Taffi with the replacement value approach. *Id.* at __, 117 S.Ct. at 1884 note 2 and 1885. The Supreme Court specifically rejected the view adopted in In re Hoskins, 102 F.3d 311 (7th Cir.1996), that a midpoint between fair market value and wholesale value should be adopted. Rash, __ U.S. at __, 117 S.Ct. at 1886. The Supreme Court also rejected as a "ruleless approach" the Second Circuit's conclusion that "no fixed value, whether it be retail, wholesale, or some combination of the two, should be imposed on every bankruptcy court conducting a § 506(a) evaluation ..... as long as the final valuation of that claim reflects § 506(a)'s dual considerations [the purpose of the valuation and the proposed disposition and use of the collateral]." *Id.* at __, 117 S.Ct. at 1886 note 5, citing General Motors Acceptance Corp. v. Valenti (In re Valenti), 105 F.3d 55, 62 (2d Cir.1997).

§ 9.251   BANKRUPTCY   Ch. 9

    (b) the debtor surrenders the property securing the claim to the secured creditor; and

6. The debtor will be able to make all payments under the plan and comply with the plan.[4]

Library References:

West's Key No. Digests, Bankruptcy ⚖3715(1)–3715(14).

§ 9.252   Chapter 13—Plan—Confirmation: Objections

If the trustee or an unsecured creditor objects to confirmation,[1] the court may not approve the plan unless, as of the effective date, either

1. The value of the property to be distributed under the plan on account of such claim is not less than the amount of such claim; or

2. The plan provides that all of the debtor's projected disposable income to be received in the three-year period beginning on the date that the first payment is due under the plan will be applied to make payments under the plan. "Disposable income" in this context means income which is received by the debtor and which is not reasonably necessary to be expended either for the maintenance or support of the debtor or the debtor's dependents, or for the payment of expenditures necessary for the continuation, preservation, and operation of the debtor's business.[2] Notably, after confirmation, the court may order any entity from whom the debtor receives income to pay all or part of such income to the trustee appointed in the debtor's chapter 13 case.[3]

Any objection to confirmation must be filed before confirmation.[4] If no objection is timely filed, the court may determine that the plan has been proposed in good faith and not by any means forbidden by law without receiving evidence on these issues.[5]

See supra, § 9.166 note 8 for a discussion of the determination of "present value."

4. 11 U.S.C.A. § 1325(a).

§ 9.252

1. *See infra*, § 9.285 for a procedural checklist for filing an objection to a chapter 13 plan.

2. 11 U.S.C.A. § 1325(b).

PRACTICE POINTER: The Fourth Circuit has held that funds that a debtor is *permitted* to withdraw from an IRA account without any tax penalty, but not *required* to withdraw, are not included in disposable income because (i) the debtor has not *received* them, and (ii) forced withdrawal "would effectively undercut the very purpose of retirement and pension plans" by depriving the debtor of funds for retirement. *See* In re Solomon, 67 F.3d 1128 (4th Cir.1995).

Courts hold that postpetition revenue received from exempt sources is income, the disposable portion of which must be paid to unsecured creditors in order for a chapter 13 plan to be confirmable. *See, e.g.*, Stuart v. Koch (In re Koch), 109 F.3d 1285, 1289 (8th Cir.1996) (worker's compensation benefits); In re Freeman, 86 F.3d 478, 480–81 (6th Cir.1996) (tax refunds); In re Hagel, 184 B.R. 793, 796–97 (9th Cir.B.A.P.1995) (social security benefits); In re Sassower, 76 B.R. 957, 960 (Bankr.S.D.N.Y.1987) (pension, welfare, and unemployment benefits).

3. 11 U.S.C.A. § 1325(c).

4. Bankr.R. 3015(f).

5. Bankr.R. 3015(f).

Library References:
West's Key No. Digests, Bankruptcy ⚖︎3715(6).

§ 9.253 Chapter 13—Plan—Confirmation: Effect

The provisions of the confirmed plan bind the debtor and each creditor, whether or not the claim of such creditor is provided for in the plan, and whether or not the creditor objected to, or accepted the confirmed plan.[1] Except as otherwise provided in the plan, the confirmation of a plan vests all property of the estate in the debtor;[2] the property so vesting in the debtor will be free and clear of any claim or interest of any creditor provided for by the plan, unless the plan or the confirmation order provide otherwise.[3]

Library References:
West's Key No. Digests, Bankruptcy ⚖︎3715(9.1)–3715(13).

§ 9.254 Chapter 13—Payments

The debtor must begin making payments within 30 days after filing the plan unless the court orders otherwise.[1] The trustee holds all payments until confirmation or denial of the plan. If the plan is confirmed, the trustee distributes all payments in accordance with the plan as soon as practicable. If confirmation is denied, the trustee returns all payments to the debtor after deducting any unpaid allowed administrative expenses.[2] Priority claims and any fees owed to a standing trustee must be paid before or at the same time as payments to creditors.[3]

Library References:
West's Key No. Digests, Bankruptcy ⚖︎3712, 3714.

§ 9.255 Chapter 13—Discharge

As soon as practicable after completion by the debtor of all payments under the plan, the court will grant the debtor a discharge of all debts provided for by the plan or disallowed under Section 502, unless the debtor has executed a court-approved waiver of discharge.[1] The discharge granted under chapter 13 after all payments under the plan are made (a "full-compliance discharge") is extremely broad and discharges the debtor from certain debts that are nondischargeable under chapter 7 or 11. In fact, the discharge under chapter 13 is sometimes called a "super-discharge" because of its inclusiveness. Unless a chapter 13 debtor fails

§ 9.253

1. 11 U.S.C.A. § 1327(a). See also H.R.Rep.No. 95–595, 95th Cong., 1st Sess. 430 (1977).
2. 11 U.S.C.A. § 1327(b).
3. 11 U.S.C.A. § 1327.

§ 9.254

1. 11 U.S.C.A. § 1326(a)(1).
2. 11 U.S.C.A. § 1326(a)(2).
3. 11 U.S.C.A. § 1326(c).

§ 9.255

1. 11 U.S.C.A. § 1328(a).

§ 9.255

to obtain a discharge based on a finding that the plan was not filed in good faith,[2] the following debts that are nondischargeable under chapter 7 or 11 may be discharged under chapter 13:[3]

- Debts obtained by false pretenses, false representation, or actual fraud;[4]
- Debts obtained by use of materially false financial statements;[5]
- Certain debts for luxury goods or services or cash advances obtained within 60 days before the order for relief;[6]
- Debts for fraud or defalcation while acting as a fiduciary;[7] and
- Debts for willful and malicious injury.[8]

Apparently, the rationale for the chapter 13 super-discharge was, in part, to encourage individual debtors to file a repayment plan under chapter 13 rather than a liquidation plan under chapter 7. The Supreme Court has explained the rationale behind the very broad discharge granted to chapter 13 debtors:

> [T]he dischargeability of debts in chapter 13 that are not dischargeable in chapter 7 represents a policy judgment that [it] is preferable for debtors to attempt to pay such debts to the best of their abilities over three years rather than for those debtors to have those debts hanging over their heads indefinitely, perhaps for the rest of their lives.[9]

Library References:

West's Key No. Digests, Bankruptcy ⇐3251–3423, 3718(1)–3718(10).

§ 9.256 Chapter 13—Discharge—Exceptions

Congress did "not intend for debtors to be able to utilize chapter 13 as an office solely to obtain discharge from certain liabilities. For example, it ... [was] not contemplated that an individual who committed a heinous crime would be able in good faith to use chapter 13 solely as a means of discharging a civil obligation owing to a harmed party."[1] Excluded from discharge under chapter 13 are debts:

2. See 11 U.S.C.A. § 1325(a)(3).

3. To obtain the entire list, compare the nondischargeable debts under 11 U.S.C.A. § 523 to the nondischargeable debts under 11 U.S.C.A. § 1328(a).

4. See 11 U.S.C.A. § 523(a)(2)(A).

5. See 11 U.S.C.A. § 523(a)(2)(B).

6. See 11 U.S.C.A. § 523(a)(2)(C).

7. See 11 U.S.C.A. § 523(a)(4).

8. See 11 U.S.C.A. § 523(a)(6). See, e.g., In re Solomon, 67 F.3d 1128 (4th Cir.1995)

($160 million in sexual misconduct claims were discharged after completion of plan payments totalling $45,000). The only basis for creditors to attack such a discharge is on the ground that the plan was not proposed in good faith. See 11 U.S.C.A. § 1325(a)(3).

9. Pennsylvania Dep't of Public Welfare v. Davenport, 495 U.S. 552, 563, 110 S.Ct. 2126, 2133, 109 L.Ed.2d 588 (1990).

§ 9.256

1. 140 Cong.Rec.H 10,765 (Oct. 4, 1994).

- Provided for under Section 1322(b)(5) (secured or unsecured debt on which the last payment is due after the final payment under the plan);[2]
- To a former spouse for child support or alimony;
- Certain student loans;
- Resulting from an injury caused by driving while intoxicated;
- For restitution or a criminal fine which was part of the debtor's criminal sentence;[3] or
- A consumer debt for property or services necessary for the debtor's performance under the plan if prior approval by the trustee of the debtor's incurring the debt was practicable and was not obtained.[4]

The court may grant a "hardship discharge" to a chapter 13 debtor who has not completed payments under the plan only if (i) the debtor's failure to make such payments is due to circumstances for which the debtor should not justly be held accountable, (ii) the value, as of the effective date of the plan, of property actually distributed under the plan on account of each allowed unsecured claim is not less than the amount that would have been paid on such claim if the debtor were liquidated under chapter 7, and (iii) modification of the plan is not "practicable."[5] In contrast to the limited exceptions to "a full-compliance" discharge upon completion of all payments under the plan (described in the preceding paragraph), a "hardship discharge" cannot discharge *any* of the debts specified in Section 523(a).[6] Therefore, in addition to the nondischargeable debts listed above, a hardship discharge will not discharge certain taxes, customs duties, unscheduled debts, fines, or debts arising from fraud or certain judgments.[7]

§ 9.257 Chapter 13—Discharge—Objections

A debtor or any creditor may file a complaint to obtain a determination of the dischargeability of any debt.[1] A complaint other than under Section 523(c) may be filed at any time, even after the case has been closed.[2] On a chapter 13 debtor's motion for a discharge under Section 1328(b), the court must set a deadline for the filing of a complaint to determine the dischargeability of any debt pursuant to Section 523(c).[3]

---

2. *See supra*, § 9.249.
3. 11 U.S.C.A. § 1328(a).
4. 11 U.S.C.A. § 1328(d).
5. 11 U.S.C.A. § 1328(b).
6. 11 U.S.C.A. § 1328(c). *See supra*, § 9.207 for a discussion of debts that are nondischargeable under 11 U.S.C.A. § 523(a).
7. *See* 11 U.S.C.A. § 523(a).

§ 9.257

1. Bankr.R. 4007(a).
2. Bankr.R. 4007(b). A case may be reopened for filing a complaint to determine the dischargeability of a debt other than under Section 523(c) without payment of an additional filing fee. *Id.*
3. Bankr.R. 4007(d).

§ 9.257   BANKRUPTCY   Ch. 9

The court must give all creditors not less than 30 days notice.[4] A creditor's complaint objecting to the discharge of a particular claim is an adversary proceeding under Bankruptcy Rule 7001.[5]

§ 9.258   Chapter 13—Discharge—Revocation

The court may revoke the discharge within one year after it was granted on the request of a party in interest, but only if the debtor obtained the discharge through fraud, and the party seeking revocation did not know of the fraud until after the discharge was granted.[1]

Library References:

West's Key No. Digests, Bankruptcy ⟲3320.1–3322.

§ 9.259   Chapter 13—Postconfirmation Modification of a Plan

The debtor, the trustee, or the holder of an allowed unsecured claim may seek to modify the plan at any time after confirmation but before the completion of payments under the plan. Specifically, the plan may be modified to increase or reduce the amount of payments on claims of a particular class provided for by the plan, extend or reduce the time for such payments, or alter the amount of distribution on a particular claim to take account of any payment on that claim other than under the plan.[1] The modified plan must comply with the provisions governing the plan and preconfirmation modification.[2] A modified plan may not provide for payments beyond three years after the first payment under the original confirmed plan was due; however, the court, for cause, may approve a longer payment period, not to exceed five years.[3]

Library References:

West's Key No. Digests, Bankruptcy ⟲3713.

§ 9.260   Chapter 13—Revocation of Confirmation Order

At any time within 180 days after the entry of the order confirming a chapter 13 plan, the court, on request of a party in interest and after notice and a hearing, may revoke the confirmation order if such order

---

4. Bankr.R. 4007(d).

5. Bankr.R. 4007(e). *See supra,* § 9.16 for a discussion of adversary proceedings and *infra,* §§ 9.266, 9.288 for procedural and drafting checklists for the commencement of an adversary proceeding. *See infra,* § 9.309 for a sample complaint to commence an adversary proceeding.

§ 9.258

1. 11 U.S.C.A. § 1328(c).

§ 9.259

1. 11 U.S.C.A. § 1329(a).

2. 11 U.S.C.A. § 1329(b)(1).

3. 11 U.S.C.A. § 1329(c). Bankr.R. 3015(g) governs requests for modification of a confirmed chapter 13 plan. *See infra,* § 9.286 for a procedural checklist to request modification of a confirmed plan.

was procured by fraud.[1] The court's power to revoke the confirmed plan for fraud is discretionary because the debtor may also have been a victim of the fraud; thus, the court may decide that it would be inequitable or unnecessary to revoke confirmation.[2] If the court revokes the confirmation order, the court will dispose of the case under Section 1307 of the Code by either dismissing the case or converting it to a chapter 7 liquidation, unless, within a time set by the court, the debtor proposes a new plan which the court then confirms.[3] A proceeding to revoke confirmation is an adversary proceeding.[4]

Library References:
West's Key No. Digests, Bankruptcy ⚖3715(14).

§ 9.261 Chapter 13—Conversion or Dismissal of Cases

A debtor may convert a chapter 13 case to a chapter 7 liquidation at any time, and any waiver of the right to convert is unenforceable.[1] Similarly, the court must dismiss the case if the debtor so requests, provided that the case has not already been converted under Section 706, 1112, or 1208 of the Code.[2] Any waiver of the right to dismiss is also unenforceable.[3]

In addition, upon the request of a party in interest or the U.S. trustee, the court may dismiss a chapter 13 case or convert it to chapter 7 for cause, whichever is in the best interests of creditors.[4] The court may not convert a chapter 13 case to a case under another chapter of the Bankruptcy Code if the debtor is a farmer unless the debtor requests such conversion.[5] Many of the same factors used to determine whether a court should convert or dismiss a chapter 11 case to a chapter 7 case,[6] also are relevant in the consideration of whether to convert a chapter 13 case to chapter 7 or to dismiss the case in its entirety; *e.g.*, unreasonable delay by the debtor that is prejudicial to creditors, failure to timely file a plan, denial of confirmation.[7] Prior to confirmation, the court also may convert a chapter 13 case to a case under either chapter 11 or 12 on

---

§ 9.260

1. 11 U.S.C.A. § 1330(a).

2. *See* § 1330 Comment (Part I Bankruptcy Code, 1996 Collier Pamphlet Edition).

3. 11 U.S.C.A. § 1330(b).

4. Bankr.R. 7001(5).

§ 9.261

1. 11 U.S.C.A. § 1307(a). A fee of $400 is required for converting a case under chapter 13 to a case under chapter 11 on the request of a debtor. 28 U.S.C.A. § 1930(a).

2. 11 U.S.C.A. § 1307(b).

3. 11 U.S.C.A. § 1307(b).

4. 11 U.S.C.A. § 1307(c).

5. 11 U.S.C.A. § 1307(e).

6. *See supra*, § 9.174 for a discussion of factors a court considers in determining whether to convert or dismiss a chapter 11 case.

7. 11 U.S.C.A. § 1307(c). Note that Section 1307(c)(9) mirrors Section 1112(e) in allowing the U.S. trustee to request that the court convert the case to a chapter 7 liquidation if the debtor fails to file within the required time period the information required by Section 521(1). *See infra*, § 9.265 for the filing requirements under Section 521(1).

§ 9.261

request of a party in interest or the U.S. trustee and after notice and a hearing.[8]

Library References:

West's Key No. Digests, Bankruptcy ⬢3716.10–3717.

§ 9.262 Chapter 13—Conversion or Dismissal of Cases—Procedure

Bankruptcy Rule 1017(d) provides that a proceeding to dismiss or convert a case to another chapter that is brought by a party in interest is a contested matter governed by Bankruptcy Rule 9014. A motion to dismiss or convert brought by the debtor must be filed and served as required by Bankruptcy Rule 9013.[1] The hearing on the dismissal of the case or the conversion of the case to another chapter requires no less than 20 days notice by mail.[2] Section 348 of the Bankruptcy Code and Bankruptcy Rule 1019 establish the effects of the conversion of a chapter 11, 12, or 13 case to a chapter 7 liquidation. For example, all claims actually filed by a creditor in the superseded case will be deemed filed in the chapter 7 case.[3] The rule "is not intended to invalidate any action taken in the superseded case before its conversion to chapter 7."[4]

§ 9.263 Chapter 13—Closing and Reopening Cases

The court will close the case after an estate is fully administered and the court has discharged the trustee.[1] However, the case may be reopened on motion of the debtor or other party in interest to administer assets, to accord relief to the debtor, or for other cause.[2]

Library References:

West's Key No. Digests, Bankruptcy ⬢3441–3445.

§ 9.264 Procedural Checklist—Commencing a Voluntary Case[1]

1. File with the clerk of the bankruptcy court a petition specifying the

---

8. 11 U.S.C.A. § 1307(d). "The court will exercise its sound discretion in determining whether to grant the request, based on the nature of the debtor's business and other similar factors." See H.Rep.No. 95-595, 95th Cong., 1st Sess. 428 (1977).

§ 9.262

1. Bankr.R. 1017(d).
2. Bankr.R. 2002(a)(5).
3. Bankr.R. 1019(3).
4. See Bankr.R. 1019, Advisory Committee Note.

§ 9.263

1. 11 U.S.C.A. § 350(a).
2. 11 U.S.C.A. § 350(b); Bankr.R. 5010. In addition, Rule 9024 exempts motions to reopen cases from the one-year limitation of F.R.C.P. 60(b). See supra, § 9.33 note 6 regarding the desirability of closing cases expeditiously to avoid the incurrence of additional fees under 28 U.S.C.A. § 1930(a).

§ 9.264

1. 11 U.S.C.A. § 301; Bankr.R. 1002, 1004, 1005, 1006, 1008, 5005. See supra, § 9.8.

chapter under which relief is sought.[2] (See § 9.8)[3] A petition generally conforming to Official Form 1 may be used for a voluntary case of an individual, partnership, or corporate debtor eligible to file under chapter 7, 11, 12, or 13. (See § 9.5 note 3)[4] A copy must be provided for the United States trustee.[5] Local rules should be consulted for the number of copies required.

2. Local rules and applicable nonbankruptcy law as well as the corporate charter and by-laws, or the partnership agreement and certificate of partnership, if appropriate, should be consulted to determine if a corporate resolution or similar authorization of the filing is required.[6]

3. A corporate debtor filing under chapter 11 also must file Official "Exhibit A"[7] to Official Form 1. (See § 9.5 note 3)

4. An individual debtor whose debts are primarily consumer debts must attach Official "Exhibit B"[8] to Official Form 1.

5. A notice of commencement of the case (Official Form 9) should be filed with the petition.

6. A petition must be verified or contain an unsworn declaration (Official Form 2) in accordance with 28 U.S.C.A. § 1746.[9]

2. 11 U.S.C.A. § 301; Bankr.R. 1002(a).

3. PRACTICE POINTER: The petition should be filed in person to be certain that all papers filed have been accepted by the clerk (or in some cases, the judge) and that the case has, in fact, been commenced. Retain a copy stamped by the bankruptcy clerk with the date and time of filing.

4. Discussing official forms.

5. Bankr.R. 1002(b).

6. CAVEAT: If proper authorization is not obtained, the court will lack jurisdiction when the petition is filed. Consequently, any relief granted may be ineffectual, and the petition may be dismissed. In the absence of a contrary provision in the debtor's certificate of incorporation, by-laws, or partnership agreement, state law governs. If the court finds that those who purport to act on behalf of a corporation (or other debtor) have not been granted proper authority to institute the proceedings, the court will have "no alternative but to dismiss the petition." Price v. Gurney, 324 U.S. 100, 65 S.Ct. 513, 89 L.Ed. 776 (1945). See, e.g., In re Berton L. Brown, 163 B.R. 596 (Bankr.N.D.Fla.1993) (petition signed by debtor's wife pursuant to a general power of attorney was dismissed for lack of express authority to file a bankruptcy petition); In re Giggles Restaurant, Inc., 103 B.R. 549 (Bankr.D.N.J.1989) (petition dismissed because corporate resolution authorizing the bankruptcy filing failed to satisfy state-law quorum requirement). However, courts have found that where authorization for the filing is challenged after the corporation has acquiesced in the filing, acquiescence ratifies the filing, and the case may not be dismissed because of the original defect in the filing of the petition. In re Martin–Trigona, 760 F.2d 1334 (2d Cir. 1985); In re Dearborn Process Service, Inc., 149 B.R. 872 (Bankr.N.D.Ill.1993).

7. "Exhibit A" requires information concerning a corporate debtor's financial condition and capital structure. It follows Official Form 1 in any volume containing the Official Forms.

8. "Exhibit B" is an Official Form which must be completed by an attorney representing an individual whose debts are primarily consumer debts. It is a declaration by such attorney that he or she has informed the petitioner that the petitioner may proceed under chapter 7 or 13 and has explained the relief available under each such chapter. It can be found with Official Form 1.

9. Bankr.R. 1008.

§ 9.264 BANKRUPTCY Ch. 9

7. The appropriate filing fee must be presented.[10] The filing fees are as follows: (1) chapter 7 or 13: $130; (2) chapter 11: $800 and (3) chapter 12: $200.[11] Upon application to the court,[12] and upon certain conditions, an individual who is unable to pay the filing fee may obtain court authorization to pay the fee in installments.[13]

Following the commencement of the case, the clerk or the debtor, if directed by the court, must send by mail to all creditors and indenture trustees:

1. Proper notice of the order for relief;[14]

2. 20 days minimum notice of the Section 341 meeting of creditors;[15] (*see* § 9.37) and

3. 30 days notice of the deadline for determining the dischargeability of debt, which is 60 days from the first date set for the Section 341 meeting (30 days under chapter 13).[16]

§ 9.265 Procedural Checklist—Lists and Schedules to Be Filed at the Commencement of a Case Under Chapter 7, 11, 12, or 13[1]

The debtor must file the following at the commencement of a case under the Bankruptcy Code[2] (see § 9.11):[3]

1. In a voluntary case, together with the petition, a list containing the names and addresses of each creditor unless the petition is accompanied by a schedule of liabilities.[4] In an involuntary case, this list must be filed within 15 days from the entry of an order for relief unless the petition is accompanied by a schedule of liabilities.[5]

2. In a chapter 11 case, unless the court orders otherwise, within 15 days after entry of the order for relief, a list of all equity

---

10. Bankr.R. 1006.
11. 28 U.S.C.A. § 1930(a).
12. Official Form 3.
13. Bankr.R. 1006(b).
14. Bankr.R. 2002(f).
15. Bankr.R. 2003(a).
16. Bankr.R. 2002(f), 4007(c), 4007(d).

§ 9.265
1. 11 U.S.C.A. § 521; Bankr.R. 1007. See *supra*, § 9.11 for a discussion of the lists and schedules that must be filed at the commencement of a case.

CAVEAT: It is imperative to consult local bankruptcy rules, as they may require the filing of additional material or set forth specific procedures or formats that must be followed.

2. 11 U.S.C.A. § 521; Bankr.R. 1007; 11 U.S.C.A. § 1106(a)(2); Bankr.R. 5005.

3. The lists, schedules, and statements must be filed with the clerk in the district where the case is pending. The judge may permit the papers to be filed with that judge. If a debtor has not done so, a trustee appointed under Section 1104 of the Bankruptcy Code must file the lists, schedules, and statements required by Section 521.

4. Bankr.R. 1007(a)(1).
5. Bankr.R. 1007(a)(2).

security holders showing the number and kind of interests held, and the last known address or place of business of each holder.[6]

3. In a voluntary chapter 11 case, as a schedule with the bankruptcy petition, a separate list of the 20 largest unsecured creditors, excluding insiders, with full names, addresses, and claims.[7] Involuntary chapter 11 cases require the filing of this list within 2 days of entry of the order for relief.[8]

4. If an individual debtor's schedule of assets and liabilities includes consumer debts secured by property of the estate, the debtor must file with the clerk, not later than 30 days after the filing of a chapter 7 petition or the date of the meeting of creditors, a statement of intention with respect to the retention or surrender of the property,[9] and must perform upon the stated intention within 45 days after filing the notice of intent.[10] (*see* § 9.186)

In a voluntary case, the schedules and statements listed below must be filed with the petition, or within 15 days thereafter if the list of all the debtor's creditors and their addresses is filed with the petition.[11] In an involuntary case, the schedules and statements must be filed within 15 days after entry of the order for relief.[12]

5. A schedule of all assets and liabilities.[13] Each claim, even if it is partly secured or partly entitled to priority, should be listed only once on Schedule D (creditors holding secured claims) or Schedule E (creditors holding unsecured priority claims) or Schedule F (creditors holding unsecured nonpriority claims).

6. A schedule of current income and expenditures.[14]

7. A statement of financial affairs.[15]

8. A statement of executory contracts and unexpired leases.[16]

Library References:

West's Key No. Digests, Bankruptcy ⚖2321–2325.

6. Bankr.R. 1007(a)(3).
7. Official Form 4.
8. Bankr.R. 1007(d).
9. Official Form 8.
10. 11 U.S.C.A. § 521(2).
11. Bankr.R. 1007(c).
12. Bankr.R. 1007(c).
13. Schedules A through F of Official Form 6.
14. Schedules I and J of Official Form 6.
15. Official Form 7.
16. Schedule G of Official Form 6.

§ 9.266 Procedural Checklist—Commencing an Adversary Proceeding[1]

1. File a complaint with the clerk of the bankruptcy court along with any extra copies required by local rules and one or two office copies. The caption of a complaint and any other pleading in an adversary proceeding filed by a debtor should conform to Official Form 16C. The caption of a complaint or any pleading in an adversary proceeding filed by a party other than the debtor should conform to Official Form 16D.

2. Include the filing fee if one is required pursuant to 28 U.S.C.A. § 1930.[2]

3. Include an Adversary Proceeding Cover Sheet.

4. Prepare a sufficient number of summonses and notices of the trial or pre-trial conference to serve on all adverse parties and for certification of service in accordance with Bankruptcy Rule 7004. There is no official form for a summons; it should comply with the local rules.

5. Personal service pursuant to Federal Rule of Civil Procedure 4(d)(1)-(6) must be made by delivery of the summons and complaint within 10 days following issuance of the summons. Service made by any authorized form of mail must be deposited in the mail within 10 days after issuance of the summons.

6. After completion of service, a certificate of service must be filed with the clerk of the bankruptcy court.[3]

§ 9.267 Procedural Checklist—Commencing a Contested Matter[1]

1. Obtain a hearing date from the judge's chambers, taking care to obtain a date that allows time to comply with the notice requirements. To ascertain notice requirements for a particular contested

§ 9.266

1. Bankr.R. 7002 and 7004. *See supra*, § 9.16. Bankr.R. 7004 sets forth the method and manner for service of a summons and complaint. Part VII of the Bankruptcy Rules incorporates those specific rules of the Federal Rules of Civil Procedure which are made applicable to adversary proceedings. *See* Bankr.R. 7002. *See* Bankruptcy Rule 2002, which sets forth notice requirements, and Bankruptcy Rule 9006, which provides information concerning the computation, enlargement, and reduction of time periods under the Bankruptcy Code. *See infra*, §§ 9.287, 9.288, respectively, for a drafting checklist of general rules and a drafting checklist for a complaint in an adversary proceeding. *See infra*, § 9.309 for a sample complaint to commence an adversary proceeding.

2. *See* 28 U.S.C.A. § 1914.

3. Bankr.R. 8008(d).

§ 9.267

1. Bankr.R. 9014. *See* Bankruptcy Rule 2002, which sets forth notice requirements, and Bankruptcy Rule 9006, which provides information concerning the computation, enlargement, and reduction of time periods under the Bankruptcy Code. *See supra*, § 9.17; *see infra*, § 9.287 for a drafting checklist of general rules.

Ch. 9   APPEAL FROM INTERLOCUTORY JUDGMENT § 9.268

matter, check the local rules and the Bankruptcy Rule that applies to the Code section under which relief is sought.

2. File the required number of copies of a notice of motion, a motion requesting the desired relief, and a proposed order with the clerk of the bankruptcy court. (See §§ 9.306–9.308)[2] The caption should conform to Official Form 16B.

3. Include a filing fee if required pursuant to 28 U.S.C.A. § 1930.

4. Serve copies on the debtor or trustee, the U.S. trustee, the creditors' committee, and those entities specified by the rules or the court. Service should be effected in the manner provided by Bankruptcy Rule 7004 for service of a summons and complaint.[3]

5. After completion of service, a certificate of service should be filed with the clerk of the bankruptcy court.[4]

§ 9.268 Procedural Checklist—Appeal From an Interlocutory Judgment, Order, or Decree of a Bankruptcy Judge[1]

1. Within 10 days of the date of entry of the judgment, order, or decree, file a notice of appeal with the clerk indicating that the named party wants to appeal a specific order.[2]

2. Together with the notice of appeal, file a motion for leave to appeal in accordance with Bankruptcy Rule 8003.

3. File proof of service in accordance with Bankruptcy Rule 8008.

4. Within 10 days of filing the notice of appeal, entry of an order granting leave to appeal, or entry of an order disposing of the last timely motion outstanding, file a designation of the items to be included in the record on appeal and a statement of the issues to be presented.

5. Within 10 days after service of the appellant's statement, the appellee may file a designation of additional items to be included in the record on appeal.[3]

---

2. Sample form of motion papers in a contested matter.

3. Bankruptcy Rule 9014 sets forth the method and manner of service and those specific rules of the Federal Rules of Civil Procedure that apply to contested matters. Notice requirements sometimes may be modified with the consent of the court.

4. Bankr.R. 8008(d).

§ 9.268

1. See supra, § 9.25; see infra, §§ 9.287, 9.289, respectively, for a drafting checklist of general rules and a drafting checklist for a motion for leave to appeal.

2. Bankr.R. 8001(b), 8002(a).

3. PRACTICE POINTER: In addition to providing a counter-designation of the additional items to be included in the record, it may be advisable for counsel to the appellee to provide a counter-statement of the issues on appeal.

§ 9.268

Library References:

West's Key No. Digests, Bankruptcy ⇔3768.

§ 9.269 Procedural Checklist—Creditor's Motion to Request Relief From the Automatic Stay[1]

1. File motion papers pursuant to Section 362 of the Bankruptcy Code and Bankruptcy Rules 4001(a) and 9014. (*See* §§ 9.17, 9.50–9.55)[2]

2. A motion for relief from the automatic stay under Section 362(d) must be accompanied by a fee of $60. (Pub.L.No. 101–162)

3. Serve the motion papers on the debtor or trustee and on any creditors' committee elected or appointed in the case or, if no committee has been appointed, on the debtor's 20 largest creditors and such other entities as the court may direct.[3]

4. After completion of service, a certificate of service should be filed with the clerk of the bankruptcy court.[4]

Library References:

West's Key No. Digests, Bankruptcy ⇔2435.1–2442.

§ 9.270 Procedural Checklist—Creditor's Motion to Obtain Adequate Protection[1]

1. File motion papers pursuant to Section 362(d) or 363(e) of the Bankruptcy Code and Bankruptcy Rule 4001(d) demonstrating the need for adequate protection or requesting approval of an agreement to provide adequate protection (attached as an exhibit to the motion).

2. Serve the motion papers on any committee elected or appointed in the case or, if no committee has been appointed, on the debtor's 20 largest creditors and such other entities as the court may direct.[2]

3. After completion of service, a certificate of service should be filed with the clerk of the bankruptcy court.[3]

§ 9.269

1. *See supra,* §§ 9.50–9.55; *see supra,* § 9.267 for a procedural checklist for commencing a contested matter and *see infra,* §§ 9.287, 9.292, respectively, for a drafting checklist of general rules and a drafting checklist for a motion to request relief from the automatic stay.

2. Discussion of contested matters, the automatic stay, and relief therefrom.

3. Bankr.R. 4001(d)(1).

4. Bankr.R. 8008(d).

§ 9.270

1. *See supra,* §§ 9.56–9.58; *see supra* § 9.267 for a procedural checklist for commencing a contested matter and *see infra,* §§ 9.287, 9.293, respectively, for a drafting checklist of general rules and a drafting checklist for a creditor's motion to obtain adequate protection.

2. Bankr.R. 4001(d)(1).

3. Bankr.R. 8008(d).

Ch. 9 USE, SELL, OR LEASE PROPERTY OF ESTATE § 9.271

Library References:

West's Key No. Digests, Bankruptcy ⚚3062.

§ 9.271 Procedural Checklist—Debtor's Motion to Use, Sell, or Lease Property of the Estate[1]

1. File motion papers pursuant to Section 363 of the Bankruptcy Code and Bankruptcy Rule 6004 requesting court authorization for the use, sale, or lease of property (other than cash collateral) that is out of the ordinary course of business.

2. Provide not less than 20 days notice to the U.S. trustee, any creditors' committee elected or appointed in the case, all creditors and indenture trustees. The notice must include the time and place of any public sale, the terms and conditions of any private sale, and the time fixed for the filing of objections.[2]

3. If the property is to be sold free and clear of all liens and other interests[3] (see § 9.63), the motion must be made in accordance with Bankruptcy Rule 9014 and served on all parties who have an interest in the property to be sold. The notice must include the date of the hearing on the motion and the deadline for filing and serving objections on the debtor or trustee.[4]

4. Objections to a proposed use, sale, or lease are governed by Bankruptcy Rule 9014 and generally are required to be filed and served not less than 5 days before the date set for the proposed action.[5]

5. When all the nonexempt property of the estate has an aggregate gross value of less than $2,500, it is sufficient to provide a general notice of the intent to sell such property outside the ordinary course of business to all parties listed in paragraph 2, *supra*.[6]

6. Objections to a sale of assets with a gross value of under $2,500 are governed by Bankruptcy Rule 9014 and generally must be filed and served within 15 days of the mailing of the notice, or within the time fixed by the court.[7]

§ 9.271

1. 11 U.S.C.A. § 363; Bankr.R. 4001, 6004, 7001. See *supra*, §§ 9.60, 9.62; see *supra*, § 9.266 for a procedural checklist for commencing an adversary proceeding and see *infra*, §§ 9.287, 9.288, and 9.294, respectively, for a drafting checklist of general rules, a drafting checklist for a complaint in an adversary proceeding, and a drafting checklist for a debtor's motion to use, sell, or lease property of the estate.

2. Bankr.R. 6004, 2002(a)(2), (c)(1), (i), (k). The court may direct that notices be transmitted only to the U.S. trustee and the creditors' committees elected or appointed in the case (or their authorized agents) and to those creditors and equity security holders who have filed and served on the debtor a request that all notices be mailed to them.

3. 11 U.S.C.A. § 363(f).

4. Bankr.R. 6004(c).

5. Bankr.R. 6004(b).

6. Bankr.R. 6004(d).

7. Bankr.R. 6004(d).

§ 9.271

7. After completion of service, a certificate of service should be filed with the clerk of the bankruptcy court.[8]

§ 9.272 Procedural Checklist—Debtor's Motion to Request Use of Cash Collateral[1]

1. File motion papers pursuant to Section 363(c)(2)(B) of the Bankruptcy Code and Bankruptcy Rules 4001 and 9014 requesting use of cash collateral.[2]

2. File with the motion papers an affidavit of the debtor's chief financial officer or accountant to support the debtor's need for use of the cash collateral and to substantiate the value of the adequate protection that is proposed. Such person should serve as a witness at the hearing.

3. Serve the motion papers in accordance with Bankruptcy Rule 9014 on each entity with an interest in the cash collateral and on any committee elected or appointed in the case or its authorized agent, or if no committee has been appointed, on the debtor's 20 largest creditors and on such other entities as the court may direct.[3]

4. After completion of service, a certificate of service should be filed with the clerk of the bankruptcy court.[4]

Library References:

West's Key No. Digests, Bankruptcy ⚖3084.

§ 9.273 Procedural Checklist—Cash Collateral Stipulation[1]

1. File motion papers pursuant to Section 363(c)(2)(A) and Bankruptcy Rule 4001(d) requesting court authorization of the cash collateral stipulation.

2. The motion papers and notice of the time within which objections may be filed and served on the debtor in possession or trustee must be mailed to the U.S. trustee, any committee elected or appointed in

---

8. Bankr.R. 8008(d).

§ 9.272

1. 11 U.S.C.A. § 363; Bankr.R. 4001(b). See supra, §§ 9.65–9.69; see supra, § 9.267 for a procedural checklist for commencing a contested matter and see infra, §§ 9.287, 9.295, respectively, for a drafting checklist of general rules and a drafting checklist for a debtor's motion to request use of cash collateral.

2. Bankr.R. 4001(b).

3. Bankr.R. 4001(b)(1); Bankr.R. 7004(h). In cases filed on or after October 22, 1994, if an insured depository institution is a respondent, it must be served by certified mail.

4. Bankr.R. 8008(d).

§ 9.273

1. 11 U.S.C.A. § 363; Bankr.R. 4001(d). See supra, §§ 9.65–9.66; see supra, § 9.267 for a procedural checklist for commencing a contested matter and see infra, §§ 9.287, 9.296, respectively, for a drafting checklist of general rules and a drafting checklist for a cash collateral stipulation. Timing requirements are set forth in Bankr.R. 4001.

the case or its authorized agent, or if no committee has been appointed, on the debtor's 20 largest creditors, any major secured creditors and lessors, and on such other entities as the court may direct.[2] Unless the court fixes a different time, objections may be filed within 15 days of the mailing of notice.[3]

3. After completion of service, a certificate of service should be filed with the clerk of the bankruptcy court.[4]

§ 9.274 Procedural Checklist—Debtor's Motion to Obtain Postpetition Financing[1]

1. File motion papers pursuant to Section 364 of the Bankruptcy Code and Bankruptcy Rules 4001 and 9014.

2. Serve the motion papers on any committee elected or appointed in the case or, if no committee has been appointed, on the debtor's 20 largest unsecured creditors, the U.S. trustee, and any major secured creditors and lessors.[2]

3. After completion of service, a certificate of service should be filed with the clerk of the bankruptcy court.[3]

Library References:

West's Key No. Digests, Bankruptcy ⟜3088.

§ 9.275 Procedural Checklist—Request to Assume, Reject, or Assign an Executory Contract or Unexpired Nonresidential Real Property Lease[1]

1. The trustee or debtor in possession must file motion papers with the bankruptcy court pursuant to Section 365 of the Bankruptcy Code and Bankruptcy Rules 6006 and 9014.[2]

---

2. Bankr.R. 4001(d)(1), 7004(h). In cases filed on or after October 22, 1994, if an insured depository institution is a respondent, it must be served by certified mail.

3. Bankr.R. 4001(d)(2). See supra, § 9.67 for a description of circumstances under which a debtor may obtain court approval for the emergency use of cash collateral on fewer than 15 days notice.

4. Bankr.R. 8008(d).

§ 9.274

1. 11 U.S.C.A. § 364; Bankr.R. 4001(c), (d). See supra, § 9.71; see supra, § 9.267 for a procedural checklist for commencing a contested matter and see infra, §§ 9.287, 9.297, respectively, for a drafting checklist of general rules and a drafting checklist for

a debtor's motion to obtain postpetition financing.

2. Bankr.R. 4001(c)(1).

3. Bankr.R. 8008(d).

§ 9.275

1. See supra, §§ 9.74–9.81; see supra, § 9.267 for a procedural checklist for commencing a contested matter and see infra, §§ 9.287, 9.298, respectively, for a drafting checklist of general rules and a drafting checklist for a motion to assume or reject an executory contract.

2. 11 U.S.C.A. § 365; Bankr.R. 6006. In a chapter 11, 12, or 13 case, unexpired leases of nonresidential real property are deemed rejected 60 days after the order for relief unless the court, for cause, extends

§ 9.275

2. Similarly, the nondebtor party to an executory contract or unexpired lease must file motion papers pursuant to Bankruptcy Rules 6006 and 9014 to request the court to shorten the time for a debtor or trustee to assume or reject a contract or lease.[3]

3. If the debtor is in default (other than a default by virtue of a bankruptcy clause or financial condition clause)[4] (*see* § 9.74 and note 4),[5] the debtor may not assume the executory contract or unexpired lease unless it fulfills the three preconditions for assumption outlined *supra*, § 9.79. (*See* § 9.248 note 4)[6]

4. Notice of the motion must be given to the other party to the contract or lease, other parties in interest as the court may direct, and to the United States trustee.[7]

5. After completion of service, a certificate of service should be filed with the clerk of the bankruptcy court.[8]

Library References:

West's Key No. Digests, Bankruptcy ⚖3117.

§ 9.276 Procedural Checklist—Debtor's Motion to Reject or Modify a Collective Bargaining Agreement[1]

1. Fulfill all requirements of Section 1113.[2] (*See* § 9.86)

2. After fulfilling all such requirements, file motion papers requesting court authorization to reject the agreement. (*See* § 9.17)[3]

3. Continue to meet and negotiate with the employees' representative in good faith until the hearing date.[4]

4. After completion of service, a certificate of service should be filed with the clerk of the bankruptcy court.[5]

the 60-day period prior to its expiration. For a discussion of this time limit and its interpretation by the courts, *see supra*, § 9.77 and note 1. If the validity of a contract is in question, a separate adversary proceeding must be commenced to determine the contractual dispute. *See supra*, § 9.74 note 3 PRACTICE POINTER.

3. 11 U.S.C.A. § 365(d)(2); Bankr.R. 6006(b).

4. 11 U.S.C.A. § 365(b)(2).

5. Discussion of the invalidity of bankruptcy clauses or financial condition clauses.

6. Discussing curing of defaults.

7. Bankr.R. 6006(c).

8. Bankr.R. 8008(d).

§ 9.276

1. *See* 11 U.S.C.A. § 1113; Bankr.R. 9014; *see supra*, § 9.267 for a procedural checklist for commencing a contested matter and *see infra*, §§ 9.287, 9.299, respectively, for a drafting checklist of general rules and a drafting checklist for a debtor's motion to reject or modify a collective bargaining agreement.

2. *See* 11 U.S.C.A. § 1113.

3. Discussion of commencing a contested matter.

4. 11 U.S.C.A. § 1113(b)(2).

5. Bankr.R. 8008(d).

§ 9.277 Procedural Checklist—Debtor's Motion to Obtain Approval of a Compromise and Settlement of a Claim[1]

1. The debtor must file motion papers pursuant to Bankruptcy Rule 9019 requesting authorization to enter into the settlement.

2. The debtor must provide at least 20 days notice of the hearing date to creditors, indenture trustees, the U.S. trustee, and any other entity as the court may direct.[2]

3. Attach affidavits of relevant parties or experts that establish evidentiary support for the settlement. Such parties may be required as witnesses at the hearing.

4. After completion of service, a certificate of service should be filed with the clerk of the bankruptcy court.[3]

Library References:

West's Key No. Digests, Bankruptcy ⇐3033.

§ 9.278 Procedural Checklist—Claiming Exemptions[1]

1. All property claimed as exempt by an individual debtor must be included as part of the schedule of assets required by Bankruptcy Rule 1007 to be filed with the petition or within 15 days from the date of entry of the order for relief (see § 9.11) unless the court orders otherwise.

2. The estimated value of the property claimed as exempt and specification of the law providing each exemption must be filed on Official Form 6, Schedule C. (See § 9.5, note 3)[2]

3. If the debtor fails to claim exemptions within the time allowed, a dependent of the debtor may file the list within 30 days thereafter.[3]

4. The schedule of exemptions may be amended at any time before the case is closed and must be served on the trustee and all creditors.[4]

§ 9.277

1. See supra, § 9.97; see supra, § 9.267 for a procedural checklist for commencing a contested matter and see infra, §§ 9.287, 9.300, respectively, for a drafting checklist of general rules and a drafting checklist for a debtor's motion to obtain approval of a compromise and settlement of claim.

2. Bankr.R. 9019, 2002.

3. Bankr.R. 8008(d).

§ 9.278

1. 11 U.S.C.A. § 522(l); Bankr.R. 4003(a), 1007(c). See supra, § 9.125.

2. Discussion of Official Forms.

3. 11 U.S.C.A. § 522(l); Bankr.R. 4003(a).

4. Bankr.R. 1009.

§ 9.278 BANKRUPTCY Ch. 9

Library References:

West's Key No. Digests, Bankruptcy ⚖2794.1–2802.

§ 9.279 Procedural Checklist—Debtor's Motion to Avoid a Judicial Lien or a Nonpossessory, Nonpurchase–Money Security Interest That Impairs Exempt Property[1]

1. File motion papers pursuant to Bankruptcy Rules 9013 and 9014.

2. File and serve the motion papers in accordance with the procedure governing contested matters. (See § 9.17)[2]

3. After completion of service, a certificate of service should be filed with the clerk of the bankruptcy court.[3]

§ 9.280 Procedural Checklist—Debtor's Motion to Obtain Court Approval of a Reaffirmation Agreement[1]

1. File motion papers pursuant to 11 U.S.C.A. § 524(c) and (d) and Bankruptcy Rules 4008 and 9014 at or before the hearing to consider the debtor's reaffirmation agreement. The agreement must have been made before the granting of a discharge under Section 727, 1141, 1228, or 1328 of the Bankruptcy Code.[2]

2. The hearing must be held no more than 30 days after the entry of an order granting or denying a discharge, or confirming a plan in a chapter 11 case concerning an individual debtor, on not less than 10 days notice to the debtor and the trustee.[3]

3. After completion of service, a certificate of service should be filed with the clerk of the bankruptcy court.[4]

Library References:

West's Key No. Digests, Bankruptcy ⚖3417.

§ 9.279

1. 11 U.S.C.A. § 522(f). See supra, §§ 9.128–9.129; see supra, § 9.267 for a procedural checklist for commencing a contested matter and see infra, §§ 9.287, 9.301, respectively, for a drafting checklist of general rules and a drafting checklist for a debtor's motion to avoid a judicial lien or nonpossessory, nonpurchase-money security interest that impairs exempt property.
2. Discussion of contested matters.
3. Bankr.R. 8008(d).

§ 9.280

1. See supra, § 9.130 for a discussion of reaffirmation and drafting requirements for a reaffirmation agreement; see supra, § 9.267 for a procedural checklist for commencing a contested matter and see infra, §§ 9.287, 9.302, and 9.303 respectively, for a drafting checklist of general rules for all motions, a drafting checklist for a reaffirmation agreement, and a drafting checklist for a motion seeking court approval for a reaffirmation agreement.

2. 11 U.S.C.A. § 524(c)(1); Bankr.R. 4008.
3. Bankr.R. 4008.
4. Bankr.R. 8008(d).

§ 9.281 Procedural Checklist—Debtor's Motion to Request an Extension of Exclusivity[1]

1. File motion papers pursuant to Section 1121(d) of the Bankruptcy Code and Bankruptcy Rule 9014.

2. File and serve the motion papers in accordance with the procedure governing contested matters. (*See* § 9.17)[2]

3. Preparation of affidavits in support of the motion is optional. It will depend upon whether objections to the motion are anticipated.[3]

4. After completion of service, a certificate of service should be filed with the clerk of the bankruptcy court.[4]

Library References:

West's Key No. Digests, Bankruptcy ⟲3534.

§ 9.282 Procedural Checklist—Filing a Chapter 11 Plan and Disclosure Statement[1]

1. File a plan in accordance with 11 U.S.C.A. § 1121 and Bankruptcy Rule 3016. The plan must satisfy all requirements set forth in Sections 1122 and 1123 of the Bankruptcy Code.

2. Date the plan and any amendment thereof and identify the name of the plan proponent(s).[2]

3. File with the plan a disclosure statement in accordance with 11 U.S.C.A. § 1125 or, for a prepackaged plan, evidence of compliance with 11 U.S.C.A. § 1126(b).[3]

4. Mail the proposed plan and disclosure statement with notice of the hearing in the form of Official Form 12 to the debtor, the U.S. trustee, any trustee or committee appointed under the Bankruptcy Code, any indenture trustees, and any party in interest who files a written request for all notices pursuant to the Bankruptcy Rule 2002.[4]

§ 9.281

1. 11 U.S.C.A. § 1121(d). See *supra*, § 9.142, and with respect to chapter 11 cases of small businesses, § 9.143; see *supra*, § 9.267 for a procedural checklist for commencing a contested matter and see *infra*, §§ 9.287, 9.304, respectively, for a drafting checklist of general rules and a drafting checklist for a debtor's motion to request an extension of exclusivity.

2. Discussion of contested matters.

3. Both parties may wish to file affidavits of appropriate persons to establish evidentiary support for their respective positions, and such persons should be available as witnesses at the hearing. The debtor bears the burden of proof that there is cause for an extension of exclusivity.

4. Bankr.R. 8008(d).

§ 9.282

1. 11 U.S.C.A. §§ 1121–1125; Bankr.R. 3016. See *supra*, §§ 9.147–9.163.

2. Bankr.R. 3016(b).

3. Bankr.R. 3016(c).

4. Bankr.R. 3017(a).

§ 9.282

5. The proponent must provide a minimum of 25 days notice of the deadline for filing objections and the hearing to consider approval of a disclosure statement.[5]

6. Objections to the disclosure statement must be filed and served on the debtor, the U.S. trustee, any trustee or committee appointed under the Bankruptcy Code, and such other entities as may be designated by the bankruptcy court. Objections may be filed at any time prior to approval of the disclosure statement or by such earlier date as the court may fix.[6]

Library References:
West's Key No. Digests, Bankruptcy ⇐3531, 3540.

§ 9.283 Procedural Checklist—Soliciting Acceptance of a Chapter 11 Plan[1]

Unless the bankruptcy court orders otherwise with respect to one or more unimpaired classes of creditors, the debtor in possession, trustee, plan proponent or clerk, as ordered by the court, must mail to all creditors, equity security holders, and the United States trustee:

1. The proposed plan, or a court approved summary thereof;

2. The court-approved disclosure statement (see § 9.162);

3. Notice of the time within which acceptances and rejections of such plan may be filed;

4. Notice of the time fixed for filing objections to confirmation and the hearing on confirmation;

5. Such other information as the court may direct, including any opinion of the court approving the disclosure statement, or a court-approved summary of the opinion;[2] and

6. A ballot conforming to Official Form 14 must be sent to all creditors and equity security holders entitled to vote on the plan (i.e., all members of impaired classes).[3] A vote may be changed if the change is approved by the court for cause after notice and a hearing.[4]

Library References:
West's Key No. Digests, Bankruptcy ⇐3541.1–3547.

---

5. Bankr.R. 2002(b)(1).
6. Bankr.R. 3017(a).

§ 9.283

1. 11 U.S.C.A. § 1126; Bankr.R. 3016, 3017. See supra, § 9.162.
2. Bankr.R. 2002(b).
3. **PRACTICE POINTER**: The language of Section 1125(b) does not prohibit the sending of materials which are not court-approved in addition to the plan or summary of the plan and disclosure statement and any other court-approved material. First American Bank of New York v. Century Glove, Inc., 81 B.R. 274 (D.Del.), aff'd 860 F.2d 94 (3d Cir.1988).

4. Bankr.R. 3018(a); see 11 U.S.C.A. § 1127; Bankr.R. 3019, the applicable local Bankruptcy Rules. See supra, § 9.164 for modification of an accepted chapter 11 plan before confirmation.

§ 9.284 Procedural Checklist—Filing a Chapter 12 or 13 Plan of Debt Adjustment[1]

1. A chapter 12 debtor may file a chapter 12 plan with the petition or no later than 90 days after entry of the order for relief, unless the court has extended the period.[2]

2. A chapter 13 debtor may file a chapter 13 plan with the petition or no later than 15 days thereafter, unless the court extends the period for cause shown and on notice. If a case is converted to chapter 13, a plan must be filed 15 days after conversion.[3]

3. Every proposed plan and any modification must be dated.[4]

4. The plan or a summary thereof must be included with each notice of the hearing on confirmation mailed pursuant to Bankruptcy Rule 2002.[5]

5. A copy of the plan and any plan modification must be filed with the clerk for transmittal to the U.S. trustee.[6]

6. After completion of service, a certificate of service should be filed with the clerk of the bankruptcy court.[7]

§ 9.285 Procedural Checklist—Objection to a Chapter 12 or 13 Plan[1]

1. An objection to confirmation is a contested matter governed by Bankruptcy Rule 9014.

2. File an objection to confirmation with the court and serve the objection on the debtor, the trustee, any other party designated by the court, and the U.S. trustee before confirmation of the plan.[2]

3. After completion of service, a certificate of service should be filed with the clerk of the Bankruptcy Court.[3]

---

§ 9.284

1. 11 U.S.C.A. §§ 1221–1222; Bankr.R. 3013, 3015. See supra, §§ 9.221–9.223 regarding a chapter 12 plan. 11 U.S.C.A. §§ 1321–1322; Bankr.R. 3013, 3015. See supra, §§ 9.246–9.249 regarding a chapter 13 plan.

2. 11 U.S.C.A. § 1221; Bankr.R. 3015(a).

3. 11 U.S.C.A. § 1321; Bankr.R. 3015(b).

4. Bankr.R. 3015(c).
5. Bankr.R. 3015(d).
6. Bankr.R. 3015(e).
7. Bankr.R. 8008(d).

§ 9.285

1. Bankr.R. 3015(f). See supra, §§ 9.226, 9.252, respectively, for a discussion of objections to a chapter 12 or 13 plan. See supra, § 9.267 for a procedural checklist for commencing a contested matter and see infra, § 9.287 for a drafting checklist of general rules.

2. Bankr.R. 3015(f).

PRACTICE POINTER: If no objection is timely filed, the court may determine that the plan has been proposed in good faith and not by any means forbidden by law without receiving evidence on such issues.

3. Bankr.R. 8008(d).

§ 9.286 Procedural Checklist—Debtor's Motion to Request Modification of a Chapter 12 or 13 Plan After Confirmation[1]

1. File a request for plan modification pursuant to Section 1229 or 1329 of the Bankruptcy Code and Bankruptcy Rule 3015(g).

2. The request must identify the proponent and be filed with the proposed modification.

3. Provide the debtor, the trustee, and all creditors (unless the court orders otherwise with respect to creditors who are not affected by the proposed modification) not less than 20 days notice by mail of the time fixed for filing objections and, if an objection is filed, the hearing to consider the proposed modification. A copy of the proposed modification or a summary thereof must be included with the notice.[2]

4. Provide the clerk with a copy of the notice for transmittal to the U.S. trustee.

5. After completion of service, a certificate of service should be filed with the clerk of the bankruptcy court.[3]

§ 9.287 Drafting Checklist—General Rules for All Motions, Applications, and Complaints[1]

1. Every application to the court for an order must be made in writing

---

§ 9.286

1. 11 U.S.C.A. § 1223; Bankr.R. 3019. See supra, § 9.224 discussing modification of a chapter 12 plan. 11 U.S.C.A. § 1323; Bankr.R. 3015. See supra, § 9.250 discussing modification of a chapter 13 plan. See supra, § 9.267 for a procedural checklist for commencing a contested matter and see infra, § 9.287 for a drafting checklist of general rules.

2. If the court directs the clerk to provide notice, the court may require the proponent to furnish a sufficient number of copies of the proposed modification or summary thereof to enable the clerk to include a copy with each notice.

3. Bankr.R. 8008(d).

§ 9.287

1. See supra, § 9.16 for a discussion of adversary proceedings and § 9.17 for a discussion of contested matters. See infra, §§ 9.306–9.308 for a sample motion, notice of motion, and proposed order for a contested matter. See infra, § 9.288 for a drafting checklist for a complaint in an adversary proceeding and § 9.309 for a sample complaint to commence an adversary proceeding.

CAVEAT: Practitioners must consult and comply with all local rules. See supra, § 9.5 for a discussion of the sources of governing law.

PRACTICE POINTER: Practitioners should make inquiry concerning the norms of practice within the relevant jurisdiction. For example, in the Southern District of New York, although Local Bankruptcy Rule 9013–1(b) requires that a memorandum of law be filed with any motion, where no novel or disputed points of law are raised, it is common practice to omit the filing of a memorandum of law and to include a statement in the motion requesting waiver of the requirement. Example: [Name of Applicant] requests that the court waive and dispense with the requirement set forth in Local Bankruptcy Rule 9013–1(b) that a motion be accompanied by a memorandum of law. This motion does not present any substantial issues of law which would require consideration of any authority other than the case law and provisions of the Bankruptcy Code cited herein. Accordingly,

Ch. 9   COMPLAINT IN AN ADVERSARY PROCEEDING § 9.288

unless made during a hearing.[2]

2. Every motion, application, or complaint should provide a brief summary of background information that includes:
   - The date the petition was filed;
   - A statement establishing the basis of the court's jurisdiction;
   - A brief statement identifying the debtor; if there are multiple debtors, whether the cases are being jointly administered;
   - If the debtor is in business, a brief description of the debtor's business;
   - A statement as to whether a statutory committee has been appointed, and if so, when; and
   - Any significant events in the proceedings, and the dates thereof.

3. Every motion should include a brief statement of the background necessary for an understanding of the basis for the relief that is sought.

4. A demand must be made for judgment for the relief that is sought stating with particularity the grounds therefor.[3]

5. Alternative forms of relief or several types of relief may be demanded.

6. All pleadings must be signed in accordance with Federal Rule of Civil Procedure 11.

§ 9.288   Drafting Checklist—Complaint in an Adversary Proceeding[1]

The complaint must include the following:

1. A specific assertion of the grounds of the bankruptcy court's jurisdiction, including a statement whether the proceeding is core or non-core;[2]
2. A concise statement of the claim;
3. A request for specific relief, including attorneys' fees, if appropriate;

[Name of Applicant] submits that waiver of the Local Bankruptcy Rule 9013–1(b) requirement is appropriate in these circumstances.

2. Bankr.R. 7007(b)(1).
3. Bankr.R. 7007(b)(1).

§ 9.288

1. Bankr.R. 7001 and Part VII of the Bankruptcy Rules. See supra, § 9.16; see supra, §§ 9.266, 9.287, respectively, for a procedural checklist for commencing an adversary proceeding and a drafting checklist of general rules. See infra, § 9.309 for a sample of a complaint in an adversary proceeding.

2. See 28 U.S.C.A. § 157.

§ 9.288   BANKRUPTCY   Ch. 9

    4. A demand for a jury trial should be made if so desired; and

    5. A request for alternate relief, if appropriate.

§ 9.289 Drafting Checklist—Motion for Leave to Appeal From an Interlocutory Judgment, Order, or Decree of a Bankruptcy Judge[1]

A motion for leave to appeal under 28 U.S.C.A. § 158(a) must contain:

1. A statement of the facts necessary for an understanding of the questions to be presented;
2. A statement of those questions and of the relief sought;
3. A statement of the reasons why an appeal should be granted; and
4. A copy of the judgment, order, or decree complained of and of any opinion or memorandum relating thereto.[2]

Library References:

West's Key No. Digests, Bankruptcy ⚖︎3768.

§ 9.290 Drafting Checklist—Motion for a Stay of a Bankruptcy Court Judgment or Order Pending Appeal[1]

A motion for a stay pending appeal should set forth:

1. The background of the case;
2. The salient facts and procedural history of the matter from which the appeal is taken;
3. The nature of the relief requested; and
4. The reasons why a stay pending appeal should be granted (*i.e.*, a substantial probability of success on the appeal, or the likelihood of irreparable harm and substantial injury in the event that a stay is not granted).

Library References:

West's Key No. Digests, Bankruptcy ⚖︎3776.5(4).

§ 9.289

1. 28 U.S.C.A. § 158(a). *See supra*, § 9.25; *see supra*, §§ 9.267, 9.268, 9.287, respectively, for a procedural checklist for commencing a contested matter, a procedural checklist for a motion for leave to appeal, and a drafting checklist of general rules.

2. Bankr.R. 8003(a).

§ 9.290

1. Bankr.R. 8005, 8007(c). *See supra*, § 9.25; *see supra*, § 9.267 for a procedural checklist for commencing a contested matter and *see supra*, § 9.287 for a drafting checklist of general rules.

§ 9.291 Drafting Checklist—Application of Debtor or Statutory Committee to Retain Professionals[1]

In a case under chapter 7, 11, 12, or 13, an application by a debtor in possession, trustee, or statutory committee appointed in the case to retain professionals pursuant to Section 327, 1103, or 1114 of the Bankruptcy Code must be filed with the court and transmitted to the United States trustee and must include the following:

1. Specific facts showing the need for the retention;
2. The name and address of the person to be retained;
3. The reasons for the selection of such person;
4. The services to be rendered;
5. The proposed compensation arrangements;
6. All of the person's connections with the debtor, creditors, any other party in interest, their respective attorneys and accountants, the U.S. trustee, or any person employed in the office of the U.S. trustee; and
7. The application must be accompanied by an affidavit of the proposed professional stating such person's connections with the debtor, creditors, any other party in interest, their respective attorneys and accountants, the U.S. trustee, or any person employed in the office of the U.S. trustee.[2]
8. The application must satisfy all requirements set forth in the guidelines issued by the U.S. trustee.

Library References:

West's Key No. Digests, Bankruptcy ⇐3024.

§ 9.292 Drafting Checklist—Creditor's Motion to Request Relief From the Automatic Stay[1]

1. A motion requesting relief from the automatic stay should specify the nature of the relief sought and state with particularity the grounds therefor.[2]

§ 9.291

1. 11 U.S.C.A. § 327. See supra, § 9.29; see supra, § 9.267 for a procedural checklist for commencing a contested matter and see supra, § 9.287 for a drafting checklist of general rules for applications. See infra, §§ 9.310, 9.311 for a sample application for retention and attorney's affidavit.

2. Bankr.R. 2014(a).

PRACTICE POINTER: A separate set of pleadings containing a notice, application, professional's affidavit, and proposed order must be filed for each professional to be retained.

§ 9.292

1. 11 U.S.C.A. § 362(d)-(g); Bankr.R. 4001. See supra, §§ 9.50, 9.52; see supra, §§ 9.267, 9.269, and 9.287, respectively, for a procedural checklist for commencing a contested matter, a procedural checklist for a motion requesting relief from the automatic stay, and a drafting checklist of general rules.

2. Bankr.R. 9013.

§ 9.292

2. The nature of the creditor's claim should be described, with security documents attached as exhibits to the motion.[3]

3. The motion must demonstrate "cause," which includes the lack of adequate protection of an interest in property.[4] To establish a lack of adequate protection, the secured creditor must demonstrate that it is not protected against a decrease in the value of the collateral securing its claim. (See §§ 9.56–9.58)[5]

4. Alternately, the motion must demonstrate both that the debtor lacks equity in the collateral securing its claim and that such collateral is not necessary to an effective reorganization.[6]

5. The party requesting relief has the burden of proof on the issue of whether the debtor has equity in the property. The party opposing the relief has the burden of proof on all other issues.[7]

Library References:

West's Key No. Digests, Bankruptcy ⟺ 2435.1–2442.

§ 9.293 Drafting Checklist—Creditor's Motion to Obtain Adequate Protection[1]

1. Describe the nature of the collateral and the financing agreement which gives rise to the secured creditor's interest in the debtor's property.

2. Explain the basis for adequate protection to be granted (e.g., the collateral in the debtor's possession has and will continue to decline in value postpetition), and describe both the reasons for, and the degree of, this decline in the collateral's value.

3. State the amount and/or the nature of the adequate protection being sought (e.g., periodic or a lump sum cash payment, an additional or replacement lien, granting an administrative expense claim, etc.) and the manner in which this adequate protection was determined (i.e., the amount of the decline in the fair market value of the collateral postpetition).[2]

---

3. **PRACTICE POINTER**: Alternatively, the motion can incorporate by reference a filed proof of claim which includes the security documents as exhibits.

4. 11 U.S.C.A. § 362(d)(1).

5. Discussion of adequate protection.

6. 11 U.S.C.A. § 362(d)(2).

7. 11 U.S.C.A. § 362(g).

§ 9.293

1. 11 U.S.C.A. § 362(d) or 363(e); Bankr.R. 4001(d). See supra, §§ 9.56–9.58;

see supra, §§ 9.267, 9.270, and 9.287, respectively, for a procedural checklist for commencing a contested matter, a procedural checklist for a motion to obtain adequate protection, and a drafting checklist of general rules.

2. The debtor bears the burden of proof that any protection to be provided is adequate. Both parties should file affidavits of appropriate persons to establish evidentiary support for their respective positions, and such persons should be available as witnesses at a hearing.

§ 9.294 Drafting Checklist—Debtor's Motion to Use, Sell, or Lease Property of the Estate[1]

1. Identify and describe the property to be leased or sold.

2. Describe why the debtor has chosen to sell or lease the property; why the proposed transaction is in the best interests of the debtor's estate; and why the proposed transaction represents a reasonable business judgment on the part of the debtor.

3. Describe any interests that third parties may have in the property; whether or not these parties have consented to the sale or lease; and whether the property will be sold or leased free and clear of all such liens pursuant to Section 363(f) (the liens would then become attached to the proceeds of the sale), or whether the property will remain subject to such liens following the transaction.[2]

4. Describe the debtor's efforts to market the property, and why the deal the debtor has selected is the best offer.

5. Describe the pertinent terms of the proposed sale or lease.

6. Propose bidding procedures for any competing offers for the property that may be made at or prior to the hearing seeking court approval of the sale or lease (for example, a minimum competing bid or the minimum increment of each successive bid), or alternatively, why the debtor believes that conducting an auction at the hearing would not be worthwhile.

7. Describe whether the transaction is exempt from transfer taxes pursuant to Section 1146(c) of the Bankruptcy Code.

8. If applicable, the motion should also seek court approval of any expense reimbursement or "break-up" fee that the debtor would have to pay to the proposed purchaser or lessor in the event that a third party makes a higher or better offer to the debtor for the property at or prior to the hearing.

9. Alternatively, the debtor could argue that the sale or lease is in the ordinary course of the debtor's business, such that notice and a hearing is not required.[3] (see §§ 9.60–9.61)

---

§ 9.294

1. 11 U.S.C.A. § 363; Bankr.R. 4001, 6004, 7001. See supra, §§ 9.60–9.63; see supra, §§ 9.266, 9.271, and 9.287, respectively, for a procedural checklist for commencing an adversary proceeding, a procedural checklist for a motion to use, sell, or lease property of the estate, and a drafting checklist of general rules.

2. See 11 U.S.C.A. § 552(b).

3. 11 U.S.C.A. § 362(c).

§ 9.295 Drafting Checklist—Debtor's Motion to Request Use of Cash Collateral[1]

1. Specify the amount of cash collateral needed, including, where appropriate, the amount to be used before a final hearing.
2. Include the names and addresses of all parties holding an interest in the cash collateral.
3. Concisely describe the facts evidencing need for use of the cash collateral.
4. If interim use of cash collateral is requested, describe facts demonstrating that: (a) there is a reasonable likelihood that the trustee or debtor in possession will prevail at the final hearing (*see* 11 U.S.C.A. § 363(c)(3)) and (b) the estate would suffer immediate and irreparable harm if it did not obtain interim use of cash collateral. (*See* Bankr.R. 4001(c)(2)).
5. Describe the nature of the adequate protection to be provided. The debtor has the burden of proving that the creditor's interest will be adequately protected.[2]

Library References:

West's Key No. Digests, Bankruptcy ⇔3084.

§ 9.296 Drafting Checklist—Cash Collateral Stipulation[1]

1. Describe the secured creditor's claim, including all principal and prepetition accrued interest, as well as the collateral securing the indebtedness.
2. Describe the basis for the secured creditor's "cash collateral" interest, including the debtor's verification of perfection of a lien on collateral and proceeds.
3. Describe the debtor's need to use cash collateral.
4. Summarize the terms of the stipulation relating to the use of cash collateral as follows:
    * Describe those cash proceeds authorized to be retained by the debtor and any basis under which it may utilize such cash (for

§ 9.295

1. 11 U.S.C.A. § 363(c)(2)(B); Bankr.R. 4001, 9014. See *supra,* §§ 9.65–9.66; *see supra,* §§ 9.267, 9.272, and 9.287, respectively, for a procedural checklist for commencing a contested matter, a procedural checklist for a motion requesting use of cash collateral, and a drafting checklist of general rules.

2. Both parties should file affidavits of appropriate persons to establish evidentiary support for their respective positions, and such persons should be available as witnesses at a hearing.

§ 9.296

1. 11 U.S.C.A. § 363(c)(2)(B); Bankr.R. 4001, 9014. See *supra,* §§ 9.65–9.66; *see supra,* §§ 9.273, 9.287, respectively, for a procedural checklist for a cash collateral stipulation and a drafting checklist of general rules.

Ch. 9   OBTAIN POSTPETITION FINANCING   § 9.297

example, any budget pursuant to which such cash may be expended);

- Describe any financial information that must be presented by the debtor to the secured creditor on a going forward basis;

- Describe any cash proceeds to be paid to the secured creditor pursuant to the stipulation, as well as the application of such monies to the reduction of principal and/or interest on the creditor's secured claim;

- Describe the duration of the cash collateral stipulation and the circumstances under which either party may terminate the agreement, as well as the remedies provided to the secured creditor under such circumstances; and

- Describe any reservation of rights provided to either party, including the ability to contest the validity and/or extent of liens, and the right to seek recovery of any prepetition payments pursuant to the debtor's avoidance powers.

5. Set forth the basis for the waiver of any rights by the debtor as part of the stipulation.

6. Include a statement to the effect that the stipulation is in the best interests of the estate and its creditors.

§ 9.297 Drafting Checklist—Debtor's Motion to Obtain Postpetition Financing[1]

1. Specify the amount and type of credit to be extended and the name and address of the lender.

2. Explain the reasons why the debtor needs credit.

3. Summarize the terms of the agreement and attach as an exhibit a draft or executed copy of the proposed agreement.

4. Describe with particularity the efforts made to obtain credit from other sources and with lower priority.[2] (See § 9.71)

5. If applicable, describe the collateral to be pledged and/or the adequate protection to be provided to existing lienholders affected by the proposed postpetition financing.[3]

---

§ 9.297

1. 11 U.S.C.A. § 364; Bankr.R. 4001; 9014. See supra, § 9.71; see supra, §§ 9.267, 9.274, and 9.287, respectively, for a procedural checklist for commencing a contested matter, a procedural checklist for a motion to obtain postpetition financing, and a drafting checklist of general rules. Timing requirements are set forth in Bankr.R. 4001.

2. See 11 U.S.C.A. § 364. Efforts to obtain postpetition financing must comply with 11 U.S.C.A. § 364.

3. Bankr.R. 4001(c) and Advisory Comm. Note to 1987 Amendment.

§ 9.297 BANKRUPTCY Ch. 9

6. Affidavits of appropriate persons may be needed to establish evidentiary support for the proposed financing.[4]

Library References:

West's Key No. Digests, Bankruptcy ⟸3038.

§ 9.298 Drafting Checklist—Motion to Assume or Reject an Executory Contract or Unexpired Non–residential Real Property Lease[1]

1. Describe with particularity the contract or lease which is the subject of the motion, including all pertinent terms and provisions therein.

2. With respect to a motion to reject an executory contract or unexpired lease:

   - Set forth the basis for the debtor's business judgment that the contract or lease is burdensome and of little or no value to the estate;

   - To the extent known, discuss why the contract or lease does not comport with the contemplated business plan of the debtor;

   - Assess the damage claim that would arise from rejection compared to any potential benefits to the estate from assuming the contract or lease; (see §§ 9.81–9.83)

   - Describe why it is in the best interest of the estate that the contract or lease be rejected;

3. With respect to a motion to assume an executory contract or unexpired lease:

   - Set forth the debtor's business judgment for determining to assume the executory contract or unexpired lease, including why the contract or lease comports with the debtor's ongoing business plan;

   - Describe all defaults under the contract or lease, including the amount of any arrearages thereunder, the manner in which such defaults will be cured or adequate assurance that the debtor will promptly cure such defaults, and the timing thereof; (see § 9.248 note 4)[2]

4. Such persons may be required to serve as witnesses at a hearing.

§ 9.298

1. 11 U.S.C.A. § 365; Bankr.R. 6006, 9014. See supra, §§ 9.74–9.82. This checklist may be used by a debtor who wishes to assume or reject an executory contract or unexpired lease or by a creditor seeking relief pursuant to Section 365. See supra, §§ 9.267, 9.275, and 9.287, respectively, for a procedural checklist for commencing a contested matter, a procedural checklist for a motion to assume or reject an executory contract or unexpired lease, and a drafting checklist of general rules.

2. Discussion of curing defaults before assuming an executory contract.

- Describe any compensation for actual pecuniary loss that will be required to be paid, and the terms thereof;

- Set forth the basis of "adequate assurance" by the debtor for the future performance of all obligations under the executory contract or unexpired lease; and

- With respect to a shopping center location, set forth the debtor's basis for "adequate assurance" of future performance of a lease of real property, including:

    (i) The source of rent and other consideration due under the lease; and in the case of an assignment, that the financial condition and operating performance of the proposed assignee shall be similar to the financial condition and operating performance of the debtor at the time the debtor became the lessee;

    (ii) That any percentage rent due will not decline substantially;

    (iii) That assumption or assignment is subject to all the provisions of the lease, including radius, location, use, or exclusivity; and

    (iv) That assumption or assignment will not disrupt any tenant mix or balance in the shopping center.

§ 9.299 Drafting Checklist—Debtor's Motion to Reject or Modify a Collective Bargaining Agreement (CBA)[1]

1. Describe the background of the debtor's overall relationship with its employees.

2. Describe the provisions of the CBA which the debtor wishes to modify or reject.

3. The debtor must demonstrate that prior to filing an application to reject a CBA, (i) the debtor made a proposal to the authorized representatives of the employees covered by such agreement, which proposal provided for modifications that were necessary to permit the reorganization of the debtor, and (ii) that the debtor provided the employees' representatives with the relevant information necessary to evaluate the proposal.[2]

---

§ 9.299
1. 11 U.S.C.A. § 1113. See supra, § 9.86; see supra, §§ 9.267, 9.276, and 9.287, respectively, for a procedural checklist for commencing a contested matter, a procedural checklist for a motion to reject or modify a collective bargaining agreement, and a drafting checklist of general rules.

2. 11 U.S.C.A. § 1113(c)(1).

§ 9.299   BANKRUPTCY   Ch. 9

4. The debtor must further demonstrate that after making such a proposal to the employees' representatives, the debtor met at reasonable times with the representative to confer in good faith in attempting to reach a mutually satisfactory modification of the CBA, but that the authorized representative has refused without good cause to accept the debtor's proposal.[3]

5. If the debtor seeks to reject the CBA, it must convince the judge that the "balance of the equities clearly favors" rejection.[4]

6. If the debtor merely seeks to modify the CBA, it must describe the nature of the proposed modifications to the CBA, the benefits to the debtor which will result from these modifications, and why these changes are necessary to ensure the success of the reorganization.

§ 9.300   Drafting Checklist—Debtor's Motion to Obtain Approval of a Compromise and Settlement of a Claim[1]

1. Include background concerning the basis of the claim.

2. Describe the position of each of the parties to the dispute.

3. Summarize the terms of the proposed settlement and attach as an exhibit the draft of the proposed settlement.

4. Provide an accounting that weighs the benefits versus the costs to the estate.

5. Affidavits of witnesses may be needed to establish evidentiary support for the settlement.

6. Include a statement that the agreement is in the best interests of the estate and its creditors.

Library References:

West's Key No. Digests, Bankruptcy ⇐3033.

3. 11 U.S.C.A. § 1113(c)(2).
4. 11 U.S.C.A. § 1113(c)(3).

§ 9.300

1. Bankr.R. 9019. See supra, § 9.97 and consult the guidelines set forth in the case cited in note 4; see supra, §§ 9.267, 9.277, and 9.287, respectively, for a procedural checklist for commencing a contested matter, a procedural checklist for a motion to obtain approval of a compromise and settle-

§ 9.301 Drafting Checklist—Debtor's Motion to Avoid a Judicial Lien or a Nonpossessory, Nonpurchase–Money Security Interest That Impairs Exempt Property[1]

1. The motion must state the amount of, and the authority for, the exemption sought.

2. Identify the property claimed as exempt and state its fair market value as of the petition date, or if it was acquired postpetition, on the date it became property of the estate (if possible, attach an appraiser's report as an exhibit).

3. Describe the lien, including its type, amount, and date.

4. Calculate the amount of the debtor's surplus equity to determine the amount of the lien that may be exempted. (*See* § 9.128)[2]

§ 9.302 Drafting Checklist—Reaffirmation Agreement[1]

1. Include the name and address of the creditor, the amount and purpose of the debt.

2. State the terms of the payment plan, including the principal amount, the interest rate, and the amount of the monthly payments.

3. Provide a description of the security, including its present fair market value.

4. Include a *clear and conspicuous statement* advising the debtor that the agreement may be rescinded by the debtor at any time before discharge or within 60 days after the agreement has been filed with the court, whichever is later, by giving notice of rescission to the creditor.[2]

5. Include a *clear and conspicuous statement* advising the debtor that the reaffirmation agreement is not required under title 11, nonbankruptcy law, or under any agreement not in accordance with the provisions of Section 524(c) of the Bankruptcy Code.[3]

6. The agreement must be signed by the debtor and the creditor.

---

ment of a claim and a drafting checklist of general rules.

§ 9.301

1. 11 U.S.C.A. § 522(f); Bankr.R. 9014. See *supra*, §§ 9.128–9.129; see *supra*, §§ 9.267, 9.279, and 9.287, respectively, for a procedural checklist for commencing a contested matter, a procedural checklist for a motion to avoid a judicial lien, and a drafting checklist of general rules.

2. Discussion of the calculation of the debtor's surplus equity.

§ 9.302

1. 11 U.S.C.A. § 524(c); Bankr.R. 4008. See *supra*, §§ 9.130–9.131; see *supra*, §§ 9.280, 9.287, respectively, for a procedural checklist for a motion seeking approval of a reaffirmation agreement and a drafting checklist of general rules; see *infra*, § 9.303 for a drafting checklist for a motion seeking approval of a reaffirmation agreement.

2. 11 U.S.C.A. § 524(c)(2)(A).

3. 11 U.S.C.A. § 524(c)(2)(B).

§ 9.303 Drafting Checklist—Debtor's Motion for Approval of a Reaffirmation Agreement[1]

1. Include the name and address of the creditor, and the amount and purpose of the debt.
2. Describe the terms of the reaffirmation agreement, including the principal amount, the interest rate, and the amount of the monthly payments. Describe the security, including its present fair market value. Attach a copy of the agreement as an exhibit.
3. Include financial information about the debtor to enable the court to determine whether the agreement would impose an undue hardship on the debtor or a dependent of the debtor. This should include the debtor's current net monthly income and current monthly expenses, including payments that would be due under the reaffirmation agreement and any other reaffirmation agreement that the debtor has entered or anticipates entering.
4. State the reasons why the agreement is in the best interest of the debtor.[2]

Library References:
West's Key No. Digests, Bankruptcy ⇨3417.

§ 9.304 Drafting Checklist—Debtor's Motion to Request an Extension of Exclusivity[1]

1. File a motion pursuant to Section 1121(d) of the Bankruptcy Code demonstrating "cause" for an extension of exclusivity. In general, the debtor should attempt to demonstrate that the extension will facilitate the debtor's reorganization efforts. Although each debtor's reasons for seeking an extension will differ, factors to be considered include:

   • The size and complexity of the debtor's business;

---

§ 9.303

1. 11 U.S.C.A. § 524(c); Bankr.R. 4008. See supra, § 9.130; see supra, §§ 9.280, 9.287, 9.302, respectively, for a procedural checklist for a motion to obtain approval of a reaffirmation agreement, a drafting checklist of general rules, and a drafting checklist for a reaffirmation agreement.

2. Description of the contents of the attorney's affidavit.

§ 9.304

1. 11 U.S.C.A. § 1121(d); Bankr.R. 9014. See supra, §§ 9.142–9.144; see supra, §§ 9.267, 9.281, and 9.287, respectively, for a procedural checklist for commencing a contested matter, a procedural checklist for a motion to extend exclusivity, and a drafting checklist of general rules.

PRACTICE POINTER: When a debtor has elected treatment under chapter 11 as a "small business," the debtor must demonstrate that the need for an extension of exclusivity has been caused by "circumstances for which the debtor should not be held accountable." 11 U.S.C.A. § 1121(e)(3)(B). See supra, § 9.143.

- The need for additional time to resolve complex claims and legal disputes;
- The need for additional time to complete and evaluate the business plan;
- Good faith progress that the debtor is making toward proposing a plan, including development of a business plan, negotiations with creditors, and submission of draft plans;
- The need for additional time to restructure management and operations;
- The need for additional time to evaluate the business;
- The need for additional time for the statutory committees to complete due diligence; and
- The debtor's achievements to date in restructuring and revitalizing its business.

2. Describe any previous extensions of exclusivity.
3. State the length of the requested extension.
4. File affidavits of witnesses to provide evidentiary support.

Library References:
West's Key No. Digests, Bankruptcy ⚖3534.

§ 9.305 Forms—Notice of Appearance and Demand for Service of Documents[1]

UNITED STATES BANKRUPTCY COURT
[NAME] DISTRICT OF NEW YORK

```
                              )
  In re                       )
[NAME OF DEBTOR ]             )
                              ) Chapter __ Case No.
             Debtor.          ) __ B _____ ([JUDGE'S INITIALS ])
                              )
Tax I.D. No.: _____         )
                              )
```

NOTICE OF APPEARANCE AND DEMAND
FOR SERVICE OF DOCUMENTS

PLEASE TAKE NOTICE that the undersigned appears for [Name of creditor or interest holder] in the above-captioned chapter [numeral] case and, pursuant to [section 1109(b) of title 11 of the United States Code

§ 9.305
1. See supra, § 9.36 note 3 PRACTICE POINTER.

§ 9.305 BANKRUPTCY Ch. 9

(the "Bankruptcy Code") and] Rules 2002, 9007, and 9010 of the Federal Rules of Bankruptcy Procedure (the "Bankruptcy Rules"), requests that all notices given or required to be given in this case, and all papers served, or required to be served, in this case be given to, and served upon:

[Name of attorney of record], Esq.
[Name of law firm]
[Address of firm]

PLEASE TAKE FURTHER NOTICE that[, pursuant to section 1109(b) of the Bankruptcy Code,] the foregoing request includes not only the notices and papers referred to in Bankruptcy Rule 2002 but also includes, without limitation, notices of any applications, motions, orders, complaints, demands, hearings, requests or petitions, answering or reply papers, memoranda and briefs in support of any of the foregoing and any other document brought before this Court with respect to this case, whether formal or informal, whether written or oral, and whether transmitted by mail, hand delivery, telephone, facsimile, telex or otherwise.

Dated: [City], New York
[Date]

———————————————
[NAME OF ATTORNEY]
(A Member of the Firm)

[NAME OF LAW FIRM]
Attorneys for [Name of creditor or interest holder]
[Address of law firm]
[Telephone number of law firm]

To: Clerk of the Bankruptcy Court
United States Bankruptcy
Court for the [Name of District]
District of New York
[Address]
[City], New York _____

Attached Service List

Ch. 9 CONTESTED MATTER—MOTION § 9.306

§ 9.306 Forms—Contested Matter[1]—Motion[2]

[NAME OF LAW FIRM]
Attorneys for [Debtor in Possession]
[Address of law firm]
[Telephone number of law firm]
[Name of attorney of record], Esq.

Return Date: [Date]
[Time]

UNITED STATES BANKRUPTCY COURT
[NAME] DISTRICT OF NEW YORK

```
_____
                        )
    In re               )
[NAME OF DEBTOR]        ) Chapter __ Case No.
                        ) __ B _____ ([JUDGE'S INITIALS])
            Debtor.     )
                        )
_____
```

MOTION OF [NAME OF DEBTOR] FOR ORDER PURSUANT TO SECTION 1121(d) OF THE BANKRUPTCY CODE EXTENDING THE EXCLUSIVE PERIODS DURING WHICH DEBTOR MAY FILE A PLAN OF REORGANIZATION AND SOLICIT ACCEPTANCES THEREOF

TO THE HONORABLE [NAME OF JUDGE],
UNITED STATES BANKRUPTCY JUDGE:

[Full name of debtor] ("[Shortened name of debtor]"), as debtor and debtor in possession in the above-captioned case (the "Debtor"), respectfully represents:

§ 9.306

1. To determine whether to commence a contested matter or an adversary proceeding, see supra, §§ 9.16, 9.17.

2. This is a "form" in the loosest sense of the word. It is provided as a sample rather than a true form, as any motion must be highly fact-specific and must cite to relevant controlling case law. In order to provide a sample that shows, in a readable manner, how a motion should be drafted, virtually all of the statements are fact-specific to the sample and must be replaced by the facts applicable to the specific circumstances. See supra, §§ 9.267, 9.287, respectively, for procedural and drafting checklists for commencing a contested matter as well as the applicable procedural and drafting checklists for the relevant type of contested matter.

For a motion to seek relief from the automatic stay, see supra, §§ 9.50, 9.52, 9.269, 9.292. For a motion to seek adequate protection, see supra, §§ 9.56–9.58, 9.270, 9.293. For a motion to request court approval to use, sell, or lease property of the estate, see supra, §§ 9.60–9.63, 9.271, 9.294. For a motion to request court approval to use cash collateral, see supra, §§ 9.65–9.66, 9.272, 9.295. For a motion to request court approval for a postpetition financing, see supra, §§ 9.71, 9.274, 9.297. For a motion to request court approval to assume or reject an executory contract or unexpired lease, see supra, §§ 9.74–9.81, 9.275, 9.298.

CAVEAT: See supra, § 9.5 and note 3 for sources of governing law. Be sure to consult all applicable law and rules, including any specific requirements for pleadings.

523

§ 9.306 BANKRUPTCY Ch. 9

Background

1. On [*Date*] (the "Petition Date"), the Debtor filed with this Court a voluntary petition for relief under chapter 11, title 11, United States Code (the "Bankruptcy Code").

2. The Debtor continues to operate its business and manage its properties as a debtor in possession pursuant to sections 1107(a) and 1108 of the Bankruptcy Code.

3. On [*Date*], pursuant to section 1102 of the Bankruptcy Code, the United States Trustee for the _____ District of New York, appointed a statutory committee of unsecured creditors (the "Creditors' Committee") for this chapter 11 case.

Description of the Business

4. [*Debtor*] is a [*form of business, e.g., partnership*] engaged in [*nature of business*]. [*Description of business*].

The Exclusive Periods

5. Section 1121(b) of the Bankruptcy Code provides for an initial period of 120 days after the commencement of a chapter 11 case during which a debtor has the exclusive right to file a plan of reorganization. Section 1121(c)(3) of the Bankruptcy Code provides that, if the debtor files a plan within the 120–day exclusive period, it has an initial period of 180 days after the commencement of the chapter 11 case to obtain acceptance of such plan, during which time periods competing plans may not be filed. The periods under sections 1121(b) and 1121(c)(3) of the Bankruptcy Code are hereinafter referred to as the "Exclusive Periods." The Debtor's Exclusive Periods will expire on [*Date*] and [*Date*], respectively.

Relief Requested

6. The Debtor believes that it has established the framework for a consensual plan through which returns to creditors can be maximized. Consequently, the Debtor is confident that it may proceed to negotiate, prepare, and file a plan of reorganization and an accompanying disclosure statement that will be supported by the Creditors' Committee and indeed, it has initiated these efforts. In order to afford the Debtor, the Creditors' Committee, and other parties in interest an opportunity to develop a consensual plan of reorganization and enable the Debtor to prepare and file such a plan, the Debtor respectfully submits that an extension of the Exclusive Periods is necessary and warranted. Although it is anticipated that the Debtor will be able to file a consensual plan by [*date*], there are critical factors affecting this timing of plan filing that are beyond the Debtor's control. Accordingly, pursuant to section

1121(d) of the Bankruptcy Code, the Debtor requests extensions of the Exclusive Periods for approximately [*number (numerals)*] days, through and including, [*Date*] and [*Date*], respectively.

7. The Debtor has discussed this motion with the Creditors' Committee, which does not object to the relief sought herein.

Sufficient Cause Exists to Extend the Debtor's Exclusive Periods

8. Section 1121(d) of the Bankruptcy Code provides:

On request of a party in interest made within the respective periods specified in subsections (b) and (c) of this section and after notice and a hearing, the court may for cause reduce or increase the 120–day period or the 180–day period referred to in this section.

11 U.S.C.A. § 1121(d). The circumstances of this chapter 11 case support the requested extensions of the Debtor's Exclusive Periods.

9. The existence of good faith progress toward reorganization and the need for more time to continue such progress has been recognized as a significant factor establishing cause for extending the exclusive periods under section 1121(d). *E.g., In re McLean Industries, Inc.*, 87 B.R. 830, 834 (Bankr.S.D.N.Y.1987) ("In finding cause, courts have relied on, in addition to the need of the creditors [sic] committee to negotiate with the debtor ... the existence of good faith progress towards reorganization").

The Debtors Have Explored All Feasible Potential Reorganization Strategies and Are Now Proceeding With the Development and Preparation of a Consensual Reorganization Plan

10. As previously reported, the Creditors' Committee has approved the key elements of the Debtor's contemplated plan. [Describe]

11. In furtherance of the Debtor's goal of maximizing creditor recoveries in these proceedings, [*Describe debtor's efforts to reorganize, such as identification of potential purchasers of assets, preparation of pertinent information for parties in interest, negotiations with such parties, development of organizational structure, efforts to obtain necessary financing, and identification and rejection of burdensome executory contracts or unexpired leases.*] These initiatives have been supported by the Creditors' Committee.

12. At the present time, the Debtor and the Creditors' Committee, with the assistance of their respective professionals, are working to finalize the foregoing reorganization proposals. [*Provide details.*]

13. The negotiation and preparation of a plan of reorganization requires substantial time and effort on the part of the Debtor, the

Creditors' Committee, and their advisors. Apart from determining the structure and governance of the reorganized entity and the means by which the plan will be implemented, many issues necessary to the formulation of a reorganization plan must be addressed and resolved by the parties, including, *inter alia*, the classification and treatment of claims and the terms of the equity and/or debt which may be issued under the plan. Additionally, the Debtor must analyze and treat complex issues involving taxation and asset valuation and must prepare detailed financial analyses and projections.

14. The Debtor currently projects that it will file a plan by [*Date*], with the goal of emerging from chapter 11 before [*Date*]. However, additional time may be necessary to ensure that the most cost effective and efficient structures are proposed and implemented. The requested extension of the Exclusive Periods will afford the Debtor and the Creditors' Committee an opportunity to accomplish these tasks and will facilitate the reorganization effort to the direct benefit of all parties in interest.

15. The Debtor is prepared and committed to continue and complete the substantial work necessary to propose, file, and confirm a reorganization plan. [*Describe availability of credit and commitment of management and employees to the reorganization process.*] The extension of the Exclusive Periods requested herein will enable the Debtor's employees, their financial advisors, and other professionals, as well as the Creditors' Committee and their professionals, to continue to focus their complete time, skills, and energies on the reorganization effort.

The Termination of the Exclusive Periods Will Impair the Debtor's Ability to Consummate Successfully the Transactions Currently Being Developed

16. The Debtor submits that the interests of all parties to these proceedings will be served by a [*number*]-day extension of the Exclusive Periods. The Debtor's reorganization is premised upon the continuation of its primary business; therefore, it is essential that the Debtor maintain normal business operations in order to preserve the value of these assets.

The Debtor Is Seeking an Extension of the Exclusive Periods to Permit It to Complete the Reorganization Process

17. The Debtor has enjoyed the support of the Creditors' Committee on all significant steps it has taken. It is evident that the Debtor is not seeking the requested extension of the Exclusive Periods as leverage or as a negotiating tactic. The Debtor's sole purpose in seeking the instant request is to permit it to complete the confirmation and consum-

mation of a consensual reorganization which maximizes returns to creditors and preserves its business to the greatest extent possible; in other words, the Debtor seeks to accomplish the primary goals and purposes of chapter 11.

18. It is in the best interests of the Debtor's estate and its creditors that exclusivity remain in effect to afford the Debtor the opportunity to complete, file and confirm a plan of reorganization. The termination of exclusivity would surely disrupt this process, as it would compel the Debtor to deal with the threat of competing plans or actually oppose such a plan or plans if filed. The Debtor respectfully submits that any such plan or plans could not conceivably maximize creditor recoveries.

[Waiver of Memorandum of Law

19. The Debtor requests that the Court waive and dispense with the requirement set forth in Rule 9013–1(b) of the Local Bankruptcy Rules that any motion filed shall have a separate memorandum of law. The Debtor submits that the relevant authorities are set forth herein and, accordingly, that waiver of the Rule 9013–1(b) requirement is appropriate under the circumstances.]*

Notice

20. Notice of this Motion is being provided to those parties required to receive notice pursuant to [*this Court's Order Establishing Administrative Procedures, dated* _____]. The Debtor submits that no other or further notice is necessary.

21. No previous application for the relief requested herein has been made to this or any other court.

WHEREFORE the Debtor respectfully requests entry of an order granting the relief requested herein and such other and further relief as is just.

Dated: [*City*], New York
      [*Date*]

[*Name of attorney of record*]

[*NAME OF LAW FIRM*]
Attorneys for [*the Debtor in Possession*]
[*Address of law firm*]
[*Telephone number of law firm*]

§ 9.307 Forms—Contested Matter—Notice of Motion[1]

[NAME OF LAW FIRM]
Attorneys for [Debtor in Possession]
[Address of law firm]
[Telephone number of law firm]
[Name of attorney of record], Esq.

Return Date: [Date]
[Time]

UNITED STATES BANKRUPTCY COURT
[NAME] DISTRICT OF NEW YORK

```
                              )
     In re                    )
[NAME OF DEBTOR]              ) Chapter __ Case No.
                              ) __ B _____ ([JUDGE'S INITIALS])
              Debtor.         )
                              )
```

NOTICE OF MOTION PURSUANT TO SECTION 1121(d) OF THE BANKRUPTCY CODE FOR EXTENSION OF THE EXCLUSIVE PERIODS DURING WHICH DEBTOR MAY FILE A PLAN OF REORGANIZATION AND SOLICIT ACCEPTANCES THEREOF

PLEASE TAKE NOTICE that, upon the annexed motion of [NAME OF DEBTOR], as debtor in possession (the "Debtor"), dated _____ (the "Motion"), the Debtor will move before the Honorable [Name of Judge], United States Bankruptcy Judge, on [Date] at [time], in Room ___ of the United States Bankruptcy Court, [address of court], for an order pursuant to section 1121(d) of title 11, United States Code (the "Bankruptcy Code"), extending the periods during which the Debtor shall have the exclusive right to (i) file a plan or plans of reorganization, to and including [Date], and (ii) solicit acceptances of such plan(s), to and including [Date].

PLEASE TAKE FURTHER NOTICE that objections, if any, to the relief requested in the Motion must be made in writing, shall conform to the Federal Rules of Bankruptcy Procedure, the Local Rules of the Bankruptcy Court and [any applicable standing orders], shall set forth the name of the objectant, the nature and amount of any claim or interest held or asserted against the Debtor's estate or properties, the basis for the objection and the specific grounds therefor, and shall be

§ 9.307

1. This is a "form" in the loosest sense of the word. It is provided as a sample rather than a true form. In order to provide a sample that shows, in a readable manner, how a notice of motion should be drafted, the title and first paragraph are fact-specific to the sample and must be replaced by the facts applicable to the specific circumstances.

CAVEAT: See supra, § 9.5 and note 3 for sources of governing law. Be sure to consult all applicable law and rules, including any specific requirements for pleadings.

Ch. 9   CONTESTED MATTER—PROPOSED ORDER   § 9.308

filed with the Court, with a copy to chambers, and be served upon (a) [*Name of law firm*], attorneys for the Debtor, [*Address of law firm*], Attn: [*Name of attorney of record*], Esq., (b) [*Name of law firm*], attorneys for the Official Committee of Unsecured Creditors, [*Address of law firm*], Attn: [*Name of attorney of record*], Esq., and (c) the Office of the United States Trustee, [*Address of Office of the U.S. Trustee*], Attn: [*Name of U.S. Trustee*], Esq., so as to be received no later than [*Date*] at [*time*].

Dated: [*City*], New York
      [*Date*]

                        [*Name of attorney of record*],

                        [*NAME OF LAW FIRM*]
                        Attorneys for [*the Debtor in Possession*]
                        [*Address of Law Firm*]
                        [*Telephone Number of Law Firm*]

TO: THE PARTIES ON THE
     ANNEXED SERVICE LIST

§ 9.308 Forms—Contested Matter—Proposed Order[1]

[*NAME OF LAW FIRM*]
Attorneys for [*Debtor in Possession*]
[*Address of law firm*]
[*Telephone number of law firm*]
[*Name of attorney of record*], Esq.

UNITED STATES BANKRUPTCY COURT
[*NAME*] DISTRICT OF NEW YORK

————————————————)
)
    In re   )
[*NAME OF DEBTOR*]   ) Chapter __ Case No.
) __ B _____ ([*JUDGE'S INITIALS*])
         Debtor.)
)
————————————————

§ 9.308

1. This is a "form" in the loosest sense of the word. It is provided as a sample rather than a true form. In order to provide a sample that shows, in a readable manner, how a proposed order should be drafted, the title and descriptions of the relief requested are fact-specific to the sample and must be replaced by the facts applicable to the specific circumstances.

CAVEAT: *See supra*, § 9.5 and note 3 for sources of governing law. Be sure to consult all applicable law and rules, including any specific requirements for pleadings.

§ 9.308

ORDER PURSUANT TO SECTION 1121(d) OF THE BANKRUPTCY CODE EXTENDING THE EXCLUSIVE PERIODS DURING WHICH THE DEBTOR MAY FILE A PLAN OF REORGANIZATION AND SOLICIT ACCEPTANCES THERETO

A hearing having been held on _____ (the "Hearing"), to consider the motion, dated _____ (the "Motion"), of [Name of debtor], as debtor and debtor in possession herein (the "Debtor"), for an order, pursuant to section 1121(d) of title 11 of the United States Code (the "Bankruptcy Code"), extending the exclusive periods during which only the Debtor may file a plan or plans of reorganization and solicit acceptances thereto to [Date] and [Date], respectively; and the Court having jurisdiction to consider the Motion and the relief requested therein in accordance with 28 U.S.C.A. §§ 157(b)(2) and 1334 [and the Standing Order of Referral of Cases to Bankruptcy Court Judges of [Court]]; and due and sufficient notice of the Motion and Hearing having been given as reflected by the affidavit of service heretofore filed with the Court; and the appearances of all interested parties having been duly noted in the record of the Hearing; and no objections to the Motion having been received; and the Statutory Committee of Unsecured Creditors having no objection to the relief requested in the Motion; and the Court having found that good cause exists to extend the periods specified in sections 1121(b) and (c) of the Bankruptcy Code, pursuant to section 1121(d) of the Bankruptcy Code; and it appearing that the extension of the exclusive periods to [Date] and [Date], respectively, is reasonable and in the best interests of the Debtor, its estate, and all parties in interest; and Court having considered the Motion; and upon the record of the Hearing and the Motion; and after due deliberation and sufficient cause appearing therefor, it is

ORDERED that the Motion is hereby granted in all respects; and it is further

ORDERED that, pursuant to section 1121(d) of the Bankruptcy Code, the 120–day period specified in section 1121(b) of the Bankruptcy Code and the 180–day period specified in section 1121(c)(3) of the Bankruptcy Code are hereby extended through and including [Date] and [Date], respectively, without prejudice to such further requests pursuant to section 1121(d) of the Bankruptcy Code as may be made by the Debtor or any party in interest within such extended periods.

Dated: [City], New York
    [Date]

                                        United States Bankruptcy Judge

Ch. 9   ADVERSARY PROCEEDING—COMPLAINT   § 9.309

§ 9.309 Forms—Adversary Proceeding[1]—Complaint[2]
💾

[NAME OF LAW FIRM]
Attorneys for [Debtor in Possession]
[Address of law firm]
[Telephone number of law firm]
[Name of attorney of record], Esq.

UNITED STATES BANKRUPTCY COURT
[NAME] DISTRICT OF NEW YORK

In re [NAME OF DEBTOR], Debtor. [NAME OF DEBTOR], Debtor–Plaintiff, v. [NAME OF DEFENDANT], Defendant.	Chapter __ Case No. __ B _____ ([JUDGE'S INITIALS]) Adv. Proc. No.

§ 9.309

1. To determine whether to commence an adversary proceeding or a contested matter, see supra, §§ 9.16, 9.17.

2. This is a "form" in the loosest sense of the word. It is provided as a sample rather than a true form, as any complaint must be highly fact-specific and must cite to relevant controlling case law. In order to provide a sample that shows, in a readable manner, how a complaint should be drafted, some of the brackets contain factual information that must be replaced by the facts applicable to the specific circumstances. See supra, §§ 9.266 and 9.287–9.288, respectively, for procedural and drafting checklists for commencing an adversary proceeding.

To commence an adversary proceeding to determine the dischargeability of a debt under 11 U.S.C.A. § 523(a)(2)(A), the complaint must specifically allege all the elements necessary to sustain a prima facie case of fraud, i.e.: (i) the debtor made the representation; (ii) the debtor knew the representation was false at the time it was made; (iii) the debtor made the representation with the intent and for the purpose of deceiving the plaintiff; (iv) the plaintiff relied on the representation and such reliance was justifiable; and (v) the false representation made by the debtor was the proximate cause of a loss sustained by the plaintiff.

To commence an adversary proceeding to recover a preference, the complaint must specifically allege all the elements set forth at 11 U.S.C.A. § 547(b) and discussed supra, § 9.117. To commence an adversary proceeding to recover a fraudulent conveyance, the complaint must specifically allege all the elements set forth at 11 U.S.C.A. § 548(a) or (b) and discussed supra, § 9.119.

CAVEAT: See supra, § 9.5 and note 3 for sources of governing law. Be sure to consult all applicable law and rules, including any specific requirements for pleadings.

§ 9.309

COMPLAINT [TO RECOVER MONEY]

Plaintiff, [Name] (the "Plaintiff"), [as debtor in possession,] as and for its complaint against [Name] (the "Defendant"), respectfully alleges:

JURISDICTION

1. This Court has subject matter jurisdiction over this proceeding pursuant to 28 U.S.C.A. §§ 157(a) and 1334 and [the Standing Order of Referral of Cases to Bankruptcy Judges dated [Date], issued by [Judge], United States District Judge for the [District] District of New York]. This Court has personal jurisdiction over the Defendant pursuant to Bankruptcy Rule 7004.

2. This proceeding constitutes a [core proceeding pursuant to 28 U.S.C.A. § 157(b)(2)(A), (E), and (O)].

3. Venue properly lies in this Court pursuant to 28 U.S.C.A. § [1409(a)].

4. This proceeding is initiated pursuant to Bankruptcy Rule 7001[(1)].

THE PARTIES

5. The Plaintiff is a [describe the plaintiff].

6. On [Date] (the "Petition Date"), [the Plaintiff] filed with this Court a [voluntary] petition for relief under chapter [11], title 11, United States Code (the "Bankruptcy Code").

7. [The Plaintiff continues to operate its business and manage its properties as a debtor in possession pursuant to sections 1107(a) and 1108 of the Bankruptcy Code.]

8. Upon information and belief, the Defendant is [Describe the Defendant].

CLAIM FOR RELIEF [(TO RECOVER MONEY)]

9. The Plaintiff repeats and realleges each and every allegation contained in paragraphs 1 through 8 of this Complaint with the same force and effect as though fully set forth herein.

10. Prior to the Petition Date, [describe the transaction upon which the complaint is based]. A copy of [the pertinent documentation supporting the complaint] is annexed hereto as Exhibit A. [Thus, the Plaintiff has a valid claim against the Defendant in an amount equal to at least $_____ for _____ and interest accrued thereon through [Date] (exclusive of costs and additional interest accruing through the date of payment).]

11. [The Plaintiff has made demand for the amount identified in paragraph 10 in respect of the Delivered Goods on various occasions,

Ch. 9 APPLICATION § 9.310

including written demand as evidenced by that certain letter dated _____, a copy of which is annexed hereto as Exhibit B. To date, the Defendant has refused to pay the Plaintiff for the Delivered Goods.]

12. [Accordingly, the Defendant is presently indebted to the Plaintiff in an amount equal to at least $_____, as discussed above.]

13. [The Plaintiff may recover $_____ together with costs and additional interest thereon, for the benefit of its estate and creditors pursuant to section 542 of the Bankruptcy Code.]

WHEREFORE, the Plaintiff requests that the Court enter judgment against the Defendant [in the amount of $_____ together with costs and additional interest thereon,] and grant such other and further relief as the Court deems proper.

Dated: [City], New York
      [Date]

                                    [Name of attorney of record]

                                    [NAME OF LAW FIRM]
                                    Attorneys for [the Debtor in Possession]
                                    [Address of law firm]
                                    [Telephone number of law firm]

§ 9.310 Forms—Retention of Professionals—Application[1]

[NAME OF LAW FIRM]
Attorneys for [Debtor in Possession]
[Address of law firm]
[Telephone number of law firm]
[Name of attorney of record], Esq.

§ 9.310

1. This is a "form" in the loosest sense of the word. It is provided as a sample rather than a true form, as any application must be highly fact-specific and must comply with the applicable local rules. In order to provide a sample that shows, in a readable manner, how an application should be drafted, the application contains sample factual information that must be replaced by the facts applicable to the specific circumstances. See supra, § 9.29 discussing the retention of professionals and supra, §§ 9.287 and 9.291, respectively, for a checklist of general rules for drafting and a drafting checklist for an application to retain professionals. This form of application and the attorney's affidavit that must be filed with it (see infra, § 9.311) may be used by a debtor or a statutory committee.

CAVEAT: See supra, § 9.5 and note 3 for sources of governing law. Be sure to consult all applicable law and rules, including any specific requirements for pleadings.

533

§ 9.310   BANKRUPTCY   Ch. 9

UNITED STATES BANKRUPTCY COURT
[NAME] DISTRICT OF NEW YORK

```
_____
                               )
   In re                       )
[NAME OF DEBTOR]               )   Chapter __ Case No.
                               )   __ B _____ ([JUDGE'S INITIALS])
              Debtor.          )
_____)
```

APPLICATION FOR ENTRY OF AN ORDER PURSUANT TO SECTION 327(a) OF THE BANKRUPTCY CODE AUTHORIZING THE EMPLOYMENT OF [NAME OF FIRM] AS ATTORNEYS FOR THE [DEBTOR]

TO THE HONORABLE UNITED STATES BANKRUPTCY JUDGE:

[Full name of debtor] ("[Shortened name of debtor]"), as debtor and debtor in possession in the above-captioned case (the "Debtor"), respectfully represents:

Background

1. On the date hereof (the "Petition Date"), the Debtor filed with this Court a voluntary petition for relief under chapter 11, title 11, United States Code (the "Bankruptcy Code").

2. The Debtor continues to operate its business and manage its properties as a debtor in possession pursuant to sections 1107(a) and 1108 of the Bankruptcy Code.

Description of the Business

3. [Debtor] is a [form of business, e.g., partnership] engaged in [nature of business—several paragraphs, if necessary to provide a reasonably detailed description of the nature of the business, its principal products or services, its location(s), market, assets, employees, and corporate structure].

Retention of [Name of Firm]

4. The Debtor has employed [Name of Firm] ("[Short form name of law firm, hereafter, Law Firm]") as its attorneys in connection with the commencement and prosecution of its chapter 11 case. Pursuant to section 327(a) of the Bankruptcy Code, the Debtor requests the Court to approve the employment of [Law Firm] under a general retainer as its attorneys to perform the extensive legal services that will be necessary during its chapter 11 case. The Debtor has been informed that [Name of attorney of record], Esq. and other members and associates of [Law Firm] who will be employed in this chapter 11 case are admitted to practice before this Court.

5. The Debtor has selected [*Law Firm*] as its attorneys because of the firm's extensive general experience and knowledge in the field of debtors' and creditors' rights and [business reorganizations] under chapter [11] of the Bankruptcy Code. Since [*Date*], [*Law Firm*] has rendered legal services and advice to the Debtor in connection with restructuring its indebtedness and exploring other alternatives to chapter 11. In connection therewith, [*Law Firm*] has become familiar with the Debtor's business and affairs. Accordingly, the firm has the necessary background to deal effectively with many of the potential legal issues and problems that may arise in the context of the chapter 11 case. The Debtor believes that [*Law Firm*] is qualified and able to represent it in this chapter 11 case.

6. The services of [*Law Firm*] under a general retainer are necessary to enable the Debtor to execute faithfully its duties as debtor and debtor in possession. Subject to further order of this Court, [*Law Firm*] will be required to render the following professional services:

(a) To take all necessary actions to protect and preserve the estate of the Debtor, including the prosecution of actions on the Debtor's behalf, the defense of any actions commenced against the Debtor, negotiations concerning all litigation in which the Debtor is involved, and the filing of objections to claims filed against the estate;

(b) To prepare on behalf of the Debtor, as debtor in possession, all necessary motions, applications, answers, orders, reports, and papers in connection with the administration of the estate herein;

(c) To negotiate and prepare on behalf of the Debtor a plan or plans of reorganization and all related documents;

(d) To perform all other necessary legal services in connection with this chapter 11 case.

7. It is necessary that the Debtor employ attorneys under a general retainer to render the foregoing professional services.

8. [*Law Firm*] has stated its desire and willingness to act in this case and render the necessary professional services as attorneys for the Debtor and debtor in possession.

9. To the best of the Debtor's knowledge, the members and associates of [*Law Firm*] do not have any connection with the Debtor, its creditors, or any other party in interest, or their respective attorneys, except as set forth herein and in the annexed affidavit of [*Name of attorney of record*], Esq., a member of [*Law Firm*] (the "[*Name of attorney of record*] Affidavit").

10. The Debtor has paid to [*Law Firm*] a retainer of $_____ for its services to be rendered and disbursements to be incurred in connection with this chapter 11 case as described above.

11. [*Law Firm*] intends to apply to the Court for allowance of compensation and reimbursement of expenses in accordance with applicable provisions of the Bankruptcy Code, the Federal Rules of Bankruptcy Procedure (the "Bankruptcy Rules"), and the local rules and orders of the Court, including the Guidelines for Fees and Disbursements for Professionals in _____ District of New York Bankruptcy Cases (the "Guidelines").

12. The Debtor, subject to the provisions of the Bankruptcy Code, the Bankruptcy Rules, and the local rules and orders of the Court, including the Guidelines, proposes to pay [*Law Firm*] its customary hourly rates in effect from time to time as set forth in the [*Name of attorney of record*] Affidavit, and submits that such rates are reasonable.

Jurisdiction

13. This Court has jurisdiction over this Motion pursuant to 28 U.S.C. §§ 157 and 1334 and [the Standing Order of Referral of Cases to Bankruptcy Court Judges of the District Court for the _____ District of New York, dated _____ (_____, Acting C.J.)]. Consideration of this Motion is a core proceeding pursuant to 28 U.S.C. § 157(b).

Notice

14. No trustee, examiner or creditors' committee has been appointed in the Debtor's chapter 11 case. Notice of this motion has been given to the United States Trustee. The Debtor submits that, given the administrative nature of the relief requested herein and the exigencies of the circumstances, no other or further notice need be given.

[Waiver of Memorandum of Law

15. The Debtor requests that the Court waive and dispense with the requirement set forth in Rule 9013–1(b) of the Local Bankruptcy Rules that any motion filed shall have an accompanying memorandum of law. The application does not present a novel issue of law. Accordingly, the Debtor submits that waiver of the Rule 9013–1(b) requirement is appropriate in these circumstances.]

16. No previous application for the relief requested herein has been made to this or any other court.

WHEREFORE the Debtor respectfully requests entry of an order granting the relief requested herein and such other and further relief as is just.

Dated: [*City*], New York
    [*Date*]

                                 [*Name of debtor*]
                             Debtor and Debtor in Possession

Ch. 9   RETENTION OF PROFESSIONALS—AFFIDAVIT § 9.311

By:_____

[Name of attorney of record]
[NAME OF LAW FIRM]
Attorneys for [the Debtor in Possession]
[Address of law firm]
[Telephone number of law firm]

Library References:

West's Key No. Digests, Bankruptcy ⇐3029.1–3030.

§ 9.311 Forms—Retention of Professionals—Affidavit[1]

[NAME OF LAW FIRM]
Attorneys for [Debtor in Possession]
[Address of law firm]
[Telephone number of law firm]
[Name of attorney of record], Esq.

UNITED STATES BANKRUPTCY COURT
[NAME] DISTRICT OF NEW YORK

_____)
     In re   )
[NAME OF DEBTOR]   ) Chapter __ Case No.
) __ B _____ ([JUDGE'S INITIALS])
          Debtor.   )
_____)

AFFIDAVIT OF PROPOSED ATTORNEY AND DISCLOSURE STATEMENT PURSUANT TO BANKRUPTCY CODE SECTIONS 329 AND 504 AND FEDERAL RULES OF BANKRUPTCY PROCEDURE 2014(a) AND 2016(b)

§ 9.311

1. This is a "form" in the loosest sense of the word. It is provided as a sample rather than a true form, as any affidavit must be highly fact-specific and must comply with the applicable local rules. In order to provide a sample that shows, in a readable manner, how an affidavit of a proposed attorney should be drafted, the affidavit contains sample factual information that must be replaced by the facts applicable to the specific circumstances. See supra, § 9.29 discussing the retention of professionals and supra, § 9.287 for a checklist of general rules for drafting. This form of attorney's affidavit may be used by a debtor or a statutory committee.

CAVEAT: The requirement that a proposed attorney make full disclosure cannot be overemphasized. See supra, § 9.29 and the related CAVEATS and cases cited.

CAVEAT: See supra, § 9.5 and note 3 for sources of governing law. Be sure to consult all applicable law and rules, including any specific requirements for pleadings.

537

§ 9.311   BANKRUPTCY   Ch. 9

STATE OF NEW YORK)
) ss.:
COUNTY OF _____)

    [NAME OF ATTORNEY OF RECORD], being duly sworn, deposes and says:

    1. I am an attorney at law admitted to practice before this Court and a member of the firm of _____ ("[Name of law firm, hereafter, short form name of Law Firm]"). [Law Firm] is a [description] law firm with its offices in this district at [address]. [List other offices, if applicable.] Unless otherwise stated, I have personal knowledge of the facts hereinafter set forth.

    2. Neither I, [Law Firm], nor any member or associate thereof, insofar as I have been able to ascertain, has any connection with the debtor in the above-captioned case (the "Debtor"), its creditors, or any other party in interest herein, or their attorneys and accountants, except as set forth in this affidavit.

    3. [Law Firm] has rendered legal services to [Name of Debtor] Since [Date]. Since such time, [Law Firm] has represented [Name of Debtor] in connection with negotiations between [Name of Debtor] and its major creditors in on-going efforts to restructure its obligations to its lenders. [Law Firm] attorneys have taken an active role in counselling the Debtor in connection with these negotiations. Most recently, [Law firm] has performed services necessary to enable the Debtor to file for protection under chapter [11] of the Bankruptcy Code.

    4. [Law Firm] and members and associates of [Law Firm] have in the past represented, currently represent, and may in the future represent entities which are claimants of the Debtor in matters totally unrelated to the pending chapter [11] case.

    5. [Law Firm] does not represent any such entity in connection with the pending chapter [11] case or have any relationship with any such entity, attorney, or accountant which would be adverse to the Debtor or its estate.

    6. In addition to the fees and expenses received by [Law Firm] for services rendered to the Debtor and in connection with the prepetition efforts to restructure the Debtor's bank credit facilities and other outstanding debt obligations, [Law Firm] has received from the Debtor the approximate aggregate sum of $_____ under a general retainer for professional services to be rendered and disbursements to be incurred in connection with [Law Firm]'s representation of the Debtor in this case under chapter [11] of the Bankruptcy Code. [Law Firm] intends to apply for compensation for professional services rendered in connection with this case and for reimbursement of expenses incurred, in accordance with Bankruptcy Code section 328(a), the Federal Rules of Bankruptcy Procedure (the "Bankruptcy Rules"), and local rules, including the

Guidelines for Fees and Disbursements for Professionals in _____ District of New York Bankruptcy Cases.

7. [*Law Firm*]'s current customary hourly rates, subject to change from time to time, are $_____ for members, $_____ for associates, and $_____ for paraprofessionals. Subject to Court approval of its retention, the Debtor has agreed that [*Law Firm*] will be paid at its customary hourly rate for all services rendered in or in connection with this case.

8. No promises have been received by [*Law Firm*] nor any member or associate thereof as to payment or compensation in connection with this case other than in accordance with the provisions of title 11 of the United States Code. [*Law Firm*] has no agreement with any other entity to share with such entity any compensation received by [*Law Firm*].

9. The foregoing constitutes the statement of [*Law Firm*] pursuant to sections 329 and 504 of the Bankruptcy Code, Bankruptcy Rule 2016(b), and Local Bankruptcy Rule _____.

10. Except as set forth herein, and based upon the information available to me, neither I, [*Law Firm*], nor any member or associate thereof, insofar as I have been able to ascertain, holds or represents any interest adverse to the Debtor or its estate in the matters upon which [*Law Firm*] is to be employed. Accordingly, I believe [*Law Firm*] is a "disinterested person," as defined in section 101(14) of the Bankruptcy Code, as modified by section 1107(b).

_____
[*Name of attorney of record*]

Sworn to before me
on _____

_____
Notary Public

§ 9.312 Forms—Plan Provision for Retention of Jurisdiction[1]

Article [*number*]
RETENTION OF JURISDICTION

The Bankruptcy Court shall have exclusive jurisdiction of all matters arising out of, and related to, the chapter 11 case and the plan

---

§ 9.312

1. *See supra*, § 9.151. This is a sample provision, rather than a "form," and should be modified as appropriate.

pursuant to, and for the purposes of, sections 105(a) and 1142 of the Bankruptcy Code and for, among other things, the following purposes:

    a. To hear and determine pending applications for the assumption or rejection of executory contracts or unexpired leases, if any are pending, and the allowance of claims resulting therefrom;

    b. To determine any and all pending adversary proceedings, applications, and contested matters.

    c. To hear and determine any objection to administrative expense claims or to claims;

    d. To enter and implement such orders as may be appropriate in the event the confirmation order is for any reason stayed, revoked, modified, or vacated;

    e. To issue such orders in aid of execution of the plan, to the extent authorized by section 1142 of the Bankruptcy Code;

    f. To consider any modifications of the plan, to cure any defect or omission, or reconcile any inconsistency in any order of the Bankruptcy Court, including, without limitation, the confirmation order;

    g. To hear and determine all applications for compensation and reimbursement of expenses of professionals under sections 330, 331, and 503(b) of the Bankruptcy Code;

    h. To hear and determine disputes arising in connection with the interpretation, implementation, or enforcement of the plan;

    i. To recover all assets of the debtor and property of the estate, wherever located;

    j. To hear and determine matters concerning state, local, and federal taxes in accordance with sections 346, 505, and 1146 of the Bankruptcy Code;

    k. To hear any other matter not inconsistent with the Bankruptcy Code; and

    l. To enter a final decree closing the chapter 11 case.

Library References:

West's Key No. Digests, Bankruptcy ⇌3570.

Chapter 10

MECHANIC'S LIENS

by
Laurence S. Tauber

Table of Sections

10.1	Scope Note.
10.2	Strategy.
10.3	Nature of Mechanic's Lien.
10.4	Creation of Mechanic's Lien—Elements.
10.5	⎯⎯ Protected Class.
10.6	⎯⎯ Improvements to Real Property.
10.7	⎯⎯ Consent or Request of Owner.
10.8	Extent of Lien—Ownership Interest at Time of Filing.
10.9	⎯ Sale of Property.
10.10	⎯ Insurance Proceeds.
10.11	⎯ Amount.
10.12	⎯ Loss of Profits.
10.13	Subcontractors and Materialmen—Derivative Rights.
10.14	⎯⎯ Statutory Protections.
10.15	Procedure—Notice of Lien.
10.16	⎯⎯ Contents.
10.17	⎯⎯ Filing.
10.18	⎯⎯ Service.
10.19	Amendment of Notice of Lien.
10.20	Lien for Private Improvements—Checklist.
10.21	Liens Under Contract for Public Improvements—Extent of Lien.
10.22	⎯ Notice of Lien.
10.23	⎯ Filing of Notice of Lien.
10.24	⎯ Notice of Completion and Acceptance.
10.25	⎯ Checklist.
10.26	Lien Priorities—Private Improvements—Parity of Mechanic's Liens.
10.27	⎯⎯ Assignments of Contract Rights.
10.28	⎯⎯ Building Loan Mortgages.
10.29	⎯⎯ Contracts of Sale.
10.30	⎯⎯ Seller's Mortgage.
10.31	⎯⎯ Deeds.
10.32	⎯ Contracts for Public Improvements.
10.33	Assignment of Liens.
10.34	Assignments of Contracts for Private Improvements and Orders to be Filed—Filing of Notice of Assignment.
10.35	⎯ Contents of Notice of Assignment.

10.36	____ Extension of Term of Notice of Assignment.
10.37	Assignment of Contracts and Orders for Public Improvements.
10.38	Duration of Lien for Private Improvements—Notice of Pendency.
10.39	____ Extensions.
10.40	Duration of Lien Under Contract for a Public Improvement—Notice of Pendency.
10.41	____ Extension of Lien.
10.42	Discharge of Lien for Private Improvement—Satisfaction of Lien.
10.43	____ Expiration of Term.
10.44	____ Termination of Notice of Pendency.
10.45	____ Failure to Prosecute.
10.46	____ Undertaking.
10.47	____ Judgment.
10.48	____ Defective Lien.
10.49	____ Deposit of Money with County Clerk or Court.
10.50	Discharge of Lien for Public Improvement—Satisfaction of Lien.
10.51	____ Expiration of Lien.
10.52	____ Satisfaction of Judgment.
10.53	____ Deposit of Money.
10.54	____ Undertaking.
10.55	____ Retention of Credit.
10.56	____ Invalidity of Lien.
10.57	____ Failure to Prosecute.
10.58	____ Procedures.
10.59	Building Loan Contracts—Filing Requirements.
10.60	____ Checklist.
10.61	Subordination of Liens—Agreement with Owner.
10.62	____ ____ Postponement of Judgments.
10.63	Subordination of Liens to Subsequent Mortgage.
10.64	Subordination of Notices of *Lis Pendens*.
10.65	Discharge of Liens on Sale of Real Property.
10.66	Limitations on Waiver of Mechanic's Lien.
10.67	Effect of Filing of Notice of Lien on Right of Arbitration.
10.68	Bond to Discharge Liens—Effect of Bond.
10.69	____ Requirements of Bond.
10.70	____ Claim Against Bond.
10.71	____ Notice of Claim.
10.72	____ Action on Bond.
10.73	____ Discharge of Liens and Notices of Claims.
10.74	Protecting the Owner—Itemized Statement.
10.75	____ Lien Wilfully Exaggerated.
10.76	Repossession of Materials Not Used.
10.77	Enforcement of Mechanic's Liens—Courts.
10.78	____ Courts of Record—Procedures.
10.79	____ ____ Necessary Parties.
10.80	____ Actions in a Court Not of Record—Summons and Complaint.
10.81	____ ____ Proceedings Upon Return of Summons.
10.82	____ ____ Judgments and Transcripts.
10.83	____ Costs and Disbursements.
10.84	____ Effect of Failure to Establish Lien.
10.85	____ Deposit of Money or Securities to Discharge Lien—Procedures.

Ch. 10 MECHANIC'S LIENS

10.86 ____ ____ Effect of Order.
10.87 ____ ____ Preference Over Contractors.
10.88 ____ ____ Delivery of Property in Lieu of Money.
10.89 ____ Deficiency Judgment.
10.90 ____ Vacating of Mechanic's Lien, Cancellation of Bond or Return of Deposit.
10.91 ____ Public Improvements.
10.92 ____ New Parties.
10.93 ____ Service of Answer on State or Public Corporation.
10.94 Trust Funds—Purpose.
10.95 ____ Creation.
10.96 ____ Contractors and Subcontractors.
10.97 ____ Beneficiaries.
10.98 Diversion of Trust Assets.
10.99 Notice of Lending.
10.100 Record Keeping Obligations.
10.101 Right of Beneficiaries to Examine Books or Records.
10.102 Action to Enforce Trust—Standing and Procedure.
10.103 ____ Remedies.
10.104 ____ Preferences.
10.105 Relief After Judgment on Obligation Constituting Trust Claim; Effect on Mechanic's Liens.
10.106 Misappropriation of Trust Funds.
10.107 Procedural Checklist.
10.108 Forms.
10.109 ____ Notice of Mechanic's Lien—General Form.
10.110 ____ Notice of Lien for Public Improvement.
10.111 ____ Form For Demand for Terms of Contract.
10.112 ____ Demand for Notice of Completion and Acceptance of Public Improvement.
10.113 ____ Petition to Amend Notice of Mechanic's Lien—Correct Name of Owner of Property.
10.114 ____ Assignment of Lien for Public Improvement.
10.115 ____ Assignment of Mechanic's Lien.
10.116 ____ Assignment of Moneys Due or to Become Due Under Public Improvement Contract.
10.117 ____ Affidavit for Continuance of Mechanic's Lien.
10.118 ____ Affidavit for Continuance of Lien for Public Improvement.
10.119 ____ Petition to Discharge Mechanic's Lien Where Notice of Lien Defective.
10.120 ____ Petition for Order Discharging Mechanic's Lien Upon Filing of Undertaking.
10.121 ____ Undertaking to Discharge Mechanic's Lien.
10.122 ____ Petition for Order Fixing Amount of Undertaking to Discharge Mechanic's Lien.
10.123 ____ Approval by Lienors of Subordination of Mechanic's Liens to Trust Bond or Note and Mortgage.
10.124 ____ Affidavit for Order Fixing Amount of Bond to Discharge All Mechanic's Liens.
10.125 ____ Petition for Order Requiring Itemized Statement.
10.126 ____ Notice of Application for Order Requiring Itemized Statement.

§ 10.1   MECHANIC'S LIENS   Ch. 10

10.127 ____ Demand for Itemized Statement.
10.128 ____ Affidavit in Support of Application to Cancel Mechanic's Lien for Failure to Furnish Itemized Statement.
10.129 ____ Notice Requiring Lienor to Commence Action to Enforce Mechanic's Lien.
10.130 ____ Affidavit in Support of Application to Cancel Notice of Mechanic's Lien for Failure to Commence Action.
10.131 ____ Notice Requiring Lienor to Commence Action to Enforce Lien for Public Improvement.
10.132 ____ Affidavit in Support of Application to Cancel Notice of Lien for Public Improvement for Failure to Commence Action.
10.133 ____ Complaint for Foreclosure of Lien for Public Improvement.
10.134 ____ Complaint for Foreclosure of Mechanic's Lien—Contractor.
10.135 ____ Defense and Counterclaim Based on Wilful Exaggeration of Mechanic's Lien.
10.136 ____ Affidavit in Support of Motion to Consolidate Actions for Foreclosure of Mechanic's Liens.
10.137 ____ Notice of Motion to Consolidate Actions to Foreclose Mechanic's Liens.
10.138 ____ Acceptance of Offer to Pay Money Into Court in Discharge of Mechanic's Lien.
10.139 ____ Offer to Pay Money Into Court in Discharge of Mechanic's Lien.
10.140 ____ Judgment of Foreclosure and Sale—Mechanic's Lien.
10.141 ____ Judgment of Foreclosure—Lien for Public Improvement—Where Lien Discharged and Fund Retained for Payment.
10.142 ____ Affidavit in Support of Motion for Summary Judgment—Foreclosure of Lien for Public Improvement.
10.143 ____ Demand for Verified Statement from Trustee.
10.144 ____ Petition for Verified Statement from Trustee of Trust Funds.
10.145 ____ Complaint by Subcontractor to Enforce Trust Against Funds Received by Contractor or Assignee of Contractor.
10.146 ____ Complaint by Surety to Have Parties Declared Trustees of Subcontract Moneys and for Accounting.
10.147 ____ Affidavit in Support of Motion to Determine if Class Action Can be Maintained—Action to Impress and Enforce Trust.

WESTLAW Electronic Research

See WESTLAW Electronic Research Guide preceding the Summary of Contents.

---

§ 10.1 Scope Note

This chapter is intended to provide a concise review of New York law concerning the creation and enforcement of mechanic's liens in connection with the improvement of real property, whether owned by private individuals or entities or properties belonging to state and local governments or public corporations.

This chapter discusses the elements of what would entitle a party to a mechanic's lien,[1] the method of creating and preserving one,[2] the rights of materialmen and subcontractors,[3] assignment of liens and contract rights,[4] duration of liens[5] and how to foreclose upon and enforce such a lien.[6] The relationship of the holders of mechanic's liens to one another as well as to the holders of other liens or interests in the property is reviewed.[7] In addition, the methods for discharging of liens,[8] either before an action is commenced or judgment is granted or upon payment of the underlying debt is also analyzed. Statutory protections for owners are discussed as well.[9] The establishment of trust funds is also covered.[10]

Several related areas which are outside the scope of this chapter include, liens related to labor for railroads, to which special rules apply under Lien Law sections 6 and 61, enforcement actions relating to funds held in trust with respect to improvements to real property which are governed by Article 3–A of the Lien Law, liens on vessels, which are governed by Article 4 of the New York Lien Law, monuments, gravestones and cemetery structures (Article 5), liens for labor on stone (Article 6), service of stallions and bulls (Article 7) and personal property (Articles 8–9).

§ 10.2 Strategy

There are two perspectives in viewing mechanic's liens; the view of the owner of the property (or with respect to a public improvement, the contractor) and the view of the contractors, subcontractors and materialman and others who undertake the improvement.

Regardless of whether a private or a public improvement is involved, the attorney for the party performing the work must first determine whether his client falls within the class of persons entitled to a lien and second that the services performed were those which fall within the type for which a lien may be created to enforce payment. The property owner (with respect to a private improvement) and the contractor (with respect to a public improvement) have similar concerns but from the opposite standpoint.

The attorney representing the party performing the services must be responsive to the formal requisites in creating a lien including the statutory time limitations in creating and enforcing liens.[1] As outlined below, such persons benefit from certain statutory protections intended

§ 10.1
1. See infra, §§ 10.2–10.6.
2. See infra, §§ 10.7–10.27.
3. See infra, §§ 20.13–10.14.
4. See infra, §§ 10.36–10.41.
5. See infra, §§ 10.42–10–46.
6. See infra, §§ 10.84–10.101.
7. See infra, §§ 10.28–10.35, 10.67–10.70.
8. See infra, §§ 10.47–10.64, 10.73–10.80.
9. See infra, §§ 10.81–10.82.
10. See infra, §§ 10.102–10.115.

§ 10.2
1. See infra, §§ 10.14–10.19.

to prevent collusive actions between owners and contractors and which provide certain priority of rights over other parties. The attorney representing the owner is also concerned with whether the lienor has complied with statutory requirements inasmuch as a failure to do so may subject a lien to attack. In addition, certain statutory protections are available to owners as well to prevent persons with baseless claims from harassing property owners.[2] All these areas are explored below.

§ 10.3 Nature of Mechanic's Lien

A lien is a claim or charge upon an interest in property which is created by law. Mechanic's liens are creations of statute, designed to protect the claims of subcontractors, architects, engineers, laborers and materialmen.[1] The right to impose such liens is granted in order to protect persons enhancing the value of real property by furnishing materials or performing labor with the owner's consent to the extent of the value of the materials or labor.[2] This protection is in addition to the right of action which such person would have to recover a money judgment for breach of contract.[3]

The protection afforded under the statute cannot be avoided. Thus, a "pay when paid" provision in a contract, which would prevent a subcontractor or materialman from seeking payment until the contractor was paid by the owner and thereby prevent imposition of a mechanic's lien for its enforcement, is void as against public policy.[4]

Library References:
West's Key No. Digests, Mechanics' Liens ⇐1.

§ 10.4 Creation of Mechanic's Lien—Elements

The creation of a mechanic's lien on private property is authorized by New York Lien Law § 3. This statute, which is the foundation for the entire statutory corpus of lien laws provides:

> A contractor, subcontractor, laborer, materialman, landscape gardener, nurseryman or person or corporation selling fruit or ornamental trees, roses, shrubbery, vines and small fruits, who performs labor or furnishes materials for the improvement of real property with the consent or at the request of the owner thereof, or of his agent, contractor or subcontractor, and any trust fund to

---

2. *See infra*, §§ 10.74–10.75.

§ 10.3

1. In re Einach's Estate, 1 Misc.2d 537, 146 N.Y.S.2d 240 (Surr.Ct., Erie County, 1955).

2. Charles C. Kellogg & Sons Co. v. DeLia, 173 Misc. 156, 17 N.Y.S.2d 330 (Sup. Ct., Oneida County, 1940), reversed 262 App.Div. 803, 28 N.Y.S.2d 4 (4th Dep't 1941).

3. Better Home Improvement Corp. v. Forovus Realty Corp., 235 N.Y.S.2d 209 (Sup.Ct., Kings County, 1962).

4. West–Fair Electric Contractors v. Aetna Casualty & Surety Company, 87 N.Y.2d 148, 638 N.Y.S.2d 394, 661 N.E.2d 967 (1995).

which benefits and wage supplements are due or payable for the benefit of such laborers, shall have a lien for the principal and interest, of the value, or the agreed price, of such labor, including benefits and wage supplements due or payable for the benefit of any laborer, or materials upon the real property improved or to be improved and upon such improvement, from the time of filing a notice of such lien as prescribed in this chapter. When the contract for an improvement is made with a husband or wife and the property belongs to the other or both, the husband or wife contracting shall also be presumed to be the agent of the other, unless such other having knowledge of the improvement shall, within ten days after learning of the contract give the contractor written notice of his or her refusal to consent to the improvement. Within the meaning of the provisions of this chapter, materials actually manufactured for but not delivered to the real property, shall also be deemed to be materials furnished.

There are three elements which must be satisfied for the statute to apply. First, the party seeking to avail itself of the right to impose a mechanic's must fall into the class of persons it is designed to protect, generally a contractor,[1] subcontractor,[2] laborer[3] or materialman,[4] although the law encompasses additional persons as well. Second, the lien must fall within the notion of an "improvement" within the meaning of the statute. Next, the services or material must have been provided "with the consent or at the request of the owner"[5] of the property.

Library References:
West's Key No. Digests, Mechanics' Liens ⚖1–21, 22–115(5).

§ 10.5 Creation of Mechanic's Lien—Elements—Protected Class

Lien Law grants the right to a mechanic's lien to a fairly broad spectrum of individuals who provide services which may improve private property. These include:

1. Contractors;
2. Subcontractors;
3. Laborers;
4. Materialman;
5. Landscape gardeners; and

§ 10.4

1. See Lien Law § 2(9) and discussion at § 10.5, *infra*.

2. See Lien Law § 2(10) and the discussion at § 10.5, *infra*.

3. See Lien Law § 2(11) and discussion at § 10.5, *infra*.

4. See Lien Law § 2(12) and discussion at § 10.5, *infra*.

5. Lien Law § 3 and discussion at § 10.7, *infra*.

§ 10.5 MECHANIC'S LIENS Ch. 10

6. Nurserymen or person or corporation selling fruit or ornamental trees, roses, shrubbery, vines and small fruits.

Other persons, not specifically delineated in the statute, fall within the protection of the statute, including draftsmen, engineers,[1] surveyors and architects.[2]

A "contractor" is defined as a person who contracts with the owner of real property for the improvement of the property or with the state or a public corporation for a public improvement.[3] A "subcontractor" contracts with a contractor or with another subcontractor for the improvement of the real property or the public improvement.[4] A "laborer" is any person who performs labor or services upon a public or private improvement.

A "materialman" is defined as any person who, in connection with the improvement, provides materials[5] or the use of machinery, tools, or equipment, or compressed gases for welding or cutting, or fuel or lubricants for the operation of machinery or motor vehicles, to the owner of the property, the contractor or a subcontractor.[6] There are certain distinctions in treatment of public and private improvements, as will be discussed below. It is worth noting that a lien may be created for the value of materials produced for a private improvement, even if not actually used, however, in the context of a public improvement, no such lien could be created.

Library References:

West's Key No. Digests, Mechanics' Liens ⇐79–93, 94–115(5).

§ 10.6 Creation of Mechanic's Lien—Elements—Improvements to Real Property

The labor performed or material furnished must be for the improvement of real property. Section 2 of the Lien Law defines improvement to include a broad range of activities such as:

1. Demolition of a structure;
2. Erection of a structure;
3. Alterations of a structure;
4. Repair of any structure upon, connected with, or beneath the surface of, any piece of real property;

---

§ 10.5

1. Atlantic Cement Company, Inc. v. St. Lawrence Cement Co., 22 A.D.2d 228, 254 N.Y.S.2d 676 (3d Dep't 1964).
2. Bralus Corp. v. Berger, 307 N.Y. 626, 120 N.E.2d 829 (1954). *See* Chas. H. Sells, Inc. v. Chance Hills Joint Venture, 163 Misc.2d 814, 622 N.Y.S.2d 422 (1995)(engineering and surveying).
3. *See* Lien Law § 2(9).
4. *See* Lien Law § 2(10).
5. A & J Buyers, Inc. v. Johnson, Drake & Piper, Inc., 25 N.Y.2d 265, 303 N.Y.S.2d 841, 250 N.E.2d 845 (1969).
6. Lien Law § 2(12).

548

5. Any work done upon a piece of real property or materials furnished for its permanent improvement;
6. Any work done or materials furnished in equipping any structure on the property with any chandeliers, brackets or other fixtures or apparatus for supplying gas or electric light;
7. Drawings by any architect or engineer or surveyor, of any plans or specifications or survey, which are prepared for or used in connection an improvement;
8. The value of materials actually manufactured for but not delivered to the real property;
9. The reasonable rental value for the use of machinery, tools and equipment and the value of compressed gases furnished for welding or cutting in connection with the demolition, erection, alteration or repair of any real property;
10. The value of fuel and lubricants consumed by machinery operating on the improvement, or by motor vehicles owned, operated or controlled by the owner, or a contractor or subcontractor while engaged exclusively in the transportation of materials to or from the improvement for the purposes of constructing the improvement; and
11. The performance of real estate brokerage services in obtaining a lessee for a term of more than three years of all or any part of real property (for other than residential purposes) pursuant to a written brokerage agreement.

Because the statute includes engineering and surveying services, it is possible for a party to obtain a lien even though no physical improvement to the property had taken place.[1]

Library References:
West's Key No. Digests, Mechanics' Liens ⇌22–34.

§ 10.7 Creation of Mechanic's Lien—Elements—Consent or Request of Owner

The next element required for the creation of a mechanic's lien is that the services or material have been provided "with the consent or at the request of the owner"[1] of the real property. Each of these terms requires evaluation. The statute defines "owner" to include a range of persons besides the holder of a fee simple interest. Thus, the term includes:

§ 10.6
1. Charles H. Sells, Inc. v. Chance Hills Joint Venture, 163 Misc.2d 814, 622 N.Y.S.2d 422 (Sup.Ct., Westchester County, 1995)(professional engineering and surveying services were provided in connection with obtaining a municipal approval).

§ 10.7
1. Lien Law § 3.

1. The owner in fee of real property or of a lesser estate in the property;
2. A lessee for a term of years;
3. A purchaser in possession under a contract for the purchase of real property;
4. All persons having any right, title or interest in the real property, which may be sold under an execution under any law relating to the enforcement of liens of judgment; and
5. All persons having any right or franchise granted by a public corporation to use the streets and public places and any right, title or interest in and to such franchise.

It should be noted that if a prospective purchaser of property at a statutory or judicial sale fails to complete the sale, any liens for improvements approved by him attaches to his deposit and not the property itself.[2]

Because the term "owner" includes not only the owner in fee but also of "a lesser estate," the statute also reaches a lessee of property,[3] and permits a mechanic's lien on a leasehold interest in property.[4]

The owner must consent to the work performed. The courts have consistently held that knowledge or mere acquiescence and even actual benefit to the owner from the work performed does not constitute "consent."[5] Rather, the owner must have taken some concrete action, *i.e.*, an affirmative act or course of conduct to procure the work is required.[6]

Library References:

West's Key No. Digests, Mechanics' Liens ⚖=55–78.

§ 10.8 Extent of Lien—Ownership Interest at Time of Filing

Lien Law § 4(1) governs the scope and extent of a mechanic's lien,[1] as well as the extent and survival of a lien on property whose ownership has changed.

The general rule is that is that the lien extends to the owner's property interest which exists at the time of the filing of the notice of

---

2. *Cf.* M & B Plumbing & Heating Company, Inc. v. Cammarota, 103 A.D.2d 879, 477 N.Y.S.2d 901 (3d Dep't 1984).

3. *See* Ombony v. Jones, 19 N.Y. 234 (1859).

4. Ingram & Greene, Inc. v. Wynne, 47 Misc.2d 200, 262 N.Y.S.2d 663 (Sup.Ct., Queens County, 1965).

5. Harner v. Schecter, 105 A.D.2d 932, 482 N.Y.S.2d 124 (3d Dep't 1984).

6. *Id.*

§ 10.8

1. Lien Law §§ 4(2), (3) deals with the extent and under what circumstances a lien will extend to oil, gas and mineral deposits on real property.

lien, and attaches to all property or improvements which are thereafter joined to the existing property.[2]

An exception to this rule is a general assignment for the benefit of creditors. In such an instance, a lien filed within thirty days of the assignment will attach itself to the assigned interests in the property.[3]

Library References:

West's Key No. Digests, Mechanics' Liens ⚖ 180–193.

§ 10.9 Extent of Lien—Sale of Property

Under Lien Law § 4(1) the removal from the property of an improvement or the sale of a portion of the property after a notice of lien has been filed, does not affect the rights of the lienor, either in respect to the real property remaining or the part so removed.

The Court of Appeals, in interpreting Lien Law § 4(1), clarified the application of the section to a sale of a portion of the improved property by the owner.[1] *Niagara Venture v. Sicoli & Massaro, Inc.*[2] concerned discharge of mechanic's liens. Niagara was the owner of 20.6 acres of land. It contracted with Sicoli & Massaro, Inc. for construction of a theme park on part of the land. After the theme park was constructed on the northerly 16.1 acres, that area was conveyed to the city; Niagara retained ownership of an unimproved 4.5 acre parcel. After the conveyance of the theme park and apparently without realizing that the conveyance had occurred, several contractors filed private liens against the entire 20.6 acre parcel. Sicoli & Massaro filed six pairs of liens for the same work and materials and in the same amounts against the entire 20.6 acre parcel as private liens, and as a lien for a public improvement. Other contractors filed public improvement liens for identical work and material and in the same amounts as their private liens.

At trial, the court refused to discharge the public improvement liens, discharged the mechanic's liens to the extent they encumbered property owned by the City, and upheld the mechanic's liens on the remaining 4.5 acres retained by the owner. The Appellate Division reversed and discharged the liens against the remaining 4.5 acres, reasoning that the owner retained no improved property that could be the subject of private improvement liens.

2. Lien Law §§ 4(2), (3); Niagara Venture v. Sicoli & Massaro, 77 N.Y.2d 175, 565 N.Y.S.2d 449, 566 N.E.2d 648 (1990); Thurber Lumber Company, Inc. v. N.F.B. Development Corp., 215 A.D.2d 551, 551, 626 N.Y.S.2d 841, 842 (2d Dep't 1995). *See* Chapter 11 "Mortgage Foreclosure," *infra* for a discussion of judicial sales of real property.

3. Lien Law § 13(1).

§ 10.9

1. In Niagara Venture v. Sicoli & Massaro, Inc., 77 N.Y.2d 175, 566 N.E.2d 648, 565 N.Y.S.2d 449 (1990).

2. *Id.*

The Court of Appeals reversed stating that "a lien filed against a unified parcel operates against the owner's interest in the entire parcel even if improvements are physically made on only a portion of the property." The Court noted that had the liens been filed before the owner had conveyed away any portion of the parcel, those liens would have encumbered its interest in the entire parcel, including the 4.5 undeveloped acres. Consequently, the Court reasoned, the owner should not be freed of the encumbrances on the 4.5–acre undeveloped portion of the tract because of its prior conveyance of the developed portion of the land.

Library References:

West's Key No. Digests, Mechanics' Liens ⇐161–201.

§ 10.10 Extent of Lien—Insurance Proceeds

Under Lien Law § 4–a, a mechanic's lien extends not only to the real property itself but also to the proceeds (in excess of premiums paid), of any insurance policy covering the property if the improvements are destroyed by fire or other casualty.

Library References:

West's Key No. Digests, Mechanics' Liens ⇐180.

§ 10.11 Extent of Lien—Amount

The statute limits the amount of the lien.[1] The amount of the lien may not exceed the contractual amount which the owner of the property agreed to pay.[2] In addition, the contractor may not recover for a sum greater than any sum actually earned.

Library References:

West's Key No. Digests, Mechanics' Liens ⇐161–164(4).

§ 10.12 Extent of Lien—Loss of Profits

Recovery under the Lien Law may not be had for breach of contract or loss of profits.[1] The lien may only be asserted for improvements covered by the statute; recovery for other items of damages,[2] such as

---

§ 10.11

1. Lien Law § 4.

2. *See* Alvaro Inc. v. Chow, 221 A.D.2d 752, 633 N.Y.S.2d 643 (3d Dep't 1995); Maycumber v. Wolfe, 10 Misc.2d 464, 171 N.Y.S.2d 44 (Sup.Ct., Onondaga County, 1958).

§ 10.12

1. Schenectady Homes Corporation v. Greenside Painting Corporation, 37 N.Y.S.2d 53 (County Ct., Schenectady County, 1942).

2. Hurd v. H. R. Day Constr. Co., 146 Misc. 103, 261 N.Y.S. 90 (Sup.Ct., Erie County, 1932).

rental of machinery, must be asserted as a separate cause of action.[3]

Library References:
West's Key No. Digests, Mechanics' Liens ⬤161–164(4).

§ 10.13 Subcontractors and Materialmen—Derivative Rights

Because subcontractors and materialmen do not contract directly with the owner of the property in which the improvements are being made but rather with the general contractor, their rights are said to be derivative in nature, that is, they derive from the rights which the general contractor has against the owner of the property and cannot exceed such rights.[1] Thus, their claims are restricted to any amount established as owing by the owner to the general contractor.[2] In addition, they must prove performance to the same extent that a general contractor is required to prove performance.[3] No lien can attach on behalf of a subcontractor if no money is due to him from the general contractor.[4]

Because the subcontractor's and materialman's rights are derivative of the rights of the general contractor, payment in full by the property owner of his obligations to the general contractor will discharge any obligations that the owner would have and prevent the attachment of any lien in favor of a subcontractor or materialman.[5]

Library References:
West's Key No. Digests, Mechanics' Liens ⬤94–115(5).

§ 10.14 Subcontractors and Materialmen—Derivative Rights—Statutory Protections

Subcontractors and materialmen are provided two statutory protections to prevent collusion between an owner and a general contractor. First, the law permits the subcontractor or materialman to demand that an owner provide a "statement of the terms of a contract made between an owner and a contractor, pursuant to which an improvement of real property is being made, and, of the amount due or to become due

3. John H. Black Co. v. Surdam Holding Corporation, 140 Misc. 113, 250 N.Y.S. 17 (3d Dep't 1931).

§ 10.13

1. *See* C.B. Strain & Son, Inc. v. Baranello & Sons, 90 A.D.2d 924, 457 N.Y.S.2d 925 (3d Dep't 1982).

2. *Id.*

3. Kalt Lumber Co. v. Sterner, 121 Misc. 505, 201 N.Y.S. 567 (Sup.Ct., N.Y. County, 1923). *See generally infra*, § 10.77 concerning enforcement of Mechanic's Liens.

4. E.F. Curialle & Co. v. Kenray Realty Corp., 25 Misc.2d 745, 202 N.Y.S.2d 677 (Sup.Ct., Kings County, 1960).

5. W.E. Blume, Inc. v. Postal Telegraph Cable Co., 265 App.Div. 1062, 39 N.Y.S.2d

thereon."[1] The demand must be in writing upon the owner, or his duly authorized agent, and may be made by "a subcontractor, laborer or materialman performing labor for or furnishing materials to a contractor, or subcontractor"[2] under the contract between the owner and general contractor.

The statute provides that if the owner refuses or neglects to furnish the statement within thirty days of the demand or falsely states the terms of such contract or the amount due or to become due thereon, "and a subcontractor, laborer or materialman has not been paid the amount of his claim against a contractor or subcontractor, under such contract, and a judgment has been obtained and execution issued against such contractor or subcontractor and returned wholly or party unsatisfied, the owner shall be liable for the loss sustained by reason of such refusal, neglect or false statement, and the lien of such subcontractor, laborer or materialman, filed as prescribed in this article, against the real property improved for the labor performed or materials furnished after such demand, shall exist to the same extent and be enforced in the same manner as if such labor and materials had been directly performed for and furnished to such owner."[3] Thus, failure to provide an accurate statement will create a direct obligation to the subcontractor or materialman.

The second protection provided to subcontractors and materialmen is contained in Lien Law § 7 which is intended to prevent collusive dealing between the owner and others in order to defeat a subcontractor's or materialman's lien. That statute provides that payments by an owner, contractor or subcontractor under a contract for the improvement of real property which are made prior to the time when due under the contract in order to prevent payment to a subcontractor, materialman or laborer, will not be effective against the lien of such parties which was created before the payment was actually due. Similarly, an owner cannot transfer title to a third party or grant a mortgage, lien or incumbrance to a third party where the grantee or mortgagee is aware that the purpose of the transfer or grant is to avoid payment to a subcontractor, materialman or laborer. Any such transfer of interest in the property will be ineffective against a claim of such parties which concerns an improvement to the property which existed prior to the transfer of title or the creation of the mortgage, lien or incumbrance interest.[4]

Lien Law § 7 states that for advance payments to be of no effect against a lien the payments made must be for "the purpose of avoiding the provisions of this article." Accordingly, a materialman or subcontrac-

539 (2d Dep't 1943).

§ 10.14
1. Lien Law § 8.
2. Lien Law § 8.
3. Lien Law § 8.
4. Lien Law § 7.

tor must prove that advance payments or mortgages were made in bad faith to avail himself of the protections of this law.[5]

A transfer of title to a good faith purchaser of real property for value whose conveyance is recorded subsequent to the commencement of the improvement but prior to the filing of a notice of lien has priority over any such lien provided the instrument of conveyance contains the lien covenant provisions mentioned in Lien Law § 13(5).

Library References:
West's Key No. Digests, Mechanics' Liens ⟲94–115(5).

§ 10.15 Procedure—Notice of Lien

To obtain a valid mechanic's lien, the contractor, subcontractor, materialman or other party entitled to a lien must file a Notice of Lien. The notice of lien is required so that the owner will have sufficient information so that he may discover whether the labor or the material has been performed or furnished and the value of the services or material provided.[1]

Library References:
West's Key No. Digests, Mechanics' Liens ⟲117–160.

§ 10.16 Procedure—Notice of Lien—Contents

Lien Law § 9 states that the notice of lien must contain the following information:

1. The name and residence of the lienor; and if the lienor is a partnership or a corporation, the business address of such firm, or corporation, the names of partners and principal place of business, and if a foreign corporation, its principal place of business within the state.

1–a. The name and address of the lienor's attorney, if any.

2. The name of the owner of the real property against whose interest therein a lien is claimed, and the interest of the owner as far as known to the lienor.

3. The name of the person by whom the lienor was employed, or to whom he furnished or is to furnish materials; or, if the lienor

---

5. Abe Schild Stone Corp. v. Apostle, 41 Misc.2d 732, 246 N.Y.S.2d 446 (Sup.Ct., N.Y. County, 1964); J.W. Van Cott & Son v. Gallon, 163 Misc. 914, 298 N.Y.S. 67 (Sup. Ct., Del. County, 1937).

§ 10.15
1. Vogel v. Luitwieler, 52 Hun 184, 5 N.Y.S. 154 (1889); see also, Application of Lycee Francais De New York, 26 Misc.2d 374, 204 N.Y.S.2d 490 (Sup.Ct., N.Y. County, 1960); Waring v. Burke Steel Co., 69 N.Y.S.2d 399 (Sup.Ct., Monroe County, 1947).

is a contractor or subcontractor, the person with whom the contract was made.

4. The labor performed or materials furnished and the agreed price or value thereof, or materials actually manufactured for but not delivered to the real property and the agreed price or value thereof.

5. The amount unpaid to the lienor for such labor or materials.

6. The time when the first and last items of work were performed and materials were furnished.

7. The property subject to the lien, with a description thereof sufficient for identification; and if in a city or village, its location by street and number, if known.

The notice must be verified by the lienor or his agent, stating that (1) the statements therein contained are true to his knowledge except as to the matters therein stated to be alleged on information and belief, and (2) with respect to those matters which are alleged on information and belief, he believes those matters to be true.[1]

The Lien Law is to be construed liberally[2] and a failure to state the name of the true owner or contractor, or a misdescription of the true owner, will not affect the validity of the lien,[3] provided no prejudice will result. A complete misdescription of an owner will invalidate a lien.[4] Omission of the name of a co-tenant will invalidate the lien as against the unnamed party but the lien against the named party will be valid to the extent of such co-tenant's interest.[5] Omission of an item, such as the nature of the labor performed and the materials provided or the date work commenced, is fatal.[6]

A description of the realty to which the lien attaches which substantially complies with the statute and adequately identifies the property will be sufficient to maintain a lien.[7] However, the description must be sufficient so as to exclude all other tracts of land.[8] Thus, a notice of lien with respect to a condominium which does not exclude common areas or limit itself to specified sublots or units is defective.[9]

§ 10.16
1. Lien Law § 9(7).
2. Lien Law § 23.
3. Lien Law § 9(7).
4. Matter of Kleet Lumber Co., Inc., 197 A.D.2d 576, 602 N.Y.S.2d 663 (2d Dep't 1993).
5. Melniker v. Grae, 82 A.D.2d 798, 439 N.Y.S.2d 409 (2d Dep't 1981).
6. See Fanning v. Belle Terre Estates, Inc., 152 App.Div. 718, 137 N.Y.S. 595 (2d Dep't 1912) with respect to labor and materials and In re Emslie, 102 Fed. 291 (2d Cir.1900) concerning date of performance.
7. See Cleg Co. v. Henry Moss & Co., 64 N.Y.S.2d 99 (Sup.Ct., Kings County, 1946).
8. Contelmo's Sand & Gravel, Inc. v. J & J Milano, Inc., 96 A.D.2d 1090, 467 N.Y.S.2d 55 (2d Dep't 1983).
9. See Matter of M.M.E. Power Enterprises, Inc., 205 A.D.2d 631, 613 N.Y.S.2d 266 (2d Dep't 1994); Application of Atlas Tile and Marble Works, Inc. and Atamco Inc., 191 A.D.2d 247, 595 N.Y.S.2d 10 (1st Dep't 1993), leave to appeal granted 82 N.Y.2d 651, 601 N.Y.S.2d 581, 619 N.E.2d 659, appeal withdrawn and discontinued 82 N.Y.2d 847, 606 N.Y.S.2d 598, 627 N.E.2d 520.

Ch. 10   PROCEDURE—NOTICE OF LIEN—FILING   § 10.17

Library References:

West's Key No. Digests, Mechanics' Liens ⚖︎122, 133–152.

§ 10.17 Procedure—Notice of Lien—Filing

A mechanic's lien attaches and becomes effective upon the filing of the notice of lien with the county clerk.[1] Prior to the filing, no lien exists.[2] Consequently, the provisions of Lien Law § 10 which govern filing must be strictly adhered to.[3]

An originally executed Notice of lien, as opposed to a copy, must be filed.[4] The statute specifies when the notice of lien must be filed. Failure to file within the prescribed period is generally fatal.[5] As a general rule, the notice of lien may be filed:

> (a) at any time during the progress of the work and the furnishing of the materials; or
>
> (b) within eight months after the completion of the contract, or the final performance of the work, or the final furnishing of the materials, dating from the last item of work performed or materials furnished.[6]

Different rules apply for single family dwellings. If the improvement is related to real property improved or to be improved with a single family dwelling, the notice of lien may be filed:

> (a) at any time during the progress of the work and the furnishing of the materials; or
>
> (b) within four months after the completion of the contract, or the final performance of the work, or the final furnishing of the materials, dating from the last item of work performed or materials furnished.[7]

For purposes of the Lien Law, a condominium unit is considered to be a single family dwelling.[8]

In all cases it should be noted that the phrase "completion of the contract, or the final performance of the work" in the statute refers to the original contract. Additional work which was not anticipated by the original contract or was not a continuance of the work performed under

---

§ 10.17

1. Beacon Construction Co., Inc. v. Matco Electric Co., 521 F.2d 392 (2d Cir.1975).

2. Home Federal Savings & Loan Association v. Four Star Heights, Inc., 70 Misc.2d 118, 333 N.Y.S.2d 334 (Sup.Ct., Kings County, 1971).

3. Lien Law § 10.

4. Terrell v. Meisenhelder, 143 Misc. 911, 257 N.Y.S. 625 (Sup. Ct., Suffolk County, 1932).

5. See Metivier v. Sarandrea, 154 Misc.2d 355, 585 N.Y.S.2d 291 (Sup.Ct., Oneida County, 1992), aff'd 187 A.D.2d 963, 592 N.Y.S.2d 938 (4th Dep't 1992).

6. Lien Law § 10(1).

7. Lien Law § 10(1).

8. City of Albany Industrial Development Agency v. Degraff–Moffly/General Contractors, Inc., 164 A.D.2d 20, 562 N.Y.S.2d 821 (3d Dep't 1990).

§ 10.17 MECHANIC'S LIENS Ch. 10

the original contract would not toll the commencement of the filing period.[9] It should also be noted that the right of a contractor or materialman to file the notice of lien within the statutorily prescribed time period is not subject to the automatic stay provisions of the Bankruptcy Code if the owner files a bankruptcy petition; rather, the filing would relate back to the time the underlying debt was created.[10]

In the case of a lien by a real estate broker, the notice of lien may be filed only after the brokerage services have been rendered and a lease has been signed by both the lessor and the lessee. A copy of the brokerage agreement must be annexed to the notice of lien. If the brokerage commission is to be paid in installments, the notice of lien may be filed within eight months after the final payment is due, but in no event later than five years after the first installment payment was made.[11]

The notice of lien is filed in the clerk's office of the county where the property is located. If the property is located in two or more counties, the notice of lien must be filed in the office of the clerk of each county in which it is located. Each county clerk is required to maintain a "lien docket" which lists the particulars of the notice under separate columns headed "owners," "lienors," "lienor's attorney," "property," "amount," "time of filing," and "proceedings had." The date, hour and minute of the filing of each notice of lien must be entered in the lien docket.[12]

There are two different types of recordation systems utilized in New York, the grantor-grantee system, and the block-lot system.[13] In counties in which the grantor-grantee system is used, the county clerk is required to arrange the names of the owners of property in the lien docket in alphabetical order.[14]

In counties in which the county clerk indexes liens in a block-lot index, every notice of lien must contain a designation of the block number of the property which is to be affected by the lien. The county clerk is then required to enter the particulars of the notice of lien under the block number of every block designated on the notice of lien. A filing which is made without the block designation or with an erroneous designation shall take effect only at the time the county clerk is presented with the correct information.[15]

---

9. *See* Nelson v. Schrank, 273 App.Div. 72, 75 N.Y.S.2d 761 (2d Dep't 1947).

10. In re James A. Phillips, Inc., 29 B.R. 391 (Bankr.S.D.N.Y.1983). *See generally*, Chapter 9, "Bankruptcy," *supra*.

11. Lien Law § 10(1).

12. Lien Law § 10(1).

13. **PRACTICE POINTER:** The county clerk in each county or a local title insurance company can be contacted for information concerning the system adopted in a particular county. For a discussion of each of these systems, *see* Chapter 12 "Purchase and Sale of Real Estate," § 12.53, *infra*.

14. *Id.*

15. Lien Law § 10(2).

The statute authorizes county clerks to adopt other indexing systems utilizing electromechanical, electronic or any other methods.[16]

It should be noted that the validity of the lien and the right to file a notice of lien is not affected by the death of the owner before the filing of the notice of lien.[17]

Library References:

West's Key No. Digests, Mechanics' Liens ⇒117–132(15), 153–156, 158–160.

§ 10.18 Procedure—Notice of Lien—Service

The Lien Law provides that a copy of the notice of lien must be served upon the owner within 30 days after the notice of lien is filed.[1] The lien will not be enforceable unless the owner is served in accordance with the statute.[2] The statute prescribes the manner of service:

1. If the owner is a natural person, service is to be effected in the following manner:

    - by delivering a copy of the notice of lien to the owner personally, or if he cannot be found, to his agent or attorney, or
    - by leaving it at the owner's last known place of residence in the city or town in which the real property or a part of it is located, with a person of suitable age and discretion, or
    - by registered or certified mail addressed to the owner's last known place of residence, or
    - if the owner has no residence in the city or town, or cannot be found, and he has no agent or attorney, by affixing a copy conspicuously on the property, between the hours of nine o'clock in the forenoon and four o'clock in the afternoon;

2. If the owner of the property is a corporation, service of a copy of the notice of lien is to be made in the following manner:

    - by delivering the notice to and leaving it with the president, vice-president, secretary or clerk to the corporation, the cashier, treasurer or a director or managing agent thereof, personally, within the State of New York, or
    - if such officer cannot be found within the State of New York by affixing a copy of the notice of lien conspicuously on the

---

16. Lien Law § 10(2).
17. Lien Law § 10(1).

§ 10.18
1. Lien Law § 11.

2. Beacon Construction Co., Inc. v. Matco Elec. Co., 521 F.2d 392 (2d Cir.1975).

§ 10.18   MECHANIC'S LIENS   Ch. 10

property between the hours of nine o'clock in the forenoon and four o'clock in the afternoon, or

- by registered or certified mail addressed to its last known place of business.

Strict compliance with the service requirements under the Lien Law is required. Service by any other manner is insufficient.[3]

Proof of service upon the owner must be filed with the county clerk within 35 days after the notice of lien is filed.[4] The lienor must comply with this requirement. Failure to do so will terminate the notice as a lien.[5]

Until the owner has been served with a copy of the notice of lien, any payment made by the owner to any contractor or other person claiming a lien, in good faith and without knowledge of the lien, shall be protected from attack by a party, such as a subcontractor, materialman or laborer, who claims to have derivative rights through the party to whom payment was made.[6]

Not only must the owner of the property be served with a copy of the notice of lien, but the contractor or subcontractor must also be served either simultaneously or within 30 days after the filing of a notice of lien. Once again, the failure to strictly comply with the statute's notice requirement will terminate the lien.[7]

Unlike the requirements concerning service on an owner, service on a contractor or subcontractor may be made by certified mail.[8] If the lienor is a contractor or subcontractor, he must serve a copy of the notice of lien to the person, firm or corporation with whom the contract was made.[9] The notice requirement is not limited to entities in which a lienor has a direct contractual relationship.[10] Thus, a lienor who has contracted with a subcontractor or a sub-subcontractor but not with a contractor must also serve a copy of the notice of lien (or any amendment of the notice) by certified mail to the contractor.[11]

Proof of service of the notice of lien on contractors and subcontractors must also be filed with the county clerk within 35 days after the notice of lien has been filed. Failure to file proof of service with the county clerk within the requisite time period shall terminate the notice as a lien.[12]

---

3. See HMB Acquisition Corp., Inc. v. F & K Supply, Inc., 209 A.D.2d 412, 618 N.Y.S.2d 422 (2d Dep't 1994) (service upon Secretary of State not valid).

4. Lien Law § 11.

5. See Podolsky v. Narnoc Corp., 196 A.D.2d 593, 601 N.Y.S.2d 320 (2d Dep't 1993).

6. Lien Law § 11. See Drachman Structurals, Inc. v. Anthony Rivara Contracting Co., Inc., 78 Misc.2d 486, 356 N.Y.S.2d 974 (Sup.Ct., Nassau County, 1974).

7. Lien Law § 11–b.

8. Lien Law § 11–b.

9. Lien Law § 11–b.

10. Lien Law § 11–b.

11. Lien Law § 11–b.

12. Lien Law § 11–b.

Library References:
West's Key No. Digests, Mechanics' Liens ⚙=123, 156.

§ 10.19 Amendment of Notice of Lien

Section 12–a of the Lien Law contains two provisions which permit the lienor to amend his lien. First, the lienor may, within 60 days of the filing of his notice of lien, file an amendment for the purposes of reducing the amount of the lien.[1] This amendment requires 20 days notice to existing lienors, mortgagees and the owner. The amendment may not be filed if an action or proceeding to enforce or cancel the mechanic's lien has been commenced. Notwithstanding the filing of any amendment to the notice of lien (including an amendment reducing the amount of the lien), issues relating to wilful exaggeration of the lien will survive.[2]

A lienor[3] may move for an order permitting it to amend a notice of lien and correct defects contained in the filing.[4] The lienor must provide existing lienors, mortgagees and owners with five days' notice of its motion. Failure to provide such notice will defeat the motion.[5] If the motion is granted, the court may order the amendment of a notice of lien upon a public or private improvement, *nunc pro tunc*, *i.e.*, with retroactive effect to the date of the original filing of the notice. The court may not order an amendment to be filed if it will prejudice the rights of an existing lienor, mortgagee or purchaser.[6]

The purpose of this section is to permit a lienor to remedy a technical defect in the original notice of lien.[7] Courts have permitted amendments of liens to be filed in cases where the true contractor was not named,[8] the date of completion of work was incorrectly stated,[9] the lot number was misidentified but the street address was correct,[10] the lienor's name was misspelled[11] or to indicate the contractor's legal name where an assumed name was listed in the notice.[12]

A court may not order an amendment to a lien where there is a

---

§ 10.19

1. Lien Law § 12–a(1).

2. See § 10.75, *infra*.

3. An owner has no right to make an application to amend a notice of lien under Lien Law § 21–a; MXP Realty Corp. v. Angrisani, 152 Misc.2d 458, 576 N.Y.S.2d 754 (Sup.Ct., Suffolk County, 1991).

4. Lien Law § 12–a(2).

5. Bennett Brothers v. Bracewood Realty No. 1, Inc., 23 A.D.2d 498, 256 N.Y.S.2d 308 (2d Dep't 1965); Application of Boulder Apartments, Inc., 14 Misc.2d 287, 155 N.Y.S.2d 520 (Sup.Ct., Westchester County, 1956).

6. Lien Law § 12–a(2).

7. Application of Upstate Builders Supply Corp., 63 Misc.2d 35, 310 N.Y.S.2d 862 (Sup.Ct., Onondaga County, 1970).

8. San Marco Construction Corp. v. Gillert, 15 Misc.2d 208, 178 N.Y.S.2d 137 (Sup. Ct., Westchester County, 1958).

9. Clifton Steel Corp. v. General Elec. Co., 80 A.D.2d 715, 437 N.Y.S.2d 735 (3d Dep't 1981).

10. Fremar Building Corp. v. Sand, 104 A.D.2d 1025, 480 N.Y.S.2d 945 (2d Dep't 1984).

11. Core Joint Concrete Pipe Corporation v. Paino Brothers, Inc., 247 App.Div. 746, 285 N.Y.S. 706 (2d Dep't 1936).

12. Corina Associates v. McManus, Longe, Brockwehl, Inc., 39 A.D.2d 613, 330 N.Y.S.2d 847 (3d Dep't 1972).

§ 10.19   MECHANIC'S LIENS   Ch. 10

substantial defect and the lien is not valid.[13] A court cannot amend a notice of lien which was not timely filed.[14] A notice of lien in which the correct owner of the property was not named may not be amended if a third party would be prejudiced.[15] A complete misdescription of the property may not be corrected by the filing of an amendment[16] nor may the amount of the lien be increased if prejudice would result.[17] A notice of lien cannot be amended to include a second distinct corporation as lienor where the period to file for such corporation had expired.[18]

Library References:

West's Key No. Digests, Mechanics' Liens ⟲124, 158.

§ 10.20   Lien for Private Improvements—Checklist

An attorney seeking to create a lien for a private improvement must be able to answer affirmatively each of the question listed below:

1. Is the client within the type of class entitled to a lien?[1] (*See also* § 10.5)

2. Did the client perform labor for or provide materials or otherwise provide the type of services covered by the statute?[2] (*See also* § 10.5)

3. Was the property improved within the meaning of the statute?[3] (*See also* § 10.6)

4. Did the owner consent to the improvement?[4] (*See also* § 10.7)

5. Is the project continuing and if it has been completed have fewer than eight months (four months for a single family dwelling) elapsed since completion and acceptance?[5] (*See also* § 10.17)

6. When preparing the notice of lien, have all the requirements of the statute been complied with?[6] (*See also* § 10.16)

13. Hilzenradt v. Breindel, 139 N.Y.S.2d 688 (Sup.Ct., Sullivan County, 1955).

14. Fish v. Anstey Construction Co., 71 Misc. 2, 130 N.Y.S. 927 (Sup.Ct., N.Y. County, 1911).

15. Kiernan Equipment Corp. v. Centre Lighting Fixture Manufacturing Co., 20 A.D.2d 895, 248 N.Y.S.2d 961 (2d Dep't 1964).

16. Matter of Clemens, 200 Misc. 772, 104 N.Y.S.2d 720 (Sup.Ct., Albany County, 1951).

17. Application of Upstate Builders Supply Corp., 63 Misc.2d 35, 310 N.Y.S.2d 862 (Sup.Ct., Albany County, 1970).

18. Onorati v. Testco Inc., 204 A.D.2d 876, 612 N.Y.S.2d 473 (3d Dep't 1994).

§ 10.20

1. Lien Law § 2.
2. Lien Law § 2(4).
3. Lien Law § 2(4).
4. Lien Law § 3.
5. Lien Law § 10.
6. Lien Law § 9.

7. Was the notice of lien verified? The original verified notice should be used for filing.[7] (*See also* § 10.16)

8. Has the notice of lien been filed with the county clerk in each county in which the property is located?[8] (*See also* § 10.17)

9. Were copies of the notice of lien served by certified mail on the contractor (if applicable) and owner?[9] (*See also* § 10.18)

10. Has a proof of service upon the owner and the contractor been filed simultaneously with the filing of the notice of lien?[10] (*See also* § 10.18)

11. If the client is a subcontractor, materialman or laborer, has a demand for terms of the contract been made?[11] (*See also* § 10.14)

§ 10.21 Liens Under Contract for Public Improvements—Extent of Lien

The procedures and scope of liens for public improvements, to a large extent, mirror those with respect to private improvements. Nevertheless, there are important differences which require some discussion.

Section 5 of the Lien Law provides the general rules governing liens for public improvements.[1] A public improvement means an improvement to property owned by the state or a public corporation.[2] Unlike Lien Law § 3 which governs liens for private improvements, Lien Law § 5 limits liens for public improvements to "[a] person performing labor for or furnishing materials to a contractor, his subcontractor or legal representative, for the construction or demolition of a public improvement ..."[3] Thus, a contractor has no lien rights under the statute.[4] Further, a materialman who provides materials to another materialman is not covered by the statute[5] nor is one whose materials, though delivered to the contractor, are ultimately not used for the improvement.[6] The lien attaches only to "the moneys of the state or of such corporation

---

7. Lien Law § 9(7).
8. Lien Law § 10.
9. Lien Law § 11.
10. Lien Law § 11.
11. Lien Law § 8.

§ 10.21
1. Lien Law § 5.
2. *See* Lien Law § 2(7).
3. Lien Law § 5.

4. *See* Anderson v. John L. Hayes Construction Co., Inc., 243 N.Y. 140, 153 N.E. 28 (1926), motion to amend requiter denied 243 N.Y. 593, 154 N.E. 619 (1926).

5. Kingston Trust Co. v. State, 57 Misc.2d 55, 291 N.Y.S.2d 208 (Sup.Ct., Ulster County, 1968).

6. Application of Wade Lupe Construction Co., Inc., 134 Misc.2d 738, 512 N.Y.S.2d 338 (Sup.Ct., Schenectady County, 1976).

§ 10.21 MECHANIC'S LIENS Ch. 10

applicable to the construction or demolition of such improvement"[7] and not to the real estate itself.[8] The lien is created by the filing of a notice of lien in accordance with Lien Law § 12.[9]

> **Library References:**
>
> West's Key No. Digests, Municipal Corporations ⚖373; Public Contracts ⚖23, 24; States ⚖108, 108.5.

§ 10.22 Liens Under Contract for Public Improvements—Notice of Lien

The notice of lien must contain the following information:

1. The name and residence of the lienor;

2. The name of the contractor or subcontractor for whom the labor was performed or materials furnished. If the name of the contractor or subcontractor is not known to the lienor, it may be so stated in the notice. A failure to correctly state the name of the contractor or subcontractor will not affect the validity of the lien;

3. The amount claimed to be due or to become due;

4. The date payment is due;

5. A description of the public improvement upon which the labor was performed and materials expended;

6. The kind of labor performed and materials furnished;

7. The kind of materials actually manufactured for but not delivered to such public improvement;

8. A general description of the contract pursuant to which such public improvement was constructed or demolished.

9. If the lienor is a partnership or a corporation, the notice must also state the lienor's business address, the names of any partners, and if a foreign corporation, its principal place of business within the state.

As is the case with a notice of lien for private improvements, a notice of lien for public improvements must be verified by the lienor or his agent, "to the effect that the statements therein contained are true to his own knowledge, except as to the matters therein stated to be alleged on information and belief, and that as to those matters he believes it to be true."[1]

> **Library References:**
>
> West's Key No. Digests, Municipal Corporations ⚖373(3); Public Contracts ⚖23, 29, 30; States ⚖108, 108.5.

7. Lien Law § 5.

8. Maryland Casualty Co. v. Board of Water Commissioners of City of Dunkirk, 66 F.2d 730 (2d Cir.1933), cert. denied 290 U.S. 702, 54 S.Ct. 346, 78 L.Ed. 603 (1933).

9. See infra § 10.22.

§ 10.22

1. Lien Law § 12.

§ 10.23 Liens Under Contract for Public Improvements—Filing of Notice of Lien

The notice of lien may be filed at any time before, or within 30 days of, completion and acceptance of the construction or demolition of a public improvement.[1] It is filed with the head of the department or bureau having charge of the construction or demolition project and with either the State Comptroller or the financial officer of the public corporation or such other officer or person who is charged with the custody and disbursements of the state or corporate funds with respect to the contract under which the claim is made.[2]

Just as each county clerk is required to maintain a lien book to record notices of liens for private improvements, the State Comptroller or the financial officer of the public corporation or other responsible officer with whom the notice is filed is obligated to maintain a "lien book" and enter into such book "the name and residence of the lienor, the name of the contractor or subcontractor, the amount of the lien and date of filing, and a brief designation of the contract under which the lien arose."[3]

As is the case with respect to liens for private improvements,[4] Lien Law § 11–c requires that simultaneously with the filing of a notice of lien for public improvements, a copy of the notice of lien must be served by certified mail on the contractor or subcontractor for whom the lienor was employed. A copy must be sent to the contractor even if the lienor has no direct contractual relationship with the contractor. Proof of service of the notice of lien upon the parties required by Lien Law § 11–c must be filed with the notice of lien. A failure to file the proof of service will nullify the notice of lien.[5]

Library References:

West's Key No. Digests, Municipal Corporations ⇌373(3); Public Contracts ⇌23, 29, 30; States ⇌108, 108.5.

§ 10.24 Liens Under Contract for Public Improvements—Notice of Completion and Acceptance

As noted above, in the case of private improvements, a subcontractor or materialman may demand of an owner a statement of the terms of the contract between the owner and the contractor.[1] In the case of public improvements, an analogous right is granted to subcontractors and materialmen under Lien Law § 11–a, which permits such persons to

---

§ 10.23
1. Lien Law § 12.
2. Lien Law § 12.
3. Lien Law § 12.
4. See supra, § 10.18.
5. Id.

§ 10.24
1. See supra § 10.14.

§ 10.24 MECHANIC'S LIENS Ch. 10

demand from the governmental agency or public corporation contracting for the improvement notice of completion and acceptance of the work being performed.[2] The demand may be filed at any time before, or within 30 days of, completion and acceptance of the construction or demolition of a public improvement.

The demand for notice of completion must be filed with the head of the department or bureau having charge of the construction or demolition. The demand must contain the following information:[3]

    1. The name and address of the party making the demand;

    2. The name of the contractor or subcontractor for whom the labor was performed or materials furnished;

    3. The estimated amount of the entire value of the materials provided or labor performed; and

    4. A description of the public improvement upon which the labor was performed or the materials were furnished.[4]

The state agency or public corporation is obligated to respond to a request for notice of completion and acceptance within five days of a request,[5] however, a failure to do so will not give rise to any cause of action, extend any period of time within which an act (including the filing of a notice of lien) must be performed or otherwise affect the rights of any party.[6]

§ 10.25 Liens Under Contract for Public Improvements—Checklist

An attorney seeking to create a lien on account of a public improvement should be able to answer affirmatively each of the question listed below:

1. Did the client perform labor for or provide materials to a contractor or subcontractor?[1] (*See* § 10.22) If yes, then the type of services fall within those covered by the statute.

2. Did the property belong to the state or a public corporation?[2] (*See* § 10.22) If yes, then the improvement is a public improvement.

3. If the client provided materials, were the materials used by the contractor or subcontractor in connection with the public improvement?[3] (*See* § 10.21)

2. Lien Law § 11–a.
3. Lien Law § 11–a(2).
4. Lien Law § 11–a(2).
5. Lien Law § 11–a(3).
6. Lien Law § 11–a(4).

§ 10.25
1. Lien Law § 5.
2. Lien Law § 5.
3. Lien Law § 5.

4. Is the project continuing and if it has been completed have fewer than 30 days elapsed since completion and acceptance?[4] (*See* § 10.21)

5. When preparing the notice of lien, have all the requirements of the statute been complied with?[5] (*See* § 10.22)

6. Was the notice of lien verified?[6] (*See also* § 10.22) The original verified notice should be used for filing.

7. Has the notice of lien been filed with the bureau or department head? Has a copy been filed with the State Comptroller or financial officer of the public corporation?[7] (*See* § 10.23)

8. Were copies of the notice of lien served by certified mail on the subcontractor (if applicable) and contractor?[8] (*See* § 10.23)

9. Has a proof of service upon the subcontractor and the contractor been filed simultaneously with the filing of the notice of lien?[9] (*See* § 10.23)

10. Has a demand for notice of completion and acceptance been made?[10] (*See* § 10.24)

§ 10.26 Lien Priorities—Private Improvements—Parity of Mechanic's Liens

A mechanic's lien may be one of many liens which encumber real property. Section 13 of the Lien Law is designed to establish priorities among lien holders. As a general rule, it follows the established principle of "first in time," that is, that the lien or encumbrance which is recorded first will have priority over subsequently recorded interests. There are, however, several important exceptions.

The statute provides that a properly filed mechanic's lien will, as a general matter, have "priority over a conveyance, mortgage, judgment or other claim against such property not recorded, docketed or filed at the time of the filing of the notice of such lien ..."[1] Subject to certain exceptions, it will also have priority over:

> 1. "advances made upon any mortgage or other encumbrance thereon" made after filing of the notice of lien;
>
> 2. "the claim of a creditor who has not furnished materials or performed labor" upon the property, if the property has been assigned "by the owner by a general assignment for the benefit of creditors, within thirty days before the filing" of the notice of lien;

---

4. Lien Law § 12.
5. Lien Law § 12.
6. Lien Law § 12.
7. Lien Law § 12.
8. Lien Law § 11–c.

9. Lien Law § 11–c.
10. Lien Law § 11–a.

§ 10.26

1. Lien Law § 13(1).

§ 10.26 MECHANIC'S LIENS Ch. 10

  3. an attachment issued after the notice of lien is filed or a money judgment thereafter recovered upon a claim, which was not for materials furnished, labor performed or moneys advanced for the improvement of the property and over any claim or lien acquired in any proceedings upon such judgment;

  4. advances made upon a contract by an owner for an improvement of real property which grants the contractor an option to purchase the property, provided the advances were made after the time when the lienor began providing labor or materials to the contractor.[2]

A properly filed mechanic's lien will, as general matter, have priority over transfers, mortgages, judgments or other claims against the property not recorded, docketed or filed at the time of the filing of the notice of lien. Except for laborers for daily or weekly wages who have preference over all other lien holders, as between those holding mechanic's liens, there are generally no priorities.[3] Rather, where a single building or piece of real estate is concerned, the liens of all such holders, regardless of when their respective notice of liens were filed, shall be on a parity.[4] However, if several buildings or properties are involved under a single contract, and there are conflicting liens, the lien of a lienor will have priority over the liens of other lienors upon the particular part of the property where his labor was performed or his materials were utilized.[5]

Library References:

  West's Key No. Digests, Mechanics' Liens ⚖︎196.

§ 10.27 Lien Priorities—Private Improvements—Assignments of Contract Rights

Section 13(1–a) governs the rights of parties, such as lenders to contractors, who have advanced funds to a contractor and received legitimate assignments of amounts due or to become due under a contract for the improvement of real property. If the assignment was duly filed prior to the filing of a notice of lien or assignment of any other party, the assignee shall have priority over such parties "to the extent of moneys advanced upon such assignment before the filing of the notice of lien or [any other] assignment ...." However, with respect to any additional funds which are subsequently advanced after a notice of lien or other assignment is filed, the assignee's lien will be on a parity with such other lienors to the extent of the additional funds advanced. If the

---

2. *See* Lien Law § 13(1).

3. *See* Lien Law § 13(1).

4. *See* Drachman Structurals, Inc. v. Anthony Rivara Contracting Co., Inc., 78 Misc.2d 486, 356 N.Y.S.2d 974 (Sup.Ct., Nassau County, 1974). The only exception being that the lien of a laborer, subcontractor or materialman will have priority over the person for whom he has performed the labor or provided the materials. *See* Lien Law § 56.

5. Lien Law § 13(1).

assignee filed its assignment after the filing of the notice of lien or assignment of another party, its lien will be on a parity with other lienors to the extent of moneys actually advanced prior to the filing of the assignment.[1]

Library References:

West's Key No. Digests, Mechanics' Liens ⚖︎194–201.

§ 10.28 Lien Priorities—Private Improvements—Building Loan Mortgages

As a general rule, mechanic's liens have priority over advances made on a recorded building loan mortgage if the advances are made after the filing of the notice of lien.[1] However, a building loan mortgage, regardless of when it was recorded, will have priority over such lien to the extent of advances made before the filing of such notice of lien, provided the mortgage (the building loan contract if the party contracting for the improvement is not the owner of the property) contains a covenant by the mortgagor that he will hold all advances received by him in trust to be applied first for the payment of the cost of improvements, and that he will apply the same first to the payment of the cost of improvement before such funds are used for any other purposes.[2]

If the party contracting for the improvement is not the owner of the property, the building loan contact must also be filed as required by Lien Law § 22.[3] A statement in the mortgage that it is "subject to the trust fund provisions of section thirteen of the lien law" will fulfill the requirement concerning inclusion of the lien covenant.[4]

A mortgage which is recorded after work on the improvement has begun but before the expiration of the period for the filing of a notice of lien, will have priority over liens which are filed after it to the extent of advances made by the mortgagee to the mortgagor before the filing of the notice of lien. The mortgage, must however, contain the lien covenant required by Lien Law § 13(3).

Library References:

West's Key No. Digests, Mortgages ⚖︎151(3), 163(3).

§ 10.27

1. **PRACTICE POINTER:** Attorneys of clients planning to advance funds to contractors should advise their clients to have a lien search conducted by a reputable title company before each advance of funds.

§ 10.28

1. Lien Law § 13(2). *See infra*, Chapter 11, "Mortgage Foreclosure," § 11.9.

2. Lien Law § 13(3).

3. *See infra*, § 10.59.

4. **CAVEAT:** Every mortgage should contain the lien covenant language mandated by Lien Law § 13(3).

§ 10.29 Lien Priorities—Private Improvements—Contracts of Sale

To the extent a prospective purchaser of property has paid sums to the owner on account of the contract prior to the filing of a notice of lien, the lien of a prospective purchaser on the property will have priority over notices of liens which are filed after the contract of sale is recorded in accordance with Real Property Law § 294.[1] The recorded contract must, however, specify the total amount of payments made by the purchaser or required by the contract to be made by the purchaser before title will pass.[2]

Library References:

West's Key No. Digests, Mechanics' Liens ⟐199.

§ 10.30 Lien Priorities—Private Improvements—Seller's Mortgage

A mortgage granted to the seller of property by the purchaser in connection with the sale of the property which is recorded prior to the filing of a notice of lien will have priority over the notice of lien,[1] provided the mortgage contains a covenant that the mortgagee will hold any funds it receives in trust to be applied first for the cost of improvements.

Library References:

West's Key No. Digests, Mortgages ⟐151(3), 163(3).

§ 10.31 Lien Priorities—Private Improvements—Deeds

A title granted under a deed recorded after commencement of the improvement, but before the expiration of the period for filing of a notice of lien after completion of the improvement, will be valid as against liens filed within a corresponding period of time (measured from the recording of the deed) provided the deed contains a covenant by the grantor that any consideration for the sale received by the seller will be held as a trust fund which will be applied first for the payment of the cost of the improvement before used for any other purpose.[1] The deed may simply state that it is "subject to the trust fund provisions of section thirteen of

---

§ 10.29

1. See Lien Law § 13(3).
2. **PRACTICE POINTER:** Because contracts of sale are rarely recorded, the general practice is that any payments to be made by the purchaser prior to closing be held in escrow. See Chapter 12, "Purchase and Sale of Real Property," infra. In the event payments are to be made directly to the seller prior to closing, the contract of sale must be recorded prior to such payment, and a search of the record by a reputable title company must be completed to ascertain that no notice of lien has been filed against the property.

§ 10.30

1. Lien Law § 13(4).

§ 10.31

1. Lien Law § 13(5).

the lien law" in order to fulfill this requirement. The purchaser has no obligation to insure the rightful application of funds by the seller. Note that this requirement does not apply to a deed given by a referee or other person appointed by the court for the sole purpose of selling real property or to transfers of title where the deed was recorded before any improvements were commenced.[2]

Library References:
West's Key No. Digests, Mechanics' Liens ⇒197.

§ 10.32 Lien Priorities—Contracts for Public Improvements

Lien Law § 25 governs priorities concerning contracts for public improvements.[1] Some of the priority rules concerning contracts for public improvements mirror those with respect to private improvements. Thus, as is the case with private improvements, laborers for daily or weekly wages who have liens have an absolute preference for the full amount of their unpaid wages over all other lienors having liens arising under the same contract, regardless of when they filed their notices of liens. Such laborers are treated as a single class. All others possessing valid mechanic's liens are also treated as a single class.

Assignees of rights to moneys due under contracts for public improvements are treated similarly to assignees of moneys due under contracts for private improvements. The lien of an assignee whose assignment was duly filed prior to the filing of a notice of lien or assignment of any other party will have priority over all such parties to the extent that the assignee made advances before the other assignments or notices of lien were filed. If he made additional advances after a notice of lien or assignment was filed, he will, to the extent of such advances, be treated as a lienor on parity with all other lienors (other than laborers for daily or weekly wages who are entitled to a preference) and will be on a parity with such lienors and receive a share of the funds which are ultimately available for payment in proportion to the amount the lienor's claim bears to the claims of all lienors.

As is the case with respect to contracts for private improvements, an assignee of moneys due under a contract for a public improvement whose assignment is filed after the filing of a notice of lien or an assignment by any other party will be treated as a lienor having a lien to the extent of advances actually made prior to the filing of his assignment.

Library References:
West's Key No. Digests, Municipal Corporations ⇒373(1); Public Contracts ⇒27; States ⇒108, 108.5.

2. Lien Law § 13(5).

§ 10.32
1. Lien Law §§ 25(1), (4).

§ 10.33 Assignment of Liens

Section 14 of the Lien Law permits the assignment of liens and the recordation of such assignments.[1] There are several formal requirements which must be adhered to:

1. The assignment must be in writing.

2. The instrument of assignment must be signed and acknowledged by the lienor before the discharge of the lien.

3. The assignment must state:

   i. the names and places of residence of the assignor and assignee;

   ii. the amount of the lien; and

   iii. the date of filing the notice of lien;

4. The assignment must be filed in the same office where the original notice of the lien assigned was filed.

The county clerk is required to enter the information concerning the assignment of the lien in the lien book where the notice of lien was originally entered. Although the validity of an assignment is not affected if it is not filed and recorded, there are certain consequences to non-filing, namely:

1. The assignee need not be made a defendant or notified if an action to foreclose a mortgage, lien or other incumbrance is commenced against the property;[2] and

2. If the owner of the real property subject to the lien assigned or the contractor of a public corporation, makes a payment to the original lienor on account of such lien, without notice of such assignment, the payment will be valid.[3]

Library References:
West's Key No. Digests, Mechanics' Liens ⇌202–206.

§ 10.34 Assignments of Contracts for Private Improvements and Orders to Be Filed—Filing of Notice of Assignment

Lien Law § 15 governs the assignment of contracts for private improvements and orders for payment. An assignment of a contract for the performance of labor or the furnishing of materials for the improvement of real property or under a building loan contract or of any amount due under such contract or order for the making of a payment pursuant to any such assignment is not valid unless a notice of assignment (or a

§ 10.33
1. Lien Law § 14.
2. Lien Law § 14.
3. Lien Law § 14.

statement containing the terms of a notice of assignment) is filed within ten days after the date of such assignment or such order, in the office of the county clerk of the county in which the real property improved or to be improved is located.[1] The county clerk must record all such assignments filed with him in the lien docket or lien book maintained by him. Each such assignment must be indexed by the name of the assignor and each order is to be indexed by the name of the drawer.[2] An assignment which is not recorded shall be void as against a subsequently filed assignment by a purchaser in good faith for valuable consideration.[3]

Library References:

West's Key No. Digests, Mechanics' Liens ⚖114.

§ 10.35 Assignments of Contracts for Private Improvements and Orders to Be Filed—Contents of Notice of Assignment

The "notice of assignment" may only be filed if funds are advanced or to be advanced to a contractor or subcontractor upon the assignment of a contract for the performance of labor or the furnishing of materials for the improvement of real property, or of any portion of the funds due or to become due under such contract. The said notice must contain the following information:

1. The names and addresses of the assignor and assignee;

2. The date of the assignment;

3. The date the assignment will terminate (which may not be more than two years after the date of the assignment);

4. The name of each county in which the real property involved in the contracts is or may be located; and

5. Either a specific description of the substance of the contract being assigned (including identification of the real property involved) or a statement that the assignment covers all or a specified class of the assignor's accounts or contract rights.[1]

Identification of the real property involved will be sufficient if the name of the record owner and the location of the real estate by street and number and town or city is included. For property located in the City of New York, the county location must be given, except that for property located in New York City, Nassau or Onondaga counties, where

---

§ 10.34

1. Lien Law § 15(1).
2. See Lien Law § 15(1).
3. Section 15(1) of the Lien Law states that "every such assignment or order, not filed shall be absolutely void as against a subsequent assignee in good faith and for valuable consideration, whose assignment or order is first duly filed."

§ 10.35

1. See Lien Law § 15(2).

the block system of recording or registering and indexing conveyances is used, the notice must also specify the block in which the property is located.[2]

Library References:

West's Key No. Digests, Mechanics' Liens ⚙114.

§ 10.36 Assignments of Contracts for Private Improvements and Orders to Be Filed—Extension of Term of Notice of Assignment

The "Notice of Assignment" may only be filed if funds are advanced or to be advanced to a contractor or subcontractor upon the assignment of a contract for the performance of labor or the furnishing of materials for the improvement of real property, or of any portion of the funds due or to become due under such contract.

The term of a "Notice of Assignment" may be extended beyond the termination date stated in the Notice of Assignment by filing within sixty days prior to the termination date, a subsequent "Notice of Assignment", which must be entitled "Second Notice of Assignment" or "Third Notice of Assignment," as the case may be. The additional Notice of Assignment must identify the prior "Notice of Assignment" to which it relates and meet all the requirements set forth above.[1] A Notice of Assignment may be amended. However, if the amendment extends the assignment to cover additional contracts, it will be effective with respect to such added contracts only from the date of the filing of the amendment.[2]

Finally, it should be noted that any assignment must contain a covenant by the assignor that he will hold any funds advanced to him by the assignee as trust funds to be first applied to the payment of trust claims.[3]

Library References:

West's Key No. Digests, Mechanics' Liens ⚙114.

2. *See* Lien Law § 15(2).

§ 10.36
1. *See* Lien Law § 15(3).
2. *See* Lien Law § 15(4).
3. *See* Lien Law § 13(6). With respect to trust assets held by a contractor or subcontractor, "trust claims" are defined under Lien Law § 71 to include:

(a) claims of subcontractors, architects, materialmen, engineers, surveyors and laborers;

(b) payroll and sales taxes;

(c) unemployment and other taxes relating to employment of the persons listed in (a), above;

(d) benefits or wage supplements;

(e) premiums on surety bonds relating to the improvements; and

(f) certain funds payable to the owner under Lien Law § 71–a.

§ 10.37 Assignment of Contracts and Orders for Public Improvements

The counterpart to the law governing assignments of private improvement contracts and orders in the sphere of public improvements is Lien Law § 16.[1] It requires all such assignments and orders to be filed within 20 days after the date of such assignment with the head of the department or bureau having charge of the improvement or with the financial or other officer or person of the public corporation responsible for the custody and disbursement of the corporate funds applicable to the contract involved. Assignments which are not filed are void as against a subsequent assignee in good faith and for valuable consideration, whose assignment or order is filed first. The financial officer of the public corporation, or other officer or person with whom the assignment or order is filed is required to record the assignment in the lien book maintained by him.[2]

As is the case with respect to assignments of contracts or orders for private improvements, any assignment of a contract or order for public improvements must contain a covenant by the assignor that he will hold any funds advanced to him by the assignee as trust funds to be first applied to the payment of trust claims.[3]

Library References:

West's Key No. Digests, Municipal Corporations ⟺373(2); Public Contracts ⟺23, 24; States ⟺108, 108.5.

§ 10.38 Duration of Lien for Private Improvements—Notice of Pendency

As a general rule, a lien created by the filing of a notice of lien will terminate after one year unless the lienor has commenced an action to foreclose the lien and has filed a notice of pendency of the foreclosure action with the county clerk of the county in which the notice of lien was originally filed.[1]

The notice of pendency must contain the following information:

1. The names of the parties to the action;

2. The object of the action;

3. A brief description of the real property affected by the action; and

4. The time of filing the notice of lien.

§ 10.37
1. Lien Law § 16.
2. Lien Law § 16.
3. *See* Lien Law § 25(5).

§ 10.38
1. See Lien Law § 17.

§ 10.38

If an action is commenced against a lienor to enforce another lien, and the plaintiff in such action or the defendant-lienor files a notice of the pendency of that action within one year time of the filing of the notice of lien, the lien will survive and continue and the action is deemed to be an action to enforce the lien of the defendant lienor.

Although the failure to file a notice of pendency of an action will result in the termination of the lien, it does not affect the lienor's cause of action or the liability of the owner for the payment of the underlying debt which gave rise to the lien. If a lien is discharged by deposit or by order,[2] a notice of pendency may not be filed.

Library References:

West's Key No. Digests, Mechanics' Liens ⇒174–179.

§ 10.39 Duration of Lien for Private Improvements—Extensions

Lien Law § 17 permits the duration of a mechanic's lien on property which is not improved or to be improved with a single family dwelling to be extended for a period of one year if an action to foreclose is not commenced within one year of the filing of the notice of lien.[1] The extension must be filed with the county clerk of the county in which the original notice of lien was filed within one year from the date of filing of the original notice of lien. The county clerk is required to redocket the lien as of the date of filing the extension. The extension must contain the following information:

1. The names of the lienor and the owner of the real property against whose interest the lien is claimed;

2. A brief description of the real property affected by the lien;

3. The amount of the lien; and

4. The date of the original filing of the original notice of lien.[2]

The extension will permit the lien to continue for an additional one year period. The lien will terminate if the lienor does not commence an action during the extension period to foreclose on the lien unless a court order continuing the lien is issued. If such an order is issued, the lien will be redocketed as of the date of the order with a statement that the lien is continued by virtue of such order. A lien on real property improved or to be improved with a single family dwelling may only be

---

2. *See infra* § 10.49.

§ 10.39

1. Lien Law § 17 provides that lien for which an action to foreclose has not been commenced shall terminate after one year unless an extension to such lien, except for a lien on real property improved or to be improved with a single family dwelling, is filed with the county clerk of the county in which the notice of lien is filed within one year from the filing of the original notice of lien, continuing such lien and such lien shall be redocketed as of the date of filing such extension.

2. Lien Law § 17.

extended by court order. The court may not order the extension of any lien for more than one year but may grant successive orders of extension in each successive year.

A lien which remains effective due to the filing of a notice of pendency will terminate if the notice of pendency is terminated or cancelled.[3] CPLR 6513 provides that a notice of pendency will terminate, unless extended by court order, after three years. CPLR 6514 provides for termination of a notice of pendency for various reasons, including, failure to serve a summons within the required time period, abatement, settlement or discontinuance of the action, expiration of time to appeal a judgment against the plaintiff, if a final judgment is rendered against the plaintiff has not been stayed and if the plaintiff has not commenced or prosecuted the action in good faith.

Library References:
West's Key No. Digests, Mechanics' Liens ⬅︎174–179.

§ 10.40 Duration of Lien Under Contract for a Public Improvement—Notice of Pendency

The provisions concerning the duration of liens for a contract for public improvements are similar to those concerning liens for private improvements. A lien created by the filing of a notice of lien will terminate after six months (as opposed to one year with respect to private improvements) unless the lienor has commenced an action to foreclose the lien and has filed a notice of pendency of the foreclosure action with the comptroller of the state or the financial officer of the public corporation with whom the notice of the lien was originally filed.[1]

If an action is commenced against a lienor to enforce another lien, and the plaintiff in such action or the defendant-lienor files a notice of the pendency of that action within one year of the filing of the notice of lien, the lien will survive and continue and the action is deemed to be an action to enforce the lien of the defendant lienor.

Library References:
West's Key No. Digests, Municipal Corporations ⬅︎373(4); Public Contracts ⬅︎23, 24; States ⬅︎108, 108.5.

§ 10.41 Duration of Lien Under Contract for a Public Improvement—Extension of Lien

Lien Law § 18 permits the duration of a lien on a contract for public improvements to be extended for a period of six months if an action to foreclose is not commenced in within six months of the filing of the

---

3. Lien Law § 17.

§ 10.40
1. See Lien Law § 18.

§ 10.41 MECHANIC'S LIENS Ch. 10

notice of lien.¹ The extension must be filed with the comptroller of the state or the financial officer of the public corporation with whom the notice of such lien was filed within six months The lien is then redocketed as of the date of filing the extension. The extension must contain the following information:

1. The names of the lienor and the contractor or subcontractor for whom the labor was performed or materials furnished;

2. A description of the public improvement upon which the labor was performed and materials expended;

3. The amount of the lien; and

4. The date of the original filing of the original notice of lien.

The extension will permit the lien to continue for an additional one year period. The lien will terminate if the lienor does not commence an action during the extension period to foreclose on the lien unless a court order continuing the lien is issued. If such an order is issued, the lien will be redocketed as of the date of the order with a statement that the lien is continued by virtue of such order. The court may not order the extension of any lien for more than one year but may grant successive orders of extension in each successive year.²

Library References:

West's Key No. Digests, Municipal Corporations ⚖373(4); Public Contracts ⚖23, 24; States ⚖108, 108.5.

§ 10.42 Discharge of Lien for Private Improvement—Satisfaction of Lien

Lien Law § 19 provides that a lien for private improvements may be terminated in several different manners. The most common method for removing the lien is for the lien to be satisfied and the lienor consent to the release of the lien.¹ This is accomplished by the filing of a certificate of the lienor, in the office of the county clerk in which the notice of lien creating the lien was originally filed, stating that the lien has been satisfied or released. If the lien is being released with respect to only a portion of the real property which it encumbers, the certificate must specify which portion of the property is being released. Upon the filing of the certificate, the county clerk must record the filing in the lien docket maintained by him under the column marked "Proceedings Had."

Library References:

West's Key No. Digests, Mechanics' Liens ⚖237–244.

§ 10.41
1. Lien Law § 18.
2. Lien Law § 18.

§ 10.42
1. Lien Law § 19(1).

§ 10.43 Discharge of Lien for Private Improvement—Expiration of Term

As noted above,[1] the lien will terminate if an action to foreclose upon the lien is not commenced within one year of the filing of the notice of lien and a notice of the pendency of the action to foreclose is not filed with the county clerk unless the lien has been extended pursuant to Lien Law § 17. The lien will not terminate if an action to foreclose on a mortgage or another mechanic's lien affecting the property has been filed and a notice of the pendency of the action to foreclose has been filed with the county clerk.[2]

Library References:
West's Key No. Digests, Mechanics' Liens ⟸174–179.

§ 10.44 Discharge of Lien for Private Improvement—Termination of Notice of Pendency

The termination of the effectiveness of the notice of pendency will result in the termination of the lien. As noted earlier,[1] CPLR 6513 provides that a notice of pendency will terminate, unless extended by court order, after three years and CPLR 6514 provides for termination of a notice of pendency for various reasons, including failure to serve a summons within the required time period, abatement, settlement or discontinuance of the action, expiration of time to appeal a judgment against the plaintiff, if a final judgment rendered against the plaintiff has not been stayed and if the plaintiff has not commenced or prosecuted the action in good faith.

Library References:
West's Key No. Digests, Mechanics' Liens ⟸268.

§ 10.45 Discharge of Lien for Private Improvement—Failure to Prosecute

Lien Law § 19 provides that the court may order the cancellation of a lien if the lienor fails to prosecute the action to foreclose. This would also be grounds to vacate the notice of pendency under CPLR 6514.

Library References:
West's Key No. Digests, Mechanics' Liens ⟸235, 260.

§ 10.46 Discharge of Lien for Private Improvement—Undertaking

If there is no basis for removal of the lien for any of the reasons set forth above, an owner or contractor may still have the lien removed by

§ 10.43
1. See supra, § 10.38.
2. Lien Law § 19(2).

§ 10.44
1. See supra, § 10.39.

having a surety undertake to pay the bond in the event the lienor succeeds in the action against the owner.[1] The amount of the undertaking will be decided by the court but may not be less than the amount of the lien.[2]

The statute states that the owner or contractor may bring in two sureties who are freeholders (*i.e.*, owners of real property) who must justify, *i.e.*, demonstrate to the court, their ability to pay at least double the amount named in the undertaking. The common method for removal of the lien is to engage an authorized surety or fidelity company to post a bond.

A copy of the undertaking, with notice that the sureties will establish their ability to pay the undertaking before the court at the time and place set forth in the undertaking, must be served upon the lienor or the lienor's attorney, not less than five days before such order is to be made. If, as is normally the case, a surety or fidelity company which has been issued a certificate of qualification by the superintendent of insurance is issuing a surety bond, no justification or notice of justification is required, and only a copy of the undertaking and notice of an application for an order to discharge the lien must be served by the owner or contractor upon the lienor or his attorney, not less than two days before the application for an order to discharge is made. When the undertaking is approved by the court, the court will order the lien discharged.

An authorized fidelity or surety company issuing a bond or undertaking must file a certified copy of a resolution adopted by the company's board of directors, authorizing the execution of the undertaking or bond.[3]

The lienor must be served with a copy of the undertaking and notice of justification, if applicable. If the lienor cannot be found, or does not appear by an attorney, service may be made by leaving a copy of the undertaking and notice at the lienor's place of residence if he is an individual residing in the state. If the lienor is a corporation, a copy of the undertaking and notice of justification may be served at its principal place of business within the state as stated in the notice of lien, upon a person of suitable age and discretion therein. If the lienor does not reside in New York or is a corporation whose place of business is not stated in the notice of lien and is not known, service of the undertaking and notice of justification may be effected in the manner directed by the court. The premises, if any, described in the notice of lien as the lienor's residence or place of business shall be deemed to be the lienor's place of residence or its place of business for the purposes of effecting service of the

§ 10.46
1. Lien Law § 19(4).
2. **CAVEAT:** An undertaking to remove a contractor's lien should also cover liens of subcontractors.
3. Lien Law § 19(4).

undertaking and notice unless the person serving the papers or directing the service had knowledge to the contrary.[4]

If the lienor has a mailing address outside the State of New York, service may be made by registered or certified mail, return receipt requested, to the lienor at the mailing address contained in the notice of lien.[5]

Library References:

West's Key No. Digests, Mechanics' Liens ⟐218–229.

§ 10.47 Discharge of Lien for Private Improvement—Judgment

The owner of the property may have the lien discharged by filing in the office of the clerk of the county where the property is located a copy of a final judgment of a court of competent jurisdiction deciding the action in favor of the owner, together with proof of service upon the lienor and notice of entry of the judgment.[1]

Library References:

West's Key No. Digests, Mechanics' Liens ⟐291(7).

§ 10.48 Discharge of Lien for Private Improvement—Defective Lien

The owner or any other party in interest, may apply to the court to have a lien discharged if the contents of the notice of lien itself indicate that no valid lien may exist.[1] There several ways this can happen:

1. The nature of the labor performed or materials furnished would not entitle the party claiming the lien to a lien under the Lien Law;

2. Where the notice of lien is invalid because of material non-compliance with Lien Law § 9 which governs the contents of the notice of lien. This could include a complete misdescription of the owner or the property.[2]

3. Where there has been material non-compliance with Lien Law § 10, which governs the filing of the notice of lien. This could include failure to file the notice of lien or proof of service within the statutorily required time periods.[3]

The owner must serve the lienor with a copy of the papers upon which application will be made together with a notice setting forth the

4. Lien Law § 19(4).
5. Lien Law § 19(4).

§ 10.47

1. Lien Law § 19(5).

§ 10.48

1. Lien Law § 19(6).
2. *See supra,* § 10.16.
3. *See supra,* § 10.18.

§ 10.48   MECHANIC'S LIENS   Ch. 10

court to whom the application will be made and the time and place of the hearing on not less than five days before such time. If the lienor cannot be found, service may be made as directed by the court.[4]

The application must be made upon a verified petition accompanied by written proof. If the application is approved, the court will issue an order discharging the lien.[5]

Library References:

West's Key No. Digests, Mechanics' Liens ⚖157.

§ 10.49 Discharge of Lien for Private Improvement— Deposit of Money With County Clerk or Court

Lien Law § 20 permits the discharge of a lien relating to a private improvement by the deposit of funds equal to the amount of the lien with the court.[1] If the notice of lien has been filed but an action to foreclose on the lien has not been commenced, the owner may deposit with the county clerk, in whose office the notice of lien is filed, an amount equal to the amount claimed in the notice of lien, together with interest to the time of the making of the deposit. After the funds are deposited with the county, the lien will be discharged, and the county treasurer or any other officer with whom the money is deposited must, within ten days, send a notice by mail to the lienor, at the address set forth in the notice of lien, that the lien has been discharged by deposit.[2]

If the lienor has commenced an action to foreclose the lien, the lien may still be discharged by the payment into court of the amount which the court, upon five days notice to all parties, determines is sufficient to pay any potential judgment in favor of the lienor.[3]

After any deposit of funds with the county or the court, the county clerk must enter the words "discharged by payment" into the lien docket and against the lien for which the funds were deposited. Either the lienor or the depositor may apply for a court order for the release of the deposited funds. If the application for such order is made by lienor, he must provide notice of the application to the depositor; if the application is made by the depositor then he must provide notice of the application to the lienor.

Library References:

West's Key No. Digests, Mechanics' Liens ⚖218–229.

4. Lien Law § 19(6).
5. Lien Law § 19(6).

§ 10.49
1. Lien Law § 20.

2. Lien Law § 20.
3. Lien Law § 20.

§ 10.50 Discharge of Lien for Public Improvement—Satisfaction of Lien

Lien Law § 21 provides for the discharge of liens relating to public improvements and closely resembles Lien Law § 19, which concerns the discharge of liens for private improvements.[1] Each circumstance is discussed below.

As is the case with private improvements, the most common method of discharge occurs upon payment in full of the amount of the lien, in which event the contractor or other party against whom the lien is filed may have the lien discharged by filing a certificate of the lienor or his successor in interest, duly acknowledged and approved, which states that the lien is discharged.[2]

Library References:

West's Key No. Digests, Municipal Corporations ⟸373(6); Public Contracts ⟸23, 31; States ⟸108, 108.5.

§ 10.51 Discharge of Lien for Public Improvement—Expiration of Lien

A lien may be discharged by demonstrating that the lien has expired under Lien Law § 18.[1] This would include:

1. When six months have elapsed since the filing of the notice of lien, unless, before the expiration of such six month period either:

    a. an order continuing said lien has been filed in the office where the notices are filed, or

    b. a notice of the pendency of an action to enforce the lien has been filed.

2. When the period of time for which the lien has been continued by order has expired, unless, before the expiration of the extension period either:

    a. an order continuing the lien for an additional period of time has been filed in the offices where the original notices were filed or

    b. a notice of the pendency of an action to enforce the lien has been filed.[2]

Library References:

West's Key No. Digests, Municipal Corporations ⟸373(6); Public Contracts ⟸23, 31; States ⟸108, 108.5.

§ 10.50
1. Lien Law § 20.
2. Lien Law § 21(1).

§ 10.51
1. Lien Law § 21(2).
2. Lien Law § 20(2).

§ 10.52 Discharge of Lien for Public Improvement— Satisfaction of Judgment

A lien may be discharged upon satisfaction of a judgment rendered in an action to foreclose upon the lien.[1]

Library References:

West's Key No. Digests, Municipal Corporations ⚖=373(6); Public Contracts ⚖=23, 31; States ⚖=108, 108.5.

§ 10.53 Discharge of Lien for Public Improvement— Deposit of Money

A contractor may obtain a court order for the discharge of a lien by depositing with the Comptroller of the State or the financial officer of the public corporation or the officer or person with whom the notice of lien is filed, funds in such amount as directed by the court, which shall not be less than the amount claimed by the lienor, with interest covering a period of one year from the time of making such deposit, together with any additional amount the judge or justice deems sufficient to cover costs and expenses.[1]

The effect of such a discharge of lien operates only to relieve the Comptroller of the State or the financial officer of the public corporation or the officer or person with whom the lien is filed of any liability imposed upon such officer by reason of the filing of the lien. The lien remains valid for all other purposes until otherwise discharged.[2]

Library References:

West's Key No. Digests, Municipal Corporations ⚖=373(6); Public Contracts ⚖=23, 31; States ⚖=108, 108.5.

§ 10.54 Discharge of Lien for Public Improvement— Undertaking

Lien Law § 21(5) provides that a lien for public improvements may also be discharged by an undertaking or posting of a bond by a surety. The contractor or subcontractor must execute the undertaking with two or more sufficient sureties, who shall be freeholders, or an authorized surety or fidelity company, to the state or the public corporation with which the notice of lien is filed, in such amount as the court thereof may direct, which may not be less than the amount claimed in the notice of lien.[1] The rules concerning justification and service of notice of justifica-

§ 10.52

1. Lien Law § 21(3). See Borges, et al., *Enforcing Judgments and Collecting Debts in New York* (West 1997) Ch.11 "Satisfaction of Judgments."

§ 10.53

1. Lien Law § 21(4).

2. Lien Law § 21(3–a).

§ 10.54

1. Lien Law § 21(5).

tion are identical to those contained in Section 19(4) with respect to private improvements.[2] The provisions of CPLR Article 25 and Justice Court Act § 18 are applicable to an undertaking given for the discharge of a lien on account of public improvements.

Library References:

West's Key No. Digests, Municipal Corporations ⚖︎373(6); Public Contracts ⚖︎23, 31; States ⚖︎108, 108.5.

§ 10.55 Discharge of Lien for Public Improvement— Retention of Credit

If a contractor has a credit with the state or with a public corporation which is withheld because a notice of lien has been filed against his interest in such funds, and the amount of the credit exceeds the amount of the lien, the contractor may apply without notice to the court for an order discharging the lien and directing the Comptroller of the State or the financial officer or person with whom the lien is filed, to retain from the credit which is be less than the amount claimed by the lienor, with interest thereon for one year, together with any additional amount the court deems necessary to cover all costs and expenses, and to immediately pay over the balance of such funds to the contractor. The amount so retained shall be held by the Comptroller or such financial officer or other officer or person until the lien is otherwise discharged as provided in this section. The application for the order to discharge the lien and release the balance of the credit may be made upon an affidavit of the contractor or his attorney. If an assignment of rights to such funds has been filed, the assignee must appear before the court and make its case.[1]

If an estimated amount is due to the contractor by the state or public corporation, and the amount of the estimate exceeds the amount of the lien by at least one and one-half times, the Comptroller of the State or the financial officer or person with whom the notice of lien is filed, may pay the estimated amount due to the contractor, after deducting an amount equal to one and one-half times the amount stated to be due in the notice of lien. The amount deducted is then withheld until the lien is otherwise discharged.[2]

Library References:

West's Key No. Digests, Municipal Corporations ⚖︎373(6); Public Contracts ⚖︎23, 31; States ⚖︎108, 108.5.

§ 10.56 Discharge of Lien for Public Improvement— Invalidity of Lien

Where the notice of lien on its face is not valid, the contractor may

2. *See supra*, § 10.42.

§ 10.55
1. Lien Law § 21(6).

2. Lien Law § 21(6–a).

§ 10.56   MECHANIC'S LIENS   Ch. 10

seek a court order to discharge the lien.[1] This would occur where:

    1. The character of the labor or materials furnished and for which a lien is claimed as stated in the notice of lien is not sufficient for creation of a valid lien; or

    2. Where the notice of lien is invalid because it does not contain the information required by Lien Law § 12, or has not been filed within the time period prescribed in Lien Law § 12 or otherwise does not comply with the requirements of such law.[2]

Library References:

    West's Key No. Digests, Municipal Corporations ⇐373(6); Public Contracts ⇐23, 31; States ⇐108, 108.5.

§ 10.57   Discharge of Lien for Public Improvement— Failure to Prosecute

The court may vacate or cancel a lien of record if the lienor fails to prosecute the action for foreclosure of the lien.[1]

Library References:

    West's Key No. Digests, Municipal Corporations ⇐373(6); Public Contracts ⇐23, 31; States ⇐108, 108.5.

§ 10.58   Discharge of Lien for Public Improvement— Procedures

In order to obtain an order of the court to vacate or cancel a lien for a public improvement, the following procedures should be followed:

    1. A notice requiring the lienor to commence an action to enforce the lien must be personally served upon the lienor or in such other manner as the court may direct, within not less than 30 days, or to show cause why the notice of lien should not be cancelled.

    2. Proof of service of the notice to commence action upon the lienor must also be filed with the court, as well proof that an action to foreclose the lien must be filed at the time the application for the court order is filed.[1]

Library References:

    West's Key No. Digests, Municipal Corporations ⇐373(6); Public Contracts ⇐23, 31; States ⇐108, 108.5.

§ 10.56
1. Lien Law § 21(7).
2. Lien Law § 21(7).

§ 10.57
1. Lien Law § 21(8).

§ 10.58
1. *See* Lien Law § 21-a.

§ 10.59 Building Loan Contracts—Filing Requirements

Another document which can be recorded under the Lien Law and which may be accorded priority over a mechanic's lien is the building loan contract.[1] As noted above, a building loan contract, regardless of when it was recorded, will have priority over a mechanic's lien to the extent of advances made before the filing of the notice of lien, provided the building loan contract contains a covenant that all advances received by the borrower under the contract will be held in trust and applied first for the payment of the cost of improvements.[2] If the building loan contract is not filed in accordance with Lien Law § 22, any lien created by the filing of any notice of lien prior to the filing of the building loan contract will have priority over the building loan contract.

The Lien Law requires building loan contracts to be filed to prevent secret arrangements between lenders and owners or contractors and enable materialmen and laborers to determine the amounts of funds available to owners and contractors for the payment of supplies and services.[3] The recorded contract also alerts contractors that they furnish materials and labor subject to claims against the property which are superior to their own.[4]

The building loan contract must be filed in the office of the county clerk of the county in which the property on which the improvements are to be made is located before the building loan mortgage made in connection with the contract is recorded.

Unless the county clerk maintains a block index, all building loan contracts and modifications of building loan contracts must be indexed in a book provided for that purpose, in the alphabetical order of the names of borrowers. If the county clerk indexes liens in a block index, each building loan contract presented for filing must indicate the number of every block, on the land map of the county, which is affected by the building loan contract. The county clerk must then enter the building loan contract in the block index, under the block number of every block so designated.

Library References:

West's Key No. Digests, Mortgages ⟺151(3), 163(3), 166–176.

§ 10.60 Building Loan Contracts—Checklist

A duly recorded building loan contract must meet the following requirements:

---

§ 10.59

1. The filing of building loan contracts is governed by Lien Law § 22.
2. Lien Law § 13(3). *See supra*, §§ 10.26–10.28.
3. *See* Nanuet National Bank v. Eckerson Terrance, Inc., 47 N.Y.2d 243, 417 N.Y.S.2d 901, 391 N.E.2d 983 (1979); In re Lynch III Properties Corp., 125 B.R. 857 (E.D.N.Y.1991).
4. *See* Osinoff v. Queens Apartments, Inc., 10 Misc.2d 762, 173 N.Y.S.2d 225 (Sup.Ct., Queens County, 1958).

§ 10.60 MECHANIC'S LIENS Ch. 10

1. It must be in writing.

2. It must be verified by the borrower under oath.

3. It must be acknowledged.

4. It must state the amount of the loan, of all expenses incurred in connection with the loan and the net sum available to the borrower for the improvements.

5. It must contain the lien covenant contained in Lien Law § 13.

6. It must be filed in the office of the clerk of the county in which the land on which the improvements are to be made is located.

7. It must be filed before the building mortgage is recorded.

8. Any modification of the building loan contract must be filed within ten days after the execution of the modification. A modification will not have retroactive effect and cannot impair existing rights of third parties.

9. A 25 dollar filing fee is payable, except in counties within the City of New York where the fee is 50 dollars.

10. If the county in which the building loan contract is to be filed utilizes the block indexing system, the contract must indicate the property's block number.[1] (See § 10.59)

§ 10.61 Subordination of Liens—Agreement With Owner

The Lien Law provides a method for the subordination of mechanic's liens to subsequently recorded trust mortgages and to mortgagor filed assignments of funds due under building loan contracts.[1] The purpose of this law and similar provisions is to facilitate new funding for a construction project by insuring the lender priority over a class of existing lien holder, i.e., the holders of mechanic's liens, provided a majority of the class consents to such priority. Such subordination may be desirable in order to complete a project which is in distress. Under the statute, if the holders of fifty-five percent of the aggregate amount of all liens filed prior to or within fifteen days of the recording of a mortgage or filing of an assignment of moneys due under a building contract approve such mortgage or assignment, all mechanic's liens which had been previously filed will be subordinated to the mortgage note or the assignment. A duly acknowledged written instrument of approval must be filed in the office of the county clerk to effectuate the subordination.

§ 10.60

1. Lien Law § 22.

§ 10.61

1. Lien Law § 26.

The mortgagee under the trust mortgage or assignee under the assignment will act as a trustee, and must advance funds under the trust mortgage or assignment for the completion of the improvements.[2]

It should be noted that under Lien Law § 33, the subordination provisions of Lien Law § 26 do not apply to laborers or materialmen for daily or weekly wages, who retain their priority status.[3]

Library References:
West's Key No. Digests, Mechanics' Liens ⟜194–201.

§ 10.62 Subordination of Liens—Agreement With Owner—Postponement of Judgments

The subordination of mechanic's liens to a newly filed trust mortgage or assignment of moneys due under a contract will also subordinate existing money judgments and attachments.[1] Judgment liens which, however, do not relate to claims for materials provided, labor performed or money loaned for the improvement of the property will be subordinated to all mechanic's liens and any judgments relating to such claims.[2]

Lien Law § 33 provides that the subordination provisions of Lien Law § 28 do not apply to judgments of laborers or materialmen for daily or weekly wages, who retain their priority status.

Library References:
West's Key No. Digests, Mechanics' Liens ⟜194–201.

§ 10.63 Subordination of Liens to Subsequent Mortgage

Section 29 of the Lien Law contains a subordination provision similar to that of Lien Law § 26.[1] Instead of the holders of fifty-five percent of the aggregate amount of liens approving the trust mortgage or assignment and agreeing to subordinate all mechanic's liens to the lien of the mortgage or assignment as provided in Lien Law § 26, Lien Law § 29 provides for the holders to designate one or more representatives to approve a new mortgage and bond and subordinate existing mechanic's liens, whether or not a notice of lien has been filed, to the lien of such mortgage.

The consent of the representatives must be in writing, acknowledged and filed with the county clerk, together with a written instrument designating the representatives. The representatives may condition their

2. Clio Realty Corp. v. Heflam Building Corp., 227 App.Div. 439, 238 N.Y.S. 127 (2d Dep't 1929).

3. Lien Law § 33.

§ 10.62

1. *See* Lien Law § 28.

2. *See also* Corbin–Kellogg Agency v. Tasker, 248 App.Div. 58, 289 N.Y.S. 156 (3d Dep't 1936).

§ 10.63

1. Lien Law § 29.

§ 10.63 MECHANIC'S LIENS Ch. 10

consent upon the deposit of funds with the county clerk. The amount of any such deposit is entered in the lien docket.[2]

As is the case under Lien Law § 26, the subordination by the representatives of the holders of mechanic's liens effects a subordination of existing judgments and attachments to the lien of the mortgage. Judgment liens which, however, do not relate to claims for materials provided, labor performed or money loaned for the improvement of the property will be subordinated to all mechanic's liens and any judgments relating to such claims.[3]

Lien Law § 33 provides that the subordination provisions of Lien Law § 29 do not apply to liens or judgments of laborers or materialmen for daily or weekly wages, who retain their priority status.

Library References:
West's Key No. Digests, Mortgages ⬄151(3), 163(3).

§ 10.64 Subordination of Notices of *Lis Pendens*

A subordination of mechanic's lien and judgments to the lien of a subsequent mortgage and bond or assignment of contract rights also effects a subordination of all actions and notices of pendency of actions in any proceeding to foreclose on a mechanic's lien and all proceedings to enforce a judgment will be subordinated in the same manner as mechanic's liens are subordinated under Lien Law §§ 26, 28 and 29.[1]

Library References:
West's Key No. Digests, Mechanics' Liens ⬄194–201, 268.

§ 10.65 Discharge of Liens on Sale of Real Property

The ability of the holders of fifty-five percent or more of the aggregate amount of liens filed against a property to designate a representative to consent to the subordination of existing mechanic's liens to the lien of a subsequent mortgage extends to the sale of the property by the owner.[1] Lien Law § 31 permits such holders to designate one or more representatives by a written acknowledged instrument who may consent in a written acknowledged instrument to the sale of the property of the owner free and clear of existing liens. Such instruments of designation and consent are to be filed in the office of the county clerk in which the property is located. The representatives may condition their consent on the deposit of funds with the county clerk in which event the liens on the property will be transferred to the deposit. The facts concerning the deposit are entered by the county clerk in the lien docket

2. Lien Law § 29.
3. Lien Law § 29.

§ 10.64
1. *See* Lien Law § 31.

§ 10.65
1. *See* Lien Law § 31.

maintained by him. The consent may be conditioned upon the transfer of other real or personal property to trustees who are to transfer any sums realized upon such property to the county clerk to be added to the deposit.[2]

The funds deposited with the county clerk are to be awarded to successful lienors in actions to foreclose upon their liens. Remaining funds are to be returned to the owner selling the property.

The subordination of liens under § 31 is similar to that under Lien Law §§ 26, 28 and 29. All mechanic's liens are on a parity. Judgments relating to actions to foreclose a lien for materials provided or labor performed or moneys advanced in connection with an improvement of the property are treated as mechanic's liens. Judgments which do not relate to materials provided or labor performed or moneys advanced in connection with an improvement of the property are subordinated to mechanic's liens. Liens of materialmen or laborers for daily or weekly wages are not discharged by the consent of the designated representative of the lien holder.

Library References:

West's Key No. Digests, Mechanics' Liens ⚷233.

§ 10.66 Limitations on Waiver of Mechanic's Lien

Lien Law § 34 prohibits any contract from requiring a party to waive its rights to file or enforce a mechanic's lien. A contract may require a party to waive the right to file a mechanic's lien simultaneously with or after payment. A party is permitted to subordinate, release or satisfy all or a portion of the lien after the notice of lien has been filed.[1]

Library References:

West's Key No. Digests, Mechanics' Liens ⚷207–217.

§ 10.67 Effect of Filing of Notice of Lien on Right of Arbitration

The filing of a notice of lien does not affect any rights of arbitration which a party may have under a contract to provide materials or perform labor in connection with the improvement of property. An award by arbitrators in an arbitration proceeding conducted in accordance with a contractual right will be binding and conclusive in any action to foreclose on the lien.[1]

2. *See* Lien Law § 31.

§ 10.66
1. Lien Law § 34.

§ 10.67
1. Lien Law § 35.

§ 10.68 Bond to Discharge Liens—Effect of Bond

An owner or the contractor with whom the owner has contracted may, at any time, post a bond with the clerk of the county in which real property is to be improved in an amount determined by the court but in no event less than the unpaid amount under the contract, which provides for payment of any judgment in an action to foreclose on a mechanic's lien with respect to the improvement.[1] The bond must be issued by a fidelity or surety company authorized to do business in the State of New York which has received a certificate of solvency from the Superintendent of Insurance.[2] A bond issued by an insurance company which cannot demonstrate that it has received the Superintendent's certificate will not be approved by the court.[3]

Upon approval of the bond by the court, the court will order existing liens of contractors, subcontractors, materialmen and laborers on the property discharged.[4] The filing of the bond will also release the owner from complying with any demand for terms of the contract as required by Lien Law § 8.

Library References:

West's Key No. Digests, Mechanics' Liens ⚖═226.

§ 10.69 Bond to Discharge Liens—Requirements of Bond

Any bond must be executed by the owner or contractor, as the case may be, principal and by the fidelity or surety company, as surety, and contain the following information:

1. The name of the owner;
2. The name of the contractor;
3. The name of the surety company;
4. The date and amount of the contract; and
5. A description of the real property upon which the improvement is to be made, is being made, or has been made. A description which is adequate for a notice of lien is sufficient.[1]

---

§ 10.68
1. Lien Law § 37(1).
2. See Lien Law § 37(2).
3. See Timal v. Kiamzon, 164 Misc.2d 159, 623 N.Y.S.2d 1016 (Sup.Ct., Queens County, 1995).
4. See Lien Law § 37(4).

§ 10.69
1. See Lien Law § 37(3).

Library References:
West's Key No. Digests, Mechanics' Liens ⇔223.

§ 10.70 Bond to Discharge Liens—Claim Against Bond

The claim of a contractor, subcontractor, laborer or materialman who performs labor or furnishes materials in connection with the contract described in the bond will attach against the bond for the principal amount of the claim plus interest or the amount agreed to by the parties.[1] Claims of materialmen for materials produced but not delivered are included.[2] Claimants must file a notice of claim with the clerk of the county in which the bond is filed. The notice must be filed within the period prescribed for the filing of a notice of lien, *i.e.*,

(a) at any time during the progress of the work and the furnishing of the materials; or

(b) within four months (for a single family dwelling) after the completion of the contract, or the final performance of the work, or the final furnishing of the materials, dating from the last item of work performed or materials furnished.[3]

An action on the bond to enforce the notice of claim may be brought in any court in which an action to foreclose on a notice of lien could be commenced.

Information concerning notices of claims and actions to enforce such claims are maintained in a lien bond docket maintained by the clerk of the county in which the notice of claim is filed.[4]

Library References:
West's Key No. Digests, Mechanics' Liens ⇔227, 228.

§ 10.71 Bond to Discharge Liens—Notice of Claim

A notice of claim against a bond must be verified and contain the following information:

(1) the name and residence of the claimant if the claimant is an individual and, if the claimant is a partnership or a corporation, the claimant's business address, the names of partners and principal place of business, and if claimant is a foreign corporation, its principal place of business within the state of New York;

(2) the names of the owner, contractor and surety named in the bond;

---

§ 10.70
1. *See* Lien Law § 37(5).
2. In contrast to claims for liens for public improvements which may not include materials not utilized in the improvements. *See supra*, § 10.21.
3. *See* Lien Law § 10 discussed at § 10.17, supra.
4. For particulars *see* Lien Law § 37(10).

(3) the name of the person who employed the claimant to whom the claimant furnished or is to furnish materials;

(4) the labor performed or materials furnished (which would include materials manufactured for but not delivered to the real property) and the agreed price or value of such materials or services;

(5) the amount unpaid to the claimant for the labor performed or materials provided or manufactured;

(6) a description of the real property.[1]

Library References:

West's Key No. Digests, Mechanics' Liens ⚖227, 228.

§ 10.72 Bond to Discharge Liens—Action on Bond

An action upon a bond must be commenced within one year after the improvement is completed or within two years after the last item of work was performed or the last item of materials was furnished by the claimant if the work was abandoned. As is the case with respect to actions to enforce a notice of lien,[1] commencement of an action by one claimant is deemed a bringing of the action by every claimant who is made a defendant in the action.[2]

The following is necessary in order to commence an action on a bond:

1. The plaintiff must first file the summons and complaint in the office of the clerk of the county where the bond is filed;

2. The summons and complaint must join as parties defendant, the principal and surety on the bond, the contractor, and all other claimants who have filed notices of claim prior to the date of the filing of such summons and complaint. A claimant who files his notice of claim on or after the date of filing of the summons and complaint may be brought into the action by amendment at any time up to and including the time and in the manner and under the conditions that a lienor who files his notice of claim may be brought into an action to foreclose a lien pursuant as provided on Lien Law § 62.[3]

The court has the power to adjust and determine the equities of all the parties to any action on a bond. If the defendant makes a counter-

§ 10.71

1. Lien Law § 37(6) also provides that: the notice of claim shall be verified by the claimant or his agent in the form required for the verification of notices in section nine.

§ 10.72

1. *See* Lien Law § 17 discussed at § 10.43, *supra*.
2. *See* Lien Law § 37(9).
3. *See* Lien Law § 37(9).

claim in the action he will be deemed to have waived a trial by jury with respect to any issues raised by the counterclaim.[4]

Library References:

West's Key No. Digests, Mechanics' Liens ⚖228.

§ 10.73 Bond to Discharge Liens—Discharge of Liens and Notices of Claims

Notices of liens filed by persons whose liens where discharged by the posting of a bond will be discharged by the court upon application by the owner together with proof that the bond secures the payment of the claim described in the notice of lien. The owner must serve a copy of the application together with a copy of the bond at least two days before the hearing.[1]

A notice of claim will be discharged under the following circumstances:

> (1) By the filing with the county clerk of a duly acknowledged certificate of the claimant stating that the claim has been satisfied and may be discharged; or

> (2) If the claimant fails to begin an action on the bond within the time provided in Lien Law § 37(9).[2]

Library References:

West's Key No. Digests, Mechanics' Liens ⚖218–229.

§ 10.74 Protecting the Owner—Itemized Statement

An owner or contractor may demand that a party who has filed a notice of lien provide a verified statement in writing listing the items of labor or services which are the subject of the lien, the value of such items and the terms of the contract under which those item were furnished. If the lienor does not comply with such request within five days, the owner or contractor, as the case may be, may, upon two days notice which is personally served upon the lienor, petition the court for an order directing the lienor to provide the statement. If the lienor is personally served with an order to supply the itemized statement and fails to do so statement within five days after such service, the court may order the lien cancelled.[1]

Library References:

West's Key No. Digests, Mechanics' Liens ⚖149.

4. *See* Lien Law § 37(8).

§ 10.73
1. *See* Lien Law § 37(11).
2. *See* Lien Law § 37(12).

§ 10.74
1. *See* Lien Law § 37(12).

§ 10.75 Protecting the Owner—Lien Wilfully Exaggerated

If the court determines in any action that the lienor has wilfully exaggerated his mechanic's lien, regardless of whether a private or public improvement is concerned, the lien will be declared void.[1] As noted above, an amendment to a notice of lien reducing the amount of a lien will not protect a lienor if the amount claimed in the original notice of lien was wilfully exaggerated. Once a lien is discharged for wilful exaggeration it may not be refiled and any notice of lien subsequently with respect to such claim may be discharged upon application to the court with two days notice.

It should be noted that wilful exaggeration does not encompass honest differences in contract interpretation.[2] The burden of proof in proving wilful exaggeration is on the owner.[3]

As an additional protection for owners against wilful exaggeration of claims in notices of claims, the owner or contractor, as the case may be, against whom the claim was made is entitled to damages equal to the premium of any bond posted to discharge the lien, attorneys's fees incurred in obtaining the discharge of the lien and an amount equal to the difference of the amount claimed and the amount to which the lienor was actually entitled.[4]

It should be noted that a finding of wilful exaggeration will not prevent the plaintiff from recovering a judgment for the value of work actually performed.[5]

Library References:
West's Key No. Digests, Mechanics' Liens ⚖︎157(3).

§ 10.76 Repossession of Materials Not Used

A contractor or subcontractor who has not been paid in full for work performed for a private or public improvement may repossess and remove unused materials he has provided from the property. Repossession shall restore his title to the materials and he will have no lien or claim against the property for the value of such materials. Although as a general rule a contractor's right of repossession is not affected by the subsequent sale, encumbrance, attachment, or transfer from the work site of the improvement itself, a purchaser or encumbrancer of the

---

§ 10.75

1. See Lien Law § 38.
2. See Howdy Jones Construction Co., Inc. v. Parklaw Realty, Inc., 76 A.D.2d 1018, 429 N.Y.S.2d 768 (1980), aff'd 53 N.Y.2d 718, 439 N.Y.S.2d 354, 421 N.E.2d 846 (1981).
3. Schenectady Homes Corporation v. Greenside Painting Corporation, 37 N.Y.S.2d 53 (County Ct., Schenectady County, 1942).
4. See Lien Law § 39–a.
5. Grimpel v. Hochman, 74 Misc.2d 39, 343 N.Y.S.2d 507 (Civ.Ct., N.Y. County, 1972).

material in good faith whose interest arose after the transfer from the site of the improvement or a creditor attaching the materials after the transfer will have priority over the right to repossess the materials. A party's right to repossession and removal does not extend to materials whose purchase price exceeds the amount due to him. However, if materials have been partly paid for, they may only be repossessed if the portion of the purchase price previously paid (less the cost of removal) is refunded.[1]

Library References:

West's Key No. Digests, Mechanics' Liens ⚖48.

§ 10.77 Enforcement of Mechanic's Liens—Courts

A lienor may bring an action to prove his claim and enforce his mechanic's lien on the real property against which the lien is filed and against the person who contracted with the lienor and is liable for the underlying debt which is the basis for the lien.[1] Similarly, a lien for labor performed or materials provided for a public improvement may be enforced against both the funds of the state or the public corporation for which the public improvement is undertaken as well as against the contractor or subcontractor who contracted with the lienor.[2] The action may be maintained in the supreme court, a county court which has jurisdiction, without regard to the amount of the debt, or in a court which would have jurisdiction in a contract action for an amount equal to the amount of the debt.

Library References:

West's Key No. Digests, Mechanics' Liens ⚖258.

§ 10.78 Enforcement of Mechanic's Liens—Courts of Record—Procedures

The procedures governing actions to enforce a mechanic's lien in a court of record,[1] are the same as those governing the foreclosure of a mortgage upon real property and the application of the proceeds of the

§ 10.76
1. See Lien Law § 39–c.

§ 10.77
1. See Lien Law § 41.
2. See Lien Law § 42.

§ 10.78
1. Courts of record are listed in Judiciary Law § 2 and include the Court of Appeals, the appellate division of the supreme court, the supreme court, all county courts (other than counties located in the City of New York), family courts, surrogate's courts, all city courts (other than New York City) and the civil and criminal courts of the City of New York. Courts of record have inherent powers, not dependant upon statute, to take any action reasonably necessary for the administration of justice within the scope of their jurisdiction. See Gabrelian v. Gabrelian, 108 A.D.2d 445, 489 N.Y.S.2d 914 (2d Dep't 1985), appeal dism'd 66 N.Y.2d 741, 497 N.Y.S.2d 365, 488 N.E.2d 111 (1985).

sale of the property.[2] In addition, if actions to foreclose upon mechanic's liens against the same property (in the case of a lien for private improvements), or the same contract fund (with respect to a lien for public improvements), the court in which the first action was filed may upon its own motion or the motion of any party to any of the actions, consolidate all of the actions.[3]

A lienor may bring an action to prove his claim and enforce his mechanic's lien against the real property against which the lien is filed and against the person who contracted with the lienor and is liable for the underlying debt which is the basis for the lien. Similarly, a lien for labor performed or materials provided for a public improvement may be enforced against both the funds of the state or the public corporation for which the public improvement is undertaken as well as against the contractor or subcontractor who contracted with the lienor. If actions to foreclose upon mechanic's liens are brought against the same property, in the case of a lien for private improvements, or the same contract fund, with respect to a lien for public improvements, the court in which the first action was filed may either upon its own motion or the motion of any party to the actions, consolidate all of the actions.

Library References:
West's Key No. Digests, Mechanics' Liens ⇌245–310(4).

§ 10.79 Enforcement of Mechanic's Liens—Courts of Record—Necessary Parties

In any action in a court of record to enforce a mechanic's lien against real property or a public improvement, the following must be made defendants:

    1. All lienors who have filed notices of lien against the same real property or public improvement, prior to the filing of the notice of *lis pendens* in the action to enforce the lien. This would include other subcontractors and materialmen;[1]

    2. All persons having liens or claims against such real property, by judgment, mortgage or otherwise which have been filed, docketed or recorded prior to the filing of the *lis pendens* in the action to enforce the lien. This would include mortgagees and judgment creditors;[2]

    3. All record owners of the property. This would include all co-owners including tenants-in-common, joint tenants and, in the case of tenancy by the entirety, both the husband and spouse;[3]

2. *See* Lien Law § 43. *See generally,* Chapter 11, "Mortgage Foreclosure," *infra* for a discussion of the New York Real Property Actions and Procedures Law.

3. *See* Lien Law § 43.

§ 10.79
1. Lien Law § 44(1).
2. Lien Law § 44(2).
3. Lien Law § 44(3).

4. If, by law, a *lis pendens* may not be filed in an action, all lienors having liens against the real property which is the subject of the action provided notices of such liens have been filed against the same property, and all persons having subsequent liens or claims against the property, whether by judgment, mortgage or otherwise;[4]

5. The State of New York, if the lien is a lien for public improvement and has been filed against funds of the state. Service of the State is effected by service upon the attorney-general.[5]

Similarly, in a mortgage foreclosure action, persons who have filed notices of lien prior to the filing of the *lis pendens* in the foreclosure action are also necessary parties to such an action.[6]

Every defendant in an action to foreclose on a lien who is a lienor must, in his answer, set forth his lien, or he will be deemed to have waived his lien unless the lien is admitted in the complaint, and not contested by any another defendant. The allegations in the answer of a defendant lienor are deemed denied by the other lienors in the action without the necessity of serving replies. If two or more lienors who have filed notices of liens against the same real property or public improvement, they may join in the action as plaintiffs.[7]

In deciding the action, the court may adjust and determine the equities of all the parties to the action and the order of priority of different liens, and determine all issues raised by any defense or counterclaim in the action. However, only the Court of Claims may decide upon an issue between the state and the contractor.[8]

It should be noted that any defendant who files a counterclaim will be deemed to have waived his right to a trial by jury of the issues raised in the counterclaim.[9]

Library References:

West's Key No. Digests, Mechanics' Liens ⚖=261–264.1.

§ 10.80 Enforcement of Mechanic's Liens—Actions in a Court Not of Record—Summons and Complaint

An action to foreclose a lien commenced in a court which is not a court record is commenced in the same manner as if it were commenced in a court of record. A verified summons and complaint is served by personal service upon the owner of the real property verified in the same manner as a complaint in an action in a court of record. The complaint

4. Lien Law § 44(4).
5. Lien Law § 44(6).
6. *See* Lien Law § 44–a.
7. Lien Law § 44(6).
8. Lien Law § 45.
9. *Id.*

§ 10.80   MECHANIC'S LIENS   Ch. 10

must contain substantially the same facts as are set forth in the notice of lien, and the substance of the agreement under which labor was performed or materials were provided. The form and contents of the summons are the same as those of a summons and complaint to begin a contract action in the same court. The summons must be returnable not less than twelve nor more than 20 days after the date of the summons. If service is of the summons is made by publication, the summons is returnable after the last publication of the summons. Service must be made at least eight days before the return date.[1]

If the plaintiff lienor is unable to effect personal service of the summons on a defendant in an action in a court not of record, because the defendant has left the state, service of the summons may be effected by leaving a copy at the defendant's last place of residence and by publishing a copy of the summons once a week for three successive weeks in a newspaper in the city or county where the property which is the subject of the suit is situated.[2]

Library References:

West's Key No. Digests, Mechanics' Liens ⚖═265, 271.

§ 10.81   Enforcement of Mechanic's Liens—Actions in a Court Not of Record—Proceedings Upon Return of Summons

If the action is commenced in a court not of record, then, on the return date set forth in the summons, the defendant must file a verified answer, containing a general denial of each allegation of the complaint, a specific denial of one or more of the material allegations contained in the complaint or any other matter which would constitute a defense to the lien or to the claim upon which the lien is founded. Judgment may be rendered for the amount claimed, together with costs, against a defendant who fails to appear on the return date, on proof by affidavit of the service of the summons and complaint on the defendant.[1]

If issue is joined in an action to foreclose upon a lien in a court not of record, it must be tried in the same manner as any other issues in that court. A judgment may be entered for the plaintiff or for the defendant in the same manner as in an action on contract in such court.[2]

If judgment is entered on behalf of a lienor plaintiff, execution may be issued upon the judgment in an action to enforce a mechanic's lien against real property in a court not of record, which shall direct the officer to sell the title and interest of the owner in the property upon which the lien set forth in the complaint existed at the time of filing the

§ 10.80
1. See Lien Law § 46.
2. Lien Law § 47.

§ 10.81
1. Lien Law § 48.
2. Lien Law § 49.

notice of lien. Execution may be issued upon a judgment obtained in an action to enforce a mechanic's lien against real property in a court not of record, which shall direct the officer to sell the title and interest of the owner in the premises, upon which the lien set forth in the complaint existed at the time of filing the notice of lien.[3]

Library References:

West's Key No. Digests, Mechanics' Liens ⌾245–310(4).

§ 10.82 Enforcement of Mechanic's Liens—Actions in a Court Not of Record—Judgments and Transcripts

A party who wishes to appeal a judgment which is rendered in a court not of record, may do so in accordance with the laws regulating appeals from judgments in actions on contract in such courts.[1]

On the entry of a judgment in a court not of record, the justice or judge of the court in which it is tried, or other person authorized to furnish transcripts of judgments shall furnish the successful party a transcript of the proceedings which he may then file with the clerk of the county with whom the notice of lien is filed. The filing of the transcript has the same effect as the filing of a transcript of any other judgment rendered in such courts.[2]

Library References:

West's Key No. Digests, Mechanics' Liens ⌾291.

§ 10.83 Enforcement of Mechanic's Liens—Costs and Disbursements

A court of record has the discretion to award costs and disbursements to the prevailing party in an action to enforce a mechanic's lien against real property.[1] A court of not record may award costs and disbursements (including any expenses incurred in service of summons by publication pursuant to Lien Law § 47) to the extent costs may be awarded in other civil actions commenced in such court.[2]

Library References:

West's Key No. Digests, Mechanics' Liens ⌾310.

§ 10.84 Enforcement of Mechanic's Liens—Effect of Failure to Establish Lien

As discussed above, the right to sue on the contract creating the debt obligation is independent from the right to a lien on the property

---

3. Lien Law § 50.

§ 10.82
1. See Lien Law § 51.
2. See Lien Law § 51.

§ 10.83
1. See Lien Law § 53.
2. See Lien Law § 53.

§ 10.84   MECHANIC'S LIENS   Ch. 10

itself. Thus, a contractor or other party who normally would be entitled to a mechanic's lien but fails to file his notice of lien or commence an action to foreclose upon the lien within the statutory periods will not be deprived of the right to bring a separate action based upon the contract for the improvement. Similarly, the failure of a lienor to establish a valid lien in an action to foreclose upon a lien will not prevent him from recovering for the obligation due under the contract.[1]

Library References:
West's Key No. Digests, Mechanics' Liens ⚖=291(7), 303.

§ 10.85   Enforcement of Mechanic's Liens—Deposit of Money or Securities to Discharge Lien— Procedures

Section 20 of the Lien Law provides for the discharge of a lien at any time upon the deposit of money with the court or county clerk. A related provision, Lien Law § 55, provides for the discharge of a lien once an action has been commenced upon the deposit of money or securities with the court.

The procedures for discharging a lien by deposit under Lien Law § 55 are simpler than those under Lien Law § 20. The owner must take the following steps:

    1. Make an offer to pay into court the sum of money stated in the notice of lien or deposit securities which should be described in the offer, to discharge the lien.[1]

    2. If the action is in a court of record, file the offer with the clerk with whom the notice of lien which is the subject of the action is filed.

    3. If the action is in a court not of record, file the offer with the court.

    4. Serve the plaintiff with a copy of the offer.

    5. If the owner receives a written acceptance of the offer from the plaintiff-lienor, the written acceptance must be filed with the clerk, or the court, as the case may be, within ten days after it was serviced.

    6. A copy of the acceptance of the offer must be served upon the owner.

    7. The court may then order that upon the depositing with such clerk, or court, as the case may be, of the sum offered or the

---

§ 10.84

1. *See* Lien Law § 54; *see also* Lien Law § 64 which provides that the court has the power to award monetary judgments and well as other judgments.

§ 10.85

1. Lien Law § 55.

securities described in the offer, that the lien be discharged, and attach instead to the money or securities deposited.[2]

Library References:

West's Key No. Digests, Mechanics' Liens ⚙=218–229.

§ 10.86 Enforcement of Mechanic's Liens—Deposit of Money or Securities to Discharge Lien—Effect of Order

If the owner's offer is to deposit money only and not securities, the court, on application by the owner and notice to the plaintiff-lienor may discharge the lien and attach it to the money deposited even without the acceptance of the offer by the plaintiff.[1]

If the action is brought in a court not of record, the deposit may be issued by the county court of the county where the action is brought upon notice.[2]

Upon the filing of the order to discharge the lien and the deposit of the funds or securities with the county clerk of such county, the clerk must discharge the notice of lien, by noting in the lien docket in writing on the margin of the record, the words "discharged by payment."[3] Any money or securities deposited upon the acceptance of an offer will be held by the clerk or the court until the final determination of the action, including an appeal.[4]

Library References:

West's Key No. Digests, Mechanics' Liens ⚙=218–229.

§ 10.87 Enforcement of Mechanic's Liens—Deposit of Money or Securities to Discharge Lien—Preference Over Contractors

As noted earlier, under Lien Law § 13 (concerning private improvements) and Lien § 25 (concerning public improvements) mechanic's liens are on a parity with one another.[1] However, this is not entirely the case, because a person who has performed services or provided materials for which he is entitled to a lien, is entitled to payment from the proceeds of the sale of the property before any payment is made to the person for whom he performed the services or provided the materials.[2]

When more than one notice of lien is filed by different parties for the same claim, such as when a contractor has filed a notice of lien for

2. Lien Law § 55.

§ 10.86
1. Lien Law § 55.
2. Lien Law § 55.
3. Lien Law § 55.
4. Lien Law § 55.

§ 10.87
1. *See supra* discussions at § 10.26 and § 10.34.
2. *See* Lien Law § 56.

§ 10.87 MECHANIC'S LIENS Ch. 10

his workman or subcontractor, and the workman or subcontractor have filed their own notices of lien, the judgment will provide for the payment of only one of the claims to the party entitled to it, *i.e.*, the workman or subcontractor.[3]

A voluntary payment by an owner with respect to the lien of one claimant will not affect the lien of another party.[4] Thus, it is essential that any settlement of the claims of a contractor provide for the settlement of claims of those providing labor or materials to the contractor or any of his subcontractors.

Library References:

West's Key No. Digests, Mechanics' Liens ⚖218–229.

§ 10.88 Enforcement of Mechanic's Liens—Delivery of Property in Lieu of Money

A judgment may provide that an owner and lienor may agree upon the owner's delivery of notes, bills, securities or other property to the court in satisfaction of the debt. The judgment may also bar the sale of the property unless the owner delivers the agreed property to the court in the time specified.[1]

Library References:

West's Key No. Digests, Mechanics' Liens ⚖218–229.

§ 10.89 Enforcement of Mechanic's Liens—Deficiency Judgment

As is the case in mortgage foreclosure actions, if the proceeds of the sale of the property are not sufficient to satisfy the plaintiff-lienor's claim, a deficiency judgment may be entered against the person liable for such claim.[1] In order to obtain a deficiency judgment, the plaintiff lienor must comply with the requirements of Real Property Actions and Proceedings Law § 1371 concerning deficiency judgments, including the ninety-day limitation period.[2]

---

3. *See* Lien Law § 56, which provides: If several notices of lien are filed for the same claim, as where the contractor has filed a notice of lien, for the services of his workmen, and the workmen have also filed notices of lien, the judgment shall provide for but one payment of the claim which shall be paid to the parties entitled thereto.

4. *See* Lien Law § 56, which provides: Payment voluntarily made upon any claim filed as a lien shall not impair or diminish the lien of any person except the person to whom the payment was made.

§ 10.88

1. *See* Lien Law § 57.

§ 10.89

1. *See* Lien Law § 59.

2. Silpin Plumbing Corp. v. A Builders Corp., 190 Misc. 598, 75 N.Y.S.2d 681 (Sup. Ct., Kings County, 1947); *see* Chapter 11, "Mortgage Foreclosure," *infra*.

§ 10.90 Enforcement of Mechanic's Liens—Vacating of Mechanic's Lien, Cancellation of Bond or Return of Deposit

An owner may serve the holder of a mechanic's lien with a notice requiring him to either commence an action to enforce the lien within not less than 30 days from the date of service or show cause why the notice of lien should not be vacated, deposit returned or bond cancelled, as the case may be.[1] The application of the owner must include proof of service of the notice and order to show cause and an affidavit that the lienor has not commenced an action to foreclose on the lien.[2] Service may be made personally or by leaving it at the lienor's last known address with a person of suitable age and discretion with directions to give it to the lienor.[3] If an action to enforce the lien is not commenced within the period prescribed in the notice, the court, in its discretion, may vacate the lien.[4]

Library References:

West's Key No. Digests, Mechanics' Liens ⟐160, 218–229.

§ 10.91 Enforcement of Mechanic's Liens—Public Improvements

When a judgment is rendered in an action to enforce a lien with respect to services rendered or materials furnished in connection with a public improvement, the judgment will direct the state or public corporation to make payments to the lienors to the extent of their claims against the contractor provided such amounts not exceed the amounts due the contractor.[1] The court has no power to enter an award in excess of amounts owed by the state or the public corporation to the contractor.[2]

If a claim can be filed against the state in the Court of Claims or the state alleges that the contractor is in breach of his contract, the court's judgment may only determine the validity of the liens and their amount.[3]

Library References:

West's Key No. Digests, Municipal Corporations ⟐373(7); Public Contracts ⟐23, 32; States ⟐108, 108.5.

§ 10.90

1. See Lien Law § 59.
2. Lien Law § 59.
3. See Lien Law § 59.
4. Application of Lasa Corp., 27 Misc.2d 495, 203 N.Y.S.2d 731 (Sup.Ct., Queens County, 1960).

§ 10.91

1. See Lien Law § 60.
2. Smith v. State, 65 Misc. 376, 118 N.Y.S. 780 (Sup.Ct, N.Y.County, 1909).
3. See Lien Law § 60.

§ 10.92 Enforcement of Mechanic's Liens—New Parties

As noted above, Lien Law § 44[1] states that all parties who have filed notices of lien are necessary parties in any action to foreclose on a mechanic's lien. Lien Law § 62 complements that section, first, by permitting any lienor who files a notice of lien after an action to foreclose on a lien has been commenced to become a party to the foreclosure action, unless the trial in the action has already commenced.[2] Second, any other party to the existing action may move the court to have such party brought into the action.[3]

An order joining such additional party will have the following provisions:

1. It will provide for time and manner of service of the new party's pleadings;

2. Will deem all prior pleadings amended and that the allegations of the new party be deemed denied by all other parties to the action.[4]

The addition of the new party is not, to the extent possible, to cause any substantial delay in the pending proceedings.[5]

Library References:
West's Key No. Digests, Mechanics' Liens ⚖=261–264.1.

§ 10.93 Enforcement of Mechanic's Liens—Service of Answer on State or Public Corporation

In an action to foreclose upon a lien with respect to labor performed or material provided in connection with a public improvement, the defendants in the action are required to serve copies of their answer within forty days after service of the complaint, upon the state, the public corporation, or, with respect to the City of New York, the Corporation Counsel.[1]

Library References:
West's Key No. Digests, Municipal Corporations ⚖=373(7); Public Contracts ⚖=23, 32; States ⚖=108, 108.5.

§ 10.94 Trust Funds—Purpose

Article 3–A of the New York Lien Law provides for the creation of a trust out of certain construction payments or other funds to insure

---

§ 10.92

1. *See* Lien Law § 60. *See supra*, discussion at § 10.79 concerning necessary parties.
2. *See* Lien Law § 62.
3. *See* Lien Law § 62.
4. Lien Law § 62.
5. *See* Lien Law § 62.

§ 10.93

1. Lien Law § 63.

payment of subcontractors, materialmen, laborers, and architects and other expenses related to construction.[1] The statute was intended to prevent an owner or general contractor from retaining construction loan proceeds for their own benefit[2] by designating such funds as trust funds and imposing a fiduciary relationship and responsibility upon the owner or contractor receiving such funds.[3]

The Lien Law provides that the following funds shall constitute assets of the Trust:

1. Funds received by an owner for or in connection with an improvement of real property, including a home improvement loan;

2. Funds received by a contractor under or in connection with a contract for an improvement of real property, or home improvement,

3. Funds received by a contractor under a contract for a public improvement;

4. Funds received by a subcontractor under or in connection with a subcontract made with the contractor for such improvement of real property including a home improvement contract or public improvement;

5. Funds received by a subcontractor under or in connection with a subcontract for the improvement of real property made with any subcontractor; and

6. Any right of action for any such funds due or earned or to become due or earned.[4]

The trustee is vested with the responsibility and the authority for the proper application of trust finds.[5]

Library References:
West's Key No. Digests, Mechanics' Liens ⚖︎115.

§ 10.95 Trust Funds—Creation

The trust fund is created any time an asset which would be a trust asset comes into existence, even if no lienors exist at such time. The trust continues and the owner's fiduciary obligations continue until all trust claims arising at any time during the improvement have been paid

---

§ 10.94
1. Caristo Const. Corp. v. Diners Financial Corp., 21 N.Y.2d 507, 289 N.Y.S.2d 175, 236 N.E.2d 461 (1968).
2. In re Grosso, 9 B.R. 815 (Bankr. N.D.N.Y.1981).
3. Eminon Acoustical Contractors Corp. v. Richkill Associates, Inc., 89 Misc.2d 992, 392 N.Y.S.2d 1007 (Sup.Ct., Queens County, 1977); Cadin Construction Corp. v. Adam Jay Associates, 86 Misc.2d 407, 382 N.Y.S.2d 671 (Sup.Ct., Nassau County, 1976).
4. Lien Law § 70(1).
5. *See* Lien Law § 74.

§ 10.95 MECHANIC'S LIENS Ch. 10

or the trust assets have been dissipated. A contractor's or subcontractor's fiduciary obligations continue with respect to all trust claims arising prior to completion of the contract or subcontract until they have been paid or all trust assets have been dissipated.[1]

The following funds received by the owner of property which is being improved will be deemed to be trust funds:

1. Funds received under a building loan contract;

2. Funds received under a building loan mortgage or a home improvement loan;

3. Funds received under a mortgage recorded after commencement of the improvement and before the expiration of four months after completion of the improvement;

4. Funds received as consideration for a conveyance recorded after commencement of the improvement and before the expiration of four months after the completion of the improvement;

5. Funds received as consideration for, or advances secured by, an assignment of rents due or to become due under an existing or future lease or tenancy of the property being improved if the assignment is executed after the commencement of the improvement and before the expiration of four months after the completion of the improvement;

6. Funds received as consideration for or advances secured by an assignment of rents executed before the commencement of the improvement and an express promise to make an improvement, or an express representation that an improvement will be made, is contained in the assignment or given in the transaction in which the assignment is made;

7. Funds received as proceeds of any insurance payable because of the destruction of the improvement or its removal by fire or other casualty, except for amounts equal to premiums paid for the insurance which are payable to the owner; and

8. Funds received under an executory contract for the sale of real property and the improvement thereof by the construction of a building thereon.[2]

Library References:

West's Key No. Digests, Mechanics' Liens ⚖115.

§ 10.96 Trust Funds—Contractors and Subcontractors

With respect to a contractor, the following funds received by a contractor in connection with an improvement are deemed to be trust funds:

§ 10.95
1. Lien Law § 70(3).

2. Lien Law § 70(5). See also Lien Law § 71–a.

1. Funds received under the contract for the improvement of real property, or home improvement or the public improvement;

2. Funds received under an assignment of funds due or earned or to become due or earned under such contract; and

3. Funds received as proceeds of any insurance payable because of destruction of the improvement of real property including a home improvement or public improvement or its removal by fire or other casualty, except for amounts equal to premiums paid by the contractor which are retained by the contractor.[1]

The following funds paid to a subcontractor in connection with the improvement of real property are deemed to be trust funds:

1. Funds received under the subcontract;

2. Funds received under an assignment or order for the payment of moneys due or earned or to become due or earned under the subcontract; and

3. The proceeds of any insurance payable because of the destruction of the improvement of real property or public improvement or its removal by fire or other casualty, except for amounts equal to premiums paid by the subcontractor which may be retained by him.[2]

Library References:

West's Key No. Digests, Mechanics' Liens ⇔115.

§ 10.97 Trust Funds—Beneficiaries

The owner of any property being improved is required to apply all trust funds received by him towards payment of the cost of the improvements.[1] Trust claims for which the owner is obligated under the trust include claims of contractors, subcontractors, architects, engineers, surveyors, laborers and materialmen arising out of the improvement, and other costs of improvement of the property.[2]

Contractors or subcontractors holding trust funds must apply such funds for the following:

1. Payment of claims of subcontractors, architects, engineers, surveyors, laborers and materialmen;

2. Payment of payroll taxes for such persons required to be withheld and sales taxes for materials or equipment required to be installed or furnished in connection with the performance of the improvement;

§ 10.96
1. Lien Law § 70(6).
2. Lien Law § 71(7).

§ 10.97
1. Lien Law § 71(1).
2. Lien Law § 71(3)(a).

609

3. Payment of taxes and unemployment insurance and other contributions due by reason of the employment out of which such claims arose;

4. Payment of any benefits or wage supplements, or the amounts necessary to provide such benefits or furnish such supplements, to the extent that the trustee, as employer, is obligated to pay or provide such benefits or furnish such supplements by any agreement to which he is a party;

5. Payment of premiums on a surety bond or bonds filed and premiums on insurance accrued during the making of the improvement, including home improvement, or public improvement; and

6. Payment to which the owner is entitled.[3]

Trust beneficiaries do not have to have a lien or become lienors to possess or retain trust claims.[4]

Library References:

West's Key No. Digests, Mechanics' Liens ⚖115.

§ 10.98 Diversion of Trust Assets

Trust assets may only be used for the purposes set forth in the statute. Accordingly, they may not be levied upon or subject to restraining notices as the individual property of the trustee. Further the trustee has a fiduciary duty to defend the trust *res* against any attempt to improperly apply such funds. Both the trustee and any trust beneficiary may intervene in any action or proceeding to defend the trust against misapplication of such funds.[1] A trustee's failure to maintain records of use of trust funds is presumptive evidence of diversion of such funds.[2] While a purchaser in good faith for value without notice that the transfer of trust funds is a diversion of trust assets acquires good title to such assets, if the acquiror receives the property with knowledge that such transfer is in violation of the trust, the assets may be reclaimed by the trustee or the trust beneficiaries.[3]

Library References:

West's Key No. Digests, Mechanics' Liens ⚖115.

§ 10.99 Notice of Lending

The Lien Law provides for the filing of a Notice of Lending with the county clerk, in the case of improvement of private property and or with

---

3. Lien Law § 71(2).
4. Lien Law § 71(4); *See* Harman v. Fairview Associates, 25 N.Y.2d 101, 302 N.Y.S.2d 791, 250 N.E.2d 209 (1969).

§ 10.98
1. Lien Law § 72.

2. Schwadron v. Freund, 69 Misc.2d 342, 329 N.Y.S.2d 945 (Sup.Ct., Rockland County, 1972).

3. *See, e.g.*, Canron Corp. v. City of New York, 89 N.Y.2d 147, 652 N.Y.S.2d 211, 674 N.E.2d 1117 (1996).

the head of the department or bureau having charge of a public improvement and the financial officer of the public corporation charged with disbursing funds under the contract. A filed Notice of Lending will protect a lender who receives funds in repayment of a loan or as security for a loan from claims that the payments constituted a diversion of trust assets.[1] The lender must require the owner or contractor, as the case may be, to hold the loan proceeds as trust funds for the payment of trust claims.

A Notice of Lending is effective with respect to advances made on or after the day of filing or not more than five days before the date of filing. The notice must contain the following information:

(1) The name and address of the person making the advances,

(2) The name and address of the person to whom or on whose behalf the advances are made, and whether he is owner, contractor or subcontractor,

(3) In the case of advances relating to one specific project for the improvement of real property including a home improvement or one specific public improvement, a description, sufficient for identification, of the improvement and of the real property involved for which the advances are made, and in the case of a notice of lending relating to several or undetermined projects for the improvement of real property including a home improvement or for public improvements, a statement of each county in which the real property is or may be situated,

(4) The date of any advance made on or before the date of filing for which the notice is intended to be effective,

(5) In the case of a notice of lending relating to several or undetermined projects, the date the notice will terminate, which termination date shall not be more than two years after the date the notice of lending is filed, and

(6) The maximum balance of advances outstanding to be permitted by the lender pursuant to the notice.[2]

Real property is deemed to be specifically identified if it includes the name of the record owner and the location of the real estate by street and number and town or city or, if the real estate is in the City of New York, by county, except that if the real estate is in the City of New York or counties of Nassau or Onondaga, where the block system of recording or registering and indexing conveyances is in use, the notice of lending must state the block in which the real estate is located.[3]

§ 10.99

1. Fleck v. Perla, 40 A.D.2d 1069, 339 N.Y.S.2d 246 (4th Dep't 1972)

2. Lien Law § 73.

3. Lien Law § 73(3)(a).

§ 10.99   MECHANIC'S LIENS   Ch. 10

A "Notice of Lending" may be continued in effect for advances made beyond the termination date set forth in the notice by filing a "Second Notice of Lending" or "Third Notice of Lending," which identifies the prior notice to which it relates. The new notice of lending must be filed within 60 days prior to the termination date set forth in the original notice of lending. If a Notice of Lending is amended to increase the maximum balance of advances outstanding to be permitted by the lender, it is effective with respect to the increased amount only with respect to advances made not more than five days before the date of filing the amended notice.[4]

A trust beneficiary may demand a verified statement of all advances actually made by the lender to the trustee. The demand must be made in writing and served either by personal service or by registered or certified mail. Failure to comply with such demand will remove the protections afforded by the notice of lien.[5]

Library References:

West's Key No. Digests, Mechanics' Liens ⚖115.

§ 10.100 Record Keeping Obligations

A trustee who deposits trust funds in a bank or other depositary must deposit the funds in his own name. Trust funds may be deposited in a single bank account provided the trustee books of account shall clearly show the allocation to each trust of the funds deposited in his bank account or accounts.[1]

A trustee is obligated to keep books or records with respect to each trust of which he is trustee. If funds of separate trusts are deposited in the same bank account, he must keep a record of the account showing the allocation to each trust of the deposits and withdrawals made with respect to such trusts.[2]

The books or records with respect to each trust created under the Lien Law must contain the following information:[3]

    a. With respect to trust assets receivable:

        (1) The name and address of each person from whom the trustee has or will have a right to receive funds which will constitute trust assets, with a statement sufficient to identify the contract or other transaction by reason of which the funds will become payable;

4. Lien Law § 73(3)(c).
5. Lien Law § 73(4).

2. Lien Law § 75.
3. Lien Law § 75.

§ 10.100
1. Lien Law § 75.

(2) the amount of each payment or advance from each such person that has become due or earned or is otherwise payable; and

(3) the date upon which the payment became due, earned or payable.

b. With respect to trust accounts payable:

(1) The name and address of each person possessing a trust claim, whether or not such claim is then due, with a statement identifying the contract or transaction out of which the trust claim arises;

(2) the amount of each trust claim that has become due, earned or otherwise payable; and

(3) the date upon which the trust claim became due, earned or payable.

c. With respect to trust funds received:

(1) The name and address of each person from whom funds constituting trust assets have been received and the form of payment (*i.e.*, cash, check or other instrument for the payment of money, bank credit or drawing account, etc.) including any instrument made payable to a trust beneficiary or any moneys paid directly to a trust beneficiary on behalf of the trustee, with a description of the form in which the funds were received;

(2) the date on which each payment or remittance from such person was received;

(3) the amount received on such date; and

(4) if such funds are deposited in a bank or other depositary, the name and address of the bank or depositary in which the deposit was made.

d. With respect to payments made with trust assets:

(1) The name and address of each person to whom a payment has been made, with moneys or other assets constituting trust assets, including payments made directly to such person on behalf of the trustee by a person from whom trust assets are receivable;

(2) the date when and place where each payment was made;

(3) the amount paid on each of such dates and a statement whether the payment was made in cash or by check and the manner of payment if made by some other person on behalf of the trustee;

(4) with respect to each payment, a description of the trust claim or if the owner is the trustee, the nature of the expendi-

ture if other than payment of a trust claim, for which the payment is made. The description must identify the payment as a payment for a trust purpose and show for what trust purpose it was expended (*i.e.*, labor, materials, taxes, insurance, performance under contract or subcontract, interest charges on mortgages, or other particular trust claim or item of cost of improvement);

(5) if the payment was made pursuant to a contract between the trustee and the recipient of the payment, the date when the contract was made, whether it was oral or in writing, and the agreed price between the parties;

(6) if a payment relates to a particular item or items of the improvement, or if any such payment for materials or services relates to materials furnished, or services (other than daily or weekly labor), rendered with respect to a particular item or items of the improvement, a description of such item or items;

(7) if a payment was made with funds received under an assignment of funds due or earned or to become due or earned under the contract or subcontract, a statement of the amount of such funds so used together with the name and address of the assignee and the date of the assignment.

e. With respect to transfers of trust assets in repayment of or to secure advances made pursuant to a "Notice of Lending:"

(1) the name and address of the person to whom the asset was transferred;

(2) the date of the transfer;

(3) a description of the asset transferred;

(4) the amount of the transfer;

(5) the amount of the consideration for the transfer or of the advances secured or repaid thereby;

(6) the date or dates when the consideration was paid or the advances were made and the manner in which the payment or advance was made.[4]

A trustee's failure to maintain records of use of trust funds is presumptive evidence of diversion of trust funds.[5]

Library References:

West's Key No. Digests, Mechanics' Liens ⚖115.

4. Lien Law § 75.

5. Lien Law § 75(4). *See also* Schwadron v. Freund, 69 Misc.2d 342, 329 N.Y.S.2d 945 (Sup.Ct., Rockland County, 1972).

§ 10.101 Right of Beneficiaries to Examine Books or Records

All trust beneficiaries are entitled, upon request, after the expiration of 30 days from the date his trust claim became payable, and thereafter not more than once a month, (a) to examine the books or records of the trustee with respect to the trust, and make copies of any part or parts thereof relating to the trust; or (b) at the beneficiary's option to receive a verified statement setting forth the entries with respect to the trust contained in such books or records.[1]

Any request for such examination of records relating to the trust and to make such copies, or for such verified statement, must be made by the beneficiary in writing served personally or by registered or certified mail.[2] The request must contain:

1. A statement of the name and address of the beneficiary,

2. A description of the improvement of real property, or home improvement, or the public improvement sufficient to identify it and to identify the trust, and

3. A statement of the nature of the trust claim sufficient to identify it, the amount then due and unpaid, and the due date thereof.[3]

Unless otherwise agreed to by the beneficiary, the examination and copying must be permitted within ten days after service of the request, at a place within the county in which the improvement, or home improvement, or public improvement is located, designated by the trustee within such ten days, and at a time during usual business hours, so designated by the trustee. The examination and copying may be made by the beneficiary or by his duly authorized agent in writing.[4]

Within ten days after service of a request for a verified statement, the trustee must serve the beneficiary with a statement, subscribed by the trustee or an officer thereof and verified on his own knowledge, setting forth the entries with respect to the trust contained in the books or records kept by the trustee and the names and addresses of the person or persons who, on behalf of or as officer, director or agent of the trustee, made or consented to the making of the payments shown in such statement.[5]

If the trustee believes that the persons requesting information concerning the trust are not entitled to such information, he may apply to any court having jurisdiction of an action to enforce the trust, to vacate the request. If a trustee refuses or fails to comply with a request for examination or copying within ten days of the request, or applies for

---

§ 10.101
1. Lien Law § 76.
2. Lien Law § 76.
3. Lien Law § 76.
4. Lien Law § 76.
5. Lien Law § 76.

§ 10.101   MECHANIC'S LIENS   Ch. 10

a court order to vacate the request, the beneficiary may apply for an order directing the trustee to comply with the request. Any such application must be made on at least three days' notice and may be determined summarily upon affidavits of the parties.[6]

Library References:

West's Key No. Digests, Mechanics' Liens ⚖115.

§ 10.102   Action to Enforce Trust—Standing and Procedure

Both the trustee and any trust beneficiary may bring an action to enforce the trust.[1] If the action is brought by a beneficiary it must be brought in a representative action on behalf of all trust beneficiaries.[2] Although the rules governing class actions under CPLR 908 apply to representative actions on behalf of trust beneficiaries, the court has the discretion to waive the requirements of CPLR 908(a)(1) in determining whether a class action may be maintained.[3] Of course, the action need not be brought in a representative capacity if there is only one trust beneficiary.[4]

An action to enforce a trust may be brought at any time while the property is being improved and thereafter but no later than one year after the improvement has been completed or, with respect to subcontractors or materialmen, after the expiration of one year from the date on which final payment under the claimant's contract became due, whichever is later. A trustee may bring an action after the one year period for a final settlement and discharge, in which event, claimants will be entitled to enforce their claims.[5] Successive actions may be maintained from time to time during the improvement provided no other action to enforce the trust is pending.[6]

Library References:

West's Key No. Digests, Mechanics' Liens ⚖115.

§ 10.103   Action to Enforce Trust—Remedies

The court may grant various types of relief to a party seeking to enforce a trust, including the following:

---

6. Lien Law § 76.

§ 10.102

1. Under Lien Law § 77(6) the court may direct that trust claims shown upon a schedule or schedules filed by the trustee shall be deemed to have been filed in the action.

2. Imperial Plumbing & Heating Corp. v. Stratford Development Corp., 26 Misc.2d 815, 208 N.Y.S.2d 174 (Sup.Ct., Nassau County, 1960).

3. See Lien Law § 77(1).

4. In re Westchester Structures, Inc., 181 B.R. 730 (Bankr.S.D.N.Y.1995).

5. Harman v. Fairview Associates, 25 N.Y.2d 101, 302 N.Y.S.2d 791, 250 N.E.2d 209 (1969).

6. Id.

Ch. 10 ACTION TO ENFORCE TRUST—REMEDIES § 10.103

1. To compel an interim or final accounting by the trustee;

2. To identify and recover trust assets in the hands of any person together with interest accruing from the time of the diversion;[1]

3. To set aside as a diversion any unauthorized payment, assignment or other transfer of trust assets to any party, whether voluntary or involuntary;

4. To enjoin a diversion of trust assets;

5. To recover damages for breach of trust;

6. To enforce on behalf of the trust any right of action constituting a trust asset;

7. To determine the existence and amount of any trust asset or of any trust claim;

8. To terminate or limit the authority of the trustee in the application of trust assets or of any trust asset or direct the time and manner of application of a trust asset;

9. To require the trustee to give security to ensure the proper distribution of the trust assets, either during the pendency of the action or thereafter, or to furnish assurance of such proper distribution, if it appears that there is danger that any trust asset will be dissipated before judgment or diverted from trust purposes;

10. To order distribution of any trust asset available for distribution, or for retention of particular trust assets for future distribution. Where the holder of any trust assets is a trustee or a transferee who received the assets with the knowledge that they were trust funds, any order for distribution and retention for future distribution of any trust assets shall include the amount of the funds plus interest from the time of the diversion to the date of the order;

11. To settle the interim or final account of the trustee;

12. To grant final discharge of the trustee at the termination of the trust, or discharge of the trustee with respect to the application of specific trust assets; and

13. To grant such other and further relief as to the court may seem necessary and proper.[2]

Where applicable, the relief granted by the court will be for the benefit of all trust beneficiaries. Unless the court directs otherwise, an order for distribution of trust assets shall be only for the benefit of persons who are trust beneficiaries at the time of entry of the judgment

---

§ 10.103

1. "Interest shall be computed at the rate equal to the underpayment rate set by the commissioner of taxation and finance pursuant to subsection (e) of section one thousand ninety-six of the tax law ..." Lien Law § 77(1).

2. Lien Law § 77(3)(a).

§ 10.103   MECHANIC'S LIENS   Ch. 10

whose claims are due and payable on the date set for distribution and either are undisputed by the trustee or have been determined in the action.[3]

If an action to enforce a trust of which the owner is trustee is commenced before the completion or abandonment of the improvement or, in an action to enforce a trust of which a contractor or subcontractor is trustee, the action is commenced before the completion or abandonment of the performance by the trustee under the contract or subcontract, the judgment shall provide for distribution of the assets then available for distribution among trust beneficiaries whose claims are then payable, and who have appeared in the action or who file their claims within such time as the court shall direct, unless the court shall determine that under the circumstances equity requires that the distribution of trust assets be deferred until other trust claims mature.[4]

If an action to enforce a trust of which a contractor or subcontractor is trustee is brought after the completion or abandonment of the performance of the contract or subcontract but before the improvement has been completed, the court may order that the action be continued until additional trust assets may become available.[5]

As is the case with respect to other class actions brought under CPLR 908, an action brought to enforce a trust shall not be compromised or discontinued nor dismissed by consent, by default or for failure to prosecute, except with the approval of the court. On any application for such approval notice shall be given in such manner as the court shall direct.[6]

Library References:

West's Key No. Digests, Mechanics' Liens ⚖115.

§ 10.104   Actions to Enforce Trust—Preferences

As a general rule, in any distribution of trust assets pursuant to order or judgment in an action to enforce a trust, the following classes of trust claims shall have preference, in the following order:

    1. Trust claims for taxes and for unemployment insurance and other contributions, due by reason of employments, and for amounts of taxes withheld or required to be withheld;

    2. Trust claims of laborers for daily or weekly wages;

    3. Trust claims for benefits and wage supplements;

    4. Trust claims for any amounts of wages of laborers (other than claims for amounts of taxes deducted and withheld, which are already trust claims as provided above) which were actually deduct-

---

3. Lien Law § 77(3)(b).
4. Lien Law § 77(4).
5. Lien Law § 77(5).
6. Lien Law § 77(7).

ed from payments to the laborer under law or agreement, for payment to a party on behalf of the laborer or in satisfaction of an obligation of the laborer, to the extent that such person is entitled to assert, as a trust claim, the claim the laborer would otherwise have had for such amount.[1]

Library References:

West's Key No. Digests, Mechanics' Liens ⚛︎115.

§ 10.105 Relief After Judgment on Obligation Constituting Trust Claim; Effect on Mechanic's Liens

If a trust beneficiary obtains a judgment against the trustee with respect to an obligation which constitutes the trust claim, he may not obtain a lien against any trust asset and, if a trust asset is to be affected by an action to enforce the judgment, the action will be deemed to be for the benefit of all other trust beneficiaries who are entitled at that time to maintain an action to enforce the trust.[1] The Lien Law's provisions concerning trust funds are not intended to affect the rights of holders of mechanic's liens. Consequently, the holder of a mechanic's lien may seek to enforce his lien for his sole benefit.[2] A payment in satisfaction of a mechanic's lien from trust assets will not be deemed to be a diversion of trust assets.[3] The claims of trust beneficiaries are junior to the claims of the holders of mechanic's liens.[4] In determining a trust beneficiary's share of a distribution of trust assets, the amount of the beneficiary's trust claim is not reduced by the amount of any lien to which he is entitled or any bond to which he is entitled because of his lien.

Library References:

West's Key No. Digests, Mechanics' Liens ⚛︎115.

§ 10.106 Misappropriation of Trust Funds

A trustee of a trust who is an owner who utilizes trust funds for his own benefit before payment of all trust claims is guilty of larceny and punishable as provided in the Penal Law. Similarly, a contractor or subcontractor who is the trustee of a trust who fails to pay from trust assets in his possession any trust claim within 31 days of the time payment is due will also be guilty of larceny.[1]

§ 10.104
1. Lien Law § 77.

§ 10.105
1. Lien Law § 78.
2. Lien Law §§ 78–79.
3. Lien Law § 79.

4. Ingalls Iron Works Co. v. Fehlhaber Corp., 337 F.Supp. 1085 (S.D.N.Y.1972).

§ 10.106
1. Lien Law § 79–a(1).

§ 10.106

There are certain exceptions to the foregoing. Thus, a contractor or subcontractor who is a trustee who disputes in good faith the existence, validity or amount of a trust claim or disputes that it is due, or in good faith disputes the application of trust funds for a purpose other than a trust purpose, will not be guilty of larceny for failure to pay such disputed claims, provided he makes any required payment within 31 days of the final determination of such dispute.[2]

Use of trust funds for repayment to another person of advances made by such person to the trustee or on his behalf as trustee where the advances were actually applied for the legitimate trust purposes of the trust is permissible. If the trustee himself made advances for trust purposes, he is permitted to be repaid for such advances or to apply trust assets for non-trust purposes up to the amount of such advances.[3]

As previously noted, a trustee's failure to keep the books or records of the trust as required by law, will be presumptive evidence that the trustee has applied or consented to the application of trust funds for other than legitimate trust purposes.[4] It should be noted that even if a deed, mortgage, building loan contract or assignment of contract contains the trust fund provisions required by law,[5] a trustee who is in compliance with Lien Law § 79-a will not be deemed to have committed larceny as a result of his application of trust assets.

Library References:

West's Key No. Digests, Mechanics' Liens ⟳115.

§ 10.107 Procedural Checklist

This section will summarize for the practitioner the steps in obtaining and enforcing a mechanic's lien in connection with the improvement of private property with cross references to more detailed coverage in the text.

1. Determine that the client falls within the type of class entitled to a lien. (See § 10.5)

2. Determine whether the client performed labor for or provide materials or otherwise provided the type of services covered by the statute. (See § 10.5)

3. Determine that the property was improved within the meaning of the statute. (See § 10.6)

4. Determine that the owner consented to the improvement. (See § 10.7)

---

2. Lien Law § 79-a(1).
3. Lien Law § 79-a(2).
4. Lien Law § 79-a(3). See supra, § 10.98.
5. See supra, §§ 10.27–10.31.

5. Determine whether the project is continuing or, if it has been completed, that fewer than eight months (four months for a single family dwelling) have elapsed since completion and acceptance. (*See* § 10.17)

6. Make certain that the notice of lien complies with all the requirements of the statute. (*See* § 10.16)

7. Have the notice of lien verified and file the original verified notice. (*See* § 10.16)

8. File the notice of lien with the county clerk in each county in which the property is located. (*See* § 10.17)

9. Serve copies of the notice of lien by certified mail on the contractor (if applicable) and the owner. (*See* § 10.18)

10. File proof of service upon the owner and the contractor simultaneously with the filing of the notice of lien. (*See* § 10.18)

11. If the client is a subcontractor, materialman or laborer, make a demand for terms of the contract. (*See* § 10.14)

12. If the lien is about to expire and a notice of pendency has not been filed, file an extension with the county clerk. (*See* § 10.39)

13. If a suit to enforce the lien has been commenced, file a notice of pendency with the clerk. (*See* § 10.38)

14. A verified summons and complaint must be served to commence an action to enforce a lien in both a Court of Record or a Court which is not of Record. (*See* §§ 10.78, 10.80)

15. Make certain that all necessary parties have been brought into the action. (*See* § 10.79).

§ 10.108 Forms

The following are representative forms which may be utilized in various actions concerning mechanic's liens. For additional forms with commentary, see *West's Forms*, Real Property Actions and Procedures Law, Article 7.

§ 10.109 Forms—Notice of Mechanic's Lien—General Form

TO THE CLERK OF THE COUNTY OF _____, STATE OF NEW YORK AND ALL OTHERS WHOM IT MAY CONCERN.

PLEASE TAKE NOTICE, that (1) _____, residing at _____, in the County of _____, State of New York, has and claims a lien for the principal and interest of the price and value of the labor and material hereinafter mentioned, upon the house, building and appurtenances, and upon the lot, premises and parcel of land upon which the same may stand, or be intended to stand, hereinafter mentioned, pursuant to the Lien Law of the State of New York and all acts amending or extending the same or providing for the filing of mechanic's liens; or in force in said County in reference to mechanic's liens; and hereby states:

(2) The name of said lienor's attorney is _____, of _____, New York.

(3) The name of the owner of the real property against whose interest therein a lien is claimed is _____ of _____, New York, and the interest of the owner as far as known to the lienor is owner in fee [or state other interest].

(4) The name of the person by whom the lienor was employed is _____. The name of the person to whom the lienor furnished or is to furnish materials is _____. The name of the person with whom the contract was made is _____.

(5) The labor performed was [specify labor performed]. The material furnished was [specify material furnished]. The material actually manufactured for but not delivered is [specify] and The agreed price and value of the labor performed is $_____. The agreed price and value of the material furnished is $_____. The agreed price and value of the material actually manufactured for _____ but not delivered is $_____. Total agreed price and value is $_____.

(6) The amount unpaid to the lienor for said labor performed is $_____. The amount unpaid to the lienor for material furnished is $_____. The amount unpaid to the lienor for the material actually manufactured for but not delivered is _____. Total amount unpaid is $_____. The total amount claimed for which this lien is filed is $_____.

(7) The time when the first items of work were performed was _____, 19__; and the time when the first items of material were furnished was _____, 19__.

The time when the last items of work were performed was _____, 19__; and the time when the last items of materials were furnished was _____, 19__.

(8) [Insert description of property subject to lien in conformity with Lien Law s 9, subd. 7].

(9) That said labor and materials were performed and furnished for and used in the improvement of the real property hereinbefore described.

(10) That four months have not elapsed dating from the last item of work performed, and dating from the last items of materials furnished, nor since the completion of the contract nor since the final performance of the work, nor since the final furnishing of the materials for which this lien is claimed.

Dated: _____, N.Y.,
           _____, 19__.

———————————————
Lienor

[*Verification*]

§ 10.110 Forms—Notice of Lien for Public Improvement

To the Comptroller of the City of _____, New York, and the Commissioner of _____ of the City of _____, New York.

PLEASE TAKE NOTICE, and the undersigned hereby states: that _____ Inc. whose business address and principal place of business is at _____, New York has and claims a lien in the principal and interest of the value and price of the labor and materials hereinafter mentioned upon the moneys of such municipal corporation applicable to the construction of the public improvement hereinafter mentioned, to the extent of the amount due or to become due in and on the contract with said municipal corporation hereinafter described, and hereby further state:

1. The name of the contractor for whom the labor was performed and materials furnished is _____ Corp. of _____ New York, contractor with the City of _____, owner.

2. The amount due the lienor is _____ ($_____) Dollars. The amount to become due the lienor is _____ ($_____) Dollars, the total amount claimed for which this lien is filed is _____ ($_____) Dollars and the date when due is _____, 19__.

3. A description of the public improvement upon which the labor was performed and materials expended is as follows: construction of _____, N.Y.

4. The kind of labor performed and materials furnished is as follows: [*specify labor performed and materials furnished*.]

5. The kind of materials actually manufactured for but not delivered to said public improvement is as follows: [*specify*.]

6. A general description of the contract pursuant to which such public improvement was constructed is as follows: Contract between _____ Corp. and the City of _____ provided that _____ Corp. would provide all labor and material to furnish and install all concrete building foundations, floors and arches, etc., on the above specified public improvement.

7. This notice is filed pursuant to the Lien Law of the State of New York, and all acts of the Legislature of the State of New York amending or extending the same, or providing for filing liens on account of public improvements. The labor and materials aforesaid were performed and furnished for the construction of said public improvement pursuant to said contract with said municipal corporation.

§ 10.110   MECHANIC'S LIENS   Ch. 10

8. Thirty days have not elapsed since the completion and acceptance of the construction of said public improvement.

Dated: _____, N.Y.,

_____, 19__.

―――――――――――

By _____

[Verification]

§ 10.111   Forms—Form for Demand for Terms of Contract

To: _____, Owner

_____, New York

PLEASE TAKE NOTICE, that the undersigned, _____ [insert name of subcontractor, laborer or materialman], pursuant to the provisions of Lien Law § 8, hereby demands that you furnish to him a statement of the terms of your contract with _____ [insert name of contractor] for the improvement of the following described real property in the City of _____, New York owned by you, and the amount due or to become due thereon:

[insert brief description of property].

The undersigned, on the _____ day of _____, 19__, entered into a contract with the said _____ [contractor] to furnish materials [or perform labor] in connection with the said contract between you and _____ [contractor].

Dated: _____, N.Y.,

_____, 19__.

―――――――――――
Subcontractor
[or Laborer
or Materialman
P.O. Address]

§ 10.112   Forms—Demand for Notice of Completion and Acceptance of Public Improvement

To: [Head of Department or bureau having charge of construction or demolition]

PLEASE TAKE NOTICE that the undersigned, _____, of _____ Street, _____, New York, having performed work for [or furnished materials to] _____, a contractor [or subcontractor] in the estimated amount of _____ ($_____) Dollars, in connection with the construction or demolition of the public improvement hereinafter described, hereby demands that you furnish to him a notice of the completion and acceptance of the said public improvement: [*set forth description of public improvement*].

This demand is made pursuant to Lien Law § 11–a of the State of New York, which requires that a written notice be mailed to me within FIVE (5) DAYS after completion and acceptance of said public improvement.

Dated: _____, N. Y., _____, 19__.

> [*Signature*]
> [*Type Name*
> *P.O. Address*]

§ 10.113 Forms—Petition to Amend Notice of Mechanic's Lien—Correct Name of Owner of Property

SUPREME COURT OF THE STATE OF NEW YORK
COUNTY OF _____

_____
)
In the Matter of the Application)
of _____, Lienor, for an Order) PETITION
Amending *Nunc Pro Tunc* a   ) TO AMEND NOTICE OF
Certain Notice of Lien Filed   ) MECHANIC'S LIEN
Against Certain Real Property) Index No. _____
of _____, Owner.   )
)
_____)

TO THE SUPREME COURT OF THE STATE OF NEW YORK, COUNTY OF _____:

The Petition of _____ respectfully shows:

1. That he is the President of _____, a domestic corporation having its place of business in _____, _____ County, New York, the corporation being the Lienor above mentioned, and claiming under notice of mechanic's lien hereinafter.

2. That upon information and belief at the time the within notice of lien was filed, lienor was informed and verily believed that the name of the owner of the premises described in the Notice of Mechanic's Lien, copy of which is annexed as part hereof and marked "Exhibit A", was The _____ Corp.

3. That during the period beginning _____, 19__, up to and including _____, 19__, lienor was employed by The _____ Corp. to perform and furnish and did in fact perform and furnish certain electric lighting and power services, systems, fixtures and machinery which were

§ 10.113   MECHANIC'S LIENS   Ch. 10

improvements of the property described in the Notice of Mechanic's Lien annexed as "Exhibit A".

4. That at the time lienor filed its Notice of Mechanic's Lien, lienor had been led to believe and did so believe, that the true owner of the premises in which he furnished the work, labor and materials was The _____ Corp., there being no other owner being indicated or revealed to lienor. That the materials and labor were ordered by The _____ Corp. who did not inform or notify lienor that its interest in the property was that of a lessee whereas in fact the true owners' names were obscured and kept unknown to lienor.

5. That thereafter lienor caused a search to be made of the title owner of record to the premises described in the annexed Exhibit A and was advised that the true owners of record of said property are _____, _____ and _____ and that The _____ Corp., now in bankruptcy, was merely a lessee of the premises, and not the true owner in fee.

6. There is a certain mortgage, originally in the amount of _____ ($_____) Dollars dated _____, 19__, and recorded _____, 19__, in the _____ County Clerk's office made by _____ Realty Corp. to _____ Bank and assigned to the _____ Savings Bank on _____, 19__, and recorded _____, 19__; and the following Notices of Mechanics Liens filed in the Office of the Clerk of _____ County:

Lien of _____, Inc. in the amount of $_____, filed _____, 19__ against _____, _____ and _____ as owners and The _____ Corp. as contractor-lessee;

Lien of _____ Division of _____ Corporation in the amount of $_____ against _____, _____ and _____, as owners, and The _____ Corp. as contractor-lessee, filed _____, 19__.

Lien of _____ Front Corporation in the amount of $_____ filed _____, 19__ against _____ Realty Corp., _____, _____ and _____, owners, and The _____ Corp. as contractor.

There are no other persons having an interest in the described premises excepting the owner, your petitioner and the persons in this paragraph mentioned.

7. No previous application for the relief hereby sought has been made.

8. The lienor will seek such further relief as may be just.

WHEREFORE, petitioner respectfully requests an order amending the Notice of Lien, nunc pro tunc, in respect of the particulars herein set forth and amending the docket and record thereof in the Office of the Clerk of _____ County, together with such further relief as the Court deems just.

Ch. 10   ASSIGNMENT OF MECHANIC'S LIEN   § 10.115

_____
Petitioner
By _____
President

§ 10.114   Forms—Assignment of Lien for Public Improvement

KNOW ALL MEN BY THESE PRESENTS, that I, _____, of _____, New York, for value received do hereby sell, assign and transfer unto _____ of _____, New York, his administrators, executors, assigns and successors, a certain public improvement lien in the amount of _____ ($_____) Dollars, created by the filing by me of notice of said lien with the Superintendent of _____ of the State of New York and with the Comptroller of the State of New York on the _____ day of _____, 19__, against moneys due or to become due from the State of New York to _____, under a contract for the construction of the public improvement known as _____, located at _____, New York, said contract being designated as Contract No. _____, together with my claim for all sums of money secured by said lien.[1]

Dated: _____, N. Y., _____, 19__.

[<i>Signature of Assignor</i>]
_____
Assignor

[<i>Acknowledgment</i>]

§ 10.115   Forms—Assignment of Mechanic's Lien

KNOW ALL MEN BY THESE PRESENTS, That I, _____, of _____, New York, for value received, do hereby sell, assign and transfer unto _____ of _____, New York, his administrators, executors, assigns and successors, a certain mechanic's lien in the sum of _____ ($_____) Dollars, created by the filing by me of a notice of said lien in the office of the Clerk of the County of _____ on the _____ day of _____, 19__, against the following described real property and _____, as owner thereof: [<i>insert description of property</i>], together with my claim for all sums of money secured by said lien.

And the assignor does hereby appoint the assignee, his administrators, executors, assigns and successors, his lawful attorney, irrevocably, with full power of substitution and revocation, to ask for, collect, demand and receive, prosecute and sue for in a court of law or equity, all sums of

---

§ 10.114   contained in the form in § 10.113.
1. Continue with second paragraph as

§ 10.115 MECHANIC'S LIENS Ch. 10

money above assigned, with full power and authority to do and perform all acts necessary in the premises.

Dated: _____, N.Y., _____, 19__.

[Signature of Assignor]

_____
Assignor

[Acknowledgment]

§ 10.116 Forms—Assignment of Moneys Due or to Become Due Under Public Improvement Contract

KNOW ALL MEN BY THESE PRESENTS, That _____, Inc. of _____, in the City of _____, State of New York, hereinafter designated as the assignor.

IN CONSIDERATION of the sum of _____ ($_____) Dollars, and other good and valuable consideration, by _____ of _____, in the City of _____, State of New York, hereinafter designated as the assignee, to the assignor in hand paid, receipt whereof is hereby acknowledged by the assignor.

The assignor has hereby assigned, sold, transferred and set-over, and by these presents does hereby assign, sell, transfer and set-over unto the assignee, administrators, executors and assigns and successors, for his own use and benefit, absolutely and forever, _____ ($_____) Dollars out of all money or moneys due or to become due to the assignor, under a certain contract made by and between _____, Inc., as party of the first part, and the Department of Parks of the City of _____, as party of the second part, dated the _____ day of _____, 19__, and bearing Contract No. _____ covering demolition of various buildings on _____ Street and _____ Avenue, _____, New York.

AND the assignor does hereby authorize, empower, and direct the Comptroller of the City of _____ or any department thereof, to pay to the assignee, his administrators, executors and assigns and successors, any and all money or moneys due or to become due to the assignor, or his administrators, assigns and executors and successors, by virtue of said contract.

AND the assignor does hereby certify that the assignor has not encumbered nor done any act or acts to lessen any rights of the assignor or his assigns, nor any security given under said contract: and that the assignor has a good right to assign said money or moneys due or to become due under said contract.

AND the assignor does hereby agree that the assignor will make, execute and deliver any and all papers, instruments and documents that may be required by the assignee, his administrators, executors and assigns and successors, and/or the Comptroller of the City of _____ or any department thereof, to effectuate the purpose hereof.

AND the assignor does hereby appoint the assignee, his administrators, executors, assigns and successors, the lawful attorney, irrevocably, with full power of substitution and revocation, to ask for, collect, demand and receive; to prosecute and sue for, by proceedings or otherwise, in a court of law or equity; to give acquittance for said money or moneys due or to become due, or any part thereof; and to withdraw any claims, suits or proceedings pertaining to or arising out of this assignment.

AND the assignor does hereby further covenant pursuant to Lien Law section 25 that the assignor receive any moneys advanced hereunder by the assignee and will hold the right to receive such moneys as a trust fund; that the assignor will first apply said fund to the payment of trust claims as defined in section 71 of the Lien Law and that the assignor will apply same to such payments only, before using any part of the advances for any other purpose.

IN WITNESS WHEREOF, the assignor does hereby set its hand and seal or cause these presents to be signed by their proper corporate officers and cause their proper corporate seal to be hereto fixed this _____ day of _____, 19__.

By _____
President.

[Seal]

[Acknowledgment]

§ 10.117 Forms—Affidavit for Continuance of Mechanic's Lien

SUPREME COURT OF THE STATE OF NEW YORK
COUNTY OF _____

```
_____
                               )
In the Matter of the Application )
of _____, Lienor, for an Order )
Extending a Certain Notice     ) Affidavit
of Lien Filed Against Certain  ) Index No. _____
Real Property of _____,       )
Owner.                         )
_____)
```

STATE OF NEW YORK)
) ss.:
COUNTY OF _____   )

629

§ 10.117   MECHANIC'S LIENS   Ch. 10

_____, being duly sworn, deposes and says:

I am an attorney at law with offices at _____, New York, and am the attorney for the lienor hereinafter mentioned.

Heretofore and on the _____ day of _____, 19__, a notice of mechanic's lien in the amount of _____ ($_____) Dollars was filed in the office of the Clerk of the County of _____, by _____, a domestic corporation, against the _____ Company, as owner, and affecting the premises described in said notice of lien, a copy of which is hereto annexed.

That an action has not been begun to foreclose said lien. That the said lien was continued by order of this Court filed herein on the _____ day of _____, 19__, for a period of six months.

That the said lien was further continued by order of this Court entered herein on the _____ day of _____, 19__, for a period of six months. That an order is sought herein continuing the said lien for a period of one year for the following reasons:

No previous application has been made for such an order.

WHEREFORE, deponent desires leave to have the mechanic's lien described herein continued for a period of one year for the purpose of enabling the persons against whom the said lien has been filed to realize on the said premises and make some just disposition thereof.

[Signature]

_____

[Type Name of Deponent]

[Jurat]

§ 10.118   Forms—Affidavit for Continuance of Lien for Public Improvement

SUPREME COURT OF THE STATE OF NEW YORK
COUNTY OF _____

_____)
In the Matter of the Application)
of _____, Lienor, for an Order)
Extending a Certain Notice)
of Lien Filed Against that) Affidavit
Certain Contract for Public) Index No. _____
Improvement between the New York)
State Department of _____ and)
and _____.)
_____)

STATE OF NEW YORK,)
) ss.:
COUNTY OF _____)

_____, being duly sworn, deposes and says:

That he is the president of _____ Corporation, a domestic corporation, which performed the labor, and furnished the materials set forth in the notice of lien, hereinafter mentioned, in and about the construction of the new dining room building and continuous flow bath building at _____, New York, pursuant to Contract No. _____, entered into between the Department of _____ and _____ Contracting Company.

On the _____ day of _____, 19__, the _____ Corporation filed in the office of the Comptroller of the State of New York and on the _____ day of _____, 19__, filed in the office of the Department of _____ of the State of New York, a notice of lien for _____ ($_____) Dollars against the said public improvement and against the contract of the said _____ Contracting Company.

The date when the said sum of _____ ($_____) Dollars became due is _____, 19__; and the name of the contractor for whom labor was performed and materials furnished, and by whom the _____ Corporation was employed as stated in said contract is _____ Contracting Company.

Said lien will expire on the _____ day of _____, 19__, and no action has been commenced or other proceedings taken to enforce this lien, and said lien has not been bonded, cancelled or discharged, and the whole amount claimed thereunder is now due and payable.

No stays have been taken to enforce the said lien for the following reasons:

The balance remaining due on said contract from the State is approximately _____ ($_____) Dollars, against which liens of approximately _____ ($_____) Dollars have been filed. The _____ Surety Company, which is the surety for the faithful performance of the contract entered into between the Department of _____ and _____ Contracting Company has completed the job at a cost of _____ ($_____) Dollars, but the State, as yet, has not finally accepted the said job. An agreement has been entered into between the [*surety company*] and the _____ Corporation, providing for the payment of the amount claimed and said [*surety company*] has requested that such action be deferred.

Deponent therefore prays that an order be entered continuing said lien for a period of one year.

No previous application for the order has been made to any court or judge.

[*Signature*]

_____

[*Type Name of Deponent*]

[*Jurat*]

§ 10.119 MECHANIC'S LIENS Ch. 10

§ 10.119 Forms—Petition to Discharge Mechanic's Lien Where Notice of Lien Defective

SUPREME COURT OF THE STATE OF NEW YORK
COUNTY OF _____

_____
)
In the Matter of The Application   ) PETITION TO DISCHARGE
of _____ for an order discharging) MECHANIC'S LIENTAKING
a certain Mechanic's Lien filed   )
by _____, Lienor   ) Index No. _____
_____   )

TO THE SUPREME COURT OF THE STATE OF NEW YORK, COUNTY OF _____:

The petition of _____, Inc., by its attorney, _____, respectfully shows:

1. That petitioner is a corporation, organized and existing under the laws of the State of New York.

2. That heretofore and on or about _____, 19__, _____ Corp., filed an alleged notice of mechanic's lien, in the sum of _____ ($_____) Dollars, against certain real property situate in the City of _____, County of _____, described therein, and against _____ Inc. as owner of said real property, to secure a claim for labor and material in connection with the improvement of said real property. A true copy of said notice of lien, marked "Exhibit A", is attached hereto and made a part hereof.

3. That said notice of lien is defective for failure to comply with the provisions of Section 9 of the Lien Law of the State of New York, in that [*specify defect*].

4. That no previous application has been made for the relief prayed for herein.

WHEREFORE, petitioner prays for an order summarily discharging of record the alleged notice of lien filed herein, and for such other and further relief as to Court may seem just and proper.

[*Attorney for Petitioner*
P.O. Address.
Tel. No.]

[*Verification*]

632

Ch. 10   DISCHARGING MECHANIC'S LIEN   § 10.120

§ 10.120 Forms—Petition for Order Discharging Mechanic's Lien Upon Filing of Undertaking

SUPREME COURT OF THE STATE OF NEW YORK
COUNTY OF _____

In the Matter of The Application) PETITION TO DISCHARGE
of _____ for an order discharging) MECHANIC'S LIEN UPON
a certain Mechanic's Lien filed) FILING OF UNDERTAKING
by _____, Lienor) Index No. _____
)

TO THE SUPREME COURT OF THE STATE OF NEW YORK, COUNTY OF _____.

The petition of _____, by his attorney _____, respectfully shows:

1. The petitioner is the owner of all those certain premises with the buildings thereon erected located at _____, in the City of _____, County of _____, [*follow with brief description of property*].

2. On or about _____, 19__, _____ filed in the office of the Clerk of the County of _____, a certain notice of mechanic's lien against the above described premises for the sum of _____ ($_____) Dollars.

3. The petitioner desires to execute pursuant to the provisions of the Lien Law an undertaking with sufficient sureties for such sum as this court might direct not less than the amount claimed in said notice of lien and conditioned for the payment of any judgment which might be rendered against the said property for the enforcement of said lien, procured upon its duly verified petition an order on or about the _____ day of _____, 19__, duly made by Mr. Justice _____, a Justice of the _____ County Supreme Court, by the terms of which order the sum of _____ ($_____) Dollars was fixed as the amount of the undertaking to be executed and given by petitioner with two or more sufficient sureties who should be freeholders or with a surety or fidelity company authorized by the laws of this State to transact business in the State of New York to the Clerk of the County of _____, to discharge the lien filed herein by said respondent as above set forth.

4. Presented with this petition is a copy of the proposed undertaking executed and acknowledged by petitioner as principal and by _____ Indemnity Co., a New York Corporation having its principal office at _____, City of _____, as surety, in the sum of _____ ($_____) Dollars, conditioned that if your petitioner, its successors and assigns should well and truly pay any judgment which might be rendered against

§ 10.120   MECHANIC'S LIENS   Ch. 10

the above mentioned property for the enforcement of said lien not exceeding the sum of _____ ($_____) Dollars, then the obligation contained in said undertaking to be void, otherwise, to remain in full force and effect.

5. Also presented with this petition is a certificate of qualification duly issued by the Superintendent of Insurance of the State of New York under Section 1110 of the Insurance Law, and which certificate has not been revoked.

WHEREFORE, petitioner prays that an order may be made and entered herein approving the undertaking given by petitioner and the aforesaid surety to discharge the said mechanic's lien and for a further order which shall provide that upon filing said undertaking in the office of the Clerk of the County of _____, the lien acquired by the filing of said notice of lien in the office of the Clerk of the County of _____, against the premises described herein shall be discharged and that the Clerk of the County of _____ be directed to cancel and discharge the same of record and to enter upon the lien docket and upon all indices an appropriate entry thereof with reference to the order prayed for and the date of entry thereof.

[Attorney for Petitioner
P. O. Address.
Tel. No.]

[Verification]

§ 10.121   Forms—Undertaking to Discharge Mechanic's Lien

KNOW ALL MEN BY THESE PRESENTS, That I, _____, as principal, and the _____ INDEMNITY COMPANY, a New York corporation having its principal office at _____, City of _____, as surety, are held and firmly bound unto the Clerk of the County of _____ in the sum of _____ ($_____) Dollars lawful money of the United States, for which payment well and truly to be made we bind ourselves, our heirs, executors, administrators, successors and assigns, jointly and severally, firmly by these presents.

Signed and sealed this _____ day of _____, 19__.

WHEREAS, on the _____ day of _____, 19__, _____ filed in the office of the Clerk of the County of _____, a notice of mechanic's lien in the sum of _____ ($_____) Dollars, against certain property of _____, situated [insert brief description of property] and known as _____, in the City and County of _____, and,

634

WHEREAS, said _____, desires to discharge said lien or claim pursuant to Section 19 of the Lien Law of the State of New York by giving an undertaking, as provided in said section; and

WHEREAS, by an order of the Supreme Court duly entered in the office of the Clerk of the County of _____ on the _____ day of _____, 19__, the amount of an undertaking to be executed for the purpose of so discharging said lien was fixed at the sum of _____ ($_____) Dollars.

NOW, THEREFORE, the condition of this obligation is such that if the above bounden _____, shall well and truly pay any judgment which may be rendered against said property for the enforcement of said lien, not exceeding the sum of _____ ($_____ Dollars), then this obligation to be void, otherwise to remain in full force and effect.

[Name of Indemnity Company]

By:_____
Name:_____
Title:_____

[Corporate Seal]

[Acknowledgment]

§ 10.122 Forms—Petition for Order Fixing Amount of Undertaking to Discharge Mechanic's Lien

SUPREME COURT OF THE STATE OF NEW YORK
COUNTY OF _____

_____
)
In the Matter of The Application) PETITION FOR ORDER FIXING
of _____ for an order discharging) AMOUNT OF UNDERTAKING
a certain Mechanic's Lien filed   )
by _____, Lienor   ) Index No. _____
_____)

TO THE SUPREME COURT OF THE STATE OF NEW YORK, COUNTY OF _____:

The petition of _____ (the "Petitioner") by his attorney, _____, respectfully shows that:

1. The Petitioner is the owner of premises located at _____, in the City of _____, [follow with brief description of property].

2. On or about the _____ day of _____, 19__, _____ filed in the office of the Clerk of the County of _____, a notice of mechanic's

§ 10.122   MECHANIC'S LIENS   Ch. 10

lien against the above described premises for the sum of _____ ($_____) Dollars.

3. The Petitioner desires to execute an undertaking with sufficient sureties for such sum as the Court may direct not less than the amount claimed in said notice of lien, conditioned for the payment of any judgment which may be rendered against the property for the enforcement of the lien pursuant to the provisions of the Lien Law.

4. No previous application has been made for the order prayed for herein.

WHEREFORE Petitioner asks that an order made by the Court fixing the amount of an undertaking which may be given by the Petitioner with sufficient sureties to discharge said lien of record.

[Attorney for Petitioner
P.O. Address.
Tel. No.]

[Verification]

§ 10.123 Forms—Approval by Lienors of Subordination of Mechanic's Liens to Trust Bond or Note and Mortgage

WHEREAS, [insert name of owner], a domestic corporation, with its principal place of business in the Borough of _____, City of _____, is the owner in fee of the premises in the Borough of _____, County of _____, City and State of New York, and bounded and described as follows:

[insert description]

and

WHEREAS, the building has been in the course of construction on the said premises under contracts with the said owner, and

WHEREAS, the said owner, [insert name of owner], has duly executed and delivered its bond [or note] in the sum of _____ ($_____) Dollars, and also a mortgage upon the aforesaid premises to secure payment of the said sum of _____ ($_____) Dollars both bearing date _____, 19__, to _____, _____, _____ and _____ as trustees for the purpose of issuing certificates of interest therein for moneys loaned, material furnished, labor performed and any other indebtedness incurred after the recording of the said mortgage for the completion of said building and of any expenses in connection with the said trust bond [or note] and mortgage and,

WHEREAS the said trust mortgage was duly recorded in the office of the Register of the County of _____ in Liber _____ at Page _____ and duly indexed under Block _____, of Section _____, on the _____ day of _____, 19__, and

WHEREAS up to and not later than fifteen days after the recording of said trust mortgage as aforesaid, we the undersigned and other lienors have duly filed in the office of the Clerk of the County of _____, mechanics liens affecting the said premises, or a part thereof, amounting in the aggregate to the sum of _____ ($_____) Dollars, and

WHEREAS none of the mechanic's liens have been discharged in the manner provided in Article 2 of the Lien Law of the State of New York, and

WHEREAS mechanic's liens were filed by the undersigned lienors as aforesaid, amounting together to _____ ($_____) Dollars and representing at least 55% of the aforesaid aggregate amount of _____ ($_____) Dollars of all mechanic's liens filed against the said premises as aforesaid.

NOW in pursuance of Section 26 of Article 2 of the Lien Law of the State of New York, we, the undersigned mechanic's lienors, hereby severally approve the aforesaid trust bond [*or note*] and mortgage.

Dated: _____, N.Y.,
_____, 19__.

[*Name of Lienor*]

By _____, Pres.

[*Acknowledgments*]

§ 10.124 Forms—Affidavit for Order Fixing Amount of Bond to Discharge All Mechanic's Liens

SUPREME COURT OF THE STATE OF NEW YORK
COUNTY OF _____

In the Matter of The Application)
of _____, Owner, to discharge all)
mechanic's liens which may be)
filed in or about the performance) AFFIDAVIT
of a certain contract with _____,)
Contractor, for the improvement) Index No. _____
of certain real property, by the)
filing of a bond pursuant to)
Section 37 of the Lien Law.)
_____)

STATE OF NEW YORK)
) ss.:
COUNTY OF _____)

§ 10.124　　　MECHANIC'S LIENS　　　Ch. 10

_____, being duly sworn, deposes and says:

1. He is the attorney for [*insert name of owner*] the applicant herein (the "Applicant").

2. The Applicant is the owner of certain real property situate in the City of _____, County of _____, which is briefly described as follows: [*insert description*].

3. On the _____ day of _____, 19__, the Applicant entered into a contract with _____ Company, Inc., contractor, for the improvement of said real property, a copy of which contract is annexed hereto.

4. The amount remaining unpaid on said contract is _____ ($_____) Dollars.

5. Pursuant to the provisions of Lien Law § 37, the Applicant wishes to obtain an order discharging said real property from the lien of each and every contractor, subcontractor, materialman or laborer performing labor or furnishing materials in or about the performance of the said contract, upon the filing of a bond in conformity with said section.

6. In pursuance thereof, deponent asks for an order fixing the amount of such bond.

7. No previous application has been made for the relief prayed for herein.

　　　　　　　　　　　　　　　　[*Signature*]

　　　　　　　　　　　　　　　　_____
　　　　　　　　　　　　　　　　[*Type Name of Deponent*]

[*Jurat*]

§ 10.125　Forms—Petition for Order Requiring Itemized Statement 💾

SUPREME COURT OF THE STATE OF NEW YORK
COUNTY OF _____

_____
　　　　　　　　　　　　　　　　)
In the Matter of the Application)
of _____ for an order directing)　PETITION FOR ORDER
_____, Lienor, to deliver the　)　REQUIRING ITEMIZED
itemized statement of labor and)　STATEMENT
material and the terms of the   )
contract required by Lien Law,   )　Index No. _____
Section 38.   )
　　　　　　　　　　　　　　　　)
_____

638

TO THE SUPREME COURT OF THE STATE OF NEW YORK:

The petition of_____ ("Petitioner"), by its attorney _____, respectfully shows:

1. Petitioner, _____, is a domestic corporation with its principal place of business at _____, City of _____, and at the times hereinafter mentioned is, was and still is the owner in fee of the following described real property:

[*insert description of property*]

2. On or about _____, 19__, _____, a domestic corporation with its principal place of business at _____, City of New York, filed a notice of mechanic's lien against the aforesaid property, in the amount of _____, in the office of the Clerk of the County of _____.

3. On _____, 19__, the Petitioner caused to be served a demand on said lienor, pursuant to New York State Lien Law § 38, demanding that it furnish a statement, in writing within five (5) days after receipt of said demand, which shall set forth the items of labor and the value thereof, and the items of material and the value thereof, which make up the amount for which the lien was claimed, which shall also set forth the terms of the contract under which such items were furnished, verified in the form required for the verification of notices of mechanic's liens. A copy of said demand so served, and the affidavit of due service thereof of _____, sworn to _____, 19__, are hereto annexed and made a part hereof.

4. Said lienor has failed and refused to comply with the said demand, in that it has failed to serve any statement whatsoever in response to said demand although more than five (5) days have passed since said demand was served on said lienor.

5. No previous application has been made for the relief prayed for herein.

WHEREFORE, Petitioner prays for an order directing the lienor to furnish said statement in compliance with said demand, within five (5) days.

> _____
> [*Attorney for Petitioner*
> *P.O. Address*
> *Tel. No.*]

[*Verification*]

§ 10.126 Forms—Notice of Application for Order Requiring Itemized Statement

SUPREME COURT OF THE STATE OF NEW YORK
COUNTY OF _____

_____)
In the Matter of the Application)
of _____ for an order directing)   NOTICE OF APPLICATION FOR
_____, Lienor, to deliver the)   ORDER REQUIRING ITEMIZED
itemized statement of labor and)   STATEMENT
material and the terms of the)
contract required by Lien Law,)   Index No. _____
Section 38.)
_____)

SIRS:

PLEASE TAKE NOTICE, that on the annexed petition of _____, duly verified _____, 19__, application will be made, pursuant to New York Lien Law § 38, at Special Term, Part _____ of the Supreme Court, to be held at the Court House, _____, City of _____, on the _____ day of _____, 19__, at _____ o'clock in the forenoon, for an order directing _____, lienor, to furnish to petitioner a specific itemized statement of its certain mechanic's lien, in the amount of _____ ($_____) Dollars, notice of which was filed in the office of the Clerk of the County of _____ on or about _____, 19__, against petitioner as owner, as required by New York Lien Law § 38, and providing that if such statement be not served, an order will be granted vacating and setting aside the said mechanic's lien; and for such other and further relief as may be just and proper.

Dated: _____, N.Y.,
_____, 19__.

Yours, etc.

_____
[*Attorney for Petitioner*
P.O. Address.
Tel. No.]

To:

_____
Lienor
P.O. Address

§ 10.127 Forms—Demand for Itemized Statement

To: _____, Lienor _____, New York.

Ch. 10 AFFIDAVIT: CANCEL LIEN § 10.128

PLEASE TAKE NOTICE, that the undersigned, Owner [or *Contractor*], hereby demands that you furnish to him a verified statement, in writing, setting forth the items of labor and/or material, and the value thereof, which make up the amount for which you claim a mechanic's lien in the amount of _____ ($_____) Dollars; the said statement, in writing, also to set forth the terms of the contract under which the items were furnished.

This demand refers to the said certain mechanic's lien in the amount of _____ ($_____) Dollars, notice of which was originally filed in the _____ County Clerk's Office on or about the _____ day of _____, 19___.

This demand is made pursuant to section 38 of the Lien Law of the State of New York, and the statement, in writing, must be furnished to the undersigned within FIVE (5) DAYS after the receipt of this demand by you.

Dated: _____, N.Y.,
_____, 19___.

[*Owner or Contractor*
P.O. Address]

§ 10.128 Forms—Affidavit in Support of Application to Cancel Mechanic's Lien for Failure to Furnish Itemized Statement

SUPREME COURT OF THE STATE OF NEW YORK
COUNTY OF _____

)
In the Matter of the Application)
of _____ for an order directing)
_____, Lienor, to deliver the) AFFIDAVIT
itemized statement of labor and)
material and the terms of the) Index No. _____
contract required by Lien Law,)
Section 38.)
)

STATE OF NEW YORK)
) ss.:
COUNTY of _____)

_____, being duly sworn, deposes and says that he is an attorney and counselor at law, residing and having his office in the City of _____, County of _____ and State of New York, and is attorney for _____, owner described in the annexed notice of motion, and the applicant herein. This proceeding was duly instituted by a demand in

641

§ 10.128   MECHANIC'S LIENS   Ch. 10

writing served on _____, lienor, and demanding an itemized statement of the items of the alleged mechanic's lien filed in the office of the Clerk of the County of _____ on the _____ day of _____, 19__, and the terms of the contract, under section 38 of the Lien Law of the State of New York. No statement was furnished pursuant to such demand. Deponent thereupon brought proceedings in the Supreme Court, _____ County, to compel the furnishing of such a statement, and secured an order on the _____ day of _____, 19__, at Special Term, Part _____, of the said court, held at the City of _____, N. Y., on that day, directing the furnishing of such a statement. Said order was duly served on the lienor on _____, 19__. The last mentioned order directed that the lienor within five days after the service of copy thereof upon him deliver to this deponent such statement as is in said order described; that no statement whatsoever has been served pursuant to said order.

WHEREFORE by reason of such failure of such lienor to comply with the terms, directions and conditions of the said order deponent prays for an order cancelling the lien in question pursuant to the provisions of the said statute.

_____
[*Type Name of Deponent*]

[*Jurat*]

§ 10.129 Forms—Notice Requiring Lienor to Commence Action to Enforce Mechanic's Lien

SUPREME COURT OF THE STATE OF NEW YORK
COUNTY OF _____

_____
)
In the Matter of The Application   ) NOTICE TO COMMENCE
of _____, requiring _____,   ) ACTION OR SHOW CAUSE
Lienor, to enforce his lien or   ) PURSUANT TO LIEN LAW,
show cause why the Notice of   ) SECTION 59
Lien should not be vacated and   )
canceled of record as prescribed   ) Index No. _____
by Section 59 of the Lien Law.   )
)
_____

SIR:

PLEASE TAKE NOTICE that pursuant to Section 59 of the Lien Law, you are hereby required to commence an action on or before the _____ day of _____, 19__, to enforce the lien filed by you in the office of the Clerk of _____ County, on _____, 19__, in the sum of _____

Ch. 10   CANCEL NOTICE OF MECHANIC'S LIEN   § 10.130

($_____) Dollars, against _____, Inc. as owner in fee and _____ Corp., as contractor and affecting premises located in the City of _____, County of _____, State of New York, and described as follows: [*insert description*]; or in the event of your failure to commence such action that you appear at a Special term, Part _____ of this Court to be held at the courthouse thereof, located at _____, on the _____ day of _____, 19__, at _____ o'clock in the _____ noon of that day, or as soon thereafter as counsel can be heard, and show cause why an order should not be made vacating and canceling said notice of lien of record.

Dated: _____, N.Y.,
       _____, 19__.

                                    _____
                                    [*Attorney for* _____, *Owner*
                                    P.O. Address
                                    Tel. No.]

To: _____ [*Lienor*
      P.O. Address]

§ 10.130 Forms—Affidavit in Support of Application to Cancel Notice of Mechanic's Lien for Failure to Commence Action

SUPREME COURT OF THE STATE OF NEW YORK
COUNTY OF _____

In the Matter of The Application of _____, requiring _____, Lienor, to enforce his lien or show cause why the Notice of Lien should not be vacated and canceled of record as prescribed by Section 59 of the Lien Law.	AFFIDAVIT IN SUPPORT APPLICATION TO CANCEL NOTICE OF LIEN Index No. _____

STATE OF NEW YORK)
) ss.:
COUNTY OF _____)

_____, being duly sworn, deposes and says:

1. I make this affidavit in support of an application to vacate and discharge the mechanic's lien hereinafter described, for failure to commence an action to foreclose the same after the service of a notice pursuant to Section 59 of the Lien Law.

2. I am the President of _____ Corp. the above named contractor described in the said notice of lien.

3. On the _____ day of _____, 19__, the lienor above named filed in the office of the Clerk of the County of _____, a notice of

§ 10.130   MECHANIC'S LIENS   Ch. 10

mechanic's lien in the sum of _____ ($_____) Dollars, claiming against _____, Inc. as owner and _____ Corp., as contractor, and affecting property therein described as follows: [*insert description*].

4. On the _____ day of _____, 19__, I caused to be duly served on said lienor a notice pursuant to Section 59 of the Lien Law, requiring _____ to commence an action to enforce said lien on or before the _____ day of _____, 19__, which was more than thirty days after such service or to show cause why the said notice of lien should not be vacated and cancelled. A copy of said notice is annexed hereto. There is also annexed hereto the affidavit of service of _____, sworn to the _____ day of _____, 19__, showing due service of said notice.

5. More than thirty days have elapsed since the service of such notice and the lienor has not commenced any action to enforce said lien.

6. No previous application has been made for the cancellation of said mechanic's lien.

WHEREFORE, I pray for an order vacating and cancelling the mechanic's lien herein.

[*Signature*]

[*Type Name of Deponent*]

[*Jurat*]

§ 10.131   Forms—Notice Requiring Lienor to Commence Action to Enforce Lien for Public Improvement

SUPREME COURT OF THE STATE OF NEW YORK
COUNTY OF _____

_____)
In the Matter of The application of)
_____ requiring _____, Lienor,) NOTICE TO COMMENCE
to commence an action to enforce) ACTION OR SHOW CAUSE
his Lien or show cause why the) PURSUANT TO LIEN LAW
Notice of Lien should not be) SECTION 21-a
vacated and canceled of record as)
prescribed by Section 21-a of the) Index No. _____
Lien Law.)
_____)

SIR:

You are hereby notified, pursuant to Section 21-a of the Lien Law of the State of New York, to commence an action on or before the _____

644

Ch. 10   FAILURE TO COMMENCE ACTION   § 10.132

day of _____, 19__, to enforce the lien filed by _____, on the _____ day of _____, 19__, with the _____ [*head of department or bureau having charge of demolition or construction*] and the Comptroller of the State of New York [*or financial officer of the public corporation, or other officer or person charged with the custody and disbursements of the state or corporate funds applicable to the contract under which the claim is made*] against moneys due or to become due _____, contractor by the State of New York [*or the public corporation*] as the result of certain work and construction upon a public improvement known as _____ in the City of _____, New York, County of _____, as described in the notice of said lien; or in the event of your failure to commence such action that you appear at a Special Term, Part _____ of this Court to be held at the Court House in the City of _____, New York, on the _____ day of _____, 19__ at the opening of Court on that day or as soon thereafter as counsel can be heard, and then and there show cause why an order should not be made, vacating, discharging and cancelling said notice of lien of record.

Dated: _____, N.Y.,

_____, 19__.

_____
[*Attorney for Contractor*
P.O. Address.
Tel. No.]

To: _____ [*Lienor*
P.O. Address]

§ 10.132 Forms—Affidavit in Support of Application to Cancel Notice of Lien for Public Improvement for Failure to Commence Action

SUPREME COURT OF THE STATE OF NEW YORK
COUNTY OF _____

_____)
In the Matter of The application of   )
_____ requiring _____, Lienor,   ) AFFIDAVIT IN SUPPORT OF
to commence an action to enforce   ) APPLICATION TO CANCEL
his Lien or show cause why the   ) NOTICE OF LIEN
Notice of Lien should not be   )
vacated and canceled of record as   ) Index No. _____
prescribed by Section 21–a of the   )
Lien Law.   )
_____)

STATE OF NEW YORK   )
) ss.:
COUNTY OF _____   )

645

§ 10.132 MECHANIC'S LIENS Ch. 10

_____, being duly sworn, deposes and says:

That he resides at _____, New York and is an attorney at law, duly licensed and qualified to practice as such with offices at _____, New York.

That deponent is the attorney for _____ who hereby applies for an order for the cancellation of the certain lien in the sum of _____ ($_____) Dollars notice of which dated _____, 19__ was filed with the _____ [head of department or bureau having charge of the demolition or construction] and the Comptroller of the State of New York [or financial officer of the public corporation, or other officer or person charged with the custody and disbursements of the state or corporate funds applicable to the contract under which the claim is made] on _____, 19__ by the above named _____, Lienor, against the moneys due _____, contractor, by the State of New York [or the public corporation] as the result of certain work and construction on a public improvement known as _____ Park, in the City of _____, County of _____.

That on _____, 19__ the deponent caused to be personally served on the said _____ [lienor] a notice requiring him, pursuant to Section 21-a of the Lien Law to commence an action to foreclose the said lien on or before _____, 19__ or to show cause at a Special Term, Part _____ of the Supreme Court to be held at the Court House in the City of _____, New York on the _____ day of _____, 19__ at the opening of Court on that day or as soon thereafter as counsel could be heard why said lien should not be vacated and cancelled of record.

A copy of said notice and the affidavit of _____ showing personal service of said notice are hereto annexed and made a part hereof to the same extent as if at length set forth herein.

Deponent further says that no action has been commenced to enforce or foreclose said lien and therefore application is now made for cancellation of the said lien.

That no previous application has been made for cancellation of such lien.

[Signature]

_____
[Type Name of Deponent]

[Jurat]

§ 10.133 Forms—Complaint for Foreclosure of Lien for Public Improvement

SUPREME COURT OF THE STATE OF NEW YORK
COUNTY OF _____

```
_____ )
                         )
_____,      )
                         )
            Plaintiff,   )   VERIFIED
                         )   COMPLAINT
         -against-       )
                         )   Index No. _____
_____,      )
                         )
            Defendant.   )
_____ )
```

Plaintiff, by his attorney, _____, complaining of defendants, alleges:

FOR A FIRST CAUSE OF ACTION:

1. Plaintiff is and was at all times mentioned herein a resident of _____ County in the State of New York.

2. That at all times mentioned herein, defendants, _____ and _____ were and still are doing business as co-partners in a joint venture under contract with the New York State _____ Authority.

3. That at all times mentioned herein, defendant, _____ Corporation of _____, New York was a domestic corporation duly organized under the laws of the State of New York, with a principal place of business at _____, New York, and was a subcontractor to _____ and _____ under contract with the New York State _____ Authority.

4. That at all times herein mentioned, upon information and belief, defendant, _____ Insurance Company was and is a corporation duly organized under the laws of the State of _____ and duly authorized to carry on business as a Surety Company in the State of New York.

5. That defendant, New York State _____ Authority is a public corporation duly organized and existing under the provisions of the _____ Law, and it and the State of New York are made defendants to this action by reason of the fact that they are in possession of funds due and owing to defendants, _____ and _____ under the contract hereinafter described.

6. That on or about the _____ day of _____, 19__, defendants, _____ and _____ entered into an agreement with the defendant, New York State _____ Authority for construction of a certain public improvement, to wit: the construction of a bridge across the _____ River

§ 10.133   MECHANIC'S LIENS   Ch. 10

at _____, New York, and the proper grading at and about the entrances to said bridge on each side of said river, and such agreement is known as contract No. _____.

7. Upon information and belief, defendants _____ and _____ have duly performed all of the terms of said contract with defendant New York State _____ Authority on their part to be performed.

8. Subsequent to the making of said contract and during the performance thereof and between the _____ day of _____, 19__ and the _____ day of _____, 19__, the plaintiff furnished to _____ and _____ through defendant, _____ Corporation under an agreement, certain materials for the construction of said public improvement, which materials were in fact used in the construction of said improvement, to wit: _____ cubic yards of gravel, and said materials were of the value and agreed price of _____ ($_____) Dollars, no part of which sum has been paid.

9. That on or about _____, 19__, prior to the time when the construction of said public improvement was completed or accepted, plaintiff duly filed in the offices of the New York State _____ Authority, the Comptroller of the State of New York and the Superintendent of Public Works of the State of New York a Notice of Lien, a true and complete copy of which is annexed hereto and made a part hereof.

10. Said Notice of Lien was in writing, verified by the lienor, and stated the name and residence of the lienor, the name of the contractors to whom the aforesaid materials were furnished, the amount claimed to be due and the date when due, a description of the public improvement upon which the materials were expended, the kind of materials furnished, and a general description of the contract pursuant to which the public improvement was constructed.

11. By reason of the foregoing, plaintiff acquired a valid lien upon said contract and upon the moneys in the control of defendant, State of New York, and defendant, New York State _____ Authority, applicable to the construction of said public improvement, to the extent of _____ ($_____) Dollars with interest as aforesaid. Upon information and belief, the amount of said moneys exceeds the amount of plaintiff's said lien.

12. Neither said lien or the claim upon which it is based has been paid, waived, canceled or discharged, and no action or proceeding has been brought to foreclose or to enforce said lien or claim.

FOR A SECOND CAUSE OF ACTION:

13. Repeats the allegations in paragraphs 1 through 12 as though the same were herein set forth in full, and further alleges:

14. On or about the _____ day of _____, 19__, pursuant to Section 137 of the State Finance Law and the requirements of the

Ch. 10   COMPLAINT FOR FORECLOSURE OF LIEN § **10.133**

Comptroller of the State of New York, defendants, _____ and _____, as principals, and defendant, _____ Insurance Co. as surety, duly executed and delivered a labor and material bond, guaranteeing prompt payment of all moneys due to all persons supplying defendants, _____ and _____, or their sub-contractors, with labor and materials employed and used in carrying out said contract.

15. By reasons of the foregoing, if the Court should find that said lien of plaintiff, though valid, cannot be satisfied because the moneys, if any, due to the defendants, _____ Corp. and _____ Co. on account of said contract are insufficient therefor, then the defendants, _____ and _____ Insurance Co. are liable to plaintiff for the payment of said lien and the claim upon which it is based, to wit: the sum of _____ ($_____) Dollars with interest from the _____ day of _____, 19__.

WHEREFORE, plaintiff demands judgment as follows:

1. That plaintiff be adjudged to have a valid lien upon the moneys of the State of New York or the New York State _____ Authority applicable to the construction of said public improvement, and due and to become due under said contract, in the sum of _____ ($_____) Dollars with interest thereon from _____, 19__.

2. That defendant, State of New York, or defendant, New York State _____ Authority, or both of said defendants, be directed to pay over to Plaintiff said sum of _____ ($_____) Dollars with interest thereon from _____, 19__, together with the costs of this action, and that plaintiff have judgment therefor.

3. That in the event the moneys, if any, due or to become due on account of said contract are insufficient for the payment of plaintiff's lien in full, plaintiff have judgment against defendants, _____ and _____ and defendant, _____ Insurance Co. for any deficiency that may remain, with costs and disbursements.

4. That if plaintiff should fail for any reason to establish a valid lien herein, he recover judgment for such sums as are due to him or for which he might recover in an action on contract against defendants, _____ and _____.

5. That plaintiff have such other, further and different relief as to the Court may seem just and proper.

>   [*Attorney for Plaintiff*
>   *P.O. Address*
>   *Tel. No.*]

[*Verification*]

§ 10.134   MECHANIC'S LIENS   Ch. 10

§ 10.134 Forms—Complaint for Foreclosure of Mechanic's Lien—Contractor

SUPREME COURT OF THE STATE OF NEW YORK
COUNTY OF _____

_____
)
_____,   )
)
          Plaintiff,   ) VERIFIED
) COMPLAINT
     -against-   )
) Index No. _____
_____,   )
)
          Defendant.   )
_____   )

The plaintiff, complaining of the defendants, by _____ its attorney, alleges:

1. That at all times hereinafter mentioned plaintiff was and still is a domestic corporation, duly organized and existing under and by virtue of the laws of the State of New York.

2. That upon information and belief the defendants, _____ and _____, are now and at all times hereinafter mentioned were domestic corporations organized and existing under the laws of the State of New York.

3. That at all the times hereinafter mentioned, the defendant, _____, was and still is the owner of certain lands and premises in the city of _____, State of New York, County of _____, more particularly bounded and described as follows:

[insert description of property]

4. That heretofore and on or about the _____ day of _____, 19__ the plaintiff and the defendant, _____, entered into an agreement in writing wherein and whereby plaintiff agreed to do certain work and furnish certain materials for the repair and alterations of the house on the property of the said defendant, _____, hereinbefore described, and the defendant, _____, promised to pay to the plaintiff therefor, in the manner set forth in the said contract, the sum of _____ ($_____) Dollars; that a copy of said contract is hereto annexed, marked Exhibit "A" and made part of this complaint.

5. That thereafter the plaintiff entered into and upon the performance of the said agreement. That while this work was progressing, the plaintiff and the defendant, _____, entered into another agreement, orally, for extra work to be done and materials to be furnished in the

Ch. 10   CONTRACTOR   § 10.134

sum of _____ ($_____) Dollars, such work and materials to be done and furnished simultaneously with the work agreed to under the written contract described in Exhibit "A". That the plaintiff had almost completed these repairs and alterations of said house as required by the said contracts and had duly performed almost all those conditions of the contracts when the plaintiff was arbitrarily denied its right to complete the contracts by the defendant, _____. That the work to be done and the materials to be furnished, which the defendant, _____, refused to permit the plaintiff to complete, total the sum of _____ ($_____) Dollars.

    6. That the first item of work was performed and the first item of material was furnished by the plaintiff on the _____ day of _____, 19__, and the last item of work was performed and the last item of material was furnished on the _____ day of _____, 19__.

    7. That the work, labor and services so performed by the plaintiff and the materials so furnished by the plaintiff were performed and furnished for the improvement of the real property hereinbefore described and were performed and furnished with the knowledge and consent and at the request of the defendant, _____.

    8. That at the time of the filing of the lien hereinafter set forth, there was and still is justly due, owing and unpaid by the defendant, _____, to the plaintiff the sum of _____ ($_____) Dollars, with interest thereon from the _____ day of _____, 19__.

    9. That on the _____ day of _____, 19__, and within four months after the final performance of the work and the final furnishing of the material dating from the last item of work performed and materials furnished, plaintiff caused to be filed in the Office of the Clerk of the County of _____, that being the county where the property hereinbefore described is situated, a notice of lien in writing, which notice did state the name and residence of the lienor and its business address and principal place of business; the name and address of the lienor's attorney; the name of the owner of the real property against whose interest therein a lien is claimed and the interest of the owner so far as known to lienor; the name of the person by whom the lienor was employed and to whom it furnished the materials and with whom the contract was made; the labor performed and materials furnished, and the agreed price and value thereof; the amount unpaid to the lienor for such labor and materials; the time when the first and last items of work were performed and materials were furnished; the property subject to the lien, with a description thereof sufficient for identification together with its location by street and number, which said notice of lien was duly verified by the plaintiff to the effect that the statements therein contained were true to his knowledge except as to the matters therein stated to be alleged on information and belief, and that as to those matters he believed it to be true.

§ 10.134 MECHANIC'S LIENS Ch. 10

10. That on or about the _____ day of _____, 19__, the said notice of lien was duly docketed in the said Clerk's office in the Lien Docket kept for the said purpose and thereafter and on or about the _____ day of _____, 19__, plaintiff caused a copy of the said notice of lien to be duly personally served upon the defendant _____, and by registered mail, return receipt requested, upon the defendants, _____.

11. That the said lien has not been paid, waived, cancelled or discharged, and that no other action or proceeding either at law or in equity has ever been brought to recover the claim of the plaintiff or any part thereof.

12. On information and belief, that all of the defendants herein have or claim to have some interest in or lien upon the said premises, which interest or lien, if any, is subsequent and subordinate, to plaintiff's lien as hereinbefore set forth.

13. That no persons other than the defendants above mentioned have or claim to have a lien upon the said premises to the knowledge of plaintiff, nor has any other lien been filed.

WHEREFORE, plaintiff demands judgment that he be adjudged to have a valid lien on the said premises for the sum of _____ ($_____) Dollars with interest thereon from the _____ day of _____, 19__, together with the costs and disbursements of this action; that the equities of the parties to this action and the order and priority of the different liens be adjusted and determined and that it be adjudged that plaintiff has a lien on said premises prior to the interest therein or lien thereon of any of the defendants; that the interest of the defendant, _____ [owner], in the premises be sold according to law and that from the proceeds of such sale the plaintiff be paid the amount of his said lien and interest thereon, together with the expenses of such sale and costs of this action, and that plaintiff have judgment for any deficiency that may remain after such payment against the defendant, _____; that the defendants and all persons claiming under or through them be forever foreclosed of all right and equity of redemption or other interest in said premises; that, in case it be determined that the plaintiff does not have a valid and subsisting lien upon said real property, the plaintiff may have a personal judgment against the defendant _____, for the sum of _____ ($_____) Dollars, with interest thereon from the _____ day of _____, 19__, together with the costs and disbursements of this action; and that plaintiff have such other and further relief as to the Court may seem just and proper.

                [Attorney for Plaintiff
                P.O. Address
                Tel. No.]

[Verification]

§ 10.135 Forms—Defense and Counterclaim Based on Wilful Exaggeration of Mechanic's Lien

AS FIRST, SEPARATE AND COMPLETE DEFENSE AND AS A COUNTERCLAIM HEREIN THE DEFENDANT, _____ CORP., ALLEGES:

12. Upon information and belief that the plaintiff at all times mentioned herein was and now is a domestic corporation organized and existing under and by virtue of the laws of the State of New York and having its principal place of business in the City of _____, New York.

13. That at all times mentioned herein, defendant, _____ Corp. was and now is a domestic corporation organized and existing under and by virtue of the laws of the State of New York, and having its principal place of business in the City of _____, New York.

14. That said defendant now is and at all times mentioned herein was the owner of the real property described in paragraph "___" of the complaint. Said parcel of real estate now is and was at all times mentioned herein commonly known as _____ Street, _____, New York.

15. That on or about _____, 19__, the plaintiff entered into a written contract with _____, a copy of which is attached hereto marked Exhibit A.

16. That pursuant to such contract _____ ($_____) Dollars was paid to the plaintiff on or about _____, 19__.

17. That on or about _____, 19__, plaintiff and defendant entered into a contract, a copy of which is attached hereto marked Exhibit B.

18. That the total fair and reasonable value of the work which the plaintiff did pursuant to such contracts was less than _____ ($_____) Dollars.

19. That the total fair and reasonable value of the work, labor and services performed by plaintiff and materials furnished by plaintiff for the improvement of real property owned by the defendant and described in paragraph "___" of the complaint was less than _____ ($_____) Dollars.

20. That on _____, 19__ plaintiff filed in the Office of the County Clerk of _____ County a Notice of Lien against the defendant and the aforesaid parcel of real property owned by the defendant, a true copy of which notice is attached to the complaint herein.

21. That the County Clerk of _____ County, in his book called "Lien Docket", entered in the column therein headed "Amount" the sum of _____ ($_____) Dollars, as the amount for which plaintiff claimed a lien against defendant's said real property as stated in such Notice of Lien.

§ 10.135 MECHANIC'S LIENS Ch. 10

22. Thereafter and on or about _____, 19__, the return date of a Notice of Motion made by the defendant for an order directing the plaintiff to serve a verified itemized statement pursuant to Section 38 of the Lien Law, plaintiff through its attorneys stated in open Court that the amount for which it was claiming a lien pursuant to aforesaid Notice of Lien was _____ ($_____) Dollars and consented that the County Clerk of _____ County change the amount stated in his docket from _____ ($_____) Dollars to _____ ($_____) Dollars and thereafter said County Clerk did change said amount of _____ ($_____) Dollars.

23. Upon information and belief that the plaintiff did wilfully exaggerate the amount for which it did claim a lien as stated in its said Notice of Lien.

24. By reason of the facts hereinbefore alleged and the statutes in such cases made and provided, particularly Sections 39 and 39–a of the Lien Law, the said lien of plaintiff is void and no recovery can be had thereon.

25. By reason of the facts hereinbefore alleged and the statutes in such cases made and provided, particularly Sections 39 and 39–a of the Lien Law, there is now due and owing to the defendant from the plaintiff the sum of _____ ($_____) Dollars including _____ ($_____) Dollars, the amount of the premium for the bond given by defendant to discharge the said lien, _____ ($_____) Dollars as reasonable attorney's fees for securing the discharge of lien on the filing of said bond and in defending and procuring in this action a judgment discharging said lien and _____ ($_____) Dollars the difference between the amount claimed to be due as stated in said Notice of Lien and the amount actually due thereon, and _____ ($_____) Dollars the amount by which the payment made as alleged in paragraph "16" hereof exceeded the total fair and reasonable value of work done and materials furnished as alleged in paragraphs "18" and "19" hereof.

WHEREFORE, defendant demands judgment:

(a) Dismissing the complaint herein.

(b) Declaring the lien alleged in the complaint herein to be void on account of wilful exaggeration.

(c) Directing that the defendant, _____ Corp. recover from the plaintiff the sum of _____ ($_____) Dollars and have judgment therefor with interest thereon.

(d) Directing that the defendants recover from the plaintiff the costs and disbursements of this action.

[Attorney for Defendant
P.O. Address
Tel. No.]

[Verification]

§ 10.136 **Forms—Affidavit in Support of Motion to Consolidate Actions for Foreclosure of Mechanic's Liens**

SUPREME COURT OF THE STATE OF NEW YORK
COUNTY OF _____

```
_____   )
                           )
_____,         )
                           )
                           )
              Plaintiff,   )
                           )  ACTION No. 1
       -against-           )
                           )  Index No. _____
                           )  [Name of Assigned Judge]
_____,         )
                           )
              Defendant.   )
_____   )
```

AFFIDAVIT IN SUPPORT OF MOTION
TO CONSOLIDATE ACTIONS

SUPREME COURT OF THE STATE OF NEW YORK
COUNTY OF _____

```
_____   )
                           )
_____,         )
                           )
                           )
              Plaintiff,   )  ACTION No. 2
                           )
       -against-           )  Index No. _____
                           )  [Name of Assigned Judge]
                           )
_____,         )
                           )
              Defendant.   )
_____   )
```

STATE OF NEW YORK   )
) ss.:
COUNTY OF _____   )

_____, being duly sworn, deposes and says: I am the attorney for the plaintiff in Action No. 1 and am making this affidavit in support of a motion to consolidate the actions entitled as above so that the trial of both these actions can be held at one and the same time.

In Action No. 1, all the defendants have been served except _____ Corp., and issue has been joined by the service of an answer by all of the defendants except _____, Inc. and _____ Inc. After the service of a summons and complaint upon the defendant, _____, Inc., which appeared by its attorney, _____, an affirmative defense was interposed stating in effect that a bond had been given to discharge the lien heretofore filed by the defendant _____, Inc., and that there was another action (Action No. 2 herein) "based upon the same cause of action as alleged by the plaintiff herein."

Your deponent thereupon communicated with _____ and _____, attorneys for _____ Corp., and ascertained that while such an action had been commenced, the action had not yet been placed upon the calendar.

Action No. 1 and Action No. 2 are both based upon essentially the same claims. _____, Inc., as well as _____, Inc., _____, Inc. and _____, Inc., were subcontractors of the defendant, _____ Corp., all of whom have claims against the said _____ Corp., as contractor and _____ Corp., as owner. These claims arise out of failure by _____ Corp., to meet its obligations and make payments as provided in its respective contracts with the said sub-contractors and is the basis of all of the claims of the said sub-contractors herein.

_____ Corp. is a surety company which bonded the lien of _____ Inc. Upon information and belief the defendant _____ Corp., has a sum of money which it is holding to apportion between the various subcontractors pursuant to a decision of the court.

It is submitted that all of the claims of the sub-contractors and lienors should be heard at the same time. In this manner all the issues can be resolved and the claims of the various lienors justly determined and apportioned. A consolidation of these actions would not only save a duplication of a trial involving the same parties and the same issues but would save considerable time and expense to all involved.

Upon information and belief, the plaintiff in Action No. 2 has noticed its case for trial for the _____ term of this court. Your deponent has been in communication with several of the defendants and upon the basis of information from the attorneys for several of the defendants, including the defendant _____ Corp., your deponent is of the opinion that all of the defendants not only consent to this motion but join in the application thereof.

That no prejudice will result but on the contrary all of the rights of all of the parties will be determined in a consolidated trial involving the same property and the same issues.

That no previous application has been made for this or similar relief.

WHEREFORE, your deponent respectfully prays that the trial of these actions be consolidated.

[*Signature*]

Ch. 10   NOTICE OF MOTION TO CONSOLIDATE   **§ 10.137**

───────────────────────
[*Type Name*]

[*Jurat*]

§ 10.137 Forms—Notice of Motion to Consolidate Actions to Foreclose Mechanic's Liens 💾

SUPREME COURT OF THE STATE OF NEW YORK
COUNTY OF _____

```
─────────────────────── )
                        )
          _____,  )
                        )
            Plaintiff,  )
                        ) Action No. 1
          -against-     )
                        ) Index No. _____
____, ____, ____,       ) [Name of Assigned Judge]
____ and ____,          )
                        )
          Defendants.   )
─────────────────────── )
```

                                   NOTICE OF MOTION TO CONSOLIDATE ACTIONS
                                   Oral argument is requested
                                   (check box if applicable) ( )

SUPREME COURT OF THE STATE OF NEW YORK
COUNTY OF _____

```
─────────────────────── )
                        )
          _____,  )
                        )
            Plaintiff,  )
                        ) Action No. 2
          -against-     )
                        ) Index No. _____
____, ____, ____,       ) [Name of Assigned Judge]
____ and ____,          )
                        )
          Defendants.   )
─────────────────────── )
```

     Upon the affidavit of _____, sworn to on _____, 19__, and upon [*list supporting papers if any*], the _____ will move this court in Room _____ at the Courthouse, _____, _____, New York, on the _____ day of _____, 19__, at _____ (a.m./p.m.) for an order, pursuant to

§ 10.137   MECHANIC'S LIENS   Ch. 10

CPLR 602 and section 43 of the Lien Law, consolidating the action above designated as Action No. 1 with the action above designated as Action No. 2, both now pending in the Supreme Court of the State of New York, County of _____, upon the ground that the said actions for foreclosure of mechanic's liens against certain real property owned by _____, of _____, New York, involve common questions of law and fact, and for such other and further relief as to the court may seem proper.

The above-entitled two actions are brought for the foreclosure of mechanic's liens.

Pursuant to CPLR 2214(b), answering affidavits, if any, are required to be served upon the undersigned at least seven days before the return date of this motion. ( ) (check box if applicable)

                                                      _____
                                                      [*Attorney for Plaintiff*
                                                      _____ (*Action No. 1*)
                                                      P.O. Address
                                                      Tel. No.]

To: _____
    [*Attorney for Plaintiff* _____
    (*Action No. 2*)
    P.O. Address
    Tel. No.]

    _____
    [*Attorney for Defendant*
    (*Actions Nos. 1 & 2*)
    P.O. Address
    Tel. No.]

§ 10.138 Forms—Acceptance of Offer to Pay Money Into Court in Discharge of Mechanic's Lien

SUPREME COURT OF THE STATE OF NEW YORK
COUNTY OF _____

```
_____
                       )
_____,       )
                       )  ACCEPTANCE OF OFFER
            Plaintiff, )  PURSUANT TO LIEN
                       )  LAW SECTION 55
    -against-          )
                       )  Index No. _____
_____,       )  [Name of Assigned Judge]
                       )
            Defendant. )
_____)
```

658

_____, the plaintiff herein, does hereby accept the offer of the defendant _____, dated _____, 19__, to pay into court the sum of _____ ($_____) Dollars to secure the discharge of that certain mechanic's lien in the sum of _____ ($_____) Dollars, which is sought to be enforced herein, and which was created by the filing of a notice of lien in the office of the Clerk of the County of _____, on the _____ day of _____, 19__, against the following described real property owned by said defendant and situate in the City of _____, County of _____:

[insert brief description],

such sum of money to take place of the above described property upon which the said lien exists and to be subject to the lien.

Dated: _____, N.Y.,
_____, 19__.

_____
[Plaintiff]

_____
[Attorney for Plaintiff
P.O. Address
Tel. No.]

To: _____
[Attorney for Defendant
P.O. Address
Tel. No.]

_____
Clerk of _____ County

§ 10.139 Forms—Offer to Pay Money Into Court in Discharge of Mechanic's Lien

SUPREME COURT OF THE STATE OF NEW YORK
COUNTY OF _____

_____)
)
_____,) OFFER TO DEPOSIT MONEY
                      Plaintiff,) PURSUANT TO LIEN LAW
) SECTION 55
             -against-   )
) Index No. _____
_____,) [Name of Assigned Judge]
)
                      Defendant.   )
_____)

§ 10.139 MECHANIC'S LIENS Ch. 10

SIRS:

Pursuant to the provisions of Lien Law, § 55, _____, the defendant herein, does hereby offer to pay into court the sum of _____ ($_____) Dollars to secure the discharge of that certain mechanic's lien in the sum of _____ ($_____) Dollars, which is sought to be enforced herein, and which was created by the filing of a notice of said lien in the office of the Clerk of the County of _____, on the _____ day of _____, 19__, against the following described real property owned by said defendant and situate in the City of _____, County of _____: [insert brief description], such sum of money to take the place of the above described property upon which the said lien exists and to be subject to the lien.

Dated: _____, N.Y.,
        _____, 19__.

_____
[*Defendant*]

_____
[*Attorney for Defendant*
P.O. Address
Tel. No.]

To: _____
[*Attorney for Plaintiff*
P.O. Address
Tel. No.]

_____
Clerk of _____ County

§ 10.140 Forms—Judgment of Foreclosure and Sale—Mechanic's Lien

At a Special Term, Part _____ of the Supreme Court of the State of New York, held in and for the County of _____, at _____, on the _____ day of _____, 19__.

Present: Hon. _____, Justice.

SUPREME COURT OF THE STATE OF NEW YORK
COUNTY OF _____

_____
_____,
               Plaintiff,   )
) JUDGMENT
        -against-   )
) Index No. _____
_____,   )
)
               Defendant.   )
_____   )

Ch. 10 JUDGMENT OF FORECLOSURE AND SALE § 10.140

The issues in this action having come on regularly for trial before _____, one of the Justices of this Court, without a jury, at a Term, Part _____ thereof, held at the _____ Courthouse, in the City of _____, on the _____ day of _____, 19__ and all of the defendants having been personally served with the summons and verified complaint herein, and the plaintiff having appeared by _____, his attorney, and the defendant _____, having appeared by _____, his attorney and the defendant, _____, having appeared by _____, its attorney, and this case having been duly tried and the Court having heard the allegations and proofs of the parties and a decision in writing dated _____, 19__, stating the grounds on which the issues were decided by the Court having been made and filed, and further stating separately findings of fact and conclusions of law directing judgment for plaintiff as hereinafter provided,

NOW, on motion of _____, attorney for the plaintiff herein, it is

ORDERED, ADJUDGED AND DECREED that the defendant, _____ [owner] is justly indebted to the plaintiff in the amount of _____ ($_____) Dollars with interest from _____, 19__ in the amount of _____ ($_____) Dollars making in all the sum of _____ ($_____) Dollars and it is further

ORDERED, ADJUDGED AND DECREED that by the filing and docketing of the lien set forth in the complaint, filed by plaintiff _____, 19__ against defendant _____'s property hereinafter described, the plaintiff acquired and now has a valid and subsisting lien against the premises described in the complaint herein in the amount of _____ ($_____) Dollars, and it is further

ORDERED, ADJUDGED AND DECREED that all the right, title and interest which the defendant, _____, had on the _____ day of _____, 19__, in the real property described in the complaint and hereinafter specifically described, be sold at public auction by and under the direction of _____ Esq., who is hereby appointed referee for that purpose, and that said referee give public notice of the time and place of such sale, according to the law and the course and practice of this Court and that the plaintiff, or any of the parties to this action, may become a purchaser or purchasers on such sale; that the referee execute to the purchaser or purchasers on such sale a deed or deeds of the premises sold, and that such referee on receiving the proceeds of sale forthwith pay therefrom the taxes, assessments and water rates which are or may become liens on the premises at the time of sale, with such interest or penalties as may have lawfully accrued to the date of payment; that said

§ 10.140　　　　　MECHANIC'S LIENS　　　　　Ch. 10

referee then deposit the balance of such proceeds of sale in _____ Bank and shall thereafter make the following payments, and his checks drawn for that purpose shall be paid by the said depository;

FIRST: A sum not exceeding _____ ($_____) Dollars to the said referee for his fees herein.

SECOND: Advertising expenses as shown on the bills presented and certified by the said referee to be correct, and duplicate copies of which shall be left with said depository.

THIRD: That said referee shall then pay to the following parties the following amounts, as far as the balance of said proceeds of sale will pay the same, in the following order of priority:

a) To the plaintiff the sum of _____ ($_____) Dollars with interest from the date hereof, and

b) To the plaintiff the sum of _____ ($_____) Dollars adjudged to the plaintiff for its costs and disbursements in this action and an additional allowance in the sum of _____ ($_____) Dollars, making a total sum due of _____ ($_____) Dollars with interest thereon from the date hereof.

FOURTH: That in case the plaintiff be the purchaser of said premises at said sale, or in the event that the rights of the purchaser at said sale and the terms of sale under this judgment shall be assigned to and acquired by plaintiff and a valid assignment thereof filed with said referee, said referee shall not require the plaintiff to pay in cash the entire amount bid at said sale but shall execute and deliver to plaintiff a deed or deeds of the premises sold upon payment to said referee of the amounts specified above in the items marked "First" and "Second", and the amounts of the aforesaid taxes, assessments and water rates, and interest and penalties thereon, or in lieu of the payment of said last mentioned amounts, upon filing with said referee the receipts of the proper municipal authorities showing the payment thereof. That the balance of the amount bid, after deducting the aforesaid amounts paid by plaintiff for referee fees, advertising expenses, taxes, assessments and water rates, shall be allowed to the plaintiff and applied by said referee upon the amount to be paid to the plaintiff as specified above in item marked "Third" Sub-division "a" and "b". That if, after so applying the balance of said amount paid, there shall be a surplus over and above said amount due to the plaintiff, the plaintiff shall pay to said referee, upon delivery to it of said referee's deed, the amount of said surplus. That said referee, on receiving said several amounts from the plaintiff, shall forthwith pay therefrom said taxes, assessments, water rates and interest or penalties thereon, unless the same have already been paid, and shall then deposit the balance with the Treasurer of the County of _____ [or City of New York]. That the said referee take the receipt of the plaintiff, or his attorney, and of the defendant, _____ [owner], or his attorney, for the amounts paid as hereinbefore directed under item marked "Third" and file same with his report of sale and that he deposit the surplus monies, if any, with the Treasurer of the County of _____ [*or City of New York*], as hereinabove directed, within five days after he receives the same, to the credit of this action, to be drawn only by order of the Court, signed by a Justice of the Court, and that he make a report of such sale and file it with the Clerk of the County of _____ with all convenient speed.

That if the proceeds of such sale be insufficient to pay the amounts in items marked "First", "Second" and "Third", that the said referee specify the amount of the deficiency on the claim of the plaintiff, and that the plaintiff may have personal judgment against the defendant, _____ [*owner*], for such deficiency so specified by the referee upon due application to the court and that said plaintiff may have execution therefor, in such amount as determined by said court, and that the purchaser or purchasers at such sale be let into possession of the premises so sold to them on production of the referee's deed or deeds of such premises, and it is further

ORDERED, ADJUDGED AND DECREED that each and all of the defendants to this action, and all persons claiming under them, or any or either of them, after the filing of the notice of the pendency of action herein, be and they hereby are forever barred and foreclosed of and from all right, title, interest, lien, claim and equity of redemption in and to said premises and each and every part thereof.

The following is a description of said premises hereinbefore mentioned:

[*insert description of property*]

Enter,

_____
J.S.C.

§ 10.141 Forms—Judgment of Foreclosure—Lien for Public Improvement—Where Lien Discharged and Fund Retained for Payment

At a Special Term, Part _____ of the Supreme Court of the State of New York, held in and for the County of _____, at _____, on the _____ day of _____, 19__.

Present: Hon. _____, Justice.

§ 10.141

SUPREME COURT OF THE STATE OF NEW YORK
COUNTY OF _____

```
                              )
_____,              )
                              )
                 Plaintiff,   )
                              )   JUDGMENT
     -against-                )
                              )   Index No. _____
_____,              )
                              )
                 Defendant.   )
                              )
```

This action having been duly commenced for the foreclosure of a lien affecting the public improvement described in the complaint, and the issues having duly come on to be tried before a Term, Part _____, of the Supreme Court held in and for the County of _____, and the allegations and evidence of the parties having been heard, and due deliberation having been had, and the decision dated _____, 19__, having been made and filed herein by the Hon. _____, before whom the action was tried, and _____, Esq., having duly appeared for plaintiff _____, Inc., and _____, Esq. having duly appeared for defendant _____ Corporation, and Honorable _____, Attorney General of the State of New York, having duly appeared for defendant The People of the State of New York,

NOW, on motion of _____, Esq., attorney for plaintiff _____, Inc. it is

ORDERED, ADJUDGED AND DECREED that plaintiff _____, Inc., by the filing of its Notice of Lien described in the Decision and herein and by its having furnished materials and performed labor in and upon the public improvement described in the Decision herein, did acquire and now has a good, valid and subsisting lien in the amount of _____ ($_____) Dollars and interest upon and against the funds retained on _____, 19__ by the Comptroller of the State of New York, pursuant to Section 21, Subdivision 6, of the Lien Law of the State of New York, said retained funds arising out of Department of _____ Contract No. _____ for the construction and completion of the public improvement provided for therein and described in the Decision herein; and it is further

ORDERED, ADJUDGED AND DECREED that there is now due and owing to plaintiff _____, Inc. from defendant _____ Corporation and should be paid to plaintiff _____, Inc. by the Comptroller of the State of New York the sum of _____ ($_____) Dollars with interest on _____ ($_____) Dollars from an average due date of _____, 19__ and on _____ ($_____) Dollars from _____, 19__; and it is further

    ORDERED, ADJUDGED AND DECREED that plaintiff _____, Inc. is granted judgment enforcing and foreclosing its said lien and in form only against defendant _____ Corporation for the sum of _____ ($_____) Dollars with interest on _____ ($_____) Dollars from an average due date of _____, 19__, amounting to the sum of _____ ($_____) Dollars, and on _____ ($_____) Dollars from _____, 19__, amounting to the sum of _____ ($_____) Dollars, and costs as taxed in the sum of _____ ($_____) Dollars, making in all the sum of _____ ($_____) Dollars; and it is further

    ORDERED, ADJUDGED AND DECREED that out of said funds, to wit: _____ ($_____) Dollars duly retained on _____, 19__ by the Comptroller of the State of New York, pursuant to Section 21, Subdivision 6 of the Lien Law of the State of New York, said retained funds arising out of said Department of _____ Contract No. _____, the Comptroller of the State of New York pay to plaintiff _____, Inc. the said sum of _____ ($_____) Dollars; and it is further

    ORDERED, ADJUDGED AND DECREED that, in the event there be any deficiency, plaintiff _____, Inc. is hereby granted personal judgment against defendant _____ Corporation for the amount of such deficiency.

                                     Enter,

                                       _____
                                       J.S.C.

§ 10.142 Forms—Affidavit in Support of Motion for Summary Judgment—Foreclosure of Lien for Public Improvement

SUPREME COURT OF THE STATE OF NEW YORK
COUNTY OF _____

_____,
                       Plaintiff,
) AFFIDAVIT
      -against-
) Index No. _____
_____,
                     Defendant.

§ 10.142   MECHANIC'S LIENS   Ch. 10

STATE OF NEW YORK)
) ss.:
COUNTY OF _____)

_____, being duly sworn, deposes and says:

1. That he is the _____ of _____ Inc., the plaintiff herein, and is fully familiar with the facts and circumstances set forth herein.

2. That heretofore and on or about _____, 19__ the plaintiff, _____ Inc. and the defendant, _____ Inc. entered into a contract under the terms of which _____ Inc. was to [describe work] for a [describe project] which the defendant, _____ Inc. was building for the defendant, the City of _____, New York. The agreed price for the work was $_____ per lineal foot (a copy of the contract is attached to the complaint as Exhibit A).

3. The total value of the work performed by _____ Inc. was $_____.

4. _____ Inc. was to be paid pursuant to Article 4 of its contract with the defendant, _____ Inc., that is, _____ Inc. was to be paid on the 25th of the month for 90% of the value of the work installed during the preceding month.

5. _____ Inc. completed its work and submitted its application for payment on or about _____, 19__, which made payment of the sum of $_____ due on _____, 19__.

6. Neither the defendant, _____ Inc. nor the defendant, The City of _____, has made any objection to the amount of the requisition for payment nor has either made any objection to the quality of work done by the plaintiff, _____ Inc.

7. Numerous demands were made for payment and on or about _____, 19__ deponent was informed by an employee of the City of _____ that the defendant, _____ Inc. at that date had received three (3) requisitions and that the payment for the piling was in the first of said requisitions, the exact date of which is unknown to your deponent.

8. When no payment was made, _____ Inc. duly caused a notice of lien to be filed with the Comptroller of the City of _____ and the City Engineer of the City of _____ on or about _____, 19__ and served on _____ Inc.

9. Deponent is informed by counsel and verily believes that said lien has been extended by order of this Court.

10. Deponent has also been shown an Order issued by this Court directing the City of _____ to retain in its possession the sum of $_____ from moneys due _____ Inc. as a sum sufficient to protect the City against any claim which the plaintiff, _____ Inc. might have by reason of the aforesaid lien.

Ch. 10   VERIFIED STATEMENT FROM TRUSTEE   § 10.143

11. That Order is based upon an affidavit of _____ who represents himself as Vice President of _____ Inc. That affidavit does not contest the value of the work done by _____ Inc. nor the fact that at least $_____ was then due.

12. Deponent further states that no check in the sum of $_____ or any other sum was tendered to deponent or any other officer or employee of _____ Inc. by the defendant, _____ Inc., the defendant, City of _____, or anyone acting on their behalf.

13. The defendant, _____ Inc., by its failure to make payment as provided in the contract between the parties, has deprived the plaintiff of the use of its money for a period in excess of one year.

14. This affidavit is made in support of a motion for summary judgment against the defendant, _____ Inc., declaring that said defendant has breached its contract with the plaintiff and that there is therefore due to the plaintiff the sum of $_____ with interest thereon from _____, 19__ or in the alternative that the defendant, _____ Inc., is now indebted to the plaintiff in the sum of $_____ with interest from _____, 19__, the balance being due on final payment by the City of _____ to the defendant, _____ Inc., further directing the defendant the City of _____ to pay said amount to the plaintiff herein out of the sum of $_____ due from the defendant, City of _____, to the defendant, _____ Inc. and for such other and further relief as to the Court may seem just and proper.

[Signature]

_____

[Type Name]

[Jurat]

§ 10.143   Forms—Demand for Verified Statement From Trustee[1]

[Add court and caption]

PLEASE TAKE NOTICE that the undersigned having been entitled for more than thirty days last past to a payment as hereinafter set forth, on account of the improvement hereinafter mentioned, hereby demands that you deliver to it a verified statement setting forth the entries with respect to the books and records maintained for the Lien Law Trust established by law for such improvement herein within ten days after the service upon you of this demand pursuant to provisions of Section 76 of the Lien Law and the names and addresses of the person or persons

---

§ 10.143
1. Trust beneficiaries are entitled to examine and copy or demand a verified statement of setting forth the entries in trust records. See Lien Law § 76.

§ 10.143 MECHANIC'S LIENS Ch. 10

who on behalf of, or as Officer, Director or Agent of the Trustee made or consented to the making of any payment shown in such statement, and in connection with this demand the undersigned states:

1. The name and address of the undersigned beneficiary is:

_____ Construction Corp.

_____ Street

_____, _____ County, New York

2. The improvement on account of which the undersigned claims the right to payment is an improvement of real property commonly known as _____, constructed on the property of _____ Development Corp., _____ Associates, and _____, situate on the west side of _____ and _____, at _____, _____ County, New York.

3. The amount due and unpaid to the undersigned is _____ ($_____) Dollars which became due and payable to it on _____, 19__, for the rental of equipment and the supplying of labor and materials, including asphalt and cinders, in connection with the paving of parking fields upon the said property.

4. The monies due _____ Construction Corp., for the aforementioned work, labor and materials at the aforementioned site are due in accordance with a contract made between _____ Corp., and the said _____ Construction Corp.

_____ CONSTRUCTION CORP.

By: _____
President

To: _____ Corp.
_____
_____, New York

§ 10.144 Forms—Petition for Verified Statement From Trustee of Trust Funds

SUPREME COURT OF THE STATE OF NEW YORK
COUNTY OF _____

In the Matter of The Demand of)
_____ Construction Corp. Upon) PETITION
_____ Corp. for a Statement)
pursuant to Section 76 of the) Index No. _____
Lien Law.)

TO THE SUPREME COURT OF THE STATE OF NEW YORK, COUNTY OF _____:

668

The petition of _____ Construction Corp., respectfully shows to the court and alleges:

FIRST: The petitioner is a domestic corporation with a principal place of business located at _____, New York.

SECOND: That petitioner was employed by _____ Corp., to pave parking fields of property hereinafter described and rent construction equipment in connection with said improvement.

THIRD: That petitioner actually did pave said parking fields and rent said equipment to the benefit of _____ Corp., a subcontractor of _____ Corp., the general contractor, and _____ Development Corp., _____ Associates, and _____, owners of the property hereinafter described.

FOURTH: The amount due and unpaid to petitioner for the aforementioned work, labor and service is _____ ($_____) Dollars.

FIFTH: That the real property upon which petitioner rendered the aforementioned work, labor and service is commonly known as _____, situated on the west side of _____ at _____, _____ County, New York, and is described on the tax maps of the County of _____ as being in Section _____, Block _____, Lot numbers _____, _____, _____, and _____.

SIXTH: That on or about the _____ day of _____, 19__, above named petitioner caused to be served upon _____ Corp., a notice pursuant to Section 76 of the Lien Law, requesting that the respondent, as Lien Law Trustee under the aforementioned improvement, serve upon the petitioner a verified statement setting forth the entries with respect to the books and records maintained for the Lien Law Trust by respondent. A copy of such Demand for Statement is annexed hereto, marked "Exhibit A", and made a part hereof.

SEVENTH: That more than ten days have elapsed since the service of said demand and _____ Corp., has failed to comply with such demand to serve such statement.

WHEREFORE, the petitioner prays for an order, pursuant to Section 76, Subdivision 5 of the Lien Law, directing _____ Corp. to serve upon petitioner within ten days of the date of said order, a verified statement drawn in accordance with the provisions of Section 76 of the Lien Law setting forth the entries with respect to the books and records maintained for the Lien Law Trusts established by law for the improvement of real property described in this petition and for such other or further relief as the court may determine is just and proper.

_____ Construction Corp.

By: _____
V.P.

[Verification]

§ 10.145 Forms—Complaint by Subcontractor to Enforce Trust Against Funds Received by Contractor or Assignee of Contractor

SUPREME COURT OF THE STATE OF NEW YORK
COUNTY OF _____

_____)
_____, individually and in behalf)
of all the lienors, claimants or)
creditors for wages or materials)
in connection with improvement)
of certain land and premises)
herein described.)
) COMPLAINT
              Plaintiff,)
) Index No. _____
        -against-)
)
_____, Corporation, _____ and)
_____,)
)
           Defendants.)
_____)

    The plaintiff, _____, by his attorney, _____, respectfully shows to this court and alleges:

    FOR A FIRST CAUSE OF ACTION AGAINST THE DEFENDANT, _____:

    FIRST: Upon information and belief, that heretofore and on or about the _____ day of _____, 19__, the defendant, _____, and the defendant, _____, entered into an agreement wherein and whereby the said _____ contracted and agreed to construct a residence building on premises of the defendant, _____, at _____ Avenue, in the Village of _____, County of _____, State of New York, and the said defendant, _____, agreed to furnish the labor and the materials in connection therewith and the defendant, _____, agreed to pay the said _____, the agreed value of such work and materials upon the completion of the construction of the said building according to contract.

    SECOND: That thereafter said _____ commenced the construction of the said house on the said premises of the defendant, _____, and in connection therewith entered into a written contract with the plaintiff, _____, for the installation of ten radiators in the said dwelling house, together with the necessary pipe to connect the same with the boiler and central heating plant, and to furnish the materials in connection therewith for the sum of _____ ($_____) Dollars, and the agreement therefor was executed by and between the plaintiff _____, and the defendant, _____, on _____, 19__.

THIRD: That thereafter the plaintiff duly performed and furnished all of the things necessary on his part to be performed and furnished according to the terms of the said contract, and has duly demanded from the defendant, _____, the sum of _____ ($_____) Dollars, being the agreed and reasonable amount of the materials furnished and services rendered, but the defendant, _____, has wholly refused and failed to pay the same.

FOURTH: That upon information and belief the said defendant _____, has received, on account of the sums due for the construction of the dwelling hereinbefore mentioned from _____, the sum of _____ ($_____) Dollars.

FIFTH: That said funds in the hands of the said _____ constitute trust funds in his hands for the benefit of any and all other persons, if any there be, who are mechanics or material men who have furnished labor or materials in connection with the work of the construction of said dwelling house on the premises of the defendant _____.

SIXTH: That the plaintiff herein sues individually on behalf of himself and in behalf of all other persons, if any there be, who are or who may claim to be, lienors, or creditors of the said defendant, _____, by reason of services rendered or materials supplied in connection with the improvement of the premises hereinbefore described or by reason of said contract for the work or materials furnished thereunder for the purpose of having such claims ascertained and determined and allocated to the persons and claimants entitled thereto ratably in accordance with the amounts of their respective claims therein.

AS A SECOND CAUSE OF ACTION AGAINST THE DEFENDANT, _____ CORPORATION:

SEVENTH: Upon information and belief that at all times hereinafter mentioned, the _____ Corporation was and is a domestic corporation, organized and existing under and by virtue of the laws of the State of New York.

EIGHTH: Realleges and reiterates, with the same force and effect as though set forth at length herein, the allegations contained in paragraphs "First", "Second", "Third", "Fourth" and "Fifth" of the complaint herein.

NINTH: Upon information and belief that on or about the _____ day of _____, 19__, the defendant, _____, assigned to the defendant, _____ Corporation, all of his right, title and interest in and to the balance of the moneys due or to become due from the defendant, _____, to the defendant, _____, in connection with the construction of the said residence building and under the contract for the construc-

§ 10.145 MECHANIC'S LIENS Ch. 10

tion thereof, on which contract there was unpaid the sum of _____ ($_____) Dollars.

TENTH: Upon information and belief, that thereafter the defendant, _____, paid unto the defendant, _____ Corporation, the sum of _____ ($_____) Dollars and the defendant, _____ Corporation, in consideration therefor executed and delivered a release of the defendant, _____, from any and all claims which the said _____, or his assignee, the defendant _____ Corporation, had against the said _____.

ELEVENTH: That the said monies received by the defendant, _____ Corporation, from the defendant, _____, in payment of the amounts owed to the defendant, _____, were trust funds for the benefit of the plaintiff and of all persons who furnished materials or services in connection with the construction of the said residence structure, and who have not been paid in full thereof, ratably in accordance with the amount of their respective claims.

TWELFTH: That the plaintiff herein sues on behalf of himself individually and on behalf of all other persons, firms, or corporations who may be or who may claim to be lienors against the premises described in paragraph "First" of the complaint herein, or creditors of the defendant, _____, by reason of services rendered or materials furnished and supplied and such other persons, firms, or corporations, if any there be, to the improvement of the said premises or pursuant to and by virtue of the contract between said defendant _____ and the defendant _____, and for the determination and allocation of the respective interests of the plaintiff and such persons, firms, or corporations, if any there be, in and to the trust funds in the hands of the defendant _____ Corporation and who have not been paid in full therefor ratably in accordance with the amounts of their respective claims.

WHEREFORE, the plaintiff demands judgment as follows:

1. For judgment against the defendant _____, determining that the sum of _____ ($_____) Dollars paid to him by the said defendant _____, be declared to constitute trust funds in his hands and that he be declared a trustee thereof for the benefit and purpose of payment of all persons, firms or corporations who have rendered services or furnished materials to the said defendant _____, and for the improvement of the real estate described in paragraph "first" of the complaint herein and for the determination and allocation of the respective rights and interests of such creditors or claimants in and to said trust funds.

2. For a judgment against the _____ Corporation declaring and imposing a trust upon the funds paid by the defendant _____, to said _____ Corporation, as assignee of the defendant _____, for the benefit of all persons, firms, or corporations who have rendered services or furnished materials to the said _____ for the improvement of the said real property and for the adjudication and allocation of the respec-

tive rights and interests in and to said trust funds of the parties entitled thereto.

3. For a judgment for the costs and disbursements of this action and such other and further relief as to the Court may seem just and proper.

[Attorney for Plaintiff
P.O. Address
Tel. No.]

[Verification]

§ 10.146 Forms—Complaint by Surety to Have Parties Declared Trustees of Subcontract Moneys and for Accounting[1]

SUPREME COURT OF THE STATE OF NEW YORK
COUNTY OF _____

_____, individually and in behalf of all the lienors, claimants or creditors for wages or materials in connection with improvement of certain land and premises herein described.

Plaintiff,

-against-

_____, Corporation, _____ and _____,

Defendants.

COMPLAINT
Index No. _____

The plaintiff, complaining of the defendants, alleges

First: That at all the times herein mentioned, the plaintiff was and now is a domestic corporation, maintaining an office for the transaction of business at No. _____ _____ Avenue, _____, New York.

Second: Upon information and belief, that the defendant, _____ Trucking, Inc., is a domestic corporation maintaining an office for the

---

§ 10.146
1. As noted in § 10.102, an action by a trust beneficiary to enforce a trust must be brought in a representative capacity. Although the rules contained in Article 9 of the CPLR apply to such actions, the court has to discretion to relax the prerequisites contained in CPLR 908.

transaction of business at No. _____ _____ Avenue, _____, New York, and that all of the other defendants are residents of _____ County, New York; that the defendants _____, _____ and _____, are officers and directors of _____ Trucking, Inc.

Third: Upon information and belief, that _____, Paving Co., Inc., is a domestic corporation with its principal office and place of business located in the Village of _____, _____ County, New York.

Fourth: Upon information and belief, that heretofore and on or about _____, 19__, said _____ Paving Co., Inc. entered into a prime contract with the State of New York, Department of Public Works, for the construction of the _____ Street Arterial Highway, in the City of _____, New York, known and described as Contract No. _____.

Fifth: Upon information and belief, that heretofore and on or about _____, 19__, said _____ Paving Co., Inc., herein referred to as the prime contractor, entered into a subcontract with the defendant, _____ Trucking, Inc., herein referred to as the subcontractor, for the furnishing of labor and materials, supplies and equipment, and performing certain of the work embraced within said prime contract, including particularly Items _____, _____, _____, and _____ of the prime contract, in accordance with the terms of the related plans and specifications of said prime contract, which contracts, plans and specifications are incorporated herein by reference.

Sixth: That as a condition of the said subcontract being awarded to the defendant subcontractor, said subcontractor was required to furnish to _____ Paving Co., Inc., two (2) surety bonds, one known and described as a labor and material payment bond, and the other known and described as a performance bond.

Seventh: That the subcontractor, upon its application to the plaintiff, applied to the plaintiff and requested the plaintiff to execute and deliver to the prime contractor, as surety, however, and not otherwise, for said subcontractor, its labor and material payment bond, and its separate performance bond; and that upon said application plaintiff made, executed and delivered to the prime contractor its said labor and material payment bond, a copy of which is annexed hereto, marked Exhibit "A", and made a part hereof, and a copy of which performance bond is annexed hereto, marked Exhibit "B", and made a part hereof.

Eighth: Upon information and belief, that the defendant subcontractor entered upon the performance of said subcontract and physically completed substantial portions thereof and received payments on the subcontract price of at least _____ ($_____) Dollars, but left unpaid substantial bills for labor, materials, services and supplies; that said subcontractor has defaulted in the performance of said subcontract, and that the plaintiff has been obliged to incur a liability on its aforesaid performance bond for the payment of labor, materials, supplies and services necessary to complete said subcontract, the precise extent of which is not known and cannot be ascertained at this time.

Ninth: That _____ Products Inc., a domestic corporation whose address is _____ Road, P.O. Box _____, _____, New York, furnished materials to said subcontractor for use, and which were used, in the construction of said improvement, in the fair and reasonable amount of _____ ($_____) Dollars, which claim became due and payable on or about _____, 19__; that after due investigation and inquiry the plaintiff paid said claim in full; that by assignment, subrogation and by operation of law, the plaintiff is now the owner and holder of all of the rights and remedies of said _____ Products Inc. as a job creditor, relating to the aforesaid contract moneys.

Tenth: Upon information and belief, that by virtue of the provisions of the Lien Law of the State of New York, the said sum of _____ ($_____) Dollars, which has been paid by the prime contractor to the defendant subcontractor on account of the aforesaid improvement, constitutes trust funds to be applied by the subcontractor first to the payment of job creditors arising out of said improvement.

Eleventh: Upon information and relief, that substantial portions of the said sum of _____ ($_____) Dollars were diverted and paid to one or more or all of the defendants, _____, _____, _____, and _____, individually and doing business as _____ Factors Co., hereinafter collectively referred to as to as transferees, and to other non-job or non-trust beneficiaries, as defined in Article 3–A of the Lien Law, _____ ($_____) Dollars of which, upon information and belief, were diverted and paid to and received by _____, doing business as _____ Factors Co., and that the amount or amounts of the balance of said diversions to the other transferees are unknown to the plaintiff at this time.

Twelfth: Upon information and belief, that the defendant _____, individually and doing business as _____ Factors Co., when he received said payments, knew or had notice and knowledge that the checks or proceeds thereof received by him were contract estimates and payments on account of work done by the defendant subcontractor and its suppliers on the subcontract job herein referred to; and knew that said trust funds were trust funds within the purview of Article 3–A of the Lien Law of the State of New York; and that the defendants, _____, _____ and _____, knew or had notice and knowledge that the checks or proceeds thereof received by them, and aggregating some _____ ($_____) Dollars were contract estimates and payments on account of work done by the defendant subcontractor and its suppliers on the subcontract job herein referred to; and knew that said funds were trust funds within the purview of Article 3–A of the Lien Law of the State of New York.

Thirteenth: Upon information and belief, that the receipt, acceptance and retention by the defendants-transferees of the proceeds of said

§ 10.146   MECHANIC'S LIENS   Ch. 10

contract moneys constituted diversions of trust funds within the purview of Article 3–A of the Lien Law of the State of New York, and that said defendants-transferees participated in the diversion of such trust funds, and by reason thereof became, by operation of law, trustees ex maleficio for the benefit of the job creditors on said job to the extent of such diversions necessary to satisfy the claim of the job creditor now owned and held by the plaintiff, as well as the claims of such other job creditors as may come in and participate in this action, and also the loss, damage and claims of the plaintiff in completing said defaulted subcontract.

Fourteenth: Upon information and belief, that some of the persons who have asserted claims against the plaintiff and claim to have furnished work, labor, services, materials or supplies, in the prosecution of said subcontract, the nature, extent and correctness of whose claims, is not presently known to the plaintiff, are set forth on Exhibit "C" attached hereto, and made a part hereof.

Fifteenth: Upon information and belief, that there are other suppliers to said subcontract job, the existence, nature, extent and correctness of whose claims are not presently known to the plaintiff, and that it is accordingly impractical to name them as parties to or interested in this action. This action, however, is brought for the benefit of all such persons, whether presently known or not.

Sixteenth: Upon information and belief, that the books of account, cancelled checks, check stubs and other accounting records of the defendant subcontractor have been withheld and secreted from the plaintiff by the defendant subcontractor and its officers, which have hindered and delayed and are hindering and delaying the plaintiff in the prompt and expeditious processing of the claims of said job creditors.

Seventeenth: Upon information and belief, that the defendants-transferees were not furnishers of labor, materials or supplies to said subcontract job and were not trust beneficiaries of said subcontract job or subcontract job moneys, or other beneficiaries under Article 3–A of the Lien Law of the State of New York.

Eighteenth: Upon information and belief, that said defendants-transferees did not file or did not properly file any assignment or proper assignment of the funds of said subcontract moneys, as required by the Lien Law of the State of New York, nor did they, or any of them, file any notice of lending, as prescribed by Article 3–A of said Lien Law.

Nineteenth: That one (1) year has not elapsed since the completion of the improvement herein referred to.

Twentieth: Upon information and belief, that no other Article 3–A action has been brought or is pending with reference to said subcontract job.

Twenty–First: That prior to the commencement of this action, the plaintiff demanded of all of the defendants the payment to the plaintiff of the amount of the job creditors claim paid by the plaintiff, but that such demand has been refused and no part thereof has been paid.

Twenty–Second: That this action is brought as a class action under Article 3–A of the Lien Law of the State of New York.

WHEREFORE, plaintiff demands judgment:

1. That the defendant, _____ Trucking, Inc., be required to account for and disclose the disposition of the several payments of subcontract moneys and the proceeds and avails thereof received by it from _____ Paving Co., Inc., growing out of the construction subcontract herein referred to, or so much thereof as shall be necessary to repay to the plaintiff the amount paid by it to said job creditor herein referred to, and also the claims of all of said other job creditors who shall have joined in this action up to the time of the entry of the final judgment to be entered herein, together with interest on such amounts as the defendant has received, from the date each sum was received by it, together with the costs and disbursements of the action.

2. That the defendants, _____, _____, _____, and _____, individually and doing business as _____ Factors Co., and each and all of them, be required to account for and disclose the receipt and disposition of the subcontract moneys and the proceeds and avails thereof received by them, and each of them, growing out of the construction subcontract herein referred to, or so much thereof as shall be necessary to repay to the plaintiff the amount paid by it to the job creditor herein referred to, and also the claims of all other job creditors who shall have joined in this action up to the time of the entry of the final judgment to be entered herein, together with such amount or amounts as the plaintiff shall be required to pay to complete or pay for the completion of the defaulted subcontract, together with interest on such amounts as each of such defendants-transferees, respectively, has received, from the date each sum was received by said defendants, respectively, together with the costs and disbursements of the action.

3. That the defendants be declared trustees of all of said subcontract moneys arising from the prosecution of the construction subcontract herein referred to, aggregating _____ ($_____) Dollars, and that the plaintiff and all others who shall have joined in this action be adjudged to have claims thereon and therein for the amounts of their respective claims, and that the plaintiff's claim presently paid to said job creditor be adjudged and fixed at _____ ($_____) Dollars with interest, together with such other claim or claims of job creditors as the plaintiff shall have paid and established prior to the entry of the judgment to be entered herein, and including also plaintiff's loss, cost, damage and liability which it may have incurred in completing said defaulted subcontract.

4. That this court make such direction as to the giving of notice to other job creditors, giving them an opportunity and notice to come in and participate in this action as may be just and proper.

5. That the court determine the shares and interests of all persons in such trust funds, including the shares and interests of persons not presently parties to this action, and require the production of the books, records and papers of the defendant _____ Trucking, Inc., to ascertain the identity of the job creditors to assist the Court in determining who are or may be job creditors, and the extent and validity of their claims arising out of the construction subcontract herein referred to.

6. That the Court take such proceedings as are necessary to bring before it and under its control all such trust funds and all property into which the same may have been diverted and to distribute the same among the parties and persons entitled thereto.

7. That the plaintiff have such other, further and different relief as may be just and proper.

[Attorney for Plaintiff
P.O. Address
Tel. No.]

[Verification]

Ch. 10   ACTION TO IMPRESS & ENFORCE TRUST § 10.147

§ 10.147 Forms—Affidavit in Support of Motion to Determine if Class Action Can Be Maintained—Action to Impress and Enforce Trust[1]

SUPREME COURT OF THE STATE OF NEW YORK
COUNTY OF _____

_____
)
_____, individually and in behalf   )
of all the lienors, claimants or   )
creditors for wages or materials   )
in connection with improvement   )
of certain land and premises   )
herein described.   ) AFFIDAVIT
)
                        Plaintiff,   ) Index No. _____
) [Name of Assigned Judge]
         -against-   )
)
_____, Corporation, _____ and   )
)
_____,   )
)
                        Defendants.   )
_____   )

STATE OF NEW YORK)
) ss:
COUNTY of _____)

_____, being duly worn, deposes and says:

1. I am an attorney at law duly licensed to practice before the courts of the State of New York, and am associated with the firm of _____, _____, _____ & _____, P.C., attorneys for plaintiff in the above entitled action. I make this affidavit in support of plaintiff's motion to have the action declared a class action and to determine the method of notice.

2. The summons and complaint were served upon the defendant, _____ ("Contractor") by service upon ___, an attorney in the Office of the Secretary of State of the State of New York on the ___ day of _____, 1996, and upon defendant ___ Bank, by service upon _____.

3. As more fully appears from a copy of the summons and complaint submitted herewith, this is an action against the defendant to

---

§ 10.147
1. As noted in § 10.102, an action by a trust beneficiary to enforce a trust must be brought in a representative capacity. Although the rules contained in Article 9 of the CPLR apply to such actions, the court has to discretion to relax the prerequisites contained in CPLR 908.

§ 10.147   MECHANIC'S LIENS   Ch. 10

impress a trust pursuant to Article 3–A of the Lien Law of the State of New York upon certain funds which prior to _____, have been maintained in a bank account with defendant _____ Bank in the name of Contractor. Said funds, upon information and belief, were received by Contractor as the result of construction projects performed on job sites located within the State of New York.

4. Annexed hereto as Exhibit "B" is a copy of an affidavit of _____, President of Contractor, submitted as Contractor's answer to interrogatories in an action for substantially the same relief requested in the above entitled action, which action was commenced in the United States District Court of the _____ District of New York and which action was dismissed for reasons other than voluntary discontinuance and neglect to prosecute. Upon information and belief, Exhibit "B" contains admissions binding on Contractor which establish the class of all creditors comprising New York Lien Law Article 3–A creditors having performed work for Contractor upon construction projects located in New York and thereby entitled to share in funds received by Contractor as general contractor and deposited in an account in the name of Contractor maintained in the _____ Bank.

5. Upon information and belief, as more fully appears from Exhibit "B" annexed hereto, there are ___ creditors belonging to the class of creditors comprising mechanic's lienors and Article 3–A creditors under the Lien Law of the State of New York and said creditors, upon information and belief, are owed the money as a result of having performed sub-contracting services for Contractor on construction projects located within the State of New York. Upon information and belief, ten of the creditors listed may have waived their rights in the aforesaid bank account.

6. Upon information and belief, as more fully appears from Exhibit "B" annexed hereto, Contractor deposited the funds it received under or in connection with the contract for the improvement of real property in New York State, portions of which work were performed by the creditors listed in Exhibit "B" annexed hereto, and in particular, portions of which were performed by plaintiff _____ & Son, Inc., and deposited such funds in the bank account in the _____ Bank which account was maintained in the name of Contractor.

7. Upon information and belief, as a result of the foregoing, the funds deposited by Contractor with the _____ Bank in an account in the name of Contractor were trust funds within the meaning of Article 3–A of the Lien Law of the State of New York.

8. Upon information and belief, defendant _____ Bank transferred funds out of the account of Contractor which monies were held by Contractor in trust for the creditors listed in Exhibit "B" annexed hereto. Upon information and belief, the aforesaid transfers by _____

Ch. 10   ACTION TO IMPRESS & ENFORCE TRUST § 10.147

Bank were in violation of Article 3-A of the Lien Law of the State of New York.

9. Upon information and belief, there are numerous and substantial questions of law and fact common to the proposed class of creditors set forth in Exhibit "B", and in particular, but in no way limiting the foregoing, the following questions of law and fact are common to the proposed class:

(a) Whether the funds deposited in the account of Contractor with the defendant _____ Bank were trust funds pursuant to the provisions of Article 3-A of the Lien Law of the State of New York;

(b) Whether the funds were transferred to the defendant _____ Bank;

(c) Whether the transfer of said funds was a violation of the provisions of Article 3-A of the Lien Law of the State of New York.

10. Upon information and belief, plaintiff will fairly and adequately protect the interests of the proposed class. Plaintiff has a substantial stake in this lawsuit in that its monetary claim as beneficiary of the said trust funds exceeds [*$20,000.00*].

11. If plaintiff succeeds in asserting its claim, upon information and belief, as a matter of law, creditors who establish valid trust claims share pro-rata in the trust funds so recovered pursuant to Article 3-A of the Lien Law of the State of New York.

12. Upon information and belief, by virtue of the aforesaid, plaintiff's claim is typical of the claims of the proposed class.

13. Upon information and belief, by virtue of the aforesaid, the questions of law and fact common to the class predominate over questions affecting individual members of the class.

14. Notwithstanding the requirements that this action be maintained as a class action, upon information and belief, a class action is superior to other available methods in that due to the size of the class it would be impracticable, difficult and inconvenient to join all members of the class. Furthermore, the maintaining of this action as a class action would obviate the risk of inconsistent determinations inherent in the prosecution of claims by the individual members of the class and maintaining this action as a class action will prevent a multiplicity of suits and will avoid the attendant and unnecessary costs and delays.

15. Upon information and belief, no other litigation concerning the controversy set forth in the above entitled action is now pending.

16. Sixty days have not elapsed after the time in which to serve a responsive pleading has expired.

17. No previous application for the relief requested herein has been made.

§ 10.147   MECHANIC'S LIENS   Ch. 10

WHEREFORE, your deponent respectfully prays this court for an order pursuant to Article 9 of the CPLR:

a) permitting plaintiff to maintain this action as a class action on behalf of itself and the class of all other persons similarly situated having performed work for Contractor upon construction projects located in the State of New York and thereby entitled to share in funds received by Contractor and deposited in an account in the name of Contractor maintained in the _____.

b) that the members of the class listed in Exhibit "B" annexed hereto, be notified that the action is being maintained as a class action by mailing a notice substantially in the same form as the one annexed hereto as Exhibit "C" to each member of the class listed in Exhibit "B" by certified mail, return receipt requested, or in such other manner as the court shall deem proper; and

c) for such other and further relief as to the court may seem just and proper in the premises.

                                            [*Signature*]

                                            [*Type Name*]

[*Jurat*]

Chapter 11

MORTGAGE FORECLOSURE

by
Robert A. Wolf
and
Suzanne M. Berger

Table of Sections

11.1	Scope Note.
11.2	Strategy—Initial Client Interview.
11.3	___ First Review of Loan Documents.
11.4	___ Foreclosure Title Certificate.
11.5	New York Mortgage Foreclosure Law.
11.6	___ Choice of Remedies: Foreclosure Action or Money Action.
11.7	___ Partial Foreclosure Action.
11.8	___ Non–Judicial Foreclosure.
11.9	Representing Subordinate Lienors.
11.10	Pre-commencement Procedure.
11.11	___ Notice of Default.
11.12	___ Notice of Acceleration.
11.13	___ Foreclosure Title Certificate.
11.14	Determining the Necessary Defendants.
11.15	___ The United States As a Necessary Defendant.
11.16	Starting the Foreclosure Action.
11.17	___ Notice of Pendency of Action.
11.18	Summons.
11.19	___ Venue.
11.20	Complaint.
11.21	___ Allegations Regarding Parties.
11.22	___ Allegations Regarding Loan, Note and Mortgage.
11.23	___ References to Pertinent Terms of Note and Mortgage.
11.24	___ Asserting Default(s).
11.25	___ Reserving Right to Add Advances Made by Plaintiff to Indebtedness Secured by Mortgage.
11.26	___ Allegation Regarding Subordinate Interest of Defendant(s).
11.27	___ Whether There Has Been or is Pending Another Action Regarding the Mortgage Debt.
11.28	___ Amendments.
11.29	Receivers.
11.30	___ Considerations in Determining Whether to Seek Appointment of Receiver.
11.31	___ *Ex Parte* Motion for Appointment of Receiver.

11.32	____ Compensation.
11.33	____ Opposing Appointment of Receiver.
11.34	____ Discharging Receiver.
11.35	Defendant's Response.
11.36	____ Motion to Dismiss Complaint.
11.37	____ Answer and Defenses.
11.38	____ Notice of Appearance and Waiver.
11.39	Obtaining Judgment.
11.40	____ Motion for Judgment.
11.41	____ Opposing Motion for Judgment.
11.42	Reference to Compute.
11.43	____ Hearing Before Referee to Compute.
11.44	____ Report of Referee to Compute.
11.45	____ Motion to Confirm Referee's Computation Report and for Judgment of Foreclosure and Sale.
11.46	Judgment of Foreclosure and Sale.
11.47	Foreclosure Sale.
11.48	____ Noticing and Advertising the Sale.
11.49	____ Conducting the Sale.
11.50	____ Vacating the Sale.
11.51	Referee's Deed, Other Closing Documents and Referee's Report of Sale.
11.52	Deficiency Judgment.
11.53	Surplus Money Proceedings.
11.54	Eviction of Tenants and Other Occupants After Foreclosure Sale.
11.55	Drafting Checklists.
11.56	____ Notice of Default.
11.57	____ Notice of Acceleration.
11.58	____ Notice of Pendency of Action.
11.59	____ Summons.
11.60	____ Complaint.
11.61	____ Order Appointing Receiver.
11.62	____ Affidavit in Support of *Ex Parte* Application for Receiver.
11.63	____ Notice of Motion for Summary Judgment and Related Relief.
11.64	____ Affidavit of Regularity and in Support of Plaintiff's Motion for Summary Judgment and Related Relief.
11.65	____ Judgment of Foreclosure and Sale.
11.66	____ Notice of Sale.
11.67	____ Terms and Memorandum of Sale.
11.68	Forms.
11.69	____ Notice of Default. 💾
11.70	____ Notice of Acceleration. 💾
11.71	____ Notice of Pendency of Action. 💾
11.72	____ Summons. 💾
11.73	____ Verified Complaint for Foreclosure of Mortgage Affecting Single Family Residence. 💾
11.74	____ Verified Complaint for Foreclosure of Mortgage Affecting Commercial, Multi–Unit Residential or Mixed Property. 💾
11.75	____ Order Appointing Receiver. 💾
11.76	____ Affidavit in Support of Motion for Appointment of Receiver. 💾
11.77	____ Notice of Motion for Summary Judgment and Related Relief. 💾

11.78 ____ Affidavit of Regularity and in Support of Motion for Summary Judgment. 💾
11.79 ____ Judgment of Foreclosure and Sale. 💾
11.80 ____ Notice of Sale. 💾
11.81 ____ Terms and Memorandum of Sale. 💾

WESTLAW Electronic Research

See WESTLAW Electronic Research Guide preceding the Summary of Contents.

---

§ 11.1 Scope Note

This chapter is designed to guide the practitioner through the judicial foreclosure of a New York real property mortgage. The first part of the chapter discusses those items which the attorney should determine during the initial client interview, the need for the attorney to review the pertinent loan documents, and the need for the "foreclosure title certificate" issued by a title insurance company.[1] Next, after discussing the statutory framework governing mortgage foreclosure in New York, the chapter discusses New York's "election of remedies" rule.[2] The chapter then proceeds to explain the concept of "partial foreclosure" and the fact that foreclosure by advertisement, a nonjudicial method of foreclosure theoretically available pursuant to statute, in fact is not used in New York.[3] A discussion then ensues as to considerations for the practitioner representing subordinate lienors who may be named defendants in a foreclosure action.[4] The final portion of the first part of the chapter sets forth the details which should be attended to prior to the commencement of the foreclosure action, including the preparation of a default and/or acceleration notice(s), ordering and reviewing the foreclosure title certificate, and the determination of the necessary defendants to the action.[5]

The second part of this chapter is a step-by-step guide to each stage of a judicial foreclosure. This part explains that, initially, the lender's lawyer should prepare and file a notice of pendency of action, the summons and complaint, and, if the property is income producing or in danger of waste, an application for the appointment of a receiver.[6] The chapter then discusses the types of defenses that are typically asserted by borrowers, guarantors, or subordinate lienors in response to a foreclosure complaint and the typical notice of appearance and waiver of service of papers sometimes served by non-contesting defendants.[7] Next, the chapter explains that if an answer denying the material allegations of

§ 11.1
1. See infra, §§ 11.2—11.4.
2. See infra, §§ 11.5—11.6.
3. See infra, §§ 11.7—11.8.
4. See infra, § 11.9.
5. See infra, §§ 11.10—11.15.
6. See infra, §§ 11.16—11.34.
7. See infra, §§ 11.35—11.38.

§ 11.1   MORTGAGE FORECLOSURE   Ch. 11

the complaint and/or containing affirmative defenses has been served, the lender must move pursuant to CPLR 3212 for summary judgment. If no defenses are interposed, the lender still must make a motion for a default judgment, but the lender can utilize RPAPL § 1321 rather than CPLR 3212. In both cases, the lender, as part of that motion, also generally seeks appointment of a referee to compute the amounts that are due to the lender.[8]

If the lender's motion for summary judgment or for a default judgment is granted, there is a hearing, sometimes by submission of an affidavit rather than through live testimony, before the court-appointed referee to compute. The referee will issue a report as to the amount due and whether the mortgaged premises should be sold in one parcel or more than one parcel.[9]

The lender must then make a motion to confirm the referee's report and for a judgment of foreclosure and sale. The chapter reviews the contents of the judgment of foreclosure and sale and the foreclosure sale procedure.[10]

The textual portion of the chapter concludes with a discussion of post-foreclosure sale proceedings—the motion to confirm the referee's report of sale, deficiency judgment proceedings, surplus money proceedings, the discharge of the receiver, and motion practice to evict foreclosed parties who try to remain in possession of the premises after the conveyance of the referee's deed.[11]

The last portion of the chapter contains a drafting checklist, together with sample foreclosure forms that can be used by the practitioner during the course of the foreclosure process.[12]

This chapter does not include a discussion of real property tax lien foreclosures,[13] strict foreclosure (permitted in New York only in the limited circumstances of a determination of claims where a prior foreclosure was void or voidable),[14] foreclosures of judgment liens,[15] foreclosures of chattel mortgages and UCC liens in connection with security interests in personal property under the Uniform Commercial Code ("UCC"),[16] the collection of a deficiency judgment against the borrower or the guarantor,[17] the effect of a bankruptcy filing on the foreclosure action,[18]

---

8. See infra, §§ 11.39—11.42.
9. See infra, §§ 11.42—11.44.
10. See infra, §§ 11.45—11.49.
11. See infra, §§ 11.50—11.54.
12. See infra, §§ 11.55—11.81.
13. RPAPL § 1521. See RPAPL § 1521(2)(b), which provides that " ... the people of the state of New York may foreclose such lien as a mortgage on real property is foreclosed, provided such lien remains unpaid after the expiration of one year from the entry of such judgment."
14. RPAPL § 1503.
15. CPLR 5233 (personal property); CPLR 5236 (real property).
16. UCC §§ 9–501, et seq.
17. Chapter 8 "Enforcement of Money Judgments," supra.
18. Chapter 9 "Bankruptcy," supra.

Ch. 11   STRATEGY—INITIAL CLIENT INTERVIEW   § 11.2

or various landlord-tenant issues that may arise in the context of a mortgage foreclosure.[19]

§ 11.2   Strategy—Initial Client Interview

Prior to or during the initial client interview, the attorney should obtain copies of:

1. The mortgage note evidencing the debt;
2. The recorded mortgage securing the note (and all modification, extension, consolidation or other agreements concerning that mortgage);[1]
3. All assignments of the mortgage note and mortgage;
4. All amendments or modifications of the mortgage note and mortgage;
5. Any guaranties of the mortgage indebtedness;
6. Record of payments made by the borrower, if any;
7. Record of advances, if any, made by the lender for items such as real estate taxes, cooperative maintenance charges, repairs or other charges which may be added to the principal balance of the debt secured by the mortgage;
8. Correspondence between the borrower and the lender;
9. Phone logs or other memoranda reflecting communications between the borrower and the lender;
10. Tenant leases concerning the mortgaged property;
11. Assignment of leases and rents to lender;
12. Rent roll for the mortgaged property;
13. If available, a recent appraisal of the mortgaged property or an estimate of its value;
14. Any environmental reports regarding the mortgaged property;
15. Current addresses of the borrower(s) and the guarantor;

---

19. Chapter 13 "Landlord–Tenant Proceedings," *infra*.

§ 11.2

1. PRACTICE POINTER: The attorney should verify that all mortgages and assignments or modifications thereof have been recorded in the office of the clerk of the county in which the mortgaged property is located because whether the mortgage sought to be foreclosed has priority over other mortgage liens depends on the date of recordation. RPL § 291. Mortgages are deemed recorded as of the date of their delivery to the recording office. RPL § 317. If a mortgage has not been recorded and subsequent lienors have no actual notice of the earlier mortgage, the subsequent mortgage probably will be held to be superior to the earlier, unrecorded mortgage. *See* Federal National Mortgage Ass'n v. Levine–Rodriguez, 153 Misc.2d 8, 579 N.Y.S.2d 975 (Sup.Ct., Rockland County, 1991); Henrietta Building Supplies, Inc. v. Rogers, 117 Misc.2d 843, 459 N.Y.S.2d 372 (Sup.Ct., Monroe County, 1983).

§ 11.2   MORTGAGE FORECLOSURE   Ch. 11

16. Information as to whether the lender has brought any other actions, or taken any other steps, to collect the amounts due under the mortgage note;

17. Information on the litigation status of the borrower, *i.e.*, whether there has been a bankruptcy filing;[2]

18. The amount of the unpaid balance of the loan, the date the last payment was made, and whether the lender has made any advances, such as payments for real estate taxes, property insurance, or repairs, that may be chargeable to the borrower.

The attorney representing the borrower should begin to explore potential defenses to the anticipated foreclosure action.[3]

§ 11.3   Strategy—First Review of Loan Documents

In reviewing the loan documents, it is essential that the lender's attorney determine the following:

1. Whether the lender has recourse against the borrower's assets generally as well as against the mortgaged property, or whether the loan is non-recourse and the lender only has recourse against the mortgaged property;

2. Whether the events of default described in the note and mortgage have occurred. The failure to make a payment when due, by itself, may be insufficient to trigger an event of default upon which to base a foreclosure action. Frequently, the loan documents provide that there cannot be an event of default justifying foreclosure until the expiration of a certain "grace" period beyond the payment due date and/or after notification by the lender to the borrower of the default. In some cases, both a written notice of the default *and* an opportunity to cure the violation of the loan covenants is required to trigger an event of default;

3. Whether the lender is permitted to accelerate the due date of the unpaid principal balance of the loan upon an event of default with or without further notice to the borrower;[1]

4. Whether the parties contractually agreed in the mortgage that, upon an event of default, the lender would be entitled, upon appropriate

---

2. PRACTICE POINTER: If the borrower, or any necessary defendant is under the protection of the Bankruptcy Code, the automatic stay, 11 U.S.C.A. § 362, may prevent the lender from taking any actions without an order from the bankruptcy court lifting or modifying that stay. See Chapter 9 "Bankruptcy," *supra*.

3. *See infra*, §§ 11.35—11.38.

§ 11.3

1. If no additional notice is required, the commencement of the foreclosure action will function to accelerate the due date of the indebtedness. *See infra*, § 11.12. If the lender does not intend to accelerate the entire indebtedness, the lender may commence a partial foreclosure action. *See infra*, § 11.7.

application, to the *ex parte* appointment of a receiver of rents and profits;[2] and

5. Whether the value of the mortgaged property is sufficient to satisfy the mortgage debt and, if it is a recourse debt, whether the borrower has other assets or means of paying the debt.

§ 11.4 Strategy—Foreclosure Title Certificate

The lender's attorney should immediately order a foreclosure report from a title company as soon as the attorney knows that the lender intends to commence, or is even just considering commencing, a foreclosure action.[1] That report will show the attorney other liens and interests recorded against the property and provide other information required to draft a proper complaint, including a listing of the necessary parties who must be named as defendants in the foreclosure action.[2]

§ 11.5 New York Mortgage Foreclosure Law

Procedures for the foreclosure of mortgages concerning New York real property are governed by RPAPL Article 13. New York mortgage foreclosure law developed during the 1930's depression and was designed to provide many protections to the property owner. As a result, lenders are required to resort to judicial proceedings in order to pursue the remedy of foreclosure. Lenders cannot maintain at the same time more than one action to recover the debt,[1] and they cannot obtain a deficiency judgment against the borrower or guarantor without a separate post-sale proceeding in the foreclosure action to determine the fair market value of the property at the time of the sale.[2]

The rules, though cumbersome and quite technical, must be adhered to or there will not be marketable title to convey to a purchaser at the foreclosure sale.

2. **PRACTICE POINTER:** See RPL § 254(10), which provides that a mortgage that contains a covenant "that the holder of this mortgage, in any action to foreclose it, shall be entitled to the appointment of a receiver," must be construed as meaning that the lender is entitled, without notice and without regard to the adequacy of any security for the debt, to the appointment of a receiver.

§ 11.4
1. **PRACTICE POINTER:** Often it is quickest to use the title company that prepared the mortgagee's title policy. The identity of this company can be obtained either from the mortgage loan closing binder, which should contain a copy of the title policy, or from the lender. Occasionally, a lender may not want to use this company if there is concern that the title company may alert the borrower to the request, or if the mortgage has changed holders and the new lender prefers to use another company.

It usually takes a week or two to obtain this report, so the attorney should order it early and leave ample time in his or her schedule to review it prior to filing to avoid having to amend the pleadings and the notice of pendency at an early stage.

2. See infra, §§ 11.14—11.15.

§ 11.5
1. See RPAPL § 1301. See infra, § 11.6.
2. See RPAPL § 1371. See infra, §§ 11.47—11.50.

§ 11.6 New York Mortgage Foreclosure Law—Choice of Remedies: Foreclosure Action or Money Action

New York law requires the lender whose borrower has defaulted to elect its remedy. The lender cannot pursue two courses of action simultaneously, and under some scenarios, an earlier action will bar a subsequent one even if the lender is not fully repaid. The lender must choose whether to (i) foreclose upon the mortgage, or (ii) sue on the note and/or the guaranty of the indebtedness.[1] There are exceptions, and if the lender can demonstrate special circumstances, the court in which the foreclosure action is pending can grant leave to commence a second action.[2] Generally, the "special circumstances" inquiry is an equitable one and is reviewed on a case-by-case basis. The inquiry focuses on whether the plaintiff could have obtained all the relief it was entitled to in the foreclosure action without the undue burden of commencing a second action against the defendant.[3]

On the other hand, if a money action on the debt has been commenced first and has resulted in a final judgment, and the execution issued in connection with that judgment has been returned wholly or partially unsatisfied, a foreclosure action may then be commenced with-

---

§ 11.6

1. See RPAPL § 1301. RPAPL § 1301 prohibits second actions not only against the maker of the note but against the guarantors for the same debt. TBS Enterprises, Inc. v. Grobe, 114 A.D.2d 445, 494 N.Y.S.2d 716 (2d Dep't 1985), appeal denied 67 N.Y.2d 602, 499 N.Y.S.2d 1028, 490 N.E.2d 556 (1986).

2. Rarely does the court find "special circumstances." For example, in Boyd v. Jarvis, 74 A.D.2d 937, 426 N.Y.S.2d 142 (3d Dep't 1980), the court held that the plaintiff's motion to maintain a second action against the borrower on a bond should have been denied for failure to demonstrate special circumstances. See also, Wand v. Saleh, 218 A.D.2d 647, 630 N.Y.S.2d 367 (2d Dep't 1995) (law office failure in timely moving for a deficiency judgment was not special circumstances); Manufacturers Hanover Trust Co. v. 400 Garden City Associates, 150 Misc.2d 247, 568 N.Y.S.2d 505 (Sup.Ct., Nassau County, 1991) (bankruptcy filing of borrower not special circumstances to proceed against guarantor).

The few cases finding "special circumstances" actually appear to determine that the second action is not an action on the mortgage debt. See, e.g., Rainbow Venture Associates, L.P. v. Parc Vendome Associates, Ltd., 221 A.D.2d 164 , 633 N.Y.S.2d 478 (1st Dep't 1995). In this case, the court held that special circumstances existed sufficient to permit the lender to commence a separate action against the property owner for physical damages to the mortgaged premises where it was improbable that the foreclosure action would satisfy the mortgage debt, and where the proposed action raised different questions of law, fact and proof than the foreclosure proceeding. See also, Pagano v. Smith, 201 A.D.2d 632, 608 N.Y.S.2d 268 (2d Dep't 1994).

3. Manufacturers Hanover Trust Co. v. 400 Garden City Associates, supra, relying on Stein v. Nellen Development Corp., 123 Misc.2d 268, 473 N.Y.S.2d 331 (Sup.Ct., Suffolk County, 1984).

out leave of court.[4]

RPAPL § 1301, the statute governing the election of remedies, has been held to apply only where the mortgaged property is located within the State of New York.[5] Thus, if the real property is located out of state, RPAPL § 1301 will not bar a money action brought in New York to collect the loan debt even though a mortgage foreclosure action regarding the same debt has been commenced by the lender in the foreign state.[6]

If the borrower has executed two separate and distinct notes to the lender, separate actions may be commenced with respect to each note. Similarly, the mortgagee may have more than one action pending against the borrower so long as only one seeks to recover on the mortgage debt.[7]

The decision whether to foreclose or to sue on the note must be made with care because the lender cannot simply change its mind after an action has been commenced. In coming to this determination, the lender must remember that a judgment creditor is precluded from enforcing a money judgment obtained in a money action on a note by executing on the mortgaged property.[8] Thus, unless the borrower has other substantial assets, the better choice is the equitable remedy of foreclosure.

On the other hand, if the mortgaged premises is environmentally contaminated or, if no environmental report was prepared, the lender may not wish to foreclose, for if it were to obtain the mortgaged property upon a foreclosure sale, it would inject itself into the chain of title and possibly subject itself to a claim for liability under the Comprehensive Environmental Response, Compensation and Liability Act ("CERCLA").[9]

---

4. RPAPL § 1301(1); Jamaica Savings Bank v. Henry, 112 A.D.2d 920, 492 N.Y.S.2d 437 (2d Dep't 1985).

5. Fielding v. Drew, 94 A.D.2d 687, 463 N.Y.S.2d 15, 16 (1st Dep't 1983).

6. **CAVEAT:** The lender's attorney must check the law of the sister state to determine whether the sister state permits the maintenance of the foreclosure action in that state at the same time a money judgment action is pending in New York.

7. Dollar Dry Dock Bank v. Piping Rock Builders, Inc., 181 A.D.2d 709, 581 N.Y.S.2d 361 (2d Dep't 1992) (action to set aside an allegedly fraudulent conveyance by borrower is not an action to recover on mortgage debt that runs afoul of RPAPL § 1301). See also, Rainbow Venture Associates, L.P. v. Parc Vendome Associates, Ltd., 221 A.D.2d 164, 633 N.Y.S.2d 478 (1st Dep't 1995) (property damage action by lender against borrower for "waste").

8. CPLR 5230(a), 5235, and 5236(b).

9. CERCLA can be found at 42 U.S.C.A. §§ 9601 et seq. See Resolution Trust Corp. v. Polmar Realty, Inc., 780 F.Supp. 177, 181 (S.D.N.Y.1991), where the court stated, "Under CERCLA a property owner is liable for the environmental cleanup of property that is contaminated if it forecloses upon it, and under recent case law, it appears that a secured lender may be precluded from suing the former owners for money damages, after it has obtained a judgment of foreclosure and sale ..." But see Northeast Doran, Inc. v. Key Bank of Maine, 15 F.3d 1 (1st Cir.1994) (secured creditor exemption applies); United States v. McLamb, 5 F.3d 69 (4th Cir.1993) (same); United States v. Fleet Factors Corp., 901 F.2d 1550 (11th Cir.1990), cert. denied 498 U.S. 1046, 111 S.Ct. 752, 112 L.Ed.2d 772 (1991).

Moreover, in a foreclosure action, assuming the loan is a recourse loan, the lender ultimately can enforce its judgment against the borrower (as well as against any guarantors) in a deficiency judgment proceeding. The effect of RPAPL § 1301 is simply to make the lender wait until the foreclosure sale has been completed to take action against the borrower (and any guarantors) for any deficiency by way of a post-sale motion in the foreclosure action for a deficiency judgment.[10]

Library References:

West's Key No. Digests, Mortgages ⟜218.4, 411, 561.2.

§ 11.7 New York Mortgage Foreclosure Law—Partial Foreclosure Action

RPAPL § 1351(2) permits a "partial" judicial foreclosure of a mortgage. A partial foreclosure action is appropriate where the debt is not all due at the time the action is commenced, either because the mortgage does not provide for acceleration or because the lender has determined not to accelerate for the full indebtedness. In such circumstances, the mortgagee may sue for so much of the debt as has become due, have the mortgaged property sold to satisfy that debt, and retain a continuing lien against the property for the balance of the mortgage debt.[1] This procedure, though authorized by statute, is rarely used in New York.

Subsequent partial foreclosure actions to recover new installments which become due do not violate the election of remedies statute, RPAPL § 1301.[2]

Library References:

West's Key No. Digests, Mortgages ⟜380-590.

§ 11.8 New York Mortgage Foreclosure Law—Non-judicial Foreclosure

In New York, virtually all foreclosures of real property are judicial foreclosures under Article 13 of the RPAPL.[1] Because even an uncontested judicial foreclosure can take six months to a year to wind its way through the court, novices in the mortgage foreclosure arena may wonder why they cannot expedite the process through the nonjudicial foreclosure procedure described in Article 14 of the RPAPL, entitled *Foreclosure of Mortgage by Advertisement*.

10. *See infra*, § 11.52.

§ 11.7

1. Golden v. Ramapo Improvement Corp., 78 A.D.2d 648, 432 N.Y.S.2d 238 (2d Dep't 1980).

2. *Id.*, 78 A.D.2d at 650–51, 432 N.Y.S.2d at 242.

§ 11.8

1. Connecticut and a minority of other states permit strict foreclosure, a much quicker remedy. In strict foreclosure states, upon application of the lender, the court sets a law day, and the mortgagor has until that day to redeem the property or else the property is sold. Conn.Gen.St. § 49–24.

As the practitioner might divine by the paucity of cases discussing foreclosure by advertisement, and despite the fact that many New York mortgages contain the requisite power of sale clause that would seemingly permit foreclosure by advertisement,[2] that remedy, for various reasons, is rarely, if ever, used in New York. First, foreclosure by advertisement is of uncertain constitutional validity. It has not been tested since the United States Supreme Court's decision in *Fuentes v. Shevin*[3] barring certain takings without a prior opportunity to be heard. Second, because there is no court involvement in a foreclosure by advertisement, the lender cannot obtain a receiver to manage the property until the foreclosure is concluded, and the asset may be "wasted" before the foreclosure can be completed. Third, foreclosure by advertisement is ineffective to extinguish liens held by the United States.[4] Finally, if a foreclosure by advertisement is used, and the occupants of the mortgaged premises remain at the conclusion of the action, a writ of assistance under RPAPL § 221 is not available to evict the occupants. The alternate eviction method provided by RPAPL § 713(5) requires, as a precondition to commencement of the summary proceeding, that the deed delivered pursuant to the foreclosure sale be exhibited to the occupant. Consequently, because foreclosure by advertisement does not result in such a deed instrument, it is unclear whether a summary proceeding under RPAPL Article 7 could be instituted.

Most importantly, from a practical standpoint, foreclosure by advertisement is not recommended because title insurers, concerned about due process challenges and about whether the lender followed strictly the many and detailed requirements of the statute, will not insure title obtained through foreclosure by advertisement; therefore, the marketability of the title will be severely impaired.

Library References:

West's Key No. Digests, Mortgages ⟐320–328, 329–379.

§ 11.9 Representing Subordinate Lienors

An attorney may be consulted to defend a foreclosure action on behalf of defendants other than borrowers and guarantors. For example, all persons or entities having a lien on the property to be foreclosed, which lien is subordinate to that of the foreclosing mortgagee, will have been made parties to the foreclosure action.[1]

Generally, liens, whether mortgage liens, judgment liens, or mechanic's liens, are subordinate if they were recorded in the County

---

2. *See* RPAPL Art. 14, titled "Foreclosure of Mortgage by Advertisement" (RPAPL §§ 1401 *et seq.*).

3. 407 U.S. 67, 92 S.Ct. 1983, 32 L.Ed.2d 556 (1972).

4. *See* 28 U.S.C.A. § 2410(c).

§ 11.9

1. *See* RPAPL § 1311. *See infra*, § 11.14.

Clerk's office after the recordation of the mortgage which the plaintiff seeks to foreclose.[2]

Prior liens may be subordinated by agreement. Therefore, the attorney should determine whether there has been any subordination agreement between the lienor and the foreclosing mortgagee which would vary the general priority rule.

Additionally, in some instances, mechanic's liens, though recorded after the mortgage sought to be foreclosed, relate back to a period prior to the recording of the mortgage and may not be subordinate.[3]

A truly subordinate lienor has no defense to a superior mortgagee's foreclosure action. At the conclusion of the foreclosure action, the subordinate lienor's lien will be extinguished, and its interest in the real property will be relegated to any surplus generated by the superior mortgagee's foreclosure sale.[4] Of course, the subordinate lienor retains its substantive claim, if any, against the owner of the property, which may be enforced through other means.[5]

The first task of the lawyer representing the subordinate lienor is to determine whether the lienor's interest is truly subordinate. The general rule of priority is one of timing. Thus, the first recorded lien is usually superior;[6] however, a mechanic's lien arising out of improvements to the property sought to be foreclosed has priority over liens not related to the improvement of that property.[7]

If the foreclosing mortgagee's liens arise out of a consolidated mortgage, the general rules of priority still apply. Consequently, a lienor with a lien which was recorded in between the recording of the original mortgage lien and the recording of the second mortgage lien, notwithstanding the subsequent consolidation of the two mortgage liens, is junior only to the extent of the unpaid balance of the original, earlier lien.[8]

The other general rule is that a leasehold estate is subordinate to a fee estate. However, in both instances, the lien being foreclosed may

---

2. RPL § 291; Lien Law § 13. See also, Chapter 10 "Mechanics' Liens," supra.

PRACTICE POINTER: Always verify that the mortgage sought to be foreclosed has been properly recorded. The date the mortgage was delivered for recording is the date that sets priority, not the date the mortgage was executed.

3. See, e.g., Lien Law § 22. See also, Chapter 10 "Mechanic's Liens," supra.

4. RPAPL §§ 1351, 1354. See infra, § 11.46, § 11.53.

5. For example, the mechanic's lienor may have a breach of contract claim, or, in the absence of privity of contract, an unjust enrichment claim, against the property owner.

6. Lacaille v. Feldman, 44 Misc.2d 370, 253 N.Y.S.2d 937 (Sup.Ct., N.Y. County, 1964) (judgment lien is superior to subsequently recorded state tax lien).

7. Lien Law § 13. See Betcher v. Rademacher, 35 Misc.2d 693, 230 N.Y.S.2d 535 (Sup.Ct., Erie County, 1962).

8. A consolidation agreement does not change priorities affecting third parties to the consolidation agreement. Societe Generale v. Charles and Company Acquisition, Inc., 157 Misc.2d 643, 597 N.Y.S.2d 1004 (Sup.Ct., N.Y. County, 1993).

have been contractually subordinated to the later lien or the tenancy. For example, tenants with substantial bargaining power often obtain nondisturbance agreements with their landlord's mortgagee in which the mortgagee agrees not to "disturb" the tenancy by naming the tenant as a defendant in a foreclosure action, provided the tenant is not in default under its lease. In such cases, if the tenant is improperly named as a defendant in the action, the nondisturbance agreement should be asserted as an affirmative defense.

The other major exception to the priority rule occurs when the mortgage being foreclosed is a construction loan mortgage and the alleged subordinate lienors are mechanic's lienors. Under certain circumstances, mechanic's liens, though filed after the mortgage was recorded, may be superior to part of the debt secured by the mortgage if the provisions of Article 3–A of the Lien Law are not carefully followed. A full discussion of this complex area of the law is beyond the scope of this chapter.[9]

Additionally, there is an exception to the priority rule in the case of a lien filed by the board of managers of a condominium against a condominium unit for unpaid common charges. Such a lien is subordinate to a first mortgage but superior to other liens.[10]

Generally, if the subordinate lienor determines that its interest is truly subordinate, the attorney should simply file a notice of appearance and waiver in foreclosure. By doing so, the subordinate lienor is deemed to have admitted the material allegations of the complaint. Further service of most of the often voluminous motion papers is waived. The subordinate lienor usually retains its right to notice of the foreclosure sale so that it can determine whether there will be a surplus for it. However, the form notice of appearance can be adapted to require service of specific additional papers of interest in a particular case. Alternatively, the defendant wishing to receive copies of all papers may simply serve a notice of appearance.

§ 11.10 Pre-commencement Procedure

Before the commencement of the foreclosure action, the lender's counsel should confirm that the default upon which the action will be based has been noticed in the manner required by the documents, that the time for curing the default has lapsed, and that a notice of acceleration has been served, if required.

---

9. *See* Chapter 10 "Mechanic's Liens," *supra*.

10. RPL §§ 339–z, 339–aa. *See* Societe Generale v. Charles and Company Acquisition, Inc., 157 Misc.2d 643, 597 N.Y.S.2d 1004 (Sup.Ct., N.Y. County, 1993), disagreeing with Dime Savings Bank of New York, F.S.B. v. Levy, 161 Misc.2d 480, 615 N.Y.S.2d 218 (Sup.Ct., Rockland County, 1994) (holding that because of RPL § 339–aa, when second mortgage was consolidated with first mortgage, and condominium lien had not yet been filed, second mortgage had priority).

§ 11.10   MORTGAGE FORECLOSURE

In addition, the lender should have in hand a foreclosure title certificate, updated by the title company to the date of the filing of the notice of pendency and the complaint (or as close to that date as possible), setting forth the holders of all the subordinate liens and/or claims on the property who should be named as defendants in the action.

Library References:

West's Key No. Digests, Mortgages ⊶391–419.

§ 11.11   Pre-commencement Procedure—Notice of Default

In preparing the notice of default, the attorney for the lender should specifically identify the nature of the borrower's default(s) and refer to the section(s) of the loan document imposing the obligation(s) as to which the borrower has defaulted. The notice should also specify the amount of time the borrower has to cure the default(s), if any, and the consequence of the borrower's failure to cure the default(s).[1]

The notice of default should be addressed to the borrower at its current address and to all other addresses provided for in the loan documents. Sometimes loan documents also provide for contemporaneous notice to the borrower's counsel or some other party. These notice provisions should be followed carefully.

The notice of default should be delivered by a method that strictly complies with the provisions of the loan documents (*e.g.*, certified mail, personal delivery, overnight courier, etc.).

Generally, a copy of the notice of default also should be sent to the guarantor(s), if any.

Library References:

West's Key No. Digests, Mortgages ⊶391–419.

§ 11.12   Pre-commencement Procedure—Notice of Acceleration

A separate notice of acceleration of the entire loan indebtedness should be sent to the borrower if the loan documents require such a separate notice to be sent. Additionally, where the mortgaged property is secured by more than one mortgage, subordination agreements or other agreements between the mortgagees may require that the other mortgagees be given notice of acceleration.

---

§ 11.11

1. **PRACTICE POINTER:** Lender's counsel should send a written notice of default even where the note and mortgage do not require one in order to establish at the outset documentary evidence that may be needed in the foreclosure action to rebut any contention by the borrower that the lender waived the borrower's default.

Where no separate notice of acceleration is required by the loan documents, the verified complaint is sufficient notice of the lender's election.[1] Additionally, a notice of acceleration is not necessary if the mortgage loan has matured and the default is the failure to pay the outstanding indebtedness upon maturity.[2]

Library References:
West's Key No. Digests, Mortgages ⚖=391–419.

§ 11.13 Pre-commencement Procedure—Foreclosure Title Certificate

Before commencing a foreclosure action, the lender's attorney should order a foreclosure certificate from a local title insurance company. In order to prepare such a certificate, the title company usually requests the address of the mortgaged property, its tax lot information, the name of the borrower, the name of the lender, and the date and recording information of the mortgage to be foreclosed.

§ 11.12

1. The statutory form of acceleration clause provides that the lender has the option to accelerate upon the borrower's default. RPL § 258, Schedule N, ¶ 4.

See Albertina Realty Co. v. Rosbro Realty Corp., 258 N.Y. 472, 476, 180 N.E. 176, 177 (1932), where the court stated that, " . . . the unequivocal overt act of the plaintiff in filing the summons and verified complaint and *lis pendens* constituted a valid election." See also Logue v. Young, 94 A.D.2d 827, 463 N.Y.S.2d 120 (3d Dep't 1983) (service of complaint sufficient to manifest election to accelerate); City Streets Realty Corp. v. Jan Jay Construction Enterprises Corp., 88 A.D.2d 558, 559, 450 N.Y.S.2d 492, 493 (1st Dep't 1982) (" . . . the mere filing of a summons and complaint with notice of pendency is sufficient indication of the intent to accelerate the mortgage"); Centerbank v. D'Assaro, 158 Misc.2d 92, 94, 600 N.Y.S.2d 1015, 1017 (Sup.Ct., Suffolk County, 1993) ("Upon service of the Summons and Complaint . . . the plaintiff indicated its intention to accelerate the mortgage . . ."). *Cf.* Gold v. Vanden Brul, 28 Misc.2d 644, 211 N.Y.S.2d 757 (Sup.Ct., Monroe County, 1961) (verification of complaint constituted election to accelerate, despite fact that summons not served until after tender of payment).

PRACTICE POINTER: Even where a formal written notice of acceleration is not required by the loan documents, the better practice is to provide such a notice to the borrower to forestall the borrower's argument later that it was relying on some unwritten agreement that the lender would not accelerate the indebtedness.

2. **PRACTICE POINTER:** As with respect to the notice of default, lender's counsel would be wise to take the additional time to provide the borrower with a notice of acceleration despite the fact that it may not be required as a matter of law or pursuant to the loan documents. The acceleration notice should be sent to the borrower in the manner provided by the "notice" section of the loan documents, *i.e.*, a copy may have to be sent to the borrower's counsel and/or to additional parties. Lender's counsel generally also should send a copy of the notice of acceleration to the guarantor(s), if any. Sending an acceleration notice, even when not required, will likely forestall any argument by the borrower in opposition to a motion for summary judgment that the lender waived its right to foreclose or agreed to forbear from foreclosing. See also, § 11.11 note 1.

CAVEAT: Lender's counsel should advise the lender that after the mortgage loan has been accelerated, lender should not accept payments of less than the full amount of the indebtedness unless it obtains the borrower's agreement that such acceptance is without prejudice. Acceptance of partial payments may be held to be a waiver of acceleration, and the lender may not be able to foreclose on the entire indebtedness. See The Dime Savings Bank of New York v. Glavey, 214 A.D.2d 419, 625 N.Y.S.2d 181 (1st Dep't 1995).

§ 11.13   MORTGAGE FORECLOSURE   Ch. 11

The foreclosure certificate will identify all subordinate liens and interests upon the mortgaged premises and will also identify all necessary defendants.[1] Thus, all junior mortgagees, judgment creditors and mechanics' lienors should be identified and must be made parties to the foreclosure action.[2] Additionally, tenants (other than residential rent-regulated tenants and tenants with non-disturbance agreements) of the premises with recorded leases or memoranda of leases may be identified in the title report.

The foreclosure certificate will contain the legal description of the mortgaged premises sought to be foreclosed. This description should match the description in the mortgage as it ultimately will be incorporated in the final foreclosure judgment.

Finally, the foreclosure certificate will contain all the recording information for the recorded mortgage(s) (*i.e.*, date recorded, book and page of the particular County Clerk's office in which recorded, and amount of mortgage tax paid upon recording). It is a necessary element of the lender's *prima facie* case that the mortgage was recorded (so as to give the mortgage lien priority *vis-a-vis* any subsequently recorded mortgage or other lien) and that the required mortgage tax was paid upon recording.[3]

If the lender's attorney prosecutes the foreclosure action in conformity with the foreclosure certificate and the applicable law, then, at the conclusion of the proceeding, the title company will insure title in the purchaser at the foreclosure sale.

Before filing the notice of pendency, the lender's attorney should obtain a continuation or "update" from the title company as close to the date of filing as possible, if not on the date of filing itself. The continuation will show any changes in the lien records since the date of the original report. This request is generally made by telephone, and the response comes that day or the next by telephone.[4] The lender's attorney should make sure that the oral response is confirmed in writing.[5]

§ 11.14 Determining the Necessary Defendants

All persons having a subordinate lien interest in the mortgaged

---

§ 11.13

1. *See infra*, § 11.14.
2. **PRACTICE POINTER:** Do not hesitate to question the title company about its certificate. Sometimes liens are incorrectly shown or only partially explained.
3. RPL § 291; Tax Law § 258. *See infra*, § 11.22.
4. **PRACTICE POINTER:** In some areas, title companies will file the notice of pendency and the complaint for the lender and will update the report by checking the real estate records immediately before that filing. Counsel may want to inquire whether the title company it is using performs that service.
5. **PRACTICE POINTER:** A week or so after filing the notice of pendency, the lender's attorney should have the title company do another update. This will serve two purposes. It will ensure that the notice of pendency has been correctly indexed and recorded, and it will also ensure that no new liens were recorded in the final moments between the last continuation and the filing of the notice of pendency.

property are necessary defendants.[1] Lienors with superior liens are not necessary parties.[2] Parties who file notices of lien after the filing of the notice of pendency are not necessary parties, as their liens automatically will be extinguished by a judgment of foreclosure as a matter of law.[3] Tenants (except tenants protected by various rent regulation statutes or tenants with nondisturbance agreements)[4] are proper but not necessary parties. However, if tenants are not named in the foreclosure action, their tenancy interests cannot be extinguished, and they will survive a foreclosure sale.[5]

Library References:

West's Key No. Digests, Mortgages ⟾433–435.

§ 11.15 Determining the Necessary Defendants—The United States as a Necessary Defendant

If the United States of America is a necessary party to the action because of judgment liens, tax liens, or other subordinate interests, special care must be taken to follow the procedures outlined in 28 U.S.C.A. § 2410. Briefly, the United States must be served as prescribed in 28 U.S.C.A. § 2410(b) and must be given 60 days to respond to the complaint.[1] Additionally, unlike other lienors, the United States, when it holds the equity of redemption, usually has one year after the foreclosure

§ 11.14

1. RPAPL § 1311(3).

2. Clark v. Fuller, 136 Misc. 151, 239 N.Y.S. 269 (Sup.Ct., Chautaugua County, 1930); Sayville Federal Savings & Loan Ass'n v. Schons, 17 Misc.2d 54, 55, 183 N.Y.S.2d 106, 107 (Suffolk County Ct.1958).

3. Lien Law § 44–a.

4. *E.g.*, Emergency Tenant Protection Act of 1974, as amended, New York City Rent Control Law, and Rent Stabilization Law of 1969. *See* Finkelstein and Ferrara, *Landlord and Tenant Practice in New York* (West 1997) Ch. 11 "Rent Regulation."

5. **PRACTICE POINTER:** If the lender is not certain at the outset of the action who all the occupants of the premises are, the prudent thing to do is to include in the caption a number of so-called "John Doe defendants." The inclusion of such "John Doe defendants" also guards against the possibility that the updated title search done after the commencement of the action will reveal a new lienor who filed just before the notice of pendency was filed. If there is such a new lienor who needs to be included as a defendant, and/or if the lender decides to join as a defendant a tenant not originally identified, lender's counsel can simply serve any such new party with the summons and complaint as a "John Doe" defendant and subsequently move to amend the caption of the action to substitute the true name of the party for the particular "John Doe."

§ 11.15

1. 28 U.S.C.A. § 2410(b) provides, in pertinent part:

In actions in the State courts service upon the United States shall be made by serving the process of the court with a copy of the complaint upon the United States attorney for the district in which the action is brought or upon an assistant United States attorney or clerical employee designated by the United States attorney in writing filed with the clerk of the court in which the action is brought and by sending copies of the process and complaint, by registered mail, or by certified mail, to the Attorney General of the United States at Washington, District of Columbia. In such actions the United States may appear and answer, plead or demur within sixty days after such service or such further time as the court may allow.

§ 11.15 MORTGAGE FORECLOSURE Ch. 11

sale to redeem.[2]

In a foreclosure action, the United States of America cannot be named as a defendant because it is a tenant, since the United States has not waived its sovereign immunity for that purpose.[3]

Library References:

West's Key No. Digests, Mortgages ⚖︎433–435.

§ 11.16 Starting the Foreclosure Action

The first steps in the foreclosure action involve the filing of the notice of pendency of action and the summons and complaint.

Library References:

West's Key No. Digests, Mortgages ⚖︎426–442, 444–459(4).

§ 11.17 Starting the Foreclosure Action—Notice of Pendency of Action

A notice of pendency of action, also known as a *lis pendens*, must be filed with the clerk of the county in which the property is located simultaneously with the commencement of a foreclosure action (or no more than thirty days before the foreclosure complaint is served).[1] The notice of pendency is the instrument that gives notice to the world that the mortgagee has commenced a foreclosure action.[2]

In order to file the notice of pendency with the county clerk, lender's counsel must purchase an index number and pay an additional fee imposed for the filing of the notice of pendency. In some counties, the charge increases if the mortgaged property covers more than one block and lot; in others, the fee increases for each defendant named, including the "John Does." Most counties require that a copy of the summons and complaint be filed together with the notice of pendency.[3]

A proper notice of pendency is critical to a successful foreclosure because only that instrument will bar all claims to the property by new lienors, as all liens that are recorded after the filing of the notice of

---

2. 28 U.S.C.A. § 2410(c).
3. Marine Midland Bank v. Marcal Enterprises, Inc., 91 Misc.2d 810, 398 N.Y.S.2d 782 (Genesee County Ct.1977), aff'd 64 A.D.2d 812, 407 N.Y.S.2d 833 (4th Dep't 1978).

§ 11.17

1. CPLR 6512.
2. CPLR 6501.
3. *See* CPLR 6511 for general, statewide statutory requirements regarding the filing, content and indexing of a notice of pendency.

CAVEAT: CPLR 6512 requires that the owner of the property sought to be foreclosed in the action be served within thirty days of the filing of the notice of pendency. If the thirty day deadline is not met, the notice of pendency is of no further force and effect. No new notice of pendency can be filed. If the lender's attorney will not be able to serve the owner within the thirty day period, the attorney must obtain a court order extending the period before it expires.

pendency are automatically extinguished by the judgment of foreclosure without the necessity of naming those new lienors as defendants. For this reason, it is important that lender's counsel obtain from the title company not only an update or so-called "continuation search" of the original foreclosure title certificate showing any new liens up to the date of filing, but a second update after the filing of the notice of pendency to confirm that the notice of pendency has been indexed properly against the mortgaged property.[4]

A notice of pendency is effective for three years from the date it is filed.[5] Counsel for the lender must move before the expiration of three years for an extension[6] and present a good explanation to the court why the action remains pending.[7]

If the foreclosure action is settled before final judgment, the parties who have appeared can stipulate to the cancellation of the notice of pendency.[8] Together with the stipulation, lender's counsel must provide an affirmation stating the names of the parties served, the date of service, and whether any of those parties have appeared. If all parties who have appeared in the foreclosure action will not stipulate, lender's counsel may move the court for an order cancelling the notice of pendency on the ground that the foreclosure action has been discontinued.[9]

Library References:

West's Key No. Digests, Lis Pendens ⚖1–26.

§ 11.18 Summons

As is true of all actions, there must be a summons which accompanies the foreclosure complaint.[1]

Library References:

West's Key No. Digests, Mortgages ⚖440.

§ 11.19 Summons—Venue

Venue in a mortgage foreclosure action is proper in the county in which the property, or any part of the property, sought to be foreclosed

---

4. PRACTICE POINTER: If the summons is amended, or the property sought to be foreclosed upon is released in part during the foreclosure action due, for example, to a partial sale, the notice of pendency should be amended. Such an amendment will not extend the three-year period during which the notice of pendency is effective. *See infra,* § 11.28.

5. CPLR 6513.

6. PRACTICE POINTER: Docket the expiration date of the notice of pendency and periodic reminders of the expiration date during the six-month period preceding expiration. This will give the attorney ample notice of the upcoming expiration date and allow the attorney to move to extend the effectiveness for another three years.

7. CPLR 6513.

8. CPLR 6514(d).

9. CPLR 6514(a).

§ 11.18

1. For a form for a summons, *see infra,* § 11.72.

is located.[1]

Where the mortgage sought to be foreclosed covers real property located in more than one county, venue is proper in either county.[2]

Library References:

West's Key No. Digests, Mortgages ⬅︎422.

§ 11.20 Complaint

The complaint in a mortgage foreclosure action must include certain essential allegations. Those key allegations, as required under the RPAPL and certain other statutory provisions, as well as pertinent case law, will be set forth in the next few sections. If the complaint contains each of those essential allegations, it will withstand a motion to dismiss.

In the case of a foreclosure upon a home (*i.e.*, a single family residence), where the attorney for the foreclosing plaintiff will generally want to keep the client's legal expenses to a minimum, a simple, concise complaint that contains those key allegations, without more, will often be the desired form of pleading.[1]

However, where the foreclosure action concerns a commercial building, a multi-unit residential property (*e.g.*, a large rental or cooperative apartment building), or a mixed-use property, and/or where the pertinent loan documents are more complex, and/or where it is expected that the defendant-borrower and/or other defendants will contest the foreclosure, a more detailed complaint with greater specificity than that required by the pertinent statutes and case law is recommended.[2] In this more detailed complaint, the attorney will want to go into greater detail in describing why each of the defendants has been made a party to the action, quote from the specific provisions of the mortgage and other loan documents that set forth the obligations of the borrower and of the guarantor(s) which have been breached and that entitle the plaintiff to foreclose, and annex copies of those pertinent documents as exhibits.

Library References:

West's Key No. Digests, Mortgages ⬅︎444–453.

§ 11.19

1. CPLR 507.
2. Dollar Dry Dock Bank v. Piping Rock Builders, Inc., 181 A.D.2d 709, 710, 581 N.Y.S.2d 361, 363 (2d Dep't 1992).

CAVEAT: When the mortgaged property is located in more than one county, make sure that the notice of pendency of action is filed in each county in which any portion of the property is located.

§ 11.20

1. For a form of a complaint for the foreclosure of a mortgage affecting a single family residence, see *infra*, § 11.73.

2. For a form of a complaint for the foreclosure of a mortgage affecting commercial, multi-unit residential or mixed property, see *infra*, § 11.74.

§ 11.21 Complaint—Allegations Regarding Parties

As is true with respect to any action, the complaint in a foreclosure action should start off with separate paragraphs establishing the identity and interest of each of the parties.

The initial paragraph should identify the plaintiff as an individual, corporation, partnership, or other entity, state the residence, state of formation and/or principal office of the plaintiff, and allege that the plaintiff is the holder of the mortgage affecting the premises which are the subject of the foreclosure action.

The next paragraph of the complaint generally should identify the defendant-borrower and set forth the basis or bases for jurisdiction over this defendant. At the very least, there should be an allegation that the defendant-borrower is the owner of the property which is the subject of the foreclosure action.[1] A metes and bounds description of the property should either appear in this paragraph or be referred to as appearing in a schedule annexed to the complaint.[2]

There should then be a separate paragraph for each of the other defendants (other than any defendant-guarantors) named in the action, setting forth the identity of each such defendant, the nature of the lien or other interest which each such defendant has or claims it has with respect to the subject property, and the allegation that any such lien or other interest is subordinate to that of the mortgage lien of the plaintiff. Under RPAPL §§ 202 and 202-a, the particular interest or lien of a governmental entity in an action affecting real property must be pleaded with specificity. As to any guarantors named as defendants in the action, the pertinent paragraph(s), after setting forth the identity of each such defendant, should allege that each is made a party for the purpose of seeking a deficiency judgment against each such defendant if a deficiency arises after the foreclosure sale.[3]

Library References:

West's Key No. Digests, Mortgages ⚞445.

§ 11.22 Complaint—Allegations Regarding Loan, Note and Mortgage

The complaint then should set forth those essential allegations that establish the existence of the mortgagee-mortgagor relationship between the plaintiff-lender and the defendant-borrower, and to establish the plaintiff's standing to foreclose upon the mortgage. Those allegations are as follows:

§ 11.21
1. CPLR 302(a)(4).
2. **CAVEAT:** Check to see that the metes and bounds description is identical to that appearing in the notice of pendency of action, in the subject mortgage and in the foreclosure title certificate.
3. See infra, § 11.52.

§ 11.22   MORTGAGE FORECLOSURE   Ch. 11

1. The extension of a loan by the plaintiff to the defendant-borrower and the principal amount of such loan;

2. The defendant-borrower's execution and delivery to the plaintiff of a note evidencing the loan (or if the plaintiff holds the note by assignment, the delivery of the note to the original lender and its subsequent assignment to the plaintiff);

3. The defendant-borrower's execution and delivery to the plaintiff of a mortgage affecting the subject property as security for the defendant-borrower's promise to repay to the plaintiff the indebtedness evidenced by the note (or if the plaintiff holds the mortgage by assignment, the delivery of the mortgage to the original lender and its subsequent assignment to the plaintiff);

4. The recording of the mortgage in the office of the Clerk (or in the case of the counties of New York City, the office of the Register) of the county in which the subject property is located, thereby establishing the priority of the mortgage lien *vis-a-vis* subsequently recorded mortgages and other liens;[1] and

5. The payment of the applicable mortgage recording tax at the time that the mortgage was recorded.[2]

Library References:

West's Key No. Digests, Mortgages ⚖446.

§ 11.23   Complaint—References to Pertinent Terms of Note and Mortgage

The complaint should make reference to those key terms of the note and the mortgage which entitle the plaintiff to a judgment of foreclosure and the attendant relief sought by plaintiff in the action. In the simple form of complaint, paraphrasing those key terms will suffice. In the more detailed pleading, the lender's attorney may want to consider quoting those pertinent terms verbatim.

Assuming that the borrower's default under the loan documents is a failure to make the requested payment(s) of interest and/or principal, the first key terms to which the complaint should make reference are the loan payment provisions, which are usually found in the note. If the default is other than one for failure to make the interest and/or principal payments required under the note (*e.g.*, a breach of an obligation under the mortgage, such as the failure to pay real estate taxes, or the failure to obtain the plaintiff's consent to enter into a new lease for a portion of

§ 11.22

1. Federal National Mortgage Ass'n v. Levine–Rodriguez, 153 Misc.2d 8, 579 N.Y.S.2d 975 (Sup.Ct., Rockland County, 1991); Henrietta Building Supplies, Inc. v. Rogers, 117 Misc.2d 843, 459 N.Y.S.2d 372 (Sup.Ct., Monroe County, 1983).

2. Tax Law § 258.

the premises), the pleading should refer to the pertinent term(s) of the mortgage.

If the note and/or mortgage provide for an increased rate of interest on the principal balance of the loan once a default occurs (often referred to as the "default rate"), that provision(s) also should be mentioned.

Next, this section of the complaint should cite to those terms of the note and/or the mortgage which establish that the borrower's failure to perform the particular obligation(s) under the document(s) constitutes an event of default which permits the plaintiff to demand payment of the entirety of the indebtedness evidenced by the note and secured by the mortgage. For example, if the obligation of the borrower is the failure to pay a monthly installment of interest when due (inclusive of any grace period allowed under the documents), then the complaint should refer to those provision(s) of the note and mortgage which entitle the plaintiff to accelerate the entirety of the indebtedness upon such a default and to pursue its remedies, including foreclosure. The same obviously holds true with regard to any other unfulfilled obligation on the borrower's part.

Assuming the plaintiff is going to seek the appointment of a receiver in the foreclosure action to collect the rents and any other income from the property, the complaint should cite to the provision in the mortgage entitling the plaintiff to such relief.[1]

Furthermore, if the mortgage entitles the plaintiff to attorneys' fees which the plaintiff incurs in seeking to collect the indebtedness from the borrower, including those fees incurred in the prosecution of the foreclosure action itself, the complaint should make reference to the attorneys' fees provision.

If there is a guaranty of the payment of the indebtedness by a guarantor-defendant(s), the complaint also should make reference to the pertinent provisions of the guaranty which make the guarantor(s) liable therefor.

Library References:

West's Key No. Digests, Mortgages ⚖︎446.

§ 11.24 Complaint—Asserting Default(s)

Having set forth the pertinent terms of the note, the mortgage and the guaranty, if any, counsel for the plaintiff should then proceed to assert the actual default(s) committed by the borrower. For example, if the default was a failure to timely pay a monthly interest installment(s), the pleading should allege the specific month(s) as to which the requisite

---

§ 11.23

1. See infra, §§ 11.29—11.34 for a discussion of the receiver in a mortgage foreclosure action.

§ 11.24 MORTGAGE FORECLOSURE Ch. 11

payment(s) was not made, the expiration of the pertinent grace period, if any, for making such payment(s), and the giving of any written notice by plaintiff to borrower of such default.[1]

The complaint also should allege that the plaintiff has elected to accelerate the loan indebtedness as a consequence of such default.

Lastly, this section of the complaint should allege the amount of the outstanding indebtedness due under the note and mortgage (*i.e.*, principal balance of loan, interest and late charges),[2] and the fact that as of the filing of the complaint, that indebtedness remains unpaid.

Library References:

West's Key No. Digests, Mortgages ⚖=448.

§ 11.25 Complaint—Reserving Right to Add Advances Made by Plaintiff to Indebtedness Secured by Mortgage

Another standard paragraph that appears toward the end of virtually every foreclosure complaint is the assertion that, during the course of the foreclosure action, it may become necessary for the plaintiff, in order to protect its security (*i.e.*, the mortgaged premises), to pay out of its own pocket monies for such items as real estate taxes, insurance premiums, repairs and the like which the borrower has not paid, and that if the plaintiff does so, the sum of such payments be deemed added to the amount of the indebtedness secured by the plaintiff's mortgage lien.[1] This allegation usually accords with a provision in the mortgage that entitles the plaintiff-lender to such relief.

Library References:

West's Key No. Digests, Mortgages ⚖=446.

§ 11.24

1. **PRACTICE POINTER:** Even where a default and/or acceleration notice is not required, it is strongly recommended that the lender send a written notice to the borrower of the default and of the borrower's consequent election to demand full payment of the loan (also known as "accelerating" the loan indebtedness). In this way, there is documentary evidence that can be used in the ensuing foreclosure action to rebut possible defenses by the borrower that it was not advised of a default and/or that the lender allegedly orally advised the borrower that it would not call the loan despite the default.

2. **PRACTICE POINTER:** The amount of the principal balance alleged should be precise to the penny. The amount of interest and late charges can, but need not be, so specific. Moreover, as interest continues to accrue on the principal balance, even if plaintiff wishes to be precise about the interest figure, that figure can only be through a date no later than the filing of the complaint. Consequently, the pleading should in any event allege that interest continues to accrue thereafter at a particular rate (often a default rate that is greater than the normal rate in the note and mortgage).

§ 11.25

1. For examples of such standard paragraphs, as used in complaints, *see infra*, § 11.73, ¶ 11 and § 11.74, ¶ 21.

§ 11.26 Complaint—Allegation Regarding Subordinate Interest of Defendant(s)

Even though the earlier section of the complaint containing allegations regarding each of the defendants already may have set forth the assertion that the particular lien or interest of each such defendant is subordinate to that of plaintiff's mortgage lien upon the premises,[1] it is typical for the plaintiff to include a "catch-all" allegation toward the end of the pleading alleging that "each of the defendants asserts a lien or interest subordinate to that of the plaintiff."[2]

Library References:

West's Key No. Digests, Mortgages ⟐452.

§ 11.27 Complaint—Whether There Has Been or Is Pending Another Action Regarding the Mortgage Debt

The final paragraph of the foreclosure complaint alleges whether or not there has been or is another action to recover all or any portion of the mortgage debt. This paragraph is required in order to show that the plaintiff, in commencing the foreclosure action, is not violating the "election of remedies" rule embodied in RPAPL § 1301.[1]

Library References:

West's Key No. Digests, Mortgages ⟐451.

§ 11.28 Complaint—Amendments

If the complaint is subsequently amended to (i) change the parties to the action, or (ii) change the description of the property sought to be foreclosed, an amended notice of pendency should be filed with the County Clerk reflecting that change.

However, no amendment to the pleadings or to the notice of pendency is required if the plaintiff merely wants to substitute previously unknown or unidentified parties in place of the "John Doe defendants" originally named in the action. Lender's counsel, having originally included "John Doe defendants" for this purpose, should serve the known new defendants with the summons and complaint, advising them by cover letter that they are named in the action by virtue of a specified interest as "John Doe" No. ___.[1]

§ 11.26

1. See supra, § 11.21.
2. For examples of such "catch-all" allegations, see infra, § 11.73, ¶ 17 and § 11.74, ¶ 22.

§ 11.27

1. See supra, § 11.6.

§ 11.28

1. See supra, § 11.14, note 5.

§ 11.28 MORTGAGE FORECLOSURE

The next time a motion is made to the court, lender's counsel should seek to amend the caption formally to reflect the name of the new party in place of the particular "John Doe" defendant.

Library References:
West's Key No. Digests, Mortgages ⚖=458.

§ 11.29 Receivers

Virtually every mortgage contains a provision entitling the plaintiff-lender, upon the commencement of a foreclosure action, to the appointment by the court of a receiver of the mortgaged premises. The same mortgage provision almost invariably permits the plaintiff to seek the appointment of a receiver *ex parte* (*i.e.*, without notice to the borrower) and without regard to the value of the mortgaged property.[1]

The court-appointed receiver is empowered to collect the rents and any other income derived from the property, to maintain the premises in a proper state of repair, and to make such other expenditures as are necessary to preserve the property, such as paying real estate taxes, insurance premiums, the salaries of building employees, electricity and fuel. The receiver usually also is empowered under the court order appointing him or her to commence legal proceedings against any tenants who fail to pay their rent, and to lease up any vacant portions of the mortgaged premises. In performing each of the foregoing functions, the receiver essentially steps into the shoes of, and takes the place of, the borrower-owner of the premises during the pendency of the foreclosure action.

Although it is the plaintiff who seeks the appointment of a receiver, from a legal standpoint, the receiver is deemed an agent and officer of the court, and not an agent of the plaintiff who procured the receiver's appointment.[2] However, as a practical matter, the receiver usually will establish a cooperative working relationship with the plaintiff and plaintiff's counsel, and will seek the consent of the plaintiff on such issues as whether to make particular repairs to the premises, whether to lease up particular portions of the premises and if so with whom as tenants, or whether to leave any of those unleased portions vacant.

Library References:
West's Key No. Digests, Mortgages ⚖=466–474.

§ 11.30 Receivers—Considerations in Determining Whether to Seek Appointment of Receiver

From the plaintiff-lender's perspective, the primary purpose in seeking the appointment of a receiver is to divert the property's income

§ 11.29

1. *See infra,* § 11.31.

2. *See, e.g.,* Jamaica Savings Bank v. Florizal Realty Corp., 95 Misc.2d 654, 407 N.Y.S.2d 1016 (Sup.Ct., Queens County, 1978).

stream away from the borrower and into the hands of a court-appointed officer. To put this purpose in blunt terms, the key desire of the lender here is to prevent the defaulting borrower, who obviously has not been making the mortgage payments, from continuing to "milk" the income stream, *i.e.*, from continuing to put rental monies derived from the property into his or her own "pocket," rather than using those monies to meet the borrower's mortgage obligations and to operate and maintain the property properly. Concomitantly, the lender seeks, via the appointment of a receiver, to have the receiver use the rental monies collected by him or her to pay expenses necessary to preserve the value of the property that serves as the lender's collateral and to prevent the deterioration of the property during the pendency of the foreclosure action.

Given the foregoing purposes for having a receiver, the plaintiff-lender generally will seek the appointment of a receiver when there is significant income, most often in the form of rental payments made by tenants, generated by the mortgaged property. In contrast, where there is no income to be collected from the property (*e.g.*, the property consists solely of vacant land, or, even if improved by a building, has no tenants), it generally will not make sense to have a receiver. Indeed, even where the property, or a portion thereof, is tenanted, if the amount of rental income is negligible, there may not be economic justification for seeking to have a receiver appointed.[1] A receiver can be a fairly expensive proposition. Receivers generally are entitled to a commission of five percent (5%) of all income collected.[2] Moreover, where there is no income for a court-appointed receiver to collect, the plaintiff-lender who procured the receiver's appointment can be compelled to advance to the receiver necessary expenditures made by the latter from the lender's own pocket to preserve the property.[3]

Where the rental income generated by the property is relatively minimal, making it difficult for the lender to justify the appointment of a receiver economically, a lender may want to consider the alternative of exercising its rights under an assignment of rents, if any, that it received from the borrower at the inception of the loan. A significant number of mortgage loan documents today, especially those with respect to commercial and multi-residential properties, include such an assignment of rents in the mortgage document itself and/or in a separate assignment document executed simultaneously with the mortgage and other attendant loan documents.

§ 11.30

1. CAVEAT: If the property is deteriorating or presents a hazard, and the foreclosure is not going to be concluded imminently, and/or if the mortgagor does not cooperate in allowing the property to be secured, a receiver may be required despite the expense to insulate the mortgaged property from liability. *See, e.g.*, Department of Housing Preservation and Development of the City of New York v. Greenpoint Savings Bank, 169 Misc.2d 61, 646 N.Y.S.2d 601 (Civ.Ct., N.Y. County, 1995).

2. CPLR 8004(a). *See infra*, § 11.32.

3. CPLR 8004(b).

If such an assignment is a so-called "absolute" one, *i.e.*, it assigns all right, title and interest of the borrower in the rents and leases to the lender as of the inception of the loan, and merely gives the borrower a license to collect the rents until there is an event of default by the borrower under the loan documents, then in accordance with the usual further terms of such an assignment, the lender can revoke the borrower's license upon a default and send notices to the tenants directing them to pay their rent directly to the lender.[4]

The one downside of using this alternative, at least where the foreclosure action is not quickly resolved, is that all the lender is doing under this scenario is collecting the rents. In the meantime, no one is operating the property. The lender generally is not going to perform that function unless it wants to take on the added role of a mortgagee-in-possession, with the attendant risks that acting in such a capacity entails,[5] and the borrower, now deprived of its rental stream, is certainly not going to continue to take on that responsibility. In contrast, with a receiver, not only would the receiver be collecting the rents, but he or she would also be making the expenditures from the rental income necessary to operate and maintain the property. Thus, while the lender's exercise of an assignment of rents may be a desirable alternative on a short-term basis (*e.g.*, it may bring the borrower to the bargaining table much more quickly and effectuate a more expeditious resolution of the foreclosure action), seeking the appointment of a receiver is in most instances the preferable alternative, particularly where the property produces a sizable amount of rental income.[6]

---

4. For an example of such an "absolute" assignment of rents, see Federal Home Loan Mortgage Corporation v. Dutch Lane Associates, 775 F.Supp. 133 (S.D.N.Y. 1991). Such an "absolute" assignment is to be contrasted with a so-called "conditional" assignment of rents, where the legal transfer to the lender of the borrower's rights in the rents does not take place at the loan's inception but only becomes effective upon some further action on the lender's part, such as a written notice to the borrower of an event of default and/or a demand that the borrower turn over the rents, followed by non-compliance on the part of the borrower. See, e.g., 1180 Anderson Avenue Realty Corp. v. Mina Equities Corp., 95 A.D.2d 169, 465 N.Y.S.2d 511 (1st Dep't 1983).

5. *See* Bankers Federal Savings Bank FSB v. Off West Broadway Developers, 224 A.D.2d 376, 638 N.Y.S.2d 72, 74 (1st Dep't 1996), where the court stated, "The immediate benefit of the appointment of a receiver of rents is that the holder of the mortgage is spared the exposure to liability which would result from assuming control of the property as a mortgagee in possession." *See also* Castillo v. Carver Federal Savings and Loan Ass'n, 125 A.D.2d 287, 508 N.Y.S.2d 574 (2d Dep't 1986) (if plaintiff were a mortgagee in possession, plaintiff would owe a duty of care with respect to the maintenance of the premises); E. Landau Industries, Inc. v. 385 McLean Corp., 58 Misc.2d 725, 296 N.Y.S.2d 707 (Sup.Ct., Westchester County, 1969).

6. PRACTICE POINTER: Often, a fairly substantial amount of time elapses between the borrower's initial default under the mortgage loan documents and the appointment of a receiver in the lender's subsequently commenced foreclosure action. The lender's exercise of its rights under an "absolute" assignment of rents during this interim period can cut off the flow of income into the borrower's "pockets" from the inception of the default. The lender can thereby have the "best of both worlds"—precluding the borrower from collecting rent from the outset of the default, and then, once a foreclosure action is commenced, having a court-appointed receiver

Library References:
West's Key No. Digests, Mortgages ⚖︎466–474.

§ 11.31 Receivers—*Ex Parte* Motion for Appointment of Receiver

Virtually all mortgages contain a provision entitling the plaintiff-lender, upon the commencement of a foreclosure action, to the appointment of a receiver *ex parte*, *i.e.*, without prior notice to the borrower or to any other defendant. Indeed, RPL § 254(10) provides that a covenant in a mortgage which merely states "that the holder of this mortgage, in any action to foreclose it, shall be entitled to the appointment of a receiver," is deemed to entitle the plaintiff-lender to the appointment of a receiver without notice and without regard to the adequacy of the security.[1] Thus, pursuant to the statutory interpretation of such a covenant in a mortgage, the plaintiff-lender not only is permitted to obtain a receiver *ex parte*, but it can do so whether or not the property has a fair market value in excess of the mortgage debt.

The constitutionality of the statutory scheme allowing for the *ex parte* appointment of a receiver has been consistently upheld by the courts.[2] The primary rationale for the decisions in these cases has been that the CPLR permits any party, once an *ex parte* order has been entered appointing a receiver, to seek to remove him or her at any time.[3]

The *ex parte* application for the appointment of a receiver is made by the submission to the court of a proposed order appointing a receiver to which there is annexed an affidavit in support of the appointment.

The form of an order appointing a receiver submitted *ex parte* to the court (the "receivership order") should contain at least the following decretal provisions:[4]

1. Authorizing the individual appointed as receiver to collect the "rents and profits" (*i.e.*, the income) from the mortgaged premises (the legal metes and bounds description of the premises should be annexed as an exhibit to the order);

2. Authorizing the receiver to collect rents from the tenants of the premises, and directing the tenants to pay their rent to the receiver during the pendency of the foreclosure action;

to take over the rent collection function from the lender and also to make the expenditures necessary to preserve the property from the income received.

§ 11.31

1. *See also*, RPAPL § 1325(1), which provides: "Where the action is for the foreclosure of a mortgage providing that a receiver may be appointed without notice, notice of a motion for such appointment shall not be required."

2. Friedman v. Gerax Realty Associates, 100 Misc.2d 820, 420 N.Y.S.2d 247 (Sup.Ct., Nassau County, 1979); Massachusetts Mutual Life Ins. Co. v. Avon Associates, Inc., 83 Misc.2d 829, 373 N.Y.S.2d 464 (Sup.Ct., N.Y. County, 1975); City Partners Ltd.-BMG v. Jamaica Savings Bank, N.Y.L.J., 1/3/79, p.13, col.2 (Sup.Ct., Nassau County).

3. CPLR 6405.

4. For a sample form of an order appointing a receiver, *see infra*, § 11.75.

§ 11.31   MORTGAGE FORECLOSURE   Ch. 11

3. Authorizing the receiver to lease any portion of the premises that are or become vacant for up to a specified maximum term;[5]

4. Directing the receiver to make the expenditures necessary for the operation of the premises, such as real estate taxes, water and sewer charges, insurance premiums, property maintenance and repairs,[6] and principal and interest on any mortgage affecting the property superior to that of the mortgage being foreclosed;

5. If the premises are a multiple dwelling in a city with a population of at least one million (*i.e.*, New York City), then in accordance with RPAPL § 1325(3), requiring the receiver to register with any municipal department as may be required under local law and to give priority in the making of expenditures to the "correction of immediately hazardous and hazardous violations of housing maintenance laws within the time set by orders of any municipal department";

6. Authorizing the receiver to commence legal proceedings respecting the mortgaged premises, such as dispossess proceedings seeking the removal of any tenant failing to pay its rent to the receiver;[7]

7. Authorizing the receiver, if the plaintiff-lender is willing to permit the receiver to do so, to retain a managing agent to assist the receiver in the performance of the receiver's duties;[8]

8. Enjoining the defendant-borrower and any other defendants from collecting rents from tenants or leasing any portion of the premises during the receivership;

5. PRACTICE POINTER: The proposed maximum term which counsel inserts in the proposed order usually will depend upon whether the premises are commercial or residential. In the case of commercial property, the proposed term generally will be longer (somewhere in the 3–5 year range), as it usually will be difficult to find a commercial tenant willing to accept a lease of shorter duration. In contrast, a residential tenant, such as one in an apartment building, usually will be more amenable to a one or two-year lease. Where the apartment in question is rent-stabilized, the pertinent statutes and regulations require that the receiver offer the tenant the option of a one or two-year lease.

6. PRACTICE POINTER: A proposed "cap" should be inserted in the proposed order to give the plaintiff-lender some degree of control over the extent of repairs being performed.

7. A receiver is not allowed to retain counsel without a court order. CPLR 6401(b). Such authorization can be set forth in the receivership order, or alternatively, the order can require the receiver to make a future application to the court in order to retain counsel.

8. A managing agent generally will be desirable when there are a substantial number of tenants of the mortgaged premises, requiring rent billing, record keeping and rendering of building services on a scale that the receiver will not usually have the capacity to perform alone. However, the managing agent does add another layer of expense to the receivership. The managing agent's fee is generally negotiable with the receiver and the lender. A set monthly fee or a set percentage of the rental income collected are the usual methods of compensation.

9. Directing the defendant-borrower to turn over all pertinent records regarding the mortgaged premises to the receiver, such as rent records, service contracts and leases, and to turn over to the receiver all security deposits of tenants and any rents collected from tenants between the date the receivership order is signed and the date the receiver qualifies by filing the receiver's bond (*see* item [10] below), other than those rental monies disbursed during that period for the necessary operation of the property;

10. Requiring the receiver, before commencing his or her duties, to obtain from a surety company and file with the court a receiver's bond, in an amount inserted by the court in the order, as security for the faithful discharge of his or her duties;[9] and

11. Directing the receiver to deposit all monies received by him or her from the premises in any amount(s) at a bank designated by the court in the order.[10]

The supporting affidavit annexed to the proposed receivership order should be by an officer or other authorized representative of the lender. That affidavit should contain, in concise form, the following information:

1. Brief background facts of the action (a copy of the complaint should be attached), including a reference to the subject mortgage (a copy of the mortgage also should be attached), the nature of the default, and the date upon which the action was commenced;

2. A reference to the provision in the mortgage which entitles the plaintiff to the *ex parte* appointment of a receiver;

3. A brief description of the mortgaged premises (*e.g.*, one or more buildings and whether the premises are of residential, commercial or mixed use), and a reference to the approximate number of tenants and the approximate amount of the monthly rent roll for the premises;[11]

4. If the plaintiff-lender wishes to recommend a particular individual as a receiver, a brief recitation of the qualifications of such

---

9. It is the filing of the receiver's bond with the court that "qualifies" the receiver to commence performing his or her responsibilities as set forth in the receivership order.

10. As the Federal Deposit Insurance Corporation insures bank accounts only up to the first $100,000, it would be prudent for the receiver to set up separate accounts for each $100,000 of funds.

11. PRACTICE POINTER: The court often multiplies the monthly rent roll by 2 or 3 to arrive at the amount of the receiver's bond. If a relatively recent rent roll is available, a copy of it should be attached as an exhibit to the affidavit. If a recent one is not available (because the borrower, contrary to its usual obligation under the mortgage, has failed to supply one), the plaintiff may want to take whatever rent roll it has in its files, however old it is, and insert in the affidavit an estimated current rent roll figure calculated to take into consideration changes in rental market conditions since the time of that older rent roll.

§ 11.31 MORTGAGE FORECLOSURE Ch. 11

individual;[12] and

5. If the plaintiff-lender wishes to recommend a particular entity as managing agent, a brief recitation of the qualifications of such entity.[13]

Library References:

West's Key No. Digests, Mortgages ⇐469.

§ 11.32 Receivers—Compensation

The compensation to which a receiver is entitled for his or her services is referred to as the receiver's "commissions." The amount of commissions which a receiver may be awarded by the court is governed by CPLR 8004. That statutory provision states in relevant part:

(a) Generally. A receiver, except where otherwise prescribed by statute, is entitled to such commissions, *not exceeding five percent upon the sums received and disbursed by him, as the court by which he is appointed allows* ... [Emphasis added.]

The above emphasized portion of CPLR 8004(a) is admittedly ambiguous and has given rise to the question, among others, whether the statute contemplates a commission of up to five percent (5%) of income received by the receiver plus up to an additional 5% of expenses disbursed by the receiver (the so-called "double recovery theory"), or whether the statute intends just a "single recovery," *i.e.*, up to 5% of the sums received by the receiver, on the theory that the sums that are received by the receiver are the same ones that are ultimately disbursed by him or her.[1]

Although there are some lower court cases which have opted for the "double recovery" theory,[2] and at least one lower court has awarded a "hybrid" commission based on 2.5% of income received plus 2.5% of expenses disbursed,[3] the prevailing judicial view, including holdings of the Appellate Divisions of the First and Fourth Departments,[4] is the

---

12. The individual recommended usually must be on the qualified list of receivers maintained by the Office of Court Administration ("OCA") and must not have received other appointments during that year which would push him or her over the permissible limit. An individual can get on the OCA list by completing an OCA application. In any event, the court is not bound to appoint the individual recommended. See Part 36 of the Rules of the Chief Judge, 22 NYCRR Part 36.

13. Again, the court is not obligated to appoint the entity recommended by the plaintiff.

§ 11.32

1. B. Bergman, *The 5 Percent Question; Receiver's Commission: Confusion Reigns Over "How Much,"* N.Y.L.J., 5/24/95, p.5, col.2.

2. *See, e.g.*, Sunrise Fed. Sav. & Loan Ass'n. v. West Park Ave. Corp., 47 Misc.2d 940, 263 N.Y.S.2d 529 (Sup.Ct., Nassau County, 1965).

3. Resolution Trust Corp. v. Preferred Entity Advancements, Inc., 157 Misc.2d 683, 598 N.Y.S.2d 437 (Sup.Ct., Queens County, 1993).

4. Eastrich Multiple Investor Fund, L.P. v. Citiwide Development Assoc., 637 N.Y.S.2d 712, 218 A.D.2d 43 (1st Dep't

"single recovery" theory, *i.e.*, a maximum 5% commission based on sums received.

The receiver's commissions generally are payable out of the account which the receiver maintains into which income is deposited and out of which expenses are disbursed. However, if at the termination of the receivership, the receiver's account has been depleted and there are no funds available to pay the receiver commissions, then CPLR 8004(b) comes into play. That statute provides that in such a situation, the receiver can apply to the court for a fixing of commissions, and the court can direct the "party who moved for the appointment of the receiver," *i.e.*, the plaintiff-lender, to pay the commissions and also to reimburse the receiver for any out-of-pocket expenses.

Although traditionally receivers have waited until they seek to be discharged at the conclusion of their receiverships[5] to be awarded their commissions, the general increase in the length of time it takes to complete a foreclosure action at present (given increasingly congested court dockets and the increasing number of contested foreclosures), has led a number of receivers to seek interim awards of commissions during the pendency of the foreclosure. While the granting of such interim requests are obviously within the discretion of the court, if the foreclosure action is expected to last for more than a year, it may be prudent for the receiver to seek such interim commissions approximately every three to six months.

Library References:
   West's Key No. Digests, Mortgages ⚭474.

§ 11.33 Receivers—Opposing Appointment of Receiver

In order successfully to oppose the appointment of a receiver in a mortgage foreclosure action, the borrower must show that the foreclosure action should be dismissed. For example, the borrower can show that service has been improperly effected, and therefore the court lacks jurisdiction. Alternatively, the borrower can attempt to demonstrate that the lender has improperly noticed the default or has frustrated the cure of the default, requiring dismissal of the action and the denial of the motion for the appointment of the receiver.[1]

1996); Coronet Capital Co. v. Spodek, 202 A.D.2d 20, 615 N.Y.S.2d 351 (1st Dep't 1994); People v. Abbott Manor Nursing Home, 112 A.D.2d 40, 490 N.Y.S.2d 411 (4th Dep't 1985).

5. Unless a court order or stipulation of the parties directs otherwise, the receivership terminates upon the delivery of a referee's deed of the premises to the successful bidder at the foreclosure sale. *See infra*, § 11.34.

§ 11.33

1. *See* City Streets Realty Corp. v. Jan Jay Construction Enterprises Corp., 88 A.D.2d 558, 559, 450 N.Y.S.2d 492, 493 (1st Dep't 1982) (denial of motion to appoint receiver where court found issue of fact as to whether lender had frustrated cure of default).

§ 11.33   MORTGAGE FORECLOSURE   Ch. 11

Library References:
West's Key No. Digests, Mortgages ⬢466–469.

§ 11.34   Receivers—Discharging Receiver

Unless the receivership is concluded sooner by reason of a settlement between the parties or an order of the court, the receivership continues until the "consummation of the foreclosure sale,"[1] *i.e.*, until the conveyance of the referee's deed to the successful bidder at the foreclosure sale.[2]

Upon the conclusion of the receivership, the receiver proceeds to prepare and serve a motion which: (i) sets forth an accounting of all income he or she collected and all disbursements he or she expended during the course of the receivership, and also sets forth the balance of funds remaining in the receiver's account; and (ii) requests the court to: (a) approve the receiver's accounting; (b) fix the amount of the receiver's commissions; (c) direct to whom the receiver is to disburse the funds remaining in the receiver's account after paying himself or herself the commissions fixed by the court;[3] and (d) discharge both the receiver and the surety company on the receiver's bond from all further responsibilities and obligations.

Library References:
West's Key No. Digests, Mortgages ⬢474.

§ 11.35   Defendant's Response

Within the twenty day time period permitted by CPLR 3012(a) for foreclosure complaints personally served within New York State, or within the thirty days permitted by CPLR 3012(c) for foreclosure complaints served outside the State or by means other than personal delivery, each defendant must respond to the foreclosure complaint by appearing, answering or moving to dismiss pursuant to CPLR 3211. Each of those alternatives is discussed below.

Library References:
West's Key No. Digests, Mortgages ⬢454–459(4).

§ 11.34

1. Allison v. Roslyn Plaza, Ltd., 86 Misc.2d 849, 385 N.Y.S.2d 454, 456 (Sup. Ct., Nassau County, 1976).

2. See *infra*, § 11.51.

3. If the foreclosure sale results in a deficiency, *i.e.*, the purchase price at the sale is less than the foreclosure judgment amount due the plaintiff, then the court will direct the receiver to pay the post-commission funds left in the receiver's account, up to the full amount of the deficiency, to the plaintiff. If there are still monies remaining in the receiver's account after payment to the plaintiff of the full deficiency, or if the foreclosure sale results in a surplus, then the monies remaining in the receiver's account will be distributed in accordance with a court order rendered in conjunction with a surplus money proceeding. See *infra*, § 11.53. Any monies still remaining in the receiver's account after the plaintiff and all surplus money claimants, if any, are fully satisfied, are remitted to the borrower-defendant.

§ 11.36 Defendant's Response—Motion to Dismiss Complaint

While motions to dismiss foreclosure complaints pursuant to CPLR 3211 are not generally favored, a motion to dismiss for lack of jurisdiction may lie where service of the complaint was improper.[1]

Additional grounds for a motion to dismiss might include the Statute of Limitations,[2] that the plaintiff corporation is a foreign corporation not authorized to do business in the State of New York,[3] failure to plead compliance with the notice provisions of the loan documents,[4] failure to plead an essential element of RPAPL § 1301(3), such as the allegation that no other actions are pending to recover the same debt, or the pendency of another action to recover the same debt.[5]

Library References:
West's Key No. Digests, Mortgages ⚖=475.

§ 11.37 Defendant's Response—Answer and Defenses

Alternatively, the defendant may interpose an answer and, if warranted, allege affirmative defenses or even counterclaims.[1]

The answer should contain admissions and denials as appropriate in any civil pleading.[2] Possible affirmative defenses to be considered by the borrower's counsel are:

1. Breach of contract by the lender;[3]
2. Duress;[4]

§ 11.36

1. See CPLR Art. 3 and NYBCL §§ 304–307.

2. The Statute of Limitations for commencement of a foreclosure action is six (6) years. CPLR 213(4).

3. NYBCL § 1312.

4. See Verna v. O'Brien, 78 Misc.2d 288, 356 N.Y.S.2d 929 (Sup.Ct., N.Y. County, 1974).

5. See supra, § 11.6.

§ 11.37

1. PRACTICE POINTER: A defendant should consider pleading the affirmative defenses in conjunction with the counterclaims. The plaintiff, in the face of counterclaims, is likely to move to sever those claims as unrelated to the foreclosure action. However, if those counterclaims are virtually identical to the defenses, the motion to sever is less likely to succeed.

2. CPLR 3018.

CAVEAT: If the complaint is verified, CPLR 3020(a) requires that the answer be verified by one of the defendants. CPLR 3020(b) also may require that the answer be verified.

3. The borrower's attorney should determine whether the lender has complied with its material obligations under the loan agreement, such as the duty to continue funding a construction loan so long as the borrower complies with its obligations or the duty to extend the maturity date upon certain terms and conditions.

4. A contract executed under duress is voidable, not void. Such a contract can be ratified, and therefore duress must be asserted promptly before the benefits of the loan are used. Hudson River Yards Corp. v. Tillotson, 144 N.Y.S.2d 183 (Sup.Ct., Westchester County, 1955).

In Marine Midland Bank N.A. v. Mitchell, 100 A.D.2d 733, 473 N.Y.S.2d 664, 665 (4th Dep't 1984), the appellate division held that the court below properly dismissed a de-

§ 11.37 MORTGAGE FORECLOSURE Ch. 11

3. The existence of a forbearance agreement or other supplemental agreement in which the lender agreed to forbear from foreclosing until the occurrence of a certain event;

4. Forgery, *i.e.*, the borrower's signature on the loan documents was forged, or the documents were signed without the borrower's permission;

5. Fraudulent inducement of the borrower to enter into the loan documents;

6. Lack of consideration;[5]

7. Oral modification of the loan documents;

8. Partial payment after acceleration constituting a waiver of the acceleration;[6]

9. Payment or tender of payment;

10. Statute of Limitations;[7]

11. Unclean hands (although a foreclosure action is an equitable action, certain equitable defenses, such as "unclean hands" are not

fense based on an alleged threat by the secured creditor to close the defendant's business unless the mortgage was executed. The alleged threat was not duress because "the threatened exercise of a legal right cannot constitute duress."

PRACTICE POINTER: The defense of duress, including the threat of criminal prosecution, must be specifically pleaded as an affirmative defense. *See* Marine Midland Bank N.A. v. Mitchell, *supra*.

5. The defense of lack of consideration is difficult to sustain. The recital of consideration in the instruments, whether in the note or the mortgage, is *prima facie* evidence to establish consideration. Blueberry Investors Company v. Ilana Realty, Inc., 184 A.D.2d 906, 907, 585 N.Y.S.2d 564, 566 (3d Dep't 1992); Gould v. McBride, 36 A.D.2d 706, 707, 319 N.Y.S.2d 125, 126 (1st Dep't), aff'd 29 N.Y.2d 768, 326 N.Y.S.2d 565, 276 N.E.2d 626 (1971).

6. Federal National Mortgage Ass'n v. Miller, 123 Misc.2d 431, 432, 473 N.Y.S.2d 743, 744 (Sup.Ct., Nassau County, 1984) (plaintiff waived acceleration of entire indebtedness when it accepted partial payments under Chapter 13 plan).

7. The Statute of Limitations for commencement of an action to foreclose a mortgage in New York is six (6) years. CPLR 213(4). The Statute of Limitations commences to run on the date the installment payment was due or on the date the default occurred. *See e.g.*, Haberkorn v. DaSilva,

210 N.Y.S.2d 391, 396 (Sup.Ct., Kings County, 1960); Boulukos v. Chresafes, 20 Misc.2d 673, 187 N.Y.S.2d 141 (Sup.Ct., Nassau County, 1959). Where the mortgagor makes an unconditional promise to pay the mortgage debt after the cause of action has accrued, the limitations period may begin to run anew. General Obligations Law § 17–105. *See* Sichol v. Crocker, 177 A.D.2d 842, 576 N.Y.S.2d 457 (3d Dep't 1991), appeal denied 79 N.Y.2d 755, 581 N.Y.S.2d 665, 590 N.E.2d 250 (1992) (written acknowledgement of debt is insufficient; must be an unconditional promise to pay). *See also* Petito v. Piffath, 85 N.Y.2d 1, 647 N.E.2d 732, 623 N.Y.S.2d 520 (1994), reversing 199 A.D.2d 252, 253, 604 N.Y.S.2d 591, 592 (2d Dep't 1993) (agreement was not sufficient to invoke General Obligations Law § 17–105).

Laches is an equitable defense which generally requires a showing that unreasonable delay by the mortgagee has misled the mortgagor. *See* Verna v. O'Brien, 78 Misc.2d 288, 356 N.Y.S.2d 929 (Sup.Ct., N.Y. County, 1974). However, laches is probably not available in a foreclosure action if the action is timely commenced under the six year Statute of Limitations. New York State Mortgage Loan Enforcement and Administration Corp. v. North Town Phase II Houses, Inc., 191 A.D.2d 151, 594 N.Y.S.2d 183 (1st Dep't 1993); Schmidt's Wholesale, Inc. v. Miller & Lehman Construction, Inc., 173 A.D.2d 1004, 569 N.Y.S.2d 836 (3d Dep't 1991).

recognized as defenses to foreclosure actions);[8]

12. Unconscionability (Courts will consider defenses of unconscionability where it appears the lender is overreaching, the default is inconsequential or inadvertent, and the borrower has made efforts to cure.[9] Nevertheless, mortgages are generally enforced according to their terms, and the mere fact that enforcement now seems unfair will not persuade the court that enforcement is unconscionable);[10]

13. Usury.[11]

Library References:

West's Key No. Digests, Mortgages ⬥454.

§ 11.38 Defendant's Response—Notice of Appearance and Waiver

Often, a defendant has no defense to the foreclosure action, particularly if the defendant merely holds a subordinate lien. In such cases, that defendant's only interest in the action is to determine whether surplus funds will be available after the sale to satisfy its lien as well as the plaintiff's lien. In such cases, it is customary to file a notice of appearance and waiver in foreclosure. The usual form provides for an appearance by counsel under CPLR 320 and generally waives notice of all further proceedings, except the notice of sale, surplus money proceedings and notice of any discontinuance of the action. Thus, the subordinate

---

8. Jo Ann Homes at Bellmore, Inc. v. Dworetz, 25 N.Y.2d 112, 122, 302 N.Y.S.2d 799, 806, 250 N.E.2d 214, 219 (1969).

9. DiMatteo v. North Tonawanda Auto Wash, Inc., 101 A.D.2d 692, 476 N.Y.S.2d 40 (4th Dep't 1984) (unconscionability is a defense in mortgage foreclosure actions); Karas v. Wasserman, 91 A.D.2d 812, 458 N.Y.S.2d 280 (3d Dep't 1982) (foreclosure may be denied in case of inadvertent, inconsequential default in order to prevent unconscionable overreaching conduct); Josephson v. Caral Real Estate Co., 200 N.Y.S.2d 1016 (Sup.Ct., N.Y. County, 1960) (allegations of specific unconscionable activity on part of plaintiff to induce breach may properly be introduced as defense to mortgage foreclosure); The Clark-Robinson Corp. v. Jet Enterprises, 159 N.Y.S.2d 214 (Sup.Ct., Bronx County, 1957) (where principal and interest were paid and tax default was cured, acceleration denied); Domus Realty Corp. v. 3440 Realty Co., 179 Misc. 749, 40 N.Y.S.2d 69 (Sup.Ct., N.Y. County), aff'd 266 App.Div. 725, 41 N.Y.S.2d 940 (1st Dep't 1943) (unconscionable means conduct that is monstrously harsh and shocking to the conscience of the court).

10. Graf v. Hope Building Corp., 171 N.E. 884, 254 N.Y. 1 (1930), where the court held that if a covenant is fair on its face, is not oppressive or unconscionable, and involves no penalty or forfeiture, the contention that enforcement is ungenerous will not avail in equity.

11. In New York, certain loans with an effective interest rate (including certain fees) that exceeds twenty-five percent (25%) per annum but that are for less than $2.5 million are criminally usurious and unenforceable. Penal Law §§ 190.40, 190.42 and General Obligations Law §§ 5–501 et seq. However, the usury defense is personal to the borrower and may not be asserted by an assignee without offering to pay a part of the sum borrowed. General Obligations Law § 5–517. Generally, corporate borrowers cannot assert the defense of usury. General Obligations Law § 5–521.

PRACTICE POINTER: Simultaneously with serving the answer, the defendant should consider serving all necessary discovery requests.

§ 11.38   MORTGAGE FORECLOSURE   Ch. 11

lienor will receive notice of the sale and will preserve its right to any surplus.

A defendant also can modify the standard form of notice to demand service of additional papers which may be of interest to that defendant. However, having appeared and not answered, the defendant cannot oppose the entry of a foreclosure judgment.

Where the defendant files a notice of appearance and waiver in foreclosure, the lender will move for judgment pursuant to RPAPL § 1321.

Library References:

West's Key No. Digests, Mortgages ⟪454(1).

§ 11.39   Obtaining Judgment

When the time of all defendants to answer or to move to dismiss has expired, the lender may move the court, pursuant to RPAPL § 1321, CPLR 3212 or CPLR 3215, for a judgment which in essence states that plaintiff is entitled to the relief requested in its complaint, including foreclosure, once a computation has been made as to the amount due under the subject mortgage. In the same motion, the lender seeks appointment of a referee to compute that amount.[1] Alternatively, the lender may seek to have the court compute the amount due where the calculations either are agreed to or are straightforward.

Library References:

West's Key No. Digests, Mortgages ⟪483–498.

§ 11.40   Obtaining Judgment—Motion for Judgment

The plaintiff, in moving for judgment, must demonstrate to the court that it is entitled to all of the relief sought in the verified complaint. Thus, the plaintiff must, by verified complaint or by affidavit of an officer of the plaintiff, show that the plaintiff is the owner and holder of the note and mortgage, that there was a properly noticed default, and that since that time, the default has not been cured.

The motion papers also must demonstrate, by affidavit, and, if necessary, by an accompanying memorandum of law, that plaintiff's lien is superior to the lien of all other defendants, either because it was recorded first, or because it is accorded priority on another ground, such as a subordination agreement.

Additionally, the plaintiff's counsel generally submits an affidavit of regularity attesting to the proper filing of the notice of pendency,[1] attesting further that all the defendants against whom judgment is

§ 11.39
1. See infra, §§ 11.42—11.45.

§ 11.40
1. RPAPL § 1331.

sought have been properly served, and reciting their status with respect to an appearance in the action.[2]

CPLR 3215, regarding default judgments, will govern the additional showings which must be made with respect to those defendants against whom a default judgment is sought. RPAPL § 1321 will govern with respect to those defendants who have appeared in the action, but not answered.

With respect to those defendants who have answered, the lender must move for summary judgment, showing why there are no material issues of disputed fact which preclude judgment in favor of the lender.

Library References:
West's Key No. Digests, Mortgages ⚖483–498.

§ 11.41 Obtaining Judgment—Opposing Motion for Judgment

The opposition to a motion for judgment will focus on the lender's failure to adhere to the statutory rules of procedure, or, in the case of a motion made pursuant to CPLR 3212, the opposition will try to create disputed issues of material fact.

For example, often a mechanic's lienor will try to demonstrate that its mechanic's lien should be accorded priority because the mortgage loan was a construction loan, and the lender did not assiduously follow the dictates of Lien Law § 22. Sometimes, a borrower will attempt to demonstrate that one or more of its affirmative defenses require a trial.

If the court denies the lender's motion for judgment, the matter will proceed through discovery to trial.

Library References:
West's Key No. Digests, Mortgages ⚖483–498.

§ 11.42 Reference to Compute

Unlike the procedure in most other plenary actions, the court's granting of summary judgment or judgment by default in a mortgage foreclosure action does not end the case. Before the final judgment of foreclosure and sale can be entered, there must be a computation of the amount due the plaintiff-lender, and a determination as to whether the mortgaged premises should be sold in one parcel or multiple parcels. While the court itself can render such a computation and determination, those functions almost always are delegated by the court, in the order granting summary judgment or default judgment, to the so-called "referee to compute".[1] A hearing is then scheduled and subsequently conduct-

---

2. For a sample form of an affidavit of regularity, see infra, § 11.78.

§ 11.42
1. RPAPL § 1321(1).

ed before the referee to compute. If only the plaintiff appears at the hearing, the evidence presented to the referee often consists merely of the submission of an affidavit from the plaintiff. Where the hearing is a contested one—*i.e.*, not only the plaintiff but one or more defendants appear at the hearing to present evidence—more formal submission of evidence via the live testimony of witnesses usually will be required. After the referee renders a report setting forth his or her computation and determination, the plaintiff-lender may move the court for confirmation of the referee's report and entry of a judgment of foreclosure and sale.

Library References:
West's Key No. Digests, Mortgages ⚖479.

§ 11.43 Reference to Compute—Hearing Before Referee to Compute

From a technical point of view, the hearing before a referee to compute in a mortgage foreclosure action is subject to the same provisions of Article 43 of the CPLR that govern a trial of any matter by a court-appointed referee. Among the pertinent requirements of CPLR Article 43 are: (1) that the hearing take place within twenty (20) days of the order of reference;[1] (2) that the venue of the hearing be in the county in which the action is pending;[2] and (3) that the referee conduct the hearing in the same manner as a court trying a case without a jury.[3]

Practically speaking, however, the hearing before the referee to compute often tends to be considerably more informal than the provisions of CPLR Article 43 dictate. The pertinent case law has lent support in this regard, holding that failures to comply with the literal provisions of Article 43 with respect to referee's hearings are to be deemed mere irregularities which, absent prejudice shown to a party, may be disregarded.[4] Where the foreclosure action is uncontested, the "hearing" before the referee to compute often consists merely of the submission to the referee of an affidavit from an officer or other representative of the plaintiff setting forth a calculation of the total mortgage indebtedness due the plaintiff (including principal, interest, late charges and advances for such items as real estate taxes), and also stating the plaintiff's position as to whether the premises should be sold in one parcel or in multiple parcels.

Once the order appointing the referee to compute has been entered, the plaintiff's attorney should contact the referee and work out a

§ 11.43
1. CPLR 4313.
2. *Cf.* CPLR 507.
3. CPLR 4318.

4. *See* Stein v. American Mortgage Banking, Ltd., 216 A.D.2d 458, 628 N.Y.S.2d 162 (2d Dep't 1995); Shultis v. Woodstock Land Development Associates, 195 A.D.2d 677, 599 N.Y.S.2d 340 (3d Dep't 1993).

mutually agreeable date for the hearing. After a date is chosen, the plaintiff's counsel should prepare and serve a notice of the date, time and place of the hearing.[5] Also, in order to determine in advance whether the hearing is going to be contested, thereby necessitating that the plaintiff's counsel bring a representative of the plaintiff to testify at the hearing, the notice should state that any defendant who intends to attend the hearing should so advise both the referee and the plaintiff's counsel in writing by a designated date (e.g., a date approximately a week in advance).

Whether or not the hearing is going to be contested, before it commences, the referee should sign a referee's oath pursuant to which the referee swears to discharge his or her duties properly. If no defendant attends the hearing, then the submission to the referee of the plaintiff's affidavit should suffice. However, if one or more defendants do attend the hearing, then a representative of the plaintiff must come to the hearing to testify both on direct examination by plaintiff's counsel and on cross-examination by counsel for any contesting defendant(s). Assuming the cost is not prohibitive, it is recommended that plaintiff's counsel arrange for a court stenographer to attend and record all testimony and statements proffered at the hearing, in case the ensuing referee's computation report is challenged by any party. The testimony proffered by the plaintiff on direct examination should be accompanied by the submission of documentary evidence supporting the computation of the outstanding mortgage indebtedness (e.g., the note, the mortgage, any other pertinent loan documents that bear on the calculation of interest, late charges and other fees, and the plaintiff's records substantiating the amounts claimed to be due). The plaintiff's testimony also should address the issue of whether the premises should be sold in a single parcel or in multiple parcels. Facts specific to the premises, such as whether the premises consist of a single or multiple tax lot(s), and whether the premises are improved by one or more buildings, will be relevant on this issue.

Library References:
West's Key No. Digests, Mortgages ⟨=479.

§ 11.44 Reference to Compute—Report of Referee to Compute

Once the hearing is completed, the referee proceeds to prepare, sign and file with the court his or her referee's report.

Where the hearing is uncontested, it is recommended that plaintiff's counsel prepare for the referee a proposed report which the referee can

5. PRACTICE POINTER: It is preferable, though not mandated by statute, that the referee sign the notice and cause it to be served, usually by plaintiff's counsel, upon all parties entitled to notice. However, it is also permissible for the notice to go out under the name of plaintiff's counsel without the referee's signature.

§ 11.44   MORTGAGE FORECLOSURE   Ch. 11

sign at the hearing itself. For this purpose, a Blumberg form entitled "Referee's Oath and Report of Amount Due,"[1] usually will suffice, subject to one caveat set forth below. That form, which as its name indicates combines both the referee's oath and referee's report, is a very concise "fill in the blanks" document into which the amount of principal, interest and any other charges that are due can be inserted, as can the documents admitted into evidence. The form also contains a preprinted sentence that indicates that the referee finds that the premises should be sold in one parcel. Obviously, if there are grounds for selling the premises in multiple parcels, the preprinted sentence should be altered accordingly. Moreover, whether the referee's recommendation is that the premises should be sold in one parcel or multiple parcels, a sentence or two should be added setting forth the factual basis for the referee's recommendation in that regard.[2]

Library References:
West's Key No. Digests, Mortgages ⚖️479.

§ 11.45 Reference to Compute—Motion to Confirm Referee's Computation Report and for Judgment of Foreclosure and Sale

Once the referee to compute has filed his or her report with the court, the plaintiff's counsel may proceed to make a motion seeking the court's confirmation of the referee's report and the entry of a judgment of foreclosure and sale, the primary relief sought in the foreclosure action. Accompanying the notice of that motion should be a new "affidavit of regularity" of plaintiff's counsel. That new affidavit of regularity essentially updates the procedural history of the foreclosure action (previously set forth in counsel's earlier affidavit of regularity submitted in support of the plaintiff's motion for judgment)[1] to include reference to the court's order granting judgment and the appointment of the referee to compute, and a summary of the referee's findings as set forth in his or her report. A copy of the referee's report should be annexed as an exhibit to the affidavit of regularity, as should a copy of the proposed judgment of foreclosure and sale which the plaintiff seeks to have the court enter. The essential terms that should be included in the judgment of foreclosure and sale are set forth below.[2]

§ 11.44

1. Form W 363—Referee's Oath and Report of Amount Due (Julius Blumberg, Inc.).

2. See CPLR 4319. See also, Rosen Trust v. Rosen, 53 A.D.2d 342, 386 N.Y.S.2d 491, 505 (4th Dep't 1976), aff'd 43 N.Y.2d 693, 401 N.Y.S.2d 66, 371 N.E.2d 828 (1977), holding that the requirement under CPLR 4213(b) that, in a non-jury trial, the court set forth the facts that are essential to its decision, is applicable to decisions of a referee.

§ 11.45

1. For a sample form of an affidavit of regularity and in support of a motion for summary judgment, see infra, § 11.78.

2. See infra, § 11.46.

724

Ch. 11   JUDGMENT OF FORECLOSURE AND SALE   § 11.46

Library References:

West's Key No. Digests, Mortgages ⚖═479.

§ 11.46 Judgment of Foreclosure and Sale

The court's entry of a judgment of foreclosure and sale (the "foreclosure judgment") grants the key relief sought by the plaintiff in the foreclosure action—namely, the foreclosure of subordinate liens and claims against the mortgaged premises (provided the holders of such liens and claims have been named and served as defendants in the action, or the lien or claim came into existence subsequent to the plaintiff's filing of the notice of pendency), and the authorization for conducting a foreclosure sale of the premises free and clear of all such subordinate liens and claims. The foreclosure judgment also, among other things, designates the publication(s) in which the sale should be advertised, the name of a referee who will conduct the sale and the place where the sale is to be conducted, and sets forth the manner in which the proceeds of the sale are to be disbursed by the referee.

The recommended form of foreclosure judgment appears in § 11.79, *infra*. That form contains each of the following decretal provisions which must be included in the foreclosure judgment:

1. A confirmation of the report of the referee to compute;

2. A fixing of the amounts due the plaintiff (as per the referee's report), which amounts[1] consist of the principal, interest and other charges, if any, due under the subject mortgage, plus any allowable costs taxed by the clerk of the court,[2] plus an allowance as of right of up to $200,[3] plus a discretionary additional allowance of up to $300 authorized by statute in a foreclosure action;[4]

3. A directive as to whether the premises should be sold in one parcel or several parcels;

4. A designation of the place where the foreclosure sale is to be held (*e.g.*, the front steps of, or other specified place within, the county courthouse, or a specified place at a particular town hall; the place is different depending on the county and sometimes, where in

---

§ 11.46

1. The aggregate of those amounts set forth in the foreclosure judgment, together with interest at the statutory rate of nine percent (9%) per annum, represents the sum which the defendant-borrower would have to pay to the plaintiff prior to the foreclosure sale in order to satisfy the mortgage indebtedness and thereby "redeem" the property, *i.e.*, avoid a foreclosure sale. Assuming the defendant-borrower does not satisfy the indebtedness, then the fixing of those amounts establishes the basis for determining whether the amount of the successful bid at the foreclosure sale results in a deficiency or a surplus.

2. If the plaintiff desires to recover those costs, it must submit with the proposed foreclosure judgment a bill of costs to be taxed by the clerk.

3. CPLR 8302(d).

4. *See* CPLR 8303(a)(1).

725

§ 11.46   MORTGAGE FORECLOSURE   Ch. 11

the county, the property is located);[5]

5. A designation of the individual who is to conduct the foreclosure sale as the "referee at sale" (that individual can, but does not have to, be the same individual who served as the referee to compute);

6. A designation of the newspaper or other publication in which notice of the sale is to be advertised;[6]

7. A statement that if either the plaintiff or its nominee becomes the purchaser at the foreclosure sale, such party shall not be required to make a deposit with the referee at the conclusion of the sale pending the closing of title;[7]

8. A directive that the referee shall execute in favor of the purchaser at the foreclosure sale a referee's deed at closing, and that, upon receiving the proceeds of the sale, the referee shall pay any real estate taxes, assessments and water rates for the premises which are outstanding (the judgment also provides that it is not necessary for the referee to do so where, as often happens, the purchaser pays such sums);

9. A directive that the referee deposit the balance of the sale proceeds in a bank designated in the foreclosure judgment, and disburse therefrom, in order of priority: (a) the sum of his or her fee as referee; (b) the expenses of advertising the sale (unless already paid by the plaintiff, which is invariably what actually happens); and (c) the judgment amount due to the plaintiff;

10. A direction that if the amount bid at the foreclosure sale is enough to fully satisfy each of the sums set forth in item (9) above, so that there is a resultant surplus, to pay those surplus moneys into the court;

11. If the amount bid at the sale results in a deficiency rather than a surplus, and the plaintiff has recourse against the borrower and/or any guarantor(s) under the pertinent loan documents, then a directive that the plaintiff will be entitled to recover a deficiency judgment against any such party or parties as may be determined by the court provided a motion for such deficiency judgment is made

---

5. CAVEAT: It is imperative that the designation of the situs of the sale be extremely specific. It is not sufficient for the foreclosure judgment merely to state "at the County Courthouse". The specific address of the courthouse or other building should be set forth, as well as the precise portion of the building at which the sale is to be conducted. If the foreclosure judgment is not that explicit, plaintiff's counsel should request the court to add the specifics to the judgment. Otherwise, there is the potential for the foreclosure sale to be voided.

6. See infra, § 11.48.

7. In contrast, a non-plaintiff purchaser is usually required to make a downpayment of ten percent (10%) of the foreclosure sale price. See infra, § 11.49.

under RPAPL § 1371;[8]

12. A directive that the purchaser at the foreclosure sale be allowed to take possession of the foreclosed premises upon production of the referee's deed;[9]

13. The key foreclosure language of the foreclosure judgment, namely, the decree that "all of the defendants in this action, and all persons claiming under them or any or either of them after the filing of the notice of pendency of this action, be and they hereby are forever barred and foreclosed of all right, claim, lien, title, interest and equity of redemption in said mortgaged premises and each and every part thereof"; and

14. A metes and bounds description of the mortgaged premises to be sold at the foreclosure sale.[10]

Library References:

West's Key No. Digests, Mortgages ⇐483–498, 502.

§ 11.47 Foreclosure Sale

As will be discussed below, there are several aspects to the foreclosure sale, including: (1) the service of a notice of the sale; (2) the advertising of the sale in accordance with the foreclosure judgment; (3) the conducting of the sale itself by the court-appointed referee at sale; (4) the delivery of the referee's deed to the individual or entity who was the successful purchaser at the sale; and (5) the preparation and filing of the referee's report of sale.

Library References:

West's Key No. Digests, Mortgages ⇐500.5–554.

§ 11.48 Foreclosure Sale—Noticing and Advertising the Sale

Once the foreclosure judgment is entered, plaintiff's counsel should serve notice of entry thereof, and then communicate with the referee at

---

8. **CAVEAT:** The inclusion of such language in the foreclosure judgment is a prerequisite to the plaintiff's ability to recover a deficiency judgment after the foreclosure sale. *See infra*, § 11.52, for a further discussion of this issue.

9. **CAVEAT:** The inclusion of this language in the foreclosure judgment is a prerequisite to the plaintiff's ability to evict any party defendant who continues in possession of the premises or any portion thereof after the foreclosure sale. *See infra*, § 11.54, for a further discussion of this issue.

10. **CAVEAT:** This metes and bounds description should be *identical* to that set forth in the mortgage, in the notice of pendency, and in the foreclosure title certificate. Accordingly, before submitting the proposed foreclosure judgment to the court, plaintiff's counsel should be sure to compare the description in the judgment to that in each of the other aforementioned documents. Any error in the description in the judgment, however small, will necessitate having to go back to the court to apply for an amendment of the judgment. If not discovered until after the foreclosure sale, the error could necessitate reconducting the sale, although in such situations, where no prejudice can be shown, courts generally are amenable to amending the foreclosure judgment retroactively.

§ 11.48 MORTGAGE FORECLOSURE Ch. 11

sale designated in the foreclosure judgment to set up a date and time for the foreclosure sale.

In scheduling the sale date, the plaintiff's counsel must take specific heed of the advertising and timing requirements as set forth in RPAPL § 231 regarding the sale. RPAPL § 231, which governs sales of real estate including foreclosure sales, requires that the notice of sale be "published," *i.e.*, advertised in the particular newspaper designated in the foreclosure judgment, either once a week for four (4) successive weeks, or twice a week for three (3) successive weeks. If the three (3) week method is used, then the sale *must* take place "on any day on or after the twenty-first [21st] day and on or before the twenty-eighth [28th] day after the day of the first publication." If the four (4) week method is used, then the sale *must* take place "on or after the twenty-eighth [28th] day and on or before the thirty-fifth [35th] day after the day of first publication."[1]

Also, pursuant to RPAPL § 231(2)(b), where the mortgaged premises are located entirely outside a city or incorporated village in which a daily, semi-weekly or tri-weekly newspaper is published, then in addition to publication in the particular newspaper, notice of the sale must be posted in three public places in the town in which the premises are located, and if the sale is to be held in a town or city other than that in which the premises are located, the notice also must be posted in three public places in that other town or city.[2]

The notice of sale that is advertised and, if necessary, posted, must set forth the day, time of day and place of the sale (which also was specified in the foreclosure judgment) and a metes and bounds description of the property to be sold.[3] It should also set forth the names of the referee at sale and the plaintiff's counsel.

It also must be emphasized that in addition to the advertising and posting, if necessary, of the notice of sale, the plaintiff's counsel should cause a copy of the notice of sale, bearing the caption of the case like any other litigation document served in the foreclosure action,[4] to be served

---

§ 11.48

1. PRACTICE POINTER: RPAPL § 231(2)(a). Plaintiff's counsel should consult with the plaintiff as to what method is preferred. Obviously, the twice a week for three weeks method, yielding a total of six advertisements, as opposed to a total of four advertisements for the once a week for four weeks method, will be somewhat more expensive. On the other hand, there may be a compelling reason why the plaintiff wishes to hold the sale as quickly as possible and is willing to pay the extra advertising expense in order to gain a week on the conducting of the sale.

2. PRACTICE POINTER: Because the requirements for advertising and posting can be hypertechnical and cumbersome, it is strongly recommended that the plaintiff's counsel seek authority from the plaintiff to retain the services of an advertising company that specializes in these matters and takes care of placing the foreclosure sale ads in the designated newspaper and posting the notice(s) where necessary.

3. RPAPL § 231(2)(a).

4. For a sample form of a notice of sale, *see infra*, § 11.80.

upon all defendants in the action entitled to such notice.[5] Failure to serve notice of the sale upon any such defendant can serve as a basis for voiding the foreclosure sale, if prejudice can be shown.[6]

When the foreclosure sale needs to be postponed, and provided the postponed sale is scheduled for a date no later than four weeks (*i.e.*, 28 days) after the original date, then RPAPL § 231(3) provides that notice of the postponed sale must be published just once, at least three days before the postponed date, in the same newspaper in which the original notice of sale was published. Where posting of the original sale was required, RPAPL § 231(3) also requires that the notice of the postponed sale be posted at least three days before the postponed date in the same place where the original notice was posted. Also, notice of the postponed sale should be served upon the same parties entitled to notice as were served with the original notice of sale. The notice of postponed sale should be headed "Legal Notice of Postponement of Sale," and should set forth the date and time of the original sale, followed by the adjourned date and time, together with the specific place of the sale.

Library References:

West's Key No. Digests, Mortgages ⬩510.

§ 11.49 Foreclosure Sale—Conducting the Sale

In preparation for conducting the foreclosure sale, the plaintiff's counsel should prepare a document, called "Terms of Sale," which is read by the referee at the foreclosure sale immediately before the commencement of the bidding process.[1]

The terms of sale set forth the various procedures and details governing the process of the sale, including the manner in which the sale is conducted, the manner in which the property is to be sold (single or multiple parcels), and the delivery of the referee's deed.[2] While the terms of sale may amplify the sale terms set forth in the foreclosure judgment, they cannot vary or contradict the provisions of the foreclosure judgment.[3]

A copy of the notice of sale, as advertised in the particular newspaper designated in the foreclosure judgment, should be annexed to the terms of sale. The terms of sale should require that the successful bidder

---

5. **CAVEAT:** Such defendants may include those who have served a notice of appearance and waiver, if they specifically enumerated a notice of sale as one of the documents as to which they did not waive service.

6. *See, e.g.*, Federal Home Loan Mortgage Corp. v. Dutch Lane Associates, 810 F.Supp. 86 (S.D.N.Y.1992); Snell v. Timmerman, 67 A.D.2d 1096, 415 N.Y.S.2d 152, 154 (4th Dep't 1979).

§ 11.49

1. RPAPL § 231(4).

2. For a sample form of the terms of sale, *see infra*, § 11.81.

3. Crisona v. Macaluso, 33 A.D.2d 569, 305 N.Y.S.2d 441 (2d Dep't 1969); Franklin National Bank v. DeGiacomo, 44 Misc.2d 518, 253 N.Y.S.2d 819 (Sup.Ct., Nassau County, 1964).

deliver at the sale to the referee a ten percent (10%) downpayment toward the successful bid in cash or certified check, unless the plaintiff or its nominee is the successful bidder, in which case the downpayment requirement is waived. It is also recommended that the document require that any bidder, other than the plaintiff or its nominee exhibit to the referee proof that it has cash or a certified check equal to at least ten percent (10%) of its bid, to guard against the discovery after the close of the auction that the supposed successful bidder does not have sufficient funds.

The terms of sale should also set forth: (1) the date by which the successful bidder needs to pay the referee the balance of the purchase price, upon payment of which the referee's deed will be delivered to the purchaser (usually on or before 30 days after the date of the sale); (2) that the referee will give the purchaser a credit for any real estate taxes, assessments or water rents affecting the premises which are paid and documented by the purchaser; (3) that if the purchaser fails to pay the balance of the purchase price by the specified date, then it will be held liable for any deficiency between its bid and the successful bid upon a resale, plus the costs and expenses of a resale; (4) that the premises will be sold in one parcel or in multiple parcels, depending on which manner is set forth in the foreclosure judgment, and subject to whatever liens and/or encumbrances are set forth in the foreclosure judgment; and (5) that the expenses of recording the referee's deed, including any real property transfer taxes and transfer or deed stamps, are the responsibility of the purchaser.

Once the referee at sale has read aloud the terms of sale, as well as the metes and bounds description of the premises to be sold, the referee should entertain bidding by any prospective purchasers, including the plaintiff. In order to expedite the bidding process, the referee may state in advance that bids must be in increments of a minimal figure (*e.g.*, $100, $1,000 or $5,000, depending on the size and value of the property).[4]

Obviously, the purchaser at the foreclosure sale will be the highest bidder, provided the purchaser delivers to the referee, unless the purchaser is the plaintiff or the plaintiff's nominee, the required ten percent (10%) downpayment. In addition to making that downpayment, the purchaser will execute at the conclusion of the sale a one-page memorandum of sale, which is typically annexed to the terms of sale document,[5] memorializing the fact that it is the purchaser and setting forth the purchase price. The memorandum of sale also contains a section, to be executed by the referee, acknowledging receipt from the purchaser of the

---

4. It would be prudent for such a procedure to be either included in the terms of sale itself or at least announced by the referee before he or she begins entertaining bids.

5. For a sample form of a memorandum of sale, *see infra*, § 11.81.

ten percent (10%) downpayment, or if the purchaser is the plaintiff or its nominee, stating that the downpayment has been waived.

Library References:

West's Key No. Digests, Mortgages ⇐500.5–525.

§ 11.50 Foreclosure Sale—Vacating the Sale

RPAPL § 231(6) provides that: "At any time within one year after the sale, but not thereafter, the court, upon such terms as may be just, may set the sale aside for failure to comply with the provisions of this section as to the notice, time or manner of such sale if a substantial right of a party was prejudiced by the defect." Thus, because on one of the six scheduled days for advertisement of a sale during a three week period, the advertisement, albeit inadvertently, did not appear in the newspaper designated in the foreclosure judgment, a sale was voided by the court for failure to comply with the publication requirements of RPAPL § 231(2)(a).[1] Similarly, a foreclosure sale was voided where notice of a postponed sale, scheduling the postponed sale for a date nine weeks after the original sale date, was only advertised once, whereas RPAPL § 231(3) only permits such a single notice when the postponed sale takes place within four weeks of the original sale date.[2]

A foreclosure sale also may be set aside where the terms of sale read by the referee at sale are contrary to, or materially different from, the provisions of the foreclosure judgment, so as to be misleading to and/or deter potential bidders.[3]

There are a number of cases dealing with the issue of whether a foreclosure sale can be vacated on the ground that the amount of the successful bid was significantly below the fair market value of the property at the time of the sale. The firmly established rule is that the mere alleged inadequacy of the bid price is a legally insufficient ground for vacating the sale and that the sale will not be set aside unless the amount bid was so low as to "shock the conscience of the court."[4] Thus, a foreclosure sale was upheld where the successful bid was only 37% of

---

§ 11.50

1. Williamsburgh Savings Bank v. McLeod, N.Y.L.J., 10/24/79, p.15, col.3 (Sup. Ct., Queens County).

2. Salvo Realty Corp. v. Rosenkrantz, 34 A.D.2d 1021, 312 N.Y.S.2d 787 (2d Dep't 1970).

3. *See, e.g.,* Muchard v. Wilmet, 84 Misc.2d 949, 378 N.Y.S.2d 332 (Sup.Ct., Livingston County, 1976) (sale vacated where terms of sale suggested that sale would be subject to lien of certain unpaid taxes, whereas foreclosure judgment provided that sale would be free of tax liens); Franklin National Bank v. DeGiacomo, 44 Misc.2d 518, 253 N.Y.S.2d 819 (Sup.Ct., Nassau County, 1964) (sale set aside where terms of sale varied from provision in foreclosure judgment directing premises to be sold in separate parcels in a specific sequence).

4. *See, e.g.,* Guardian Loan Company, Inc. v. Early, 47 N.Y.2d 515, 419 N.Y.S.2d 56, 392 N.E.2d 1240 (1979); Polish National Alliance of Brooklyn, USA v. White Eagle Hall Co., Inc., 98 A.D.2d 400, 470 N.Y.S.2d 642 (2d Dep't 1983) ("Polish National Alliance").

§ 11.50   MORTGAGE FORECLOSURE   Ch. 11

the fair market value of the property.[5] However, where the only bid at the sale was that of the plaintiff for $1.00, as compared to a judgment of nearly $1.9 million, the court set aside the sale upon a finding that the purchase price was "so grossly inadequate as to shock the conscience of the Court."[6]

Library References:
West's Key No. Digests, Mortgages ⇔529.

§ 11.51   Referee's Deed, Other Closing Documents and Referee's Report of Sale

The successful bidder at the foreclosure sale is entitled to receive from the referee at sale a referee's deed of the premises sold at foreclosure upon the payment to the referee of the balance of its successful bid amount (unless the plaintiff or its nominee or assignee was the successful bidder for an amount less than that due the plaintiff under the foreclosure judgment, in which case no money need change hands).

Conceivably, the delivery of the referee's deed can be effectuated immediately upon the conclusion of the sale; however, such delivery usually takes place at some point within 30 days after the sale as part of a formal closing at the referee's office or some other mutually agreed place.[1]

The referee's deed delivered at the closing can be, and most often is, a standard printed form.[2]

In addition to the referee's deed, the documents signed at the closing often also will include the following:

1. State Board of Equalization and Assessment Real Property Transfer Report (Form EA–5217) for properties other than those located in New York City; for New York City properties, the New York City Real Property Transfer Tax Return ("NYC RPT Form") must be executed by the Referee as grantor and the purchaser as grantee;[3]

---

5. Polish National Alliance, *supra*. See also, Frank Buttermark Plumbing & Heating Corp. v. Sagarese, 119 A.D.2d 540, 500 N.Y.S.2d 551 (2d Dep't), appeal denied 68 N.Y.2d 607, 506 N.Y.S.2d 1031, 498 N.E.2d 433 (1986) (sale upheld where bid price was only 30% of property's fair market value).

6. Central Trust Company, Rochester v. Alcon Developers, Inc., 93 Misc.2d 686, 403 N.Y.S.2d 396, 397 (Sup.Ct., Wayne County, 1978).

§ 11.51

1. Moreover, provided there is no objection from any other party, the referee at sale generally will be amenable to an adjournment of the closing beyond the 30–day period if requested by the successful bidder and consented to by plaintiff.

2. Form 1697—Referee's Deed (Julius Blumberg, Inc.).

3. In order to record a referee's deed for a New York City property, the purchaser at the foreclosure sale must file the NYC RPT Form and pay the applicable transfer tax. N.Y.C.Admin. Code, Chapter 21. The regulations governing the amount of such tax, which are dependent upon such factors as the type of property (residential or commercial), the amount of the mortgage debt

2. New York State Real Estate Transfer Tax form documents. The purchaser at foreclosure was and is liable for the payment of the New York State Real Estate Transfer Tax (the "Transfer Tax"), the computation of which is set forth in Tax Law Article 31 §§ 1400–1421. The purchaser at foreclosure was *not* liable for the New York State Real Property Transfer Gains Tax (the so-called "Cuomo Tax"), formerly Tax Law Article 31–B, §§ 1440–1449(c), which Cuomo Tax in any event was repealed by the New York State Legislature effective as of June 15, 1996 (Chapter 309 of the Laws of 1996). When the Cuomo Tax was still in effect, a purchaser of real estate, be it at foreclosure or otherwise, completed a Combined Real Property Transfer Tax Affidavit, Real Estate Transfer Tax Return and Credit Line Mortgage Certificate, known as Form TP–584. Practitioners should inquire of the New York State Department of Taxation or of a title insurance company as to whether the current version of the Form TP–584 or a newly promulgated form will now be used for the still effective Transfer Tax. In any event, the purchaser must also complete the New York State Real Estate Transfer Tax Return Supplemental Schedules (Form TP–584.1);[4] and

3. Multiple Dwelling Registration Statement or Affidavit in Lieu of Registration Statement. For a multiple dwelling property in New York City, the referee's deed, like any other deed, cannot be recorded without a Multiple Dwelling Registration Statement completed by the purchaser. For non-multiple dwelling properties, an affidavit in lieu of registration is required. N.Y.C.Admin. Code § 27–2099(c). Certain municipalities outside of New York City may require similar documents, and absent counsel's familiarity with such requirements, consultation with a title company is strongly recommended.

While not required, the purchaser of the premises pursuant to the foreclosure sale may want to have a title company present at the closing to insure the title to the premises so purchased. Typically, particularly where the plaintiff (or its nominee or assignee) is the purchaser, the title company will be the same one which did the original foreclosure search and issued the certificate of necessary party defendants.

In connection with the closing, the purchaser's counsel will usually prepare for signature by the referee at the sale. RPAPL § 1355(1) requires that the referee's report of sale be filed with the clerk of the court within 30 days of the delivery of the referee's deed to the

and/or the amount bid at the sale, are set forth in N.Y.C.Admin. Code § 11–2102.

4. Pursuant to Tax Law § 1402–a, Part II of Schedule C of those Supplemental Schedules requires calculation of the so-called "mansion tax," an additional transfer tax of one per cent (1%) for the conveyance of residential property for which the consideration is $1 million or more.

§ 11.51   MORTGAGE FORECLOSURE   Ch. 11

purchaser, unless such time is extended by the court within the thirty (30) day period.

The referee's report of sale will recite the fact that proper notice was given of the sale, will annex a copy of the advertisement of the sale, and will identify the successful bidder at the sale and the amount of its bid. The report also will set forth the date upon which the referee's deed was conveyed to the purchaser. Finally, the report will contain a statement that calculates the amount of the deficiency or surplus resulting from the sale, after taking into consideration the amount of the foreclosure judgment, the costs of advertising the sale, and the amount of the referee at sale's fees (typically $500, pursuant to CPLR 8003(b)).

Once the report of sale is filed, the plaintiff, or, if the purchaser is other than the plaintiff or the latter's nominee or assignee, then the non-plaintiff purchaser, can make a motion for confirmation of the report. RPAPL § 1355(2) governs the timing for making such a motion. Where there are no surplus monies resulting from the foreclosure sale, the motion to confirm can be made at any time "after the report shall have been filed eight [8] days." Where there are surplus monies, the motion to confirm cannot be made *earlier* than three months, nor *later* than four months, after the delivery of the referee's deed.

If a deficiency judgment is sought, RPAPL § 1371(2) requires that such a motion be made simultaneously with the motion for confirmation of the referee's report of sale and within 90 days after the delivery of the referee's deed.[5]

Library References:
West's Key No. Digests, Mortgages ⚖=525, 554.

§ 11.52 Deficiency Judgment

If the foreclosure sale results in a deficiency (*i.e.*, the successful bid price is less than the amount due the plaintiff under the foreclosure judgment), and the plaintiff has recourse under the loan documents against the defendant-borrower and/or the defendant-guarantor(s), if any, for any deficiency, then the plaintiff may seek to recover a deficiency judgment in the foreclosure action against the borrower and/or the guarantor(s).[1]

There are two essential procedural prerequisites that the plaintiff must comply with in order to be able to seek a deficiency judgment. First, under RPAPL § 1371(1), the right of the plaintiff to seek a deficiency judgment must be preserved by an explicit decretal paragraph

---

5. For a further discussion of deficiency judgments, *see infra*, § 11.52.

§ 11.52

1. Obviously, the borrower and/or the guarantor(s) would have had to be previously named and served as defendants in the foreclosure action. Absent special circumstances, a separate action for the deficiency would be barred by the election of remedies provision contained in RPAPL § 1301(3).

in the foreclosure judgment which adjudges the plaintiff entitled to recovery of a deficiency judgment against the specific defendant(s) named therein, subject to the plaintiff's making of a motion for such judgment, and the court's determination as to the amount of such judgment, all in accordance with RPAPL § 1371.[2] The absence of such a provision from the foreclosure judgment precludes the plaintiff from pursuing a deficiency judgment.[3]

Second, pursuant to RPAPL § 1371(2), the plaintiff must make the motion for a deficiency judgment simultaneously with the making of the motion for confirmation of the referee's report of sale,[4] and within *ninety (90) days* of the delivery of the referee's deed to the purchaser. It is essential to note that in order to comply with this requirement, the plaintiff's counsel must *effect service of the motion* within the 90-day period.[5] RPAPL § 1371(2) requires that the motion be served personally upon the attorney who has appeared in the action for the party against whom the deficiency judgment is sought, or upon the party itself, unless the court permits some other manner of service. Failure to comply with the prerequisites contained in RPAPL § 1371(2) precludes the plaintiff from obtaining a deficiency judgment.[6]

Assuming that the plaintiff has satisfied each of these procedural prerequisites, the court must determine the amount of the deficiency judgment which the plaintiff may recover. Here again, RPAPL § 1371(2) sets forth the parameters. The final sentence of that statutory subsection provides that the deficiency judgment amount is calculated by first taking: (i) the amount set forth in the foreclosure judgment, together with accrued interest thereon, plus any sums due on any prior liens and encumbrances, plus the costs and disbursements of the foreclosure action; and subtracting therefrom (ii) the *higher of* the fair market value of the premises as of the date of the foreclosure sale (or as close to that date as possible) or the successful bid price at the sale.

The penultimate sentence of RPAPL § 1371(2) states that the court can determine the fair market value of the premises for purposes of the deficiency judgment calculation "upon affidavit or otherwise." Where there is no opposition to the motion, an affidavit of a real estate appraiser or broker attesting to the fair market value usually will

2. For a sample form of a judgment of foreclosure and sale, *see infra*, § 11.79.

3. *See, e.g.*, Cassia Corp. v. North Hills Holding Corp., 281 App.Div. 709, 118 N.Y.S.2d 220 (2d Dep't 1952), aff'd 305 N.Y. 837, 114 N.E.2d 39 (1953).

4. The requests for confirmation of the referee's report of sale and for a deficiency judgment can be included within the same motion.

5. *See* CPLR 2211, which provides that, "A motion on notice is made when a notice of the motion or an order to show cause is served."

6. *See, e.g.*, Voss v. Multifilm Corporation of America, 112 A.D.2d 216, 491 N.Y.S.2d 434 (2d Dep't 1985); Amsterdam Savings Bank v. Amsterdam Pharmaceutical Development Corporation, 106 A.D.2d 797, 484 N.Y.S.2d 217 (3d Dep't 1984).

§ 11.52 MORTGAGE FORECLOSURE Ch. 11

suffice.[7] However, where a triable issue of fact has been raised by virtue of a defendant's submission of a conflicting affidavit or valuation, a hearing generally will be required at which both sides will present testimony of their respective experts as to the fair market value of the property at the time of sale.[8]

Finally, it should be noted that even if the plaintiff fails to or is barred from pursuing a motion for a deficiency judgment, or the motion has been denied, there is still a possible "consolation prize" for the plaintiff at the conclusion of the foreclosure action. The potential "consolation prize" is set forth in RPAPL § 1371(4). The provision states that whether or not a deficiency judgment motion has been made, or, if made, has been denied, the court "shall direct that all moneys remaining in the hands of a receiver of the rents and profits appointed in the action, after the payment of the receiver's fees and the expenses of the receivership, ... shall be paid to the plaintiff to the extent of the amount, if any, by which the judgment of foreclosure and sale exceeds the amount paid for the property upon the sale." Thus, if the foreclosure sale results in a deficiency, any sums remaining in the receiver's account at the conclusion of the receivership (less the receiver's commissions and expenses) get paid over to the plaintiff to the extent necessary to cover the deficiency.

Library References:
West's Key No. Digests, Mortgages ⇐555–562.

§ 11.53 Surplus Money Proceedings

If the amount bid at the foreclosure sale results in a surplus rather than a deficiency, then generally there will need to be a surplus money proceeding to determine the disposition of that surplus.

The threshold question of whether there is in fact a surplus requires reference to RPAPL § 1354, which governs the distribution of the proceeds of the foreclosure sale. RPAPL § 1354(1) and (2), read together, indicate that unless the foreclosure judgment directs otherwise, the referee at sale must first pay out of the sale proceeds the expenses of the sale (which would include advertising costs and the referee's fees), the amount of taxes, assessments and water charges which are liens upon the foreclosed premises (e.g., unpaid real estate taxes), and the amount due the plaintiff under the foreclosure judgment.[1]

---

7. See, e.g., Turner v. Meierdiercks, 106 A.D.2d 445, 482 N.Y.S.2d 538 (2d Dep't 1984).

8. See, e.g., Ogdensburg Savings and Loan Association v. Moore, 100 A.D.2d 679, 473 N.Y.S.2d 877 (3d Dep't 1984); Broward National Bank of Fort Lauderdale v. Starzec, 30 A.D.2d 603, 290 N.Y.S.2d 112 (3d Dep't 1968).

§ 11.53

1. The foreclosure judgment typically provides that the purchaser at foreclosure sale will be given a credit, or "allowance," against the purchase price for any expenses of the sale or taxes, assessments and/or water charges which the purchaser pays instead of the referee. See infra, § 11.79, for a sample form of a judgment of foreclo-

If there are still sale proceeds remaining after the distribution of the sums set forth in RPAPL § 1354(1) and (2), then RPAPL § 1354(3) directs the referee at sale, if the foreclosure judgment so states, to then give distribution priority to the holder, if any, of a subordinate second mortgage on the premises. This provision requires a cross-reference to RPAPL § 1351(3), which states that the foreclosure judgment can only contain such a provision if the court finds that the second mortgage is the only other mortgage affecting the premises that is subordinate to the first mortgage of the plaintiff, and that the second mortgage is itself superior to all other liens and encumbrances upon the property (other than real estate tax liens and other municipal liens set forth in RPAPL § 1354(2)). RPAPL § 1351(3) requires that the second mortgagee make a motion for inclusion of such a provision in the foreclosure judgment (although it is a not uncommon practice for the plaintiff-first mortgagee and the second mortgagee to stipulate to the inclusion of such a provision in the judgment). The practical effect of such a provision is to obviate the necessity of the second mortgagee participating in a formal surplus money proceeding (the mechanics of which will be discussed below) as a prerequisite to its obtaining any proceeds from the sale.

If, after all the distributions authorized under RPAPL § 1354(1)-(3) are made, there are still funds remaining from the sale proceeds, such funds are deemed "surplus moneys" under RPAPL § 1354(4), which must be deposited by the referee at sale into court within five days after the referee has received them (*i.e.*, within five days after the delivery of the referee's deed to the purchaser, at which time the purchaser would have paid the balance of the purchase price to the referee).

Pursuant to RPAPL § 1355(2), where there are surplus moneys, a motion to confirm the referee's report of sale must be made no sooner than three months and no later than four months after the filing of the report.[2] Moreover, that statutory section requires the moving party to include with its motion papers: (i) a voucher showing that the referee has paid the surplus moneys into court; (ii) a certificate of the court clerk reciting the existence of any notices of claims to the surplus moneys which have been filed; and (iii) an affidavit showing any other unsatisfied lien on the property.

RPAPL § 1361 sets forth the general procedures regarding the filing of a notice of claim to the surplus moneys and the determination as to who is entitled to such moneys. RPAPL § 1361(1) authorizes anyone (whether or not a named party to the foreclosure action), at any time before the confirmation of the referee's report of sale, to file a written notice of a claim to the surplus moneys with the clerk of the court,

---

sure and sale. However, whether it is the referee who pays such items out of the sale proceeds, or the purchaser who pays for them out of its own pocket and then gets a credit against the purchase price, the resultant amount of the balance remaining from the sale proceeds will be the same.

2. See *supra*, § 11.51.

stating the nature and extent of the claim and the address of the claimant or the claimant's attorney.

RPAPL § 1361(2) states that upon the motion to confirm the referee's report of sale, or at any time within three (3) months thereafter, upon the motion of any party to the foreclosure action or anyone who has filed a claim upon the surplus moneys, and with notice to all parties who have appeared in the action and all persons who have filed such surplus money claims, the court, by itself or by reference, is to ascertain and report the respective amount(s) due to those entitled to the surplus moneys, to prioritize the rights of the claimants thereto, and to order distribution of the moneys accordingly.

Typically, the court will delegate these functions to a referee, often the same person who has served as the referee at sale. If the court or the referee desires to hold a hearing in order to make the requisite determinations, RPAPL § 1361(3) requires that notice of such hearing be given by mail, or in such other manner as the court may order, to the owner of the equity of redemption (*i.e.*, the defendant-former owner of the foreclosed premises), all parties who have appeared in the action, all others who have filed a notice of claim to the surplus moneys and anyone else with a recorded lien against the premises.[3]

The surplus moneys stand in the place of the foreclosed premises for the benefit of those whose subordinate liens or other vested interests affecting those premises have been extinguished as a result of the plaintiff's foreclosure sale.[4] Therefore, in order to be able to share in the surplus moneys, one's lien or interest must be as to the foreclosed premises. For example, a creditor whose judgment against the defendant-owner of the mortgaged premises has been docketed in the county in which the premises are located has a valid lien against the premises which, upon foreclosure, entitles the creditor to claim against the surplus.[5] However, where the creditor obtained its judgment in another county, and never filed a transcript of that judgment in the county of the mortgaged premises, the creditor does not have a valid claim to the surplus.[6]

A discussion of the relative priorities of surplus money claimants could consume a separate chapter by itself. For purposes of this chapter, a few brief general points on the issue of priorities will have to suffice.

---

3. Although not expressly stated in the statute, the notice requirements contained in RPAPL § 1361(2) and (3), in not limiting notice to those who have filed written notices of their claims pursuant to RPAPL § 1361(1), evidence a statutory intent that the filing of such a written claim notice, while a prudent thing to do, is not a precondition to one's ability to prove entitlement to a distribution from the surplus.

4. First Federal Savings and Loan Association of Rochester v. Brown, 78 A.D.2d 119, 434 N.Y.S.2d 306, 310 (4th Dep't 1980).

5. CPLR 5203(a).

6. Sadow v. Poskin Realty Corp., 63 Misc.2d 499, 312 N.Y.S.2d 901, 908 (Sup. Ct., Queens County, 1970).

Generally, the claimants' relative priorities as to the surplus moneys will be the same as they were with respect to the mortgaged premises prior to the foreclosure thereof. Thus, for example, among competing subordinate mortgagees, the second mortgagee will have a claim to the surplus superior to that of each of the other mortgagees. Similarly, competing judgment creditors will share in the distribution of the surplus in the order of priority in which their judgments were docketed in the county of the subject premises.[7]

Where the competing claimants are a mortgagee and a judgment creditor, the "first in time, first in right" scenario has a slight twist. This is owing to the fact that although pursuant to the statutory recording provisions of RPL §§ 290 and 291, an unrecorded mortgage does not have priority as to a subsequently recorded mortgage, such priority does not inure to the benefit of creditors holding subsequently docketed judgments. Therefore, a mortgage, albeit unrecorded, is still deemed a lien upon the premises as of the date of its execution, giving the holder of such a mortgage priority as to surplus moneys vis-a-vis a judgment creditor whose judgment was docketed after the execution of the mortgage.[8]

Finally, if there is still a balance remaining from the foreclosure sale proceeds after all other surplus money claimants have been paid, the defendant-former owner of the premises, as the owner of the now-foreclosed equity of redemption, is entitled to that remaining surplus.[9]

Library References:

West's Key No. Digests, Mortgages ⚭563–569.

§ 11.54 Eviction of Tenants and Other Occupants After Foreclosure Sale

The delivery of the referee's deed to the successful purchaser at the foreclosure sale vests the purchaser with title to the foreclosed premises free and clear of all subordinate liens and claims of those parties named and served as defendants in the foreclosure action, and of all subordinate liens and claims which came into existence after the filing of the notice of pendency of action. However, the possibility exists that notwithstanding the foreclosure of all of those subordinate interests, a foreclosed tenant, owner or other occupant may continue to physically occupy some or all of the premises after the delivery of the referee's deed. How does the purchaser go about evicting such an occupant?

[7] See, e.g., Valley National Bank of Long Island v. Levy, 45 A.D.2d 771, 356 N.Y.S.2d 1003 (2d Dep't 1974).

[8] Dime Savings Bank of New York v. Roberts, 167 A.D.2d 674, 563 N.Y.S.2d 253, 255 (3d Dep't 1990), appeal dismissed 77 N.Y.2d 939, 569 N.Y.S.2d 612, 572 N.E.2d 53 (1991).

[9] See, e.g., First Federal Savings & Loan Association of Rochester v. Brown, 86 A.D.2d 963, 448 N.Y.S.2d 302 (4th Dep't 1982).

§ 11.54

There are two alternate eviction methods available to the purchaser. One is to make a motion in the foreclosure action under RPAPL § 221 which asks the court to issue a writ of assistance to the sheriff directing the latter to oust the occupant and put the purchaser into possession. The alternate method is for the purchaser to commence a separate special proceeding under RPAPL § 713(5), akin to a landlord-tenant proceeding,[1] in whichever court has jurisdiction over such a proceeding in the county in which the premises are located.

RPAPL § 221 provides as follows:

> *Where a judgment affecting the title to, or the possession, enjoyment or use of, real property* allots to any person a distinct parcel of real property, or contains a direction for the sale of real property, or confirms such an allotment or sale, *it also may direct the delivery of the possession of the property to the person entitled thereto.* If a party, or his representative or successor, who is bound by the judgment, withholds possession from the person thus declared to be entitled thereto, *the court, by order, in its discretion*, besides punishing the disobedience as a contempt, *may require the sheriff to put that person into possession.* Such an order shall be executed as if it were an execution for the delivery of the possession of the property. [Emphasis added.]

Provided the foreclosure judgment contains a direction, as required under RPAPL § 221, that the purchaser at the foreclosure sale be put into possession of the foreclosed premises,[2] then the purchaser can use RPAPL § 221 to evict the occupant.

The proper way for the purchaser to use the RPAPL § 221 remedy is to make a motion for the relief afforded under that statute (which relief is commonly referred to as a "writ of assistance") in the foreclosure action itself.[3] While there is nothing in the language of that statute which requires it, it is prudent for the purchaser to deliver to the occupant a copy of the referee's deed along with a written demand that the occupant vacate the premises.[4] In so doing, the purchaser can avoid an argument by the occupant in opposition to the motion that the occupant was not aware that title had been conveyed to the purchaser pursuant to the foreclosure sale.

The court does have a certain degree of discretion in adjudicating a motion under RPAPL § 221. Thus, where the occupant can show that his or her children will be "thrown out onto the street" if compelled to vacate immediately, the court may be inclined to grant the occupant

---

§ 11.54

1. *See* Chapter 13, "Landlord Tenant Proceedings," *infra. See also*, Finkelstein and Ferrara, *Landlord and Tenant Practice in New York* (West 1997) Ch. 15 "Holdover Proceedings."

2. For a sample form of a judgment of foreclosure and sale, *see infra*, § 11.79.

3. Lincoln First Bank, N.A. v. Polishuk, 86 A.D.2d 652, 446 N.Y.S.2d 399 (2d Dep't 1982).

4. *Id.*

some reasonable period of time within which to locate alternate living quarters, usually subject to the condition that reasonable use and occupancy be paid to the purchaser in the interim. However, it has been held that a court does not have so much discretion as to permit a foreclosed occupant to remain at the premises indefinitely.[5]

In accordance with the purpose of the notice of pendency of action,[6] it has been held that the writ of assistance remedy under RPAPL § 221 is available as against a tenant whose lease for a term of six years did not come into existence until after the filing of the *lis pendens*, on the ground that under CPLR 6501, a person whose "conveyance" is recorded after the filing of the *lis pendens* is bound by the foreclosure judgment to the same extent as a named party, and that RPL § 290(3) defines a "conveyance" to include a lease for a term of more than three (3) years.[7] However, at least two relatively recent lower court decisions have held that where the post-*lis pendens* tenant whose eviction under RPAPL § 221 was sought allegedly had a lease or tenancy for less than three (3) years, the purchaser could not avail itself of that statutory remedy.[8]

The alternative post-foreclosure sale remedy for evicting a foreclosed occupant is set forth in RPAPL § 713(5), which provides:

> A special proceeding may be maintained under this article after a *ten-day notice to quit has been served upon the respondent in the manner prescribed in section 735*, upon the following grounds:
>
> * * *
>
> 5. The property has been sold in foreclosure and *either the deed delivered pursuant to such sale, or a copy of such deed, certified as provided in the civil practice law and rules, has been exhibited to him*. [Emphasis added.]

Unlike the RPAPL § 221 remedy, which is exercised by the making of a motion in the pending foreclosure action, the RPAPL § 713(5) remedy requires the commencement of a new special proceeding in a court that has jurisdiction to entertain such a proceeding (*e.g.*, a landlord-tenant court, county court, district court or justice court).

Before the proceeding is commenced, the purchaser must serve a ten-day written notice to quit upon the occupant in the same manner as that prescribed for service of a notice of petition and petition under RPAPL § 735.[9] Failure properly to serve the ten-day notice to quit

---

5. Mykap Realty Corp. v. Goodman, 5 A.D.2d 780, 169 N.Y.S.2d 956 (2d Dep't 1958).

6. See *infra*, § 11.17.

7. Chemical Bank v. Columbia Asphalt Corp., 70 A.D.2d 925, 417 N.Y.S.2d 756 (2d Dep't 1979).

8. Bowery Savings Bank v. Giannattasio, N.Y.L.J., 5/10/95, p.25, col.3 (Sup.Ct., Suffolk County); Green Point Savings Bank v. Leselrod, N.Y.L.J., 7/31/91, p.25, col.3 (Sup.Ct., Suffolk County).

9. CAVEAT: Particular attention should be paid to the manner of service required under RPAPL § 735, as it differs

§ 11.54   MORTGAGE FORECLOSURE   Ch. 11

mandates denial of the relief sought by the petitioner-purchaser.[10] Simultaneously with the service of the ten-day notice, a certified copy of the referee's deed should be served upon the occupant. The fact that both items have been properly served upon the occupant should be alleged by the purchaser in the petition filed to commence the special proceeding.[11]

As can be seen from the discussion above regarding these two alternative eviction remedies, the RPAPL § 713(5) method has more stringent requirements than its RPAPL § 221 counterpart. Moreover, because a new proceeding must be commenced under RPAPL § 713(5), and because such a proceeding, particularly if brought in courts like the landlord-tenant courts of the counties of New York City, which have extremely congested dockets, can be prolonged for extensive periods of time, the generally preferred route for foreclosure purchasers is to employ the eviction method authorized by RPAPL § 221.

Library References:
West's Key No. Digests, Mortgages ⟐544.

§ 11.55   Drafting Checklists

The following sections, §§ 11.56–11.67, contain checklists which enumerate the key provisions that should be included in the foreclosure action form documents that appear in §§ 11.69–11.81.

§ 11.56   Drafting Checklists—Notice of Default

The notice of default (*see* § 11.69, for a sample form of a notice of default) should include the following:

1. A specific identification of the subject loan, the note and the mortgage, plus any other pertinent loan documents.

2. Specific identification of the nature of the borrower's default(s) (*e.g.*, failure to pay interest in a specified amount for a specified month or months).

3. A reference to the section(s) of the pertinent loan document(s) imposing the obligation as to which the borrower has defaulted.

4. A statement as to the number of days within which the borrower must cure the default(s).

5. The consequences of the borrower's failure to cure the default(s).

---

from that applicable to service of process in plenary proceedings pursuant to CPLR 308–311.

10. Federal National Mortgage Association v. Graham, 67 Misc.2d 735, 324 N.Y.S.2d 827 (Sup.Ct., Kings County, 1971).

11. Plander v. Rappalyea, N.Y.L.J., 10/20/72, at p.18, col.4 (2d Dep't); Stier v. Don Mar Operating Co., 33 A.D.2d 816, 305 N.Y.S.2d 397 (3d Dep't 1969).

6. An indication as to the manner in which the notice of default is being sent (certified mail, Federal Express and/or whatever other method(s) is required under the loan documents).

7. If required by the loan documents, an indication by the designation "cc" (carbon copy) at the foot of the letter that a copy of the notice of default is being sent to the borrower's attorneys and/or any other parties, such as the guarantor and/or any other attorneys, entitled to notice. (*See* § 11.11)

§ 11.57 Drafting Checklists—Notice of Acceleration

The notice of acceleration (*see* § 11.70, for a sample form of a notice of acceleration) should include the following:

1. The same references to the subject loan, note, mortgage and other pertinent loan documents as for the notice of default. (*See* § 11.56)

2. A reference to the notice of default and a summary of the notice given thereunder regarding the nature of the defaults and the time within which to cure.

3. A statement that the borrower has failed to cure those defaults within the time specified. (*See* § 11.12)

4. Consequently, the election by the lender to declare the full amount of the indebtedness under the loan immediately due and payable, specifying the respective amounts of principal, interest and other charges (such as late charges) due (collectively referred to as the "accelerated indebtedness").

5. A demand that the full amount of the accelerated indebtedness be paid immediately, absent which the lender will proceed with all of its rights and remedies.

6. The same indication as to the method(s) of transmittal of the notice of acceleration as for the notice of default. (*See* § 11.56)

7. The same indication as to those also receiving copies of the notice of acceleration, as enumerated with respect to the notice of default. (*See id.*)

§ 11.58 Drafting Checklists—Notice of Pendency of Action

The notice of pendency of action, commonly known as the *lis pendens* (*see* § 11.71, for a sample form of a notice of pendency of action) should include the following:

1. Identification of the mortgage(s) sought to be foreclosed, including the parties thereto, the date of execution, the principal sum thereof and the date, liber/reel and page of recordation. (*See* § 11.17)

2. A metes and bounds description of the mortgaged premises.

§ 11.58   MORTGAGE FORECLOSURE   Ch. 11

3. Identification of the action that has been commenced. (*See id.*)

4. A direction to the clerk of the particular county in accordance with that county's practice to index the *lis pendens* against the specified section, block and lot number(s) for the premises or in such other manner as the particular county clerk requires. (*See id.*)

§ 11.59 Drafting Checklists—Summons

The summons (*see* § 11.72, for a sample form of a summons) should include the following:

1. Directly below the index number, a statement that the basis for venue is that a judgment in the action would affect the title to, or the use and enjoyment of, property located in the county in which the action has been filed.

2. A notice to the defendants that they must serve an answer to plaintiff's complaint within 20 days of service of the summons in the case of personal service, or within 30 days after service of the summons is complete if not personally served within New York State, or a default judgment will be taken.

3. A list at the end of the summons of the names and addresses of each defendant. (*See* § 11.18)

§ 11.60 Drafting Checklists—Complaint

The complaint (*see* §§ 11.73 and 11.74, for sample forms of complaints) should include the following allegations:

1. In separate paragraphs, the identification and interest of each of the parties, and with respect to each of the defendants a statement as to the lien or other interest which each such defendant has or claims to have with respect to the subject property, which lien or interest is subordinate to that of plaintiff's mortgage lien. (*See* § 11.20)

2. Allegations regarding the subject loan, note and mortgage of the action, including the recordation information regarding the mortgage and an allegation that the requisite mortgage recording tax was paid at the time of recordation. (*See id.*)

3. References to (or verbatim quotations of) the pertinent terms of the note and of the mortgage entitling the plaintiff to a judgment of foreclosure and the attendant relief sought in the action. (*See* § 11.23)

4. Assertion of the default(s) committed by the defendant-borrower, the election of the plaintiff to accelerate the mortgage loan indebtedness as a consequence of such default, and the amount of the outstanding indebtedness due under the note and mortgage. (*See* § 11.24)

Ch. 11 ORDER APPOINTING RECEIVER § 11.61

5. A reservation of the plaintiff's right to add advances made for such items as real estate taxes and insurance premiums to the indebtedness secured by the mortgage. (*See* § 11.25)

6. A general allegation that the lien or interest of each of the defendants in and to the subject premises is subordinate to that of the plaintiff's mortgage lien. (*See* § 11.26)

7. An allegation that either there has been no other action or proceeding commenced to recover all or any portion of the mortgage debt, or, if there has, the nature and disposition of any such action. (*See* § 11.27)

§ 11.61 Drafting Checklists—Order Appointing Receiver

The order appointing a receiver (*see* § 11.75, for a sample form of an order appointing a receiver) should contain the following decretal provisions:

1. Authorization for the individual appointed as receiver to collect the rents and profits from the mortgaged premises. (*See* § 11.31)

2. Authorization for the receiver to collect rents from the tenants of the mortgaged premises, together with a direction that the tenants continue to pay their rent to the receiver during the foreclosure action. (*See id.*)

3. Authorization for the receiver to lease any portion of the premises that is or becomes vacant, for up to a specified maximum term. (*See id.*)

4. A direction that the receiver make expenditures for the operation and maintenance of the premises (including payments for real estate taxes, insurance premiums, repairs up to a specified maximum amount, and principal and interest on any mortgage superior to that of the subject mortgage of the action). (*See id.*)

5. If the mortgaged premises are a multiple dwelling in New York City, the requisite direction under RPAPL § 1325(3) that the receiver give priority in the making of expenditures for the correction of immediately hazardous and hazardous violations. (*See id.*)

6. Authorization for the receiver to commence dispossess proceedings seeking to remove any defaulting tenant.

7. If desired, authorization for the receiver to retain a managing agent.

8. An injunction against the defendant-borrower and any other defendants from collecting rents from any tenants during the receivership. (*See id.*)

9. A direction that the defendant-borrower turn over all pertinent records regarding the mortgaged premises, all security deposits of tenants, and any rents collected from tenants between the date the receivership order is signed and the date that the receiver qualifies by filing the receiver's bond (other than those rental monies expended by the defendant-borrower for the necessary operation of the property).

10. A fixing of the amount of the receiver's bond.

11. A direction for the receiver to deposit all monies collected in a bank designated by the court.

12. A description of the metes and bounds of the mortgaged premises, usually annexed as an exhibit to the receivership order.

§ 11.62 Drafting Checklists—Affidavit in Support of *Ex Parte* Application for Receiver

The affidavit in support of the *ex parte* application for the appointment of a receiver (*see* § 11.76, for a sample form of an affidavit in support of a motion for the appointment of a receiver) should include the following information:

1. Brief background facts of the action, with a copy of the complaint annexed as an exhibit. (*See* § 11.31)

2. Reference to the provision in the mortgage entitling the plaintiff to the *ex parte* appointment of a receiver. (*See id.*)

3. A brief description of the mortgaged premises (*i.e.*, residential, commercial or other).

4. The approximate number of tenants in the building and the approximate amount of the monthly rent roll.

5. If the plaintiff desires to recommend a particular individual as a receiver and/or a particular entity as managing agent, a brief recital of the qualifications of such individual and/or entity. (*See id.*)

§ 11.63 Drafting Checklists—Notice of Motion for Summary Judgment and Related Relief

The notice of motion for summary judgment and related relief (*see* § 11.77, for a sample form of a notice of motion for summary judgment and related relief) should include the following:

1. The return date of the motion and the location of the courthouse at which the motion will be heard.

2. A recitation of the papers, including affidavits and memoranda of law, being submitted in support of the motion.

3. An enumeration of each of the specific items of relief sought, including summary judgment, dismissal of the defendants' affirma-

tive defenses and/or counterclaims, the appointment of a referee to compute, the amendment of the caption and any other applicable relief.

4. A request that answering papers be served in accordance with CPLR 2214(b).

§ 11.64 Drafting Checklists—Affidavit of Regularity and in Support of Plaintiff's Motion for Summary Judgment and Related Relief

The affidavit of regularity submitted by the plaintiff's attorney in support of the plaintiff's motion for summary judgment and related relief (see § 11.78, for a sample form of an affidavit of regularity and in support of a motion for summary judgment) should include the following:

1. An enumeration of the items of relief sought in the motion. (See § 11.40)

2. A summary of the facts of the action (the subject mortgage, the subject premises, the defaults under the mortgage, the commencement date of the action and the procedural status of the action to date, including a recitation of any answers or appearances by any of the defendants). (See id.)

3. A brief summary of why the plaintiff is entitled to summary judgment as a matter of law (noting that the accompanying affidavit of plaintiff's officer sets forth the facts entitling plaintiff to summary judgment in more detail).

4. A brief recitation of why the plaintiff is entitled to the related relief requested.

5. A statement that all of the proceedings to date in the foreclosure action have been in conformity with all statutory and other required procedures. (See id.)

§ 11.65 Drafting Checklists—Judgment of Foreclosure and Sale

The foreclosure judgment (see § 11.79, for a sample form of a judgment of foreclosure and sale) should include the following decretal provisions:

1. A confirmation of the report of the referee to compute.

2. The fixing of the amounts due to the plaintiff.

3. A directive as to whether the premises should be sold in one parcel or several parcels.

§ 11.65   MORTGAGE FORECLOSURE   Ch. 11

4. A blank insert for the court's designation of the place at which the foreclosure sale is to be conducted.

5. A blank insert for the court's designation of the individual who is to conduct the foreclosure sale as the referee at sale.

6. A blank insert for the court's designation of the newspaper or other publication in which notice of the sale is to be advertised.

7. A provision indicating that if the plaintiff or its nominee becomes the purchaser at the foreclosure sale, then such party shall not be required to make a deposit with the referee towards the purchase price.

8. Directions as to the payments, in order of priority, that the referee is to make from the proceeds of the foreclosure sale.

9. The direction for the referee to deposit any surplus monies into the court.

10. If there is recourse against the borrower and/or any guarantor(s), a directive that the plaintiff will be entitled to recover a deficiency judgment provided the requisite motion is subsequently made under RPAPL § 1371.

11. A directive that the purchaser at the foreclosure sale be allowed to take possession of the foreclosed premises upon the referee's conveyance of the referee's deed.

12. The key decretal paragraph that all defendants in the action and all other persons whose claimed interests in the mortgaged premises came after the filing of the notice of pendency, are forever barred and foreclosed from all rights, claims, liens, interests and/or equity of redemption in the premises.

13. A metes and bounds description of the mortgaged premises.

§ 11.66   Drafting Checklists—Notice of Sale

The notice of sale (*see* § 11.80, for a sample form of a notice of sale) should including the following:

1. The precise date, time and place of the sale (the place should be that specified in the foreclosure judgment, which judgment should be specified in the notice).

2. A metes and bounds description of the property to be sold or summary thereof.

3. A recitation of any encumbrances, liens or other restrictions subject to which the premises will be sold (this should conform precisely with the corresponding terms of the foreclosure judgment).

Ch. 11   TERMS AND MEMORANDUM OF SALE   § 11.67

4. The approximate amount of the plaintiff's mortgage lien.
5. The name of the referee at sale.
6. The name of plaintiff's counsel.

§ 11.67 Drafting Checklists—Terms and Memorandum of Sale

The terms and memorandum of sale (*see* § 11.81, for a sample form of the terms and memorandum of sale) should include the following:

1. A copy of the advertisement of sale attached as an exhibit.
2. A requirement that the successful bidder deliver at the sale to the referee a ten percent (10%) downpayment toward the successful bid with the qualification that if the plaintiff or its nominee is the successful bidder, the deposit requirement is waived.
3. A requirement that any bidder, other than the plaintiff or its nominee exhibit to the referee that it has cash or a certified check(s) equal to at least ten percent (10%) of its bid.
4. The date by which the successful bidder needs to close with the referee.
5. A statement that the referee will give the purchaser credit for any real estate taxes, assessments or water rents which are paid by the purchaser.
6. A statement as to the potential liability of the purchaser if it fails to pay the balance of the purchase price by the specified closing date.
7. A statement as to the manner in which the premises will be sold (*i.e.*, in one parcel or in multiple parcels).
8. A recitation of the liens, encumbrances and/or restrictions subject to which the premises will be sold in accordance with the foreclosure judgment.
9. A statement that the expenses of recording the referee's deed, including any real property transfer taxes and transfer or deed stamps, will be borne by the purchaser.
10. A memorandum of sale, to be filled in at the conclusion of the bidding at the foreclosure sale. The purchaser signs the upper portion of the memorandum, with the amount of the purchaser's successful bid filled in. On the lower half of the memorandum, which lower half is labeled "Receipt," if the purchaser is not the plaintiff or its nominee, the referee fills in and signs the pertinent information regarding the referee's receipt of the ten percent (10%) downpayment from the purchaser. If the purchaser is the plaintiff

§ 11.68 Forms

Set forth in §§ 11.69–11.81, *infra*, are sample forms for the pre-foreclosure notices of default and of acceleration and for certain key documents that are filed and served during the course of the foreclosure action.

§ 11.69 Forms—Notice of Default

[ABC SAVINGS BANK

1234 FORECLOSURE PATH

EMPIRE, NEW YORK 00002]

_____, 19__

NOTICE OF DEFAULT

CERTIFIED MAIL/RETURN RECEIPT REQUESTED

[DEF Borrower Associates
5678 Foreclosure Road
Empire, New York 00001]

Attention: [*Individual Principal of Borrower*]

Re: Loan from [*ABC Savings Bank*] to [*DEF Borrower Associates*]

[*To Whom it May Concern*]

Reference is hereby made to a certain note in the consolidated principal amount of $_____ dated _____, 19__, from [*DEF Borrower Associates*] to [*ABC Savings Bank*] (the "Note") and to the mortgage and other documents of even date therewith securing same (respectively, the "Mortgage" and "Loan Documents").

You are hereby advised that you are in default of Section _____ of the Note and Section _____ of the Mortgage by reason of your failure to make payment of the monthly interest payments in the amount of $_____ each due thereunder on [*January 1, 19__, February 1, 19__, March 1, 19__ and April 1, 19__,*] together with late payment charges (collectively, the "Arrearages") as set forth in Section _____ of the Note.

You are hereby further advised that in the event you fail to make full payment of the Arrearages within ten (10) days of the sending of this notice, the undersigned shall proceed to declare the entire principal balance of the Note and Mortgage in the amount of $_____, together with all accrued interest, and charges, including interest from the date hereof at the Involuntary Rate as defined in the Note, immediately due and payable.

Nothing contained in this Note shall be deemed a waiver of the undersigned's right to pursue all remedies available to it pursuant to the Note, Mortgage and Loan Documents and applicable law, as in its discretion, it deems appropriate.

Very truly yours,

[ABC SAVINGS BANK]

By:_____
[Print name], [Vice President]

/jal

By Certified Mail/Return Receipt Requested

cc:
1. [Robert A. Guarantor]
2. [Attorneys for borrower, if note, mortgage and/or loan documents require same]
3. [Attorneys for guarantor, if guaranty requires same]

§ 11.70 Forms—Notice of Acceleration

[ABC SAVINGS BANK
1234 FORECLOSURE PATH
EMPIRE, NEW YORK 00002]

_____, 19__

NOTICE OF ACCELERATION

CERTIFIED MAIL/RETURN RECEIPT REQUESTED

[DEF Borrower Associates
5678 Foreclosure Road
Empire, New York 00001]

Attention: [Individual Principal of Borrower]

Re: Loan from [ABC Savings Bank] to [DEF Borrower Associates]

[*To Whom it May Concern*]

Reference is hereby made to a certain note in the consolidated principal amount of $_____ dated _____, 19__ from [*DEF Borrower Associates*] to [*ABC Savings Bank*] (the "Note") and to the mortgage and other documents of even date therewith securing same (respectively, the "Mortgage" and "Loan Documents").

Reference is also made to the undersigned's Notice of Default to you dated _____, 19__, pursuant to which you were advised that you were in default of the Note and the Mortgage by reason of your failure to make payment of the monthly interest payments in the amount of $_____ each due thereunder on [*January 1, 19__, February 1, 19__, March 1, 19__ and April 1, 19__,*] together with late payment charges (collectively, the "Arrearages") as set forth in the Note, and that if you failed to make full payment of the arrearages within ten (10) days of the sending of that Notice of Default, the undersigned would proceed to declare the entire indebtedness under the Note and Mortgage, including interest at the Involuntary Rate (as defined in the Note) immediately due and payable.

You are hereby further advised that, by reason of your failure to make full payment of the Arrearages within said ten (10)-day period, the undersigned hereby declares the entire principal balance of the Note and Mortgage in the amount of $_____, together with all accrued interest, and charges, including interest from the date hereof at the Involuntary Rate (collectively, the "Accelerated Indebtedness") immediately due and payable.

Upon your failure to make immediate payment of the Accelerated Indebtedness in full, the undersigned shall proceed to pursue all remedies available to it pursuant to the Note, Mortgage and Loan Documents and applicable law, as in its discretion, it deems appropriate.

Very truly yours,

[ABC SAVINGS BANK]

By:_____
   [*Print name*], [*Vice President*]

/jal

By Certified Mail/Return Receipt Requested

cc:

1. [*Robert A. Guarantor*]
2. [*Attorneys for borrower, if note, mortgage and/or loan documents require same*]
3. [*Attorneys for guarantor, if guaranty requires same*]

§ 11.71 Forms—Notice of Pendency of Action

SUPREME COURT OF THE STATE OF NEW YORK
COUNTY OF _____

[ABC SAVINGS BANK],)) Plaintiff,)) -against-)) [DEF BORROWER ASSOCIATES,) ROBERT A. GUARANTOR, SUB-) ORDINATE MORTGAGEE COM-) PANY, INC., MECHANIC'S LIEN) CORP., THE PEOPLE OF THE) STATE OF NEW YORK, THE) COMMISSIONER OF TAXATION) AND FINANCE OF THE STATE) OF NEW YORK, THE CITY OF) EMPIRE, THE DEPARTMENT OF) FINANCE OF THE CITY OF) EMPIRE, THE ENVIRONMENTAL) CONTROL BOARD OF THE CITY) OF EMPIRE, and JOHN DOE #1) through JOHN DOE #20, said John) Doe defendants being fictitious, it) being intended to name all other) parties who may have some interest) in or lien upon the premises sought) to be foreclosed],)) Defendants.))	NOTICE OF PENDENCY OF ACTION Index No. _____

NOTICE IS HEREBY GIVEN that an action has been commenced and is now pending in this court upon the verified complaint of the above-named plaintiff against the above-named defendants for the foreclosure of a certain mortgage dated _____, 19__ made by defendant [DEF Borrower Associates] to plaintiff [ABC Savings Bank] to secure payment of the principal sum of _____ ($_____) dollars with interest, which mortgage was recorded in the Office of the [Clerk or Register] of the County of _____ in Reel _____, Page _____ on _____, 19__.

The premises affected by said mortgage at the time of the commencement of this action are situated in the City of [Empire], County of _____, State of New York, and are more particularly described in Schedule A annexed hereto.

Dated: _____, New York
_____, 19__

    [*SMITH & JONES, LLP*]
    Attorneys for Plaintiff
    [*Address and Phone Number*]

TO THE CLERK OF _____ COUNTY:

You are hereby directed to index the within Notice against the following section, block, and lot numbers of the County of _____ affected thereby:

    Section ____; Block ____; Lots ____ and ____.

Dated: _____, New York
_____, 19__

    [*SMITH & JONES, LLP*]
    Attorneys for Plaintiff
    [*Address and Phone Number*]

SCHEDULE A

ALL THAT CERTAIN lot, place or parcel of land, situate, lying and being in the City of [*Empire*], County of _____ and State of New York, bounded and described as follows:

[*Set forth metes and bounds description contained in mortgage.*]

§ 11.72 Forms—Summons

SUPREME COURT OF THE STATE OF NEW YORK
COUNTY OF _____

[*ABC SAVINGS BANK*],
 	
      Plaintiff,
 	
   -against-
 	
[*DEF BORROWER ASSOCIATES, ROBERT A. GUARANTOR, SUBORDINATE MORTGAGEE COMPANY, INC., MECHANIC'S LIEN CORP., THE PEOPLE OF THE STATE OF NEW YORK, THE COMMISSIONER OF TAXATION AND FINANCE OF THE STATE OF NEW YORK, THE CITY OF EMPIRE, THE DEPARTMENT OF FINANCE OF THE CITY OF EMPIRE, THE ENVIRONMENTAL CONTROL BOARD OF THE CITY OF EMPIRE, and JOHN DOE #1 through JOHN DOE #20, said John Doe defendants being fictitious, it being intended to name all other parties who may have some interest in or lien upon the premises sought to be foreclosed*],
 	
      Defendants.
	SUMMONS
	
	Date of Filing _____
	
	The basis of the venue is that a judgment in this action would affect the title to, or the enjoyment of, real property located in the County of _____.

TO THE ABOVE–NAMED DEFENDANTS:

 YOU ARE HEREBY SUMMONED to answer the Verified Complaint in this action and to serve a copy of your Answer on the plaintiff's attorneys within twenty (20) days after the service of this Summons, exclusive of the day of service (or within thirty (30) days after the service is complete if this Summons is not personally delivered to you within the State of New York). In case of your failure to answer, judgment will be taken against you by default for the relief demanded herein.

TYPE OF ACTION: FORECLOSURE OF MORTGAGE.

Dated: _____, New York

   _____, 19__

§ 11.72   MORTGAGE FORECLOSURE   Ch. 11

[SMITH & JONES, LLP]
Attorneys for Plaintiff
[Address and Phone Number]

Defendants' Addresses:
[Set forth names and addresses of each defendant.]

§ 11.73   Forms—Verified Complaint for Foreclosure of Mortgage Affecting Single Family Residence

SUPREME COURT OF THE STATE OF NEW YORK
COUNTY OF _____

_____

[ABC SAVINGS BANK],

            Plaintiff,

       -against-

[JACK BORROWER and JILL BORROWER, PENULTIMATE CREDIT CORP., and "JOHN DOE #1" through "JOHN DOE #12," the last twelve names being fictitious and unknown to plaintiff, the persons or parties intended being the tenants, occupants, persons or corporations if any, having or claiming an interest in or lien upon the premises described in the complaint],

            Defendants.

_____

COMPLAINT

Index No. _____

Plaintiff, [ABC Savings Bank], by its attorneys, [Smith & Jones, LLP], hereby alleges upon information and belief:

    1. Plaintiff is a banking corporation duly organized and existing under the laws of the State of New York, having a principal place of business located at _____ [street address], _____ [city], New York.

    2. Defendant(s) [Jack Borrower and Jill Borrower] are residents of the State of New York who are owners of the real property located within the County of _____, State of New York, which property is to be the subject of this foreclosure action and is more particularly described in Schedule A hereto (the "Premises").

3. Upon information and belief, defendant [*Penultimate Credit Corp.*] is a New York corporation having a principal place of business at _____ [*street address*], _____ [*city*], New York.

4. On or about _____, 19__, defendants [*Jack Borrower and Jill Borrower*] borrowed the sum of _____ ($_____) DOLLARS from plaintiff's assignor, _____, a licensed mortgage banker, as evidenced by a certain note dated the same date. Pursuant to the terms of the note, the loan was repayable as follows: the sum of $_____ on _____, 19__ and a like sum of $_____ on the _____ day of each and every month thereafter until _____, 19__. The monthly payments were to be applied first to the payment of interest at the rate of __% per annum, and the balance of the monthly payments was to be applied in reduction of principal. Interest was to continue at the above rate or the default rate, if applicable, pending satisfaction of the indebtedness.

5. The note provided, among other things, that if the makers of the note, [*Jack Borrower and Jill Borrower*], defaulted in the payment of any of the above described payments for fifteen (15) days, the entire balance under the note would be immediately due and payable without notice or demand.

6. In order to collaterally secure their obligation, defendants [*Jack Borrower and Jill Borrower*], on the same day, executed, acknowledged and delivered to the plaintiff's assignor a mortgage by which said defendants mortgaged the Premises to the plaintiff's assignor.

7. The mortgage contains, among other things, the following provisions:

    a. The holder of this mortgage in any action to foreclose it shall be entitled to the appointment of a receiver without notice and without regard to the security.

    b. In case of foreclosure sale said premises or so much thereof as may be affected by this mortgage may be sold in one parcel.

    c. The mortgagor will pay all taxes, assessments, sewer rents or water rates and in default thereof, the mortgagee may pay the same.

    d. If the mortgagor fails to pay any installment of principal or interest on any prior mortgage ... the mortgagee may pay the same and the mortgagor on demand will repay the amount so paid with interest thereon at the contract rate and the same shall be added to the mortgage indebtedness and be secured by this mortgage.

    e. If the holder of this mortgage is required to retain legal counsel for the purpose of commencing proceedings hereunder, a sum equal to __% of the unpaid balance collaterally secured hereby shall be added to said indebtedness as fair and reasonable legal fees and deemed secured hereby in addition to costs, allowances and additional allowances as provided by law.

f. The whole of said principal sum and interest shall become due at the option of the mortgagee after default in the payment of any installment of principal or of interest for fifteen (15) days; ...

8. The mortgage was duly recorded in _____ of Mortgages at Page _____ in the Office of the _____ [*Clerk or Register*] of the County of _____ on the _____ day of _____, 19__, and the New York State recording tax was duly paid thereon.

9. The subject mortgage ultimately was assigned by written agreement therefor to plaintiff [*ABC Savings Bank*], the latter now being the owner and holder of the mortgage.

10. Defendants [*Jack Borrower and Jill Borrower*] are the owners of the equity of redemption herein foreclosed and are joined as necessary party defendants to foreclose all of the right, title and interest and equity of redemption in the mortgaged premises and are liable for any deficiency judgment as may be directed by this Court.

11. Plaintiff verily believes that during the pendency of this action, in order to protect the security of the within mortgage, it may be compelled to make advances to prior mortgagees, if any, for installments of principal and interest, taxes, assessments, water rates, and/or fire insurance premiums that are or may become due under said prior mortgage or to the receiver of taxes, or to the fire insurance company, which advances are to be included in the balance due to plaintiff, plus interest, as provided for in the within mortgage foreclosed and deemed further secured thereby.

12. [*Jack Borrower and Jill Borrower*] have defaulted under their note for $_____ owing to plaintiff, and no payment thereof has been made to plaintiff from either Jack Borrower or Jill Borrower despite demand, by failing to make monthly payments due on _____, 19__ and thereafter, to date. By virtue thereof, plaintiff has elected and hereby elects to accelerate the entire principal balance of $_____ to be immediately due and payable under the mortgage herein foreclosed, plus interest at the rate of __% per annum from _____, 19__, together with $_____ representing late charges accrued prior to this action, and $_____ representing legal fees pursuant to the mortgage, for a total of $_____ due and payable, plus interest, together with any advances made or to be made to protect plaintiff's mortgage.

13. Plaintiff is still the owner and holder of the mortgage herein foreclosed and of the note secured thereby.

14. Any defendant captioned as a corporation is a New York corporation.

15. Plaintiff is a New York corporation [*or partnership or other*].

16. No other action has been commenced for the recovery of the sum secured by the subject note and mortgage.

17. Each and all of the defendants herein have or claim to have some interest in, or lien upon the mortgaged premises or some part thereof, which interest or lien if any, has accrued subsequently to the lien of the subject mortgage, and is subject and subordinate thereto.

18. The plaintiff shall not be deemed to have waived, altered, released or changed the election previously made by reason of any payments made after the date of commencement of this action.

WHEREFORE, the plaintiff demands judgment that:

1. The defendants here and all persons claiming under them or any or either of them subsequent to the commencement of this action be forever barred and foreclosed of all right, claim, lien and equity of redemption in the mortgaged premises.

2. The premises be decreed to be sold according to law in "as is" physical order and condition, subject to the following: (a) any covenants, easements, restrictions and reservations of record; (b) violations of record; (c) any state of facts an accurate survey may show; (d) assessments and water rates with interest and penalties accrued; (e) rights of tenants or persons in possession of the subject premises; (f) prior mortgage lien(s) of record held by _____ and any advances or arrears thereunder; (g) prior lien(s) of record held by _____ and any other prior liens or record, if any; and (h) any equity of redemption of the United States of America to redeem the premises within 120 days from the date of sale.

3. This Court forthwith appoint a receiver of the rents and profits of the premises during the pendency of this action with the usual powers and duties.

4. The monies arising from the sale be brought into court.

5. The plaintiff be paid the amount due on the note and mortgage with interest to the time of such payment, attorney's fees as set forth in the mortgage, the costs of this action and the expenses of the sale so far as the amount of such monies properly applicable thereto will pay the same.

6. The defendants [*Jack Borrower and Jill Borrower*] be adjudged to pay the whole residue, or so much thereof as the Court may determine to be just and equitable, of the debt remaining unsatisfied after the sale of the mortgaged premises and the application of the proceeds pursuant to the provisions contained in such judgment, the amount thereof to be determined by the Court as provided in Section 1371 of the Real Property Actions and Proceedings Law.

Dated: _____, New York

_____, 19__

[*SMITH & JONES, LLP*]
[Address and Phone Number]

§ 11.74 Forms—Verified Complaint for Foreclosure of Mortgage Affecting Commercial, Multi-unit Residential or Mixed Property

SUPREME COURT OF THE STATE OF NEW YORK
COUNTY OF _____

_____

[ABC SAVINGS BANK],)
)
Plaintiff,)
)
-against-)
)
[DEF BORROWER ASSOCIATES,)
ROBERT A. GUARANTOR, SUB-)
ORDINATE MORTGAGEE COM-)
PANY, INC., MECHANIC'S LIEN)
CORP., THE PEOPLE OF THE)
STATE OF NEW YORK, THE)
COMMISSIONER OF TAXATION) VERIFIED COMPLAINT
AND FINANCE OF THE STATE)
OF NEW YORK, THE CITY OF) Index No. _____
EMPIRE, THE DEPARTMENT OF)
FINANCE OF THE CITY OF)
EMPIRE, THE ENVIRONMENTAL)
CONTROL BOARD OF THE CITY)
OF EMPIRE, and JOHN DOE #1)
through JOHN DOE #20, said John)
Doe defendants being fictitious, it)
being intended to name all other)
parties who may have some interest)
in or lien upon the premises sought)
to be foreclosed],)
)
Defendants.)
_____)

Plaintiff, [ABC Savings Bank] (the "Bank"), by its attorneys [Smith & Jones, LLP] complaining of the defendants herein, alleges as follows:

THE PARTIES

1. At all relevant times, plaintiff Bank was and still is a banking corporation duly organized and existing under the laws of the State of New York, having a principal place of business located at _____ [street address], _____ [city], New York. The Bank is the holder of a real

property mortgage (the "Mortgage") more particularly described below affecting the premises set forth below which are the subject of this foreclosure action.

2. Upon information and belief, at all relevant times, defendant [*DEF Borrower Associates*] ("Borrower") (i) was and still is a limited partnership organized and existing under the laws of the State of New York; (ii) has maintained and still maintains a principal place of business located at _____ [*street address*], _____ [*city*], New York; and (iii) was and still is the owner of real property located within the State of New York, which property is sought to be foreclosed herein, and which property is located in the City of [*Empire*], County of _____, and is more particularly described as follows (the "Premises"):

ALL THAT CERTAIN lot, piece or parcel of land, situate, lying and being in the City of [*Empire*], County of _____ and State of New York, bounded and described as follows:

[*Set forth here metes and bounds description of premises contained in the mortgage.*]

3. Upon information and belief, at all relevant times, defendant [*Robert A. Guarantor*] ("Guarantor"): (i) was and still is a resident of the State of New York; (ii) was and still is transacting and/or doing business within the State of New York; and (iii) has submitted to the personal jurisdiction of the courts of the State of New York in connection with this action pursuant to a certain Guaranty of Payment (the "Guaranty") dated _____, 19__, executed and delivered by Guarantor to the Bank. Guarantor is named as a defendant herein by virtue of the Guaranty, pursuant to which Guarantor will be liable for any deficiency judgment which may result after a foreclosure sale in this action.

4. Upon information and belief, at all relevant times, defendant [*Subordinate Mortgage Company, Inc.*] (the "Subordinate Mortgagee"): (i) was and still is a corporation organized and existing under the State of New York; (ii) was and still is transacting and/or doing business in the State of New York; and (iii) has maintained and still maintains a principal place of business at _____ [*street address*], _____ [*city*], New York. Subordinate Mortgagee is named as a defendant herein by virtue of a mortgage it holds affecting the Premises, dated _____, 19__, executed and delivered by Borrower and recorded in the Office of the _____ [*Clerk or Register*] of _____ County on _____, 19__, in Reel ___, page ___ (the "Subordinate Mortgage"). The lien of the Subordinate Mortgage is subject and subordinate to the lien of the Bank's Mortgage sought to be foreclosed herein.

5. Upon information and belief, at all relevant times, defendant [*Mechanic's Lien Corp.*] ("Mechanic's"): (i) was and still is a corporation organized and existing under the laws of the State of New York; (ii) was and still is transacting and/or doing business in the State of New York; and (iii) has maintained and still is maintaining a principal place of

business at _____ [*street address*], _____ [*city*], New York. Defendant Mechanic's is named a defendant herein by virtue of the fact that on or about _____, 19__, Mechanic's filed a notice of mechanic's lien against the Premises (No. _____) in the office of the _____ [*Clerk or Register*] of _____ County in the amount of $_____, which lien is subject and subordinate to the lien of the Bank's Mortgage sought to be foreclosed herein.

6. Defendants The People of the State of New York and The Commissioner of Taxation and Finance of the State of New York are made defendants herein by virtue of unpaid franchise taxes [*set forth precise dates and amounts, if known*], if any, that may be due from Borrower, which taxes, if any, may be a lien upon the Premises by virtue of the provisions of the Tax Law of the State of New York, and which lien, if any, is subordinate to the lien of the Bank's Mortgage sought to be foreclosed herein.

7. Defendants The City of [*Empire*] and The Department of Finance of the City of [*Empire*] are made defendants herein by virtue of unpaid city business taxes [set forth precise dates and amounts, if known], if any, that may be due from Borrower, which taxes, if any, may be a lien upon the Premises, and which lien, if any, is subordinate to the lien of the Bank's Mortgage sought to be foreclosed herein.

8. Defendant The Environmental Control Board of the City of [*Empire*] is made a defendant herein by virtue of an unpaid judgment against Borrower in connection with Environmental Control Board Lien Violation No. _____, filed _____, 19__, in the amount of $_____, the lien as to which, if any, is subordinate to the lien of the Bank's Mortgage sought to be foreclosed herein.

9. Defendants John Doe #1 through John Doe #20 (fictitious names) are named as defendants herein to represent all other parties who may have some interest in or lien upon the Premises subordinate to the lien of the Bank's Mortgage sought to be foreclosed herein.

THE NOTE, THE MORTGAGE AND THE GUARANTY

10. On _____, 19__, for the purpose of securing the repayment of a loan by the Bank to Borrower in the amount of $_____, [*Associates*] executed, acknowledged and delivered to the Bank a mortgage note (the "Note"), a copy of which is annexed as Exhibit A, under which Borrower acknowledged its indebtedness to the Bank in the aforesaid amount.

11. As additional security for the repayment of the indebtedness evidenced by the Note, Borrower, on or about _____, 19__, executed, acknowledged and delivered to the Bank the Mortgage, a copy of which is annexed as Exhibit B, under which Borrower mortgaged the Premises to the Bank.

Ch. 11   VERIFIED COMPLAINT FOR FORECLOSURE   **§ 11.74**

12. Upon information and belief, the Mortgage was duly recorded in the Office of the _____ [*Clerk or Register*] of the County of _____ on _____, 19__ in Reel _____, page _____.

13. Upon information and belief, at the time of the recording of the Mortgage, there was paid to the _____ [*Clerk or Register*] of the County of _____ the amount of tax imposed on the Mortgage.

14. As further security for the repayment of the indebtedness evidenced by the Note, defendant Guarantor, on or about _____, 19__, executed, acknowledged and delivered to the Bank the absolute, unconditional, present and continuing Guaranty, a copy of which is annexed as Exhibit C.

PERTINENT TERMS OF THE LOAN DOCUMENTS

15. The Note provides, *inter alia*:

FOR VALUE RECEIVED, [*DEF BORROWER ASSOCIATES*] (the "Borrower"), _____ [*street address*], _____ [*city*], New York does hereby covenant and promise to pay to the order of [*ABC SAVINGS BANK*], or its successors or assigns (collectively, the "Bank"), on the Maturity Date of _____, 19__, at its office at _____ [*street address*], _____ [*city*], New York, or at such other place as the Bank may designate to the Borrower in writing in legal tender of the United States, the principal sum of $_____ (the Principal Amount), together with interest on the unpaid principal balance at the rate of ___ percent (___%) per annum, which interest shall be payable monthly in arrears on the _____ day of each month hereafter and, together with the Principal Amount, on the Maturity Date.

1. Interest on the Principal Amount shall be computed on the basis of a 360-day year for the actual number of days outstanding. The Principal Amount, together with any accrued interest thereon payable on the Maturity Date, shall be paid in immediate federal funds.

2. Interest on any part of the Principal Amount not paid when due and, to the extent permitted by applicable law, on any overdue interest, shall be payable on demand at a rate equal to ___% per month (the "Involuntary Rate") until such overdue payment is made, but shall in no event exceed the maximum rate allowed by law. In addition, if any installment of interest and/or principal is not received by Payee within ten (10) calendar days after the installment is due, Maker shall pay Payee a late charge of _____ (___%) percent of such installment, such late charge to be immediately due and payable without demand by Payee.

16. The Mortgage contains, among other things, the following provisions:

ARTICLE I
PARTICULAR COVENANTS, WARRANTIES AND REPRESENTATIONS OF THE MORTGAGOR

* * *

Section 1.04. *Payment of Debt.* The Mortgagor will punctually pay the principal and interest and all other sums to become due in respect of the Note at the time and place and in the manner specified in the Note, according to the true intent and meaning thereof and without offset or counterclaim, all in any coin or currency of the United States of America which at the time of such payment shall be legal tender for the payment of public and private debts.

* * *

ARTICLE II
EVENTS OF DEFAULT AND REMEDIES

Section 2.01. If one or more of the following Events of Default shall happen, that is to say:

(a) *if (i) a default shall be made in the payment of any interest on the Note, when and as the same shall become due and payable, and such default shall have continued for a period of ten (10) days after written notice that the payment is due shall have been given by Mortgagee to Mortgagor*, or (ii) default shall be made in any payment of principal on the Note, when and as the same shall become due and payable, and such default shall have continued for a period of ten (10) days after written notice that the payment is due shall have been given by Mortgagee to Mortgagor (except that no notice or cure period shall be given with respect to default in payment of principal due at maturity or by acceleration or otherwise), in each case, as in the Note and this Mortgage provided, or (iii) default shall be made in the payment of any tax or tax escrow payment, as applicable and said default shall have continued for a period of ten (10) days after written notice that the payment is due shall have been given by Mortgagee to Mortgagor, or (iv) default shall be made in the due observance or performance of any covenant or agreement on the part of the Mortgagor contained in Sections _____, _____, _____, _____, or ____ hereof [emphasis added];

* * *

then and in every such case:

I. The Mortgagee may declare the entire principal of the Note then outstanding (if not then due and payable), and all accrued and unpaid interest thereon, to be due and payable immediately, and upon any such declaration the principal of the Note and said accrued and unpaid interest shall become and be immediately due and payable, anything in the Note or in this Mortgage to the contrary notwithstanding;

* * *

III. The Mortgagee, with or without entry, personally or by its agents or attorneys, insofar as applicable, may:

(1) *institute proceedings for the complete or partial foreclosure of this Mortgage* [emphasis added]; or

(2) take such steps to protect and enforce its rights whether by action, suit or proceeding in equity or at law for the specific performance of any covenant, condition or agreement in the Note, this Mortgage, or the other Documents or in aid of the execution of any power herein granted, or for any foreclosure hereunder, or for the enforcement of any other appropriate legal or equitable remedy or otherwise as the Mortgagee shall elect.

* * *

Section 2.04. After the happening of any Event of Default and immediately upon the commencement of any action, suit or other legal proceedings by the Mortgagee to obtain judgment for the principal of, or interest on, the Note and other sums required to be paid by the Mortgagor pursuant to any provisions of this Mortgage, or of the Documents, or of any nature in aid of the enforcement of the Note or of this Mortgage, the Mortgagor does hereby (a) waive personal service of process and also consents to service by certified mail to the address of the Mortgagor set forth on the cover page of this Mortgage (with copies to be sent as provided in Section _____), and (b) if required by the Mortgagee, consent to the appointment of a receiver or receivers of the Mortgaged Property or any part thereof or any business or businesses conducted thereon and of all the earnings, revenues, rents, issues, profits and income thereof. *After the happening of any Event of Default, or upon the commencement of any proceedings to foreclose this Mortgage* or to enforce the specific performance hereof or in aid thereof or upon the commencement of any other judicial proceeding to enforce any right of the Mortgagee, the *Mortgagee shall be entitled, as a matter of right, if it shall so elect, without the giving of notice to any other party and without regard to the adequacy or inadequacy of any security for the Mortgage indebtedness, forthwith either before or after declaring the unpaid principal of the Note to be due and payable, to the appointment of such receiver or receivers* [emphasis added].

17. The Guaranty, executed by Guarantor in favor of the Bank, provides in relevant part as follows:

2. Guarantor unconditionally guarantees to you [*the Bank*] and to any purchaser from you, the due performance and prompt payment, whether at maturity or by acceleration or otherwise, of all of Borrower's obligations under the Loan Documents [*including the Note and Mortgage*], together with interest on such obligations to the extent provided for in said documents, including all legal and other costs or expenses paid or incurred by you in the enforcement thereof against either the Borrower or any of us.

3. Guarantor's liability hereunder shall be unaffected by (i) any amendment or modification of the provisions of the Loan Documents or any other instrument made to or with you by the Borrower. Guarantor waives any right or claim of right to cause a marshaling of the Borrower's assets or to cause you to proceed against any of the security for the Loan Documents before proceeding against Guarantor or to proceed against Guarantor in any particular order, and Guarantor agrees that any payments required to be made by Guarantor hereunder shall become due on demand in accordance with the terms hereof and of the Loan Documents immediately upon the happening of any default under the Loan Documents and without presentment of the Loan Documents to the Borrower, demand for payment or protest hereof, or notice of non-payment or protest thereof, and Guarantor expressly waives and relinquishes all rights and remedies accorded by applicable law to guarantors.

THE DEFAULTS UNDER THE LOAN DOCUMENTS

18. Borrower has failed to comply with the terms and conditions of the Note and the Mortgage by failing to make payment to the Bank of the interest payments in the amount of $_____ each due thereunder on [*January 1, 19__, February 1, 19__, March 1, 19__ and April 1, 19__,*] together with late payment charges as set forth in the Note.

19. By letter dated _____, 19__ (the "Default Notice"), sent by certified mail, return receipt requested, the Bank advised Borrower of its defaults as set forth above and further advised Borrower that upon its failure to make payment in full of the aggregate amount of $_____ in outstanding interest and late charges on or before ten (10) days from the sending of the Default Notice to Borrower, the entire principal balance of the Note in the amount of $_____, together with all accrued interest at the Involuntary Rate and late charges, would automatically be accelerated and immediately be due and payable without further notice. A copy of the Default Notice was also sent by certified mail, return receipt requested, to Guarantor at the same time it was sent to Borrower. A copy of the Default Notice and copies of the return receipts evidencing Borrower's and Guarantor's receipt of same, are collectively annexed as Exhibit D.

20. More than ten (10) days have expired since the sending of the Default Notice to Borrower and Guarantor, and both Borrower and Guarantor have failed to make any of the payments described in the Default Notice. As a result, pursuant to the provisions of the Note and Mortgage, the aforesaid principal balance of the Note and Mortgage in the amount of $_____, together with accrued interest at the Involuntary Rate and late charges, has been accelerated. Accordingly, there is now due and owing to the Bank the outstanding principal balance under the Note and Mortgage in the sum of $_____, with accrued interest at the Involuntary Rate and late charges thereon.

21. In order to protect its security, the Bank may be compelled further during the pendency of this action to pay taxes, assessments, water rates, sewer rents, insurance premiums, and other charges affecting the Premises, or some part thereof, and the Bank requests that any such sum or sums paid be added to the Note and be deemed secured by the Mortgage and be further deemed a valid lien on the Premises.

22. Each of the above-named defendants has or claims to have some interest in or lien upon said Premises, or some part thereof, which interest or lien, if any, is subject and subordinate to the lien of the Mortgage held by the Bank and sought to be foreclosed in this action.

23. The Bank requests that if this action proceeds to judgment of foreclosure and sale, the Premises be sold subject to covenants and restrictions, easements and agreements of record, to any state of facts an accurate survey might show, and to taxes, assessments, sewer rents and water charges, if any.

24. No other action has been brought to recover the sum of money or any part thereof secured by the Note or the Mortgage.

WHEREFORE, plaintiff demands judgment that:

(i) defendants and all persons claiming under them or any of them subsequent to the commencement of this action and the filing of a notice of pendency thereof, be barred and foreclosed of and from all estate, right, title and interest, claim, lien and equity of redemption of, in and to the Premises more particularly described in this Verified Complaint, including any personal property appurtenant thereto;

(ii) the Premises be ordered sold according to law; that the monies arising from the sale thereof be brought into Court; that from the net proceeds of such sale, plaintiff be paid (a) the amount due on the Note, together with the accrued interest and late charges thereon as set forth above; (b) costs, allowances and disbursements of this action; (c) a sum in respect of reasonable attorneys' fees incurred by plaintiff in connection with the collection of the indebtedness secured by the Mortgage, and the foreclosure thereof; and (d) any amounts advanced and paid pursuant to the terms and provi-

§ 11.74   MORTGAGE FORECLOSURE   Ch. 11

sions of the Mortgage and Note, including, without limitation, taxes, water rates and sewer rents, insurance premiums and all other charges and liens upon the aforesaid Premises, with interest on said amounts from the dates of the respective payments and advances thereof;

(iii) defendants [*DEF Borrower Associates*] and [*Robert A. Guarantor*] be adjudged to pay the whole residue, if any, of the debt of the Note and Mortgage remaining unsatisfied after a foreclosure sale of the Premises and the application of the proceeds pursuant to the directions contained in such judgment;

(iv) upon plaintiff's application therefor, this Court appoint a receiver of the rents and profits of the Premises during the pendency of this action with the usual powers and duties; and

(v) plaintiff have such other, further and different relief as may be just and equitable.

Dated: _____, New York
       _____, 19__

[SMITH & JONES, LLP]
Attorneys for Plaintiff
[*Address and Phone Number*]

VERIFICATION

STATE OF NEW YORK   )
) ss.:
COUNTY OF _____   )

_____, being duly sworn, deposes and says:

1. I am a [*Vice President*] of plaintiff [*ABC Savings Bank*] in this action. I have read the foregoing Verified Complaint, know the contents thereof, and state that the same are true to my knowledge, except as to those matters therein stated to be alleged on information and belief, and as to those matters, I believe them to be true.

2. The ground of my belief as to all matters in said Verified Complaint not stated upon my knowledge are information acquired from the books and records of plaintiff.

_____
[*Name*]

Sworn to before me this
day of _____, 19__

_____
NOTARY PUBLIC

§ 11.75 Forms—Order Appointing Receiver

At an Ex Parte Motion Part of the Supreme Court of the State of New York held in and for the County of _____ at the County Courthouse, _____, New York on the ___ day of _____, 19__.

PRESENT:
HON. _____, Justice.

_____

[ABC SAVINGS BANK],)
)
)
            Plaintiff,)
)
         -against-)
)
[DEF BORROWER ASSOCIATES,)
ROBERT A. GUARANTOR, SUB-)
ORDINATE MORTGAGEE COM-)
PANY, INC., MECHANIC'S LIEN)
CORP., THE PEOPLE OF THE)
STATE OF NEW YORK, THE)
COMMISSIONER OF TAXATION) ORDER APPOINTING A
AND FINANCE OF THE STATE) RECEIVER
OF NEW YORK, THE CITY OF)
EMPIRE, THE DEPARTMENT OF) Index No. _____
FINANCE OF THE CITY OF)
EMPIRE, THE ENVIRONMENTAL)
CONTROL BOARD OF THE CITY)
OF EMPIRE, and JOHN DOE #1)
through JOHN DOE #20, said John)
Doe defendants being fictitious, it)
being intended to name all other)
parties who may have some interest)
in or lien upon the premises sought)
to be foreclosed],)
)
            Defendants.)
_____)

Upon the Summons, Verified Complaint and Notice of Pendency of Action filed in the office of the Clerk of _____ County on the _____ day of _____, 19__, and upon reading and filing the annexed affidavit of _____ [Bank's officer], sworn to the _____ day of _____, 19__, and upon motion of [Smith & Jones, LLP], the attorneys for the plaintiff; it is

769

§ 11.75 MORTGAGE FORECLOSURE Ch. 11

ORDERED, that _____ be and [s]he hereby is appointed Receiver during the pendency of this action for the benefit of the plaintiff herein, of all the rents and profits of the mortgaged premises known as _____ [*set forth here address and/or commonly known name of property*], located in the City of [*Empire*], County of _____, State of New York, and more particularly described in Schedule A annexed hereto; and it is

FURTHER ORDERED, that the said Receiver be and [s]he hereby is authorized and directed to collect from the tenants of said mortgaged premises or from any persons liable therefor all the rents thereof now due and unpaid or hereafter and during the pendency of this action to become due, and that said tenants be, and they hereby are, directed to pay over to the said Receiver all the rents now due and unpaid or hereafter and during the pendency of this action to become due, and that all persons in possession other than lawful tenants be, and they hereby are, directed to surrender possession to the said Receiver, subject to the Emergency Rent Laws, if any; and it is

FURTHER ORDERED, that the said Receiver be and [s]he hereby is authorized to lease for a term not exceeding [ ] year(s) or such other term as may be mandated by statute, said premises or any part thereof which is or may become vacant; to keep the premises in a proper state of repair in compliance with law and insured against loss or damage by fire, and to make the expenditures necessary for said purposes and for the purpose of paying the necessary running expenses of the said premises subject, however, to the qualification that the Receiver shall not expend in excess of $_____ for any repair without further application to this Court; to pay any taxes, water rates or assessments now due upon said premises or hereafter and during the pendency of this action to become due; to pay the principal and interest and other charges in connection with any prior encumbrances of the Premises; and to institute and carry on such legal proceeding(s) as may be necessary for the protection or recovery of said mortgaged premises, for the collection of the rents and profits thereof, or for the removal of any tenant or other person from the premises, subject, however, to the qualification that the Receiver shall not retain counsel without further application to this Court; [*if the subject property is a multiple dwelling in New York City, then in accordance with RPAPL § 1325(3), the receivership order also must provide that the Receiver shall register with any municipal department as provided by applicable law, and that with regard to the Receiver's expenditures, the Receiver shall give priority "to the correction of immediately hazardous and hazardous violations of housing maintenance laws within the time set by orders of any municipal department, or, if not practicable, seek a postponement of the time for compliance"*]; and it is

FURTHER ORDERED, that the Receiver be permitted to appoint _____ as the managing agent of the Premises and to compensate said managing agent the fair and reasonable value of the managing agent's services solely out of the rents and profits of the Premises, subject, however, to the qualification that if the rents and profits are insufficient to compensate the managing agent, the managing agent shall be so notified and shall perform no further services without further order of this Court; and it is

FURTHER ORDERED, that during the pendency of this action the defendants and their agents be, and they hereby are, enjoined and restrained from leasing, renting or collecting the rents or profits of the said premises, and from interfering with the said Receiver or in any way with the premises or its possession, and that all lawful tenants of the said premises and any persons liable for such rents be, and they hereby are, enjoined and restrained from paying the same to any of the said defendants or to anyone except the said Receiver; and it is

FURTHER ORDERED, that the said Receiver be and [s]he is hereby authorized to receive, and the defendants, [*DEF Borrower Associates*] and [*Robert A. Guarantor*] be, and they hereby are directed, to turn over to said Receiver, all leases, rent rolls, security deposits of tenants of the premises, and any and all records, service contracts and agreements relating to the management of the premises held by said defendants, together with any and all monies held or received by said defendants in connection with the premises during the period commencing with the date of this Order to and including the date upon which said Receiver files with the Clerk of this Court [her] his bond as set forth below, except for those monies disbursed by said defendants during said period for the reasonable operation of the premises; and it is

FURTHER ORDERED, that the said Receiver be and [s]he hereby is directed to retain the moneys which may come to [her] his hands as such Receiver, except such moneys as [s]he is hereinbefore authorized to expend, until the said mortgaged premises are sold under a judgment to be entered herein, and then, after deducting therefrom [her] his disbursements and all other payments directed by the order of this Court, [s]he retain the said moneys in [her] his hands until further order of this Court; and it is

FURTHER ORDERED, that before entering upon [her] his duties as such Receiver, [s]he execute to the People of the State of New York, and file with the Clerk of this Court, a bond in the form prescribed by law, in the sum of $_____, with a surety company as surety, for the faithful discharge of [her] his duties as such Receiver; and it is

FURTHER ORDERED, that in accordance with the provisions of Section 202.52(a) and (b) of the Uniform Civil Rules for the Supreme Court and the County Court, the Receiver shall promptly deposit all monies received by [her] him in a checking account [*or an interest-bearing account*] at _____ (the "Depository"), such account to be in [her] his name, as Receiver, and to show the name of the instant case; the Depository shall furnish monthly statements regarding such account to the Receiver and said Receiver's counsel, if any; [*and no funds shall*

§ 11.75   MORTGAGE FORECLOSURE   Ch. 11

be withdrawn from the Receiver's account, and no check thereon shall be honored, unless directed by further order of this Court or unless the check is countersigned by the Receiver's surety on [her] his bond]; and it is

FURTHER ORDERED, that the appointee named as Receiver herein shall comply with the provisions of Section 35(a) of the Judiciary Law, Sections 6401–6405 of the Civil Practice Law and Rules, and Article 13 of the Real Property Actions and Proceedings Law.

ENTER

_____
J.S.C.

SCHEDULE A

[Set forth here legal metes and bounds description of Premises contained in Mortgage.]

§ 11.76   Forms—Affidavit in Support of Motion for Appointment of a Receiver

SUPREME COURT OF THE STATE OF NEW YORK
COUNTY OF _____

_____

[ABC SAVINGS BANK],   )
)
                                    Plaintiff,   )
)
            -against-   )
)
[DEF BORROWER ASSOCIATES,   )
ROBERT A. GUARANTOR, SUB-   )
ORDINATE MORTGAGEE COM-   )
PANY, INC., MECHANIC'S LIEN   )
CORP., THE PEOPLE OF THE   )
STATE OF NEW YORK, THE   )   AFFIDAVIT IN SUPPORT
COMMISSIONER OF TAXATION   )   OF APPLICATION FOR
AND FINANCE OF THE STATE   )   APPOINTMENT OF A
OF NEW YORK, THE CITY OF   )   RECEIVER
EMPIRE, THE DEPARTMENT OF   )
FINANCE OF THE CITY OF   )   Index No. _____
EMPIRE, THE ENVIRONMENTAL   )
CONTROL BOARD OF THE CITY   )
OF EMPIRE, and JOHN DOE #1   )
through JOHN DOE #20, said John   )
Doe defendants being fictitious, it   )
being intended to name all other   )
parties who may have some interest   )
in or lien upon the premises sought   )
to be foreclosed],   )

Ch. 11 MOTION FOR APPOINTMENT OF A RECEIVER § 11.76

)
       Defendants.)
_____)

STATE OF NEW YORK)
) ss:
COUNTY OF _____)

_____, being duly sworn, deposes and says:

1. I am a [*Vice President*] of [*ABC Savings Bank*] (the "Bank"), the plaintiff in the above-entitled action, and am familiar with the facts and circumstances stated herein. I submit this affidavit in support of the Bank's application for an order of this Court: (i) appointing *ex parte* a Receiver of the rents and profits of the premises located at _____, [*Empire*], New York, commonly known as _____ (the "Premises"), which are the subject of this mortgage foreclosure action; (ii) designating a qualified officer of the Court to serve as such Receiver; and (iii) permitting the Receiver to employ _____ as the managing agent of the Premises.

BACKGROUND

2. This is an action to foreclose upon a mortgage (the "Mortgage") affecting the Premises, which mortgage is more particularly described in the Verified Complaint dated _____, 19__, filed herein and annexed hereto as Exhibit 1.

3. The Mortgage and an accompanying mortgage note (the "Note"), both dated _____, 19__, were made by defendant, [*DEF Borrower Associates*] ("Borrower") to the Bank to secure repayment of a loan in the amount $_____. The Mortgage was recorded in the Office of the _____ [*Clerk or Register*] of _____ County, in Reel _____, page ___ on _____, 19__.

4. As appears from the Complaint, there is now due and unpaid to the Bank under the Note and Mortgage, the principal sum of $_____ with accrued interest thereon at the Involuntary Rate (as defined in the Note) and such other charges and expenses due or to become due thereunder as a result of the failure of the Borrower to make payment to the Bank of monthly interest due on [*January 1, 19__, February 1, 19__, March 1, 19__ and April 1, 19__,*] together with late payment charges as set forth in the Note.

5. The Summons, Complaint and Notice of Pendency of Action were filed in the Office of the Clerk of _____ County on _____, 19__. As evidenced by the Affidavits of Service, copies of which are annexed hereto as Exhibit 2, service of the Summons and Complaint was effected upon the following defendants on _____, 19__: _____, _____, _____, and _____.

THIS COURT SHOULD APPOINT A RECEIVER
FOR THE PREMISES

6. The Mortgage provides:

Section 2.04. After the happening of any Event of Default and immediately upon the commencement of any action, suit or other legal proceedings by the Mortgagee to obtain judgment for the principal of, or interest on, the Note and other sums required to be paid by the Mortgagor pursuant to any provisions of this Mortgage, or of the Documents, or of any nature in aid of the enforcement of the Note or of this Mortgage, the Mortgagor does hereby (a) waive personal service of process and also consents to service by certified mail to the address of the Mortgagor set forth on the cover page of this Mortgage (with copies to be sent as provided in Section ____), and (b) if required by the Mortgagee, consent to the appointment of a receiver or receivers of the Mortgaged Property or any part thereof or any business or businesses conducted thereon and of all the earnings, revenues, rents, issues, profits and income thereof. *After the happening of any Event of Default, or upon the commencement of any proceedings to foreclose this Mortgage or to enforce the specific performance hereof or in aid thereof or upon the commencement of any other judicial proceeding to enforce any right of the Mortgagee, the Mortgagee shall be entitled, as a matter of right, if it shall so elect, without the giving of notice to any other party and without regard to the adequacy or inadequacy of any security for the Mortgage indebtedness, forthwith either before or after declaring the unpaid principal of the Note to be due and payable, to the appointment of such receiver or receivers* [emphasis added].

7. Thus, the Bank is entitled to the appointment of a Receiver in the event of a foreclosure action, without regard to the adequacy of the security for the subject indebtedness and without notice to Borrower.

THE PREMISES

8. The Premises are improved by a ____ story building consisting of [*give details regarding the number of commercial and residential units, and/or other pertinent facts regarding the nature and composition of the property*].

9. Upon information and belief, the Premises are occupied by approximately ____ tenants, paying an aggregate monthly rental income of approximately $____ as set forth on the Schedule annexed hereto as Exhibit 3.

10. [*Optional*] The Bank believes that absent the appointment of a Receiver, the Premises may be materially injured or destroyed or will deteriorate to such an extent that on a sale at public auction the

Ch. 11 MOTION FOR APPOINTMENT OF A RECEIVER § 11.76

Premises will not realize a sum sufficient to satisfy the indebtedness due to the Bank with interest, costs and arrears of taxes.

11. [*Optional*] The Bank respectfully submits that the security is insufficient to protect the Bank's Mortgage with interest, water charges, sewer rent, taxes, and foreclosure expenses unless the Premises are judicially managed pending adjudication of this suit. It is therefore necessary that a Receiver be appointed to collect the rents and profits of the Premises so that the same may not be dissipated.

[*Set forth here any recommendation of the plaintiff regarding who should be appointed as Receiver.*]

THE BANK RECOMMENDS THAT THIS COURT AUTHORIZE THE RECEIVER TO APPOINT _____ AS THE MANAGING AGENT OF THE PREMISES

12. In addition, it is respectfully requested that this Court authorize the Receiver to appoint as managing agent of the Premises, _____, a company highly experienced in the management of properties similar to the Premises. As the Premises are occupied by numerous tenants and also have a number of vacancies, it is essential that a qualified managing agent be appointed to manage the property.

13. [*State here pertinent facts as to experience and expertise of recommended managing agent in managing property in general, and managing properties similar to Premises in particular.*] (A copy of _____'s resume is annexed hereto as Exhibit __.) Accordingly, it is respectfully requested that the Receiver be authorized to appoint _____ as managing agent of the Premises.

CONCLUSION

14. No previous application has been made for any of the relief requested herein.

WHEREFORE, for all of the foregoing reasons, this Court should grant the Bank's motion in all respects and should enter an Order Appointing Receiver in the proposed form annexed hereto.

_____
[*Name of Bank Officer*]

Sworn to before me this day of _____, 19__

_____
Notary Public

§ 11.77 Forms—Notice of Motion for Summary Judgment and Related Relief

SUPREME COURT OF THE STATE OF NEW YORK
COUNTY OF _____

_____
[ABC SAVINGS BANK],

                Plaintiff,

-against-

[DEF BORROWER ASSOCIATES, ROBERT A. GUARANTOR, SUBORDINATE MORTGAGEE COMPANY, INC., MECHANIC'S LIEN CORP., THE PEOPLE OF THE STATE OF NEW YORK, THE COMMISSIONER OF TAXATION AND FINANCE OF THE STATE OF NEW YORK, THE CITY OF EMPIRE, THE DEPARTMENT OF FINANCE OF THE CITY OF EMPIRE, THE ENVIRONMENTAL CONTROL BOARD OF THE CITY OF EMPIRE, and JOHN DOE #1 through JOHN DOE #20, said John Doe defendants being fictitious, it being intended to name all other parties who may have some interest in or lien upon the premises sought to be foreclosed],

                Defendants.

NOTICE OF MOTION FOR SUMMARY JUDGMENT AND RELATED RELIEF

Index No. _____

Motion By:

    Plaintiff, [*ABC Savings Bank*] (the "Bank")

Date, Time and Place of Hearing:

    _____, 19__ at _____ a.m. at an IAS Part __ of the Supreme Court, _____ County, at the Courthouse, _____, [*Empire*], New York.

Papers Submitted:

    (1) Affidavit of Regularity of _____, Esq.

    (2) Affidavit of _____, [*Vice President*] of Plaintiff, [*ABC Savings Bank*].

    (3) Exhibits referred to in the aforesaid affidavits.

(4) Memorandum of Law.

(5) All other papers heretofore filed herein.

Relief Requested:

An order and/or judgment:

1. Pursuant to New York Civil Practice Law and Rules ("CPLR") 3212, granting summary judgment in favor of the Bank and against all of the defendants on the grounds that there are no triable issues of fact in this proceeding, and that accordingly, the Bank is entitled to all of the relief requested in its Verified Complaint, including judgment of foreclosure and sale, as a matter of law;

2. Pursuant to CPLR 3211(b), dismissing each of the affirmative defenses asserted in the Answers of defendants [*DEF Borrower Associates*] ("Borrower"), [Subordinate Mortgagee Company, Inc.] ("Subordinate Mortgagee") and [*Mechanic's Lien Corp.*] ("Mechanic's") on the grounds that each of said defenses lacks merit and fails to state a valid defense to foreclosure;

3. Pursuant to CPLR 3211(a)(7), dismissing each of the counterclaims asserted in the Answers of defendants Borrower, Subordinate Mortgagee and Mechanic's on the ground that each of said counterclaims fails to state a cause of action; or, alternatively, pursuant to CPLR 3212, granting summary judgment in favor of the Bank and against each of said defendants with respect to each such counterclaim on the grounds that each such counterclaim raises no material triable issues of fact;

4. Referring this action to some suitable person as a referee (the "Referee") to ascertain and compute the amount due the Bank for principal and interest under the mortgage as set forth in the Bank's Verified Complaint, and for any other amounts due and owing the Bank, including any sums advanced by the Bank under the terms of the mortgage, and directing that upon presentation and coming in of the Referee's Report, the Bank have the usual judgment of foreclosure and sale;

5. Amending the caption of this proceeding by directing that the names of the "John Doe" defendants be deleted from the caption; and

6. For such other, further and different relief as this Court may deem just and proper.

PLEASE TAKE FURTHER NOTICE that, pursuant to CPLR 2214(b), answering papers, if any, must be personally served at least seven (7) days before the return date of this motion.

§ 11.77 MORTGAGE FORECLOSURE Ch. 11

Dated: _____, New York
       _____, 19__

[SMITH & JONES, LLP]
Attorneys for Plaintiff
[Address and Phone Number]

To: [Service List]

§ 11.78 Forms—Affidavit of Regularity and in Support of Motion for Summary Judgment 💾

SUPREME COURT OF THE STATE OF NEW YORK
COUNTY OF _____

_____)
)
[ABC SAVINGS BANK],   )
)
                  Plaintiff,   )
)
       -against-   )
)
[DEF BORROWER ASSOCIATES,   )
ROBERT A. GUARANTOR, SUB-   )
ORDINATE MORTGAGEE COM-   )
PANY, INC., MECHANIC'S LIEN   )
CORP., THE PEOPLE OF THE   ) AFFIDAVIT OF REGULARITY
STATE OF NEW YORK, THE   ) AND IN SUPPORT OF
COMMISSIONER OF TAXATION   ) PLAINTIFF'S MOTION FOR
AND FINANCE OF THE STATE   ) SUMMARY JUDGMENT AND
OF NEW YORK, THE CITY OF   ) RELATED RELIEF
EMPIRE, THE DEPARTMENT OF   )
FINANCE OF THE CITY OF   ) Index No. _____
EMPIRE, THE ENVIRONMENTAL   )
CONTROL BOARD OF THE CITY   )
OF EMPIRE, and JOHN DOE #1   )
through JOHN DOE #20, said John)
Doe defendants being fictitious, it)
being intended to name all other)
parties who may have some interest)
in or lien upon the premises sought)
to be foreclosed],   )
)
                  Defendants.)
_____)

STATE OF NEW YORK)
) ss.:
COUNTY OF _____   )

_____, Esq., being duly sworn, deposes and says:

1. I am a member of the firm of [*Smith & Jones, LLP*], attorneys for [*ABC Savings Bank*] ("the Bank"), the plaintiff in the instant mortgage foreclosure action. I am fully familiar with the facts and circumstances stated herein, and I submit this affidavit in support of the Bank's motion for an order and/or judgment:

   (i) Pursuant to New York Civil Practice Law and Rules ("CPLR") 3212, granting summary judgment in favor of the Bank and against all of the defendants on the grounds that there are no triable issues of fact in this proceeding, and that accordingly, the Bank is entitled to all of the relief requested in its Verified Complaint, including judgment of foreclosure and sale, as a matter of law;

   (ii) Pursuant to CPLR 3211(b), dismissing each of the affirmative defenses asserted in the Answers of defendants [*DEF Borrower Associates*] ("Borrower"), [*Subordinate Mortgage Company, Inc.*] ("Subordinate Mortgagee") and [*Mechanic's Lien Corp.*] ("Mechanic's") on the ground that each of said defenses lacks merit and fails to state a valid defense to foreclosure;

   (iii) Pursuant to CPLR 3211(a)(7), dismissing each of the counterclaims asserted in the answers of defendants Borrower, Subordinate Mortgagee and Mechanic's on the ground that each of said counterclaims fails to state a cause of action; or, alternatively, pursuant to CPLR 3212, granting summary judgment in favor of the Bank and against each of said defendants with respect to each such counterclaim on the grounds that each such counterclaim raises no material triable issues of fact;

   (iv) Referring this action to some suitable person as a referee (the "Referee") to ascertain and compute the amount due the Bank for principal and interest under the mortgage as set forth in the Bank's Verified Complaint, and for any other amounts due and owing the Bank, including any sums advanced by the Bank under the terms of the mortgage, and directing that upon presentation and coming in of the Referee's Report, the Bank have the usual judgment of foreclosure and sale;

   (v) Amending the caption of this proceeding by directing that the names of the "John Doe" defendants be deleted from the caption; and

   (vi) For such other, further and different relief as this Court may deem just and proper.

2. In view of the fact that part of the relief requested by the Bank is for an order appointing a Referee to compute, this affidavit should also

§ 11.78　　　MORTGAGE FORECLOSURE　　　Ch. 11

be deemed the Bank's Affidavit of Regularity upon a motion for an order appointing such a Referee.

THE FORECLOSURE PROCEEDING TO DATE

3. This is an action to foreclose upon a first fee mortgage dated _____, 19__, in the amount of $_____, made by defendant [*DEF Borrower Associates*] ("Borrower"), as mortgagor, in favor of the Bank, as mortgagee (the "Mortgage"). The Mortgage was duly recorded in the Office of the _____ [*Clerk or Register*] of _____ County on _____, 19__ in Reel ___, Page ___. A copy of the Mortgage is annexed hereto as Exhibit ___. The Mortgage secures a mortgage note (the "Note") in the amount of $_____, dated _____, 19__, made and delivered by Borrower to the Bank. A copy of the Note is annexed hereto as Exhibit ___.

4. The Mortgage constitutes a first mortgage lien upon the fee estate in and to the premises located in the City of [*Empire*], County of _____ and State of New York commonly known by the address _____, [*Empire*], New York (the "Premises"). The Premises are more particularly described in Exhibit ___ hereto. As stated in the Verified Complaint, and as set forth in further detail below and in the accompanying Affidavit of _____, [*Vice President*] of the Bank, by reason of monetary defaults under the Mortgage, there is now due and owing thereunder the accelerated principal sum of $_____, together with all interest accrued thereon at the Involuntary Rate, no part of which has been paid.

5. The Summons and Verified Complaint commencing this action (Exhibit __) were filed in the office of the Clerk of _____ County (the "County Clerk") on _____, 19__. At approximately the same time or immediately thereafter, and more than twenty (20) days ago, a Notice of Pendency of this Action (Exhibit __) was filed in the County Clerk's Office containing the date of the Mortgage, the time and place of recording of same, the parties thereto, the names of the parties to this action, the object of this action, and a description of all of the property in _____ County affected thereby.

6. The defendants are of full age and competence and are not absentees. Each of the defendants (other than the "John Doe" defendants, who are sought to be deleted from this action) has been properly served with the Summons and Verified Complaint as evidenced by the Affidavits of Service, copies of which are collectively annexed hereto as Exhibit ___.

7. The statutory time periods prescribed under CPLR 3012 and any extended time period thereto granted by the Bank have elapsed since completion of service of the Summons and Verified Complaint upon each of the defendants and none of the defendants has appeared, answered or moved with respect to the Verified Complaint within said time periods or any extended time periods thereto granted by the Bank except the following:

(a) Borrower, on or about _____, 19__, served a Verified Answer to the Verified Complaint (Exhibit __);

(b) Defendant Subordinate Mortgagee, on or about _____, 19__, served a Verified Answer to the Verified Complaint (Exhibit __);

(c) Defendant Mechanic's, on or about _____, 19__, served a Verified Answer to the Verified Complaint (Exhibit __);

(d) Defendants The People of the State of New York and The Commissioner of Taxation and Finance of the State of New York appeared herein on or about _____, 19__, by serving a Notice of Appearance in response to the Verified Complaint (Exhibit __);

(e) Defendants The City of [Empire] and The Department of Finance of The City of [Empire], on or about _____, 19__, appeared herein by serving a Notice of Appearance and Waiver in Foreclosure in response to the Verified Complaint (Exhibit __);

(f) Defendant The Environmental Control Board of the City of [Empire], on or about _____, 19__, appeared herein by serving a Notice of Appearance and Waiver in response to the Verified Complaint (Exhibit __).

8. To date, defendant [Robert A. Guarantor] ("Guarantor") has not interposed a responsive pleading, served a notice of appearance, or attempted to contact the Bank directly or through counsel with respect to the Verified Complaint.

THE BANK IS ENTITLED TO SUMMARY JUDGMENT AS A MATTER OF LAW

9. The Bank respectfully submits that this Court should grant summary judgment in favor of the Bank with respect to all of the relief requested in the Verified Complaint on the grounds that there are no material issues of fact in this proceeding and, accordingly, the Bank is entitled to judgment as a matter of law pursuant to CPLR 3212(b).

10. As clearly shown in the Bank's Verified Complaint (Exhibit __), and in the [Bank Vice President's] Affidavit accompanying this motion, the indebtedness under the Mortgage was properly accelerated by reason of the Borrower's monetary defaults under the Note and Mortgage, and to date, payment has not been made of the accelerated principal balance due under the Note and Mortgage in the aggregate amount of $_____, or of the interest accrued thereon, or of any additional charges and expenses payable pursuant to the Mortgage, Note, and other pertinent loan documents.

11. Specifically, the Borrower defaulted under the Note and Mortgage by failing to make payment of the monthly interest installments of $_____ each that were due on [January 1, 19__, February 1, 19__,

March 1, 19__ and April 1, 19__,] together with late payment charges due thereunder.

12. Accordingly, the Bank sent to Borrower and Guarantor, by certified mail, return receipt requested, a written notice of default (the "Notice of Default," Exhibit __) dated _____, 19__, apprising Borrower and Guarantor of Borrower's defaults and advising Borrower and Guarantor that upon their failure to make payment full of the aggregate amount of $_____ in outstanding interest and late charges on or before ten (10) days from the sending of the Default Notice, the entire principal balance of the Note, together with all accrued interest at the default rate and late charges would automatically be accelerated and immediately be due and payable without further notice. Thereafter, the applicable time periods prescribed by the pertinent loan documents for Borrower and Guarantor to cure Borrower's defaults elapsed and Borrower and Guarantor failed to cure said defaults. Accordingly, the Bank elected to declare the entire principal balance of the Note and Mortgage in the amount of $_____, together with all accrued interest and charges, immediately due and payable.

13. To date, Borrower has not made payment of all or any portion of the accelerated principal balance of $_____, together with accrued interest and additional charges and expenses. Nor has defendant Guarantor made payment of any of said sums as required under the Guaranty of Payment (the "Guaranty," Exhibit __) executed by Guarantor on _____, 19__.

14. None of the answering defendants can in good faith dispute the foregoing facts comprising the defaults by Borrower and Guarantor under the pertinent loan documents, which defaults clearly entitle the Bank to foreclose upon the Mortgage.

15. Accordingly, the Bank is entitled, as a matter of law, to judgment for all of the relief requested in the Verified Amended Complaint.

NONE OF THE AFFIRMATIVE DEFENSES AND COUNTERCLAIMS ALLEGED BY THE ANSWERING DEFENDANTS CONSTITUTES A VALID DEFENSE TO FORECLOSURE

16. The answering defendants have asserted several frivolous "affirmative defenses" and "counterclaims," none of which, as is demonstrated below, in the [*Bank Vice President's*] Affidavit, and in the Memorandum of Law accompanying this motion, constitute a valid defense to the Bank's clearly established entitlement to judgment.

[*Set forth in this section a brief discussion of each affirmative defense and counterclaim and why each should be dismissed—a more detailed discussion of the foregoing should be contained in the accompanying Bank Vice President's Affidavit and in the accompanying Memorandum of Law.*]

Ch. 11 JUDGMENT OF FORECLOSURE AND SALE § 11.79

THE ADDITIONAL ITEMS OF REQUEST RELIEF SHOULD BE GRANTED

Appointment of Referee to Compute

17. In view of all of the foregoing, including, without limitation, the Bank's clearly established right and entitlement to summary judgment, the Bank respectfully submits that it is also entitled to an order of this Court referring this action to some suitable person as Referee to ascertain and compute the amounts due the Bank for principal and interest on the Mortgage as set forth in the Verified Complaint, and for any other amounts due and owing the Bank, including any sums advanced by the Bank under the terms of the Mortgage and for reasonable attorneys' fees, and directing that upon presentation and coming in of the Referee's Report, the Bank have the usual judgment of foreclosure and sale.

Amendment of Caption of This Proceeding

18. The Bank also respectfully requests that this Court direct the deletion from the caption of "John Doe #1 through John Doe #20, said John Doe defendants being fictitious, it being intended to name all other parties who may have some interest in or lien upon any of the premises sought to be foreclosed herein" (the "John Doe defendants"). Since the commencement of this action, the Bank has ascertained that, upon information and belief, no parties other than the defendants previously served in this action have an interest in or lien upon the Premises. Accordingly, this Court should direct that the names of the John Doe defendants be deleted from the title of this proceeding.

CONCLUSION

19. No previous application has been made for any of the relief requested herein.

WHEREFORE, for all of the foregoing reasons, the motion of plaintiff Bank should be granted in all respects.

_____, Esq.

Sworn to before me _____, 19__

_____
Notary Public

§ 11.79 Forms—Judgment of Foreclosure and Sale

At an IAS Part ___ of the Supreme Court of the State of New York, County of _____, located at _____, [Empire], New York on the _____ day of _____, 19__.

783

§ 11.79   MORTGAGE FORECLOSURE   Ch. 11

PRESENT:
HON. _____, Justice.

_____

[ABC SAVINGS BANK],

                Plaintiff,

        -against-

[DEF BORROWER ASSOCIATES, ROBERT A. GUARANTOR, SUBORDINATE MORTGAGEE COMPANY, INC., MECHANIC'S LIEN CORP., THE PEOPLE OF THE STATE OF NEW YORK, THE COMMISSIONER OF TAXATION AND FINANCE OF THE STATE OF NEW YORK, THE CITY OF EMPIRE, THE DEPARTMENT OF FINANCE OF THE CITY OF EMPIRE, THE ENVIRONMENTAL CONTROL BOARD OF THE CITY OF EMPIRE],

             Defendants.

_____

JUDGMENT OF FORE-
CLOSURE AND SALE

Index No. _____

Upon the Summons, Verified Complaint, and Notice of Pendency of Action filed herein on _____, 19__; upon the Affidavits of Service upon the defendants previously filed herein; upon the Notice of Motion to Confirm Referee's Computation Report and for Judgment of Foreclosure and Sale (the "Confirmation and Judgment Motion") dated _____, 19__; and upon the Affidavit of Regularity of _____, Esq., sworn to _____, 19__ in support of the Confirmation and Judgment Motion; upon the Order of the Honorable _____ dated _____, 19__, which *inter alia*, appointed _____ as Referee to ascertain and compute the amount due to the plaintiff [*ABC Savings Bank*] for principal, interest, and otherwise on the note and mortgage referred to in the Verified Complaint, and to examine and report whether the mortgaged premises can be sold in parcels; and upon all other proceedings previously had herein, from all of which it appears that this action was brought to foreclose upon a first mortgage on real property situated in the City of [*Empire*], County of _____ and State of New York, and that the entire balance of the principal sum secured by the mortgage, to wit, the sum of $_____, together with interest thereon and various late charges and other charges expended by the plaintiff is now due and payable; that all of the defendants herein have been duly served with the Summons and

Verified Complaint in this action; that the time to answer or move with respect to the Verified Complaint has expired as to each of the defendants and that no answer or motion directed to the Verified Complaint or otherwise has been interposed by or on behalf of any defendant and that the time to do so has not been extended by consent or by Order of this Court, except that: (i) defendant [*DEF Borrower Associates*] ("Borrower"), on or about _____, 19__, served a Verified Answer to the Verified Complaint; (ii) defendant [*Subordinate Mortgagee Company, Inc.*] ("Subordinate Mortgagee"), on or about _____, 19__, served a Verified Answer to the Verified Complaint; and (iii) defendant [*Mechanic's Lienor Corp.*] ("Mechanic's"), on or about _____, 19__, served a Verified Answer to the Verified Complaint; and upon the aforesaid Order of the Honorable _____ dated _____, 19__, in which this Court (i) entered summary judgment in favor of the plaintiff for all of the relief requested in plaintiff's Verified Complaint; (ii) dismissed each of the affirmative defenses and counterclaims asserted by defendants Borrower, Subordinate Mortgagee and Mechanic's; (iii) referred this action to _____ as Referee to compute the amount due to plaintiff as sought in plaintiff's Verified Complaint, and to examine and report whether the mortgaged premises can be sold in parcels; (iv) amended the caption of this action to delete therefrom the names of the "John Doe" defendants; and (v) ordered that upon presentation and coming in of the Referee's Report, and on motion for confirmation thereof, the plaintiff have the usual judgment of foreclosure and sale, together with the costs, disbursements, and allowances of this action; and it appearing that none of the defendants herein is an infant, incompetent, or absentee, and that the Notice of Pendency filed in this action on _____, 19__ contains truly and correctly all of the particulars required by law to be stated in such notice; and upon the report of the Referee, _____, on file with this Court, a copy of which is annexed hereto, from which it appears that the sum of $_____ was due to the plaintiff on _____, 19__, the date of the Report, and that the mortgaged premises should be sold in one parcel.

NOW, on motion of [*Smith & Jones, LLP*], attorneys for the plaintiff herein, it is

ORDERED, that the motion be and the same hereby is granted; and it is further

ORDERED AND ADJUDGED, that the report of the Referee be and the same hereby is in all respects ratified and confirmed; and it is further

ORDERED AND ADJUDGED, that the plaintiff is entitled to have judgment herein for the sum of $_____ together with interest thereon from the date of the Report, _____, 19__, besides the sum of $_____ as taxed by the Clerk of the Court and hereby adjudged to the plaintiff for costs and disbursements in this action, with interest thereon from the date hereof, together with an additional allowance of $300 hereby

§ 11.79   MORTGAGE FORECLOSURE   Ch. 11

awarded to the plaintiff in addition to costs and disbursements, with interest thereon from the date hereof; and it is further

ORDERED AND ADJUDGED, that the mortgaged premises described in the Verified Complaint and as hereinafter described, be sold in one parcel subject to existing encumbrances, covenants, and restrictions of record, if any, leases of tenants not made parties to this action, if any, and any projections and state of facts, if any, as an accurate survey may show, at public auction at _____ under the direction of _____, who is hereby appointed Referee for that purpose; that the Referee give public notice of the time and place of the sale according to law and the practice of this Court, namely, in the _____ [*name of newspaper in which sale to be advertised to be inserted by Court*]; that the plaintiff or its nominee or any other parties to this action may become the purchaser or purchasers at such sale; that in case the plaintiff or its nominee shall become the purchaser at the same it shall not be required to make any deposit thereon; that the Referee execute to the purchaser or purchasers on such sale a deed of the premises sold; that the Referee on receiving the proceeds of such sale forthwith pay therefrom the taxes, assessments or water rates which are or may become liens on the premises at the time of sale with such interest or penalties which may be lawfully accrued thereon to the date of payment; that the Referee then deposit the balance of the proceeds of sale in his/her own name as Referee in _____ [*name of Bank to be inserted by Court*]; and shall thereafter make the following payments, and his/her checks drawn for that purpose shall be paid by the depository:

1. A sum not exceeding $_____ to the Referee for his/her fees herein.

2. The expenses of the sale and advertising expenses as shown in the bills presented and certified by the Referee to be correct, and duplicate copies of which shall be left with the depository.

3. The sum of $_____ to the plaintiff or its attorneys, adjudged to the plaintiff for its costs and disbursements in this action (as taxed by the Clerk of the Court), with interest thereon from the date of entry hereof, together with an additional allowance of $300 hereby awarded to the plaintiff in addition to costs, with interest thereon from the date of entry hereof; and also the sum of $_____, the amount so reported due as aforesaid, together with the legal interest thereon from _____, 19__, the date of the Report, or so much thereof as the purchase money of the mortgaged premises will pay of the same.

If plaintiff or its nominee is the purchaser of the mortgaged premises at the sale, or if the rights of the purchaser at the same and the terms of sale under this judgment shall be assigned to and be acquired by the plaintiff or its nominee, and a valid assignment thereof filed with the Referee, the Referee shall not require plaintiff or its nominee to pay in cash the entire amount bid at such sale, but shall execute and deliver to the plaintiff or its nominee a deed or deeds of the premises sold upon the payment to said Referee of the amounts specified above in items marked "1" and "2" and the amount of the aforesaid taxes, assessments and water rates and interest or penalties thereon, or in lieu of the payment of the last mentioned amount, upon filing with the Referee receipts of the proper municipal authorities, showing the payment thereof; that the balance of the amount bid after deducting therefrom the aforesaid amount paid by the plaintiff for Referee's fees, advertising expenses and taxes, assessments and water rates, shall be allowed to the plaintiff or its nominee and applied by the Referee upon the amounts due to the plaintiff as specified above in item marked "3"; that if after so applying the balance of the amount bid there shall be a surplus over and above the amounts due to the plaintiff, the plaintiff or its nominee shall pay to the Referee upon delivery to him/her of the Referee's deed the amount of such surplus; that the Referee on receiving the several amounts from the plaintiff shall forthwith pay therefrom the taxes, assessments, water rates and interest or penalties thereon, unless the same shall have already been paid, and shall pay the surplus money into court.

The Referee is directed to take the receipt of the plaintiff or its attorneys for the amounts paid as hereinbefore directed, in item marked "3" and file it with his/her report of sale; to pay into Court the surplus moneys, if any, within five days after the same shall be received and be ascertainable, to the credit of this action, to be withdrawn only on the order of the Court signed by a Justice of this Court; and to make a report of such sale and file it with the Clerk of _____ County, with all convenient speed; and it is further

ORDERED AND ADJUDGED that if the proceeds of such sale be insufficient to pay the amount reported due to the plaintiff with interest and costs as aforesaid, the plaintiff shall recover from the defendants [*ABC Borrower Associates*] and [*Robert A. Guarantor*], the whole deficiency or so much thereof as the Court may determine to be just and equitable of the residue of the mortgaged debt remaining unsatisfied after the sale of the mortgaged premises and the application of the proceeds thereof, provided a motion for a deficiency judgment shall be made as prescribed by Section 1371 of the Real Property Actions and Proceedings Law within the time limited therein, and the amount thereof is determined and awarded by an order of this Court as provided for in said statutory provision; and it is further

ORDERED AND ADJUDGED that the purchaser or purchasers at said sale be let into possession on production of the Referee's deed or deeds; and it is further

ORDERED AND ADJUDGED that each and all of the defendants in this action and all persons claiming under them or any or either of them after the filing of the Notice of the Pendency of this action, be and they hereby are forever barred and foreclosed of all right, claim, lien, title,

§ 11.79   MORTGAGE FORECLOSURE   Ch. 11

interest and equity of redemption in said mortgaged premises and each and every part thereof.

The following is a description of the mortgaged premises hereinbefore mentioned:

[*Set forth here legal metes and bounds description contained in Mortgage.*]

E N T E R:

_____
J.S.C.

§ 11.80   Forms—Notice of Sale

SUPREME COURT OF THE STATE OF NEW YORK
COUNTY OF _____
_____

[ABC SAVINGS BANK],   )
)
              Plaintiff,   )
)
         -against-   )
)
[DEF BORROWER ASSOCIATES,   )
ROBERT A. GUARANTOR, SUB-   )
ORDINATE MORTGAGEE COM-   )
PANY, INC., MECHANIC'S LIEN   )   NOTICE OF SALE
CORP., THE PEOPLE OF THE   )
STATE OF NEW YORK, THE   )   Index No. _____
COMMISSIONER OF TAXATION   )
AND FINANCE OF THE STATE   )
OF NEW YORK, THE CITY OF   )
EMPIRE, THE DEPARTMENT OF   )
FINANCE OF THE CITY OF   )
EMPIRE, THE ENVIRONMENTAL   )
CONTROL BOARD OF THE CITY   )
OF EMPIRE],   )
)
              Defendants.   )
_____)

In pursuance of a judgment of foreclosure and sale entered in the above entitled action and bearing date of _____, 19__, I, _____, Esq., the undersigned, the Referee in said judgment named, will sell in one parcel, at public auction, at the _____ County Courthouse, _____, New York, on _____, 19__, at _____ a.m. [*or p.m.*], on that date, the

788

premises described by said judgment to be sold and therein described as follows:

[*Set forth legal metes and bounds description.*]

Also known on the Official Tax Map of the Town of _____, County of _____ as Section _____; Block _____; Lot _____, commonly known as _____, New York, and shall be offered as a whole and sold off to the highest bidder who will offer the highest price under the following terms:

Subject to any encumbrances, to covenants and restrictions of record, if any; leases of tenants not made parties to this action, if any; and any projections and state of facts, if any, an accurate survey may disclose.

The approximate amount of the lien due to the plaintiff pursuant to the judgment, with costs and allowances, excluding the expenses of the sale, is $_____.

Dated: _____, 19__

[_____]
Referee
[*Address and Phone Number*]

§ 11.81 Forms—Terms and Memorandum of Sale

SUPREME COURT OF THE STATE OF NEW YORK
COUNTY OF _____

_____

[ABC SAVINGS BANK],)
)
Plaintiff,)
)
-against-)
)
[DEF BORROWER ASSOCIATES,)
ROBERT A. GUARANTOR, SUB-)
ORDINATE MORTGAGEE COM-)
PANY, INC., MECHANIC'S LIEN) TERMS AND MEMORANDUM
CORP., THE PEOPLE OF THE) OF SALE
STATE OF NEW YORK, THE)
COMMISSIONER OF TAXATION) Index No. _____
AND FINANCE OF THE STATE)
OF NEW YORK, THE CITY OF)
EMPIRE, THE DEPARTMENT OF)
FINANCE OF THE CITY OF)
EMPIRE, THE ENVIRONMENTAL)
CONTROL BOARD OF THE CITY)
OF EMPIRE],)
)
Defendants.)
_____)

The premises described in the annexed advertisement of sale will be sold under the direction of _____, Esq., Referee, upon the following terms:

1. Ten (10%) per cent of the purchase price in cash or certified check will be required to be paid to the Referee at the time and place of sale and for which the Referee's receipt will be given unless plaintiff or its nominee is the successful bidder, in which case the deposit requirement is waived.

2. At or before the time of making a bid, the bidder, other than plaintiff, shall exhibit to the Referee cash or a certified check(s) for at least ten (10%) per cent of the amount of the bid.

3. The residue of the purchase money will be required to be paid to the Referee at [her] his office, _____, [*Empire*], New York, on or before [*generally 30th day after date of foreclosure sale*] at _____ a.m. [*or p.m.*] when and where the Referee's Deed will be ready for delivery.

4. The Referee is not required to send any notice to the purchaser and if the purchaser neglects to call at the time and place above specified to receive [her] his deed, the purchaser will be charged with interest thereafter on the whole amount of its purchase unless the Referee shall deem it proper to extend the time for the completion of the purchase.

5. All taxes, assessments and water rents, which, at the time of sale, are liens or encumbrances upon the premises, will be allowed by the Referee out of the purchase money, provided the purchaser shall, previous to the delivery of the deed, produce to the Referee proofs of such liens, and duplicate receipts for the payment thereof.

6. The purchaser of the premises, or any portion thereof, will at the time and place of the sale, sign a memorandum of its purchase.

7. The bidding will be kept open after the property is struck down; and in case any purchaser shall fail to comply with any of the above conditions of sale, the premises so struck down to it will be again put up for sale under the direction of the Referee under the same terms of sale, without application to the court, unless the plaintiff's attorney shall elect to make such application and such purchaser will be held liable for any deficiency there may be between the sum for which the premises shall be struck down upon the sale, and that for which they may be purchased on the resale, and also for any costs or expenses occurring on such resale.

8. The premises will be sold in one parcel subject to existing restrictions, encumbrances and covenants of record if any, subject to leases of tenants not made parties to this action, if any, and subject to any projections and state of facts as an accurate survey may show.

9. All expenses of recording the Referee's Deed, including real property transfer tax and transfer stamps, shall be borne by the purchaser.

Dated: [*Empire*], New York
_____, 19__

_____
Referee

MEMORANDUM OF SALE

I have this _____ day of _____, 19__, purchased the premises described in the annexed printed advertisement of sale for the sum of $_____ and hereby promise and agree to comply with the terms and conditions of the sale of said premises, as above-mentioned and set forth.

Dated: _____, New York
_____, 19__

_____
Purchaser

RECEIPT

_____, 19__ received from _____ [*Insert Purchaser's name*] the sum of $ _____ being 10% of the amount bid by _____ [*Insert Purchaser's name*] for the property sold under the Judgment of Foreclosure and Sale in this action.

_____
Referee

–or–

[in case of plaintiff being successful bidder]

The deposit of 10% is hereby waived.

_____
Referee

Chapter 12

PURCHASE AND SALE OF REAL ESTATE

by
Bernard M. Rifkin

Table of Sections

12.1	Scope Note.
12.2	Strategy.
12.3	____ Pre-contract Checklist.
12.4	Contract of Sale.
12.5	____ Preparation and Delivery
12.6	____ Recordation.
12.7	Residential Contract of Sale.
12.8	____ Parties.
12.9	____ Premises.
12.10	____ Personal Property.
12.11	____ Purchase Price and Method of Payment.
12.12	____ ____ Down Payment.
12.13	____ ____ Assumption of Existing Mortgage.
12.14	____ ____ Purchase Money Mortgage.
12.15	____ ____ Mortgage Contingency.
12.16	____ ____ Acceptable Funds.
12.17	____ Permitted Exceptions.
12.18	____ Governmental Violations and Orders.
12.19	____ Seller's Representations.
12.20	____ Condition of Property.
12.21	____ Insurable and Marketable Title.
12.22	____ Closing, Deed and Title.
12.23	____ Closing Date and Place.
12.24	____ Conditions to Closing.
12.25	____ Deed Transfer and Recording Taxes.
12.26	____ Apportionments.
12.27	____ Allowance for Unpaid Taxes.
12.28	____ Title Examination; Seller's Inability to Convey; Limitation of Liability.
12.29	____ Defaults and Remedies.
12.30	____ Assignment.
12.31	____ Broker.
12.32	____ Risk of Loss.
12.33	Condominium Contract of Sale.
12.34	____ Comparisons to the Residential Contract of Sale.

Ch. 12   PURCHASE & SALE OF REAL ESTATE

12.35 ___ Homeowner's Associations.
12.36 Contract of Sale for Office, Commercial and Multi-family Residential Premises.
12.37 Contract of Sale for Cooperative Apartment
12.38 ___ Standard Form.
12.39 Contract of Sale for New Construction.
12.40 Title Insurance.
12.41 ___ The Buyer's Obligation.
12.42 ___ Role of the Title Insurer.
12.43 ___ Duration and Cost.
12.44 ___ Basic and Extended Coverage.
12.45 Title Insurance Policy.
12.46 ___ Loan Policy Coverage.
12.47 ___ New York Modifications of Loan Policy.
12.48 ___ Owner's Policy Coverage.
12.49 ___ New York Modifications of Owner's Policy.
12.50 ___ Standard Exceptions.
12.51 ___ Endorsements.
12.52 ___ Exclusions.
12.53 Title Examination: Recording Title and the Torrens System.
12.54 ___ Objections to Be Disposed of Prior to Closing.
12.55 ___ ___ Checklist.
12.56 The Survey Map.
12.57 ___ What it May Disclose.
12.58 ___ Effect on Marketability of Title.
12.59 ___ ___ Where Contract Is Silent on the Matter of Survey.
12.60 ___ ___ Where Contract Subject to Any State of Facts an Accurate Survey May Show.
12.61 ___ ___ Where Contract Subject to Any State of Facts an Accurate Survey May Show Provided Same Does Not Render Title Unmarketable.
12.62 ___ ___ Where Contract Subject to Specific Encroachments or to Facts Shown on a Specific Survey.
12.63 ___ ___ Suggested Clause.
12.64 Marketability of Title.
12.65 ___ What Renders Title Unmarketable.
12.66 ___ ___ Encroachments Due to Adverse Possession.
12.67 ___ ___ Party Walls.
12.68 ___ Driveway Easements.
12.69 ___ Other Covenants and Restrictions.
12.70 ___ Reservations for Public Utilities.
12.71 ___ Land Abutting Bodies of Water and the Federal Navigational Servitude.
12.72 Closing of Title.
12.73 ___ Checklist.
12.74 ___ Recording Fees and Filings.
12.75 ___ Disclosure and Other Requirements.
12.76 ___ ___ Foreign Investors Real Property Tax.
12.77 ___ ___ Form 1099–S Federal Requirement for One to Four Family Residence.

§ 12.1 PURCHASE & SALE OF REAL ESTATE Ch. 12

12.78 ___ ___ Form 1099–S Federal Requirement for One to Four Family Residence—Checklist.
12.79 ___ ___ Cash Payments Received by Businesses in Excess of $10,000.
12.80 ___ ___ Lead Paint Hazards.
12.81 ___ ___ Agricultural Foreign Investment Disclosure Act.
12.82 ___ Payment of Taxes.
12.83 ___ ___ New York State Real Estate Transfer Tax and Mansion Tax.
12.84 ___ ___ Article 31–B—Real Property Transfer Gains Tax.
12.85 ___ ___ New York City Real Property Transfer Tax.
12.86 ___ ___ Cities of Mount Vernon and Yonkers.
12.87 ___ ___ Real Estate Investment Trusts.
12.88 ___ ___ Mortgage Recording Tax Outside New York City.
12.89 ___ ___ Mortgage Recording Tax Rate in New York City.
12.90 ___ Method of Payment.
12.91 ___ Other Required Forms and Information.
12.92 Forms.
12.93 ___ Residential Contract of Sale.
12.94 ___ Contract of Sale—Condominium Unit.
12.95 ___ ___ Office, Commercial and Multi–Family Residential Premises.
12.96 ___ ___ Cooperative Apartment.
12.97 ___ Durable General Power of Attorney. 💾
12.98 ___ Power of Attorney to Take Effect at a Later Time. 💾

WESTLAW Electronic Research

See WESTLAW Electronic Research Guide preceding the Summary of Contents.

§ 12.1 Scope Note

This chapter examines all aspects of the purchase and sale of real estate in the State of New York, including the contract of sale;[1] title insurance;[2] issues affecting title and marketability of title; closing of title;[3] and transfer taxes.[4] The checklist and in-depth analysis of the residential contract of sale included in this chapter use, as a starting point, a published form approved by the New York State Land Title Association, the Real Property Section of the New York State Bar Association, the Real Property Committee of the Association of the Bar of the City of New York and the Real Property Committee of the New York County Lawyers Association ("Approved Residential Contract").[5] *See* the discussion in Sections 12.7 through 12.32. The Approved Residential Contract provides, at a minimum, a standard or a checklist for those clauses which ought to be considered in drafting a contract for the

---

§ 12.1
1. *See infra,* §§ 12.7–12.39.
2. *See infra,* §§ 12.40—12.52.
3. *See infra,* §§ 12.53—12.71.
4. *See infra,* §§ 12.82—12.91.

5. The joint efforts of these committees of the Bar and the title insurers have resulted in the publication of the most commonly used forms which will be referenced in this chapter as "Approved" forms.

794

purchase and sale of real estate. Similar forms have been adopted for use in Condominiums and Cooperative transactions as well as for Office, Commercial and Multi-Family Residential Premises transactions ("Approved Standard Contracts"). A brief overview of each of these contracts, along with a comparison to the Approved Residential Contract follows in Sections 12.33 through 12.38. The complete text of each form appears in this chapter in Sections 12.93 through 12.96 with the permission of the publisher, Julius Blumberg, Inc. The forms were designed to be fair and well-balanced, and not to constitute either a "seller's" or "buyer's" contract. Nevertheless, clauses need to be added or modified to adjust each form to the facts of the transaction at hand.[6]

It is important to keep in mind that the preparation for entering into a contract for the sale of real property involves a great deal of planning and the collection of information. What follows in the various sections throughout the chapter must be carefully considered, even if a particular issue appears to be a "post-contract" issue. For example, in a conveyance of commercial property, the rent roll and the status of rent collection should be known prior to the execution of the contract. In all transactions, the condition of the property, as well as the existence or potential existence of violations imposed by governmental authorities, should be considered.[7] Moreover, actual or potential environmental and zoning issues should be addressed in the contract. For a discussion of these issues, *see infra* Chapter 15 "Environmental Law" and Chapter 16 "Land Use."

After the contract has been executed and the down payment or escrow has been arranged, the title must be examined. Title examination and issues involving surveys and marketability of title are dealt with in Sections 12.53 through 12.71. An examination of the issues to be taken up at the closing follows, with analysis of recording and regulatory requirements set forth in Sections 12.72 through 12.91. The chapter concludes with reprints of general power of attorney forms[8] and the standard forms of contract of sale.[9]

§ 12.2 Strategy

In a transaction involving the conveyance of real property the perspective is somewhat different depending on whether you are repre-

---

6. For a more complete discussion and analysis of the Real Estate Contract of Sale, *see* Rudolph deWinter, Real Estate Contracts and Conveyances in New York, A Practitioner's Handbook, Cal. No. 150, Julius Blumberg (1992); Milton R. Friedman, Contracts and Conveyances of Real Property (P.L.I. 5th ed. 1995).

7. CAVEAT: Counsel should also be aware of the Visual Artists Rights Act ("VARA")(17 U.S.C.A. § 106A) and its implications. VARA protects the artist's right to prevent modification of a work of art and there is an issue as to whether it operates as an easement or a negative covenant that runs with the property. *See* B. Rifkin, *Visual Artists Rights Act: An Easement or a Negative Covenant*, 24 New York Real Property Law Journal (Fall 1996). Accordingly, counsel should always investigate whether property contains art subject to VARA's protection.

8. *See infra*, §§ 12.97, 12.98.

9. *See infra*, §§ 12.93–12.96.

senting a seller, a buyer or a lender. Prior to utilizing the standard contract form set forth in this chapter or any other form contract and negotiating its terms, as much information as possible must be gathered from your client. For example, in representing the seller in a contract for the sale of residential real estate, the deed should be reviewed to ascertain the legal owners of the property and whether your client has the authority to convey title in fee simple, if the legal description of the property is accurately stated, and whether the deed was properly recorded. This information is also vital to the buyer's attorney, who will need to verify that the seller has the ability to convey free and clear title to the buyer.

Any survey that the seller may have should also be reviewed and passed on to the buyer's attorney. The buyer's attorney will want to confirm that the property being conveyed is the property that the buyer intended to buy. Similarly, the attorney for the lending institution will need to ensure the exact description and location of the mortgaged property so as to properly secure its interest in the land. The seller's attorney should also inquire as to the status of the structures on the premises and confirm that the seller has a certificate of occupancy for the premises and for any improvements made thereon. The lending institution and the title company will request copies of these certificates and the originals will be given to the seller at closing, as is usually required by the terms of the contract of sale.

Attorneys must also consider engineering or environmental concerns or matters relating to the occupancy of the premises which may not necessarily show up in the public records.

The attorney for the seller should inquire as to the client's plans upon transfer of title to determine whether it is necessary to include a possessory agreement in the contract of sale. Attorneys representing both parties will also want to identify any real estate brokers involved in the transaction so as to avoid a future claim by an undisclosed agent who was somehow involved in bringing the parties together or in the original negotiations. The point is, simply, to gather as much information as possible to ensure that all relevant issues and contingencies are properly addressed in the contract of sale. The information gathered will be critical not only for negotiating and drafting purposes, but for ensuring that all pre-closing issues are addressed and that all requirements of the lending institution and the title company will be satisfied.

Regardless of how familiar the practitioner is with the standard form contract, the issues must be considered anew with each transaction based on the particular circumstances surrounding the transfer. Use the checklist below as part of the information gathering process.

§ 12.3 Strategy—Pre-contract Checklist

Attorney for Seller. Seller's counsel should ascertain whether the seller has a properly executed and recorded deed in the seller's name, all proper certificates of occupancy and compliance for the structures to be conveyed, and a proper legal description of the premises. Counsel should also ascertain the names and addresses of all parties to the contract, the names of any real estate brokers involved in the transaction, the already agreed upon terms such as the purchase price, the down payment, the financing arrangements, the personal property to be specifically included or excluded in the sale, and any other facts peculiar to the particular transaction.

The seller's attorney should establish that the seller has made alternate living arrangements upon vacating the premises and whether there are any tenants occupying the premises that need to be removed prior to the conveyance. With this information in hand, the seller's attorney will be prepared to draft the proposed contract of sale.

The following documents should be gathered by the seller's attorney:

1. The contract pursuant to which seller acquired the property.
2. The title report which was marked up at the prior closing. (See §§ 12.53—12.55)
3. The survey of the property, if one exists. (See §§ 12.56—12.63) If none is available the seller's title company may be able to supply one for a modest charge.
4. The previous title policy, if any was issued (See §§ 12.45—12.52)
5. The original Owner's Duplicate Certificate of Title ("ODC") if the property is subject to the Torrens System. (See § 12.55)
6. The deed (See § 12.22)
7. A certificate of occupancy for all structures and improvements. (See § 12.24)
8. The rent roll, if applicable, and a list of the rents that are being collected and whether any are in arrears. (See § 12.36)
9. Any leases of any part or all of the premises, if applicable, whether or not recorded in the land records. (See § 12.36)
10. Existing mortgages to which title may be taken subject by the buyer (to determine any conditions in the mortgage which must be dealt with in the contract.) (See § 12.13)
11. Any agreement that has been entered into with a real estate broker, either between seller and broker or buyer and broker. (See § 12.31)
12. All underlying documents creating the condominium or cooperative (where appropriate). (See §§ 12.33—12.38)

Before drafting the contract, the seller's attorney should also obtain the following information:

13. Who currently occupies the premises and who may occupy the premises after the sale. (*See* §§ 12.7, 12.38)

14. Which personal fixtures are to be specifically included or excluded in the contract of sale. (*See* § 12.10)

15. The agreed upon method of payment, the amount of the down payment, whether a mortgage will be obtained by purchaser, etc. (*See* § 12.11)

16. Whether any governmental (federal, state, local, municipal) violations or notices of violation have been issued or received. (*See* § 12.18)

17. Whether any additions, improvements or structural changes have been made to the land or buildings since title was acquired by the seller. (*See* § 12.24)

18. The status of the seller as tenant in common, joint tenant, tenant by the entirety, corporation, Limited Partnership, Limited Liability Company, General Partnership, Trust, Executor, or operating under a Power of Attorney. Any documents necessary to establish the power to act must be obtained. (*See* §§ 12.8, 12.55)

Attorney for Purchaser. The purchaser's attorney should review the terms of the proposed contract of sale and the above documentation and confirm all of the agreed upon terms with his or her client. Purchaser's counsel will also discuss the financing details with the purchaser so as to ensure that the purchaser is adequately protected if the contract of sale includes a mortgage contingency clause and the details of any inspection done by the purchaser or an engineer to ascertain whether there are any potential problems regarding the structures being conveyed. In addition, purchaser's attorney will need to determine:

1. Engineering or other structural concerns that might warrant further investigation by a professional engineer.

2. Whether the premises is in compliance with environmental regulations.

3. For residential property compliance with lead paint hazard disclosure. (*See* § 12.80)

§ 12.4 Contract of Sale

The contract of sale is the single most critical document in any real estate transaction. It is the contract that fixes the rights and obligations of the parties from the date on which it is executed through the closing of title, and, in some cases, for a period of time beyond the closing.

A contract for the sale of real estate must be in writing.[1] To satisfy the Statute of Frauds, a contract must state the price, designate the parties, identify and describe the premises to be conveyed and state all the essential and material terms of the agreement.[2] A party will not be bound by any contract not signed by him or his duly authorized agent.[3]

§ 12.5 Contract of Sale—Preparation and Delivery

The contract for the sale of real property is ordinarily prepared by the seller's attorney, therefore any ambiguity in the language used in the contract of sale is generally resolved against the seller.[1]

Ordinarily, in a transaction of moderate proportions, the standard form of contract, appropriately adapted to the particular transaction, is used. The standard form of contract ("Approved Standard Contract") is a published form approved by the New York State Land Title Association, the Real Property Section of the New York State Bar Association, the Real Property Committee of the Association of the Bar of the City of New York and the Real Property Committee of the New York County Lawyers' Association. Approved Standard Contracts have been adopted for use in residential, condominium and cooperative transactions as well as for transactions involving office, commercial and multi-family residential premises.[2]

Five copies of the contract should be prepared for the convenience of all concerned. The original is usually retained by the seller, three copies are given to the purchaser and one is given to the real estate broker to substantiate his or her claim to a commission. The purchaser will, in turn, provide a copy of the contract to both the title insurance company and the lending institution. Note that a contract will not become effective until it is unconditionally delivered.[3]

§ 12.4

1. General Obligations Law § 5–703(2). However, General Obligations Law § 5–703(4) adds that, "Nothing contained in this section abridges the powers of courts of equity to compel the specific performance of agreements in cases of part performance." See Chapter 5, "Commercial Sales Contracts," *supra*.

2. Lerand Corp. v. Meltzer, 267 N.Y. 343, 196 N.E. 283, rearg. denied 268 N.Y. 546, 198 N.E. 396 (1935); Irvmor Corp. v. Rodewald, 253 N.Y. 472, 171 N.E. 747 (1930); Cooley v. Lobdell, 153 N.Y. 596, 47 N.E. 783 (1897); 160 Chambers St. Realty Corp. v. Register of the City of New York, et al., 226 A.D.2d 606, 641 N.Y.S.2d 351 (2d Dep't 1996); Marder's Nurseries, Inc. v. Hopping, 171 A.D.2d 63, 573 N.Y.S.2d 990 (2d Dep't 1991).

3. Mazzochetti v. Cassarino, 49 A.D.2d 695, 370 N.Y.S.2d 765 (4th Dep't 1975); Coppola v. Fredstrom, 45 A.D.2d 857, 358 N.Y.S.2d 538 (2d Dep't 1974); Crosson v. Mielcarek, 27 A.D.2d 690, 276 N.Y.S.2d 910 (4th Dep't 1967).

§ 12.5

1. Lo Biondo v. D'Auria, 45 A.D.2d 735, 356 N.Y.S.2d 679 (2d Dep't 1974).

2. The full text of these forms appear in §§ 12.93—12.96, *infra*. They are reprinted with the permission of the publisher, Julius Blumberg.

3. Senzamici v. Young, 174 A.D.2d 831, 570 N.Y.S.2d 760 (3d Dep't 1991); Manhattan Theatre Club, Inc. v. Bohemian Benevolent and Literary Assoc. of City of New York, 102 A.D.2d 788, 478 N.Y.S.2d 274 (1st Dep't 1984), aff'd 64 N.Y.2d 1069, 489 N.Y.S.2d 877, 479 N.E.2d 222 (1985); Besser v. K.L.T. Assocs., Inc., 42 A.D.2d 725, 345 N.Y.S.2d 659 (2d Dep't), aff'd 34 N.Y.2d

§ 12.6 Contract of Sale—Recordation

The best way for a purchaser to protect his or her interest in the real estate during the time between contract and closing is to record the contract. Sellers, however, will generally not want a contract to be recorded because it creates a potential cloud on title. The contract should provide specifically whether it may or may not be recorded.

By statute, a contract for the sale of real property or an instrument canceling a contract may be recorded in the office of the recording officer of any county in which any of the real property to which it relates is situated.[1] In lieu of recording the entire contract, a memorandum executed by the parties, and containing at least the names of the parties, the time fixed by the contract for the conveyance of title, and a description of the property, may be recorded.[2] A contract for the sale of real property that is not recorded is void as against any person who subsequently purchases, in good faith and for a valuable consideration, the same property or any portion of it from the same seller.[3]

A duly recorded contract is enforceable against a person who, subsequent to the recording and while the recording is effective, purchases the same real property or any part of it, even if in good faith and for valuable consideration. If the recorded contract provides for a down payment to be made prior to the conveyance of title, the lien of the purchaser arising from the payment is enforceable against any person who, subsequent to the recording and while it is effective purchases the same real property. The lien will be enforceable to the extent of any payment made, not exceeding the total amount specified in the recorded contract or memorandum.[4]

The recording is effective up to and including the thirtieth day after the day fixed by the contract for the conveyance of title. An agreement extending the time for the conveyance of title that is acknowledged and certified may be recorded and is then effective up to and including the thirtieth day after the day fixed by that agreement for the conveyance of title.[5] Note that once the recording has ceased to be effective, the contract becomes (1) void as against a subsequent purchaser in good faith and for a valuable consideration, who has no other notice of an interest of the contract vendee in the premises or of any claim thereof, and (2) ineffective to give notice to a subsequent purchaser of any interest of the contract vendee in the premises, or of any claim thereof, or to create any duty of inquiry.[6]

687, 356 N.Y.S.2d 295, 312 N.E.2d 478 (1974); Balsam v. Axelrod, 102 Misc.2d 1000, 424 N.Y.S.2d 814 (Sup.Ct., N.Y. County, 1979).

§ 12.6
1. RPL § 294(1).
2. RPL § 294(2).
3. RPL § 294(3).
4. RPL § 294(4).
5. RPL § 294(5).
6. RPL § 294(8)(a).

A contract will not be deemed recorded if it is recorded more than one year prior to the date on which the vendor acquired title to the real property to which the contract relates. Nor will an executory contract recorded before the date when the vendor acquired title be deemed recorded as against a person to whom the real property is conveyed or contracted to be sold or exchanged, by a conveyance or contract which is part of the transaction in which the vendor acquired title.[7]

Library References:
>West's Key No. Digests, Vendor and Purchaser ⚍26.

§ 12.7 Residential Contract of Sale

The following sections contain a discussion of the basic terms and conditions of the residential real estate contract, using the standard form Residential Contract of Sale (hereinafter also referred to as the Blumberg A125) as an illustration. The form is reprinted in Section 12.93, *infra*.

Riders are often used to elaborate on the mortgage contingency clause set forth in the standard form contract so as to clarify the rights and obligations of the parties (*e.g.*, when a purchaser applies for a mortgage in good faith, but subsequently does not qualify due to job loss), or to specify what constitutes a breach and when the seller will be entitled to keep the down payment as liquidated damages, or when the contract will be void and the purchaser entitled to a refund of the down payment.[1] Often times, a rider will also include a provision that the contract will be contingent upon an engineering, environmental or other type of inspection, as the circumstances may warrant. In addition, riders ordinarily provide that the contract will be contingent upon a satisfactory inspection of the premises by the purchaser within 24 hours of closing. Another common clause in a rider is to the effect that the contract will be subject to any facts that any accurate survey might show. Counsel for the purchaser must be careful with this clause so that the purchaser is not required to take title where a survey reveals facts which may render title unmarketable.[2] Another common use of the rider is to supplement the provisions set forth in the Approved Residential Contract as to the rights and obligations of each party if the seller is unable to convey marketable title.[3] It may also be necessary to include in a rider, a possessory agreement if there is a possibility that the seller will remain in possession after the purchaser has closed on the mortgage loan. The agreement should set forth a daily, weekly or monthly rate to be charged to the seller in possession, specify how adjustments are to be

---

7. RPL § 294(6).

§ 12.7
1. *See infra*, § 12.15.

2. *See infra*, §§ 12.56—12.63.
3. *See infra*, §§ 12.28, 12.29.

calculated at closing for items such as taxes or fuel and address the issue of risk of loss during the tenancy.

§ 12.8 Residential Contract of Sale—Parties

A contract for the sale of real property must be executed by parties who are legally competent and who have the legal capacity to sign the contract. Various parties and entities, such as fiduciaries, guardians, corporations, partnerships, and limited liability companies, have the legal capacity to convey real property in accordance with strict statutory requirements.[1] When a guardian *ad litem* is appointed, the party represented by the guardian must consent to the property transfer unless incapacity can be documented.

A party purchasing property from an attorney-in-fact for a principal must carefully examine the power of attorney to make certain that it authorizes the conveyance of the real property in question. For a power of attorney to be effective, it must be in writing, acknowledged and recorded in the same manner as a conveyance of real property.[2]

Powers of attorney are strictly construed,[3] and a practitioner must make certain that the instrument specifically authorizes whatever acts are being conducted on behalf of the principal. A power of attorney once granted continues to be effective until it is revoked by the principal. Any revocation must be in writing and acknowledged and must be known to the third party relying on the power. If relying upon a power of attorney, it is important to make certain that, at each step of the proceedings from the contract through the closing, the power of attorney has not been revoked and the principal is still living.[4] Indeed, title insurers will require proof or some form of verification that the grantor of the power of attorney is alive and competent at the time of closing. The most frequently used method of verification is a telephone call from the grantor in the presence of the relying party and a person who recognizes the voice of the grantor. An affidavit submitted by counsel who has spoken recently to the grantor will also suffice.

§ 12.8

1. *See infra,* § 12.55 for further discussion of the specific conveyance requirements for each party or entity listed.

2. *See* General Obligations Law §§ 5–1501 *et seq. See also* RPL §§ 294, 326; Davis v. Dunnet, 239 N.Y. 338, 146 N.E. 620 (1925).

CAVEAT: The power of attorney form must strictly adhere to the requirements set forth in the General Obligations Law, which even detail the point type size required. Laws governing the short form powers of attorney were amended in 1996. There is no grandfathering of prior executed forms of power of attorney to take effect at a future date.

There are two statutory short forms of powers of attorney—the Statutory Short Form of Power of Attorney (Attorney in Fact) and the Statutory Short Form of power of Attorney to Take Effect at a Later Time. They are reproduced *infra* in §§ 12.97, 12.98.

3. N.Y. Jur.2d § 68.

4. Weber v. Bridgman, 113 N.Y. 600, 21 N.E. 985 (1889). *See* General Obligations Law § 3–501 as to powers granted by persons in the military service.

There are two statutory short forms of powers of attorney—the Statutory Short Form Power of Attorney (Attorney in Fact) and the Statutory Short Form of Power of Attorney Effective at a Future Date. The first form is used to create a power of attorney that is unaffected by the subsequent disability or incompetence of the principal.[5] The second form, referred to as a "springing" power of attorney, is used to create a power of attorney that is to take effect upon the occurrence of a contingency, including but not limited to the incapacity of the principal.[6] The springing power of attorney must designate in writing the person or persons who may declare that such contingency occurred. The power granted takes effect upon the written declaration of the person or persons that the contingency has occurred without regard to whether or not it actually occurred.

The enumerated powers in the statutory forms are to be authorized by initialing the granted powers. Alternatively, the authorized powers may be listed by letter followed by the statement: "( ). Each of the above identified by the following letters." This statement must be initialed.[7]

Library References:

West's Key No. Digests, Vendor and Purchaser ⚚9–11, 59.

§ 12.9 Residential Contract of Sale—Premises

A contract for the sale of real property must describe the property to be conveyed. The description should be sufficient as to evidence a common intent of the parties to deal with a particular piece of property as distinguished from another property.[1] To accomplish this, the Approved Residential Contract (Blumberg A125) includes the following in the contract: the street address; the tax map designation (where one exists);[2] and a metes and bounds description.

5. General Obligations Law § 5–1501.
6. General Obligations Law §§ 5–1505, 5–1506.
7. Ch.499, L. 1996; General Obligations Law § 5–1501.

CAVEAT: Note that this form, which was amended in 1996 differs from the original version which required that the powers not granted be crossed out. Forms of power of attorney executed prior to October 1994 continue to remain effective under the preexisting law.

§ 12.9

1. Cooley v. Lobdell, 153 N.Y. 596, 47 N.E. 783 (1897) (a writing that is so indefinite in its description of the land that the intention of the parties cannot be gathered from it, is insufficient).
2. **CAVEAT**: Tax assessors are required to use tax maps for their assessment work pursuant to Real Property Tax Law § 503(1)(a). The preparation and maintenance of these maps are governed by Section 503(1)(b). For a discussion of the methods of preparation and filing requirements, see N.Y.Jur., Tax and Assessments, §§ 283—286. Although the taxpayer is chargeable for real estate taxes in the tax assessment records, the taxpayer is not chargeable for errors in the underlying description. Needless to say, discrepancies between the tax map and the filed map or metes and bounds can create serious problems which need to be resolved. This tax map is not the same as the filed map referred to above. The filed map recorded pursuant to RPL §§ 333 et seq. has the same effect as the metes and bounds description. Nevertheless, many counties are now requiring a notation of the tax map on recorded documents.

§ 12.9   PURCHASE & SALE OF REAL ESTATE   Ch. 12

The most important of the three is the metes and bounds description. A street address will generally not prevail over a metes and bounds description since it does nothing to identify the quantity of the property being conveyed.[3] Moreover, real property title records are not officially indexed according to house and street numbers, but rather according to the names of grantors and grantees, or to official section, block and lot numbers. A tax map designation must refer to a filed map.[4] The Approved Residential Contract form contains blanks in which to insert the street address of the premises and the tax map designation. Should any ambiguity arise as to the premises to be conveyed, the street address and tax map designation may be referenced to ascertain the intent of the parties.

The essential features of the metes and bounds description are clarity, definiteness and uniqueness. In other words, it should describe the parcel in clear, unambiguous language that could not apply to any other portion of the earth's surface. First the geographical area is pinpointed. Then, from a permanent starting point or monument, which may be a street corner, a mountain peak, a concrete monument or anything else that is reasonably immovable, the beginning point is fixed. From that point on, the courses and distances (or "metes and bounds") may be stated with greater or less difficulty depending upon the shape of the parcel—*i.e.*, the kind and number of angles and curves it involves, whether any line is parallel to any other line involved and so forth. Whenever possible, fixed monuments such as street corners, the sides of streets or lots on a filed map, and so forth, are referred to. This is important because if there is a conflict between the course and distance and the location of a fixed monument, the latter will generally govern.[5] If the land is improved, the description generally refers to "the buildings and improvements thereon."

The metes and bounds description is placed on a separate page marked "Schedule A," which is attached to the contract. Putting the description on a separate page and not in the body of the contract is a matter of convenience. Often a photocopy of the description from some other source, such as a prior deed or title report, can be obtained, thus

---

3. *See e.g.*, Huggins v. Castle Estates, 44 A.D.2d 25, 352 N.Y.S.2d 719 (4th Dep't 1974).

4. McPherson v. Schade, 149 N.Y. 16, 43 N.E. 527 (1896) (if the conveyance contains no other description than the lot number on a map which is not filed, title is unmarketable).

CAVEAT: A copy of the filed map should be examined to verify the dimensions of the property.

5. *See, e.g.*, Muhlker v. Ruppert, 124 N.Y. 627, 26 N.E. 313 (1891) (where the beginning point was said to be a point opposite the center of a party wall, a stated number of feet from the corner, and this distance was incorrectly stated, the center of the party wall controlled). *See also* Vaughan v. Commonwealth Land Title Ins. Co., 133 A.D.2d 626, 519 N.Y.S.2d 734 (2d Dep't 1987) (where the courses and distances description does not close, it is appropriate to conclude that the parties intended a conveyance of the parcel as described by monumentation).

obviating the need for re-typing and avoiding the chance of error in the description.[6]

Where the language in a description is susceptible of more than one interpretation and leaves the intent of the parties uncertain, parol evidence is admissible to prove the particular property to which the ambiguous description applies.[7] If a definitive identification can be made by the use of parol or extrinsic evidence, that is, if the writing can be expanded with exactitude, then the Statute of Frauds has been satisfied.[8] Note that the "rules" of construction with respect to legal descriptions are not harmonious in every case.[9]

The Approved Residential Contract also provides that along with the premises, the seller shall convey any interests in any land adjoining the premises, such as the bed of any street or highway, including any right to unpaid awards payable by reason of condemnation or damage.[10]

---

6. CAVEAT: The description as well as the deed by which the seller took title, should be carefully examined. The attorney should avoid thoughtless copying of a description from an old deed or contract inasmuch as there may have been a taking of a portion of the property for a street widening or other purpose. It is strongly urged that a "same as" clause (a clause reciting that the property to be transferred is the same as the property described in the recorded deed by which the seller took title) be used after a description which might well be helpful in curing a defect therein.

7. Smith v. Town of Warwick, 71 A.D.2d 618, 418 N.Y.S.2d 141 (2d Dep't 1979); Smith v. Slocum, 71 A.D.2d 1058, 420 N.Y.S.2d 814 (4th Dep't 1979) (parol evidence admissible where contract of sale described the property to be sold merely as property in the Town of Lima, Livingston County "on the west side of Route 15A (Rochester Road) consisting of a one-story metal building which houses the Robert Slocum Snowmobile Enterprise").

8. Piazza v. Sutherland, 53 Misc.2d 726, 279 N.Y.S.2d 640 (Sup.Ct., Suffolk County, 1967) (contract designated the realty as "the oval track," "the drag strip," 17 acres adjoining them, and another five-foot strip adjoining to the extent of about three acres, the description was sufficiently exact to satisfy the Statute of Frauds); Boyajian v. Casey, 52 A.D.2d 1014, 383 N.Y.S.2d 714 (3d Dep't 1976) (the description of the property was as follows: "approx. 106 Acres Book 488. Page 527 Recorded Saratoga Co. Clerks off. House and Barn. Except camp with Approx. 2 ½ Acres Seller gives right of way in front of camp on river bank." The court said that the main parcel was adequately described. As to the excluded property, the court held that, while standing alone, the description of same as a 2 ½ acre camp might possibly be too vague to satisfy the Statute of Frauds, the complete contract further specifies the general location of the camp, thereby warranting parol evidence to indicate its exact location).

But see Snay v. Wood, 50 A.D.2d 651, 374 N.Y.S.2d 809 (3d Dep't 1975) (where separate writings, constituting the memorandum, were devoid of any attempt to describe the property in question, the memorandum was insufficient). *See* Chapter 5 "Commercial Sales Contracts," *supra* for a discussion of the Statute of Frauds.

9. Shay v. Mitchell, 50 A.D.2d 404, 378 N.Y.S.2d 334 (4th Dep't 1976), aff'd 40 N.Y.2d 1040, 391 N.Y.S.2d 856, 360 N.E.2d 356 (1976) (a contract of sale and the conveyance delivered pursuant thereto described the subject property by metes and bounds, but concluded with the clause, "said parcel of land contains 40 acres of land, more or less." The court found that contract could not be rescinded by the buyer a year and a half later after finding out that the property contained only 31 acres.); D'Antoni v. Goff, 52 A.D.2d 973, 383 N.Y.S.2d 117 (3d Dep't 1976) (rescission was appropriate where the parties believed that about 15 acres were being sold when, in fact, and by mutual mistake, 68.38 acres were being conveyed).

10. *See* Chapter 14, "Eminent Domain Proceedings," *infra*.

§ 12.10 Residential Contract of Sale—Personal Property

It is important to specifically list all items of personal property and fixtures that are to be included or excluded in the sale. Real property generally includes land and things attached to or considered to be part of the land, such as buildings, fixtures, trees and shrubbery, minerals beneath and airspace above the land, and incidental rights such as a right to cross over other land for purposes of access to a public street. Since fixtures are attached to the real property and thus considered to be part of the conveyance, the seller must specifically exclude in the contract those fixtures that were not intended to be conveyed. The Approved Residential Contract lists a variety of fixtures such as plumbing, heating, lighting and cooking fixtures; cabinets and mantels; switch plates and door hardware; window treatments, storm windows and storm doors; TV aerials and cable facilities; shrubbery, fencing and tool sheds; kitchen and laundry appliances; and carpeting. The standard form states that these items are to be included in the sale unless specifically stricken from the contract.

Personal property is all other types of property, and generally means physical objects that can be moved or transported easily from one place to another, such as a television set or household furnishings and furniture. Personal property is not considered to be part of the real property being sold unless specifically included in the contract. The Blumberg A125 contains space to be filled in by the preparer indicating what specifically is to be included and excluded from the terms of the sale.

The practitioner should review this clause with the client prior to the preparation or execution of the contract. While these terms are ordinarily spelled out in the binder agreement, if there is one, the attorney is not always given this agreement and the parties may have made other agreements during negotiations. A binder is sometimes only a deposit contemplating a more formal contract. It has, however, sometimes been construed as an enforceable contract. A court may even provide the missing terms which are not essential to the determination that a contract was entered into.[1] It is best to clarify this in advance and be as specific as possible in the contract of sale so to avoid any surprises on the day of the closing.

---

§ 12.10
1. N.Y.Jur.2d § 179; Keystone Hardware Corp. v. Tague, 246 N.Y. 79, 158 N.E. 27 (1927).

§ 12.11 Residential Contract of Sale—Purchase Price and Method of Payment

The contract must specify the purchase price in order to satisfy the Statute of Frauds. The method of payment should also be stated in the contract even though this is not a requirement of the Statute of Frauds. If the contract is silent as to method of payment, it will be presumed that payment of the full amount will be paid in cash at the time of the closing.[1]

Library References:
West's Key No. Digests, Vendor and Purchaser ⟜12–15, 69–78, 168–187.

§ 12.12 Residential Contract of Sale—Purchase Price and Method of Payment—Down Payment

In a contract for the sale of residential property the parties generally agree that the down payment will be held in escrow, usually by the seller's attorney, until title actually closes or at least until the purchaser obtains a firm mortgage commitment. The down payment usually represents ten percent of the purchase price, although any amount may be agreed upon by the parties. Attorneys representing buyers should object to contract clauses allowing for the release of escrow funds prior to closing. Sometimes, however, builders will demand that the escrow funds be released, in which case the buyer will acquire a lien on the property for the amount of the deposit. This is known as a vendee's lien.[1]

A contract which requires that a down payment be held in escrow must identify the escrow agent and the bank in which the down payment is to be deposited during the term of the escrow.[2] The escrow agent has a fiduciary obligation to segregate and safeguard the down payment in a special bank account that cannot be commingled with the agent's personal or business funds. The agent is not required, however, to maintain a down payment in a bank account which is separate from all other bank accounts, provided that the agent's books of account and banking records accurately show the allocation to each owner of all funds that are deposited in the escrow agent's special bank account and all transactions relating to the receipt and disbursement of escrow funds.[3] Unless the contract provides otherwise, an escrow agent is not required to deposit

---

§ 12.11

1. 160 Chambers St. Realty Corp. v. Register of the City of New York, et al., 226 A.D.2d 606, 641 N.Y.S.2d 351 (2d Dep't 1996).

§ 12.12

1. *See* Lien Law § 71–a. *See infra*, § 12.39.

2. General Business Law Art. 36–C.

CAVEAT: These statutory provisions may be modified by a written agreement signed by the buyer, seller and escrow agent. The provisions are not exclusive and do not relieve a buyer, seller or escrow agent from compliance with all other applicable provisions of law, or from civil or criminal liability imposed by other applicable provisions of law.

3. General Business Law § 778–a.

the down payment in an interest-bearing bank account. If the agent is an attorney admitted to practice in New York, a bank account authorized by Judiciary Law § 497 is considered to be a lawful depository for down payments held in escrow.[4]

The Approved Residential Contract (Blumberg A125) calls for a "down payment" payable on the signing of the contract. The check is payable to the escrowee, or the seller's attorney, and is held in escrow until closing or termination of the contract. Whether or not interest is to be held for the parties is to be specified. Income taxes on any interest must be paid by the party entitled to the down payment. The form further provides that the down payment is to be paid to the seller at closing. If the closing does not take place and the escrowee receives notice demanding the down payment, the escrowee must give notice to the other party. If the escrowee does not receive an objection within ten days of notice, the escrowee is authorized to make payment as demanded. If, however, the escrowee does receive objection, the escrowee must continue to hold the down payment until otherwise directed by the parties or final court order or may pay it into court and be relieved of all further obligation.

Library References:

West's Key No. Digests, Vendor and Purchaser ⚖︎12–15, 69–78, 168–187.

§ 12.13 Residential Contract of Sale—Purchase Price and Method of Payment—Assumption of Existing Mortgage

If the seller has an assumable mortgage, the contract may provide for the purchaser to assume the obligation to pay the unpaid principal on the existing mortgage by joinder in deed. If the purchaser is to take title to the property subject to an existing mortgage, the purchaser will want assurance that the outstanding mortgage amount is not larger than the seller represented it would be at the date of the closing. To accomplish this, the seller is required to furnish at the title closing an estoppel certificate in recordable form, made by the holder of the mortgage, verifying the important facts as to unpaid principal and interest, maturity date, etc.[1] If the holder of the mortgage is holding an escrow fund for the payment of taxes and fire insurance, the certificate should also specify the amount of the fund, as the buyer will be required to purchase an assignment thereof from the seller. However, sellers' attorneys are cautioned that institutional lenders have almost universally refused to furnish formal estoppel certificates in recordable form but will issue informal letters instead. These letters are generally accepted by buyers'

4. *Id.*

§ 12.13
1. *See* RPL § 274–a.

attorneys and title insurance companies.[2] While the statutory obligation of a mortgage-holder to furnish an estoppel certificate or letter arises only if a demand is made in writing by registered or certified mail, reputable holders normally comply with informal written requests.

The Approved Residential Contract sets forth the amounts of principal, interest and escrows, if any, and specifies the monthly installment payment and due date. The form further provides for adjustments to be made for payments on the existing mortgage between contract and closing and that the escrow on the existing mortgage is to be assigned to the purchaser upon payment of the amount of the escrow by the purchaser to the seller at the closing. Seller is required to provide either a certificate in recordable form from the mortgagee stating the amount due. If the mortgagee is an institutional lender, a letter signed by a duly authorized officer, employee or agent may be substituted. The certificate or letter is to be furnished not more than 30 days before closing. The Approved Residential Contract form also requires the seller to represent and warrant that true copies of the existing mortgage, note and any extensions and modifications thereof have been delivered to the purchaser, that the existing mortgage is not in default and will not be at the time of closing, and that there is no due on sale clause.[3]

Library References:
West's Key No. Digests, Mortgages ⇔279–285; Vendor and Purchaser ⇔168–187.

§ 12.14 Residential Contract of Sale—Purchase Price and Method of Payment—Purchase Money Mortgage

The contract may provide that the seller will hold a mortgage on the property to be sold. The Approved Residential Contract requires that the mortgage be attached to the contract and drafted by the seller's attorney or that the standard form of the New York State Land Title Association be used. The purchaser is required to pay the mortgage recording tax, recording fees and attorney's fees.[1] Note that it is customary for the borrower to pay all expenses in connection with a mortgage, including the fee of the lender's attorney for drawing the mortgage instruments.

---

2. *But see* Grace v. Nappa, 46 N.Y.2d 560, 415 N.Y.S.2d 793, 389 N.E.2d 107 (1979) (purchaser did not have to accept less than a certificate executed and acknowledged in recordable form where the seller presented the purchaser canceled checks, an amortization schedule and a letter from the mortgagee which indicated among other things, that the mortgagee did not personally consider the mortgage to be "in good standing"; court found failure to deliver a certificate to be a material breach of the contract since, in light of the letter from the mortgagee, the purchaser could have reasonably anticipated that litigation with respect to the mortgage might ensue).

3. PRACTICE POINTER: A "due on sale" or "due on transfer" provision in a mortgage effectively would prohibit or at least make more difficult the assumption of a mortgage by a purchaser.

§ 12.14

1. *See infra*, §§ 12.74—12.89.

§ 12.14   PURCHASE & SALE OF REAL ESTATE   Ch. 12

If the seller is to take a purchase-money mortgage which is subordinate to a prior mortgage, it is important from the buyer's point of view that there be flexibility as to extending, refinancing or consolidating the prior lien. It is also important from the seller-junior-mortgagee's point of view that his or her position not be made less favorable. Hence, the form contains a provision regulating the interest rate of any extension, or replacement or consolidated mortgage, and the amount thereof. The maximum interest rate specified would normally be that of the prior mortgage. The clause also provides that if the principal amount exceeds the amount of the existing prior lien at the time of placing such new mortgage or consolidated mortgage, the excess must be paid to the junior mortgagee in reduction of his lien. However, such reduction shall not alter or affect the regular installments, if any, of principal payable thereunder. Thus, the junior mortgagee's relative position is maintained as he originally agreed. He is always "behind" the same amount of debt at the same rate of interest and the chance of default on the part of the owner is not made more likely by an increased prior obligation.

The standard form further provides that a purchase money mortgage will be subject and subordinate to any existing mortgage and extensions, modification, replacements or consolidations of that mortgage provided that the interest rate is not be greater than a stated percentage per annum and the total debt service not greater than a stated amount per annum. If the principal exceeds the amount of principal and interest owing on the existing mortgage at the time of placing the new or consolidated mortgage, the excess is to be paid to the holder of the purchase money mortgage in reduction of the principal and that payment will not alter regular installments of the purchase money mortgage and the holder will execute further subordination without charge.

Library References:

West's Key No. Digests, Vendor and Purchaser ⇔79, 168–187.

§ 12.15 Residential Contract of Sale—Purchase Price and Method of Payment—Mortgage Contingency

The purchase of most real estate is financed by the issuance of a mortgage by a lending institution; thus, contracts often provide for a mortgage contingency. The mortgage contingency clause is one of the most significant provisions in the contract and practitioners often supplement the contingency terms provided in the Approved Residential Contract by an additional rider.[1] The standard form states that the

§ 12.15
1. **CAVEAT**: Note that one of the faults of the Approved Standard Residential Contract (Blumberg A125) is that the purchaser is not protected once a conditional commitment is issued. Additional language may be

810

obligations of the purchaser to fulfill the terms of the contract are conditioned upon the purchaser obtaining a written mortgage commitment from an institutional lender[2] by a certain date, known as the Commitment Date. The agreed upon date is often 45 days from the contract date, the amount of time that it is usually anticipated to take to receive such a commitment. However, as a practical matter, so long as the purchaser has applied for the loan in good faith and has furnished the lending institution with all the required documentation, the parties usually will not cancel the contract if a commitment has not been issued by the date set.[3] The purpose behind this provision is to protect the buyer from being required to fulfill an obligation that he or she cannot fulfill[4] and conversely, to protect the seller from a buyer who is unwilling to pursue a mortgage in good faith so that the property is not tied up in a binding contract and thus can go back on the market for sale.

The Approved Residential Contract states the amount of the loan, as well as the interest rate, usually the prevailing rate, and that it not to exceed a certain amount so as to protect the buyer from having to accept mortgage terms that do not reflect the current market. The contract also indicates the length of the mortgage. Usually a buyer will state the maximum amount that he will apply for so as to protect himself and that the mortgage will be for a term of 30 years, even if he ultimately decides to commit himself to a higher payment under a 15 year program. In that way he will be in a position to turn down any unfavorable terms that are offered and avoid liability under the contract.[5]

---

necessary to provide for certain contingencies between commitment and closing. As a practical matter, if the purchaser's job is lost, the loan will not be closed on but the purchaser is not relieved of his obligation under the terms of the contract.

2. *See* Delsack v. Cumella, 189 A.D.2d 640, 593 N.Y.S.2d 2 (1st Dep't 1993) (court noted that definition of institutional lender, as defined by RPL § 274a, did not include a mortgage broker).

3. PRACTICE POINTER: The extension of time should be confirmed in writing.

4. *See, e.g.,* Aurrichio v. Rinaldi, 56 Misc.2d 663, 289 N.Y.S.2d 808 (Sup.Ct., Suffolk County, 1968) (after purchaser's application was denied, an extension of time for the purchasers to obtain a mortgage commitment was granted and subsequently, the purchasers made an application to another bank which was also disapproved. The purchasers then demanded the return of their down payment, but the sellers refused and wanted the purchasers to make a third application for a mortgage. The court held that the purchasers were under no obligation to proceed with a third application, particularly in the absence of any indication that the requirements of lending institutions had become more lenient, and upon the sale of the property to another, the purchasers were entitled to the return of their down payment, even though the contract period for cancellation for failure to obtain a mortgage had expired).

5. *See, e.g.,* Donato v. Baltrusaitis, 56 Misc.2d 935, 290 N.Y.S.2d 659 (Sup.Ct., Queens County, 1958). The purchasers were excused from performance and were entitled to the return of their deposit where a 20 year mortgage was specified and the only firm commitment made available to the purchasers was for 25 years. The court also held that where the purchasers had twice been refused a 20 year commitment and such a commitment could not have been obtained elsewhere within two days, the fact that the purchasers demanded return of their down payment two days before the date by which the commitment was to be obtained was not fatal to their action for return of their deposit.

§ 12.15   PURCHASE & SALE OF REAL ESTATE   Ch. 12

The Approved Residential Contract further provides that the purchaser shall make prompt application; furnish accurate information; pay all fees in connection with obtaining the loan; pursue the loan application with diligence; cooperate with the lender in furnishing all required information and documentation; promptly give notice to seller of the name of the lender or lenders to which the purchaser has made application; comply with all the requirements set forth in the conditional commitment; and promptly send a copy of the conditional commitment to the seller. In addition, if the purchaser fails to give notice or accepts a commitment that does not comply with the terms of the contract, the purchaser waives its right to cancel the contract and receive return of the down payment.

If, however, after good faith application is made, and a commitment is not issued by the commitment date, the purchaser may cancel the contract within five business days after the stated commitment date and the contract will be deemed canceled, along with all rights and obligations made by the parties, and the down payment will be returned.

The conditions under which the mortgage must be obtained and when the contract shall become void under this provision should be carefully drawn in an attached rider.[6]

Library References:
West's Key No. Digests, Vendor and Purchaser ⚖︎79, 168–187.

§ 12.16 Residential Contract of Sale—Purchase Price and Method of Payment—Acceptable Funds

The Approved Residential Contract states that payment of the purchase price will be made in cash, but not to exceed $1,000, and that the remainder shall be paid by certified or bank check of the purchaser unendorsed and payable to the order of the seller unless the seller otherwise directs on not less than three business days notice. Note that it is common practice for the purchaser to obtain a certified check payable to his or her own order and then to endorse it to the seller's order at the title closing. A purchaser's attorney may therefore question the desirability of the clause as it now reads and may prefer to have the requirement that the check be payable to the order of seller deleted. However, this method creates a problem of negotiability by the seller who may need the funds immediately after closing for another purchase. The requirement that the funds be paid by certified or bank check is important to the seller, particularly if he or she is simultaneously

---

6. *See, e.g.*, Loper v. O'Rourke, 86 Misc.2d 441, 382 N.Y.S.2d 663 (Sup.Ct., Suffolk County, 1976) (the language in the rider stated that the contract was conditioned upon the buyers' obtaining a *firm* mortgage commitment (as opposed to a conditional commitment) within 45 days from the contract date and that "the contract shall immediately become null and void, unless the time is extended by the parties by written agreement").

purchasing another home, because if the funds are not certified or in the form of a cashier's check, they cannot be drawn against until they have cleared. Therefore, this is an essential element of the contract and failure to comply will result in breach.[1]

The Approved Residential Contract further provides that money due to the seller other than the purchase price shall be by personal check in an amount not to exceed an agreed upon dollar amount. Finally, any other provisions for payment may be made and agreed to by the parties in writing.

Library References:

West's Key No. Digests, Vendor and Purchaser ⚖ 12–15, 69–78, 168–187.

§ 12.17 Residential Contract of Sale—Permitted Exceptions

The Approved Residential Contract allows the seller to convey title to the premises with certain permitted exceptions to title. These exceptions do not render title unmarketable and do not affect the purchaser's ability to obtain title insurance. The premises are conveyed subject to the following exceptions: zoning and subdivision laws and regulations, provided there is no violation; landmark, historic or wetlands designation, provided there is no violation; consents for the erection of structures on, under or above streets; encroachments of stoops upon any street or highway; real estate taxes that are a lien but are not yet due and payable; and any survey exception or other matters agreed upon by the parties.

§ 12.18 Residential Contract of Sale—Governmental Violations and Orders

Notices of building, fire, labor, health, etc., codes or regulations do not amount to encumbrances and do not affect marketability of title unless the contract provides that they will.[1] The Approved Residential Contract requires that the seller comply with all notices of governmental violations and orders issued as of the contract date and clear all such violations against or affecting the premises as of the date of the contract,

---

§ 12.16

1. *See, e.g.,* Colonial Diversified, Inc. v. Assured Holding Corp., 71 A.D.2d 1011, 420 N.Y.S.2d 419 (2d Dep't 1979) (where purchaser agreed to pay balance due at closing by "cash or good certified check," but prior to closing indicated to vendors that it would tender a check of the Small Business Administration drawn on the United States Treasury and that such check could not be certified, purchaser was defaulting party; consequently, purchaser was barred from recovering down payment, and was also liable for damages sustained by vendors by virtue of the default).

§ 12.18

1. Manhattan Life Ins. Co. v. Wall Investing Corp., 131 Misc. 363, 226 N.Y.S. 717 (Sup.Ct., Onondaga County, 1928), aff'd 223 App.Div. 833, 228 N.Y.S. 845 (1st Dep't 1928).

§ 12.18   PURCHASE & SALE OF REAL ESTATE   Ch. 12

prior to closing.[2] Therefore, the premises are to be conveyed free of violations at closing. The seller is required to furnish to the purchaser any authorizations that are necessary to make the searches that could disclose these matters.

A buyer's attorney might well try to induce the seller's attorney to amend this clause to apply to those violations in existence at the date of closing. However, the seller's attorney will most likely resist this point, as sellers have no desire to open the door to the buyers' having the premises inspected by all departments having jurisdiction, prior to the closing. If the seller does agree, a provision should be added to the effect that, should compliance exceed a stated maximum cost, the seller might cancel the contract upon return to the buyer of any payments made thereunder.

§ 12.19   Residential Contract of Sale—Seller's Representations

The seller makes very few representations in a real estate contract. The purchaser buys the premises as is, as discussed in the next section. The Approved Residential Contract does provide for a few standard representations as to the premises and as to the seller. With respect to the premises, the seller(s) represents that he, she or they are the sole owner(s) of the premises and has the right to convey the premises, that the premises abut or have access to a public road, and that the premises are not affected by exemptions or abatements of taxes. The seller also represents that the seller is not a foreign person as defined by FIRPTA[1] and that the seller has not been known by any other name for the past ten years, except any name inserted into the contract. This last requirement is really for the title company. The title company searches the chain of title and searches to ensure that there are no liens on the premises or judgments against the seller which need to be cleared before title can be properly conveyed to the purchaser. In order to complete a proper search, the title company needs to be aware of all names used by the seller.[2]

§ 12.20   Residential Contract of Sale—Condition of Property

There are no warranties as to the physical condition of the premises in a contract for the sale of real estate; therefore, even in the absence of

---

2. **CAVEAT**: If the premises are located in New York City, all obligations affecting the premises pursuant to N.Y.C. Administrative Code incurred prior to closing and payable in money shall be discharged by the seller prior to closing. Note that there is no survival provision.

§ 12.19
1. See infra, § 12.76.
2. See infra, § 12.55.

a clause so providing, every sale is made "as is."[1] The "as is" clause in the Approved Residential Contract provides that the purchaser has inspected the property, is aware of its physical condition, and agrees to purchase the property "as is" subject to reasonable wear and tear before closing. The form further provides that the purchaser will have the right to inspect the premises, after reasonable notice to the seller, prior to closing. This clause is ordinarily used to make it clear to the buyer that there will be no liability on the part of the seller (barring fraud) for defects which might later be discovered, and to negate the existence of any representations by the seller as to the particular condition, fitness, or type of construction of the premises. Note that the form contains a merger clause and a provision that the contract may not be changed (or terminated) orally, thereby foreclosing any possibility of the buyer asserting an alleged oral warranty made prior to, contemporaneously with, or subsequent to, the written contract.

The "as is" clause means that the purchaser must take that which he bargained for, reasonable use, wear, tear and natural deterioration excepted. It does not mean that the purchaser must accept property changed by intervening acts of destruction. Therefore, liabilities for risk of loss set forth in General Obligations Law § 5–1311 (Uniform Vendor and Purchaser Risk Act) will still govern.[2]

§ 12.21 Residential Contract of Sale—Insurable and Marketable Title

The Approved Residential Contract requires that the Seller convey, and the Purchaser accept, "insurable title" as the designated title company will approve and insure in accordance with its standard form of policy coverage as approved by the State Insurance Department.[1] The standard title insurance policy insures "marketable" title except for those matters to which exception is taken in the policy.[2]

§ 12.20

1. Salerno v. D'Alessandro, 213 A.D.2d 391, 623 N.Y.S.2d 305 (2d Dep't 1995) (purchasers barred from claiming fraudulent inducement where contract contained comprehensive and specific merger clauses pursuant to which the buyers agreed, among other things, that they were fully acquainted with the physical condition of the premises based on their own inspection and investigation, that they entered into the contract based solely on their own inspection and investigation, that they did not rely upon any representations written or oral as to the physical condition of the premises, that they were accepting the premises "as is" and, as to the property, neither party was relying on any statement not specifically contained in the contract).

2. *See* Approved Properties, Inc. v. City of New York, 52 Misc.2d 956, 277 N.Y.S.2d 236 (Sup.Ct., Richmond County, 1966). *See infra* § 12.32.

See also Citibank v. Plapinger, 66 N.Y.2d 90, 495 N.Y.S.2d 309, 485 N.E.2d 974 (1985); Danann Realty Corp. v. Harris, 5 N.Y.2d 317, 320–321, 184 N.Y.S.2d 599, 601–602, 157 N.E.2d 597 (1959); Risbano v. 3rd & 60th Assocs., 200 A.D.2d 658, 606 N.Y.S.2d 335 (2d Dep't 1994); Weiss v. Shapolsky, 161 A.D.2d 707, 708, 555 N.Y.S.2d 843, 844 (2d Dep't 1990).

§ 12.21

1. *See infra*, §§ 12.45—12.52.
2. *See infra*, § 12.50.

§ 12.21   PURCHASE & SALE OF REAL ESTATE   Ch. 12

This is probably the most important clause in the contract because unless there is good title to convey, the obligations under the contract cannot be fulfilled. Once the parties execute the contract, a title search is ordered to determine that the seller does indeed have good and unencumbered title to the premises described in the contract and thus, the ability to convey title to the purchaser and fulfill the obligations set forth in the contract.

Although, for practical purposes marketable and insurable title often are the same, they are not necessarily so. For example, if a title company has previously insured a title and overlooked a defect, it probably will insure title again even though the title may not be marketable, especially if it is a matter that time will cure. Thus, a contract should provide that title shall be marketable. Further discussion of marketable title and what renders title unmarketable is found in Sections 12.64 through 12.71.

Library References:

West's Key No. Digests, Vendor and Purchaser ⟶128–144(3).

§ 12.22 Residential Contract of Sale—Closing, Deed and Title

The Approved Residential Contract defines closing as the settlement of obligations of the parties, including payment of the purchase price and delivery of the type of deed specified in the contract in proper statutory form for recording, free of all encumbrances, except as otherwise stated, so as to provide the purchaser with fee simple title to the premises. The deed must be duly executed and acknowledged. The deed is to contain a covenant in compliance with Lien Law § 13.

In the New York City metropolitan area, a bargain and sale deed, with or without a covenant against the grantor's acts, is usually specified in the contract, while in some other areas of New York State a full covenant and warranty deed is generally specified. Bargain and sale deeds take two forms. They can be with or without covenants. In either case, the grantor conveys no greater estate than that which he or she owns. Most bargain and sale deeds contain a covenant as to grantor's acts to the effect that the grantor has done no act to encumber the land or affect title.

A full covenant and warranty deed contains six covenants: the covenant of *seisin*; the covenant of the right to convey; the covenant against encumbrances; the covenant of general warranty; the covenant of quiet enjoyment; and the covenant of further assurances. In addition to the six covenants, there is a warranty that the seller warrants only against the claims or the demands of those claiming through him or her but not against the paramount title, unless fraud can be proven by the buyer.

816

A quitclaim deed is a deed with no representations or covenants. It merely states that the grantor conveys whatever rights the grantor might have in the property.

Since almost all real estate transactions involve title insurance and most buyers substitute reliance on a title insurance policy for reliance on the grantor, a bargain and sale deed with covenants against grantor's acts is the most prevalent form of deed in use today. If the seller is a corporation, it must deliver to the purchaser at the time of closing a resolution of the board of directors authorizing the sale and delivery of the deed and a certificate executed by the corporate secretary certifying the resolution and that the transfer is in conformity with the requirements of Section 909 of the Business Corporation Law.[1] The deed itself must contain a recital sufficient to establish compliance with Section 909.

Library References:

West's Key No. Digests, Vendor and Purchaser ⚖145–159.

§ 12.23 Residential Contract of Sale—Closing Date and Place

A contract of sale should state the time and date of closing. If it does not, the law will imply a reasonable time and place. The Approved Residential Contract provides space to designate the time and place of closing. It is common practice to specify that a closing will take place "on or about" a specified date because, as a practical matter, the time of closing will most frequently be dictated by the lending institution and not the parties. The "on or about" clause is usually interpreted as being within 30 days of the closing date designated in the contract. The closing usually takes place at the offices of legal counsel for the lending institution.

If a "time is of the essence" clause is added to the contract, the failure of either party to perform on that date will excuse the other from performance, and will be a breach of the contract.[1] If the contract does not make time of the essence, one of the parties may make time of the essence by notice to the other party. If reasonable notice is given, the failure of either party to perform on that date will be considered a breach of contract. For a notice to be reasonable, it must bear a reasonable relation to the time elapsed after the closing date set forth in the contract of sale. There is no predetermined number of days that is required for such a notice. Each case must be examined on its own facts. A time of the essence notice should not be given until after the expira-

§ 12.22

1. *See infra*, § 12.54. *See* Chapter 1 "Business Organizations: Corporations," *supra*.

§ 12.23

1. **PRACTICE POINTER:** Note that the use of "on or before" for a closing date makes time of the essence.

tion of the closing date set forth in the contract. For example, if an "on or about" clause is used, notice that time is of the essence should not be sent until 30 days after the specified date. The time is of the essence notice should state the exact time of day, the date and the place of the closing. The notice should be given to the other party as well as to the other party's attorney.

Library References:
West's Key No. Digests, Vendor and Purchaser ⟐78, 145–159.

§ 12.24 Residential Contract of Sale—Conditions to Closing

The contract is subject to the fulfillment of certain conditions, as set forth in the Approved Residential Contract. The first condition is that the representations and warranties made by the seller at the time of the execution of the contract will still be accurate as of the date of the closing. The next condition requires the seller to deliver to the purchaser a valid certificate of occupancy or other certificate of compliance covering the building or buildings and all improvements located on the premises being conveyed and, if applicable, authorizing its use as a multi-family residence.[1]

Formerly a duly executed and sworn Real Property Gains Tax Law affidavit was required as well but the law was repealed effective June 16, 1996.[2] Additional documents that are to be delivered at the time of closing by the seller include the following:

- A certification that seller is not a foreign person;[3]
- A smoke alarm affidavit if the premises include a one or two family house;[4] and
- Any other affidavits required as a condition of recording the deed[5]

These documents are provided by the representative of the title company and are executed at the time of the closing.

The premises are to be delivered, with keys, broom clean, vacant, and free of tenancies. Plumbing (including water supply and septic systems, if any), heating and air conditioning, electrical and mechanical

---

§ 12.24

1. PRACTICE POINTER: The buyer will want to include language in the contract requiring the delivery of a certificate of occupancy for all structures on the premises requiring such certificate. *See, e.g.,* Masi v. Iwanski, 136 A.D.2d 609, 523 N.Y.S.2d 588 (2d Dep't 1988) (where seller's attorney had deleted language requiring delivery of certificate of occupancy for all structures requiring one and merely stated that the seller would deliver the original certificate of occupancy, and the seller did not deliver a certificate for a one-car garage that was converted into a family room or for a constructed two-car garage, the court found that the seller was not obligated to under the contract).

2. *See* Tax Law Art. 31–B; *see infra*, § 12.84.

3. *See infra*, § 12.76.

4. *See infra*, § 12.90.

5. *See infra*, §§ 12.75—12.90.

systems and equipment and all appliances are to be in working order as of the date of closing. The purchaser has the right to inspect the premises prior to closing at reasonable times and upon reasonable notice to the seller.

Library References:

West's Key No. Digests, Vendor and Purchaser ⚖︎145–159.

§ 12.25 Residential Contract of Sale—Deed Transfer and Recording Taxes

Articles 31 and 31-B of the Tax Law require that the seller pay a transfer tax upon the transfer of real property. In addition, the cities of Yonkers and Mount Vernon require the payment of a separate and additional transfer tax.[1] New York State imposes a mansion tax upon the purchase of a one, two, or three family dwelling (cooperative apartment or condominium unit) where the purchase price is one million dollars or more. The Approved Residential Contract requires that the seller pay the tax at closing by certified or bank check, and submit any required tax returns, duly acknowledged and executed. The seller must make certain that any check and return required to be delivered is delivered promptly after the closing. The obligation to pay any additional tax or deficiency and any interest or penalties survives the closing. As a practical matter, the seller makes payment to the representative of the title insurance company, who, in turn, ensures proper delivery to the appropriate officer.

Article 11 of the Tax Law[2] requires the payment of a mortgage recording tax. The Approved Residential Contract imposes on the borrower the same requirements as are imposed on the seller, as discussed above, with respect to the payment of transfer taxes.

§ 12.26 Residential Contract of Sale—Apportionments

There are certain costs that must be adjusted between the buyer and the seller at the closing of title. Typically, real estate taxes, water and sewer charges, rents, and home heating are items that are adjusted at closing.

The Approved Residential Contract provides for apportionments of the following, to the extent they are applicable, as of the day before the date of closing: taxes; water charges and sewer rents, to be made on the basis of the fiscal period for which they are assessed; fuel; interest on existing mortgage; premiums on existing transferable insurance policies; vault charges; and rents, as and when collected.

§ 12.25
1. *See infra*, §§ 12.82—12.85.

2. Tax Law §§ 250 *et seq. See infra*, §§ 12.86, 12.87.

§ 12.26   PURCHASE & SALE OF REAL ESTATE   Ch. 12

The contract further provides that if closing occurs before a new tax rate has been fixed, the apportionment of taxes shall be based on the tax rate for the immediately preceding fiscal period applied to the latest assessed valuation. If there is a water meter on the premises, the seller is required to furnish a reading not more than 30 days before the date of closing and apportionments are made on the basis of that reading. If the premises are affected by an annual installment assessment and the first installment is a lien or has been paid, the seller is required to pay the entire assessment at or prior to closing.

If the property is being conveyed with tenants-in-possession, the rents must be adjusted. Since most rents are payable monthly, adjustments are typically prorated based on the number of days in the month. If a tenant has posted a security deposit, the security deposit should be assigned or credited to the purchaser at the time of closing.[1]

§ 12.27 Residential Contract of Sale—Allowance for Unpaid Taxes

The seller may credit the purchaser with unpaid taxes, water charges and sewer rents at the time of closing. The credit to the purchaser must have added to it interest and penalties to a date not less than five business days after the closing.

If, at the date of closing, there are liens or encumbrances which the seller is obligated to pay and discharge, the seller may use any portion of the balance of the purchase price to satisfy them. To exercise this option, the Blumberg A125 provides that the seller must deliver to the purchaser, at the closing, satisfaction instruments in recordable form, along with any recording or filing fee. In addition, the seller must notify the purchaser upon three days prior notice so that the purchaser may provide separate certified or bank checks as requested to clear up these matters.

Alternatively, the seller may make arrangements with the title company employed by the purchaser in advance of closing, to deposit with the company sufficient moneys required to assure discharge, but only if the title insurance company will insure title to the purchaser and the lending institution free of any such liens and encumbrances, or with insurance against enforcement of them out of the insured premises.[1]

§ 12.26

1. **CAVEAT**: The collection and keeping of security deposits should be in compliance with applicable laws. *See* General Obligations Law §§ 7–101 *et seq.*

§ 12.27

1. **CAVEAT**: This provision accommodates a seller who may not wish to or be in a position to fully satisfy a lien or encumbrance at the time of the closing, but who is willing to make an escrow deposit with the purchaser's title company to assure its eventual satisfaction of record. Obviously the title is unmarketable, even though it has been insured as stated, until the lien or encumbrance is satisfied of record. In the meantime, a purchaser in this situation will very likely have difficulty if he wishes to sell or mortgage the premises. Buyers' at-

§ 12.28 Residential Contract of Sale—Title Examination; Seller's Inability to Convey; Limitation of Liability

A real estate contract will almost always be contingent upon the seller's ability to convey, at the very least, insurable title. The Approved Residential Contract provides that the purchaser must order a title examination[1] promptly after execution of the contract, or, if the contract contains a mortgage contingency clause, after the commitment has been issued and accepted by the purchaser. The purchaser must then deliver a copy of the title report to the seller's attorney promptly after receipt. If the examination reveals defects in title (*i.e.*, liens, encumbrances or objections), so that the seller is unable to convey in accordance with the requirements of the contract or the purchaser has valid grounds for refusing to accept title, the seller may take action to remove the defects or cancel the contract. If the seller elects to cancel the contract, the seller is then obligated to refund to the buyer the amount paid on the purchase price and to pay the net cost of examining title and other costs incurred in connection with examination of title, such as survey costs. If the seller elects to take action to remove the defects, the seller may adjourn the closing for a period not exceeding 60 days but not beyond the expiration of the purchaser's mortgage commitment. If the seller does not remove the defects by the expiration of the adjournment date, either party may cancel on 10 days notice. In any case, any existing mortgage (unless assumed) and any matter created by the seller after the date of the contract must be satisfied by the seller at or prior to the closing. Note that any obligation to a broker will survive termination of the contract.

This clause may be supplemented in the rider to provide additional options for the purchaser or to further limit the seller's liability. For example, the purchaser may want the option to elect to accept whatever title the seller is able to convey. A seller may want to include language to the effect that the seller will not be required to bring any action or proceeding or to incur any expense in excess of a specified amount to cure any title defect or to enable the seller to otherwise comply with the provisions of the contract.[2]

As discussed in the next section, courts will *carefully* construe this clause when determining the extent of the seller's liability in cases where title is defective.

torneys should approach this provision with the utmost circumspection.

§ 12.28
1. See *infra*, §§ 12.53—12.55.

2. See *infra*, § 12.93. The clause contained in this contract is more comprehensive and may be incorporated into the rider attached to the Approved Residential Contract.

§ 12.28   PURCHASE & SALE OF REAL ESTATE   Ch. 12

Library References:

West's Key No. Digests, Abstracts of Title ⊙–1–3; Vendor and Purchaser ⊙–145–159, 334–353.

§ 12.29 Residential Contract of Sale—Defaults and Remedies

The Approved Residential Contract provides that if the purchaser defaults, the seller's sole remedy is retention of the down payment as liquidated damages. If the seller defaults, the purchaser is entitled to specific performance and any other remedies to which the purchaser is entitled at law or in equity.

Notwithstanding that a buyer may have established his or her substantive right to enforcement of a contract for the sale of real property, where the remedy sought is specific performance rather than damages, the courts will not grant the equitable remedy unless it appears that it would lie within the capability of the seller to comply with the court's direction. The court will not make what may prove to be a futile order. That the seller may not have been able to convey good title when the action was commenced is irrelevant if the seller is able to do so when the court makes its order.[1]

The parties to a contract for the sale of real property may agree to restrict the liability consequent upon a breach or may agree that no damages will be payable at all once the *status quo* has been restored. Implicit in such a limitation is the obligation to act in good faith and the existence of a situation beyond the control of the parties.[2]

In determining the extent of the seller's liability upon the inability to convey marketable title, the courts will look to the facts of the case and the language of the contract. For example, in a case where the vendee agreed to accept insurable title subject to the facts shown on the survey and the survey failed to reveal the existence of an encroachment from the adjoining premises which the title company excepted from coverage, the vendor could not convey insurable title as called for in the contract, and was required to refund the vendee's down payment pursu-

---

§ 12.29

[1]. S.E.S. Importers, Inc. v. Pappalardo, 53 N.Y.2d 455, 442 N.Y.S.2d 453, 425 N.E.2d 841 (1981). *But see* Shepard v. Spring Hollow at Sagaponack, 87 A.D.2d 126, 450 N.Y.S.2d 547 (2d Dep't 1982) (here, the answer admitted to nonconformance and the seller had tendered return of the down payment; thus, there was no need for judicial resolution as there was in S.E.S. The court reasoned that since the seller's inability to deliver was not self-created, its right to limit its liability should not be further inhibited; thus, the buyer's exclusive remedy was the return of the down payment and reimbursement for survey and title examination costs).

[2]. Mancini–Ciolo, Inc. v. Scaramellino, 118 A.D.2d 761, 500 N.Y.S.2d 276 (2d Dep't 1986) (on the closing date, the vendors were unable to convey the property in accordance with the contract because of the exercise of a right of first refusal of third parties; thus, the liability of the vendors was limited by the contract clause).

ant to the contract.[3] Similarly, where there was a valid objection to title under the contract, which the court held required a certificate of occupancy to be obtained by the seller, and the certificate could not be obtained because there was a natural slope of the dwelling that created a hazardous condition, specific performance was denied. The court held that the contract did not impose an affirmative duty on the seller to secure the certificate by performing the work required to correct the condition. Thus, specific performance was denied and the purchaser was limited to the recovery of his deposit and the net cost of title examination.[4]

However, where the contract provides that a purchaser may accept such title as the seller is able to convey, specific performance may be the appropriate remedy. In a case where a paragraph in the contract of sale provided that if the seller was unable to transfer to the purchaser in accordance with the contract, the seller's sole liability was to refund moneys paid on account of the contract plus charges, specific performance in favor of the purchasers was not precluded upon the inability of the vendor to obtain a certificate of occupancy since the rider to the contract specifically provided that the purchasers possessed the right to accept such title to the premises as the seller was able to convey.[5] The court noted that the contract provision did not provide the seller with the unilateral right to cancel the contract, but rather was solely intended to limit his liability in the event that he was unable to transfer title to the premises to the purchasers.

In another case, where the contract made its cancellation and return of purchaser's down payment, together with title search expenses, a consequence of the seller's failure to obtain a proper certificate of occupancy on the adjourned closing date, the question of whether the seller was able to cure the defect within a reasonable time after that date

---

[3]. Costa v. District Nursing Assoc. of Northern Westchester, Inc., 175 A.D.2d 274, 572 N.Y.S.2d 727 (2d Dep't 1991).

[4]. Sloan v. Pinafore Homes, Inc., 34 A.D.2d 681, 310 N.Y.S.2d 731 (2d Dep't 1970).

[5]. Knight v. McClean, 148 A.D.2d 421, 538 N.Y.S.2d 576 (2d Dep't 1989); *see also* Caira v. Bell Bay Properties, Inc., 143 A.D.2d 870, 533 N.Y.S.2d 550 (2d Dep't 1988). *But see* Armstrong Properties, Inc. v. Glasso, 141 A.D.2d 687, 529 N.Y.S.2d 572 (2d Dep't 1988) (purchaser was not entitled to specific performance of the contract for sale of a lot where the vendor represented that the conveyance would be a legal building plot and a building permit could not be issued unless a variance was obtained. The vendor refused to apply for a variance claiming it was unnecessary and offered to terminate the contract. The purchaser refused and sought to have the vendor specifically perform by conveying a legal building plot. The court held that the purchaser was not entitled to specific performance of the contract. Assuming, arguendo, that a variance was necessary in order for the subject property to constitute a legal building plot, the contract did not require the defendant to obtain such a variance. Further, the contract provided that if the defendant was unable to transfer title in accordance with the contract, his sole obligation was to refund all moneys paid by the plaintiff on account of the contract, plus all the costs of the title examination and the survey. Although this paragraph was similar to the paragraph in Knight, there was no clause allowing the purchaser to accept such title as could be conveyed).

was irrelevant. The court found that, because the contract provided for its cancellation, it did not allow any further adjournments, however reasonable the period.[6] Specific performance was also denied where a contract provided that the sole remedy available to the purchaser, under the terms of the contract prepared by him, was the return of the deposit and the reasonable costs of examining title. The court found that it was within the power of the parties to provide for such limitation of liability.[7]

Contracts may provide for other damages as well. A vendor, whose title was defective for lack of a sufficient description, was held liable for a surveyor's fee for a consultation which disclosed the defect, although no survey was in fact actually made.[8] However, in a case where a contract did not provide for the recovery of counsel fees by the buyer, such fees were held not to be recoverable.[9]

Damages for lost profits based on the seller's breach of contract for the sale of real property are available for the failure to convey real property pursuant to a contract in cases of bad faith or willful disregard of the contract.[10] If the vendee knows of the vendor's inability to convey title when the parties entered into the contract, however, the vendee's damages are not measurable by the loss of his bargain.[11]

Library References:

West's Key No. Digests, Vendor and Purchaser ⬢246–331, 334–353.

§ 12.30 Residential Contract of Sale—Assignment

A contract should specify whether it is assignable. The Approved Residential Contract prohibits the purchaser from assigning the contract without the prior written consent of the seller. This serves to protect the seller where there is a mortgage contingency clause. A purchaser may be either pre-qualified or certain that he or she will qualify for the intended financing, but the financial status and ability of an assignee to qualify will not necessarily be known and the assignee may not qualify.

Library References:

West's Key No. Digests, Vendor and Purchaser ⬢207, 214.

---

6. Delegated Properties, Ltd. v. Lewis, 36 A.D.2d 766, 321 N.Y.S.2d 234 (2d Dep't 1971).

7. Scerbo v. Robinson, 63 A.D.2d 1096, 406 N.Y.S.2d 370 (3d Dep't 1978).

8. Iannelli Bros., Inc. v. Muscarella, 30 A.D.2d 698, 291 N.Y.S.2d 851 (2d Dep't 1968).

9. Atlas Realty of East Meadow, Inc. v. Ostrofsky, 56 Misc.2d 787, 289 N.Y.S.2d 784 (Sup.Ct., Nassau County, 1967).

10. Camperlino and Fatti Builders, Inc. v. Dimovich Constr. Corp., 198 A.D.2d 803, 604 N.Y.S.2d 389 (4th Dep't 1993), leave to appeal dismissed 83 N.Y.2d 906, 614 N.Y.S.2d 388, 637 N.E.2d 279 (1994).

11. Kessler v. Rae, 40 A.D.2d 708, 336 N.Y.S.2d 680 (2d Dep't 1972); Diamond Central, Inc. v. Gilbert, 13 A.D.2d 931, 216 N.Y.S.2d 609 (1st Dep't 1961).

§ 12.31 Residential Contract of Sale—Broker

The Approved Residential Contract includes a representation that the parties have not dealt with any broker other than the one named in the contract and an agreement that the parties will indemnify each other against costs arising out of breach of their respective representations. The purpose of the clause printed in the standard form of contract of sale is to protect the seller against the buyer's subsequently taking the position that a broker other than the one named brought about the sale. The representation on the part of the buyer is for the protection of the seller and not the broker. The latter may not sue the buyer on the contract of sale; the broker's remedy is by action upon his brokerage contract.[1] It is beyond the purview of this chapter to examine brokerage agreements.

Library References:

West's Key No. Digests, Brokers ⚖1–106.

§ 12.32 Residential Contract of Sale—Risk of Loss

The contract for the sale of real property should contain a risk of loss clause. As a practical matter, sellers are willing to assume the risk of loss because they have casualty insurance to cover that risk. A risk of loss clause will typically allow a buyer to cancel a contract if there is damage beyond some agreed upon amount such as a percentage of the purchase price. The clause should also provide that ordinary wear and tear between the date of contract and the date of closing is an acceptable condition and not covered by the risk of loss clause.

Risk of loss of real property is governed by the General Obligations Law,[1] while risk of loss of personal property is governed by the Uniform Commercial Code.[2] This distinction may be significant in a contract involving the sale of both real and personal property. In a case where the real property for sale included a sculpture which disappeared between contract and closing, and the contract did not state which party was to bear the risk of loss, the court held that the risk of loss was governed by the rules relating to personal property rather than by the rules relating to real property.[3] The court did state, however, that it was mindful of the anomaly which may be implicit in applying different risk of loss rules to real property and personal property sold under the same contract and indicated that the finding as to which rules should govern might vary if

---

§ 12.31

1. Warsawer v. Burghard, 234 App.Div. 346, 254 N.Y.S. 749 (1st Dep't 1932).

§ 12.32

1. General Obligations Law § 5–1311.

2. UCC § 2–509(3).

3. Deitch v. Shamash, 56 Misc.2d 875, 290 N.Y.S.2d 137 (Civ.Ct., N.Y. County, 1968).

the lost or destroyed property was that which customarily accompanies realty, such as blinds, refrigerators, etc.[4]

Library References:

West's Key No. Digests, Vendor and Purchaser ⇌203.

§ 12.33 Condominium Contract of Sale[1]

While it is beyond the scope of this chapter to discuss the creation and administration of a condominium, practitioners should be aware of the special considerations involved in the transfer of a condominium unit. It should also be recognized that many of the inspection clauses in a typical contract for sale may be of less importance in a condominium purchase since the common elements are maintained by the condominium association. The practitioner representing a party in the transfer of a condominium unit must read the underlying documents creating the condominium inasmuch as they may contain easements, restrictions, the mechanism for making common assessments, and other matters that are of critical importance to a buyer.

Library References:

West's Key No. Digests, Condominium ⇌4, 15.

§ 12.34 Condominium Contract of Sale—Comparisons to the Residential Contract of Sale

The contract of sale of a condominium unit is for all practical purposes very similar to the Approved Residential Contract. The form contract of sale referred to in this section, the Approved Condominium Contract, was drafted by a committee of the Association of the Bar of the City of New York.

The principal differences between the Approved Condominium Contract and the Approved Residential Contract are those provisions and representations dealing with (1) the validity of the formation of the Condominium regime pursuant to Article 9B of the Real Property Law; (2) compliance with Section 352(e) of the General Business Law ("the Martin Act"); (3) requisite actions required of the Board of Managers in connection with a sale; (4) waivers of a right of first refusal of the condominium association with respect to a contemplated purchase; and

---

4. *Id.*, 56 Misc.2d at 877, 290 N.Y.S.2d at 138.

§ 12.33

1. *See infra*, § 12.94, Form of Condominium Contract of Sale (Julius Blumberg Inc.).

(5) payment of common charges by the seller.[1]

Another significant difference between the contracts is the description of the property. The description includes reference to the specific condominium unit number to be conveyed and the percentage interest in the common elements, as set forth in the Condominium Declaration, the filed instrument by which the condominium property is declared to be in compliance with the Real Property Law,[2] and its bylaws as it is or may be amended. No specific provision is made for a description of the overall property or for a tax map designation, although the latter should be included along with the street address. There is also no reference to the conveyance of any interest in streets or unpaid awards.

There are also differences in the closing adjustments clauses in the two contracts. The adjustment clause in the condominium contract provides for the apportionment of the following: common charges, which are typically due monthly; water charges and sewer rents, if separately assessed for the unit; fuel, if separately stored for the unit; and any unpaid assessments. Listed as a condition to closing is a waiver of the right of first refusal exercisable by the board of managers.

Another important distinction is that the condominium contract does not provide either for marketable or insurable title *per se*, but requires the seller to comply with the reasonable requirements of a licensed New York title insurer to omit an exception.

Note also that unlike the Approved Residential Contract, the Approved Condominium Contract has no space for an escrowee's signature.

Library References:

West's Key No. Digests, Condominium ⊕4, 15.

§ 12.35 Condominium Contract of Sale—Homeowner's Associations

Homeowners' Associations are a common law form of arrangement between two or more property owners bearing some similarity to the common elements aspects of a condominium. The Homeowners' Association may be a part of a condominium or separate from it; accordingly, transfer and title issues may be separate.[1] In fact, the Homeowners'

---

§ 12.34

1. For a more complete discussion of the condominium requirements, *see* Certilman and Adler, Real Estate Titles, Ch. 25 (N.Y.S.B.A. 1994).

2. The Condominium Act is set forth in Article 9–B of the RPL.

§ 12.35

1. The Approved Condominium Contract in § 12.94 *infra*, does not contain any special language with respect to Erie County. Paragraph 6 of the Erie County Bar Association 1992 Combined Condominium and Homeowners' Association Contract provides the following language:

DEED (a) If the property is part of a Homeowners' Association and not part of a Condominium, at closing, seller shall

Association may not be related to a condominium but to a group of separate property owners who may want to share the expenses and costs of a common facility including recreation, road maintenance or other amenities. The typical documents of creation of a homeowner's association will include (1) covenants and restrictions, (2) clustering of lots, (3) the organizational framework of the association, (4) easements of use and enjoyment, and (5) obligation to pay assessments.

A purchaser should obtain copies of the most recent bylaws and certification from an appropriate authority that assessments and *ad valorem* taxes, if any, have been paid. It should also be ascertained if the association is structured as a not-for-profit entity. In addition, it would be prudent to examine the most recent six month period of board of directors' minutes. The lien status of any assessments should be ascertained together with the financial status of the Association as a whole.

The homeowners' association must also comply with the requirements of Section 352-e of the General Business Law and file its declaration with the Attorney General of New York. However, the current policy of the Attorney General's office is to issue a no action letter. This means neither approval nor disapproval, but the enforcement provisions of the General Business Law (the Martin Act) are applicable.

Library References:

West's Key No. Digests, Condominium ⚖8.

§ 12.36 Contract of Sale for Office, Commercial and Multi-family Residential Premises

The standard form Commercial Contract of Sale was approved by the Real Property Committee of the Association of the Bar of the City of New York ("Approved Commercial Contract").[1]

One of the unique features of the Approved Commercial Contract is that except for the purchase price and the signatures of the parties (seller and purchaser) and the escrowee, all of the specific information and details of the transaction are inserted on the last page. Highlights of the Approved Commercial Contract include the following:

deliver to purchaser a warranty deed (or fiduciary deed where appropriate) with lien covenant giving good and marketable title in fee simple, free and clear of all encumbrances, except as stated in this Contract. In the event seller is a corporation, seller may deliver to purchaser a bargain and sale deed with covenant against grantors' acts.

(b) If the property is part of a condominium, seller shall tender to purchaser at closing a bargain and sale deed with lien covenant conveying insurable title and free of all encumbrances, except as otherwise provided herein or except where affirmative coverage is available. The deed must comply with the requirements of 339-o of the Real Property Law.

§ 12.36

1. *See infra*, § 12.95, Form of Contract of Sale—Office, Commercial and Multi-Family (Julius Blumberg Inc).

Ch. 12 CONTRACT OF SALE FOR OFFICE § 12.36

1. Description. The description of the premises includes a more detailed and expanded definition than in the Residential Contract of Sale discussed in §§ 12.7 et seq. The description is contained in Schedule A and includes a tax map designation.

2. Personal Property. The sale includes all personal property. Any exclusions should be separately provided for.

3. Purchase Price. The purchase price is payable in compliance with the terms of an attached Schedule C. There are also extensive provisions with respect to the contents of a purchase money mortgage.[2]

4. Mortgage Contingency. There is no mortgage contingency clause. Each transaction has its own special circumstances.

5. Permitted Exceptions. These are included in an attached Schedule B.

6. Governmental Violations and Orders. There is additional language with respect to the responsibilities of the parties for the clearing of governmental violations and orders than is contained in the Residential Contract of Sale.

7. Seller's Representations. These are much more extensive than in the Residential Contract of Sale. There is also a limitation date specified for certain representations which survive closing. No action can be brought after the specified date.

8. Condition of Property: There is additional language which deals with destruction damage and condemnation.

9. Title Company Approval—Insurable Title. The concept used is acceptable fee simple title, subject to permitted exceptions set forth in Schedule B.

10. Closing Deed and Title. This clause is substantially more sophisticated than those of the contracts discussed above.

11. Conditions to Closing. The seller is required to deliver a bargain and sale deed without covenants, and all leases, security deposits, rent schedule and service contracts, among other and more extensive provisions. The purchaser's closing obligations are also more extensive and include the delivery of checks adjusted for apportionments, the delivery in proper recordable form of any purchase money mortgage, and the delivery of an indemnification agreement against any claims made by tenants with respect to security deposits to the extent paid, credited or assigned to the purchaser.

---

[2] Note that the standard form refers to the New York Board of Title Underwriters ("NYBTU"); but that organization no longer exists. The forms have been issued by Title Insurance Rating Service Association ("TIRSA").

§ 12.36   PURCHASE & SALE OF REAL ESTATE   Ch. 12

12. Deed Transfer and Recording Taxes. The Approved Commercial Contract contains extensive provisions.

13. Title Examination, Sellers Inability to Convey, Limitations of Liability. The Approved Commercial Contract includes limitation on abatement of purchase price and unpaid taxes.[3] The contract also gives the purchaser a vendee's lien on the premises for the amount of the down payment but provides that the lien will not continue after the purchaser defaults on the contract.

14. No Assignment of Contract Without Written Consent of Seller. There is no provision to this effect in the Approved Commercial Contract. However, note the contract provides for various possibilities of termination of the contract if an existing mortgage cannot be assumed by the purchaser.

15. Gains Tax and Miscellaneous Provisions. Subparagraph 17.09 of Section 17 requires compliance with the requirements of Article 31B (The Gains Tax). Effective June 15, 1996, this Article was repealed (see § 12.84 infra). The subparagraph should be stricken.

The Approved Commercial Contract also contains an extensive provision on the seller's obligations with respect to existing and new leases on the premises to be conveyed between the time of contract and the time of closing. Another significant difference between this contract and the Residential Contract of Sale pertains to covenants of the seller between the date of contract and closing as to the premises, *i.e.*, the seller will not remove any fixtures, equipment or personal property located on the premises. Finally, the Approved Commercial Contract contains an extensive provision on apportionments concerning fuel, service contracts, changes in tax rate, etc.

Practitioners representing parties in commercial transactions are cautioned that commercial contracts are heavily negotiated and drafted around specific circumstances. The standard form contract discussed in this section serves the purpose, at the very least, of being an excellent checklist.[4]

---

3. **PRACTICE POINTER**: The seller might agree to provide a limit on the amount of abatement that the seller would be required to accept, otherwise the seller would have no obligation to deliver title.

4. **PRACTICE POINTER**: There is perhaps no substitute for experience; however, in doing a commercial transaction, attorneys for both sides must become knowledgeable about the economics of the transaction. Form books, articles and consultation with colleagues will frequently yield insights into appropriate drafting to obtain clauses which are unambiguous. Consultation with title counsel may also provide insights into what to consider.

§ 12.37 Contract of Sale for Cooperative Apartment[1]

The Contract of Sale of a Cooperative Apartment is substantially different from the contract for the sale of real property. The transfer of a unit of a cooperative involves the transfer of shares of stock, together with a long-term proprietary lease. The Court of Appeals, in *Tax Commission v. Shor*,[2] held that this interest is, for most purposes, an interest in personalty. The ramifications of that decision were significant, to say the least.[3]

It is important to bear the following in mind when considering the issues involved with the contract of sale of a cooperative unit. Copies of the proprietary leases are almost never recorded. The purchaser should ascertain from the seller who holds the leases and should obtain verification from the cooperative board of directors. The cooperative entity which grants the proprietary leases is usually the holder of the fee title and acts as lessor. The fee title is generally subject to one or more mortgages.

The proprietary lessee may obtain financing either privately or institutionally. The secured interest is created by filing pursuant to the Uniform Commercial Code. Maintenance charges paid by the proprietary lessee include charges for the common elements and for the underlying mortgage on the fee. The search and examination of title to the underlying fee forms a significant part of the information required by the purchaser of a cooperative unit. Note that it is now possible to create a tenancy by the entirety for the ownership of the cooperative unit.[4]

Library References:

West's Key No. Digests, Landlord and Tenant ⚖=352–354, 359–360.

§ 12.38 Contract of Sale for Cooperative Apartment—Standard Form

The standard form contract was prepared by the Committee on Condominiums and Cooperatives of the Real Property Section of the New York State Bar Association ("Approved Cooperative Contract").[1] There are some significant differences between the provisions set forth in Approved Cooperative Contract and those contained in the Approved

---

§ 12.37

1. See infra, § 12.94, Form of Contract of Sale—Cooperative Apartment (Julius Blumberg Inc.).

2. 43 N.Y.2d 151, 371 N.E.2d 523, 400 N.Y.S.2d 805 (1977).

3. See Bernard M. Rifkin, *Co-op Proprietary Leases Revisited*, N.Y.S.B.J., Vol. 60, No. 6, at p. 12. (Dec. 1988).

4. EPTL § 6–2.2 has been amended to add a new subparagraph (c) which states that on and after January 1, 1996 "a disposition ... of the shares of stock of a cooperative apartment corporation allocated to an apartment or unit together with the appurtenant proprietary lease to a husband and wife creates in them a tenancy by the entirety."

§ 12.38

1. See infra, § 12.96, Form of Contract of Sale—Cooperative (Julius Blumberg Inc.).

Residential Contract. The Approved Cooperative Contract includes the names of the managing agent of the cooperative and the cooperative housing corporation. The contract provides for identification of the unit and the shares of the unit. There is no provision for a description of the overall premises, which is identified by apartment number and unit and street address. There is no tax map designation and no mention of any interest in streets and unpaid awards. The contract requires identification of the "proposed occupants," and the relation of the occupant to the purchaser, as well as pets.

Personal property that is specifically included is listed, but is subject to the rights of the cooperative corporation.[2] There is also no provision for existing mortgages or for a purchase money mortgage, although such a financing provision may be considered. Since the conveyance involves shares of stock and not realty, there is a financing contingency clause for the purchaser to obtain a "Loan Commitment" rather than a mortgage commitment.

The Approved Cooperative Contract contains extensive seller representations, such as that the shares and lease are free and clear of liens, the shares were duly issued, paid for and are non-assessable, and the seller has not made any alteration to the cooperative unit without the prior written consent of the cooperative corporation. These representations and covenants survive closing for a period of one year. There is also a provision in the contract stating that the purchaser has examined and is satisfied with or has waived the examination of the proprietary lease and the cooperative corporation's certificate of incorporation, by-laws, house rules, and most recent audit financial statement and statement of tax deductions. Counsel for purchasers should carefully review all of these documents and contact the cooperative corporation or its counsel to discuss any concerns or to request further documentation prior to execution of the contract.

There is no provision for title company approval or insurable title. Similarly, there is no requirement for title examination or limitations of liability on the part of the seller for an inability to convey marketable title.[3] There is no transfer by deed. Rather, the seller is required to transfer a duly executed stock certificate representing the shares to be transferred, as well as the seller's proprietary lease and a written statement of consent to the transfer by an officer of the cooperative corporation, among other required documents. The purchaser is required to execute and deliver an assumption of lease agreement.[4]

There are other additional conditions. For example, the purchaser will not be obligated to close unless the cooperative corporation is duly incorporated and in good standing and has fee or leasehold title to the

---

2. *See supra*, §§ 12.13, 12.14.

3. *See supra*, §§ 12.21, 12.28.

4. **PRACTICE POINTER**: This document is presented to the purchaser at the closing by the cooperative board.

premises at the time of closing. Moreover, sale of the cooperative unit to the purchaser is subject to the approval of the corporation. The purchaser is required to make a good faith application to the corporation, including attending one or more interviews and furnishing any required documentation, references or other data. If the purchaser has applied in good faith and the corporation denies the application, the contract is canceled.

The Approved Cooperative Contract does not provide for the payment or adjustment of real estate taxes since all taxes imposed on the cooperative by the state, county, town, village or municipality are part of the monthly maintenance charge. Maintenance charges are adjusted at closing. Pending assessments are paid by the party who owned the shares on the date specified by the corporation for payment. Any transfer fee imposed by the corporation, known as a flip tax, is paid by the party upon whom the corporation imposes such a fee. The seller is required to pay transfer and processing fees and taxes. The purchaser pays any fee imposed by the corporation relating to the purchaser's financing.

There are also extensive provisions in the Approved Cooperative Contract for defaults, remedies and indemnities. These should be carefully reviewed. Paragraph 13 of the contract provides for indemnities, including court costs and attorney's fees resulting from either party's representations, and covenants which the contract states shall survive the closing.

§ 12.39 Contract of Sale for New Construction

While it is beyond the scope of this chapter to provide complete analysis of new construction contracts, the attorney representing the purchaser is cautioned that the proposed contract must be carefully reviewed. This section serves to provide a brief overview of the kinds of issues that may arise. In addition, refer to the discussion in Sections 12.4 through 12.32, *supra*.

There are essentially two kinds of contracts involving new construction. The first involves the purchase of a home that includes the land and the finished house and other improvements. This typically involves a property sold out of a subdivision. The second involves a situation in which a homeowner already owns the land, or separately purchases it, and signs a separate construction contract with a builder. In those cases involving the purchase of the land and house simultaneously, the buyer will typically be presented with a standard contract used throughout the subdivided development. Most of these forms are extremely one-sided. Among those clauses about which the purchaser's attorney should be most concerned are the following:

1) release of deposit to the builder prior to closing of title,
2) right of builder to substitute materials,

§ 12.39   PURCHASE & SALE OF REAL ESTATE   Ch. 12

3) eliminate or limit the right of builder to reconfigure plans for house,

4) right of builder to reenter property for a period of time after closing of title to complete any unfinished items, and

5) builder's unilateral right to set the closing date with *per diem* penalties imposed upon buyer for not closing in accordance with the builder's set date.

The purchaser's attorney should negotiate to have these clauses removed. If the builder refuses to make any concessions, the purchaser's attorney must advise the purchaser of the risks of proceeding. In those cases in which the purchaser already owns the lot on which the home is to be constructed, additional issues arise with respect to construction financing, and are raised by subcontractors, suppliers and others placing liens on the property. *See* Chapter 10 "Mechanics' Liens," *supra*.

§ 12.40 Title Insurance

Title insurance serves to protect the investment of the purchaser of real property and the security of the lending institution providing a mortgage or deed of trust on that property. It is common practice for purchasers and lenders to obtain a title insurance policy prior to closing. Indeed, all lenders require that a title insurance policy be issued as a condition to closing on the mortgage loan.

There are different types of title insurance, designed to cover a variety of risks and different forms of coverage, depending on the needs or requirements of the insured. It should be emphasized that the discussion that follows is meant to impart general information only, with the understanding that title policies and practices will vary, even within New York State.

Library References:

West's Key No. Digests, Vendor and Purchaser ⚖═199.

§ 12.41 Title Insurance—The Buyer's Obligation

It is the responsibility of a prospective buyer or lender to inquire into the condition and status of title to the real property before the sale or loan is consummated.[1] A purchaser of real property needs to ascertain whether the seller has the ability to convey the property, free and clear of all encumbrances, liens and all other limitations or restrictions, such as the levying of a special assessment. Once the property is accepted by

---

§ 12.41

1. General Obligations Law § 5–703 requires real estate contracts to be in writing, signed by the party to be charged. In addition, contracts usually contain representations about the status of title to be delivered and the personal property or fixtures included in the sale. (*See, e.g., infra,* § 12.93, Par. 2 Personal Property, Par. 12 Condition of Property and Par. 1 Premises of the Residential Contract of Sale.)

the buyer, in the absence of mutual mistake or fraud and deceit, a seller will not be responsible for matters that might affect the title to the property.[2] The only exception might be for possible liability on warranties if a warranty deed is used.

Information regarding the status and condition of the property can be gathered from various public records. Interests in real property are made a matter of public record by recording documents in the county recorder's office or other appropriate offices in the county where the real property is located. These documents include deeds, mortgages, leases, grants or reservations of easements, deed restrictions, abstracts of judgments, tax liens, notices of pendency and others. By recording evidence of a claim of interest in real property, a person gives notice to the world of that interest. This notice is called constructive notice, which means that all persons are presumed to know the facts even though they don't have actual notice.[3] Accordingly, a prospective buyer is charged with the responsibility of knowing what has been recorded against the property being acquired.[4] However, the process doesn't stop here. A physical inspection of the property should be made to determine whether there is any evidence of another person's right in the property based on such factors as adverse possession, an unrecorded lease, an unrecorded contract of sale or rights of way not of record. Additionally, a survey of the land should be obtained in order to determine the exact location of the boundaries and physical conditions such as roadways.[5]

Library References:
West's Key No. Digests, Vendor and Purchaser ⚖︎199.

§ 12.42 Title Insurance—Role of the Title Insurer

The title insurer assumes the responsibility of the buyer or lender in ascertaining the condition of title to the real property and further assumes the responsibility for determining the validity and genuineness of documents in the chain of title. When requested, the title insurer can usually extend its responsibility to include matters ascertainable from an inspection of the land itself or from an inquiry of persons in possession of the land.

2. Absent provisions in the contract to the contrary, covenants and obligations contained therein merge into and do not survive the deed. See RPL § 251. See also infra, § 12.93, Par. 12 and 28(a) of the Residential Contract of Sale. In newly constructed residential dwellings the non-merger doctrine has been substantially modified by case law. See N.Y.Jur.2d, Real Property Sales and Exchanges §§ 182, 183 and Fraud and Deceit § 98.
3. RPL §§ 290 et seq.
4. RPL §§ 290 et seq.

5. See infra, §§ 12.56—12.63.

PRACTICE POINTER: Considerable help in interpretation can be obtained from the title insurer, and from both past and future surveyors should a survey become necessary. If the survey is not a current one, i.e., more than one or two months old, it may be necessary to update the survey, with either a new one or an inspection. Where new financing is to be obtained, the requirements of the lending institution will have to be complied with. Here again, the title insurer can be of considerable help.

§ 12.42   PURCHASE & SALE OF REAL ESTATE   Ch. 12

When all the necessary inquiries are made, the title insurer will reflect its findings in a preliminary report, which may be in the form of a "commitment for title insurance." Once the buyer or lender is willing to accept those items which have been reported against the property, the transaction can then be consummated. As a condition for closing, the buyer or lender will require that the title company issue its policy of title insurance, giving assurances as to the ownership of the land, and the priority and validity of a mortgage or deed of trust on the land. This policy will show who owns the land and what the title is subject to by way of taxes and assessments, mineral reservations, and other such matters, including any liens, encumbrances, rights and reservations appearing of record.

The public records that must be examined generally include those in the following offices:

- The county recorder of the county in which the property is located;
- Any taxing authority that levies taxes or assessments on real property;
- The clerk of the county courts; and
- The surrogate's court where appropriate.

To adequately search the records, it is necessary for the title insurer to examine, summarize and classify every instrument affecting real property and the status of the various owners. Ordinarily, all documents recorded since the organization of the state government up to the most recent filings must be considered, and their effect upon the title to the land must be determined. In actuality, the title search period is subject to compliance with local standards which may mean the search will be conducted for a span of 40 to 60 years. These records are often voluminous.

§ 12.43   Title Insurance—Duration and Cost

Unlike other types of insurance, such as life, fire or public liability, which insure against loss or damage in the event of a future occurrence, title insurance protects the insured against the possibility of loss or damage from defects in the title existing on the date of the policy, but asserted at a later time.[1] Another important distinction is that title insurance is written for a one-time premium that need not be renewed. The protection afforded in an owner's policy continues until the interest of the insured is transferred or conveyed. Even when an insured dies, his

---

§ 12.43

1. ALTA 1992 owner's and lender's policy contains a specific provision limiting liability to matters existing at Date of Policy.

heirs or devisees remain protected under the terms of the policy.[2] If the insured is a corporation or other entity, it is possible to obtain coverage in favor of its successors by dissolution, merger or consolidation. A lender's policy is not only for the benefit of the insured lender but also for subsequent assignees under most circumstances.[3] When the loan has been paid or otherwise satisfied, liability under the lender's policy is extinguished.

The amount of liability which a title insurance company assumes under a policy of title insurance is determined basically by the type of policy issued and by the value of the property insured. An owner's policy is ordinarily written for the selling price of the property, including mortgages and other liens. A lender's policy is written for the amount of the loan. The amount of insurance an insured obtains, in addition to the stated amount in the policy, includes costs, attorney's fees and expenses which the insurer may become obligated to pay in connection with litigation and investigation should the title or interest of an insured become the subject of litigation.

The cost of a policy of title insurance is based not only on the risk factor, but also on the cost of producing the policy, including maintenance of a title plant, a facility for the storage of old records and inventory, and the many steps involved in the search, examination and evaluation of a title. As in other businesses or professions, rates are subject to change, depending upon the prevailing cost of goods and services. There is a strict schedule of rates applicable in New York that is approved by the New York State Department of Insurance.[4]

Library References:

West's Key No. Digests, Vendor and Purchaser ⟐199.

§ 12.44 Title Insurance—Basic and Extended Coverage

A policy of title insurance may provide standard coverage or extended coverage. A standard coverage policy is more limited in its coverage. It basically insures against defects that are ascertainable from an examination of the public records plus certain off-record risks. Off-record risks are included in standard and extended coverage policies. These risks include the following: forgery or false personation or the transferring of title by a name other than that in which title was acquired; minority, incapacity, insanity, death or disappearance of any interested person in the chain of title; the ability of the person, entity or agent to deliver title;

---

2. ALTA 1992 owner's policy, conditions and stipulations, Par. 1(a) provides for continuation of coverage as of the original policy date for successors to the title by operation of law.

3. ALTA 1992 loan policy—conditions and stipulations Par. 1, definition of terms, Subpar. (a)(i).

4. **PRACTICE POINTER**: For a minimum charge, the Title Insurance Rating Association will provide a copy of its rate manual. Any insurer would also be willing to provide a copy.

and the actual delivery and effectiveness of each deed in the chain of title.[1]

An extended coverage policy includes all of the protection of a standard coverage policy plus coverage of additional risks. As the name implies, it extends the coverage of a standard policy to include within its scope coverage of other possible defects that are ascertainable not only from the records, but also from an inspection of the land itself, or from making inquiry of persons in actual possession of the land, or from a correct survey. The issuance of such extended coverage is based upon an off-record investigation sufficient to ascertain whether any matters exist that could affect the lender's security. A survey may or may not be required, depending upon the type and location of the property or the nature of the transaction itself.

Inspections made for these policies, particularly those made in older neighborhoods, often disclose a variety of encroachments, overhanging buildings or architectural details, party-walls, boundary fences, community driveways, faulty surveys, improperly located improvements, and the like. If any matters of a material nature are found to exist, an exception is specifically shown in the extended coverage policy when it is written, unless the matter can be corrected prior to the issuance of the policy.

Extended coverage policies of title insurance are available to both lenders and owners. However, the use of extended coverage policies by lenders is most prevalent.

Library References:
West's Key No. Digests, Vendor and Purchaser ⇐199.

§ 12.45 Title Insurance Policy

The only form of policy utilized in New York State is the American Land Title Policy form ("ALTA").[1] However the New York State Department of Insurance has authorized some variations to accommodate the requirements and differences in New York law. The insuring provisions of the New York policies and their modifications are set forth in the following four sections.[2] These title insurance policies are the major policies offered in New York State. In addition, there are Owner Leasehold and Lender's Leasehold policies, as well as similar policies covering

§ 12.44

1. J. Pedowitz, Real Estate Titles, Ch. 27, Pt IB, Nature of Title Insurance (2d ed. 1996 Supp.).

§ 12.45

1. These forms were adopted by ALTA on October 17, 1992. The discussion reflects the content of these forms.

2. See infra, § 12.46 (loan policy), § 12.47 (loan policy modifications), § 12.48 (owner's policy) and § 12.49 (owner's policy modifications). Exclusions from coverage are discussed infra at § 12.52. Conditions and stipulations, which contain definitions of terms and matters related to the measure of damages and claim notification are discussed supra at §§ 12.40–12.44.

cooperative interests. All of the policies have a common format: there is a jacket cover page which includes the affirmative coverages, and a Schedule "A" which describes the premises which is the subject of the interests of the insured, (usually a part of Schedule "A" describes the interest insured, *i.e.*, fee title, first mortgage, lessee, etc.) In most every case, there is a Schedule "B" which includes those matters which the title insurer or its agent has discovered from the public records which may affect the interest insured and which becomes the subject of performance according to the contract of sale or the loan commitment.

It is important to note that the exclusions[3] from coverage are essentially not negotiable but may be modified to some extent by approval endorsements,[4] if appropriate facts and assurances can be provided to the underwriter.

There are two issues in coverages that require some amplification. First is coverage provided over the gap,[5] namely after the date of delivery of the conveyance (whether a deed, mortgage or lease) but prior to its recordation. In the case where the judgment entered against the former owner was filed *after* the delivery of the deed but prior to its recordation, the judgment cannot be enforced against the purchaser for a valuable consideration.[6] The second issue is the treatment of mechanic's liens which are filed after the delivery of the deed but prior to the recording of the conveyance or mortgage or the making an advance of funds after the recordation of the mortgage.[7] The Lien Law in New York differs from that law in any other jurisdiction. That difference is predicated on the application of the trust fund sections of the New York Lien Law.[8] These sections provide that a mortgage delivered and funds advanced by the lender prior to the filing of a mechanic's lien will retain priority even though the lien is filed prior to the recordation of the mortgage.[9]

Library References:

West's Key No. Digests, Insurance ⟐417.5–429.2, 493–508.2.

§ 12.46 Title Insurance Policy—Loan Policy Coverage

The basic form of lender's policy coverage provided by ALTA contains the following provisions regarding:

3. *See infra*, § 12.52.

4. *See infra*, § 12.51.

5. *See infra*, §§ 12.47, Par. 3, 12.49, Par. 3.

6. *See also* Schlesinger v. Sanford Main Shopping Center, Inc., 37 Misc.2d 840, 237 N.Y.S.2d 190 (Sup.Ct., Queens County, 1962). A judgment creditor is not a purchaser under the New York recording act. RPL § 290.

7. *See infra*, §§ 12.47, Par. 1, 12.49, Par. 3.

8. *See* Lien Law §§ 10, 13(3), (5), with respect to the trust fund. *See* Lien Law §§ 2(13), (14), 22 regarding building loans.

9. Suffolk County Federal Savings and Loan Association v. Geiger, 57 Misc.2d 184, 291 N.Y.S.2d 982 (Sup.Ct., Suffolk County, 1968). *See* Chapter 10 "Mechanic's Liens," *supra*.

§ 12.46 PURCHASE & SALE OF REAL ESTATE Ch. 12

1. Title to the estate or interest described in Schedule A being vested other than stated therein;
2. Any defect in or lien or encumbrance on the title;
3. Unmarketability of the title;
4. Lack of a right to access to and from the land;
5. Invalidity or unenforceability of the lien of the insured mortgage upon the title;
6. Priority of any lien or encumbrance over the lien of the insured mortgage;

Outside of New York State the following provision on mechanics' liens is part of the ALTA loan policy coverage:

7. Lack of priority of the lien of the insured mortgage over any statutory lien for services, labor or material:
    (a) arising from an improvement or work related to the land which is contracted for or commenced subsequent to Date of Policy;
    (b) arising from an improvement or work related to the land which is contracted for or commenced subsequent to Date of Policy and which is financed in whole or in part by proceeds of the indebtedness secured by the insured mortgage which at Date of Policy the insured has advanced or is obligated to advance;[1]
8. The invalidity or unenforceability of any assignment of the insured mortgage, provided the assignment is shown in Schedule A, or the failure of the assignment shown in Schedule A to vest title to the insured mortgage in the named insured assignee free and clear of all liens.
9. The Company will also pay the costs, attorney's fees and expenses incurred in defense of the title, or the lien of the insured mortgage, as insured only to the extent provided in the conditions and stipulations
10. This policy shall not be valid or binding until countersigned below by a validating signatory of the Company.

§ 12.47 Title Insurance Policy—New York Modifications of Loan Policy

The following modifications are made to the ALTA form of coverage for the New York loan policy because in New York State recording a

---

§ 12.46

1. The foregoing provision 7 is deleted from the New York policy and the following provision on mechanic's liens is part of the New York loan policy coverage:

7. Any statutory lien for services, labor or materials furnished prior to the date hereof, and which has now gained or which may hereafter gain priority over the estate or interest of the insured as shown in Schedule A of this policy.

mortgage will not necessarily assure that funds advanced will have priority over a subsequently filed mechanic's lien.[1]

1. Insuring provision Number 7 is deleted and the following is substituted:

>7. Any statutory lien for services, labor or materials furnished prior to the date hereof, and which has now gained or which may hereafter gain priority over the estate or interest of the insured as shown in Schedule A of this policy.

2. Paragraph number 6 of the Exclusions From Coverage is deleted.[2]

3. The following is added to Paragraph 7 of the Conditions and Stipulations of this policy:

>(d) If the recording date of the instruments creating the insured interest is later than the policy date, such policy shall also cover intervening liens or encumbrances, except real estate taxes, assessments, water charges or sewer rents.[3]

Nothing herein contained shall be construed as extending or changing the effective date of said policy, unless otherwise expressly stated.

§ 12.48 Title Insurance Policy—Owner's Policy Coverage

The basic form of owner's policy coverage provided by ALTA contains provisions regarding:

1. Title to the estate or interest described in Schedule A being vested other than stated therein;
2. Any defect in or lien or encumbrance on the title;
3. Unmarketability of the title;
4. Lack of a right to access to and from the land;

The Company will also pay the costs, attorneys' fees and expenses incurred in defense of the title, as insured, but only to the extent provided in the conditions and stipulations.[1]

This policy shall not be valid or binding until countersigned below by a validating signatory of the Company.

---

§ 12.47

1. See Lien Law §§ 2(13), 13(3),(5), 22.

2. The Exclusion is eliminated based upon New York Lien Law, explained in § 12.45 in the text at notes 5–7.

3. See § 12.45 and footnote 5 which explain the gap coverage provided in New York State.

§ 12.48

1. Note that this paragraph and the one that follows are unnumbered.

§ 12.49   PURCHASE & SALE OF REAL ESTATE   Ch. 12

§ 12.49   Title Insurance Policy—New York Modifications of Owner's Policy

The following modifications are made to the ALTA form of coverage for the New York owner's policy.

1. The following provision is added to the insuring provisions on the face page of the policy:

    "5. Any statutory lien for services, labor or materials furnished prior to the date hereof, and which has now gained or which may hereafter gain priority over the estate of interest of the insured as shown on Schedule A of this policy."[1]

2. Paragraph number 6 of the Exclusions From Coverage is deleted.

3. The following is added to Paragraph 7 of the Conditions and Stipulations of this policy:

    "(d) If the recording date of the instruments creating the insured interest is later than the policy date, such policy shall also cover intervening liens and encumbrances, except real estate taxes assessments, water charges and sewer rents."[2]

§ 12.50   Title Insurance Policy—Standard Exceptions

The following standard five exceptions to coverage appear in Schedule "B" of the ALTA Title Report for both the owner's policy and the loan policy.

1. Taxes or assessments which are not shown as existing liens by the records of any taxing authority that levies taxes or assessments on real property or by the public records.[1]

2. Any facts, rights, interest or claims which are not shown by the public records but which could be ascertained by an inspection of the land or by making inquiry of persons in possession thereof.[2]

---

§ 12.49

1. See supra, § 12.47 note 2.
2. The gap coverage, which includes liens and judgments against an owner or a lender after delivery of the conveyance but prior to recordation, is discussed at § 12.45 notes 5–7.

§ 12.50

1. PRACTICE POINTER: This includes proceedings by a public agency which may result in taxes or assessments, or notices of such proceedings whether or not shown by a recording or by the public records. This includes such matters as an assessment for the installation of underground utilities which becomes a lien by virtue of a statute and without recording any notice in the county recorder's office.

2. PRACTICE POINTER: Item 2 would include such matters as violations of deed restrictions or any rights or claims of persons in possession of the land. For example, loss or damage is not insured against if based on a right to occupy the land by a tenant under an unrecorded lease or by a

842

Ch. 12   ENDORSEMENTS   § 12.51

3. Easements, liens or encumbrances or claims thereof, which are not shown by the public records. This item would include such matters as unrecorded utility easements, public or private roads and community driveways or, unrecorded mechanic's liens whose priority will relate back to date of commencement of work though recorded after the date of policy.

4. Discrepancies, conflicts in boundary lines, shortage in area, encroachments or any other facts which a correct survey would disclose and which are not shown by the public records.

5. (a) Unpatented mining claims; (b) reservations or exceptions in patents or in Acts authorizing the issuance thereof; (c) water rights, claims or title to water.

§ 12.51   Title Insurance Policy—Endorsements

Title insurance policies will usually include endorsements. Certain endorsements are included in the basic coverage discussed above and are provided at no additional charge.[1] Other endorsements, known as special endorsements, provide additional assurances to an insured. They can be used to expand the coverage of either a standard coverage policy or an extended coverage policy. Some special risk endorsements are provided at no additional charge[2] and some cost a nominal fee of $25.[3] Need for a third party claiming title by adverse possession.

§ 12.51

1. The following Endorsements are automatically part of the basic policy:

Standard New York Endorsement (Loan Policy) (For ALTA 10/17/92)

Standard New York Endorsement (Owner's Policy) (For ALTA 10/17/92)

TIRSA Leasehold Endorsement (Loan Policy) (For ALTA 10/17/92)

TIRSA Leasehold Endorsement (Owner's Policy) (For ALTA 10/17/92)

TIRSA Cooperative Endorsement (Loan Policy) (8/17/95)

TIRSA Cooperative Endorsement (Owner's Policy) (8/17/95).

2. The following are Special Risk Endorsements (varying premium rates apply):

ALTA Endorsement 9 (Restrictions, Encroachments, Minerals) (10/17/92) NY (9/1/93)

TIRSA Survey Endorsement (Loan Policy) (9/1/93)

TIRSA New York Fairway Endorsement (9/1/93)

TIRSA Non–Imputation Endorsement (Partnership Form) (8/15/94)

TIRSA Non–Imputation Endorsement (Stock Acquisition) (8/15/94)

TIRSA Residential Revolving Credit Endorsement (9/1/93)

TIRSA Commercial Revolving Credit Endorsement (9/1/93)

TIRSA Market Value Policy Rider Endorsement (9/1/93)

TIRSA Joint & Several Liability Endorsement (9/1/93)

TIRSA Swap Endorsement (1/31/95)

TIRSA Additional Interest Endorsement (1/31/95)

TIRSA First Loss Endorsement (5/1/96)

TIRSA Last Dollar Endorsement (5/1/96)

TIRSA Contract Vendee Endorsement (1/31/95)

3. ALTA Endorsement 6 (Variable Rate Mortgage) (6/1/87) NY (9/1/93)

ALTA Endorsement 7 (Manufactured Housing Unit) (6/1/87) NY (9/1/93)

TIRSA Fannie Mae Balloon Mortgage Endorsement (9/1/93)

843

§ 12.51   PURCHASE & SALE OF REAL ESTATE   Ch. 12

special endorsement may depend on the particular circumstances, such as the need for protection against: priority of unrecorded mechanic's liens; forced removal of buildings which encroach upon adjoining land; or loss by reason of existing violation of private building restrictions. There is also a form of coverage which provides that if the recording date of the instrument creating the insured interest is later than the policy date, the policy will cover intervening liens or encumbrances, except for real estate taxes, assessments, water charges and sewer rents. This is known as gap coverage.

§ 12.52   Title Insurance Policy—Exclusions

Like other types of insurance policies, a policy of title insurance contains certain printed exclusions. Note that if the examination of title discloses specific matters that would constitute a lien or encumbrance or would have an adverse effect on the title, they would need to be excepted from the policy unless the parties can eliminate such matters by appropriate documents or possible court action. If not eliminated, such items would be specifically set forth as matters not insured against by the policy. These matters would appear in Schedule B of the title report.[1] As a practical matter, most property is affected in some way by matters of record, but in many cases a buyer or a lender would have no objections to certain of these items being shown as exclusions in the policy of title insurance. Such items might include an easement for public utility purposes along the side or across the rear few feet of the property, or covenants, conditions and restrictions set forth on a recorded declaration of restrictions.

TIRSA Endorsement 4 (Condominium) (9/1/93)

TIRSA 5.1 (Planned Unit Development) Endorsement (9/1/93)

TIRSA Land Same As Survey Endorsement (9/1/93)

TIRSA New York City "Air Rights" Endorsement (9/1/93)

TIRSA Variable Rate Mortgage Endorsement (Fixed Rate Conversion) (9/1/93)

TIRSA Endorsement 6.2 (Variable Rate Mortgage—Negative Amortization) (9/1/93)

TIRSA Environmental Protection Lien Endorsement 8.1 (9/1/93)

TIRSA Environmental Protection Lien Endorsement 8.1 (New York City Only) (8/15/94)

TIRSA Environmental Protection Lien Endorsement 8.1 (Governmental Agencies) (5/1/96)

TIRSA Waiver of Arbitration Endorsement (Owner's Policy) (9/1/93)

TIRSA Waiver of Arbitration Endorsement (Loan Policy) (9/1/93)

TIRSA Residential Mortgage Endorsement (8/15/94)

TIRSA Successor in Ownership of Indebtedness Endorsement (8/15/94)

TIRSA Reverse Mortgage Endorsement (1/31/95)

TIRSA Cluster Endorsement (1/31/95) NYSID REQUIRES TITLE INSURER APPROVAL PRIOR TO ISSUANCE.

TIRSA Limited Liability Company and Limited Liability Partnership Endorsement (1/31/95).

§ 12.52

1. See §§ 12.53—12.55 for title objections raised by the title insurer which are not part of the exclusions.

Exclusions 1 through 3, below, are contained in the owner's and loan policies:

1. (a) Any law, ordinance or governmental regulation (including but not limited to building and zoning laws, ordinance, or regulation) restricting, regulating, prohibiting or relating to:

    (i) the occupancy, use, or enjoyment of the land, (ii) the character, dimensions or locations of any improvement now or hereafter erected on the land; (iii) a separation in ownership or a change in the dimensions or area of the land or any parcel of which the land is or was a part; or (iv) environmental protection, or the effect of any violation of these laws, ordinances or governmental enforcement thereof or a notice of defect, lien or encumbrance resulting from a violation or alleged violations affecting the land has been recorded in the public records at Date of Policy.

    (b) Any governmental police power not excluded by (a) above, except to the extent that a notice of the exercise thereof or a notice of defect, lien or encumbrance resulting from a violation or alleged violation affecting the land has been recorded in the public records at Date of Policy.

2. Rights of eminent domain unless notice of the exercise thereof has been recorded in the public records at Date of Policy, but not excluding from coverage any taking which has occurred prior to Date of Policy which would be binding on the rights of a purchaser for value without knowledge.

3. Defects, liens, encumbrances, adverse claims or other matters:

    (a) created, suffered, assumed or agreed to by the insured claimant;

    (b) not known to the Company, not recorded in the public records at Date of Policy, but known to the insured claimant and not disclosed in writing to the Company by the insured claimant prior to the date the insured claimant became an insured under this policy;

    (c) resulting in no loss or damage to the insured claimant;

    (d) attaching or created subsequent to Date of Policy (except to the extent that this policy insures the priority of the lien of the insured mortgage over any statutory lien for services, labor or material); or

    (e) resulting in loss or damage which would not have been sustained if the insured claimant had paid value for the insured mortgage.

§ 12.52   PURCHASE & SALE OF REAL ESTATE   Ch. 12

Note that the following exclusion appears only in the owner's policy:

4. Any claim, which arises out of the transaction vesting in the insured the estate or interest insured by this policy, by reason of the operation of federal bankruptcy, state insolvency, or similar creditors' rights laws, that is based on:

   (i) the transaction creating the estate or interest insured by this policy being deemed a fraudulent conveyance or fraudulent transfer; or

   (ii) the transaction creating the estate or interest insured by this policy being deemed a preferential transfer except where the preferential transfer results from the failure:

   (a) to timely record the instrument of transfer; or

   (b) of such recordation to impart notice to a purchaser for value or a judgment or lien creditor.

The following exclusions appear only in the lender's policy:

4. Unenforceability of the lien of the insured mortgage because of the inability or failure of the insured at Date of Policy or the inability or failure of any subsequent owner of the indebtedness, to comply with applicable doing business laws of the state in which the land is situated.

5. Invalidity or unenforceability of the lien of the insured mortgage, or claim thereof, which arises out of the transaction evidenced by the insured mortgage and is based upon usury or any consumer credit protection or truth in lending law.

6. Any statutory lien for services, labor or materials (or the claim of priority of any statutory lien for services, labor or materials over the lien of the insured mortgage) arising from an improvement or work related to the land which is contracted for and commenced subsequent to Date of Policy and is not financed in whole or in part by proceeds of the indebtedness secured by the insured mortgage which at Date of Policy the insured has advanced or is obligated to advance.[2]

7. Any claim, which arises out of the transaction creating the interest of the mortgagee insured by this policy, by reason of the operation of federal bankruptcy, state insolvency, or similar creditors' rights laws, that is based on:

   (i) the transaction creating the interest of the insured mortgagee being deemed a fraudulent conveyance or fraudulent transfer; or

---

[2]. This paragraph is deleted from the New York loan policy. See § 12.47 regarding New York State mechanics' lien law.

846

(ii) the subordination of the interest of the insured mortgagee as a result of the application of the doctrine of equitable subordination; or

(iii) the transaction creating the interest of the insured mortgagee being deemed a preferential transfer except where the preferential transfer results from the failure:

(a) to timely record the instrument of transfer; or

(b) of such recordation to impart notice to a purchaser for value or a judgment or lien creditor.

§ 12.53 Title Examination—Recording Title and the Torrens System

The contract of sale will require that the purchaser order a title examination either after the execution of the contract or after the buyer obtains a mortgage commitment.[1] The practitioner needs to have a basic knowledge of New York State's system for recognizing land ownership. New York State utilizes a grantor/grantee title recording system[2] as well as a title registration or a Torrens System.[3] Most title in New York passes under the recording system and title is examined by tracing the chain of title instruments recorded in the county clerk's office where the property is located.[4]

New York is phasing out the Torrens System.[5] However, practitioners need to be aware of the special requirements of the Torrens System and the law governing the phase-out.

Under the Torrens System, all instruments must be filed with the Registrar of the county in which premises are located. The original instruments are retained by the Registrar. Each instrument should recite the Certificate of Title Number under which the premises are registered. Recording memos should be clearly marked "File with Registrar." Filing fees vary from recording fees.

Title to county clerked property does not pass until the deed is *county clerked* in the Registrar's office.[6] The *original* Owner's Duplicate Certificate of Title ("ODC") must be produced at closing and forwarded together with closing instruments, otherwise the closing instruments will not be accepted for filing. The whereabouts of the ODC should be ascertained in advance of closing.

§ 12.53
1. *See supra*, § 12.15.
2. RPL § 291.
3. RPL Art. 12. The goal of the Torrens System is to provide a vehicle where all matters relating to title were to be registered in one place, on the owner's duplicate certificate of ownership located in the Registrar's office.
4. RPL § 291.
5. Ch. 227, L.1996.
6. RPL § 406.

§ 12.53   PURCHASE & SALE OF REAL ESTATE   Ch. 12

All memorials of liens and encumbrances shown on the ODC must be dealt with at the closing. Liens and encumbrances must be filed in the Registrar's office in order to be effective against registered property. Federal liens, bankruptcies and federal judgments remain outside and are not required to comply with the Torrens Registration system in order to be effective.

Torrens System: Deed Requirements. Names of grantors must conform exactly to names on ODC and the deed must recite source of grantor's title, and the registration number of grantor's ODC. Corporate deeds must contain the recitals "normal course of business" or "stockholders consent." Individual grantor-date of acknowledgement must be within 30 days of filing, otherwise an affidavit proving delivery during the lifetime of the grantor must be forwarded with closing instruments to the Registrar.

Torrens System: Deeds into an Inter Vivos Trust. The trust agreement must be filed. A deed from a trustee should recite the filing document number of the trust agreement. In case one or more of the county clerked owners has died, or in case of any other transfer by operation of law, or otherwise, (such as foreclosure, etc.) a petition will have to be made to the supreme court and a new certificate issued in the name or names of the proposed grantor(s).

Torrens System: Mortgages. The original mortgage is retained by the Registrar. A "Registration Copy" will be forwarded to the party designated in the "Record and Return" instructions on the mortgage.[7]

Article 12 of the RPL was amended effective January 1, 1992. These amendments are summarized as follows:

(a) Survey, map or plan to be filed has been amended to require any new map being filed, to designate all Torrens property by markings which are easily discernable on microfilm.[8]

(b) Owner's Duplicate Certificate of Title.[9] This section now requires the owner of the property to make a written request for the Owner's Duplicate Certificate of Title. In addition, the form for the request is part of this section.

(c) At the time of filing, two copies of the deed must be submitted. The extra copy will be conformed and returned to the party indicated in the return address box.

---

[7] Submission of a duplicate original mortgage for use as the Registration Copy will save some fees.

PRACTICE POINTER: The Registration Copy of the mortgage must be submitted together with any satisfaction, release or assignment of the mortgage. In addition, the ODC must be submitted with a satisfaction or release. Although not mandatory, it is recommended that the ODC be submitted even with assignments so that the ODC can be conformed to the original Certificate to reflect the assignment.

[8] RPL § 381.

[9] RPL § 396.

(d) Memorials to be carried forward has been amended to require a written request by the mortgagee who has become the fee owner, NOT to merge said mortgage with the fee title, otherwise the Registrar shall delete the mortgage from the memorials.

(e) Certificate as to part of property remaining after transfer has been amended to require a survey to be submitted when filing a deed for a portion of property being conveyed. No survey will be required when transferring whole lots, and designated (*e.g.*, north 50 feet) parts of lots. This will assist the Registrar's office in issuing a certificate of title with the correct description.[10]

(f) Loss of duplicate certificate has been amended as to the procedure for issuance of new Owner's Duplicates. A form has been included in this section of the law. Your attention is called to the fact that only the owner of the property can apply.[11]

(g) Assignment of mortgage, lease or other lien or charge has been amended to eliminate the requirement for the submission of the registration copy of the mortgage when submitting satisfactions or releases.[12]

(h) Release, discharge or surrender of charge or incumbrance has been amended to eliminate the requirement for the submission of the registration copy of the mortgage when submitting satisfactions or releases.[13]

(i) Death of owner of county clerked property: transfer of property has been amended: The forms to transfer the property to the surviving spouse are a portion of this law. Transferring property to the surviving spouse no longer requires the consent of the Attorney General or submission to the court.[14]

(j) Joint tenant with right of survivorship—same as surviving spouse.

(k) Executor/Administrator—The forms to transfer the property to the Executor/Administrator are a portion of this law. Transferring property to the Executor/Administrator no longer requires the consent of the Attorney General or submission to the court.

(*l*) Heirs-at-law—must submit a petition, order and verification to the Attorney General, and the Registrar, for their consent, and submit same to the supreme court for the judge's signature. (There is no change in the procedure.)

Phase-out of Torrens System. Effective January 1, 1997 the Torrens Registration Act is amended to phase out the Torrens System

10. RPL § 407.
11. RPL § 414.
12. RPL § 418.
13. RPL § 419.
14. RPL § 423.

§ 12.53 PURCHASE & SALE OF REAL ESTATE Ch. 12

and to move all property into the recording system. Provisions of the amended law include the following:

(a) On or after January 1, 1997, no property may be county clerked[15] under Article 12 of the RPL. Provided, however, that certificates of title affecting title prior to January 1, 1997 shall be county clerked pursuant to Article 12.

(b) Until January 1, 2000, only adverse instruments (defined as judgments, mechanic's liens, notices of pendency and other nonconsensual instruments which encumber but do not convey the fee title to county clerked property) may be accepted for filing by the Registrar.

(c) On or after January 1, 1997, the Registrar shall refuse to accept for filing any voluntary instrument (defined as deeds, including tax deeds, sheriff's or marshall's deeds, mortgages, leases, easements and other consensual instruments). Instead, on payment of the recording charges the Registrar is required to record the certificate of title with the county clerk or with the city county clerk in the counties of New York, Kings, Queens and the Bronx.

(d) On or before January 1, 2000, the Registrar will be required to record all remaining unrecorded certificates of title with the county clerk or city county clerk.

(e) Upon recordation of the certificate of title, the county clerked property will be "subject only to incumbrances, charges, trusts, liens and transfers as may be memorialized by the certificate" and free from all others except those set forth in Section 400 of the RPL (*e.g.*, liens arising under federal law or U.S. Constitution, real estate taxes and assessments, tenants in possession under leases under one year ... etc.).

(f) After recordation of the certificate, the county clerked property shall be conveyed or encumbered in the same manner as property governed by Article 9 of the RPL (*i.e.*, the Recording Acts). All instruments noted or memorialized on the certificate of title so recorded are given the same force and effect as if they were filed or recorded with the county clerk on the date memorialized or noted on the certificate.

(g) No instruments filed or recorded with the county clerk (or with the city county clerk in the counties of New York, Kings, Queens and the Bronx) prior to the recordation of the certificate but not memorialized or noted thereon shall affect the title to the county clerked property unless said instrument is re-recorded, re-filed or re-docketed after the recordation of the certificate, provided,

---

15. In four counties within New York City (New York, Kings, Queens and Bronx Counties), this function was performed by the City Registrar; in all other counties the county clerk performed this function.

however, that a judgment docketed by the county clerk prior to the time a certificate of title is recorded shall be valid against such land if the land owner received notice of such judgment.

(h) Recordation of the certificate of title will not disturb the effect of any determinations of title made pursuant to registration proceedings under Article 12 of the RPL.

(i) Prescriptive easements or title by adverse possession can only be asserted against the property based upon possession arising after the date when the certificate of title is recorded. Possession prior to that date may not be tacked on or added to any period of future adverse possession.

(j) Nothing contained in this legislation will terminate, diminish, or impair any existing right to resort to the Assurance Fund created under Sections 426 to 429 of the RPL.

Library References:
West's Key No. Digests, Records ⚖9; Vendor and Purchaser ⚖220–245.

§ 12.54 Title Examination—Objections to Be Disposed of Prior to Closing

After the title examination has been completed, the title insurance company will send a report to the purchaser and the purchaser will send a copy to the seller. This report will reveal any objections that there may be to title, as discussed below. Most if not all of these issues should have been dealt with or disclosed in the course of preparation of the contract, or the issues should have been anticipated and a means of dealing with them planned by the seller's attorney. Note that investigations or inspections of the premises under contract, or a title examination or report, may disclose additional matters not known prior to contract. Attorneys must also consider the need for addressing engineering or environmental concerns or matters relating to the occupancy of the premises which may not necessarily show up in the public records.

Upon the receipt of the objections to title, the attorney for the seller must make an initial evaluation as to the means of eventual disposition. The proper objections must be disposed of at or prior to the closing (unless the contract specifically provides that some of the matters disclosed will not be deemed objections). The objections not deemed proper or appropriate should be argued out and agreed upon prior to closing.

The attorney for the purchaser should actively seek resolution of the objections, and should not assume that the seller's attorney will do whatever is necessary to dispose of them. Unless assurances are received indicating that disposition of exceptions is under control, there is a better than even chance that the closing will take far more time than planned, or that the buyer will ultimately accept something less than

§ 12.54 PURCHASE & SALE OF REAL ESTATE Ch. 12

what should have been received because of the pressures that exist at the time of the closing. In some cases, it may become necessary to adjourn the closing to a later date.

As the attorney for the buyer, it is important to contact the attorney for the seller to confirm that these matters are being properly addressed. In some areas, the local Bar Association has established standards for closing which, among other things, provide that if the search sets forth judgments, tax liens, bankruptcy proceedings or disability proceedings that may refer to the sellers, the seller's attorney must deliver to the buyer's attorney before the date of closing an appropriate affidavit agreeing to dispose of the exceptions before the closing.

§ 12.55 Title Examination—Objections to Be Disposed of Prior to Closing—Checklist

Examples of the types of objections which should be disposed of in advance of closing or by prior arrangements made for disposition at closing are listed below. Some guidance on methods of clearing objective is provided. However, a complete discussion as to how to clear each of these objections is beyond the purview of this chapter. Counsel should consult the title company for further guidance.

1. Violations of restrictive covenants or conditions, or of easements or other agreements affecting the plot or the existing improvements, or their present use.

2. Restrictive covenants, easements or agreements affecting the premises, but not excepted in the contract of sale.

3. Subdivision compliance—where required.

4. Lack of legal access.

5. Encroachments and other exceptions (including adverse possession or description disclosed by an accurate survey, including boundary line agreements, encroachment agreements, etc.)[1]

6. Possessory interest and other rights disclosed by a personal inspection.

7. Confirmatory, correction, or quitclaim deeds, and/or release or surrenders as to outstanding interests or by reason of defects in prior instruments.

8. Liens, such as mortgages, money judgments (including New York City Parking Violation Judgments), federal tax liens, (especially if they are against prior owners in the chain of title); mechanics' Liens (and supplementary instruments); UCC filings that require

---

§ 12.55

1. See RPAPL § 881, as to access over adjoining property to make repairs and improvements.

termination or release; state and city franchise tax liens (especially if they are against corporations not currently in the chain of title); maintenance charges imposed as liens by covenants, restrictions or agreements of record; estate taxes (state and federal); real estate tax liens (including old tax leases or other old tax sales); possible bankruptcies against names similar to that of the current owner, or some prior owner; lien of debts of a decedent (applicable in New York within 18 months after the issuance of Letters); New York City vault tax; municipal emergency repair liens[2] and Transit Adjudication Bureau liens.[3]

9. Leases and tenancies, recorded or unrecorded.

10. Contingent or terminable interests. Proof of death of a life tenant or holder of interest is required.

11. Options and rights of first refusal (*e.g.*, to buy or lease).[4]

12. Notice of Pendency of any action to be canceled or discontinued. Cancellation may be by stipulation, or if no appearances, by affidavit of plaintiff's attorney without a court order.[5] A bond is permitted in actions other than to foreclose a mortgage, partition or dower.[6]

13. Defects in actions or proceedings in the chain of title, such as foreclosure, partition, an action to bar claims,[7] probate, proceedings for leave to sell, bankruptcy or insolvency proceedings. These defects must be cured.

14. Legacies that may be a charge on the realty. Proof of payment is required.

15. Right of election by a surviving spouse. Proof of non-exercise by the surviving spouse within the statutory period of a right of election or of its release is required. The effect of possible ante-nuptial agreement waiving the right of election should be considered.

16. After-born or posthumous children with rights as against a Last Will and Testament in the chain of title.[8] Proof that none exists is required.

17. Dower, curtesy and proof as to marital status, when applicable.

---

2. N.Y.C. Administrative Code §§ 17–151 *et seq.*

3. Public Authorities Law § 1209–a.

4. CAVEAT: In some cases, data showing termination or disposition may need to be in recordable form.

5. CPLR 6514(d), (e).

6. CPLR 6515.

7. See RPAPL Art. 15.

8. *See* EPTL § 11–1.1, which permits exercise of power of sale by a fiduciary to supersede. *See also* Preminger, *et al.*, *Trusts and Estates Practice in New York* (West 1997).

§ 12.55   PURCHASE & SALE OF REAL ESTATE   Ch. 12

Dower is applicable only where the coupled married before September 1, 1930. If the husband owns the property in his name only, the wife must join in a deed of conveyance unless either has died. There is no dower right in a joint tenancy.

The matter of curtesy is largely academic. However, it is possible that if property was owned by a married woman who died before September 1, 1930, and her husband is still living, he may still have curtesy rights.

18. Proof as to other names by which a party may have been known.

19. Proof as to family history and genealogy.

20. Proof of due delivery of deeds during the lifetime of the grantor. This is usually raised if there is a hiatus of over 30 days between date and recording date of deed.

21. Effect of restricted use imposed by statutory provisions.[9]

22. Defects in, or proof of compliance with, statutory prerequisites to conveyance by municipal corporations, etc.

23. Limitation on capacity to take, such as limitation on devises to charity.

24. Right of redemption by federal government.[10]

25. Recorded contracts[11] and outstanding unrecorded contracts of sale of which there is notice.

26. Bankruptcy. A lien of judgment is not discharged unless a proceeding is brought under Section 150 of the Debtor and Creditor Law, or unless there is an order in the Bankruptcy Court to sell free and clear.[12]

27. Conveyance by fiduciary. Three or more fiduciaries, whether they be Trustees, Executors or Administrators, unless contrary to the express provisions of an instrument conferring the power, may act by a majority (or the majority of the survivors).[13] There is an exception in the case of a power of appointment. Wills probated in another state require ancillary probate in the county where the New York property is located. Ancillary letters will not be required if the

---

9. See, e.g., General City Law § 35; Town Law § 279; Village Law § 7-734.

10. Under the Federal Tax Lien Act of 1966, the right of redemption is up to 120 days as to federal tax liens. As to other federal liens, the period lasts up to one year. Note that the right of redemption also applies to liens filed by the government after *lis pendens*.

11. See RPL § 294(5); see also supra, § 12.6.

12. Carman v. European American Bank & Trust Co., 78 N.Y.2d 1066, 576 N.Y.S.2d 90, 581 N.E.2d 1345 (1991).

13. EPTL § 10-10.7.

executor was properly appointed in the state of original probate. In all cases the full consideration must be shown.[14]

28. **Conveyance by a guardian—Mental Hygiene Law.** The entire structure of the Mental Hygiene Law was changed effective April 1, 1993. Sections 77 and 78 which dealt with conservators and committees was repealed on the same dates that Section 81 became effective.[15]

The entire thrust of the law was to provide a mechanism so that a court order could be tailor made to fit the needs of an incapacitated person according to the degree of incapacity. The persons operating as conservators or committees may continue to perform under the existing orders until modified or abrogated by a court. Any other statutes referring to conservators or committees are deemed to refer to guardians.

The courts which have jurisdiction under the new law are:

(a) In New York City—the Supreme Court.

(b) Outside New York City—the Supreme Court.

(c) The Surrogate's Court where a guardian is needed to receive money or property.

There are provisions for hearings and trials where necessary. The persons who may be involved include:

(a) The affected party.

(b) Members of the family.

(c) Heirs designated by Will.

(d) A court appointed evaluator.

(e) In certain circumstances a special guardian *ad litem*.

The affected party has the right to have counsel. The petitioner has the burden of proving the necessity to appoint a guardian or co-guardians by clear and convincing evidence. The basic policy of law is to provide for the least restrictive order possible. There is provision for a bond unless waived. The appointment of a guardian does not create the presumption that the incapacitated party is not required to consent to property transfer. Accordingly, title insurers will most likely consider the documents on which the court order is based together with the clarity of the terms of the court order.

29. **Conveyance by entities.**

---

14. SCPA Art. 16.

15. For a full discussion of the changes to the Mental Hygiene Law affecting guardians, *see* Chapter 22, "Guardianship," *infra*.

(a) Corporation.[16]

(1) Sale of real property

(i) In the absence of any specific provision in the Certificate of Incorporation, the consent of two-thirds of the stockholders and the majority of the board of directors is required.

(ii) The document to be executed is a corporate resolution made by the Corporate Secretary indicating such action at a duly called regular or special meeting.

(iii) A statement contained in the deed or other conveyance that the shareholders have duly authorized the conveyance or that it was made in the ordinary course of business is presumptive evidence of that fact. No action to set aside the conveyance may be made after one year of the recordation of the conveyance.

(2) Mortgage of real property—The same rules apply as above unless the certificate of incorporation provides that the consent of the stockholders is not required, in which case the action of the directors alone is sufficient.

The authorization of a mortgage on the real property lease or pledge of a security interest may be authorized by the vote of the board of directors unless the certificate of incorporation also requires a vote of the stockholders.

(b) The Limited Partnership.

The Limited Partnership Law was amended effective April 1, 1991. Although the legislation completely revised the old law by adopting a new Article 8A, it permitted the continued operation of the Limited Partnership under Article 8 if the entity opted to do so.

(1) The Limited Partnership governed by original Article 8

The original Article 8 provided that the sale or mortgages of its property, if not a sale of all or substantially all of its assets, could be done by the action of the general partner together with any approvals that might be required by the limited partnership agreement. The same requirements applied to mortgages.

If the sale of the property involved the sale of all or substantially all of its assets, the law technically required the consent of all of the limited partners in addition to the

---

16. 15 NYBCL §§ 615, 909, 911.

general partner(s).[17] A title company may consider consent from less than all of the limited partners if (a) obtaining the consents of all limited partners is impractical, (b) the limited partnership agreement requires something other than the consents of all limited partners, or (c) not all the limited partners respond. Any combination of the foregoing may be considered with the approval of counsel.

(2) The limited partnership formed on or after April 1, 1991 or a previously formed limited partnership which opted to be governed by the new Article 8A:

(i) Unless the agreement provides otherwise, the consent of all of the general partners and

(ii) The consent of two thirds of each class of limited partners is required to convey or to mortgage property.[18]

(c) The General Partnership.

The sale of or mortgaging by a partnership owning real property generally requires the consent of whichever partners are granted the authority to do so in the partnership agreement. In the absence of such a provision in the partnership agreement, any partner can cause the dissolution of the partnership by transferring such interests.[19] However, if any partner transfers the entire partnership property without the consent of the other partners (unless provided for in the agreement), the other partners' interests may not have been transferred if the sale:

(1) prevents the carrying on of the usual business of the partnership or

(2) is a power which is prohibited by the partnership agreement.[20]

The NYPL deals with defenses by third parties who have no knowledge of an unauthorized partnership act. A title company will insist upon an examination of the last amended partnership agreement in order to determine the source of authority to act. In other words, the partnership agreement, as last amended, must be the source for authority.

(d) The Limited Liability Company ("LLC").[21]

The LLC has the authority to "sell, convey, assign, encumber, mortgage, pledge, lease, exchange, transfer, create a security interest in or otherwise dispose of all or part of its property

---

17. NYPL Art. 8, § 98.
18. NYPL Art. 8A, § 121–801(c).
19. NYPL § 62.
20. NYPL §§ 20, 21.
21. See NYLLCL §§ 202(c), 601.

or assets." The LLC's property is owned by the LLC with none of its members having any separate interest in it. In addition, the membership interest in the LLC is considered to be personal property. The title company would need to examine the operating agreement to determine where authority to convey real property resides.

(e) Not-for-Profit, Religious Corporations and Education Corporations (purchase, sale, mortgage or lease of real property).[22]

(1) No court order is required to authorize the purchase, sale, lease or mortgage of real property, except as noted *infra*, in paragraph (3). However, the transaction must be authorized by the vote of two-thirds of the entire board of directors, provided that if there are twenty-one or more directors the vote of a majority of the entire board is sufficient if it complies with the certificate of incorporation and by-laws.

(2) A sale, lease, exchange or other disposition of "all, or substantially all" of the assets of the corporation must comply with the following:

(i) If there are members entitled to vote thereon, the board of directors must adopt a resolution recommending the sale, lease, exchange or other disposition, specifying the terms and conditions and the eventual disposition of the consideration, together with a statement that the dissolution of the corporation is or is not contemplated thereafter.

(ii) If there are members entitled to vote thereon, the resolution of the board containing all essential facts must be approved by a two-thirds vote at an annual or special meeting after notice to all members whether or not entitled to vote and to the holders of any bonds or subvention certificates of the corporation.

(iii) If there are no members entitled to vote, the resolution of the board of directors as set forth above, in paragraph (e)(2)(i) will suffice.

(3) Such a sale, lease, exchange or other disposition by a Type B or Type C corporation also requires a court order based upon a petition in compliance with the Not-for-Profit Corporation Law.[23]

22. *See generally* Not-for-Profit Corporation Law §§ 210, 504, 509, 510, 511; Religious Corporation Law §§ 2–b, 12.

23. The Not-for-Profit Corporation Law creates four types of corporations: A, B, C and D. Not-for-Profit Corporation Law § 201. The requisite approval required for

(4) In addition sales, mortgages (other than purchase money) and leases for a term exceeding five years by religious corporations continue to require a court order as mandated by the Religious Corporations Law and requires notice of the application to the Attorney General. There is presently no provision for any confirmatory order to cover transactions consummated without the required court order.

(f) Other Types of Corporations

The Not-for-Profit Corporation Law provides for the creation of four types of not-for-profit corporations.[24] The ability of each of these to transfer interests in real property is governed by the specific provisions of the Not-for-Profit Corporation Law.

Type A is intended to cover the usual non-business membership corporations where activities by or for members are the predominant aspect. They would include civic, patriotic, social, fraternal, professional, trade or service associations. Type B covers the charity, educational, cultural, scientific and literary corporations, those to prevent cruelty to children or animals, and Religious and Education Corporations. In these cases, court approval will be required and notice must be given to the Attorney General. Type C is a new type whose purposes are ordinarily carried on for profit, but is intended to be non-profit. Type D is intended to cover the formation of corporations for purposes as provided in some other law, and may also include purposes included within Types A, B and/or C.

Another type of corporation is the legislatively chartered corporation.[25] Practitioners who are handling a transaction in which one of these corporations is a party must know that these entities are governed by the specific requirements of the legislation that created them, and may also be subject to the requirements of the Not-for-Profit Corporation Law.

§ 12.56 The Survey Map

The purpose of a survey is to obtain a representation in a diagrammatic form of the physical location of the property, and ultimately to ascertain the usability of the property for the purpose for which it is being purchased. The survey should show the dimensions and angles of the property, the improvements thereon, and encroachments, if any.[1]

conveyancing or borrowing vary with the type of Not-for-Profit Corporation. Not-for-Profit Corporation Law § 510. See infra, paragraph (f).

24. Not-for-Profit Corporation Law § 201.

25. An example of a legislatively chartered corporation is Columbia University.

§ 12.56

1. Under New York law, "the practice of the profession of land surveying is defined

§ 12.56   PURCHASE & SALE OF REAL ESTATE   Ch. 12

There are different types of surveys[2] and standards subscribed to and utilized by surveyors vary to a very significant degree. Title insurers in New York, through the New York State Land Title Association, have adopted a set of standards to consider when offering survey coverage,[3] especially those authorized pursuant to the Rate Manual of the Title Insurance Rating Service Association ("TIRSA"). Additionally, various organizations of land surveyors have adopted sets of minimum standards to which their members subscribe.[4] The attorney representing a client, especially where new development is likely to take place, should make inquiry and know what survey standards will be employed by the surveyor[5] and what will actually be shown on the survey.

as practicing that branch of the engineering profession and applied mathematics which includes the measuring and plotting of the dimensions and areas of any portion of the earth, including all naturally placed and man-or-machine-made structures and objects thereon, the lengths and directions of boundary lines, the contour of the surface and the application of rules and regulations in accordance with local requirements incidental to subdivisions for the correct determination, description, conveying and recording thereof or for the establishment or reestablishment thereof." Education Law § 7203.

2. Aerial Survey—A technique of obtaining photographic topographical data, which when used together with survey measurements on the ground, can within reasonable limits, be of great value in plotting the physical location of property.

Perimeter Map—Map of the survey of the perimeter of a large tract of land that eventually may be subdivided into building lots.

Perimeter Survey—Survey of the perimeter of a parcel of land only. Interior walls, buildings, fences, etc. are not shown.

Survey in Possession—Same as perimeter survey, but in some cases interior walls, buildings, fences, etc.—will be located and shown on survey.

Tape Location Survey—The survey map is based upon measurements made without the use of angle measuring instruments and may not be based upon objective monumentation.

Topographical Survey—Same as survey in possession with additional information such as ground elevations, sewer mains, electric and telephone service to be used by an architect for the design of new buildings.

U.S. Coast & Geodetic (now known as National Ocean Survey). Stone monuments placed by the National Ocean Survey that control the state plane coordinate system. From these monuments the various counties can set their own monuments to lay out the street system. This is the core of information on which most surveying is based. Nevertheless the coordinate system established by the National Ocean Survey may not be the final arbiter of the boundaries of real property.

Section 8 of Chapter 151 of the Unconsolidated Laws of New York states as follows:

8. Interpretation of Act. Nothing contained in this act shall be interpreted as requiring any purchaser or mortgagee to rely wholly on a description based upon aforementioned (coordinate) system.

3. Survey coverage is not part of the title policy, and such coverage should be considered if the client wants to assure the lender of the stability of those matters which may effect the interests of the insured relating to the boundaries of the insured property.

4. See, for example, Standards Adopted by New York State Association of Professional Land Surveyors, Inc. dated October 19, 1966 as revised November 19, 1977 and more recently the 1992 standards adopted by the American Congress of Surveying and Measurement and the American Land Title Association.

5. CAVEAT: Surveyors in various areas may subscribe to the standards of their state association or may subscribe to local standards. These local standards may be more or less onerous than the state standards. The notes placed on a survey, including the seal of the surveyor, are of great importance and should be carefully read

The professional surveyor is also subject to state regulation and licensing requirements which may dictate the functions that may be performed by the surveyor. New York State regulates the licensing of land surveyors pursuant to the Education Law.[6] The statute specifically provides that a survey may be made by professional engineers "except that the determination of real property boundaries may be done only by a licensed land surveyor."[7] A certificate of a licensed engineer who lacks a land surveyor's license is not sufficient.[8]

Although the survey is an important tool to be understood by counsel dealing with real property, the survey is not the creator of title. Title is evidenced by the chain of title. The survey can identify the monuments and locations, but the quantum of the title depends upon the chain of title, as evidenced in the land and other collateral records.[9]

In the absence of specific notations to the contrary, the number of degrees, minutes and seconds shown on a survey are measured with regard to due north and due south. Minor variation or deflection errors can result in description variation of significant amounts of land.[10]

It is beyond the purview of this section to discuss the issue of surveyor's liability. Several American Law Report articles on the subject discuss the tort and contract aspects of the surveyor's liability.[11] Note that a surveyor's liability may depend upon the contractual basis upon which the surveyor was hired.[12]

and understood by the attorney and the client.

6. *See* Education Law §§ 7200–7209.

7. Education Law § 7208(e). *See also* RPL § 334 and 1970 Op. Att'y Gen. 210 (informal opinion).

8. Nassau–Suffolk Civil Eng'rs. Inc. v. Albertson, No. 194780 (Sup.Ct., Suffolk County, June 10, 1979) (which held that the certificate of the surveyor required by RPL § 375, on subdivision maps accepted for filing in the Suffolk County Clerk's office, means a certificate filed by a licensed land surveyor, not by a person who is only a licensed professional engineer). *See also* Scarano v. Board of Regents, 57 A.D.2d 991, 394 N.Y.S.2d 322 (3d Dep't 1977).

9. Such as probate and litigation records establishing adverse possession or actions to quiet title.

10. Deflection differentials

Degree 1—1.75 feet per 100 feet

Minute 1 degree—0.03 feet per 100 feet (60 minutes=1 minute)

Seconds 20 inches—0.01 feet per 100 feet (60 minutes=1 minute)

These deflections indicate that where a description contains an error in the above amounts there will be a loss or gain of a substantial quantum of real estate, thereby affecting title.

11. *See* 72 A.L.R. 4th 132 (1989) (Dispute or doubt as to boundary); 35 A.L.R.3d 504 (1971) (Surveyor's liability for mistake in, or misrepresentation as to accuracy of survey of real property); 3 A.L.R.2d 577 (1949) (Recording unrecordable instrument); 130 A.L.R. 1034 (1941) (Property rights in respect of building, fence, or other structure placed upon another's land through mistake as to boundary or location); 40 A.L.R. 1358 (1926) (Personal liability of municipal officer or employee in performance of duty) (engineer or surveyor).

12. Wetzler v. O'Brien, 81 A.D.2d 517, 437 N.Y.S.2d 343 (1st Dep't 1981) (where the court reinstated a verdict for the defendant that indicated the metes and bounds of the property had to be shown for a subdivision map and only the entrance and exit of the water traversing the property had to be shown and not all of the topographical features including the course of the brook which, if detailed in the survey, would have indicated that a contemplated

§ 12.57 **The Survey Map—What It May Disclose**

The proper utilization of a "good" survey is indispensable to making proper evaluations of the quality of title. A survey may disclose matters such as variations between record and actual courses, dimensions, angles, street lines, widenings and the location of easements. It may also disclose the location of setbacks from streets and possible non-compliance with setbacks from side and rear lines which violate either zoning ordinances or other recorded restrictions. All of these matters may impinge on the marketability of the title or its value to the purchaser or mortgagee.

A survey may also disclose "open and visible matters" such as advertising signs, exposed water meters indicating underground pipes, cesspool covers, drainage ditches or ponds indicating unrecorded but adverse prescriptive rights or even adverse possession. In a most unusual case,[1] an advertising sign, which was the subject of an unrecorded lease for twenty years, was placed upon property well before the premises were contracted to be sold. The lessee of the sign was the owner of property which did not abut the property where the sign was located. The court held that because of the actual notice of the sign, the buyer was not protected by the recording act, and that the property interest of the sign owner was protected for the full length of the lease. The court further found that the lessee's interest had ripened into an easement in gross, even though it was not appurtenant to that owner's property,[2] and was enforceable for the full twenty year term of the lease so long as the rent was paid. This case could be rationalized as protecting the right of a tenant in possession.

Another problem which may be uncovered by a property survey is one relating to the location of streets, roads or highways and the problem of access to and from a legally opened road or the existence of a public or private easement of access. For example, roads laid out prior to 1664 (the date of the Dutch surrender to the British) vested title in the sovereign absolutely but roads laid out thereafter belong to the owner of the underlying land.[3]

access road could not have been built by the plaintiffs without moving the brook).

§ 12.57
1. XAR Corp. v. Di Donato, 76 A.D.2d 972, 429 N.Y.S.2d 59 (3d Dep't 1980).

2. An easement in gross can only be a personal covenant benefitting only the party to whom it is granted. See 2 Warren's Weed, New York Real Property, § 28.04 (4th ed. 1981).

3. Appleton v. City of New York, 219 N.Y. 150, 114 N.E. 73 (1916); Dunham v. Williams, 37 N.Y. 251 (1867). Consider also the effect of General Municipal Law § 35. This Section provides that where the city map indicates a proposed street widening the city may, through board action, permit construction of buildings in the area designated for possible widening subject to restrictions which include a limitation on future condemnation awards.

It is worth noting that property lines which appear to be stable and established for many years may be called into question. For example, there is a federal program which seeks to accurately locate the boundaries of federal land and protect the land so located. Whether or not the title to governmental lands not held in a public capacity can be subject to adverse possession is a question that is usually resolved in favor of the sovereign. The United States has been conducting a federal program which has been given added impetus by virtue of the Federal Land Policy and Management Act of 1976.[4]

§ 12.58 The Survey Map—Effect on Marketability of Title

A contract for the sale of real property is based upon the seller's agreeing to deliver "marketable title." This may be defined as title that is of such quality that the buyer does not have to go to unusual lengths or efforts or indulge in litigation to prove its validity.[1] The effect of a survey condition on the marketability of title may depend on whether the contract contains a provision waiving objections to all or some facts which a survey might disclose that would render title unmarketable. The discussion which follows will indicate some of the situations which typically give rise to marketability problems in relation to the facts disclosed by a survey.

Library References:

West's Key No. Digests, Vendor and Purchaser ⇔130.

§ 12.59 The Survey Map—Effect on Marketability—Where Contract Is Silent on the Matter of Survey

A purchaser will not be required to accept unmarketable title where the contract is silent as to the survey conditions to which the buyer is subject. In the landmark case of *McPherson v. Schade*,[1] the building on the subject property encroached on the abutting property to the extent of 5 feet for a distance of 25 feet. Additionally, a portion of the premises was used by the abutting owner as an alleyway for ingress and egress. While the contract was silent as to survey conditions, the dimensions of the property were described pursuant to a survey. However, the contract still required the seller to deliver a marketable title. The Court of

---

4. 90 Stat. 2743 (codified in scattered sections of Titles 5, 15, 16, 30, 31, 40, 42, 43 U.S.C.A.).

§ 12.58

1. Marketability may be defined as a title whose validity is not open to serious doubt. Brokaw v. Duffy, 165 N.Y. 391 59 N.E. 196 (1901); Kirkwall Corp. v. Sessa, 60 A.D.2d 563, 400 N.Y.S.2d 349 (1st Dep't 1977); Caselli v. Messina, 148 Misc.2d 671, 567 N.Y.S.2d 972 (Sup.Ct., App. Term, 1990), aff'd 193 A.D.2d 775, 598 N.Y.S.2d 265 (1993).

§ 12.59

1. 149 N.Y. 16, 43 N.E. 527 (1896).

§ 12.59 PURCHASE & SALE OF REAL ESTATE Ch. 12

Appeals held that the buyer was not required to accept the title proffered.

Library References:
West's Key No. Digests, Vendor and Purchaser ⚖=130.

§ 12.60 The Survey Map—Effect on Marketability—Where Contract Subject to Any State of Facts an Accurate Survey May Show

A purchaser may inadvertently waive the requirement of marketability by means of a contract provision. For example, if a contract states that the property is being sold "subject to any state of facts an accurate survey may show" and an encroachment is found to exist, the purchaser will be required to accept title because of this provision.[1] However, the purchaser of property pursuant to a judicial sale may be relieved from taking title even when the sale is announced or advertised as "subject to any state of facts an accurate survey may show."[2] This is based upon the theory that had the buyer entered into a formal contract it might have provided that the transfer of title would be made subject to a marketability provision.

Furthermore, where the contract provides that it is subject to any state of facts a survey might show, a buyer will not have to accept a title which contains a shortage or deficiency of land.[3]

Library References:
West's Key No. Digests, Vendor and Purchaser ⚖=130.

§ 12.61 The Survey Map—Effect on Marketability—Where Contract Is Subject to Any State of Facts an Accurate Survey May Show Provided Same Does Not Render Title Unmarketable

This is probably the most dangerous clause to use in a contract since it undoubtedly gives an unwilling buyer the opportunity to reject the title. No doubt many conditions shown on a survey would render a title unmarketable but would not normally deter a willing buyer. A case which illustrates this point rather cogently is *Laba v. Carey*.[1] A prior

§ 12.60
1. McCarter v. Crawford, 245 N.Y. 43, 156 N.E. 90 (1927).
2. Lane v. Chantilly Corp., 251 N.Y. 435, 167 N.E. 578 (1929) (notice of sale in foreclosure provided title was subject to facts disclosed by survey).
3. Meehan v. Newman Improvement Corp., 262 N.Y. 682, 188 N.E. 119 (1933); Kaplan v. Bergmann, 122 App.Div. 876, 107 N.Y.S. 423 (2d Dep't 1907).

§ 12.61
1. 29 N.Y.2d 302, 327 N.Y.S.2d 613, 277 N.E.2d 641 (1971), rev'g 36 A.D.2d 823, 321 N.Y.S.2d 159 (2d Dep't 1971)(covenant whereby owner of the property could be required to raise the level of the sidewalk did not render title unmarketable).

owner had entered into a covenant with the City of New York by which it was granted a waiver of a legal grade requirement. The prior owner built the sidewalk one foot below grade in order to be consistent with abutting owners and covenanted with the City to restore the sidewalk to grade at any time the Commissioner of Highways may direct. The contract which the seller entered into contained the following two provisions:

> Subject to covenants, restrictions, utility agreements and easements of record, if any now in force, provided same are not now violated.
>
> Subject to any state of facts an accurate survey may show provided same does not render title unmarketable.

The court held the title marketable "where a purchaser agrees to take title subject to easements and restrictive covenants of record which [were] not violated."[2] The court explained "this is the precise kind of title that the seller is obligated to tender and we are not persuaded that, absent an expression of a contrary intent in the contract, that obligation is broadened by the existence of the usual 'insurance' clause."[3]

In another case where the contract of sale was "subject to any state of facts an accurate survey may show, provided same does not render title unmarketable," the court held that the buyers were precluded from alleging that the sellers misrepresented the boundaries of the property in question.[4] A survey conducted by the buyers prior to closing contained a clear description of the boundaries of the property being sold, and did not serve to render title unmarketable. The court held that the buyers were, therefore, precluded from alleging, four years after the closing and in conclusory fashion, that the sellers misrepresented the boundaries of the property in question.

Library References:

West's Key No. Digests, Vendor and Purchaser ⚖=130.

§ 12.62 The Survey Map—Effect on Marketability—Where Contract Subject to Specific Encroachments or to Facts Shown on a Specific Survey

Despite what would ordinarily render a title unmarketable, where a contract provides that it is subject to a specific encroachment, the contract will be enforceable.[1] A contract will also be enforceable where it is subject to facts shown on a specific survey. Where a contract contained

---

2. Laba, 29 N.Y.2d at 308–309, 327 N.Y.S.2d at 618–619.

3. Id.

4. Eisenthal v. Wittlock, 198 A.D.2d 395, 603 N.Y.S.2d 586 (2d Dep't 1993).

§ 12.62

1. 401 East 72nd Street Realty Co., Inc. v. Ebling Realty Co., 222 App.Div. 388, 226 N.Y.S. 58 (1st Dep't 1928), aff'd mem. 248 N.Y. 545, 162 N.E. 518 (1928).

§ 12.62   PURCHASE & SALE OF REAL ESTATE   Ch. 12

a clause referring to a specific survey and stating that the buyer would accept the encroachments shown on that survey, *e.g.*, a wall that encroached from 1/4 inch to 1 3/4 inches, the buyer could not contend that the contract was unenforceable due to alleged misrepresentation.[2] However, where the encroachments are more substantial than that shown on the named survey, the court may not enforce the contract.[3] For example, where a bay window encroached two feet on the street and the contract provided that it was subject to a survey which showed an encroachment of 12 inches, the contract was held not to be enforceable.[4]

Library References:
West's Key No. Digests, Vendor and Purchaser ⇨130.

§ 12.63   The Survey Map—Effect on Marketability— Suggested Clause

Where a survey is available, a satisfactory clause to include in the Contract of Sale would be:

"Subject to the facts shown on the survey made by _____ dated _____ (and redated _____) and to any state of facts shown in the said survey, brought down to date, would show, provided the additional facts that would be disclosed by reason of said survey being brought down to date do not render title unmarketable."

§ 12.64   Marketability of Title

The conveyance of marketable title is probably the most critical aspect of the real estate transaction and the requirement that the seller is to convey marketable title should be specified in the contract, along with the rights and obligations of the parties if the seller is unable to transfer such title. Indeed, a purchaser is entitled to a marketable title unless the parties stipulate otherwise in the contract. A buyer will not be compelled to take property that the buyer may be obliged to defend by litigation, or to receive a title that is subject to probable claims by another.[1] Similarly, where a defect in the record title can be cured only by a resort to parol evidence, or an apparent encumbrance can be removed or defeated only by such evidence, marketable title becomes a question of fact and the purchaser will not be compelled to take title

---

2. Kreshover v. Berger, 135 App.Div. 27, 119 N.Y.S. 737 (1st Dep't 1909).

3. Fineman v. Callahan, 222 App.Div. 752, 225 N.Y.S. 401 (2d Dep't 1927).

4. Heyman v. Steich, 134 App.Div. 176, 114 N.Y.S. 603 (Sup.Ct., Kings County, 1908), aff'd 118 N.Y.S. 1113 (2d Dep't 1909), aff'd mem. 201 N.Y. 578, 95 N.E. 1130 (1911).

§ 12.64

1. Boecher v. Borth, 51 A.D.2d 598, 377 N.Y.S.2d 781 (3d Dep't 1976) (involving a certain remainder interest under a Will; the apparent interest of the remainderman in the property was a sufficient cloud on the title to have rendered it unmarketable).

which an ordinarily prudent person would be justified in hesitating to accept or loan money on.[2]

The Court of Appeals has set forth the general rules as to what constitutes marketable title.[3] Marketable title is title that can be readily sold or mortgaged to a person of reasonable prudence. The test of marketability is whether there is an objection to title so as to interfere with a sale or with the market value of the property.[4] Keep in mind, however, that while the law assures to a buyer a title free from reasonable doubt, it need not necessarily be free from every doubt.[5] For example, the mere possibility, such as a very remote or improbable contingency, or suspicion of a defect, which according to ordinary experience has no probable basis, does not render a title unmarketable.

Mere marketability of a title is no guarantee that a title company will be willing to insure it. Such companies are entitled to choose their own risks.[6] On the other hand, the fact that a title company is willing to insure a title does not mean that it is marketable. Marketability is a legal question; insurability is a commercial decision. If the contract provides that the purchaser agrees to accept a title such as a designated title company will approve and insure, the named title company is the final judge of title and, if it is willing to insure in accordance with the contract, no further requirement need be met by the seller.[7] Of course, the parties may agree to stipulate to the delivery of both marketable and insurable title.[8]

Generally, where the contract provides that the purchaser agrees to accept a title such as any reputable title company would approve and insure, the seller assumes the burden of delivering a title that the title company will approve and insure unconditionally and without exceptions.[9] However, this rule is not absolute, but is tempered by the exigencies of the particular contract. For example, in a case where the title company insured subject to a telephone easement and a covenant to raise the sidewalk of the premises to legal grade at any time as the

2. Cerf v. Diener, 210 N.Y. 156, 104 N.E. 126 (1914).

3. Voorheesville Rod and Gun Club v. E.W. Tompkins Co., 82 N.Y.2d 564, 606 N.Y.S.2d 132, 626 N.E.2d 917 (1993); Regan v. Lanze, 40 N.Y.2d 475, 387 N.Y.S.2d 79, 354 N.E.2d 818 (1976).

4. Voorheesville Rod and Gun Club, 82 N.Y.2d at 571, 606 N.Y.S.2d at 135, 626 N.E.2d at 920.

5. Id.

6. Gilchrest House, Inc. v. Guaranteed Title and Mortgage Co., 277 App.Div. 788, 97 N.Y.S.2d 226 (2d Dep't 1950), aff'd 302 N.Y. 852, 100 N.E.2d 46 (1951).

7. Haar v. Daly, 232 App.Div. 423, 250 N.Y.S. 59 (2d Dep't 1931), aff'd 258 N.Y. 623, 180 N.E. 360 (1931); Creative Living, Inc. v. Steinhauser, 78 Misc.2d 29, 355 N.Y.S.2d 897 (Sup.Ct., Bronx County, 1974) (by contracting for an insurable title, the parties had abrogated the general rule requiring marketability).

8. New York Investors v. Manhattan Beach Bathing Parks Corp., 229 App.Div. 593, 243 N.Y.S. 548 (2d Dep't 1930), aff'd 256 N.Y. 162, 176 N.E. 6 (1930).

9. Newmark v. Weingrad, 43 A.D.2d 983, 352 N.Y.S.2d 660 (2d Dep't 1974), aff'd 35 N.Y.2d 832, 362 N.Y.S.2d 863, 321 N.E.2d 784 (1974) (title company refused to insure one of the lots involved in the sale); Atlas Realty of East Meadow, Inc. v. Ostrofsky, 56 Misc.2d 787, 289 N.Y.S.2d 784 (Sup. Ct., Nassau County, 1967).

§ 12.64   PURCHASE & SALE OF REAL ESTATE   Ch. 12

Commissioner of Highways might direct, the seller was not in breach of the contract since the purchaser had specifically agreed to take title subject to easements and restrictive covenants of record which were not violated and there was no showing of any violation. The court reasoned that the "insurance" clause and the "subject to" clause were to be read together.[10]

Moreover, this requirement may be waived by the buyer if the buyer is aware of the objection to marketability at the time of the contract.[11] The buyer will also waive the opportunity to place the seller in default for failure to provide clear title if he or she fails to tender performance and demand good title.[12] Tender is excused only if the title defect is not curable.[13] Where time is not made of the essence in the contract to convey realty, a buyer cannot object to the title without giving the seller a reasonable opportunity to cure a defect when found and the seller cannot be placed in default without the purchaser also making demand for the deed and tendering the purchase price.[14] For an interesting case on the seller's liability, see *Leder v. Dry Dock Savings Institution.*[15] The court held that the failure of a seller to communicate known encroachments to a broker may result in seller's liability for the broker's commission if the sale is not consummated because of the encroachments. In this case, the one half inch encroachment was deemed to be minimal, but the court indicated that if the title was clearly unmarketable and that fact was known to the defendant, there might be liability.

Library References:

West's Key No. Digests, Vendor and Purchaser ⚖ 130.

§ 12.65   Marketability of Title—What Renders Title Unmarketable

Marketability of title is concerned with impairments on title to a property, *i.e.*, the right to unencumbered ownership and possession, and

---

10. Laba v. Carey, 29 N.Y.2d 302, 327 N.Y.S.2d 613, 277 N.E.2d 641 (1971).

11. *See* Rose v. Spa Realty Associates, 60 A.D.2d 937, 400 N.Y.S.2d 919 (3d Dep't 1978) (the purchasers' early prior knowledge of the sewer easement and their failure to raise any objection thereto by suit or otherwise until after judgment, appeals and resettled judgment in a specific performance action precluded the purchasers from refusing to close under the doctrines of estoppel and laches); *see also* Ilemar Corp. v. Krochmal, 58 A.D.2d 853, 396 N.Y.S.2d 676 (2d Dep't), aff'd 44 N.Y.2d 702, 405 N.Y.S.2d 444, 376 N.E.2d 917 (1978); *but see* Patten of New York Corporation v. Geoffrion, 193 A.D.2d 1007, 598 N.Y.S.2d 355 (3d Dep't), leave to appeal denied 82 N.Y.2d 654, 602 N.Y.S.2d 803, 622 N.E.2d 304 (1993) (mere knowledge of a utility easement did not defeat the buyer's right to object to the marketability of title where on the merits title really was unmarketable and the title company was unwilling to insure without exception).

12. Willard v. Mercer, 83 A.D.2d 656, 442 N.Y.S.2d 200 (3d Dep't 1981); Ilemar Corp. v. Krochmal, 58 A.D.2d 853, 396 N.Y.S.2d 676 (2d Dep't 1977), aff'd 44 N.Y.2d 702, 405 N.Y.S.2d 444, 376 N.E.2d 917 (1978); Bord v. Brindisi, 49 A.D.2d 695, 370 N.Y.S.2d 766 (4th Dep't 1975).

13. Gentile v. Kim, 101 A.D.2d 939, 475 N.Y.S.2d 631 (3d Dep't 1984).

14. Bord v. Brindisi, 49 A.D.2d 695, 370 N.Y.S.2d 766 (4th Dep't 1975).

15. 8 N.Y.S.2d 68 (City Ct., N.Y. County, 1938).

not with legal public regulation of the use of the property. Accordingly, a zoning ordinance in existence at the time of the contract which regulates only the use of the property, will generally not be considered an encumbrance making the title unmarketable. Where, however, a contract expressly provides that the seller warrants and represents that, upon purchase, the property will not be in violation of any zoning ordinance, the purchaser is entitled to demand that the vendor rectify any violation or return the down payment.[1]

Lack of legal access will render title unmarketable.[2] However, in a case where an undeveloped tract of land was bounded on three sides by public streets and, before the adjourned date for closing of title the village erected a barrier at one intersection with the net result of making access to the tract more difficult or burdensome but still allowing an individual on any part of the property to proceed to each and every public street exactly as he could before the barrier was erected, the title was not rendered unmarketable by the placement of the barrier.[3]

An easement over the seller's property in favor of an adjoining land owner, which had not been excepted by the seller's agreement to convey marketable title, rendered title unmarketable, even though there was no showing that the encumbrance actually diminished the market value of the property.[4] The existence of an easement providing the purchaser with use of adjoining property, however, does not render title to the property being purchased unmarketable.[5]

Street encroachments may affect marketability of title. A one and one-half foot encroachment of the front of a garage upon a public street

---

§ 12.65

1. Voorheesville Rod and Gun Club v. E.W. Tompkins Co., 82 N.Y.2d 564, 606 N.Y.S.2d 132, 626 N.E.2d 917 (1993)(but where there was no such warranty or representation and the buyer agreed to purchase the property subject to the zoning laws and the seller failed to obtain subdivision approval, title was not rendered unmarketable. The court noted that the proper method for avoiding such problems is not for the courts to expand the conditions which render title unmarketable, thereby altering the concept of marketability of title, but for the parties to real estate contracts to include specific provisions dealing with the duty to obtain subdivision approval).

2. Barasky v. Huttner, 210 A.D.2d 367, 620 N.Y.S.2d 121 (2d Dep't 1994), citing Pollak v. State of New York, 41 N.Y.2d 909, 394 N.Y.S.2d 617, 363 N.E.2d 342 (1977).

3. Kirkwall Corp. v. Sessa, 48 N.Y.2d 709, 422 N.Y.S.2d 368, 397 N.E.2d 1172 (1979)(plaintiff, by written contract, had agreed to purchase the property in question subject to all zoning regulations and ordinances, and therefore, could not then argue that the vendor's promise to provide insurable title was in some way violated solely because of the title insurance company's refusal to insure the right of ingress and egress which was limited by a preexisting ordinance).

4. Rhodes v. Astro–Pac, Inc., 51 A.D.2d 656, 378 N.Y.S.2d 195 (4th Dep't 1976), aff'd 41 N.Y.2d 919, 394 N.Y.S.2d 623, 363 N.E.2d 347 (1977)(an easement is an encumbrance, and obviously a purchaser need not accept title subject to an encumbrance if the contract specifies conveyance of title free of all encumbrances).

5. DeJong v. Mandelbaum, 122 A.D.2d 772, 505 N.Y.S.2d 659 (2d Dep't 1986); Lippes v. Bradley, 203 A.D.2d 959, 612 N.Y.S.2d 719 (4th Dep't 1994) (fact that a portion of the deck and the brick patio extended into a common area owned by the condominium association did not constitute an encroachment upon the property of the sellers that rendered title unmarketable).

§ 12.65   PURCHASE & SALE OF REAL ESTATE   Ch. 12

was held to be an incurably defective bar to clear title.[6] Similarly, the four foot encroachment of a stoop and a twelve inch encroachment of a bay window onto a public street rendered title unmarketable even though the applicable building code allowed for the erection of the subject building with a one foot encroachment.[7] Other encroachments that may render title unmarketable include encroachments of roof cornices, trim, fire escapes, cellar doors and the like.[8] It should also be noted that some legislative authority permits front wall encroachments up to six inches, depending upon when the walls were erected,[9] and that in these situations, title insurance will still be available. Note that if the contract provides that the buyer shall take title subject to such conditions, the buyer may be required to accept title. Moreover, although an unwilling buyer may get relief from an imprecisely drawn contract, as a practical matter these types of encroachments will not discourage willing buyers or lenders.

The existence of certain unlocated burial reservations, which were not excepted from the contract and which inhibited development of the property for residential use, rendered the sellers' title unmarketable.[10]

A railroad easement also rendered title unmarketable where the clear and unequivocal wording of the contract required the vendor to convey title "except for utility easements and except none."[11]

Library References:
West's Key No. Digests, Vendor and Purchaser ⬅130.

6. Sydelman v. Marici, 56 A.D.2d 866, 392 N.Y.S.2d 333 (2d Dep't 1977)(however, the seller's proposed remedy of removing the encroachment and adding 1½ feet to the rear of the garage would constitute an alteration from, and a substitute for, what was contracted for). *Cf.* O. W. Siebert Co., Inc. v. Kramer, 107 Misc.2d 520, 435 N.Y.S.2d 476 (Sup.Ct., Queens County, 1980)(where five feet of the subject property's frontage lay in the bed of a mapped street, title was not rendered unmarketable).

7. Acme Realty Co. v. Schinasi, 215 N.Y. 495, 109 N.E. 577 (1915); *see also* Ravine Point Corp. v. Kott, 254 N.Y. 580, 173 N.E. 875 (1930)(building encroached into street by four feet).

8. *See* Jennings v. Baumann, 214 App. Div. 361, 212 N.Y.S. 334 (2d Dep't 1925), aff'd. 243 N.Y. 532, 154 N.E. 593 (1926)(where building projected into the street); Lencrif Realty Corp. v. Cappelen, 247 N.Y. 566, 161 N.E. 184 (1928)(where building encroached on highway).

9. Front wall encroachments on street permitted:

In cities—up to six inches if built before January 1, 1960. After January 1, 1960, one year notice to municipality of the encroachment is required. Local legislative permission to maintain encroachment may be granted if wall was built before January 1, 1979. General City Law § 38–a . .

In towns and villages—up to six inches if built before January 11, 1940. After January 1, 1940, one year notice to municipality of the encroachment is required. Local legislative permission may be granted if wall was built prior to January 1, 1965. Town Law § 130(7); Village Law § 6–632.

Within New York County (limits as of May 25, 1899)—ten inches if built before same date. N.Y.C. Administrative Code § 692h–6.0(a) (1977).

10. Patten of New York Corporation v. Geoffrion, 193 A.D.2d 1007, 598 N.Y.S.2d 355, (3d Dep't 1993), leave to appeal denied 82 N.Y.2d 654, 602 N.Y.S.2d 803, 622 N.E.2d 304 (1993).

11. Tanners Realty Corp. v. Ruggerio, 111 A.D.2d 974, 490 N.Y.S.2d 73 (3d Dep't 1985).

§ 12.66 Marketability of Title—What Renders Title Unmarketable—Encroachments Due to Adverse Possession

Encroachments on property due to adverse possession may render title unmarketable. The existence for the required period of time of fences and hedges may result in a finding of adverse possession.[1] Note that hostile possession is a condition of adverse possession. Thus, when an agreement exists, there is no adverse possession since consent obviated a condition of adverse possession.[2] Adverse possession was also found in a case where a stone wall and new hedges were at issue.[3] A property owned by a municipality in its proprietary capacity is also subject to being lost by adverse possession.[4]

Adverse possession does not begin to run against a recorded easement unless it is an existing right of way and fencing will not be deemed adverse until such time as the need for the right of way arises, a demand is made by the owner of the dominant estate that the easement be opened, and the owner of the servient estate refuses to do so.[5]

In *Mylott v. Sisca*,[6] the plaintiff sought an injunction to compel removal of a deck that extended three feet over the southerly leg of a parking easement for approximately eleven feet. The plaintiff commenced the action seven years after the deck was built. The court rejected a defense of laches inasmuch as the ten year period for prescriptive easement rights had not yet run. The court nevertheless refused to grant injunctive relief and remitted the case to the trial court to determine whether the imposition of monetary damages would be a just remedy and to what extent the plaintiff's easement to park two vehicles was impaired. The court, while rejecting laches, applied the concept of balancing the equities.

Library References:

West's Key No. Digests, Vendor and Purchaser ⇨130.

§ 12.66

1. *See* RPAPL §§ 501–551.

2. Devyr v. Schaefer, 55 N.Y. 446 (1874).

3. Rusoff v. Engel, 89 A.D.2d 587, 452 N.Y.S.2d 250 (2d Dep't 1982).

4. Town of Hempstead v. Bonner, 77 A.D.2d 567, 429 N.Y.S.2d 739 (2d Dep't 1980), app. denied 51 N.Y.2d 707, 433 N.Y.S.2d 1027, 414 N.E.2d 402 (1980).

5. Castle Associates v. Schwartz, 63 A.D.2d 481, 407 N.Y.S.2d 717 (2d Dep't 1978). The distinction between prescriptive rights and adverse possession is that a prescriptive right allows the use of property. Adverse possession is a method of acquisition of title to real property by possession for a statutory period under certain conditions. The period for the acquisition of rights by adverse possession and prescriptive rights is 10 years. CPLR 212(a) and RPAPL § 511. *See also* Warren's Weed, New York Law of Real Property (4th ed. 1981) "Inspection of Property."

6. 168 A.D.2d 852, 564 N.Y.S.2d 523 (3d Dep't 1990).

§ 12.67 Marketability of Title—What Renders Title Unmarketable—Party Walls

Much old construction was more economically erected with the use of common walls, more commonly known as party walls. In some instances, however, the so-called party wall was located solely on the property of one of the owners.

A case involving a problem akin to this was *O'Neil v. Van Tassel*,[1] involving a contract which made no mention of an attached party wall. However, as the premises were described in the contract, to the effect that "the northerly wall of number twenty-four (Renwick Street) being a party wall ...", the dimension could not be justified unless the party wall was included in the computation to arrive at the figure represented in the contract. The court held that the recorded party wall agreement rendered title unmarketable. The court distinguished the earlier case of *Hendricks v. Stark*[2] where the property was sold at auction and was described as being forty-four feet on West Street and eighty feet on Hoboken. No mention was made of party walls. The premises in fact measured accurately to the center of party walls as described. The court held that the fact that there was in effect a mutual easement did not diminish the value of the property.

The problem of beam rights is directly related to party walls. In *Soma Realty Company v. Romeo*,[3] the court held that in the absence of proof of any license, it would be presumed that a grant of beam rights to an owner of an adjoining building was given and that such grant ripened into a prescriptive right on the passage of the requisite period (in this case, twenty years) based upon the doctrine of lost grant.[4] Furthermore, the party having the benefit of the beam rights would thereafter have rights similar to that created where a party wall existed.

Library References:
West's Key No. Digests, Vendor and Purchaser ⚷130.

§ 12.68 Marketability of Title—What Renders Title Unmarketable—Driveway Easements

An easement to pass over a defendant's property in favor of an adjoining owner has been held to be an encumbrance which rendered the seller's title unmarketable.[1] The encumbrance was an objection to title

---

§ 12.67

1. 137 N.Y. 297, 33 N.E. 314 (1893) (per curiam).
2. 37 N.Y. 106 (1867).
3. 31 Misc.2d 20, 220 N.Y.S.2d 752 (Sup.Ct., Onondaga County, 1961).
4. The court indicates that the beams were in existence almost 100 years and "absent any proof of a license it must be presumed that a grant was given and lost." 17 N.Y.2d at 339, 270 N.Y.S.2d at 757.

§ 12.68

1. Rhodes v. Astro–Pac, 51 A.D.2d 656, 378 N.Y.S.2d 195 (4th Dep't 1976), aff'd mem. 41 N.Y.2d 919, 363 N.E.2d 347, 394 N.Y.S.2d 623 (1977).

not covered by the contract. There is a line of cases which indicates that a driveway or private road abutting or affecting two properties used by adjoining owners for a ten year period can result in the acquisition of an easement as a matter of prescriptive right.[2] However, until the prescriptive right is declared, the title would still be considered unmarketable.[3]

Library References:

West's Key No. Digests, Vendor and Purchaser ⚖=130.

§ 12.69 Marketability of Title—What Renders Title Unmarketable—Other Covenants and Restrictions

Other covenants and restrictions which are not disclosed may render the title unmarketable. The First Department has held[1] that an affirmative covenant to erect a dwelling house was not violated by the construction of an apartment house. However, the prior common owner of the tract had validly placed setback restrictions which were violated by the erection of the structure five feet beyond the line established. Despite the existence of undisclosed covenants and restrictions, utilization of the premises for the purposes for which the property was intended may be acquired by the insured in two different ways depending on the particular facts; the seller may have acquired rights with a prescriptive easement or even by way of an actual easement.[2] It should also be noted that even sporadic use of an easement over a period of time may ripen into a prescriptive easement.[3] Neither of these methods will make the title marketable, but may provide the opportunity for a title insurer to provide coverage that will satisfy the insured and enable the transaction to proceed.

Alternatively, Section 2001 of the RPAPL may offer some help in relieving the effect of the violation of the covenant and restriction to which an adjoining owner may be a beneficiary by way of a short Statute of Limitations for an action to enjoin the violation. In this instance, title insurers will frequently be willing to provide coverage that despite the violations of the restrictions, the building and improvements may be utilized in their present state for so long as these buildings stand.[4] In summary, neither solution necessarily addresses the problem of market-

---

2. See supra, § 12.66.

3. Mission of the Immaculate Virgin for the Protection of Homeless and Destitute Children v. Cronin, 143 N.Y. 524, 38 N.E. 964 (1894); Roe v. Strong, 119 N.Y. 316, 23 N.E. 743 (1890).

§ 12.69

1. Holt v. Fleischman, 75 App.Div. 593, 78 N.Y.S. 647 (1st Dep't 1902).

2. Rahabi v. Morrison, 81 A.D.2d 434, 440 N.Y.S.2d 941 (2d Dep't 1981) (the prescriptive requirement is ten years).

3. Beutler v. Maynard, 80 A.D.2d 982, 437 N.Y.S.2d 463 (4th Dep't 1981) (the right of way to a cabin was used only over a consistent period during the summers and was held to be continual use).

4. RPAPL § 2001.

§ 12.69   PURCHASE & SALE OF REAL ESTATE   Ch. 12

able title, but does provide the purchaser or lender with satisfactory insurability.

Library References:

West's Key No. Digests, Vendor and Purchaser ⚖ 130.

§ 12.70 Marketability of Title—What Renders Title Unmarketable—Reservations for Public Utilities

Public utility easements may also present marketability problems. If a sale is not made conditional on the purchaser accepting title to land where there is a grant allowing telephone and electric companies the right to install wires across the premises, the purchaser may have the right to opt out of the contract. However, this would not be the result if there were easements granted allowing the use of the street for the laying of gas pipes or sewers and for paving.[1]

Many contracts provide for the purchaser to take subject to utility easements, either recorded or unrecorded. This may be dangerous, especially where main underground easements of great depth may not be easily ascertained from the public record. The practice in certain areas is for title companies to take standard exceptions to unrecorded underground and non-visible easements. This could be of very serious concern where the buyer is acquiring large tracts or where properties may be located near major underground easements such as aqueducts. Aqueduct land, park lands and the like may not be alienable without state legislation, thereby perpetuating marketability problems into the indefinite future. Adverse possession against a government instrumentality where the title is held for public benefit may not exist at all. The fact that an easement has not been utilized by the government does not give the fee owner title to the easement area by adverse possession.[2]

Library References:

West's Key No. Digests, Vendor and Purchaser ⚖ 130.

§ 12.71 Marketability of Title—What Renders Title Unmarketable—Land Abutting Bodies of Water and the Federal Navigational Servitude

This section does not purport to consider the many problems that may be raised in connection with land under water and the boundaries of title bordering on water. Suffice it to say that surveys in many cases do call attention to problems related to title where such matters as the

§ 12.70
1. Warren's Weed, New York Law of Real Property (4th ed. 1981) "Marketability of Title."

2. See supra, § 12.66 note 5.

former boundaries of bodies of water may be indicated. Where a line in a survey shows that the former high water mark may be inland of the property, it calls into question whether or not the title to the land presently not under water is owned by the sovereign, be it city, town or state; it also calls into question the matter of the federal navigational servitude. Both of these matters are beyond the purview of this section.

Library References:
West's Key No. Digests, Vendor and Purchaser ⚖130.

§ 12.72 Closing of Title

At the closing of title, the representative from the title company will review all documentation in connection with the mortgage loan and the conveyance of title to ensure that all requirements are satisfied, the documents are properly executed, acknowledged and in recordable form, and the appropriate taxes and filing fees are paid. The title closer will subsequently arrange for proper recordation and payment. The following sections provide an overview of the required documentation, taxes and fees. Note that certain costs, such as real estate taxes, will be apportioned between the parties to the transaction and paid for at the closing. Additionally, there will be a host of other documents and fees in connection with the bank loan, such as processing fees, and bank attorney fees and points on the loan. Counsel should review the schedule of mortgage loan fees prior to closing and contact the lending institution's attorney with any questions prior to the closing. The attorney for the seller will also have to request from the bank that issued the *seller's* loan on the premises to be conveyed (if there is an outstanding loan) a letter indicating the amount due to satisfy the mortgage, with accrued interest up to the day of the closing. The seller must be prepared to pay that amount at closing by certified or bank check. This will often be deducted from the proceeds of the purchase price and the seller's attorney can arrange in advance with the purchaser's bank to have a bank check drawn in the amount necessary to satisfy the mortgage. A fee may be imposed with respect to preparation of the mortgage satisfaction and filing.

Library References:
West's Key No. Digests, Vendor and Purchaser ⚖145–159.

§ 12.73 Closing of Title—Checklist

New York State real estate closing practices are not uniform. In the metropolitan area of New York City, an agent or employee of the title company will probably be at the closing, take the documents to be recorded, and even mark up the title report which ultimately becomes the basis for the issuance of the title policy. In other areas, attorneys approved by the title company will serve the same function. In either

§ 12.73 PURCHASE & SALE OF REAL ESTATE Ch. 12

case, the orderly completion of the closing process requires compliance, at a minimum, with documents indicating authority and recording requirements set forth in the following checklist.

1. Proof of continuance of authority as to closing instruments executed by an attorney-in-fact. A durable power will survive disability of the grantor. Proof that the grantor is alive is required. (*See* § 12.8)[1]

2. Proof of proper execution by any party not present at the closing, and as to authority to effect delivery.

3. Questions as to competence and capacity of a party executing a closing instrument: (*See* § 12.55)

   - Corporate stockholder consents, where required by the certificate of incorporation, or other special circumstances, such as a sale of the principal asset of the corporation. (*See* § 12.55, No. 29 of Checklist)
   - Authority of executing partner(s) to act, *e.g.*, limitation in the partnership certificate; sale of only asset; virtual dissolution, etc. (*See* § 12.55, No. 29 of Checklist)
   - Infancy,[2] mental incapacity, impaired persons, etc.
   - Requisite court approval whenever required—including, but not limited to, sales, mortgages and leases by religious, charitable or membership corporations, benevolent orders, or by fiduciaries or for sales by trustees in bankruptcy, or other court appointed officers recital of authority in closing instruments.
   - Proof that a corporate party has in fact been incorporated, or that a partnership or a limited partnership has been duly formed in compliance with statutory requirements, or that a Trustee has been duly appointed, etc.[3] (*See* § 12.55)

4. Disposition of possible fiduciary or equitable conflicts, *e.g.*, an executor or a trustee dealing personally with estate or trust property or a partner with partnership property, etc.

5. Rights of creditors where there is not a "valuable" consideration to the grantor or mortgagor; or where there is a potential insolvency or a preferential transfer.

6. Compliance with usury laws, Truth-in-Lending Law, Real Estate Settlement Procedures Act, etc.[4]

§ 12.73

1. This may be accomplished by affidavit or telephone call by persons able to establish voice recognition.

2. As to married infants, see General Obligations Law § 3–101.

3. Title insurers will raise questions of authority as to trusts, executors and the like and will check public records where available. See Preminger, et al., *Trusts and Estates Practice in New York* (West 1997).

4. PRACTICE POINTER: General Obligations Law § 5–501 has eliminated

Ch. 12 RECORDING FEES AND FILINGS **§ 12.74**

7. Compliance with Lien Law provisions or other appropriate precautions to assure statutory priority or enforceability.[5] (*See* § 12.46)

8. Closing instruments to recite full consideration if executed by fiduciary, attorney-in-fact, or others where this information should be of record. (*See* § 12.55, Checklist No. 27)

9. Recitals and "subject to" clauses in closing instruments.

10. Medium of payment—avoidance of use of checks of parties other than parties to the transaction, endorsed checks, etc.—possible equitable vendors' and vendees' liens.

11. Compliance with zoning and building ordinances (when required by the contract). (*See* § 12.18)

12. Personal property:
    - Sales tax compliance
    - Bill of sale
    - Filing of UCC documents

13. N.Y. State, N.Y.C., Yonkers, Mount Vernon Transfer and Stamp Taxes, Mortgage Taxes, payment of recording charges and filing fees. (*See* §§ 12.74–12.89)

14. The Administrative Code of the City of New York[6] requires an affidavit signed by the transferor and transferee of a one or two family dwelling that premises are equipped with an approved and operable single station smoke detecting alarm device. Such affidavit must be submitted upon payment of New York City Real Property Transfer Tax. New York State also has a smoke alarm affidavit requirement,[7] but it is not required to be submitted with payment of the New York Real Property Transfer Tax.

§ 12.74 Closing of Title—Recording Fees and Filings

In New York State, recording fees vary from county to county.[1] The recording officers of New York State are the county clerks, except for four of the five counties of New York City (New York, Kings, Queens and Bronx), where recording is done in the office of the City Register.[2]

---

need for the yo-yo deal (into and out of a corporation) by removing loans of $250,000 or over from usury law except for one and two family houses and except for criminal usury.

5. *See* Lien Law §§ 13, 22.

6. N.Y.C. Administrative Code § 11-2105 (g). *See also infra*, § 12.90.

7. Education Law § 378(5). *See also infra*, § 12.90.

§ 12.74

1. *See, e.g.,* the Schedule of Property Recording Fees and Real Estate Taxes issued by the City of New York, which serves as a useful guide even for other counties. The Guide is issued by the New York State Department of Finance as compiled by the City Register.

2. RPL § 290(4).

§ 12.74   PURCHASE & SALE OF REAL ESTATE   Ch. 12

The recording system is based upon a Block Indexing system in several of the counties in New York State, including the entire City of New York. This is known as a geographical system. In many of the other counties, the system is based upon a grantor/grantee indexing system.[3]

In New York State, the following documents must be filed with the deed:

- In all counties outside of the City of New York, the Equalization Form EA5217.[4]

- The TP-584 (New York State Real Property Transfer Form and Credit Line Mortgage Certificate) and where necessary the TP-584.1 (Supplemental Schedule to the Real Estate Transfer Tax Return);[5]

- N.Y.C. Real Estate Property Transfer Tax Return (In New York City this serves as a substitute for the EA5217);

- The Cities of Yonkers and Mount Vernon each have a special Real Property Transfer Tax Return;

- Registration Multiple Dwelling, New York City or Alternate Non-Multiple Dwelling.

Various cities, towns and counties also have requirements for filing and recording. Counsel should consult with the title company as to specific recording requirements for towns, cities and villages.

UCC filings may be required to perfect liens or secured interests in the county where the property is located or in some instances in the Office of the Secretary of State in Albany. In any event, the filing of a security in a cooperative must be filed in the county where the property is located. The same requirement also applies to fixture filings.[6] The basic charge for filing a UCC(1) form[7] or an assignment or a release is $7.00, plus additional charges for indexing against additional debtors and for supplementary affidavits or riders.[8]

In all recording matters, title insurers impose additional charges for the service of filing or recording or the payment of *ad valorem* and water and sewer charges. Counsel for both parties should ask the title company or agent what the various recording, filing and services charges will be prior to closing so as to ensure that their clients are prepared to make these additional payments at the time of closing.

---

3. *See* Bernard M. Rifkin, Real Estate Titles, Ch. 2 (2d ed. NYSBA 1996 Supp.), for a more complete discussion of the search procedure and the chain of title concept.

4. *See infra*, § 12.90.

5. *See infra*, § 12.83.
6. *See supra*, §§ 12.37, 12.38.
7. The UCC(1) form is filed to acquire a lien on personalty.
8. *See* Executive Law § 96–a; General Obligations Law §§ 9–401—9–410.

§ 12.75 Closing of Title—Disclosure and Other Requirements

Certain disclosures may be required in connection with a transaction involving the conveyance of real property. The sections below provide an overview of these requirements and a discussion as to when they are applicable.

§ 12.76 Closing of Title—Disclosure and Other Requirements—Foreign Investors Real Property Tax Act

The Foreign Investors Real Property Tax Act ("FIRPTA") provides the United States with the means to collect real property capital gains tax from aliens or entities that are not U.S. taxpayers. Under this Act, foreign persons, as specifically defined, are subject to various information reporting requirements.[1] "A foreign person" is defined in the regulations in several ways, the most illuminating definition is "a foreign person is a nonresident alien individual, foreign corporation, foreign partnership, foreign trust or foreign estate, but not a resident." Foreign as used here means alien, not sister state.

As of January 1, 1986, as part of the Tax Reform Act of 1984, the purchaser of real property (the transferee) is required to deduct a withholding tax of 10% of the total amount realized by the seller (transferor) on the disposition of a United States Real Property Interest ("USRPI") as defined in the Internal Revenue Code.[2] USRPI means an interest in real property including an interest in a mine, well, or other natural deposit located in the United States, or the Virgin Islands or an interest in any domestic corporation, other than solely as a creditor.

"Total amount realized" means the sum of (1) the cash paid or to be paid plus (2) the fair market value of other property transferred or to be transferred added to the amount outstanding of any liability assumed by the transferee or to which the USRPI is subject immediately before and after the transfer.

The requirement that the purchaser withhold 10% of the amount realized is subject to five exceptions:

1. Non–Foreign Certification. The seller of real or personal property furnishes to the purchaser a certificate under penalties of perjury, setting out the seller's U.S. taxpayer identification number ("TIN") and stating in the certificate that the seller is not a foreign person.

2. Non–USRPHC Certification. The purchaser of an interest in a non-publicly traded U.S. Corporation receives a certificate from the corporation that the latter is not and has not been a United States

---

§ 12.76
1. 26 U.S.C.A. § 6039C.

2. 26 U.S.C.A. § 1446; 26 U.S.C.A. §§ 861(a)(5), 897, 6039(c), 6652(g).

§ 12.76   PURCHASE & SALE OF REAL ESTATE   Ch. 12

Real Property Holding Corporation ("USRPHC") during the applicable time period, *i.e.*, the shorter of

(a) the period following FIRPTA's general effective date, June 19, 1980, or

(b) the five year period ending on the date of disposition of the stock or other interest. This certification also must be provided under penalties of perjury. Thus, under the 1984 Act and FIRPTA, a purchaser of non-publicly traded stock in a U.S. Corporation may be liable for withholding unless they obtain either a non-USRPHC certificate from the corporation or a non-foreign certificate from the seller.

3. Qualifying Statement. The purchaser has received a "qualifying statement" as defined in Internal Revenue Code § 1445 (hereafter "I.R.C."). A "qualifying statement" is a statement issued by the I.R.S. officially confirming that either:

(a) The seller or the purchaser has reached an agreement or provided security, with or to the I.R.S. for the payment of any tax due on any gain recognized by the seller on the disposition of real property, or

(b) the seller is exempt from tax on the disposition.

4. Residence. If the property is acquired by the purchaser for use as a residence, and the total amount realized by the seller does not exceed $300,000, no withholding is required.

5. Publicly Traded Stock. The disposition is of a share of stock that is regularly traded on an established securities market. If the buyers rely on certificates to insulate them against withholding, they must retain the certificates until the end of the fifth taxable year following the taxable year in which the transfer takes place. Failure to produce the certificate or reliance on a knowingly false affidavit will strip away the insulation.

If taxes are to be withheld, Forms 8288 and 8288A must be filed and the amount withheld paid within 10 days by mailing to Internal Revenue Center, Philadelphia, PA 19255.

§ 12.77 Closing of Title—Disclosure and Other Requirements—Form 1099–S Federal Requirement One to Four Family Residence

In 1986, Congress enacted Section 6045(c) of the I.R.C., which requires reporting of real estate transactions. Transactions subject to reporting are those consisting in whole or in part of the sale or exchange of one to four family real estate for money, indebtedness, property or services or any present or future ownership interest. One to four family real estate includes the following:

- Any structure designed principally for the occupancy of one to four families, such as a house, townhouse, duplex or four unit apartment building, and any accessory fixtures, land, and any associated structures (for example, a detached garage or tool shed) transferred with the structure.

- A condominium unit designed principally for the occupancy of one to four families, and any accessory fixtures as well as common elements, including land.

- Stock in a cooperative housing corporation (as defined in I.R.C. § 216).

- Improved or unimproved land, including air space.

- Inherently permanent structures, including any residential, commercial, or industrial building.

Form 1099–S is used to report the sale or exchange of reportable real estate. A flow chart is attached to the form to assist in determining who is responsible for the filing of Form 1099–S, and the specific requirements of completion and filing. Whether the seller is actually subject to tax on the sale or exchange is not relevant. For example, regardless whether an individual seller of a personal residence may defer the gain under the rollover provisions of Section 1034 of the I.R.C., the transaction is a sale under federal tax principles, and thus is reportable on Form 1099–S. Similarly, like-kind exchanges and other gain deferrable transactions remain "exchanges" and in accordance with the rules prescribed are reportable transactions.

Form 1099–S is not required to be filed in the following cases:

- Sales of mobile homes that include wheels and axles;
- Refinancing;
- Foreclosures or abandonments;
- Transactions where the seller is a corporation or government unit; and
- Volume sellers—selling twenty-five or more units per year.

While in most situations the Code of Federal Regulations, ("Regulations")[1] would require the buyer's attorney to file Form 1099–S, it is important for all parties involved in real estate transactions to recognize filing responsibility.[2]

1. The person required to file Form 1099–S is listed in the following order of priority:

    (a) The person listed as the settlement agent on the closing statement.

§ 12.77
1. 26 C.F.R. §§ 1.6045–4 et seq.
2. 26 C.F.R. § 1.6045–4 (b)(2).

PRACTICE POINTER: As a practical matter, the Form 1099–S is filed by the lender's counsel.

§ 12.77   PURCHASE & SALE OF REAL ESTATE   Ch. 12

(b) If no settlement agent is listed on the closing statement, the person who prepared the closing statement.

2. If no closing statement is used for the transaction, then the Regulations provide that the person responsible for filing Form 1099–S is:

(a) The buyer's (or transferee's) attorney, if that attorney actively participates in the transaction. An example of active participation is where the attorney prepares or reviews the preparation of documents transferring legal or equitable ownership.

(b) The seller's (or transferor's) attorney, if that attorney actively participates in the transaction. An example of active participation is where the attorney is present at the delivery of the buyer's note, or a significant part of the cash proceeds to the seller.

(c) The title or escrow company that disburses the most money.

3. If no one individual is responsible or has assumed responsibility pursuant to a written agreement for closing the transaction, as discussed above in paragraphs 1 and 2, then the person responsible pursuant to the Code of Federal Regulations for filing Form 1099–S is:

1. The mortgage lender.
2. The seller's broker.
3. The buyer's broker.
4. The buyer.

The Regulations provide for the use of a designation agreement between the parties to the transaction which may, by mutual agreement, identify an individual as being responsible to file the Form 1099–S other than the person who would normally be required to file the Form.

When the transaction involves more than one seller, the sellers should provide an allocation of the proceeds. A Form 1099–S must be filed for each seller, with the gross proceeds being divided as per the sellers' allocation. If the sellers do *not* provide an allocation, the Form 1099–S filed for each seller must reflect the full proceeds. An allocation is not required when the seller is: (1) a partnership or (2) a husband and wife who held the property as community property, joint tenants, tenants-in-common, or tenants by the entirety.

Transfers of real property by foreign transferors are generally subject to reporting, as are transfers of U.S. Real Property Interest ("U.S.R.P.I.").[3] Information returns can be required for both federal

---

3. *See supra,* § 12.76 for a discussion of the Foreign Investors Real Property Tax Act.

income tax withholding (Form 8288) and the transfer or sale of real property (Form 1099-S).

It is important to note that it is unlawful for the person required to report the transaction to make a separate charge to any customer for complying with the information reporting requirements.

As a general rule, the reporting person must file the required Form 1099-S by means of magnetic media.[4] There are two exceptions—where the reporting person is filing fewer than 250 information returns for the year, or, where the reporting person shows undue hardship would result from having to file by magnetic media. Undue hardship may be shown by filing Form 8508—Request for Waiver from Filing Information Returns on Magnetic Media, or by submitting a written statement requesting such a waiver.[5]

Form 1099-S must be filed with the Internal Revenue Service after December 31st of the calendar year in which the closing took place, but on or before February 28th of the calendar year following the closing. A copy must be sent to the transferor on or before January 31st of the calendar year immediately following the calendar year of the sale.

A substitute form may be used in place of Form 1099-S if it contains identical provisions to those of Form 1099-S, and all applicable revenue procedures are complied with.

The reporting person is exposed to civil penalties for the following types of noncompliance:

- Failure to file a correct information return (I.R.C. § 6721).

- Failure to furnish a correct payee statement (I.R.C. § 6722).

- Failure to comply timely with a specified information requirement (I.R.C. § 6723).

The reporting person may also be subject to at least two criminal penalties for willful noncompliance:

- Willful failure to file an information return, or supply information (I.R.C. § 7203).

- Fraudulent returns, statements, or other documents (I.R.C. § 7207).

A transferor may be subject to a civil penalty for failure to comply with information reporting requirements under I.R.C. § 6723, if a Tax Identification Number or other required information is not given to the reporting person. Criminal penalties may be imposed for willful failure to supply a Tax Identification Number (I.R.C. § 7203), and for fraudulent statements under penalty of perjury (I.R.C. § 7206).

---

4. This means milar tape.

5. Requests are submitted to the Martinsburg Computing Center in Martinsburg, West Virginia, 25401.

§ 12.77   PURCHASE & SALE OF REAL ESTATE

The real estate reporting person must request a Tax Identification Number from the transferor at or before the time of closing. This solicitation may be made in person or in writing. Form W-9 may be used for recording the seller's Tax Identification Number.

§ 12.78   Closing of Title—Disclosure and Other Requirements—Form 1099-S Federal Requirement for One to Four Family Residence—Checklist

1. The information required to be reported in Form 1099-S includes:

   - The seller's name, address and taxpayer identification number;
   - A general description of the real estate transferred;
   - The date of closing;
   - The amount of the "gross proceeds" of the transaction;
   - An indication as to whether the transferor will receive any non-cash property or services;
   - The name, address and tax identification number of the real estate reporting person;
   - An indication as to whether the seller's financing was federally-subsidized;
   - Any real property tax imposed against the purchaser of a residence; and
   - Any other information required by Form 1099-S or its instructions.

The reporting person must report on the Form 1099-S, in box 5, that part of the real property tax that is treated as a tax imposed on the buyer. The seller is treated as paying taxes up to the date of sale, and the buyer is treated as paying the taxes beginning with the date of sale.

§ 12.79   Closing of Title—Disclosure and Other Requirements—Cash Payments Received by Businesses in Excess of $10,000[1]

Any person who receives more than $10,000 in cash or foreign currency in a single transaction must file a Form 8300 to the IRS no later than the 15th day after the receipt of the cash. If multiple cash payments are made within one year for a related transaction and the total of the payments exceeds $10,000, Form 8300 must be filed within 15 days of receipt of $10,000 or more.

---

§ 12.79
1. I.R.C. § 6050I; 26 C.F.R. §§ 1.6050I-1(c)(1) *et seq.* This summary was provided by Bill Auerbach of the Real Estate Board of New York, Inc.

The definition of cash is broadened for "designated reporting transactions" to include cashier's checks, bank drafts, traveler's checks and money orders. Designated reporting transactions are retail sales of consumer durables, and collectibles or travel and entertainment activities. Limited exceptions are permitted for loans, installment sales, and down payment plans if the recipient does not know that the instrument is being used to escape the rules.

An agent is exempt from filing a Form 8300 if the agent receives cash in excess of $10,000 from a principal and then remits all the cash as instructed by the principal within 15 days. The agent must disclose the identity of the principal to the cash recipient.

Form 8300 provides that the recipient of the cash payment report:

- The individual from whom the cash was received;
- The person (or persons) on whose behalf the transaction was conducted;
- The description of the transaction and method of payment; and
- The business reporting the transaction.

Any person named in a Form 8300 filed with the IRS must receive a written statement from the company filing the form on or before January 31st of the year following the calendar year in which the cash is received. The statement must show:

- The name and address of the business filing Form 8300;
- The total amount of reportable cash received; and
- That the transaction was reported to the IRS.

In addition to reporting cash transactions in excess of $10,000, a Form 8300 may be used to report any transaction of a suspicious nature under $10,000.[2]

§ 12.80 Closing of Title—Disclosure and Other Requirements—Lead Paint Hazards

On October 28, 1992, the Housing and Community Development Act was signed into law.[1] This bill, among other things, contains requirements involving disclosure of information concerning lead paint upon any transfer or lease of residential property built prior to 1978. Regulations for the disclosure of lead-based paint hazards have since been

---

2. Instructions Form § 8300 issued 8/94. This form may be filed voluntarily for any suspicious transaction (see Definitions), even if it does not exceed $10,000.

§ 12.80
1. 15 U.S.C.A. §§ 2681 et seq.

§ 12.80   PURCHASE & SALE OF REAL ESTATE   Ch. 12

issued by the Housing and Urban Development ("HUD") and the Environmental Protection Agency ("EPA").[2]

The target properties are those containing residential units, including single family, multi-family, cooperatives, mixed use, residential hotels, and boarding houses, which were constructed prior to 1978 and with paint or other surface containing lead equal to or in excess of 1.0 milligram per square centimeter or 0.5 percent by weight.

In connection with the sale or lease of a target property, a seller or landlord, as the case may be, must permit the purchaser or tenant a ten day or other period specified by mutual agreement to conduct an inspection for the presence of lead based paint hazards. A seller or landlord is also required to disclose known lead based paint hazards and provide available reports to buyers or tenants. Additionally, sellers and landlords must give buyers and tenants the pamphlet developed by the EPA, HUD, and the Consumer Product Safety Commission entitled "Protect Your Family From Lead In Your Home."

The disclosure requirements must occur prior to contract ratification. Failure to disclose will not create a defect in title or affect the validity of the subsequent contract or lease. The remedies available to purchasers and tenants are those available in Section 1018 of Title X[3] and include compensatory damages and punitive damages.

This Act does not apply to the following:

Foreclosure sales;

Premises that are certified to be lead free by a certified inspector;[4]

Reletting;

Purchase, sale or servicing of mortgages;

0-bedroom leases (hotel rooms and efficiency units) not separated from living area; and

Lease terms for less than 100 days

Note that oral leases and playgrounds and abutting properties of target properties, as defined above, are not exempt from the Act.

---

2. These regulations were issued by HUD and EPA on March 8, 1996. See 24 C.F.R. Pt. 35; 40 C.F.R., Pt. 74 (Mar. 8, 1996). Effective dates for compliance are as follows: (1) September 6, 1996, for premises containing more than four residential units; and (2) December 6, 1996, for premises containing four or fewer residential units. The EPA has issued a fact sheet detailing most of the requirements for compliance with the statute, entitled "Prevention Pesticides and Toxic Substances (7404) EPA 747-96-002."

3. 42 U.S.C.A. § 4852d.

4. PRACTICE POINTER: No list of federally certified inspectors is currently provided for obtaining such certification, although there are published state approved lists of organizations who can provide certification.

§ 12.81 Closing of Title—Disclosure and Other Requirements—Agricultural Foreign Investment Disclosure Act[1]

This Act establishes a detailed set of requirements for filing disclosure forms with the Agricultural Stabilization and Conservation Service Office in Washington, D.C. upon the sale of land used for agriculture within the previous five years before acquisition. There is an exemption from filing requirements if the land is less than ten acres in size and the annual receipts from sales of products is less than $1,000. The law affects foreign persons and entities where foreign persons hold more than 10 percent of the equity.[2]

§ 12.82 Closing of Title—Payment of Taxes[1]

The sections that follow provide an overview of the taxes charged in conjunction with the conveyance of, or transfer of an interest in, real property or the issuance of a mortgage loan. The discussion includes the rates charged for each tax, computation of the rate when necessary and the appropriate method of payment for each tax.

§ 12.83 Closing of Title—Payment of Taxes—New York State Real Estate Transfer Tax and Mansion Tax

The New York State Transfer Tax is $2.00 per $500 consideration or fraction thereof.[1] In computing the tax, existing liens (mortgages) will be deductible from the consideration paid for the property only where the transfer is of a 1, 2 or 3 family house or individual residential condominium unit or cooperative apartment, or where the consideration is less than $500,000.[2] Transfers to cooperative sponsors are taxed on the basis of gross consideration, without deduction of existing liens (mortgages).[3] Resales of commercial units are taxed on the basis of gross consideration and the proportionate share of underlying mortgages.[4]

§ 12.81

1. 7 U.S.C.A. §§ 3501–3508, and accompanying regulations in 7 C.F.R. Pt. 781.

2. For a more detailed analysis of the requirements and exclusions, see D. A. Richards, *Reporting and Disclosure Requirements For the Foreign Investor in U.S. Real Estate*, U.S. Real Property, Real Property Probate and Trust Journal, Vol. 25, No. 2, at p. 221 (ABA Summer 1990).

§ 12.82

1. For a fuller discussion of New York income tax, see Chapter 35, "Income Tax," *infra*.

§ 12.83

1. *But see infra*, § 12.87 for special rates for real estate investment trusts.
2. Tax Law § 1402.
3. 20 NYCRR Pts. 572, 575(6), 666.
4. Tax Law § 1402.

§ 12.83   PURCHASE & SALE OF REAL ESTATE   Ch. 12

The present tax rate became effective May 1, 1983 but does not apply to transfers of property made on or after such date pursuant to contracts entered into prior to such date. Copies of contracts and assignments are required to obtain the benefit for earlier rates (.55 cents per $500 of consideration).

Section 1401 of the Tax Law applies the transfer tax to a lease or sublease with an option to purchase. The consideration is measured by the value of the rental stream up to the point where the option is exercisable to which is also added any payment made for the option right.

A special additional tax of 1% of gross consideration (commonly referred to as the "Mansion Tax") is imposed on the purchase of a 1, 2 or 3 family house or individual residential condominium or cooperative apartment when the purchase price is $1,000,000 or more. This tax is paid by the grantee unless exempt; in which case it is payable by the grantor. This tax and the basic transfer tax on co-ops became effective July 1, 1989 but do not apply to transfers made on or after such date pursuant to contracts entered into on or before February 16, 1989. This tax is paid by the grantee unless exempt, in which case it is payable by the grantor. However, this tax is paid in addition to the $2.00 per $500 of consideration and must be paid by the fifteenth day after transfer.[5]

Erie County has imposed a surcharge of $5.00 per $1,000 of consideration, making the total transfer tax due $9.00 per $1,000. This surcharge is in all respects similar to the Real Estate Transfer Tax except that there is an exemption for 1 or 2 family dwellings owned and occupied by at least one person over the age of 62, provided the premises were owned and occupied by that person for at least one year prior to transfer. If the grantor qualifies for exemption, the tax is not payable by the grantee.

Broome County increased the New York State Real Property Transfer Tax by .50 cents for each $500 of consideration or fraction thereof, making the effective tax rate $5.00 per thousand. Contracts dated prior to October 1, 1994 are grandfathered, but copies must be submitted with Form TP 584. In addition, Broome County will charge an additional $5.00 for filing a duplicate Form TP 584.

Note that the transfer of air and development rights is taxable, as is a negative covenant or easement unless it is stated that it is given for no consideration.[6]

A deed in lieu of foreclosure is also subject to New York State Transfer Tax, based upon the principal amount then due on the mortgage plus accrued interest regardless of the recital of non-merger language.[7] In a conveyance pursuant to foreclosure, the New York State

---

5. Tax Law § 1402(a).
6. Tax Law § 1402(f).
7. 20 NYCRR § 575.11.

Transfer Tax is based on the consideration paid, which is either the judgment amount or the bid price plus the amount of any other liens or encumbrances to which the property is taken subject. If the debt is recourse, the consideration may reflect the fair market value and the tax is then based upon the lesser of either the fair market value or the actual amount paid.

In a conveyance in lieu of foreclosure to a lienor, the tax is based on the consideration paid on the unpaid balance of debt plus any other liens or encumbrances to which the property is taken subject to.[8] If recourse debt, the consideration may be based upon the lesser of the amount paid or the fair market value.[9]

Where the transfer of a cooperative unit is involved, and the unit is not individually owned (*e.g.*, a transfer of the sponsor's shares) the proportional amount of the mortgage on the underlying fee must be added to the consideration.[10] Where the transfer of the cooperative unit is from an individually owned unit, the proportional amount of the mortgage on the underlying fee title is not added.[11]

§ 12.84 Closing of Title—Payment of Taxes—Article 31-B—Real Property Transfer Gains Tax

Effective March 28, 1983, a gains tax was imposed by Article 31-B of the Tax Law.[1] This tax was repealed effective June 15, 1996.[2] Taxpayers who paid the gains tax for transactions occurring on or after June 15, 1996 will be entitled to a refund. For transactions which take place after the effective date there is no requirement to complete Schedule B of Form TP584 (The Omnibus Transfer Tax Form) or to file the Tentative Assessment which may have been issued prior to repeal.

For transactions involving successive transfers of condominium and cooperative units, special problems are presented. An application for refund (Form TP165.8) can be filed for transfers prior to June 15, 1996 of units aggregating less than $1,000,000. For transfers prior to June 15, 1996, of units aggregating more than $1,000,000, the gains tax paid is not refundable. However, for gains tax paid for transfers made *on or after June 15, 1996*, payment will be refunded when Form DTF701 is filed.

---

8. 20 NYCRR § 575.11(2).
9. *See* 20 NYCRR § 575.11(2).
10. *See* 20 NYCRR §§ 575.11(15), 575.1(d)(6).
11. Tax Law § 1402(a).

§ 12.84

1. A 10% tax was imposed on the gain derived form the transfer of an interest in real property or the transfer of a controlling interest in an entity which owned real property located in New York State and where the gross consideration was one million dollars or more. This also affected certain transactions leases, assignments or leases, terminations of leases, regardless of the stated consideration.

2. Ch. 309 §§ 171–180, L.1996.

§ 12.85 Closing of Title—Payment of Taxes—New York City Real Property Transfer Tax

New York City imposes real property transfer taxes.[1] The tax rate varies depending upon the type of real property and the amount of consideration paid to acquire the real property.[2] The following is a summary of the rates:

1. 1, 2 or 3 family, individual condo or co-op
   (a) consideration $500,000 and under. 1% gross consideration
   (b) consideration over $500,000. 1.425% gross consideration
2. Consideration $500,000. and less other than for 1, 2 or 3 family, condo or co-op, including controlling interests in entities and grant, assignment or surrender of leases. 1.425% gross consideration
3. All other property consideration over $500,000. 2.625% gross consideration
4. Commercial cooperative unit by sponsor.
   (a) consideration $500,000 and under. 1.425% gross consideration
   (b) consideration over $500,000. 2.625% gross consideration
5. Subsequent transfer of commercial cooperative unit.
   (a) consideration $500,000 and under. 1% gross consideration
   (b) consideration over $500,000. 1.425% gross consideration

Effective for transfers on or after August 28, 1997, Tax Law § 1201 and Section 11–2102 of the New York City Administrative Code have been amended to reduce or eliminate the tax on transfers of real property (or interests in real property) consisting of a one, two or three family house, or an individual condominium or cooperative unit. The foregoing does not apply to:

1. Conveyances to a mortgagee, lienor or encumbrancer regardless of whether the grantor was personally liable;
2. Conveyances or transfers made to a real estate investment trust.
3. Mortgages or deferred payment arrangements placed on the property in anticipation of the sale of the property.

§ 12.85

1. N.Y.C. Administrative Code § 11–2106.
2. See infra, § 12.86 for a special rate for real estate investment trusts.

Note that when a cooperative unit used solely for commercial purposes is transferred, a proportionate share of the underlying mortgage is included in the consideration to be taxed. Conveyances subject to tax include transferable development rights.

The New York City transfer tax must be paid by the 30th day after the transfer.[3] However, as a practical matter, because the state transfer tax must be paid by the 15th day after the transfer,[4] this 30 day period benefits only the transfer of a cooperative apartment or other economic interest where no recording is necessary.

Transfers involving no change in beneficial interests are exempt from taxation.[5]

The taxable consideration for a transfer by a referee or receiver under foreclosure or execution is the amount bid for the property and the costs paid by the purchaser, plus the amount of any preexisting mortgages, liens or other encumbrances remaining on the property after the transfer, whether or not the underlying indebtedness is assumed.[6]

For a transfer by deed in lieu of foreclosure, the consideration is the amount of outstanding debt plus any liens to which the property is subject.[7]

§ 12.86 Closing of Title—Payment of Taxes—Cities of Mount Vernon and Yonkers

In Mount Vernon the tax is 1% of consideration in excess of $100,000 payable by purchaser.[1] In Yonkers, effective January 1, 1990, the tax is 2.75% of gross consideration if the purchase price exceeds $25,000. The tax is payable by the seller.[2]

§ 12.87 Closing of Title—Payment of Taxes–Real Estate Investment Trusts

New York State Real Property Transfer Tax for real estate investment trusts ("REIT") is governed by Section 1402(b) of the Tax Law which provides:

(a) The rate of transfer tax is $1.00 per $500 or fraction of consideration. This rate is one half of the normal rate.

---

3. N.Y.C. Administrative Code § 11-2104.

4. Tax Law § 1410.

5. N.Y.C. Administrative Code § 11-2106(8).

6. Amended Regulations, New York City Department of Finance, 3/27/89, Art. 24(b), (d).

7. See id.

§ 12.86

1. City of Mount Vernon Local Law 4 (Effective Sept. 1, 1986).

2. City of Yonkers Code of Ordinances, Art. VI, as amended October 10, 1989 by Tax Law § 1230(b).

§ 12.87   PURCHASE & SALE OF REAL ESTATE   Ch. 12

   (b) REIT has the same meaning as in Section 856 of the I.R.C.[1]

   (c) The taxable conveyances include conveyances of real property or an interest in an entity, corporation or partnership owning real property whereby the REIT acquires a controlling interest in the entity and the conveyance occurs in connection with the initial formation of the REIT.[2]

   (d) The value of the equity interest received by the REIT is subject to various qualifying requirements among which are a continuity of interest test and a use of proceeds test.[3]

New York City Real Property Transfer Tax of REITS is at the rate of one half of the normal city rate for qualifying REIT transfers.[4] The previously existing sunset provision with respect to the REITS was repealed effective June 15, 1996. In its place the law now provides:[5]

   (a) The New York State and New York City tax rates for REITS was extended permanently. This includes the 50% reduction in rates and applies to transfers occurring in connection with the initial formation of the REIT.

   (b) Existing REITS will be able to utilize the reduced rates through September 1, 1999.

§ 12.88   Closing of Title—Payment of Taxes—Mortgage Recording Tax Outside New York City

The following counties only impose the basic and special additional tax. The rate is for each $100 and remaining major fraction of principal debt secured by a mortgage:[1]

Allegany	.75	Fulton	.75	Ontario	.75
Chautauqua	.75	Greene	.75	Orleans	.75
Chemung	.75	Hamilton	.75	Otsego	.75
Chenango	.75	Herkimer	.75	St. Lawrence	.75
Clinton	.75	Jefferson	.75	Schoharie	.75
Columbia	.75	Lewis	.75	Schulyer	.75
Cortland	.75	Madison	.75	Seneca	.75
Delaware	.75	Montgomery	.75	Steuban	.75
Franklin	.75	Oneida	.75	Sullivan	.75

§ 12.87

1. Tax Law § 1402(b)(2)(A).
2. Tax Law § 1402(b)(2)(B).
3. Tax Law §§ 1402(b)(2)(A), (b)(2)(B)(i) and (ii). Consideration is measured pursuant to Tax Law § 1402(b)(3).
4. Tax Law § 1201(b)(xi).
5. Chapter 309 of the Laws of 1996 provides tax benefits for REITS. There are requirements for transferor's retention of equity in the property for two years in various proportions depending on when the REIT was formed. It is conceivable that the failure to comply with this requirement might result in the loss of the benefit of the transfer tax reduction.

§ 12.88

1. *See infra* for the derivation of the various tax rates and their application to various localities.

Ch. 12   MORTGAGE RECORDING TAX OUTSIDE NYC   § 12.88

Tioga	.75	Ulster	.75	Yates	.75
Tompkins	.75	Warren	.75		

The following counties impose the basic and special additional tax. The rate is for each $100 and remaining major fraction of principal debt secured by a mortgage:

Albany	$1.00	Monroe	1.00	Saratoga	1.00
Broome	1.00	Nassau	1.00	Schenectady	1.00
Cattaraugus	1.00	Niagara	1.00	Suffolk	1.00
Cayuga	1.00	Onondaga	1.00	Washington	1.00
Dutchess	1.00	Orange	1.00	Wayne	1.00
Erie	1.00	Oswego	1.00	Westchester	1.00 [2]
Essex	1.00	Putnam	1.00	Wyoming	1.00
Greene	1.00	Rensselaer	1.00		
Livingston	1.00	Rockland	1.00		

Explanation of the Levels and Method of Computation of Mortgage Recording Tax. In all counties in New York State, a basic mortgage tax of $0.50 per $100,[3] as well as a special additional Tax of $0.25 per $100 is charged.[4] The Tax Law further provides that where the premises are principally improved, or are to be improved, by a structure containing not more than six residential dwelling units having their own separate cooking facilities, the special additional tax is to be paid by the mortgagee, unless the mortgagee is a natural person in which case the mortgagee is exempt from this tax.[5] Where the premises are not improved as described above, the special additional tax is to be paid by the mortgagor.[6]

Section 275 of the RPL requires that a new mortgage recording tax be paid if at the time of the assignment of mortgage the principal amount is "due and payable" and both principal and interest has been paid to the lender.[7]

In all counties shown as charging $1.00 or more per $100.00 of obligation, an additional mortgage recording tax of $0.25 per $100 of obligation is imposed. A special exemption of $0.25 per $100 is allowed up to the first $10,000 of mortgage obligation to a maximum of $25.00 if the mortgage is on a property principally improved or to be improved by

---

2. If the real property covered by the mortgage is located in whole or in part in the City of Yonkers, the rate is $1.50

3. Tax Law § 253.

4. Tax Law § 253(1–a)(a).

5. Tax Law § 253(1–a)(a), (b) (an affidavit is required).

6. If the mortgagor is an organization exempt from federal income taxation pursuant to Section 501 of the I.R.C., then the mortgagor is exempt from this special additional tax. Tax Law § 253(1–a)(b). If this is the case, then the tax is to be paid by the mortgagee. If the mortgagee is an organization exempt from federal income taxation pursuant to Section 501 of the I.R.C. then the mortgagee is exempt from this special additional tax. If this is the case, then the tax is to be paid by the mortgagor regardless of whether the property is residential or not. Tax Law § 253(1–a)(b).

7. *See* New York State Tax Bulletin TSB–M–89(6.1)R relating to dormant mortgages.

§ 12.88   PURCHASE & SALE OF REAL ESTATE   Ch. 12

a one or two family residential dwelling.[8] This claimed exemption must appear in the body of the mortgage.

Section 281 of the Real Property Law and Section 253(b) of the Tax Law create special provisions for credit line mortgages. Section 281 deals with lien priority issues which create a priority for future advances over intervening liens other than mechanics liens. The law does not deal with federal lien priorities which may intervene over future advances. For residential credit line mortgages (principally improved by one to six family owner occupied residences the tax is based on the maximum principal amount secured by the mortgage regardless of the number of advances and pay backs.)[9] Non-residential qualifying credit line mortgages of less than $3,000,000 will be taxed at the rates applicable to the principal amount secured regardless of the number of advances or readvances.[10]

§ 12.89   Closing of Title—Payment of Taxes—Mortgage Recording Tax Rate in New York City

Mortgages securing less than $500,000 per $100 of principal debt or obligation are subject to tax at the following rates per $100 of principal debt or obligation.:

New York City	Basic	Additional	Special Additional	TOTAL
$1.00	$.50	$.25	$.25	$2.00

All mortgages of 1, 2 or 3 family dwelling, individual condominium units individual cooperative apartments securing $500,000 or more are subject the rates below per $100 of principal debt or obligation.:

New York City	Basic	Additional	Special Additional	TOTAL
$1.125	$.50	$.25	$.25	$2.125

For all other mortgages securing $500,000 or more are taxed at the following rates per $100 of principal debt or obligation.

New York City	Basic	Additional	Special Additional	TOTAL
$1.75	$.50	$.25	$.25	$2.75

Explanation of the Levels and Method of Computation of Mortgage Recording Tax. In the counties of New York City, the total mortgage tax rate may be $2.00, $2.125 or $2.75 per $100 of principal debt or obligation or major fraction. The following is an explanation of the total mortgage recording tax.

---

8. Tax Law § 253(2)(a).
9. Tax Law § 253–b(1–a).
10. Tax Law § 253(1–a) was adopted pursuant to Chs. 89 and 490, L.1996, effective for mortgages recorded on or after November 6, 1996.

In all counties, including New York City, a basic mortgage tax of $0.50 per $100,[1] as well as a special additional Tax of $0.25 per $100 is charged.[2] New York City also imposes the following tax on the recording of real estate mortgages (or assignment of rent which is not part of an existing mortgage) in New York City:

(a) $1.00 for each $100 of indebtedness on mortgages for less than $500,000 (a total of $2.00 per $100), or

(b) $1.125 for each $100 of indebtedness with respect to mortgages for $500,000 or more securing a 1, 2, 3–family house, an individual condominium unit (a total of $2.125 per $100), or $1.75 for each $100 of all other mortgages securing a principal debt or obligation of $500,000 or more (a total of $2.75 per $100).[3]

The Tax Law further provides that where the premises are principally improved, or are to be improved, by a structure containing not more than six residential dwelling units having their own separate cooking facilities, the special additional tax is to be paid by the mortgagee, unless the mortgagee is a natural person in which case the mortgage is exempt from this tax.[4] Where the premises are not improved as described above, the special additional tax is to be paid by the mortgagor.[5]

A new mortgage recording tax must be paid if, at the time of the assignment of mortgage, the principal amount is "due and payable" and both principal and interest has been paid to the lender.[6]

In all counties shown as charging $1.00 or more per $100.00 of obligation, an additional mortgage recording tax of $0.25 per $100 of obligation is imposed. A special exemption of $0.25 per $100 is allowed up to the first $10,000 of mortgage obligation to a maximum of $25.00 if the mortgage is on a property principally improved or to be improved by a one or two family residential dwelling.[7] This claimed exemption must appear in the body of the mortgage.

Section 281 of the RPL and Section 253(b) of the Tax Law create special provisions for credit line mortgages. Section 281 deals with lien priority issues which create a priority for future advances over interven-

§ 12.89

1. Tax Law § 253.

2. Tax Law § 253(1–a)(a).

3. Tax Law § 253–a; Administrative Code of City of New York § 11–2601 as amended effective August 1, 1990.

4. Tax Law § 253(1–a)(a), (b) (an affidavit is required).

5. If the mortgagor is an organization exempt from federal income taxation pursuant to Section 501 of the I.R.C., then the mortgagor is exempt from this special additional tax. Tax Law § 253(1–a)(b). If this is the case, then the tax is to be paid by the mortgagee. If the mortgagee is an organization exempt from federal income taxation pursuant to Section 501 of the I.R.C. then the mortgagee is exempt from this special additional tax and the tax is to be paid by the mortgagor regardless of whether the property is residential or not. Tax Law § 253(1–a)(b).

6. RPL § 275. See New York State Tax Bulletin TSB–M–89(6.1)R relating to dormant mortgages.

7. Tax Law § 253(2)(a).

ing liens other than mechanics liens. The law does not deal with federal lien priorities which may intervene over future advances. For residential credit line mortgages (principally improved by one to six family owner occupied residences the tax is based on the maximum principal amount secured by the mortgage regardless of the number of advances and pay backs.)[8] Non-residential qualifying credit line mortgages of less than $3,000,000 will be taxed at the rates applicable to the principal amount secured regardless of the number of advances or readvances.[9]

§ 12.90 Closing of Title—Payment of Taxes—Method of Payment

Payment of transfer and mortgage recording taxes must be by certified check or bank (teller's) check, payable as follows.[1] New York State Gains Tax is payable to the New York State Department of Taxation and Finance, P.O. Box 5045, Albany, New York 12205–5045. If a courier service is used, the address is;

NYS Tax Department, TTB-[Specify Tax]
West Mall Office Plaza, 855 Central Avenue–2nd Floor
Albany, New York 12206–1579.

Although the gains tax was repealed, some payments will be due for transactions where the consideration aggregated over a period of time prior to June 15, 1996, when the tax was repealed.

New York State Real Estate Transfer Tax (including the mansion tax): Outside New York City the tax is payable to the county clerk of the County where the property is located. Inside New York City the tax is payable to the New York City Department of Finance.[2]

Mortgage Recording Tax: Outside New York City the tax is payable to the county clerk of the County where the property is located. Inside New York City the tax is payable to the New York City Department of Finance.

New York City Real Property Transfer Tax is payable to the New York City Department of Finance.

Note that the amount of fees charged for filing documents which are collateral to, but essential in, the recording system varies from county to county. These documents may include affidavits, registration forms, and tax forms. The local office of the county clerk or the City Register of New

---

8. Tax Law § 253–b.
9. Tax Law § 253(1–a) was adopted pursuant to Chs. 89 and 490, L.1996, effective for mortgages recorded on or after November 6, 1996.

§ 12.90
1. PRACTICE POINTER: Some counties outside New York City will accept funds other than certified or bank checks for New York State real estate transfer tax and mortgage recording tax. Inquiry should be made of the appropriate county clerk to ascertain the practice in any particular county.

2. New York City Department of Finance, 345 Adams Street, 5th Floor, Brooklyn, New York 11201.

York City should be consulted in such cases. In some instances the City Register or the county clerk will accept a trust or escrow check held in an attorney's account which is specifically titled as such.

§ 12.91 Closing of Title—Other Required Forms and Information

The following additional forms and affidavits must also be collected by the title closer at the time of closing.

Allocation of Special Additional Mortgage Tax. Every mortgage offered for recording must indicate whether or not it covers real property improved or to be improved by one or more structures containing in the aggregate not more than six residential dwelling units, each having their own separate cooking facilities. This recital may be stated on the mortgage instrument itself or it may be done through the attachment of a separate page to the mortgage. The statement may be made by any person having knowledge of the nature of the improvements. It does not have to be sworn or subscribed to, but it must be signed by the person making the statement.

The purpose of this requirement is to facilitate the segregation and distribution, by the county clerk or register, of the special additional mortgage recording tax of $.25 for each $100 and each remaining major fraction thereof of principal debt or obligation which may be secured by the mortgage.[1] It is important to stress that this requirement in no way changes the rate of tax or the amount to be collected by the recording officer. However, mortgages may not be accepted for recording unless they make the required disclosure as to the type of real property it covers.

The segregation of the tax proceeds collected by the county clerk or register's office is intended to provide funds for the Metropolitan Transit Authority and the Niagara Frontier Transportation Authority. It is only applicable in the following counties: Bronx, Dutchess, Erie, Kings, Nassau, New York, Orange, Putnam, Queens, Richmond, Rockland, Suffolk and Westchester.

Smoke Alarm. An affidavit is required in connection with the sale of a one or two family dwelling, a condominium or a cooperative apartment to the effect that a smoke alarm in operable condition is contained in the premises.[2]

Statement for One or Two Family Residence. A statement in the mortgage itself that the real property is improved or will be improved by a one or two family residence or dwelling is sufficient to claim the $10,000 deduction from the additional mortgage recording tax im-

§ 12.91
1. Tax Law § 253(1–a)(a).

2. Executive Law § 378(5); N.Y.C. Administrative Code, Tit. 27, Ch. 1, Subch. 17, Art. 6.

§ 12.91   PURCHASE & SALE OF REAL ESTATE   Ch. 12

posed by Tax Law Section 253.2(a). The recital to qualify for the $10,000 exemption must, however, be made within the mortgage text itself and may not be made on a separate form.

New York State Equalization and Assessment Form. The EA 5217 Assessment and Equalization Form is a recording requirement in every county (except those counties located in New York City) where a deed of real property is to be recorded. It is required for the sale of all real property, residential or commercial, including condominiums.

The EA 5217 is a four part preprinted form available from most title companies as well as from the office of the county clerk. A $25.00 fee is payable to the county clerk where the deed is recorded.

The form requires information about whether the property is in an agricultural district. The number of agricultural districts varies from county to county. There are fifty counties across New York State with agricultural districts. Those counties that do *not* presently have an agricultural district are Hamilton, Nassau, Putnam, Rockland, Warren, Westchester and the five counties in New York City.

If the property is in fact within such a district, Section 310 of the Agricultural and Markets Law requires the grantor to give a notice to the grantee that the property being delivered to the grantee is in an agricultural district. In some counties the real estate tax assessment records reflect whether the assessed property is in an agricultural district while some counties have not yet adjusted the tax assessment records to reflect that information. In order to determine the boundaries of an agricultural district reference should be made to the town clerk's office which has a detailed map for each district in the town. The town assessor is also a source of information about agricultural boundaries.

§ 12.92   Forms

What follows are reprints of the standard form contracts of sale and general powers of attorney discussed in the text. They provide, at the very least, a checklist of all the essential issues involved in the various transactions. Additional Riders may be necessary, as negotiations may warrant in specific circumstances of the transaction.

§ 12.93 Residential Contract of Sale[1]

Jointly prepared by the Real Property Section of the New York State Bar Association, the New York State Land Title Association, the Committee on Real Property Law of the Association of the Bar of the City of New York and the Committee on Real Property Law of the New York County Lawyers' Association.

WARNING: NO REPRESENTATION IS MADE THAT THIS FORM OF CONTRACT FOR THE SALE AND PURCHASE OF REAL ESTATE COMPLIES WITH SECTION 5-702 OF THE GENERAL OBLIGATIONS LAW ("PLAIN LANGUAGE").

CONSULT YOUR LAWYER BEFORE SIGNING THIS AGREEMENT

NOTE: FIRE AND CASUALTY LOSSES AND CONDEMNATION.
This contract form does not provide for what happens in the event of fire, or other casualty loss or condemnation before the title closing. Unless different provision is made in this contract, Section 5-1311 of the General Obligations Law will apply. One part of that law makes a Purchaser responsible for fire and casualty loss upon taking possession of the Premises before the title closing.

Residential Contract of Sale

Contract of Sale made as of   19   BETWEEN

Address:
Social Security Number (Fed. I. D. No(s):
                                                                                 hereinafter called "Seller" and

Address:
Social Security Number; Fed. I. D. No(s).
                                                                                 hereinafter called "Purchaser".

The parties hereby agree as follows:

1. **Premises.** Seller shall sell and convey and Purchaser shall purchase the property, together with all buildings and improvements thereon (collectively the "Premises"), more fully described on a separate page marked "Schedule A", annexed hereto and made a part hereof and also known as

Street Address:

Tax Map Designation:

Together with Seller's ownership and rights, if any, to land lying in the bed of any street or highway, opened or proposed, adjoining the Premises to the center line thereof, including any right of Seller to any unpaid award by reason of any taking by condemnation and/or for any damage to the Premises by reason of change of grade of any street or highway. Seller shall deliver at no additional cost to Purchaser, at Closing (as hereinafter defined), or thereafter, on demand, any documents that Purchaser may reasonably require for the conveyance of such title and the assignment and collection of such award or damages

2. **Personal Property.** This sale also includes all fixtures and articles of personal property now attached or appurtenant to the Premises, unless specifically excluded below. Seller represents and warrants that at Closing they will be paid for and owned by Seller, free and clear of all liens and encumbrances, except any existing mortgage to which this sale may be subject. They include, but are not limited to, plumbing, heating, lighting and cooking fixtures, bathroom and kitchen cabinets, mantels, door mirrors, switch plates and door hardware, venetian blinds, window treatments, shades, screens, awnings, storm windows, storm doors, window boxes, mail box, TV aerials, weather vane, flagpole, pumps, shrubbery, fencing, outdoor statuary, tool shed, dishwasher, washing machine, clothes dryer, garbage disposal unit, range, oven, refrigerator, freezer, air conditioning equipment and installations, wall to wall carpeting and built-ins not excluded below (*strike out inapplicable items*).

Excluded from this sale are furniture and household furnishings and

3. **Purchase Price.** The purchase price is
                                                                                 $
payable as follows:
(a) on the signing of this contract, by Purchaser's check payable to the Escrowee (as hereinafter defined), subject to collection, the receipt of which is hereby acknowledged, to be held in escrow pursuant to paragraph 6 of this contract (the "Downpayment"):
                                                                                 $
(b) by allowance for the principal amount unpaid on the existing mortgage on the date hereof, payment of which Purchaser shall assume by joinder in the deed $
(c) by a purchase money note and mortgage from Purchaser to Seller $
(d) balance at Closing in accordance with paragraph 7: $

4. **Existing Mortgage.** (*Delete if inapplicable*) If this sale is subject to an existing mortgage as indicated in paragraph 3(b) above:
(a) The Premises shall be conveyed subject to the continuing lien of the existing mortgage, which is presently payable, with interest at the rate of   percent per annum, in monthly installments of $ which include principal, interest and escrow amounts, if any, and with any balance of principal being due and payable on

(b) To the extent that any required payments are made on the existing mortgage between the date hereof and Closing which reduce the unpaid principal amount thereof below the amount shown in paragraph 3(b), then the balance of the price payable at Closing under paragraph 3(d) shall be increased by the amount of the payments of principal. Seller represents and warrants that the amount shown in paragraph 3(b) is substantially correct and agrees that only payments required by the existing mortgage will be made between the date hereof and Closing

(c) If there is a mortgage escrow account, Seller shall assign it to Purchaser, if it can be assigned, and in that case Purchaser shall pay the amount in the escrow account to Seller at Closing.

(d) Seller shall deliver to Purchaser at Closing a certificate dated not more than 30 days before Closing signed by the holder of the existing mortgage, in form for recording, certifying the amount of the unpaid principal, the date to which interest has been paid and the amounts, if any, claimed to be unpaid for principal and interest, itemizing the same. Seller shall pay the fees for recording such certificate. If the holder of the existing mortgage is a bank or other institution as defined in Section 274-a of the Real Property Law it may, instead of the certificate, furnish a letter signed by a duly authorized officer, employee or agent, dated not more than 30 days before Closing, containing the same information.

(e) Seller represents and warrants that (i) Seller has delivered to Purchaser true and complete copies of the existing mortgage, the note secured thereby and any extensions and modifications thereof, (ii) the existing mortgage is not now, and at the time of Closing will not be, in default, and (iii) the existing mortgage does not contain any provision that permits the holder of the mortgage to require its immediate payment in full or to change any other term thereof by reason of the sale or conveyance of the Premises.

5. **Purchase Money Mortgage.** (*Delete if inapplicable*) If there is to be a purchase money mortgage as indicated in paragraph 3(c) above:
(a) The purchase money note and mortgage shall be drawn by the attorney for Seller in the form attached or, if not, in the standard form adopted by the New York State Land Title Association. Purchaser shall pay at Closing the mortgage recording tax, recording fees and the attorney's fees in the amount of $ for its preparation
(b) The purchase money note and mortgage shall also provide that it is subject and subordinate to the lien of the existing mortgage and any extensions, modifications, replacements or consolidations of the existing mortgage, provided that (i) the interest rate thereof shall not be greater than   percent per annum and the total debt service thereunder shall not be greater than $ per annum, and (ii) if the principal amount thereof shall exceed the amount of principal owing and unpaid on the existing mortgage at the time of placing such new mortgage or consolidated mortgage, the excess be paid to the holder of such purchase money mortgage in reduction of the principal thereof. The purchase money mortgage shall also provide that such payment to the holder thereof shall not alter or affect the regular installments, if any, of principal payable thereunder and that the holder thereof will, on demand and without charge therefor, execute, acknowledge and deliver any agreement or agreements further to effectuate such subordination.

6. **Downpayment in Escrow.** (a) Seller's attorney ("Escrowee") shall hold the Downpayment for Seller's account in escrow in a segregated bank account at   until Closing or sooner termination of this contract and shall pay over or apply the Downpayment in accordance with the terms of this paragraph. Escrowee shall (*not*) (*Delete if inapplicable*) hold the Downpayment in an interest-bearing account for the benefit of

---

§ 12.93
1. Forms may be purchased from Julius Blumberg, Inc. NYC 10013, or any of its dealers. Reproduction prohibited.

899

the parties. If interest is held for the benefit of the parties, it shall be paid to the party entitled in the Downpayment and the party receiving the interest shall pay any income taxes thereon. If interest is not held for the benefit of the parties, the Downpayment shall be placed in an IOLA account or as otherwise permitted or required by law. The Social Security or Federal Identification numbers of the parties shall be furnished to Escrowee upon request. At Closing, the Downpayment shall be paid by Escrowee to Seller. If for any reason Closing does not occur and either party gives Notice (as defined in paragraph 25) to Escrowee demanding payment of the Downpayment, Escrowee shall give prompt Notice to the other party of such demand. If Escrowee does not receive Notice of objection from such other party to the proposed payment within 10 business days after the giving of such Notice, Escrowee is hereby authorized and directed to make such payment. If Escrowee does receive such Notice of objection within such 10 day period or if for any other reason Escrowee in good faith shall elect not to make such payment, Escrowee shall continue to hold such amount until otherwise directed by Notice from the parties to this contract or a final, nonappealable judgment, order or decree of a court. However, Escrowee shall have the right at any time to deposit the Downpayment and the interest thereon with the clerk of a court in the county in which the Premises are located and shall give Notice of such deposit to Seller and Purchaser. Upon such deposit or other disbursement in accordance with the terms of this paragraph, Escrowee shall be relieved and discharged of all further obligations and responsibilities hereunder.

(b) The parties acknowledge that, although Escrowee is holding the Downpayment for Seller's account, for all other purposes Escrowee is acting solely as a stakeholder at their request and for their convenience and that Escrowee shall not be liable to either party for any act or omission on its part unless taken or suffered in bad faith or in willful disregard of this contract or involving gross negligence on the part of Escrowee. Seller and Purchaser jointly and severally agree to defend, indemnify and hold Escrowee harmless from and against all costs, claims and expenses (including reasonable attorneys' fees) incurred in connection with the performance of Escrowee's duties hereunder, except with respect to actions or omissions taken or suffered by Escrowee in bad faith or in willful disregard of this contract or involving gross negligence on the part of Escrowee.

(c) Escrowee may act or refrain from acting in respect of any matter referred to herein in full reliance upon and with the advice of counsel which may be selected by it (including any member of its firm) and shall be fully protected in so acting or refraining from action upon the advice of such counsel.

(d) Escrowee acknowledges receipt of the Downpayment by check subject to collection and Escrowee's agreement to the provisions of this paragraph by signing in the place indicated on the signature page of this contract.

(e) Escrowee or any member of its firm shall be permitted to act as counsel for Seller in any dispute as to the disbursement of the Downpayment or any other dispute between the parties whether or not Escrowee is in possession of the Downpayment and continues to act as Escrowee.

7. Acceptable Funds. All money payable under this contract, unless otherwise specified, shall be paid by:

(a) Cash, but not over $1,000.00;

(b) Good certified check of Purchaser drawn on or official check issued by any bank, savings bank, trust company or savings and loan association having a banking office in the State of New York, unendorsed and payable to the order of Seller, or as Seller may otherwise direct upon not less than 3 business days notice (by telephone or otherwise) to Purchaser;

(c) As to money other than the purchase price payable to Seller at Closing, uncertified check of Purchaser up to the amount of $_____ and

(d) As otherwise agreed to in writing by Seller or Seller's attorney.

8. Mortgage Contingency. (Delete if inapplicable) (a) The obligations of Purchaser hereunder are conditioned upon issuance on or before _____, 19__, (the "Commitment Date") of a written commitment from any Institutional Lender pursuant to which such Institutional Lender agrees to make a first mortgage loan, other than a VA, FHA or other governmentally insured loan, to Purchaser, at Purchaser's sole cost and expense, of $_____ or such lesser sum as Purchaser shall be willing to accept, at the prevailing fixed rate of interest not to exceed _____ or initial adjustable rate of interest not to exceed _____ for a term of at least _____ years and on other customary commitment terms, whether or not conditional upon any factors other than an appraisal satisfactory to the Institutional Lender. For purposes of this contract, the term "Institutional Lender" shall mean any bank, savings bank, private banker, trust company, savings and loan association, credit union or similar banking institution whether organized under the laws of this state, the United States or any other state; foreign banking corporation licensed by the Superintendent of Banks of New York or the Comptroller of the Currency to transact business in New York State; insurance company duly organized or licensed to do business in New York State; mortgage banker licensed pursuant to Article 12-D of the Banking Law; and any instrumentality created by the United States or any state with the power to make mortgage loans. Purchaser shall (i) make prompt application to an Institutional Lender for such mortgage loan, (ii) furnish accurate and complete information regarding Purchaser and members of Purchaser's family, as required, (iii) pay all fees, points and charges required in connection with such application and loan, (iv) pursue such application with diligence, (v) cooperate in good faith with such Institutional Lender to obtain such commitment and (vi) promptly give Notice to Seller of the name and address of each Institutional Lender to which Purchaser has made such application. Purchaser shall comply with all requirements of such commitment (or any other commitment accepted by Purchaser) and shall furnish Seller with a copy thereof promptly after receipt thereof. If such commitment is not issued on or before the Commitment Date, then, unless Purchaser has accepted a commitment that does not comply with the requirements set forth above, Purchaser may cancel this contract by giving Notice to Seller within 5 business days after the Commitment Date, in which case this contract shall be deemed cancelled and thereafter neither party shall have any further rights against, or obligations or liabilities to, the other by reason of this contract, except that the Downpayment shall be promptly refunded to Purchaser and except as set forth in paragraph 27. If Purchaser fails to give notice of cancellation or if Purchaser shall accept a commitment that does not comply with the terms set forth above, then Purchaser shall be deemed to have waived Purchaser's right to cancel this contract and to receive a refund of the Downpayment by reason of the contingency contained in this paragraph. (Delete if inapplicable) (b) Purchaser and Seller agree that the submission of an application to a mortgage broker registered pursuant to Article 12-D of the New York Banking Law ("Mortgage Broker") shall constitute full compliance with the terms and conditions set forth in paragraph 8(a)(i) of this contract, and that Purchaser's cooperation in good faith with such Mortgage Broker to obtain a commitment from an Institutional Lender (together with Purchaser's cooperation in good faith with any Institutional Lender to which Purchaser's application has been submitted by such Mortgage Broker), and the prompt giving of Notice by Purchaser to Seller of the name and address of each Mortgage Broker to which Purchaser has submitted such an application shall constitute full compliance with the terms and conditions set forth in paragraph 8(a)(v) and (vi) of this contract.

9. Permitted Exceptions. The Premises are sold and shall be conveyed subject to:

(a) Zoning and subdivision laws and regulations, and landmark, historic or wetlands designation, provided that they are not violated by the existing buildings and improvements erected on the property or their use;

(b) Consents for the erection of any structures on, under or above any streets on which the Premises abut;

(c) Encroachments of stoops, areas, cellar steps, trim and cornices, if any, upon any street or highway.

(d) Real estate taxes that are a lien, but are not yet due and payable; and

(e) The other matters, if any, including a survey exception, set forth in a Rider attached.

10. Governmental Violations and Orders. (a) Seller shall comply with all notes or notices of violations of law or municipal ordinances, orders or requirements noted or issued as of the date hereof by any governmental department having authority as to lands, housing, buildings, fire, health, environmental and labor conditions affecting the Premises. The Premises shall be conveyed free of them at Closing. Seller shall furnish Purchaser with any authorizations necessary to make the searches that could disclose these matters.

(b) (Delete if inapplicable) All obligations affecting the Premises pursuant to the Administrative Code of the City of New York incurred prior to Closing and payable in money shall be discharged by Seller at or prior to Closing.

11. Seller's Representations. (a) Seller represents and warrants to Purchaser that:

(i) The Premises abut or have a right of access to a public road;

(ii) Seller is the sole owner of the Premises and has the full right, power and authority to sell, convey and transfer the same in accordance with the terms of this contract;

(iii) Seller is not a "foreign person", as that term is defined for purposes of the Foreign Investment in Real Property Tax Act, Internal Revenue Code ("IRC") Section 1445, as amended, and the regulations promulgated thereunder (collectively "FIRPTA");

(iv) The Premises are not affected by any exemptions or abatements of taxes; and

(v) Seller has been known by no other name for the past ten years, except

(b) Seller covenants and warrants that all of the representations and warranties set forth in this contract shall be true and correct at Closing.

(c) Except as otherwise expressly set forth in this contract, none of Seller's covenants, representations, warranties or other obligations contained in this contract shall survive Closing.

12. Condition of Property. Purchaser acknowledges and represents that Purchaser is fully aware of the physical condition and state of repair of the Premises and of all other property included in this sale, based on Purchaser's own inspection and investigation thereof, and that Purchaser is entering into this contract based solely upon such inspection and investigation and not upon any information, data, statements or representations, written or oral, as to the physical condition, state of repair, use, cost of operation or any other matter related to the Premises or the other property included in the sale, given or made by Seller or its representatives, and shall accept the same "as is" in their present condition and state of repair, subject to reasonable use, wear, tear and natural deterioration between the date hereof and the date of Closing (except as otherwise set forth in paragraph 16(f)), without any reduction in the purchase price or claim of any kind for any change in such condition by reason thereof subsequent to the date of this contract. Purchaser and its authorized representatives shall have the right, at reasonable times and upon reasonable notice (by telephone or otherwise) to Seller, to inspect the Premises before Closing.

900

13. Insurable Title. Seller shall give and Purchaser shall accept such title as _____ shall be willing to approve and insure in accordance with its standard form of title policy approved by the New York State Insurance Department, subject only to the matters provided for in this contract.

14. Closing, Deed and Title. (a) "Closing" means the settlement of the obligations of Seller and Purchaser to each other under this contract, including the payment of the purchase price to Seller, and the delivery to Purchaser of a _____ deed in proper statutory short form for record, duly executed and acknowledged, so as to convey to Purchaser fee simple title to the Premises, free of all encumbrances, except as otherwise herein stated. The deed shall contain a covenant by Seller as required by subd. 5 of Section 13 of the Lien Law.

(b) If Seller is a corporation, it shall deliver to Purchaser at the time of Closing (i) a resolution of its Board of Directors authorizing the sale and delivery of the deed, and (ii) a certificate by the Secretary or Assistant Secretary of the corporation certifying such resolution and setting forth facts showing that the transfer is in conformity with the requirements of Section 909 of the Business Corporation Law. The deed in such case shall contain a recital sufficient to establish compliance with that Section.

15. Closing Date and Place. Closing shall take place at the office of _____ at _____ o'clock on _____ 19 _____ or, upon reasonable notice (by telephone or otherwise) by Purchaser, at the office of _____

16. Conditions to Closing. This contract and Purchaser's obligation to purchase the Premises are also subject to and conditioned upon the fulfillment of the following conditions precedent:

(a) The accuracy, as of the date of Closing, of the representations and warranties of Seller made in this contract.

(b) The delivery by Seller to Purchaser of a valid and subsisting Certificate of Occupancy or other required certificate of compliance, or evidence that none was required, covering the building(s) and all of the other improvements located on the property authorizing their use as a _____ family dwelling at the date of Closing.

(c) The delivery by Seller to Purchaser of a duly executed and sworn affidavit (in form prescribed by law) claiming exemption of the sale contemplated hereby, if such be the case, under Article 31-B of the Tax Law of the State of New York and the Regulations promulgated thereunder, as the same may be amended from time to time (collectively the "Gains Tax Law"); or if such sale shall not be exempt under the Gains Tax Law, Seller and Purchaser agree to comply in a timely manner with the requirements of the Gains Tax Law and, at Closing, Seller shall deliver to Purchaser (i) an official return showing no tax due, or (ii) an official return accompanied by a certified or official bank check drawn on a New York State banking institution payable to the order of the New York State Department of Taxation and Finance in the amount of the tax shown to be due thereon. Seller shall (x) pay promptly any additional tax that may become due under the Gains Tax Law, together with interest and penalties thereon, if any, which may be assessed or become due after Closing, and or execute any other documents that may be required in respect thereof, and (y) indemnify, defend and save Purchaser harmless from and against any of the foregoing and any damage, liability, cost or expense (including reasonable attorneys' fees) which may be suffered or incurred by Purchaser by reason of the nonpayment thereof. The provisions of this subparagraph (c) shall survive Closing.

(d) The delivery by Seller to Purchaser of a certification stating that Seller is not a foreign person, which certification shall be in the form then required by FIRPTA. If Seller fails to deliver the aforesaid certification or if Purchaser is not entitled under FIRPTA to rely on such certification, Purchaser shall deduct and withhold from the purchase price a sum equal to 10% thereof (or any lesser amount permitted by law) and shall at Closing remit the withheld amount with the required forms to the Internal Revenue Service.

(e) The delivery of the Premises and all building(s) and improvements comprising a part thereof in broom clean condition, vacant and free of leases or tenancies, together with keys to the Premises.

(f) All plumbing (including water supply and septic systems, if any), heating and air conditioning, if any, electrical and mechanical systems, equipment and machinery in the building(s) located on the property and all appliances which are included in this sale being in working order as of the date of Closing.

(g) If the Premises are a one or two family house, delivery by the parties at Closing of affidavits in compliance with state and local law requirements to the effect that there is installed in the Premises a smoke detecting alarm device or devices.

(h) The delivery by the parties of any other affidavits required as a condition of recording the deed.

17. Deed Transfer and Recording Taxes. At Closing, certified or official bank checks payable to the order of the appropriate State, City or County officer in the amount of any applicable transfer and or recording tax payable by reason of the delivery or recording of the deed or mortgage, if any, shall be delivered by the party required by law or by this contract to pay such transfer and or recording tax, together with any required tax returns duly executed and sworn to, and such party shall cause any such checks and returns to be delivered to the appropriate officer promptly after Closing. The obligation to pay any additional tax or deficiency and any interest or penalties thereon shall survive Closing.

18. Apportionments and Other Adjustments; Water Meter and Installment Assessments. (a) To the extent applicable, the following shall be apportioned as of midnight of the day before the day of Closing:

(i) taxes, water charges and sewer rents, on the basis of the fiscal period for which assessed; (ii) fuel; (iii) interest on the existing mortgage; (iv) premiums on existing transferable insurance policies and renewals of those expiring prior to Closing; (v) vault charges; (vi) rents as and when collected.

(b) If Closing shall occur before a new tax rate is fixed, the apportionment of taxes shall be upon the basis of the tax rate for the immediately preceding fiscal period applied to the latest assessed valuation.

(c) If there is a water meter on the Premises, Seller shall furnish a reading to a date not more than 30 days before Closing and the unfixed meter charge and sewer rent, if any, shall be apportioned on the basis of such last reading.

(d) If at the date of Closing the Premises are affected by an assessment which is or may become payable in annual installments, and the first installment is then a lien, or has been paid, then for the purposes of this contract all the unpaid installments shall be considered due and shall be paid by Seller at or prior to Closing.

(e) Any errors or omissions in computing apportionments or other adjustments at Closing shall be corrected within a reasonable time following Closing. This subparagraph shall survive Closing.

19. Allowance for Unpaid Taxes, etc. Seller has the option to credit Purchaser as an adjustment to the purchase price with the amount of any unpaid taxes, assessments, water charges and sewer rents, together with any interest and penalties thereon to a date not less than five business days after Closing, provided that official bills therefor computed to said date are produced at Closing.

20. Use of Purchase Price to Remove Encumbrances. If at Closing there are other liens or encumbrances that Seller is obligated to pay or discharge, Seller may use any portion of the cash balance of the purchase price to pay or discharge them, provided Seller shall simultaneously deliver to Purchaser at Closing instruments in recordable form and sufficient to satisfy such liens or encumbrances of record, together with the cost of recording or filing said instruments. As an alternative Seller may deposit sufficient monies with the title insurance company employed by Purchaser acceptable to and required by it to assure their discharge, but only if the title insurance company will insure Purchaser's title clear of the matters or insure against their enforcement out of the Premises and will insure Purchaser's Institutional Lender clear of such matters. Upon notice (by telephone or otherwise), given not less than 3 business days before Closing, Purchaser shall provide separate certified or official bank checks as requested to assist in clearing up these matters.

21. Title Examination; Seller's Inability to Convey; Limitations of Liability. (a) Purchaser shall order an examination of title in respect of the Premises from a title company licensed or authorized to issue title insurance by the New York State Insurance Department or any agent for such title company promptly after the execution of this contract or, if this contract is subject to the mortgage contingency set forth in paragraph 8, after a mortgage commitment has been accepted by Purchaser. Purchaser shall cause a copy of the title report and of any additions thereto to be delivered to the attorney(s) for Seller promptly after receipt thereof.

(b)(i) If at the date of Closing Seller is unable to transfer title to Purchaser in accordance with this contract, or Purchaser has other valid grounds for refusing to close, whether by reason of liens, encumbrances or other objections to title or otherwise (herein collectively called "Defects"), other than those subject to which Purchaser is obligated to accept title hereunder or which Purchaser may have waived and other than those which Seller has herein expressly agreed to remove, remedy or discharge and if Purchaser shall be unwilling to waive the same and to close title without abatement of the purchase price, then, except as hereinafter set forth, Seller shall have the right, at Seller's sole election, either to take such action as Seller may deem advisable to remove, remedy, discharge or comply with such Defects or to cancel this contract; (ii) if Seller elects to take action to remove, remedy or comply with such Defects, Seller shall be entitled from time to time, upon Notice to Purchaser, to adjourn the date for Closing hereunder for a period or periods not exceeding 60 days in the aggregate (but not extending beyond the date upon which Purchaser's mortgage commitment, if any, shall expire), and the date for Closing shall be adjourned to a date specified by Seller not beyond such period. If for any reason whatsoever, Seller shall not have succeeded in removing, remedying or complying with such Defects at the expiration of such adjournment(s), and if Purchaser shall still be unwilling to waive the same and to close title without abatement of the purchase price, then either party may cancel this contract by Notice to the other given within 10 days after such adjourned date. (iii) notwithstanding the foregoing, the existing mortgage (unless this sale is subject to the same) and any matter created by Seller after the date hereof shall be released, discharged or otherwise cured by Seller at or prior to Closing.

(c) If this contract is cancelled pursuant to its terms, other than as a result of Purchaser's default, this contract shall terminate and come to an end, and neither party shall have any further rights, obligations or liabilities against or to the other hereunder or other-

§ 12.93   PURCHASE & SALE OF REAL ESTATE   Ch. 12

wise, except that: (i) Seller shall promptly refund or cause the Escrowee to refund the Downpayment to Purchaser and, unless cancelled as a result of Purchaser's default or pursuant to paragraph 8, to reimburse Purchaser for the net cost of examination of title, including any appropriate additional charges related thereto, and the net cost, if actually paid or incurred by Purchaser, for updating the existing survey of the Premises or of a new survey; and (ii) the obligations under paragraph 27 shall survive the termination of this contract.

22. Affidavit as to Judgments, Bankruptcies, etc. If a title examination discloses judgments, bankruptcies or other returns against persons having names the same as or similar to that of Seller, Seller shall deliver an affidavit at Closing showing that they are not against Seller.

23. Defaults and Remedies. (a) If Purchaser defaults hereunder, Seller's sole remedy shall be to receive and retain the Downpayment as liquidated damages, it being agreed that Seller's damages in case of Purchaser's default might be impossible to ascertain and that the Downpayment constitutes a fair and reasonable amount of damages under the circumstances and is not a penalty.

(b) If Seller defaults hereunder, Purchaser shall have such remedies as Purchaser shall be entitled to at law or in equity, including, but not limited to, specific performance.

24. Purchaser's Lien. All money paid on account of this contract, and the reasonable expenses of examination of title to the Premises and of any survey and survey inspection charges, are hereby made liens on the Premises, but such liens shall not continue after default by Purchaser under this contract.

25. Notices. Any notice or other communication ("Notice") shall be in writing and either (a) sent by either of the parties hereto or by their respective attorneys who are hereby authorized to do so on their behalf or by the Escrowee, by registered or certified mail, postage prepaid, or

(b) delivered in person or by overnight courier, with receipt acknowledged, to the respective addresses given in this contract for the party and the Escrowee, to whom the Notice is to be given, or to such other address as such party or Escrowee shall hereafter designate by Notice given to the other party or parties and the Escrowee pursuant to this paragraph. Each Notice mailed shall be deemed given on the third business day following the date of mailing the same, except that any notice to Escrowee shall be deemed given only upon receipt by Escrowee and each Notice delivered in person or by overnight courier shall be deemed given when delivered.

26. No Assignment. This contract may not be assigned by Purchaser without the prior written consent of Seller in each instance and any purported assignment(s) made without such consent shall be void.

27. Broker. Seller and Purchaser each represents and warrants to the other that it has not dealt with any real estate broker in connection with this sale other than

("Broker") and Seller shall pay Broker any commission earned pursuant to a separate agreement between Seller and Broker. Seller and Purchaser shall indemnify and defend each other against any costs, claims and expenses, including reasonable attorneys' fees, arising out of the breach on their respective parts of any representation or agreement contained in this paragraph. The provisions of this paragraph shall survive Closing or, if Closing does not occur, the termination of this contract.

28. Miscellaneous. (a) All prior understandings, agreements, representations and warranties, oral or written, between Seller and Purchaser are merged in this contract, it completely expresses their full agreement and has been entered into after full investigation, neither party relying upon any statement made by anyone else that is not set forth in this contract.

(b) Neither this contract nor any provision thereof may be waived, changed or cancelled except in writing. This contract shall also apply to and bind the heirs, distributees, legal representatives, successors and permitted assigns of the respective parties. The parties hereby authorize their respective attorneys to agree in writing to any changes in dates and time periods provided for in this contract.

(c) Any singular word or term herein shall also be read as in the plural and the neuter shall include the masculine and feminine gender, whenever the sense of this contract may require it.

(d) The captions in this contract are for convenience of reference only and in no way define, limit or describe the scope of this contract and shall not be considered in the interpretation of this contract or any provision hereof.

(e) This contract shall not be binding or effective until duly executed and delivered by Seller and Purchaser.

(f) Seller and Purchaser shall comply with IRC reporting requirements, if applicable. This subparagraph shall survive Closing.

(g) Each party shall, at any time and from time to time, execute, acknowledge where appropriate and deliver such further instruments and documents and take such other action as may be reasonably requested by the other in order to carry out the intent and purpose of this contract. This subparagraph shall survive Closing.

(h) This contract is intended for the exclusive benefit of the parties hereto and, except as otherwise expressly provided herein, shall not be for the benefit of, and shall not create any rights in, or be enforceable by, any other person or entity.

IN WITNESS WHEREOF, this contract has been duly executed by the parties hereto.

_____ Seller   _____ Purchaser

_____ Seller   _____ Purchaser

Attorney for Seller: **Attorney for Purchaser:**

Address: Address:

Tel.:   Fax: Tel.:   Fax:

Receipt of the Downpayment is acknowledged and the undersigned agrees to act in accordance with the provisions of paragraph 6 above.

_____ Escrowee

Contract of Sale   PREMISES

Title No. _____   Section
                                         Block
                                         Lot
                                         County or Town
                                         Street Number Address

TO

EPA and HUD Lead Paint Regulations: Owners of pre-1978 housing must disclose known lead-based paint hazards to purchasers. Use the following BLUMBERG LAW PRODUCTS (800 LAW MART) to comply:

3140 Information Booklet   3142 Disclosure Form, Sale of Residence   3143WIN Disclosure form software

§ 12.94 Contract of Sale—Condominium Unit[1]

CONSULT YOUR LAWYER BEFORE SIGNING THIS AGREEMENT

Contract of Sale — Condominium Unit

Agreement made as of   19   between

residing at

and   ("Seller")

residing at

                                                                                                      ("Purchaser")

1. Unit: Seller agrees to sell and convey, and Purchaser agrees to purchase, Unit No.   ("Unit") in the building ("Building") known as   Condominium ("Condominium") and located at   , New York, together with a   percent undivided interest in the Common Elements (as defined in para. 6) appurtenant thereto, all upon and subject to the terms and conditions set forth herein. The Unit shall be as designated in the Declaration of Condominium Ownership (as the same may be amended from time to time, the "Declaration") of the Condominium, recorded in   County, New York or the By-Laws (as the same may be amended from time to time, the "By-Laws") of the Condominium.

2. Personal Property: (a) The sale includes all of Seller's right, title and interest, if any, in and to:

(i) the refrigerators, freezers, ranges, ovens, dishwashers, washing machines, clothes dryers, cabinets and counters, lighting and plumbing fixtures, air conditioning equipment, venetian blinds, shades, screens, storm windows and other window treatments, wall-to-wall carpeting, bookshelves, switchplates, door hardware, built-ins and articles of property and fixtures attached to or appurtenant to the Unit, except those listed in subpara. 2(b), all of which included property and fixtures are represented to be owned by Seller, free and clear of all liens and encumbrances other than those encumbrances ("Permitted Exceptions") set forth on Schedule A annexed hereto and made a part hereof (strike out inapplicable items); and

(ii)

(b) Excluded from this sale are:

(i) furniture and furnishings (other than as specifically provided in this Contract); and

(ii)

(c) The property referred to in subpara. 2(a)(i) and (ii) may not be purchased if title to the Unit is not conveyed hereunder.

3. Purchase Price: (a) The purchase price ("Purchase Price") is $, payable as follows:

(i) $ ("Downpayment") on the signing of this Contract by check subject to collection, the receipt of which is hereby acknowledged, to be held in escrow pursuant to para. 16; and

(ii) $, constituting the balance of the Purchase Price, by certified check of Purchaser or official bank check (except as otherwise provided in this Contract) on the delivery of the deed as hereinafter provided.

(b) All checks in payment of the Purchase Price shall represent United States currency and be drawn on or issued by a bank or trust company authorized to accept deposits in New York State. All checks in payment of the Downpayment shall be payable to the order of Escrowee (as hereinafter defined). All checks in payment of the balance of the Purchase Price shall be payable to the order of Seller (or as Seller otherwise directs pursuant to subparas. 6(a)(ix) or 19(b)).

(c) Except for the Downpayment and checks aggregating not more than one-half of one percent of the Purchase Price, including payment for closing adjustments, all checks delivered by Purchaser shall be certified or official bank checks as hereinabove provided.

4. Closing of Title: The closing documents referred to in para. 6 shall be delivered, and payment of the balance of the Purchase Price shall be made, at the closing of title ("Closing"), to be held on   19   at   M. at the offices of

or at the office of Purchaser's lending institution or its counsel; provided, however, that such office is located in either the City or County in which either (a) Seller's attorney maintains an office or (b) the Unit is located.

5. Representations, Warranties and Covenants: Seller represents, warrants and covenants that

(a) Seller is the sole owner of the Unit and the property referred to in subpara. 2(a), and Seller has the full right, power and authority to sell, convey and transfer the same;

(b) The common charges (excluding separately billed utility charges) for the Unit on the date hereof are $ per month.

(c) Seller has not received any written notice of any intended assessment or increase in common charges not reflected in subpara. 5(b). Purchaser acknowledges that it will not have the right to cancel this Contract in the event of the imposition of any assessment or increase in common charges after the date hereof of which Seller has not heretofore received written notice.

(d) The real estate taxes for the Unit for the fiscal year of   through   are $

(e) Seller is not a "sponsor" or a nominee of a "sponsor" under any plan of condominium organization affecting the Unit;

(f) All refrigerators, freezers, ranges, dishwashers, washing machines, clothes dryers and air conditioning equipment included in this sale will be in working order at the time of Closing.

(g) If a copy is attached to this Contract, the copy of the Certificate of Occupancy covering the Unit is a true and correct copy; and

(h) Seller is not a "foreign person" as defined in para. 18. (If inapplicable, delete and provide for compliance with Code Withholding Section, as defined in para. 18.)

6. Closing Documents: (a) At the Closing, Seller shall deliver to Purchaser the following:

(i) Bargain and sale deed with   covenant against grantor's acts ("Deed"), complying with RPL § 339-0 and containing the covenant required by LL § 13(5), conveying to Purchaser title to the Unit, together with its undivided interest in the Common Elements (as such term is defined in the Declaration and which term shall be deemed to include Seller's right, title and interest in any limited common elements attributable to or used in connection with the Unit) appurtenant thereto, free and clear of all liens and encumbrances other than Permitted Exceptions. The Deed shall be executed and acknowledged by Seller and, if requested by the Condominium, executed and acknowledged by Purchaser, in proper statutory form for recording;

(ii) If a corporation and if required pursuant to BCL § 909, Seller shall deliver to Purchaser (1) a resolution of its board of directors authorizing the delivery of the Deed and (2) a certificate executed by an officer of such corporation certifying as to the adoption of such resolution and setting forth facts demonstrating that the delivery of the Deed is in conformity with the requirements of BCL § 909. The Deed shall also contain a recital sufficient to establish compliance with such law;

(iii) A waiver of right of first refusal of the board of managers of the Condominium ("Board") if required in accordance with para. 8.

(iv) A statement by the Condominium or its managing agent that the common charges and any assessments then due and payable to the Condominium have been paid to the date of the Closing;

(v) All keys to the doors of, and mailbox for, the Unit;

(vi) Such affidavits and/or other evidence as the title company ("Title Company") from whom Purchaser has ordered a title insurance report and which is authorized to do business in New York State shall reasonably require in order to omit from its title insurance policy all exceptions for judgments, bankruptcies or other returns against Seller and persons or entities whose names are the same as or are similar to Seller's name;

(vii) Official New York State Real Property Transfer Gains Tax Tentative Assessment and Return (or, if applicable, Official Statement of No Tax Due) duly completed by the New York State Department of Taxation and Finance (or, if applicable, a duly

---

§ 12.94

1. Forms may be purchased from Julius Blumberg, Inc. NYC 10013, or any of its dealers. Reproduction prohibited.

executed and acknowledged affidavit of Seller in form required pursuant to the Gains Tax Law (as hereinafter defined) claiming exemption therefrom;

(viii) New York City Real Property Transfer Tax Return, if applicable, and combined Real Property Transfer Gains Tax Affidavits, prepared, executed and acknowledged by Seller in proper form for submission;

(ix) Checks in payment of all applicable real property transfer taxes except a transfer tax which by law is primarily imposed on the purchaser ("Purchaser Transfer Tax") and any New York State Real Property Transfer Gains Tax ("Gains Tax") due in connection with the sale. In lieu of delivery of such checks, Seller shall have the right, upon not less than 3 business days notice to Purchaser, to cause Purchaser to deliver said checks at the Closing and to credit the amount thereof against the balance of the Purchase Price. Seller shall pay the additional transfer taxes and Gains Taxes, if any, payable after the Closing by reason of the conveyance of the Unit, which obligation shall survive the Closing;

(x) Certification that Seller is not a foreign person pursuant to para.18. *(If inapplicable, delete and provide for compliance with Code Section, as defined in para. 18.)*; and

(xi) Affidavit that a single station smoke detecting alarm device is installed pursuant to New York Executive Law §378(5).

(b) At the Closing, Purchaser shall deliver to Seller the following:

(i) Checks in payment of (y) the balance of the Purchase Price in accordance with subpara. 3(b) and (z) any Purchaser Transfer Tax;

(ii) If required by the Declaration or By-Laws, power of attorney to the Board, prepared by Seller, in the form required by the Condominium. The power of attorney shall be executed and acknowledged by Purchaser and, after being recorded, shall be sent to the Condominium;

(iii) New York City Real Property Transfer Tax Return executed and acknowledged by Purchaser and an Affidavit in Lieu of Registration pursuant to New York Multiple Dwelling Law, each in proper form for submission, if applicable, and combined Real Property Transfer Gains Tax Affidavits; and

(iv) If required, New York State Equalization Return executed and acknowledged by Purchaser in proper form for submission.

(c) It is a condition of Purchaser's obligation to close title hereunder that:

(i) All notes or notices of violations of law or governmental orders, ordinances or requirements affecting the Unit and noted or issued by any governmental department, agency or bureau having jurisdiction which were noted or issued on or prior to the date hereof shall have been cured by Seller;

(ii) Any written notice to Seller from the Condominium (or its duly authorized representative) that the Unit is in violation of the Declaration, By-Laws or rules and regulations of the Condominium shall have been cured; and

(iii) The Condominium is a valid condominium created pursuant to RPL Art. 9-B and the Title Company will so insure.

7. Closing Adjustments: (a) The following adjustments shall be made as of 11:59 P.M. of the day before the Closing:

(i) Real estate taxes and water charges and sewer rents, if separately assessed, on the basis of the fiscal period for which assessed, except that if there is a water meter with respect to the Unit, apportionment shall be based on the last available reading, subject to adjustment after the Closing, promptly after the next reading is available; provided, however, that in the event real estate taxes have not, as of the date of Closing, been separately assessed to the Unit, real estate taxes shall be apportioned on the same basis as provided in the Declaration or By-Laws or, in the absence of such provision, based upon the Unit's percentage interest in the Common Elements;

(ii) Common charges of the Condominium; and

(iii) If fuel is separately stored with respect to the Unit only, the value of fuel stored with respect to the Unit at the price then charged by Seller's supplier (as determined by a letter or certificate to be obtained by Seller from such supplier), including any sales taxes.

(b) If at the time of Closing the Unit is affected by an assessment which is or may become payable in installments, then, for the purposes of this Contract, only the unpaid installments which are then due shall be considered due and are to be paid by Seller at the Closing. All subsequent installments at the time of Closing shall be the obligation of Purchaser.

(c) Any errors or omissions in computing closing adjustments shall be corrected. This subpara. 7(c) shall survive the Closing.

(d) If the Unit is located in the City of New York, the "customs in respect to title closings" recommended by The Real Estate Board of New York, Inc., as amended and in effect on the date of Closing, shall apply to the adjustments and other matters therein mentioned, except as otherwise provided herein.

8. Right of First Refusal: If so provided in the Declaration or By-Laws, this sale is subject to and conditioned upon the waiver of a right of first refusal to purchase the Unit held by the Condominium and exercisable by the Board. Seller agrees to give notice promptly to the Board of the contemplated sale of the Unit to Purchaser, which notice shall be given in accordance with the terms of the Declaration and By-Laws, and Purchaser agrees to provide promptly all applications, information and references reasonably requested by the Board. If the Board shall exercise such right of first refusal, Seller shall promptly refund to Purchaser the Downpayment (which term, for all purposes of this Contract, shall be deemed to include interest, if any, earned thereon) and upon the making of such refund this Contract shall be deemed cancelled and of no further force or effect and neither party shall have any further rights against, or obligations or liabilities to, the other by reason of this Contract. If the Board shall fail to exercise such right of first refusal within the time and in the manner provided for in the Declaration or By-Laws or shall declare in writing its intention not to exercise such right of first refusal (a copy of which writing shall be delivered to Purchaser promptly following receipt thereof), the parties hereto shall proceed with this sale in accordance with the provisions of this Contract.

9. Processing Fee: Seller shall, at the Closing, pay all fees and charges payable to the Condominium (and/or its managing agent) in connection with this sale, including, without limitation, any processing fee, the legal fees, if any, of the Condominium's attorney in connection with this sale and, unless otherwise agreed to by Seller and Purchaser in writing, all "flip taxes," transfer or entrance fees or similar charges, if any, payable to or for the Condominium or otherwise for the benefit of the Condominium unit owners, which arise by reason of this sale.

10. No Other Representations: Purchaser has examined and is satisfied with the Declaration, By-Laws and rules and regulations of the Condominium, or has waived the examination thereof. Purchaser has inspected the Unit, its fixtures, appliances and equipment and the personal property, if any, included in this sale, as well as the Common Elements of the Condominium, and knows the condition thereof and, subject to subpara. 5(f), agrees to accept the same "as is," i.e., in the condition they are in on the date hereof, subject to normal use, wear and tear between the date hereof and the Closing. Purchaser has examined or waived examination of the last audited financial statements of the Condominium, and has considered or waived consideration of all other matters pertaining to this Contract and to the purchase to be made hereunder, and does not rely on any representations made by any broker or by Seller or anyone acting or purporting to act on behalf of Seller as to any matters which might influence or affect the decision to execute this Contract or to buy the Unit, or said personal property, except those representations and warranties which are specifically set forth in this Contract.

11. Possession: Seller shall, prior to the Closing, remove from the Unit all furniture, furnishings and other personal property not included in this sale, shall repair any damage caused by such removal, and shall deliver exclusive possession of the Unit at the Closing, vacant, broom-clean and free of tenancies or other rights of use or possession.

12. Access: Seller shall permit Purchaser and its architect, decorator or other authorized persons to have the right of access to the Unit between the date hereof and the Closing for the purpose of inspecting the same and taking measurements, at reasonable times and upon reasonable prior notice to Seller (by telephone or otherwise). Further, Purchaser shall have the right to inspect the Unit at a reasonable time during the 24-hour period immediately preceding the Closing.

13. Defaults and Remedies: (a) If Purchaser defaults hereunder, Seller's sole remedy shall be to retain the Downpayment as liquidated damages, it being agreed that Seller's damages in case of Purchaser's default might be impossible to ascertain and that the Downpayment constitutes a fair and reasonable amount of damages under the circumstances and is not a penalty.

(b) If Seller defaults hereunder, Purchaser shall have such remedies as Purchaser shall be entitled to at law or in equity, including, but not limited to, specific performance.

14. Notices: Any notice, request or other communication ("Notice") given or made hereunder (except for the notice required by para. 12), shall be in writing and either (a) sent by any of the parties hereto or their respective attorneys, by registered or certified mail, return receipt requested, postage prepaid, or (b) delivered in person or by overnight courier, with receipt acknowledged, to the address given at the beginning of this Contract for the party to whom the Notice is to be given, or to such other address for such party as said party shall hereafter designate by Notice given to the other party pursuant to this para. 14. Each Notice mailed shall be deemed given on the third business day following the date of mailing the same and each Notice delivered in person or by overnight courier shall be deemed given when delivered.

15. Purchaser's Lien: The Downpayment and all other sums paid on account of this Contract and the reasonable expenses of the examination of title to, and departmental violation searches in respect of, the Unit are hereby made a lien upon the Unit, but such lien shall not continue after default by Purchaser hereunder.

16. Downpayment in Escrow: (a) Seller's attorney ("Escrowee") shall hold the Downpayment for Seller's account in escrow in a segregated bank account at the depository identified at the end of this Contract until Closing or sooner termination of this Contract and shall pay over or apply the Downpayment in accordance with the terms of this para. 16. Escrowee shall *(not)* (*Delete if inapplicable*) hold the Downpayment in an interest-bearing account for the benefit of the parties. If interest is held for the benefit of the parties, it shall be paid to the party entitled to the Downpayment and the party receiving the interest shall pay any income taxes thereon. If interest is not held for the benefit of the parties, the Downpayment shall be placed in an IOLA account or as otherwise permitted or required by law. The Social Security or Federal Identification numbers of the parties shall be furnished to Escrowee upon request. At Closing, the Downpayment shall be paid by Escrowee to Seller. If for any reason Closing does not occur and either party gives Notice (as defined in paragraph 14) to Escrowee demanding payment of the Downpayment, Escrowee shall give prompt Notice to the other party of such demand. If Escrowee does not receive Notice of objection from such other party to the proposed payment within 10 business days after the giving of such Notice, Escrowee is hereby authorized and directed to make such payment. If Escrowee does receive such Notice of objection within such 10 day period or if for any other reason Escrowee in good faith shall elect not to make such payment, Escrowee shall continue to hold such amount until otherwise directed by Notice from the parties to this Contract or a final, nonappealable judgment, order or decree of a court. However, Escrowee shall have the right at any time to deposit the Downpayment with the clerk of a court in the county in which the Unit is located and shall give Notice of such deposit to Seller and Purchaser. Upon such deposit or other disbursement in accordance with the terms of this para. 16, Escrowee shall be relieved and discharged of all further obligations and responsibilities hereunder.

(b) The parties acknowledge that, although Escrowee is holding the Downpayment for Seller's account, for all other purposes Escrowee is acting solely as a stakeholder at their request and for their convenience and that Escrowee shall not be liable to either party for any act or omission on its part unless taken or suffered in bad faith or in willful disregard of this Contract or involving gross negligence on the part of Escrowee. Seller and Purchaser jointly and severally agree to defend, indemnify and hold Escrowee harmless from and against all costs, claims and expenses (including reasonable attorneys' fees) incurred in connection with the performance of Escrowee's duties hereunder, except with respect to actions or omissions taken or suffered by Escrowee in bad faith or in willful disregard of this Contract or involving gross negligence on the part of Escrowee.

(c) Escrowee may act or refrain from acting in respect of any matter referred to herein in full reliance upon and with the advice of counsel which may be selected by it (including any member of its firm) and shall be fully protected in so acting or refraining from action upon the advice of such counsel.

(d) Escrowee acknowledges receipt of the Downpayment by check subject to collection and Escrowee's agreement to the provisions of this para. 16 by signing in the place indicated in this Contract.

(e) Escrowee or any member of its firm shall be permitted to act as counsel for Seller in any dispute as to the disbursement of the Downpayment or any other dispute between the parties whether or not Escrowee is in possession of the Downpayment and continues to act as Escrowee.

17. New York State Gains Tax: (a) Seller and Purchaser agree to comply in a timely manner with the requirements of article 31-B of the Tax Law and the regulations applicable thereto, as the same from time to time may be amended (collectively, the "Gains Tax Law"). Purchaser agrees to deliver to Seller a duly executed and acknowledged Transferee Questionnaire simultaneously with the execution of this Contract or within 5 business days after subsequent written request from Seller or Seller's attorney. At the Closing, Seller shall deliver (i) an Official Statement of No Tax Due or (ii) an Official Tentative Assessment and Return accompanied by a certified or official bank check drawn on any banking institution described in subpara. 3(b), payable to the order of the State Tax Commission, in the amount of the tax shown to be due thereon, or (iii) if applicable, a duly executed and acknowledged affidavit in form permitted under the Gains Tax Law claiming exemption therefrom.

(b) Seller agrees (i) to pay promptly any tax due under the Gains Tax Law and any interest and penalties thereon which may be assessed or due after the Closing, (ii) to indemnify and save Purchaser harmless from and against any of the foregoing and any cost, claim and expense (including reasonable attorneys' fees) incurred by Purchaser by reason of the non-payment thereof, and (iii) to make any other payments and execute, acknowledge and deliver such further documents as may be necessary to comply with the Gains Tax Law.

(c) The obligations under this para. 17 shall survive the Closing.

18. FIRPTA: Seller represents and warrants to Purchaser that Seller is not a "foreign person" as defined in IRC § 1445, as amended, and the regulations issued thereunder ("Code Withholding Section"). At the Closing Seller shall deliver to Purchaser a certification stating that Seller is not a foreign person in the form then required by the Code Withholding Section. In the event Seller fails to deliver the aforesaid certification or in the event that Purchaser is not entitled under the Code Withholding Section to rely on such certification, Purchaser shall deduct and withhold from the Purchase Price a sum equal to 10% thereof and shall at Closing remit the withheld amount with the required forms to the Internal Revenue Service.

19. Title Report; Acceptable Title: (a) Purchaser shall, promptly after the date hereof, or after receipt of the mortgage commitment letter, if applicable, order a title insurance report from the Title Company. Promptly after receipt of the title report and thereafter of any continuations thereof and supplements thereto, Purchaser shall forward a copy of each such report, continuation or supplement to the attorney for Seller. Purchaser shall further notify Seller's attorney of any other objections to title not reflected in such title report of which Purchaser becomes aware following the delivery of such report, reasonably promptly after becoming aware of such objections.

(b) Any unpaid taxes, assessments, water charges and sewer rents, together with the interest and penalties thereon to a date not less than two days following the date of Closing, and any other liens and encumbrances which Seller is obligated to pay and discharge or which are against corporations, estates or other persons in the chain of title, together with the cost of recording or filing any instruments necessary to discharge such liens and encumbrances of record, may be paid out of the proceeds of the monies payable at the Closing if Seller delivers to Purchaser at the Closing official bills for such taxes, assessments, water charges, sewer rents, interest and penalties and instruments in recordable form sufficient to discharge any other liens and encumbrances of record. Upon request made not less than 3 business days before the Closing, Purchaser shall provide at the Closing separate checks for the foregoing payable to the order of the holder of any such lien, charge or encumbrance and otherwise complying with subpara. 3(b). If the Title Company is willing to insure Purchaser that such charges, liens and encumbrances will not be collected out of or enforced against the Unit and is willing to insure the lien of Purchaser's Institutional Lender (as hereinafter defined) free and clear of any such charges, liens and encumbrances, then Seller shall have the right in lieu of payment and discharge to deposit with the Title Company such funds or to give such assurances or to pay such special or additional premiums as the Title Company may require in order to so insure. In such case the charges, liens and encumbrances with respect to which the Title Company has agreed so to insure shall not be considered objections to title.

(c) Seller shall convey and Purchaser shall accept fee simple title to the Unit in accordance with the terms of this Contract, subject only to, (a) the Permitted Exceptions and (b) such other matters as (i) the Title Company or any other title insurer licensed to do business by the State of New York shall be willing, without special or additional premium, to omit as exceptions to coverage or to except with insurance against collection out of or enforcement against the Unit and (ii) shall be accepted by any lender described in RPL § 274-a ("Institutional Lender") which has committed in writing to provide mortgage financing to Purchaser for the purchase of the Unit ("Purchaser's Institutional Lender"), except that if such acceptance by Purchaser's Institutional Lender is unreasonably withheld or delayed, such acceptance shall be deemed to have been given.

(d) Notwithstanding any contrary provisions in this Contract express or implied, or any contrary rule of law or custom, if Seller shall be unable to convey the Unit in accordance with this Contract (provided that Seller shall release, discharge or otherwise cure at or prior to Closing any matter created by Seller after the date hereof and any existing mortgage, unless this sale is subject to it) and if Purchaser elects not to complete this transaction without abatement of the Purchase Price, the sole obligation and liability of Seller shall be to refund the Downpayment to Purchaser, together with the reasonable cost of the examination of title to, and departmental violation searches in respect of, the Unit, and upon the making of such refund and payment, this Contract shall be deemed cancelled and of no further force or effect and neither party shall have any further rights against, or obligations or liabilities to, the other by reason of this Contract. However, nothing contained in this subpara. 19(d) shall be construed to relieve Seller from liability due to a willful default.

20. Risk of Loss; Casualty: (a) The risk of loss or damage to the Unit or the personal property included in this sale, by fire or other casualty, until the earlier of the Closing or possession of the Unit by Purchaser, is assumed by Seller, but without any obligation of Seller to repair or replace any such loss or damage unless Seller elects to do so as hereinafter provided. Seller shall notify Purchaser of the occurrence of any such loss or damage to the Unit or the personal property included in this sale within 10 days after such occurrence or by the date of Closing, whichever first occurs, and by such notice shall state whether or not Seller elects to repair or restore the Unit and/or the personal property, as the case may be. If Seller elects to make such repairs and restorations, Seller's notice shall set forth an adjourned date for the Closing, which shall be not more than 60 days after the date of the giving of Seller's notice. If Seller either does not elect to do so or, having elected to make such repairs and restorations, fails to complete the same on or before said adjourned date for the Closing, Purchaser shall have the following options:

(i) To declare this Contract cancelled and of no further force or effect and receive a refund of the Downpayment in which event neither party shall thereafter have any further rights against, or obligations or liabilities to, the other by reason of this Contract; or

(ii) To complete the purchase in accordance with this Contract without reduction in the Purchase Price, except as provided in the next sentence. If Seller carries hazard insurance covering such loss or damage, Seller shall turn over to Purchaser at the Closing the net proceeds actually collected by Seller under the provisions of such hazard insurance policies to the extent that they are attributable to loss of or damage to any property included in this sale, less any sums theretofore expended by Seller in repairing or replacing such loss or damage or in collecting such proceeds, and Seller shall assign (without recourse to Seller) Seller's right to receive any additional insurance proceeds which are attributable to the loss of or damage to any property included in this sale.

(b) If Seller does not elect to make such repairs and restorations, Purchaser may exercise the resulting option under (i) or (ii) of (a) above only by notice given to Seller within 10 days after receipt of Seller's notice. If Seller elects to make such repairs and restorations and fails to complete the same on or before the adjourned closing date, Purchaser may exercise either of the resulting options within 10 days after the adjourned closing date.

(c) In the event of any loss of or damage to the Common Elements which materially and adversely affects access to or use of the Unit, arising after the date of this Contract but prior to the Closing, Seller shall notify Purchaser of the occurrence thereof within 10 days after such occurrence or by the date of Closing, whichever occurs first, in which event Purchaser shall have the following options:

(i) To complete the purchase in accordance with this Contract without reduction in the Purchase Price, or

(ii) To adjourn the Closing until the first to occur of (1) completion of the repair and restoration of the loss or damage to the point that there is no longer a materially adverse effect on the access to or use of the Unit or (2) the 60th day after the date of the giving of Seller's aforesaid notice. In the event Purchaser elects to adjourn the Closing as aforesaid and such loss or damage is not so repaired and restored within 60 days after the date of the giving of Seller's aforesaid notice, then Purchaser shall have the right either to (x) complete the purchase in accordance with this Contract without reduction in the Purchase Price or (y) declare this Contract cancelled and of no further force or effect and receive a refund of the Downpayment, in which latter event neither party shall thereafter have any further rights against, or obligations or liabilities to, the other by reason of this Contract.

§ 12.94 PURCHASE & SALE OF REAL ESTATE Ch. 12

(d) In the event of any loss of or damage to the Common Elements which does not materially and adversely affect access to or use of the Unit, Purchaser shall accept title to the Unit in accordance with this Contract without abatement of the Purchase Price.

21. Internal Revenue Service Reporting Requirement: Each party shall execute, acknowledge and deliver to the other party such instruments, and take such other actions, as such other party may reasonably request in order to comply with IRC § 6045(e), as amended, or any successor provision or any regulations promulgated pursuant thereto, insofar as the same requires reporting of information in respect of real estate transactions. The provisions of this para. 21 shall survive the Closing. The parties designate _____ as the attorney responsible for reporting this information as required by law.

22. Broker: Seller and Purchaser represent and warrant to each other that the only broker with whom they have dealt in connection with this Contract and the transaction set forth herein is _____ and that they know of no other broker who has claimed or may have the right to claim a commission in connection with this transaction. The commission of such broker shall be paid by Seller pursuant to separate agreement. If no broker is specified above, the parties acknowledge that this Contract was brought about by direct negotiation between Seller and Purchaser and each represents to the other that it knows of no broker entitled to a commission in connection with this transaction. Seller and Purchaser shall indemnify and defend each other against any costs, claims or expenses (including reasonable attorneys' fees) arising out of the breach on their respective parts of any representation, warranty or agreement contained in this para. 22. The provisions of this para. 22 shall survive the Closing or, if the Closing does not occur, the termination of this Contract.

23. Mortgage Contingency: *(Delete if inapplicable)* The obligations of Purchaser hereunder are conditioned upon issuance on or before _____ (the "Commitment Date") of a written commitment from any Institutional Lender pursuant to which such Institutional Lender agrees to make a loan, other than a VA, FHA or other governmentally insured loan to Purchaser, at Purchaser's sole cost and expense, of $ _____ or such lesser sum as Purchaser shall be willing to accept, at the prevailing fixed rate of interest not to exceed _____ or initial adjustment rate of interest not to exceed _____ for a term of at least _____ years and on other customary commitment terms, whether or not conditioned upon any factors other than an appraisal satisfactory to the Institutional Lender, secured by a first mortgage on the Unit together with its undivided interest in the Common Elements. Purchaser shall (a) make prompt application to an Institutional Lender for such mortgage loan, (b) furnish accurate and complete information on Purchaser and members of Purchaser's family, as required, (c) pay all fees, points and charges required in connection with such application and loan, (d) pursue such application with diligence, (e) cooperate in good faith with such Institutional Lender to the end of securing such first mortgage loan and (f) promptly give Notice to Seller of the name and address of each Institutional Lender to which Purchaser has made such application. Purchaser shall comply with all requirements of such commitment (or of any commitment accepted by Purchaser) and shall furnish Seller with a copy thereof promptly after receipt thereof. If such commitment is not issued on or before the Commitment Date, then, unless Purchaser has accepted a commitment that does not comply with the requirements set forth above, Purchaser may cancel this Contract by giving Notice to Seller within 5 business days after the Commitment Date, in which case this Contract shall be deemed cancelled and thereafter neither party shall have any further rights against, or obligations or liabilities to, the other by reason of this Contract except that the Downpayment shall be promptly refunded to Purchaser and except as set forth in para. 22. If Purchaser fails to give Notice of cancellation or if Purchaser shall accept a commitment that does not comply with the terms set forth above, then Purchaser shall be deemed to have waived Purchaser's right to cancel this Contract and to receive a refund of the Downpayment by reason of the contingency contained in this para. 23.

24. Gender, Etc.: As used in this Contract, the neuter includes the masculine and feminine, the singular includes the plural and the plural includes the singular, as the context may require.

25. Entire Contract: All prior understandings and agreements between Seller and Purchaser are merged in this Contract and this Contract supersedes any and all understandings and agreements between the parties and constitutes the entire agreement between them with respect to the subject matter hereof.

26. Captions: The captions in this Contract are for convenience and reference only and in no way define, limit or describe the scope of this Contract and shall not be considered in the interpretation of this Contract or any provision hereof.

27. No Assignment by Purchaser: Purchaser may not assign this Contract or any of Purchaser's rights hereunder.

28. Successors and Assigns: Subject to the provisions of para. 27, the provisions of this Contract shall bind and inure to the benefit of both Purchaser and Seller and their respective distributees, executors, administrators, heirs, legal representatives, successors and permitted assigns.

29. No Oral Changes: This Contract cannot be changed or terminated orally. Any changes or additional provisions must be set forth in a rider attached hereto or in a separate written agreement signed by both parties to this Contract.

30. Contract Not Binding Until Signed: This Contract shall not be binding or effective until properly executed and delivered by Seller and Purchaser.

In Witness Whereof, the parties hereto have duly executed this Contract on the day and year first above written.

_____ (Soc. Sec. No. _____)   _____ (Soc. Sec. No. _____)
Seller   Purchaser

_____ (Soc. Sec. No. _____)   _____ (Soc. Sec. No. _____)
Seller   Purchaser

Agreed to as to para. 16: _____   Escrow Depository: _____
                    Escrowee

SCHEDULE A — Permitted Exceptions

1. Zoning laws and regulations and landmark, historic or wetlands designation which are not violated by the Unit and which are not violated by the Common Elements to the extent that access to or use of the Unit would be materially and adversely affected.

2. Consents for the erection of any structure or structures on, under or above any street or streets on which the Building may abut.

3. The terms, burdens, covenants, restrictions, conditions, easements and rules and regulations set forth in the Declaration, By-Laws and rules and regulations of the Condominium, the Power of Attorney from Purchaser to the board of managers of the Condominium and the floor plans of the Condominium, all as may be amended from time to time.

4. Rights of utility companies to lay, maintain, install and repair pipes, lines, poles, conduits, cable boxes and related equipment on, over and under the Building and Common Elements, provided that none of such rights imposes any monetary obligation on the owner of the Unit or materially interferes with the use of or access to the Unit.

5. Encroachments of stoops, areas, cellar steps, trim, cornices, lintels, window sills, awnings, canopies, ledges, fences, hedges, coping and retaining walls projecting from the Building over any street or highway or over any adjoining property and encroachments of similar elements projecting from adjoining property over the Common Elements.

6. Any state of facts which an accurate survey or personal inspection of the Building, Common Elements or Unit would disclose, provided that such facts do not prevent the use of the Unit for dwelling purposes. For the purposes of this Contract, none of the facts shown on the survey, if any, identified below, shall be deemed to prevent the use of the Unit for dwelling purposes, and Purchaser shall accept title subject thereto.

7. The lien of any unpaid common charge, real estate tax, water charge, sewer rent or vault charge, provided the same are paid or apportioned at the Closing as herein provided.

8. The lien of any unpaid assessments to the extent of installments thereof payable after the Closing.

9. Liens, encumbrances and title conditions affecting the Common Elements which do not materially and adversely affect the right of the Unit owner to use and enjoy the Common Elements.

10. Notes or notices of violations of law or governmental orders, ordinances or requirements (a) affecting the Unit and noted or issued subsequent to the date of this Contract by any governmental department, agency or bureau having jurisdiction and (b) any such notes or notices affecting only the Common Elements which were noted or issued prior to or on the date of this Contract or at any time hereafter.

11. Any other matters or encumbrances subject to which Purchaser is required to accept title to the Unit pursuant to this Contract.

The survey referred to in No. 6 above was prepared by _____ dated _____ 19___ and last revised _____ 19___

906

Ch. 12   OFFICE, COMMERCIAL & MULTI–FAMILY   § 12.95

§ 12.95 Contract of Sale—Office, Commercial and Multi-family Residential Premises[1]

154 Contract of sale for New York office, commercial and multi-family residential premises. 2-95

Distributed by Julius Blumberg, Inc.
NYC 10013

Prepared by the Real Property Committee of the Association of the Bar of the City of New York

NOTE: This form is intended to cover matters common to most transactions. Provisions should be added, altered or deleted to suit the circumstances of a particular transaction.

Contract of Sale — Office, Commercial and Multi-Family Residential Premises

Table of Contents

Section 1. Sale of premises and acceptable title
Section 2. Purchase price, acceptable funds, existing mortgages, purchase money mortgage, escrow of downpayment and foreign persons
Section 3. The closing
Section 4. Representations and warranties of seller
Section 5. Acknowledgements of purchaser
Section 6. Seller's obligations as to leases
Section 7. Responsibility for violations
Section 8. Destruction, damage or condemnation
Section 9. Covenants of seller
Section 10. Seller's closing obligations
Section 11. Purchaser's closing obligations
Section 12. Apportionments
Section 13. Objections to title, failure of seller or purchaser to perform and vendee's lien
Section 14. Broker
Section 15. Notices
Section 16. Limitations on survival of representations, warranties, covenants and other obligations
Section 17. Gains tax and miscellaneous provisions
Signatures and receipt by escrowee
Schedule A. Description of premises (to be attached)
Schedule B. Permitted exceptions
Schedule C. Purchase price
Schedule D. Miscellaneous
Schedule E. Rent schedule (to be attached)

CONTRACT dated   19   between

("Seller") and

("Purchaser").

Seller and Purchaser hereby covenant and agree as follows:

Section 1. Sale of Premises and Acceptable Title

§1.01. Seller shall sell to Purchaser, and Purchaser shall purchase from Seller, at the price and upon the terms and conditions set forth in this contract: (a) the parcel of land more particularly described in Schedule A attached hereto ("Land"); (b) all buildings and improvements situated on the Land (collectively, "Building"); (c) all right, title and interest of Seller, if any, in and to the land lying in the bed of any street or highway in front of or adjoining the Land to the center line thereof and to any unpaid award for any taking by condemnation or any damage to the Land by reason of a change of grade of any street or highway; (d) the appurtenances and all the estate and rights of Seller in and to the Land and Building; and (e) all right, title and interest of Seller, if any, in and to the fixtures, equipment and other personal property attached or appurtenant to the Building (collectively, "Premises"). The Premises are located at or known as

§1.02. Seller shall convey and Purchaser shall accept fee simple title to the Premises in accordance with the terms of this contract, subject only to: (a) the matters set forth in Schedule B attached hereto (collectively, "Permitted Exceptions"); and (b) such other matters as (i) the title insurer specified in Schedule D attached hereto (or if none is so specified, then any title insurer licensed to do business by the State of New York) shall be willing, without special premium, to omit as exceptions to coverage or to except with insurance against collection out of or enforcement against the Premises and (ii) shall be accepted by any lender described in Section 274-a of the Real Property Law ("Institutional Lender") which has committed in writing to provide mortgage financing to Purchaser for the purchase of the Premises ("Purchaser's Institutional Lender"), except that if such acceptance by Purchaser's Institutional Lender is unreasonably withheld or delayed, such acceptance shall be deemed to have been given.

Section 2. Purchase Price, Acceptable Funds, Existing Mortgages, Purchase Money Mortgage, Escrow of Downpayment and Foreign Persons

§2.01. The purchase price ("Purchase Price") to be paid by Purchaser to Seller for the Premises as provided in Schedule C attached hereto is $

§2.02. All monies payable under this contract, unless otherwise specified in this contract, shall be paid by (a) certified checks of Purchaser or any person making a purchase money loan to Purchaser drawn on any bank, savings bank, trust company or savings and loan association having a banking office in the State of New York or (b) official bank checks drawn by any such banking insitution, payable to the order of Seller, except that uncertified checks of Purchaser payable to the order of Seller up to the amount of one-half of one percent of the Purchase Price shall be acceptable for sums payable to Seller at the Closing.

---

§ 12.95
1. Forms may be purchased from Julius Blumberg, Inc. NYC 10013, or any of its dealers. Reproduction prohibited.

907

§2.03. (a) If Schedule C provides for the acceptance of title by Purchaser subject to one or more existing mortgages (collectively, "Existing Mortgage(s)"), the amounts specified in Schedule C with reference thereto may be approximate. If at the Closing the aggregate principal amount of the Existing Mortgage(s), as reduced by payments required thereunder prior to the Closing, is less than the aggregate amount of the Existing Mortgage(s) as specified in Schedule C, the difference shall be added to the monies payable at the Closing, unless otherwise expressly provided herein.

(b) If any of the documents constituting the Existing Mortgage(s) or the note(s) secured thereby prohibits or restricts the conveyance of the Premises or any part thereof without the prior consent of the holder or holders thereof ("Mortgagee(s)") or confers upon the Mortgagee(s) the right to accelerate payment of the indebtedness or to change the terms of the Existing Mortgage(s) in the event that a conveyance is made without consent of the Mortgagee(s), Seller shall notify such Mortgagee(s) of the proposed conveyance to Purchaser within 10 days after execution and delivery of this contract, requesting the consent of such Mortgagee(s) thereto. Seller and Purchaser shall furnish the Mortgagee(s) with such information as may reasonably be required in connection with such request and shall otherwise cooperate with such Mortgagee(s) and with each other in an effort expeditiously to procure such consent, but neither shall be obligated to make any payment to obtain such consent. If such Mortgagee(s) shall fail or refuse to grant such consent in writing on or before the date set forth in Schedule D or shall require as a condition of the granting of such consent (i) that additional consideration be paid to the Mortgagee(s) and neither Seller nor Purchaser is willing to pay such additional consideration or (ii) that the terms of the Existing Mortgage(s) be changed and Purchaser is unwilling to accept such change, then unless Seller and Purchaser mutually agree to extend such date or otherwise modify the terms of this contract, Purchaser may terminate this contract in the manner provided in §13.02. If Schedule C provides for a Purchase Money Mortgage (as defined in §2.04), Seller may also terminate this contract in the manner provided in §13.02 if any of the foregoing circumstances occur or if Seller is unwilling to accept any such change in the terms of the Existing Mortgage(s).

§2.04. (a) If Schedule C provides for payment of a portion of the Purchase Price by execution and delivery to Seller of a note secured by a purchase money mortgage ("Purchase Money Mortgage"), such note and Purchase Money Mortgage shall be drawn by the attorney for the Seller on the most recent forms of the New York Board of Title Underwriters for notes and for mortgages of like lien, as modified by this contract. At the Closing, Purchaser shall pay the mortgage recording tax and recording fees therefor and the filing fees for any financing statements delivered in connection therewith.

(b) If Schedule C provides for the acceptance of title by Purchaser subject to Existing Mortgage(s) prior in lien to the Purchase Money Mortgage, the Purchase Money Mortgage shall provide that it is subject and subordinate to the lien(s) of the Existing Mortgage(s) and shall be subject and subordinate to any extensions, modifications, renewals, consolidations, substitutions or replacements thereof (collectively, "Refinancing" or "Refinanced Mortgage"), provided that (i) the rate of interest payable under a Refinanced Mortgage shall not be greater than that specified in Schedule D as the Maximum Interest Rate or, if no Maximum Interest Rate is specified in Schedule D, shall not be greater than the rate of interest that was payable on the refinanced indebtedness immediately prior to such Refinancing, and (ii) if the principal amount of the Refinanced Mortgage plus the principal amount of other Existing Mortgage(s), if any, remaining after placement of a Refinanced Mortgage exceeds the amount of principal owing and unpaid on all mortgages on the Premises superior to the Purchase Money Mortgage immediately prior to the Refinancing, an amount equal to the excess shall be paid at the closing of the Refinancing to the holder of the Purchase Money Mortgage in reduction of principal payments due thereunder in inverse order of maturity. The Purchase Money Mortgage shall further provide that the holder thereof shall, on demand and without charge therefor, execute, acknowledge and deliver any agreement or agreements reasonably required by the mortgagor to confirm such subordination.

(c) The Purchase Money Mortgage shall contain the following additional provisions:

(i) "The mortgagor or any owner of the mortgaged premises shall have the right to prepay the entire unpaid indebtedness together with accrued interest, but without penalty, at any time on or after [insert the day following the last day of the fiscal year of the mortgagee in which the Closing occurs or, if a Prepayment Date is specified in Schedule D, the specified Prepayment Date], on not less than 10 days' written notice to the holder hereof."

(ii) "Notwithstanding anything to the contrary contained herein, the obligation of the mortgagor for the payment of the indebtedness and for the performance of the terms, covenants and conditions contained herein and in the note secured hereby is limited solely to recourse against the property secured by this mortgage, and in no event shall the mortgagor or any principal of the mortgagor, disclosed or undisclosed, be personally liable for any breach of or default under the note or this mortgage or for any deficiency resulting from or through any proceedings to foreclose this mortgage, nor shall any deficiency judgment, money judgment or other personal judgment be sought or entered against the mortgagor or any principal of the mortgagor, disclosed or undisclosed, but the foregoing shall not adversely affect the lien of this mortgage or the mortgagee's right of foreclosure."

(iii) "In addition to performing its obligations under Section 274-a of the Real Property Law, the mortgagee, if other than one of the institutions listed in Section 274-a, agrees that, within 10 days after written request by the mortgagor, but not more than twice during any period of 12 consecutive months, it will execute, acknowledge and deliver without charge a certificate of reduction in recordable form (a) certifying as to (1) the then unpaid principal balance of the indebtedness secured hereby, (2) the maturity date thereof, (3) the rate of interest, (4) the last date to which interest has been paid and (5) the amount of any escrow deposits then held by the mortgagee, and (b) stating, to the knowledge of the mortgagee, whether there are any alleged defaults hereunder and, if so, specifying the nature thereof."

(iv) "All notices required or desired to be given under this mortgage shall be in writing and shall be delivered personally or shall be sent by prepaid registered or certified mail, addressed to the mortgagor and mortgagee at the addresses specified in this mortgage or to such other parties or at such other addresses, not exceeding two, as may be designated in a notice given to the other party or parties in accordance with the provisions hereof."

(v) The additional provisions, if any, specified in a rider hereto.

§2.05. (a) If the sum paid under paragraph (a) of Schedule C or any other sums paid on account of the Purchase Price prior to the Closing (collectively, "Downpayment") are paid by check or checks drawn to the order of and delivered to Seller's attorney or another escrow agent ("Escrowee"), the Escrowee shall hold the proceeds thereof in escrow in a special bank account (or as otherwise agreed in writing by Seller, Purchaser and Escrowee) until the Closing or sooner termination of this contract and shall pay over or apply such proceeds in accordance with the terms of this section. Escrowee need not hold such proceeds in an interest-bearing account, but if any interest is earned thereon, such interest shall be paid to the same party entitled to the escrowed proceeds, and the party receiving such interest shall pay any income taxes thereon. The tax identification numbers of the parties are either set forth in Schedule D or shall be furnished to Escrowee upon request. At the Closing, such proceeds and the interest thereon, if any, shall be paid by Escrowee to Seller. If for any reason the Closing does not occur and either party makes a written demand upon Escrowee for payment of such amount, Escrowee shall give written notice to the other party of such demand. If Escrowee does not receive a written objection from the other party to the proposed payment within 10 business days after the giving of such notice, Escrowee is hereby authorized to make such payment. If Escrowee does receive such written objection within such 10 day period or if for any other reason Escrowee in good faith shall elect not to make such payment, Escrowee shall continue to hold such amount until otherwise directed by written instructions from the parties to this contract or a final judgment of a court. However, Escrowee shall have the right at any time to deposit the escrowed proceeds and interest thereon, if any, with the clerk of the Supreme Court of the county in which the Land is located. Escrowee shall give written notice of such deposit to Seller and Purchaser. Upon such deposit Escrowee shall be relieved and discharged of all further obligations and responsibilities hereunder.

(b) The parties acknowledge that Escrowee is acting solely as a stakeholder at their request and for their convenience, that Escrowee shall not be deemed to be the agent of either of the parties, and that Escrowee shall not be liable to either of the parties for any act or omission on its part unless taken or suffered in bad faith, in willful disregard of this contract or involving gross negligence. Seller and Purchaser shall jointly and severally indemnify and hold Escrowee harmless from and against all costs, claims and expenses, including reasonable attorneys' fees, incurred in connection with the performance of Escrowee's duties hereunder, except with respect to actions or omissions taken or suffered by Escrowee in bad faith, in willful disregard of this contract or involving gross negligence on the part of Escrowee.

(c) Escrowee has acknowledged agreement to these provisions by signing in the place indicated on the signature page of this contract.

§2.06. In the event that Seller is a "foreign person", as defined in Internal Revenue Code Section 1445 and regulations issued thereunder (collectively, the "Code Withholding Section"), or in the event that Seller fails to deliver the certification of non-foreign status required under §10.12(c), or in the event that Purchaser is not entitled under the Code Withholding Section to rely on such certification, Purchaser shall deduct and withhold from the Purchase Price a sum equal to ten percent (10%) thereof and shall at Closing remit the withheld amount with Forms 8288 and 8288A (or any successors thereto) to the Internal Revenue Service; and if the cash balance of the Purchase Price payable to Seller at the Closing after deduction of net adjustments, apportionments and credits (if any) to be made or allowed in favor of Seller at the Closing as herein provided is less than ten percent (10%) of the Purchase Price, Purchaser shall have the right to terminate this contract, in which event Seller shall refund the Downpayment to Purchaser and shall reimburse Purchaser for title examination and survey costs as if this contract were terminated pursuant to §13.02. The right of termination provided for in this §2.06 shall be in addition to and not in limitation of any other rights or remedies available to Purchaser under applicable law.

Section 3. The Closing

§3.01. Except as otherwise provided in this contract, the closing of title pursuant to this contract ("Closing") shall take place on the scheduled date and time of closing specified in Schedule D (the actual date of the Closing being herein referred to as "Closing Date") at the place specified in Schedule D.

Section 4. Representations and Warranties of Seller

Seller represents and warrants to Purchaser as follows:

§4.01. Unless otherwise provided in this contract, Seller is the sole owner of the Premises.

§4.02. If the Premises are encumbered by an Existing Mortgage(s), no written notice has been received from the Mortgagee(s) asserting that a default or breach exists thereunder which remains uncured and no such notice shall have been received and remain uncured on the Closing Date. If copies of documents constituting the Existing Mortgage(s) and note(s) secured thereby have been exhibited to and initialed by Purchaser or its representative, such copies are true copies of the originals and the Existing Mortgage(s) and note(s) secured thereby have not been modified or amended except as shown in such documents.

§4.03. The information concerning written leases (which together with all amendments and modifications thereof are collectively referred to as "Leases") and any tenancies in the Premises not arising out of the Leases (collectively, "Tenancies") set forth in Schedule E attached hereto ("Rent Schedule") is accurate as of the date set forth therein or, if no date is set forth therein, as of the date hereof, and there are no Leases or Tenancies of any space in the Premises other than those set forth therein and any subleases or subtenancies. Except as otherwise set forth in the Rent Schedule or elsewhere in this contract:

(a) all of the Leases are in full force and effect and none of them has been modified, amended or extended;

(b) no renewal or extension options have been granted to tenants;

(c) no tenant has an option to purchase the Premises;

(d) the rents set forth are being collected on a current basis and there are no arrearages in excess of one month;

(e) no tenant is entitled to rental concessions or abatements for any period subsequent to the scheduled date of closing;

(f) Seller has not sent written notice to any tenant claiming that such tenant is in default, which default remains uncured;

(g) no action or proceeding instituted against Seller by any tenant of the Premises is presently pending in any court, except with respect to claims involving personal injury or property damage which are covered by insurance; and

(h) there are no security deposits other than those set forth in the Rent Schedule.

If any Leases which have been exhibited to and initialed by Purchaser or its representative contain provisions that are inconsistent with the foregoing representations and warranties, such representations and warranties shall be deemed modified to the extent necessary to eliminate such inconsistency and to conform such representations and warranties to the provisions of the Leases.

§4.04. If the Premises or any part thereof are subject to the New York City Rent Stabilization Law, Seller is and on the Closing Date will be a member in good standing of the Real Estate Industry Stabilization Association, and, except as otherwise set forth in the Rent Schedule, there are no proceedings with any tenant presently pending before the Conciliation and Appeals Board in which a tenant has alleged an overcharge of rent or diminution of services or similar grievance, and there are no outstanding orders of the Conciliation and Appeals Board that have not been complied with by Seller.

§4.05. If the Premises or any part thereof are subject to the New York City Emergency Rent and Rehabilitation Law, the rents shown are not in excess of the maximum collectible rents, and, except as otherwise set forth in the Rent Schedule, no tenants are entitled to abatements as senior citizens, there are no proceedings presently pending before the rent commission in which a tenant has alleged an overcharge of rent or diminution of services or similar grievance, and there are no outstanding orders of the rent commission that have not been complied with by Seller.

§4.06. If an insurance schedule is attached hereto, such schedule lists all insurance policies presently affording coverage with respect to the Premises, and the information contained therein is accurate as of the date set forth therein or, if no date is set forth therein, as of the date hereof.

§4.07. If a payroll schedule is attached hereto, such schedule lists all employees presently employed at the Premises, and the information contained therein is accurate as of the date set forth therein or, if no date is set forth therein, as of the date hereof, and, except as otherwise set forth in such schedule, none of such employees is covered by a union contract and there are no retroactive increases or other accrued and unpaid sums owed to any employee.

§4.08. If a schedule of service, maintenance, supply and management contracts ("Service Contracts") is attached hereto, such schedule lists all such contracts affecting the Premises, and the information set forth therein is accurate as of the date set forth therein or, if no date is set forth therein, as of the date hereof.

§4.09. If a copy of a certificate of occupancy for the Premises has been exhibited to and initialed by Purchaser or its representative, such copy is a true copy of the original and such certificate has not been amended, but Seller makes no representation as to compliance with any such certificate.

§4.10. The assessed valuation and real estate taxes set forth in Schedule D, if any, are the assessed valuation of the Premises and the taxes paid or payable with respect thereto for the fiscal year indicated in such schedule. Except as otherwise set forth in Schedule D, there are no tax abatements or exemptions affecting the Premises.

§4.11. Except as otherwise set forth in a schedule attached hereto, if any, if the Premises are used for residential purposes, each apartment contains a range and a refrigerator, and all of the ranges and refrigerators and all of the items of personal property (or replacements thereof) listed in such schedule, if any, are and on the Closing Date will be owned by Seller free of liens and encumbrances other than the lien(s) of the Existing Mortgage(s), if any.

§4.12. Seller has no actual knowledge that any incinerator, boiler or other burning equipment on the Premises is being operated in violation of applicable law. If copies of a certificate or certificates of operation therefor have been exhibited to and initialed by Purchaser or its representative, such copies are true copies of the originals.

§4.13. Except as otherwise set forth in Schedule D, Seller has no actual knowledge of any assessment payable in annual installments, or any part thereof, which has become a lien on the Premises.

§4.14. Seller is not a "foreign person" as defined in the Code Withholding Section.

Section 5. Acknowledgments of Purchaser

Purchaser acknowledges that:

§5.01. Purchaser has inspected the Premises, is fully familiar with the physical condition and state of repair thereof, and, subject to the provisions of §7.01, §8.01, and §9.04, shall accept the Premises "as is" and in their present condition, subject to reasonable use, wear, tear and natural deterioration between now and the Closing Date, without any reduction in the Purchase Price for any change in such condition by reason thereof subsequent to the date of this contract.

§5.02. Before entering into this contract, Purchaser has made such examination of the Premises, the operation, income and expenses thereof and all other matters affecting or relating to this transaction as Purchaser deemed necessary. In entering into this contract, Purchaser has not been induced by and has not relied upon any representations, warranties or statements, whether express or implied, made by Seller or any agent, employee or other representative of Seller or by any broker or any other person representing or purporting to represent Seller, which are not expressly set forth in this contract, whether or not any such representations, warranties or statements were made in writing or orally.

Section 6. Seller's Obligations as to Leases

§6.01. Unless otherwise provided in a schedule attached to this contract, between the date of this contract and the Closing, Seller shall not, without Purchaser's prior written consent, which consent shall not be unreasonably withheld: (a) amend, renew or extend any Lease in any respect, unless required by law; (b) grant a written lease to any tenant occupying space pursuant to a Tenancy; or (c) terminate any Lease or Tenancy except by reason of a default by the tenant thereunder.

§6.02. Unless otherwise provided in a schedule attached to this contract, between the date of this contract and the Closing, Seller shall not permit occupancy of, or enter into any new lease for, space in the Building which is presently vacant or which may hereafter become vacant without first giving Purchaser written notice of the identity of the proposed tenant, together with (a) either a copy of the proposed lease or a summary of the terms thereof in reasonable detail and (b) a statement of the amount of the brokerage commission, if any, payable in connection therewith and the terms of payment thereof. If Purchaser objects to such proposed lease, Purchaser shall so notify Seller within 4 business days after receipt of Seller's notice if such notice was personally delivered to Purchaser, or within 7 business days after the mailing of such notice by Seller to Purchaser, in which case Seller shall not enter into the proposed lease. Unless otherwise provided in a schedule attached to this contract, Purchaser shall pay to Seller at the Closing, in the manner specified in §2.02, the rent and additional rent that would have been payable under the proposed lease from the date on which the tenant's obligation to pay rent would have commenced if Purchaser had not so objected until the Closing Date, less the amount of the brokerage commission specified in Seller's notice and the reasonable cost of decoration or other work required to be performed by the landlord under the terms of the proposed lease to suit the premises to the tenant's occupancy ("Reletting Expenses"), prorated in each case over the term of the proposed lease and apportioned as of the Closing Date. If Purchaser does not so notify Seller of its objection, Seller shall have the right to enter into the proposed lease with the tenant identified in Seller's notice and Purchaser shall pay to Seller, in the manner specified in §2.02, the Reletting Expenses, prorated in each case over the term of the lease and apportioned as of the later of the Closing Date or the rent commencement date. Such payment shall be made by Purchaser to Seller at the Closing. In no event shall the amount so payable to Seller exceed the sums actually paid by Seller on account thereof.

§6.03. If any space is vacant on the Closing Date, Purchaser shall accept the Premises subject to such vacancy, provided that the vacancy was not permitted or created by Seller in violation of any restrictions contained in this contract. Seller shall not grant any concessions or rent abatements for any period following the Closing without Purchaser's prior written consent. Seller shall not apply all or any part of the security deposit of any tenant unless such tenant has vacated the Premises.

§6.04. Seller does not warrant that any particular Lease or Tenancy will be in force or effect at the Closing or that the tenants will have performed their obligations thereunder. The termination of any Lease or Tenancy prior to the Closing by reason of the tenant's default shall not affect the obligations of Purchaser under this contract in any manner or entitle Purchaser to an abatement of or credit against the Purchase Price or give rise to any other claim on the part of Purchaser.

§6.05. Seller hereby indemnifies and agrees to defend Purchaser against any claims made pursuant to §7-107 or §7-108 of the General Obligations Law (the "GOL") by tenants who resided in the Premises on or prior to the Closing Date other than (a) claims with respect to tenants' security deposits paid, credited or assigned to Purchaser pursuant to §10.03, (b) claims made pursuant to §7-107 of the GOL with respect to funds for which Seller was not liable, and (c) claims made pursuant to §7-108 of the GOL by tenants to whom Purchaser failed to give the written notice specified in §7-108(c) of the GOL within thirty days after the Closing Date. The foregoing indemnity and agreement shall survive the Closing and shall be in lieu of any escrow permitted by §7-108(d) of the GOL and Purchaser hereby waives any right it may have to require any such escrow.

Section 7. Responsibility for Violations

§7.01. Except as provided in §7.02 and §7.03, all notes or notices of violations of law or governmental ordinances, orders or requirements which were noted or issued prior to the date of this contract by any governmental department, agency or bureau having jurisdiction as to conditions affecting the Premises and all liens which have attached to the Premises prior to the Closing pursuant to the Administrative Code of the City of New York, if applicable, shall be removed or complied with by Seller. If such removal or compliance has not been completed prior to the Closing, Seller shall pay to Purchaser at the Closing the reasonably estimated unpaid cost to effect or complete such removal or compliance, and Purchaser shall be required to accept title to the Premises subject thereto, except that Purchaser shall not be required to accept such title and may terminate this contract as provided in §13.02 if (a) Purchaser's Institutional Lender reasonably refuses to provide financing by reason thereof or (b) the Building is a multiple dwelling and either (i) such violation is rent impairing and causes rent to be unrecoverable under Section 302-a of the Multiple Dwelling Law or (ii) a proceeding has been validly commenced by tenants and is pending with respect to such violation for a judgment directing deposit and use of rents under Article 7-A of the Real Property Actions and Proceedings Law. All such notes or notices of violations noted or issued on or after the date of this contract shall be the sole responsibility of Purchaser.

§7.02. If the reasonably estimated aggregate cost to remove or comply with any violations or liens which Seller is required to remove or comply with pursuant to the provisions of §7.01 shall exceed the Maximum Amount specified in Schedule D (or if none is so specified, the Maximum Amount shall be one-half of one percent of the Purchase Price), Seller shall have the right to cancel this contract, in which event the sole liability of Seller shall be as set forth in §12.02, unless Purchaser elects to accept title to the Premises subject to all such violations or liens, in which event Purchaser shall be entitled to a credit of an amount equal to the Maximum Amount against the monies payable at the Closing.

§7.03. Regardless of whether a violation has been noted or issued prior to the date of this contract, Seller's failure to remove or fully comply with any violations which a tenant is required to remove or comply with pursuant to the terms of its lease by reason of such tenant's use or occupancy shall not be an objection to title. Purchaser shall accept the Premises subject to all such violations without any liability of Seller with respect thereto or any abatement of or credit against the Purchase Price, except that if Purchaser's Institutional Lender reasonably refuses to provide financing by reason of a violation described above, Purchaser shall not be required to accept the Premises subject thereto and Purchaser shall have the right to terminate this contract in the manner provided in §13.02.

§7.04. If required, Seller, upon written request by Purchaser, shall promptly furnish to Purchaser written authorizations to make any necessary searches for the purposes of determining whether notes or notices of violations have been noted or issued with respect to the Premises or liens have attached thereto.

Section 8. Destruction, Damage or Condemnation

§8.01. The provisions of Section 5-1311 of the General Obligations Law shall apply to the sale and purchase provided for in this contract.

Section 9. Covenants of Seller

Seller covenants that between the date of this contract and the Closing:

§9.01. The Existing Mortgage(s) shall not be amended or supplemented or prepaid in whole or in part. Seller shall pay or make, as and when due and payable, all payments of principal and interest and all deposits required to be paid or made under the Existing Mortgage(s).

§9.02. Seller shall not modify or amend any Service Contract or enter into any new service contract unless the same is terminable without penalty by the then owner of the Premises upon not more than 30 days' notice.

§9.03. If an insurance schedule is attached hereto, Seller shall maintain in full force and effect until the Closing the insurance policies described in such schedule or renewals thereof for no more than one year of those expiring before the Closing.

§9.04. No fixtures, equipment or personal property included in this sale shall be removed from the Premises unless the same are replaced with similar items of at least equal quality prior to the Closing.

§9.05. Seller shall not withdraw, settle or otherwise compromise any protest or reduction proceeding affecting real estate taxes assessed against the Premises for any fiscal period in which the Closing is to occur or any subsequent fiscal period without the prior written consent of Purchaser, which consent shall not be unreasonably withheld. Real estate tax refunds and credits received after the Closing Date which are attributable to the fiscal tax year during which the Closing Date occurs shall be apportioned between Seller and Purchaser, after deducting the expenses of collection thereof, which obligation shall survive the Closing.

§9.06. Seller shall allow Purchaser or Purchaser's representatives access to the Premises, the Leases and other documents required to be delivered under this contract upon reasonable prior notice at reasonable times.

Section 10. Seller's Closing Obligations

At the Closing, Seller shall deliver the following to Purchaser:

§10.01. A statutory form of bargain and sale deed without covenant against grantor's acts, containing the covenant required by Section 13 of the Lien Law, and properly executed in proper form for recording so as to convey the title required by this contract.

§10.02. All Leases initialed by Purchaser and all others in Seller's possession.

§10.03. A schedule of all security deposits (and, if the Premises contains six or more family dwelling units, the most recent reports with respect thereto issued by each banking organization in which they are deposited pursuant to GOL §7-103) and a check or credit to Purchaser in the amount of any cash security deposits, including any interest thereon, held by Seller on the Closing Date or, if held by an Institutional Lender, an assignment to Purchaser and written instructions to the holder of such deposits to transfer the same to Purchaser, and appropriate instruments of transfer or assignment with respect to any security deposits which are other than cash.

§10.04. A schedule updating the Rent Schedule and setting forth all arrears in rents and all prepayments of rents.

§10.05. All Service Contracts initialed by Purchaser and all others in Seller's possession which are in effect on the Closing Date and which are assignable by Seller.

§10.06. An assignment to Purchaser, without recourse or warranty, of all of the interest of Seller in those Service Contracts, insurance policies, certificates, permits and other documents to be delivered to Purchaser at the Closing which are then in effect and are assignable by Seller.

§10.07. (a) Written consent(s) of the Mortgagee(s), if required under §2.03(b), and (b) certificate(s) executed by the Mortgagee(s) in proper form for recording and certifying (i) the amount of the unpaid principal balance thereof, (ii) the maturity date thereof, (iii) the interest rate, (iv) the last date to which interest has been paid thereon and (v) the amount of any escrow deposits held by the Mortgagee(s). Seller shall pay the fees for recording such certificate(s). Any Mortgagee which is an Insitutional Lender may furnish a letter complying with Section 274-a of the Real Property Law in lieu of such certificate.

§10.08. An assignment of all Seller's right, title and interest in escrow deposits for real estate taxes, insurance premiums and other amounts, if any, then held by the Mortgagee(s).

§10.09. All original insurance policies with respect to which premiums are to be apportioned or, if unobtainable, true copies or certificates thereof.

§10.10. To the extent they are then in Seller's possession and not posted at the Premises, certificates, licenses, permits, authorizations and approvals issued for or with respect to the Premises by governmental and quasi-governmental authorities having jurisdiction.

§10.11. Such affidavits as Purchaser's title company shall reasonably require in order to omit from its title insurance policy all exceptions for judgments, bankruptcies or other returns against persons or entities whose names are the same as or similar to Seller's name.

§10.12(a) Checks to the order of the appropriate officers in payment of all applicable real property transfer taxes and copies of any required tax returns therefor executed by Seller, which checks shall be certified or official bank checks if required by the taxing authority, unless Seller elects to have Purchaser pay any of such taxes and credit Purchaser with the amount thereof, (b) the Tentative Assessment and Return or Statement of No Tax Due or affidavit (whichever is applicable) and the checks and other items (if any) required under §17.09(a), and (c) a certification of non-foreign status, in form required by the Code Withholding Section, signed under penalty of perjury. Seller understands that such certification will be retained by Purchaser and will be made available to the Internal Revenue Service on request.

§10.13. To the extent they are then in Seller's possession, copies of current painting and payroll records. Seller shall make all other Building and tenant files and records available to Purchaser for copying, which obligation shall survive the Closing.

§10.14. An original letter, executed by Seller or by its agent, advising the tenants of the sale of the Premises to Purchaser and directing that rents and other payments thereafter be sent to Purchaser or as Purchaser may direct.

§10.15. Notice(s) to the Mortgagee(s), executed by Seller or by its agent, advising of the sale of the Premises to Purchaser and directing that future bills and other correspondence should thereafter be sent to Purchaser or as Purchaser may direct.

§10.16. If Seller is a corporation and if required by Section 909 of the Business Corporation Law, a resolution of Seller's board of directors authorizing the sale and delivery of the deed and a certificate executed by the secretary or assistant secretary of Seller certifying as to the adoption of such resolution and setting forth facts showing that the transfer complies with the requirements of such law. The deed referred to in §10.01 shall also contain a recital sufficient to establish compliance with such law.

§10.17. Possession of the Premises in the condition required by this contract, subject to the Leases and Tenancies, and keys therefor.

§10.18. Any other documents required by this contract to be delivered by Seller.

Section 11. Purchaser's Closing Obligations

At the Closing, Purchaser shall:

§11.01. Deliver to Seller checks in payment of the portion of the Purchase Price payable at the Closing, as adjusted for apportionments under Section 12, plus the amount of escrow deposits, if any, assigned pursuant to §10.08.

§11.02. Deliver to Seller the Purchase Money Mortgage, if any, in proper form for recording, the note secured thereby, financing statements covering personal property, fixtures and equipment included in this sale and replacements thereof, all properly executed, and Purchaser shall pay the mortgage recording tax and recording fees for any Purchase Money Mortgage.

§11.03. Deliver to Seller an agreement indemnifying and agreeing to defend Seller against any claims made by tenants with respect to tenants' security deposits to the extent paid, credited or assigned to Purchaser under §10.03.

§11.04. Cause the deed to be recorded, duly completed all required real property transfer tax returns and cause all such returns and checks in payment of such taxes to be delivered to the appropriate officers promptly after the Closing.

§11.05. Deliver any other documents required by this contract to be delivered by Purchaser.

Section 12. Apportionments

§12.01. The following apportionments shall be made between the parties at the Closing as of the close of business on the day prior to the Closing Date:

(a) prepaid rents and Additional Rents (as defined in §12.03);

(b) interest on the Existing Mortgage(s);

(c) real estate taxes, water charges, sewer rents and vault charges, if any, on the basis of the fiscal period for which assessed, except that if there is a water meter on the Premises, apportionment at the Closing shall be based on the last available reading, subject to adjustment after the Closing when the next reading is available;

(d) wages, vacation pay, pension and welfare benefits and other fringe benefits of all persons employed at the Premises whose employment was not terminated at or prior to the Closing;

(e) value of fuel stored on the Premises, at the price then charged by Seller's supplier, including any taxes;

(f) charges under transferable Service Contracts or permitted renewals or replacements thereof;

(g) permitted administrative charges, if any, on tenants' security deposits;

(h) dues to rent stabilization associations, if any;

(i) insurance premiums on transferable insurance policies listed on a schedule hereto or permitted renewals thereof;

(j) Reletting Expenses under §6.02, if any; and

(k) any other items listed in Schedule D.

If the Closing shall occur before a new tax rate is fixed, the apportionment of taxes at the Closing shall be upon the basis of the old tax rate for the preceding period applied to latest assessed valuation. Promptly after the new tax rate is fixed, the apportionment of taxes shall be recomputed. Any discrepancy resulting from such recomputation and any errors or omissions in computing apportionments at Closing shall be promptly corrected, which obligations shall survive the Closing.

§12.02. If any tenant is in arrears in the payment of rent on the Closing Date, rents received from such tenant after the Closing shall be applied in the following order of priority: (a) first to the month preceding the month in which the Closing occurred; (b) then to the month in which the Closing occurred; (c) then to any month or months following the month in which the Closing occurred; and (d) then to the period prior to the month preceding the month in which the Closing occurred. If rents or any portion thereof received by Seller or Purchaser after the Closing are payable to the other party by reason of this allocation, the appropriate sum, less a proportionate share of any reasonable attorneys' fees, costs and expenses of collection thereof, shall be promptly paid to the other party, which obligation shall survive the Closing.

§12.03. If any tenants are required to pay percentage rent, escalation charges for real estate taxes, operating expenses, cost-of-living adjustments or other charges of a similar nature ("Additional Rents") and any Additional Rents are collected by Purchaser after the Closing which are attributable in whole or in part to any period prior to the Closing, then Purchaser shall promptly pay to Seller Seller's proportionate share thereof, less a proportionate share of any reasonable attorneys' fees, costs and expenses of collection thereof, if and when the tenant paying the same has made all payments of rent and Additional Rent then due to Purchaser pursuant to the tenant's Lease, which obligation shall survive the Closing.

Section 13. Objections to Title, Failure of Seller or Purchaser to Perform and Vendee's Lien

§13.01. Purchaser shall promptly order an examination of title and shall cause a copy of the title report to be forwarded to Seller's attorney upon receipt. Seller shall be entitled to a reasonable adjournment or adjournments of the Closing for up to 60 days or until the expiration date of any written commitment of Purchaser's Institutional Lender delivered to Purchaser prior to the scheduled date of Closing, whichever occurs first, to remove any defects in or objections to title noted in such title report and any other defects or objections which may be disclosed on or prior to the Closing Date.

§13.02. If Seller shall be unable to convey title to the Premises at the Closing in accordance with the provisions of this contract or if Purchaser shall have any other grounds under this contract for refusing to consummate the purchase provided for herein, Purchaser, nevertheless, may elect to accept such title as Seller may be able to convey with a credit against the monies payable at the Closing equal to the reasonably estimated cost to cure the same (up to the Maximum Expense described below), but without any other credit or liability on the part of Seller. If Purchaser shall not so elect, Purchaser may terminate this contract and the sole liability of Seller shall be to refund the Downpayment to Purchaser and to reimburse Purchaser for the net cost of title examination, but not to exceed the net amount charged by Purchaser's title company therefor without issuance of a policy, and the net cost of updating the existing survey of the Premises or the net cost of a new survey of the Premises if there was no existing survey or the existing survey was not capable of being updated and a new survey was required by Purchaser's Institutional Lender. Upon such refund and reimbursement, this contract shall be null and void and the parties hereto shall be relieved of all further obligations and liability other than any arising under Section 14. Seller shall not be required to bring any action or proceeding or to incur any expense in excess of the Maximum Expense specified in Schedule D (or if none is so specified, the Maximum Expense shall be one-half of one percent of the Purchase Price) to cure any title defect or to enable Seller otherwise to comply with the provisions of this contract, but the foregoing shall not permit Seller to refuse to pay off at the Closing, to the extent of the monies payable at the Closing, mortgages on the Premises, other than Existing Mortgages, of which Seller has actual knowledge.

§13.03. Any unpaid taxes, assessments, water charges and sewer rents, together with the interest and penalties thereon to a date not less than two days following the Closing Date, and any other liens and encumbrances which Seller is obligated to pay and discharge or which are against corporations, estates or other persons in the chain of title, together with the cost of recording or filing any instruments necessary to discharge such liens and encumbrances of record, may be paid out of the proceeds of the monies payable at the Closing if Seller delivers to Purchaser on the Closing Date official bills for such taxes, assessments, water charges, sewer rents, interest and penalties and instruments in recordable form sufficient to discharge any other liens and encumbrances of record. Upon request made a reasonable time before the Closing, Purchaser shall provide at the Closing separate checks for the foregoing payable to the order of the holder of any such lien, charge or encumbrance and otherwise complying with §2.02. If Purchaser's title insurance company is willing to insure both Purchaser and Purchaser's Institutional Lender, if any, that such charges, liens and encumbrances will not be collected out of or enforced against the Premises, then, unless Purchaser's Institutional Lender reasonably refuses to accept such insurance in lieu of actual payment and discharge, Seller shall have the right in lieu of payment and discharge to deposit with the title insurance company such funds or assurances or to pay such special or additional premiums as the title insurance company may require in order to so insure. In such case the charges, liens and encumbrances with respect to which the title insurance company has agreed so to insure shall not be considered objections to title.

§13.04. If Purchaser shall default in the performance of its obligation under this contract to purchase the Premises, the sole remedy of Seller shall be to retain the Downpayment as liquidated damages for all loss, damage and expense suffered by Seller, including without limitation the loss of its bargain.

§13.05. Purchaser shall have a vendee's lien against the Premises for the amount of the Downpayment, but such lien shall not continue after default by Purchaser under this contract.

Section 14. Broker

§14.01. If a broker is specified in Schedule D, Seller and Purchaser mutually represent and warrant that such broker is the only broker with whom they have dealt in connection with this contract and that neither Seller nor Purchaser knows of any other broker who has claimed or may have the right to claim a commission in connection with this transaction, unless otherwise indicated in Schedule D. The commission of such broker shall be paid pursuant to separate agreement by the party specified in Schedule D. If no broker is specified in Schedule D, the parties acknowledge that this contract was brought about by direct negotiation between Seller and Purchaser and that neither Seller nor Purchaser knows of any broker entitled to a commission in connection with this transaction. Unless otherwise provided in Schedule D, Seller and Purchaser shall indemnify and defend each other against any costs, claims or expenses, including attorneys' fees, arising out of the breach on their respective parts of any representations, warranties or agreements contained in this paragraph. The representations and obligations under this paragraph shall survive the Closing or, if the Closing does not occur, the termination of this contract.

Section 15. Notices

§15.01. All notices under this contract shall be in writing and shall be delivered personally or shall be sent by prepaid registered or certified mail, addressed as set forth in Schedule D, or as Seller or Purchaser shall otherwise have given notice as herein provided.

Section 16. Limitations on Survival of Representations, Warranties, Covenants and other Obligations

§16.01. Except as otherwise provided in this contract, no representations, warranties, covenants or other obligations of Seller set forth in this contract shall survive the Closing, and no action based thereon shall be commenced after the Closing. The representations, warranties, covenants and other obligations of Seller set forth in §4.03, §6.01 and §6.02 shall survive until the Limitation Date specified in Schedule D (or if none is so specified, the Limitation Date shall be the date which is six months after the Closing Date), and no action based thereon shall be commenced after the Limitation Date.

§16.02. The delivery of the deed by Seller, and the acceptance thereof by Purchaser, shall be deemed the full performance and discharge of every obligation on the part of Seller to be performed hereunder, except those obligations of Seller which are expressly stated in this contract to survive the Closing.

Section 17. Gains Tax and Miscellaneous Provisions

§17.01. If consent of the Existing Mortgagee(s) is required under §2.03(b), Purchaser shall not assign this contract or its rights hereunder without the prior written consent of Seller. No permitted assignment of Purchaser's rights under this contract shall be effective against Seller unless and until an executed counterpart of the instrument of assignment shall have been delivered to Seller and Seller shall have been furnished with the name and address of the assignee. The term "Purchaser" shall be deemed to include the assignee under any such effective assignment.

§17.02. This contract embodies and constitutes the entire understanding between the parties with respect to the transaction contemplated herein, and all prior agreements, understandings, representations and statements, oral or written, are merged into this contract. Neither this contract nor any provision hereof may be waived, modified, amended, discharged or terminated except by an instrument signed by the party against whom the enforcement of such waiver, modification, amendment, discharge or termination is sought, and then only to the extent set forth in such instrument.

§17.03. This contract shall be governed by, and construed in accordance with, the law of the State of New York.

§17.04. The captions in this contract are inserted for convenience of reference only and in no way define, describe or limit the scope or intent of this contract or any of the provisions hereof.

§17.05. This contract shall be binding upon and shall inure to the benefit of the parties hereto and their respective heirs or successors and permitted assigns.

§17.06. This contract shall not be binding or effective until properly executed and delivered by Seller and Purchaser.

§17.07. As used in this contract, the masculine shall include the feminine and neuter, the singular shall include the plural and the plural shall include the singular, as the context may require.

§17.08. If the provisions of any schedule or rider to this contract are inconsistent with the provisions of this contract, the provisions of such schedule or rider shall prevail. Set forth in Schedule D is a list of any and all schedules and riders which are attached hereto but which are not listed in the Table of Contents.

§17.09. (a) Seller and Purchaser agree to comply in a timely manner with the requirements of Article 31-B of the Tax Law of the State of New York and the regulations applicable thereto, as the same from time to time may be amended (collectively, the "Gains Tax Law"). Purchaser agrees to deliver to Seller a duly executed and acknowledged Transferee Questionnaire simultaneously with the execution of this contract or within five (5) business days after subsequent written request from Seller or Seller's attorney. At the Closing, Seller shall deliver (i) an official Statement of No Tax Due or (ii) an official Tentative Assessment and Return accompanied by a certified check or official bank check drawn on any banking institution described in §2.02(a), payable to the order of the State Tax Commission in the amount of the tax shown to be due thereon (it being understood, however, that if Seller has duly elected to pay such tax in installments, the amount so required to be paid shall be the minimum installment of such tax then permitted to be paid), or (iii) if applicable, a duly executed and acknowledged affidavit in form permitted under the Gains Tax Law claiming exemption therefrom.

(b) Seller agrees (i) to pay promptly any installment(s) or additional tax due under the Gains Tax Law, and interest and penalties thereon, if any, which may be assessed or due after the Closing, (ii) to indemnify and save the Purchaser harmless from and against any of the foregoing and any damage, liability, cost or expense (including reasonable attorneys' fees) which may be suffered or incurred by Purchaser by reason of the non-payment thereof, and (iii) to make any other payments and execute, acknowledge and deliver such further documents as may be necessary to comply with the Gains Tax Law.

(c) If this contract is assignable by Purchaser, no assignment of any rights hereunder shall be effective unless every assignor and assignee complies in a timely manner with the requirements of the Gains Tax Law applicable to the assignment transaction and unless an assignor or assignee delivers to Seller at or before the Closing the applicable items referred to in subparagraph (a) of this Section, all as may be required as a prerequisite to the recording of the deed. In addition to making the payments and delivering the instruments and documents referred to above, Purchaser and any assignor or assignee of this contract shall promptly (i) make any other payments and (ii) execute, acknowledge and deliver such further documents and instruments as may be necessary to comply with the Gains Tax Law.

(d) Purchaser, if request is made within a reasonable time prior to the Closing Date, shall provide at the Closing a separate certified or official bank check drawn on any banking institution described in §2.02(a) in the amount of the tax shown to be due on the official Tentative Assessment and Return, which amount shall be credited against the balance of the Purchase Price payable at the Closing.

(e) The provisions of this §17.09 shall survive the delivery of the deed.

IN WITNESS WHEREOF, the parties hereto have executed this contract as of the date first above written.

Seller:

Purchaser:

Receipt by Escrowee

The undersigned Escrowee hereby acknowledges receipt of $, by check subject to collection, to be held in escrow pursuant to §2.05.

Schedule A

DESCRIPTION OF PREMISES

(to be attached separately and to include tax map designation)

Schedule B

PERMITTED EXCEPTIONS

1. Zoning regulations and ordinances which are not violated by the existing structures or present use thereof and which do not render title uninsurable.
2. Consents by the Seller or any former owner of the Premises for the erection of any structure or structures on, under or above any street or streets on which the Premises may abut.
3. The Existing Mortgage(s) and financing statements, assignments of leases and other collateral assignments ancillary thereto.
4. Leases and Tenancies specified in the Rent Schedule and any new leases or tenancies not prohibited by this contract.
5. Unpaid installments of assessments not due and payable on or before the Closing Date.
6. Financing statements, chattel mortgages and liens on personalty filed more than 5 years prior to the Closing Date and not renewed, or filed against property or equipment no longer located on the Premises or owned by Tenants.

7. (a) Rights of utility companies to lay, maintain, install and repair pipes, lines, poles, conduits, cable boxes and related equipment on, over and under the Premises, provided that none of such rights imposes any monetary obligation on the owner of the Premises.

(b) Encroachments of stoops, areas, cellar steps, trim cornices, lintels, window sills, awnings, canopies, ledges, fences, hedges, coping and retaining walls projecting from the Premises over any street or highway or over any adjoining property and encroachments of similar elements projecting from adjoining property over the Premises.

(c) Revocability or lack of right to maintain vaults, coal chutes, excavations or sub-surface equipment beyond the line of the Premises.

(d) Any state of facts that an accurate survey would disclose, provided that such facts do not render title unmarketable. For the purposes of this contract, none of the facts shown on the survey, if any, identified below shall be deemed to render title unmarketable, and Purchaser shall accept title subject thereto:

§ 12.95   PURCHASE & SALE OF REAL ESTATE   Ch. 12

Schedule C

PURCHASE PRICE

The Purchase Price shall be paid as follows:

   (a) By check subject to collection, the receipt of which is hereby acknowledged by Seller: $

   (b) By check or checks delivered to Seller at the Closing in accordance with the provisions of §2.02:

   (c) By acceptance of title subject to the following Existing Mortgage(s):

   (d) By execution and delivery to Seller by Purchaser or its assignee of a note secured by a Purchase Money Mortgage on the Premises, payable as follows:

Purchase Price $ _____

Schedule D

MISCELLANEOUS

1. Title insurer designated by the parties (§1.02):

2. Last date for consent by Existing Mortgagee(s) (§2.03(b)):

3. Maximum Interest Rate of any Refinanced Mortgage (§2.04(b)):

4. Prepayment Date on or after which Purchase Money Mortgage may be prepaid (§2.04(c)):

5. Seller's tax identification number (§2.05):

6. Purchaser's tax identification number (§2.05):

7. Scheduled time and date of Closing (§3.01):

8. Place of Closing (§3.01):

9. Assessed valuation of Premises (§4.10):
   Actual Assessment:
   Transition Assessment:

10. Fiscal year and annual real estate taxes on Premises (§4.10):

11. Tax abatements or exemptions affecting Premises (§4.10):

12. Assessments on Premises (§4.13):

13. Maximum Amount which Seller must spend to cure violations, etc. (§7.02):

14. Maximum Expense of Seller to cure title defects, etc. (§13.02):

15. Broker, if any (§14.01):

16. Party to pay broker's commission (§14.01):

17. Address for notices (§15.01):
   If to Seller:

   with a copy to Seller's attorney:

   If to Purchaser:

   with a copy to Purchaser's attorney:

18. Limitation Date for actions based on Seller's surviving representations and other obligations (§16.01):

19. Additional Schedules or Riders (§17.08):

Schedule E

RENT SCHEDULE

(to be attached separately)

914

§ 12.96 Contract of Sale—Cooperative Apartment[1]

CONSULT YOUR LAWYER BEFORE SIGNING THIS AGREEMENT
Contract of Sale — Cooperative Apartment

This Contract is made as of   between the "**Seller**" and the "**Purchaser**" identified below.

1. Certain Definitions and Information
1.1 The "Parties" are:
Seller:

Address:

Prior names
used by Seller:
Soc. Sec. No

Purchaser:

Address:

Soc. Sec. No

1.2. The "Attorneys" are (name, address and telephone)
For Seller

For Purchaser:

1.3 The "Escrowee" is (name, address and telephone)

1.4 The "Managing Agent" is (name, address and telephone)

1.5 The name of the cooperative housing corporation ("Corporation") is

1.6 The "Unit" number is
1.7 The Unit is located in "Premises" known as

1.8 The "Shares" are the   shares of the Corporation allocated to the Unit.
1.9 The "Lease" is the proprietary lease for the Unit given by the Corporation.
1.10 The "Broker" (see Par. 12) is

1.11 The "Closing" is the transfer of ownership of the Shares and Lease, which is scheduled to occur on
           19   at   M. (see Pars. 9 and 10)
1.12 The "Purchase Price" is $
   1.12.1 the "Contract Deposit" is $
   1.12.2 the "Balance" of the Purchase Price due at Closing is $ (see Par. 2)

1.13 The "Maintenance" charge is the rent payable under the Lease which at the date of this Contract is in the monthly amount of
$ (see Par. 4)
1.14 The "Assessment" is the additional rent payable under the Lease which at the date of this Contract is
$ payable as follows:

1.15 The Party upon whom the Corporation imposes a "Flip Tax" or similar transfer fee, if any, is
              (see Par. 11.3)
1.16 If Par. 19 (Financing Contingency) applies:
   1.16.1 the "Loan Terms" are:
Amount Financed: $ or any lower amount applied for or acceptable to Purchaser.
Payment Terms and Charges: The customary payment terms (including prevailing fixed or adjustable interest rate, prepayment provisions and maturity) and charges (including points, origination and other fees) then currently being offered to purchasers of cooperative apartments by the Institutional Lender (defined in Par. 19.5.1) to which Purchaser applies.
Security: Pledge of the Shares and Lease.
   1.16.2 the period for Purchaser to obtain a Loan Commitment Letter is   business days after a fully executed counterpart of this Contract is given to Purchaser.
1.17 The "Proposed Occupants" of the Unit are the following:
   1.17.1 persons and relationship to Purchaser.

   1.17.2 pets.

1.18 The Contract Deposit shall be held in a   interest bearing escrow account. Interest shall be payable to the
              The escrow
account shall be a   type
account held at
              (See Par. 28)

2. Agreement to Sell and Purchase; Purchase Price; Escrow
2.1 Seller agrees to sell and assign to Purchaser, and Purchaser agrees to purchase and assume from Seller, the Seller's Shares and Lease for the Purchase Price and upon the other terms and conditions stated in this Contract.
2.2 The Purchase Price is payable to Seller by Purchaser as follows:
   2.2.1 the Contract Deposit at the time of signing this Contract, by Purchaser's collectible check to the order of Escrowee.
   2.2.2 the Balance at Closing, only by cashier's, official bank or certified check of Purchaser made payable to the direct order of Seller. These checks shall be drawn on and payable by a branch of a commercial or savings bank, savings and loan association or trust company located in the same City or County as the Unit. Seller may direct, on not less than 3 business days' Notice (defined in Par. 17) prior to Closing, that all or a portion of the Balance shall be made payable to persons other than Seller.

3. Personal Property
3.1 Subject to any rights of the Corporation or any holder of a mortgage to which the Lease is subordinate, this sale includes all of Seller's ownership, if any, of the following "Property" to the extent existing in the Unit on the date hereof: the refrigerator, freezer, range, oven, microwave oven, dishwasher, cabinets and counters, lighting fixtures, chandeliers, wall-to-wall carpeting, plumbing fixtures, central air-conditioning and/or window or sleeve units, washing machine, dryer, screens and storm windows, window treatments, switch plates, door hardware, built-ins not excluded in Par. 3.2 and

3.2 Specifically excluded from this sale is all personalty not included in Par. 3.1 and

§ 12.96
1. Forms may be purchased from Julius Blumberg, Inc. NYC 10013, or any of its dealers. Reproduction prohibited.

915

3.3 The Property shall not be purchased if Closing does not occur.

3.4 No consideration is being paid for the Property. Seller makes no representation as to the condition of the Property. Purchaser shall take the Property "as is" on the date of this Contract, except for reasonable wear and tear, and except further, the appliances shall be in working order at Closing.

3.5 At or prior to the time of Closing, Seller shall remove from the Unit all the furniture, furnishings and other personalty not included in this sale, and repair any damage caused by such removal.

4. Representations and Covenants

4.1 Subject to any matter affecting title to the Premises (as to which Seller makes no representations or covenants), Seller represents and covenants that:

4.1.1 Seller is and shall at Closing be the sole owner of the Shares and Lease with the full right and power to sell and assign them;

4.1.2 the Shares and Lease will at Closing be free and clear of liens (other than the Corporation's general lien on the Shares, for which no monies shall be owed), encumbrances and adverse interests ("Liens"); or Seller will deliver to Purchaser at Closing all requisite terminations, releases and or satisfactions executed in form suitable for filing and or recording, so as to remove of record, at Seller's expense, any such Liens;

4.1.3 the Shares were duly issued, fully paid for and are non-assessable;

4.1.4 the Lease is, and will at Closing be, in full force and effect and no notice of default under the Lease will be in effect at Closing;

4.1.5 the Maintenance and Assessments payable as of the date hereof are as specified in Pars. 1.13 and 1.14. All sums due to the Corporation will be fully paid by Seller to the end of the payment period immediately preceding the date of Closing;

4.1.6 as of this date, Seller neither has actual knowledge nor has received any written notice of (a) any increase in Maintenance or (b) any proposed Assessment which has been either adopted or is under consideration by the Board of Directors of the Corporation and not reflected in the amounts set forth in Pars. 1.13 and 1.14;

4.1.7 Seller will not at Closing be indebted for labor or material which might result in the filing of a notice of mechanic's lien against the Unit or the Premises;

4.1.8 there are and at closing will be no violations of record which the owner of the Shares and Lease would be obligated to remedy under the terms of the Lease;

4.1.9 Seller has not made any alterations or additions to the Unit, without any required consent of the Corporation;

4.1.10 Seller has not entered and will not enter into, and has no actual knowledge of, any agreement (other than the Lease) affecting the use and or occupancy of the Unit which would be binding on or adversely affect Purchaser; and

4.1.11 Seller has been known by no other name for the past 10 years except as set forth in Par. 1.1.

4.2 Purchaser represents and covenants that Purchaser is acquiring the Shares and Lease solely for residential occupancy of the Unit by the Proposed Occupants only and will so represent to the Corporation in connection with Purchaser's application to the Corporation for approval of this transaction by the Corporation.

4.3 The representations and covenants contained in Par. 4.1 shall survive Closing, but any action based thereon must be instituted within 1 year from Closing.

5. Corporate Documents

Purchaser has examined and is satisfied with or has waived the examination of the Lease, and the Corporation's certificate of incorporation, bylaws, house rules, most recent audited financial statement and most recent statement of tax deductions available to the Corporation's shareholders under Internal Revenue Code ("IRC") § 216 (or any successor statute).

6. Required Approval and References

6.1 This sale is subject to the approval of the Corporation.

6.2 Purchaser shall in good faith:

6.2.1 submit to the Corporation or its Managing Agent, within 10 business days after the receipt of a fully executed counterpart of this Contract, an application for approval of this sale on the form required by the Corporation containing such data and together with such documents as the Corporation reasonably requires except for the Loan Commitment Letter (defined in Par. 19.5.2), if applicable, which shall be submitted by Purchaser within 3 business days after it is obtained;

6.2.2 attend (and cause any person who will reside in the Unit to attend) one or more personal interviews, as requested by the Corporation; and

6.2.3 promptly submit to the Corporation such further references, data and documents reasonably requested by the Corporation.

6.3 Either Party, after learning of the approval or denial by the Corporation of the application, shall promptly send Notice to the other Party of the Corporation's decision. If approval or denial has not been issued on or before the date set for Closing, the Closing shall be adjourned for 30 business days for the purpose of obtaining such approval unless otherwise agreed to by the Parties. If the approval of this sale is not obtained by said adjourned date, either Party may cancel this Contract on Notice to the other provided that the Corporation's approval is not issued before Notice of cancellation is given. In the event of a denial other than for Purchaser's bad faith conduct, this contract shall be deemed cancelled. In the event of cancellation pursuant to this Par. 6, the Escrowee shall refund the Contract Deposit to Purchaser. In case of a denial or lack of approval due to Purchaser's bad faith conduct, Purchaser shall be in default and Par. 13.1 shall govern.

7. Condition of Unit and Possession

7.1 Seller makes no representation as to the condition of the Unit. Purchaser has inspected the Unit and shall take the same "as is", on the date of this Contract, reasonable wear and tear excepted.

7.2 Seller shall deliver possession of the Unit at the Closing, vacant, broom-clean and free of all occupants and rights of possession.

8. Risk of Loss

8.1 While Seller has legal title and is in possession of the Unit, Seller assumes all risk of loss or damage ("Loss") to the Unit and Property from fire or other cause not due to the fault of Purchaser or Purchaser's contractors, agents or servants. In the event of a Loss, Seller shall have the option (but not the obligation) to restore the Unit and Property to as near as reasonably possible to the condition immediately prior to the Loss.

8.2 Within 10 calendar days after the Loss occurs, Seller shall give Notice to Purchaser of the Loss and whether or not Seller elects to restore ("Election Notice").

8.3 If Seller elects to restore, Seller must do so within 60 calendar days after sending the Election Notice or by the Closing, whichever is later ("Restoration Period").

8.4 If the Closing is before such 60 calendar day period expires, then the Closing shall be adjourned to a date and time fixed by Seller on not less than 10 calendar days' prior Notice to Purchaser, but in no event shall the Closing be adjourned for more than 70 calendar days after giving of the Election Notice.

8.5 If Seller elects not to restore or fails, in a timely manner, to send the Election Notice or, having sent the Notice, Seller fails to complete the restoration within the Restoration Period, then Purchaser's sole remedy is either to:

8.5.1 cancel this Contract in accordance with Par. 16 and recover all sums theretofore paid on account of the Purchase Price; or

8.5.2 complete the purchase in accordance with this Contract, without reduction in the Purchase Price or claim against Seller, but with the right to receive any "Net Insurance Proceeds" as defined in Par. 8.6 together with an assignment to Purchaser, without recourse to Seller, of any uncollected proceeds, which assignment shall be delivered by Seller at Closing.

8.6 "Net Insurance Proceeds" are proceeds of Seller's insurance covering the Loss which is attributable to the Unit and Property after deducting legal and other collection expenses incurred by Seller and any sums paid or incurred by Seller for restoration.

8.7 If Purchaser fails to exercise one of Purchaser's options pursuant to Par. 8.5 by Notice to Seller within 7 business days after Seller gives the Election Notice or within 7 business days after the Restoration Period expires (in the event Seller fails to complete the restoration within the Restoration Period), then Purchaser will be deemed to have conclusively elected the option to complete the purchase pursuant to Par. 8.5.2.

8.8 If Purchaser is given possession of the Unit prior to Closing:

8.8.1 Purchaser assumes all risk of Loss to the Unit and Property prior to Closing from fire or other cause not the fault of Seller or Seller's contractors, agents, employees or servants; and

8.8.2 Purchaser shall be obligated to complete the purchase in accordance with this Contract, without reduction in the Purchase Price or claim against Seller and without delay.

8.9 Notwithstanding anything to the contrary in Par. 8.1, Purchaser shall have the right to cancel this Contract in accordance with Par. 16 if, prior to Closing and while Seller is in possession, through no fault of Purchaser or Purchaser's contractors, agents, employees and servants, either:

8.9.1 a Loss occurs to the Unit which would cost more than 10% of the Purchase Price to restore; or

8.9.2 more than 10% of the units in the Premises are damaged and rendered uninhabitable by fire or other cause, regardless of whether the Unit is damaged.

8.10 Purchaser shall be deemed to have waived Purchaser's right to cancel under Par. 8.9 if Purchaser fails to elect to cancel by Notice to Seller given within 7 business days after Seller gives Notice to Purchaser of the event which gives rise to Purchaser's right to cancel. In the event Purchaser waives or is deemed to have waived this right to cancel, the provisions of Par. 8.5.2 shall apply.

9. Closing Location

The Closing shall be held at the location designated by the Corporation, or (if none is designated), at the office of Seller's attorney.

10. Closing

10.1 At Closing, Seller shall deliver:

10.1.1 Seller's certificate for the Shares duly endorsed for transfer to Purchaser or accompanied by a separate duly executed stock power to Purchaser, and in either case, with any guarantee of Seller's signature required by the Corporation;

10.1.2 Seller's counterpart original of the Lease and a duly executed assignment thereof to Purchaser in the form required by the Corporation;

10.1.3 a written statement by an officer of the Corporation or its authorized agent consenting to the transfer of the Shares and Lease to Purchaser and setting forth the amounts and payment status of the Maintenance and any Assessments;

10.1.4 executed FIRPTA document(s) (defined in Par. 26),

10.1.5 keys to the Unit, building entrances, garage, mailbox and any locks in the Unit;

10.1.6 if requested, an assignment to Purchaser of Seller's interest in the Property;

10.1.7 Net Insurance Proceeds and/or assignment of any uncollected Net Insurance Proceeds, if applicable, and

10.1.8 instruments or other documents required under Par. 4.1.2, if any.

10.2 At Closing, Purchaser shall:

10.2.1 pay the Balance in accordance with Par. 2.2.2;

10.2.2 execute and deliver to Seller and the Corporation an agreement assuming the Lease, in the form required by the Corporation; and

10.2.3 if requested by the Corporation, execute and deliver counterparts of a new lease substantially the same as the Lease, for the balance of the Lease term, in which case the Lease shall be cancelled and surrendered to the Corporation together with Seller's assignment thereof to Purchaser.

10.3 At Closing, the Parties shall provide the information necessary for Internal Revenue Service ("IRS") Form 1099 S or other similar form required

10.4 At Closing, Seller shall provide, and the Parties shall execute, all documents necessary to comply with any applicable transfer and/or gains tax filings.

11. Closing Fees, Taxes and Apportionments

11.1 At Closing, Seller shall pay, if applicable:

11.1.1 the processing fee(s) of the Corporation, its attorneys, and/or agents, except as set forth in Par. 11.2.1;

11.1.2 the cost of stock transfer stamps; and

11.1.3 the transfer tax and transfer gains tax, except a transfer tax which by its terms imposes primary liability on the purchaser.

11.2 At Closing, Purchaser shall pay

11.2.1 the sales taxes, if any, on this sale, other than the transfer stamps as provided for in Par. 11.1.2;

11.2.2 the cost of any title search;

11.2.3 any fee to the Corporation or its agents and/or attorneys relating to Purchaser's financing; and

11.2.4 a transfer tax which by law is primarily imposed on the purchaser.

11.3 At Closing, the Flip Tax, if any, shall be paid by the Party specified in Par. 1.15.

11.4 At Closing, the Parties shall apportion as of 11:59 P.M. of the day preceding the Closing, the Maintenance and any other periodic charges due the Corporation (other than Assessments).

11.5 Assessments, whether payable in a lump sum or installments, shall not be apportioned, but shall be paid by the Party who is the owner of the Shares on the date specified by the Corporation for payment. Purchaser shall pay any installments payable after Closing provided Seller had the right to and elected to pay the Assessments in installments.

11.6 Each party covenants to the other that it will timely pay any taxes for which it is primarily liable pursuant to law. This Par. 11.6 shall survive Closing.

12. Broker

12.1 Each Party represents to the other that such Party has not dealt with any other person acting as a broker, whether licensed or unlicensed, in connection with this transaction other than the Broker named in Par. 1.10

12.2 Seller shall pay the Broker's commission pursuant to a separate agreement. The Broker shall not be deemed to be a third-party beneficiary of this provision.

12.3 This Par. 12 shall survive the Closing

13. Defaults, Remedies and Indemnities

13.1 In the event of a default or misrepresentation by Purchaser, Seller's sole remedy shall be to terminate this Contract and retain the Contract Deposit as liquidated damages, except there shall be no limitation on Seller's remedies for a breach of Par. 12.1. In case of Purchaser's misrepresentation or default, Seller's damages would be impossible to ascertain and the Contract Deposit constitutes a fair and reasonable amount of compensation.

13.2 In the event of a default or misrepresentation by Seller, Purchaser shall have such remedies as Purchaser is entitled to at law or in equity, including specific performance, because the Unit and possession thereof cannot be duplicated.

13.3 Each Party indemnifies and holds harmless the other against and from any claim, judgment, loss, liability, cost or expense resulting from the indemnitor's breach of any of the representations or covenants stated to survive Closing. This indemnity includes, without limitation, reasonable attorneys' fees and disbursements, court costs and litigation expenses. This Par. 13.3 shall survive the Closing.

13.4 Purchaser indemnifies and holds harmless Seller against and from any claim, judgment, loss, cost or expense resulting from the Lease obligations assumed by Purchaser. This indemnity includes, without limitation, reasonable attorneys' fees and disbursements, court costs and litigation expenses. This indemnity does not include or excuse a breach of any representation or covenant by Seller in Par. 4.1. This Par. 13.4 shall survive the Closing.

13.5 In the event any instrument for the payment of the Contract Deposit fails of collection, Seller shall have the right to sue on the uncollected instrument. In addition, such failure of collection shall be a default under this Contract, provided Seller gives Purchaser Notice of such failure of collection and, within 3 business days after Notice is given, Escrowee does not receive from Purchaser an unendorsed certified check, bank check or immediately available funds in the amount of the uncollected funds. Failure to cure such default shall entitle Seller to the remedy in Par. 13.1 and to retain all sums as may be collected and/or recovered.

14. Entire Agreement; Modification

14.1 All prior oral or written representations, understandings and agreements had between the Parties with respect to the subject matter of this Contract, and with the Escrowee as to Par. 28, are merged in this Contract, which alone fully and completely expresses their agreement.

14.2 A provision of this Contract may be changed or waived only in writing signed by the Party (or Escrowee) to be charged.

14.3 The Attorneys may extend in writing any of the time limitations stated in this Contract.

15. No Assignment by Purchaser

15.1 Purchaser may not assign this Contract or any of Purchaser's rights hereunder and any purported assignment shall be null and void.

15.2 This Contract shall bind and inure to the benefit of the Parties hereto and their respective heirs, personal and legal representatives and successors in interest.

16. Cancellation for Other than Default or Misrepresentation

If Seller shall be unable to transfer the Lease and the Shares in accordance with this Contract for any reason not due to Seller's willful acts or omissions, then the sole obligation of Seller shall be to refund to Purchaser the Contract Deposit and reimburse Purchaser for the actual costs incurred for Purchaser's title or abstract search, except such reimbursement shall not be required if a cancellation is pursuant to Par. 6 or 19. Upon making such refund, this Contract shall be cancelled and neither Party shall have any further claim against the other hereunder.

17. Notices

17.1 Any notice or demand ("Notice") shall be in writing and either delivered by hand or overnight delivery or sent by certified or registered mail to the Party and simultaneously, in like manner, to such Party's Attorney, if any, and to Escrowee at the addresses set forth in Par. 1, or to such other address as shall hereafter be designated by Notice given pursuant to this Par. 17.

17.2 Each Notice shall be deemed given on the same day if delivered by hand or on the following business day if sent by overnight delivery, or the second business day following the date of mailing.

17.3 The Attorneys are authorized to give any Notice specified in this Contract on behalf of their respective clients.

17.4 Failure to accept a Notice does not invalidate the Notice.

18. Margin Headings

The margin headings do not constitute part of the text of this Contract.

19. Financing Contingency (delete if inapplicable)

19.1 Purchaser may cancel this Contract and recover the Contract Deposit by following the procedure in Par. 19.4 if after complying with Purchaser's "Financing Obligations" in Par. 19.2 below and Purchaser's other obligations under this Contract:

19.1.1 Purchaser fails through no fault of Purchaser to obtain from an "Institutional Lender" (defined in Par. 19.5.1) a "Loan Commitment Letter" (defined in Par. 19.5.2) for financing on the Loan Terms and within the time period stated in Par. 1.16 (the "Loan"); or

19.1.2 the Institutional Lender and the Corporation cannot agree on the terms of an agreement for the protection of the Institutional Lender (commonly called a recognition agreement), if required by the Institutional Lender.

19.2 Purchaser's right to cancel under Par. 19.1 and recover the Contract Deposit is conditioned upon Purchaser's diligent compliance with all of the following "Financing Obligations":

19.2.1 Purchaser must apply in good faith for the Loan from an Institutional Lender within 7 business days after a fully executed counterpart of this Contract is given to Purchaser;

19.2.2 the Loan application must contain truthful, accurate and complete information as required by the Institutional Lender; and

19.2.3 Purchaser must comply with all requirements of the Institutional Lender to obtain the Loan Commitment Letter and to close the Loan.

19.3 Purchaser may also cancel this Contract and recover the Contract Deposit in accordance with the procedure in Par. 19.4 if:

19.3.1 the Closing is adjourned by Seller or the Corporation for more than 30 business days from the date set for Closing in Par. 1.11; and

19.3.2 the Loan Commitment Letter expires on a date more than 30 business days after the date set for Closing in Par. 1.11 and before the new date set for Closing pursuant to Par. 19.3.1; and

19.3.3 Purchaser is unable in good faith to obtain from the Institutional Lender an extension or a new Loan Commitment Letter for the Amount Financed stated in Par. 1.16 or the same principal amount stated in the expired Loan Commitment Letter, whichever is lower, without paying any additional fees to the Institutional Lender (unless Seller, within 5 business days after receipt of Notice of such fees, gives Notice that Seller will pay such fees and pays them when due). All other substantive Loan terms may be materially no less favorable than in the expired Loan Commitment Letter.

19.4 In order to cancel pursuant to Par. 19.1 or 19.3, Purchaser shall give Notice of cancellation to Seller within 7 business days after the right to cancel arises. Purchaser's failure to timely give such Notice of cancellation will be deemed a conclusive waiver of such right to cancel. In case of cancellation pursuant to Par. 19.1, a copy of any loan refusal letter or non-complying Loan Commitment Letter (as the case may be) issued by the Institutional Lender shall accompany the Notice of cancellation, if available, or if not then available, shall be provided promptly after receipt. In case of cancellation pursuant to Par. 19.3, a copy of all written communications between the Institutional Lender and Purchaser concerning the extension or new loan commitment shall accompany the Notice of cancellation (or a copy of any letter refusing to extend the loan commitment or make a new loan commitment received by Purchaser after sending the cancellation Notice shall be sent to Seller promptly after receipt). Purchaser's obligation under this Par. 19.4 shall survive the cancellation of this Contract.

19.5 The definitions for certain terms used in this Par. 19 are:

19.5.1 an "Institutional Lender" is any bank, savings bank, savings and loan association, trust company, credit union of which Purchaser is a member, insurance company or governmental entity which is duly authorized to issue a loan secured by the Shares and Lease in the state where the Unit is located and is then currently extending similarly secured loan commitments; and

19.5.2 a "Loan Commitment Letter" is a written offer to make the Loan with or without recourse, and whether or not conditional upon any factor other than an appraisal satisfactory to the Institutional Lender. An offer to make the Loan which is conditional on obtaining a satisfactory appraisal shall only become a Loan Commitment Letter upon such condition being met.

20. Singular/Plural and Joint/Several

The use of the singular shall be deemed to include the plural, and vice versa, whenever the context so requires. If more than one entity is selling or purchasing the Unit, their obligations shall be joint and several.

21. No Survival

No representation and/or covenant contained herein shall survive Closing except as expressly provided. Computational errors shall survive and be corrected after Closing.

22. Inspections

Purchaser shall have the right to inspect the Unit at reasonable times upon reasonable request to Seller, and within 48 hours prior to Closing.

23. Governing Law

This Contract shall be governed by the laws of the State of New York. Any action or proceeding arising out of this Contract shall be brought in the county where the Unit is located and the Parties hereby consent to said venue.

24. Removal of Liens

24.1 Purchaser shall deliver or cause to be delivered to Seller or Seller's Attorney, not less than 10 calendar days prior to Closing, a list of Liens, if any, which may violate Par. 4.1.

24.2 Seller shall have a reasonable period of time to remove any such Lien.

25. Cooperation of Parties

25.1 The Parties shall each cooperate with the other, the Corporation, Purchaser's Institutional Lender and title company, if any, and obtain, execute and deliver such documents as are reasonably necessary to close.

25.2 The Parties shall timely file or pre-file all required documents in connection with all governmental filings that are required by law. Each Party represents to the other that its statements in such filings will be true and complete. This Par. 25.2 shall survive the Closing.

26. FIRPTA and Gains Tax

26.1 The Parties shall comply with IRC §§ 897, 1445 and related provisions, as amended, and any substitute provisions of any successor statute and the regulations thereunder ("FIRPTA"). The Seller shall furnish to the Purchaser at or prior to Closing a Certification of Nonforeign Status in accordance with FIRPTA. If the Seller fails to deliver such certification by Closing, the Purchaser shall deduct and withhold from the Purchase Price such sum required by law and remit such amount to the IRS. In the event of such withholding by Purchaser, Seller's obligations hereunder, including (but not limited to) the transfer of ownership of the Shares and Lease, shall not be excused or otherwise affected. In the event of any claimed over-withholding, Seller shall be limited solely to an action against the IRS for a refund. Seller hereby waives any right of action against Purchaser on account of such withholding. This Par. 26.1 shall survive the Closing.

26.2 If a Real Property Transfer Gains Tax pre-filing is required by law, Purchaser shall simultaneously herewith deliver to Seller a completed and executed Transferee Questionnaire or the equivalent thereof.

27. Additional Conditions

27.1 Purchaser shall not be obligated to close unless at the time of the Closing:

27.1.1 the Corporation is duly incorporated and in good standing; and

27.1.2 the Corporation has fee or leasehold title to the Premises, whether or not marketable or insurable; and

27.1.3 there is no pending *in rem* action or foreclosure action of any underlying mortgage affecting the Premises.

27.2 Purchaser shall give Seller Notice of any failure of any of the conditions in Par. 27.1. If any condition in Par. 27.1 is not true and is not cured within a reasonable period of time after giving said Notice, then either Seller or Purchaser shall have the option to cancel this Contract pursuant to Par. 16.

28. Escrow Terms

28.1 Escrowee acknowledges receipt of the check for the Contract Deposit, subject to collection.

28.2 The check for the Contract Deposit shall be deposited by Escrowee in an escrow account as described in Par. 1.18 and the proceeds held and disbursed in accordance with the terms of this Contract. Upon Closing, Escrowee shall deliver the Contract Deposit to Seller. In all other cases, if either Party makes a demand upon Escrowee for delivery of the Contract Deposit, Escrowee shall give Notice to the other Party of such demand. If a Notice of objection to the proposed payment is not received from the other Party within 7 business days after the giving of Notice by Escrowee, time being of the essence, Escrowee is hereby authorized to deliver the Contract Deposit to the Party who made the demand. If Escrowee receives a Notice of objection within said period, or if for any other reason Escrowee in good faith elects not to deliver the Contract Deposit, then Escrowee shall continue to hold the Contract Deposit and thereafter pay it to the Party entitled when Escrowee receives (a) a Notice from the objecting Party withdrawing the objection, or (b) a Notice signed by both Parties directing disposition of the Contract Deposit or (c) a judgment or order of a court of competent jurisdiction.

28.3 In the event of any dispute or doubt as to the genuineness of any document or signature, or uncertainty as to Escrowee's duties, then Escrowee shall have the right either to continue to hold the Contract Deposit in escrow or to pay the Contract Deposit into court pursuant to relevant statute.

28.4 The parties agree jointly to defend (by attorneys selected by Escrowee), indemnify and hold harmless Escrowee against and from any claim, judgment, loss, liability, cost or expense resulting from any dispute or litigation arising out of or concerning Escrowee's duties or services hereunder. This indemnity includes, without limitation, disbursements and reasonable attorneys' fees either paid to retain attorneys or representing the fair value of legal services rendered by Escrowee to itself.

28.5 Escrowee shall not be liable for any error in judgment or for any act done or step taken or omitted in good faith, or for any mistake of fact or law, except for Escrowee's own gross negligence or willful misconduct.

28.6 The Parties acknowledge that Escrowee is merely a stakeholder. Upon payment of the Contract Deposit pursuant to Par. 28.2 or 28.3, Escrowee shall be fully released from all liability and obligations with respect to the Contract Deposit.

28.7 In the event Escrowee is the attorney for either Party, Escrowee shall be entitled to represent such Party in any lawsuit.

28.8 Escrowee shall serve without compensation.

28.9 The signing of this Contract by Escrowee is only to evidence Escrowee's acceptance of the terms and conditions of this Par. 28.

29. Binding Effect

This Contract shall not be binding unless a fully executed counterpart thereof has been delivered to each of the Parties.

In Witness Whereof, the Parties hereto have duly executed this Contract as of the date first above written.

ESCROW TERMS AGREED TO: _____ SELLER: _____ PURCHASER: _____

Escrowee

§ 12.97 Durable General Power of Attorney

DURABLE GENERAL POWER OF ATTORNEY
NEW YORK STATUTORY SHORT FORM[1]

THE POWERS YOU GRANT BELOW CONTINUE TO BE EFFECTIVE SHOULD YOU BECOME DISABLED OR INCOMPETENT

CAUTION: THIS IS AN IMPORTANT DOCUMENT. IT GIVES THE PERSON WHOM YOU DESIGNATE (YOUR "AGENT") BROAD POWERS TO HANDLE YOUR PROPERTY DURING YOUR LIFETIME, WHICH MAY INCLUDE POWERS TO MORTGAGE, SELL, OR OTHERWISE DISPOSE OF ANY REAL OR PERSONAL PROPERTY WITHOUT ADVANCE NOTICE TO YOU OR APPROVAL BY YOU. THESE POWERS WILL CONTINUE TO EXIST EVEN AFTER YOU BECOME DISABLED OR INCOMPETENT. THESE POWERS ARE EXPLAINED MORE FULLY IN NEW YORK GENERAL OBLIGATIONS LAW, ARTICLE 5, TITLE 15, SECTIONS 5–1502A THROUGH 5–1503, WHICH EXPRESSLY PERMIT THE USE OF ANY OTHER OR DIFFERENT FORM OF POWER OF ATTORNEY.

THIS DOCUMENT DOES NOT AUTHORIZE ANYONE TO MAKE MEDICAL OR OTHER HEALTH CARE DECISIONS. YOU MAY EXECUTE A HEALTH CARE PROXY TO DO THIS.

IF THERE IS ANYTHING ABOUT THIS FORM THAT YOU DO NOT UNDERSTAND, YOU SHOULD ASK A LAWYER TO EXPLAIN IT TO YOU.

THIS IS intended to constitute a DURABLE GENERAL DURABLE POWER OF ATTORNEY, pursuant to Article 5, Title 15 of the New York General Obligations Law:

I, _____

(insert YOUR name and address)

do hereby appoint:

_____
_____

---

§ 12.97

1. Every statutory short form DURABLE power of attorney, to be valid, must be written, typed or printed using letters which are in legible writing of or clear type of no less than twelve-point in size or if in writing a reasonable equivalent thereof and must contain, in bold face UPPER CASE OR UPPER AND LOWER CASE type or a reasonable equivalent thereof the "CAUTION" which is printed in bold face type at the beginning of the statutory form printed above and the "DIRECTIONS" which ARE printed in bold face type immediately before subdivisions (A) through (Q) of the statutory form printed above.

§ 12.97   PURCHASE & SALE OF REAL ESTATE   Ch. 12

(If 1 person is to be appointed agent, insert the name and address of YOUR agent above)

_____
_____
_____
_____

(If 2 or more persons are to be appointed agents, BY YOU insert THEIR NAMES and ADDRESSES above)

my attorney(s)-in-fact TO ACT

(If more than one agent is designated, CHOOSE ONE OF THE FOLLOWING TWO CHOICES BY PUTTING YOUR INITIALS IN ONE OF THE BLANK SPACES TO THE LEFT OF YOUR CHOICE:)

( ) EACH AGENT MAY SEPARATELY ACT.

( ) ALL AGENTS MUST ACT TOGETHER.

(IF NEITHER BLANK SPACE IS INITIALED, THE AGENTS WILL BE REQUIRED TO ACT TOGETHER)

IN MY NAME, PLACE AND STEAD in any way which I myself could do, if I were personally present, with respect to the following matters as each of them is defined in Title 15 of Article 5 of the New York General Obligations Law to the extent that I am permitted by law to act through an agent:

(DIRECTIONS: Initial in the BLANK SPACE TO THE LEFT OF YOUR CHOICE any one or more of the FOLLOWING LETTERED subdivisions as to which YOU WANT to give YOUR agent authority. If the blank space TO THE LEFT OF any particular LETTERED subdivision is NOT initialed, NO AUTHORITY WILL BE GRANTED for matters that are included in that subdivision. ALTERNATIVELY, THE LETTER CORRESPONDING TO EACH POWER YOU WISH TO GRANT MAY BE WRITTEN OR TYPED ON THE BLANK LINE IN SUBDIVISION "(Q)", AND YOU MAY THEN PUT YOUR INITIALS IN THE BLANK SPACE TO THE LEFT OF SUBDIVISION "(Q)" IN ORDER TO GRANT EACH OF THE POWERS SO INDICATED)

( ) (A) real estate transactions;
( ) (B) chattel and goods transactions;
( ) (C) bond, share and commodity transactions;
( ) (D) banking transactions;
( ) (E) business operating transactions;
( ) (F) insurance transactions;
( ) (G) estate transactions;
( ) (H) claims and litigation;
( ) (I) personal relationships and affairs;

( ) (J) benefits from military service;
( ) (K) records, reports and statements;
( ) (L) RETIREMENT BENEFIT TRANSACTIONS;
( ) (M) MAKING GIFTS TO MY SPOUSE, CHILDREN AND MORE REMOTE DESCENDANTS, AND PARENTS, NOT TO EXCEED IN THE AGGREGATE $10,000 TO EACH OF SUCH PERSONS IN ANY YEAR;
( ) (N) TAX MATTERS;
( ) (O) ALL OTHER MATTERS;
( ) (P) full and unqualified authority to my attorney(s)-in-fact to delegate any or all of the foregoing powers to any person or persons whom my attorney(s)-in-fact shall select;
( ) (Q) EACH OF THE ABOVE MATTERS IDENTIFIED BY THE FOLLOWING LETTERS:

_____

(Special provisions and limitations may be included in the statutory short form DURABLE power of attorney only if they conform to the requirements of Section 5–1503 of the New York General Obligations Law.)

_____
_____
_____

THIS DURABLE POWER OF ATTORNEY SHALL NOT BE AFFECTED BY MY SUBSEQUENT DISABILITY OR INCOMPETENCE.

IF EVERY AGENT NAMED ABOVE IS UNABLE OR UNWILLING TO SERVE, I APPOINT

_____
_____

(INSERT NAME AND ADDRESS OF SUCCESSOR)

TO BE MY AGENT FOR ALL PURPOSES HEREUNDER.

TO INDUCE ANY THIRD PARTY TO ACT HEREUNDER, I HEREBY AGREE THAT ANY THIRD PARTY RECEIVING A DULY EXECUTED COPY OR FACSIMILE OF THIS INSTRUMENT MAY ACT HEREUNDER, AND THAT REVOCATION OR TERMINATION HEREOF SHALL BE INEFFECTIVE AS TO SUCH THIRD PARTY UNLESS AND UNTIL ACTUAL NOTICE OR KNOWLEDGE OF SUCH REVOCATION OR TERMINATION SHALL HAVE BEEN RECEIVED BY SUCH THIRD PARTY, AND I FOR MYSELF AND FOR MY HEIRS, EXECUTORS, LEGAL REPRESENTATIVES AND ASSIGNS, HEREBY AGREE TO INDEMNIFY AND HOLD HARMLESS ANY SUCH THIRD PARTY FROM AND AGAINST ANY AND ALL CLAIMS THAT MAY ARISE AGAINST SUCH THIRD PARTY BY REASON OF SUCH

§ 12.97   PURCHASE & SALE OF REAL ESTATE   Ch. 12

THIRD PARTY HAVING RELIED ON THE PROVISIONS OF THIS INSTRUMENT.

THIS DURABLE GENERAL POWER OF ATTORNEY MAY BE REVOKED BY ME AT ANY TIME.

In Witness Whereof I have hereunto signed my name this _____ day of _____, 19__.

(YOU SIGN HERE:) ==>   _____
                                (SIGNATURE OF PRINCIPAL)

STATE OF NEW YORK)
) ss.:
COUNTY OF   )

On the _____ day of _____, 19__, before me personally came _____, to me known and known to be the individual described in and who executed the foregoing instrument and (s)he acknowledged to me that (s)he executed the same.

_____
Notary Public

§ 12.98   Power of Attorney to Take Effect at a Later Time

**DURABLE GENERAL POWER OF ATTORNEY
EFFECTIVE AT A FUTURE TIME
NEW YORK STATUTORY SHORT FORM**[1]

(CAUTION: THIS IS AN IMPORTANT DOCUMENT. IT GIVES THE PERSON WHOM YOU DESIGNATE (YOUR "AGENT") BROAD POWERS TO HANDLE YOUR PROPERTY DURING YOUR LIFETIME, WHICH MAY INCLUDE POWERS TO MORTGAGE, SELL, OR OTHERWISE DISPOSE OF ANY REAL OR PERSONAL PROPERTY WITHOUT ADVANCE NOTICE TO YOU OR APPROVAL BY YOU. THESE POWERS MAY ONLY BE USED AFTER A CERTIFICATION THAT YOU HAVE BECOME DISABLED, INCAPACITATED, OR INCOMPETENT OR THAT SOME OTHER EVENT HAS OCCURRED. THESE POWERS ARE EXPLAINED MORE FULLY IN NEW YORK GEN-

---

§ 12.98

1. Every statutory short form power of attorney effective at a future time, to be valid, must be written, typed or printed using letters which are in legible writing of or clear type of no less than twelve-point in size or if in writing a reasonable equivalent thereof and must contain, in bold face UPPER CASE OR UPPER AND LOWER CASE type or a reasonable equivalent thereof the "CAUTION" which is printed in bold face type at the beginning of the statutory form printed above and the "DIRECTIONS" which ARE printed in bold face type immediately before subdivisions (A) through (Q) of the statutory form printed above.

ERAL OBLIGATIONS LAW, ARTICLE 5, TITLE 15, SECTIONS 5–1502A THROUGH 5–1506, WHICH EXPRESSLY PERMITS THE USE OF ANY OTHER OR DIFFERENT FORM OF POWER OF ATTORNEY.

THIS DOCUMENT DOES NOT AUTHORIZE ANYONE TO MAKE MEDICAL OR OTHER HEALTH CARE DECISIONS. YOU MAY EXECUTE A HEALTH CARE PROXY TO DO THIS.

IF THERE IS ANYTHING ABOUT THIS FORM THAT YOU DO NOT UNDERSTAND, YOU SHOULD ASK A LAWYER TO EXPLAIN IT TO YOU.)

THIS IS intended to constitute a POWER OF ATTORNEY EFFECTIVE AT A FUTURE TIME pursuant to Article 5, Title 15 of the New York General Obligations Law:

I, _____

(insert YOUR name and address)

do hereby appoint:

_____

(If 1 person is to be appointed agent, insert the name and address of YOUR agent above)

_____
_____
_____

(If 2 or more persons are to be appointed agents BY YOU, insert THEIR NAMES and ADDRESSES above)

MY ATTORNEY(S)-IN–FACT TO ACT

(IF MORE THAN ONE AGENT IS DESIGNATED, CHOOSE ONE OF THE FOLLOWING TWO CHOICES BY PUTTING YOUR INITIALS IN ONE OF THE BLANK SPACES ( ) TO THE LEFT BY YOUR CHOICE:)

( ) EACH AGENT MAY SEPARATELY ACT.

( ) ALL AGENTS MUST ACT TOGETHER.

(IF NEITHER BLANK SPACE IS INITIALED, THE AGENTS WILL BE REQUIRED TO ACT TOGETHER)

TO TAKE EFFECT upon the occasion of the signing of a written statement EITHER:

(INSTRUCTIONS: COMPLETE OR OMIT SECTION (I)—OR—SECTION (II) BELOW BUT NEVER COMPLETE BOTH SECTION (I) AND (II) BELOW. IF YOU DO NOT COMPLETE EITHER SECTION (I) OR SECTION (II) BELOW, IT SHALL BE PRESUMED THAT YOU WANT THE PROVISIONS OF SECTION (I) BELOW TO APPLY)

(I) by a physician or physicians named herein by ME at this point:

§ 12.98   PURCHASE & SALE OF REAL ESTATE   Ch. 12

Dr. _____

(Insert Full Name(s) and Address(es) of Certifying Physician(s) Chosen BY YOU)

or if no physician or physicians are named hereinabove, OR IF THE PHYSICIAN OR PHYSICIANS NAMED HEREINABOVE ARE UNABLE TO ACT, by MY regular physician, or by a physician who has treated ME within one year preceding the date of such signing, or by a licensed psychologist or psychiatrist, certifying that I AM suffering from diminished capacity that would preclude ME from conducting MY affairs in a competent manner;

(II) by a person or persons named herein by ME at this point:

_____
_____

(Insert Full Name(s) and Address(es) of Certifying Person(s) Chosen BY YOU)

CERTIFYING that the following specified event has occurred:

_____
_____
_____
_____

(Insert hereinabove the specified event the certification of which will cause THIS POWER OF ATTORNEY to take effect)

IN MY NAME, PLACE AND STEAD in any way which I myself could do, if I were personally present, with respect to the following matters as each of them is defined in Title 15 of Article 5 of the New York General Obligations Law to the extent that I am permitted by law to act through an agent:

(DIRECTIONS: Initial in the BLANK SPACE TO THE LEFT OF YOUR CHOICE any one or more of the FOLLOWING LETTERED subdivisions as to which YOU WANT to give YOUR agent authority. If the blank space TO THE LEFT OF any particular LETTERED subdivision is NOT initialed, NO AUTHORITY WILL BE GRANTED for matters that are included in that subdivision. ALTERNATIVELY, THE LETTER CORRESPONDING TO EACH POWER YOU WISH TO GRANT MAY BE WRITTEN OR TYPED ON THE BLANK LINE IN SUBDIVISION "(Q)", AND YOU MAY THEN PUT YOUR INITIALS IN THE BLANK SPACE TO THE LEFT OF SUBDIVISION "(Q)" IN ORDER TO GRANT EACH OF THE POWERS SO INDICATED)

( ) (A) real estate transactions;
( ) (B) chattel and goods transactions;
( ) (C) bond, share and commodity transactions;
( ) (D) banking transactions;
( ) (E) business operating transactions;
( ) (F) insurance transactions;
( ) (G) estate transactions;
( ) (H) claims and litigation;
( ) (I) personal relationships and affairs;
( ) (J) benefits from military service;
( ) (K) records, reports and statements;
( ) (L) RETIREMENT BENEFIT TRANSACTIONS;
( ) (M) MAKING GIFTS TO MY SPOUSE, CHILDREN AND MORE REMOTE DESCENDANTS, AND PARENTS, NOT TO EXCEED IN THE AGGREGATE $10,000 TO EACH OF SUCH PERSONS IN ANY YEAR;
( ) (N) TAX MATTERS;
( ) (O) ALL OTHER MATTERS;
( ) (P) full and unqualified authority to my attorney(s)-in-fact to delegate any or all of the foregoing powers to any person or persons whom my attorney(s)-in-fact shall select;
( ) (Q) EACH OF THE ABOVE MATTERS IDENTIFIED BY THE FOLLOWING LETTERS: _____

(Special provisions and limitations may be included in the statutory short form power of attorney effective at a future time only if they conform to the requirements of Section 5–1503 of the New York General Obligations Law.)

_____
_____
_____

IF EVERY AGENT NAMED ABOVE IS UNABLE OR UNWILLING TO SERVE, I APPOINT

_____

(INSERT NAME AND ADDRESS OF SUCCESSOR)

TO BE MY AGENT FOR ALL PURPOSES HEREUNDER.

TO INDUCE ANY THIRD PARTY TO ACT HEREUNDER, I HEREBY AGREE THAT ANY THIRD PARTY RECEIVING A DULY EXECUTED COPY OR FACSIMILE OF THIS INSTRUMENT TOGETHER WITH A DULY EXECUTED COPY OR FACSIMILE OF THE WRITTEN STATEMENT OR STATEMENTS OF CERTIFICATION REQUIRED FOR THIS INSTRUMENT TO BE EFFECTIVE MAY ACT HEREUNDER, AND THAT THE SUSPENSION, REVOCATION OR TERMINATION HEREOF SHALL BE INEFFECTIVE AS TO SUCH THIRD PARTY UNLESS AND UNTIL ACTUAL NOTICE OR KNOWL-

EDGE OR SUCH SUSPENSION, REVOCATION OR TERMINATION SHALL HAVE BEEN RECEIVED BY SUCH THIRD PARTY, AND I FOR MYSELF AND FOR MY HEIRS, EXECUTORS, LEGAL REPRESENTATIVES AND ASSIGNS, HEREBY AGREE TO INDEMNIFY AND HOLD HARMLESS ANY SUCH THIRD PARTY FROM AND AGAINST ANY AND ALL CLAIMS THAT MAY ARISE AGAINST SUCH THIRD PARTY BY REASON OF SUCH THIRD PARTY HAVING RELIED ON THE PROVISIONS OF THIS INSTRUMENT.

THIS GENERAL POWER OF ATTORNEY EFFECTIVE AT A FUTURE TIME MAY BE REVOKED BY ME AT ANY TIME.

In Witness Whereof, I have hereunto signed my name this _____ day of _____, 19__.

(YOU SIGN HERE:) ==>   _____
                                        (SIGNATURE OF PRINCIPAL)

STATE OF NEW YORK)
) ss.:
COUNTY OF   )

On the _____ day of _____, 19__, before me personally came _____, to me known and known to be the individual described in and who executed the foregoing instrument and (s)he acknowledged to me that (s)he executed the same.

                              _____
                                        Notary Public

GENERAL PRACTICE IN NEW YORK

Volume 21

By

ROBERT L. OSTERTAG
HON. JAMES D. BENSON

Sections 7.1 to 12.98

1999 Pocket Part

Insert this Pocket Part in back of Volume

ST. PAUL, MINN.
WEST GROUP
1999

GENERAL PRACTICE IN NEW YORK
FORMS ON DISK™

The **Forms on Disk**™ which accompany these volumes provide instant access to WordPerfect 5.1/5.2 versions of the forms included in *General Practice in New York*. These electronic forms will save you hours of time drafting legal documents. The electronic forms can be loaded into your word processing software and formatted to match the document style of your law firm. These electronic forms become templates for you to use over and over without having to retype them each time.

The forms in Volumes 20, 21, 22, 23, 24 and 25 that are included on the accompanying disks are marked with the following disk icon for easy identification.

COPYRIGHT © 1999
By
WEST GROUP

This is the 1999 Pocket Part to Volume 21 of WEST'S NEW YORK PRACTICE SERIES

West's New York Practice Series

Vol. 1	Walker, et al., New York Limited Liability Companies and Partnerships: A Guide to Law and Practice
Vols. 2-4	Haig, et al., Commercial Litigation in New York State Courts
Vol. 5	Barker and Alexander, Evidence in New York State and Federal Courts
Vol. 6	Greenberg, Marcus, et al., New York Criminal Law
Vol. 7	Marks, et al., New York Pretrial Criminal Procedure
Vol. 8	Davies, Stecich, Gold, et al., New York Civil Appellate Practice
Vol. 9	Ginsberg, Weinberg, et al., Environmental Law and Regulation in New York
Vol. 10	Sobie, et al., New York Family Court Practice
Vols. 11-12	Scheinkman, et al., New York Law of Domestic Relation

Vol. 13	Taber, et al., Employment Litigation in New York
Vols. 14-16	Kreindler, Rodriguez, et al., New York Law of Torts
Vols. 17-19	Field, Moskin, et al., New York and Delaware Business Organizations: Choice, Formation, Operation, Financing and Acquisitions
Vols. 20-25	Ostertag, Benson, et al., General Practice in New York
Vol. 26	Borchers, Markell, et al., New York State Administrative Procedure and Practice
Vol. A	Borges, et al., Enforcing Judgments and Collecting Debts in New York
Vols. B-C	Bensel, Frank, McKeon, et al., Personal Injury Practice in New York
Vols. D-E	Preminger, et al., Trusts and Estates Practice in New York
Vols. F-G	Finkelstein and Ferrara, Landlord and Tenant Practice in New York

FOREWORD

Here is the first update to *General Practice in New York*, volume 21 of the New York Practice Series. The pocket part covers the significant changes in the applicable law from publication of the original volume until 1999. Many of the updates were prepared by one or more of the original chapter authors; others were editorially prepared in-house by West and are so indicated. With respect to chapters of the book not updated at all, West makes no representations with respect to the current status of ther material therein.

December 1999

COORDINATED RESEARCH IN NEW YORK FROM WEST

New York Practice 2d
David D. Siegel

Handling the DWI Case in New York
Peter Gerstenzang

New York Elder Law Practice
Vincent J. Russo and Marvin Rachlin

WEST'S McKINNEY'S FORMS

Civil Practice Law and Rules

Uniform Commercial Code

Business Corporation Law

Matrimonial and Family Law

Real Property Practice

Estates and Surrogate Practice

Criminal Procedure Law

Not-For-Profit Corporation Law

Tax Practice and Procedure

Local Government Forms

Selected Consolidated Law Forms

McKinney's Consolidated Laws of New York Annotated

West's New York Legal Update

New York Digest

New York Law Finder

PAMPHLETS

New York Civil Practice Law and Rules

New York Sentence Charts

Westlaw®

COORDINATED RESEARCH FROM WEST GROUP

WEST*Check*® and WESTMATE®

West CD–ROM Libraries™

To order any of these New York practice tools, call your West Group Representative or 1–800–328–9352.

NEED RESEARCH HELP?

If you have research questions concerning Westlaw or West Group Publications, call West Group's Reference Attorneys at 1–800–733–2889.

WESTLAW® ELECTRONIC RESEARCH GUIDE

Coordinating Legal Research with Westlaw

The *New York Practice Series* is an essential aid to legal research. Westlaw provides a vast, online library of over 8000 collections of documents and services that can supplement research begun in this publication, encompassing:

- Federal and state primary law (statutes, regulations, rules, and case law), including West's editorial enhancements, such as headnotes, Key Number classifications, annotations

- Secondary law resources (texts and treatises published by West Group and by other publishers, as well as law reviews)

- Legal news

- Directories of attorneys and experts

- Court records and filings

- Citators

Specialized topical subsets of these resources have been created for more than thirty areas of practice.

In addition to legal information, there are general news and reference databases and a broad array of specialized materials frequently useful in connection with legal matters, covering accounting, business, environment, ethics, finance, medicine, social and physical sciences.

This guide will focus on a few aspects of Westlaw use to supplement research begun in this publication, and will direct you to additional sources of assistance.

Databases

A database is a collection of documents with some features in common. It may contain statutes, court decisions, administrative materials, commentaries, news or other information. Each database has a unique identifier, used in many Westlaw commands to select a database of interest. For example, the database containing New York cases has the identifier NY-CS.

The Westlaw Directory is a comprehensive list of databases with information about each database, including the types of documents each contains. The first page of a standard or customized Westlaw Directory is displayed upon signing on to Westlaw, except when prior, saved re-

WESTLAW ELECTRONIC RESEARCH GUIDE

search is resumed. To access the Westlaw Directory at any time, enter DB.

Databases of potential interest in connection with your research include:

NY-AG	New York Attorney General Opinions
NYETH-EO	New York Ethics Opinions
NYETH-CS	Legal Ethics & Professional Responsibility - New York Cases
WLD-NY	West's Legal Directory - New York
LAWPRAC	The Legal Practice Database

For information as to currentness and search tips regarding any Westlaw database, enter the SCOPE command SC followed by the database identifier (e.g., SC NY-CS). It is not necessary to include the identifier to obtain scope information about the currently selected database.

Westlaw Highlights

Use of this publication may be supplemented through the Westlaw Bulletin (WLB), the Westlaw New York State Bulletin (WSB-NY) and various Topical Highlights. Highlights databases contain summaries of significant judicial, legislative and administrative developments and are updated daily; they are searchable both from an automatic list of recent documents and using general Westlaw search methods for documents accumulated over time. The full text of any judicial decision may be retrieved by entering FIND.

Consult the Westlaw Directory (enter DB) for a complete, current listing of highlights databases.

Retrieving a Specific Case

The FIND command can be used to quickly retrieve a case whose citation is known. For example:

FI 616 A.2d 1336

Updating Case Law Research

There are a variety of citator services on Westlaw for use in updating research.

KeyCite[SM] is an enhanced citator service that integrates all the case law on Westlaw. KeyCite provides direct and negative indirect history for any case within the scope of its coverage, citations to other decisions and secondary materials on Westlaw that have mentioned or discussed the cited case, and a complete integration with West Group's Key Number System so that you can track a legal issue explored in a case. KeyCite is as current as Westlaw and includes all cases on Westlaw, including unpublished opinions. To view the KeyCite history of a displayed

WESTLAW ELECTRONIC RESEARCH GUIDE

case, enter the command KC. To view the KeyCite information for a selected case, simply enter a command in the following form:

KC 113 SCT 2786

To see a complete list of publications covered by KeyCite, enter the command KC PUBS. To ascertain the scope of coverage, enter the command SC KC. For the complete list of commands available enter KC CMDS.

Retrieving Statutes, Court Rules and Regulations

Annotated and unannotated versions of the New York statutes are searchable on Westlaw (identifiers NY-ST-ANN and NY-ST), as are New York court rules (NY-RULES) and New York Administrative Code (NY-ADC).

The United States Code and United States Code - Annotated are searchable databases on Westlaw (identifiers USC and USCA, respectively), as are federal court rules (US-RULES) and regulations (CFR).

In addition, the FIND command may be used to retrieve specific provisions by citation, obviating the need for database selection or search. To FIND a desired document, enter FI, followed by the citation of the desired document, using the full name of the publication, or one of the abbreviated styles recognized by Westlaw.

If Westlaw does not recognize the style you enter, you may enter one of the following, using US, NY, or any other state code in place of XX:

FI XX-ST	Displays templates for codified statutes
FI XX-LEGIS	Displays templates for legislation
FI XX-RULES	Displays templates for rules
FI XX-ORDERS	Displays templates for court orders

Alternatively, entering FI followed by the publication's full name or an accepted abbreviation will normally display templates, useful jump possibilities, or helpful information necessary to complete the FIND process. For example:

FI USCA	Displays templates for United States Code - Annotated
FI FRAP	Displays templates for Federal Rules of Appellate Procedure
FI FRCP	Displays templates for Federal Rules of Civil Procedure
FI FRCRP	Displays templates for Federal Rules of Criminal Procedure
FI FRE	Displays templates for Federal Rules of Evidence
FI CFR	Displays templates for Code of Federal Regulations
FI FR	Displays templates for Federal Register

To view the complete list of FINDable documents and associated prescribed forms, enter FI PUBS.

WESTLAW ELECTRONIC RESEARCH GUIDE

Updating Research in re Statutes, Rules and Regulations

When viewing a statute, rule or regulation on Westlaw after a search or FIND command, it is easy to update your research. A message will appear on the screen if relevant amendments, repeals or other new material are available through the UPDATE feature. Entering the UPDATE command will display such material.

Documents used to update New York statutes are also searchable in New York Legislative Service (NY-LEGIS). Those used to update rules are searchable in New York Orders (NY-ORDERS).

Documents used to update federal statutes, rules, and regulations are searchable in the United States Public Laws (US-PL), Federal Orders (US-ORDERS) and Federal Register (FR) databases, respectively.

When documents citing a statute, rule or regulation are of interest, Shepard's Citations on Westlaw may be of assistance. That service covers federal constitutional provisions, statutes and administrative provisions, and corresponding materials from many states. The command SH PUBS displays a directory of publications which may be Shepardized on Westlaw. Consult the Westlaw manual for more information about citator services.

Using Westlaw as a Citator

For research beyond the coverage of any citator service, go directly to the databases (cases, for example) containing citing documents and use standard Westlaw search techniques to retrieve documents citing specific constitutional provisions, statutes, standard jury instructions or other authorities.

Fortunately, the specific portion of a citation is often reasonably distinctive, such as 22:636.1, 301.65, 401(k), 12-21-5, 12052. When it is, a search on that specific portion alone may retrieve applicable documents without any substantial number of inapplicable ones (unless the number happens to be coincidentally popular in another context).

Similarly, if the citation involves more than one number, such as 42 U.S.C.A. §1201, a search containing both numbers (e.g., 42 +5 1201) is likely to produce mostly desired information, even though the component numbers are common.

If necessary, the search may be limited in several ways:

A. Switch from a general database to one containing mostly cases within the subject area of the cite being researched;

WESTLAW ELECTRONIC RESEARCH GUIDE

B. Use a connector (&, /S, /P, etc.) to narrow the search to documents including terms which are highly likely to accompany the correct citation in the context of the issue being researched;

C. Include other citation information in the query. Because of the variety of citation formats used in documents, this option should be used primarily where other options prove insufficient. Below are illustrative queries for any database containing New York cases:

> N.Y.Const.! Const.! Constitution /s 6 VI +3 3

will retrieve cases citing the New York State Constitution, Art. 6, §3; and

> "Criminal Procedure Law" CPL /s 30.30

will retrieve cases citing Criminal Procedure Law §30.30.

Alternative Retrieval Methods

WIN® (Westlaw Is Natural™) allows you to frame your issue in plain English to retrieve documents:

> Does new trial motion extend (toll) the time for filing (taking) appeal?

Alternatively, retrieval may be focused by use of the Terms and Connectors method:

> TO(30) /P DI(NEW +1 TRIAL /P EXTEND!
> EXTENSION TOLL! /P APPEAL)

In databases with Key Numbers, either of the above examples will identify Appeal and Error ⟹345.1 as a Key Number collecting headnotes relevant to this issue if there are pertinent cases.

Since the Key Numbers are affixed to points of law by trained specialists based on conceptual understanding of the case, relevant cases that were not retrieved by either of the language-dependent methods will often be found at a Key Number.

Similarly, citations in retrieved documents (to cases, statutes, rules, etc.) may suggest additional, fruitful research using other Westlaw databases (e.g., annotated statutes, rules) or services (e.g., citator services).

Key Number Search

Frequently, case law research rapidly converges on a few topics, headings and Key Numbers within West's Key Number System that are likely to contain relevant cases. These may be discovered from known, relevant reported cases from any jurisdiction; Library References in West publications; browsing in a digest; or browsing the Key Number System on Westlaw using the JUMP feature or the KEY command.

WESTLAW ELECTRONIC RESEARCH GUIDE

Once discovered, topics, subheadings or Key Numbers are useful as search terms (in databases containing reported cases) alone or with other search terms, to focus the search within a narrow range of potentially relevant material.

For example, to retrieve cases with at least one headnote classified to Appeal and Error ⟲345.1, sign on to a caselaw database and enter

30k345.1 [use with other search terms, if desired]

The topic name (Appeal and Error) is replaced by its numerical equivalent (30) and the ⟲ by the letter k. A list of topics and their numerical equivalents is in the Westlaw Reference Manual and is displayed in Westlaw when the KEY command is entered.

Using JUMP

Westlaw's JUMP feature allows you to move from one document to another or from one part of a document to another, then easily return to your original place, without losing your original result. Opportunities to move in this manner are marked in the text with a JUMP symbol (▶). Whenever you see the JUMP symbol, you may move to the place designated by the adjacent reference by using the Tab, arrow keys or mouse click to position the cursor on the JUMP symbol, then pressing Enter or clicking again with the mouse.

Within the text of a court opinion, JUMP arrows are adjacent to case cites and federal statute cites, and adjacent to parenthesized numbers marking discussions corresponding to headnotes.

On a screen containing the text of a headnote, the JUMP arrows allow movement to the corresponding discussion in the text of the opinion,

▶ (3)

and allow browsing West's Key Number System beginning at various heading levels:

- ▶ 30   APPEAL AND ERROR
- ▶ 30VII   Transfer of Cause
- ▶ 30VII(A)   Time of Taking Proceedings
- ▶ 30k343   Commencement of Period of Limitation
- ▶ 30k345.1 k.   Motion for new trial.

To return from a JUMP, enter GB (except for JUMPs between a headnote and the corresponding discussion in opinion, for which there is a matching number in parenthesis in both headnote and opinion). Returns from successive JUMPs (e.g., from case to cited case to case cited by cited case) without intervening returns may be accomplished by repeated entry of GB or by using the MAP command.

WESTLAW ELECTRONIC RESEARCH GUIDE

General Information

The information provided above illustrates some of the ways Westlaw can complement research using this publication. However, this brief overview illustrates only some of the power of Westlaw. The full range of Westlaw search techniques is available to support your research.

Please consult the Westlaw Reference Manual for additional information or assistance or call West's Reference Attorneys at 1-800-REF-ATTY (1-800-733-2889).

For information about subscribing to Westlaw, please call 1-800-328-9352.

SUMMARY OF CONTENTS

Volume 20

Chapter	Page
1. Business Organizations: Corporations	2
2. Non-corporate Entities	16
3. Municipal Law	19
4. Municipal Law	21
6. Buying and Selling a Small Business	25

Volume 21

7. Consumer Law	2
8. Enforcement of Money Judgments	4
9. Bankruptcy	5
11. Mortgage Foreclosure	11
12. Purchase and Sale of Real Estate	25

Volume 22

14. Eminent Domain	2
15. Environmental Law	5
16. Land Use Law	8
17. Employment Law	14
18. Civil Rights Law	15
19. Immigration and Nationality Law Permanent Residence Applications	39
20. Adoptions	52

Volume 23

21. Domestic Relations	2
22. Guardianship	9
23. Elder Law	21
24. Estate Planning	30
25. Probate and Estate Administration	37
26. Personal Injury	51

Volume 24

28. Legal Malpractice	2
29. Medical Malpractice	20
30. Damages	21

SUMMARY OF CONTENTS

Chapter | **Page**
31. Insurance — 31
32. Workers' Compensation — 34
33. Local Criminal Court Practice — 39
34. Social Security Disability Cases — 50
35. Income Tax — 55
37. Civil Appellate Practice Before the Appellate Division and Other Intermediate Appellate Courts — 58

Volume 25

38. Criminal Appellate Practice Before the Appellate Division and Other Intermediate Appellate Courts — 2
39. Civil and Criminal Appeals to the Court of Appeals — 4

Table of Statutes — 5
Table of Rules and Regulations — 15
Table of Cases — 17
Index — 31

WEST'S NEW YORK PRACTICE SERIES

General Practice in New York

Volume 21

Chapter 7

CONSUMER LAW

(update prepared in-house)

Table of Sections

7.21   Automobile Leasing—The Consumer Leasing Act
7.25   Repossession—Prevention and Avoidance
7.26   ____ Defending Deficiency Claims
7.31   Credit Reporting—Consumer Rights
7.33   ____ Litigating Credit Reporting Matters

Westlaw Electronic Research

See Westlaw Electronic Research Guide preceding the Summary of Contents.

§ 7.21   Automobile Leasing—The Consumer Leasing Act

PAGE 34:

[*Re-write* **CAVEAT** *in note 14 as follows.*]

14. The Statute of Limitations under the CLA is one year from termination of the lease. 15 U.S.C.A. § 1667d(c).

§ 7.25 Repossession—Prevention and Avoidance

PAGE 48:

[*In note 7 and the* **PRACTICE POINTER**, *replace citations to Personal Property Law § 403(4) with citations to Personal Property Law § 403(2)(b).*]

§ 7.26 Repossession—Defending Deficiency Claims

PAGE 50:

[*In note 3, replace citation to Personal Property Law § 403(4) with citation to Personal Property Law § 403(2)(b).*]

[*In note 8, in the* **PRACTICE POINTER**, *the citation to Personal Property Law § 339 should be to Personal Property Law § 340(1).*]

§ 7.31 Credit Reporting—Consumer Rights

PAGE 61:

[*Add to end of note 5.*]

5. The 1996 amendments to 15 U.S.C.A. § 1681c(b) have changed the cited dollar figure from $50,000 to $150,000. Note that General Business Law § 380–j(f)(1)-(2) keeps the $50,000 figure and also allows bankruptcies to be reported for fourteen years.

[*Replace first paragraph of note 6 with the following.*]

6. 15 U.S.C.A. § 1681b permits credit reporting agencies to disclose credit reports only to a party designated by the consumer to whom it relates (15 U.S.C.A. § 1681b(b)(2)) or to any other person who intends to use the information in connection with a credit transaction, employment, or an insurance policy involving the consumer, or who "otherwise has a legitimate business need for the information ... in connection with a business transaction that is initiated by the consumer" (15 U.S.C.A. § 1681b(a)(3)(F)). *See also*, General Business Law § 380–b.

PAGE 63:

11. *See* Sepulvado v. CSC Credit Services, Inc., 158 F.3d 890, 896 (5th Cir.1998), *cert. denied*, ___ U.S. ___, 119 S.Ct. 1344, 143 L.Ed.2d 507 (1999) (holding that completeness is not required for its own sake, but merely to ensure accuracy; an accurate though incomplete report is acceptable).

§ 7.33 Credit Reporting—Litigating Credit Reporting Matters

PAGE 66:

[*Updated citation is 56 F.3d 469 (2d Cir.1995), cert. denied 517 U.S. 1150, 116 S.Ct. 1452, 134 L.Ed.2d 571 (1996).*]

Chapter 8

ENFORCEMENT OF MONEY JUDGMENTS

(update prepared in-house)

Table of Sections

8.1 Scope Note

Westlaw Electronic Research

See Westlaw Electronic Research Guide preceding the Summary of Contents.

§ 8.1 Scope Note

PAGE 184:

[*Replace note 20 with the following.*]

20. *See* Chapter 12 "Purchase and Sale of Real Property," *infra*.

[*Replace note 21 with the following.*]

21. CPLR Article 50–A. *See* Chapter 29 "Medical Malpractice," *infra*.

[*Replace note 22 with the following.*]

22. CPLR Article 50–B. *See* Chapter 26 "Personal Injury," *infra*.

Chapter 9

BANKRUPTCY

(update prepared in-house)

Table of Sections

9.1	Scope Note
9.2	Strategy
9.3	___ Checklist for Representing a Debtor
9.7	Eligibility to File
9.18	Jurisdiction of the Bankruptcy Court
9.19	___ Types of Jurisdiction
9.49	Property of the Estate
9.62	Use, Sale, or Lease of Property—Outside Ordinary Course of Business
9.102	Claims Procedures—Interest on Claims and Charges Against Secured Claims
9.107	Subordination
9.109	Setoff
9.138	Chapter 11—Appointment of a Trustee
9.170	___ Discharge
9.208	Chapter 7—Discharge—Procedure for Objections to Discharge of Particular Debts
9.209	___ Conversion or Dismissal of Cases
9.249	Chapter 13—Plan—Discretionary Provisions: Debtor's Principal Residence
9.251	___ Plan—Confirmation

Westlaw Electronic Research

See Westlaw Electronic Research Guide preceding the Summary of Contents.

---

§ 9.1 Scope Note

PAGE 259:

[*Insert at beginning of section.*]

NOTE: Chapter 12 of Title 11 has been repealed, effective 1998 (with temporary re-enactment through April 1999) "but that all cases commenced or pending under this chapter, and all matters and proceedings in and related to such cases, shall be conducted and determined under this chapter as if such chapter had not been repealed." 11 U.S.C.A. Ch. 12, Refs and Annos. Please delete all references and citations to Chapter 12, including §§ 9.212–9.235, in this chapter.

§ 9.2 Strategy

PAGE 265:

[Replace last full sentence of note 6 with the following.]

6. The amount of the fee ranges from $250 through $10,000 and depends upon the total amount of disbursements made by the debtor for each quarter.

§ 9.3 Strategy—Checklist for Representing a Debtor

PAGE 268:

4. *But see* In re Shea & Gould, 214 B.R. 739, 744 (Bankr.S.D.N.Y.1997) (holding that a partnership that is in dissolution is eligible to file for Chapter 11 relief if it is in dissolution in order to "to wind up its affairs and liquidate its assets—not to reorganize them;" the court also rejected as dictum the part of the opinion in In re C–TC 9th Avenue Partnership that said that any partnership in dissolution is ineligible for Chapter 11). Shea & Gould is not unanimously accepted. In In re Hagerstown Fiber Ltd. Partnership, 226 B.R. 353, 358 (Bankr. S.D.N.Y.1998), the court approved C–TC's "bright line" rule over Shea & Gould.

§ 9.7 Eligibility to File

PAGE 272:

3. However, In re Shea & Gould, 214 B.R. 739 (Bankr.S.D.N.Y.1997) rejected as dictum the part of the opinion in In re C–TC 9th Avenue Partnership that said that any partnership in dissolution is ineligible for Chapter 11. Shea held that whereas a partnership seeking to reorganize may not file for Chapter 11 relief, a partnership seeking to wind up its affairs may file. Shea & Gould is not unanimously accepted. In In re Hagerstown Fiber Ltd. Partnership, 226 B.R. 353, 358 (Bankr.S.D.N.Y.1998), the court approved C–TC's "bright line" rule over Shea & Gould.

§ 9.18 Jurisdiction of the Bankruptcy Court

PAGE 280:

[In footnote 2, in page's first full paragraph, first updated citation is Seminole Tribe of Florida v. Florida, 517 U.S. 44, 116 S.Ct. 1114, 134 L.Ed.2d 252 (1996). Second updated citation is Ohio Agricultural Commodity Depositors Fund v. Mahern, 517 U.S. 1130, 116 S.Ct. 1411, 134 L.Ed.2d 537 (1996).]

[In footnote 2, in page's second full paragraph, in first sentence, eliminate the phrase "...in the only circuit court decision to date implementing Seminole in the bankruptcy context".]

[Add to end of footnote 2.]

2. Cases decided after Creative Goldsmiths have gone the other way, and the Fourth Circuit remains the only circuit to date that has declared Bankruptcy Code § 106 unconstitutional. In re Willis, 230 B.R. 619, 623 (Bankr.E.D.Okla.1999), declined to follow Creative Goldsmiths and held that since "the Bankruptcy Code has a vast number of privileges and immunities which are enforceable through the Fourteenth Amendment," Congress had the power to abrogate the states' sovereign immunity through the Bankruptcy Code. In re Arecibo Community Health Care, Inc., 233 B.R. 625, 630 (D.Puerto Rico 1999) has distinguished between states' immunity being abrogated and being deemed waived. Interpreting Creative Goldsmiths as holding only that abrogations of state immunity unconstitutional, the Arecibo opinion held that Bankruptcy Code § 106 could still be constitutional if viewed as a waiver. A state's immunity would be deemed waived if it filed a proof of claim and affirmatively became involved in bankruptcy proceedings. This is because "it

would be highly inequitable for a state to be able to reap the benefits of filing a proof of claim and receiving monies from the estate, if unlike all other creditors, it would not be liable for any amounts that it owed to the estate." However, a state could preserve its immunity by not affirmatively acting and not filing a proof of claim in the first place. *See also* In re Straight, 143 F.3d 1387, 1392 (10th Cir.1998).

§ 9.19 Jurisdiction of the Bankruptcy Court—Types of Jurisdiction

PAGE 283:

4. The bankruptcy court also has jurisdiction where claims on other grounds are inseparable from the bankruptcy claim. *See* In re Southmark Corp., 163 F.3d 925, 930 (5th Cir.1999), *cert. denied* ___ U.S. ___, 119 S.Ct. 2339, 144 L.Ed.2d 236 (1999) (holding that since professional malpractice claims alleged against accountant were inseparable from bankruptcy context, the bankruptcy court could take jurisdiction).

6. *But see* Matter of FedPak Systems, Inc., 80 F.3d 207, 213 (7th Cir.1996) (limiting bankruptcy court jurisdiction and redefining "related to" jurisdiction to "dispute[s] affect[ing] the amount of property for distribution ... or the allocation of property among creditors") (internal citations and quotations omitted); In re White Trailer Corp., 222 B.R. 322, 325 (Bankr. N.D.Ind.1998) (attacking the "could conceivably have any effect" language as too broad and requiring instead "a direct effect upon either the assets of the estate or their distribution to creditors").

[*In note 8, updated citation is In re Dow Corning Corp., 86 F.3d 482 (6th Cir.1996), cert. denied 519 U.S. 1071, 117 S.Ct. 718, 136 L.Ed.2d 636 (1997).*]

§ 9.49 Property of the Estate

PAGE 310:

[*In note 1, add to end of carryover paragraph on page 310.*]

1. *But see* In re Dubroff, 119 F.3d 75 (2d Cir.1997) (holding that IRAs are exempt from distribution under the Bankruptcy Code; a subsequent statutory amendment failed to prove that IRAs were not exempt under previous statute, so IRA in case arising under old statute was exempt).

[*Replace quoted paragraph with the following.*]

[A]ll trusts, custodial accounts, annuities, insurance contracts, monies, assets or interests established as part of, and all payments from, either any trust or plan, which is qualified as an individual retirement account under section four hundred eight or section four hundred eight A of the United States Internal Revenue Code of 1986, as amended, or a Keogh (HR-10), retirement or other plan established by a corporation, which is qualified under section 401 of the United States Internal Revenue Code of 1986, as amended, or created as a result of rollovers from such plans pursuant to sections 402 (a) (5), 403 (a) (4), 408 (d) (3) or 408A of the Internal Revenue Code of 1986, as amended ... shall be conclusively presumed to be spendthrift trusts under this section and the common law of the state of New York for all purposes, including ... all cases arising under or related to a case arising under ... the United States Bankruptcy Code.

§ 9.62 Use, Sale, or Lease of Property—Outside Ordinary Course of Business

PAGE 320:

4. Add to the end of the footnote: *But see* Matter of Tiara Motorcoach Corp., 212 B.R. 133 (Bankr.N.D.Ind.1997) (rejecting Integrated Resources standard in favor of standard set out in S.N.A. Nut Company, 186 B.R. 98, 104 (Bankr.N.D.Ill.1995); that rule determined the propriety of break-up fees in bankruptcy cases by asking "whether the interests of all concerned parties are best served by such a fee").

§ 9.102 Claims Procedures—Interest on Claims and Charges Against Secured Claims

PAGE 355:

[*In note 10, updated citation is* Orix Credit Alliance, Inc. v. Delta Resources, Inc. (In re Delta Resources, Inc.), *54 F.3d 722 (11th Cir.1995), cert. denied 516 U.S. 980, 116 S.Ct. 488, 133 L.Ed.2d 415 (1995).*]

§ 9.107 Subordination

PAGE 362:

[*In note 21, updated citation is* United States v. Noland, *517 U.S. 535, 116 S.Ct. 1524, 134 L.Ed.2d 748 (1996).*]

PAGE 363:

[*In note 21, updated citation is* United States v. Reorganized CF & I Fabricators, *518 U.S. 213, 116 S.Ct. 2106, 135 L.Ed.2d 506 (1996).*]

[*In note 22, updated citation is* In re Envirodyne Indus., Inc., *79 F.3d 579 (7th Cir.1996), cert. denied 519 U.S. 821, 117 S.Ct. 77, 136 L.Ed.2d 36 (1996).*]

§ 9.109 Setoff

PAGE 366:

3. *See* In re Holden, 217 B.R. 161, 166 (D.Vt.1997) (holding that even under Strumpf, "a temporary freeze on funds in which a creditor has a good faith basis for asserting a right of setoff, and which is promptly followed by a request for relief from stay, maintains the status quo" and therefore is not a violation of the automatic stay).

§ 9.138 Chapter 11—Appointment of a Trustee

PAGE 393:

1. *But see* In re Altman, 230 B.R. 6, 16 (Bankr.D.Conn.1999) (applied preponderance of evidence standard; following Grogan v. Garner, 498 U.S. 279, 286–291, 111 S.Ct. 654, 659–661, 112 L.Ed.2d 755 (1991), the court held that "in the absence of an express congressional direction to apply a higher standard of proof, the test should generally be the preponderance of the evidence").

§ 9.170 Chapter 11—Discharge

PAGE 429:

[*In* note 2, updated citation is Resorts International, Inc. v. Lowenschuss (In re Lowenschuss), 67 F.3d 1394, 1401 (9th Cir.1995), cert. denied 517 U.S. 1243, 116 S.Ct. 2497, 135 L.Ed.2d 189 (1996).]

§ 9.208 Chapter 7—Discharge—Procedure for Objections to Discharge of Particular Debts

PAGE 456:

[*In* the carryover paragraph beginning on page 456, the updated citation is American Express Travel Related Services v. Hashemi (In re Hashemi), 104 F.3d 1122 (9th Cir.1996), cert. denied 520 U.S. 1230, 117 S.Ct. 1824, 137 L.Ed.2d 1031 (1997).]

§ 9.209 Chapter 7—Conversion or Dismissal of Cases

PAGE 459:

[*In* note 9, add to the left hand column, 2 lines from the bottom, right before "A court in New York has noted...".]

9. *See* In re Gomes, 220 B.R. 84, 87 (Bankr.Cal.1998) (citing In re Kelly, 841 F.2d at 915, held that a debtor's ability to pay his debts, standing alone, can support the conclusion of substantial abuse; also held that "Congress did not specify a threshold percentage or formula for determining what constitutes the "ability" to pay one's debts").

§ 9.249 Chapter 13—Plan—Discretionary Provisions: Debtor's Principal Residence

PAGE 481:

1. *But see* In re Reeves, 221 B.R. 756, 760 (Bankr.C.D.Ill.1998) (holding that § 1322(c)(2), while not completely superseding Nobleman, does permit "the bifurcation of an undersecured mortgage on a Chapter 13 debtor's principal residence when the last payment on the original payment schedule is due before the final payment under the [debtors'] plan is due").

§ 9.251 Chapter 13—Plan—Confirmation

PAGE 485:

[*In* note 3, insert right before the last paragraph on the page.]

3. *See* In re Donley, 217 B.R. 1004, 1006 (Bankr.S.D.Ohio 1998) (holding that the replacement-value standard for valuing retained collateral does not apply in context of redemption under Chapter 7 because "application of the replacement value standard does not reflect the purpose of the valuation and the proposed disposition or use of such property in the context of redemption under chapter 7") (internal punctuation omitted). Donley applied its own standard in place of the replacement-value standard: the retained collateral would be valued at "what [a creditor] would receive if the redemption did not occur and it were forced to repossess and to sell the [property]in the most beneficial manner it could." *Id.* at 1007.

§ 9.251 BANKRUPTCY Ch. 9

[*The updated citation for the Taffi case in the last paragraph on the page is Taffi v. United States (In re Taffi), 96 F.3d 1190 (9th Cir.1996) (en banc), cert. denied 521 U.S. 1103, 117 S.Ct. 2478, 138 L.Ed.2d 987 (1997).*]

Chapter 11

MORTGAGE FORECLOSURE

by
Robert A. Wolf

Table of Sections

11.8a Non–Judicial Foreclosure of Commercial Mortgages: The New Article 14 of the Real Property Actions and Proceedings Law
11.8b The New RPAPL Article 14—When Applicable
11.8c ____ When Not Applicable
11.8d Commencement of the Non–Judicial Foreclosure Proceeding—Purchase of Index Number and Filing of Notice of Pendency
11.8e The Notice of Intention to Foreclose
11.8f The Non–Judicial Foreclosure—Notice of Sale
11.8g ____ Service of the Notice of Sale
11.8h ____ Publication of the Notice of Sale
11.8i ____ Conducting of the Sale
11.8j Conveyance of the Property by "Power of Sale Deed"
11.8k Distribution of the Proceeds of the Non–Judicial Sale
11.8l Report of the Non–Judicial Foreclosure Sale
11.8m Surplus Money and Deficiency Judgment Proceedings Under Article 14
11.8n Receivership Under RPAPL Article 14
11.8o The Right to Convert the Article 14 Non–Judicial Foreclosure to a Judicial Foreclosure Under Article 13

Westlaw Electronic Research
See Westlaw Electronic Research Guide preceding the Summary of Contents.

PAGE 701:

[*Add as new sections.*]

§ 11.8a Non–Judicial Foreclosure of Commercial Mortgages: The New Article 14 of the Real Property Actions and Proceedings Law

On July 7, 1998, Governor Pataki signed into law a new Article 14 of the New York Real Property Actions and Proceedings Law ("RPAPL") authorizing non-judicial foreclosure of commercial mortgages under certain delineated circumstances.[1] The new Article 14, labeled "Foreclosure of Mortgage by Power of Sale," replaced the rarely used former version of RPAPL Article 14 that had been titled "Foreclosure of Mortgage by Advertisement."

§ 11.8a

The impetus for the new legislation was the growing concern, exacerbated by the experience of the real estate recession during the late 1980's and early 1990's, that the myriad of time-consuming steps and procedures required to complete a judicial mortgage foreclosure under Article 13 of the RPAPL, even in instances where the foreclosure was uncontested, was dissuading lenders from continuing to invest in mortgage lending on New York real estate.[2]

Accordingly, a special task force of the New York State Bar Association's Real Property Section took the initiative in drafting proposed legislation to allow non-judicial foreclosure of mortgages under certain specified conditions.[3] The ultimate new statutory scheme that was enacted after refinement of the initial drafts, provides for an expedited, non-judicial foreclosure alternative with respect to commercial mortgages, while at the same time furnishing judicial safeguards for borrowers and other interested parties possessing legitimate defenses to foreclosure. Moreover, the new Article 14 contains a statutorily-approved form of "power of sale" foreclosure deed that enables a purchaser of property foreclosed non-judicially under the statute to obtain marketable, insurable title.

Obviously wishing to give the new statute a trial period, the Legislature provided therein that the new Article 14 is to remain in effect until July 1, 2001, when, unless it is renewed, it shall be deemed repealed.[4]

Set forth below is a discussion of the salient provisions of the new RPAPL Article 14.

1. Richard S. Fries, "Amendment to RPAPL Article 14 Allows Non-Judicial Foreclosure of Commercial Mortgages," *New York State Bar Journal* (Dec. 1998) at 50.
2. *Id.*
3. *Id.*
4. 1998 N.Y. Laws ch. 231, § 2.

§ 11.8b The New RPAPL Article 14—When Applicable

The new Article 14 of the RPAPL is applicable essentially to those mortgages affecting commercial property which contain a so-called "power of sale" provision, i.e., a provision stating that upon a default under the mortgage or under the note or bond secured thereby, the mortgagee has the right to sell the mortgaged property.[1] Most commercial mortgages, including those entered into even before the enactment of the new RPAPL Article 14, contain such a simple, straightforward provision, which, without more, suffices to bring the mortgage under the rubric of the statute. Nevertheless, so that there is no question as to the availability of the new non-judicial foreclosure remedy, it is strongly suggested that practitioners, in henceforth drafting commercial mortgages, add to their standard "power of sale" provision language authorizing the lender to avail itself of the procedures set forth in RPAPL Article 14.

1. RPAPL § 1401(1).

§ 11.8c The New RPAPL Article 14—When Not Applicable

Making clear that the new Article 14 is only applicable to commercial mortgages, RPAPL § 1401(1) specifically excludes mortgages upon the following residential properties from the scope of the statutory scheme:

1. A residential building containing fewer than six (6) dwelling units.[1]

2. A residential condominium unit in a residential condominium building.[2]

3. A residential cooperative building.[3]

4. A building containing 65% or more residential tenancies located in a city containing a population of one million or more (i.e., New York City).[4]

An additional provision of the statute states that non-judicial foreclosure is also not available where the mortgagee seeks to foreclose the interests of any tenants in any leases for residential units at the mortgaged property.[5]

1. RPAPL § 1401(1)(A).
2. RPAPL § 1401(1)(B).
3. RPAPL § 1401(1)(C).
4. RPAPL § 1401(1)(D).
5. RPAPL § 1401(2).

§ 11.8d Commencement of the Non-Judicial Foreclosure Proceeding—Purchase of Index Number and Filing of Notice of Pendency

Notwithstanding the non-judicial nature of the foreclosure proceeding under RPAPL Article 14, the statute provides for the existence of a court file in which all of the requisite papers during the course of the proceeding will be filed and maintained. Accordingly, as in the case of a judicial foreclosure, the mortgagee must purchase an index number from the court of the county in which the mortgaged property is located in order to set up the file for the non-judicial proceeding.[1]

The mortgagee then files with the clerk of the county in which the mortgaged property is located a Notice of Pendency of the non-judicial foreclosure proceeding.[2] The filing of the Notice of Pendency commences the non-judicial foreclosure proceeding.[3]

The Notice of Pendency must specify the following:

1. The date of the mortgage.
2. The parties to the mortgage.
3. The time and place of the recordation of the mortgage.
4. The name of the record owner of the mortgaged property.
5. The name of any subordinate liens or holders of subordinate interests in the mortgaged property entitled to service of notice of the non-judicial foreclosure sale (see *infra*, § 11.8g).

§ 11.8d MORTGAGE FORECLOSURE Ch. 11

6. That the object of the non-judicial proceeding is for foreclosure of the mortgage by power of sale.

7. A designation of the mortgaged property, including the number of each block and lot on the county land or tax map which is the subject of the foreclosure proceeding.[4]

The Notice of Pendency binds all of those who acquire liens and/or other interests in the mortgaged property subsequent to the filing of such Notice to the non-judicial foreclosure of their liens and interests without the necessity of having to serve them with a notice of the non-judicial foreclosure sale.[5]

1. RPAPL § 1403(1).
2. RPAPL § 1403(1).
3. RPAPL § 1403(2).
4. RPAPL § 1403(1).
5. RPAPL § 1403(4).

§ 11.8e The Notice of Intention to Foreclose

Within ten (10) days of the filing of the Notice of Pendency, the mortgagee must serve, along with a copy of the Notice of Pendency, a written Notice of Intention to Foreclose. The latter Notice must be served upon the mortgagor, the obligor on the mortgage note, the owner of the mortgaged property (if different than the mortgagor) and any other person or entity having a subordinate lien or interest in the property. Such service must be effected either by (i) both certified or registered mail and ordinary first-class mail, or by (ii) personal service in the same manner as service of a summons.[1]

The Notice of Intention to Foreclose is required to set forth, among other things, the following matters:

- the identification of the mortgage by the parties thereto, the execution and recordation dates thereof, and any recorded amendments and modifications thereof;[2]

- the nature of, and if monetary, also the amounts of, the defaults under the mortgage;[3]

- a statement that the mortgagee has made demand for curing of the default(s), if such demand is required under the loan documents, and that the mortgagee has declared the entire loan indebtedness immediately due and payable (i.e., that the mortgagee has accelerated the loan indebtedness), by written notice to the mortgagor;[4]

- the amount of the outstanding principal balance, the amount of accrued interest thereon and the approximate amount of other sums due under the mortgage;[5]

- a statement that the interests in the mortgaged property of the mortgagor and of all others having subordinate interests therein who have been served with a copy of the Notice of Intention to Foreclose will be terminated by foreclosure of the mortgage by power of sale pursuant to Article 14 and that such persons and entities may thereafter be evicted from the property by judicial process;[6]

- a statement that the mortgagor and any subordinate interest holders may have a right to surplus monies from the foreclosure sale proceeds in accordance with RPAPL § 1418, and if a deficiency judgment is available under the loan documents, that the mortgagee shall have a right to seek same pursuant to RPAPL § 1419 (see *infra*, § 11.8m);[7]

- a statement of the rights and remedies that the mortgagor and subordinate lienors and interest holders have under RPAPL § 1421 in certain circumstances, to convert the non-judicial foreclosure to a judicial foreclosure proceeding conducted in accordance with RPAPL Article 13 (see *infra*. § 11.8o);[8] and

- where a governmental entity is entitled to such notice, specificity as to the nature of the governmental entity's interest or lien in the mortgaged property.[9]

Affidavits of service of the Notice of Intention to Foreclose upon all those served with same must be filed prior the date of the foreclosure sale with the appropriate county clerk under the index number of the non-judicial proceeding.[10]

1. RPAPL § 1402(1).
2. RPAPL § 1402(2)(A).
3. RPAPL § 1402(2)(B).
4. RPAPL § 1402(2)(C).
5. RPAPL § 1402(2)(D).
6. RPAPL § 1402(2)(E).
7. RPAPL § 1402(2)(F).
8. RPAPL § 1402(2)(G).
9. RPAPL § 1402(2)(H).
10. RPAPL § 1402(3).

§ 11.8f The Non-Judicial Foreclosure—Notice of Sale

The next set of steps in this non-judicial foreclosure process involves the service, filing and advertising of the Notice of Sale, followed by the conducting of the non-judicial sale itself.

The Notice of Sale in an Article 14 proceeding must specify the following:

1. The names of the mortgagor, the record owner of the mortgaged property (if different than the mortgagor), the mortgagee and any assignee of the mortgagee;[1]

2. The execution date of the mortgage, the recordation date thereof, the place of recordation, the book and page numbers in which it was recorded and recordation information as to any assignment(s) of the mortgage;[2]

3. The identity of holders of subordinate liens and interests in the mortgaged property and the nature of such liens and interests;[3]

4. The outstanding principal sum claimed due under the mortgage, the amount of accrued interest thereon, the amount of late charges, other sums due under the mortgage and any sums advanced by the mortgagee recoverable under the mortgage, including the costs of sale and reasonable attorneys' fees and disbursements;[4]

5. The legal description of the mortgaged property, the street address thereof and the tax block and lot or other tax map identification;[5]

§ 11.8f MORTGAGE FORECLOSURE Ch. 11

6. In the event the mortgaged property is comprised of two or more distinct parcels, then, unless the mortgage provides that the parcels shall be sold as one, a specification as to the order in which the parcels shall be sold at foreclosure;[6]

7. The right of the owner of the mortgaged property to redeem same up to the time of the sale, by paying to the mortgagee each of the amounts and sums set forth in item 4 above;[7] and

8. The date, place and time of the foreclosure sale.[8]

1. RPAPL § 1404(1).
2. RPAPL § 1404(2).
3. RPAPL § 1404(3).
4. RPAPL § 1404(4).
5. RPAPL § 1404(5).
6. RPAPL § 1404(6).
7. RPAPL § 1404(7).
8. RPAPL § 1404(8).

§ 11.8g The Non-Judicial Foreclosure—Service of the Notice of Sale

A copy of the Notice of Sale has to be served upon the mortgagor, the obligor on the mortgage note, the owner of the mortgaged property (if different than the mortgagor), any holder of a subordinate lien or interest in the mortgaged property whom the mortgagee seeks to foreclose and any other person or entity designated by the terms of the mortgage to receive such notice.[1]

Service upon each of the foregoing must be effected at least thirty (30) days prior to the date of the foreclosure sale by delivering a copy of the Notice of Sale in the manner prescribed for personal service of a summons and by mailing an additional copy by first class mail in an envelope bearing the legend "Personal and Confidential" and not indicating on the outside of the envelope that the communication is from an attorney or concerns an action or proceeding against the one being served.[2] Alternatively, service of the Notice of Sale upon the mortgagor, the mortgagor's assigns or a subsequent grantee of the mortgaged property from the mortgagor in accordance with the service method prescribed in the mortgage is an acceptable method of service.[3] Service of the Notice of Sale upon the United States of America or any agency thereof must be in accordance with applicable federal statute(s).[4]

Affidavits of service of the Notice of Sale must be filed prior to the date of the sale under the index number of the non-judicial proceeding.[5]

1. RPAPL § 1405(1).
2. RPAPL § 1406(1).
3. RPAPL § 1406(2).
4. RPAPL § 1406(3).
5. RPAPL § 1405(1).

§ 11.8h The Non-Judicial Foreclosure—Publication of the Notice of Sale

A copy of the Notice of Sale must be published at least once a week during the five (5) successive weeks immediately preceding the date of the sale, or alternatively, at least twice a week during the four (4) successive weeks immediately preceding the sale date. Such publication is required to appear in a newspaper of general circulation distributed in the county in which the mortgage property is located, or if no such newspaper is distributed in such county, then in such a paper distributed in an adjoining county. The statutory exception to the foregoing is for the counties of New York City, as to which publication is required to be made in the same manner as a notice of a judicial proceeding in a newspaper within the particular county of the city to be designated by the clerk of that county.[1]

Also, a copy of the Notice of Sale must be filed on or before the date of the first publication thereof with the clerk of the county or counties in which the mortgaged property is located.[2]

1. RPAPL § 1405(2).
2. RPAPL § 1405(3).

§ 11.8i The Non-Judicial Foreclosure—Conducting of the Sale

The non-judicial foreclosure sale must be held at any courthouse located in the county which is the situs of the mortgaged property. The one exception to the foregoing is once again for the counties of New York City, as to which the pertinent statutory provision requires that the sale take place at the courthouse of the Supreme Court for the particular New York City county.[1]

The sale must be conducted by a licensed auctioneer, sheriff, marshal or court-appointed official for that purpose. The sale must take place during reasonable business hours, on a day other than a Saturday, a Sunday or a public holiday.[2]

With regard to scheduling, if publication of the Notice of Sale was twice a week for four (4) weeks, then the sale must take place between, inclusively, the twenty-eighth (28th) day and the thirty-fifth (35th) day after the first publication date. If publication was once a week for five (5) weeks, then the sale must take place between, inclusively, the thirty-fifth day (35th) and the forty-second (42nd) day after the first publication date.[3]

The statutorily-authorized person conducting the sale is obligated to announce the terms thereof at the outset of the auction sale. A copy of the terms of sale must be made available by the mortgagee or person conducting the sale at or prior to the sale.[4]

If the successful bidder at the sale is other than the mortgagee, that bidder must deposit at the sale's conclusion at least ten per cent (10%) of the bid price, in cash, certified check or bank check, with the person who conducted the sale. At the same time, a memorandum of the sale, incorporating the terms of the sale, must be executed by the person conducting the sale and by the successful bidder. This memorandum must also state the identity of the successful bidder, the amount of this successful bid, the amount of the deposit and the date, time and place of

§ 11.8i MORTGAGE FORECLOSURE Ch. 11

the scheduled closing for a conveyance of the "power of sale" deed to the successful bidder (see *infra*, § 11.8j). Pending the conveyance to the successful bidder of title to the foreclosed property, the person who conducted the sale is required to deposit the bid price down payment in a separate account in a commercial bank or savings bank located in New York State.[5]

1. RPAPL § 1408(1).
2. RPAPL § 1408(1).
3. RPAPL § 1408(2).
4. RPAPL § 1408(3).
5. RPAPL § 1408(4).

§ 11.8j Conveyance of the Property by "Power of Sale Deed"

One of the most laudatory features of the new RPAPL Article 14 is that it sets forth verbatim in one of its provisions the precise form of the deed instrument that is to be executed and delivered by the authorized person who conducted the non-judicial foreclosure sale to the purchaser at the sale.[1] The form of that deed instrument, which is labeled in the statute a "Power of Sale Deed," is as follows:

POWER OF SALE DEED

THIS DEED, made as of the _____ day of _____, _____, between _____, in the capacity of auctioneer/sheriff/marshal/referee, having an office at _____, _____, New York ("Grantor") and _____, a _____ having an address at _____, _____ ("Grantee"),

WITNESSETH:

That _____ ("Mortgagee"), the owner and holder of the mortgage described in Exhibit A attached hereto encumbering the property described hereinbelow (the "Property"), and the note, bond or other obligation secured thereby, has foreclosed the lien of said mortgage pursuant to article fourteen of the real property actions and proceedings law of the state of New York;

That Grantor has been designated by Mortgagee or by the court in the county in which the sale has taken place to conduct the sale of the Property;

That the sale was duly held on _____ _____, _____, and the memorandum of sale attached hereto as Exhibit B was executed at the conclusion of the sale;

And that pursuant thereto and in consideration of _____ Dollars ($_____) paid by Grantee, being the highest sum bid at the sale, Grantor does hereby grant and convey to Grantee:

(Land Description of the Property)

TOGETHER with all right, title and interest, if any, of the Grantor in and to any streets and roads abutting the above-described premises to the center lines thereof; **TOGETHER** with the appurtenances and all the estate and rights of the grantor in and to said premises; to have and to hold the premises herein granted to the grantee, the heirs or successors and assigns of the Grantee forever.

IN WITNESS WHEREOF, Grantor has hereunto set the Grantor's hand and seal the date first above written.

(ACKNOWLEDGMENT)[2]

In providing for a deed instrument to be utilized in a non-judicial foreclosure sale, the new RPAPL Article 14 rectifies a key shortcoming of the old Article 14, which explicitly provided that a conveyance instrument was not necessary to vest title in a purchaser at foreclosure sale. That defect, among others, rendered the Foreclosure of Mortgage by Advertisement scheme of the old Article 14 virtually useless, as title companies would rarely ever insure title in a purchaser of a property foreclosed under that former statute.[3]

The new Article 14 cures that problem, not only by providing for a specific form of deed instrument that is patently acceptable to title insurance companies, but in also explicitly setting forth that the purchaser, upon a non-judicial sale conducted and a deed conveyance delivered in accordance with the statutory provisions, "obtains marketable title" in the same manner and to the same extent as a purchaser at a judicial foreclosure sale conducted pursuant to RPAPL Article 13.[4]

1. RPAPL § 1412(1).
2. RPAPL § 1412(1).
3. 21 West's New York Practice Series, *General Practice in New York*, § 11.8 at 693 (West Group 1998).
4. RPAPL § 1412(3).

§ 11.8k Distribution of the Proceeds of the Non-Judicial Sale

The statute directs the person who conducted the non-judicial foreclosure sale to distribute and pay from the proceeds of the sale (*i.e.*, the amount paid by the purchaser of the foreclosed property) in a prioritized order[1] similar to that set forth in the standard judgment of foreclosure and sale in an RPAPL Article 13 judicial foreclosure action[2].

The prioritized order of distribution and payment under RPAPL Article 14 is as follows:

1. All real estate taxes, water rates, sewer rents and other local governmental liens and encumbrances having priority over the foreclosed mortgage.[3]
2. The costs and expenses of the non-judicial foreclosure sale.[4]
3. The amount due to the mortgagee, including principal, interest, late charges, sums advanced by the mortgagee pursuant to the terms of the mortgage, and reasonable attorneys' fees and disbursements.[5]

Any surplus monies remaining after distribution and payment of the foregoing items must be deposited, by the person who conducted the

§ 11.8k

sale, with the County Treasurer of the county in which the sale took place, within five (5) days after receipt of same (which receipt would presumably occur at the closing of the sale, at which the Power of Sale Deed would be conveyed in exchange for the purchaser's tender of the balance of the sale price).[6]

1. RPAPL § 1413(1).
2. 21 West's New York Practice Series, *General Practice in New York*, § 11.46 at 726 (West Group 1998).
3. RPAPL § 1413(1)(A).
4. RPAPL § 1413(1)(B). This provision incorporates by reference RPAPL § 1417, which statutory section includes, as items comprising the costs and expenses of the sale, the advertisement of the Notice of Sale, the service of the Notice of Sale and the fees of the person conducting the sale.
5. RPAPL § 1413(1)(C). With regard to reasonable attorneys' fees, RPAPL § 1417(G) states that such fees shall not exceed $2,500.00, unless the court authorizes more.
6. RPAPL § 1413(2).

§ 11.8l Report of the Non–Judicial Foreclosure Sale

Within fifteen (15) days of executing and conveying to the purchaser the Power of Sale Deed, the person who conducted the non-judicial foreclosure sale must render a Report of the Sale which must state: the date, time and place of the sale; the sum bid for each distinct parcel separately offered for sale (if the foreclosure involved just one parcel, the Report will obviously so state); the sum bid for each parcel; the name of each purchaser of each parcel; and the name of each person or entity to whom proceeds of the sale were paid and the amount of any such payment.[1]

The Report must also contain: an original affidavit of publication of the Notice of Sale by a representative of the publisher of the newspaper in which the publication appeared; copies of the affidavits of service of the Notice of Intention to Foreclose and of the Notice of Pendency previously filed; and the original Terms of Sale and the executed Memorandum of Sale.[2]

Also, the Report must specify the amount claimed by the mortgagee to be due under the foreclosed mortgage (an original affidavit by the mortgagee attesting to the amount must also be contained within the Report), the sums distributed from the sale proceeds and to whom and the amount of any resulting deficiency or surplus.[3]

Finally, each aforementioned affidavit required to be contained in the Report must have annexed thereto a copy of the Notice of Sale.[4]

The Report of the Sale is required to be filed, within thirty (30) days after the delivery of the Power of Sale Deed, in the County Clerk's office of the county in which the sale took place.[5]

1. RPAPL § 1414(1).
2. RPAPL § 1414(2).
3. RPAPL § 1414(3).
4. RPAPL § 1414(4).
5. RPAPL § 1415(1).

§ 11.8m Surplus Money and Deficiency Judgment Proceedings Under Article 14

With respect to surplus monies or deficiencies that arise pursuant to the non-judicial foreclosure sale, RPAPL Article 14 contains the seeming paradox of requiring judicial intervention in what is statutorily labeled as a non-judicial proceeding. The foregoing statement is not in any way intended to be critical of the new statute, but rather to highlight some commendable examples of how Article 14, while allowing a lender, at least under specified circumstances, to have a foreclosure sale in an expeditious, non-judicial manner, also occasionally provides for court intervention to protect the rights and interests of borrowers, subordinate lienors and other claimants.

In the event of a surplus arising from the sale, any person or entity asserting a claim thereto should file a notice of the claim under the index number assigned to the non-judicial proceeding within twenty (20) days of the filing of the Report of the Sale. Thereafter, an application to the court may be made by any claimant for payment out of the surplus. Such application must be served upon all persons or entities who have been served with the Notice of Sale or who have filed a notice of claim.[1]

As is true with respect to a surplus money proceeding under RPAPL Article 13,[2] the court, by itself or by a court-appointed referee, will proceed to determine the respective amounts due to those entitled to the surplus moneys, to prioritize their respective rights and to decree distribution of the moneys by the County Treasurer in such prioritized manner.[3]

In the event of a deficiency arising from the sale and the existence of a right granted to the mortgagee under the loan documents to obtain a deficiency judgment, Article 14 requires the mortgagee to make an application for such a judgment in the non-judicial proceeding within ninety (90) days of the delivery of the Power of Sale Deed. Notice of the application must be served upon the persons or entities liable therefor by personal service "or in such other manner as the court may direct."[4]

The court then proceeds to determine the fair market value of the foreclosed property as of the date of the foreclosure sale or the nearest earlier date for which there was a market value. In coming to such determination, the court may rely upon the appraisal of a New York State-licensed real estate appraiser or otherwise as the court may direct. The court will then enter an order directing the entry of a deficiency judgment in an amount equal to the aggregate amount of the indebtedness due to the mortgagee, plus costs and expenses set forth in the Report of Sale, less the greater of (i) the court-determined fair market value of the property, or (ii) the purchase price for the property bid at the foreclosure sale.[5]

1. RPAPL § 1418(1).

2. See 21 West's New York Practice Series, General Practice in New York, § 11.53 at 738-39 (West Group 1998).

§ 11.8m   MORTGAGE FORECLOSURE   Ch. 11

3. RPAPL § 1418(3).
4. RPAPL § 1419(2).
5. RPAPL § 1419(2).

§ 11.8n   Receivership Under RPAPL Article 14

Another example of potential judicial involvement in an Article 14 foreclosure proceeding relates to the right of the mortgagee to seek the appointment of a receiver. Although the rapidity with which a mortgagee can complete a non-judicial foreclosure under the statute would seem to militate against the need for the expense of a receiver, there may be special circumstances, such as where the mortgaged property yields a significant amount of rental income each month, when a receiver is nevertheless desired.

In such situations, Article 14 authorizes the mortgagee, so long as the mortgage contains the requisite language permitting same,[1] to make an *ex parte* application to the court, under the index number of the non-judicial proceeding, for the appointment of a receiver.[2] The application can be made at any time after the filing of the Notice of Pendency of the Article 14 proceeding[3] and should be accompanied by a form of order appointing a receiver to be submitted to the court for signature.[4]

1. *See* discussion in 21 West's New York Practice Series, *General Practice in New York*, § 11.31 at 711 as to the language in a mortgage which suffices to permit the mortgagee's *ex parte* application for the appointment of a receiver.

2. RPAPL § 1420(1).
3. RPAPL § 1420(1).
4. RPAPL § 1420(2).

§ 11.8o   The Right to Convert the Article 14 Non–Judicial Foreclosure to a Judicial Foreclosure Under Article 13

The ultimate version of Article 14 adopted by the Legislature was designed to effectuate a significant compromise between the desires of the lender community for an expeditious procedure by which to complete foreclosure proceedings, and those of borrowers, subordinate lienors and other interested parties for the availability of judicial safeguards, particularly where there are legitimate defenses to foreclosure. The final statutory section of Article 14 effectively underscores that compromise by setting forth certain circumstances pursuant to which an Article 14 non-judicial foreclosure proceeding can be converted to a judicial one under RPAPL Article 13.[1]

In this regard, the statutory section, RPAPL § 1421, makes a distinction between mortgage documents executed prior to the effective date of the statute (i.e., July 7, 1998), and those executed after that date.

As to mortgage documents executed prior to July 7, 1998 (whether the document is the original or a modification, amendment, extension or consolidation thereof), the mortgagor has the automatic right to request that any further foreclosure proceedings be conducted judicially pursuant to RPAPL Article 13, by giving written notice of such request to the mortgagee within forty (40) days of receipt of the mortgagee's Notice of Intention to Foreclose. Such written notice must be given by certified or registered mail or by any other method authorized in the mortgage documents.[2]

In contrast, as to mortgage documents executed after July 7, 1998, the mortgagor does not have such an automatic right. Rather, in such instance, if the mortgagor seeks to convert the non-judicial proceeding to a judicial one, the mortgagor is required to apply by order to show cause, in the State Supreme Court of the county in which the mortgaged property is located, asking for an order for such a conversion and for a temporary restraining order staying any further non-judicial foreclosure proceedings pending a hearing on the application. Such application must be made within forty (40) days of the mortgagor's receipt of the mortgagee's Notice of Intention to Foreclose.[3]

The statutory provision further requires that the mortgagor's application include one or more affidavits that state facts to support one or more of the following grounds allegedly entitling the mortgagor to have the foreclosure proceeding conducted judicially under RPAPL Article 13:

1. That the subject mortgage document(s) do not contain language permitting foreclosure by power of sale or other non-judicial means;[4]

2. That the obligation secured by the mortgage is invalid or not otherwise due;[5]

3. That the mortgagor is not in default under the mortgage or otherwise has a meritorious defense to foreclosure;[6]

4. That the mortgagee has not complied with the terms and conditions of Article 14;[7] or

5. That under the facts and circumstances, to permit the foreclosure to proceed non-judicially under Article 14 "would cause an undue hardship to the mortgagor."[8]

Obviously, if the court, after considering the mortgagor's application and any opposition papers from the mortgagee, finds that the mortgagor has satisfactorily proved any of the above grounds and therefore grants the application, the foreclosure must proceed as a judicial one under RPAPL Article 13.[9] Conversely, if the application is denied, the foreclosure may proceed to sale as a non-judicial proceeding under Article 14.[10]

The statutory section also provides that any interested party other than the mortgagor can also make application to the court for conversion to judicial foreclosure, but in such instance the application must be made under the injunctive relief provisions of Article 63 of the Civil Practice Law and Rules. Furthermore, the court is directed to apply the standards for preliminary injunctive relief in determining such an application and to consider whether granting the requested relief will prejudice the "substantial rights of any party or unduly delay the adjudication of such rights."[11]

§ 11.80   MORTGAGE FORECLOSURE   Ch. 11

1. RPAPL § 1421.

2. RPAPL § 1421(1). This automatic conversion right granted to borrowers with regard to pre–July 7, 1998 mortgage documents could, in theory, render it extremely rare for a pre–July 7, 1998 mortgage to be the subject of an Article 14 non-judicial proceeding, as such borrowers, even those without legitimate defenses, will likely seek to "buy time" by invoking the significantly longer process of an RPAPL Article 13 judicial foreclosure. However, in those instances of pre–July 7, 1998 mortgages where the lender is able to consummate a "quick deal" with a borrower, e.g., a consensual foreclosure in consideration of the borrower and its guarantors being released from any liability for a deficiency judgment, an Article 14 non-judicial foreclosure will be a most desirable and expeditious remedy.

3. RPAPL § 1421(2).
4. RPAPL § 1421(2)(B)(1).
5. RPAPL § 1421(2)(B)(2).
6. RPAPL § 1421(2)(B)(3).
7. RPAPL § 1421(2)(B)(4).

8. RPAPL § 1421(2)(B)(5). The vagueness of this "undue hardship" factor is one that has received particular criticism from legal commentators who have addressed the new RPAPL Article 14. See, e.g., Huck Qavanaugh, "Ambiguity Diminishes Efficacy of Non–Judicial Foreclosure Law," *New York Law Journal*, October 15, 1998, at 1, col. 1. Bruce Bergman, "Non–Judicial Actions: Statutory Ambiguities Could Cause Delays in Default Cases," *New York Law Journal*, February 10, 1999, at 5, col. 2. It remains to be seen how courts will interpret this provision with respect to which the legislative history offers virtually no guidance.

9. RPAPL § 1421(3).
10. RPAPL § 1421(4).
11. RPAPL § 1421(6).

Chapter 12

PURCHASE AND SALE OF REAL ESTATE

by
Bernard M. Rifkin

Table of Sections

12.15	Residential Contract of Sale—Purchase Price and Method of Payment—Mortgage Contingency
12.23	____ Closing Date and Place
12.25	____ Deed Transfer and Recording Taxes
12.51	Title Insurance Policy—Endorsements
12.74	Closing of Title—Recording Fees and Filings
12.85	____ Payment of Taxes—New York City Real Property Transfer Tax
12.86	____ ____ Cities of Mount Vernon and Yonkers
12.86a	____ ____ Peconic Bay Region Transfer Taxes, County of Suffolk, Towns of East Hampton, Riverhead, Shelter Island, Southampton and Southold
12.89	____ ____ Mortgage Recording Tax Rate in New York City
12.93	Residential Contract of Sale
12.99	Forms—Acknowledgments and Proofs of Conveyances of Real Property Situated in New York

Westlaw Electronic Research

See Westlaw Electronic Research Guide preceding the Summary of Contents.

§ 12.15 Residential Contract of Sale—Purchase Price and Method of Payment—Mortgage Contingency

PAGE 812:

[Insert at end of section.]

NOTE: On May 4, 1999, the Joint Committee of the Mortgage Contingency Clause published a set of instructions which are very helpful in understanding the changes made in the text of the approved form of contract for the sale of residential real property.[7] The intention of the changes are to make more certain what was the original intention of Paragraph 8.

---

7. The text of the Amended Paragraph 8 of the Approved Contract of Sale appears as an addendum to Section 12. The Joint Committee consisted of New York State Bar Association, Real Property Section, New York County Real Property Section, the

§ 12.15   PURCHASE AND SALE OF REAL ESTATE   Ch. 12

Real Property Committee of the Association of the Bar of the City of New York and the Real Property Committee.

§ 12.23   Residential Contract of Sale—Closing Date and Place

PAGE 818:

[*Insert at end of section.*]

The model contract of sale provides for a requirement that all notices to be given in the contract must be made in writing and may be given by the respective attorneys for the parties to each other.[1] This requirement is contained in paragraph 25 of the model contract. A new clause will be added to permit delivery by ordinary mail.

1. *See* General Obligations Law, Section 15-301(subd. 5).

§ 12.25   Residential Contract of Sale—Deed Transfer and Recording Taxes

PAGE 819:

[*Add as fourth sentence of section.*]

A new transfer tax is also imposed on the purchaser or seller of property in Peconic Bay in Suffolk County (*See* § 12.86.1 for the method of imposition.)

§ 12.51   Title Insurance Policy—Endorsements

PAGE 843:

[*Replace note 2 with the following.*]

2. The following are Special Risk Endorsements (varying premium rates apply):

ALTA Endorsement 9 (Restrictions, Encroachments, Minerals)   Sept. 1, 1993
(3/27/92)
NY (9/1/93)

TIRSA Additional Interest Endorsement (1/31/95)   Jan. 31, 1995
   NYSID REQUIRES TITLE INSURER APPROVAL PRIOR TO ISSUANCE

TIRSA Contract Vendee Endorsement (1/31/95)   Jan. 31, 1995

TIRSA New York Fairway Endorsement (9/1/93)   Sept. 1, 1993

TIRSA First Loss Endorsement (5/1/96)   May 1, 1996
   NYSID REQUIRES TITLE INSURER APPROVAL PRIOR TO ISSUANCE

TIRSA Joint & Several Liability Endorsement (9/1/93)   Sept. 1, 1993

TIRSA Last Dollar Endorsement (5/1/96)   May 1, 1996
   NYSID REQUIRES TITLE INSURER APPROVAL PRIOR TO ISSUANCE

Ch. 12   PURCHASE AND SALE OF REAL ESTATE   § 12.51

TIRSA Market Value Policy Rider Endorsement (9/1/93)	Sept. 1, 1993
TIRSA Non-Imputation Endorsement (10/21/97)	Oct. 21, 1997
TIRSA RCE-1 (10/21/97)	Oct. 21, 1997
TIRSA RCE-2 (10/21/97)	Oct. 21, 1997
TIRSA RCE-3 (10/21/97) NYSID REQUIRES TITLE INSURER APPROVAL PRIOR TO ISSUANCE	Oct. 21, 1997
TIRSA RCE-4 (10/21/97) NYSID REQUIRES TITLE INSURER APPROVAL PRIOR TO ISSUANCE	Oct. 21, 1997
IRSA Survey Endorsement (Loan Policy) (9/1/93)	Sept. 1, 1993
TIRSA Swap Endorsement (1/31/95) NYSID REQUIRES TITLE INSURER APPROVAL PRIOR TO ISSUANCE	Jan. 31, 1995

[*Replace note 3 with the following.*]

3. The following endorsements are offered at a charge of $25:

TIRSA Fannie Mae Balloon Mortgage Endorsement (9/1/93)	Sept. 1, 1993
TIRSA Cluster Endorsement (1/27/97) NYSID REQUIRES TITLE INSURER APPROVAL PRIOR TO ISSUANCE	Jan. 27, 1997
TIRSA Endorsement 4 (Condominium) (9/1/93)	Sept. 1, 1993
TIRSA 8.1 EPL (10/21/97)	Oct. 21, 1997
TIRSA 8.1. EPL (Governmental Agencies) (10/21/97)	Oct. 21, 1997
TIRSA 8.1. EPL (New York City Only) (10/21/97)	Oct. 21, 1997
TIRSA Junior Loan Policy Endorsement 1 (10/21/97)	Oct. 21, 1997
TIRSA Land Same As Survey Endorsement (9/1/93)	Sept. 1, 1993
TIRSA Limited Liability Company and Limited Liability Partnership Endorsement (1/31/95)	Jan. 31, 1995
ALTA Endorsement 7 (Manufactured Housing Unit) (6/1/87) NY (9/1/93)	Sep. 1, 1993
TIRSA New York City "Air Rights" Endorsement (9/1/93)	Sep. 1, 1993
TIRSA 5.1 (Planned Unit Development) Endorsement (9/1/93)	Sep. 1, 1993
TIRSA Residential Mortgage Endorsement (8/15/94)	Aug. 15, 1994
TIRSA Reverse Mortgage Endorsement (1/31/95)	Jan. 31, 1995
TIRSA Successor in Ownership of Indebtedness Endorsement (8/15/94)	Aug. 15, 1994
ALTA Endorsement 6 (Variable Rate Mortgage) (6/1/87) NY (9/1/93)	Sep. 1, 1993

§ 12.51 PURCHASE AND SALE OF REAL ESTATE Ch. 12

TIRSA Variable Rate Mortgage Endorsement (Fixed Rate Conversion) (9/1/93) — Sep. 1, 1993

TIRSA Endorsement 6.2 (Variable Rate Mortgage–Negative Amortization) (9/1/93) — Sep. 1, 1993

TIRSA Waiver of Arbitration Endorsement (Loan Policy) (9/1/93) — Sep. 1, 1993

TIRSA Waiver of Arbitration Endorsement (Owner's Policy) (9/1/93) — Sep. 1, 1993

TIRSA IDA Endorsement (1/28/99) — Jan. 28, 1999

§ 12.74 Closing of Title—Recording Fees and Filings

PAGE 878:

[*Add following first paragraph on page.*]

Proper recording is essential to the creation of the appropriate constructive notice which assures the priority of the instrument for an owner, lender or other party offering the instrument for recordation. Among the most significant laws to be complied with are the requirements for acknowledgments which are established pursuant to Section 290 et. seq. of the Real Property Law. (*See infra* § 12.99)

[*Replace note 3 with the following.*]

3. See Bernard M. Rifkin, Real Estate Titles, Ch. 2 (2d ed. NYSBA 1998 Supp.), for a more complete discussion of the search procedure and the chain of title concept.

[*Replace paragraph reading "N.Y.C. Real Estate Property Transfer Tax Return (In New York City this serves as a substitute for the EA5217); " with the following.*]

N.Y.C. Real Estate Property Transfer Tax Return (RPTTNYC) (In New York City this serves as a substitute for the EA5217);[5.1]

5.1 See infra, § 12.85.

[*Add to note 7.*]

7. Articles 8 and 9 of the UCC, §§ 8–103 and 8–106 of the U.C.C., together with filing requirements of §§ 9–115 304(7) have created new rules for determining whether certain obligations and interests in entities are securities or finance assets. Whether the interest is perfected by possession of the instrument or by filing and the place of filing are important matters to be determined by the documents themselves.

§ 12.85 Closing of Title—Payment of Taxes—New York City Real Property Transfer Tax

PAGE 890:

[*Insert at bottom of page as #4.*]

4. There are proposed regulatory provisions which will further elaborate the applicable rule for this credit. On the whole the prospect is not very favorable for the ability to utilize the credit. For example

there are proposed severe restrictions on preconveyancing financing and a maximum ten percent limit on interest rate variations either for the benefit or detriment of the new owner.[2.1]

2.1 19 N.Y.C.R.R. § 23–03(k).

§ 12.86 Closing of Title—Payment of Taxes—Cities of Mount Vernon and Yonkers

PAGE 891:

[*Re-write section as follows.*]

In Mount Vernon the tax is 1% of consideration in excess of $100,000 payable by purchaser.[1] In Yonkers, effective January 1, 1999, the tax is 1.4% of gross consideration if the purchase price exceeds $25,000. The tax is payable by the seller.[2]

1. City of Mount Vernon Local Law 4 (Effective Sept. 1, 1986).
2. City of Yonkers Code of Ordinances, as amended June 23, 1998 by Tax Law § 1230(b). Gen'l Ord. No. 3–1998 Special City Council, effective Jan. 1, 1999.

[*Insert new section.*]

§ 12.86a Closing of Title—Payment of Taxes—Peconic Bay Region Transfer Taxes, County of Suffolk, Towns of East Hampton, Riverhead, Shelter Island, Southampton and Southold[1]

PAGE 891:

1. Section 1449–aa uses the same definitions applicable to taxable interests which are transferred as is contained in the transfer tax applicable to transfers pursuant to Article 31 of the Tax Law. The tax is collected by the recording officer (the County Clerk).

    The tax is imposed on the Peconic Bay Region, consisting of the towns of East Hampton, Riverhead, Shelter Island, Southampton and Southold.

2. The tax is imposed in addition to any other transfer tax imposed (Section 1449–bb).

    The tax rate pursuant to Section 1449–bb is two percent (2%) of the consideration paid for the conveyance for the interest in the property transferred as indicated above.

    Consideration is modified by the provisions of Section 1449–bb(3) and in the case of cooperative transfers by Section 1449–ff and gg.

    Other than these matters consideration is defined as including all liens whether assumed or purchase money (Section 1449–cc(4)).

§ 12.86a PURCHASE AND SALE OF REAL ESTATE   Ch. 12

3. The tax is for the benefit of the Community Preservation Fund and may be collected by the Treasurer of the County or the recording officer (the County Clerk) acting on his agent. It is payable at the same time as the Article 31 Real Property Transfer Tax is paid. A return similar to the TP 584 is to be prepared by the County Treasurer.

4. Section 1449-dd provides that the grantee is liable for the tax but if the grantee is exempt the grantor pays. There is a presumption that the tax applies and the burden of proof to the contrary is upon the party who is liable for the payment.

5. Exemptions—Section 1449-ee of the Tax Law

    The Community Preservation Transfer Tax does not apply to the following conveyance and does not shift to the grantor where the grantee is:

    a. The United Nations, The United States of America, The State of New York or any of their instrumentalities, agencies or any public (benefit) corporations including such entities created by agreement or compact with another state or Canada.

    NOTE: If any of these entities or instrumentalities are the grantor the tax will apply to the grantee.

    b. Conveyances to secure debt or other obligation

    c. Conveyance pursuant to a tax sale

    d. Conveyances to effect a mere change in identity except for conveyances to a cooperative housing corporation or dwelling unit (See paragraph 7(b) for the tax as it applies to cooperative housing corporation transactions).

    e. A deed of partition

    f. Contracts of sale without use or occupancy or an option without use or occupancy

    g. Conveyances where the property is already subject to certain restrictions, set forth in Section 1449-ee (Subdivision (j), (k), and (l). The Section exempts property to be conveyed if it is the subject of one or more of a number of development restrictions (i.e.) agricultural, conservation, scenic and open space easements. Additional exemptions other than those stated in this section can be created by locally adopted laws.

6. Exemptions relating to consideration Section 1449-ee(3)

    a. In East Hampton, Shelter Island and Southampton there is a $250,000.00 exemption for the conveyance of improved real property and an exemption of $100,000.00 for the conveyance of an improved land.

Ch. 12 PURCHASE AND SALE OF REAL ESTATE § 12.86a

 b. In Riverhead and Southold the exemption for the conveyance of improved real property is $150,000.00 and an exemption $75,000.00 for unimproved real property.

7. Credits allowed—Section 1449-ff Tax Law

 a. Where a tax was paid on the same real property by the grantor in a prior taxable transaction involving a lease or option on all or a portion of the property. The statute sets forth a formula for apportionment.

 b. Section 1449-gg governs the transfer tax imposed on the transfer of property to and from a cooperative housing corporation or partnership.

 The statute's definition of a controlling interest is not applicable to the proprietary lease or shares of stock.

 The transfer tax applies to the original conveyance into the cooperative housing corporation and to the transfer of proprietary leases by the corporation or by the sponsor. It also applies to any subsequent transfers by the owner of an individual residential unit and shall exclude the value of any liens affecting the cooperative, corporation and/or the proprietary lease, which liens continue to survive after the transfer.

 In addition, a proportional credit is allowed for the tax paid on the conveyance to the cooperative corporation. No credit may be allowed below zero. There can be no credit allowed for a tax paid more than 24 months prior to the transfer of the first of a series of transfers made by the cooperative housing corporation.

 There is also a provision for cooperation housing corporations to file information returns regarding the transfer of shares including social security numbers of the grantors and grantee returns must be filed by January 15 of each year.

8. The remaining sections of the statute contain provisions with respect to the following subjects:

 a. Section 1449-hh–Designation of Agents (To collect the tax (the County Treasurer) is authorized to designate the County Clerk).

 b. Section 1449-ii–Liability of the Recording Officer

 c. Section 1449-jj–Refunds

 d. Section 1449-kk–Deposit and Disposition of Revenue

 e. Section 1449-ll–Judicial Review

 f. Section 1449-mm–Apportionment (Between towns and areas not subject to the tax)

§ 12.86a PURCHASE AND SALE OF REAL ESTATE Ch. 12

g. Section 1449–nn–Miscellaneous–includes authority to the towns to adopt measures of Administration of the tax consistent with the enforcement of Article 31 of the Tax Law

h. Section 1449–oo–Returns to be secret

The Effective Date and Sunset Provision

(1) The effective date of the imposition of Peconic Bay Regional Town Transfer Tax is April 1, 1999 in all towns except Southold where it is effective March 1, 1999. The referendum requirement was complied with by the inclusion of the issue on the ballot of the election held November 3, 1998.

(2) The tax remains in effect until December 31, 2010 after which date it is automatically repealed.

1. N.Y. Tax Law Article 31D, §§ 1449-aa, et seq.

§ 12.89 Closing of Title—Payment of Taxes—Mortgage Recording Tax Rate in New York City

PAGE 896:

[Add to end of section.]

In a ruling dated April 7, 1999, the Tax Commission stated in response the following questions:

(1) Whether a mortgage, in the principal amount of less than $3 million, executed to secure the repayment of advances and re-advances made to reimburse the borrower for expenses incurred in making improvements upon real property and without the execution of a building loan agreement would qualify as a credit line mortgage;

(2) Whether a mortgage, in the principal amount of less than $3 million, executed to secure the repayment of advances and re-advances made to fund—but not reimburse the borrower for—the making of improvements upon real property and without the execution of a building loan agreement would qualify as a credit line mortgage;

(3) If the answer in issue (2) is that such a mortgage would qualify as a credit line mortgage, whether such mortgage would still qualify if the mortgage or other loan documents contains an express promise to make an improvement upon real property.

The response was negative. In all three cases, the mortgage tax rate would not be based on the credit line exemption.[10]

10. Tax Commission Opinion TSB A 99 (2)R, April 7, 1999.

§ 12.93 Residential Contract of Sale

PAGE 902:

[Add at end of section.]

MODEL MORTGAGE CONTINGENCY CLAUSE (NYSBA T & T COM Draft)
for
RESIDENTIAL CONTRACT OF SALE
(Jointly prepared by NYSBA, NYSLTA, ABCNY, NYCLA)
(Blumberg form A 125 dated 11–96)

8. Mortgage Commitment Contingency. (Delete *paragraph* if inapplicable)

(a) The obligation of Purchaser to purchase under this contract is conditioned upon issuance, on or before days after a fully executed copy of this contract *is given to Purchaser in the manner set forth in paragraph 25 or subparagraph 8(1)* (the "Commitment Date"), of a written commitment from an Institutional Lender pursuant to which such Institutional Lender agrees to make a first mortgage loan, other than a VA, FHA or other governmentally insured loan, to Purchaser, at Purchaser's sole cost and expense, of $, at the prevailing fixed or adjustable rate of interest for a term of at least years (or such lesser sum or shorter term as Purchaser shall be willing to accept) and on other customary commitment terms (the "Commitment"). To the extent a Commitment is conditioned on sale of Purchaser's current home, payment of any outstanding debt or line of credit or any other customary conditions, Purchaser accepts the risk that such conditions may not be met; however, a commitment conditioned on the Institutional Lender's approval of an appraisal shall not be deemed a "Commitment" hereunder until an appraisal is approved (if that does not occur before the Commitment Date, Purchaser may cancel under paragraph 8(3) unless the Commitment Date is extended). Purchaser's obligations hereunder are conditioned only on issuance of a Commitment. Once a Commitment is issued, Purchaser is bound under this contract even if the lender fails or refuses to fund the loan for any reason.

(b) Purchaser shall (i) make prompt application to one or, at Purchaser's election, more than one Institutional Lender for such mortgage loan, (ii) furnish accurate and complete information regarding Purchaser and members of Purchaser's family, as required, (iii) pay all fees, points and charges required in connection with such application and loan, (iv) pursue such application with diligence, and (v) cooperate in good faith with such Institutional Lender(s) to obtain such Commitment. Purchaser shall accept a Commitment meeting the terms stated in (a) above and shall comply with all requirements of such Commitment (or any other commitment accepted by Purchaser). Purchaser shall furnish Seller with a copy thereof promptly after receipt thereof.

§ 12.93 PURCHASE AND SALE OF REAL ESTATE Ch. 12

(c) (Delete this subparagraph if inapplicable) Prompt submission by Purchaser of an application to a mortgage broker registered pursuant to Article 12–D of the New York Banking Law ("Mortgage Broker") shall constitute full compliance with the terms and conditions set forth in paragraph 8(b)(i), provided that such Mortgage Broker promptly submits such application to such Institutional Lender(s). Purchaser shall cooperate in good faith with such Mortgage Broker to obtain a Commitment from such Institutional Lender(s).

(d) If the Institutional Lender denies such application in writing prior to the Commitment Date, Purchaser may cancel this contract by giving Notice thereof to Seller, with a copy of such denial, provided that Purchaser has complied with all its obligations under this all its obligations under this *paragraph 8*.

(e) If such Commitment is not issued by the Institutional Lender on or before the Commitment Date, then, unless Purchaser has accepted a written commitment from an Institutional Lender that does not comply with the terms set forth in paragraph 8(a), Purchaser may cancel this contract by giving notice to Seller within 5 business days after the Commitment Date, provided that such Notice includes the name and address of the Institutional Lender(s) to which application was made and that Purchaser has complied with all its obligations under this *paragraph 8*.

(f) If Purchaser fails to give Notice of cancellation or if Purchaser shall accept a written commitment from an Institutional Lender that does not conform to the terms set forth in (a) above, to cancel this contract and to receive a refund of the Downpayment by reason of the contingency continued in this *paragraph 8*.

(g) If Seller has not received a copy of a commitment accepted by Purchaser by the Commitment Date, Seller may cancel this contract by giving Notice to Purchaser within 5 business days after the Commitment Date, which cancellation shall become effective if Purchaser does not deliver a copy of such commitment to Seller within 10 business days after the Commitment Date. After such cancellation neither party shall have any further rights against, or obligations or liabilities to, the other by reason of this contract, except that the Downpayment shall be promptly refunded to Purchaser (provided Purchaser has complied with all its obligations under this *paragraph 8*) and except as set forth in paragraph 27.

(h) If *Seller requests an adjournment of the Closing* to a date beyond the expiration date of a commitment accepted by Purchaser and Purchaser is unable in good faith to obtain an extension of such expiration date *for a loan on materially no less favorable terms* or to obtain the same without paying additional fees to the Institutional Lender (unless Seller, within 5 business days after receipt of Notice of such fees, gives Notice to Purchaser that Seller will pay such fees and pays them when due), Purchaser may *either refuse such request or* cancel this contract by giving Notice to Seller within 5 business days after the right to cancel arises, provided that Purchaser has complied with all its obligations under this *paragraph 8*.

(i) If this contract is canceled by Purchaser pursuant to paragraphs 8(d), (e) or (h), thereafter neither party shall have any further rights against, or obligations or liabilities to, the other by reason of this contract, except that the Downpayment shall be promptly refunded to Purchaser and except as set forth in paragraph 27. *If this contract is canceled by Purchaser pursuant to paragraph 8(H), Seller shall reimburse Purchaser for any non-refundable financing and inspection expenses and other sums reimbursable under paragraph 21.*

(j) The respective attorneys of the parties to this contract are hereby authorized to give and receive on behalf of their clients all Notices and deliveries under this paragraph 8.

(k) For purposes of this contract, the term "Institutional Lender" shall mean any bank, savings bank, private banker, trust company, savings and loan association, credit union or similar banking institution whether organized under the laws of this state, the United States or any other state; foreign banking corporation licensed by the Superintendent of Banks of New York or regulated by the Comptroller of the Currency to transact business in New York State; insurance company duly organized or licensed to do business in New York State; mortgage banker licensed pursuant to Article 12–D of the Banking Law; and any instrumentality created by the United States or any state with the power to make mortgage loans.

(*l*) For purposes of subparagraph (a), Purchaser shall be deemed to have been given a fully executed copy of this contract on the fifth day following the date of ordinary ore regular mailing, postage prepaid.

4/14/99

NOTES ON MORTGAGE COMMITMENT CONTINGENCY CLAUSE
for
RESIDENTIAL CONTRACT OF SALE
(Jointly prepared by NYSBA, NYSLTA, ABCNY, NYCLA)
(Blumberg form A 125 dated 11–96)

1. WARNING: the mortgage commitment contingency clause for the Residential Contract of Sale is a bar association form that attempts to provide a mechanism that makes the rights and obligations of the parties clear in sales of residences in ordinary circumstances. It should be reviewed carefully by Seller and Purchaser and their attorneys in each and every transactions to make sure that all the provisions are appropriate for that transaction. Negotiated modifications should be made whenever necessary.

2. Under the clause, the obligation of Purchaser to purchase under the contract of sale is contingent on Purchaser's obtaining a mortgage commitment letter from an Institutional Lender within the number of days specified for the amount specified. This refers to calendar days.

§ 12.93 PURCHASE AND SALE OF REAL ESTATE Ch. 12

Seller's attorney should state his/her calculation of the Commitment Date in the letter delivering the executed contract to Purchaser's attorney, to prevent confusion later. *Purchaser should promptly confirm or correct that date. In applying for a loan, Purchaser should inform its lender of the scheduled date of closing in the contract and request that the expiration date of the commitment occur after the scheduled date of closing.* Purchaser must comply with deadlines and pursue the application in good faith. The commitment contingency is satisfied by issuance of a commitment in the amount specified on or before the Commitment Date, unless the commitment is conditioned on approval of an appraisal. If the commitment is conditioned on approval of an appraisal and such approval does not occur prior to the Commitment Date, Purchaser should either cancel the contract or obtain an extension of the Commitment Date. IF the commitment is later withdrawn or not honored, Purchaser runs the risk of being in default under the contract of sale with Seller.

3. If there are loan terms and conditions that are required or would not be acceptable to Purchaser, such as the interest rate, term of the loan, points, fees or a condition requiring sale of the current home, those terms and conditions should *be* specified in a rider.

4. This clause assumes that initial review and approval of Purchaser's credit will occur before the commitment letter is issued. Purchaser should confirm with the lender that this is the case before applying for the commitment.

5. If, as has been common, the commitment letter itself is conditioned on sale of Purchaser's home or payment of any outstanding debt or line of credit, such a commitment will satisfy the contract contingency nonetheless, and Purchaser will take the risk of fulfilling those commitment conditions, including forfeiture of the downpayment if Purchaser defaults on its obligation to close. Under New York case law, a defaulting purchaser may not recover any part of the downpayment, *and Seller does not have* to prove any damages. If Purchaser is not willing to take that risk, the clause must be modified accordingly.

6. Purchaser may submit an application to a registered mortgage broker instead of applying directly to an Institutional Lender.

7. This clause allows Seller to cancel if a commitment is not accepted by Purchaser by the Commitment Date, unless Purchaser timely supplies a copy of the commitment, to allow Seller the option to avoid having to wait until the scheduled date of closing to see if Purchaser will be able to close. Seller may prefer to cancel rather than to wait and settle for forfeiture of the downpayment if Purchaser defaults. *Because of Seller's right to cancel, Purchaser may not waive this contingency clause. This clause means that Purchaser is subject to cancellation by Seller even if Purchaser is willing to risk that he/she will obtain the Commitment after the Commitment Date. Some Purchaser may not want to be subject to such cancellation by Seller.*

8. Purchaser may want to add to paragraph 22 that Purchaser's *reimbursement* should *include non-refundable financing and inspection* expenses of Purchaser, which should be refunded by Seller if Seller willfully defaults under the contract of sale [alternative: if Seller is unable to transfer title under the contract of sale].

Joint Committee on the Mortgage Contingency Clause:

Real Property Section of the New York State Bar Association

Real Property Law Committee of the Association of the Bar of the City of New York

Real Property Committee of the New York County Lawyers Association

PAGE 926:

[*Insert new section.*]

§ 12.99 Forms—Acknowledgments and Proofs of Conveyances of Real Property Situated in New York

I. THE UNIFORM FORMS OF CERTIFICATES OF ACKNOWLEDGMENT OR PROOFS

Two new Chapters of New York Law (179 of 1997 and 596 of 1998) have made substantive changes in the method of taking acknowledgments and proofs.

(I) ACKNOWLEDGMENT IN NEW YORK STATE (RPL 309-a)

Section 309(a) Real Property Law provides that:

The certificate or an acknowledgment, *within* this state, of a conveyance or other instrument in respect to *real property situate in this state,* by a person, may conform substantially with the following form, the blanks being properly filled:

State of New York   )
) SS.:
County of   )

On _____ before me, the undersigned, personally appeared

personally known to me or proved to me on the basis of satisfactory evidence to be the individual(s) whose name(s) is (are) subscribed to the within instrument and acknowledged to me that he/she/they executed the same in his/her/their capacity(ies), and that by his/her/their signature(s) on the instrument, the individual(s), or the person upon behalf of which the individual(s) acted, executed the instrument.

(signature and office of person taking acknowledgment)

(2) ACKNOWLEDGMENT OUTSIDE NEW YORK STATE (RPL 309–a(2))

Section 309–a(2) Real Property Law

The Certificate of Acknowledgment, taken without this state, of a conveyance or other instrument with respect to *real property situate in this state*, by a person, may conform substantially with the following form, the blanks being property filled: in that State, District of Columbia, Territory, Possession, or Foreign Country.

State of New York)
) SS:
County of   )

On _____ before me, the undersigned, personally appeared

personally known to me or proved to me on the basis of satisfactory evidence to be the individual(s) whose name(s) is (are) subscribed to the within instrument and acknowledged to me that he/she/they executed the same in his/her/their capacity(ies), and that by his/her/their signature(s) on the instrument, the individual(s), or the person upon behalf of which the individual(s) acted, executed the instrument, the individual(s), or the person upon behalf of which the individual(s) acted, executed the instrument, and that such individual(s) made such appearance before the undersigned in

(insert city or political subdivision and state or country or other place acknowledgment taken).

_____

_____
(signature and office of person taking acknowledgment)

(3) SUBSCRIBING WITNESS ACKNOWLEDGMENTS

The acknowledgment or proofs of execution by a subscribing witness taken inside and outside the State of New York are also modified as follows:

Section 309–a(2) Real Property Law provides that:

The certificate for a proof of execution by a subscribing witness, taken within this state, of a conveyance or other instrument made by any person in respect to *real property situate in this state*, may conform substantially with the following form, the blanks being properly filled by a subscribing witness:

ACKNOWLEDGMENT IN NEW YORK STATE (RPL 309–a(2))

State of New York   )
) SS:
County of   )

On _____ before me, the undersigned, personally appeared

the subscribing witness(es) to the foregoing instrument, with whom I am personally acquainted, who, being by me duly sworn, did depose and say that he/she/they reside(s) in (*if the place of residence is in a city, include the street and street number, if any, thereof*):

that he/she/they know(s)

to be the individual(s) described in and who executed the foregoing instrument; that said subscribing witness(es) was (were) present and saw said

execute the same; and that said witness(es) at the same time subscribed his/her/their name(s) as witness(es) thereto.

_____
_____*(signature and office*
of person taking acknowledgment)

(4) GENERAL REQUIREMENTS AND NOTES ON AUTHENTICATION AND PROOFS

The new Uniform Laws do not modify the existing laws with respect to acknowledgments which conform either to the laws of New York or to the place where the acknowledgments is taken. (See Sections 299–a and 301–a of the Real Property Law)

(i) Section 299–a RPL provides for acknowledgments or proofs, if taken pursuant to the laws of another jurisdiction, it must be accompanied by a certificate of authentication that it does comply with the laws of that jurisdiction.

(ii) The person authorized to provide a certificate to the effect that it conforms with the laws of that a state may be made by a variety of persons which include lawyers admitted to practice in New York but resident in the other state or jurisdiction or an attorney at law in the jurisdiction where the certificate is executed. There is also provision for New York judicial certification of other parties who are deemed qualified by a New York State Court.

(iii) Section 301–a—Acknowledgments or Proofs Taken in a Foreign Country

Such acknowledgments or proofs taken in a foreign country with respect to real property located in New York State may be made by an attorney, consular officer of the United States resident in such country, a foreign consular officer in

§ 12.99   PURCHASE AND SALE OF REAL ESTATE   Ch. 12

New York under the seal of their office, or any other person deemed qualified by a New York judge. (See Section 301–a subd. 2(a), (b) and (c)).

(iv) The Uniform Laws adopted by Chapters 179 of the Laws of 1997 and 596 of the Laws of 1998 did not amend various stringent rules governing acknowledgments and proofs relating to requirements of the right to introduce documents into evidence. These rules are set out in Sections 311.

(v) Section 313 RPL defines the term Notary Public.

(vi) Section 314 RPL deals with proofs in the event of the death of the grantor, mortgagor and/or the party who had taken the acknowledgment.

(vii) Section 314–a RPL deals with the death of witnesses to the document.

(vii) Section 318 RPL deals with the requirement that the acknowledgment or proof of the execution of the document must be recorded with the document or it cannot be entered into evidence.

(ix) Nothing in the Chapters 179 of 1997 and 596 of 1998 modify any provision in the Laws of another state, District of Columbia or territory or possession or foreign country.

(x) The definition of "person" contained in Section 309–a of the RPL is the key provision which enables the new Uniform Acknowledgment and Proofs to be viable for individuals and entities.

II. OTHERS AUTHORIZED TO TAKE ACKNOWLEDGMENTS AND PROOFS WITHIN THE STATE OF NEW YORK

A. AUTHORITY TO TAKE ACKNOWLEDGMENTS AND PROOFS

Section 298 of the Real Property Law provides that an acknowledgment or proof of a conveyance of real property situated in New York may be made at any place within the state before one of the following persons:

(a) a Justice of the Supreme Court

(b) an Official Examiner

(c) an Official Referee

(d) a Notary Public.

Section 298 further provides that such an acknowledgment or proof may be made before any of the following officers, if made within the district wherein such officer is authorized to perform official duties:

(a) a Judge or Clerk of any court of record

(b) a Commissioner of Deeds[5]

(c) the Mayor or Recorder of a city.

(d) a Surrogate, Special Surrogate, or Special County Judge

(e) the County Clerk or other recording officer of a county

Section 298 also provides that such an acknowledgment or proof may be taken by one of the following officers anywhere within the county containing the town, village, or city in which that officer is authorized to perform his official duties:

(a) a Justice of the Peace

(b) a Town Councilman

(c) a Village Police Justice

(d) a Judge of any inferior local jurisdiction.[6]

B. CERTIFICATES OF AUTHENTICATION

A certificate of acknowledgment or proof taken within the state pursuant to Section 298 is required in certain limited instances to be authenticated by the certificate of the clerk of the county where the officer who took the acknowledgment or proof is authorized to act before such an acknowledgment or proof can be read into evidence or recorded in any other county than the one in which the officer is authorized to act. Section 310 requires such authentication when the acknowledgment or proof was made by any of the following officers:

(a) a Commissioner of Deeds

(b) a Justice of the Peace

(c) a Town Councilman

(d) a Village Police Justice

(e) a Judge of any court of inferior local jurisdiction

Such a certificate of authentication made pursuant to Section 310 must fulfill the following requirements under Section 312 as to the contents of the certificate of authentication. The requirements set forth in Section 312, subdivision 2, paragraph 2 are that all certificates of authentication must state in the substance:

(a) that, at the time when such original certificate purports to have been made, the person whose name is subscribed to the original certificate was such officer as he is therein represented to be;

(b) that the authenticating officer is acquainted with the handwriting of the officer making the original certificate, or has compared the signature of such officer upon the original certificate with a specimen of his signature filed or deposited in the office of such authenticating officer, or recorded, filed, or deposited, pursuant to law, in any other place, and believes the signature upon the original certificate is genuine;

(c) if the original certificate is required to be under seal, that the authenticating officer has compared the impression of the seal affixed thereto with a specimen impression thereof filed or deposited in his office, or recorded, filed, or deposited, pursuant to law, in any other place, and believes the impression of the seal upon the original certificate is genuine.

C. CERTIFICATE OF ACKNOWLEDGMENT—SUBSTANTIVE NEW YORK REQUIREMENTS

An acknowledgment or proof taken pursuant to the laws of New York must fulfill the following statutory requirements. First, Section 303 of the Real Property Law prohibits the taking of an acknowledgment by any officer unless he knows or has satisfactory evidence that the person making it is the person described in and who executed the agreement. Thus, the officer taking the acknowledgment must know or have satisfactory evidence that the person making it is both the person described in the instrument, as well as the person who is executing it. Second, the person taking the acknowledgment or proof must indorse thereupon or attach thereto, a certificate signed by that person, stating all the matters required to be done, known, or proved on the taking of such acknowledgment or proof; together with the name and substance of the testimony of each witness examined before him, and if a subscribing witness, his place of residence. Section 306.

Acknowledgments taken by a New York authorized notary public must comply with Section 137 of the Executive Law. Although no seal is required, the notary must state the venue of his act and below his signature, in black ink, either print, type or stamp the words, "Notary Public, State of New York," the name of the county in which he originally qualified, and the date upon which his commission expires. A notary public who is duly licensed as an attorney and counselor at law in New York may, in his discretion, substitute the words, "Attorney and Counselor at Law" for the words, "Notary Public." Note, while Section 298 of the Real Property Law authorizes a notary public to take acknowledgments at any place within the state, Section 130 of the Executive Law limits that authority to the state of New York by making a New York notary's jurisdiction coextensive with the boundaries of the state. Further note that under no circumstances is a certificate of authentication required to record or read into evidence an acknowledgment made by a notary public duly authorized by New York. Section 310, subdivision 2, New York Real Property Law.

III. ACKNOWLEDGMENTS AND PROOFS TAKEN OUTSIDE NEW YORK BUT WITHIN THE SOVEREIGNTY OF THE UNITED STATES

A. AUTHORITY TO TAKE ACKNOWLEDGMENTS AND PROOFS

Under Section 299 an out of New York acknowledgment or proof of conveyance of real property situated in New York if made in the following places:

(a) without the state but within the United States

(b) within any territory, possession, or dependency of the United States, or

(c) within any place over which the United States, at the time when such acknowledgment or proof is taken, has or exercises jurisdiction, sovereignty, control, or a protectorate,

may be made by any of the following officers acting within his territorial jurisdiction or within that of the court of which he is an officer:

(1) A judge or other presiding officer of any court having a seal or the clerk or other certifying officer thereof.[7]

(2) A mayor or other chief civil officer of any city or other political subdivision.

(3) A notary public.

(4) A commissioner of deeds appointed pursuant to the laws of this state to take acknowledgments or proofs without this state[8]

(5) Any person authorized, by the laws of the state, District of Columbia, territory, possession, dependency, or other place where the acknowledgment or proof is made, to take the acknowledgment or proof of deeds to be recorded therein.

Section 299–a of the RPL further imposes requirements upon the use of acknowledgments and proofs authorized without the state under Section 299. Under § 299–a such an acknowledgment or proof may be taken in the manner prescribed by New York law or by the laws of the jurisdiction in which the acknowledgment or proof was taken. An acknowledgment taken in the manner prescribed by the law of New York must meet the requirements set forth in Section I, (a) of this bulletin. If it was so taken according to the law of the out of state jurisdiction, it must be accompanied by a certificate to the effect that it conforms with such laws. Such a certificate of conformity may be made by:

(a) An attorney-at-law admitted to practice in the state of New York, resident in the place where the acknowledgment or proof is taken, or by

(b) An attorney-at-law admitted to practice in the state, District of Columbia, territory, possession, dependency, or other place where the acknowledgment or proof is taken, or by

(c) Any other person deemed qualified by any court of the state of New York, any action, proceeding, or other matter pending before such court, it be necessary to determine that such acknowledgment or proof conforms with the laws of such state, District of Columbia, territory, possession, dependency, or other place; or by the supreme court of the state of New York, on application for such determination. The justice, judge, surrogate, or other presiding judicial officer shall append to the instrument so acknowledged or proved his signed statement that he deemed such person qualified to make such certificate.

B. CERTIFICATES OF AUTHENTICATION

Section 311, subsection one of the Real Property Law requires a certificate of acknowledgment taken outside New York by a commissioner of deeds appointed pursuant to the laws of New York to be authenticated by the certificate of the Secretary of State of New York. This authentication is necessary before such an acknowledgment or proof can be recorded or read into evidence in New York.

A certificate of authentication is also required by Real Property Law Section 311, subdivision 4 when a certificate of acknowledgment or proof is made pursuant to the "any person authorized" provision of RPL Section 299, subdivision 5 by an officer or person who is not elsewhere in said section specifically designated to take acknowledgments or proofs. A certificate of authentication is required before such an acknowledgment or proof can be read into evidence or recorded in New York. Such authentication can be made:

(a) by the certificate of the secretary of state of a state, or of the secretary of a territory, of the United States, or

(b) by the certificate of any officer designated in subdivision three of this section to authenticate certificates of acknowledgment or proof, or

(c) by the certificate of any officer designated in clauses (a) or (b) of subdivision two of this section to authenticate certificates of acknowledgment or proof, or

(d) by the certificate of the officer having charge of the official records showing that the person taking the acknowledgment or proof is such officer as he purports to be, or having a record of the signature of such person.

A certificate of authentication, made pursuant to Section 311, subdivision (4), i.e. a certificate authenticating a certificate of acknowledgment made pursuant to Section 299, subdivision 5 must meet additional requirements imposed by Section 312, subsection 3. Under 312, subdivision 3 a certificate of authentication of a certificate of acknowledgment made pursuant to Section 299, subdivision 5 must specify that the person making the certificate of acknowledgment was authorized by the laws of the jurisdiction within the United States where the acknowledgment or proof was taken to take the acknowledgment or proof.

The above requirements of Section 312, subdivision 3 are in addition to the statutory requirements imposed by Section 312, subdivision 2, paragraph 2, on *all* certificates of authentication. Note, paragraph one is no longer applicable since Section 311, subdivision 2 has been amended to no longer require a certificate of authentication to be attached to a certificate of acknowledgment made by a notary public within the sovereignty of the United States. The requirements of Section 312, subdivision 2, paragraph 2 are that all certificates of authentication must state in substance:

(a) that, at the time when such original certificate purports to have been made, the person whose name is subscribed to the original certificate was such officer as he is therein represented to be;

(b) that the authenticating officer is acquainted with the handwriting of the officer making the original certificate, or has compared the signature of such officer upon the original certificate with a specimen of his signature filed or deposited in the office of such authenticating officer, or recorded, filed, or deposited, pursuant to law, in any other place, and believes the signature upon the original certificate is genuine.

(c) if the original certificate is required to be under seal, that the authenticating officer has compared the impression of the seal affixed thereto with a specimen impression thereof filed or deposited in his office, or recorded, filed, or deposited, pursuant to law, in any other place, and believes the impression of the seal upon the original certificate is genuine.

C. REQUIRED SEALS

In addition to a certificate of authentication being required in certain instances by Section 311 before an out of state acknowledgment or proof of a conveyance of real property situated in New York can be read into evidence or recorded in New York, Section 308 further requires that such an acknowledgment or proof be under seal in the following cases:

(a) if made by a judge or other presiding officer of a court having a seal, or by the clerk or other certifying officer

§ 12.99 PURCHASE AND SALE OF REAL ESTATE Ch. 12

thereof, such certificate must be under the seal of such court;

(b) if made by a commissioner of deeds appointed pursuant to the laws of this state to take acknowledgments or proofs without this state, such certificate must be under his seal of office;

(c) if made by any officer specified in subdivision one of section three hundred one of this chapter, such certificate must be under the seal of the legation or consulate to which such officer is attached.

D. USE OF APOSTILLES

Effective October 15, 1981, the United States of America joined with various foreign countries in changing the procedures to be used for the authentications of documents executed before a foreign notary.

In one of the documents, the Secretary of State of the United States appends a note which clarifies the purpose of the legislation. It states:

"The scope of this convention is limited to the legalization of public documents, i.e. authentications, which is a governmental act. The convention will have no effect on the consular performance of notarial functions, i.e. those functions performed by a notary public in the United States (oaths, affirmations, affidavits, acknowledgments and attestations.). *Consular officers should continue to perform these functions*". (Emphasis added)

With respect to documentation, translation and modernization of documents, state recording laws continue to govern; the Apostille only makes easier the authentication of the signature of the official before whom the acknowledgment is taken.

IV. ACKNOWLEDGMENTS AND PROOFS TAKEN OUTSIDE OF NEW YORK AND OUTSIDE THE SOVEREIGNTY OF THE UNITED STATES

A. Authority to Take Acknowledgments and Proofs

Under Section 301 an acknowledgment or proof of a conveyance of real property situated in New York may be taken in a foreign country "before any of the following officers acting within his territorial jurisdiction or within that of the court of which he is an officer."

(1) An ambassador, envoy, minister, charge d'affaires, secretary of legation, consul-general, consul, vice-consul, consular agent, vice consular agent, or any other diplomatic or consular agent or representative of the United States, appointed or accredited to, and residing within, the country where the acknowledgment or proof is taken.

(2) A judge or other presiding officer of any court having a seal, or the clerk or other certifying officer thereof.

(3) A mayor or other chief civil officer of any city or other political subdivision.

(4) A notary public.

(5) A commissioner of deeds appointed pursuant to the laws of this state to take acknowledgments or proofs without this state.

(6) A person residing in, or going to, the country where the acknowledgment or proof is to be taken, and specially authorized for that purpose by a commission issued to him under the seal of the supreme court of the state of New York.

(7) Any person authorized, by the laws of the country where the acknowledgment or proof is made, to take acknowledgments of conveyances of real estate or to administer oaths in proof of the execution thereof.

Section 301-a further states that an acknowledgment or proof made pursuant to Section 300 may be taken in the manner prescribed by the laws of New York or by the laws of the foreign country where said acknowledgment or proof was taken. An acknowledgment taken in the manner prescribed by the law of New York must meet the requirements set forth in Section I, (a) of the bulletin. If it was taken in the manner prescribed by the laws of the foreign country, then it must be accompanied by a certificate to the effect that it conforms with such laws. Such a certificate of conformity may be made by:

(a) An attorney-at-law admitted to practice in the state of New York, resident in such foreign country, or by

(b) A consular officer of the United States, resident in such foreign country, under the seal of his office, or by

(c) A consular officer of such foreign country, resident in the state of New York, under the seal of his office, or by

(d) Any other person deemed qualified by any court of the state of New York, if, in any action, proceeding, or other matter pending before such court, it be necessary to determine that such acknowledgment or proof conforms with the laws of such foreign country; or by the supreme court of the state of New York, on application for such determination.

The justice, judge, surrogate, or other presiding judicial officer shall append to the instrument so acknowledged or proved his signed statement that he deemed such person qualified to make such certificate.

B. CERTIFICATES OF AUTHENTICATION

Before a certificate of acknowledgment or proof made by a notary public pursuant to Section 301 in a foreign country other than Canada can be read into evidence or recorded in New York, Section 311, subdivision 2 further requires that the certificate be authenticated. Such authentication may be made:

(a) by the certificate of the clerk or other certifying officer of a court in the district in which such acknowledgment or proof was made, under the seal of such court, or

(b) by the certificate of the clerk, register, recorded, or other recording officer of the district in which such acknowledgment or proof was made, or

(c) by the certificate of the officer having charge of the official records of the appointment of such notary, or having a record of the signature of such notary, or

(d) by the certificate of a consular officer of the United States resident in such country.

It is important to note that the Section 311 requirement of authentication of an acknowledgment made by a notary public in a foreign country other than Canada does not apply to acknowledgments and proofs taken by notary publics within the sovereignty of the United States. Prior to 1975, Section 311, subdivision 2 did impose such a requirement upon out of state notaries who acted within the sovereignty of the United States. The statute was amended by the Laws of 1975, Chapter 412, to omit the provisions requiring such authentication of a certificate of acknowledgment made by a notary public within the sovereignty of the United States.

A certificate of authentication is also required by Section 311, subdivision 3 when a certificate of acknowledgment or proof has been made outside of New York by a mayor or other chief civil officer of a city or other political subdivision and said acknowledgment or proof was not made under seal. Before such a certificate of acknowledgment or proof may be read in evidence or recorded in New York, a certificate of authentication must be issued by the clerk of such city or political subdivision or by a consular officer of the United States resident in the country where the acknowledgment or proof was made.

A certificate of authentication is also required by Real Property Law, Section 311, subdivision 4 when a certificate of acknowledgment or proof is made pursuant to the "any person authorized" provision of Real Property Law, Section 301, subdivision 7 by an officer or person who is not elsewhere in said section specifically designated to take acknowledgments or proofs. A certificate of authentication is required before such an acknowledgment or proof can be read into evidence or recorded in New York. Such authentication can be made:

(a) by the certificate of the secretary of state of a state, or of the secretary of a territory, of the United States, or

(b) by the certificate of any officer designated in subdivision three of this section to authenticate certificates of acknowledgment or proof, or

(c) by the certificate of any officer designated in clauses (a) or (b) of subdivision two of this section to authenticate certificates of acknowledgment or proof, or

(d) by the certificate of the officer having charge of the official records showing that the person taking the acknowledgment or proof is such officer as he purports to be, or having a record of the signature of such person.

A certificate of authentication, made pursuant to Section 311, subdivision (4), i.e., a certificate authenticating a certificate of acknowledgment made pursuant to Section 301, subdivision 7, must meet additional requirements imposed by Section 312, subsection 4. Under Section 312, subdivision 4 a certificate of authentication of a certificate of acknowledgment or proof made pursuant to Section 301, subdivision 7 must specify that the person making the certificate of acknowledgment was authorized by the laws of the foreign country, where the certificate of acknowledgment or proof was made, to take the acknowledgment or to administer oaths in proof of execution thereof.

The above requirements of Section 312, subdivision 4 are in addition to the statutory requirements imposed by Section 312, subdivision 2, paragraph 2, on *all* certificates of authentication. The requirements of Section 312, subdivision 2, paragraph 2 are that all certificates of authentication must state in substance:

(a) that, at the time when such original certificate purports to have been made, the person whose name is subscribed to the original certificate was such officer as he is therein represented to be;

(b) that the authenticating officer is acquainted with the handwriting of the officer making the original certificate, or has compared the signature of such officer upon the original certificate with a specimen of his signature filed or deposited in the office of such authenticating officer, or recorded, filed, or deposited, pursuant to law, in any other place, and believes the signature upon the original certificate is genuine;

(c) if the original certificate is required to be under seal, that the authenticating officer has compared the impression of the seal affixed thereto with a specimen impression thereof filed or deposited in his office, or recorded, filed, or deposited, pursuant to law, in any other place, and believes the impression of the seal upon the original certificate is genuine.

C. REQUIRED SEALS

In addition to a certificate of authentication being required in certain instances by Section 311 before an out of state acknowledgment or proof of a conveyance of real property situated in New York can be read into evidence or recorded in New York, Section 308 further requires that such an acknowledgment or proof be under seal in the following cases:

(a) if made by a judge or other presiding officer of a court having a seal, or by the clerk or other certifying officer thereof, such certificate must be under the seal of such court;

(b) if made by a commissioner of deeds appointed pursuant to the laws of this state to take acknowledgments or proofs without this state, such certificate must be under his seal of office:

(c) if made by an officer specified in subdivision 1 of section 301 of this section, such certificate must be under the seal of the legation or consulate to which such officer is attached.

D. USE OF APOSTILLES

Effective October 15, 1981, the United States of America joined with various foreign countries in changing the procedures to be used for the authentications of documents executed before a foreign notary.

In one of the documents, the Secretary of State of the United States appends a note which clarifies the purpose of the legislation. It states:

> "The scope of this convention is limited to the legalization of public documents, i.e. authentications, which is a governmental act. The convention will have no effect on the consular performance of notarial functions, i.e. those functions performed by a notary public in the United States (oaths, affirmations, affidavits, acknowledgments and attestations.). *Consular officers should continue to perform these functions*". (Emphasis added)

With respect to documentation, translation and modernization of documents, state recording laws continue to govern; the Apostille only makes easier the authentication of the signature of the official before whom the acknowledgment is taken. The acknowledgment taken before a foreign notary may be authenticated in the following form of an Apostille.

You will note that the Apostille is acceptable as a form of authentication in no matter what language it appears as long as it bears the same format as it is shown. This does *not* mean that the acknowledgment itself may be written in a foreign language. It means that only the Apostille may be in a foreign language. The Apostille and the acknowledgment are two different instruments. All of the numbered lines in the Apostille must be completed. The Apostille must have the seal or stamp of the official executing the Apostille affixed to the Apostille.

The following countries and territories are signataries of the Hague Convention Abolishing the Requirement of Legislation for Foreign Public Documents. Acknowledgments taken in these states may be authenticated in the form of an Apostille.

Contracting State	*Territories Covered*
Austria	
Bahamas	
Belgium	
Botswana	
Cyprus	
Fiji	
France	Departments in Europe and Overseas Departments:
	French Guiana
	Guadeloupe
	Martinique
	Reunion
	Overseas Territories:
	Affars and the Issas
	Anglo–French Condominium of the New Hebrides (Vanuatu)*
	Comoro Islands*
	French Polynesia
	New Caledonia
	St. Pierre and Miquelon
	Wallis and Futuna
Germany, Federal Republic of	Land Berlin (Western Sectors of Berlin)

§ 12.99 PURCHASE AND SALE OF REAL ESTATE Ch. 12

Hungary

Israel

Italy

Japan

Lesotho

Liechtenstein

Luxembourg

Malawi

Malta

Mauritisu

Netherlands   the Kingdom in Europe

                                      Netherlands Antilles

                                      Suriname**

Portugal   Angola*

                                      Mozambique*

                                      the other overseas departments

Seychelles

Spain

Suriname

Swaziland

Switzerland

Tonga

United Kingdom of Great Britain and Northern Ireland   Antigua

                                      Bahama Islands**

                                      the Bailiwick of Guernsey

                                      Barbados

                                      Basutoland (Lesotho)**

                                      Bechuanaland Protectorate (Botswana)

Bermuda

British Antarctic Territory***

British Guiana (Guyana)*

British Solomon Islands Protectorate (Solomon Islands)*

Brunei

Cayman Islands

Dominica*

Falkland Islands

Fiji**

Gibraltar

Gilbert and Ellice Islands (Kiribat)

Grenada*

Hong Kong

the Isle of Man

Jersey

Mauritius**

Montserrat

New Hebrides (Vanuatu)*

St. Helena

Saint Christopher, Nevis and Anguilla

Saint Lucia*

Saint Vincent*

Seychelles**

Southern Rhodesia (Zimbabwe)*

Swaziland**

Tonga**

Turks and Caicos Islands

Virgin Islands

§ 12.99   PURCHASE AND SALE OF REAL ESTATE   Ch. 12

Yugoslavia

* Now independent
** Now independent and party to the Convention.
*** The United States does not recognize claims in Antarctica.

APOSTILLE
(Convention de La Haye du 5 octobre 1961)

1. Country: United States of America
This public document

2. has been signed by ....

3. acting in the capacity of ....

4. bears the seal/stamp of ....

CERTIFIED

5. at .... 6. the ....

7. by ....

8. No ....
9. Seal/Stamp   10. Signature:
   ....

ANNEX TO THE CONVENTION

E. SAMPLE ACKNOWLEDGMENT TAKEN IN FOREIGN COUNTRY WHERE THE APOSTILLE IS NOT AUTHORIZED

)
) SS.:
)

I,_____, _____,
   (name of officer)   (title of officer)
of the United States of America at _____,
duly commissioned and qualified, do hereby certify that on this
_____ day of _____,19___, before me personally _____
known to be the person described in and who executed the foregoing
_____,
and being informed by me of the contents of said instrument he duly acknowledged to me that he had executed the same.

IN WITNESS WHEREOF, I have hereunto set my hand and official seal this _____ day of _____, 19_____.

                             _____
                             Notary Public

Ch. 12   PURCHASE AND SALE OF REAL ESTATE   § 12.99

V. AUTHENTICATIONS AND PROOFS OF PERSONS IN THE MILITARY OR ARMED FORCES

Section 300 of the RPL governs this subject what follows is a model of acknowledgment which conforms to its requirements. No authentication is required. In addition for the conveyance of real property all the other methods provided by law may be used.

COUNTRY OF (OR)   )
STATE OF   )
) SS.:
COUNTY OF   )

I, _____,
hereby certify that I am a commissioned officer in active service; to wit
_____;
(insert rank, serial number and command)

that on the _____ day of _____,19_____, before me personally appeared _____, to me known to be the person described in and who executed the foregoing instrument and acknowledged to me that he executed the same; and I further certify that the said _____, who made such aforesaid acknowledgment, was at the time of the making of the same, (enlisted or commissioned or serving in or with the armed forces of the United States or the dependent of such a person, or a person attached to or accompanying the armed forces of the United States (state the applicable facts); and that the serial number of said _____, (the person who makes this acknowledgment, or whose dependent makes this acknowledgment) is _____.

_____
(affix rank and serial number)

5. Section 307 of the RPL requires the acknowledgment or proof taken by a Commissioner of Deeds to state the day on which and the city or political subdivision the acknowledgment or proof was taken.	7. Section 307 of the RPL requires the acknowledgment or proof taken by a Commissioner of Deeds to state the day on which and the city or political subdivision the acknowledgment was taken.
6. Section 308 of the RPL requires the seal of the court or a clerk of that court.	8. Section 308 of the RPL requires the seal of that court or of a clerk of that court.